Fodor's

D0068556

JAPAN

18th Edition

**Where to Stay and Eat
for All Budgets**

**Must-See Sights
and Local Secrets**

Ratings You Can Trust

Fodor's Travel Publications   New York, Toronto, London, Sydney, Auckland
www.fodors.com

FODOR'S JAPAN

EDITORS: Josh McIlvain, Alexis Kelly, Deborah Kaufman

Editorial Contributors: Josh Bisker, Brett Bull, Allison Burke, Nicholas Coldicott, Jon Davies, Justin Ellis, Amanda Harlow, Oscar Johnson, James Klar, Deidre May, Oliver Ormrod, Katherine Pham Do, Krista Kim Pickard, and John Malloy Quinn

Editorial Production: Linda K. Schmidt

Maps: David Lindroth, *cartographer*; Rebecca Baer and Robert Blake, *map editors*

Design: Fabrizio La Rocca, *creative director;* Guido Caroti, *art director;* Moon Sun Kim, *cover designer;* Melanie Marin, *senior picture editor*

Production/Manufacturing: Robert B. Shields

Cover Photograph (cherry blossoms, Tōkyō): Corbis

Eighteenth Edition

ISBN 978–1–4000–1779–9

ISSN 0736–9956

SPECIAL SALES

This book is available for special discounts for bulk purchases for sales promotions or premiums. Special editions, including personalized covers, excerpts of existing books, and corporate imprints, can be created in large quantities for special needs. For more information, write to Special Markets/Premium Sales, 1745 Broadway, MD 6-2, New York, New York 10019, or e-mail specialmarkets@randomhouse.com.

IMPORTANT TIP & AN INVITATION

Although all prices, opening times, and other details in this book are based on information supplied to us at press time, changes occur all the time in the travel world, and Fodor's cannot accept responsibility for facts that become outdated or for inadvertent errors or omissions. So **always confirm information when it matters,** especially if you're making a detour to visit a specific place. Your experiences—positive and negative—matter to us. If we have missed or misstated something, **please write to us.** We follow up on all suggestions. Contact the Japan editor at editors@fodors. com or c/o Fodor's at 1745 Broadway, New York, New York 10019.

PRINTED IN THE UNITED STATES OF AMERICA

10 9 8 7 6 5 4 3 2 1

Be a Fodor's Correspondent

Your opinion matters. It matters to us. It matters to your fellow Fodor's travelers, too. And we'd like to hear it. In fact, we *need* to hear it.

When you share your experiences and opinions, you become an active member of the Fodor's community. That means we'll not only use your feedback to make our books better, but we'll publish your names and comments whenever possible. Throughout our guides, look for "Word of Mouth," excerpts of your unvarnished feedback.

Here's how you can help improve Fodor's for all of us.

Tell us when we're right. We rely on local writers to give you an insider's perspective. But our writers and staff editors—who are the best in the business—depend on you. Your positive feedback is a vote to renew our recommendations for the next edition.

Tell us when we're wrong. We're proud that we update most of our guides every year. But we're not perfect. Things change. Hotels cut services. Museums change hours. Charming cafés lose charm. If our writer didn't quite capture the essence of a place, tell us how you'd do it differently. If any of our descriptions are inaccurate or inadequate, we'll incorporate your changes in the next edition and will correct factual errors at fodors.com *immediately*.

Tell us what to include. You probably have had fantastic travel experiences that aren't yet in Fodor's. Why not share them with a community of like-minded travelers? Maybe you chanced upon a beach or bistro or B&B that you don't want to keep to yourself. Tell us why we should include it. And share your discoveries and experiences with everyone directly at fodors.com. Your input may lead us to add a new listing or highlight a place we cover with a "Highly Recommended" star or with our highest rating, "Fodor's Choice."

Give us your opinion instantly at our feedback center at www.fodors.com/feedback. You may also e-mail editors@fodors.com with the subject line "Japan Editor." Or send your nominations, comments, and complaints by mail to Japan Editor, Fodor's, 1745 Broadway, New York, NY 10019.

You and travelers like you are the heart of the Fodor's community. Make our community richer by sharing your experiences. Be a Fodor's correspondent.

Itterasshai! (Or simply: Happy traveling!)

Tim Jarrell, Publisher

CONTENTS

UNDERSTANDING JAPAN

MAPS

CONTENTS

ABOUT THIS BOOK

Our Ratings

Sometimes you find terrific travel experiences and sometimes they just find you. But usually the burden is on you to select the right combination of experiences. That's where our ratings come in.

As travelers we've all discovered a place so wonderful that its worthiness is obvious. And sometimes that place is so unique that superlatives don't do it justice: you just have to be there to know. These sights, properties, and experiences get our highest rating, **Fodor's Choice,** indicated by orange stars throughout this book.

Black stars highlight sights and properties we deem **Highly Recommended,** places that our writers, editors, and readers praise again and again for consistency and excellence.

By default, there's another category: any place we include in this book is by definition worth your time, unless we say otherwise. And we will.

Disagree with any of our choices? Care to nominate a place or suggest that we rate one more highly? Visit our feedback center at www.fodors.com/feedback.

Budget Well

Hotel and restaurant price categories from ¢ to $$$$ are defined in the opening pages of each chapter. For attractions, we always give standard adult admission fees; reductions are usually available for children, students, and senior citizens. Want to pay with plastic? **AE, D, DC, MC, V** following restaurant and hotel listings indicate whether American Express, Discover, Diner's Club, MasterCard, and Visa are accepted.

Restaurants

Unless we state otherwise, restaurants are open for lunch and dinner daily. We mention dress only when there's a specific requirement and reservations only when they're essential or not accepted—it's always best to book ahead.

Hotels

Hotels have private bath, phone, TV, and air-conditioning and operate on the European Plan (aka EP, meaning without meals), unless we specify that they use the Continental Plan (CP, with a Continental breakfast), Breakfast Plan (BP, with a full breakfast), or Modified American Plan (MAP, with breakfast and dinner) or are all-inclusive (AI, including all meals and most activities). We always

list facilities but not whether you'll be charged an extra fee to use them, so when pricing accommodations, find out what's included.

Many Listings

★	Fodor's Choice
★	Highly recommended
⊠	Physical address
✛	Directions
⌖	Mailing address
☎	Telephone
🖷	Fax
⊕	On the Web
✎	E-mail
🗐	Admission fee
☉	Open/closed times
►	Start of walk/itinerary
Ⓜ	Metro stations
▭	Credit cards

Hotels & Restaurants

🏨	Hotel
🛏	Number of rooms
♨	Facilities
❍	Meal plans
✕	Restaurant
✍	Reservations
🏛	Dress code
⌇	Smoking
⅋	BYOB
✕🏨	Hotel with restaurant that warrants a visit

Outdoors

🏌	Golf
⛺	Camping

Other

☙	Family-friendly
🚹	Contact information
⇨	See also
⊠	Branch address
☞	Take note

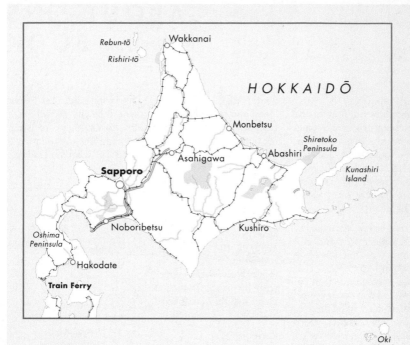

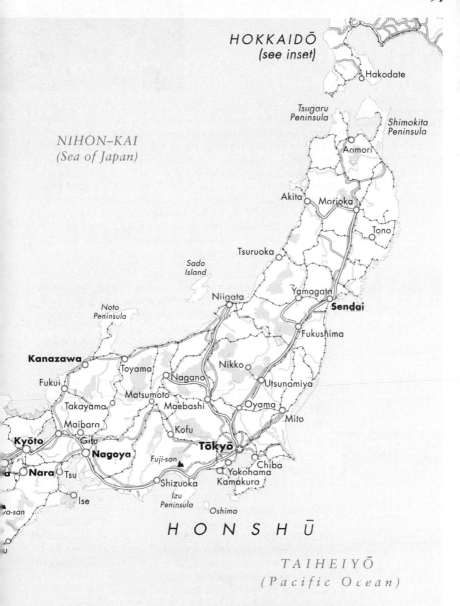

HOKKAIDŌ
(see inset)

Hakodate

*Tsugaru
Peninsula*

*Shimokita
Peninsula*

*NIHON–KAI
(Sea of Japan)*

Aomori

Akita Morioka

Tono

Tsuruoka

*Sado
Island*

Yamagata

Niigata

Sendai

*Noto
Peninsula*

Fukushima

Kanazawa

Toyama

Nikko

Fukui

Nagano

Utsunomiya

Takayama

Matsumoto

Maebashi

Oyama

Maibara

Kofu

Mito

Kyōto

Gifu

Tōkyō

Nagoya

Fuji-san ▲

Chiba

Nara

Tsu

Yokohama

Ise

Shizuoka

Kamakura

*Izu
Peninsula*

Oshima

a-san

H O N S H Ū

*TAIHEIYŌ
(Pacific Ocean)*

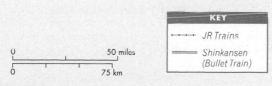

KEY

JR Trains

Shinkansen
(Bullet Train)

50 miles

75 km

Japan

WHAT'S
WHERE

TŌKYŌ 	Tōkyō is the big brother of modern Asian metropolises. This sprawling city, home to 10% of Japan's population, would take a lifetime to fully explore. The subway and rail map has all the order of a plate of spaghetti, and rather than any coherent center there is a mosaic of colorful neighborhoods—Shibuya, Asakusa, Ginza, Tsukiji, Shinjuku, and dozens more—each with its own texture. Stay long enough to get your bearings and you may start to appreciate the intertwined strands of life—from strictly conservative to outrageously avant-garde—that make Tōkyō almost a parallel universe even within the context of Japan.
SIDE TRIPS FROM TŌKYŌ 	Yokohama's Chinatown has more than 150 restaurants representing every major regional Chinese cuisine, and shops tucked in narrow lanes selling silks, spices, and herbal medicines. The Tōshō-gū shrine complex at Nikkō is stirring in its scale and flamboyance. Hakone, an expansive national park and resort area, puts you close to majestic Fuji-san (Mount Fuji), which can be climbed in summer without special gear. In Hase the 37-foot Daibutsu—the Great Buddha—has sat for seven centuries, gazing inward. The temples and shrines of nearby Kamakura, the calm 13th-century capital of Japan, remind you that this was an important religious as well as political center.
NAGOYA, ISE-SHIMA & THE KII PENINSULA 	The most important site of Japan's national religion, Shintō, is Ise Jingū (Grand Shrines of Ise). These refined wooden buildings with impressive thatched roofs sit amid groves of ancient trees and, in accordance with tradition, are rebuilt with new wood every 20 years. A loop around the Kii Peninsula winds past magnificent coastal scenery and fishing villages. Inland, the mountain monastery of Kōya-san, founded in 816, looms mythically with 120 temples, and Yoshino-san is home to perhaps the finest springtime display of cherry blossoms in Japan. Japan's fourth-largest city, Nagoya, is easy to navigate and a good place to sample aspects of contemporary Japan such as festivals, shopping, and sports events if you are on a tight schedule. The city's Tokugawa Art Museum displays the 12th century illustrated scrolls of *The Tale of Genji,* widely considered the world's first novel. In summer, *u-kai,* the ancient practice of fishing with cormorants, can be seen at nearby Gifu or Inuyama.

THE JAPAN ALPS & THE NORTH CHŪBU COAST	Travelers looking for soaring mountains, slices of old Japan, and superb hiking, skiing, and *onsen* soaking should come here, where the city of Nagano can serve as your base. Yudanaka Onsen's thermal springs are popular with people and snow monkeys, who gather near them for warmth. In the friendly city of Kanazawa are museums, shrines, traditional crafts, Nagamachi (Samurai District), and Kenroku Garden, one of the three finest in the country. Traditional Japan remains alive in Takayama, which draws the crowds for its ancient festivals each April and October. A trip around the north Chūbu coast and the Noto-hantō (Noto Peninsula) rewards you with dreamlike seascapes and charming villages such as Wajima, renowned for its lacquerware.
KYŌTO	Beyond Kyōto's ultramodern station and a city center typical of modern Japan, 12 centuries of history and tradition echo in beautiful gardens, castles, and museums, and nearly 2,000 temples and shrines. This ancient capital is the city that gave birth to classical Japanese customs, aesthetics, and arts. Glorious sights abound here, the gold-leaf Kinkaku-ji and steep hillside of Kiyomizu-dera topping most itineraries. Secular, but no less devoted to ceremony, are the geisha of the Gion district. Rituals are also observed with a near religious fanaticism at the city's gastronomic shrines serving *kaiseki ryōri,* an elegant meal that engages all senses. Like the food, Kyōto's crafts approach perfection: dolls, fans, ceramics, and creations by masters of the Kyō-yūzen silk-dyeing technique.
NARA	Ancient Nara may not match Kyōto's abundance of sacred sites, but its coherently arranged shrines and parks count among Japan's finest, and are matched by the local crafts and cuisine. Head for Nara Kōen, a splendid park with about 1,200 tame deer, and to the Kasuga Taisha temple complex. Near the park are the resplendent Tōdai-ji and the Daibutsu-den, which houses a 53-foot bronze Buddha. The finest temple in western Nara is Hōryū-ji, with its Great Treasure Hall and 7th-century wooden buildings.
ŌSAKA	On the south shore of western Honshū, Ōsaka dazzles with bright lights rather than tradition. However it does have Ōsaka-jō, a match for any castle in the country, and sumō wrestling at the Ōsaka Furitsu Taiikukaikan. Osakans are among sumō's biggest fans. Despite the bulk of the wrestlers, their quickness is amazing. Bunraku puppet masters ply a gen-

WHAT'S WHERE

tler art at the National Bunraku Theater. Ōsaka is famous for the perfection of this dramatic form. For neon and nightlife, hop on a subway to Dōtombori-dōri. Dine among the food-loving locals, whose unreserved nature is sure to make for some memorable moments. Be sure to sample specialties like *okonomiyaki,* grilled pancakes with vegetables and meat.

KŌBE

For a break from traditional Japan, try Kōbe—typified more by its harbor skyline than by sights like Ikuta Jinja, a Shintō shrine. European and Japanese influences have long mingled in this city on Ōsaka Bay. One result is Kitano-chō, with its old Western-style homes. Shopping is one of Kōbe's strong points, and at the Tasaki Shinju company you can learn how pearls get from mollusk to necklace. International accents are detectable in the culinary scene, where pride of place goes to pricey, world-famous Kōbe beef.

WESTERN HONSHŪ

Mountains divide this region into an urban south and a rural north. Today Hiroshima is the modern stronghold in the south, where the sobering remnants of the charred A-Bomb Dome testify to darker times. Offshore at Miyajima, the famous Ō-torii appears to float on the water. In nearby Bizen, masters craft the famous local pottery, and Kurashiki, with its buildings and willow-shaded canals, envelops you in an earlier time. On the northern coast, don't miss history-rich Hagi and the rare beauty of Tsuwano and Matsue.

SHIKOKU

Thanks to its isolation, the southern island of Shikoku has held on to its traditions and staved off the industry that blights parts of Japan. Leaving the beaten path rewards you with great hiking and dramatic scenery, some of the freshest seafood in the country, and a chance to make a fool of yourself (that's the idea) at the rollicking Awa Odori festival in Tokushima. Visit the mellow city of Kōchi, rugged Shōdo-shima island, and the superb Takamatsu gardens. Take to the waters at Dōgo Onsen Hon-kan and at the beach.

KYŪSHŪ

Rich in history and blessed with a balmy climate, lush Kyūshū is the southernmost of Japan's four main islands. At Aso National Park you can look into the steaming caldera of Mt. Nakadake, an active volcano. Not far from the artsy spa of Yufuin, volcanic grandeur accents pastoral views. With its quiet hills and streetcars, the harbor town Nagasaki is often called the San Francisco of Japan, testament to the city's resurrection

	from the second atomic bomb. The roots of Japanese civilization were cultivated in Kyūshū, and a visit to this energetic island provides an insight into the national character.
OKINAWA 	Okinawa is known as the Hawaii of Japan. Beaches upon beaches of soft, white sand slope gently into calm, shallow bodies of water. Relaxation and water sports are the main attractions of this archipelago that stretches for some 435 mi south of Kyūshū. A paradise for snorkelers and scuba divers, the islands teem with reefs, canyons, and shelves of coral under less than 10 meters (30 feet) of some of the clearest, cleanest, warmest waters in the world. They are also home to some 20,000 U.S. troops on bases established at the end of World War II. The battle of Okinawa was the bloodiest of the Pacific War, lasting 82 days, and is commemorated by a beautiful, expansive park outside the islands' chief city of Naha.
TŌHOKU 	Life slows down here, where rural ways and natural beauty abound. Zaō-san draws skiing enthusiasts in winter, and even nonskiers come for the *juhyō,* snow-covered fir trees that resemble fairy-tale monsters. At warmer times of year the mountaintop caldera is easily reachable by car or public transport. A short hop east is Sendai, Tōhoku's largest city and a good base for trips to Zaō-san and Matsu-shima, a bay studded with 250 pine-clad islands. Up north you can let your hair down at the lively Nebuta Festival in Aomori and the Kantō Festival in Akita. Make time for traditional Kakunodate, particularly in spring when cherry blossoms line its curving riverbanks, and nearby alpine Tazawa-ko, Japan's deepest lake.
HOKKAIDŌ 	Japan's northernmost island is also its last frontier. Glorious landscapes, hiking, and skiing adventures await, as well as the island's attractive capital, Sapporo, home of the beer. In February the Sapporo Snow Festival dazzles with huge ice sculptures. To the south are the famous hot springs of Noboribetsu Onsen and Jigokudani (Valley of Hell), a volcanic crater that belches boiling water and sulfurous vapors. The town of Nibutani is the last toehold of the indigenous Ainu people. Northeast lie three great national parks: wild Shiretoko by the sea, lake-filled Akan, and mountainous Daisetsu-zan. The northern tip of Japan is marked by a white lighthouse at Sōya-misaki.

QUINTESSENTIAL JAPAN

Seafood

As might be expected of a nation consisting of 3,000 islands, Japan is synonymous with the fruits of the sea. Sashimi and sushi have gained popularity with restaurant goers around the world, but it's hard to imagine some other so-called delicacies catching on. The northern island of Hokkaidō boasts of the quality of its *uni* (sea urchin), for example, while Akita Prefecture is famous for *shiokara* (raw squid intestines). Domestic tourism and television schedules are dominated by food, and city dwellers travel the length and breadth of the country on weekend excursions to taste regional specialties. However, as prices rise due to overfishing, most Japanese are more familiar with ¥100 plates at franchised conveyor-belt restaurants than visits to traditional sushi bars. Families consume countless varieties of tuna and shrimp, squid, and fish roe of such freshness that you are guaranteed to be leery of your local deli when you return home.

Baseball

Japan was crowned world champion of the nation's favorite sport at the inaugural Baseball Classic in 2006. Yakyū (baseball) is often said to epitomize the Japanese character. Players are subject to punishing preseason training regimes that test their stamina and will, the sacrifice bunt is a key tactic, and teams have names such as Nippon Ham Fighters and Hiroshima Carp. Japanese fans never insult opposition players, and home teams rarely hear any dissatisfaction from the stands. The prized quality of group harmony is evident as ballparks reverberate to repetitive theme songs created for each batter and fall into silence when the other team is at bat. Real emotion is reserved for championship wins, when fans crowd into city streets for a night—or, if its Ōsaka's Hanshin Tigers, jump from a bridge into a river—and hit the victory sales at local stores the next morning.

Onsen

Stepping carefully into the milky, sulfuric water, your skin tingles and then goes numb. Your fellow bathers are mere silhouettes in the steam, and the only sounds are the occasional splash or sigh as someone enters or leaves the communal tub. Onsen (hot spring baths) are one of Japan's great pleasures, and they also serve an important role as a social leveler—nakedness has the same function as the tiny doors of traditional teahouses that force all guests to duck down regardless of their social status. The bathhouse is an alternate world in which company directors, construction workers, and salarymen can forget the strict hierarchies and associated stresses of everyday life. In mountain regions *rotenburo* (outdoor baths) ease the aches and pains of hikers and skiers, and onsen across the country are said to contain minerals with healing qualities, easing ailments such as rheumatism and hypertension.

Depāto

Towering palaces catering to the every whim of the kings and queens of global consumerism, department stores in major Japanese cities give the retail experience a sophisticated shake. From the ultrapolite elevator attendants to the expert wrapping of your purchases, the attention to detail is extraordinary. Established stores follow a convenient pattern in their layout. In the basement is an expansive array of elaborately presented food, ranging from handmade sweets to bentō boxes. The first floor has cosmetics, and the next floors offer the latest in female fashion. Farther up you will find designer suits for men, ornate stationery, and refined home decorations. Finally, on the top floor, often with excellent urban views, is a restaurant area. The choice is always wide, and in even the most lavish of depāto the prices are reasonable.

WHEN TO GO

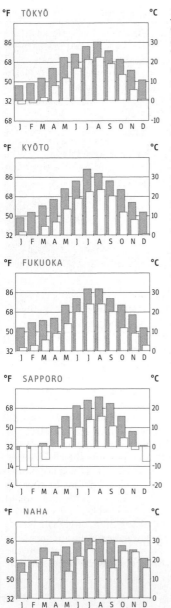

Japan's best seasons are spring and fall. In spring the country is warm, with occasional showers, and flowers grace landscapes in both rural and urban areas. The first harbingers of spring are plum blossoms in early March; *sakura* (cherry blossoms) follow, beginning in Kyūshū and usually arriving in Tōkyō by mid-April. Summer brings the rainy season, with particularly heavy rains and stifling humidity in July. Avoid July and August, unless you're visiting Hokkaidō, where temperatures are more bearable. Fall relieves with clear blue skies and glorious foliage. A few surprise typhoons may occur in early fall, but the storms are usually quick to leave. Winter is gray and chilly, with little snow in most areas along the Pacific Ocean side of the country, where temperatures rarely fall below freezing. Hokkaidō and the Japan Sea side of the country (facing Korea and Russia) are a different story, with heavy snowfalls in the winter months.

To avoid crowds, **be aware of times when most Japanese are vacationing.** Usually, Japanese vacation on the same holiday dates. As a result, airports, planes, trains, and hotels are booked far in advance. Many businesses, shops, and restaurants are closed during these holidays. Holiday periods include the few days before and after New Year's; Golden Week, which follows Greenery Day (April 29); and mid-August at the time of the Ōbon festivals, when many Japanese return to their hometowns.

⊞ Forecasts **Weather Channel** (⊕ www.weather.com).

IF YOU LIKE

Nightlife

Cocktails with pizzazz or chicken on a stick, dreamy jazz or thumping techno beats—you'll find it all under urban Japan's neon-soaked night sky. Walking the bar- and club-crazy streets at night is a great way to discover a city's character. Tipping is not customary, but upscale establishments may have extra service charges ranging from a few hundred yen to a few thousand. Karaoke clubs and *izakaya*, the traditional watering holes of office workers, are ubiquitous and a great way to mix with locals. All-night revelers might want to consider the likes of Roppongi in Tōkyō or Dōtombori in Ōsaka, while the more culturally inclined will find theaters and cinemas in every major city.

- **Susukino,** Sapporo. Wander this northern city's entertainment district for a taste of how many Japanese wind down after work. Bars, clubs, restaurants, and karaoke joints abound.

- **Kabuki-za,** Ginza, Tōkyō. There's no better place to catch a Kabuki performance than at this theater.

- **Sweet Basil 139,** Roppongi, Tōkyō. Come for dinner or just a drink at this upscale club featuring a variety of musical performances, considered to be Tōkyō's best.

- **Metro,** Kyōtō. A wide range of events and guest DJs make this one of Kansai's top clubs.

- **Bears,** Osaka. This live venue features the best of Japan's underground music.

Garden Life

Gardens are an obsession in Japan. Many urban homes have a couple of topiary trees, and Buddhist temples nationwide have immaculately maintained grounds. The best Japanese gardens are like the canvasses of master painters, in which nature is ingeniously manipulated and represented in subtly rearranged forms. Some re-create entire landscapes in miniature, and are designed for viewing from one optimal position. Others skillfully integrate immense backdrops of mountains or forest, always managing to add to the innate beauty of the natural environment. Kyōtō is home to Zen gardens, minimalist affairs of raked sand, moss, and meaningfully arranged rocks.

- **Imperial Palace East Garden,** Tōkyō. An oasis of tree-lined paths, rhododendrons, and water features that provides great views of the Imperial Palace buildings.

- **Kenrokuen,** Kanazawa. Originally landscaped in 1676, 25-acre Kenrokuen looks good all year round thanks to a wide variety of seasonal plants and trees.

- **Koinzan Saihō-ji,** Kyōtō. Escape the modern city by losing yourself in this remarkable world of verdant green and blue created by more than 120 species of moss planted on a number of levels.

- **Suizenji Kōen,** Kumamoto. Part of this garden re-creates the 53 stations of the old Tōkaidō post road that was immortalized by Hiroshiga Ando in a series of woodblock prints.

IF YOU LIKE

Outdoor Adventure

For many people modern Japan conjures images of the concrete, neon-lighted urban jungles of Kantō and Kansai. The country's wealth of natural attractions is easily overlooked, but outdoor enthusiasts will find their every whim catered to. In winter generous snowfall makes Hokkaidō and Nagano ideal destinations for skiers and snowboarders. The Japan Alps mountain range that stretches along the north side of Honshū offers excellent hiking trails, and Shikoku is well suited to cyclists. To the south, Okinawa boasts tropical temperatures for much of the year, and its clear waters are excellent for scuba diving and snorkeling.

- **Niseko,** Hokkaidō. Australians in the know head here by the tens of thousands each winter for arguably the best skiing in Japan.

- **Kamikōchi,** Nagano. En route to this small mountain village you pass though some stunning scenery, and upon arrival a series of trails provides access to the upper reaches of the surrounding peaks.

- **Shikoku.** The best way to enjoy this picturesque island in the Inland Sea is from the seat of a bicycle. Slow down to local pace and spend time exploring unexpected diversions.

- **Manta Way,** Okinawa. From April to June divers can observe rarely seen manta feeding on plankton in this strait between Iriomote and Kohama islands.

Holy Sites

Most modern Japanese would not express an affiliation with one religion, and both Shintō and Buddhism play important roles in many people's lives. Shintō architecture, with the exception of Nikko's colorful shrines, tends to be plain and simple, in the style of the nation's most sacred site at Ise, emphasizing natural materials such as wood and thatch. Temples run the gamut from austere to gaudy, both in color and design. Kyōto boasts many of the finest examples of religious architecture, while in mountain areas the act of pilgrimage and supplication to the elements is almost as important as the shrines and temples themselves.

- **Sensō-ji,** Asakusa, Tōkyō. Proof positive that even Japan's largest metropolis can preserve tradition. Sensō-ji has a tangible Old Tōkyō atmosphere from the first entrance gate, with its immense red lantern, through the narrow pedestrian streets to the huge incense burners of the temple.

- **Ise-jingū,** Mie prefecture. Home of Shintō, the national religion, the Grand Shrines of Ise are majestic thatched wooden buildings concealed in expansive forested grounds.

- **Tōdai-ji,** Nara. This temple's Daibutsu-den (Hall of the Great Buddha) is the largest wooden building in the world, and houses Japan's biggest Buddha figure, cast in bronze.

- **Kiyomizu-dera,** Kyōto. The Golden Pavilion of Kinkaku-ji may feature on more postcards, but this temple's large-scale wood construction is stunning. The steep approach to Kiyomizu-dera is lined with hundreds of craft, souvenir, and food shops.

GREAT ITINERARIES

7 DAYS IN TŌKYŌ

Day 1

Start *very* early (5 AM) with a visit to the **Tōkyō Central Wholesale Market** (Tōkyō Chūō Oroshiuri Ichiba) in the Tsukiji district. Direct train service starts around 5 AM from Shinjuku (Toei Oedo line) or Roppongi (Hibiya subway line) and gets you to Tsukuji or Tsukujishijo stations respectively in under 20 minutes. Or take a taxi. Then use the rest of the day for a tour of the **Imperial Palace** and environs.

Day 2

Spend the morning at **Sensō-ji** and adjacent **Asakusa Jinja** in Asakusa. If you're looking for souvenir gifts—sacred or secular— allow time and tote space for the abundant selection local vendors have to offer. From there go to **Ueno** for an afternoon of museums, vistas, and historic sites.

Day 3

Take a morning stroll through **Ginza** to explore its fabled shops and *depāto* (department stores). Then hit a chic restaurant or café for lunch (more reasonably priced ones are found on the upper floor of most department stores). In the afternoon see the Shintō shrine, **Meiji Jingū** and walk through the nearby Harajuku and Omotesandō fashion districts to the **Nezu Institute of Fine Arts**.

Day 4

Spend the morning browsing in **Akihabara**, Tōkyō's electronics quarter, and see the nearby Shintō shrine **Kanda Myōjin**. Spend the afternoon on the west side of **Shinjuku**, Tōkyō's 21st-century model city; and savor the view from the observation deck of architect Kenzō Tange's monumental **Tōkyō Metropolitan Government Office;** cap off the day visiting **Shinjuku Gyo-en National Garden.**

Day 5

Fill in the missing pieces: the Buddhist temple, **Sengaku-ji** in Shinagawa, the remarkable **Edo-Tōkyō Hakubutsukan** in **Ryōgoku,** a tea ceremony, Kabuki play, or see a sumō tournament, if one is in town. Or visit the **Kokugikan**, National Sumō Arena, in the Ryōgoku district, and some of the sumō stables in the neighborhood.

Days 6 & 7

You can make Tōkyō your home base for a series of side trips (⇨ Chapter 2). Take a train out to **Yokohama**, with its scenic port and Chinatown. A bit farther is **Kamakura**, the 13th-century military capital of Japan. The **Great Buddha** (Daibutsu) of the **Kōtoku-in** in nearby Hase is among the many National Treasures of art and architecture that draw millions of visitors a year.

Still farther off, but again an easy train trip, is **Nikkō**, where the founder of the Tokugawa Shogun dynasty is enshrined. **Tōshō-gū** is a monument unlike any other in Japan, and the picturesque **Lake Chūzen-ji** is in a forest above the shrine. Two full days, with an overnight stay, allows you an ideal, leisurely exploration of both. Yet another option is a trip to **Hakone**, where you can soak in a traditional onsen or climb to the summit of **Fuji-san** (Mt. Fuji).

GREAT ITINERARIES

HIGHLIGHTS OF CENTRAL JAPAN

Yes, Japan is a modern country with its skyscrapers, lightning-fast train service, and neon. But it's also rich in history, culture, and tradition. Japan is perhaps most fascinating when you see these two faces at once: a 17th-century shrine sitting defiantly by a tower of steel and glass and a geisha chatting on a cell phone.

Day 1: Ise & Koya-san
Ise-jingū (Grand Shrines of Ise), with their harmonious architecture and cypress-forest setting, provide one of Japan's most spiritual experiences.

Day 2: Kōya-san
More than 100 temples belonging to the Shingon sect of Buddhism stand on one of Japan's holiest mountains, 30 mi south of Ōsaka. An exploration of the atmospheric cemetery of Okuno-in takes you past headstone art and 300-year-old cedar trees.

Day 3: Nara
During the 8th century Nara was the capital of Japan, and many cultural relics of that period, including some of the world's oldest wooden structures, still stand among forested hills and parkland. Be sure to visit Nara's 53-foot-high, 1,300-year-old bronze Daibutsu (Great Buddha) in Tōdai-ji temple and to make friends with the deer of Nara Kōen.

Days 4–6: Kyōto
For many visitors Kyōto is Japan, and few leave disappointed. Wander in and out of temple precincts like Ginkaku-ji, spot geisha strolling about Gion, and dine on *kaiseki ryōri*, an elegant culinary event that engages all the senses. Outside the city center, day-trip to hillside Arashiyama, the gardens of the Kat-

sura Rikyū, and the temple of Enryaku-ji atop Hiei-zan. With nearly 2,000 temples and shrines, exquisite crafts, and serene gardens, Kyōto embodies traditional Japan.

Day 7: Ōsaka
Although by no means picturesque, Ōsaka provides a taste of urban Japan outside the capital, along with a few traditional sights. The handsome castle Ōsaka-jo nestles among skyscrapers, and the neon of Dōtombori flashes around the local Kabuki theater. Ōsakans are passionate about food, and you'll find some of the finest in the country here.

Day 8: Kōbe
Kōbe has recovered from the dark day in 1995 when it was struck by an earthquake that killed more than 5,000 people. Some of the first foreigners to live in Japan after the Meiji Restoration built homes in Kitano-chō, near the station, and the area retains an interesting mix of architectural styles.

Day 9: Himeji
The Western Honshū city's most famous sight, Himeji-jō, also known as the White Egret Castle (Shirasag-jō), dominates the skyline. The castle takes only an afternoon to see, but museums near the train station are worthy examples of Japan's modern architecture. Kenzō Tange designed the informative Hyōgo Prefectural Museum of History, and boxer-turned-architect Tadao Andō is responsible for the Himeji Museum of Literature, which is celebrated more for its unique minimalist exterior than for the exhibits inside.

HIGHLIGHTS OF SOUTHERN JAPAN

South and west of the tourist centers of Kyoto and Nara, Japan takes on a different feel. The farther you go, the more relaxed people become. Shikoku is a side step from Honshū in more ways than one, with a character very much its own. Behind the historical significance of Hiroshima lies one of the Japan's more attractive large cities, and nearby Miyajima is almost a theme park of mountains and shrines. Kyūshū boasts some of the most interactive scenery in the country, with active volcanoes, hot-sand baths, and steaming geysers. Hundreds of kilometers from Japan's main islands, the stark divide between the tropical beaches of Okinawa and Honshū's concrete metropolises is reflected in a different culture and cuisine.

Days 1 & 2: Shikoku

The Iya Valley may be slightly difficult to access, but it offers untouched, deep canyons, the best river rafting in Japan, and good walking trails. For a break from Japan—and the rest of the world—visit the Chichu Art Museum. This experimental project on Naoshima island, near Takamatsu, integrates art works into everyday locations, often with inspiring results.

Day 3: Kurashiki

This rustic town, an important trading port in centuries past, retains its picturesque 17th-century buildings. The 1930s classical-style Ōhara Art Museum houses a fine collection of European art. The Kurashiki Craft Museum displays crafts from around the world, including pottery from nearby Bizen.

Days 4 & 5: Hiroshima

A quick glance at the busy, attractive city of Hiroshima gives no clue to the events of August 6, 1945. Only the city's Peace Memorial Park (Heiwa Kinen Kōen)—with its memorial museum and its A-Bomb Dome (Gembaku Dōmu), a twisted, half-shattered structural ruin—serves as a reminder of the horror of the atomic bomb. From Hiroshima, make a quick trip to the island of Miyajima to see the famous floating torii of Itsukushima Jinja, a shrine built on stilts above a tidal flat.

Days 6 & 7: Yufuin & Mt. Aso

You don't need to be shaken by an earthquake to realize that Japan is seismically active. One of the locals' favorite pastimes is relaxing in an *onsen* (hot spring), and in the artsy little spa town of Yufuin, on the southernmost island of Kyūshū, you can soak in mineral water or bubbling mud. Nearby, five volcanic cones combine to create Japan's largest caldera at Mt. Aso. An immense 18 km (11 mi) by 24 km (15 mi), the stark volcanic peak contrasts vividly with the surrounding green hills. One crater, Nakadake, is still active, and reaching it on foot or via cable car affords views of a bubbling, steaming lake.

Days 8 & 9: Okinawa

Check out cosmopolitan Naha, which gives a feel for how Okinawan culture and cuisine differ from those of "mainland" Japan. Take a boat to one of the smaller Kerama islands to relax on uncrowded, unspoiled beaches. And to truly appreciate the beauty of the ocean, get into the water—there are plenty of scuba diving and snorkeling centers, with Nishibama Beach on Aka-jima highly rated.

GREAT ITINERARIES

HIGHLIGHTS OF NORTHERN JAPAN

With 80% of Japan's surface covered by mountains, the country is a dream for hikers and lovers of the great outdoors. Unfortunately, even rural areas are often spoiled by the nation's obsession with concrete, but the wilds of Hokkaidō, quietly impressive Tōhoku, and the vertiginous Japan Alps frequently reward exploration with spectacular scenery and experiences of traditional Japanese culture that have long-since been lost from urban areas.

Days 1 & 2: Sapporo

Sapporo is a pleasant and accessible city that serves as a good base for exploring the dramatic landscape of Hokkaidō. Mountains encircle Sapporo, drawing Japanese and increasing numbers of Australian skiers in winter. Take day trips out to **Tōya-ko** or **Shikotsu-ko**, picturesque caldera lakes where you can boat or fish, and the excellent **Nibutani Ainu Culture Museum** for an insight into the island's original inhabitants.

Days 3 & 4: Daisetsu-zan National Park

Japan's largest National Park, **Daisetsu-zan** is one of the nation's most popular spots for hiking and skiing, and reflects the essence of Hokkaidō: soaring mountain peaks, hidden gorges, cascading waterfalls, forests, and hot springs. Sheer cliff walls and stone spires make for a stunning drive through the **Sōun-kyō** ravine. Take a cable car up to the top of Hokkaidō's tallest mountain, **Asahi-dake**; hike or ski for a couple of hours, then unwind at a hot spring below.

Days 5 & 6: Haguro-san

This mountain, the most accessible of the Dewa-san range, a trio of sacred mountains in Tōhoku, is worth the trip not only for the lovely climb past cedars, waterfalls, and shrines but also for the thatched shrine at the top. You may even happen upon one of the many festivals and celebrations that take place at the shrine throughout the year. The rigorous climb itself, up 2,446 stone steps to the summit, is the main draw; however, it's possible to take a bus up or down the mountain.

Days 7–9: Japan Alps & North Chubu Coast

Nagano Prefecture, host of the 2000 Winter Olympics, is home to the backbone of the Japan Alps. Visit **Zenkō-ji** temple in Nagano City before heading to the hot springs of **Yudanaka Onsen** or **Kusatsu**. Alternatively, **Kamikōchi** allows you to really get away from it all—no cars are allowed into this mountain retreat. Farther west the cities of **Kanazawa** and **Takayama** offer some of the best-preserved traditional architecture in Japan, including old samurai family houses and sake breweries. Located conveniently between the two is **Shirakawago**, where steep-roofed thatched farmhouses sit snugly in a mountain valley. Stay a night to see the buildings at their best while sharing a meal around an *irori* fireplace with your fellow guests.

Tōkyō

WORD OF MOUTH

"There are many things that I love about Tōkyō, especially the food and the juxtaposition of the new and old."

—KMLoke

"One of my favorite memories of Tōkyō is that one minute you can be in the middle of the most up-to-date, high-tech, high-fashion, high-everything shopping districts, and then you can wander down a small street and come to a 1,000-year-old temple or even just a tiny traditional *okonomiyaki* restaurant."

—jules39

Updated by
Brett Bull,
Nicholas
Coldicott,
Oscar Johnson,
Krista Kim-
Pickard, and
Katherine
Pham Do

TŌKYŌ IS A CITY OF CONSTANT STIMULI. Complex, big, and always on the move, it's a place where opposites attract, and new trends come and go like the tide. The Japanese like harmony, which is reflected in a city that is both ancient and modern. It's a place where youth culture affects world trends; yet age-old traditions are deeply rooted.

Greater Tōkyō incorporates 23 wards, 26 smaller cities, 7 towns, and 8 villages—altogether sprawling 88 km (55 mi) from east to west and 24 km (15 mi) from north to south with a population of 35 million people. The wards alone enclose an area of 590 square km (228 square mi), which comprises the city center and houses 8 million residents. Because of the easy access to the public transportation system, 48% of residents are transit commuters; only 32% drive to work. Most people live in the suburbs and average a 56-minute commute. During rush hour, an immense wave of people floods all major transportation hubs, through which approximately 3 million people pass each day.

Tōkyō is a state-of-the-art financial marketplace, where billions of dollars are whisked electronically around the globe at the blink of an eye. However, most ATMs in the city shut down by 9 PM, so be sure to get enough cash when you find one. Most Citibank, Shinsei Bank (in most subway stations), and Japan Postal Savings ATMs allow international bank card transactions, but they are not always accessible. Tōkyō is a safe city, so you may carry cash without fear of street crime.

It's also a city of astonishing beauty, with a strong sense of tradition. On the flip side, it's also the center of futuristic design, lifestyle, and cutting-edge urban trends. Widespread postwar construction had given the city an uneven look that is being replaced with large-scale, designer architectural projects. Mori Building is at the forefront with its progressive Roppongi Hills (2003) and Omotestando Hills (2006) developments, and Mitsui Fudosan Co. Ltd., has joined in with the Midtown Project (2007) in Roppongi.

Tōkyō is a vanguard of international cultural events and entertainment, attracting stars like Tom Cruise and Madonna, and world-class performances like the Berlin Philharmonic. Michelin-star chefs like Alain Ducasse and Pierre Gagnaire have launched restaurants here, making this city a top gourmet destination. If you're a foodie, artist, design lover, or cultural adventurer, then Tōkyō, a city of inspiration and ideas, is for you.

EXPLORING TŌKYŌ

Tōkyō is densely packed into 23 municipal wards each with their own distinct neighborhoods. Each city ward has its own pace and style, which is refected in its history, architecture, by-laws, and atmosphere. You may smoke on the streets of Shinjuku, but not on the streets of Ginza (there's a ¥50,000 fine). Residents of Roppongi wear European designer fashion and drive luxury cars; residents of Asakusa are more traditional and ride the subway.

At the heart of the city is the Imperial Palace district near Otemachi and Tōkyō train stations, a major hub of the city's public transportation sys-

CLOSE UP

Top Reasons to Visit

1

SHOP 'TIL YOU DROP

On weekends, the main roads of Ginza are closed for pedestrians who explore the small side streets of this old shopping district. Check out the trendy togs of Tōkyo's young fashionistas on Harajuku Street. Need souvenirs? From rice crackers to *kiriko* (traditionally cut and colored glassware), you'll find it in the more than 80 shops on Asakusa's Nakamise-dori. An eccentric collection of toys, electronic gagets, and hobby items awaits you at Akihabara's Radio Kaiken. Or you can browse an impressive variety of specialty bookstores in Jimbō-chō.

WACKY-YŌ TŌKYŌ

Holy Hounddog! See the large group of dancing Elvis impersonators who gather at the entrance of Shibuya's Yoyogi Park to shake, rattle, and roll every Sunday. What's with the loud half-naked drunken people? It's all part of Asakusa's Sanja festival in May. Want to be a superhero? Cosa Gee Store in Akihabara has the greatest collection of Japanese comic character costumes. Also in Akihabara, check out the Maid Cafés where waitresses in maid costumes address patrons as *master* to cater to the festishes of Japanese *otaku* (nerds). Then meet ASIMO, Honda's humanoid robot, at the National Museum of Emerging Science and Innovation in Odaiba.

SIGHTS & THE CITY

Ueno's Tōshō-gū Shrine houses a priceless collection of historical art and is one of the city's few last remaining early-Edo-period buildings. While you're there, swing by the Ueno Zoo. Even without kids in tow, it's hard to pass up the chance to see the resident Giant Pandas, Tong Tong and Ling Ling. Need a wish granted? Visit Asakusa Jinja, the largest surviving building in the Sensō-ji temple complex, write your wish on a wooden placard and leave it for the gods. Escape the mad rush of the city in the Imperial Palace East Gardens. Or, you can escape to Odaiba's Hot Spring Theme Park for a memorable onsen experience in Edo-era surroundings—if you don't mind being naked in a crowd.

FOOD & FROLIC

For a tea ceremony, visit Hasumi Chaya, a charming teahouse on the bank of the Shinobazu Pond in Ueno, which is open in summer when lotus flowers cover the pond. For the opposite experience, the city's hard-core outsiders are found in Golden Gai, a Shinjinku district of tiny, unpretentious, even seedy *nomiya* (bars). Stop by the basement food halls in Mitsukoshi department store, in Nihombashi and Ginza, for the hundreds of delicious desserts and prepared foods. Or, head to the Tsukiji fish market for the freshest sushi in the world. But don't eat the plastic food found in the Kappabashi section of Asakusa—it's considered Pop Art.

ART ABOUNDS

The National Museum of Modern Art, near the Imperial Palace, houses the finest collection of Japanese modern art. For other exceptional museums, go to Ueno for the Tōkyō National Museum and the National Museum of Western Art. For ceramics, visit the Idemitsu Museum of Art in Yūraku-chō. If you're still not satisfied, stop by the Seiji Tōgō Memorial Sompo Japan Museum of Art in Shinjuku to see Van Gogh's *Sunflowers*.

tem. From here, it is relatively easy to plot courses to famed areas such as Ueno and Asakusa to the northeast, east to Tsukiji or Tōkyō Disney, Roppongi in the southwest and westward to Shibuya and Shinjuku. The efficient and user-friendly train and subway systems connect them all and are the best way to get around. With myriad major thoroughfares and byways that are often neither parallel nor perpendicular to one another, proximity to train stations or other major landmarks are relied upon in Tōkyō far more than street names and addresses.

Imperial Palace & Government District

The district of Nagata-chō is the core of Japan's government. It is primarily comprised of the Imperial Palace (*Kōkyo-gaien*), the Diet (national parliament building), the Prime Minister's residence (*Kantei*), and the Supreme Court. The Imperial Palace and the Diet are both important to see, but the Supreme Court is nondescript. Unfortunately, the Prime Minister's residence is only viewable from afar, hidden behind fortified walls and trees.

The Imperial Palace was built by the order of Ieyasu Tokugawa, who chose the site for his castle in 1590. The castle had 99 gates (36 in the outer wall), 21 watchtowers (three are still standing), and 28 armories. The outer defenses stretched from present-day Shimbashi Station to Kanda. Completed in 1640 (and later expanded), it was the largest castle in the world. The Japanese Imperial Family still resides in heavily blockaded sections of the palace grounds. Tours are conducted by reservation only, and restricted to designated outdoor sections, namely, the palace grounds and the East gardens. The grounds are open to the general public only twice a year: on January 2 and December 23 (the Emperor's Birthday), when thousands of people assemble under the balcony to offer their good wishes to the Imperial Family.

Numbers in the text correspond to numbers in the margin and on the Imperial Palace map.

Orientation & Planning

ORIENTATION The Imperial Palace is located in the heart of central Tōkyō and the city's other neighborhoods branch out from here. The palace is surrounded by a moat that connects through canals to Tōkyō Bay and Sumida river (*Sumida-gawa*) to the east. Outside the moat, large four-lane roads trace its outline, as if the city expanded from this primary location.

PLANNING The best way to discover the Imperial Palace is to take part in one of the free tours offered by the **Imperial Household Agency** (☎ 03/

DISCOUNTED MUSEUM ADMISSION

If you plan on visiting a lot of the city's sites, purchasing a **GRUTT Pass** (🌐 www.museum.or.jp/grutto) is the way to go. The pass, which is only ¥2,000, gives visitors free or discounted admission to 49 sites throughout the city including museums, zoos, aquariums, and parks. Passes can be purchased at all participating sites, as well as the Tōkyō Tourist Information Center, or Family Mart and 7-11 convenience stores. Keep in mind that passes expire two months after date of purchase.

3213–1111 ⊕ www.kunaicho.go.jp), which manages matters of the state. There are four different tours: Imperial Palace Grounds, the East Gardens (*Higashi Gyoen*), Sannomaru Shozokan, and Gagaku Performance (in autumn only). All tours require registration a day in advance and hours change according to the season.

If you are exploring on your own, allow at least an hour for the East Garden and Outer Garden of the palace itself. Plan to visit Yasukuni Jinja after lunch and spend at least an hour there. The Yūshūkan (at Yasukuni Jinja) and Kōgeikan museums are both small and should engage you for no more than a half hour each, but the modern art museum requires a more leisurely visit—particularly if there's a special exhibit. The best time to visit is during the spring when the *ōhanami* (cherry trees) are in bloom between late March and early April, or during the Yasukuni Spring festival (April 21–23), which pays homage to the war-dead and shrine dieties.

■ TIP➔ Avoid visiting the Imperial Palace on Monday, when the East Garden and museums are closed; the East Garden is also closed Friday. In July and August, heat will make the palace walk grueling—bring hats and bottled water.

The best way to get to the Imperial Palace is by subway. Take the Nijubashimae (Chiyoda line) Exit 6 or Tōkyō (JR line) Exit to Maranouchi Central. There are three entrance gates—Ōte-mon, Hirakawa-mon, and Kita-hane-bashi-mon. You can easily get to any of the three from the Ōte-machi or Takebashi subway station.

What to See

⑪ **Chidori-ga-fuchi National Memorial Garden.** High on the edge of the Imperial Palace moat, this park is famous for its cherry blossoms, which appear in spring. The most popular activity in this garden is renting row boats on the moat at the **Chidori-ga-fuchi Boathouse.** The entrance to the garden is near Yasukuni Jinja. ⊠ *Chiyoda-ku* ☏ *03/3234–1948* 🎟 *Park free, boat rental ¥500 for 30 min during regular season, and ¥800 for 30 min during cherry blossom season* ☉ *Park daily sunrise–sunset, boathouse daily 9:30–4, usually late Mar.–early Apr.* Ⓜ *Hanzō-mon and Shinjuku subway lines, Kudanshita Station (Exit 2).*

❽ **Hanzō-mon** (Hanzō Gate). The house of the legendary Hattori Hanzō (1541–96) once sat at the foot of this small wooden gate. Hanzō was a legendary leader of Ieyasu Tokugawa's private corps of spies and infiltrators—and assassins, if need be. They were the menacing, black-clad ninja—perennial material for historical adventure films and television dramas. The gate is a minute's walk from the subway. ⊠ *Chiyoda-ku* Ⓜ *Hanzō-mon subway line, Hanzō-mon Station (Exit 3).*

⑭ **Hirakawa-mon** (Hirakawa Gate). The approach to this gate crosses the only wooden bridge that spans the Imperial Palace moat. The gate and bridge are reconstructions, but Hirakawa-mon is especially beautiful, looking much as it must have when the shōgun's wives and concubines used it on their rare excursions from the seraglio. ⊠ *Chiyoda-ku* Ⓜ *Tōzai subway line, Takebashi Station (Exit 1A).*

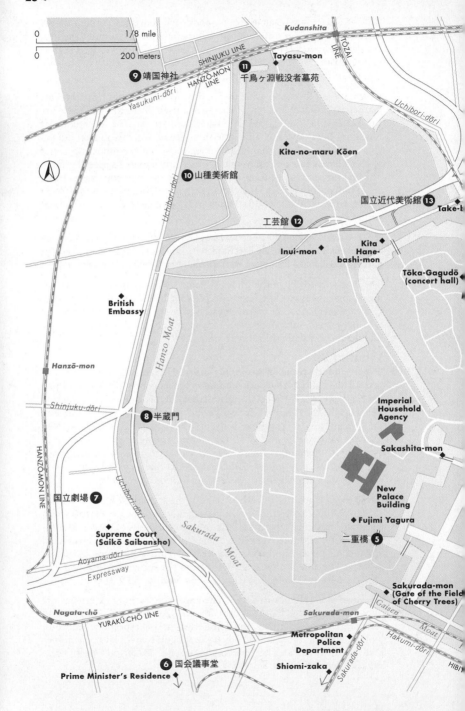

Kudanshita

1/8 mile
200 meters

SHINJUKU LINE

TŌZAI LINE

Tayasu-mon

HANZO-MON LINE

Yasukuni-dōri

9 靖国神社

11 千鳥ヶ淵戦没者墓苑

Uchibori-dōri

Kita-no-maru Kōen

Uchibori-dōri

10 山種美術館

国立近代美術館 **13**

Take-

工芸館 **12**

Inui-mon

Kita Hane- bashi-mon

Tōka-Gagudō (concert hall)

British Embassy

Hanzo Moat

Hanzō-mon

Shinjuku-dōri

Imperial Household Agency

8 半蔵門

Sakashita-mon

Uchibori-dōri

国立劇場 **7**

Sakurada Moat

New Palace Building

Supreme Court (Saikō Saibansho)

Fujimi Yagura

二重橋 **5**

Aoyama-dōri

Expressway

HANZO-MON LINE

Sakurada-mon (Gate of the Field of Cherry Trees)

Nagata-chō

YURAKŪ-CHŌ LINE

Sakurada-mon

Gaisen

Hakumi-dōri

Moat

Metropolitan Police Department

HIBI

6 国会議事堂

Sakurada-dōri

Prime Minister's Residence ↓

Shiomi-zaka

Imperial Palace & Government District

❸ Imperial Palace East Garden (Kōkyo Higashi Gyo-en). The entrance to
Fodor'sChoice the East Garden is the ⇨ **Ōte-mon,** once the main gate of Ieyasu Toku-
★ gawa's castle. Here, you will come across National Police Agency dōjō
(martial arts hall) and the Ōte Rest House, where for ¥100 you can buy
a simple map of the garden.

The **Hundred-Man Guardhouse** was once defended by four shifts of 100
soldiers each. Past it is the entrance to what was once the **ni-no-maru,**
the "second circle" of the fortress. It's now a grove and garden. At the
far end is the **Suwa Tea Pavilion,** an early-19th-century building relocated here from another part of the castle grounds.

Halfway along the steep stone walls of the **hon-maru** (the "inner circle") is **Shio-mi-zaka,** which translates roughly as "Briny View Hill,"
so named because in the Edo period the ocean could be seen from here.

Head to the wooded paths around the garden's edges for shade, quiet,
and benches to rest your weary feet. In the southwest corner is the Fujimi Yagura, the only surviving watchtower of the hon-maru; farther along
the path, on the west side, is the **Fujimi Tamon,** one of the two remaining armories.

The odd-looking octagonal tower is the **Tōka-Gagudō** (concert hall).
Its mosaic tile facade was built in honor of Empress Kojun in 1966.
⊠ *Chiyoda-ku* ▱ *Free* ☉ *Mar.–Oct., weekends and Tues.–Thurs. 9–4;
Nov.–late Dec. and early Jan. and Feb., weekends and Tues.–Thurs. 9–3:30*
Ⓜ *Tōzai, Marunouchi, and Chiyoda subway lines, Ōte-machi Station
(Exit C13b).*

❹ Imperial Palace Outer Garden (Kōkyo-Gaien). When the office buildings
of the Meiji government were moved from this area in 1899, the whole
expanse along the east side of the palace was turned into a public promenade and planted with 2,800 pine trees. The Outer Garden affords the
best view of the castle walls and their Tokugawa-period fortifications:
Ni-jū-bashi and the Sei-mon, the 17th-century Fujimi Yagura watchtower,
and the Sakurada-mon. ⊠ *Chiyoda-ku* ▱ *Free* Ⓜ *Chiyoda subway
line, Ni-jū-bashi-mae Station (Exit 2).*

⓬ Kōgeikan (Crafts Gallery of the National Museum of Modern Art). For
those who are interested in modern and traditional Japanese crafts, this
museum is worth seeing. Built in 1910, the Kōgeikan, once the headquarters of the Imperial Guard, is a Gothic-revival redbrick building.
The exhibits are all too few, but many master artists are represented here
in the traditions of lacquerware, textiles, pottery, bamboo, and metalwork. The most direct access to the gallery is from the Takebashi subway station on the Tōzai Line (Exit 1B). ⊠ *1–1 Kita-no-maru Kōen,
Chiyoda-ku* ☎ *03/3211–7781* ▱ *¥200, admission to National Museum
of Modern Art is separate; additional fee for special exhibits; free 1st
Sun. of month* ☉ *Tues.–Sun. 10–5* Ⓜ *Hanzō-mon and Shinjuku subway lines, Kudanshita Station (Exit 2); Tōzai subway line, Takebashi
Station (Exit 1b).*

❻ National Diet Building (Kokkai-Gijidō). This building, which houses the
Japanese parliament, is the perfect example of post–WWII Japanese ar-

chitecture; on a gloomy day it seems as if it might have sprung from the screen of a German Expressionist movie. Started in 1920, construction took 17 years to complete. The Prime Minister's residence, *Kantei,* is across the street. ✉ *1–7–1 Nagata-chō, Chiyoda-ku* Ⓜ *Marunouchi subway line, Kokkai-Gijidō-mae Station (Exit 2).*

⑬ **National Museum of Modern Art, Tōkyō** (Tōkyō Kokuritsu Kindai Bijutsukan). Founded in 1952 and moved to its present site in 1969, this was Japan's first national art museum. Twentieth- and 21st-century Japanese and Western art is featured throughout the year, but the museum tends to be rather bland about how these exhibitions are organized and presented, and they're seldom on the cutting edge. The second through fourth floors house the permanent collection, which includes the painting, prints, and sculpture by Rousseau, Picasso, Tsuguji Fujita, Ryūzaburo Umehara, and Taikan Yokoyama. ✉ *3–1 Kita-no-maru Kōen, Chiyoda-ku* ☎ *03/3214–2561* ⊕ *www.momat.go.jp* 🎟 *¥420, includes admission to Kōgeikan); free 1st Sun. of month* ☉ *Tues.–Thurs. and weekends 10–5, Fri. 10–8* Ⓜ *Tōzai subway line, Takebashi Station (Exit 1b); Hanzō-mon and Shinjuku subway lines, Kudanshita Station (Exit 2).*

❼ **National Theater** (Kokuritsu Gekijō). Architect Hiroyuki Iwamoto's winning entry in the design competition for the National Theater building (1966) is a rendition in concrete of the ancient *azekura* (storehouse) style, invoking the 8th-century Shōsōin Imperial Repository in Nara. The large hall seats 1,746 and presents primarily Kabuki theater, ancient court music, and dance. The small hall seats 630 and is used mainly for Bunraku puppet theater and traditional music. The building is nice to see, but all performances are in Japanese, so it can be difficult to sit through an entire show. Catch a show at the ⇨ **Kabukiza** in Ginza, where English earphones are offered. ✉ *4–1 Hayabusa-chō, Chiyoda-ku* ☎ *03/ 3265–7411* 🎟 *Varies depending on performance* Ⓜ *Hanzō-mon subway line, Hanzō-mon Station (Exit 1).*

❷ **Ōte-mon** (Ōte Gate). The main entrance to the Imperial Palace East Garden, Ōte-mon was in former days the principal gate of Ieyasu Tokugawa's castle. Most of the gate was destroyed in 1945 but was rebuilt in 1967 on the original plans. The outer part of the gate survived, and today it houses a fascinating photo collection of before-and-after photographs of the castle, taken about 100 years apart. ✉ *Chiyoda-ku* Ⓜ *Tōzai, Marunouchi, and Chiyoda subway lines, Ōte-machi Station (Exit C10).*

❶ **Tōkyō Station.** The work of Kingo Tatsuno, one of Japan's first modern architects, Tōkyō Station was completed in 1914. Tatsuno modeled his creation on Amsterdam's railway station. The building lost its original top story in the air raids of 1945, but was promptly repaired. In the late 1990s, a plan to demolish the station was impeded by public outcry. Inside, it has been deepened and tunneled and redesigned any number of times to accommodate new commuter lines, but the lovely old redbrick facade remains untouched. The best thing about the place is the historical **Tōkyō Station Hotel,** on the west side on the second and third floors. ✉ *1–9–1 Marunouchi, Chiyoda-ku* ☎ *03/3231–2511.*

Stretch Your Legs

THE VENUE OF CHOICE for runners is the **Imperial Palace Outer Garden.** At the west end of the park, Sakurada-mon's (Gate of the Field of Cherry Trees) small courtyard is the traditional starting point for the 5-km (3-mi) run around the palace—though you can join in anywhere along the route. Jogging around the palace is a ritual that begins as early as 6 AM and goes on throughout the day, no matter what the weather. Almost everybody runs the course counterclockwise, but now and then you may spot someone going the opposite way.

Looking for a challenge? Japan is a marathon mecca and one of the most famous is the **Tōkyō Big Marathon,**

(⊕ www.tokyo42195.org), held every February. Plan ahead if you're going to sign up, because the registration deadline is in August of the previous year (most of the country's running events require signing up and qualifying far more in advance than their counterparts on other shores). The Big Marathon starts at one of Tōkyō's most prominent landmarks, the Tōkyō Metropolitan Government Office in Shinjuku-ku, winds its way through the Imperial Palace, past the Tōkyō Tower and Asakusa Kaminarimon Gate, and finishes at Tōkyō Big Sight Exhibition Center in Ariake-ku. Remember to pack your long johns—the weather is harsh.

NEED A BREAK?

Stop by the **Wadakura Fuusui Koen Restaurant** for pasta, sandwiches, and soup with lovely water fountain views. English menus are available by request, but the signs are only in Japanese. Lunch set menus range from ¥1,000 to ¥2,000. ⊠ *3-1 Imperial Palace Outer Garden, Chiyoda-ku* Ⓜ *Otemachi Station (Exit D2, D3)* ☏ *03/3214-2286.*

❺ **Two-Tiered Bridge** (Ni-jū-bashi). Making a graceful arch across the moat, this bridge is surely the most photogenic spot on the grounds of the former Edo Castle. Mere mortals may pass through only on December 23 and January 2 to pay their respects to the Imperial family. The guards in front of their small, octagonal, copper-roof sentry boxes change every hour on the hour—alas, with nothing like the pomp and ceremony of Buckingham Palace. ⊠ *Chiyoda-ku* Ⓜ *Chiyoda subway line, Ni-jū-bashi-mae Station (Exit 2).*

❿ **Yamatane Museum of Art** (Yamatane Bijutsukan). The museum, which specializes in *Nihon-ga*—traditional Japanese painting—from the Meiji period and later, has a private collection of masterpieces by such painters as Taikan Yokoyama, Gyoshū Hayami, Kokei Kobayashi, and Gyokudō Kawai. The exhibits, which sometimes include works borrowed from other collections, change every two months. The decor and displays make this museum an oasis of quiet elegance. Buy the lavish catalog of the collection as a stylish coffee-table souvenir. The interior garden was designed by architect Yoshio Taniguchi, who also did the Museum of Modern Art. ⊠ *2 Samban-chō, Chiyoda-ku* ☏ *03/3239-5911* 🖷 *03/*

3239–5913 🚇 ¥500 ⏰ *Tues.–Sun. 10–4:30* Ⓜ *Tōzai and Shinjuku subway lines, Kudanshita Station (Exit 2).*

★ ❾ **Yasukuni Jinja** (Shrine of Peace for the Nation). This shrine is not as impressive as Asakusa Shrine and Meiji Jingu Shrine, so if you must choose among the three, visit the latter. Founded in 1869, this shrine is dedicated to approximately 2.5 million Japanese, Taiwanese, and Koreans who have died since then in war or military service. Since 1945 Yasukuni has been a center of stubborn political debate given that the Japanese constitution expressly renounces both militarism and state sponsorship of religion. Several Prime Ministers have visited the shrine since 1979, causing a political chill between Japan and its close neighbors, Korea and China—who suffered under Japanese colonialism. Despite all this, hundreds of thousands of Japanese come here every year, simply to pray for the repose of friends and relatives they have lost.

The shrine is not one structure but a complex of buildings that include the **Main Hall** and the **Hall of Worship**—both built in the simple, unadorned style of the ancient Shintō shrines at Ise—and the **Yūshūkan,** a museum of documents and war memorabilia. Also here are a Nō theater and, in the far western corner, a sumō-wrestling ring. Sumō matches are held at Yasukuni in April, during the first of its three annual festivals. You can pick up a pamphlet and simplified map of the shrine, both in English, just inside the grounds. ✉ *3–1–1 Kudankita, Chiyoda-ku* ☎ *03/3261–8326* 🚇 ¥800 ⏰ *Grounds daily, usually 9–9. Museum Mar.–Oct., daily 9–5; Nov.–Feb., daily 9–4:30* Ⓜ *Hanzō-mon and Shinjuku subway lines, Kudanshita Station (Exit 1).*

Akihabara & Jimbō-chō

Also known as Akihabara Electric Town, Akihabara is techno-geek heaven and is becoming a wacky fetish district where *otaku* (nerds) can indulge in Japanese anime computer game fantasies, hang out in kinky cafés, and buy anime comics. Visitors don't just come here to buy digital cameras, but to observe the bizarre subculture of this tech-savvy country.

If you're looking for something a little more cerebral, head to Jimbō-chō where family-run specialty bookstores of every genre abound including rare antiquarian and Japanese manga. The area is also home to Meiji University and Nihon Daigaku (university).

Numbers in the text correspond to numbers in the margin and on the Akihabara & Jimbō-chō map.

Orientation & Planning

ORIENTATION Akihabara is east of the Imperial Palace, right below Ueno and Asakusa. Akihabara Station is north of Tōkyō Station, on the JR Yamanote line, Hibiya line, and Tsukuba line. It is right below Asakusa and Ueno districts.

Just west of Akihabara, Jimbō-chō should be a short stopover either before or after an excursion to Akihabara. The best way to get there is by taxi, which costs about ¥800 to or from Akihabara station.

CLOSE UP

Etiquette & Behavior

PROPRIETY IS AN IMPORTANT part of Japanese society. Many Japanese expect foreigners to behave differently and are tolerant of faux pas, but they are pleasantly surprised when people acknowledge and observe their customs. The easiest way to ingratiate yourself with the Japanese is to take time to learn and respect Japanese ways.

Bow upon meeting someone.

Don't be offended if you're not invited to someone's home. Most entertaining is done in restaurants and bars.

Upon entering a home, **remove your shoes** and put on the slippers that are provided.

Oshibori is a small hot towel provided in Japanese restaurants. **This is to wipe your hands but not your face.** If you must use it on your face, wipe your face first, then your hands and never toss it on the table: fold or roll it up.

When eating with chopsticks, **do not use the part that has entered your mouth to pick up food.** Instead, use the end that you have been holding in your hand. Always rest chopsticks on the edge of the tray, bowl, or plate; sticking upright in your food is how rice is arranged at funerals.

Meishi **(business cards) are mandatory.** Remember to place those you have received in front of you during the meeting. It's also good to have one side of your business card printed in Japanese.

Be prompt for social and business occasions.

Stick to last names and use the honorific *-san* **after the name,** as in *Tanaka-san* (Mr. or Mrs. Tanaka). Also, respect the hierarchy, and as much as possible address yourself to the most senior person in the room.

Don't express anger or aggression. Losing one's temper is equated with losing face.

Stick to neutral subjects in conversation. The weather doesn't have to be your only topic, but you should take care not to be nosy.

It's not customary for Japanese businessmen to bring wives along. If you are traveling with your spouse, **do not assume that an invitation includes both of you.** If you must ask if it's acceptable to bring your spouse along, do so in a way that eliminates the need for a direct, personal refusal.

Don't pour your own drink, and always fill a companion's empty glass. If you would rather not drink, do not refuse a refill, but rather sip, keeping your glass at least half full.

Remember that because many Japanese women do not have careers, many Japanese businessmen still don't know how to interact with Western businesswomen. Be patient and, if the need arises, gently remind them that, professionally, you expect to be treated as any man would be.

Avoid too much eye contact when speaking. Direct eye contact is a show of spite and rudeness.

Refrain from speaking on your mobile phone in restaurants or public transportation.

Avoid physical contact. A slap on the back or hand on the shoulder would be uncomfortable for a Japanese person.

Do not blow your nose in public. Seriously.

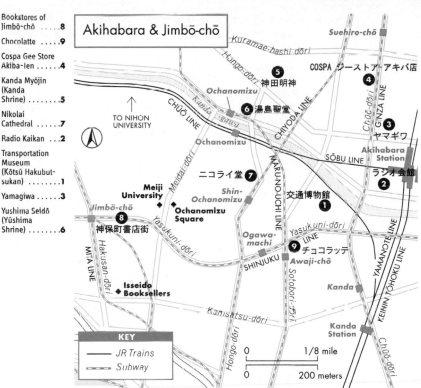

Akihabara & Jimbō-chō

PLANNING   Take the train to Akihabara Station on the JR Yamanote line. Akihabara is a 30- to 40-minute ride from most tourist hotels in Shinjuku or Minato-ku. This is a rougher part of Tōkyō, so mind your bags and wallets. Credit cards are accepted at all major electronics superstores, but bring enough cash to get around, because ATMs are difficult to find. Keep in mind that most stores in Akihabara do not open until 10 AM. Weekends draw hordes of shoppers, especially on Sunday, when the four central blocks of Chūō-dōri are closed to traffic and become a pedestrian mall. That's when the geeks come out.

What to See

8 **Bookstores of Jimbō-chō.** For the ultimate browse through art books, catalogs, scholarly monographs, secondhand paperbacks, and dictionaries in almost any language, the bookstores of Jimbō-chō are the places to go. A number of the antiquarian booksellers here carry rare typeset editions, wood-block-printed books of the Edo period, and individual prints. At shops like **Isseidō** and **Ohya Shōbō,** both open Monday–Saturday 10–6, it's still possible to find genuine 19th- and 20th-century prints—not always in the best condition—at affordable prices. Many of Japan's most prestigious publishing houses make their home in this area as well. The bookstores run for ½ km (¼ mi) on Yasukuni-dōri beginning at the Surugadai-shita intersection. ⊠ *Isseidō: 1–7–4 Kanda*

Jimbō-chō, Chiyoda-ku ☎ *03/3292–0071* ✉ *Ohya Shōbō: 1–1 Kanda Jimbō-chō, Chiyoda-ku, Jimbō-chō* ☎ *03/3291–0062* Ⓜ *Shinjuku and Mita subway lines, Jimbō-chō Station (Exit A7).*

❾ Chocolatte. This maid café is not exceptional by any standards, but it is a glimpse inside the otaku world. Beer, cocktails, tea, pasta, coffee, and desserts are served on the second floor and are cheap by Tōkyō standards. If you need to check in with the folks at home, be sure to stop by the relaxing Internet café on the third floor. This is definitely a one-of-a-kind Tōkyō experience. Coffee is ¥400 and pasta ¥800. ✉ *1–2–1 Suda-chō Kanda-ku* ☎ *03/3251–7755* ☉ *Weekdays 7:30–10, weekends 10–9.*

❹ Cospa Gee Store Akiba-Ten. Fans of anime will enjoy this zany Japanese costume shop experience. It's like no other in the world and is a good place to pick up an original costume for Halloween. ✉ *2F MN bldg., 3–15–5 Soto-Kanda, Chiyoda-ku* ☎ *03/3526–6877* ☉ *Daily 11–7.*

❺ Kanda Myōjin. (Kanda Shrine). You will never be able to see every shrine in the city and the ones in Akihabara are of minor interest, unless you are around for the Kanda festival. This shrine is said to have been founded in 730 in a village called Shibasaki, where the Ōte-machi financial district stands today. The shrine itself was destroyed in the Great Kantō Earthquake of 1923, and the present buildings are reproductions of the 1616 originals.

Some of the smaller buildings you see as you come up the steps and walk around the main hall contain the *mikoshi*—the portable shrines that are featured in one of Tōkyō's three great blowouts, the **Kanda Festival.** (The other two are the Sannō Festival of Hie Jinja in Nagata-chō and the Sanja Festival of Asakusa Shrine.) Kanda Myōjin is on Kuramae-bashi-dōri, about a five-minute walk west of the Suehiro-chō subway stop. ✉ *2–16–2 Soto Kanda, Chiyoda-ku* ☎ *03/3254–0753* Ⓜ *Ginza subway line, Suehiro-chō Station (Exit 3).*

❼ Nikolai Cathedral. It is curious that a Russian Orthodox Cathedral was built in Tōkyō's Electric Town, but Tōkyō Resurrection Cathedral is a great place to stop for a quick snapshot. Its common name, Nikolai Cathedral, was derived from its founder, St. Nikolai Kassatkin (1836–1912), a Russian missionary who came to Japan in 1861 and spent the rest of his life here. The building, planned by a Russian engineer and executed by a British ar-

SHRINE FESTIVAL

The shrine festival is a procession in which the gods, in their mikoshi, are passed through the streets to get a breath of fresh air. The mid-May Kanda Festival (www.kandamyoujin.or.jp) began in the early Edo period. Today the procession's lead floats move on carts, attended by the priests and officials of the shrine dressed in Heian-period (794–1185) costume. The mikoshi, some 70 of them, follow behind, bobbing and weaving, carried on the shoulders of the townspeople. Shrine festivals are a competitive form of worship: piety is a matter of who can shout the loudest, drink the most, and have the best time.

chitect, was completed in 1891. Heavily damaged in the earthquake of 1923, the cathedral was restored with a dome much more modest than the original. Even so, it endows this otherwise featureless part of the city with unexpected charm. ⊠ *1 1 Surugadai, Chiyoda-ku* ☎ *03/3291–1885* Ⓜ *Chiyoda subway line, Shin-Ochanomizu Station (Exit B1).*

❷ Radio Kaikan. Eight floors featuring a variety of vendors selling mini-spy cameras, cell phones disguised stun guns, anime comics, adult toys, gadgets, and odd-ball hobby supplies is a shopping mecca for otaku and visitors alike. Start browsing from the top floor and work your way down. ⊠ *1–15–16 Soto-Kanda, Chiyoda-ku* ⊘ *Daily 11–7.*

❶ Transportation Museum (Kōtsū Hakubutsukan). There seems to be a niche museum on almost every topic in Japan, including their transportation system. It's an activity for families in Akihabara district—displays explain the early development of the railway system and include a miniature layout of the rail services, as well as Japan's first airplane, which took off in 1903. To get here from JR Akihabara Station, cross the bridge on Chūō-dōri over the Kanda River, and turn right at the next corner. ⊠ *1–25 Kanda Sudachō, Chiyoda-ku* ☎ *03/3251–8481* 💴 *¥310* ⊘ *Tues.–Sun. 9:30–5* Ⓜ *JR Akihabara Station (Denki-gai Exit).*

❸ Yamagiwa. This discount superstore is for die-hard electronic shoppers. Entire floors of this discount electronics giant are devoted to computer hardware and software, fax machines, and copiers. Yamagiwa has a particularly good selection of lighting fixtures, most of them 220 volts, but the annex has export models of the most popular appliances and devices, plus an English-speaking staff to assist you with selections. You should be able to bargain prices down a bit—especially if you're buying more than one big-ticket item. ⊠ *1–5–10 Soto Kanda, Chiyoda-ku* ☎ *03/3253–5111* ⊘ *Weekdays 11–7:30, weekends 10:30–7:30* Ⓜ *JR Akihabara Station (Nishi-guchi/West Exit).*

❻ Yushima Seido (Yushima Shrine). Again, Akihabara shrines are of minor interest in comparison to the Asakusa Shrine, Yasukuni Shrine, and Meiji Jingu Shrine. If you have time to kill, then perhaps a short stroll through this shrine, which dates to 1632, will do. It started as a school for the study of Chinese Confucian classics and later became an academy for the ruling elite. In a sense, nothing has changed: in 1872 the new Meiji government established the country's first teacher-training institute here, and that, in turn, evolved into Tōkyō University—the graduates of which still make up much of the ruling elite. The hall looks like nothing else you're likely to see in Japan: painted black, weathered and somber, it could almost be in China. ⊠ *1–4–25 Yushima, Bunkyō-ku* ☎ *03/3251–4606* 💴 *Free* ⊘ *Apr.–Sept., Fri.–Wed. 10–5; Oct.–mid-Dec. and Jan.–Mar., Fri.–Wed. 10–4* Ⓜ *Marunouchi subway line, Ochanomizu Station (Exit B2).*

Ueno

JR Ueno Station is Tōkyō's version of the Gare du Nord: the gateway to and from Japan's northeast provinces. Since its completion in 1883, the station has served as a terminus in the great city migration by villagers pursuing a better life.

Ueno was a place of prominence long before the coming of the railroad. Since Ieyasu Tokugawa established his capital here in 1603, 36 subsidiary temples were erected surrounding the Main Hall, and the city of Edo itself expanded to the foot of the hill where Kan-ei-ji's main gate once stood.

The Meiji government turned Ueno Hill into one of the nation's first public parks. It served as the site of trade and industrial expositions and has a national museum, a library, a university of fine arts, and a zoo. The modernization of Ueno still continues, but the park is more than the sum of its museums. The Shōgitai failed to take everything with them: some of the most important buildings in the temple complex survived or were restored and should not be missed.

Numbers in the text correspond to numbers in the margin and on the Ueno map.

Orientation & Planning

ORIENTATION Ueno and Asakusa make up the historical enclave of Tōkyō. Traditional architecture and way of life are preserved here at the northeastern reaches of the city. Both areas can be explored in a single day, though if you have the time, it is also a good idea to devote an entire day to this place to fully appreciate its many museum exhibits and shrines.

PLANNING Exploring Ueno can be one excursion or two: an afternoon of cultural browsing or a full day of discoveries in one of the great centers of the city. ■ TIP→ **Avoid Monday, when most of the museums are closed.** Ueno out of doors is no fun at all in February or the rainy season (late June–mid-July); mid-August can be brutally hot and muggy. In April, the cherry blossoms of Ueno Kōen are glorious.

Ueno Station can be accessed by train on the Hibiya line, Ginza line, and JR Yamanote line (Kōen Entrance). Be sure to avoid morning (8–9) and evening rush hour (7–9) and bring plenty of cash for admission fees to museums and food for the day; there are no ATMs. To purchase souvenirs, museum stores accept all major credit cards.

What to See

⑭ Ame-ya Yoko-chō Market. Not much besides Ueno Station survived the bombings of World War II and anyone who could make it here from the countryside with rice and other small supplies of food could sell them at exorbitant black-market prices. Sugar was a commodity that couldn't be found at any price in postwar Tōkyō. Before long, there were hundreds of stalls in the black market selling various kinds of *ame* (confections), most of them made from sweet potatoes. These stalls gave the market its name Ame-ya Yoko-chō (often shortened to Ameyoko), which means "Confectioners' Alley." Shortly before the Korean War, the market was legalized, and soon the stalls were carrying watches, chocolate, ballpoint pens, blue jeans, and T-shirts that had somehow been "liberated" from American PXs. In years to come the merchants of Ameyoko diversified still further—to fine Swiss timepieces and fake designer luggage, cosmetics, jewelry, fresh fruit, and fish. The market became especially famous for the traditional prepared foods of the New Year, and during the last few days of December, as many as half a million people

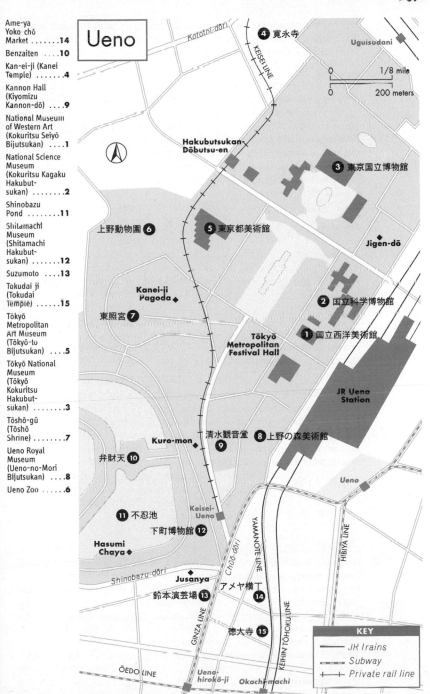

Ueno

Kototoi-dōri

KEISEI LINE

4 寛永寺

Uguisudani

0   1/8 mile
0   200 meters

**Hakubutsukan-
Dōbutsu-en**

3 東京国立博物館

上野動物園 **6**

5 東京都美術館

Jigen-dō

**Kanei-ji
Pagoda** ◆

東照宮 **7**

2 国立科学博物館

**Tōkyō
Metropolitan
Festival Hall**

1 国立西洋美術館

**JR Ueno
Station**

Kuro-mon

清水観音堂
9

8 上野の森美術館

弁財天 **10**

Ueno

11 不忍池

Keisei-
Ueno

下町博物館 **12**

**Hasumi
Chaya** ◆

YAMANOTE LINE

Chūō-dōri

HIBIYA LINE

Shinobazu-dōri

◆ **Jusanya**

アメヤ横丁

鈴本演芸場 **13**

14

KEIHIN TŌHOKU LINE

徳大寺 **15**

GINZA LINE

KEY	
——	JR Trains
-----	Subway
+—+—	Private rail line

ŌEDO LINE

**Ueno-
hirokō-ji**

Okachimachi

crowd into the narrow alleys under the railroad tracks to stock up for the holiday. ✉ *Ueno 4-chōme, Taitō-ku* ◷ *Most shops and stalls daily 10–7* Ⓜ *JR Ueno Station (Hirokō-ji Exit).*

⑩ **Benzaiten.** Perched in the middle of Shinobazu Pond, this shrine is dedicated to the goddess Benten, one of the Seven Gods of Good Luck that evolved from a combination of Indian, Chinese, and Japanese mythology. As matron goddess of the arts, she is depicted holding a lutelike musical instrument called a *biwa.* The shrine was destroyed in the bombings of 1945, but the present version, with its distinctive octagonal roof, is a faithful copy. You can rent rowboats and pedal boats at a nearby boathouse. ✉ *Taitō-ku* ☎ *03/3828–9502 for boathouse* 💴 *Rowboats ¥600 for 1 hr, pedal boats ¥600 for 30 min, swan boats ¥700 for 30 min* ◷ *Boathouse daily 10–5:30* Ⓜ *JR Ueno Station (Kōen-guchi/ Park Exit); Keisei private rail line, Keisei Ueno Station (Ikenohata Exit).*

④ **Kan-ei-ji** (Kanei Temple). In 1638 the second Tokugawa shōgun, Hidetada, commissioned Abbot Tenkai to build a temple on the hill known as Shinobu-ga-oka to defend his city from evil spirits. The only remarkable remaining structure here is the ornately carved vermilion gate to what was the mausoleum of Tsunayoshi, the fifth shōgun. Tsunayoshi is famous for his disastrous fiscal mismanagement and his *Shōrui Awaremi no Rei* (Edicts on Compassion for Living Things), which, among other things, made it a capital offense for a human being to kill a dog. ✉ *1–14–11 Ueno Sakuragi, Taitō-ku* ☎ *03/3821–1259* 💴 *Free, contributions welcome* ◷ *Daily 9–5* Ⓜ *JR Ueno Station (Kōen-guchi/ Park Exit), JR Uguisudani Station.*

⑨ **Kannon Hall** (Kiyomizu Kannon-dō). This National Treasure was a part of Abbot Tenkai's attempt to build a copy of Kyōto's magnificent Kiyomizu-dera in Ueno. His attempt was honorable, but failed to be as impressive as the original. The principal Buddhist image of worship here is the Senjū Kannon (Thousand-Armed Goddess of Mercy). Another figure, however, receives greater homage. This is the Kosodate Kannon, who is believed to answer the prayers of women having difficulty conceiving children. If their prayers are answered, they return to Kiyomizu and leave a doll, as both an offering of thanks and a prayer for the child's health. In a ceremony held every September 25, the dolls that have accumulated during the year are burned in a bonfire. ✉ *1–29 Ueno Kōen, Taitō-ku* ☎ *03/3821–4749* 💴 *Free* ◷ *Daily 7–5* Ⓜ *JR Ueno Station (Kōen-guchi/Park Exit).*

★ ① **National Museum of Western Art** (Kokuritsu Seiyō Bijutsukan). Along with castings from the original molds of Rodin's *Gate of Hell, The Burghers of Calais,* and *The Thinker,* the wealthy businessman Matsukata Kojiro (1865–1950) acquired some 850 paintings, sketches, and prints by such masters as Renoir, Monet, Gauguin, van Gogh, Delacroix, and Cézanne. Matsukata kept the collection in Europe, but he left it to Japan in his will. The French government sent the artwork to Japan after World War II, and the collection opened to the public in 1959 in a building designed by Swiss-born architect Le Corbusier. Since then, the museum has diversified a bit; more recent acquisitions include works by

Reubens, Tintoretto, El Greco, Max Ernst, and Jackson Pollock. The Seiyō is one of the best-organized, most pleasant museums to visit in Tōkyō. ⊠ *7–7 Ueno Kōen, Taitō-ku* ☎ *03/3828–5131* ⊕ *www.nmwa. go.jp* ⌨ *¥420; additional fee for special exhibits* ⊗ *Tues.–Thurs. and weekends 9:30–4:30, Fri. 9:30–7:30* Ⓜ *JR Ueno Station (Kōen-guchi/ Park Exit).*

🐾 ❷ **National Science Museum** (Kokuritsu Kagaku Hakubutsukan). The six buildings of the complex house everything from fossils to moon rocks—the 30-meter model of a blue whale perched at the museum's entrance is a huge hit with kids. And what self-respecting institution of its kind would be without a dinosaur collection? Look for them in the B2F Exhibition Hall, in the newest annex. Although the museum occasionally outdoes itself with special exhibits, it's pretty conventional, and provides relatively little in the way of hands-on learning experiences. Kids seem to like it anyway—but this is not a place to linger if your time is short. ⊠ *7–20 Ueno Kōen, Taitō-ku* ☎ *03/3822–0111* ⊕ *www.kahaku. go.jp* ⌨ *¥420; additional fees for special exhibits* ⊗ *Tues.–Thurs. 9–5, Fri. 9–8, weekends 9–6* Ⓜ *JR Ueno Station (Kōen-guchi/Park Exit).*

🐾 ⓫ **Shinobazu Pond.** Shinobazu was once an inlet of Tōkyō Bay. When the area was reclaimed, it became a freshwater pond. Abbot Tenkai had an island made in the middle of it, which he built for ⇨ **Benzaiten** the goddess of the arts. Later improvements included a causeway to the island, embankments, and even a racecourse (1884–93). Today the pond is in three sections. The first, with its famous lotus plants, is a wildlife sanctuary. Some 5,000 wild ducks migrate here from as far away as Siberia, sticking around from September to April. The second section, to the north, belongs to Ueno Zoo; the third, to the west, is a small lake for boating. ⊠ *Shinobazu-dōri, Taitō-ku* ⌨ *Free* ⊗ *Daily sunrise–sunset* Ⓜ *JR Ueno Station (Kōen-guchi/Park Exit); Keisei private rail line, Keisei-Ueno Station (Higashi-guchi/East Exit).*

NEED A BREAK?

Hasumi Chaya, a charming Japanese teahouse located on the bank of the pond, is only opened during the summer when the lotus flowers cover Shinobazu Pond. It is an open, airy café that offers perfect views of the flowers and serves lunch and dinner sets: for lunch, you can get a set of tea and snacks for ¥900; for dinner you can get a set of cold beer and snacks for ¥1,000. English is not spoken, but sets are displayed in plastic models at the entrance to make ordering easier. ⊠ *Shinobazu-dōri, Taitō-ku* ☎ *03/3833–0030 (Mon.–Sat.)* ⊗ *June 17–Aug. 31, daily noon–4, 5–9.* Ⓜ *Toei Oedo line, Ueno-Okachimachi Station (Exit 2), JR Yamanote line, Ueno Station (Exit 6).*

★ 🐾 ⓬ **Shitamachi Museum** (Shitamachi Hakubutsukan). Japanese society in the days of the Tokugawa shōguns was rigidly stratified. Some 80% of the city's land was allotted to the warrior class, temples, and shrines. The remaining 20%—between Ieyasu's fortifications on the west, and the Sumida-gawa on the east—was known as Shitamachi, literally, "downtown" or the "lower town" (as it expanded, Shitamachi came to include what today constitutes the Chūō, Taitō, Sumida, and Kōtō wards). It was here that the common, hardworking, free-spending folk, who made up more than half the population, lived. The Shitamachi Museum preserves and exhibits what remained of that way of life as late as 1940.

The two main displays on the first floor are a merchant house and a tenement, intact with all their furnishings. This is a hands-on museum: you can take your shoes off and step up into the rooms. On the second floor are displays of toys, tools, and utensils donated, in most cases, by people who had grown up with them and used them all their lives. There are also photographs and video documentaries of craftspeople at work. Occasionally various traditional skills are demonstrated, and you're welcome to take part. This don't-miss museum makes great use of its space, and there are even volunteer guides (available starting at 10) who speak passable English. ⊠ *2–1 Ueno Kōen, Taitō-ku* ☎ *03/3823–7451* ✆ *¥300* ⊙ *Tues.–Sun. 9:30–4:30* Ⓜ *JR Ueno Station (Kōen-guchi/Park Exit); Keisei private rail line, Keisei-Ueno Station (Higashi-guchi/East Exit).*

⓲ **Suzumoto.** Originally built around 1857 for Japanese comic monologue performances called rakugo, Suzumoto is the oldest theater operation of its kind in Tōkyō. The theater is on Chūō-dōri, a few blocks north of the Ginza Line's Ueno Hirokō-ji stop. ⊠ *2–7–12 Ueno, Taitō-ku* ☎ *03/ 3834–5906* ✆ *¥2,000* ⊙ *Continual performances daily 12:20–4:30 and 5:20–9:10* Ⓜ *Ginza subway line, Ueno Hirokō-ji Station (Exit 3).*

⓯ **Tokudai-ji** (Tokudai Temple). This is a curiosity in a neighborhood of curiosities: a temple on the second floor of a supermarket. Two deities are worshipped here. One is the bodhisattva Jizō, and the act of washing this statue is believed to safeguard your health. The other is of the Indian goddess Marici, a daughter of Brahma; she is believed to help worshippers overcome difficulties and succeed in business. ⊠ *4–6–2 Ueno, Taitō-ku* Ⓜ *JR Yamanote and Keihin-tōhoku lines, Okachi-machi Station (Higashi-guchi/East Exit) or Ueno Station (Hirokō-ji Exit).*

❺ **Tōkyō Metropolitan Art Museum** (Tōkyō-to Bijutsukan). The museum displays its own collection of modern Japanese art on the lower level and rents out the remaining two floors to various art institutes and organizations. At any given time, there can be at least five exhibits in the building: international exhibitions, work by local young painters, or new forms and materials in sculpture or modern calligraphy. ⊠ *8–36 Ueno Kōen, Taitō-ku* ☎ *03/3823–6921* ⊕ *www.tobikan.jp* ✆ *Permanent collection free; fees vary for other exhibits (usually ¥800–¥1,400)* ⊙ *Daily 9–5; closed 3rd Mon. of month* Ⓜ *JR Ueno Station (Kōen-guchi/Park Exit).*

❸ **Tōkyō National Museum** (Tōkyō Kokuritsu Hakubutsukan). This complex is one of the world's great repositories of East Asian art and archaeology. Altogether, the museum has some 87,000 objects in its permanent collection, with several thousand more on loan from shrines, temples, and private owners.

Fodor'sChoice
★

The Western-style building on the left (if you're standing at the main gate), with bronze cupolas, is the **Hyōkeikan.** Built in 1909, it was devoted to archaeological exhibits; aside from the occasional special exhibition, the building is closed today. The larger **Heiseikan,** behind the Hyōkeikan, was built to commemorate the wedding of crown prince

Naruhito in 1993 and now houses Japanese archaeological exhibits. The second floor is used for special exhibitions.

In 1878 the 7th-century Hōryū-ji (Hōryū Temple) in Nara presented 319 works of art in its possession—sculpture, scrolls, masks, and other objects—to the Imperial Household. These were transferred to the National Museum in 2000 and now reside in the **Hōryū-ji Hōmotsukan** (Gallery of Hōryū-ji Treasures), which was designed by Yoshio Taniguchi. There's a useful guide to the collection in English, and the exhibits are well explained. Don't miss the hall of carved wooden *gigaku* (Buddhist processional) masks.

The central building in the complex, the 1937 **Honkan,** houses Japanese art exclusively. The Honkan rotates the works on display several times during the year. It also hosts two special exhibitions annually (April and May or June, and October and November), which feature important collections from both Japanese and foreign museums. These, unfortunately, can be an ordeal to take in: the lighting in the Honkan is not particularly good, the explanations in English are sketchy at best, and the hordes of visitors make it impossible to linger over a work you especially want to study. The more attractive **Tōyōkan,** to the right of the Honkan, completed in 1968, is devoted to the art and antiquities of China, Korea, Southeast Asia, India, the Middle East, and Egypt. ✉ 13–9 *Ueno Kōen, Taito-ku* ☎ *03/3822–1111* ⊕ *www.tnm.go.jp* ✉ *Regular exhibits ¥420, special exhibits approx. ¥1,500* ☉ *Tues.–Sat. 9:30–5, Sun. 9:30–6* Ⓜ *JR Ueno Station (Kōen-guchi/Park Exit).*

★ ❼ **Tōshō-gū** (Tōshō Shrine). This shrine, built in 1627, is dedicated to Ieyasu, the first Tokugawa shōgun. It miraculously survived all major disasters that destroyed most of Tōkyō's historical structures—the fires, the 1868 revolt, the 1923 earthquake, the 1945 bombings—making it one of the only early-Edo-period buildings left in Tōkyō. The shrine and most of its art are designated National Treasures.

Two hundred *ishidorō* (stone lanterns) line the path from the stone entry arch to the shrine itself. One of them, just outside the arch to the left, is more than 18 feet high, called *obaketōrō* (ghost lantern). Legend has it that one night a samurai on guard duty slashed at a ghost (*obake*) that was believed to haunt the lantern. His sword was so strong, it left a nick in the stone, which can be seen today.

The first room inside the shrine is the **Hall of Worship;** the four paintings in gold on wooden panels are by Tan'yū, a member of the famous Kano family of artists, during the 15th century. Behind the Hall of Worship, connected by a passage called the *haiden,* is the sanctuary, where the spirit of Ieyasu is said to be enshrined.

JUNE JOYS

During the first week of June, a path along the Shinobazu Pond is lined on both sides with the stalls of the annual All-Japan Azalea Fair, a spectacular display of flowering bonsai shrubs and trees. Gardeners in *happi* (work coats) sell plants, seedlings, bonsai vessels, and ornamental stones.

CLOSE UP

A Day on the Green

TŌKYŌ HAS 21 GOLF COURSES within its borders and a vast selection beyond city limits. Though some are private, private doesn't always mean nonmembers can't play. Bear in mind that you may pay twice what you would on weekdays for weekends and holidays and just because facilities are open to tourists doesn't mean they have bilingual staff. Luckily, most have self-service systems or friendly staff. Looking for courses or to book tee-times? Visit the online guide *Golf in Japan* (⊕ www.golf-in-japan.com). Don't feel like lugging your clubs? Most courses rent sets.

IN TOWN

Showanomori Golf Course, Akishima-shi. Originally built during the U.S. occupation, this public course offers wide fairways, a remote control monorail cart, and some English-speaking staff, but no caddies. 🏌 *18 holes, Par 72* ☎ *042/543-1273* ⛳ *Fees ¥11,000–¥16,500; club rentals ¥2,000* Ⓜ *JR Ome Line, Akishima Station.*

Yomiuri Golf Club, Inagi-shi. Expect a strict dress code at this private club, which hosts the annual Salonpas World Ladies Championships in May. It's open to the public, you can rent golf carts, and caddies are a must, but don't count on a bilingual staff. 🏌 *18 holes, Par 72* ⛳ *Fees ¥26,850–¥40,000; club rentals ¥5,250* ☎ *044/966-1141* Ⓜ *Odakyu Line Semi Express, Shin Yurigaoka Station.*

Wakasu Golf Links, Koto-ku. If convenience is what you seek, this centrally located public course is for you. Reservations are required, but carts and caddies are optional. 🏌 *18 holes, Par 72* ⛳ *Fees ¥13,745–¥22,745; club rentals ¥5,250* ☎ *03/3647-9111* Ⓜ *Yūracuchō Line, Shin Kiba Station.*

OUT OF TOWN

Gotemba and Belle View Nagao golf clubs, Gotemba-shi, Shizuoka. Located at the foot of Mt. Fuji, these courses will challenge your skills and stamina, especially on foggy days when the mountain and your ball will be hard to see. 🏌 *18 holes, Par 72* ⛳ *Fees ¥5,000 for 9 holes; ¥19,000 for 18 holes; club rentals ¥3,675* ☎ *090-9892-4319* Ⓜ *Odakyu Asagiri Romance car from Shinjuku Station to Gotemba Station, 1 hour and 40 minutes.*

Kasumigaura Country Club, Kasumigaura, Ibaraki. Loaded with water hazards and sand traps, this course will make you curse and sweat. The spacious clubhouse, high-end restaurant, and other luxurious facilities will make up for it though. 🏌 *18 holes, Par 72* ⛳ *Fees ¥8,000–¥13,000; club rentals ¥4,200* ☎ *029-55-2311* Ⓜ *JR Fresh Hitachi No.48 from Ueno Station to Ishioka Station, 1 hour.*

ANOTHER OPTION

Can't make it to a course? Try one of the city's 78 driving ranges. Most are open from 11 AM to 7 or 8 PM and will rent you a club for around ¥200. The granddaddy of them all, **Lōttè Kasai Golf,** sports 300 bays and a 250-yard field. (✉ 2-4-2 Rinkai-cho, Edogawa-ku ☎ 03/5658-5600 ⛳ Ground-level bays ¥80 per ball; 3 stories up ¥60 per ball; prepaid cards ¥3,000–¥20,000 ☉ Daily 24 hours Ⓜ JR Keiyō line, Kasai-Rinkai-Koen Station). No weekday wait and an easy-to-navigate self-service system make **Meguro Gorufu-jō** another great choice. (✉ 5-6-22 Kami-Meguro, Meguro-ku ☎ 03/3713-2805 ⛳ Prepaid card for 50 balls ¥2,000 Ⓜ Hibiya Line, Naka-Megurō Station).

The real glories of Tōshō-gu are its so-called **Chinese Gate,** which you reach at the end of the building, and the fence on either side that has intricate carvings of birds, animals, fish, and shells of every description. The two long panels of the gate, with their dragons carved in relief, are attributed to Hidari Jingoro—a brilliant sculptor of the early Edo period whose real name is unknown (*hidari* means "left"; Jingoro was reportedly left-handed). The lifelike appearance of his dragons has inspired a legend. Every morning they were found mysteriously dripping with water and it was believed that the dragons were sneaking out at night to drink from the nearby Shinobazu Pond. Wire cages were put up to curtail this disquieting habit. ✉ *9–88 Ueno Kōen, Taitō-ku* ☎ *03/3822–3455* 🖃 *¥200* ✪ *Daily 9–5* Ⓜ *JR Ueno Station (Kōen-guchi/Park Exit).*

❽ **Ueno Royal Museum** (Ueno-no-Mori Bijutsukan). Although the museum has no permanent collection of its own, it makes its galleries available to various groups, primarily for modern painting and calligraphy. ✉ *1–2 Ueno Kōen, Taitō-ku* ☎ *03/3833–4191* 🖃 *Prices vary depending on exhibition, but usually ¥400–¥1500* ✪ *Sun.–Wed. 10–5, Thurs.–Sat. 10–7:30* Ⓜ *JR Ueno Station (Kōen-guchi/Park Exit).*

Ⓒ ❻ **Ueno Zoo** (Onshi Ueno Dōbutsuen). First built in 1882, this is Japan's first zoo. It houses more than 900 species including an exotic mix of gorillas, tigers, and the main attraction, Tong Tong and Ling Ling the Giant Pandas. The resident Giant Pandas are so popular that the Ueno JR station third-floor connection concourse has a panda statue, which is a landmark meeting spot. On a pleasant Sunday afternoon, you can expect upward of 20,000 Japanese clamoring to see the pandas, so be prepared for large crowds and lines. The process of the zoo's expansion somehow left within its confines the 120-foot, five-story Kan-ei-ji Pagoda, built in 1631 and rebuilt after a fire in 1639. ✉ *9–83 Ueno Kōen, Taitō-ku* ☎ *03/3828–5171* 🖃 *¥600. Free on Mar. 20, Apr. 29, and Oct. 1* ✪ *Tues.–Sun. 9:30–4* Ⓜ *JR Ueno Station (Kōen-guchi/Park Exit); Keisei private rail line, Ueno Station (Dōbutsu-en Exit).*

Asakusa

Historically, Asakusa has been the hub of the city's entertainment. The area blossomed when Ieyasu Tokugawa made Edo his capital, becoming the 14th-century city that never slept. For the next 300 years it was the wellspring of almost everything we associate with Japanese culture. In the mid-1600s, it became a pleasure quarter in its own right with stalls selling toys, souvenirs, and sweets; acrobats, jugglers and strolling musicians; and sake shops and teahouses—where the waitresses often provided more than tea. Then, in 1841, the Kabuki theaters moved to Asakusa. It was only for a short time, but that was enough to establish it as *the* entertainment quarter of the city—a reputation it held unchallenged until World War II, when most of the area was destroyed. Though it never fully recovered as an entertainment district, the area today is home to artisans and small entrepreneurs, children and grandmothers, hipsters, hucksters, and priests. If you have any time to spend in Tōkyō, make sure you devote at least a day to exploring Asakusa.

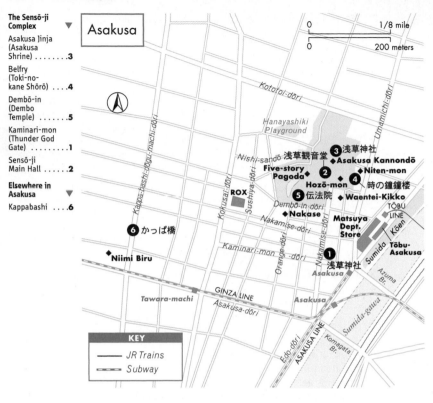

Numbers in the text correspond to numbers in the margin and on the Asakusa map.

Orientation & Planning

ORIENTATION   Rich in history and traditional culture, this northeastern area of Tōkyō should be top on your list of destinations. Asakusa is a border city ward that separates central Tōkyō from suburban areas beyond. It is a unique spiritual and commercial, tourist and residential area, where locals walk their dogs on the Askasua Jinja grounds or give offerings and pray at Kannon Temple. Life in this area is slow-paced and uncomplicated.

Asakusa is just east of Ueno and can be explored thoroughly in a half-day, whether you go straight from Ueno or on a separate excursion. Getting there by subway from Ueno Station (Ginza line, Ueno Station to Asakusa Station, ¥160) or taxi (approximately ¥900) is most convenient. Asakusa is the last stop (eastbound) on the Ginza subway line.

PLANNING   Unlike most of the other areas to explore on foot in Tōkyō, Sensō-ji is admirably compact. You can easily see the temple and environs in a morning. The garden at Dembō-in is worth a half hour. If you decide to include Kappabashi, allow yourself an hour more for the tour. Some of the shopping arcades in this area are covered, but Asakusa is essentially an outdoor experience. Be prepared for rain in June and heat and humidity in July and August.

Another way to get to Asakusa is by river bus ferry from Hinode Pier, which stops at the southwest corner of Sumida Kōen.

The Asakusa Tourist Information Center (Asakusa Bunka Kankō Center) is across the street from Kaminari-mon. A volunteer with some English knowledge is on duty daily 10–5.

The Sensō-ji Complex

Fodor's Choice
★
Dedicated to the goddess Kannon, the Sensō-ji Complex is the heart and soul of Asakusa. Come for its local and historical importance, its garden, its 17th-century Shintō shrine, and the wild Sanja Festival in May. ⊠ *2–3–1 Asakusa, Taitō-ku* ☎ *03/3842–0181* ⊡ *Free* ☾ *Temple grounds daily 6–sunset* Ⓜ *Ginza subway line, Asakusa Station (Exit 1/ Kaminari-mon Exit).*

❸ **Asakusa Jinja** (Asakusa Shrine). Several structures in the temple complex survived the bombings of 1945. The largest, to the right of the Main Hall, is this Shintō shrine to the Hikonuma brothers and their master, Naji-no-Nakamoto—the putative founders of Sensō ji. In Japan, Buddhism and Shintōism have coexisted comfortably since the former arrived from China in the 6th century. The shrine, built in 1649, is also known as Sanja Sama (Shrine of the Three Guardians). Near the entrance to Asakusa Shrine is another survivor of World War II: the east gate to the temple grounds, **Niten-mon,** built in 1618 for a shrine to Ieyasu Tokugawa and designated by the government as an Important Cultural Property. ⊠ *Taitō-ku.*

DID YOU KNOW?
Kuremutusu, the first drinking establishment in Japan to call itself a "bar," was started in Asakusa in 1880. It still stands today, under new ownership (of course) and a new name, **Waentei-Kikko.**

❹ **Belfry** (Toki-no-kane Shōrō). The tiny hillock Benten-yama, with its shrine to the goddess of good fortune, is the site of this 17th-century belfry. The bell here used to toll the hours for the people of the district, and it was said that you could hear it anywhere within a radius of some 6 km (4 mi). The bell still sounds at 6 AM every day, when the temple grounds open. It also rings on New Year's Eve—108 strokes in all, beginning just before midnight, to "ring out" the 108 sins and frailties of humankind and make a clean start for the coming year. Benten-yama and the belfry are at the beginning of the narrow street that parallels Nakamise-dōri. ⊠ *Taitō-ku.*

★ ❺ **Dembō-in** (Dembo Temple). Believed to have been made in the 17th century by Kōbori Enshū, the genius of Zen landscape design, the garden of Dembō-in, part of the living quarters of the abbot of Sensō-ji, is the best-kept secret in Asakusa. The garden of Dembō-in is usually empty and always utterly serene. Spring, when the wisteria blooms, is the ideal time to be here.

A sign in English on Dembō-in-dōri, about 150 yards west of the intersection with Nakamise-dōri, indicates the entrance, through the side door of a large wooden gate. ■ **TIP→** For permission to see the abbot's garden, you must apply at the temple administration building, between Hōzō-mon and the Five-Story Pagoda, in the far corner. ⊠ *Taitō-ku* ☎ *03/3842–0181 for reservations* 🎫 *Free* ☉ *Daily 9–4; may be closed if abbot has guests.*

┌──
│ **NEED A**
│ **BREAK?**

Nakase is a lovely retreat from the overbearing crowds at Asakusa Kannon. The building, which is 130 years old, lends to a truly authentic Japanese experience: food is served in lacquerware bento boxes and there's an interior garden and pond, which is filled with carp and goldfish. Across Orange-dōri from the red-brick Asakusa Public Hall, Nakase is expensive (lunch at the tables inside starts at ¥3,000; more elaborate meals by the garden start at ¥7,000), but the experience is worth it. ⊠ *1–39–13 Asakusa, Taitō-ku* ☎ *03/3841–4015* ▤ *No credit cards* ☉ *Open Wed.–Mon. 11–3, 5–8.*

❶ **Kaminari-mon** (Thunder God Gate). This is the proper Sensō-ji entrance, with its huge red-paper lantern hanging in the center—a landmark of Asakusa, and picture perfect. The original gate was destroyed by fire in 1865; the replica you see today was built after World War II. Two fearsome guardian gods are installed in the alcoves of Buddhist temple gates to ward off evil spirits. The Thunder God (Kaminari-no-Kami) is on the left with the Wind God (Kaze-no-Kami) on the right. ■ **TIP→** Looking to buy some of Tōkyō's most famous souvenirs? Stop at Tokiwa-dō, the shop on the west side of the gate for *kaminari okoshi* (thunder crackers), made of rice, millet, sugar, and beans.

Kaminari-mon also marks the southern extent of **Nakamise-dōri**, the Street of Inside Shops. The area from Kaminari-mon to the inner gate of the temple was once composed of stalls leased to the townspeople who cleaned and swept the temple grounds. This is now kitsch-souvenir central, so be prepared to buy a few key chains and snacks. ⊠ *Taitō-ku.*

❷ **Sensō-ji Main Hall.** The Main Hall and Five-Story Pagoda of Sensō-ji are both faithful copies of originals that burned down in 1945. During a time when most of the people of Asakusa were still rebuilding after the fire raids, it took 13 years to raise money for the restoration of their beloved Sensō-ji. To them, and those in the entertainment world, this is much more than a tourist attraction: Kabuki actors still come here before a new season of performances, and sumō wrestlers visit before a tournament to pay their respects. The large lanterns in the Main Hall were donated by the geisha associations of Asakusa and nearby Yanagibashi. Most Japanese stop at the huge bronze incense burner, in front of the Main Hall, to bathe their hands and faces in the smoke—it's a charm to ward off illnesses—before climbing the stairs to offer their prayers.

The Main Hall, about 115 feet long and 108 feet wide, is not an especially impressive work of architecture. Unlike in many other temples, part of the inside has a concrete floor, so you can come and go without removing your shoes. In this area hang Sensō-ji's chief claims to artistic importance: a collection of 18th- and 19th-century votive paintings on wood. Plaques of this kind, called *ema,* are still offered to the gods at shrines and temples, but they are commonly simpler and smaller. The worshipper buys a little tablet of wood with the picture already painted on one side and a prayer inscribed on the other. The temple owns more than 50 of these works, which were removed to safety in 1945 to escape the air raids. Only eight of them, depicting scenes from Japanese history and mythology, are on display. A catalog of the collection is on sale in the hall, but the text is in Japanese only.

Lighting is poor in the Main Hall, and the actual works are difficult to see. One thing that visitors cannot see at all is the holy image of Kannon itself, which supposedly lies buried somewhere deep under the temple. Not even the priests of Sensō-ji have ever seen it, and there is in fact no conclusive evidence that it actually exists.

Hōzō-mon, the gate to the temple courtyard, is also a repository for sutras (Buddhist texts) and other treasures of Sensō-ji. This gate, too, has its guardian gods; should either god decide to leave his post for a stroll, he can use the enormous pair of sandals hanging on the back wall—the gift of a Yamagata Prefecture village famous for its straw weaving. ⊠ *Taitō-ku.*

Elsewhere in Asakusa

★ ❻ **Kappabashi.** In the 19th century, according to local legend, a river ran through the present-day Kappabashi district. The surrounding area was poorly drained and was often flooded. A local shopkeeper began a project to improve the drainage, investing all his own money, but met with little success until a troupe of *kappa*—mischievous green water sprites— emerged from the river to help him. A more prosaic explanation for the name of the district points out that the lower-ranking retainers of the local lord used to earn extra money by making straw raincoats, also called *kappa,* that they spread to dry on the bridge.

Today, Kappabashi's more than 200 wholesale dealers sell everything from paper supplies and steam tables to their main attraction, plastic food. ⊠ *Nishi-Asakusa 1-chōme and 2-chōme, Taitō-ku* ☉ *Most shops daily 9–6* Ⓜ *Ginza subway line, Tawara-machi Station (Exit 1).*

Tsukiji & Shiodome

Although it's best known today as the site of the largest fish market in Asia, Tsukiji is also a reminder of the awesome disaster of the great fire of 1657. In the space of two days, it killed more than 100,000 people and leveled almost 70% of Ieyasu Tokugawa's new capital. Ieyasu was not a man to be discouraged by mere catastrophe, however; he took it as an opportunity to plan an even bigger and better city, one that would incorporate the marshes east of his castle. Tsukiji, in fact, means "reclaimed land," and a substantial block of land it was, laboriously drained and filled, from present-day Ginza to the bay.

To the west of Tsukiji lie Shiodome and Shimbashi. In the period after the Meiji Restoration, Shimbashi was one of the most famous geisha districts of the new capital. Its reputation as a pleasure quarter is even older. In the Edo period, when there was a network of canals and waterways here, it was the height of luxury to charter a covered boat (called a *yakata-bune*) from one of the Shimbashi boathouses for a cruise on the river; a local restaurant would cater the excursion, and a local geisha house would provide companionship. Almost nothing remains in Shimbashi to recall that golden age, but as its luster has faded, adjacent Shiodome has risen—literally—in its place as one of the most ambitious redevelopment projects of 21st-century Tōkyō.

Shiodome (literally "where the tide stops") was an area of saltwater flats on which in 1872 the Meiji government built the Tōkyō terminal—the original Shimbashi Station—on Japan's first railway line, which ran for 29 km (18 mi) to nearby Yokohama. The area eventually became Japan Rail's (JR) most notorious white elephant: a staggeringly valuable hunk of real estate, smack in the middle of the world's most expensive city that JR no longer needed and couldn't seem to sell. By 1997 the land was auctioned off. Among the buyers were Nippon Television and Dentsū, the largest advertising agency in Asia and the fourth largest in the world.

In 2002 Dentsū consolidated its scattered offices into the centerpiece of the Shiodome project: a 47-story tower and annex designed by Jean Nouvel. With the annex, known as the Caretta Shiodome, Dentsū aspired not just to a new corporate address, but an "investment in community": a complex of cultural facilities, shops, and restaurants that has turned Shiodome into one of the most fashionable places in the city to see and be seen. The 1,200-seat Dentsū Shiki Theater SEA has become one of Tōkyō's major venues for live performances; its resident repertory company regularly brings long-running Broadway hits like *Mamma Mia* to eager Japanese audiences.

Numbers in the text correspond to numbers in the margin and on the Tsukiji & Shiodome map.

Orientation & Planning

ORIENTATION Shiodome is the southeastern transportation hub of central Tōkyō and the area is easily accessed by public transport: JR Yurikome Line Shimbashi Station, Toei-Ōedo Shiodome Line Station, Toei-Asakusa Line Shimbashi Station, and Ginza Line Shimbashi Station. The connection station to the Yuikamome Monorail, a scenic ride that takes you to Odaiba in approximately 30 minutes, is also here. You can also get around quite easily on foot. There are sophisticated walkways in the sky that connect all the major buildings and subway and train stations.

Tsukiji, east of Shiodome, is a sushi-lover's dream. Perhaps getting up at 5 AM to eat fish at the market isn't your idea of breakfast, but this is definitely an excellent place to taste the freshest sushi on earth.

PLANNING Tsukiji has few places to spend time *in*; getting from point to point, however, can consume most of a morning. The backstreet shops will probably require no more than an hour. Allow yourself about an hour to explore the fish market; if fish in all its diversity holds a special fascination for you, take two hours. Remember that in order to see the fish auction in action, you need to get to the market before 6:30 AM; by 9 AM the business of the market is largely finished for the day.

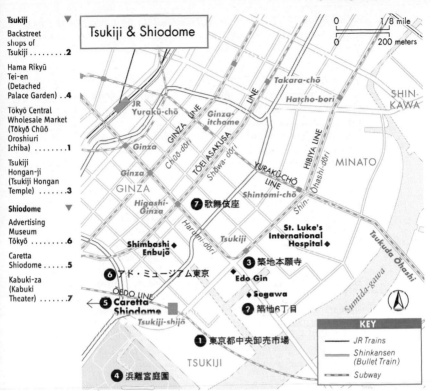

Take the subway to Tsukiji Station, which will always be the more dependable and cost-efficient option. To take the train there and back (depending on where you are staying), it will cost between ¥160 and ¥600. Sushi and sashimi will be cheaper here than in other parts of Tōkyō, with sushi sets at most sushi stalls costing between ¥1,000 to ¥2,100.

This part of the city can be brutally hot and muggy in August; during the O-bon holiday, in the middle of the month, Tsukiji is comparatively lifeless. Mid-April and early October are best for strolls in the Hama Rikyū Tei-en.

What to See

❻ Advertising Museum Tōkyō. ADMT puts the unique Japanese gift for graphic and commercial design into historical perspective, from the sponsored "placements" in 18th-century wood-block prints to the postmodern visions of fashion photographers and video directors. The museum is maintained by a foundation established in honor of Hideo Yoshida, fourth president of the mammoth Dentsū Advertising Company, and includes a digital library of some 130,000 entries on everything you ever wanted to know about hype. There are no explanatory panels in English—but this in itself is a test of how well the visual vocabulary of consumer media can communicate across cultures. ✉ *1–8–2 Higashi Shimbashi, Caretta*

Shiodome B1F–B2F, Chūo-ku ☎ *03/6218–2500* ⊕ *www.admt.jp* ✉ *Free* ⊙ *Tues.–Fri. 11–6:30, Sat. 11–4:30* Ⓜ *Ōedo subway line, Shiodome Station (Exit 7); JR (Shiodome Exit) and Asakusa and Ginza lines (Exit 4), Shimbashi Station.*

❷ Backstreet shops of Tsukiji. Tōkyō's markets provide a vital counterpoint to the museums and monuments of conventional sightseeing: they let you see how people really live in the city. If you have time for only one market, this is the one to see. The three square blocks between the Tōkyō Central Wholesale Market and Harumi-dōri have scores of fishmongers, shops, and restaurants. Stores sell pickles, tea, crackers and snacks, cutlery (what better place to pick up a professional sushi knife?), baskets, and kitchenware. Hole-in-the-wall sushi bars here have set menus ranging from ¥1,000 to ¥2,100; look for the plastic models of food in glass cases out front. The area includes the row of little counter restaurants, barely more than street stalls, under the arcade along the east side of Shin-Ōhashi-dōri, each with its specialty. If you haven't had breakfast by this point in your walk, stop at **Segawa** for *maguro donburi*—a bowl of fresh raw tuna slices served over rice and garnished with bits of dried seaweed (Segawa is in the middle of the arcade, but without any distinguishing features or English signage; your best bet is to ask someone.) ■ TIP➔ **Some 100 of the small retailers and restaurants in this area are members of the Tsukiji Meiten-kai (Association of Notable Shops), and promote themselves by selling illustrated maps of the area for ¥50; the maps are all in Japanese, but with proper frames they make great souvenirs.** ⊠ *Tsukiji 4-chōme, Chūo-ku* Ⓜ *Ōedo subway line, Tsukiji-shijō Station (Exit A1); Hibiya subway line, Tsukiji Station (Exit 1).*

❺ Caretta Shiodome. This 51-story skyscraper (⊙ 11–8) houses the offices of advertising giant Dentsu, as well as other offices, restaurants, and shopping. The sky restaurants on the buildings' top floors have scenic views of Tōkyō Bay and are a good place to have lunch or dinner. Try Bice Tōkyō (☎ 03/5537–1926 ⊙ Weekdays lunch 11–5, dinner 5:30–9:30, weekend dinner starts at 5:30) on the 47th floor, which serves a European set lunch ¥4,000 and dinner ¥12,000 menus. ⊠ *1–8–1 Higashi Shimbashi Minato-ku.*

★ ❹ Hama Rikyū Tei-en (Detached Palace Garden). Like a tiny sanctuary of Japanese tradition and nature that's surrounded by towering glass buildings, this garden is worth a visit. The land here was originally owned by the Owari branch of the Tokugawa family from Nagoya, and it extended to part of what is now the fish market. The garden became a public park in 1945, although a good portion of it is fenced off as a nature preserve. None of the original buildings have survived, but on the island in the large pond is a reproduction of the pavilion where former U.S. president Ulysses S. Grant and Mrs. Grant had an audience with the emperor Meiji in 1879. The building can now be rented for parties. The path to the left as you enter the garden leads to the "river bus" ferry landing, from which you can leave this excursion and begin another: up the Sumida-gawa to Asakusa. ⚠ **Note that you must pay the admission to the garden even if you're just using the ferry.** ⊠ *1–1 Hamarikyū–Teien,*

Chūō-ku ☎ *03/3541-0200* 🎫 *¥300* ☉ *Daily 9–4:30* Ⓜ *Ōedo subway line, Shiodome Station (Exit 8).*

★ ❼ **Kabuki-za** (Kabuki Theater). If you want to see what all of the hype is about, this is the place to see a Kabuki show. English Earphone Guides are available for a small fee and provide explanations and comments in English about the performance. Reservations by phone are recommended. ✉ *4–12–15 Ginza, Chūō-ku* ☎ *03/5565–6000* 🎫 *¥2,500 to ¥17,000* ☉ *Box office open daily 10–4* ⊕ *www.shochiku.co.jp/play/kabukiza/theater* Ⓜ *Hibiya subway line, Higashi-Ginza Station (Exit 3).*

NEED A BREAK?

Edo-Gin, one of the area's older sushi bars, founded in 1924, is legendary for its portions—slices of raw fish that almost hide the balls of rice on which they sit. The set menu at lunch is a certifiable *bāgen* (bargain) at ¥1,050, and dinner sushi dinner sets are only ¥2,800, including beer or sake. Walk southwest on Shin-Ōhashi-dōri from its intersection with Harumi-dōri. Take the first right and look for Edo-Gin just past the next corner, on the left. ✉ *4–5–1 Tsukiji, Chūō-ku* ☎ *03/3543-4401* 🎟 *AE, MC, V* ☉ *Closed early Jan.* Ⓜ *Hibiya subway line, Tsukiji Station (Exit 1); Ōedo subway line, Tsukiji-shijō Station (Exit A1).*

★ ❶ **Tokyo Central Wholesale Market** (Tōkyō Chūō Oroshiuri Ichiba). The city's fish market used to be farther uptown, in Nihombashi. It was moved to Tsukiji after the Great Kantō Earthquake of 1923, and it occupies the site of what was once Japan's first naval training academy. Today the market sprawls over some 54 acres of reclaimed land and employs approximately 15,000 people, making it the largest fish market in the world. Its warren of buildings houses about 1,200 wholesale shops, supplying 90% of the seafood consumed in Tōkyō every day—some 2,400 tons of it. Most of the seafood sold in Tsukiji comes in by truck, arriving through the night from fishing ports all over the country. ✉ *5–2–1 Tsukiji, Chūō-ku* ☎ *03/3542–1111* ⊕ *www.shijou.metro.Tōkyō.jp* 🎫 *Free* ☉ *Business hrs Mon.–Sat. (except 2nd and 4th Wed. of month)* 5 AM–3 PM Ⓜ *Ōedo subway line, Tsukiji-shijō Station (Exit A1); Hibiya subway line, Tsukiji Station (Exit 1).*

❸ **Tsukiji Hongan-ji** (Tsukiji Hongan Temple). Disaster seemed to follow this temple, the main branch in Tōkyō of Kyōto's Nishi Hongan-ji, since it was first located here in 1657: it was destroyed at least five times, and reconstruction in wood was finally abandoned after the Great Kantō Earthquake of 1923. The present stone building dates from 1935. The evocations of classical Hindu architecture in the temple's domes and ornaments were designer Chūta Ito's homage to India as the cradle of Buddhism. But with stained-glass windows and a pipe organ as well, the building is nothing if not eclectic. ✉ *3–15–1 Tsukiji, Chūō-ku* ☎ *03/3541–1131* 🎫 *Free* ☉ *Daily 6 AM–4 PM* Ⓜ *Hibiya subway line, Tsukiji Station (Exit 1).*

Nihombashi, Ginza & Yūraku-chō

Tōkyō is a city of many centers. The municipal administrative center is in Shinjuku. The national government center is in Kasumigaseki. Ni-

Fishmongers Wanted

WHY GO TO THE TSUKIJI FISH market? Quite simply, because of how the fish is sold–auction. The catch–more than 100 varieties of fish in all, including whole frozen tuna, Styrofoam cases of shrimp and squid, and crates of crabs–is laid out in the long covered area between the river and the main building. Then the bidding begins. Only members of the wholesalers' association can take part. Wearing license numbers fastened to the front of their caps, they register their bids in a kind of sign language, shouting to draw the attention of the auctioneer and making furious combinations in the air with their fingers. The auctioneer keeps the action moving in a hoarse croak that sounds like no known language, and spot quotations change too fast for ordinary mortals to follow.

Different fish are auctioned off at different times and locations, and by 6:30 AM or so, this part of the day's business is over, and the wholesalers fetch their purchases back into the market in barrows. Restaurant owners and retailers arrive about 7, making the rounds of favorite suppliers for their requirements. Chaos seems to reign, but everybody here knows everybody else, and they all have it down to a system.

⚠ **The 52,000 or so buyers, wholesalers, and shippers who work at the market may be a lot more receptive to casual visitors than they were in the past, but they are not running a tourist attraction.** They're in the fish business, moving more than 600,000 tons of it a year to retailers and restaurants all over the city, and this is their busiest time of day. The cheerful banter they use with each other can turn snappish if you get in their way. Also bear in mind that you are not allowed to take photographs while the auctions are under way (flashes are a distraction). The market is kept spotlessly clean, which means the water hoses are running all the time. Boots are helpful, but if you don't want to carry them, bring a pair of heavy-duty trash bags to slip over your shoes and secure them above your ankles with rubber bands.

hombashi is the center of banking and finance and Ginza is the center of commerce.

When Ieyasu Tokugawa had the first bridge constructed at Nihombashi, he designated it the starting point for the five great roads leading out of his city, the point from which all distances were to be measured. His decree is still in force: the black pole on the present bridge, erected in 1911, is the Zero Kilometer marker for all the national highways and is considered the true center of Tōkyō.

The early millionaires of Edo built their homes in the Nihombashi area. Some, like the legendary timber magnate Bunzaemon Kinokuniya, spent everything they made in the pleasure quarters of Yoshiwara and died penniless. Others founded the great trading houses of today—Mitsui, Mitsubishi, Sumitomo—which still have warehouses nearby.

When Japan's first corporations were created and the Meiji government developed a modern system of capital formation, the Tōkyō Stock Exchange (Shōken Torihikijo) was established on the west bank of the Nihombashi-gawa (Nihombashi River). The home offices of most of the country's major securities companies are only a stone's throw from the exchange.

In the Edo period there were three types of currency in circulation: gold, silver, and copper. Ieyasu Tokugawa started minting his own silver coins in 1598 in his home province of Suruga, even before he became shōgun. In 1601 he established a gold mint; the building was only a few hundred yards from Nihombashi, on the site of what is now the Bank of Japan. In 1612 he relocated the Suruga plant to a patch of reclaimed land west of his castle. The area soon came to be known informally as Ginza (Silver Mint).

Currency values fluctuated during this time and eventually businesses fell under the control of a few large merchant houses. One of the most successful of these merchants was a man named Takatoshi Mitsui, who by the end of the 17th century created a commercial empire—in retailing, banking, and trading—known today as the Mitsui Group. Not far from the site of Echigo-ya stands its direct descendant: Mitsukoshi department store.

The district called Yūraku-chō—the Pleasure (*yūraku*) Quarter (*cho*) lies west of Ginza's Sukiya-bashi, stretching from Sotobori-dōri to Hibiya Kōen and the Outer Garden of the Imperial Palace. The "pleasures" associated with this district in the early postwar period stemmed from a number of the buildings that survived the air raids of 1945 and requisitioned by the Allied forces. Yūraku-chō quickly became the haunt of the so-called *pan-pan* women, who kept the GIs company. Because it was so close to the military post exchange in Ginza, the area under the railroad tracks became one of the city's largest black markets. Later, the black market gave way to clusters of cheap restaurants, most of them little more than a counter and a few stools, serving *yakitori* (skewered grilled chicken) and beer. Office workers on meager budgets and journalists from the nearby *Mainichi, Asahi,* and *Yomiuri* newspaper headquarters would gather here at night. Yūraku-chō-under-the-tracks was smoky, loud, and friendly—a kind of open-air substitute for the local taproom. The area has long since become upscale, and no more than a handful of the yakitori stalls remain.

Numbers in the text correspond to numbers in the margin and on the Nihombashi, Ginza & Yūraku-chō map.

Orientation & Planning

ORIENTATION   The combined areas of Yūraku-chō, Ginza, and Nihombashi are located beside the Imperial Palace district, to the southeast side of central Tōkyō. Yūraku-chō lies west of Ginza's Sukiya-bashi, stretching from Sotobori-dōri to Hibiya Kōen and the Outer Garden of the Imperial Palace.

PLANNING   There's something about this part of Tōkyō—the traffic, the number of people, the way it urges you to keep moving—that can make you feel you've covered a lot more ground than you really have. Attack this area early in the morning but avoid rush hour (8–9) if you plan on taking the subway. None of the area's sites, with the possible exception of the

Bridgestone and Idemitsu museums, should take you more than 45 minutes. The time you spend shopping, of course, is up to you. In summer make a point of starting early or in the late afternoon, because by midday the heat and humidity can be brutal. Make sure to carry bottled water. On weekend afternoons (October–March, Saturday 3–5 and Sunday noon–5; April–September, Saturday 2–6 and Sunday noon–6), Chūō-dōri is closed to traffic from Shimbashi all the way to Kyō-bashi and becomes a pedestrian mall with tables and chairs set out along the street. Keep in mind that some of the museums and other sights in the area close on Sunday.

What to See

❶ Bank of Japan (Nihon Ginkō). The older part of the Bank of Japan is the work of Tatsuno Kingo, who also designed Tōkyō Station. Completed in 1896, on the site of the old Edo-period gold mint, the bank is one of the city's few surviving Meiji-era Western buildings. The annex building houses the **Currency Museum,** a historical collection of rare gold and silver coins from Japan and other East Asian countries. There's little English information here, but the setting of muted lighting and plush red carpets evokes the days when the only kind of money around was heavy, shiny, and made of precious metals. ⊠ *2–1–1 Nihombashi Hongoku-chō, Chūō-ku* ☎ *03/3279–1111 bank, 03/3277–3037 museum* ⊕ *www.boj.or.jp* 🎫 *Free* ⊘ *Tues.–Sun. 9:30–4:30* Ⓜ *Ginza (Exit A5) and Hanzō-mon (Exit B1) subway lines, Mitsukoshi-mae Station.*

❻ Bridgestone Museum of Art (Burijisuton Bijutsukan). This is one of Japan's best private collections of French impressionist art and sculpture and of post-Meiji Japanese painting in Western styles by such artists as Shigeru Aoki and Tsuguji Fujita. The collection, assembled by Bridgestone Tire Company founder Shōjiro Ishibashi, also includes work by Rembrandt, Picasso, Utrillo, and Modigliani. The small gallery devoted to ancient art has a breathtaking Egyptian cat sculpture dating to between 950 and 660 BC. The Bridgestone also puts on major exhibits from private collections and museums abroad. ⊠ *1–10–1 Kyō-bashi, Chūō-ku* ☎ *03/3563–0241* ⊕ *www.bridgestone-museum.gr.jp* 🎫 *¥800* ⊘ *Tues.–Sat. 10–8, Sun. 10–6 (entrance up to 30 min before closing)* Ⓜ *Ginza subway line, Kyō-bashi Station (Meijiya Exit) or Nihombashi Station (Takashimaya Exit).*

⓫ Dai-ichi Mutual Life Insurance Company Building. Built like a fortress, this edifice survived World War II virtually intact and was taken over by the Supreme Command of the Allied powers. From his office here, General Douglas MacArthur directed the affairs of Japan from 1945 to 1951. The room is kept exactly as it was then. Individuals and small groups can visit without appointment; you need only to sign in at the reception desk in the lobby. ⊠ *1–13–1 Yūraku-chō, Chiyoda-ku* ☎ *03/ 3216–1211* 🎫 *Free* ⊘ *Weekdays 10–4:30* Ⓜ *Hibiya subway line, Hibiya Station (Exit B1).*

❼ Ginza. With more history as a shopping district than trendier Omotesando and Harajuku, Ginza is where high end shopping first took root in Japan and now it's where Japanese "ladies who lunch" shop. But this area didn't always have the cachet of wealth and style. In fact, it

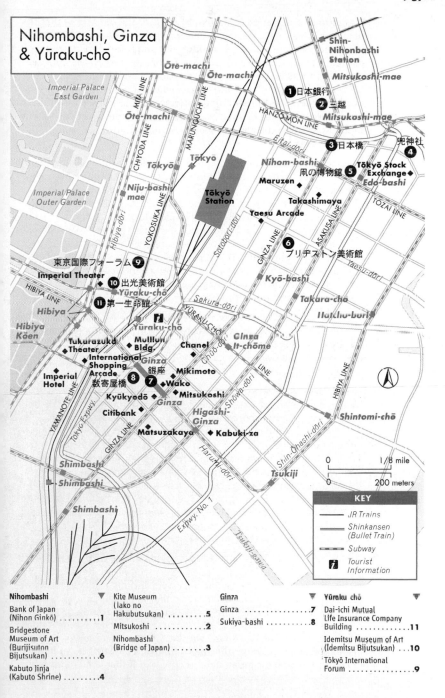

Nihombashi, Ginza & Yūraku-chō

wasn't until a fire in 1872 destroyed most of the old houses that the area was rebuilt as a Western quarter. It had two-story brick houses with balconies, the nation's first sidewalks and horse-drawn streetcars, gaslights, and, later, telephone poles. Before the turn of the 20th century, Ginza was home to the great mercantile establishments that still define its character. The **Wako** department store, for example, on the northwest corner of the 4-chōme intersection, established itself here as Hattori, purveyors of clocks and watches. The clock on the present building was first installed in the Hattori clock tower, a Ginza landmark, in 1894.

Many of the nearby shops have lineages almost as old, or older, than Wako's. A few steps north of the intersection, on Chūō-dōri, **Mikimoto** sells the famous cultured pearls first developed by Kōkichi Mikimoto in 1883. His first shop in Tōkyō dates to 1899. South of the intersection, next door to the Sanai Building, **Kyūkyodō** carries a variety of hand-made Japanese papers and traditional stationary goods. Kyūkyodō has been in business since 1663 and on Ginza since 1880. Across the street and one block south is the **Matsuzakaya** department store, which began as a kimono shop in Nagoya in 1611. And connected to the Ginza line Ginza Station is the **Mistukoshi** department store, where the basement food markets are a real attraction.

There's even a name for browsing this area: Gin-bura, or "Ginza wandering." The best times to wander here are Saturday afternoons and Sunday from noon to 5 or 6 (depending on the season), when Chūō-dōri is closed to traffic between Shimbashi and Kyō-bashi. ✉ *Chūō-ku* Ⓜ *Ginza and Hibiya subway lines, Ginza Station.*

★ ⑩ **Idemitsu Museum of Art** (Idemitsu Bijutsukan). The strength of the collection in these four spacious, well-designed rooms lies in the Tang- and Song-dynasty Chinese porcelain and in the Japanese ceramics—including works by Nonomura Ninsei and Ogata Kenzan. On display are masterpieces of Old Seto, Oribe, Old Kutani, Karatsu, and Kakiemon ware. The museum also houses outstanding examples of Zen painting and calligraphy, wood-block prints, and genre paintings of the Edo period. Of special interest to scholars is the resource collection of shards from virtually every pottery-making culture of the ancient world. The museum is on the ninth floor of the Teikoku Gekijō building. ✉ *3–1–1 Marunouchi, Chiyoda-ku* ☎ *03/3213–9402* 💰 *¥800* ⊙ *Tues.–Sun. 10–4:30* Ⓜ *Yūraku-chō subway line, Yūraku-chō Station (Exit A1).*

④ **Kabuto Jinja** (Kabuto Shrine). This is a minor shrine, so if you have had your fill of shrine-viewing, this one can be overlooked. But like the Nihombashi itself, it is another bit of history lurking in the shadows of the expressway. Legend has it that a noble warrior of the 11th century, who had been sent by the Imperial Court in Kyōto to subdue the barbarians of the north, stopped here and prayed for assistance. His expedition was successful, and on the way back he buried a *kabuto*, a golden helmet, on this spot as an offering of thanks. Few Japanese are aware of this legend, and the monument of choice in Kabuto-chō today is the nearby Tōkyō Stock Exchange. ⊠ 1–8 Kabuto-chō, Nihombashi, Chūō-ku Ⓜ Tōzai subway line, Kayaba-chō Station (Exit 10).

❺ **Kite Museum** (Tako no Hakubutsukan). Kite flying is an old tradition in Japan. The collection here includes examples of every shape and variety from all over the country, hand-painted in brilliant colors with figures of birds, geometric patterns, and motifs from Chinese and Japanese mythology. You can call ahead to arrange a kite-making workshop (in Japanese) for groups of children. ⊠ 1–12–10 Nihombashi, Chūō-ku ☎ 03/3271–2465 ⊕ www.tako.gr.jp ☜ ¥210 ⊙ Mon.–Sat. 11–5 Ⓜ Tōzai subway line, Nihombashi Station (Exit C5).

★ ❷ **Mitsukoshi.** Takatoshi Mitsui made his fortune by revolutionizing the retail system for kimono fabrics. The emergence of Mitsukoshi as Tōkyō's first *depāto* (department store), also called *hyakkaten* (hundred-kinds-of-goods emporium), actually dates to 1908, with the construction of a three-story Western building modeled on Harrods of London. This was replaced in 1914 by a five-story structure with Japan's first escalator. The present flagship store is vintage 1935. Even if you don't plan to shop, this branch merits a visit. Two bronze lions, modeled on those at London's Trafalgar Square, flank the main entrance and serve as one of Tōkyō's best known meeting places. Inside, a sublime statue of Magokoro, a Japanese goddess of sincerity, rises four stories through the store's central atrium. Check out the basement floors for a taste of the food market culture of Japanese department stores and grab a quick meal-to-go while you're there. ⊠ 1–4–1 Nihombashi Muro-machi, Chūō-ku ☎ 03/3241–3311 ⊙ Daily 10–7:30 Ⓜ Ginza and Hanzō-mon subway lines, Mitsukoshi-mae Station (Exits A3 and A5).

❸ **Nihombashi** (Bridge of Japan). Why the expressway *had* to be routed directly over this lovely old landmark back in 1962 is one of the mysteries of Tōkyō and its city planning—or lack thereof. There were protests and petitions, but they had no effect. At that time, Tōkyō had only two years left to prepare for the Olympics, and the traffic congestion was out of control. So the bridge, originally built in 1603, with its graceful double arch, ornate lamps, and bronze Chinese lions and unicorns, was doomed to bear the perpetual rumble of trucks overhead—its claims overruled by concrete ramps and pillars. ⊠ Chūō-ku Ⓜ Tōzai and Ginza subway lines, Nihombashi Station (Exits B5 and B6); Ginza and Hanzō-mon subway lines, Mitsukoshi-mae Station (Exits B5 and B6).

❽ **Sukiya-bashi.** The side streets of the Sukiya-bashi area are full of art galleries. A few, like the venerable **Nichidō** (5–3–16 Ginza), **Gekkōso** (7–2–8 Ginza), **Yoseidō** (5–5–15 Ginza), and **Kabuto-ya** (8–8–7 Ginza), actually function as dealers, representing particular artists, as well as acquiring and selling art. The majority, however, are rental spaces. Artists or groups pay for the gallery by the week, publicize their shows themselves, and in some cases even hang their own work. You might suspect, and with good reason, that some of these shows are vanity exhibitions by amateurs with money to spare, even in a prestigious venue like Ginza; thankfully, that's not always the case. ⊠ Chiyoda-ku Ⓜ Ginza, Hibiya, and Marunouchi subway lines, Ginza Station (Exit C4).

★ ❾ **Tōkyō International Forum.** This postmodern masterpiece, the work of Uruguay-born American architect Raphael Viñoly, is the first major convention and art center of its kind in Tōkyō. Viñoly's design was selected in a 1989 competition that drew nearly 400 entries from 50 countries. The plaza of the Forum is that rarest of Tōkyō rarities: civilized open space. There's a long central courtyard with comfortable benches shaded by trees. Freestanding sculpture, triumphant architecture, and people strolling—actually *strolling*—are all here. The Forum itself is actually two buildings. On the east side of the plaza is Glass Hall, the main exhibition space, and the west building has six halls for international conferences, exhibitions, receptions, and concert performances. ☒ *3–5–1 Marunouchi, Chiyoda-ku* ☏ *03/5221–9000* ⊕ *www.t-i-forum.co.jp* Ⓜ *Yūraku-chō subway line, Yūraku-chō Station (Exit A-4B).*

NEED A BREAK? Amid all of Tōkyō's bustle and crush, you actually can catch your breath in the Tōkyō International Forum—cafés and Italian, Japanese, and French restaurants are located throughout the complex. Maps are available, so pick and choose. There are also ATM machines on the third floor. A reasonably priced and delicious Kyoto-style vegetarian restaurant to try is Tsuruhan. Lunch sets start at ¥1,000 and dinner ¥3,000. ☒ *3-5-1 Marunouchi, Chiyoda-ku* ☏ *03/3214-2260* ⊕ *www.t-i-forum.co.jp.*

Aoyama, Harajuku & Shibuya

As late as 1960, this was as unlikely a candidate as any area in Tōkyō to develop into the chic capital of Tōkyō. Between Meiji shrine and the Aoyama Cemetery to the east, the area was so boring that the municipal government zoned a chunk of it for low-cost public housing. Another chunk, called Washington Heights, was being used by U.S. occupation forces who spent their money elsewhere. The few young Japanese people in Harajuku and Aoyama were either hanging around Washington Heights to practice their English or attending the Methodist-founded Aoyama Gakuin (Aoyama University)—seeking entertainment farther south in Shibuya.

When Tōkyō won its bid to host the 1964 Olympics, Washington Heights was turned over to the city for the construction of Olympic Village. Aoyama-dōri, the avenue through the center of the area, was renovated and the Ginze Line subway and Hanzō-mon Line were built under it. Suddenly, Aoyama became attractive for its Western-style fashion houses, boutiques, and design studios, and it became a hip neighborhood. Today, most of the low-cost public housing along Omotesandō are long gone, and in their place are the glass-and-marble emporia of *the* preeminent fashion houses of Europe: Louis Vuitton, Chanel, Armani, and Prada. Superb shops, restaurants, and amusements in this area target a population of university students, wealthy socialites, young professionals, and people who like "to see and be seen."

Numbers in the text correspond to numbers in the margin and on the Aoyama, Harajuku & Shibuya map.

Orientation & Planning

ORIENTATION   Aoyama, Omotestando, and Harajuku, west of the Imperial Palace and just north of Roppongi, are the trendsetting areas of youth culture and fashion. Omotestando and Aoyama contain a laundry list of European fashion houses' flagship stores. Harajuku is a bohemian and younger fashion district that inspired Gwen Stefani to write a hit song, "Harajuku Girls," and create a "Harajuku Lovers" fashion line.

Just north of Omotesando and Aoyama, in front of the Harajuku JR Station, is Harajuku's Meji Jingu Shrine, which is a famous hangout for dressed-up teens and crowds of onlookers.

Because it is the entertainment district for Japanese youth, Shibuya is not as clean or sophisticated as Tōkyō's others neighborhoods. Rarely will you see an elderly person on the streets. Shops, cheap restaurants, karaoke lounges, bars, theaters, concert halls, and nightclubs are everywhere. With Shibuya station connecting thousands of passengers from the suburbs into the heart of the city, it is the western frontier of central Tōkyō, and the last stop of the Ginza Line.

PLANNING   Trying to explore Aoyama and Harajuku together will take a long time because there is a lot of area to cover. Ideally, you should devote an entire day here, giving yourself plenty of time to browse in shops. You can see Meji Shrine in less than an hour; the Nezu Institute warrants a leisurely two-hour visit. Spring is the best time of year for the Meiji Jingu Inner Garden. Just like everywhere else in this city, June's rainy season is horrendous, and the humid heat of midsummer can quickly drain your energy and add hours to the time you need to comfortably explore. The best way to enjoy this area is to explore the tiny shops, restaurants, and cafés in the back streets.

Shibuya seems chaotic and intimidating at first, but it is fairly compact, so you can easily cover it in about two hours. Be prepared for huge crowds and some shoulder bumping. Shibuya crossing is one of the busiest in the world and at one light change, hundreds rush to reach the other side. Unless you switch into shopping mode, no particular stop along the way should occupy you for more than a half hour; allow a full hour for the NHK Broadcasting Center, however, if you decide to take the guided tour. Spring is the best time of year for Yoyogi Kōen. The area will be crowded, but Sunday affords the best opportunity to observe Japan's younger generation on display. Two subway lines, three private railways, the JR Yamanote Line, and two bus terminals move about a million people a day through Shibuya.

What to See

🔟 **Bunka-mura.** One of the liveliest venues in Tōkyō for music and art, this six-story theater-and-gallery complex, a venture of the next-door Tōkyū department store, hosts everything from science-fiction film festivals and opera to ballet and big bands. The museum on the lower-level Garden Floor often has well-planned, interesting exhibits on loan from major European museums. ⊠ *2–24–1 Dōgen-zaka, Shibuya-ku* ☎ *03/ 3477–9111, 03/3477–9999 ticket center* 📧 *Theater admission and ex-*

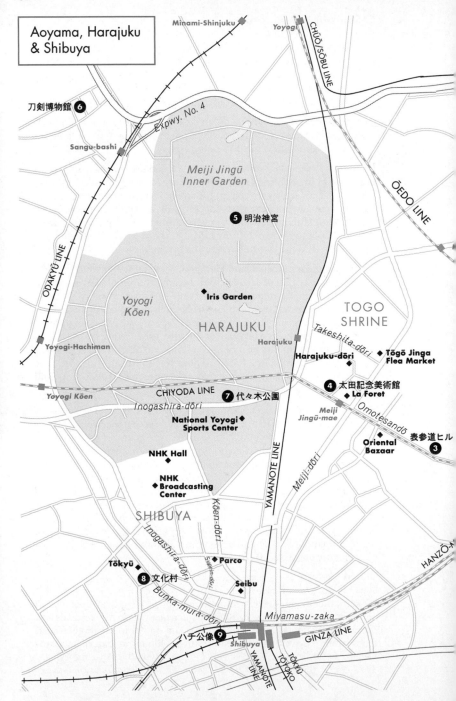

Aoyama, Harajuku & Shibuya

Minami-Shinjuku

Yoyogi

CHŪŌ/SŌBU LINE

刀剣博物館 ❻

Expwy. No. 4

Sangu-bashi

ŌEDO LINE

Meiji Jingū Inner Garden

❺ 明治神宮

ODAKYŪ LINE

Yoyogi Kōen

◆ Iris Garden

TOGO SHRINE

HARAJUKU

Takeshita-dōri

Yoyogi-Hachiman

Harajuku

◆ Tōgō Jinga Flea Market

Harajuku-dōri ◆

Yoyogi Kōen

CHIYODA LINE

❼ 代々木公園

❹ 太田記念美術館

Inogashira-dōri

◆ La Foret

Meiji Jingū-mae

Omotesandō

表参道ヒル

National Yoyogi ◆
Sports Center

◆ Oriental Bazaar

❸

NHK Hall ◆

YAMANOTE LINE

Meiji-dōri

NHK
◆ Broadcasting
Center

SHIBUYA

Kōen-dōri

Inogashira-dōri

Supin-dōri

◆ Parco

HANZŌ

Tōkyū ◆

❽ 文化村

◆ Seibu

Bunka-mura-dōri

Miyamasu-zaka

GINZA LINE

ハチ公像 ❾

Shibuya

YAMANOTE LINE

TŌKYŪ TOYOKO

hibit prices vary with events ☉ *Lobby ticket counter daily 10–7* Ⓜ *JR Yamanote Line, Ginza and Hanzō-mon subway lines, and private rail lines; Shibuya Station (Exits 5 and 8 for Hanzō-mon subway line, Kita-guchi/North Exit for all others).*

▌**NEED A BREAK?**

Les Deux Magots, sister of the famed Paris café, in the Bunka-mura complex, serves a good selection of beers and wines, sandwiches, salads, quiches, tarts, and coffee. There's a fine art bookstore next door, and the tables in the courtyard are perfect for people-watching. ✉ *Bunka-mura, lower courtyard, 2-24-1 Dōgen-zaka, Shibuya-ku* ☎ *03/3477-9124* Ⓜ *JR Yamanote Line, Ginza and Hanzō-mon subway lines, and private rail lines; Shibuya Station (Exits 5 and 8 for Hanzō-mon subway line, Kita-guchi/North Exit for all others).*

★ ❻ **Japanese Sword Museum** (Tōken Hakubutsukan). It's said that in the late 16th century, before Japan closed its doors to the West, the Spanish tried to establish a trade here in weapons made from famous Toledo steel. The Japanese were politely uninterested; they had been making blades of incomparably better quality for more than 600 years. At one time there were some 200 schools of sword-making in Japan; swords were prized not only for their effectiveness in battle but for the beauty of the blades and fittings and as symbols of the higher spirituality of the warrior caste. There are few inheritors of this art today. ✉ *4-25-10 Yoyogi, Shibuya-ku* ☎ *03/3379-1386* 🎫 *¥525* ☉ *Tues.–Sun. 10–4:30* Ⓜ *Odakyū private rail line, Sangū-bashi Station.*

★ ❺ **Meiji Shrine** (Meiji Jingū). The Meiji Shrine honors the spirits of Emperor Meiji, who died in 1912, and Empress Shōken. It was established by a resolution of the Imperial Diet the year after the emperor's death to commemorate his role in ending the long isolation of Japan under the Tokugawa Shogunate and setting the country on the road to modernization. Completed in 1920 and virtually destroyed in an air raid in 1945, it was rebuilt in 1958.

A wonderful spot for photos, the mammoth entrance gates (*torii*), rising 40 feet high, are made from 1,700-year-old cypress trees from Mt. Ari in Taiwan; the crosspieces are 56 feet long. The buildings in the shrine complex, with their curving green copper roofs, are also made of cypress wood. The surrounding gardens have some 100,000 flowering shrubs and trees.

An annual festival at the shrine takes place on November 3, Emperor Meiji's birthday, which is a national holiday. On the festival and New Year's Day, as many as 1 million people come to offer prayers and pay their respects. Several other festivals and ceremonial events are held here throughout the year; check by phone or on the shrine Web site to see what's scheduled during your visit.

The peaceful **Inner Garden** (Jingū Nai-en), where the irises are in full bloom in the latter half of June, is on the left as you walk in from the main gates. Beyond the shrine is the **Treasure House,** a repository for the personal effects and clothes of Emperor and Empress Meiji—perhaps of less interest to foreign visitors than to the Japanese. ✉ *1–1 Kami-*

zono-chō, Yoyogi, Shibuya-ku ☎ *03/3379–9222* ⊕ *www.meijijingu. or.jp* ✉ *Shrine free, Inner Garden ¥500, Treasure House ¥500* ☉ *Shrine daily sunrise–sunset; Inner Garden Mar.–Nov., daily 9–4; Treasure House daily 10–4; closed 3rd Fri. of month* Ⓜ *Chiyoda subway line, Meiji-jingū-mae Station; JR Yamanote Line, Harajuku Station (Exit 2).*

❶ **Meiji Shrine Outer Gardens** (Meiji Jingū Gai-en). This rare expanse of open space is devoted to outdoor sports of all sorts. The Yakult Swallows play at **Jingū Baseball Stadium** (✉ 13 Kasumigaoka, Shinjuku-ku ☎ 03/3404–8999); the Japanese baseball season runs from April to October. The main venue of the 1964 Summer Olympics, **National Stadium** (✉ 10 Kasumigaoka, Shinjuku-ku ☎ 03/3403–1151) now hosts soccer matches. Some of the major World Cup matches were played here when Japan co-hosted the event with Korea in 2002. The **Meiji Memorial Picture Gallery** (Kaigakan) (✉ 9 Kasumigaoka, Shinjuku-ku, Aoyama ☎ 03/3401–5179), across the street from the National Stadium, doesn't hold much interest unless you're a fan of Emperor Meiji and don't want to miss some 80 otherwise undistinguished paintings depicting events in his life. It's open daily 9–4:30 and costs ¥500. ✉ *Shinjuku-ku* Ⓜ *Ginza and Hanzō-mon subway lines, Gai-en-mae Station (Exit 2); JR Chūō Line, Shina-no-machi Station.*

❷ **Nezu Institute of Fine Arts** (Nezu Bijutsukan). This museum houses the private art collection of Meiji-period railroad magnate and politician Kaichirō Nezu. The permanent display in the main building and the annex includes superb examples of Japanese painting, calligraphy, and ceramics—some of which are registered as National Treasures—plus Chinese bronzes, sculpture, and lacquerware. The institute also has one of Tōkyō's finest gardens, with more than 5 acres of shade trees and flowering shrubs, ponds, and waterfalls, as well as seven tea pavilions. ✉ *6–5–1 Minami-Aoyama, Minato-ku* ☎ *03/3400–2536* ⊕ *www.nezu-muse.or.jp* ✉ *¥1,000* ☉ *Tues.–Sun. 9–4* Ⓜ *Ginza and Hanzō-mon subway lines, Omotesandō Station (Exit A5).*

FodorśChoice
★

★ ❸ **Omotesando Hills.** This curious shopping mall was designed by Pritzker Prize–winning architect Tadao Ando. Despised and adored with equal zeal, this controversial project demolished the charming, yet antiquated Dojunkai Aoyama Apartments along the Omotesando Avenue. Filled with high-end boutiques and designer flagship stores for Dolce & Gabbana and Yves Saint Laurent, it has the latest in Japanese haute couture. Restaurants and cafés can be found, but beware of long lines. ✉ *4–12–10 JingumaeShibuya-ku* ☎ *03/3497–0310* ☉ *Daily 11–9* Ⓜ *Ginza Line, Chiyoda Line, Hanzomon Line Omotesando Station (Exit A2).*

NEED A BREAK?

Relax "Omotesando style" at **Anniversaire**—it's just like stepping into a Parisian café. This charming venue is part of a wedding center and hall and has outdoor seating under a red awning. It's a perfect resting spot in spring and early summer. On weekends, the chapel doors open and newlyweds walk in procession in front of onlookers sitting the café, who ring little bells to wish them well. Champagne by the glass costs ¥1,000; strong coffee, ¥1,000; delicious sandwiches, ¥1,200;

and desserts ¥800. ✉ *3-5-30 Kita Aoyama, Minato-ku* ☎ *03/5411-5988* Ⓜ *Ginza, Chiyoda, and Hanzō-mon subway lines, Omotesandō Station (Exit A2).*

★ ❹ **Ōta Memorial Museum of Art** (Ōta Kinen Bijutsukan). The gift of former Tōhō Mutual Life Insurance chairman Seizō Ōta, this is probably the city's finest private collection of *ukiyo-e,* traditional Edo-period woodblock prints that flourished in the 18th and 19th centuries. The works on display are selected and changed periodically from the 12,000 prints in the collection, which include some extremely rare work by artists such as Hiroshige, Hokusai, Sharaku, and Utamaro. Be sure to verify opening hours on their official Web site or call ahead. ✉ *1–10–10 Jingū-mae, Shibuya-ku* ☎ *03/3403-0880* ⊕ *www.ukiyoe-ota-muse.jp* ☑ *¥700–¥1,000, depending on exhibit* ⊙ *Tues.–Sun. 10:30–5; closed from 26th or 27th to last day of each month.*

❾ **Statue of Hachiko.** Hachiko is the Japanese version of Lassie; he even starred in a few heart-wrenching films. Every morning, Hachiko's master, a professor at Tōkyō University, would take the dog with him as far as Shibuya Station and Hachiko would go back every evening to greet him on his return. In 1925 the professor died. Every evening for the next seven years, Hachiko would go to Shibuya and wait there until the last train had pulled out of the station. When loyal Hachiko died, his story made headlines. A handsome bronze statue of Hachiko was installed in front of the station, funded by fans from all over the country. The present version is a replica—the original was melted down for its metal in World War II. ✉ *JR Shibuya Station, West Plaza, Shibuya-ku.*

☾ ❼ **Yoyogi Kōen** (Yoyogi Park). This is the perfect spot to have a picnic on a sunny day. On Sunday, people come here to play music, practice martial arts, and ride bicycles on the bike path (rentals are available). Be sure to look out for a legendary group of dancing Elvis impersonators, who meet at the entrance every Sunday and dance to classic rock-and-roll music. There is also a community of homeless people who live in orderly, clean camps along the periphery. Sunday and holidays, there's a flea market along the main thoroughfare that runs through the park, opposite the National Yoyogi Sports Center. ✉ *Jinnan 2-chōme, Shibuya-ku* Ⓜ *Chiyoda subway line, Meiji Jingū-mae Station (Exit 2); JR Yamanote Line, Harajuku Station (Omotesandō Exit).*

Roppongi & Azabu-Jūban

During the last quarter of the 20th century, Roppongi was a better-heeled, better-behaved version of Shinjuku or Shibuya, without the shopping: not much happens by day, but by night the area is an irresistible draw for young clubbers with foreign sports cars and disposable income.

Today, this area has become an entertainment capital, attracting tourists to its bustling bar, restaurant, and nightclub scenes; English is spoken at most restaurants and shops. It's also the most prestigious address in town including the developments known as Roppongi Hills and Tōkyō Midtown, where residents are rumored to be politicians, celebrities, and businessmen. The famous Mori Tower houses the headquarters for high-rolling banking and IT companies like Goldman Sachs Japan, Lehman Brothers Japan, and Livedoor, founded by disgraced renegade businessman, Takafumi Horie.

Azabu-Jūban is a prestigious residential district with many embassies. Before the fire raids of 1945, Azabu-Jūban, like Roppongi, was a famous entertainment disctrict with department stores, a red-light quarter, and theaters. The fires destroyed the entire neighborhood, and it was reborn as a residential area. Though the apartments are small and dilapidated, this is one of the city's most expensive areas and many famous celebrities, artists, and businesspeople reside here.

Numbers in the text correspond to numbers in the margin and on the Roppongi & Azabu-Jūban map.

Orientation & Planning

ORIENTATION Roppongi is located just south of Shibuya and Aoyama, and west of the Imperial Palace. The best way to get to Roppongi is by subway, though the trains stop running at midnight. Azabu-Jūban is located just south of Roppongi, within seven-minute walking-distance from Roppongi Hills, or a short subway ride on the Toei Ōedo line to Azabu-Jūban station.

PLANNING Roppongi is a very central area, located in between Shibuya and the Imperial Palace. The best way to get here is by subway, and there are two stations: Hibiya line Roppongi Station (takes you right into the complex of Roppongi Hills), and Toei Ōedo Line Roppongi Station. At Roppongi Hills Complex, there are ATMs and Currency Exchange services, as well as family- and kid-friendly activities.

Azabu-Jūban is a quick visit, and a good place to sit in a café and people-watch. The best time to visit is in August, during the **Azabu-Jūban Summer Festival,** one of the biggest festivals in Minato-ku. The streets, which are closed to car traffic, are lined with food vendors selling delicious international fare and drinks. Everyone wears their nicest summer kimonos and watches live performances. Check the online *Minato Monthly* newsletter (⊕ www.city.minato.tokyo.jp) in August for a list of summer festivals. Only a short 10-minute walk from Roppongi, you can also take the Toei Ōedo Line from Roppongo, to Azabu-Jūban Station (exit 5), one stop away ¥160.

What to See

❺ Don Quijote. This is perhaps the weirdest 24-hour discount store on earth, complete with aquariums featuring the ugliest giant fish you've ever seen; a half-pike roller coaster on the rooftop that has never operated (angry neighbors signed a petition, forcing them to drop the idea); the constantly looping "Don Quixote" theme song; and cheesy merchandise like vinyl pants and wigs. Not convinced that you can find almost anything here? They also have secondhand Louis Vuitton bags and deodorant. ✉ *3–14–10 Roppongi Minato-ku* ☎ *03/5786–0811* ⊕ *www.donki. com* ☉ *Daily 11–10.*

❶ The Mori Tower promenade encircles three of the nine galleries of the **Mori Art Museum,** which is now one of the leading contemporary art showcases in Tōkyō. You enter the six main galleries, where the major exhi-

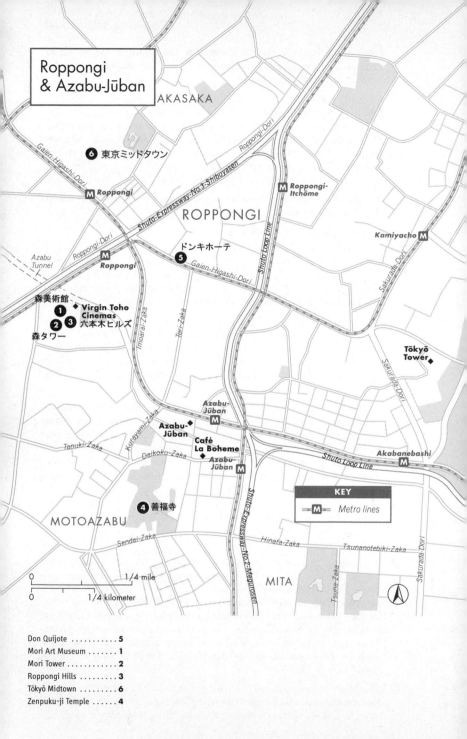

Roppongi & Azabu-Jūban

AKASAKA

ROPPONGI

6 東京ミッドタウン

Ⓜ *Roppongi*

Ⓜ *Roppongi-Itchōme*

Kamiyacho Ⓜ

Azabu Tunnel

Ⓜ *Roppongi*

5 ドンキホーテ

森美術館

1 ◆ **Virgin Toho Cinemas**

2 **3** 六本木ヒルズ

森タワー

Tōkyō Tower ◆

Azabu-Jūban Ⓜ

Azabu-Jūban ◆

Café La Boheme

◆ *Azabu-Jūban* Ⓜ

Akabanebashi Ⓜ

4 善福寺

MOTOAZABU

MITA

Gaien-Higashi-Dori
Shuto-Expressway-No.3-Shibuyasen
Roppongi-Dori
Roppongi-Dori
Gaien-Higashi-Dori
Shuto Loop Line
Sakurada-Dori
Imoarai-Zaka
Tori-Zaka
Kurayami-Zaka
Tanuki-Zaka
Daikoku-Zaka
Sendai-Zaka
Shuto-Expressway-No.2-Meguurosen
Hinata-Zaka
Tsunanotebiki-Zaka
Tsuta-Zaka
Sakurada-Dori
Shuto Loop Line

KEY
Ⓜ *Metro lines*

0 ————— 1/4 mile
0 ————— 1/4 kilometer

bitions are mounted, from the floor above. The Mori is well-designed, intelligently curated, diverse in its media, and hospitable to big crowds. ⊠ *Minato-ku* ☎ *03–5777–8600* ⊕ *http://mori.art.museum/jp* ☞ *Admission fees vary with each exhibit* ⊙ *Wed.–Mon. 10–10, Tues. 10–5* Ⓜ *Hibiya subway line, Roppongi Station (Exit 1C).*

② At the center of Roppongi Hills is the 54-story **Mori Tower.** On a clear day, you can see Mt. Fuji in the distance from the Tōkyō City View observation promenade on the 52nd floor, and by night the panoramic view of the city is spectacular. ⊠ *Minato-ku* ☎ *03/5777–8600* ⊕ *www.tokyocityview.com* ☞ *¥1,500* ⊙ *Daily 9 AM–1 PM* Ⓜ *Hibiya subway line, Roppongi Station (Exit 1C).*

☕ ③ **Roppongi Hills.** In 2003, Mori Building Company—Japan's biggest commercial landlord—created Roppongi Hills, a complex of shops, restaurants, residential and commercial towers, a nine-screen cineplex, the Grand Hyatt hotel, and a major art museum—all wrapped around the TV Asahi studios and sprawled out in five zones from the Roppongi intersection to Azabu-Jūban. To navigate this minicity, go to the information center to retrieve a 12-page floor guide with color-coded maps in English; most of the staff members speak a modicum of English as well. **English Tours** are available from the information center; you must book seven days in advance online or by phone. (☎ *03/6406–6677* ⊙ *Daily 9–6* ☞ Roppongi Hills walking tour (45 min) ¥1,500, Quick tour (30 min) ¥1,000) ⊠ *6–10–1 Roppongi, Minato-ku* ⊕ *www.roppongihills.com* Ⓜ *Hibiya subway line, Roppongi Station (Exit 1C).*

⑤ **Tōkyō Midtown.** The trend toward luxury minicity development projects, which started with Roppongi Hills in 2003, is improving the dynamic of the city. With Tōkyō Midtown, Mitsui Fudosan aims to create the tallest building in Tōkyō, using a collaboration of international architects. The complex will include a Ritz-Carlton and the Midtown Tower and will house Tōkyō businesses, upscale residences, museums, restaurants, shops, and convention halls in adjacent buildings. The top floor of the Midtown Tower will offer a spectacular view of Tōkyō. For locals, the new medical center associated with Johns Hopkins University is a welcome addition. ⊠ *9-chōme Akasaka Minato-ku* ⊕ *www.tokyo-midtown.com* Ⓜ *Toei Ōedo Line Roppongi Station, Hibiya Line Roppongi Station.*

NEED A BREAK?

Café La Boheme. A popular local hangout at all hours of the day, this café is open until 5 AM. They serve Western food for lunch, a coffee break, or dinner in 19th-century Czech dining surroundings. Coffee is ¥420, pasta lunch sets are around ¥1,000, and dinner sets are approximately ¥5,250. All major credit cards accepted. ⊠ *2-3-7 Azabu-juban, Minato-ku* ☎ *03/6400–3060* ⊕ *www. boheme.jp* ⊙ *Daily: lunch 11:30–2, dinner 2 PM–5 AM.*

④ **Zenpuku-ji Temple.** This temple, just south of the Ichinohashi Crossing, dates back to the 800s. In the 1200s, the temple was converted to the Shinran school of Buddhism. When Consul-General Townsend Harris arrived from the America in 1959, he lived on the temple grounds. ⊠ *1–6 Moto-Azabu, Minato-ku* ☎ *03/3451–7402* Ⓜ *Toei Ōedo Line Azabu-Juban Station (Exit 1).*

Shinjuku

If you love big cities, you're bound to love Shinjuku. Come here, and for the first time Tōkyō begins to seem *real:* all the celebrated virtues of Japanese society—its safety and order, its grace and beauty, its cleanliness and civility—fray at the edges.

To be fair, the area has been on the fringes of respectability for centuries. When Ieyasu, the first Tokugawa shōgun, made Edo his capital, Shinjuku was at the junction of two important arteries leading into the city from the west. It became a thriving post station, where travelers would rest and refresh themselves for the last leg of their journey; the appeal of this suburban pit stop was its "teahouses," where the waitresses dispensed a good bit more than sympathy with the tea.

When the Tokugawa dynasty collapsed in 1868, 16-year-old Emperor Meiji moved his capital to Edo, renaming it Tōkyō, and modern Shinjuku became the railhead connecting it to Japan's western provinces. As the haunt of artists, writers, and students, it remained on the fringes of respectability; in the 1930s Shinjuku was Tōkyō's bohemian quarter. The area was virtually leveled during the firebombings of 1945—a blank slate on which developers could write, as Tōkyō surged west after the war. By the 1970s property values in Shinjuku were the nation's highest, outstripping even those of Ginza.

After the Great Kantō Earthquake of 1923, Nishi-Shinjuku was virtually the only part of Tōkyō left standing; the whims of nature had given this one small area a gift of better bedrock. That priceless geological stability remained largely unexploited until the late 1960s, when technological advances in engineering gave architects the freedom to soar. Some 20 skyscrapers have been built here since then, including the Tōkyō Metropolitan Government Office complex, and Nishi-Shinjuku has become Tōkyō's 21st-century administrative center.

By day the quarter east of Shinjuku Station is an astonishing concentration of retail stores, vertical malls, and discounters of every stripe and description. By night it's an equally astonishing collection of bars and clubs, strip joints, hole-in-the-wall restaurants, pinball parlors, and peep shows—just about anything that amuses, arouses, alters, or intoxicates is for sale in Higashi-Shinjuku. Drunken fistfights are hardly unusual, and petty theft is not unknown. Not surprisingly, Higashi-Shinjuku has the city's largest—and busiest—police substation.

Numbers in the text correspond to numbers in the margin and on the Shinjuku map.

Orientation & Planning

ORIENTATION By day, Shinjuku is a bustling center of business and government where office workers move in droves during rush hour. By night, people are inundated with flashing signs, and a darker side of Tōkyō emerges, where drunken hordes leave their offices to go out for drinks, food, and sometimes, sex. Perhaps this is a rougher side of town, but Shinjuku is a fascinating place to discover at night.

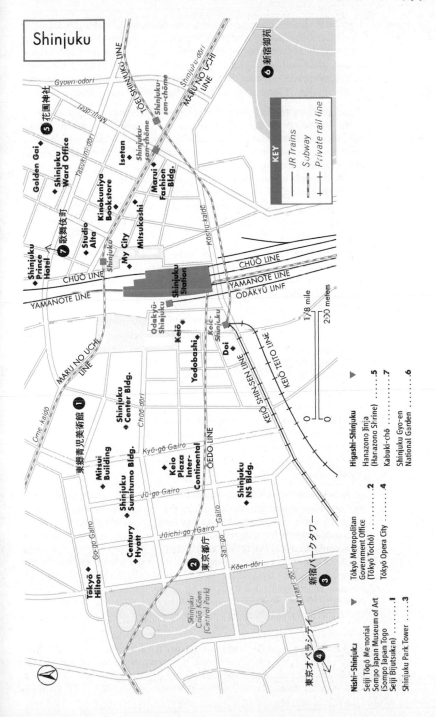

Shinjuku

Gyoen-odori

Meiji-dōri

Yasukuni-dōri

Shinjuku-dōri

TOEI SHINJUKU LINE

MARU NO UCHI LINE

5 花園神社

6 新宿御苑

⑥ Shinjuku-san-chôme

Shinjuku-san-chôme

Golden Gai

Shinjuku Ward Office

Isetan

Marui Fashion Bldg.

Kinokuniya Bookstore

Mitsukoshi

7 歌舞伎町

Studio Alta

My City

Shinjuku

Shinjuku Prince Hotel

CHŪO LINE

Shinjuku Station

CHŪO LINE

YAMANOTE LINE

ODAKYŪ LINE

YAMANOTE LINE

Kōshu-kaidō

Odakyū-Shinjuku

Keiō

Keiō-Shinjuku

Doi

Yodobashi

KEIŌ SHINSEN LINE

KEIŌ TEITO LINE

1/8 mile

200 meters

MARU NO UCHI LINE

Ōme-kaidō

1 東郷青児美術館

Shinjuku Center Bldg.

Chūō-dōri

Mitsui Building

Shinjuku Sumitomo Bldg.

Kyū-gō Gairo

Keio Plaza Inter-Continental

Jū-gō Gairo

ŌEDO LINE

Shinjuku NS Bldg.

Century Hyatt

Jūichi-gō Gairo

Tōkyō Hilton

Go-gō Gairo

 Roku-gō Gairo

Shi-go Gairo

San-go Gairo

2 東京都庁

Kōen-dōri

3 新宿パークタワー

Minami-dōri

Shinjuku Chūō Kōen (Central Park)

東京オペラシティ

4

KEY

— JR Trains

☐ Subway

—+— Private rail line

▶ **Nishi-Shinjuku**

Seiji Togō Memorial
Sompo Japan Museum of Art
(Sompo Japan Togo
Seiji Bijutsukan) **1**

Shinjuku Park Tower **3**

Tōkyō Metropolitan
Government Office
(Tōkyō Tochō) **2**

Tōkyō Opera City **4**

▶ **Higashi-Shinjuku**

Hanazono Jinja
(Harazono Shrine) **5**

Kabuki-chō **7**

Shinjuku Gyo-en
National Garden **6**

PLANNING   Every day three subways, seven railway lines, and more than 3 million commuters coverge on Shinjuku Station, making this the city's busiest and most heavily populated commercial center. The hub at Shinjuku—a vast, interconnected complex of tracks and terminals, department stores and shops—divides the area into two distinctly different subcities, Nishi-Shinjuku (West Shinjuku) and Higashi-Shinjuku (East Shinjuku).

Plan a full day for Shinjuku if you want to see both the east and west sides. Subway rides can save you time and energy, but don't rule out walking. The Shinjuku Gyo-en National Garden is worth at least an hour, especially if you come in early April during *sakura* (cherry blossom) season. The Tōkyō Metropolitan Government Office complex can take longer than you might expect; lines for the elevators to the observation decks are often excruciatingly long. Sunday, when shopping streets are closed to traffic, is the best time to tramp around Higashi-Shinjuku. The rainy season in late June and the sweltering heat of August are best avoided.

What to See

❺ **Hanazono Jinja** (Hanazono Shrine). Constructed in the early Edo period, Hanazono is not among Tōkyō's most imposing shrines, but it does have one of the longest histories. Prayers offered here are believed to bring prosperity in business. The shrine is a five-minute walk north on Meiji-dōri from the Shinjuku-san-chōme subway station. The block just to the west (5-chōme 1) has the last embattled remaining bars of the "Golden-Gai": a district of tiny, unpretentious, even seedy, nomiya (bars) that in the '60s and '70s commanded the fierce loyalty of fiction writers, artists, free-lance journalists, and expat Japanophiles. ⊠ *5–17–3 Shinjuku, Shinjuku-ku* ☎ *03/3209–5265* 🎟 *Free* ☉ *Daily sunrise–sunset* Ⓜ *Marunouchi subway line, Shinjuku-san-chōme Station (Exits B2 and B3).*

❼ **Kabuki-chō.** In 1872 the Tokugawa-period formalities governing geisha entertainment were dissolved, and Kabuki-chō became Japan's largest center of prostitution. Later, when vice laws got stricter, prostitution just went a bit deeper underground, where it remains—deeply deplored and widely tolerated.

⚠ **Kabuki-chō means unrefined nightlife at its best and raunchy seediness at its worst. Neon signs flash; shills proclaim the pleasures of the places you particularly want to shun. Even when a place looks respectable, ask about prices first:** *bottakuri*—**overcharging for food and drink—is the regional sport here, and watered-down drinks can set you back ¥5,000 or more in a hostess club. Avoid the cheap nomiya under the railway tracks; chances are there's a client in one of them looking for a fight. All that said, you needn't be intimidated by the area: use your street smarts, and it** *can* **be fun.** ⊠ *Shinjuku-ku* Ⓜ *JR (Higashi-guchi/East Exit) and Marunouchi subway line (Exits B10, B11, B12, and B13), Shinjuku Station.*

In an attempt to change the area's image after World War II, plans were made to replace Ginza's fire-gutted Kabuki-za with a new one in Shinjuku. The plans were never realized, however, as the old theater was rebuilt. But the project gave the area its present name. Kabuki-chō's own multipurpose theater is the 2,000-seat **Koma Gekijō** (⊠ *1–19–1 Kabuki-*

chō, Shinjuku-ku ☎ 03/3200–2213). The building, which also houses several discos and bars, is a central landmark for the quarter.

❶ **Seiji Tōgō Memorial Sompo Japan Museum of Art** (Sompo Japan Togo Seiji Bijutsukan). The painter Seiji Tōgō (1897–1978) was a master of putting on canvas the grace and charm of young maidens. More than 100 of his works from the museum collection are on display here at any given time, along with other Japanese and Western artists. The museum also houses van Gogh's *Sunflowers*. The gallery has an especially good view of the old part of Shinjuku. ☒ *Yasuda Fire and Marine Insurance Bldg., 42nd fl., 1–26–1 Nishi-Shinjuku, Shinjuku-ku* ☎ *03/5777–8600* ⊕ *www. sompo-japan.co.jp/museum* ☒ *¥500; additional fees for special exhibits* ☉ *Tues.–Sun. 10–6* Ⓜ *Marunouchi and Shinjuku subway lines, JR, and Keiō Shin-sen and Teitō private rail lines; Shinjuku Station (Exit A18 for subway lines, Nishi-guchi/West Exit or Exit N4 from underground passageway for all others).*

★ ❻ **Shinjuku Gyo-en National Garden.** This lovely 150-acre park was once the estate of the powerful Naitō family of feudal lords, who were among the most trusted retainers of the Tokugawa shōguns. After World War II, the grounds were finally opened to the public. It's a perfect place for leisurely walks: paths wind past ponds and bridges, artificial hills, thoughtfully placed stone lanterns, and more than 3,000 kinds of plants, shrubs, and trees. There are different gardens in Japanese, French, and English styles, as well as a greenhouse (the nation's first, built in 1885) filled with tropical plants. The best times to visit are April, when 75 different species of cherry trees—some 1,500 trees in all—are in bloom, and the first two weeks of November, during the chrysanthemum exhibition. ☒ *11 Naitō-chō, Shinjuku-ku* ☎ *03/3350–0151* ☒ *¥200* ☉ *Tues.–Sun. 9–4; also open Mon. 9–4 in cherry-blossom season (Mar. 25–Apr. 24) and for chrysanthemum show (Nov. 1–15)* Ⓜ *Marunouchi subway line, Shinjuku Gyo-en-mae Station (Exit 1).*

❸ **Shinjuku Park Tower Building.** The Shinjuku Park Tower provides any number of opportunities to rest and refuel. Some days there are free chamber-music concerts in the atrium. There are many restaurants to choose from in the building, with a variety of international and Japanese restaurants. In the afternoon, you can ride up to the skylighted bamboo garden of the Peak Lounge on the 41st floor of the **Park Hyatt Hotel** (☎ 03/5322–1234). This is the set location of the Oscar-winning film, *Lost in Translation*; the rates at Park Hyatt skyrocketed after the film became a hit and Sofia Coppola accepted the Oscar in 2003 for best screenplay. Just for kicks, have a Suntory whiskey at the New York Bar on the 41st floor. Also come for high tea, allegedly the best Sunday brunch in the city, and a spectacu-

---

HE SAID WHAT?

Yasuda Fire & Marine Insurance Company CEO Yasuo Gotō acquired *Sunflowers* in 1987 for ¥5.3 billion—at the time the highest price ever paid at auction for a work of art. He later created considerable stir in the media with the ill-considered remark that he'd like the painting cremated with him when he died.

lar view. ⊠ *3–7–1 Nishi-Shinjuku, Shinjuku-ku* Ⓜ *JR Shinjuku Station (Nishi-guchi/West Exit).*

★ ❷ **Tōkyō Metropolitan Government Office** (Tōkyō Tochō). Dominating the western Shinjuku skyline and built at a cost of ¥157 billion, Kenzō Tange's grandiose city hall complex is clearly meant to remind observers that Tōkyō's annual budget is bigger than that of the average developing country. The late-20th-century complex consists of a main office building, an annex, the Metropolitan Assembly building, and a huge central courtyard, often the venue of open-air concerts and exhibitions. Tōkyōites either love it or hate it. On a clear day, from the observation decks on the 45th floors of both towers, you can see all the way to Mt. Fuji and to the Bōsō Peninsula in Chiba Prefecture. Several other skyscrapers in the area have free observation floors, but city hall is the best of the lot. The Metropolitan Government Web site, incidentally, is an excellent source of information on sightseeing and current events in Tōkyō. ⊠ *2–8–1 Nishi-Shinjuku, Shinjuku-ku* ☎ *03/5321–1111* ⊕ *www.metro.tokyo.jp* ✇ *Free* ☉ *North observation deck daily 9:30–10:30; south observation deck daily 9:30–5:30* Ⓜ *Marunouchi and Shinjuku subway lines, JR, Keiō Shin-sen and Teitō private rail lines; Shinjuku Station (Nishi-guchi/West Exit).*

❹ **Tōkyō Opera City.** Completed in 1997, this is certain to be the last major cultural project in Tōkyō for the foreseeable future. The west side of the complex is the New National Theatre (Shin Kokuritsu Gekijō), consisting of the 1,810-seat opera house, the 1,038-seat playhouse, and an intimate performance space called the Pit, with seating for 468. Architect Helmut Jacoby's design for this building, with its reflecting pools, galleries, and granite planes of wall, deserves real plaudits.

The east side of the complex consists of a 54-story office tower flanked by a sunken garden and art museum on one side and a concert hall on the other. The museum focuses rather narrowly on post–World War II Japanese abstract painting. The 1,632-seat concert hall is arguably the most impressive classical-music venue in Tōkyō, with tiers of polished-oak panels, and excellent acoustics despite the venue's daring vertical design. ⊠ *3–20–2 Nishi-Shinjuku, Shinjuku-ku* ☎ *03/5353–0700 concert hall, 03/5351–3011 New National Theater* ⊕ *www.operacity.jp* Ⓜ *Keiō Shin-sen private rail line, Hatsudai Station (Higashi-guchi/East Exit).*

Odaiba

Tōkyō's "offshore" leisure and commercial-development complex rises on more than 1,000 acres of landfill, connected to the city by the Yurikamome monorail from Shimbashi. People come here for the arcades, shopping malls, and museums, as well as the city's longest (albeit artificial) stretch of sand beach, along the boat harbor—swimming is not recommended because of high levels of pollution. There's also the Great Ferris Wheel of Diamonds and Flowers—a neon phantasmagoric beacon for anyone driving into the city across the Rainbow Bridge. With hotels and apartment buildings as well, this is arguably the most successful of the megaprojects on Tōkyō Bay.

Orientation & Planning

ORIENTATION   Located on the southernmost point of Tōkyō, this is a popular weekend destination for families. The lack of historical monuments or buildings in Odiaba separates it from Tōkyō's other districts.

PLANNING   If you can, visit Odaiba during the week, as weekends are frenzied and crammed with families. The best way to get here is by monorail, which will also be packed on weekends. From Shimbashi Station you can take the JR, Karasumori Exit; Asakusa subway line, Exit A2; or the Ginza subway line, Exit 4—follow the blue seagull signs to the monorail. You can pick up a map of Odaiba in English at the entrance. The Yurikamome Line makes 10 stops between Shimbashi and the terminus at Ariake; fares range from ¥310 to ¥370, but the best strategy is to buy a ¥1,000 prepaid card that allows you to make multiple stops at different points in Odaiba. The monorail runs every three to five minutes from 5:46 AM to 11:56 PM.

What to See

The first monorail stop on the island is **Odaiba Kaihin Kōen,** the closest point to the beach and the site of two massive shopping complexes. Aqua City has four floors of boutiques, movie theaters, cafés, and eateries—including Hanashibe, an excellent sake-brewery restaurant on the third level. Overlooking the harbor is Decks Tōkyō Beach, a five-story complex of shops, restaurants, and boardwalks in two connected malls. Daiba Little Hong Kong, on the sixth and seventh floors of the Island Mall, has a collection of Cantonese restaurants and dim sum joints on neon-lighted "streets." At the Seaside Mall, a table by the window in any of the restaurants affords a delightful view of the harbor, especially at sunset, when the *yakatabune* (traditional roofed pleasure boats) drift down the Sumida-gawa from Yanagibashi and Ryōgoku.

Architecture buffs should make time for Daiba, the second stop on the monorail, if only to contemplate the futuristic **Fuji Television Nippon Broadcasting Building.** From its fifth-floor Studio Promenade, you can watch programs being produced. The observation deck on the 25th floor affords a spectacular view of the bay and the Rainbow Bridge. ✉ *2–4–8 Daiba, Minato-ku* ☎ *03/5500–8888* ⊕ *www.fujitv.co.jp* 💴 *¥500* ⊙ *Tues.–Sun. 10–8.*

The third stop on the monorail from Shimbashi is the **Museum of Maritime Science** (Fune-no-Kagakukan), which is built in the shape of an ocean liner and houses an impressive collection of models and displays on the history of Japanese shipbuilding and navigation. If you're interested in ships, plan at least an hour here to do it justice. There are no English-language explanations at the museum. Anchored alongside the museum are the ferries: *Yotei-maru,* which for some 30 years plied the narrow straits between Aomori and Hokkaidō, and the icebreaker *Sōya-maru,* the first Japanese ship to cross the Arctic Circle. ✉ *3–1 Higashi-Yashio, Shinagawa-ku* ☎ *03/5500–1111* ⊕ *www.funenokagakukan.or.jp* 💴 *¥1,000* ⊙ *Weekdays 10–5, weekends 10–6.*

The **National Museum of Emerging Science and Innovation,** (Nihon Gagaku Miraikan), known locally as Miraikan, is the third stop on the monorail from Shimbashi. Make sure to stop by the third floor, where you will meet the most famous intelligent robot in the world, ASIMO, and a host of other experimental robots in development. This museum has four different themes, "Earth, Environment and Frontiers," "Innovation and the Future," "Information Science and Technology for Soceity," and "Life Science." The rest of the museum is what the Japanese call ō-*majime* (deeply sincere)—five floors of thematic displays on environment-friendly technologies, life sciences, and the like with high seriousness and not much fun. The director of this facility, Dr. Mamoru Mohri, was Japan's first astronaut, who in 1992 logged some 460 hours in space aboard the NASA Spacelab-J Endeavor. Some of the exhibits have English-language explanations. It's a short walk here from the Museum of Maritime Science. ⊠ *2–41 Aomi, Kōtō-ku* ☎ *03/3570–9151* ⊕ *www.miraikan.jst.go.jp* ☞ *¥500* ⊙ *Mon. and Wed.–Sat. 10–7, Sun. 10–5.*

A two-minute walk south from the fourth stop on the monorail, Telecom Center, brings you to **Odaiba's Hot Spring Theme Park** (Ōedo Onsen Monogatari). Once upon a time, when bathtubs in private homes were a rarity, the great defining social institution of Japanese urban life was the *sento*: the local public bath. At the end of a hard day of work, there was no pleasure like sinking to your neck in hot water with your friends and neighbors, soaking your cares away, and sitting around afterward for soba, beer, and gossip. And if the sento was also an *onsen* with waters drawn from some mineral-rich underground supply, the delight was even greater. No more than a handful of such places survive in Tōkyō, but the Ōedo Onsen managed to tap a source some 4,600 feet below the bay. Visitors can choose from several indoor and outdoor pools, each with different temperatures and motifs—but remember that you must soap up and rinse off (including your hair) before you enter any of them. Follow your soak with a massage and a stroll through the food court— modeled after a street in Yoshiwara, the licensed red-light district of the Edo period—for sushi or noodles and beer. Charges include the rental of a *yukata* (cotton robe) and a towel. ⊠ *2–57 Ōmi, Kōtō-ku* ☎ *03/ 5500–1126* ⊙ *Daily 11 AM–9 AM; front desk closes at 2 AM* ☞ *¥2,700; ¥1,500 surcharge for entrance after midnight.*

The fifth stop on the monorail circuit of Odaiba is Aomi, gateway to **Palette Town,** a complex of malls and amusements at the east end of the island. The uncontested landmark here is the the 377-foot-high Giant Sky Wheel, modeled after the London Eye, the biggest in the world; it's open daily 10–10 and costs ¥900. Adjacent to the Sky Wheel is Mega Web, a complex of rides and multimedia amusements that's also a showcase for the Toyota Motor Corporation. You can ride a car (hands off—the ride is electronically controlled) over a 1-km (½-mi) course configured like a roller coaster but moving at a stately pace. You can drive any car you want, of course, as long as it's a Toyota. The shopping mall **Venus Fort** (⊠ Palette Town 1-chōme, Aomi, Kōtō-ku ☎ 03/3599–0700) at Aomi consists of galleries designed to suggest an Italian Renaissance palazzo, with arches and cupolas, marble fountains and statuary, and painted vault ceilings. The mall is chock-full of boutiques by the likes of Jean Paul Gaultier, Calvin Klein, and Ralph Lauren.

Elsewhere in Tōkyō

The sheer size of the city and the diversity of its institutions make it impossible to fit all of Tōkyō's interesting sights into neighborhoods. Plenty of worthy places—from Tōkyō Disneyland to sumō stables to the old Ōji district—fall outside the city's neighborhood repertoire. Yet no guide to Tōkyō would be complete without them.

Amusement Centers

Ⓒ **Kasai Seaside Park.** With two artificial beaches, a bird sanctuary, and the ⇨ **Tōkyō Sea Life Park** aquarium spread over a stretch of landfill between the Arakawa and the Kyū-Edogawa rivers, Kasai Seaside Park is one of the major landmarks in the vast effort to transform Tōkyō Bay into Fun City. The **Diamonds and Flowers Ferris Wheel** (Daia to Hana no Dai-kanransha), the tallest Ferris wheel in Japan, takes passengers on a 17-minute ride to the apex, 384 feet above the ground, for a spectacular view of the city. One rotation takes 70 minutes. On a clear day you can see all the way to Mt. Fuji; at night, if you're lucky, you reach the top just in time for a bird's-eye view of the fireworks over the Magic Kingdom, across the river. To get here, take the JR Keiyō Line local train from Tōkyō Station to Kasai Rinkai Kōen Station; the park is a five-minute walk from the south exit. ✉ *Rinkai-chō, Edogawa-ku* ☎ *03/3686-6911* 💲 *Free, Ferris wheel ¥700* ⊘ *Ferris wheel Sept.–July, Tues.–Fri. 10–8, weekends 10–9; Aug., weekdays 10–8, weekends 10–9.*

Ⓒ **Tōkyō Dome City.** The Kōrakuen stop on the Marunouchi subway line, about 10 minutes from Tōkyō Station, lets you out in front of the **Tōkyō Dome**, Japan's first air-supported indoor stadium, built in 1988 and home to the Tōkyō Yomiuri Giants baseball team. Across from the stadium is Tōkyō Dome City, a combination of family amusement park, shopping mall, restaurants, and a natural spring spa. The **Amusement Park** (⊘ Mon.–Sat. 10–8:30; Sat. and holidays 9–8:30 💲 Four roller-coaster rides are ¥600–¥800) has three stomach-churning roller coasters, a haunted house, and a merry-go-round. The **La Qua Shopping Center** holds 70 shops and restaurants. Shops are open daily 11–9, and restaurants are open 11–11. La Qua Spa (💲 ¥2,565; ¥315 more on holidays; ¥1,890 surcharge midnight–6 AM; ¥525 surcharge for Healing Room ⊘ Daily 11 AM–9 AM) is a natural hot spring for adults. There are four floors of pampering and hot springs with high concentrations of sodium-chloride, which is believed to increase blood circulation. ✉ *1–3–61 Kōraku, Bunkyō-ku* ☎ *03/5800–9999* ⊕ *www.tokyo-dome.co.jp.*

Ⓒ **Tōkyō Disneyland.** At Tōkyō Disneyland, Mickey-san and his coterie of Disney characters entertain just the way they do in the California and Florida Disney parks. When the park was built in 1983 it was much smaller than its counterparts in the United States, but the construction in 2001 of the adjacent DisneySea, with its seven "Ports of Call" with different nautical themes and rides, added more than 100 acres to this Magic Kingdom.

There are several types of admission tickets. Most people buy the One-Day Passport (¥5,800), which gives you unlimited access to the attractions and shows at one or the other of the two parks; also available are a weekday after–6 PM pass, at ¥3,100, and a weekend (and national holiday) after–3 PM pass, at ¥4,700 (check online for updates). There's also a two-day pass, good for both parks, for ¥10,000. You can buy tickets in advance in Tōkyō Station, near the Yaesu North Exit—look for red-jacketed attendants standing outside the booth—or from any travel local agency, such as the Japan Travel Bureau (JTB).

The simplest way to get to Disneyland is by JR Keiyō Line from Tōkyō Station to Maihama; the park is just a few steps from the station exit. From Nihombashi you can also take the Tōzai subway line to Urayasu and walk over to the Tōkyō Disneyland Bus Terminal for the 25-minute ride, which costs ¥230. ⊠ *1–1 Maihama, Urayasu-shi* ☎ *0570/ 00–8632 information, 045/683–3333 reservations* ⊕ *www. tokyodisneyresort.co.jp* ⊙ *Daily 9–10; seasonal closings in Dec. and Jan. may vary, so check before you go.*

Ⓒ **Tōkyō Tower.** In 1958 Tōkyō's fledgling TV networks needed a tall antenna to transmit signals. Trying to emerge from the devastation of World War II, the nation's capital was also hungry for a landmark—a symbol for the aspirations of a city still without a skyline. The result was the 1,093-foot-high Tōkyō Tower, an unabashed knockoff of Paris's Eiffel Tower, but with great views of the city. The Grand Observation Platform, at an elevation of 492 feet, and the Special Observation Platform, at an elevation of 820 feet, quickly became major tourist attractions; they still draw some 3 million visitors a year. A modest art gallery and a wax museum round out the tower's appeal as an amusement complex. Enjoy live music and stunning views on the main observation floor café during **Club 333,** an in-house radio show, featuring live jazz, R&B, and bossa nova performances on Wednesday evenings and a live DJ show on Friday evenings; both are 7–9 and at no extra charge. ⊠ *4–2–8 Shiba-Kōen, Minato-ku* ☎ *03/3433–5111* ☞ *¥920 for Grand Observation Platform, ¥600 extra for Special Observation Platform; aquarium ¥1,000; wax museum ¥870* ⊙ *Tower, daily 9–10. Wax museum, daily 10–9. Aquarium, Sept.–July, daily 10–7; Aug., daily 10–8* Ⓜ *Hibiya subway line, Kamiyachō Station (Exit 2).*

Ⓒ **Toshima-en.** This large, well-equipped amusement park in the northwestern part of Tōkyō has four roller coasters, a haunted house, and seven swimming pools. What makes it special is the authentic Coney Island carousel—left to rot in a New York warehouse, discovered and rescued by a Japanese entrepreneur, and lovingly restored down to the last gilded curlicue on the last prancing unicorn. From Shinjuku, the Ōedo subway line goes directly to the park. ⊠ *3–25–1 Koyama, Nerima-ku* ☎ *03/3990–3131* ☞ *Day pass ¥3,800* ⊙ *Thurs.–Mon. 10–6.*

Zoo & Aquariums

Ⓒ **Shinagawa Aquarium** (Shinagawa Suizokukan). The fun part of this aquarium in southwestern Tōkyō is walking through an underwater glass tunnel while some 450 species of fish swim around you. There are no pamphlets or explanation panels in English, however, and do your best to avoid Sunday, when the dolphin and sea lion shows draw crowds in impossible numbers. Take the local Keihin-Kyūkō private rail line from

Shinagawa to Ōmori-kaigan Station. Turn left as you exit the station and follow the ceramic fish on the sidewalk to the first traffic light; then turn right. You can also take the JR Tōkaidō Line to Oimachi Station; board a free shuttle to the aquarium from the No. 6 platform at the bus terminal just outside Oimachi Station. ✉ *3–2–1 Katsushima, Shinagawa-ku* ☎ *03/3762–3431* 🎫 *¥1,100* ☉ *Wed.–Mon. 10–4:30; dolphin and sea lion shows 3 times daily, on varying schedule.*

🐦 **Sunshine International Aquarium.** This aquarium has some 750 kinds of sea creatures on display, plus sea lion performances four times a day (except when it rains). An English-language pamphlet is available, and most of the exhibits have some English explanation. If you get tired of the sea life, head to the newly refurbished Sunshine Starlight Dome planetarium, where you can see 400,000 stars. And if that isn't enough to keep you occupied, head to the 60th floor observatory to take in some great views of the city. To get there, take the JR Yamanote Line to Ikebukuro Station (Exit 35) and walk about eight minutes west to the Sunshine City complex. You can also take the Yūraku-chō subway to Higashi-Ikebukuro Station (Exit 2); Sunshine City and the aquarium are about a three-minute walk north. ✉ *3–1–3 Higashi-Ikebukuro, Toshima-ku* ☎ *03/3989–3331* 🎫 *Aquarium ¥1,600; planetarium ¥800; observatory ¥620; tickets may be purchased in combination* ☉ *Aquarium open weekdays 10–6, weekends 10–6:30; Planetarium open daily 11–7; Observation deck open daily 10–9:30.*

🐦 **Tama Zoo** (Tama Dōbutsu Kōen). More a wildlife park than a zoo, this facility in western Tōkyō gives animals room to roam; moats typically separate them from you. You can ride through the Lion Park in a minibus. To get here, take a Keiō Line train toward Takao from Shinjuku Station and transfer at Takahata-Fudō Station for the one-stop branch line that serves the park. ✉ *7–1–1 Hodokubo, Hino-shi* ☎ *0425/91–1611* 🎫 *¥600* ☉ *Thurs.–Tues. 9:30–4.*

OFF THE BEATEN PATH

ASAKURA SCULPTURE GALLERY – Outsiders have long since discovered the Nezu and Yanaka areas of Shitamachi—much to the dismay of the handful of foreigners who have lived for years in this charming, inexpensive section of the city. Part of the areas' appeal lie in the fact that some of the giants of modern Japanese culture lived and died here, including novelists Ōgai Mori, Sōseki Natsume, and Ryūnosuke Akutagawa; scholar Tenshin Okakura, who founded the Japan Art Institute; painter Taikan Yokoyama; and sculptors Kōun Takamura and Fumio Asakura. If there's one single attraction here, it's probably Asakura's home and studio, which was converted into a gallery after his death in 1964 and now houses many of his most famous pieces. The tearoom on the opposite side of the courtyard is a quiet place from which to contemplate his garden.

From the north wicket (Nishi-guchi/West Exit) of JR Nippori Station, walk west—Tennō-ji temple will be on the left side of the street—until you reach a police box. Turn right, then right again at the end of the street. The gallery is a three-story black building on the right, a few hundred yards from the corner. ✉ *7–18–10 Yanaka, Taitō-ku* ☎ *03/3821–4549* 🎫 *¥400* ☉ *Tues.–Thurs. and weekends 9:30–4:30.*

Fodor'sChoice **Ryōgoku.** Two things make this working-class Shitamachi neighbor-
★ hood worth a special trip: this is the center of the world of sumō
wrestling as well as the site of the extraordinary Edo-Tōkyō Museum.
Five minutes from Akihabara on the JR Sōbu Line, Ryōgoku is easy to
get to, and if you've budgeted a leisurely stay in the city, it's well worth
a morning's expedition.

The **Edo-Tōkyō Museum** opened in 1993, more or less coinciding with
the collapse of the economic bubble that had made the project possible. Much of the large museum site is open plaza—an unthinkably lavish use of space. From the plaza the museum rises on massive pillars to
the permanent exhibit areas on the fifth and sixth floors. The escalator
takes you directly to the sixth floor—and back in time 300 years. You
cross a replica of the Edo-period Nihombashi Bridge into a truly remarkable collection of dioramas, scale models, cutaway rooms, and even whole
buildings: an intimate and convincing experience of everyday life in the
capital of the Tokugawa shōguns. Equally elaborate are the fifth-floor
re-creations of early modern Tōkyō, the "enlightenment" of Japan's head-
long embrace of the West, and the twin devastations of the Great Kantō
Earthquake and World War II. If you only visit one non–art museum in
Tōkyō, make this it. ⊠ *1–4–1 Yokoami, Sumida-ku* ☎ *03/3626–9974*
⊕ *www.edo-tokyo-museum.or.jp* ☒ *¥600; additional fees for special
exhibits* ☉ *Tues., Wed., and weekends 9:30–5; Thurs. and Fri. 9:30–8;
closed Tues. when Mon. is a national holiday.*

Walk straight out to the main street in front of the west exit of Ryōgoku
station, turn right, and you come almost at once to the Kokugikan (National Sumō Arena), with its distinctive copper-green roof. If you can't
attend one of the Tōkyō sumō tournaments, you may want to at least
pay a short visit to the **Sumō Museum** (⊠ *1–3–28 Yokoami, Sumida-
ku* ☎ *03/3622–0366* ☒ *Free* ☉ *Weekdays 10–4:30*), in the south
wing of the arena. There are no explanations in English, but the museum's collection of sumō-related wood-block prints, paintings, and
illustrated scrolls includes some outstanding examples of traditional
fine art.

Wander this area when the wrestlers are in town (January, May, and September are your best bets) and you're more than likely to see some of
them on the streets, in their wood clogs and kimonos. Come 7 AM–11
AM, and you can peer through the doors and windows of the stables to
watch them in practice sessions. One of the easiest to find is the **Tat-
sunami Stable** (⊠ 3–26–2 Ryōgoku), only a few steps from the west end
of Ryōgoku Station (turn left when you go through the turnstile and
left again as you come out on the street; then walk along the station building to the second street on the right). Another, a few blocks farther south,
where the Shuto Expressway passes overhead, is the **Izutsu Stable** (⊠
2–2–7 Ryōgoku).

★ **Sengaku-ji** (Sengaku Temple). In 1701, a young provincial baron named
Asano Takumi-no-Kami attacked and seriously wounded a courtier
named Yoshinaka Kira. Asano, for daring to draw his sword in the confines of Edo Castle, was ordered to commit suicide so his family line

Destination Sumo

SUMŌ WRESTLING DATES BACK some 1,500 years. Originally it was not just a sport but a religious rite performed at shrines to entertain the harvest gods. To the casual spectator, a match may seem like a fleshy free-for-all, but to the trained eye, it's a refined battle. Two wrestlers square off in a dirt ring about 15 feet in diameter and charge straight at each other in nothing but silk loincloths. There are various techniques of pushing, gripping, and throwing, but the rules are simple: except for hitting below the belt (which is nearly all a sumō wrestler wears), grabbing your opponent by the hair (which would certainly upset the hairdresser that accompanies every sumō ringside), or striking with a closed fist, almost anything goes. If you are thrown down or forced out of the ring, you lose. There are no weight divisions and a runt of merely 250 pounds can find himself facing an opponent twice his size.

To compete, you must belong to one of the 30 *heya* (stables) based in Tōkyō; there are no free agents. The stables are run by retired wrestlers who have purchased the right from the Japan Sumō Association. Sumō is very much a closed world, where hierarchy and formality rule. Youngsters recruited into the sport live in the stable dormitory and do all the community chores, as well as wait on their seniors. When they rise high enough in tournament rankings, they acquire servant-apprentices of their own.

When: Of the six Grand Sumō Tournaments (called *basho*) that take place during the year, Tōkyō hosts three: in early January, mid-May, and mid-September. Matches go from early afternoon, when the novices wrestle, to the titanic clashes of the upper ranks at around 6 PM.

Where: The tournaments are held in the Kokugikan, the National Sumō Arena, in Ryōgoku, a district in Sumida-ku also famed for its clothing shops and eateries that cater respectively to sumō sizes and tastes. ✉ *1-3-28 Yokoami, Sumida-ku* ☎ *03/3623-5111* ⊕ *www.sumo.or.jp* Ⓜ *JR Sōbu Line, Ryōgoku Station (West Exit).*

How. The price of admission buys you a whole day of sumō; the most expensive seats, closest to the ring, are tatami-carpeted loges for four people, called *sajiki*. The loges are terribly cramped, but the cost (¥9,200–¥11,300 per person) includes all sorts of food and drink and souvenirs, brought around to you by Kokugikan attendants in traditional costume. The cheapest seats cost ¥3,600 for advance sales, ¥2,100 for same-day box office sales. The latter includes discount children's tickets, which makes for an ideal family adventure. For same-day box office sales you should line up an hour in advance of the tournament. You can also reserve tickets through **Playguide** (☎ 03/5802–9999) or at Seven-Eleven, Family Mart, or Lawson convenience stores.

was abolished and his fief confiscated. Forty-seven of Asano's loyal retainers vowed revenge; the death of their leader made them *rōnin*—masterless samurai. On the night of December 14, 1702, Asano's rōnin stormed Kira's villa in Edo, cut off his head, and brought it in triumph to Asano's tomb at Sengaku-ji, the family temple. The rōnin were sentenced to commit suicide—which they accepted as the reward, not the price, of their honorable vendetta—and were buried in the temple grave-yard with their lord.

Through the centuries this story has become a national epic and the last word on the subject of loyalty and sacrifice, celebrated in every medium from Kabuki to film. The temple still stands, and the graveyard is wreathed in smoke from the bundles of incense that visitors still lay rev-erently on the tombstones. There is a collection of weapons and other memorabilia from the event in the temple's small museum. One of the items dispels forever the myth of Japanese vagueness and indirection in the matter of contracts and formal documents. Kira's family, naturally, wanted to give him a proper burial, but the law insisted this could not be done without his head. They asked for it back, and Ōishi—mirror of chivalry that he was—agreed. He entrusted it to the temple, and the priests wrote him a receipt, which survives even now in the corner of a dusty glass case. "Item," it begins, "One head."

Take the Asakusa subway line to Sengaku-ji Station (Exit A2), turn right when you come to street level, and walk up the hill. The temple is past the first traffic light, on the left. ⊠ *2–11–1 Takanawa, Minato-ku* ☎ *03/3441–5560* ☜ *Temple and grounds free, museum ¥200* ⊙ *Tem-ple Apr.–Sept., daily 7–6; Oct.–Mar., daily 7–5. Museum daily 9–4.*

Sōgetsu Ikebana School (Sōgetsu Kaikan). The schools of ikebana, like those of other traditional arts, are highly stratified organizations. Stu-dents rise through levels of proficiency, paying handsomely for lessons and certifications as they go, until they can become teachers themselves. At the top of the hierarchy is the *iemoto,* the head of the school, a title usually held within a family for generations. The Sōgetsu School of flower arrangement is a relative newcomer to all this. It was founded by Sōfū Teshigahara in 1927, and, compared to the older schools, it espouses a style flamboyant, free-form, and even radical. Introductory lessons in flower arrangement are given in English on Monday from 10 to noon. Reservations must be made a day in advance. The main hall of the Sōgetsu Kaikan, created by the late Isamu Noguchi, one of the masters of mod-ern sculpture, is well worth a visit. It's a 10-minute walk west on Aoyama-dōri from the Akasaka-mitsuke intersection or east from the Aoyama-itchōme subway stop. ⊠ *7–2–21 Akasaka, Minato-ku* ☎ *03/ 3408–1151* ⊕ *www.sogetsu.or.jp* Ⓜ *Ginza and Marunouchi subway lines, Akasaka-mitsuke Station; Ginza and Hanzō-mon subway lines, Aoyama-itchōme Station (Exit 4).*

Toden Arakawa Line. Take a trip back in time by riding the Toden Arakawa Line—Tōkyō's last surviving trolley. Heading east, for ¥160 one-way, the trolley takes you through the back gardens of old neigh-borhoods on its way to Ōji—once the site of Japan's first Western-style paper mill, built in 1875 by Ōji Paper Company, the nation's oldest joint-stock company. The mill is long gone, but the memory lingers on at the **Asuka-yama Ōji Paper Museum.** Some exhibits show the process of milling paper from pulp. Others illustrate the astonishing variety of products that can be made from paper. The museum is a minute's walk from the trolley stop at Asuka-yama Kōen: you can also get here from the JR Ōji Station (Minami-guchi/South Exit) on the Keihin–Tōhoku Line, or the Nishigahara Station (Asuka-yama Exit) on the Namboku subway line. ⊠ *1–1–3 Ōji, Kita-ku* ☎ *03/3916–2320* 💴 *¥300* 🕐 *Tues.–Sun. 10–4:30.*

WHERE TO EAT

The Japanese are world-champion modifiers. Only the most serious restaurateurs refrain from editing some of the authenticity out of foreign cuisines; in areas like Shibuya, Harajuku, and Shinjuku, too many of the foreign restaurants cater to students and young office workers who come mainly for the fun'iki (atmosphere). Choose a French bistro or Italian trattoria in these areas carefully, and expect to pay dearly. Several of France's two- and three-star restaurants have established branches and joint ventures in Tōkyō, and they regularly send their chefs over to supervise. More and more, you find interesting fusions of French and Japanese culinary traditions served in poetically beautiful presentations. The prevailing style is nouvelle cuisine: small portions, with picture-perfect garnishes and light sauces.

There's superb Japanese food all over the city, but sushi aficionados swear by Tsukiji, where the fish market supplies the neighborhood's restaurants; the restaurants in turn serve the biggest portions and charge the most reasonable prices. Asakusa takes pride in its tempura restaurants, but tempura is reliable almost everywhere, especially at branches of the well-established, citywide chains like Tenya and Tsunahachi. The farther "downtown" you go—into Shitamachi—the less likely you are to find the real thing in foreign (that is, non-Japanese) cuisine.

Beware: Standard restaurants may not have signs in English, but picture menus are often displayed in front windows (as well as plastic replicas of the dishes), so you can point to what you want.

Dress
Dining out in Tōkyō does not ordinarily demand formal attire. If it's a business meal and your hosts or guests are Japanese, dress conservatively: for men, a suit and tie; for women, a dress or suit in a basic color and a minimum of jewelry. On your own, follow the unspoken dress codes you'd observe at home and you won't go wrong. We mention dress only when men are required to wear a jacket or a jacket and tie.

For Japanese-style dining on tatami floors, keep two things in mind: wear shoes that slip on and off easily and presentable socks, and choose comfortable clothing for the few hours with your legs gathered under you.

Prices
Tōkyōites love to wine and dine at first-rate establishments, some of

---

CHECK IT OUT!

English OK! (🌐 www.englishok.jp) lists restaurants where English is spoken so people with limited or no Japanese can order food without worrying about the language barrier. Before heading out, check the Web site for maps, sample menus, and printable coupons.

which are grotesquely expensive. But have no fear: the city has a fair number of bargains, too. Restaurant concourses of department stores, usually on the first and/or second basement levels and the top floors, are good places for moderately priced dining. Food and drink, even at street stalls, are safe wherever you go. ■ TIP→ **When in doubt, note that Tōkyō's top-rated international hotels also have some of the city's best places to eat and drink.**

Price-category estimates are based on the cost of a main course at dinner, excluding drinks, taxes, and service charges. Japanese-style restaurants often serve set meals, which may include rice, soup, and pickled vegetables in addition to the main course. Credit cards are generally accepted at cheaper establishments, but check before sitting down.

WHAT IT COSTS In yen				
$$$$	**$$$**	**$$**	**$**	**¢**
AT DINNER over 3,000	2,000–3,000	1,000–2,000	800–1,000	under 800

Prices are per person for a main course.

Akasaka

Indian

★ **$$** ✕ **Moti.** Vegetarian dishes at Moti, especially the lentil and eggplant curries, are very good; so is the chicken masala, cooked in butter and spices. The chefs here are recruited from India by a family member who runs a restaurant in Delhi. As its reputation for reasonably priced North Indian cuisine grew, Moti established branches in nearby Akasaka-mitsuke, Roppongi, and farther away in Yokohama. They all have the inevitable Indian friezes, copper bowls, and white elephants, but this one—popular at lunch with the office crowd from the nearby Tōkyō Broadcasting System headquarters—puts the least into decor. ⊠ *Kimpa Bldg., 3rd fl., 2–14–31 Akasaka, Minato-ku* ☎ *03/3584–6640* 🖃 *AE, DC, MC, V* Ⓜ *Chiyoda subway line, Akasaka Station (Exit 2).*

Italian

$$$–$$$$ ✕ **La Granata.** Located in the Tōkyō Broadcasting System Garden building, La Granata is very popular with the media crowd, and deservedly so: the chefs prepare some of the most accomplished Italian food in town. La Granata is decked out in trattoria style, with brickwork arches, red-checker tablecloths, and a display of antipasti to whet the appetite. Whether you order the *tagliolini* (thin ribbon noodles) with porcini mushrooms, the spaghetti with garlic and red pepper, or any of the other menu offerings as your main meal, start with the wonderful batter-fried zucchini flowers filled with mozzarella and asparagus as an appetizer. ⊠ *TBS Garden, 1F, 5–1–3 Akasaka, Minato-ku* ☎ *03/3582–3241* 🖃 *AE, MC, V* Ⓜ *Chiyoda subway line, Akasaka Station (Exit 1A).*

Japanese

$$$$ ✕ **Jidaiya.** Like the Jidaiya in Roppongi, these two Akasaka branches serve various prix-fixe courses, including shabu-shabu, tempura, sushi, and steamed rice with seafood. The food isn't fancy, but it's delicious and filling. ✉ *Naritaya Bldg. 1F, Akasaka 3–14–3, Minato-ku* ☎ *03/3588–0489* ☰ *AE, DC, MC, V* ⊘ *No lunch weekends* Ⓜ *Ginza and Marunouchi subway lines, Akasaka-mitsuke Station (Belle Vie Akasaka Exit)* ✉ *Isomura Bldg. B1, Akasaka 5–1–4, Minato-ku* ☎ *03/3224–1505* ☰ *AE, DC, MC, V* ⊘ *No lunch weekends* Ⓜ *Chiyoda subway line, Akasaka Station (Exit 1A).*

$$$$ ✕ **Kisoji.** The specialty here is shabu-shabu: thin slices of beef boiled at your table and dipped in sauce. Normally this is an informal meal; after all, you do get to play with your food a bit. Kisoji, however, adds a dimension of posh to the experience, with all the tasteful appointments of a traditional ryōtei—tatami seating adds a 10% surcharge. ✉ *3–10–4 Akasaka, Minato-ku* ☎ *03/3588–0071* ☰ *AE, MC, V* ⊘ *Closed Sun.* Ⓜ *Ginza and Marunouchi subway lines, Akasaka-mitsuke Station (Belle Vie Akasaka Exit).*

THE QUINTESSENTIAL JAPANESE RESTAURANT

Most often walled off from the outside world, a *ryōtei* is like a villa that has been divided into several small, private dining rooms. These rooms are traditional in style, with tatami-mat floors, low tables, and a hanging scroll or a flower arrangement in the alcove. Servers are assigned to each room to present the meal's many dishes (which likely contain foods you've never seen before), pour sake, and provide light conversation. Many parts of the city are proverbial for their ryōtei; the top houses tend to be in Akasaka, Tsukiji, Asakusa and nearby Yanagi-bashi, and Shimbashi.

Akasaka-mitsuke

Japanese

$$$–$$$$ ✕ **Ninja.** In keeping with the air of mystery you'd expect from a ninja-theme restaurant, a ninja-costumed waiter leads you through a dark underground maze to your table in an artificial cave. The menu has more than 100 choices, including some elaborate set courses that are extravagant in both proportion and price. Among the impressively presented dishes are "jack-in-the-box" seafood salad, tuna and avocado tartar with mustard and vinegar-miso paste, and the life-size bonsai-tree dessert made from cookies and green-tea ice cream. Magical tricks are performed at your table during dinner—it's slightly kitschy but entertaining nonetheless. ✉ *Akasaka Tokyu Plaza, 2–14–3 Nagata-cho, Minato-ku* ☎ *03/5157–3936* ⌖ *Reservations essential* ☰ *AE, MC, V* Ⓜ *Ginza and Marunouchi subway lines, Akasaka-mitsuke Station (Tokyo Plaza Exit).*

¢–$$ ✕ **Sawanoi.** The homemade udon noodles, served in a broth with seafood, vegetables, or chicken, make a perfect light meal or midnight snack. Try the *inaha* (country style) udon, which has bonito, seaweed flakes, radish shavings, and a raw egg dropped in to cook in the hot broth. For a heartier meal, choose the *tenkama* set: hot udon and shrimp tempura with a delicate soy-based sauce. A bit rundown, Sawanoi is one of the last remaining neighborhood shops in what is now an upscale business and entertainment district. It stays open until 3 AM, and a menu is available in English. ✉ *Shimpo Bldg., 1st fl., 3–7–13 Akasaka, Minato-ku* ☎ *03/*

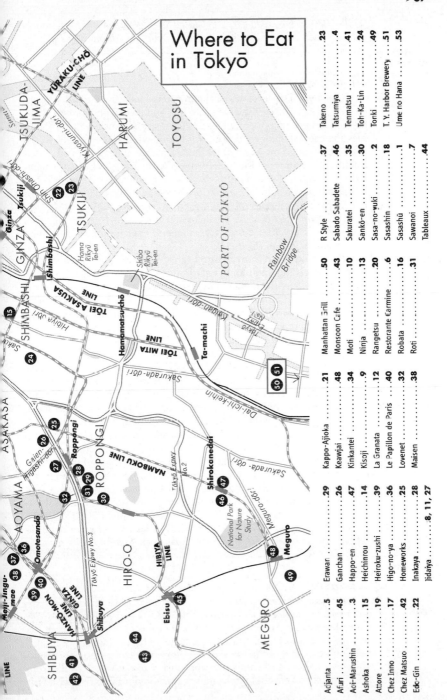

Where to Eat in Tōkyō

3582–2080 ▭ *No credit cards* ⊗ *Closed Sun.* Ⓜ *Ginza and Marunouchi subway lines, Akasaka-mitsuke Station (Belle Vie Akasaka Exit).*

Aoyama

Japanese

$$$ ✗**Higo-no-ya.** The specialty of the house is *kushi-yaki*: small servings of meat, fish, and vegetables cut into bits and grilled on bamboo skewers. There's nothing ceremonious or elegant about kushi-yaki; it resembles the more familiar yakitori, with somewhat more variety to the ingredients. Higo-no-ya's helpful English menu guides you to other delicacies like shiitake mushrooms stuffed with minced chicken; bacon-wrapped scallops; and bonito, shrimp, and eggplant with ginger. The restaurant is a postmodern–traditional cross, with wood beams painted black, paper lanterns, and sliding paper screens. ✉ *AG Bldg. B1, 3–18–17 Minami-Aoyama, Minato-ku* ☎ *03/3423–4461* ▭ *AE, DC, MC, V* ⊗ *No lunch* Ⓜ *Ginza, Chiyoda, and Hanzō-mon subway lines, Omotesandō Station (Exit A4).*

$$–$$$ ✗**Maisen.** Converted from a *sentō* (public bathhouse), Maisen still has the old high ceiling (built for ventilation) and the original signs instructing bathers where to change. Bouquets of seasonal flowers help transform the large, airy space into a pleasant dining room. Maisen's specialty is the *tonkatsu* set: tender, juicy, deep-fried pork cutlets served with a spicy sauce, shredded cabbage, miso soup, and rice. A popular alternative is the *Suruga-zen*set, a main course of fried fish served with sashimi, soup, and rice. There are no-smoking rooms upstairs. ✉ *4–8–5 Jingū-mae, Shibuya-ku* ☎ *03/3470–0071* ▭ *AE, DC, MC, V* Ⓜ *Ginza, Chiyoda, and Hanzō-mon subway lines, Omotesandō Station (Exit A2).*

¢–$$ ✗**Ume no Hana.** The exclusive specialty is tofu, prepared in more ways
Fodor'sChoice than you can imagine—boiled, steamed, stir-fried with minced crabmeat,
★ served in a custard, wrapped in thin layers around a delicate whitefish paste. Tofu is touted as the perfect high-protein, low-calorie health food; at Ume no Hana it is raised to the elegance of haute cuisine. Enter this restaurant from a flagstone walk lined with traditional stone lanterns, and remove your shoes when you step up to the main room. Latticed wood screens separate the tables. Private dining rooms have tatami seating with recesses under the tables so you can stretch your legs. Prix-fixe meals include a complimentary aperitif. ✉ *2–14–6 Kita-Aoyama, Bell Commons 6F, Minato-ku* ☎ *03/3475–8077* ▭ *AE, DC, MC, V* ⊻ *No smoking except in private rooms* Ⓜ *Ginza Line, Gaien-mae Station (Exit 3).*

Asakusa

Japanese

$$ ✗**Aoi-Marushin.** Tempura *teishoku* (an assortment of batter-fried seafood
Fodor'sChoice and fresh vegetables) is the specialty of Asakusa and a must-try at Aoi-
★ Marushin, the largest tempura restaurant in Tōkyō. There are six floors of tables, tatami seating, and English menus. This is a family restaurant, but don't expect much in the way of decor—just lots of food at reasonable prices. Aoi-Marushin's location, just a few minutes' walk from the entrance to Senṣō-ji temple, makes it an obvious choice after a visit

to the temple. ⊠ *1–4–4 Asakusa, Taitō-ku* ☎ *03/3841–0110* ▤ *AE, MC, V* Ⓜ *Ginza and Asakusa subway lines, Asakusa Station (Exit 1).*

$$ ╳ **Tatsumiya.** Neither inaccessible nor outrageously expensive, Tatsumiya is adorned — nay, cluttered—with antique chests, braziers, clocks, lanterns, bowls, utensils, and craft work, some for sale. The evening meal is in the *kaiseki* style, with seven courses: tradition demands that the meal include something raw, something boiled, something vinegary, and something grilled. The kaiseki dinner is served only until 8:30, and you must reserve ahead. Tatsumiya also serves a light lunch, plus a variety of *nabe* (one-pot seafood and vegetable stews, prepared at your table) until 10. The pork nabe is the house specialty. ⊠ *1–33–5 Asakusa, Taitō-ku* ☎ *03/3842–7373* ▤ *MC, V* Ⓜ *Ginza and Asakusa subway lines, Asakusa Station (Exits 1 and 3).*

Azabu-jūban

American-Casual

$–$$ ╳ **Homeworks.** Every so often, even on alien shores, you've got to have a burger. When the urge strikes, the Swiss-and-bacon special at Homeworks is an incomparably better choice than anything you can get at one of the global chains. Hamburgers come in three sizes on white or wheat buns, with a variety of toppings. There are also hot teriyaki chicken and pastrami sandwiches and vegetarian options like hummus and eggplant. With its hardwood banquettes and French doors open to the street in good weather, Homeworks is a pleasant place to linger over lunch. There are also branches in Hiro-o and Kyō-bashi. ⊠ *Vesta Bldg. 1F, 1–5–8 Azabu-jūban, Minato-ku* ☎ *03/3405–9884* ▤ *AE, MC, V* Ⓜ *Namboku and Ōedo subway lines, Azabu-jūban Station (Exit 4).*

Korean

$$–$$$$ ╳ **Sankō-en.** With the embassy of South Korea a few blocks away, Sanko-en stands out in a neighborhood thick with Korean-barbecue joints. Customers—not just from the neighborhood but from nearby trendy Roppongi as well—line up at all hours (from 11:30 AM to midnight) to get in. Korean barbecue is a smoky affair; you cook your own food, usually thin slices of beef and vegetables, on a gas grill at your table. The *karubi* (brisket), which is accompanied by a great salad, is the best choice on the menu. ⊠ *1–8–7 Azabu-jūban, Minato-ku* ☎ *03/3585–6306* ⌚ *Reservations not accepted* ▤ *MC, V* ⊘ *Closed Wed.* Ⓜ *Namboku and Ōedo subway lines, Azabu-jūban Station (Exit 4).*

Daikanyama

Contemporary

$$–$$$$ ╳ **Tableaux.** The mural in the bar depicts the fall of Pompeii, the banquettes are upholstered in red leather, and the walls are papered in antique gold. Tableaux may lay on more glitz than is necessary, but the service is cordial and professional, and the food is superb. Try Zuwai-crab-and red shrimp spring rolls; filet mignon with creamed potatoes, seasonal vegetables, and merlot sauce; or, for dessert, the chocolate soufflé cake. The bar is open until 1:30 AM. ⊠ *Sunroser Daikanyama*

Fodor'sChoice ★

Bldg. B1, 11–6 Sarugaku-chō, Shibuya-ku ☎ *03/5489–2201* ⊟ *AE, DC, MC, V* ⊙ *No lunch* 🍴 *Jacket and tie* Ⓜ *Tōkyū Tōyoko private rail line, Daikanyama Station (Kita-guchi/North Exit).*

Pan-Asian

¢–$$ ✕ **Monsoon Cafe.** With several locations, Monsoon Cafe meets the demand in Tōkyō for "ethnic" food—which by local definition means spicy and primarily Southeast Asian. Complementing the eclectic Pan-Asian food are rattan furniture, brass tableware from Thailand, colorful papier-mâché parrots on gilded stands, Balinese carvings, and ceiling fans. Here, at the original Monsoon, the best seats in the house are on the balcony that runs around the four sides of the atrium-style central space. Try the *satay* (grilled, skewered cubes of meat) platter, coconut-flavored deep-fried calamari, or *nasi goring* (Indonesian fried rice). ✉ *15–4 Hachiyama-chō, Shibuya-ku* ☎ *03/5489–3789* ⊕ *www. monsoon-cafe.jp* ⊟ *AE, DC, MC, V* Ⓜ *Tōkyū Tōyoko private rail line, Daikanyama Station (Kita-guchi/North Exit).*

Ebisu

Japanese

$ ✕ **Afuri.** Ramen is the quintessential Japanese fast food in a bowl: thick Chinese noodles in a savory broth, with soybean paste, diced leeks, grilled *chashu* (pork loin), and spinach. No neighborhood in Tōkyō is without at least one ramen joint—often serving only at a counter. In Ebisu, the hands-down favorite is Afuri. Using the picture menu, choose your ramen by inserting coins into a ticket machine, find a seat, and hand over your ticket to the cooks who will prepare your ramen then and there. There's limited seating, and at lunch and dinner, the line of waiting customers extends down the street. ✉ *1–1–7 Ebisu, Shibuya-ku* ☎ *03/ 3571–0957* ⊟ *No credit cards* Ⓜ *JR Yamanote Line (Nishi-guchi/West Exit) and Hibiya subway line (Exit 1), Ebisu Station.*

Ginza

Indian

$$–$$$$ ✕ **Ashoka.** Since 1968, Ashoka has staked out the high ground for Indian cuisine in Tōkyō—with a dining room suited to its fashionable Ginza location. The room is hushed and spacious, incense perfumes the air, the lighting is recessed, the carpets are thick, and the servers wear spiffy uniforms. The best thing to order here is the *thali,* a selection of curries, tandoori chicken, and naan served on a figured brass tray. The Goan fish curry is also excellent, as is the chicken tikka: boneless chunks marinated and cooked in the tandoor. ✉ *Ginza Inz Bldg. 1, 2nd fl., 3–1 Nishi Ginza, Chūō-ku* ☎ *03/3567–2377* ⊟ *AE, DC, MC, V* Ⓜ *Marunouchi and Ginza subway lines, Ginza Station (Exit C9).*

Japanese

$$$$ ✕ **Kappo-Ajioka.** When prepared incorrectly, fugu, the highly poisonous puffer fish, is fatal, yet this doesn't stop people from trying it at this Tōkyō

What's a Vegetarian to Do?

TŌKYŌ IS A GREAT GASTRONOMIC center, but it can be a bit daunting for vegetarians. Most Japanese recipes use fish stock, and it's almost unheard of to ask chefs to tweak their recipes. If you do find a flexible eatery, your choice might still arrive with ham, bacon, or chicken, because in Japanese, none of these words fall semantically under the term "meat."

There are a handful of restaurants in Tōkyō (such as Sasa-no-yuki) that specialize in *shōjin ryōri*. This traditional zen vegetarian food emphasizes natural flavors and fresh ingredients without using heavy spices or rich sauces. The variety and visual beauty of a full-course shōjin ryōri meal offers new dining dimensions to the vegetarian gourmet. *Goma-dōfu*, or sesame flavored bean curd, for example, is a tasty treat, as is *nasu-dengaku*, grilled eggplant covered with a sweet miso sauce.

The number of veggie-friendly oases is growing, but another safe bet is one of the city's numerous Italian and Indian joints. For a list of vegetarian restaurants, visit **Tōkyō Vegetarian Guide** (⊕ www.vegietokyo.com). Here are four favorites:

Itosho. At this zen restaurant, food arrives in a procession of 13 tiny dishes, each selected according to season, texture, and color. Dinner costs between ¥8,400 and ¥10,500, and reservations must be made at least two days in advance. ⊠ *3-4-7 Azabu-jūban, Minato-ku* ☎ *03/ 3454-6538* ▭ *No credit cards accepted* Ⓜ *Namboku and Ōedo subway lines, Azabu-jūban Station (Exit 1).*

Brown Rice Café. Tucked inside a Neal's Yard Remedies store, this café has just 10 tables and closes by 9 PM, but if you're shopping in Harajuku, it's a great place to stop for a tempeh burger or stuffed tofu pouch. In good weather, try the outdoor patio. ⊠ *5-1-17 Jingu-mae, Shibuya-ku* ☎ *03/5778-5416* ⊕ *www.brown.co.jp* ▭ *No credit cards* Ⓜ *Ginza and Hanzō-mon subway lines, Omotesandō Station (Exit A1).*

Pure Café. Though this airy vegan café's menu is limited, the nutritious, organic fare never disappoints. Try the samosas, veggie burgers, or wholesome soups. Pure Café, which is a stone's throw from the upscale fashion hub of Omotesandō, serves breakfast. ⊠ *5-5-21 Minami-Aoyama, Minato-ku* ☎ *03/5466-2611* ▭ *No credit cards* Ⓜ *Ginza and Hanzō-mon subway lines, Omotesandō Station (Exit B3).*

Café 8. A short walk from the trendy neighborhood of Naka-Meguro, this cute café serves an inventive fusion of Eastern and Western cuisines. The menu changes often, but might include spring rolls, nutritious curries and soups, or couscous salads. ⊠ *3-17-7 Aobadai, Meguro-ku* ☎ *03/5458-5262* ▭ *AE, DC, MC, V* Ⓜ *Denentoshi subway and private rail lines, Ikejiri-Ohashi Station.*

If you plan on staying in town long term, check out **Alishan** (⊕ www. alishan-organic-center.com), a vegetarian mail-order specialist that delivers local and imported food.

branch of the Kansai fugu ryōtei (puffer-fish restaurant). Licensed chefs prepare the fish in every way imaginable—raw, fried, stewed—using the fresh catch flown in straight from Shimonoseki, a prime fugu-fishing region. The overall flavor is subtle and somewhat nondescript—people are drawn more to the element of danger than the taste (fatalities are rare, but a few people in Japan die each year from fugu poisoning). Try the house specialty of *suppon* (Japanese turtle) and fugu nabe, fugu sashimi, or fugu *no arayaki* (grilled head and cheeks). ✉ *New Comparu Bldg. 6F, 7–7–12 Ginza, Chūō-ku* ☎ *03/3574–8844* ✍ *Reservations essential* ▤ *AE, MC, V* Ⓜ *Ginza, Hibiya, and Marunouchi subway lines, Ginza Station (Exit A5).*

$$$–$$$$ ✘ **Rangetsu.** Japan enjoys a special reputation for its lovingly raised, tender, marbled domestic beef. Try it, if your budget will bear the weight, at Rangetsu, in the form of this elegant Ginza restaurant's signature shabu-shabu or sukiyaki course. Call ahead to reserve a private alcove, where you can cook for yourself, or have a kaiseki meal brought to your table by kimono-clad attendants. Rangetsu is a block from the Ginza 4-chōme crossing, opposite the Matsuya Department Store. ✉ *3–5–8 Ginza, Chūō-ku* ☎ *03/3567–1021* ▤ *AE, DC, MC, V* Ⓜ *Marunouchi and Ginza subway lines, Ginza Station (Exits A9 and A10).*

Higashi-Shinjuku

Japanese

¢–$$ ✘ **Kinkantei.** Opened more than 200 years ago, this hole-in-the-wall soba and udon joint in Tōkyō's gay nightlife area is still a local favorite. The menu changes constantly; when in doubt, order the daily special, or hearty *hoto* (Yamanashi-style udon with vegetables), if it's available. Vegetarian and vegan choices are on the menu, which is rare for Japanese restaurants. The place seats fewer than 30 people, and from the counter you can watch the cooks at work. Open until 4 AM, Kinkantei is a fitting pit stop after a late night out. ✉ *Sunflower Bldg. 1F, 2–17–1 Shinjuku Shinjuku-ku* ☎ *03/3356–6556* ▤ *No credit cards* ◷ *Closed Sun.* Ⓜ *Shinjuku Station (Higashi-guchi/East Exit).*

Ichiyaga

Italian

$$ ✘ **Restorante Carmine.** Everybody pitched in, so the story goes, when chef Carmine Cozzolino left his job at an upscale restaurant in Aoyama and opened this unpretentious neighborhood bistro in 1987: friends designed the logo and the interior, painted the walls (black and white), and hung the graphics, swapping their labor for meals. The five-course dinner (¥3,800–¥5,000) could be the best deal in town. The menu changes weekly; specialties of the house include risotto primavera and Tuscan-style *filetto di pesce* (fish fillet) parmigiano. The wine list is well chosen, and the *torta al cioccolata* (chocolate cake) is a serious dessert. ✉ *Nishikawa Bldg. 1F, 1–19 Saiku-chō, Shinjuku-ku* ☎ *03/3260–5066* ▤ *AE, MC, V* Ⓜ *Ōedo subway line, Ushigome-Kagurazaka Station (Exit 1).*

Ikebukuro

Japanese

$$–$$$ ✕ **Sasashū.** This traditional-style pub stocks only the finest and rarest,
Fodor'sChoice the Latours and Mouton-Rothschilds, of sake: these are the rice wines
★ that take gold medals in the annual sake competition year after year. It
also serves some of the best izakaya food in town—the Japanese would-
n't dream of drinking well without eating well. Sasashū purports to be
the only restaurant in Tōkyō that serves wild duck; the chefs brush the
duck with sake and soy sauce and broil it over a hibachi. It's in a rambling, two-story, traditional-style building, with thick beams and tatami
floors. ✉ *2–2–6 Ikebukuro, Toshima-ku* ☎ *03/3971–6796* 🖃 *AE, DC,
V* ⊘ *Closed Sun. No lunch* Ⓜ *JR Yamanote Line; Yūraku-chō,
Marunouchi, and Ōedo subway lines: Ikebukuro Station (Exit 19).*

Kyō-bashi

French

$$$$ ✕ **Chez Inno.** Chef Noboru Inoue studied at Maxim's in Paris and Les
Frères Troisgros in Roanne; the result is brilliant, innovative French food.
Try fresh lamb in wine sauce with truffles and finely chopped herbs, or
lobster with caviar. The main dining room has velvet banquettes, white
stucco walls, and stained-glass windows. The elegant Hotel Seiyō Ginza
is nearby—making this area the locus of the very utmost in Tōkyō upscale. ✉ *Meiji Seika Honsha Bldg. 1F, 2–4–16 Kyō-bashi, Chūō-ku*
☎ *03/3274–2020* ⌕ *Reservations essential* 🎩 *Jacket and tie* 🖃 *AE, DC,
MC, V* ⊘ *Closed Sun.* Ⓜ *Ginza subway line, Kyō-bashi Station (Exit
2); Yūraku-chō subway line, Ginza-Itchōme Station (Exit 7).*

Italian

$$–$$$ ✕ **Attore.** This Italian restaurant in the elegant Hotel Seiyō Ginza is di-
vided into two sections. The "casual" side has a bar counter, banquettes, and a see-through glass wall to the kitchen; the "formal" side
has mauve wall panels and carpets, armchairs, and soft recessed lighting. On either side, you get some of the best Italian cuisine in Tōkyō,
though the menu is simpler and cheaper on the casual side. Try pâté of
pheasant and porcini mushrooms with white-truffle cheese sauce or the
walnut-smoked lamb chops with sun-dried tomatoes. ✉ *Hotel Seiyō
Ginza, 1–11–2 Ginza, Chūō-ku* ☎ *03/3535–1111* ⌕ *Reservations essential* 🖃 *AE, DC, MC, V* Ⓜ *Ginza subway line, Kyō-bashi Station (Exit
2); Yūraku-chō subway line, Ginza-Itchōme Station (Exit 7).*

Meguro

Japanese

★ **¢–$$** ✕ **Tonki.** Meguro, a neighborhood distinguished for almost nothing else
culinary, has arguably the best tonkatsu restaurant in Tōkyō. It's a fam-
ily joint, with Formica-top tables and a server who comes around to take
your order while you wait the requisite 10 minutes in line. And people
do wait in line, every night until the place closes at 10:45. Tonki is a
success that never went conglomerate or added frills to what it does best:

deep-fried pork cutlets, soup, raw-cabbage salad, rice, pickles, and tea. That's the standard course, and almost everybody orders it, with good reason. ✉ *1–1–2 Shimo-Meguro, Meguro-ku* ☎ *03/3491–9928* 🖃 *DC, V* ☉ *Closed Tues. and 3rd Mon. of month* Ⓜ *JR Yamanote and Namboku subway lines, Meguro Station (Nishi-guchi/West Exit).*

Thai

★ **\$\$** ✕ **Keawjai.** Blink and you miss the faded sign of this little basement restaurant a minute's walk from Meguro Station. Keawjai is one of the few places in Tōkyō to specialize in the subtle complexities of Royal Thai cuisine, and despite its size—only eight tables and four banquettes—it serves a remarkable range of dishes in different regional styles. The spicy beef salad is excellent (and *really* spicy), as are the baked rice and crabmeat served in a whole pineapple, and the red-curry chicken in coconut milk with cashews. The service is friendly and unhurried. ✉ *Meguro Kōwa Bldg. B1, 2–14–9 Kami Ōsaki, Meguro-ku* ☎ *03/5420–7727* 🖃 *AE, DC, MC, V* Ⓜ *JR Yamanote and Namboku subway lines, Meguro Station (Higashi-guchi/East Exit).*

Niban-chō

Indian

\$\$ ✕ **Adjanta.** In the mid-20th century, the owner of Adjanta came to Tōkyō to study electrical engineering. He ended up establishing what is today one of the oldest and best Indian restaurants in town. There's no decor to speak of at this 24-hour restaurant. The emphasis is on the variety and intricacy of South Indian cooking—and none of its dressier rivals can match Adjanta's menu for sheer depth. The curries are hot to begin with, but you can order them even hotter. Try the masala *dosa* (a savory crepe), *keema* (minced beef), or mutton curry. A small boutique in one corner sells saris and imported Indian foodstuffs. ✉ *3–11 Niban-chō, Chiyoda-ku* ☎ *03/3264–6955* 🖃 *AE, DC, MC, V* Ⓜ *Yūraku-chō subway line, Kōji-machi Station (Exit 5).*

Nihombashi

Japanese

\$\$ ✕ **Sasashin.** Like most izakaya, Sasashin spurns the notion of decor: there's a counter laden with platters of the evening's fare, a clutter of rough wooden tables, and not much else. It's noisy, smoky, crowded—and great fun. Like izakaya fare in general, the food is best described as professional home cooking, and is meant mainly as ballast for the earnest consumption of beer and sake. Try the sashimi, the grilled fish, or the fried tofu; you really can't go wrong by just pointing your finger at anything on the counter that takes your fancy. ✉ *2–20–3 Nihombashi-Ningyōchō, Chūō-ku* ☎ *03/3668–2456* 🖄 *Reservations not accepted* 🖃 *No credit cards* ☉ *Closed Sun. and 3rd Sat. of month. No lunch* Ⓜ *Hanzō-mon subway line, Suitengū-mae Station (Exit 7); Hibiya and Asakusa subway lines, Ningyōchō Station (Exits A1 and A3).*

Omotesandō

French

$$$$ ✕ **Le Papillon de Paris.** This fashion-minded restaurant is a joint venture of L'Orangerie in Paris and couturier Mori Hanae. Muted elegance marks the dining room, with cream walls and deep brown carpets; mirrors add depth to a room that seats only 40. The ambitious prix-fixe menus change every two weeks; the recurring salad of sautéed sweetbreads is excellent, as is the grilled Atlantic salmon. This is a particularly good place to be on Sunday between 11 and 2:30, for the buffet brunch (¥3,500), during which you can graze what is arguably the best dessert tray in town; try the pear tart or the daily chocolate-cake special. ⊠ *Hanae Mori Bldg., 5th fl., 3–6–1 Kita-Aoyama, Minato-ku* ☏ *03/3407–7461* ⌕ *Reservations essential* ▤ *AE, DC, MC, V* ⊘ *No dinner Sun.* Ⓜ *Ginza, Chiyoda, and Hanzō-mon subway lines, Omotesandō Station (Exit A1).*

Japanese

¢–$$ ✕ **R Style.** Even in some of the swankiest restaurants, Japanese *wagashi* (sweets) aren't up to par. To sample authentic handmade wagashi while sipping green tea, head to this café. The main ingredients in wagashi are adzuki beans, rice, and other grains sweetened slightly by sugarcane— making these treats a fairly healthful dessert. These intricate morsels of edible art are almost too perfectly presented to eat—almost but not quite. Try the *konomi* (rice dumpling with adzuki conserve) or *koyomi* (bracken dumpling with soy custard) set. ⊠ *Omotesando Hills Main Bldg. 3F, 4–12–10 Jingū-mae, Shibuya-ku* ☏ *03/3423–1155* ▤ *AE, MC, V* Ⓜ *Ginza, Chiyoda, and Hanzō-mon subway lines, Omotesandō Station (Exit A2); Chiyoda subway line, Meiji-Jingū-mae Station (Exit 5).*

$$–$$$ ✕ **Sakuratei.** Unconventionally located inside an art gallery, Sakuratei defies other conventions as well: eating here doesn't always mean you don't have to cook. At this do-it-yourself *okonomiyaki* (a kind of pancake made with egg, meat, and vegetables) restaurant, you choose ingredients and cook them on the *teppan* (grill). Okonomiyaki is generally easy to make, but flipping the pancake to cook the other side can be challenging—potentially messy but still fun. Fortunately, you're not expected to do the dishes. Okonomiyaki literally means "as you like it," so experiment with your own recipe or try the house special, *sakurayaki* (with pork, squid, and onions), or *monjayaki* (a watered-down variation of okonomiyaki from the Kanto region). ⊠ *3–20–1 Jingū-mae, Shibuya-ku* ☏ *03/3479–0039* ▤ *DC, MC, V* Ⓜ *Chiyoda subway line, Meiji-Jingū-mae Station (Exit 5).*

Sushi

$$ ✕ **Heiroku-zushi.** Ordinarily, a meal of sushi is a costly indulgence. The rock-bottom alternative is a *kaiten-zushi,* where sushi is literally served assembly-line style. The chefs inside the circular counter maintain a constant supply on the revolving belt on plates color-coded for price; just choose whatever takes your fancy as dishes pass by. Heiroku-zushi is a bustling, cheerful example of the genre, with fresh fish and no pretensions at all to decor. When you're done, the server counts up your plates and calculates your bill (¥126 for staples like tuna and squid to ¥367 for delicacies like eel and salmon roe). ✉ *5–8–5 Jingū-mae, Shibuya-ku* ☎ *03/3498–3968* 🚫 *No credit cards* Ⓜ *Ginza, Chiyoda, and Hanzō-mon subway lines, Omotesandō Station (Exit A1).*

Roppongi

Contemporary

$$$–$$$$ ✕ **Lovenet.** Within the 33 private theme rooms of Lovenet, you can dine and enjoy Japan's national pastime: karaoke. Go not just for the food but the entire experience. Request the intimate Morocco suite, the colorful Candy room, or the Aqua suite, where you can eat, drink, and take a dip in the hot tub while belting out '80s hits. The Italian-trained chefs prepare Mediterranean and Japanese cuisine in the form of light snacks and full-course meals, which you order via a phone intercom system. Try the duck confit with wine sauce or a salmon-roe rice bowl. The bill is calculated based on what room you use, how long you stay, and what you order. Note that there's a two-person minimum for each room. ✉ *Hotel Ibis 3F–4F, 7–14–4 Roppongi, Minato-ku* ☎ *03/5771–5511* ⊕ *www.lovenet-jp.com* ⌂ *Reservations essential* 🚫 *AE, MC, V* Ⓜ *Ōedo and Hibiya subway lines, Roppongi Station (Exit 4A).*

$$–$$$ ✕ **Roti.** Billing itself a "modern American brasserie," Roti takes pride in the creative use of simple, fresh ingredients, and a fusing of Eastern and Western elements. For an appetizer, try the Vietnamese sea-bass carpaccio with crisp noodles and roasted garlic, or the calamari batter-fried in ale with red-chili tartar sauce. Don't neglect dessert: the espresso-chocolate tart is to die for. Roti stocks some 60 Californian wines, microbrewed ales from the famed Rogue brewery in Oregon, and Cuban cigars. The best seats in the house are in fact outside at one of the dozen tables around the big glass pyramid on the terrace. ✉ *Piramide Bldg. 1F, 6–6–9 Roppongi, Minato-ku* ☎ *03/5785–3671* 🚫 *AE, MC, V* Ⓜ *Hibiya subway line, Roppongi Station (Exit 1).*

Japanese

$$–$$$$ ✕ **Inakaya.** The style here is *robatayaki,* a dining experience that segues
Fodor'sChoice into pure theater. Inside a large U-shape counter, two cooks in traditional
★ garb sit on cushions behind a grill, with a cornucopia of food spread out in front of them: fresh vegetables, seafood, skewers of beef and chicken. You point to what you want, and your server shouts out the order. The cook bellows back your order, plucks your selection up out of the pit, prepares it, and hands it across on an 8-foot wooden paddle. Inakaya is open from 5 PM to 5 AM, and fills up fast after 7. ✉ *Reine Bldg., 1st fl., 5–3–4 Roppongi, Minato-ku* ☎ *03/3408–5040* ⌂ *Reservations not accepted* 🚫 *AE, DC, MC, V* ☽ *No lunch* Ⓜ *Hibiya subway line, Roppongi Station (Exit 3).*

$$ ✕ **Ganchan.** The Japanese expect their yakitori joints—restaurants that
Fodor'sChoice specialize in bits of charcoal-broiled chicken and vegetables—to be just
★ like Ganchan: smoky, noisy, and cluttered. The counter seats barely 15, and you have to squeeze to get to the chairs in back. Festival masks, paper kites and lanterns, and greeting cards from celebrity patrons adorn the walls. The cooks yell at each other, fan the grill, and serve enormous schooners of beer. Try the *tsukune* (balls of minced chicken)

and the fresh asparagus wrapped in bacon. It stays open until 1:30 AM (midnight on Sunday). ⊠ 6–8–23 Roppongi, Minato-ku ☎ 03/3478–0092 ⊟ AE, MC, V Ⓜ Hibiya subway line, Roppongi Station (Exit 1A).

Thai

$$–$$$ ✕ **Erawan.** Window tables at this sprawling Thai "brasserie" on the top floor of a popular Roppongi vertical mall afford a wonderful view of the Tōkyō skyline at night. Black-painted wood floors, ceiling fans, Thai antiques, and rattan chairs establish the mood, and the space is nicely broken up into large and small dining areas and private rooms. The service is cheerful and professional. Specialties of the house include deep-fried prawn and crabmeat cakes, spicy roast-beef salad, sirloin tips with mango sauce, and a terrific dish of stir-fried lobster meat with cashews. For window seating, it's best to reserve ahead. ⊠ Roi Bldg. 13F, 5–5–1 Roppongi, Minato-ku ☎ 03/3404–5741 ⊟ AE, DC, MC, V Ⓜ Hibiya subway line, Roppongi Station (Exit 3).

Shibuya

Japanese

★ **$$–$$$** ✕ **Tenmatsu.** The best seats in the house at Tenmatsu, as in any tempura-ya, are at the immaculate wooden counter, where your tidbits of choice are taken straight from the oil and served immediately. You also get to watch the chef in action. Tenmatsu's brand of good natured professional hospitality adds to the enjoyment of the meal. Here you can rely on a set menu or order à la carte tempura delicacies like lotus root, shrimp, unagi (eel), and kisu (a small white freshwater fish). Call ahead to reserve counter seating or a full-course kaiseki dinner in a private tatami room. ⊠ 1–6–1 Dōgen-zaka, Shibuya-ku ☎ 03/3462–2815 ⊟ DC, MC, V Ⓜ JR Yamanote Line, Shibuya Station (Minami-guchi/South Exit); Ginza and Hanzō-mon subway lines, Shibuya Station (Exit 3A).

Shinagawa

Contemporary

$$–$$$$ ✕ **Manhattan Grill.** Only in Japan can you have a French-Indonesian meal at a restaurant called the Manhattan Grill in a food court dubbed the "Foodium." Chef Wayan Surbrata, who trained at the Four Seasons Resort in Bali, has a delicate, deft touch with such dishes as spicy roast-chicken salad, and steak marinated in cinnamon and soy sauce, served with shiitake mushrooms and gado-gado (shrimp-flavor rice crackers). One side of the minimalist restaurant is open to the food court; the floor-to-ceiling windows on the other side don't afford much of a view. ⊠ Atré Shinagawa 4F, 2–18–1 Konan, Minato-ku ☎ 03/6717–0922 ⊟ AE, MC, V Ⓜ JR Shinagawa Station (Higashi-guchi/East Exit).

★ **$$–$$$** ✕ **T. Y. Harbor Brewery.** A converted warehouse on the waterfront houses this restaurant, a Tōkyō hot spot for private parties. Chef David Chiddo refined his signature California-Thai cuisine at some of the best restaurants in Los Angeles. Don't miss his grilled mahimahi with green rice and mango salsa, or the grilled jumbo-shrimp brochettes with tabbouleh. True to its name, T. Y. Harbor brews its own beer, in a tank that reaches all the way to the 46-foot-high ceiling. The best seats in the house are on the bay-side deck, open from May to October. Reservations are a good idea on weekends. ⊠ *2–1–3 Higashi-Shinagawa, Shinagawa-ku* ☎ *03/5479–4555* ⊟ *AE, DC, MC, V* Ⓜ *Tōkyō Monorail or Rinkai Line, Ten-nōz Isle Station (Exit B).*

Shirokanedai

Japanese

$$$$ ✕ **Happo-en.** A 300-year-old Japanese garden wrapped around a lake is the setting for the palatial complex that houses this upscale restaurant, a shrine, and a traditional teahouse. Beautiful scenery aside, the food is what draws locals and visitors again and again. The grand exterior and pristine banquet rooms are somewhat uninviting and overly formal, but the tables overlooking the garden provide a tranquil backdrop for an unforgettable meal. Among the pricey prix-fixe dinners are kaiseki, shabu-shabu, sukiyaki, and tempura, and there's also a buffet dinner. Go in the afternoon for a tour of the grounds, *sado* (tea ceremony), and a seasonal Japanese set lunch for ¥4,500. ⊠ *1–1–1 Shirokanedai, Minato-ku* ☎ *03/5401–2820* 🏛 *Jacket and tie* ✍ *Reservations essential* ⊟ *AE, MC, V* Ⓜ *Mita and Namboku subway lines, Shirokanedai Station (Exit 2).*

Spanish

$$ ✕ **Sabado Sabadete.** Catalan jewelry designer Mañuel Benito used to rent a bar in Aoyama on Saturday nights and cook for his friends, just for the fun of it. Word got around: eventually there wasn't room in the bar to lift a fork. Inspired by this success, Benito opened this Spanish restaurant. The highlight of every evening is still the moment when the chef, in his bright red cap, shouts out "Gohan desu yo!"—the Japanese equivalent of "Soup's on!"—and dishes out his bubbling-hot paella. Don't miss the empanadas or the *escalivada* (Spanish ratatouille with red peppers, onions, and eggplant). ⊠ *Genteel Shirokanedai Bldg., 2nd fl., 5–3–2 Shirokanedai, Minato-ku* ☎ *03/3445–9353* ⊟ *No credit cards* ☉ *Closed Sun. and Mon.* Ⓜ *Mita and Namboku subway lines, Shirokanedai Station (Exit 1).*

Shōtō

French

$$$$ ✕ **Chez Matsuo.** With its stately homes, Shōtō, a sedate Beverly Hills, is the kind of area you don't expect so close to Shibuya Station. In the middle of it all is Chez Matsuo, in a lovely two-story Western-style house. The dining rooms overlook the garden, where you can dine by candlelight on spring and autumn evenings. Owner-chef Matsuo studied as a sommelier in London and perfected his culinary finesse in Paris. His pricey French food is nouvelle; among the house specialties are *suprême* (breast and wing) of duck, clam-and-tomato mousse, and a fish of the day. ⊠ *1–23–15 Shōtō, Shibuya-ku* ☎ *03/3485–0566* ✍ *Reservations essential* ⊟ *AE, DC, MC, V* Ⓜ *JR Yamanote Line, Ginza and Hanzō-mon subway lines, and private rail lines: Shibuya Station (Exits 5 and 8 for Hanzō-mon, Kita-guchi/North Exit for all others).*

Tora-no-mon

Chinese

$$–$$$$ ✗ **Toh-Ka-Lin.** Business travelers consider the Ōkura to be one of the best hotels in Asia. That judgment has to do with its polish, its human scale, its impeccable service, and, to judge by Toh-Ka-Lin, the quality of its restaurants. The cuisine is eclectic; two stellar examples are the Peking duck and the sautéed quail wrapped in lettuce leaf. The restaurant also has a not-too-expensive midafternoon meal ($$) of assorted dim sum and other delicacies—and one of the most extensive wine lists in town. ⊠ *Hotel Ōkura Main Bldg. 6F, 2–10–4 Tora-no-mon, Minato-ku* ☎ *03/ 3505–6068* ⊟ *AE, DC, MC, V* Ⓜ *Hibiya subway line, Kamiya-chō Station (Exit 4B); Ginza subway line, Tora-no-mon Station (Exit 3).*

Tsukiji

Sushi

★ **$$–$$$** ✗ **Edo-Gin.** In an area that teems with sushi bars, this one maintains its reputation as one of the best. Edo-Gin serves generous slabs of fish that drape over the vinegared rice rather than perch demurely on top. The centerpiece of the main room is a huge tank where the day's ingredients swim about until they are required; it doesn't get any fresher than this. Set menus here are reasonable, especially for lunch, but a big appetite for specialties like sea urchin and *ōtoro* tuna can put a dent in your budget. ⊠ *4–5–1 Tsukiji, Chūō-ku* ☎ *03/3543–4401* ⊟ *AE, DC, MC, V* ⊘ *Closed Sun and Jan. 1–4* Ⓜ *Hibiya subway line, Tsukiji Station (Exit 1); Ōedo subway line, Tsukiji-shijō Station (Exit A1).*

¢–$ ✗ **Takeno.** Just a stone's throw from the Tōkyō fish market, Takeno is a rough-cut neighborhood restaurant that fills up at noon with the market's wholesalers and auctioneers and personnel from the nearby Asahi Newspaper offices. There's nothing here but the freshest and the best— big portions of it, at very reasonable prices. Sushi and sashimi are the staples, but there's also a wonderful *tendon* bowl, with shrimp and eel tempura on rice. Prices are not posted because they vary with the costs that morning in the market. To make a reservation, you must telephone before 6:30 PM. ⊠ *6–21–2 Tsukiji, Chūō-ku* ☎ *03/3541–8698* ⊟ *No credit cards* ⊘ *Closed Sun.* Ⓜ *Hibiya subway line, Tsukiji Station (Exit 1); Ōedo subway line, Tsukiji-shijō Station (Exit A1).*

Uchisaiwai-chō

Chinese

★ **$$–$$$$** ✗ **Heichinrou.** A short walk from the Imperial Hotel, this branch of one of Yokohama's oldest and best Chinese restaurants commands a spectacular view of the Imperial Palace grounds. Call ahead to reserve a table by the window. The cuisine is Cantonese; pride of place goes to the *kaisen ryōri*, a banquet of steamed sea bass, lobster, shrimp, scallops, abalone, and other seafood dishes. Much of the clientele comes from the law offices, securities firms, and foreign banks in the building. The VIP room at Heichinrou, with its soft lighting and impeccable linens, is a popular venue for power lunches. ⊠ *Fukoku Seimei Bldg., 28th fl., 2–2–2*

Uchisaiwai-chō, Chiyoda-ku ☎ *03/3508–0555* ▤ *AE, DC, MC, V* ☉ *Closed Sun.* Ⓜ *Mita Line, Uchisaiwai-chō Station (Exit A6).*

Ueno

Japanese

$$$$ ✕ **Sasa-no-yuki.** In Shitamachi, Tōkyō's old downtown working-class neighborhood, Sasa-no-yuki has served meals based on homemade tofu for the past 300 years. The food is inspired in part by shōjin ryōri (Buddhist vegetarian cuisine). The basic three-course set menu includes *ankake* (bean curd in sweet soy sauce), *uzumi* tofu (scrambled with rice and green tea), and *unsui* (a creamy tofu crepe filled with sea scallops, shrimp, and minced red pepper). For bigger appetites, there's also an eight-course banquet. The seating is on tatami, and the garden has a waterfall. ✉ *2–15–10 Negishi, Taitō-ku* ☎ *03/3873–1145* ▤ *AE, DC, V* ☉ *Closed Mon.* Ⓜ *JR Uguisudani Station (Kita-guchi/North Exit).*

Yūraku-chō

Japanese

$$–$$$
Fodor's Choice
★

✕ **Robata.** Old, funky, and more than a little cramped, Robata is a bit daunting at first. But fourth-generation chef-owner Takao Inoue holds forth here with an inspired version of Japanese home cooking. He's also a connoisseur of pottery; he serves his food on pieces acquired at famous kilns all over the country. There's no menu; just tell Inoue-san (who speaks some English) how much you want to spend, and leave the rest to him. A meal at Robata—like the pottery—is simple to the eye but subtle and fulfilling. Typical dishes include steamed fish with vegetables, stews of beef or pork, and seafood salads. ✉ *1–3–8 Yūraku-chō, Chiyoda-ku* ☎ *03/3591–1905* ▤ *No credit cards* ☉ *Closed some Sun. each month. No lunch* Ⓜ *JR Yūraku-chō Station (Hibiya Exit); Hibiya, Chiyoda, and Mita subway lines, Hibiya Station (Exit A4).*

WHERE TO STAY

Tōkyō's developers build big. When the project is a hotel—more often than not, on the upper floors of an office tower—it's invariably at the high end of the market. Developers are taking the spare-no-expense approach to hotels: soaring atriums, concierges, oceans of marble, interior decorators fetched in from London, New York, and Milan. The results rival luxury accommodations anywhere in the world.

Though there are international (full-service) and business hotels, as well as hostels and apartment and home rentals and exchanges, there are also plenty of Japanese accommodations: *ryokan, minshuku,* "capsule" hotels, homes, and temples.

What to Expect

There are three things you can take for granted almost anywhere you set down your bags in Tōkyō: cleanliness, safety, and good service. Unless otherwise specified, all rooms at the hotels listed in this book have private baths and are Western-style. In listings, we always name the facilities that are available, but we don't specify whether they cost extra.

When pricing accommodations, try to find out what's included and what entails an additional charge.

Assume that hotels operate on the European Plan (EP, with no meals) unless we specify that they use the Continental Plan (CP, with a continental breakfast), Breakfast Plan (BP, with a full breakfast), Modified American Plan (MAP, with breakfast and dinner), or the Full American Plan (FAP, with all meals).

Prices

Deluxe hotels charge a premium for good-size rooms, lots of perks, great service, and central locations. More-affordable hotels aren't always in the most convenient places, have

HOTEL VOCABULARY

Some useful words when checking into a hotel:

- air-conditioning: *eakon*
- double beds: *daburubeddo*
- king bed: *kingu saizu-no-beddo.*
- private baths: *o-furo*
- pushed together: *kuttsukerareta*
- queen bed: *kuīn saizun-no-beddo*
- separate: *betsu*
- showers: *shawā*
- twin beds: *tsuinbeddo*

small rooms, and fewer amenities. That said, many moderately priced accommodations are still within the central wards; some have an old-fashioned charm and personal touch the upscale places can't offer. And, wherever you're staying, Tōkyō's subway and train system—comfortable (except in rush hours), efficient, inexpensive, and safe—will get you back and forth.

WHAT IT COSTS In yen					
	$$$$	$$$	$$	$	¢
FOR 2 PEOPLE	over 40,000	30,000–40,000	20,000–30,000	10,000–20,000	under 10,000

Price categories are assigned based on the range between the least and most expensive standard double rooms in nonholiday high season. Taxes (5%, plus 3% for bills over ¥15,000) are extra.

Akasaka-mitsuke

$$$–$$$$ ⊞ **Akasaka Prince Hotel.** Rooms from the 20th to the 30th floor of this hotel, designed by world-renowned architect Kenzō Tange, offer the best views of the city. A white-and-pale-gray color scheme accentuates the light from the wide windows that run the length of the rooms. This affords a feeling of spaciousness, though the rooms—oddly shaped because of Tange's attempt to give every accommodation a "corner" location—are a bit small compared to those in other deluxe hotels. The marble and off-white reception areas on the ground floor are pristine—maybe even a bit sterile. ⊠ *1–2 Kioi-chō, Chiyoda-ku 102-8585* ☎ *03/3234-1111* ⊕ *www.princehotelsjapan.com* ⇆ *693 rooms, 68 suites* ⌂ *9 restaurants, room service, refrigerators, cable TV with movies, pool, massage, 2 bars, laundry service, concierge, in-room broadband, business services, no-smoking floors* ▤ *AE, DC, MC, V* Ⓜ *Ginza and Marunouchi subway lines, Akasaka-mitsuke Station (Exit 7).*

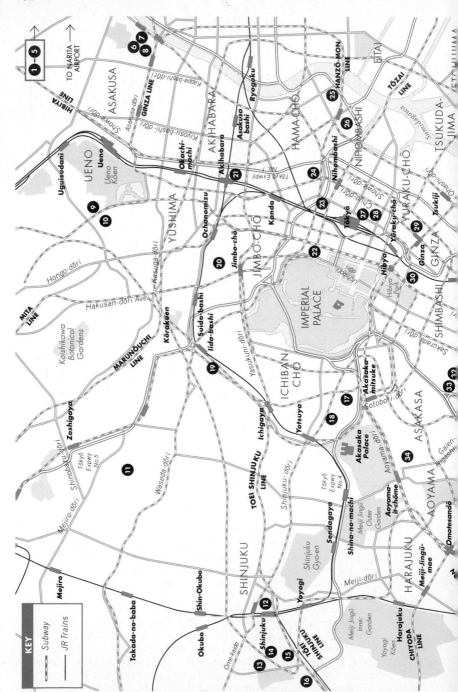

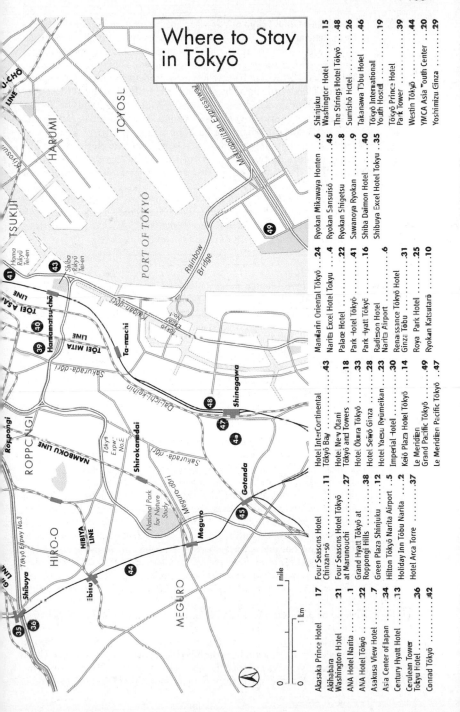

Where to Stay in Tōkyō

\$\$\$–\$\$\$\$ ▦ **Hotel New Ōtani Tōkyō and Towers.** The New Ōtani is a bustling complex in the center of Tōkyō. When the house is full and all the banquet facilities are in use, the traffic in the restaurants and shopping arcades seems like rush hour at a busy railway station. The hotel's redeeming feature is its spectacular 10-acre Japanese garden, complete with a pond and a red-lacquer bridge. The rooms in the main building are in pleasant pastels, but they lack the outstanding views of those in the Tower, many of which overlook the garden's ponds and waterfalls. Among the many restaurants and bars are La Tour d'Argent, Japan's first Trader Vic's, and The Bar, housed within a revolving lounge on the 40th floor that offers supreme city views. ✉ *4–1 Kioi-chō, Chiyoda-ku 102-0094* ☎ *03/3265–1111, 0120/227–021 toll-free* ⊕ *www.newotani.co.jp* ⤳ *1,600 rooms, 51 suites* ♨ *38 restaurants, room service, in-room safes, refrigerators, cable TV with movies, indoor pool, health club, 5 bars, babysitting, laundry service, in-room broadband, business services, meeting rooms, no-smoking rooms* ▤ *AE, DC, MC, V* Ⓜ *Ginza and Marunouchi subway lines, Akasaka-mitsuke Station (Exit 7).*

Akihabara

\$ ▦ **Akihabara Washington Hotel.** This arch-shape hotel is an inexpensive choice near Akihabara—Tōkyō's geek paradise containing the city's largest collection of electronic shops and trendy cafés staffed by waitresses in maid uniforms. The small rooms, which are big enough to include a work desk, are simple but comfortable. The subway station is two minutes away on foot. ✉ *1–8–3 Sakumacho, Chiyoda-ku 101-0025* ☎ *03/ 3255–3311* ⊕ *www.wh-rsv.com* ⤳ *312 rooms* ♨ *4 restaurants, room service, laundry service, business services* ▤ *AE, DC, MC, V* Ⓜ *JR; Hibiya subway line, Akihabara Station (Exit 5).*

Asakusa

\$\$–\$\$\$ ▦ **Asakusa View Hotel.** Upscale Western-style accommodations are rare in Asakusa, so the Asakusa View pretty much has this end of the market to itself. Off the smart marble lobby, a harpist plays in the tea lounge, and expensive boutiques line the second floor. The communal *hinoki* (Japanese-cypress) baths on the sixth floor, which also houses the Japanese-style tatami suites, overlook a Japanese garden. The best of the Western-style rooms are on the 22nd and 23rd floors, with a view of the Sensō-ji pagoda and temple grounds. There's a top-floor lounge with live entertainment. ✉ *3–17–1 Nishi-Asakusa, Taitō-ku 111-8765* ☎ *03/3847–1111* ⊕ *www.viewhotels.co.jp/asakusa* ⤳ *330 Western-style rooms, 7 Japanese-style suites* ♨ *4 restaurants, pool, health club, Japanese baths, 2 bars, no-smoking rooms* ▤ *AE, DC, MC, V* Ⓜ *Ginza subway line, Tawara-machi Station (Exit 3).*

★ \$ ▦ **Ryokan Shigetsu.** Just off Nakamise-dōri and inside the Sensō-ji grounds, this small inn could not be better located for a visit to the temple. The best options are the rooms with futon bedding and tatami floors; the Western rooms, plain but comfortably furnished, are less expensive. All rooms have private baths; there's also a Japanese-style wooden communal bath on the sixth floor with a view of the Sensō-ji pagoda.

1

✉ *1–31–11 Asakusa, Taitō-ku 111-0032* ☎ *03/3843–2345* ⊕ *www.roy.hi-ho.ne.jp/shigetsu* ⇥ *14 Western-style rooms, 10 Japanese-style rooms* ⚑ *Restaurant, Japanese baths* ▭ *AE, MC, V* Ⓜ *Ginza subway line, Asakusa Station (Exit 1/Kaminari-mon Exit).*

★ ¢ ⌂ **Ryokan Mikawaya Honten.** In the heart of Asakusa, this concrete ryokan is just behind the Kaminari-mon, the gateway to the Sensō-ji complex. Nearby are the Nakamise souvenir market and the Kappa-bashi restaurant-supply street, two popular tourist spots. The Japanese-style rooms are small for two people and lack sizable storage areas, but are very clean. Though English-challenged, the staff is attentive and friendly. ✉ *1–30–12 Asakusa, Taitō-ku 111-0032* ☎ *03/3844–8807* ⇥ *19 Japanese-style rooms, 1 Western-style room* ▭ *AE, MC, V* Ⓜ *Ginza subway line, Asakusa Station (Exit 1/Kaminari-mon Exit).*

Ebisu

$$$$ ⌂ **Westin Tōkyō.** In the Yebisu Garden Place development, the Westin provides easy access to Mitsukoshi department store, the Tōkyō Metropolitan Museum of Photography, the elegant Ebisu Garden concert hall, and the Taillevent-Robuchon restaurant (in a full-scale reproduction of a Louis XV château). The style of the hotel is updated art nouveau, with an excess of marble and bronze. The rooms are spacious—with bathrooms large enough to accommodate families—and the suites are huge by Japanese standards. The beds are very comfortable. Note, however, that communication with the hotel staff in English can at times be difficult. ✉ *1–4 Mita 1-chōme, Meguro-ku 153-0062* ☎ *03/5423–7000* ⊕ *www.westin-tokyo.co.jp/* ⇥ *438 rooms, 20 suites* ⚑ *6 restaurants, room service, in-room safes, refrigerators, cable TV with movies, gym, massage, bar, dry cleaning, laundry service, in-room broadband, business services, meeting rooms, no-smoking rooms* ▭ *AE, DC, MC, V* Ⓜ *JR, Hibiya subway line; Ebisu Station (Higashi-guchi/East Exit).*

Ginza

$$–$$$ ⌂ **Renaissance Tōkyō Hotel Ginza Tōbu.** Relatively reasonable prices, friendly service, and comfortable rooms make the Renaissance something of a bargain for the Ginza area. The standard rooms are small and have blond-wood furniture and pastel quilted bedspreads. Larger rooms can be found on the pricier Renaissance Floor. Breakfast, afternoon coffee/tea, and in-room high-speed Internet access are complimentary. Trendy and traditional shopping and the lively Tsukiji fish market are within a short walking distance. ✉ *6–14–10 Ginza, Chūō-ku 104-0061* ☎ *03/3546–0111* ⊕ *http://marriott.com* ⇥ *197 rooms, 9 suites* ⚑ *3 restaurants, room service, refrigerators, cable TV with movies, massage, bar, dry cleaning, laundry service, in-room broadband, business services, no-smoking rooms* ▭ *AE, DC, MC, V* ⦿ *CP* Ⓜ *Hibiya and Asakusa subway lines, Higashi-Ginza Station (Exit A1).*

$$ ⌂ **Yoshimizu Ginza.** You're expected to fold up your own futon at this **Fodor'sChoice** modest traditional inn, which was inspired by owner Yoshimi Naka- ★ gawa's experience living the simple life at a commune in Woodstock, New York, in the 1970s. The money that isn't spent on service has been

spent—with exquisite taste—on simple, natural appointments: wooden floors dyed pale indigo, hand-painted shōji screens, basins of Shigaraki ware in the washrooms. The two stone communal Japanese baths on the ninth floor can be reserved for a private relaxing soak for two. The inn is a few minutes' walk from the Kabuki-za and the fashionable heart of Ginza. Book early. ⊠ *3–11–3 Ginza, Chūō-ku 104-0061* ☎ *03/ 3248-4432* ⊕ *www.yoshimizu.com* ⤳ *11 Japanese-style rooms without bath* ♿ *2 restaurants, Japanese baths; no room phones, no room TVs, no smoking* ⊟ *AE, DC, MC, V* ℟ *BP* Ⓜ *Hibiya subway line, Higashi-Ginza Station (Exit 3 or A2).*

Hakozaki

$$$–$$$$ 🏨 **Royal Park Hotel.** For stopovers at Narita, this hotel can't be beat for its airport access and proximity to central Tōkyō. A passageway connects the hotel to the Tōkyō City Air Terminal, where you can catch a bus to Narita without hassle. The comfortable, spacious, marble-clad lobby has wood-panel columns and brass trim. Neutral grays and browns decorate the well-proportioned rooms. The best rooms are those on the executive floors (16–18) with a view of the Sumida River, and those on floors 6–8 overlooking the hotel's delightful Japanese garden. The shopping of Ginza and the Marunouchi business district are a short cab ride away. ⊠ *2–1–1 Nihombashi, Kakigara-chō, Chūō-ku 103-0014* ☎ *03/3667–1111* ⊕ *www.rph.co.jp* ⤳ *450 rooms, 9 suites* ♿ *6 restaurants, room service, refrigerators, cable TV with movies, massage, bar, dry cleaning, laundry service, in-room broadband, business services, no-smoking rooms* ⊟ *AE, DC, MC, V* Ⓜ *Hanzō-mon subway line, Suitengū-mae Station (Exit 4).*

Hibiya

$$$–$$$$ 🏨 **Imperial Hotel.** You can't beat the location of these prestigious quarters: in the heart of central Tōkyō, between the Imperial Palace and Ginza. The finest rooms, on the 30th floor in the New Tower, afford views of the palace grounds. The Old Imperial Bar incorporates elements from the 1923 version of the hotel, which Frank Lloyd Wright designed. The Imperial opened its doors in 1890, and from the outset the hotel has been justly proud of its Western-style facilities and personalized Japanese service. Rooms, complete with walk-in closets and flat-panel TVs, range from standard doubles to suites that are larger than many homes. ⊠ *1–1–1 Uchisaiwai-chō, Chiyoda-ku 100-8558* ☎ *03/3504–1111* ⊕ *www.imperialhotel.co.jp* ⤳ *1,005 rooms, 54 suites* ♿ *13 restaurants, cable TV with movies, indoor pool, health club, massage, 2 bars, in-room broadband, business services, no-smoking rooms* ⊟ *AE, DC, MC, V* Ⓜ *Hibiya subway line, Hibiya Station (Exit 5).*

Higashi-Gotanda

¢ 🏨 **Ryokan Sansuisō.** Budgeteers appreciate this basic ryokan, a two-story building near Gotanda Station and the Meguro River, where *sakura* (cherry) trees bloom each April. The proprietor will greet you with a warm smile and a bow and escort you to a small tatami room with a pay TV, a yukata, a Japanese tea set, and a rather noisy heater–air-conditioner mounted on the wall. Some rooms are stuffy, and only two have private baths, but the Sansuisō is clean, easy to find, and only 20 minutes by train from Tōkyō Station or Ginza. The midnight curfew poses a problem for night owls. The Japan National Tourist Organization (JNTO) can help you make reservations at this Japanese Inn Group property. ⊠ *2–9–5 Higashi-Gotanda, Shinagawa-ku 141-0022* ☎ *03/3441–7475, 03/3201–3331 for JNTO* ⊕ *www.sansuiso.net* ⤴ *9 rooms, 2 with bath* ⚬ *Room TV with movies, Japanese baths, business services* ▤ *AE, V* Ⓜ *Asakusa subway line (Exit A3) and JR Yamanote Line (Higashi-guchi/East Exit), Gotanda Station.*

Higashi-Shinjuku

¢ ▥ **Green Plaza Shinjuku.** Male budget travelers in Shinjuku willing to throw claustrophobia to the wind can settle in for a night at the Green Plaza, a capsule hotel in the entertainment district of Kabuki-chō. (As with most capsule hotels, there are no accommodations for women.) Like bees in a honeycomb, patrons sleep in yellow capsules stacked in rows along the halls of each floor. Korean-style massage (on the fifth floor) is an added option not common in the capsule world. Vending machines on three floors dispense drinks, soup, and snacks. Underwear, slacks, and neckties are available for emergency purchases. The environment is not tranquil, but it's clean, safe, and cheap. If you want to try a capsule hotel, this is the place to do it. ⊠ *1–29–3 Kabuki-chō, Shinjuku-ku 160–0021* ☎ *03/3207–4923* ⊕ *www.hgpshinjuku.jp* ⤴ *660 capsules without bath* ⚬ *Massage, sauna, laundry service; no room phones* ▤ *AE, MC, V* Ⓜ *Shinjuku Station (Higashi-guchi/East Exit).*

Kyō-bashi

$$$$ ▥ **Hotel Seiyō Ginza.** The grand marble staircase, the thick pile of the carpets, the profusion of cut flowers, the reception staff in coats and tails: all combine to create an atmosphere more like an elegant private club than a hotel. Along with this elegance, location and personalized service are the best reasons to choose the exclusive Seiyō, tucked away on a side street a few minutes from Ginza. Individually decorated rooms have walk-in closets, huge shower stalls, and a direct line to a personal secretary who takes care of your every need. The accommodations, however, are smaller than what you might expect. ⊠ *1–11–2 Ginza, Chūō-ku 104-0061* ☎ *03/3535–1111* ⊕ *www.seiyo-ginza.com* ⤴ *51 rooms, 26 suites* ⚬ *4 restaurants, room service, in-room safes, refrigerators, cable TV with movies, health club, 2 bars, babysitting, dry cleaning, laundry service, concierge, in-room broadband, business services, no-smoking rooms* ▤ *AE, DC, MC, V* Ⓜ *Ginza subway line, Kyō-bashi Station (Exit 2); Yūraku-chō Line, Ginza-Itchōme Station (Exit 7).*

Marunouchi

$$$$ ▥ **Four Seasons Hotel Tōkyō at Marunouchi.** A departure from the typical large scale of the chain, this Four Seasons, set within the glistening

Pacific Century Place, has the feel of a boutique hotel. The muted beige-and-bronze reception area resembles a comfortable private club, with deep-pile carpets, plush brocade sofas, and sumptuous armchairs. Chic black-lacquer doors lead to spacious guest rooms, which actually occupy the five floors below the seventh-floor reception area. Beds have brown-leather-covered headboards that continue partway across the ceiling for a canopy effect. Design really *matters* here—but so does high-tech luxury, in touches like plasma-screen TVs and variable lighting. The staff speaks fluent English, and the service is spot-on. ✉ *1–11–1 Marunouchi, Chiyoda-ku 100-6277* ☎ *03/5222–7222* ⊕ *www. fourseasons.com/marunouchi* ⟿ *48 rooms, 9 suites* ⚭ *Restaurant, room service, in-room safes, refrigerators, cable TV with movies, in-room DVDs, health club, Japanese baths, spa, steam room, bar, dry cleaning, laundry service, concierge, Wi-Fi, business services, meeting rooms, no-smoking rooms* ▤ *AE, DC, MC, V* Ⓜ *JR Tōkyō Station (Yaesu South Exit).*

$$$–$$$$ 🏨 **Palace Hotel.** The service is extremely helpful and professional; most of the staff has been with the hotel for more than 10 years. And you're only a moat away from the outer gardens of the Imperial Palace, and Ginza and the financial districts of Marunouchi are both a short taxi or subway ride away. An aura of calm conservatism bespeaks the Palace's half century as an accommodation for the well-to-do. The tasteful, low-key guest rooms are spacious; ask for one on the upper floors, facing the Imperial Palace. ✉ *1–1–1 Marunouchi, Chiyoda-ku 100-0005* ☎ *03/3211–5211* ⊕ *www.palacehotel.co.jp* ⟿ *384 rooms, 5 suites* ⚭ *7 restaurants, room service, in-room safes, refrigerators, cable TV with movies, in-room VCRs, indoor pool, health club, massage, sauna, bar, dry cleaning, laundry service, concierge, in-room broadband, business services, no-smoking floors* ▤ *AE, DC, MC, V* Ⓜ *Chiyoda, Marunouchi, Hanzō-mon, Tōzai, and Mita subway lines; Ōte-machi Station (Exit C-13B).*

Nihombashi

★ $$$$ 🏨 **Mandarin Oriental Tōkyō.** Occupying seven floors of the glistening Nihombashi Mitsui Tower is this hotel, a blend of harmony and outright modernity. The Mandarin's amazing rooms, decorated in dark and light browns, feature large bay windows with exquisite nighttime views of the city lights. The 45-inch flat-panel TVs, 2.1 surround-sound systems, and iPod-docking stations should please tech fans. Corner rooms have sunken marble tubs that allow you to gaze out windows while soaking. The spa devotes nine rooms to the hotel's signature body scrubs and massages. The restaurants are top-of-the-line, but guests weary from overload of superlatives might consider a short stroll toward Tōkyō Station, with its variety of tiny watering holes and *izakaya* (Japanese pubs). ✉ *2–1–1 Nihombashi Muromachi, Chūō-ku 103-8328* ☎ *03/3270–8950* ⊕ *www.mandarinoriental.com/tokyo* ⟿ *157 rooms, 22 suites* ⚭ *4 restaurants, in-room safes, in-room DVDs, gym, spa, bar, concierge, in-room broadband, Wi-Fi, business center* ▤ *AE, DC, MC, V* Ⓜ *Ginza and Hanzō-mon subway lines, Mitsukoshi-mae Station (Exit A7).*

Ningyō-chō

$ ⊞ **Sumishō Hotel.** This hotel, in a down-to-earth, friendly neighborhood, is popular with budget-minded foreign visitors who prefer to stay near the small Japanese restaurants and bars of Ningyō-chō. Even the biggest twin rooms are long and narrow, and the bathrooms are tiny units with low ceilings. The best accommodations are the three tatami rooms on the second floor overlooking a small Japanese garden. Full-course Japanese meals are available in the restaurant. The hotel is a bit hard to find: from Exit A5 of Ningyō-chō Station, turn right and take the first small right-hand street past the second traffic light; the Sumishō is on the left. ⊠ *9–14 Nihombashi-Kobunachō, Chūo-ku 103-0024* ☎ *03/3661–4603* ⊕ *www.sumisho-hotel.co.jp* ⇋ *72 Western-style rooms, 11 Japanese-style rooms* ⚒ *Restaurant, cable TV, Japanese baths, dry cleaning, laundry facilities, in-room data ports, business services, meeting rooms, no-smoking rooms* ☰ *AE, DC, MC, V* Ⓜ *Hibiya and Asakusa subway lines, Ningyō-chō Station (Exit A5).*

Nishi-Shinjuku

$$$$ ⊞ **Park Hyatt Tōkyō.** An elevator whisks you to the 41st floor, where the
Fodor'sChoice hotel—immortalized in the film *Lost in Translation*—begins with an
★ atrium lounge enclosed on three sides by floor-to-ceiling plate-glass windows. The panorama of Shinjuku, gaudy as it can be in the daytime, spreads out in front. Check-in formalities take place at sit-down desks, reached by a pleasant walk through an extensive library. Service is efficient and personal, and the mood of the hotel is contemporary and understated. King-size beds have Egyptian-cotton sheets and down-feather duvets; other appointments include an in-bath TV visible from the tub, black-lacquer cabinets, and huge plasma-screen TVs. Among the hotel's several restaurants is the popular New York Grill, with its open kitchen and steak-and-seafood menu. ⊠ *3–7–1–2 Nishi-Shinjuku, Shinjuku-ku 163-1090* ☎ *03/5322–1234* ⊕ *http://tokyo.park.hyatt. com* ⇋ *155 rooms, 23 suites* ⚒ *4 restaurants, room service, in-room safes, refrigerators, cable TV with movies, in-room DVDs, indoor pool, health club, spa, 2 bars, dry cleaning, laundry service, concierge, in-room broadband, business center, airport shuttle, no-smoking rooms* ☰ *AE, DC, MC, V* Ⓜ *JR Shinjuku Station (Nishi-guchi/West Exit).*

$$$ ⊞ **Century Hyatt Hotel.** The Century, set amid Shinjuku's skyscrapers, has the trademark Hyatt atrium-style lobby: seven stories high, with open-glass elevators soaring upward and three huge chandeliers suspended from above. The rooms are spacious for the price, though unremarkable in design; the best choices are the View Rooms (10th–26th floors), which overlook Shinjuku Koen (Shinjuku Park). Tochō-mae Station, beneath the hotel, allows swift access to the nightlife in Roppongi and Shiodome's business towers. ⊠ *2–7–2 Nishi-Shinjuku, Shinjuku-ku 160-0023* ☎ *03/3349–0111* ⊕ *http://tokyo.century.hyatt.com* ⇋ *750 rooms, 16 suites* ⚒ *6 restaurants, room service, in-room safes, refrigerators, cable TV with movies, indoor pool, gym, massage, bar, dry cleaning, laundry service, in-room broadband, business services, no-smoking* *rooms* ☰ *AE, DC, MC, V* Ⓜ *Marunouchi subway line, Nishi-Shinjuku Station (Exit C8); Ōedo subway line, Tochō-mae Station (all exits).*

$$–$$$ ▦ **Keiō Plaza Hotel Tōkyō.** This cereal-box-shape hotel, which has a reputation as a business destination, serves its guests with a classic touch. A greeter sporting a black top hat, for example, welcomes you into a lobby of generous marble and high ceilings. Equipped with spacious closets and dressing tables, the standard rooms are plenty big, and the Plaza Premier rooms have the latest in modern furniture design—no shortage of curved wood and metal here. The Sky Pool is actually two pools, one rectangular for laps and the other circular for lounging; both afford views of Shinjuku's steel-and-concrete skyscrapers. ✉ *2–2–1 Nishi-Shinjuku, Shinjuku-ku 160-8330* ☎ *03/3344–0111* ⊕ *www.keioplaza.co.jp* ↬ *1,431 rooms, 19 suites* ♨ *13 restaurants, room service, refrigerators, TV with movies, 2 pools, fitness room, massage, 3 bars, babysitting, in-room broadband, business center, meeting rooms, no-smoking rooms* ☰ *AE, DC, MC, V* Ⓜ *Shinjuku Station (Nishi-guchi/West Exit).*

$ ▦ **Shinjuku Washington Hotel.** Both the undulating tower and stouter annex of the Shinjuku Washington represent the typical Japanese business hotel: service is computerized as much as possible, and the rooms—utterly devoid of superfluous features—are just about big enough for the furniture and your luggage. In-room massage chairs, however, are a nice touch. The third-floor lobby has an automated check-in and check-out system; you are assigned a room and provided with a plastic card that opens the door and the minibar. The price is a bargain, but the staff speaks limited English and Shinjuku Station is 10 minutes away or more on foot. ✉ *3–2–9 Nishi-Shinjuku, Shinjuku-ku 160-0023* ☎ *03/3343–3111* ⊕ *www.wh-rsv.com* ↬ *1,630 rooms, 3 suites* ♨ *3 restaurants, room service, refrigerators, TV with movies, in-room VCRs, massage, some in-room broadband, bar, no-smoking rooms* ☰ *AE, DC, MC, V* Ⓜ *Shinjuku Station (Minami-guchi/South Exit).*

Odaiba

$$$–$$$$ ▦ **Hotel InterContinental Tōkyō Bay.** Wedged between Tōkyō Bay and an expressway, the InterContinental affords pleasant views in a slightly isolated setting. Rooms overlooking the river to the north run ¥7,000 more than those pointing to the bay. All of the rooms are large, and the bathrooms include separate showers and tubs. The surrounding area is filled with industrial complexes, offering nothing in the way of immediate entertainment options, but the sixth-floor Sunset Lounge is a relaxing place to unwind and view the Rainbow Bridge and surrounding Odaiba. ✉ *1–16–2 Kaigan, Minato-ku 105-8576* ☎ *03/5404–2222* ⊕ *www.ichotelsgroup.com* ↬ *331 rooms, 8 suites* ♨ *5 restaurants, refrigerators, fitness room, bar, dry cleaning, in-room broadband, business services, meeting rooms* ☰ *AE, DC, MC, V* Ⓜ *Yurikamome rail line, Takeshiba Station.*

$$$–$$$$ ▦ **Le Meridien Grand Pacific Tōkyō.** A sprawling complex at the tip of a human-made peninsula in Tōkyō Bay, the Meridien is a good choice for conventioneers at the nearby Tōkyō Big Site. European-inspired columns, pedestals, and flowery furnishings fill the entrance hall. This theme carries over to the rather sizeable rooms, decorated in shades of gold and brown. Rooms facing Haneda Airport and the Museum of Maritime Science (which resembles a large ship) are ¥6,000 less than those overlooking the Rainbow Bridge and the flat-roofed boats ferrying passengers within the harbor. ⊠ *2–6–1 Daiba, Minato-ku 135-8701* ☎ *03/5500–6711* ⊕ *www.meridien-grandpacific.com* ⟐ *796 rooms, 88 suites* ⚹ *8 restaurants, room service, 2 pools, gym, 3 bars, concierge, business center, no-smoking rooms* ⊟ *AE, DC, MC, V* Ⓜ *Yurikamome rail line, Daiba Station.*

Roppongi

$$$$ 🏨 **Grand Hyatt Tōkyō at Roppongi Hills.** The Grand Hyatt is designed with
Fodor'sChoice every imaginable convenience and comfort. A drawer in the mahogany
★ dresser in each room, for example, has laptop cables and adaptors. The showers have two delivery systems, one through a luxurious "rain-shower" head affixed to the ceiling. No expense has been spared on materials, from the Egyptian-cotton bed linens to the red-granite pool in the spa. Rooms are huge, with high ceilings, touch-panel lighting systems, remote-control black-out blinds, and muted earth tones of brown, beige, and yellow. Guests staying in Grand Club rooms receive complimentary breakfast and evening drinks. The complicated layout of the facilities can make moving around seem like a game of Chutes and Ladders. ⊠ *6–10–3 Roppongi, Minato-ku 106-0032* ☎ *03/4333–8800* ⊕ *www.tokyo.grand.hyatt.com* ⟐ *361 rooms, 28 suites* ⚹ *6 restaurants, room service, in-room safes, refrigerators, cable TV with movies, in-room DVDs, indoor pool, health club, Japanese baths, spa, 2 bars, babysitting, dry cleaning, laundry service, concierge, in-room broadband, business services, airport shuttle, no-smoking rooms* ⊟ *AE, DC, MC, V* Ⓜ *Hibiya subway line, Roppongi Station (Exit 1A); Ōedo subway line, Roppongi Station (Exit 3).*

$ 🏨 **Hotel Arca Torre.** This European-style hotel sits on a coveted location in one of Tōkyō's premier nightlife quarters, just a few minutes' walk from the Tōkyō Midtown and Roppongi Hills shopping-and-entertainment complexes. Red hanging flags and a faux-stone exterior greet you at the entry. The accommodations are ample for the price (twins are much roomier than doubles), with nice little touches like built-in hot plates for making tea and coffee, and retractable clotheslines in the bathrooms. There are, however, no closets—just some coat hooks on the wall. In keeping with the wild and wooly surroundings, adult channels are offered free of charge. ⊠ *6–1–23 Roppongi, Minato-ku 106-0032* ☎ *03/3404–5111* ⊕ *www.arktower.co.jp* ⟐ *77 rooms* ⚹ *2 restaurants, refrigerators, cable TV, some in-room broadband, no-smoking floor* ⊟ *AE, MC, V* Ⓜ *Hibiya and Ōedo subway lines, Roppongi Station (Exit 3).*

★ **¢–$** 🏨 **Asia Center of Japan.** Established mainly for Asian students and travelers on limited budgets, these accommodations have become generally popular with many international travelers for their good value and easy access (a 15-minute walk) to the nightlife of Roppongi. The "semi-doubles" here are really small singles, but twins and doubles are quite spacious for the price. Appointments are a bit spartan—off-white walls, mass-market veneer furniture—but the rooms have plenty of basic amenities like hair dryers, electric kettles, and yukatas. ⊠ *8–10–32*

Akasaka, Minato-ku 107-0052 ☎ *03/3402–6111* ⊕ *www.asiacenter.or. jp* ⬥ *172 rooms, 1 suite* ⟨ *Restaurant, refrigerators, cable TV with movies, massage, dry cleaning, laundry service, in-room data ports, meeting rooms, no-smoking rooms* ⊟ *AE, MC, V* Ⓜ *Ginza and Hanzō-mon subway lines, Aoyama-itchōme Station (Exit 4).*

Sekiguchi

$$$$ 🖫 **Four Seasons Hotel Chinzan-sō.** Where else can you sleep in a million-
Fodor'sChoice dollar room? That's about what it costs, on average, to build and fur-
★ nish each spacious room in this elegant hotel. Modern touches in the
rooms include 32-inch LCD TVs and a bedside control panel for
draperies; the large bathrooms have soaking tubs and separate showers. The spectacular fifth-floor Conservatory guest rooms have bay windows overlooking private Japanese-garden terraces. The solarium pool,
with its columns, tropical plants, and retractable glass roof, is straight
out of Xanadu. Built on the former estate of an imperial prince, Chinzan-sō rejoices in one of the most beautiful settings in Tōkyō; in summer the gardens are famous for their fireflies. Since the hotel occupies
a rather isolated section of Tōkyō, a complimentary shuttle service connects to the subway and Tōkyō Station. ⊠ *2–10–8 Sekiguchi, Bunkyō-
ku 112-0014* ☎ *03/3943–2222* ⊕ *www.fourseasons.com/tokyo* ⬥ *283
rooms, 51 suites* ⟨ *4 restaurants, room service, in-room safes, refrigerators, cable TV with movies, indoor pool, health club, Japanese baths,
spa, babysitting, dry cleaning, laundry service, concierge, in-room broadband, business services, no-smoking floors* ⊟ *AE, DC, MC, V* Ⓜ *Yūraku-
chō subway line, Edogawa-bashi Station (Exit 1A).*

Shiba Kōen

$$–$$$ 🖫 **Tōkyō Prince Hotel Park Tower.** The surrounding parkland and no ad-
jacent buildings make the Park Tower a peaceful setting. The atrium lobby
is impressive, with two glass elevators giving a clear view of the building's hollow core. Covering almost the entire exterior wall, the guest-
room windows afford nice views of nearby Tōkyō Tower and/or Shiba
Kōen (Shiba Park). Large flat-panel TVs and bathrooms with full-stall
showers and Jacuzzi tubs are nice, modern touches. The relative seclusion limits restaurant choices in the immediate area, though many can
be found at the nearby JR Hamamatsu-cho Station, less than 10 minutes away on foot. ⊠ *4–8–1 Shiba-kōen, Minato-ku 105-8563* ☎ *03/
5400–1111* ⊕ *www.princehotelsjapan.com* ⬥ *633 rooms, 40 suites* ⟨ *8
restaurants, room service, refrigerators, massage, 2 bars, in-room broadband, business center, no-smoking rooms* ⊟ *AE, DC, MC, V* Ⓜ *Ōedo
subway line, Akabanebashi Station (Akabanebashi Exit).*

$ 🖫 **Shiba Daimon Hotel.** This moderately priced hotel a minute's walk from
Zōjō-ji temple is popular with Japanese travelers. The staff is a bit ill
at ease with guests who cannot speak Japanese but no less willing to
help. The ubiquitous blond-veneer-on-pressboard furniture and floral-
print bedspreads fill the unremarkable rooms, which are reasonably spacious for the price. A good restaurant on the ground floor serves Japanese
and Chinese breakfasts and Chinese fare in the evening. ⊠ *2–3–6 Shiba-
kōen, Minato-ku 105-0011* ☎ *03/3431–3716* ⬥ *92 Western-style*

rooms, 4 Japanese-style rooms ☐ Restaurant, refrigerators, TV with movies, massage, laundry service, some in-room data ports, no-smoking rooms ☐ AE, DC, MC, V Ⓜ JR Hamamatsu-chō Station (Kita-guchi/ North Exit); Asakusa subway line, Daimon Station (Exit A3).

Shibuya

$$$$ 🏨 **Cerulean Tower Tokyu Hotel.** The pricey Cerulean Tower, perched on a slope above Shibuya's chaos, has a cavernous yet bustling lobby filled with plenty of attentive, English-speaking staffers. The rooms afford generous views of Tōkyō, but considering the price, the furnishings are rather plain. Some rooms include windows in the bathroom to allow for bathtime city gazing. Fans of the original, Japanese *Iron Chef* TV program might want to dine at Szechwan Restaurant Chen, whose menu is directed by one of the show's combatants, Kenichi Chen. There's a charge (¥2,100 per day) to use the pool, which is off-limits to people with tattoos. ☒ 26–1 Sakuragaoka-cho, Shibuya-ku 150-8512 ☎ 03/5457–0109 ⊕ www.ceruleantower-hotel.com ⬧ 405 rooms, 9 suites ☐ 6 restaurants, room service, refrigerators, massage, 2 bars, in-room broadband, business center, no-smoking rooms ☐ AE, DC, MC, V Ⓜ JR Shibuya Station (South Exit).

$$–$$$ 🏨 **Shibuya Excel Hotel Tokyu.** The key to this unremarkable hotel within the towering Mark City complex is access: local shopping options are aplenty, Shinjuku is a five-minute train ride to the north, and the Narita Express departs from nearby Shibuya Station frequently. The rooms, decorated in shades of beige and yellow, are plain but comfortable. North-facing rooms on the 10th floor and above (including the two "ladies-only" floors on levels 23 and 24) afford views of the Shinjuku skyline. The vibrant Estacion Café, above Shibuya's insanely busy intersection, serves drinks and small snacks. Perhaps equally enjoyable is the lobby vending machine, with its robot-arm dispenser. ☒ 1–12–2 Dogenzaka, Shibuya-ku 150-0043 ☎ 03/5457–0109 ⊕ www.tokyuhotels.co.jp ⬧ 407 rooms, 1 suite ☐ 3 restaurants, refrigerators, massage, in-room broadband, business services, no-smoking rooms ☐ AE, DC, MC, V Ⓜ JR Shibuya Station (Hachiko Exit).

Shinagawa

★ $$$$ 🏨 **The Strings Hotel Tōkyō.** Like the Conrad up the road in Shiodome, the Strings is all about blending modernity with traditional Japanese aesthetics. From Shinagawa Station, an elevator leads up to the hotel atrium, where a glass bridge spans a pond and cut stone mixes with dark wood. Guest rooms include LCD TVs and awesome views of the Tokyo skyline, (make sure you check it out at night), and the large bathrooms have separate showers and tubs. Prices in the hotel restaurants tend to be high, so a trip to a nearby Western steak house or coffee shop might make your wallet smile. ☒ 2–16–1 Konan, Minato-ku 108-8282 ☎ 03/ 4562–1111 ⊕ www.stringshotel.com ⬧ 200 rooms, 6 suites ☐ 2 restaurants, room service, refrigerators, TV with movies, fitness room, massage, bar, in-room broadband, business center, meeting room ☐ AE, DC, MC, V Ⓜ JR Yamanote Line, Shinagawa Station (Konan Exit).

$$–$$$ 🏨 **Le Meridien Pacific Tōkyō.** Just across the street from JR Shinagawa Station, the Meridien sits on grounds that were once part of an imperial-family estate. The hotel gears much of its marketing effort toward booking banquets, wedding receptions, conventions, and tour groups; the small, unremarkable rooms are quiet and comfortable, but public spaces carry a lot of traffic. The Sky Lounge on the 30th floor has a fine view of Tōkyō Bay. The entire back wall of the ground-floor lounge is glass, the better to contemplate a Japanese garden, sculpted with rocks and waterfalls. ⊠ *3–13–3 Takanawa, Minato-ku 108-8567* ☎ *03/3445–6711* ⊕ *www.pacific-tokyo.com* ⤳ *900 rooms, 40 suites* ⚙ *6 restaurants, room service, refrigerators, cable TV with movies, pool, massage, bar, dry cleaning, laundry service, concierge, in-room broadband, business services, no-smoking rooms* ☰ *AE, DC, MC, V* Ⓜ *JR Yamanote Line, Shinagawa Station (Nishi-guchi/West Exit).*

> ### BODY ART BEWARE
>
> Think twice about taking a dip in Tōkyō if you have a tattoo. These personal expressions are strictly forbidden in many of the city's pools, fitness clubs, hot springs, and onsen because of the association between tattoos and the *yakuza* (Japanese mafia). Some places even post signs reading, PEOPLE WITH TATTOOS ARE NOT ALLOWED.

$–$$ 🏨 **Takanawa Tōbu Hotel.** The Takanawa Tōbu, a five-minute walk from JR Shinagawa Station, provides good value for the price—particularly since the rate includes a buffet breakfast. Rooms are smallish and uninspired, the bathrooms are the claustrophobic prefabricated plastic units beloved of business hotels, and there's no proper sitting area in the lobby, but the hotel atones for these shortcomings with a friendly staff (which speaks a bit of English) and a cozy bar. There's also a small Western restaurant, the Boulogne. ⊠ *4–7–6 Takanawa, Minato-ku 108-0074* ☎ *03/3447–0111* ⊕ *www.tobuhotel.co.jp* ⤳ *190 rooms* ⚙ *Restaurant, refrigerators, TV with movies, bar, some in-room broadband, meeting room, no-smoking rooms* ☰ *DC, V* ❏❘ *BP* Ⓜ *JR Yamanote Line, Shinagawa Station (Nishi-guchi/West Exit).*

Shiodome

$$$$
Fodor'sChoice
★

🏨 **Conrad Tōkyō.** The Conrad welcomes you to the space age with a Japanese twist. Elevators shoot upward in the slick, green-hue Tōkyō Shiodome Building to the 28th floor, the location of a lobby of dark oak paneling and bronze lattices. Straight-edge counters in shades of blue and Japanese-lantern illumination come together in the bar areas. The high-ceiling rooms allow for nice views of the bay or the city from a pair of low-back sofas. Motorized blinds and 37-inch plasma TVs with DVD players housed in lacquer boxes are thoughtful touches. Highlights in the bathrooms include dual sinks, rain-shower showerheads, and separate tubs (complete with rubber ducks). ⊠ *1–9–1 Higashi-Shimbashi, Minato-ku 105-7337* ☎ *03/6388–8000* ⊕ *http://tokyo.conradmeetings. com* ⤳ *222 rooms, 68 suites* ⚙ *4 restaurants, room service, in-room safes, refrigerators, in-room DVDs, pool, health club, spa, bar, in-room broadband, Wi-Fi, business center, meeting rooms, no-smoking rooms*

➡ *AE, DC, MC, V* Ⓜ *JR Yamanote Line, Shimbashi Station (Shiodome Exit); Oedo subway line, Shiodome Station (Exit 9).*

★ **$$** 🏨 **Park Hotel Tōkyō.** A panorama of Tōkyō or a bay view, comfortable beds, and large bathrooms greet you in the rooms of this reasonably priced hotel. As is the current trend in Tōkyō, a 10-story atrium of dark-wood paneling sits below a hexagonal skylight ceiling in the lobby. A pillow-fitting service provides advice on how you can change your sleeping habits to get a better night's sleep. If that doesn't work, take a walk to the nearby fish market in Tsukiji—the activity gets started at 5 AM. ✉ *1–7–1 Higashi Shimbashi, Minato-ku 105-7227* ☎ *03/6252–1111* ⊕ *www. parkhoteltokyo.com* 🛏 *272 rooms, 1 suite* ⚒ *5 restaurants, room service, in-room safes, refrigerators, bar, concierge, in-room broadband, business center* ➡ *AE, DC, MC, V* Ⓜ *JR Yamanote Line, Shimbashi Station (Shiodome Exit); Oedo subway line, Shiodome Station (Exit 10).*

Tora-no-mon

★ **$$$$** 🏨 **Hotel Ōkura Tōkyō.** Understatedly sophisticated and human in its scale, this hotel is a Tōkyō favorite. Dark wood in the public areas and the tiered exterior architecture at the entry retain the feel of the hotel's early days in the 1960s. Amenities in the tasteful, spacious rooms include remote-control draperies and terry robes. The odd-number rooms, 871–889 inclusive, overlook a small Japanese landscaped garden. The on-site museum houses fine antique porcelain, mother-of-pearl, and ceramics; tea ceremonies take place here Monday–Saturday 11–4 (¥1,000). The main building is preferable to the south wing, which you reach by an underground shopping arcade. ✉ *2–10–4 Tora-no-mon, Minato-ku 105-0001* ☎ *03/3582–0111, 0120/003–751 toll-free* ⊕ *www.okura.com/ tokyo* 🛏 *762 rooms, 96 suites* ⚒ *10 restaurants, room service, in-room safes, refrigerators, cable TV with movies and VCR, indoor pool, health club, spa, 3 bars, dry cleaning, laundry service, concierge, in-room broadband, business services, no-smoking rooms* ➡ *AE, DC, MC, V* Ⓜ *Hibiya subway line, Kamiya-chō Station (Exit 4B); Ginza subway line, Tora-no-mon Station (Exit 3).*

$$$ 🏨 **ANA Hotel Tōkyō.** The ANA typifies the ziggurat-atrium style that seems to have been a requirement for hotel architecture from the mid-1980s. The reception floor, with its two-story fountain, is clad in enough marble to have depleted an Italian quarry. In general, though, the interior designers have made skillful use of artwork and furnishings to take some of the chill off the hotel's relentless modernism. Guest rooms are sleek and spacious. The Astral Lounge on the top (37th) floor and the Executive Floors provide superb views of the city and Mt. Fuji (on clear days). The hotel is a short walk from the U.S. Embassy. ✉ *1–12–33 Akasaka, Minato-ku 107-0052* ☎ *03/3505–1111, 0120/029–501 toll-free* ⊕ *www. anahoteltokyo.jp* 🛏 *882 rooms, 19 suites* ⚒ *14 restaurants, room service, refrigerators, cable TV with movies, indoor pool, health club, massage, sauna, 4 bars, dry cleaning, laundry service, in-room broadband, business services, meeting room, no smoking floors* ➡ *AE, DC, MC, V* Ⓜ *Ginza and Namboku subway lines, Tameike-Sannō Station (Exit 13); Namboku subway line, Roppongi-itchō Station (Exit 3).*

Ueno

¢ ▦ **Ryokan Katsutarō.** This small economical hotel is a five-minute walk from the entrance to Ueno Kōen (Ueno Park) and a 10-minute walk from the Tōkyō National Museum. The rather spacious rooms, of which the quietest are in the back, away from the main street, have traditional tatami flooring and sliding doors. A simple breakfast of toast, eggs, and coffee is only ¥500. To get here, leave the Nezu subway station by Exit 2, cross the road, take the street running northeast, and turn right at the "T" intersection; Ryokan Katsutarō is 25 yards along Dōbutsuen-uramon-dōri, on the left-hand side. ✉ *4–16–8 Ikenohata, Taitō-ku 110-0008* 🕾 *03/3821–9808* ⊕ *www.katsutaro.com/ryokan_index.html* ⇨ *7 Japanese-style rooms, 4 with bath* ঐ *Japanese baths, laundry facilities, in-room data ports; no a/c in some rooms, no TV in some rooms* ▤ *AE, MC, V* Ⓜ *Chiyoda subway line, Nezu Station (Exit 2).*

Yaesu

★ $ ▦ **Hotel Yaesu Ryūmeikan.** It's amazing that this ryokan near Tōkyō Station has survived in the heart of the city's financial district, where the price of real estate is astronomical. A friendly, professional staff goes the extra mile to make you feel comfortable; weekday evenings, someone who speaks English is usually on duty. Amenities are few, but for price and location this inn is hard to beat. Room rates include a Japanese-style breakfast; ¥800 per person is deducted from your bill if you'd rather skip it. Checkout is at 10 AM sharp; there's a ¥1,500 surcharge for each hour you overstay. ✉ *1–3–22 Yaesu, Chūo-ku 103-0028* 🕾 *03/3271–0971* ⊕ *www.ryumeikan.co.jp* ⇨ *21 Japanese-style rooms, 9 Western-style rooms* ঐ *2 restaurants, refrigerators, Japanese baths, in-room broadband* ▤ *AE, DC, MC, V* ⊙| *BP* Ⓜ *JR Line and Marunouchi subway line, Tōkyō Station (Yaesu North Exit); Tōzai subway line, Nihombashi Station (Exit A3).*

Yanaka

¢ ▦ **Sawanoya Ryokan.** The Shitamachi area is known for its down-to-earth
Fodor'sChoice friendliness, which you get in full measure at Sawanoya. This little inn
★ is a family business: everybody pitches in to help you plan excursions and book hotels for the next leg of your journey. The inn is very popular with budget travelers, so reserve online well in advance. On occasion, the staffers, who keep the facilities and rooms very clean, perform various traditional dances and ceremonies in full costume in the lobby. To get here from Nezu Station, walk 300 yards north along Shinobazu-dōri and take the street on the right; Sawanoya is 180 yards ahead on the right. ✉ *2–3–11 Yanaka, Taitō-ku 110-0001* 🕾 *03/3822–2251* ⊕ *www.sawanoya.com* ⇨ *12 Japanese-style rooms, 2 with bath* ঐ *Japanese baths, bicycles, laundry facilities, in-room data ports, Internet room* ▤ *AE, MC, V* Ⓜ *Chiyoda subway line, Nezu Station (Exit 1).*

Hostels

¢–$ ▦ **YMCA Asia Youth Center.** Both men and women can stay here, and all rooms are private and have private baths. Discounts are given to YMCA members, pastors, and students taking university entrance exams. Breakfast is available for ¥200. The hostel is an eight-minute walk from Suidō-bashi Station. ⊠ *2–5–5 Saragaku, Chiyoda-ku 101-0064* ☎ *03/3233–0611* ⊕ *ymcajapan.org/ayc* ☏ *55 rooms* ⚬ *Laundry facilities, Internet room, meeting rooms* ⊟ *DC, MC, V* Ⓜ *JR Mita Line, Suidō-bashi Station.*

¢ 🏨 **Tōkyō International Youth Hostel.** In typical hostel style, you're required to be off the premises between 10 AM and 3 PM. Less typical is the fact that for an additional ¥1,200 over the standard rate, you can eat breakfast and dinner in the hostel cafeteria. For those hitting the town, the 11 PM curfew could pose a problem. The hostel is a few minutes' walk from Iidabashi Station. ⊠ *Central Plaza Bldg., 18th fl., 1–1 Kagura-kashi, Shinjuku-ku 162-0823* ☎ *03/3235–1107* ⊕ *www.tokyo-ih.jp* ☏ *138 bunk beds* ⚬ *Japanese baths, Internet room, meeting room* ⊟ *AE, MC, V* Ⓜ *JR; Tōzai, Namboku, and Yūraku-chō subway lines: Iidabashi Station (Exit B2b).*

Near Narita Airport

Transportation between Narita Airport and Tōkyō proper takes at least an hour and a half. A sensible strategy for visitors with early-morning flights home would be to spend the night before at a hotel near the airport; all have courtesy shuttles to the departure terminals; these hotels are also a boon to visitors with layovers in Narita.

$$ 🏨 **Narita Excel Hotel Tokyu.** Airline crews rolling their bags through the lobby are a common sight at the Excel, a hotel with reasonable prices and friendly service. The rooms, which are outfitted with standard water kettles and yukatas, are soundproofed but tend to be small. The Japanese garden and nearby Shinsho-ji temple are pleasant for walks. ⊠ *31 Oyama, Chiba-ken, Narita-shi 286-0131* ☎ *0476/33–0109* ⊕ *www.narita-e.tokyuhotels.co.jp* ☏ *710 rooms, 2 suites* ⚬ *3 restaurants, cable TV, 2 pools, gym, bar, airport shuttle* ⊟ *AE, DC, MC, V.*

$–$$ 🏨 **Radisson Hotel Narita Airport.** Set on 28 spacious, green acres, this modern hotel feels somewhat like a resort, with massive indoor and outdoor pools. The standard rooms are comfortable, and those rooms in the hotel's four towers have views of the expansive property. A shuttle bus runs between the Radisson and the airport every 20 minutes or so; the hotel also operates ten buses daily directly to and from Tōkyō Station. ⊠ *650–35 Nanae, Inaba-gun, Chiba-ken, Tomisato-shi 286-0221* ☎ *0476/93–1234* ⊕ *www.radisson.com/tokyojp_narita* ☏ *493 rooms* ⚬ *2 restaurants, room service, refrigerators, cable TV with movies, indoor-outdoor pool, gym, sauna, bar, dry cleaning, laundry service, in-room broadband, meeting rooms, business services, airport shuttle, no-smoking rooms* ⊟ *AE, DC, MC, V.*

$ 🏨 **ANA Hotel Narita.** With its brass and marble, this hotel aspires to architecture in the grand style. The rooms are small, but the amenities measure up, and the proximity to the airport (about 15 minutes by shuttle bus) makes this a good choice if you're in transit. If you're flying an ANA flight bound for anywhere other than North America, you can check in at a special counter in the lobby. Room views are of the airport or surrounding greenery. ⊠ *68 Hori-no-uchi, Chiba-ken, Narita-shi 286-0107* ☎ *0476/33–1311, 0120/029–501 toll-free* ⊕ *www.anahotel-narita.com* ⟳ *434 rooms, 8 suites* ⟳ *4 restaurants, room service, cable TV with movies, indoor pool, gym, sauna, in-room data ports, Internet room, airport shuttle, no-smoking rooms* ▭ *AE, DC, MC, V.*

$ ⊞ **Hilton Tōkyō Narita Airport.** Given its proximity to the airport (a 10-minute drive), this C-shape hotel is a reasonable choice for people in transit. The deluxe rooms on the three upper floors feature funky orange blackout curtains, a work desk and ergonomic chair, kanji wall art, and a flat-screen TV. The bland furnishings in the remaining rooms, however, could use an upgrade. The top-floor banquet facilities provide a view of the landings and takeoffs on the airport runway. Complimentary buses depart for the airport or the nearby Narita train station a few times each hour. ⊠ *456 Kosuge, Chiba-ken, Narita-shi 286-0127* ☎ *0476/33–1121* ⊕ *www.hilton.com* ⟳ *548 rooms* ⟳ *3 restaurants, pool, gym, spa, bar, in-room broadband, business center, meeting rooms, airport shuttle, no-smoking rooms* ▭ *AE, DC, MC, V.*

¢–$ ⊞ **Holiday Inn Tōbu Narita.** The modern, Western-style accommodations at this hotel, which is a five-minute ride by shuttle bus from the airport, are some of the cheapest around. Inquire about specials when making a reservation. ⊠ *320–1 Tokkō, Chiba-ken, Narita-shi 286-0106* ☎ *0476/32–1234* ⊕ *www.holidayinntobunarita.com* ⟳ *484 rooms, 5 suites* ⟳ *3 restaurants, pool, massage, steam room, in-room broadband, bar, airport shuttle, no-smoking rooms* ▭ *AE, DC, MC, V.*

NIGHTLIFE & THE ARTS

An evening out in Tōkyō can be as civilized as a night of Kabuki or as rowdy as a Roppongi nightclub. In between there are dance clubs, a swingin' jazz scene, theater, cinema, live venues, and more than enough bars to keep the social lubricant flowing past millions of tonsils nightly. Rickety street stands sit yards away from luxury hotels, and wallet-depleting hostess clubs are found next to cheap and raucous rock bars.

The Arts

An astonishing variety of dance and music, both classical and popular, is found in Tōkyō, alongside the must-see traditional Japanese arts of Kabuki, Nō, and Bunraku. Eric Clapton, Yo-Yo Ma, Wynton Marsalis: whenever you visit, the headliners will be here. Tōkyō also has modern theater—in somewhat limited choices, unless you can follow dialogue in Japanese, but Western repertory companies find receptive audiences for plays in English. And it doesn't take long for a hit show from New York or London to open. Musicals such as *The Lion King* have found enormous popularity here—although you'll find Simba speaks Japanese.

INFORMATION & TICKETS *Metropolis* is a free English-language weekly magazine that has up-to-date listings of what's going on in the city; it's available at hotels, book and music stores, some restaurants and cafés, and other locations. Another source, rather less complete, is the *Tour Companion*, a tabloid visitor guide published every two weeks, available free of charge at hotels and at Japan National Tourist Organization (JNTO) offices. For coverage of all aspects of the performing-arts scene, visit ⊕ www.artindex. metro.tokyo.jp.

If your hotel can't help with concert and performance bookings, call **Ticket Pia** (☎ 03/5237–9999) for assistance in English. The **Playguide Agency** (✉ Playguide Bldg., 2–6–4 Ginza, Chūō-ku ☎ 03/3561–8821 Ⓜ Yūraku-chō subway line, Ginza Itchōme Station, Exit 4) sells tickets to cultural events via outlets in most department stores and in other locations throughout the city; you can stop in at the main office and ask for the nearest counter, but you may not find someone who speaks English. Agencies normally do not have tickets for same-day performances.

Dance

Traditional Japanese dance is divided into dozens of styles, ancient of lineage and fiercely proud of their differences. In truth, only the aficionado can really tell them apart. They survive not so much as performing arts but as schools, offering dance as a cultured accomplishment to interested amateurs. At least once a year, these teachers and their students hold a recital, so that on any given evening there's very likely to be one somewhere in Tōkyō. Truly professional performances are given at the Kokuritsu Gekijō and the Shimbashi Enbujō; the most important of the classical schools, however, developed as an aspect of Kabuki, and if you attend a play at the Kabuki-za, you are almost guaranteed to see a representative example.

Ballet began to attract a Japanese following in 1920, when Anna Pavlova danced *The Dying Swan* at the old Imperial Theater. Touring companies like the Metropolitan, the Bolshoi, Sadler's Wells, and the Bayerische Staatsoper find Tōkyō a very compelling venue—as well they might when even seats at ¥30,000 or more sell out far in advance. One domestic company that's making a name for itself is the Asami Maki Ballet, whose dancers are known for their technical proficiency and expressiveness; the company often performs at the Tōkyō Metropolitan Festival Hall. Latin dance also has a strong following too, and flamenco heartthrob Joaquín Cortés visits regularly to wide acclaim and packed houses.

The modern Japanese dance form known as Butō, with its contorted and expressive body movements, is acclaimed internationally and domestically. Butō performances are held periodically on a variety of stages. For details, check with ticket agencies and the local English-language press.

Film

Fortunately for film fans, Japan's distributors invariably add Japanese subtitles rather than dub their offerings. Exceptions include kids' movies and big blockbusters that are released in both versions—if there are two screenings close to each other, that's a sign that one may be dubbed. Tickets are expensive: around ¥1,800 for general admission and ¥2,500–¥3,000 for a reserved seat, called a *shitei-seki*. Slightly discounted tickets, usually ¥1,200–¥1,600, can be purchased from the ticket counters found in many department stores.

Although the major Japanese studios struggle to compete with big-budget U.S. fare, anime remains strong and each year sees several major domestic successes. Unless your Japanese is top-notch, most domestic films will be off-limits, but if you happen to be in town during one of the many film festivals you may be able to catch a screening with English subtitles. Festival season is in the fall, with the Tōkyō International Film Festival taking over the Shibuya district in October and a slew of other more specialized festivals screening more outré fare.

First-run theaters that have new releases, both Japanese and foreign, are clustered for the most part in three areas: Shinjuku, Shibuya, and Yūraku-chō-Hibiya-Ginza. At most of them, the last showing of the evening starts at around 7. This is not the case with the best news on the Tōkyō film scene: the handful of small theaters that take special interest in classics, revivals, and serious imports. Somewhere on the premises will also be a chrome-and-marble coffee shop, a fashionable little bar, or even a decent restaurant. Most of these small theaters have a midnight show—at least on the weekends.

Chanter Cine. A three-screen cinema complex, Chanter Cine tends to show British and American films by independent producers but also showcases fine work by filmmakers from Asia and the Middle East. ⊠ *1–2–2 Yūraku-chō, Chiyoda-ku* ☎ *03/3591–1511* Ⓜ *Hibiya, Chiyoda, and Mita subway lines, Hibiya Station (Exit A5).*

Haiyūza. This is primarily a repertory theater, but on the irregularly scheduled Haiyūza Talkie Nights it screens notable foreign films. ⊠ *4–9–2 Roppongi, Minato-ku* ☎ *03/3401–4073* Ⓜ *Hibiya subway line, Roppongi Station (Exit 4A).*

Virgin Cinemas. In Roppongi Hills, this complex offers comfort, plus six screens, VIP seats, and late shows on weekends. There are plenty of bars in the area for postmovie discussions. ⊠ *Keyakizaka Complex, 6–10–2 Roppongi, Minato-ku* ☎ *03/5775–6090* 💲 *Regular theater ¥1,800; Premier theater ¥3,000* Ⓜ *Hibiya and Ōedo subway lines, Roppongi Station (Roppongi Hills Exit).*

Music

Information in English about venues for traditional Japanese music (koto, shamisen, and so forth) can be hard to find; check newspaper listings, particularly the Friday and Saturday editions, for concerts and school recitals. Western music poses no such problem. The following are a few of the most important.

Casals Hall. The last of the fine small auditoriums built for chamber music, before the Japanese bubble economy burst in the early '90s, was designed by architect Arata Isozaki—justly famous for the Museum of Contemporary Art in Los Angeles. In addition to chamber music, Casals draws piano, guitar, cello, and voice soloists. ⊠ *1–6 Kanda Surugadai, Chiyoda-ku* ☎ *03/3294–1229* Ⓜ *JR Chūō Line and Marunouchi subway line, Ochanomizu Station (Exit 2).*

Iino Hall. Built before Japan fell in love with marble, Iino Hall maintains a reputation for comfort, intelligent programming, and excellent acoustics. The venue hosts chamber music and Japanese concert soloists. ⊠ *2–1–1 Uchisaiwai-chō, Chiyoda-ku* ☎ *03/3506–3251* Ⓜ *Chiyoda and Hibiya* *subway lines, Kasumigaseki Station (Exit C4); Marunouchi subway line, Kasumigaseki Station (Exit B2); Ginza subway line, Toranomon Station (Exit 9); Mita subway line, Uchisaiwai-chō Station (Exit A7).*

Nakano Sun Plaza. Everything from rock to Argentine tango is staged at this hall. ⊠ *4–1–1 Nakano, Nakano-ku* ☎ *03/3388–1151* Ⓜ *JR and Tōzai subway lines, Nakano Station (Kita-guchi/North Exit).*

New National Theater and Tōkyō Opera City Concert Hall. With its 1,810-seat main auditorium, this venue nourishes Japan's fledgling efforts to make a name for itself in the world of opera. The Opera City Concert Hall has a massive pipe organ and hosts visiting orchestras and performers. The Pit and Playhouse theaters showcase musicals and more intimate dramatic works. Ticket prices range from ¥1,500 to ¥21,000. The complex also includes an art gallery. ⊠ *3–20–2 Nishi-Shinjuku, Shinjuku-ku* ☎ *03/5353–0788, 03/5353–9999 for tickets* ⊕ *www.operacity.jp* Ⓜ *Keiō Shin-sen private rail line, Hatsudai Station (Higashi-guchi/East Exit).*

NHK Hall. The home base for the Japan Broadcasting Corporation's NHK Symphony Orchestra is probably the auditorium most familiar to Japanese lovers of classical music, as performances here are routinely rebroadcast on NHK-TV, the national TV station. ⊠ *2–2–1 Jinnan, Shibuya-ku* ☎ *03/3465–1751* Ⓜ *JR Yamanote Line, Shibuya Station (Hachiko Exit); Ginza and Hanzō-mon subway lines, Shibuya Station (Exits 6 and 7).*

Suntory Hall. This lavishly appointed concert auditorium in the Ark Hills complex has one of the best locations for theatergoers who want to extend their evening out: there's an abundance of good restaurants and bars nearby. ⊠ *1–13–1 Akasaka, Minato-ku* ☎ *03/3505–1001* Ⓜ *Ginza and Namboku subway lines, Tameike-Sannō Station (Exit 13).*

Tōkyō Dome. A 55,000-seat sports arena, the dome hosts big-name Japanese pop acts and the occasional international star. ⊠ *1–3–61 Kōraku, Bunkyō-ku* ☎ *03/5800–9999* Ⓜ *Marunouchi and Namboku subway lines, Kōraku-en Station (Exit 2); Ōedo and Mita subway lines, Kasuga Station (Exit A2); JR Suidō-bashi Station (Nishi-guchi/West Exit).*

Traditional Theater

BUNRAKU   Bunraku puppet theater is one of Japan's most accessible traditional arts. Its origins date to the 10th century, but the golden age occurred in the 18th century when most of the great plays were written and the puppets evolved to their present form.

Elaborately dressed in period costume, each puppet is made up of interchangeable parts: a head, shoulder piece, trunk, legs, and arms. Various puppet heads are used for roles of different sex, age, and character, and a certain hairstyle will indicate a puppet's position in life. To operate one puppet, three puppeteers must act in unison. The *omozukai* controls the expression on the puppet's face and its right arm and hand. The *hidarizukai* controls the puppet's left arm and hand along with any props that it's carrying. The *ashizukai* moves the puppet's legs. The most difficult task belongs to the omozukai.

It takes about 30 years to become an expert. A puppeteer must spend 10 years as ashizukai, an additional 10 as hidarizukai, and then 10 more years as omozukai. These master puppeteers not only manipulate the puppets' arms and legs but also roll the eyes and move the lips so that the puppets express fear, joy, and sadness.

The spiritual center of Bunraku today is Ōsaka, rather than Tōkyō, but there are a number of performances in the small hall of the Kokuritsu Gekijō. Consult *Metropolis* magazine or check with one of the English-speaking ticket agencies for performance schedules.

KABUKI   Kabuki emerged as a popular form of entertainment by women dancing lewdly in the early 17th century; before long, the authorities banned it as a threat to public order. Eventually it cleaned up its act, and by the latter half of the 18th century it had become popular with common folks—especially the townspeople of bustling Edo. Kabuki had music, dance, and spectacle; it had acrobatics and sword fights; it had pathos and tragedy, historical romance and social satire. It no longer had bawdy beauties, however—women have been banned from the Kabuki stage since 1629—but in recompense it developed a professional role for female impersonators, who train for years to project a seductive, dazzling femininity. It had—and still has—superstars and quick-change artists and legions of fans, who bring their lunch to the theater, stay all day, and shout out the names of their favorite actors at the stirring moments in their favorite plays.

The Kabuki repertoire does not really grow or change, but stars like Ennosuke Ichikawa and Tamasaburo Bando have put exciting, personal stamps on their performances that continue to draw audiences young and old. If you don't know Japanese, you can still enjoy a performance: Tōkyō's Kabuki-za (Kabuki Theater) has simultaneous English translation of its plays available on headphones.

Fodor's Choice   **Kabuki-za.** The best place to see Kabuki is at this theater, built especially
★   for this purpose, with its *hanamichi* (runway) passing diagonally through the audience to the revolving stage. Built in 1925, the Kabuki-za was destroyed in an air raid in 1945 and rebuilt in identical style in 1951. Matinees usually begin at 11 and end at 4; evening performances start at 4:30 and end around 9. Reserved seats are expensive and can be hard to come by on short notice (reserve tickets by at least 6 PM the day before you wish to attend). For a mere ¥800 to ¥1,000, however, you can buy an unreserved ticket that allows you to see one act of a play from the topmost gallery. Bring binoculars—the gallery is very far from the stage. You might also want to rent an earphone set (¥650; deposit ¥1,000) to follow the play in English, but for some this can be more of an intrusion than a help—and you can't use the set in the topmost galleries. ✉ *4–12–15 Ginza, Chūō-ku* ☎ *03/5565–6000 or 03/3541–3131* ⊕ *www.shochiku.co.jp/play/kabukiza/theater* Ⓜ *Hibiya and Asakusa subway lines, Higashi-Ginza Station (Exit 3).*

Kokuritsu Gekijō. This theater hosts visiting Kabuki companies; it also has a training program for young people who may not have the hereditary family connections but want to break into this closely guarded profession. Debut performances, called *kao-mise*, are worth watching to catch the stars of the next generation. Reserved seats are usually ¥1,500–¥9,000. Tickets can be reserved by phone up until the day of the performance by calling the theater box office between 10 and 5. ✉ *4–1 Hayabusa-chō, Chiyoda-ku* ☎ *03/3230–3000* Ⓜ *Hanzō-mon subway line, Hanzō-mon Station (Exit 1).*

Shimbashi Enbujō. Dating to 1925, this theater was built for the geisha of the Shimbashi quarter to present their spring and autumn performances of traditional music and dance. It's a bigger house than the Kabuki-za, and it presents a lot of traditional dance, *kyogen* (traditional Nō-style comic skits), and conventional Japanese drama as well as Kabuki. Reserved seats commonly run ¥2,100–¥16,800, and there's no gallery. ✉ *6–18–2 Ginza, Chūō-ku* ☎ *03/5565–6000* Ⓜ *Hibiya and Asakusa subway lines, Higashi-Ginza Station (Exit A6).*

NŌ Nō is a dramatic tradition far older than Kabuki: it reached a point of formal perfection in the 14th century and survives virtually unchanged from that period. Many of the plays in the repertoire are drawn from classical literature or tales of the supernatural, and the texts are richly poetic. Some understanding of the plot of each play is necessary to enjoy a performance, which moves at a nearly glacial pace—the pace of ritual time—as it's solemnly chanted. The major Nō theaters often provide synopses of the plays in English.

The principal character wears a carved wooden mask, which may appear expressionless until the actor "brings it to life," at which point the mask seems to convey a considerable range of emotions. The various roles of the Nō repertoire all have specific costumes—robes of silk brocade with intricate patterns that are works of art in themselves.

■ TIP→ *Kyōgen* are shorter, lighter plays that are often interspersed in between Nō performances and are much more accessible than Nō. If Nō doesn't appeal to you, consider taking advantage of opportunities to see kyōgen instead.

Nō is not very *accessible*: its language is archaic, its conventions are obscure, and its pace can put even Japanese audiences to sleep. That said, the best way to see Nō is in the open air, at torchlight performances called Takigi Nō, held in the courtyards of temples. The setting and the aesthetics of the drama combine to produce an eerie theatrical experience. Consult the *Tour Companion* listings. Tickets to Takigi Nō (held outdoors in temple courtyards) sell out quickly and are normally available only through the temples.

Kanze Nō-gakudō. Founded in the 14th century, this is among the most important of the Nō family schools in Tōkyō. The current *iemoto* (head) of the school is the 26th in his line. ✉ *1–16–4 Shōtō, Shibuya-ku* ☎ *03/3469–5241* Ⓜ *Ginza and Hanzō-mon subway lines, Shibuya Station (Exit 3A).*

National Nō Theater. This is one of the few public halls to host Nō performances. ✉ *4–18–1 Sendagaya, Shibuya-ku* ☎ *03/3423–1331* Ⓜ *JR Chūō Line, Sendagaya Station (Minami-guchi/South Exit); Ōedo subway line, Kokuritsu-Kyōgijō Station (Exit A4).*

RAKUGO   A *rakugo* comedian sits on a cushion and, ingeniously using a fan as a prop for all manner of situations, relates stories that have been handed down for centuries. With different voices and facial expressions, the storyteller acts out the parts of different characters within the stories. There's generally no English interpretation, and the monologues, filled with puns and expressions in dialect, can even be difficult for the Japanese themselves. A performance of rakugo is still worth seeing, however, for a slice of traditional pop culture.

Suzumoto. Built around 1857, Suzumoto is the oldest rakugo theater in Tōkyō. It's on Chūō-dōri, a few blocks north of the Ginza Line's Ueno Hirokō-ji stop. Tickets cost ¥2,800, and performances run continually throughout the day 12:20–4:30 and 5:20–9:10. ✉ *2–7–12 Ueno, Taitō-ku* ☎ *03/3834–5906* Ⓜ *Ginza subway line, Ueno Hirokō-ji Station (Exit 3).*

Nightlife

Most bars and clubs in the main entertainment districts have printed price lists, often in English. Drinks generally cost ¥600–¥1,200, although some small exclusive bars and clubs will set you back a lot more. Be wary of establishments without visible price lists. Hostess clubs and small backstreet bars known as "snacks" or "pubs" can be particularly treacherous territory. That drink you've just ordered could set you back a reasonable ¥1,000; you might, on the other hand, have wandered unknowingly into a place that charges you ¥15,000 up front for a whole bottle—and slaps a ¥20,000 cover charge on top. If the bar has hostesses, it's often unclear what the companionship of one will cost you, or whether she is there just for conversation. Ignore the persuasive shills on the streets of Roppongi and Kabuki-chō, who will try to hook you into their establishment. There is, of course, a certain amount of safe ground: hotel lounges, jazz clubs, and the rapidly expanding Irish pub scene are pretty much the way they are anywhere else. But elsewhere it's best to follow the old adage: if you have to ask how much it costs, you probably can't afford it.

There are five major districts in Tōkyō that have extensive nightlife, and each has a unique atmosphere, clientele, and price level.

Akasaka. Nightlife in Akasaka concentrates mainly on two streets—Tamachi-dōri and Hitotsugi-dōri—and the small alleys connecting them. The area has several cabarets and nightclubs, plus wine bars, coffee shops, late-night restaurants, pubs, and "snacks"—counter bars that will serve (and charge you for) small portions of food with your drinks, whether you order them or not. Akasaka is sophisticated and upscale—which is not surprising for an old geisha district—but not as expensive as Ginza.

Ginza. Unless you have a bottomless expense account, Ginza is best considered as a window-shopper's destination. Affordable bars and restaurants do exist, but most close around 11 PM. The late-night entertainment spots tend to be exclusive hostess clubs where kimono-clad women pander to politicians and high-rolling businessmen.

The Red Lights of Kabuki-chō

TŌKYŌ HAS MORE THAN its fair share of red-light districts, but the leader of the pack is Kabuki-chō, located just north of Shinjuku Station. The land was once a swamp, although its current name refers to an aborted post–World War II effort to bring culture to the area in the form of a landmark Kabuki theater. Nowadays, most of the entertainment is of the insalubrious kind, with strip clubs, love hotels, host and hostess clubs, and thinly disguised brothels all luridly advertising their presence.

The area is also home to Japanese and Chinese gangsters, giving rise to its image domestically as a danger zone. But in truth, Kabuki-chō poses little risk to even the solo traveler. The sheer volume of people in the area each night, combined with a prominent security-camera presence, means that crime stays mostly indoors.

Despite its sordid reputation, Kabuki-chō does offer something beyond the red lights. There are eateries galore ranging from chain diners to designer restaurants. The impressive 16th-century shrine **Hanazono Jinja**

(✉ 5-17-3 Shinjuku, Shinjuku-ku ☎ 03/3209-5265 ✆ Free ⊙ Daily sunrise-sunset Ⓜ Marunouchi subway line, Shinjuku-san-chōme Station, Exits B2 and B3) hosts several events throughout the year, but comes alive with two must-see colorful festivals on its grounds. The weekend closest to May 28 brings a shrine festival, in which portable shrines are paraded through the streets. The November Tori-no-Ichi festival (the exact days vary each year) is held here and at several shrines throughout Tōkyō, but Hanazono is the most famous place to buy the festival's *kumade*: big rakes decorated with money, mock fruit, and other items people would like to "rake in." People buy them for luck, and replace them every year.

Also here is Golden Gai, probably Tōkyō's most atmospheric drinking area. The quirky **Koma Gekijō** (Koma Stadium Theater ✉ 1-19-1 Kabuki-chō, Shinjuku-ku ☎ 03/3200-2213) is a favorite of the pension-drawing crowd, offering variety stage shows starring fading entertainers.

–Nicholas Coldicott

Roppongi. Roppongi developed to serve the needs of the post–World War II American occupiers, who picked the area as their base. Some would say little has changed since then, as the area remains a hotspot for American soldiers looking to unwind. Roppongi was traditionally ghostly quiet by day, boisterous and crude by night. But the upscale Roppongi Hills complex now draws a more urbane crowd to the area.

Shibuya. Shibuya is the heart of Tōkyō's vibrant youth culture, with shopping and nightlife geared to the teen and twentysomething crowd.

Shinjuku. Long a favorite drinking spot for artists and businesspeople alike, Shinjuku offers everything from glamorous high-rise bars to sleazy dens. The Golden-Gai area is the haunt of writers, artists, and filmmakers. Nearby Kabuki-chō is the city's most notorious red-light district, where English-speaking touts offer myriad sordid experiences. The Ni-chōme area (near Shinjuku Gyo-en National Garden) is the center of Tōkyō's vibrant gay and lesbian scene. The compact area is deserted during the day, but each night more than 250 bars, clubs, and restaurants bring Ni-chōme to life. Thanks to its diminutive dimensions, Ni-chōme is said to have more gay bars per block than any other city in the world.

Bars

Absolut Ice Bar. When the world's fourth Ice Bar opened in Tōkyō in 2006, it proved to be a big hit. The walls, bar counter, and glasses are all crafted from ice shipped from northern Sweden (it's purer, apparently), and the experience is somewhere between Lapland fantasy and being locked in a freezer. Visits are limited to 45 minutes, but only the hardiest will last that long. The Absolut-vodka-only bar serves a wide range of inventive cocktails. The entrance fee of ¥3,500 includes an ice glass, cocktail, and warming cape. If your glass breaks while you're there and you're in the mood for another cocktail, you have to buy another ice glass for ¥800. And no, you don't get to keep the cloak. ⊠ *4–2–4 Nishi-Azabu, Minato-ku* ☎ *03/5464–2160* ⊕ *www.icebartokyo.com* ☉ *Sun.–Thurs. 6 PM–midnight, Fri. and Sat. 6 PM–4:15 AM* Ⓜ *Hibiya and Ōedo subway lines, Roppongi Station (Exit 1).*

Agave. This authentic Mexican cantina treats tequila with respect, and your palate will be tempted by a choice of more than 400 tequilas and mescals. A single shot can cost between ¥800 and ¥10,000, but most of the varieties aren't available anywhere else in Japan. ⊠ *7–15–10 Roppongi, Minato-ku* ☎ *03/3479–0229* ☉ *Mon.–Thurs. 6:30 PM–2 AM, Fri. and Sat. 6:30 PM–4 AM* Ⓜ *Hibiya and Ōedo subway lines, Roppongi Station (Exit 3).*

Heartland. Depending on your outlook, this is either a stylish bar for those who've outgrown the cheap thrills of mainstream Roppongi, or a pickup joint for male-expat-banker types and foreigner-infatuated Japanese women. Either way, Heartland is relentlessly popular and features a spacious patio and delicious eponymous microbrew. Drinks start at ¥500. ⊠ *Roppongi Hills West Walk, 1F, 6–10–1 Roppongi, Minato-ku* ☎ *03/5772–7600* ☉ *Daily 11 AM–5 AM* Ⓜ *Hibiya and Ōedo subway lines, Roppongi Station (Roppongi Hills Exit).*

Fodor'sChoice
★ **Montoak.** Positioned halfway down the prestigious shopping street Omotesandō-dōri, within spitting distance of such fashion giants as Gucci, Louis Vuitton, and Tod's, this hip restaurant-bar is a great place to rest after testing the limits of your credit card. With smoky floor-to-ceiling windows, cushy armchairs, and a layout so spacious you won't believe you're sitting on one of Tōkyō's toniest streets, the place attracts a hipper-than-thou clientele but never feels unwelcoming. The bar food consists of canapés, salads, cheese plates, and the like. Drinks start at ¥700. ⊠ *6–1–9 Jingū-mae, Shibuya-ku* ☎ *03/5468–5928* ☉ *Daily 11:30 AM–midnight* Ⓜ *Chiyoda subway line, Meiji Jingū-mae Station (Exit 4).*

★ **Old Imperial Bar.** Comfortable and sedate, this is the pride of the Imperial Hotel, decorated with elements saved from Frank Lloyd Wright's earlier version of the building—alas, long since torn down. Drinks start

CLOSE UP

Golden Gai

1

TUCKED AWAY ON THE EASTERN side of Tōkyō's sordid Kabuki-chō district, Golden Gai is a ramshackle collection of more than 200 Lilliputian bars that survived the rampant construction of Japan's bubble-economy years. In the 1980s, when the *yakuza*, Japan's crime syndicate, was torching properties to sell the land to big-thinking developers, Golden Gai's supporters took turns guarding the area each night.

Each bar occupies a few square meters, and some accommodate fewer than a dozen drinkers. With such limited space, many of the bars rely on their regulars—and give a frosty welcome and exorbitant bill to the casual visitor. The timeworn look of Golden Gai captures the imagination of most visitors, but many of the establishments are notoriously unfriendly to foreigners. But times change, as do leases, and a new generation of owners is gradually emerging to offer the same intimate drinking experience and cold beers without the unwelcome reception. For a guaranteed warm welcome, try one of the following:

La Jetée. It should come as no surprise that French cinema is the proprietor's big passion: La Jetée is covered in French-cinema posters and was named after a French movie. It struggles to seat 10 customers, but that means intimate conversations—in Japanese, French, and sometimes English—usually about movies. If you want to discuss European cinema with Wim Wenders or sit toe to toe with Quentin Tarantino, this is your best bet. The music, naturally, comes exclusively from film sound tracks. The seating charge is ¥1,000. ⊠ *1-1-8 Kabuki-chō, Shinjuku-ku* ☎ *03/ 3208-9645* ☾ *Mon.-Sat. 7-early morning* Ⓜ *Marunouchi subway line, Shinjuku-san-chōme Station (Exit B3).*

Albatross G. When it opened in summer 2005, Albatross G quickly built a following with its friendliness and, in Golden Gai terms, affordability. The ¥300 seating charge and drinks starting at ¥600 are a marked contrast to most of its neighbors. ⊠ *5th Ave., 1-1 Kabuki-chō, Shinjuku-ku* ☎ *03/3202-3699* ☾ *Mon.-Sat. 8 PM-5 AM* Ⓜ *Marunouchi subway line, Shinjuku-san-chōme Station (Exit B3.*

– Nicholas Coldicott

at ¥1,000. ⊠ *Imperial Hotel, 1–1–1 Uchisaiwai-chō, Chiyoda-ku* ☎ *03/ 3504–1111* ☾ *Daily 11:30 AM–midnight* Ⓜ *Hibiya Line, Hibiya Station (Exit 5).*

Fodor'sChoice
★ **Sekirei.** This is simply the best place in Tōkyō to sink a cold one. The picture-perfect summertime beer garden looks like a budget buster, but it's run by the Asahi brewery and offers refreshments at a price anyone can afford. Most evenings, kimono-clad *nihon-buyō* dancers perform to the strains of shamisen music. Sekirei serves Japanese- and Western-style food to a demure after-work crowd. Drinks start at ¥700. ⊠ *2–2–23 Moto-Akasaka, Minato-ku* ☎ *03/3746–7723* ☾ *June–Sept., weekdays 4:30 PM–10:30 PM, weekends 5:30 PM–10:30 PM; dancers perform 2 or 3 times nightly at varying times* Ⓜ *JR Chūō Line, Shinanomachi Station.*

Vive La Vie. Vive La Vie is exactly what a bar should be: relaxing, friendly, and stylish, with quality cocktails and good music. You can relax on the sofas without any risk of disturbance or sit at the bar and join the banter. Some weekends the bar hosts local DJs and charges an entrance fee (average ¥1,500). Drinks start at ¥700. ⊠ 2–4–6 Shibuya, Shibuya-ku ☎ 03/5485–5498 ⊙ Mon.–Thurs. 7 PM–1 AM, Fri. and Sat. 7 PM–3 AM Ⓜ Ginza subway line, Omotesandō Station (Exit B1).

Beer Halls & Pubs

Clubhouse. Rugby is the sport of choice at this pub, but even those with no interest in watching the game will enjoy the decent food and amiable atmosphere. With a good mix of locals and foreigners, the bar is more hospitable than many similar venues. ⊠ 3–7–3 Shinjuku 3F, Shinjuku-ku ☎ 03/3359–7785 ⊙ Daily 5 PM–midnight Ⓜ Marunouchi subway line, Shinjuku-san-chōme Station (Exit 3).

Ginza Lion. This bar, in business since 1899 and occupying the same stately Chūō-dōri location since 1934, is remarkably inexpensive for one of Tōkyō's toniest addresses. Ginza shoppers and office workers alike drop by for beer and ballast—anything from yakitori to spaghetti. Beers start at ¥590. ⊠ 7–9–20 Ginza, Chūō-ku ☎03/3571–2590 ⊙ Mon.–Sat. 11:30 AM–11 PM Ⓜ Ginza, Hibiya, and Marunouchi subway lines, Ginza Station (Exit A3).

What the Dickens. This spacious pub is nearly always packed with a fun-seeking mix of locals and foreigners. It's in a former Aum Shinri Kyō (the cult held responsible for the gas attack in the Tōkyō subway in 1995) headquarters in Ebisu. Most Sundays, Mondays, and Tuesdays feature a mix of live music and DJs. ⊠ Roob 6 Bldg., 4th fl., 1–13–3 Ebisu-Nishi, Shibuya-ku ☎ 03/3780–2099 ⊙ Tues. and Wed. 5 PM–1 AM, Thurs.–Sat. 5 PM–2 AM, Sun. 5 PM–midnight Ⓜ Hibiya subway line, Ebisu Station (Nishi-guchi/West Exit).

Dance Clubs

★ **Ageha.** This massive bay-side venue has the city's best sound system and most diverse musical lineup. The cavernous Arena hosts well-known house and techno DJs, the bar plays hip-hop, a summer-only swimming-pool area has everything from reggae to break beats, and inside a chill-out tent there's usually ambient or trance music. Because of its far-flung location and enormous capacity, Ageha can be either a throbbing party or an embarrassingly empty hall, depending on the caliber of the DJ. Free buses to Ageha depart every half hour between 11 PM and 4:30 AM from the Shibuya police station on Roppongi-dōri, a three-minute walk from Shibuya Station (there are also return buses every half hour from 11:30 PM to 5 AM). ⊠ 2–2–10 Shin-Kiba, Kotō-ku ☎ 03/5534–1515 ⊕ www.ageha.com ⊠ Around ¥3,500 ⊙ 10 PM–early morning Ⓜ Yūraku-chō subway line, Shin-Kiba Station.

La Fabrique. A Continental crowd gathers at the late-night parties at this small, dressy, French restaurant–cum–club in Shibuya's Zero Gate complex. The music is predominantly house. ⊠ B1F, 16–9 Udagawachō, Shibuya-ku ☎ 03/5428–5100 ⊠ ¥3,000–¥3,500 ⊙ Daily 11 AM–5 AM

Ⓜ *JR Yamanote Line, Ginza and Hanzō-mon subway lines, Shibuya Station (Hachiko Exit for JR and Ginza, Exit 6 for Hanzō-mon).*

Lexington Queen. To Tōkyō's hipster club kids, Lexington Queen is something of an embarrassment: the music hasn't really changed since the place opened in 1980. But to visiting movie stars, fashion models, and other members of the international jet set, the Lex is the place to party hard and go wild—and be seen doing it. ✉ *3–13–14 Roppongi, Minato-ku* ☎ *03/3401–1661* ⊕ *www.lexingtonqueen.com* 🎫 *Admission varies* ⊘ *Daily 8 PM–5 AM* Ⓜ *Hibiya and Ōedo subway lines, Roppongi Station (Exit 5); Namboku subway line, Roppongi-Itchōme Station (Exit 1).*

911. A great central-Roppongi location and no cover charge make 911 popular as a singles' spot. Across from the Roi Building, this is a good starting point for a night of barhopping. ✉ *3–14–12 Roppongi, B1F, Minato-ku* ☎ *03/5772–8882* 🎫 *No cover charge* ⊘ *Daily 6 PM–6 AM* Ⓜ *Hibiya and Ōedo subway lines, Roppongi Station (Exit 3).*

Space Lab Yellow. This club is the granddaddy of the capital's dance scene. The club—popularly known as just "Yellow"—has been knocked from its perch as young clubbers' venue of choice by Womb, but still regularly draws A-list house DJs (Fatboy Slim, François K, Gilles Peterson) who pack the dancers in like sardines. ✉ *1–10–11 Nishi-Azabu, Minato-ku* ☎ *03/3479–0690* ⊕ *www.club-yellow.com* 🎫 *¥3,500–¥4,000* ⊘ *10 PM–early morning* Ⓜ *Chiyoda subway line, Nogizaka Station (Exit 5); Hibiya and Ōedo subway lines, Roppongi Station (Exit 2).*

★ **Womb.** Well-known techno and break-beat DJs make a point of stopping by this Shibuya überclub on their way through town. The turntable talent, including the likes of Danny Howells and Richie Hawtin, and four floors of dance and lounge space make Womb Tōkyō's most consistently rewarding club experience. ✉ *2–16 Maruyama-chō, Shibuya-ku* ☎ *03/5459–0039* ⊕ *www.womb.co.jp* 🎫 *Around ¥3,500* ⊘ *Daily 10 PM–early morning* Ⓜ *JR Yamanote Line, Ginza and Hanzō-mon subway lines, Shibuya Station (Hachiko Exit for JR and Ginza, Exit 3a for Hanzō-mon).*

Drinks with a View

Bellovisto. This 40th-floor lounge bar atop the Cerulean Tower draws a mixed crowd of tourists and local couples, who come for the grand views out over Shibuya and beyond. Drinks start at ¥1,000. ✉ *26–1 Sakura-gaoka-chō, Shibuya-ku* ☎ *03/3476–3398* ⊘ *Daily 4 PM–midnight* Ⓜ *JR, Ginza and Hanzō-mon subway lines, Shibuya Station (Minami-guchi/South Exit for JR and Ginza, Exit 8 for Hanzō-mon).*

★ **New York Bar.** Even before *Lost in Translation* introduced the Park Hyatt's signature lounge to filmgoers worldwide, New York Bar was a local Tōkyō favorite. All the style you would expect of one of the city's top hotels combined with superior views of Shinjuku's skyscrapers and neon-lighted streets make this one of the city's premier nighttime venues. The quality of the jazz on offer equals that of the view. Drinks start at ¥800, and there's a cover charge of ¥2,000 after 8 PM (7 PM on Sunday). ✉ *Park Hyatt Hotel 52F, 3–7–1–2 Nishi-Shinjuku, Shinjuku-ku* 🖀 *03/5322–1234* ◷ *Sun.–Wed. 5 PM–midnight, Thurs.–Sat. 5 PM–1 AM* Ⓜ *JR Shinjuku Station (Nishi-guchi/West Exit).*

Top of Akasaka. On the 40th floor of the Akasaka Prince Hotel, you can enjoy some of the finest views of Tōkyō. If you time your visit for dusk, the price of one drink gets you two views—the daylight sprawl of buildings and the twinkling lights of evening. Drinks start at ¥1,000, and there's a table charge of ¥800 per person. ✉ *Akasaka Prince, 1–2 Kioi-chō, Chiyoda-ku* 🖀 *03/3234–1111* ◷ *Mon.–Sat. 5 PM–1 AM, Sun. 5 PM–11 PM* Ⓜ *Ginza and Marunouchi subway lines, Akasaka-mitsuke Station (Exit D).*

Izakaya

Izakaya (literally "drinking places") are Japanese pubs that can be found on just about every block in Tōkyō. These drinking dens are often noisy, bright, and smoky, but for a taste of authentic Japanese-style socializing, a visit to an izakaya is a must—this is where young people start their nights, office workers gather on their way home, and students take a break to grab a cheap meal and a drink.

Amataro. The Center Gai location of this ubiquitous izakaya chain impresses with a huge, dimly lighted interior. On weekends the crowd is young, boisterous, and fun. ✉ *2–3F Tōkyō Kaikan Bldg., 33–1 Udagawachō, Shibuya-ku* 🖀 *03/5784–4660* ◷ *Daily 5 PM–5 AM* Ⓜ *JR Yamanote Line, Ginza and Hanzō-mon subway lines, Shibuya Station (Hachiko Exit for JR and Ginza, Exit 3a for Hanzō-mon).*

Takara. This high-class izakaya in the sumptuous Tōkyō International Forum is a favorite with foreigners because of its English-language menu and extensive sake list. ✉ *B1, 3–5–1 Marunouchi, Chiyoda-ku* 🖀 *03/5223–9888* ◷ *Weekdays 11:30–2:30 and 5–11, weekends 11:30–3:30 and 5–10* Ⓜ *Yūraku-chō subway line, Yūraku-chō Station (Exit A-4B).*

Watami. One of Tōkyō's big izakaya chains—with a half-dozen branches in the youth entertainment district of Shibuya alone—Watami is popular for its seriously inexpensive menu. Seating at this location ranges from a communal island bar to Western-style tables to more private areas. ✉ *Satose Bldg., 4F, 13–8 Udagawachō, Shibuya-ku* 🖀 *03/6415–6516* ◷ *Sun.–Thurs. 5 PM–3 AM, Fri. and Sat. 5 PM–5 AM* Ⓜ *JR Yamanote Line, Ginza and Hanzō-mon subway lines, Shibuya Station (Hachiko Exit for JR and Ginza, Exit 6 for Hanzō-mon).*

Jazz Clubs

Tōkyō jazz clubs attract world-class performers and innovative local acts. The weekly English-language magazine *Metropolis* has listings for the major clubs. For information on jazz events at small venues, a visit to the record shop **Disk Union** (✉ 3–31–2 Shinjuku, Shinjuku-ku 🖀 03/5379–3551 Ⓜ Marunouchi subway line, Shinjuku-san-chōme Station (Exit A1) is essential. The store has flyers (sometimes in English) for smaller gigs, and the staff can make recommendations.

Blue Note Tōkyō. The Blue Note sees everyone from the Count Basie Orchestra to Herbie Hancock perform to packed houses. The "Sunday Spe-

All That Tōkyō Jazz

1

THE TŌKYŌ JAZZ SCENE is one of the world's best, surpassing Paris and New York with its number of venues playing traditional, swing, bossa nova, R & B, and free jazz. Though popular in Japan before World War II, jazz really took hold of the city after U.S. forces introduced Charlie Parker and Thelonius Monk in the late 1940s. The genre had been banned in wartime Japan as an American vice, but even at the height of the war, fans were able to listen to their favorite artists on Voice of America radio. In the 1960s Japan experienced a boom in all areas of the arts, and jazz was no exception. Since then, the Japanese scene has steadily bloomed, with several local stars—such as Sadao Watanabe in the 1960s and contemporary favorites Keiko Lee and Hiromi Uehara—gaining global attention.

Today more than 120 bars and clubs host live music, plus hundreds play recorded jazz. Shinjuku, Takadanobaba, and Kichijōji are the city's jazz enclaves. Famous international acts regularly appear at big-name clubs such as the Blue Note, but the smaller, lesser-known joints usually have more atmosphere. There's an incredible diversity to enjoy, from Louis Armstrong tribute acts to fully improvised free jazz—sometimes on successive nights at the same venue.

If you time your visit right, you can attend one of the city's more than 20 annual jazz festivals. The festivals vary in size and coverage, but two to check out are the Tōkyō Jazz Festival and the Asagaya Jazz Street Festival.

In September, the **Tōkyō Jazz Festival** (☎ 03/5777-8600 ⊕ www.tokyo-jazz. com) takes over the Tōkyō International Forum in Marunouchi. Past acts have included Chick Corea, Dave Koz, Hiromi Uehara, and Sadao Watanabe.

The **Asagaya Festival** (☎ 03/5305-5075), held the last weekend of October, is a mainstream affair, with venues ranging from a Shinto shrine to a Lutheran church (most venues are within walking distance of Asagaya Station). Look for festival staff at the station to help guide you (note that they may not speak English, however). Previous headliners have included the Mike Price Jazz Quintet and vocalist Masamichi Yanō. The festival gets crowded, so come early.

— James Catchpole

cial" series showcases fresh Japanese talent. Prices here are typically high; expect to pay upward of ¥12,000 to see major acts, and be prepared for shorter sets than you would get at a club in the United States or Europe. ⊠ 6–3–16 Minami-Aoyama, Minato-ku ☎ 03/5485–0088 ⊙ Shows usually Mon.–Sat. at 7 and 9:30, Sun. at 6:30 and 9 ⊕ www.bluenote. co.jp Ⓜ Chiyoda, Ginza, and Hanzō-mon subway lines, Omotesandō Station (Exit A3).

Hot House. This could very well be the world's smallest jazz club. An evening here is like listening to live jazz in your living room with five or six other jazz lovers on your sofa. It's so small, in fact, that you can't get through the front door once the pianist is seated, so don't show up late. Live acts are trios at most, with no space for drums or amplifiers. ✉ *B1 Liberal Takadanobaba, 2–14–8 Takadanobaba, Shinjuku-ku* ☎ *03/3367–1233* ◷ *Daily 8:30* PM*–early morning* Ⓜ *JR Takadanobaba Station (Waseda Exit).*

Intro. This small basement bar features one of the best jazz experiences in Tōkyō: a Saturday "jam session" that stretches until 5 AM (¥1,000 entry fee). Other nights of the week occasionally bring unannounced live sets by musicians just dropping by, but usually it's the owner's extensive vinyl and CD collection that the regulars are listening to. Simple Japanese and Western food is available. ✉ *B1, NT Bldg., 2–14–8 Takadanobaba, Shinjuku-ku* ☎ *03/3200–4396* ◷ *Sun.–Thurs. 6:30* PM*–midnight, Fri.–6:30* PM*–1* AM*, Sat 5* PM*–5* AM Ⓜ *JR Takadanobaba Station (Waseda Exit).*

Shinjuku Pit Inn. Most major jazz musicians have played in this classic Tōkyō club. The veteran Shinjuku Pit stages mostly mainstream fare with the odd foray into the avant-garde. Afternoon admission is ¥1,300 weekdays, ¥2,500 weekends; evening entry is typically ¥3,000. Better-known local acts are often a little more. ✉ *B1 Accord Shinjuku Bldg., 2–12–4 Shinjuku, Shinjuku-ku* ☎ *03/3354–2024* ◷ *Daily, hrs vary* Ⓜ *Marunouchi subway line, Shinjuku-san-chōme Station.*

Fodor'sChoice **Sweet Basil 139.** An upscale jazz club near Roppongi Crossing, Sweet
★ Basil 139 (no relation to the famous New York Sweet Basil) is renowned for local and international acts that run the musical gamut from smooth jazz and fusion to classical. A large, formal dining area serves Italian dishes that are as good as the jazz, making this spot an excellent choice for a complete night out. With a spacious interior and standing room for 500 on the main floor, this is one of the largest and most accessible jazz bars in town. Prices range from ¥2,857 to ¥12,000 depending on who's headlining. ✉ *6–7–11 Roppongi, Minato-ku* ☎ *03/5474–0139* ⊕ *http://stb139.co.jp* ◷ *Mon.–Sat. 6–11; shows at 8* Ⓜ *Hibiya and Ōedo subway lines, Roppongi Station (Exit 3).*

Karaoke

In buttoned-down, socially conservative Japan, karaoke is one of the pressure valves. The phenomenon started in the 1970s when cabaret singer Daisuke Inoue made a coin-operated machine that played his songs on tape so that his fans could sing along. Unfortunately he neglected to patent his creation, thereby failing to cash in on one of Japan's favorite pastimes.

In Japan the singing usually takes place in the seclusion of private rooms that can accommodate groups. Basic hourly charges vary but are usually less than ¥1,000. Most establishments have a large selection of English songs, stay open late, and serve inexpensive food and drink, which you order via a telephone on the wall.

Big Echo. One of Tōkyō's largest karaoke chains, Big Echo has dozens of locations throughout the city. Cheap hourly rates and late closing times make it popular with youngsters. The Roppongi branch is spread over three floors. ✉ *7–14–12 Roppongi, Minato-ku* ☎ *03/5770–7700* ✉ *¥500–¥600 per hr* ◷ *Daily 6* PM*–5* AM Ⓜ *Hibiya and Ōedo subway lines, Roppongi Station (Exit 4).*

★ **Lovenet.** Despite the erotic name, Lovenet is actually the fanciest karaoke box in town. Luxury theme rooms of all descriptions create a fun and classy setting for your dulcet warbling. Mediterranean and Japanese food is served. ⊠ 7–14–4 Roppongi, Minato-ku ☎ 03/5771–5511 ⌷ From ¥2,000 per hr ⊙ Daily 6 PM–5 AM ⊕ www.lovenet-jp.com Ⓜ Hibiya and Ōedo subway lines, Roppongi Station (Exit 4A).

Pasela. This 10-story entertainment complex on the main Roppongi drag of Gaien-Higashi-dōri has seven floors of karaoke rooms with more than 10,000 foreign-song titles. A Mexican-theme bar and a restaurant are also on-site. ⊠ 5–16–3 Roppongi, Minato-ku ☎ 0120/911–086 ⌷ ¥500 per hr ⊙ Daily 5 PM–10 AM Ⓜ Hibiya and Ōedo subway lines, Roppongi Station (Exit 3).

Smash Hits. If karaoke just isn't karaoke to you without drunken strangers to sing to, Smash Hits has the answer. An expat favorite, it offers thousands of English songs and a central performance stage. The cover charge gets you two drinks and no time limit. ⊠ 5–2–26 Hiro-o, Shibuya-ku ☎ 03/3444–0432 ⌷ ¥3,000 ⊙ Mon.–Sat. 7 PM–3 AM ⊕ www.smashhits.jp Ⓜ Hibiya Line, Hiro-o Station.

Live Houses

Tōkyō has numerous small music clubs known as "live houses." These basement spots range from the very basic to miniclub venues, and they showcase the best emerging talent on the local scene. Many of the best live houses can be found in the Kichijōji, Kōenji, and Nakano areas, although they are tucked away in basements citywide. One of the great things about the live house scene is the variety: a single "amateur night" set can include everything from experimental ethnic dance to thrash rock. Cover charges vary depending on who's performing but are typically ¥3,000–¥5,000.

Manda-la. Relaxed and intimate, this local favorite in Kichijōji attracts an eclectic group of performers. Cover charges range from ¥1,800 to ¥4,000. ⊠ 2–8–6 Kichijōji-Minami-cho, Musashino-shi ☎ 0422/42–1579 ⊙ 6:30 PM–varying closing times Ⓜ Keiō Inokashira private rail line, JR Chūō and JR Sōbu lines, Kichijōji Station (Kōen-guchi/Park Exit, on Suehiro-dōri).

Milk. One of the city's larger live houses—it can handle 400 music fans—has three levels and more of a clublike vibe than other venues, right down to the snooty staff. Ticket prices are in the ¥2,500–¥3,000 range. ⊠ 1–13–3 Nishi-Ebisu, Shibuya-ku ☎ 03/5458–2826 ⊙ Weekends 9 PM–early morning Ⓜ JR Yamanote Line and Hibiya subway line, Ebisu Station (Nishi-guchi/West Exit).

Showboat. A small, basic venue that's been going strong for more than a decade, Showboat attracts both amateur and semiprofessional performers. Ticket prices vary by act but are typically around ¥2,000 and often include one drink. ⊠ B1 Oak Bldg. Kōenji, 3–17–2 Kita Kōenji, Suginami-ku ☎ 03/3337 5745 ⊙ Daily 6 PM—early morning Ⓜ JR Sōbu and JR Chūō lines, Kōenji Station (Kita-guchi/North Exit).

SHOPPING

You didn't fly all the way to Tōkyō to buy European designer clothing, so shop for items that are Japanese-made for Japanese people and sold in stores that don't cater to tourists. The crazy clothing styles, obscure electronics, and new games found here are capable of setting trends for the rest of the country—and sometimes the world.

Also, don't pass up the chance to purchase Japanese crafts. Color, form, and superb workmanship make these items exquisite and well worth the price. Japanese lacquerware carries a hefty price tag, but if you like the shiny boxes, bowls, cups, and trays and consider that quality lacquerware is made to last a lifetime, the cost is justified.

The Japanese approach to shopping can be feverish; on the weekends, some of the hipper, youth-oriented stores will have lines that wind down the street. But shopping here can also be an exercise in elegance and refinement. Note the care taken with items after you purchase them, especially in department stores and boutiques. Goods will be wrapped, wrapped again, bagged, and sealed. This focus on presentation also influences salespeople who are invariably helpful and polite. In the larger stores they greet you with a bow when you arrive, and many of them speak enough English to help you find what you're looking for. There's a saying in Japan: *o-kyaku-sama wa kami-sama,* "the customer is a god"—and it's taken to heart.

Japan has been slow to embrace the use of credit cards, and even though plastic is now accepted at big retailers, some smaller shops only take cash. So when you go souvenir hunting, take a decent amount of cash; Tōkyō's low crime rates make this a low-risk proposition. The dishonor associated with theft is so strong, in fact, that it's considered bad form to count change in front of cashiers.

Japan has an across-the-board 5% value-added tax (V.A.T.) imposed on luxury goods as well as on restaurant and hotel bills. This tax can be avoided at some duty-free shops in the city (don't forget to bring your passport).

Stores in Tōkyō generally open at 10 or 11 AM and close at 8 or 9 PM.

Shopping Districts

Akihabara & Jimbō-chō. Akihabara was once the only place Tōkyōites would buy cutting-edge electronic gadgets, but the area has lost its aura of exclusivity thanks to the Internet and the big discount chains around the city. Still, for its sheer variety of products and foreigner-friendliness, Akihabara has the newcomers beat—and a visit remains essential to any Tōkyō shopping spree. Salesclerks speak decent English at most of the major shops (and many of the smaller ones), and the big chains offer duty-free and export items. Be sure to poke around the backstreets for smaller stores that sell used and unusual electronic goods. The area has become the center of the *otaku* (nerd) boom, with loads of shops offering enough video games and *manga* (comic books) to satisfy even the most fastidious geek. West of Akihabara, in the used-bookstore district of Jimbō-chō, you'll find pretty much whatever you're looking for in dictionaries and art books, rare and out-of-print editions (Western and Japanese), and prints. Ⓜ *For Akihabara: JR Yamanote, Keihin Tōhoku and Sōbu lines, Akihabara Station (Electric Town Exit); Hibiya subway line, Akihabara Station. For Jimbō-chō: Hanzō-mon, Shinjuku, and Mita subway lines, Jimbō-chō Station.*

Aoyama & Omotesandō. You can find boutiques by many of the leading Japanese and Western designers in Aoyama, as well as elegant, but pricey, antiques shops on Kottō-dōri. Aoyama is a showcase not merely of high fashion but also of the latest concepts in commercial architecture and interior design. The centerpiece of Omotesandō (a short stroll from Aoyama) is the long, wide avenue running from Aoyama-dōri to Meiji Jingū. Known as the Champs-Elysées of Tōkyō, the sidewalks are lined with cafés and designer boutiques. There are also several antiques and souvenir shops. Omotesandō is perfect for browsing, window-shopping, and lingering over a café au lait. Ⓜ *Chiyoda, Ginza, and Hanzō-mon subway lines, Omotesandō Station (Exits A4, A5, B1, B2, and B3).*

Asakusa. Take time to stroll through Asakusa's arcades. Many of the goods are the kinds of souvenirs found in any tourist trap, but look a little harder and you can find small backstreet shops that have been making beautiful wooden combs, delicate fans, and other items of fine traditional craftsmanship for generations. Also here are the cookware shops of Kappabashi, where you can load up on everything from sushi knives to plastic lobsters. Ⓜ *Asakusa subway line, Asakusa Station (Kaminari-mon Exit); Ginza subway line, Asakusa Station (Exit 1) and Tawara-machi Station (Exit 3).*

Daikanyama. Unleash your inner fashionista in Daikanyama. Wedged between Shibuya and Ebisu, this area is a boutique heaven: shelves of funky shoes, stacks of retro t-shirts, and assortments of skate-punk wear. Ⓜ *Tōkyū Tōyoko Line, Daikanyama Station.*

Ginza. This world-renowned entertainment and shopping district dates to the Edo period (1603–1868), when it consisted of long, willow-lined avenues. The willows have long since gone, and the streets are now lined with department stores and boutiques. The exclusive shops in this area—including flagship stores for major jewelers like Tiffany & Co., Harry Winston, and Mikimoto—sell quality merchandise at high prices. On Sunday the main strip of Chuo-dōri is closed to car traffic and umbrella-covered tables dot the pavement; it's a great place for shoppers to rest their weary feet. Ⓜ *Marunouchi, Ginza, and Hibiya subway lines, Ginza Station (Exits A1–A10); Yūraku-chō subway line, Ginza Itchōme Station; JR Yamanote Line, Yūraku-chō Station.*

Harajuku. The average shopper in Harajuku is under 20; a substantial percentage is under 16. Most stores focus on moderately priced clothing and accessories, with a lot of kitsch mixed in, but there are also several upscale fashion houses in the area and more on the way. This shopping and residential area extends southeast from Harajuku Station along both sides of Omotesandō and Meiji-dōri; the shops that target the youngest consumers concentrate especially on the narrow street

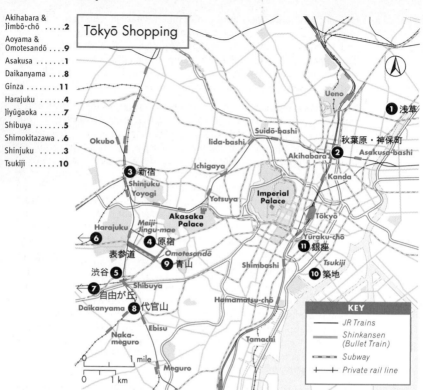

Tōkyō Shopping

called Takeshita-dōri. Tōkyō's most exciting neighborhood for youth fashion and design lies along the promenade known as Kyū Shibuya-gawa Hodō, commonly referred to as Cat Street. Ⓜ *Chiyoda subway line, Meiji Jingū-mae Station (Exits 1–5); JR Yamanote Line, Harajuku Station.*

Jiyūgaoka. Jiyūgaoka is located at the edge of the well-to-do Meguro Ward. Big chain stores are in abundance here, but the real attractions are the boutiques offering unique bedding, crockery, and furniture items. Ⓜ *Tōkyū Tōyoko line or Oimachi lines, Jiyūgaoka Station.*

Shibuya. This is primarily an entertainment and retail district geared toward teenagers and young adults. The shopping scene in Shibuya caters to these groups with many reasonably priced smaller shops and a few department stores that are casual yet chic. Ⓜ *JR Yamanote Line; Tōkyū and Keiō lines; Ginza and Hanzō-mon subway lines, Shibuya Station (Nishi-guchi/West Exit for JR, Exits 3–8 for subway lines).*

Shimokitazawa. Arguably Tokyo's hippie bastion, the twisting streets and alleyways of Shimokitazawa boast used-clothing shops, record stores, and knickknack outlets that generally offer low prices. Fans of anime or manga, and their character good offshoots, will be glad that neither is in short supply. Just follow the scent of patchouli oil from the station. Ⓜ *Keiō Inokashira or Odakyū lines, Shimokitazawa Station.*

Shinjuku. Shinjuku is not without its honky-tonk and sleaze, but it also has some of the city's most popular department stores. The shopping crowd is a mix of Tōkyō youth and office ladies. Surrounding the station are several discount electronics and home-appliance outlets. Ⓜ *JR Yamanote Line; Odakyū and Keiō lines; Marunouchi, Shinjuku, and Ōedo subway lines, Shinjuku Station.*

Tsukiji. Best known for its daily fish-market auctions, Tsukiji also has a warren of streets that carry useful, everyday items that serve as a window onto the lives of the Japanese. This is a fascinating area to poke around after seeing the fish auction and before stopping in the neighborhood for a fresh-as-can-be sushi lunch. Ⓜ *Ōedo subway line, Tsukiji-shijō Station (Exit A1); Hibiya subway line, Tsukiji Station (Exit 1).*

Shopping Streets & Arcades

Most Japanese villages have pedestrian shopping streets known as *shotengai,* and Tōkyō, a big city made up of smaller neighborhoods, is no different. But Tōkyō's shotengai are thick with boutiques, accessory shops, and cafés. Just like their surrounding neighborhoods, these streets can be classy, trendy, or a bit shabby.

Ame-ya Yoko-chō Market. Everything from fresh fish to cheap import clothing is for sale on the side streets between Okachi-machi and Ueno stations. In the days leading up to New Year's, the area turns into mosh-pit mayhem as shoppers fight for fish and snacks to serve over the holidays. The name of the market is often shortened to Ameyoko. Most shops and stalls are open daily 10–7. ✉ *Ueno 4-chōme, Taitō-ku* Ⓜ *JR Ueno Station (Hirokō-ji Exit), JR Okachi-machi Station (Exit A7).*

Kyū Shibuya-gawa Hodō. With its avant-garde crafts stores, funky T-shirt shops, and hipster boutiques, this pedestrian strip serves as a showcase for Japan's au courant designers and artisans. Cat Street is the place to experience bohemian Tōkyō in all its exuberance. ✉ *Between Jingū-mae 3-chōme and Jingū-mae 6-chōme, Shibuya-ku* Ⓜ *Chiyoda subway line, Meiji Jingū-mae Station (Exits 4 and 5).*

Nishi-Sandō. Kimono and *yukata* (cotton kimono) fabrics, traditional accessories, swords, and festival costumes at very reasonable prices are all for sale at this Asakusa arcade. It runs east of the area's movie theaters, between Rok-ku and the Sensō-ji complex. ✉ *Asakusa 2-chōme, Taitō-ku* Ⓜ *Ginza subway line, Asakusa Station (Exit 1).*

Takeshita-dōri. Teenybopper fashion is all the rage along this Harajuku mainstay, where crowds of high school kids look for the newest addition to their ever-changing, outrageous wardrobes. ✉ *Jingū-mae 1-chōme Shibuya-ku* Ⓜ *JR Harajuku Station (Takeshita-dōri Exit).*

Malls & Shopping Centers

★ **Axis.** Classy and cutting-edge housewares, fabrics, and ceramics are sold at this multistory design center on the main Roppongi drag of Gaien-Higashi-dōri. Living Motif is a home-furnishings shop with exquisite foreign and Japanese goods. Savoir Vivre has an excellent selection of ceramics. The small Yoshikin sells its own brand of professional-grade cutlery. ✉ *5–17–1 Roppongi, Minato-ku* ☎ *03/3587–2781* ☉ *Most shops Mon.–Sat. 11–7* Ⓜ *Hibiya and Ōedo subway lines, Roppongi Station (Exit 3); Namboku subway line, Roppongi Itchōme Station (Exit 1).*

Coredo. Unlike other big stores in the Ginza and Nihombashi areas, this sparkling mall has an open layout and extensive use of glass and wood. Housewares, toys, and fashion can be found here. ✉ *1–4–1 Nihombashi, Chūō-ku* ☎ *03/3272–4939* ☉ *Mon.–Sat. 11–9, Sun. 11–8* Ⓜ *Ginza, Tōzai, and Asakusa subway lines, Nihombashi Station (Exit B10).*

Glassarea. Virtually defining Aoyama elegance is this cobblestone shopping center, which draws well-heeled Aoyama housewives to its boutiques, restaurants, and housewares shops. ✉ *5–4–41 Minami-Aoyama, Minato-ku* ☎ *03/5778–4450* ☉ *Most shops daily 11–8* Ⓜ *Ginza, Chiyoda, and Hanzō-mon subway lines, Omotesandō Station (Exit B1).*

Omotesandō Hills. Architect Tadao Ando's latest adventure in concrete is Tōkyō's newest monument to shopping. The six wedge-shaped floors include some brand-name heavy hitters (Yves Saint Laurent and Harry Winston) and a wide range of smaller stores whose shelves showcase high-end shoes and bags. ✉ *4–12–10 Jingū-mae, Shibuya-ku* ☎ *03/ 3497–0293* ☉ *Daily 11–8* Ⓜ *Hanzō-mon, Ginza, and Chiyoda subway lines, Omotesandō Station (Exit A2).*

Roppongi Hills. You could easily spend a whole day exploring the retail areas of Tōkyō's newest minicity. The shops here emphasize eye-catching design and chi-chi brands. Finding a particular shop, however, can be a hassle given the building's Escher-like layout. ✉ *6–10–1 Roppongi, Minato-ku* ☎ *03/6406–6000* ☉ *Most shops daily 11–8* Ⓜ *Hibiya and Ōedo subway lines, Roppongi Station (Roppongi Hills Exit).*

Shibuya 109. This nine-floor outlet is a teenage girl's dream. It's filled with small stores whose merchandise scream kitsch and trend. Many weekend afternoons will see dance groups and fashion shows at the first-floor entrance. ✉ *2–29–1 Dōgenzaka, Shibuya-ku* ☎ *03/3477–5111* ☉ *Daily 10–9* Ⓜ *JR Yamanote Line; Ginza and Hanzō-mon subway lines: Shibuya Station (Hachiko Exit for JR, Exit 3 for subway lines).*

Department Stores

A visit to a Japanese department store is not merely a shopping excursion—it's a lesson in Japanese culture. Plan to arrive just before it opens: promptly on the hour, immaculately groomed young women face the customers from inside, bow ceremoniously, and unlock the doors. As you walk through the store, all the sales assistants stand at attention, in postures of nearly reverent welcome. Notice the uniform angle of incline: many stores have training sessions to teach their new employees the precise and proper degree at which to bend from the waist.

Most Japanese *depāto* (department stores) are parts of conglomerates that include railways, real estate, and leisure industries. The stores commonly have travel agencies, theaters, and art galleries on the premises, as well as reasonably priced restaurants and cafés.

The top floor of many department stores offer gift packages containing Japan's best-loved brands of sake, rice crackers, and other food items. Department stores also typically devote one floor to traditional Japanese crafts, including ceramics, paintings, and lacquerware. If you're pressed for time, these are great places to pick up a variety of souvenirs.

Don't miss the *depachika* (food departments) on the lower levels, where you'll encounter an overwhelming selection of Japanese and Western delacacies. Though no locals in their right minds would shop here regularly for their groceries—the price tags on the imported cheeses and hams will cause your jaw to hit the floor—a brief exploration will give you a pretty good picture of what people might select for a special occasion. Many stalls have small samples out on the counter, and nobody will raise a fuss if you help yourself, even if you don't make a purchase.

Major department stores accept credit cards and provide shipping services. Some salesclerks speak English. If you're having communication difficulties, someone will come to the rescue. On the first floor will be a general information booth with useful maps of the store in English. Some department stores close one or two days a month.

Ginza, Nihombashi & Yūraku-chō

Fodor'sChoice ★ **Matsuya.** On the fourth floor, the gleaming Matsuya houses an excellent selection of Japanese fashion, including Issey Miyake, Yohji Yamamoto, and Comme Ça Du Mode. The Louis Vuitton shops on the first and second floors are particularly popular with Tōkyō's brand-obsessed shoppers. ⊠ *3–6–1 Ginza, Chūō-ku* ☎ *03/3567–1211* ⊗ *Sat.–Thurs. 10–8:30, Fri. 10–9:30* Ⓜ *Ginza, Marunouchi, and Hibiya subway lines, Ginza Station (Exits A12 and A13).*

Matsuzakaya. The Matsuzakaya conglomerate was founded in Nagoya and still commands the loyalties of shoppers with origins in western Japan. Style-conscious Tōkyōites tend to find the sense of fashion a bit countrified. ⊠ *6–10–1 Ginza, Chūō-ku* ☎ *03/3572–1111* ⊗ *Sun.–Wed. 10:30–7:30; Thur., Fri., and Sat. 10:30–8* Ⓜ *Ginza, Marunouchi, and Hibiya subway lines, Ginza Station (Exits A3 and A4).*

★ **Mitsukoshi.** Founded in 1673 as a dry-goods store, Mitsukoshi later played a leading role in introducing Western merchandise to Japan. It has retained its image of quality and excellence, with a strong representation of Western fashion designers. The store also stocks fine traditional Japanese goods—don't miss the art gallery and the crafts area on the sixth floor. With its own subway stop, bronze lions at the entrance, and an atrium sculpture of the Japanese goddess Magokoro, the remarkable Nihombashi flagship store merits a visit even if you're not buying anything. ⊠ *1–4–1 Nihombashi Muro-machi, Chūō-ku* ☎ *03/3241–3311* ⊗ *Daily 10–7:30* Ⓜ *Ginza and Hanzō-mon subway lines, Mitsukoshi-mae Station (Exits A3 and A5)* ⊠ *4–6–16 Ginza, Chūō-ku* ☎ *03/ 3562–1111* ⊗ *Mon.–Sat. 10–8* Ⓜ *Ginza, Marunouchi, and Hibiya subway lines, Ginza Station (Exits A6, A7, A8).*

Fodor'sChoice ★ **Muji.** This chain features generically branded housewares and clothing at reasonable prices. You'll find a large selection of Bauhaus-influenced furniture, appliances, and bedding at the massive flagship branch in

Yūraku-chō. If you're overwhelmed by all the options, relax at the dining area that boasts–What else?–Muji meals. ✉ *3–8–3 Marunouchi Muro-machi, Chiyoda-ku* ☎ *03/5208–8241* ☉ *Daily 10–9* Ⓜ *JR Yamanote Line; Yūraku-chō subway line, Yūraku-chō Station (JR Kyobashi Exit, subway Exit A9).*

Takashimaya. In Japanese, *taka* means "high"—a fitting word for this store, which is beloved for its superior quality and prestige. The second floor, with shops by Christian Dior, Prada, Chanel, Cartier, and many others, is one of the toniest retail spaces in a shopping district celebrated for its exclusivity. The seventh floor has a complete selection of traditional crafts, antiques, and curios. The lower-level food court carries every gastronomic delight imaginable, from Japanese crackers and green tea to Miyazaki beef and plump melons. ✉ *2–4–1 Nihombashi, Chūō-ku* ☎ *03/3211–4111* ☉ *Daily 10–8* Ⓜ *Ginza subway line, Nihombashi Station (Exits B1 and B2)* ✉ *Takashimaya Times Sq., 5–24–2 Sendagaya, Shibuya-ku* ☎ *03/5361–1111* ☉ *Sun.–Fri. 10–8, Sat. 10–8:30* Ⓜ *JR Yamanote Line, Shinjuku Station (Minami-guchi/South Exit).*

Wako. Wako is well-known for its high-end glassware, jewelry, and accessories, as well as having some of the handsomest, most sophisticated window displays in town. The clock atop this curved 1930s-era building is illuminated at night, making it one of Tōkyō's more recognized landmarks. ✉ *4–5–11 Ginza, Chūō-ku* ☎ *03/3562–2111* ☉ *Mon.–Sat. 10:30–6* Ⓜ *Ginza, Marunouchi, and Hibiya subway lines, Ginza Station (Exits A9 and A10).*

Ikebukuro

Parco. Parco, owned by the Seibu conglomerate, is actually four vertical malls filled with small retail shops and boutiques, all in walking distance of one another in the commercial heart of Shibuya. Parco Part 1 and Part 4 (Quattro) cater to a younger crowd and stock unbranded casual clothing, crafts fabrics, and accessories; Quattro even has a club that hosts live music. Part 2 is devoted mainly to interiors and fashion, and Part 3 sells a mixture of men's and women's fashions, tableware, and household furnishings. The nearby Zero Gate complex houses the basement restaurant-nightclub La Fabrique. ✉ *15–1 Udagawa-chō, Shibuya-ku* ☎ *03/3464–5111* ☉ *Parts 1, 2, and 3 daily 10–9; Quattro daily 11–9* Ⓜ *Ginza and Hanzō-mon subway lines, Shibuya Station (Exits 6 and 7).*

Shinjuku

Isetan. One of Tōkyō's oldest and largest department stores, Isetan is known for its mix of high-end and affordable fashions, and its selection of larger sizes not found in most Tōkyō stores. The basement's food selection, which includes prepared salads and dried fish, is one of the city's largest in a department store. ✉ *3–14–1 Shinjuku, Shinjuku-ku* ☎ *03/3352–1111* ☉ *Daily 10–8* Ⓜ *JR Yamanote Line, Marunouchi subway line (Higashi-guchi/East Exit for JR, Exits B2, B3, B4, and B5 for subway line).*

Marui. Marui, easily recognized by its red-and-white OI logo, burst onto the department store scene in the 1980s by introducing an in-store credit card—one of the first stores in Japan to do so. Branches typically occupy separate buildings near busy train stations; there are a handful of big shops in Shinjuku with names like Marui Young, Marui City, and Marui Men. Youngsters flock to the stores in search of petite clothing, accessories, and sportswear. ☒ *5–16–4 Shinjuku, Shinjuku-ku* ☎ *03/ 3354–0101* ☉ *Daily 11–9* Ⓜ *JR Yamanote Line, Shinjuku Station (Higashi-guchi/East Exit); Marunouchi subway line, Shinjuku San-chōme Station (Exit B2).*

Specialty Stores

Antiques

From ornate *tansu* (traditional chests used to store clothing) to Meiji-era Nō masks, Tōkyō's antiques shops are stocked with fine examples of traditional Japanese craftsmanship. The two best areas for antiques are Nishi-Ogikubo (also known as Nishiogi), which is just outside of Shinjuku, and Aoyama. The elegant shops along Kottō-dōri—Aoyama's "Antiques Road"—are the places to hunt down exquisite ¥100,000 vases and other pricey items. The slapdash array of more than 60 antiques shops in Nishi-Ogikubo has an anything-goes feel. When visiting Nishi-Ogikubo, which you can reach by taking the Sōbu Line to Nishi-Ogikubo Station, your best bet is to pick up the free printed area guide available at the police box outside the train station's north exit. Even though it's mostly in Japanese, the map provides easy-to-follow directions to all stores. Dealers are evenly clustered in each of the four districts around the station. Antiquers can also find great buys at Tōkyō's flea markets, which are often held on the grounds of the city's shrines.

★ **Fuji-Torii.** An English-speaking staff, a central Omotesandō location, and antiques ranging from ceramics to swords are the big draws at this shop, in business since 1948. In particular, Fuji-Torii has an excellent selection of folding screens, lacquerware, painted glassware, and *ukiyo-e* (wood-block prints). ☒ *6–1–10 Jingū-mae, Shibuya-ku* ☎ *03/ 3400–2777* ☉ *Wed.–Mon. 11–6; closed 3rd Mon. of month* Ⓜ *Chiyoda subway line, Meiji Jingū-mae Station (Exit 4).*

Morita. This Aoyama shop carries antiques and new *mingei* (Japanese folk crafts) in addition to a large stock of textiles from throughout Asia. ☒ *5–12–2 Minami-Aoyama, Minato-ku* ☎ *03/3407–4466* ☉ *Daily 10–7* Ⓜ *Ginza, Chiyoda, and Hanzō-mon subway lines, Omotesandō Station (Exit B1).*

Tōgō Jinja. One of the city's biggest flea markets—where you can often find antiques and old yakuza movie posters—takes place at this shrine near Harajuku's Takeshita-dōri, on the first Sunday of the month from sunrise to sunset. ☒ *1–5 Jingū-mae, Shibuya-ku* ☎ *03/3425–7965* Ⓜ *Chiyoda subway line, Meiji-jingu-mae Station; JR Yamanote Line, Harajuku Station (Takeshita-dori Exit).*

Yasukuni Jinja. Every second and third Sunday of the month, from sunrise to sunset, antique-hunters can search and explore this large flea market. It's located near the Yasukuni shrine, so when you're finished shopping, stroll over to the shrine to learn about the controversy that surrounds it. ☒ *3–1 Kudan-Kita, Chiyoda-ku* ☎ *03/3791–0006* Ⓜ *Hanzō-mon and Shinjuku subway lines, Kudanshita Station (Exit 1).*

Books

Bookstores of Jimbō-chō. The site of one of the largest concentrations of used bookstores in the world, the Jimbō-chō area is a bibliophile's dream. In the ½-km (¼-mi) strip along Yasukuni-dōri and its side streets you can find centuries-old Japanese prints, vintage manga, and even complete sets of the *Oxford English Dictionary*. Most shops have predominately Japanese-language selections, but almost all stock some foreign titles, with a few devoting major floor space to English books. The stores in the area are usually open 9 or 9:30 to 5:30 or 6, and many of the smaller shops close on Sunday or Monday. Ⓜ *Mita, Shinjuku, and Hanzō-mon subway lines, Jimbō-chō Station (Exit A5).*

Kinokuniya. This mammoth bookstore near the south exit of Shinjuku Station devotes most of its sixth floor to English titles, with an excellent selection of travel guides, magazines, and books on Japan. ✉ *Takashimaya Times Sq., 5–24–2 Sendagaya, Shibuya-ku* ☎ *03/5361–3300* ◷ *Sun.–Fri. 10–8, Sat. 10–8:30* Ⓜ *JR Yamanote Line, Shinjuku Station (Minami-guchi/South Exit).*

Maruzen. There are English titles on the fourth floor, as well as art books; this recently relocated flagship branch of the Maruzen chain also hosts the occasional art exhibit. ✉ *1–6–4 Marunouchi, Chiyoda-ku* ☎ *03/5288–8881* ◷ *Daily 9–9* Ⓜ *JR Yamanote Line, Tōkyō Station (North Exit); Tozai subway line, Otemachi Station (Exit B2C).*

Yaesu Book Center. English-language paperbacks, art books, and calendars are available on the seventh floor of this celebrated bookstore. ✉ *2–5–1 Yaesu, Chūō-ku* ☎ *03/3281–1811* ◷ *Mon.–Sat. 10–9, Sun. 10–8* Ⓜ *JR Yamanote Line, Tōkyō Station (Yaesu South Exit 5).*

Ceramics

At first glance, Japanese ceramics may seem priced for a prince's table, but if you keep shopping, you can find reasonably priced items that are generally far superior in design to what is available back home. Sale items are often amazingly good bargains. Vases, sake sets, and chopstick rests all make good gifts.

Noritake. The Akasaka showroom of this internationally renowned brand carries fine china and glassware in a spacious setting. ✉ *7–8–5 Akasaka, Minato-ku* ☎ *03/3586–0267* ◷ *Weekdays 10–6* Ⓜ *Chiyoda subway line, Akasaka Station (Exit 7).*

Savoir Vivre. In Roppongi's ultratrendy Axis Building, this store sells contemporary and antique tea sets, cups, bowls, and glassware. ✉ *Axis Bldg., 3F, 5–17–1 Roppongi, Minato-ku* ☎ *03/3585–7365* ◷ *Mon.–Sat. 11–7, Sun. 11–6:30* Ⓜ *Hibiya and Ōedo subway lines, Roppongi Station (Exit 3).*

Tsutaya. *Ikebana* (flower arrangement) and *sadō* (tea ceremony) goods are the only items sold at this Kottō-dōri shop, but they come in such stunning variety that a visit is definitely worthwhile. Colorful vases in surprising shapes and traditional ceramic tea sets make for unique souvenirs. ✉ *5–10–5 Minami-Aoyama, Minato-ku* ☎ *03/3400–3815* ◷ *Daily 10–6:30* Ⓜ *Ginza, Chiyoda, and Hanzō-mon subway lines, Omotesandō Station (Exit B1).*

Clothing Boutiques

Japanese boutiques pay as much attention to interior design as they do to the clothing they sell. Although many mainstream Japanese designers are represented in the major upscale department stores, you may enjoy your shopping more in the elegant boutiques of Aoyama and Omotesandō—most of which are within walking distance of one another.

Bape Exclusive Aoyama. Since the late 1990s, no brand has been more coveted by Harajuku scenesters than the A Bathing Ape label (shortened to Bape) from DJ–fashion designer Nigo. At the height of the craze, hopefuls would line up outside Nigo's well-hidden boutiques for the chance to plop down ¥7,000 for a T-shirt festooned with a simian visage or a *Planet of the Apes* quote. Bape has since gone above-ground, with Nigo expanding his business empire to Singapore, Hong Kong, and London. Here in Tōkyō, you can see what all the fuss is about at a spacious boutique that houses the Bape Gallery on the second floor. ⊠ *5–5–8 Minami-Aoyama, Minato-ku* ☎ *03/3407–2145* ⊙ *Daily 11–7* Ⓜ *Ginza and Hanzō-mon subway lines, Omotesandō Station (Exit A5).*

Busy Workshop Harajuku. This Harajuku spot sells the trendy Bape clothing line and has an avant-garde interior by noted local designers Wonderwall. ⊠ *B1F, 4–28–22 Jingū-mae, Minato-ku* ☎ *03/5474–0204* ⊙ *Daily 11–7* Ⓜ *Chiyoda line, Meiji-jingū-mae Station (Exit 5); JR Yamanote Line, Harajuku Station (Takeshita-dori Exit).*

★ **Comme des Garçons.** Sinuous low walls snake through Rei Kawakubo's flagship store, a minimalist labyrinth that houses the designer's signature clothes, shoes, and accessories. Staff members will do their best to ignore you, but that's no reason to stay away from one of Tōkyō's funkiest retail spaces. ⊠ *5–2–1 Minami-Aoyama, Minato-ku* ☎ *03/3406–3951* ⊙ *Daily 11–8* Ⓜ *Ginza, Chiyoda, and Hanzō-mon subway lines, Omotesandō Station (Exit A5).*

Issey Miyake. The otherworldy creations of internationally renowned designer Miyake are on display at her flagship store in Aoyama, which carries the full Paris line. ⊠ *3–18–11 Minami-Aoyama, Minato-ku* ☎ *03/3423–1407* ⊙ *Daily 11–8* Ⓜ *Ginza, Chiyoda, and Hanzo-mon subway lines, Omotesandō Station (Exit A4).*

10 Corso Como Comme des Garçons. Milanese lifestyle guru Carla Sozzani helped create this spacious boutique for designer Rei Kawakubo's Comme des Garçons lines, which include Junya Watanabe menswear and womens wear. Also on offer are Vivienne Westwood and Balenciaga brands, and the staff isn't too busy being hip to help you out. ⊠ *5–3 Minami-Aoyama, Minato-ku* ☎ *03/5774–7800* ⊙ *Daily 11–8* Ⓜ *Ginza, Chiyoda, and Hanzō-mon subway lines, Omotesandō Station (Exit A5).*

Under Cover. This stark shop houses Paris' darling Jun Takahashi's cult clothing, with enormously high racks of men's and women's clothing with a tatty punk look. ⊠ *5–3–18 Minami-Aoyama, Minato-ku* ☎ *03/3407–1232* ⊙ *Daily 11–8* Ⓜ *Ginza, Chiyoda, and Hanzō-mon subway lines, Omotesandō Station (Exit A5).*

Y's Roppongi Hills. With its glossy surfaces and spare lines, the interior of this Ron Arad–designed shop on Roppongi's Keyakizaka-dōri serves as a suitable showcase for Yohji Yamamoto's austere fashions. ✉ *6–12–4 Roppongi, Minato-ku* ☏ *03/5413–3434* ◷ *Daily 11–9* Ⓜ *Hibiya and Ōedo subway lines, Roppongi Station (Roppongi Hills Exit).*

Clothing Chains

Beams. Beams stores provide Japan's younger men and women with extremely hip threads. Shopping here will ensure that you or your kids will be properly attired in street-ready T-shirts and porter bags. ✉ *19–6 Sarugakuchō, Shibuya-ku* ☏ *03/5428–5951* ◷ *Daily 11–8* Ⓜ *Tōkyū Tōyoko line, Daikanyama Station (Komazawa-dōri Exit).*

★ **Journal Standard.** This is not a chain dedicated to outfitting reporters in shirts and ties. In fact, this branch is frequented by young couples looking for the season's *it* fashions. ✉ *1–5–6 Jinnan, Shibuya-ku* ☏ *03/5457–0700* ◷ *Daily 11–8* Ⓜ *JR Yamanote Line; Ginza and Hanzō-mon subway lines, Shibuya Station (Hachiko Exit for JR, Exits 6 and 7 for subways).*

Uniqlo. Uniqlo offers customers a chance to wrap themselves in simple, low-priced items from the company's own brand. The vibe of the chain fits well within the relaxed attitudes of the Jiyūgaoka area, but there are locations all over the city as well as overseas. The store focuses on simple men's and women's clothing from its own label. ✉ *1–8–21 Jiyūgaoka, Meguro-ku* ☏ *03/5731–8273* ◷ *Daily 11–8* Ⓜ *Tōkyū Tōyoko and Oimachi lines, Jiyugaoka Station (South Exit).*

Dolls

There are many types of traditional dolls available in Japan, and each one has its own charm. Kokeshi dolls, which date from the Edo period, are long, cylindrical, painted, and made of wood, with no arms or legs. Daruma, papier-mâché dolls with rounded bottoms and faces, are often painted with amusing expressions. Legend has it they are modeled after a Buddhist priest who remained seated in the lotus position for so long that his arms and legs atrophied. Hakata dolls, from Kyūshū, are ceramic figurines in traditional costume, such as geisha, samurai, or festival dancers.

Beishu. Colorful and often made from precious metals, the delicate dolls hand-crafted at this shop have found their way into some of Japan's larger department stores, museums, and even the Imperial Palace. ✉ *2–3–12 Taitō-Higashi, Taitō-ku* ☏ *03/3834–3501* ◷ *Sun.–Fri. 10–6* Ⓜ *Ōedo subway line, Shin-okachimachi Station (Exit A2).*

Kyūgetsu. In business for more than a century, Kyūgetsu sells every kind of doll imaginable. ✉ *1–20–4 Yanagibashi, Taitō-ku* ☏ *03/5687–5176* ◷ *Weekdays 9:15–6, weekends 9:15–5:15* Ⓜ *Asakusa subway line, Asakusa-bashi Station (Exit A3).*

Electronics

The area around Akihabara Station has more than 200 stores with discount prices on stereos, digital cameras, computers, DVD players, and anything else that runs on electricity. The larger shops have sections or floors (or even whole annexes) of goods made for export. Products come with instructions in most major languages, and if you have a tourist visa in your passport, you can purchase them duty-free.

1

★ **Apple Store.** This stylish showroom displays the newest models from Apple's line of computer products. The Genius Bar on the second floor offers consulting services should you need advice on how to resuscitate a comatose iPod or MacBook. ✉ *3–5–12 Ginza, Chūō-ku* ☎ *03/5159–8200* ☉ *Daily 10–9* Ⓜ *Ginza, Hibiya, and Marunouchi subway lines, Ginza Station (Exit A13).*

LAOX. One of the big Akihabara chains, LAOX has several locations in the area. The "Duty Free Akihabara" branch on the main Chūō-dōri strip carries a full six floors of export models. English-speaking staff members are always on call. ✉ *1–15–3 Soto-Kanda, Chiyoda-ku* ☎ *03/3255–5301* ☉ *Daily 8–9* Ⓜ *JR Yamanote Line, Akihabara Station (Electric Town Exit).*

☯ **Sony Building.** Test drive the latest Sony gadgets at this retail and entertainment space in the heart of Ginza. Kids will enjoy trying out the not-yet-released PlayStation games, while their parents fiddle with digital cameras and stereos from Japan's electronics leader. ✉ *5–3–1 Ginza, Chūō-ku* ☎ *03/3573–2371* ☉ *Daily 11–7* Ⓜ *JR Yamanote Line, Yūraku-chō Station (Ginza Exit); Ginza, Hibiya, and Marunouchi subway lines, Ginza Station (Exit B9).*

Sukiya Camera. The cramped Nikon House branch of this two-store operation features enough Nikons—old and new, digital and film—that it could double as a museum to the brand. Plenty of lenses and flashes are available as well. ✉ *4–2–13 Ginza, Chūō-ku* ☎ *03/3561–6000* ☉ *Mon.–Sat. 10–7:30, Sun. 10–7* Ⓜ *JR Yamanote Line, Yūraku-chō Station (Ginza Exit); Ginza, Hibiya, and Marunouchi subway lines, Ginza Station (Exit B10).*

★ **Y.K. Musen.** Welcome to a world that would truly be Maxwell Smart's dream. From pinhole cameras hidden in cigarette packs to microphones capable of picking up sound through concrete, Y.K. Musen supplies the latest and greatest in snoop technology. ✉ *1–14–2 Soto-Kanda, Chiyoda-ku* ☎ *03/3255–3079* ☉ *Daily 10–6:45* Ⓜ *JR Yamanote Line, Akihabara Station (Electric Town Exit).*

Yodobashi Camera. This discount-electronics superstore near Shinjuku Station carries a selection comparable to Akihabara's big boys. ✉ *1–11–1 Nishi-Shinjuku, Shinjuku-ku* ☎ *03/3346–1010* ☉ *Daily 9:30–10* Ⓜ *Marunouchi and Shinjuku subway lines; JR Yamanote Line; Keiō and Odakyū lines, Shinjuku Station (Nishi-guchi/West Exit).*

Folk Crafts

Japanese folk crafts, called mingei—among them bamboo vases and baskets, fabrics, paper boxes, dolls, and toys—achieve a unique beauty in their simple and sturdy designs. Be aware, however, that simple does not mean cheap. Long hours of labor go into these objects, and every year there are fewer craftspeople left, producing their work in smaller and smaller quantities.

Printed fabric, whether by the yard or in the form of finished scarves, napkins, tablecloths, or pillow coverings, is another item worth purchasing. The complexity of the designs and the quality of the printing make the fabric, both silk and cotton, special. *Furoshiki*—square pieces of cloth used for wrapping, storing, and carrying things—make great wall hangings.

The Power of Tea

GREEN TEA IS UBIQUITOUS IN Japan. But did you know that besides being something of the national drink, it's also good for you? Green tea contains antioxidants twice as powerful as those in red wine; these help reduce high blood pressure, lower blood sugar, and fight cancer. Whether drinking green tea for its healing properties, good taste, or as a manner of habit, you'll have plenty of choices in Japan. Pay attention to tea varietals, which are graded by the quality and parts of the plant used, because price and quality runs the spectrum within these categories. For the very best Japanese green tea, take a trip to the Uji region of Kyoto.

Gyokuro (jewel dew). Developed from a grade of green tea called *tencha* (divine tea), the name is derived from the light green color the tea adopts when brewed. Gyokuro is grown in the shade, an essential condition to develop just this type and grade.

Matcha (rubbed tea). Most often used in the tea ceremony, matcha is a high-quality, but hard to find, powdered green tea. It has a thick, paintlike consistency when mixed with hot water. It is also a popular flavor of ice cream and other sweets in Japan.

Sencha (roasted tea). This is the green tea you are most likely to try at the local noodle or bento shop. Its leaves are grown under direct sunlight, giving it a different flavor from cousins like Gyokuro.

Genmai (brown rice tea). This is a mixture, usually in equal parts, of green tea and roasted brown rice.

Bancha (common tea). This second harvest variety ripens between summer and fall, producing leaves larger than those of Sencha and a weaker tasting tea.

Genmaicha (popcorn tea). This is a blend of bancha and genmai teas.

Kabusecha (covered tea). Similar to Gyokuru, Kabusecha leaves are grown in the shade, though for a shorter period, giving it a refined flavor.

Hōjicha (pan fried tea). A pan-fried or oven-roasted green tea.

Kukicha (stalk tea). A tea made from stalks by harvesting one bud and three leaves.

Bingo-ya. You may be able to complete all of your souvenir shopping in one trip to this tasteful four-floor shop, which carries traditional handicrafts—including ceramics, toys, lacquerware, Nō masks, fabrics, and lots more—from all over Japan. ✉ *10–6 Wakamatsu-chō, Shinjuku-ku* ☎ *03/3202–8778* ✆ *Tues.–Sun. 10–7* Ⓜ *Ōedo subway line, Wakamatsu Kawada Station (Wakamatsu-chō Exit)*.

★ **Oriental Bazaar.** The four floors of this popular tourist destination are packed with just about anything you could want as a traditional Japanese (or Chinese or Korean) handicraft souvenir: painted screens, pottery, chopsticks, dolls, and more, all at very reasonable prices. ✉ *5–9–13 Jingū-mae, Shibuya-ku* ☎ *03/3400–3933* ✆ *Fri.–Wed. 10–7* Ⓜ *Chiyoda subway line, Meiji Jingū-mae Station (Exit 4)*.

Foodstuffs & Wares

This hybrid category includes everything from crackers and dried sea-weed to cast-iron kettles, paper lanterns, and essential food kitsch like plastic sushi sets.

Backstreet Shops of Tsukiji. In Tsukiji, between the Central Wholesale Market and Harumi-dōri, among the many fishmongers, you can also find stores selling pickles, tea, crackers, kitchen knives, baskets, and crockery. The area is a real slice of Japanese life. ✉ *Tsukiji 4-chōme, Chūō-ku* Ⓜ *Ōedo subway line, Tsukiji-shijō Station (Exit A1); Hibiya subway line, Tsukiji Station (Exit 1).*

Tea-Tsu. Some people ascribe Japanese longevity to the beneficial effects of green tea. Tea-Tsu, which has five branches in Tōkyō, sells a variety of leaves in attractive canisters. The main Aoyama branch also sells tea sets and other ceramics, and the staff will serve you a complimentary cup of *cha* (tea) as you make your selection. ✉ *3–18–3 Minami-Aoyama, Minato-ku* ☎ *03/5772–2662* ⊙ *Tues.–Sun. 11–8* Ⓜ *Ginza, Chiyoda, and Hanzō-mon subway lines, Omotesandō Station (Exit A4).*

Tokiwa-dō. Come here to buy some of Tōkyō's most famous souvenirs: *kaminari okoshi* (thunder crackers), made of rice, millet, sugar, and beans. It's on the west side of Asakusa's Thunder God Gate, the Kaminari-mon entrance to Sensō-ji. ✉ *1–3 Asakusa, Taitō-ku* ☎ *03/3841 5656* ⊙ *Daily 9–8:45* Ⓜ *Ginza subway line, Asakusa Station (Exit 1).*

Yamamoto Noriten. The Japanese are resourceful in their uses of products from the sea. Nori, the paper-thin dried seaweed used to wrap maki sushi and *onigiri* (rice balls), is the specialty here. If you plan to bring some home with you, buy unroasted nori and toast it yourself at home; the flavor will be far better than that of the preroasted sheets. ✉ *1–6–3 Nihombashi Muro-machi, Chūō-ku* ☎ *03/3241–0261* ⊙ *Daily 9–6:30* Ⓜ *Hanzō-mon and Ginza subway lines, Mitsukoshi-mae Station (Exit A1).*

Housewares

Tōkyōites appreciate fine design, both the kind they can wear and the kind they can display in their homes. This passion is reflected in the exuberance of the city's *zakka* shops—retailers that sell small housewares. The Daikanyama and Aoyama areas positively brim with these stores, but trendy zakka can be found throughout the city.

Idee Shop. Local design giant Teruo Kurosaki's shop, located on the sixth floor of Takashimaya's Futako Tamagawa branch, carries housewares, fabrics, and ceramics by some of Japan's most celebrated young craftspeople. ✉ *3–17–1 Tamagawa, Setagaya-ku* ☎ *03/5797–3024* ⊙ *Daily 10–9* Ⓜ *Tōkyū Denentoshi and Oimachi lines, Futako Tamagawa Station (West Exit).*

Sempre. Playful, colorful, and bright describe both the products and the space of this Kottō-dōri housewares dealer. Among the great finds here are interesting tableware, glassware, lamps, office goods, and jewelry. ✉ *5–13–3 Minami-Aoyama, Minato-ku* ☎ *03/5464–5655* ⊙ *Mon.–Sat. 11–8, Sun 11–7* Ⓜ *Ginza, Chiyoda, and Hanzō-mon subway lines, Omotesandō Station (Exit B1).*

Kappabashi

A WHOLESALE-RESTAURANT-supply district might not sound like a promising shopping destination, but Kappabashi, about a 10-minute walk west of the temples and pagodas of Asakusa, is worth a look. Ceramics, cutlery, cookware, folding lanterns, and even kimonos can all be found here, along with the kitschy plastic food models that appear in restaurant windows throughout Japan. The best strategy is to stroll up and down the 1-km (½-mi) length of Kappabashi-dōgu-machi-dōri and visit any shop that looks interesting. Most Kappabashi shops are open until 5:30; some close on Sunday. To get here, take the Ginza subway line to Tawara-machi Station.

Kappabashi Sōshoku. Come here for *aka-chōchin* (folding red-paper lanterns) like the ones that hang in front of inexpensive bars and restaurants. ⊠ *3-1-1 Matsugaya, Taitō-ku* ☎ *03/3844-1973* ⊙ *Mon.–Sat. 9:30–5:30* Ⓜ *Ginza subway line, Tawara-machi Station (Exit 3).*

Kawahara Shōten. The brightly colored bulk packages of rice crackers, shrimp-flavored chips, and other Japanese snacks sold here make offbeat gifts. ⊠ *3-9-2 Nishi-Asakusa, Taitō-ku* ☎ *03/3842-0841* ⊙ *Mon.–Sat. 9–5:30* Ⓜ *Ginza subway line, Tawara-machi Station (Exit 3).*

Maizuru. This perennial tourist favorite manufactures the plastic food that's displayed outside almost every Tōkyō restaurant. Ersatz sushi, noodles, and even beer cost just a few hundred yen. You can buy tiny plastic key holders and earrings, or splurge on a whole Pacific lobster, perfect in coloration and detail down to the tiniest spines on its legs. ⊠ *1-5-17 Nishi-Asakusa, Taitō-ku* ☎ *03/3843-1686* ⊙ *Daily 9–6* Ⓜ *Ginza subway line, Tawara-machi Station (Exit 3).*

Noren-no-Nishimura. This Kappabashi shop specializes in *noren*—the curtains that shops and restaurants hang to announce they're open. The curtains are typically cotton, linen, or silk, most often dyed-to-order for individual shops. Nishimura also sells premade noren of an entertaining variety—from white-on-blue landscapes to geisha and sumō wrestlers in polychromatic splendor—for home decorating. ⊠ *1-10-10 Matsugaya, Taitō-ku* ☎ *03/3841-6220* ⊙ *Mon.–Sat. 10–6* Ⓜ *Ginza subway line, Tawara-machi Station (Exit 3).*

Soi Furniture. The selection of lacquerware, ceramics, and antiques sold at this Kappabashi shop is modest, but Soi displays the items in a primitivist setting of stone walls and and wooden floor planks, with up-tempo jazz in the background. ⊠ *3-17-3 Matsugaya, Taitō-ku* ☎ *03/3843-9555* ⊙ *Daily 10–7* Ⓜ *Ginza subway line, Tawara-machi Station (Exit 3).*

Sputnik Pad. Sputnik, another of Kurosaki's shops, is Tōkyō's ultimate housewares destination. It carries funky and functional interiors products from big international designers like Marc Newson. Low, a trendy "rice café," is in the basement, and the Vision Network entertainment complex is across the street. ⊠ *5–46–14 Jingū-mae, Minato-ku* ☎ *03/*

6418–1330 ☉ *Daily 11–7* Ⓜ *Ginza, Chiyoda, and Hanzō-mon subway lines, Omotesandō Station (Exit B1).*

☺ **Tōkyū Hands.** This housewares chain provides the do-it-yourselfer with all the tools, fabrics, and supplies he or she may need to tackle any job. The selection of plastic models and rubber Godzilla action figures on the seventh floor of the Shibuya branch is amazingly comprehensive. ⊠ *12–18 Udagawa-chō, Shibuya-ku* ☎ *03/5489–5111* ☉ *Daily 10–8:30* Ⓜ *JR Yamanote Line; Ginza and Hanzō-mon subway lines, Shibuya Station (Hachiko Exit for JR, Exits 6 and 7 for subway).*

Jewelry

Japan has always been known for its craftspeople who possess the ability to create finely detailed work. Jewelry is no exception, especially when cultured pearls are used. Pearls, which have become something of a national symbol, are not inexpensive, but they are a whole lot cheaper in Japan than elsewhere.

Ginza Tanaka. From necklaces to precious metals shaped into statues, this chain of jewelry stores has crafted a reputation as one of Japan's premier jewelers since its founding in 1892. ⊠ *1–7–7 Ginza, Chuo-ku* ☎ *03/5561–0491* ☉ *Daily 10:30–7* Ⓜ *Yūraku-chō subway line, Ginza 1-Chome Station (Exit 7).*

★ **Mikimoto.** Kōkichi Mikimoto created his technique for cultured pearls in 1893. His name has since been associated with the best quality in the industry. Mikimoto's flagship store in Ginza is less a jewelry shop than a boutique devoted to nature's ready-made gems. ⊠ *4–5–5 Ginza, Chūō-ku* ☎ *03/3535–4611* ☉ *Daily 11–7; occasionally closed on Wed.* Ⓜ *Ginza, Hibiya, and Marunouchi subway lines, Ginza Station (Exit A9).*

Fodor'sChoice **Shinjuku Watch Kan.** Standing a full seven stories, this watch emporium
★ has just about any import brand as well as a wide selection of Casio and Seiko models that are not sold abroad. The top floor offers repair services. ⊠ *3–29–11 Shinjuku, Shinjuku-ku* ☎ *03/3226–6000* ☉ *Daily 10–9* Ⓜ *Marunouchi and Shinjuku subway lines; JR Yamanote Line; Keiō and Odakyū lines, Shinjuku Station (Higashi-guchi/East Exit).*

Tasaki Pearl Gallery. Tasaki sells pearls at slightly lower prices than Mikimoto. The store has several showrooms and hosts an English-language tour that demonstrates the technique of culturing pearls and explains how to maintain them. ⊠ *1–3–3 Akasaka, Minato-ku* ☎ *03/5561–8880* ☉ *Daily 9–6* Ⓜ *Ginza subway line, Tameike-Sannō Station (Exit 9).*

Kimonos

Traditional clothing has experienced something of a comeback among Tōkyō's youth, but most Japanese women, unless they work in traditional restaurants, now wear kimonos only on special occasions. Like tuxedos in the United States, they are often rented, not purchased outright, for social events such as weddings or graduations. Kimonos are extremely expensive and difficult to maintain. A wedding kimono, for example, can cost as much as ¥1 million.

Most visitors, naturally unwilling to pay this much for a garment that they probably want to use as a bathrobe, settle for a secondhand or antique silk kimono. You can pay as little as ¥1,000 in a flea market, but to find one in decent condition, you should expect to pay about ¥10,000. However, cotton summer kimonos, called yukata, in a wide variety of colorful and attractive designs, can be bought new for ¥7,000–¥10,000.

Hayashi. This store in the Yūraku-chō International Arcade specializes in ready-made kimonos, sashes, and dyed yukata. ⊠ *2–1–1 Yūraku-chō, Chiyoda-ku* ☎ *03/3501–4012* ⊘ *Mon.–Sat. 10–7, Sun. 10–6* Ⓜ *JR Yamanote Line, Yūraku-chō Station (Ginza Exit); Hibiya subway line, Hibiya Station (Exit A5).*

Kawano Gallery. Kawano, in the high-fashion district of Omotesandō, sells kimonos and kimono fabric in a variety of patterns. ⊠ *4–4–9 Jingū-mae, Shibuya-ku* ☎ *03/3470–3305* ⊘ *Daily 11–6* Ⓜ *Ginza, Chiyoda, and Hanzō-mon subway lines, Omotesandō Station (Exit A2).*

Tansu-ya. This small but pleasant Ginza shop has attractive used kimonos, yukata, and other traditional clothing in many fabrics, colors, and patterns. The helpful staff can acquaint you with the somewhat complicated method of putting on the garments. ⊠ *3–4–5 Ginza, Chūō-ku* ☎ *03/3561–8529* ⊘ *Mon.–Sat. 11–8, Sun. 11–7* Ⓜ *Ginza, Hibiya, and Marunouchi subway lines, Ginza Station (Exit A13).*

Lacquerware

For its history, diversity, and fine workmanship, lacquerware rivals ceramics as the traditional Japanese craft nonpareil. One warning: lacquerware thrives on humidity. Cheaper pieces usually have plastic rather than wood underneath. Because these won't shrink and crack in dry climates, they make safer—and no less attractive—buys.

Kasumisou Gallery. The gallery's jewelry and collectors boxes are handcrafted from fine wood and make great, but expensive, gifts. ⊠ *5–3–29 Minami-Azabu, Minato-ku* ☎ *03/3473–6058* ⊘ *Mon.–Sat. 9:30–5:30, Sun. 10:30–6:30* Ⓜ *Hibiya subway line, Hiroo Station (Exit 3).*

Fodor'sChoice **Yamada Heiando.** With a spacious, airy layout and lovely lacquerware
★ goods, this fashionable Daikanyama shop is a must for souvenir hunters—and anyone else who appreciates fine design. Rice bowls, sushi trays, *bento* lunch boxes, *hashioki* (chopstick rests), and jewelry cases come in traditional blacks and reds, as well as patterns both subtle and bold. Prices are fair—many items cost less than ¥10,000—but these are the kinds of goods for which devotees of Japanese craftsmanship would be willing to pay a lot. ⊠ *Hillside Terrace G Block, 18–12 Sarugakuchō, Shibuya-ku* ☎ *03/3464–5541* ⊘ *Mon.–Sat. 10:30–7, Sun. 10:30–6:30* Ⓜ *Tōkyū Tōyoko line, Daikanyama Station (Komazawa-dōri Exit).*

Paper

What packs light and flat in your suitcase, won't break, doesn't cost much, and makes a great gift? The answer is traditional handmade *washi* (paper), which the Japanese make in thousands of colors, textures, and designs and fashion into an astonishing number of useful and decorative objects. Delicate sheets of almost-transparent stationery, greeting cards, money holders, and wrapping paper are available at traditional crafts stores, stationery stores, and department stores. Small washi-

1

covered boxes (suitable for jewelry and other keepsakes) and pencil cases are also strong candidates for gifts and personal souvenirs.

Kami Hyakka. Operated by the Ōkura Sankō wholesale paper company, which was founded in the late 19th century, this showroom displays some 512 different types and colors of paper—made primarily for stationery, notes, and cards rather than as crafts material. You can pick up three free samples when you visit. ⊠ *2–4–9 Ginza, Chūō-ku* ☎ *03/3538–5025* ◷ *Tues.–Sat. 10:30–7* Ⓜ *Yūraku-chō subway line, Ginza-Itchōme Station (Exit 5); Ginza, Hibiya, and Marunouchi subway lines, Ginza Station (Exit B4).*

Kami-no-Takamura. Specialists in washi and other papers printed in traditional Japanese designs, this shop also carries brushes, inkstones, and other tools for calligraphy. ⊠ *1–1–2 Higashi-Ikebukuro, Toshima-ku* ☎ *03/3971–7111* ◷ *Daily 11–6:45* Ⓜ *JR Yamanote Line; Marunouchi subway line, Ikebukuro Station (East Exit for JR, Exit 35 for subway).*

★ **Kyūkyodō.** Kyūkyodō has been in business since 1663—in Ginza since 1880—selling its wonderful handmade Japanese papers, paper products, incense, brushes, and other materials for calligraphy. ⊠ *5–7–4 Ginza, Chūō-ku* ☎ *03/3571–4429* ◷ *Mon.–Sat. 10–7:30, Sun. 11–7* Ⓜ *Ginza, Hibiya, and Marunouchi subway lines, Ginza Station (Exit A2).*

Origami Kaikan. In addition to shopping for paper goods at Yushima no Kobayahi's store, you can also tour a papermaking workshop and learn the art of origami. ⊠ *1–7–14 Yushima, Bunkyō-ku* ☎ *03/3811–4025* ◷ *Mon.–Sat. 9–6* Ⓜ *JR Chūō and Sōbu lines, Ochanomizu Station (West Exit); Chiyoda subway line, Yushima Station (Exit 5).*

Record Stores

Tōkyō is perhaps the premier location in the world to purchase music. The big chains will have all the standard releases, but it is the smaller specialty stores that are the real treat: local music and wide selections of imports from around the world are usually available on both vinyl and CD. For out-of-print editions and obscurities on vinyl, the prices can run well over ¥10,000.

Cisco. This small chain offers everything from techno and house to reggae, but at this branch, hip-hop and R&B reign. Make sure you take advantage of the six turntables where you can hone your DJ skills. Well, actually, they are for previewing potential purchases, but feel free to give it a shot. ⊠ *11–1 Udagawa-chō, Shibuya-ku* ☎ *03/3462–0366* ◷ *Mon.–Sat. noon–10, Sun. 11–9* Ⓜ *JR Yamanote Line; Ginza and Hanzō-mon subway lines, Shibuya Station (Hachiko Exit for JR, Exits 6 and 7 for subway).*

Fodor'sChoice **Disk Union.** Vinyl junkies rejoice. The Shinjuku flagship of this chain of-
★ fers Latin, rock, and indie at 33 rpm. Other stores clustered within the nearby blocks have punk, metal, and jazz. Be sure to grab a store flyer that lists all of their branches since each usually specializes in one music genre. CDs are available, too. ⊠ *3–31–4 Shinjuku, Shinjuku-ku* ☎ *03/ 3352–2691* ◷ *Daily 11–9* Ⓜ *Marunouchi and Shinjuku subway lines; JR Yamanote Line; Keiō and Odakyū lines, Shinjuku Station (Higashi-guchi/East Exit).*

Manhattan Records. The hottest hip-hop, reggae, and R&B vinyl can be found here and a DJ booth pumps out the jams from the center of the room. Don't expect a lot advice from the staff—no one can hear you over the throbbing tunes. ✉ *10–1 Udagawa-chō, Shibuya-ku* ☎ *03/ 3477–7166* ⏰ *Daily noon–9* Ⓜ *JR Yamanote Line; Ginza and Hanzō- mon subway lines, Shibuya Station (Hachiko Exit for JR, Exits 6 and 7 for subway).*

Swords & Knives

Supplying the tools of the trade to samurai and sushi chefs alike, Japan- ese metalworkers have played a significant role in the nation's military and culinary history. For swords, you can pay thousands of dollars for a good-quality antique, but far more reasonably priced reproductions are available as well. Consult with your airline on how best to trans- port these items home.

Ichiryō-ya Hirakawa. A small, cluttered souvenir shop in the Nishi-Sandō arcade, Ichiryō-ya carries antique swords and reproductions and has some English-speaking sales clerks. ✉ *2–7–13 Asakusa, Taitō-ku* ☎ *03/ 3843–0051* ⏰ *Wed. and Fri.–Mon. 11–6* Ⓜ *Ginza subway line, Asakusa Station (Exit 1) or Tawara-machi Station (Exit 3).*

Kiya. Workers shape and hone blades in one corner of this Ginza shop, which carries cutlery, pocketknives, saws, and more. Scissors with han- dles in the shape of Japanese cranes are among the many unique gift items sold here, and custom-made knives are available on the second floor. ✉ *1–5–6 Nihombashi-Muromachi, Chūō-ku* ☎ *03/3241–0110* ⏰ *Mon.–Sat. 10–6, Sun. 11:15–5:45* Ⓜ *Ginza subway line, Mitsukoshi- mae Station (Exit A4).*

Fodor'sChoice **Nippon Tōken** (Japan Sword). Wannabe samurai can learn how to tell ★ their *tōshin* (blades) from their *tsuka* (sword handles) with help from the English-speaking staff at this small shop, which has been open since the Meiji era (1868–1912). Items that range from a circa-1390 samu- rai sword to inexpensive reproductions will allow you to take a trip back in time, but make sure your wallet is ready for today's prices. ✉ *3–8–1 Toranomon, Minato-ku* ☎ *03/3434–4321* ⏰ *Weekdays 9:30–6, Sat. 9:30–5* Ⓜ *Hibiya and Ginza subway lines, Toranomon Station (Exit 2).*

★ **Tsubaya Hōchōten.** Tsubaya sells high-quality cutlery for professionals. Its remarkable selection is designed for every imaginable use, as the art of food presentation in Japan requires a great variety of cutting imple- ments. The best of these carry the Traditional Craft Association seal: hand-forged tools of tempered blue steel, set in handles banded with deer horn to keep the wood from splitting. Be prepared to pay the premium: a cleaver just for slicing soba can cost as much as ¥50,000. ✉ *3–7–2 Nishi-Asakusa, Taitō-ku* ☎ *03/3845–2005* ⏰ *Mon.–Sat. 9–5:45, Sun. 9–5* Ⓜ *Ginza subway line, Tawara-machi Station (Exit 3).*

Toys

☺ **Hakuhinkan.** The plethora of homegrown-character goods like Hello Kitty make this is one of Japan's biggest stores for toys. But the real treat is outside, where a massive vending machine allows shoppers, or customers of one of the nearby hostess clubs, to pick up a stuffed doll or model plane afterhours. It's on Chūō-dōri, the main axis of the Ginza shopping area. ⊠ *8–8–11 Ginza, Chūō-ku* ☎ *03/3571–8008* ⊗ *Daily 11–8* Ⓜ *Ginza and Asakusa subway lines, Shimbashi Station (Exit 1).*

⚲ **Kiddy Land.** Commonly regarded as Tōkyō's best toy store, Kiddy Land also carries kitsch items that draw in Harajuku's teen brigade. ⊠ *6–1 Jingū-mae, Shibuya-ku* ☎ *03/3409–3431* ⊗ *Daily 11–9* Ⓜ *JR Yamanote Line: Harajuku Station (Omotesandō Exit); Chiyoda subway line, Meiji Jingū-mae Station (Exit 4).*

Traditional Wares

★ **Fuji-ya.** Master textile creator Keiji Kawakami's cotton *tenugui* (teh-*noo-goo-ee*) hand towels are collector's items, as often as not are framed instead of used as towels. Kawakami is an expert on the hundreds of traditional towel motifs that have come down from the Edo period: geometric patterns, plants and animals, and scenes from Kabuki plays and festivals. When Kawakami feels he has made enough of one pattern of his own design, he destroys the stencil. The shop is near the corner of Dembō-in-dōri on Naka-mise-dōri. ⊠*2–2–15 Asakusa, Taitō-ku* ☎*03/3841–2283* ⊗ *Fri.–Wed. 10–6* Ⓜ *Ginza subway line, Asakusa Station (Exit 6).*

Hyaku-suke. This is the last place in Tōkyō to carry government-approved skin cleanser made from powdered nightingale droppings. Ladies of the Edo period—especially the geisha—swore by the cleanser. These days this 100-year-old-plus cosmetics shop sells little of the nightingale powder, but its theatrical makeup for Kabuki actors, geisha, and traditional weddings—as well as unique items like seaweed shampoo, camellia oil, and handcrafted combs and cosmetic brushes—makes it a worthy addition to your Asakusa shopping itinerary. ⊠ *2–2–14 Asakusa, Taitō-ku* ☎*03/3841–7058* ⊗ *Wed.–Mon. 11–5* Ⓜ *Ginza subway line, Asakusa Station (Exit 6).*

Jusan-ya. A shop selling handmade boxwood combs, this business was started in 1736 by a samurai who couldn't support himself as a feudal retainer. It has been in the same family ever since. Jusan-ya is on Shinobazu-dōri, a few doors west of its intersection with Chūō-dōri in Ueno. ⊠ *2–12–21 Ueno, Taitō-ku* ☎ *03/3831–3238* ⊗ *Mon.–Sat. 10–6:30* Ⓜ *Ginza subway line, Ueno Hirokō-ji Station (Exit 3); JR Yamanote Line: Ueno Station (Shinobazu Exit).*

Yono-ya. Traditional Japanese coiffures and wigs are very complicated, and they require a variety of tools to shape them properly. Tatsumi Minekawa, the current master at Yono-ya—the family line goes back 300 years—deftly crafts and decorates very fine boxwood combs. Some combs are carved with auspicious motifs, such as peonies, hollyhocks, or cranes, and all are engraved with the family benchmark. ⊠ *1–37–10 Asakusa, Taitō-ku* ☎ *03/3844–1755* ⊗ *Daily 10–7; occasionally closed on Wed.* Ⓜ *Ginza subway line, Asakusa Station (Exit 1).*

TŌKYŌ ESSENTIALS

Tōkyō Travel Tools

HELPFUL WEB SITES

The Tōkyō Convention and Visitors Bureau (⊕ www.tcvb.or.jp) regularly updates details about the city's events, lodging, and more on its Web site. J Mode (⊕ www.jmode.com) offers up-to-date cultural and entertainment news. Japan Guide (⊕ www.japan-guide.com) contains a wealth of information on Tōkyō as well as listing vital resources, while Picture Tōkyō (⊕ www.picturetokyo.com) has well-cataloged facts, photos, and a whole lot more on the city.

Metropolis (⊕ http://metropolis.co.jp) and *Tōkyō Journal* (⊕ www.tokyo.to) are slick online magazines for the English expat community and will catch you up on the latest capital city goings-on—both have up-to-date arts, events, and dining listings.

VISITOR INFORMATION

When you arrive, stop by one of the Tourist Information Centers (TIC), which can advise you on trips and provide information on popular tourist destinations and lodging (same- and subsequent-day bookings can be made for some area hotels at the JNTO center).

The TICs are independently run but Tōkyō's two main TICs are located in the JNTO headquarters and the Tōkyō Metropolitan Government building. Both are great places to get free maps and brochures and have helpful, English-speaking staff. You can also find TICs at Narita International and Haneda airports. Many are open weekdays 9–5 and Saturday 9–noon; the JNTO center is open 9–5 every day except January 1. The list of TICs is too extensive (and some say unreliable) to list, so check out the Web site below.

NTT (Japanese Telephone Corporation) can help you find information in English, such as telephone numbers, museum openings, and other information available from its databases. It's open weekdays 9–5.

🚺 **Japan National Tourist Organization (JNTO) Japan:** ✉ 10th fl., Tōkyō Kotsu Kaikan Building, 2-10-1 Yurakucho, Chiyoda-ku, Tōkyō ☎ 03/3201-3331 Ⓜ Yūrakūchō and JR Yamanōtē lines, Yūrakūchō.

🚺 **Tourist Information Centers (TIC) Tōkyō Metropolitan Government Head Office TIC** ✉ 1st fl., Tōkyō Metropolitan Government No. 1 Bldg., 8-1 Nishi-Shinjuku 2-chome, Shinjuku-ku, Tōkyō ☎ 03/5321-3077 or 03/5321-3079 Ⓜ Tōei Ōedō line, Tōchōmaé. **Narita Airport TIC** ✉ 1st fl. passenger terminal No. 2 ☎ 0476-34-6251 Ⓜ Keisei, Sobu/Narita and JR Rappid Airport lines, Airport Terminal 2 station. **Haneda Airport TIC** ✉ 1st fl. Big Bird Bldg. ☎ 03/5757-9345 Ⓜ Keikyu-Kuko and Tōkyō p Monorail lines, Haneda Airport Terminal 1 station.

Transportation

BY AIR

AIRPORTS Tōkyō has two airports, Narita (NRT) and Haneda (HND). Narita, officially the New Tōkyō International Airport in Narita, is the major gateway to Japan, serving all international flights, except those operated by (Taiwan's) China Airways, which berths at Haneda. Narita is 80 km (50 mi) northeast of Tōkyō and has two fairly well-developed terminals, plus a central building of shops and restaurants. Traffic in and out of the airport is high, especially in December and August, when millions of Japanese take holidays abroad. Both terminals at Narita have ATMs and money exchange counters in the lobbies near Customs. Both terminals also have a Japan National Tourist Organization's Tourist Information Center, where you can get free maps, brochures, and other visitor information. If flight delays give you more time than you know what to do with, a 15-minute bus ride from terminal 2 will get you to the Aviation Museum, which sports a fifth-floor observation deck, restaurants, and open air deck. It's open from 10 AM to 5 PM.

Haneda is just 20 km (12.5 mi) from Tōkyō and despite being relegated to mainly domestic flights, it is one of the five busiest airports in the world. In addition to an array of restaurants and other amenities, its Bird View platforms are open 8 to 8 and offer travelers a chance to watch planes come and go.

🛈 Airport Information **Haneda Airport (HND)** ☎ 03/5757-8111 ⊕ www.tokyo-airport-bldg.co.jp. **Narita Airport (NRT)** ☎ 0476/34-5000 ⊕ www.narita-airport.or.jp.

FROM NARITA Directly across from the customs-area exits at both terminals are the
AIRPORT TO ticket counters for buses to Tōkyō. Buses leave from platforms just out-
TŌKYŌ side terminal exits, exactly on schedule; the departure time is on the ticket. The Friendly Airport Limousine offers the only shuttle bus service from Narita to Tōkyō. Different buses stop at various major hotels in the $$$$ category and at the JR Tōkyō and Shinjuku train stations.

Japan Railways trains stop at both Narita Airport terminals. The fastest and most comfortable is the Narita Limited Express (NEX), which makes 23 runs a day in each direction. Trains from the airport go directly to the central Tōkyō station in just under an hour, then continue to Yokohama and Ōfuna.

The Keisei Skyliner train runs every 20–30 minutes between the airport terminals and Keisei-Ueno station. The trip takes 57 minutes and costs ¥1,920 ($17). The first Skyliner leaves Narita for Ueno at 9:21 AM, the last at 9:59 PM. There's also an early train from the airport, called the Morning Liner, which leaves at 7:49 AM and costs ¥1,400. From Ueno to Narita, the first Skyliner is at 6:32 AM, the last at 5:21 PM. All Skyliner seats are reserved. It only makes sense to take the Keisei, however, if your final destination is in the Ueno area; otherwise, you must change to the Tōkyō subway system or the Japan Railways loop line at Ueno (the station is adjacent to Keisei-Ueno station) or take a cab to your hotel.

You can take a taxi from Narita Airport to central Tōkyō, but it'll cost you ¥20,000 (about $180) or more, depending on traffic and where you're going. Private car service is also very expensive; from Narita Airport to the Imperial Hotel downtown, for example, will set you back about ¥35,000.

⊡ Friendly Airport Limousine aka Airport Limousine ☎ 03/3665–7232, 03/3665–7220 in Tōkyō, 0476/32–8080 for Terminal 1, 0476/34–6311 for Terminal 2 ⊕ www.limousinebus. co.jp. **IAE Co.** ☎ 0476/32–7954 for Terminal 1, 0476/34–6886 for Terminal 2. **Japan Railways** ☎ 03/3423–0111 for JR East InfoLine ⊘ Weekdays 10–6. **Keisei Railway** ☎ 03/3831–0131 for Ueno information counter, 0476/32–8505 at Narita Airport.

FROM HANEDA
AIRPORT TO
TŌKYŌ

The monorail from Haneda Airport to Hamamatsu-chō station in Tōkyō is the fastest and cheapest way into town; the journey takes about 30 minutes, and trains run approximately every four to five minutes; the fare is ¥470 ($4). From Hamamatsu-chō station, change to a JR train or take a taxi to your destination.

A taxi to the center of Tōkyō takes about 40 minutes; the fare is approximately ¥8,000 ($73).

⊡ Tōkyō Monorail Co., Ltd. ☎ 03/3434–3171.

BETWEEN
AIRPORTS

The most convenient and affordable way to shuttle between the two airports is by way of **Airport Transport Service Co,** which is known as Friendly Airport Limousine buses or just Airport Limousine bus. The service runs hourly throughout the day and costs ¥3,000. The Narita Express train from Narita Airport or the Keikyu-Kuko Line Express and Tōkyō Monorail from Haneda will get you from one airport to the other in 90 minutes for around ¥3,300 but expect to navigate at least two transfers to different train lines in crowded unfamiliar stations. A taxi will make the trip for about ¥35,000.

⊡ Airport Transport Service Co. ☎ 03/3665–7232 or 03/3665–7220 in Tōkyō, 0476/32–8080 for Terminal 1, 0476/34–6311 for Terminal 2 ⊕ www.limousinebus.co.jp.

BY BOAT

The best ride in Tōkyō, hands down, is the *suijō basu* (river bus), operated by the Tōkyō Cruise Ship Company from Hinode Pier, from the mouth of the Sumida-gawa upstream to Asakusa. The glassed-in double-decker boats depart roughly every 20–40 minutes, weekdays 9:45–7:10, weekends and holidays 9:35–7:10 (with extended service to 7:50 July 9–September 23). The trip takes 40 minutes and costs ¥660. The pier is a seven-minute walk from Hamamatsu-chō station on the JR Yamanote Line.

Another place to catch the ferry is at the Hama Rikyū Tei-en (Detached Palace Garden: open daily 9–4:30), a 15-minute walk from Ginza. Once part of the imperial estates, the gardens are open to the public for a separate ¥300 entrance fee—which you have to pay even if you are only using the ferry landing. The landing is a short walk to the left as you enter the main gate. Boats depart every 35–45 minutes every weekday 10:25–4:10; the fare between Asakusa and Hama Rikyū is ¥620.

BY BUS

Bus routes within Tōkyō are impossibly complicated. The Tōkyō Municipal Government operates some of the lines; private companies run

1

the rest. There's no telephone number even native Japanese can call for help. And buses all have tiny seats and low ceilings. Unless you are a true Tōkyō veteran, forget about taking buses.

BY CAR

Driving in Tōkyō is not recommended, as there are many narrow, one-way streets and little in the way of English road signs except on major arteries. Gas is expensive, as is parking—if you're lucky enough to find a spot. Hiring cars with a driver is common. (⇨ Rental Cars *in* Japan Essentials)

PARKING Parking in Tōkyō is hard to find and ranges anywhere from ¥100 to ¥800 for an hour or two in a lot or on-street parking to ¥1,500 or more for an off-the-beaten-path overnight lot. Meters in lots usually take bills to facilitate long-term parking. ⚠ **On-street meters often have an electronic eye to prevent re-feeding the meter for longer stays; meters won't reboot until the car is moved.**

BY RAIL

Tōkyō's subways and trains are the most efficient, safe, and affordable way to get around town. Well maintained with heating and air-conditioning, they are inviting enough to nap in, which seated commuters can do with surprising ease. Avoid traveling during rush hours (about 7 AM 9:30 AM and 5 PM–7 PM) when trains can be so crowded attendants must push commuters into cars to close the doors. The Metro subway and JR train systems are integrated with mutual, connected, or adjacent stations that make it easy to transfer from one to the other. One transfer—two at most—will take you, in less than an hour, to any part of the city you're likely to visit. At some stations—such as Ōte-machi, Ginza, and Iidabashi—long underground passageways connect the various lines.

Free English-language subway and train maps are available at most stations. Trains and subways run from 5 AM to 12:30 AM (give or take a half hour depending on the line). Times for the first and last trains are posted outside most stations. It will be in Japanese but it's relatively easy to figure out as the early time will be first train and the late time will be the last (stations where more than one line stops will require Japanese reading or guessing).

Tickets are valid only on the day you buy them. ■ TIP➔ **Remember to keep your ticket while traveling; you'll need it to exit the turnstiles.** All stations have charts above the ticket vending machines to check the fare for your destination but those in smaller (especially JR) stations may not be in English. If in doubt, buy the cheapest ticket and pay the difference at the other end.

⚠ **Electric signboards displaying departure information at platforms or terminals alternate between Japanese and English; be sure the final destination shown matches the direction you want to travel.**

BY SUBWAY The Metro uses color-coded lines (the subways are not colored-coded); a Roman letter and number (such as G 9 for Ginza Station) mark the entrance and interiors of stations along with their names in Japanese and English. Metro help desks offer help in English from 9 AM to 5 PM at Ginza, Shinjuku, Harajuku, and Asakusa stations. Thirteen subway lines serve Tōkyō; nine of them are operated by Tōkyō Metro Co. Ltd. and four by the Tōkyō Municipal Authority (Toei). Subway trains run roughly every five minutes (5 AM–midnight); except during rush hours, the intervals are slightly longer on the newer Toei lines.

Subway fares begin at ¥160. From Ueno across town to Shibuya on the Ginza Line (orange), for example, is ¥190. Metro has inaugurated an electronic card of its own, called Metro Card.The denominations are ¥1,000, ¥3,000, and ¥5,000. Automatic card dispensers are installed at some subway stations. For ¥710, you can purchase a one-day open ticket at Metro offices or ticket dispensers that gives you unlimited use of all Metro trains.

BY TRAIN Japan Railways (JR) trains in Tōkyō are color-coded, making it easy to identify the different lines. The Yamanote Line (green or silver with green stripes) makes a 35-km (22-mi) loop around the central wards of the city in about an hour. The 29 stops include the major hub stations of Tōkyō, Yūraku-chō, Shimbashi, Shinagawa, Shibuya, Shinjuku, and Ueno.

The Chūō Line (orange) runs east to west through the loop from Tōkyō to the distant suburb of Takaō. During the day, however, these are limited express trains that don't stop at most of the stations inside the loop. For local cross-town service, which also extends east to neighboring Chiba Prefecture, you have to take the Sōbu Line (yellow). The Keihin Tōhoku Line (blue) goes north to Ōmiya in Saitama Prefecture and south to Ōfuna in Kanagawa, running parallel to the Yamanote Line between Tabata and Shinagawa.

JR Yamanote Line fares start at ¥130; you can get anywhere on the loop for ¥260 or less. If you plan to use the JR often, pick up an Orange Card, which is available at any station office. The cards come in ¥1,000 and ¥3,000 denominations. Use your card at vending machines with orange panels: you punch in the cost of the ticket and that amount is automatically deducted.

Japan Railways Hotline is an English-language information service, open weekdays 10–6.

Jorudan is an invaluable easy-to-use online source for plotting inner-city train, subway, and bus commutes.

🚄 **Japan National Tourist Organization Tourist Information Center** ☎ 03/3201-3331. **Japan Railways Group** ✉ New York ☎ 212/332-8686. **Japan Railways Hotline** ☎ 03/3423-0111 ⊕ www.jreast.co.jp. **Jorudan** ⊕ www.jorudan.co.jp. **Tōkyō Metro** ⊕ www.tokyometro.jp ☎ 03/3941-2004.

BY TAXI

Tōkyō taxi fares remain among the highest in the world. Most meters start at ¥660 and after the first 2 km (1 mi) tick away at the rate of ¥80 every 274 meters (about ⅕ mi). There is no bargaining or negotiating; you pay the fare indicated on the meter. There's no need to tip.

There are also smaller cabs, called *kogata,* that charge ¥640 and then ¥80 per 290 meters (⅕ mi). If your cab is caught in traffic—hardly an uncommon event—the meter registers another ¥80 for every 1½ minutes of immobility. Between 11 PM and 5 AM, a 30% surcharge is added to the fare.

Japanese taxis have automatic door-opening systems, so do not try to open the taxi door. When you leave the cab, do not try to close the door; the driver will do it automatically. Only the curbside rear door opens.

Hailing a taxi during the day is seldom a problem. In Ginza, drivers are allowed to pick up passengers only in designated areas; look for short lines of cabs. Elsewhere, step off the curb and raise your arm. A red light on the dashboard indicates an available taxi, and a green light indicates an occupied taxi. At night, when everyone's been out drinking and wants a ride home, the rules change. Don't be astonished if a cab with a red light doesn't stop for you: refusing a fare is against the law but it's done all the time. Between 11 PM and 2 AM on Friday and Saturday nights, you have to be very lucky to get a cab in any of the major entertainment districts; in Ginza it's almost impossible.

TRAIN TRAVEL TO TŌKYŌ

The Shinkansen (bullet train), one of the fastest trains in the world, connects major cities north and south of Tōkyō. It's only slightly less expensive than flying but is in many ways more convenient because train stations are more centrally located than airports (and, if you have a Japan Rail Pass, it's extremely affordable). On the main line that runs west from Tōkyō, there are three types of Shinkansen. The *Nozomi* makes the fewest stops, which can cut as much as an hour from long, cross-country trips; it's the only Shinkansen on which you cannot use a JR Pass. The *Hikari* makes just a few more stops than the Nozomi. The *Kodama* is the equivalent of a Shinkansen local, making all stops along the Shinkansen lines.

Other trains, though not as fast as the Shinkansen, are just as convenient and substantially cheaper. There are three types of train services: *futsū* (local service), *tokkyū* (limited express service), and *kyūkō* (express service). Both the tokkyū and the kyūkō offer a first-class compartment known as the Green Car. Smoking is allowed only in designated carriages on long-distance and Shinkansen trains. Local and commuter trains are entirely non-smoking and it is enforced.

Most clerks at train stations know a few basic words of English. Moreover, they are invariably helpful in plotting your route. You can get an English-language train schedule from the Japan National Tourist Organization (JNTO). JNTO's booklet *The Tourist's Handbook* provides helpful information about purchasing tickets in Japan.

Contacts & Resources

EMBASSY

U.S. Embassy (✉ 1–10–5 Akasaka, Minato-ku, Toranomon ☎ 03/3224–500 ⊕ tokyo.usembassy.gov/ Ⓜ Namboku Line, Tameike-Sannō station).

EMERGENCIES

Assistance in English is available 24 hours a day on the Japan Helpline. The Tōkyō English Life Line (TELL) is a telephone service available daily

9 AM–4 PM and 7 PM–11 PM for anyone in distress who cannot communicate in Japanese. The service will relay your emergency to the appropriate authorities. Operators who answer the 119 and 110 hotlines rarely speak English.

The International Catholic Hospital (Seibō Byōin) accepts emergencies and takes regular appointments Monday–Saturday 8 AM–11 AM; outpatient services are closed the third Saturday of the month. The International Clinic also accepts emergencies. Appointments there are taken weekdays 9–noon and 2:30–5 and on Saturday 9–noon. St. Luke's International Hospital is a member of the American Hospital Association and accepts emergencies. Appointments are taken weekdays 8:30 AM–11 AM. The Tōkyō Medical and Surgical Clinic takes appointments weekdays 9–5 and Saturday 9–noon.

The Yamauchi Dental Clinic, a member of the American Dental Association, is open weekdays 9–12:30 and 3–5:30, Saturday 9–noon.

🆘 **General Emergency Contacts Ambulance and Fire** ☎ 119. **Japan Helpline** ☎ 0120/461-997 or 0570/000-911. **Police** ☎ 110. **Tōkyō English Life Line** (TELL) ☎ 03/5774-0992.

🆘 **Hospitals & Clinics International Catholic Hospital** (Seibō Byōin) ✉ 2-5-1 Naka Ochiai, Shinjuku District ☎ 03/3951-1111 Ⓜ Seibu Shinjuku Line, Shimo-Ochiai station (Nishi-guchi/West Exit). **International Clinic** ✉ 1-5-9 Azabu-dai, Minato-ku, Roppongi District ☎ 03/3582-2646 or 03/3583-7831 Ⓜ Hibiya Line, Roppongi station (Exit 3). **St. Luke's International Hospital** ✉ 9-1 Akashi-chō, Chūō-ku, Tsukiji District ☎ 03/3541-5151 Ⓜ Hibiya Line, Tsukiji station (Exit 3); Yūraku-chō Line, Shintomichō station (Exit 6). **Tōkyō Medical and Surgical Clinic** ✉ 32 Mori Bldg., 3-4-30 Shiba Kōen, Minato-ku ☎ 03/3436-3028 Ⓜ Toei Mita Line, Onarimon station (Exit A1); Hibiya Line, Kamiyachō station (Exit 1); Toei Ōedo Line, Akabane-bashi station. **Yamauchi Dental Clinic** ✉ Shirokanedai Gloria Heights, 1st fl., 3-16-10 Shirokanedai, Minato-ku ☎ 03/3441-6377 Ⓜ JR Yamanote Line, Meguro station (Higashi-guchi/East Exit); Namboku and Toei Mita lines, Shirokanedai station (Exit 1).

PHARMACIES No drugstores in Tōkyō are open 24 hours a day. The American Pharmacy stocks nonprescription Western products; it's open weekdays 9 AM–9 PM and weekends 9 AM–8 PM. The Koyasu Drug Store in the Hotel Okura also offers some Western products and is open Monday–Saturday 8:30 AM–9 PM, Sunday and holidays 10–9. Many grocery and convenience stores carry basics such as aspirin and ibuprofen.

Nagai Yakkyoku is open daily (except Tuesday) 10–7 and will mix a Chinese and/or Japanese herbal medicine for you after a consultation. You can't have a doctor's prescription filled here, but you can find something for a headache or stomach pain. A little English is spoken.

🆘 **American Pharmacy** ✉ Maru Bldg. B1F, 2-4-1 Marunouchi Chiyoda-ku ☎ 03/5220-7716. **Koyasu Pharmacy** ✉ Hotel Okura, main bldg. 1 F, 2-10-4 Toranomon Minato-ku ☎ 03/3583-7958. **Nagai Yakkyoku** ✉ 1-8-10 Azabu Ju-ban, Minato-ku ☎ 03/3583-3889.

INTERNET, MAIL & SHIPPING

INTERNET These days, Internet access is as easy to find as water, and many Internet cafés operate into the wee hours of the morn. Prices range from free online access for paying patrons to ¥500 or more per half hour.

Despite its name-brand popularity, Yahoo Café has no available phone numbers and the Web site is only in Japanese, but it has locations in Narita and Haneda airports, as well as the Shingawa Prince Hotel.

Manga Land is another popular Internet café chain that has more than two dozen locations throughout the city.

For a list of Internet café locations in and around the city, visit Enjoy Tokyo's Web site, which is listed below.

🔁 **Cybercafes** ⊕ www.cybercafes.com lists more than 4,000 Internet cafés worldwide. **Manga Land** ☎ 03/3408-3750. **Enjoy Tōkyō** ⊕ www009.upp.so-net.ne.jp/enjoytokyo/culture/internetcafe2.html.

MAIL   Most hotels have stamps and will mail your letters and postcards; they will also give you directions to the nearest post office, or *Yūbinkyoku.* Post offices are open weekdays 9–5 and Saturday 9–noon. Some of the central post offices have longer hours, such as the one in Tōkyō, located near Tōkyō Eki (train station), which is open 24 hours year-round. The main International Post Office is on the Imperial Palace side of JR Tōkyō station. You can also buy stamps at convenience stores.

It costs ¥110 (98¢) to send a letter by air to North America and Europe. An airmail postcard costs ¥70 (63¢). Aerograms cost ¥90 (81¢).

To get mail, have parcels and letters sent "poste restante" to the central post office in major cities; unclaimed mail is returned after 30 days. 🔁 **Main Branch International Post Office** ✉ 2-3-3 Ōte-machi, Chiyoda-ku ☎ 03/3241-4891 Ⓜ Tōkyō station.

SHIPPING   The Japanese Post Office is very efficient. To ship a 5 kg/11 lb parcel PACKAGES   to the U.S. costs ¥10,150 ($91) if sent by airmail, ¥7,300 ($65) by SAL (economy airmail) and ¥4,000 ($36) by sea. Allow a week for airmail, two to three weeks for SAL, and up to six weeks for packages sent by sea. Large shops usually ship domestically, but not overseas.

FedEx has drop-off locations at branches of Kinko's all over Tōkyō. A 1 kg/2.2 lb package from central Tōkyō to Washington D.C. would cost about ¥7,200 ($64) and take two days to be delivered. 🔁 **Express Services FedEx** ☎ 0120/00-320 toll-free, 043/298-1919 ⊕ www.fedex.com/jp.

MEDIA

Two free weekly magazines, the *Tour Companion* and *Metropolis,* available at hotels, book and music stores, and some restaurants and cafés, feature up-to-date announcements of what's going on in the city. *Metropolis* breaks the listings down into separate sections for Art & Exhibitions, Movies, TV, Music, and After Dark.

A monthly magazine with listings similar to *Metropolis*, the *Tōkyō Journal* (¥600) is available at Narita Airport newsstands and at many bookstores that carry English-language books. The Friday edition of the *Japan Times,* a daily English-language newspaper, is yet another resource for entertainment reviews and schedules.

TOURS

The Tōkyō Cruise Ship Company also operates four other lines from Hinode Pier. The Harbor Cruise Line stern-wheeler makes a 50-minute circuit under the Rainbow Bridge and around the inner harbor. Departures are at 10:30, 12:30, 1:30, and 3:30 (and 4:45 in August). The fare is ¥800. If you visit in August you should definitely opt for the evening cruise; the lights on the Rainbow Bridge and neighboring Odaiba are spectacular. Two lines connect Hinode to Odaiba itself, one at 20-minute intervals from 10:10 to 6:10 to Odaiba Seaside Park and the Museum of Maritime Science at Aomi Terminal (¥400–¥520), the other every 25 minutes from 9 to 5:40 to the shopping/amusement center at Palette Town and on to the Tōkyō Big Sight exhibition grounds at Ariake (¥350). The Kasai Sealife Park Line cruise leaves Hinode hourly from 10 to 4 and travels through the network of artificial islands in the harbor to the beach and aquarium at Kasai Rinkai Kōen in Chiba; the one-way fare is ¥800. The Canal Cruise Line connects Hinode with Shinagawa Suizokukan aquarium, south along the harborside. There are six departures daily except Tuesday between 10:15 and 4:50; the one-way fare is ¥800.

Tōkyō Cruise Ship Company ☎ 03/3457–7830 at Hinode, 03/3841–9178 at Asakusa ⊕ www.suijobus.co.jp.

EXCURSIONS Sunrise Tours, a division of the Japan Travel Bureau, runs a one-day bus tour to Nikkō on Monday, Tuesday, and Friday between April and October, at ¥13,500 (lunch included). Japan Amenity Travel and the Japan Gray Line conduct Mt. Fuji and Hakone tours, with return either by bus or train; one-day trips cost from ¥12,000 to ¥15,000 (lunch included), and two-day tours cost ¥26,500 (meals and accommodation included). Some of these tours include a quick visit to Kamakura. There are also excursions to Kyōto via Shinkansen that cost from ¥49,500 to ¥82,100; you can arrange these Shinkansen tours through Japan Amenity Travel or Japan Gray Line.

GUIDED TOURS Nippon Travel Agency America has theme-focused packages, for Tōkyō alone or in conjunction with Kyōto and Nara as well as an à la carte menu for piecing together custom tours. Travel Oriented offers a variety of package tours to Tōkyō and other Japan destinations. JTB USA has branch offices throughout the U.S. including New York, Chicago, and San Francisco that offer their own five-day package deals to Tōkyō at rock-bottom prices.

Recommended Companies Nippon Travel Agency America ⊠ 1 Harmon Plaza, Secaucus NJ ☎ 800/682–7872 ⊕ www.japanvacation.net. **Travel Oriented** ⊠ 15490 S. Western Ave., Gardena CA ☎ 800/984–8728 ⊕ www.japandeluxetour.com. **JTB USA** ☎ 800/235–3523 in New York, 800/669–5824 in Chicago, 800/882–3884 in San Francisco ⊕ www.jtbusa.com.

ORIENTATION TOURS April–June and mid-September–November, Sunrise Tours conducts a Thursday-morning (8–12:30) "Experience Japanese Culture" bus-and-walking tour (¥7,000), which includes a calligraphy demonstration, a tea ceremony, and a visit to the Edo-Tōkyō Hakubutsukan. Both Sunrise Tours and the Japan Gray Line operate a number of other bus excursions around Tōkyō with English-speaking guides. The tours vary with the current demands of the market. Most include the Tōkyō Tower

Observatory, the Imperial East Garden, a demonstration of flower arrangement at the Tasaki Pearl Gallery, and/or a Sumida-gawa cruise to Sensō-ji in Asakusa. These are for the most part four-hour morning or afternoon tours; a full day tour (seven hours) combines most of what is covered in half-day excursions with a tea ceremony at Happō Garden and lunch at the traditional Chinzan-sō restaurant. Costs range from ¥4,000 to ¥12,900. Tours are conducted in large, air-conditioned buses that set out from Hamamatsu-chō Bus Terminal, and there's also free pickup and return from major hotels.

SPECIAL-INTEREST TOURS   It's only possible to visit parts of the Imperial Palace Grounds by making online reservations in advance with the Imperial Household Agency. The guided tour (in Japanese, but with a useful pamphlet and audio guide in English) takes about an hour and 15 minutes, and covers 11 of the buildings and sites on the west side of the Palace grounds, including the Fushimi Yagura watchtower and the Fujimi Tamon armory. Log on to the Imperial Household Agency Web site to make a reservation; do this well in advance, as the available slots fill up quickly. Visitors under 18 must be accompanied by an adult. The tours are given weekdays at 10:30 AM and 1:30 PM; admission is free. Tours start at the Ni-jūbashi Bridge, a minute's walk north of the subway; follow the moat to the courtyard in front of the gate.

🔢 Recommended Agencies **Imperial Household Agency** ⊕ http://sankan.kunaicho. go.jp. **Japan Amenity Travel** ✉ Chūō-ku ☎ 03/3542-7200. **Japan Gray Line** ✉ Minato-ku ☎ 03/3433-5745. **Japan Guide Association** ☎ 03/3213-2706. **Japan National Tourist Organization** ✉ Chiyoda-ku ☎ 03/3201-3331. **Sunrise Tours Reservation Center, Japan Travel Bureau** ☎ 03/5620-9500.

Points of Interest

SITES/AREAS	JAPANESE CHARACTERS
Advertising Museum Tōkyō	アド・ミュージアム東京
Akihabara	秋葉原
Ame-ya Yoko-chō Market	アメヤ横丁
Aoyama, Harajuku & Shibuya	青山・原宿・渋谷
Asakura Sculpture Gallery	朝倉彫刻館
Asakusa	浅草
Asakusa Shrine (Asakusa Jinja)	浅草神社
Azabu-Jūban	麻布十番
Backstreet shops of Tsukiji	築地6丁目
Bank of Japan (Nihon Ginkō)	日本銀行
Belfry (Toki-no-kane Shōrō)	時の鐘鐘楼
Benzaiten	弁財天
Bookstores of Jimbō-chō	神保町書店街
Bridge of Japan (Nihombashi)	日本橋
Bridgestone Museum of Art (Burijisuton Bijutsukan)	ブリヂストン美術館
Bunka-mura	文化村
National Memorial Garden (Chidori-ga-fuchi)	千鳥ヶ淵戦没者墓苑
Chocolatte	ショコラッテ
Crafts Gallery of the National Museum of Modern Art (Kōgeikan)	工芸館
Dai-ichi Mutual Life Insurance Company Building	第一生命館
Dembō Temple (Dembō-in)	伝法院
Detached Palace Garden (Hama Rikyū Tei-en)	浜離宮庭園
Edo-Gin	江戸銀
Fuji Television Nippon Broadcasting Building	フジテレビ
Ginza	銀座
Hanazono Shrine (Hanazono Jinja)	花園神社
Hanzō Gate (Hanzō-mon)	半蔵門
Hasumi Chaya	蓮見茶屋
Hirakawa Gate (Hirakawa-mon)	平川門

Idemitsu Museum of Art (Idemitsu Bijutsukan)	出光美術館
Imperial Palace and Government District	皇居近辺
Imperial Palace East Garden (Kōkyo Higashi Gyo-en)	皇居東御苑
Imperial Palace Outer Garden (Kōkyo-Gaien)	皇居外苑
Japanese Sword Museum (Tōken Hakubutsukan)	刀剣博物館
Jimbō-chō	神保町
Kabuki-chō	歌舞伎町
Kabuki Theater (Kabuki-za)	歌舞伎座
Kabuto Shrine (Kabuto Jinja)	兜神社
Kanda Shrine (Kanda Myōjin)	神田明神
Kan-ei Temple (Kan-ei-ji)	寛永寺
Kannon Hall (Kiyomizu Kannon-dō)	清水観音堂
Kappabashi	かっぱ橋
Kasai Seaside Park	葛西臨海公園
Kite Museum (Tako no Hakubutsukan)	凧の博物館
Les Deux Magots	ドウ・マゴ・パリ
Meiji Shrine (Meiji Jingū)	明治神宮
Meiji Shrine Outer Gardens (Meiji Jingū Gai-en)	明治神宮外苑
Mitsukoshi	三越
Mori Tower	森タワー
Museum of Maritime Science (Fune-no-Kagakukan)	船の科学館
Nakase	中瀬
National Diet Building (Kokkai-Gijidō)	国会議事堂
National Museum of Emerging Science and Innovation (Nihon Kagaku Miraikan)	日本科学未来館
National Museum of Modern Art, Tōkyō (Tōkyō Kokuritsu Kindai Bijutsukan)	国立近代美術館
National Museum of Western Art (Kokuritsu Seiyō Bijutsukan)	国立西洋美術館
National Science Museum (Kokuritsu Kagaku Hakubutsukan)	国立科学博物館
National Theater (Kokuritsu Gekijō)	国立劇場
Nezu Institute of Fine Arts (Nezu Bijutsukan)	根津美術館

Nikolai Cathedral	ニコライ堂
Ōta Memorial Museum of Art (Ōta Kinen Bijutsukan)	太田記念美術館
Ōte Gate (Ōte-mon)	大手門
Odaiba	お台場
Odaiba Kaihin Kōen	お台場海浜公園
Odaiba's Hot Spring Theme Park (Ōedo Onsen Monogatari)	大江戸温泉物語
Roppongi	六本木
Roppongi Hills	六本木ヒルズ
Ryōgoku	両国
Seiji Tōgō Memorial Sompo Japan Museum of Art (Sompo Japan Tōgō Seiji Bijutsukan)	東郷青児美術館
Sengaku Temple (Sengaku-ji)	泉岳寺
Sensō-ji Complex	浅草寺
Sensō-ji Main Hall	浅草観音堂
Shinagawa Aquarium (Shinagawa Suizokukan)	しながわ水族館
Shinjuku	新宿
Shinjuku Gyo-en National Garden	新宿御苑
Shinjuku Park Tower Building	新宿パークタワー
Shinobazu Pond (Shinobazu-ike)	不忍池
Shiodome	汐留
Shitamachi Museum (Shitamachi Hakubutsukan)	下町博物館
Shrine of Peace for the Nation (Yasukuni Jinja)	靖国神社
Sōgetsu Ikebana School (Sōgetsu Kaikan)	草月会館
Statue of Hachikō	ハチ公像
Sukiya-bashi	数寄屋橋
Sunshine International Aquarium	サンシャイン国際水族館
Suzumoto	鈴本演芸場
Tama Zoo (Tama Dōbutsu Kōen)	多摩動物公園
Thunder God Gate (Kaminari-mon)	雷門
Tōkyō Central Wholesale Market (Tōkyō Chūō Oroshiuri Ichiba)	東京都中央卸売市場

Tōkyō Disneyland	東京ディズニーランド
Tōkyō International Forum	東京国際フォーラム
Tōkyō Metropolitan Art Museum (Tōkyō-to Bijutsukan)	東京都美術館
Tōkyō Metropolitan Government Office (Tōkyō Tochō)	東京都庁
Tōkyō National Museum (Tōkyō Kokuritsu Hakubutsukan)	東京国立博物館
Tōkyō Opera City	東京オペラシティ
Tōkyō Sea Life Park	葛西臨海水族園
Tōkyō Station	東京駅
Tōkyō Tower	東京タワー
Tōshō Shrine (Tōshō-gū)	東照宮
Toden Arakawa Line	都電荒川線
Tokudai Temple (Tokudai-ji)	徳大寺
Toshima-en	としまえん
Transportation Museum (Kōtsū Hakubutsukan)	交通博物館
Tsukiji	築地
Tsukiji Hongan Temple (Tsukiji Hongan-ji)	築地本願寺
Two-Tiered Bridge (Ni-jū-bashi)	二重橋
Ueno	上野
Ueno Royal Museum (Ueno-no-Mori Bijutsukan)	上野の森美術館
Ueno Zoo (Onshi Ueno Dōbutsuen)	上野動物園
Wadakura Fuusui Koen Restaurant	和田倉噴水公園レストラン
Waenti-Kikko	和えん亭 吉幸
Yamagiwa	ヤマギワ
Yamatane Museum of Art (Yamatane Bijutsukan)	山種美術館
Yoyogi Park (Yoyogi Kōen)	代々木公園
Yūraku-chō	有楽町
Yushima Shrine (Yushima Seidō)	湯島聖堂
Zenpuku Temple (Zenpuku-ji)	麻布山善福寺

RESTAURANTS

Adjanta	アジャンタ
Afuri	阿夫利
Akasaka	赤坂
Akasaka-mitsuke	赤坂見附
Aoi-Marushin	葵丸進
Ashoka	アショカ
Attore	アトーレ
Brown Rice Café	ブラウンライスカフェ
Café 8	カフェエイト
Chez Inno	シェ・イノ
Chez Matsuo	シェ・松尾
Daikanyama	代官山
Ebisu	恵比寿
Edo-Gin	江戸銀
Erawan	エラワン
Ganchan	がんちゃん
Happō-en	八芳園
Heichinrou	聘珍楼
Heiroku-zushi	平禄寿司
Higashi-Shinjuku	東新宿
Higo-no-ya	肥後の屋
Homeworks	ホームワークス
Ichiyaga	市ヶ谷
Ikebukuro	池袋
Inakaya	田舎屋
Itoshō	いと正
Kappō-Ajioka	割烹 味岡
Keawjai	ゲウチャイ
Kinkantei	きんかん亭
Kisoji	木曽路

Kyō-bashi	京橋
La Granata	ラ・グラナータ
Le Papillon de Paris	ル・パピヨン・ド・パリ
Lovenet	ラブネット
Maison	まい泉
Manhattan Grill	マンハッタングリル
Meguro	目黒
Monsoon Cafe	モンスーンカフェ
Moti	モティ
Niban-chō	二番町
Ninja	忍者
Omotesandō	表参道
Pure Café	ピュアカフェ
R Style	アールスタイル
Rangetsu	らん月
Restorante Carmine	カルミネ
Robata	炉端
Roti	ロティ
Sabado Sabadete	サバドサバデテ
Sakuratei	さくら亭
Sankō-en	三幸園
Sasa-no-yuki	笹の雪
Sasashin	笹新
Sasashū	笹周
Sawanoi	澤乃井
Shibuya	渋谷
Shirokanedai	白金台
Shōtō	松濤
T. Y. Harbor Brewery	T.Y.ハーバーブルワリーレストラン
Tableaux	タブロ　ズ
Takeno	たけの

Tatsumiya	たつみや
Tenmatsu	天松
Toh-Ka-Lin	桃花林
Tonki	とんき
Tora-no-mon	虎ノ門
Uchisaiwai-chō	内幸町
Ume no Hana	梅の花
HOTELS	
Akasaka Prince Hotel	赤坂プリンスホテル
Akihabara Washinton Hotel	秋葉原ワシントンホテル
ANA Hotel Narita	成田全日空ホテル
ANA Hotel Tōkyō	東京全日空ホテル
Asakusa View Hotel	浅草ビューホテル
Asia Center of Japan	アジア会館
Century Hyatt Hotel	センチュリーハイアット東京
Cerulean Tower Tokyu Hotel	セルリアンタワー東急ホテル
Conrad Tōkyō	コンラッド東京
Four Seasons Hotel Chinzan-sō	フォーシーズンズホテル椿山荘
Four Seasons Hotel Tōkyō at Marunouchi	フォーシーズンズホテル丸の内東京
Grand Hyatt Tōkyō at Roppongi Hills	グランドハイアット東京
Green Plaza Shinjuku	グリーンプラザ新宿
Hakozaki	箱崎
Hibiya	日比谷
Higashi-Gotanda	東五反田
Hilton Tōkyō Narita Airport	ヒルトン成田
Holiday Inn Tōbu Narita	イン東武成田
Hotel Arca Torre	ホテルアルカトーレ
Hotel InterContinental Tōkyō Bay	ホテル インターコンチネンタル 東京ベイ
Hotel New Ōtani Tōkyō and Towers	ホテルニューオータニ
Hotel Ōkura Tōkyō	ホテルオークラ

Hotel Seiyō Ginza	ホテル西洋銀座
Hotel Yaesu Ryūmeikan	ホテル八重洲龍名館
Kayaba-chō Pearl Hotel	帝国ホテル
Keio Plaza Hotel Tōkyō	京王プラザホテル
Le Meridien Grand Pacific Tōkyō	ホテル グランパシフィック メリディアン
Le Meridien Pacific Tōkyō	ホテルパシフィック東京
Mandarin Oriental Tōkyō	マンダリン オリエンタル 東京
Marunouchi	丸の内
Narita Excel Hotel Tokyu	成田エクセルホテル東急
Ningyō-chō	人形町
Nishi-Shinjuku	西新宿
Palace Hotel	パレスホテル
Park Hotel Tōkyō	パークホテル東京
Park Hyatt Tōkyō	パークハイアット東京
Radisson Hotel Narita Airport	ラディソンホテル成田エアポート
Renaissance Tōkyō Hotel Ginza Tōbu	銀座東武ホテル・ルネッサンス東京
Royal Park Hotel	ロイヤルパークホテル
Ryokan Katsutarō	旅館勝太郎
Ryokan Mikawaya Honten	旅館三河屋本店
Ryokan Shigetsu	旅館指月
Sawanoya Ryokan	澤の屋旅館
Sekiguchi	関口
Shiba Daimon Hotel	芝大門ホテル
Shiba Kōen	芝公園
Shibuya Excel Hotel Tokyu	渋谷エクセルホテル東急
Shinjuku Washington Hotel	新宿ワシントンホテル
Sumishō Hotel	住庄ほてる
Takanawa Tōbu Hotel	高輪東武ホテル
The Strings Hotel	ストリングスホテル東京
Tōkyō International Youth Hostel	東京国際ユースホステル

Tōkyō Prince Hotel Park Tower	東京プリンスホテルパークタワー
Westin Tōkyō	ウエスティンホテル東京
Yaesu	八重洲
Yanaka	谷中
YMCA Asia Youth Center	YMCAアジア青少年センター
Yoshimizu Ginza	銀座吉水

Side Trips from Tōkyō

WORD OF MOUTH

"Nikko's temples and shrines are much grander than those of Kamakura and are somewhat unusual for Japan; Kamakura's temples are older and more humble and more typical of Japan. Kamakura is in a pretty setting by the bay; Nikko is near Lake Chuzenji and the impressive Kegon waterfall."

—kja

"Take a train ride to Yokohama and visit Chinatown and have a wonderful Chinese lunch!"

—peppersalt

Updated by
Katherine
Pham Do

NIKKŌ MEANS "SUNLIGHT" and is the site of the Tokugawa shrine as well as the national park, Nikkō Kokuritsu Kōen, on the heights above it. The centerpiece of the park is Chūzenji-ko, a deep lake some 21 km (13 mi) around, and the 318-foot-high Kegon Falls, Japan's most famous waterfall. "Think nothing is splendid," asserts an old Japanese proverb, "until you have seen Nikkō."

One caveat: the term "national park" does not quite mean what it does elsewhere in the world. In Japan, pristine grandeur is hard to come by; there are few places in this country where intrepid hikers can go to contemplate the beauty of nature for very long in solitude. If a thing's worth seeing, it's worth developing. This world view tends to fill Japan's national parks with bus caravans, ropeways and gondolas, scenic overlooks with coin-fed telescopes, signs that tell you where you may or may not walk, fried-noodle joints and vending machines, and shacks full of kitschy souvenirs. That's true of Nikkō, and it's true as well of Fuji-Hakone-Izu National Park, southwest of Tōkyō, another of Japan's most popular resort areas.

The park's chief attraction is, of course, Fuji-san—spellbinding in its perfect symmetry, immortalized by centuries of poets and artists. South of Mt. Fuji, the Izu Peninsula projects out into the Pacific, with Suruga Bay to the west and Sagami Bay to the east. The beaches and rugged shoreline of Izu, its forests and highland meadows, and its numerous hot-springs inns and resorts (*izu* means "spring") make the region a favorite destination for the Japanese.

Kamakura and Yokohama, both close enough to Tōkyō to provide ideal day trips, could not make for more contrasting experiences. Kamakura is an ancient city—the birthplace, one could argue, of the samurai way of life. Its place in Japanese history begins late in the 12th century, when Minamoto no Yoritomo became the country's first shōgun and chose this site, with its rugged hills and narrow passes, as the seat of his military government. The warrior elite of the Kamakura period took much of their ideology—and their aesthetics—from Zen Buddhism, endowing splendid temples that still exist today. A walking tour of Kamakura's Zen temples and Shintō shrines is a must for anyone with a day to spend out of Tōkyō. Yokohama, too, can lay claim to an important place in Japanese history: in 1869, after centuries of isolation, this city became the first important port for trade with the West and the site of the first major foreign settlement. Twice destroyed, the city retains very few remnants of that history, but it remains Japan's largest port and has an international character that rivals—if not surpasses—that of Tōkyō. Its waterfront park and its ambitious Minato Mirai bay-side development project draw visitors from all over the world.

ORIENTATION & PLANNING

Orientation

The areas discussed in this chapter are all within a day's trip of Tōkyō, though some will require more time than others. Located Southwest of

Top Reasons to Visit

1

MT. FUJI

More than 196,000 people climb the 12,388′, white-capped, Japanese icon every year. **The Ultimate Shrine.** The elaborate, gold-covered 17th-century Tōshō-gū shrine encompasses the Five-Story Pagoda, the Sutra Library, the Gate of Sunlight, and other magnificently ornate buildings.

LIVING HISTORY

Experience 18th-century life at Nikkō Edo Village, which features a re-created period-village with everything from traditional buildings to samurai and geisha re-enactors.

DRAMATIC WATERFALLS

Kegon Falls at Chuzenji, near Nikkō, falls 318 feet into a rugged gorge. During the winter, these great falls create a cascade of giant, glistening icicles.

GET YOUR ZEN ON

Containing 50 buildings at one point, the largest Zen monastery is Engaku-ji in Kamakura. Nearby, you'll find Japan's oldest Zen temple, Kenchō-ji, built in 1250, and the Tōkei Temple, also known as the Divorce Temple as it was a safe haven for women in unhappy marriages.

Tōkyō, both Kamakura and Yokohama are close enough to be ideal day trips, with no overnights required. North of the city, Nikkō has a charming country feel about it, making it a popular vacation spot for the Japanese. Watch out for the monkeys! Southwest of Tōkyō, between Suruga and Sagami bays, is Fuji-Hakone-Izu National Park, one of Japan's most popular resort areas. Izu is defined by its dramatic rugged coastline, beaches, and *onsen* (hot springs). Hakone has mountains, volcanic landscapes, and lake cruises, plus onsen of its own. The Five Lakes form a recreational area with some of the best views of Mt. Fuji.

Nikkō

Nikkō has breathtaking sights like Kegon Falls and Lake Chūzen-ji, as well as one of the country's best-known shrines, Tōshō-gū.

Kamakura

The military capital of Japan during the 12th century is where you'll find many National Treasures, including the Great Buddha and five great Zen temples.

Yokohama

Yokohama, one of Japan's great port cities, is large but manageable and has the country's best Chinatown.

Fuji-Hakone-Izu National Park

This is the home of Mt. Fuji (Fuji-san). Besides the mountain, the park has three other areas—the Izu Peninsula, Hakone and environs, and the Five Lakes region.

Planning

If you can only take one day trip from Tōkyō, make it Kamakura, which is 25 mi southwest. It's accessible by train, which makes it quite a popular trip. If you can, go during the week and leave as early as you can, but make sure you avoid rush hour. Yokohama is another great day trip and is also accessible by train. If you have a few days and are looking to spend an overnight, jump on the train and head to Nikkō. Another option for an overnight or two is Fuji-Hakone-Izu National Park.

Concerning Restaurants

The local specialty in Nikkō is a soy-bean-based concoction known as *yuba* (tofu skin); dozens of restaurants in Nikkō serve it in a variety of dishes you might not have believed possible for so prosaic an ingredient. Other local favorites are soba (buckwheat) and udon (wheat-flour) noodles—both inexpensive, filling, and tasty options for lunch.

Three things about Kamakura make it a good place to dine. It's on the ocean (properly speaking, on Sagami Bay), which means that fresh seafood is everywhere; it's a major tourist stop; and it has long been a prestigious place to live among Japan's worldly and well-to-do (many successful writers, artists, and intellectuals call Kamakura home). On a day trip from Tōkyō, you can feel confident picking a place for lunch almost at random.

Yokohama, as befits a city of more than 3 million people, lacks little in the way of food: from quick-fix lunch counters to elegant dining rooms, you'll find almost every imaginable cuisine. Your best bet is Chinatown—Japan's largest Chinese community—with more than 100 restaurants representing every regional style. If you fancy Italian, Indian, or even Scandanavian, this international port is still guaranteed to provide an eminently satisfying meal.

Concerning Hotels

Yokohama and Kamakura are treated here as day trips, and as it's unlikely that you'll stay overnight in either city, no accommodations are listed for them. Nikkō is something of a toss-up: you can easily see Tōshō-gū and be back in Tōkyō by evening. But when the weather turns glorious in spring or autumn, why not spend some time in the national park, staying overnight at Chūzenji, and returning to the city the next day? Mt. Fuji and Hakone, on the other hand—and more especially the Izu Peninsula—are pure resort destinations. Staying overnight is an intrinsic part of the experience, and it makes little sense to go without hotel reservations confirmed in advance.

In both Nikkō and the Fuji-Hakone-Izu area, there are modern, Western-style hotels that operate in a fairly standard international style. More common, however, are the traditional ryokan (inns) and the Japanese-style *kankō* (literally, "sightseeing") hotels. The main difference between these lodging options is that kanko often have Western-style rooms and are situated in prime tourist locations whereas ryokans stick strictly to Japanese-style rooms and are found in less touristy locations. The undisputed pleasure of a ryokan is to return to it at the end of a hard day of sightseeing, luxuriate for an hour in a hot bath with your own garden view, put on the *yukata* (cotton kimono) provided for you, and sit down to a catered private dinner party. There's little point to staying at a kankō. These places do most of their business with big, boisterous tour groups; the turnover is ruthless and the cost is way out of proportion to the service they provide.

The price categories listed below are for double occupancy, but you'll find that most kankō and ryokan normally quote per-person rates, which include breakfast and dinner.

Remember to stipulate whether you want a Japanese or Western breakfast. If you don't want dinner at your hotel, it's usually possible to renegotiate the price, but the management will not be happy about it; the two meals are a fixture of their business. The typical ryokan takes great pride in its cuisine, usually with good reason: the evening meal is an elaborate affair of 10 or more different dishes, based on the fresh produce and specialties of the region, served to you—nay, *orchestrated*—in your room on a wonderful variety of trays and tableware designed to celebrate the season.

WHAT IT COSTS In yen					
	$$$$	$$$	$$	$	¢
RESTAURANTS	over 3,000	2,000–3,000	1,000–2,000	800–1,000	under 800
HOTELS	over 22,000	18,000–22,000	12,000–18,000	8,000–12,000	under 8,000

Restaurant prices are per person for a main course at dinner. Hotel price categories reflect the range of least- to most-expensive standard double rooms in non-holiday high season. Taxes (5%) are included.

NIKKŌ

Nikko is a popular vacation spot for the Japanese, for good reason: its gorgeous sights include a breathtaking waterfall and one of the country's best-known shrines. In addition, Nikkō combines the rustic charm of a countryside village (complete with wild monkeys that have the run of the place) with a convenient location not far from Tōkyō.

Getting Around

The town of Nikkō is essentially one long avenue—Sugi Namiki (Cryptomeria Avenue)—extending for about 2 km (1 mi) from the railway stations to Tōshō-gū. You can easily walk to most places within town. Tourist inns and shops line the street, and if you have time, you might want to make this a leisurely stroll. The antiques shops along the way may turn up interesting—but expensive—pieces like armor fittings, hibachi, pottery, and dolls. The souvenir shops here sell ample selections of local wood carvings.

Buses and taxis can take you from Nikkō to the village of Chūzenji and nearby Lake Chūzenji.

CLOSE UP

Ieyasu's Legacy

IN 1600, IEYASU TOKUGAWA (1543–1616) won a battle at a place in the mountains of south-central Japan called Seki-ga-hara that left him the undisputed ruler of the archipelago. He died 16 years later, but the Tokugawa Shogunate would last another 252 years.

The founder of such a dynasty required a fitting resting place. Ieyasu (ee-eh-*ya*-su) had provided for one in his will: a mausoleum at Nikkō, in a forest of tall cedars, where a religious center had started more than eight centuries earlier. The year after his death, in accordance with Buddhist custom, he was given a *kaimyō*—an honorific name to bear in the afterlife. Thenceforth, he was Tōshō-Daigongen: the Great Incarnation Who Illuminates the East. The imperial court at Kyōto declared him a god, and his remains were taken in a procession of great pomp and ceremony to be enshrined at Nikkō.

Tōshō-gū was built by his grandson, the third shōgun, Iemitsu (it was Iemitsu who established the policy of national isolation, which closed the doors of Japan to the outside world for more than 200 years). The mausoleum and shrine required the labor of 15,000 people for two years (1634–36). Craftsmen and artists of the first rank were assembled from all over the country. Every surface was carved and painted and lacquered in the most intricate detail imaginable. Tōshō-gū shimmers with the reflections of 2,489,000 sheets of gold leaf. Roof beams and rafter ends with dragon heads, lions, and elephants in bas-relief; friezes of phoenixes, wild ducks, and monkeys; inlaid pillars and red-lacquer corridors: Tōshō-gū is everything a 17th-century warlord would consider gorgeous, and the inspiration is very Chinese.

Numbers in the text correspond to numbers on the Nikkō Area map.

Tōshō-gū Area

The Tōshō-gu area encompasses three UNESCO World Heritage sights—Tōshō-gu Shrine, Futarasan Shrine, and Rinnōji Temple. These are known as *nisha-ichiji* (two shrines and one temple) and are Nikkō's main draw. Signs and maps clearly mark a recommended route that will allow you to see all the major sights, which are within walking distance of each other. You should plan for half a day to explore the area.

A multiple-entry ticket is the best way to see the Tōshō-gū precincts. The ¥1,000 pass gets you entrance to Rinnō-ji (Rinnō Temple), the Taiyū-in Mausoleum, and Futara-san Jinja (Futara-san Shrine); for an extra ¥300 you can also see the Sleeping Cat and Ieyasu's tomb at Taiyū-in (separate fees are charged for admission to other sights). There are two places to purchase the multiple-entry ticket: one is at the entrance to Rinnō Temple, in the corner of the parking lot, at the top of the path called the Higashi-sandō (East Approach) that begins across the highway from the Sacred Bridge; the other is at the entrance to Tōshō-gū,

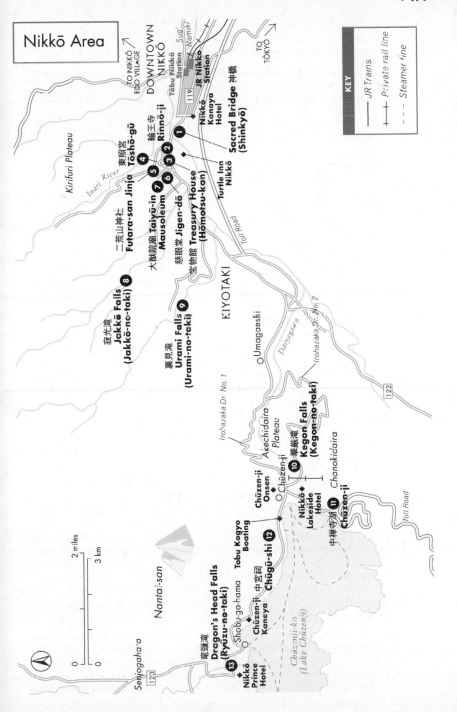

Nikkō Area

KEY
—— JR Trans
—+— Private rail line
––– Steamer line

DOWNTOWN NIKKŌ

TO NIKKŌ EDO VILLAGE
TO NIKKŌ

Tobu Nikkō Station
JR Nikkō Station
TO TOKYO

Namiki
Sugi

Nikkō Kanaya Hotel

Sacred Bridge 神橋 (Shinkyō)

輪王寺 Rinnō-ji ❶

❷ ❸

Turtle Inn Nikkō

東照宮 Tōshō-gū ❹

❺ ❻

Kirifuri Plateau

Inari River

二荒山神社 Futara-san Jinja

大猷院廟 Taiyū-in Mausoleum ❼

慈眼堂 Jigen-dō

宝物館 Treasury House (Hōmotsu-kan)

Toll Road

KIYOTAKI

寂光滝 Jakkō Falls (Jakkō-no-taki) ❽

裏見滝 Urami Falls (Urami-no-taki) ❾

Irohazaka Dr. No. 1

Irohazaka Dr. No. 2

Umagaeshi

Daiyagawa

122

Akechidaira Plateau

Chūzen-ji Onsen
Chūzen-ji

華厳滝 Kegon Falls (Kegon-no-taki) ❿

Chanokidaira

Nikkō Lakeside Hotel

中禅寺湖 Chūzen-ji ⓫

Toll Road

Tobu Kogyo Boating

Chūzen-ji Kaneya

中宮祠 Chūgū-shi ⓬

Shōbu-ga-hama

Nantai-san

竜頭滝 Dragon's Head Falls (Ryūzu-no-taki) ⓭

Nikkō Prince Hotel

Chūzenji-ko (Lake Chūzenji)

Senjogahara

122

2 miles
3 km

at the top of the broad Omote-sandō (Central Approach), which begins about 100 yards farther west.

❶ Built in 1636 for shōguns and imperial messengers visiting the shrine, the original **Sacred Bridge** (Shinkyō) was destroyed in a flood; the present red-lacquer wooden structure dates to 1907. Buses leaving from either railway station at Nikkō go straight up the main street to the bridge, opposite the first of the main entrances to Tōshō-gū. The fare is ¥190. The Sacred Bridge is just to the left of a modern bridge, where the road curves and crosses the Daiya-gawa (Daiya River).

SEEKING YOUR FORTUNE?

Make sure you visit **Gohōten-dō**, in the northeast corner of Rinnō Temple, behind the Sanbutsu-dō. Three of the Seven Gods of Good Fortune are enshrined here. These three Buddhist deities are Daikoku-ten and Bishamon-ten, who bring wealth and good harvests, and Benzai-ten, patroness of music and the arts. You might leave Tōkyō rich and musical.

The **Monument to Masatuna Matsudaira**—opposite the Sacred Bridge, at the east entrance to the grounds of Tōshō-gū—pays tribute to one of the two feudal lords charged with the construction of Tōshō-gū. Matsudaira's great contribution was the planting of the wonderful cryptomeria trees (Japanese cedars) surrounding the shrine and along all the approaches to it. The project took 20 years, from 1628 to 1648, and the result was some 36 km (22 mi) of cedar-lined avenues—planted with more than 15,000 trees. Fire and time have taken their toll, but thousands of the trees still stand in the shrine precincts, creating a setting of solemn majesty. Thousands more line Route 119 east of Nikkō on the way to Shimo-Imaichi.

★ ❷ Rinnō-ji (Rinnō Temple) belongs to the Tendai sect of Buddhism, the head temple of which is Enryaku-ji, on Mt. Hiei near Kyōto. The main hall of Rinnō Temple, called the **Sanbutsu-dō,** is the largest single building at Tōshō-gū.

In the southwest corner of the Rinnō Temple compound, behind the abbot's residence, is an especially fine Japanese garden called **Shōyō-en,** created in 1815 and thoughtfully designed to present a different perspective of its rocks, ponds, and flowering plants from every turn on its path. To the right of the entrance to the garden is the **Treasure Hall** (Hōmotsu-den) of Rinnō Temple, a rather small museum with a collection of some 6,000 works of lacquerware, painting, and Buddhist sculpture. ✉ *Rinnō Temple ¥1,000, multiple-entry ticket includes admission to Taiyū-in Mausoleum and Futara-san Shrine; Shōyō-en and Treasure Hall ¥300 ☉ Apr.–Oct., daily 8–5, last entry at 4; Nov.–Mar., daily 8–4, last entry at 3.*

❸ An unhurried visit to the precincts of Tōshō-gū should include the **Treasury House** (Hōmotsu-kan), which contains a collection of antiquities from its various shrines and temples. From the west gate of Rinnō Temple, turn left off Omote-sandō, just below the pagoda, onto the cedar-lined avenue to Futara-san Jinja. A minute's walk will bring you to the

museum, on the left. ☞ ¥500
🕑 *Apr.–Oct., daily 9–5; Nov.–Mar., daily 9–4.*

❹ With its riot of colors and carvings, inlaid pillars, red-lacquer corridors, and extensive use of gold leaf, **Tōshō-gū**, the 17th-century shrine to Ieyasu Tokugawa, is magnificent, astonishing, and never dull.

Fodor$Choice ★

The west gate of Rinnō Temple brings you out onto Omote-sando, which leads uphill to the stone torii of the shrine. The **Five-Story Pagoda** of Tōshō-gū—a reconstruction dating from 1818—is on the left as you approach the shrine. The 12 signs of the zodiac decorate the first story. The black-lacquer doors above each sign bear the three hollyhock leaves of the Tokugawa family crest.

THREE LITTLE MONKEYS

While in the Sacred Stable, take a look at the second panel from the left. Recognize the three monkeys? The trio, commonly referred to as "Hear no evil, Speak no evil, See no evil," is something of a Nikkō trademark and has been reproduced on plaques, bags, and souvenirs. The true origins of this phrase are much debated, scholars and legend suggest it originated from this shrine as a visual interpretation of the phrase, "If we do not hear, see, or speak evil, we ourselves shall be spared all evil." As for the monkeys, it's been said that a Chinese Buddhist monk introduced the image to Japan in the 8th century.

A flight of stone steps brings you to the front gate of the shrine—the Omote-mon, also called the Nio-mon (Gate of the Deva Kings), with its fearsome pair of red-painted guardian gods. In the first group of buildings on the left is the 17th-century **Sacred Stable** (Shinkyū). Housed here is the white horse—symbol of purity—that figures in many of the shrine's ceremonial events. Carvings of pine trees and monkeys adorn the panels over the stable. And where the path turns to the right, you'll find a granite font where visitors can purify themselves before entering the inner precincts of Tōshō-gū. The **Sutra Library** (Rinzō), just beyond the font, is a repository for some 7,000 Buddhist scriptures, kept in a huge revolving bookcase nearly 20 feet high; it's not open to the public.

As you pass under the second (bronze) torii, you'll see a belfry and a tall bronze candelabrum on the right and a drum tower and a bronze revolving lantern on the left. The two bronze works were presented to the shrine by the Dutch government in the mid-17th century. Behind the drum tower is the **Yakushi-dō**, which enshrines a manifestation of the Buddha as Yakushi Nyorai, the healer of illnesses.

The centerpiece of Tōshō-gū is the **Gate of Sunlight** (Yōmei-mon), at the top of the second flight of stone steps. A designated National Treasure, it's also called the **Twilight Gate** (Higurashi-mon)—implying that you could gape at its richness of detail all day, until sunset. And rich it is indeed: 36 feet high and dazzling white, the gate has 12 columns, beams, and roof brackets carved with dragons, lions, clouds, peonies, Chinese sages, and demigods, painted vivid hues of red, blue, green, and gold. On one of the central columns, there are two carved tigers; the natural grain of the wood is used to bring out the "fur." As you enter the

Yōmei-mon, there are galleries running east and west for some 700 feet; their paneled fences are also carved and painted with nature motifs.

The portable shrines that appear in the Tōshō-gū Festival, held yearly May 17–18, are kept in the **Shin-yosha,** a storeroom to the left as you come through the Twilight Gate into the heart of the shrine. The paintings on the ceiling are of *tennin* (Buddhist angels) playing harps.

Mere mortals may not pass through the **Chinese Gate** (Kara-mon), which is the "official" entrance to the Tōshō-gū inner shrine. Like its counterpart, the Yomei-mon, on the opposite side of the courtyard, the Kara-mon is a National Treasure—and, like the Yomei-mon, is carved and painted in elaborate detail with dragons and other auspicious figures. The Main Hall of Tōshō-gū is enclosed by a wall of painted and carved panel screens; opposite the right-hand corner of the wall, facing the shrine, is the **Kitō-den,** a hall where annual prayers were once offered for the peace of the nation.

The **Main Hall** (Hon-den) of Tōshō-gū is the ultimate purpose of the shrine. Remove and store your shoes in the rows of lockers at the far end of the enclosure, step up into the shrine, and follow a winding corridor to the Oratory (Hai-den)—the anteroom, resplendent in its lacquered pillars, carved friezes, and coffered ceilings bedecked with dragons. Over the lintels are paintings by Mitsuoki Tosa (1617–91) of the 36 great poets of the Heian period, with their poems in the calligraphy of Emperor Go-Mizuno-o. Deeper yet, at the back of the Oratory, is the Inner Chamber (Nai-jin)—repository of the Sacred Mirror that represents the spirit of the enshrined deity. To the right is a room that was reserved for members of the three principal branches of the Tokugawa family; the room on the left was for the chief abbot of Rinnō Temple, who was always a prince of the imperial line.

Behind the Inner Chamber is the Innermost Chamber (Nai-Nai-jin). No visitors come this far. Here is the gold-lacquer shrine where the spirit of Ieyasu resides—along with two other deities, whom the Tokugawas later decided were fit companions. One was Hideyoshi Toyotomi, Ieyasu's mentor and liege lord in the wars of unification at the end of the 16th century. The other was Minamoto no Yoritomo, brilliant military tactician and founder of the earlier (12th-century) Kamakura Shogunate (Ieyasu claimed Yoritomo for an ancestor).

■ TIP→ Don't forget to recover your shoes when you return to the courtyard. Between the Goma-dō and the **Kagura-den** (a hall where ceremonial dances are performed to honor the gods) is a passage to the **Gate at the Foot of the Hill** (Sakashita-mon). Above the gateway is another famous symbol of Tōshō-gū, the Sleeping Cat—a small panel said to have been carved by Hidari Jingoro (Jingoro the Left-handed), a late-16th-century master carpenter and sculptor credited with important contributions to numerous Tokugawa-period temples, shrines, and palaces. A separate admission charge (¥520) is levied to go beyond the Sleeping Cat, up the flight of 200 stone steps through a forest of cryptomeria to **Ieyasu's tomb.** The climb is worth making for the view of the Yomei-mon and Kara-mon from above; the tomb itself is unimpressive. 🎫 *Free; Ieyasu's tomb* ¥520 ☼ *Apr.–Oct. daily 9–5; Nov.–Mar. daily 9–4.*

★ ⑤ The 8th-century **Futara-san Jinja** (Futara-san Shrine) is sacred to the Shinto deities Okuni-nushi-no-Mikoto (god of the rice fields, bestower of prosperity), his consort Tagorihime-no-Mikoto, and their son Ajisukitaka-hikone-no-Mikoto. Futara-san actually has three locations: the Main Shrine at Tōshō-gū; the Chūgū-shi (Middle Shrine), at Chūzenji-ko; and the Okumiya (Inner Shrine), on top of Mt. Nantai.

The bronze torii at the entrance to the shrine leads to the **Chinese Gate** (Kara-mon), gilded and elaborately carved; beyond it is the **Hai-den,** the shrine's oratory. The Hai-den, too, is richly carved and decorated, with a dragon-covered ceiling. From the oratory of the Taiyū-in a connecting passage leads to the **Sanctum** (Hon-den)—the present version of which dates from 1619. Designated a National Treasure, it houses a gilded and lacquered Buddhist altar some 9 feet high, decorated with paintings of animals, birds, and flowers, in which resides the object of this veneration: a seated wooden figure of Iemitsu. To get to Futara-san, take the avenue to the left as you're standing before the stone torii at Tōshō-gū and follow it to the end. ✉ *¥200, ¥1,000 multiple-entry ticket includes admission to Rinnō Temple and Taiyū-in Mausoleum* ☉ *Apr.–Oct., daily 8 5; Nov.–Mar., daily 9–4.*

⑥ Tenkai (1536–1643), the first abbot of Rinnō Temple, has his own place of honor at Tōshō-gū: the **Jigen-dō.** The hall, founded in 848, now holds many of Rinnō Temple's artistic treasures. To reach it, take the path opposite the south entrance to Futara-san Shrine that passes between the two subtemples called Jōgyō-dō and Hokke-dō. Connected by a corridor, these two buildings are otherwise known as the Futatsu-dō (Twin Halls) of Rinnō Temple and are designated a National Cultural Property. The path between the Twin Halls leads roughly south and west to the Jigen-dō compound; the hall itself is at the north end of the compound, to the right. At the west end sits the Go-ōden, a shrine to Prince Yoshihisa Kitashirakawa (1847–95), the last of the imperial princes to serve as abbot. Behind it are his tomb and the tombs of his 13 predecessors. ✉ *Free* ☉ *Apr.–Nov., daily 8–5; Dec.–Mar., daily 9–4.*

★ ⑦ The grandiose **Taiyū-in Mausoleum** is the resting place of the third Tokugawa shōgun, Iemitsu (1604–51), who imposed a policy of national isolation on Japan that lasted more than 200 years. Iemitsu, one suspects, wanted to upstage his illustrious grandfather; he marked the approach to his own tomb with no fewer than six different decorative gates. The first is another Niō-mon—a Gate of the Deva Kings—like the one at Tōshō-gū. The dragon painted on the ceiling is by Yasunobu Kanō. A flight of stone steps leads to the second gate, the Niten-mon, a two-story structure protected front and back by carved and painted images of guardian gods. Beyond it, two more flights of steps lead to the middle courtyard. As you climb the last steps to Iemitsu's shrine, you pass a bell tower on the right and a drum tower on the left; directly ahead is the third gate, the remarkable **Yasha-mon,** named for the figures of *yasha* (she-demons) in the four niches. This structure is also known as the Peony Gate (Botan-mon) because of its carvings.

As you exit the shrine, you come to the fifth gate: the **Kōka-mon,** built in the style of the late Ming dynasty of China. The gate is normally closed, but from here another flight of stone steps leads to the sixth and last gate—the cast copper **Inuki-mon,** inscribed with characters in Sanskrit—and Iemitsu's tomb. ⚅ *¥1,000 multiple-entry ticket includes admission to Rinnō Temple and Futara-san Shrine* ⊗ *Apr.–Oct., daily 8–5; Nov.–Mar., daily 8–4.*

ↄ **Nikkō Edo Village** (Nikkō Edo Mura), a living-history theme park a short taxi ride from downtown, re-creates an 18th-century Japanese village. The complex includes sculpted gardens with waterfalls and ponds and 22 vintage buildings, where actors in traditional dress stage martial arts exhibitions, historical theatrical performances, and comedy acts. You can even observe Japanese tea ceremony rituals in gorgeous tatami-floored houses, as well as people dressed as geisha and samurai. Strolling stuffed animal characters and acrobatic ninjas keep kids happy. Nikkō Edo Mura has one large restaurant and 15 small food stalls serving period cuisine like *yakisoba* (fried soba) and *dango* (dumplings). ✉ *470–2 Egura, Fujiwara-chō, Shiodani-gun* ☎ *0288/77–1777* ⚅ *¥2,300 general admission, plus extra for rides and shows; ¥6,300 unlimited day pass includes rides and shows* ⊗ *Mid-Mar.–Nov., daily 9–5; Dec.–mid-Mar., daily 9:30–4.*

┌─
│ **DID YOU**
│ **KNOW?**
└─

Under the policy of national seclusion, only the Dutch retained trading privileges with Japan. Even then, they were confined to the tiny artificial island of Dejima, in the port of Nagasaki. They regularly sent tokens of their esteem to the shōgunate to keep their precarious monopoly, including the two bronze items found in the Sacred Stable, which were sent in 1636. The 200-year-plus monopoly dissolved when Japan opened its borders to other Western countries in 1858.

Chūzenji-ko (Lake Chūzen-ji)

More than 3,900 feet above sea level, at the base of the volcano known as Nantai-san, is Lake Chūzen-ji. People come to boat and fish on the lake and to enjoy the surrounding scenic woodlands, waterfalls, and hills. If you're looking to sightsee, check out **Tobu Kogyo Boating,** which offers chartered boat rides for 60 minutes. ✉ *2478 Chugushi, Nikkō, Tochigi-ken* ☎ *0288/55–0360* ⚅ *¥150–¥1,500 depending on route chosen* ⊗ *9:30 AM–3:30 PM* ⊗ *Dec.–Mar.*

Falling water is one of the special charms of the Nikkō National Park area; people going by bus or car from Tōshō-gū to Lake Chūzenji often ➑ stop off en route to see **Jakkō Falls** (Jakkō-no-taki), which descend in a series of seven terraced stages, forming a sheet of water about 100 feet high. About 1 km (½ mi) from the shrine precincts, at the Tamozawa bus stop, a narrow road to the right leads to an uphill walk of some 3 km (2 mi) to the falls.

➒ "The water," wrote the great 17th-century poet Bashō about the **Urami Falls** (Urami-no-taki), "seemed to take a flying leap and drop a hundred feet from the top of a cave into a green pool surrounded by a thousand rocks. One was supposed to inch one's way into the cave and enjoy the falls from behind." It's a steep climb to the cave, which begins at the Arasawa bus stop, with a turn to the right off the Chūzenji road. The falls and the gorge are striking—but you should make the climb only if you have good hiking shoes and are willing to get wet in the process.

The real climb to Lake Chūzen-ji begins at **Umagaeshi** (literally, "horse return"). In the old days, the road became too rough for horseback riding, so riders had to proceed on foot. The lake is 4,165 feet above sea level. From Umagaeshi the bus climbs a one-way toll road up the pass; the old road has been widened and is used for the traffic coming down. The two roads are full of steep hairpin turns, and on

> ## FEELING ADVENTUROUS?
>
> If you want to avoid the hairpin turns, try the **ropeway** that runs from Akechi-daira station directly to the Akechi-daira lookout. It takes 3 minutes and has panoramic views of Nikko and Kegon Falls. ⚏ *¥390* ✉ *709–5 Misawa, Hosoo-machi, Nikko* ☎ *028/855-0331* ⊘ *Apr.–Oct., daily 8:30–4; Nov.–Mar., daily 9–3* ⊘ *Mar. 1–15.*

a clear day the view up and down the valley is magnificent—especially from the halfway point at **Akechi-daira** (Akechi Plain), where you can see the summit of **Nantai-san** (Mt. Nantai), reaching 8,149 feet. Hiking season lasts from May through mid-October; if you push it, you can make the ascent in about four hours. ⚠ **Wild monkeys make their homes in these mountains, and they've learned the convenience of mooching from visitors. Be careful—they have a way of not taking no for an answer.** Umagaeshi is about 10 km (6 mi) from Tōbu Station in Nikkō, or 8 km (5 mi) from Tōshō-gū.

❿ More than anything else, **Kegon Falls** (Kegon-no-taki), the country's most famous falls, are what draw the crowds of Japanese visitors to Chūzen-ji. Fed by the eastward flow of the lake, the falls drop 318 feet into a rugged gorge; an elevator (¥530) takes you to an observation platform at the bottom. The volume of water over the falls is carefully regulated, but it's especially impressive after a summer rain or a typhoon. In winter the falls do not freeze completely but form a beautiful cascade of icicles. The elevator is just a few minutes' walk east from the bus stop at Chūzen-ji village, downhill and off to the right at the far end of the parking lot. ✉ *2479–2 Chugushi Nikkō* ☎ *028/855-0030* ⊘ *Daily 8–5.*

FodorsChoice ★

The bus trip from Nikkō to the national park area ends at Chūzenji village, which shares its name with the temple established here in 784. **Chūzen-ji** (Chūzen Temple) is a subtemple of Rinnō Temple, at Tōshō-gū. The principal object of worship at Chūzen-ji is the **Tachi-ki Kannon**, a 17-foot-tall standing statue of the Buddhist goddess of mercy, said to have been carved more than 1,000 years ago by the priest Shōdō from the living trunk of a single Judas tree. You reach the temple grounds by turning left (south) as you leave the village of Chūzenji and walking about 1½ km (1 mi) along the eastern shore of the lake. ⚏ *¥300* ⊘ *Apr.–Oct., daily 8–5; Mar. and Nov., daily 8–4; Dec.–Feb., daily 8–3:30.*

⓫

⓬ **Chūgū-shi,** a subshrine of the Futara-san Shrine at Tōshō-gū, is the major religious center on the north side of Lake Chūzenji, about 1½ km (1 mi) west of the village. The **Treasure House** (Hōmotsu-den) contains an interesting historical collection, including swords, lacquerware, and medieval shrine palanquins. ✉ *Shrine free, Treasure House ¥300* ⊙ *Apr.–Oct., daily 8–5; Nov.–Mar., daily 9–4.*

NEED A BREAK? Take a breather at the **Ryūzu-no-taki Chaya** (✉ 2485 Chugushi Nikkō ☎ 028/ 855-0157 ⊙ Daily 11–5): a charming, but rustic tea shop near the waterfalls. Enjoy a cup of green tea, a light meal, or sweets like rice cakes boiled with vegetables and *dango* (sweet dumplings).

If you've budgeted an extra day for Nikkō, you might want to consider a walk around the lake. A paved road along the north shore extends for about 8 km (5 mi), one-third of the whole distance, as far as the "beach" at Shōbu-ga-hama. Here, where the road branches off to the north for Senjōgahara, are the lovely cascades of **Dragon's Head Falls** (Ryūzu-no-taki). To the left is a steep footpath that continues around the lake to Senju-ga-hama and then to a campsite at Asegata. The path is well marked but can get rough in places. From Asegata it's less than an hour's walk back to Chūzen-ji village.

Where to Eat

Chūzen-ji

$$–$$$ ✕ **Nantai.** The low tables, antiques, and pillows scattered on tatami flooring makes visitors feel like they're dining in a traditional Japanese living room. Try the Nikkō specialty, *yuba* (tofu skin), which comes with the *nabe* (hot pot) for dinner. It is the quintessential winter family meal. The seafood here is fresh and both the trout and salmon are recommended. Each meal comes with rice, pickles, and selected side dishes like soy-stewed vegetables, tempura, udon, and a dessert. ✉ *2478–8 Chugushi Nikkō* ☎ *028/855–0201* ▭ *MC, V.*

Nikkō

$$$$ ✕ **Gyōshintei.** This is the only restaurant in Nikkō devoted to *shōjin ryōri*, the Buddhist-temple vegetarian fare that evolved centuries ago into haute cuisine. Gyōshintei is decorated in the style of a *ryōtei* (traditional inn), with all-tatami seating. It differs from a ryōtei in that it has one large, open space where many guests are served at once, rather than a number of rooms for private dining. Dinner is served until 7. ✉ *2339–1 Sannai, Nikkō* ☎ *0288/53–3751* ▭ *AE, DC, MC, V* ⊙ *Closed Thurs.*

$$$–$$$$ ✕ **Masudaya.** Masudaya started out as a sake maker more than a century ago, but for four generations now, it has been the town's best-known restaurant. The specialty is yuba, which the chefs transform, with the help of local vegetables and fresh fish, into sumptuous high cuisine. The building is traditional, with a lovely interior garden; the assembly-line-style service, however, detracts from the ambiance. Masudaya serves one nine-course kaiseki-style meal; the kitchen simply stops serving when the food is gone. Meals here are prix fixe. ✉ *439–2 Ishiya-machi, Nikkō* ☎ *0288/54–2151* ⚐ *Reservations essential* ▭ *No credit cards* ⊙ *Open 11–3* ⊙ *Closed Thurs.*

$$$–$$$$ ✕ **Meiji-no-Yakata.** Not far from the east entrance to Rinnō Temple, Meiji-no-Yakata is an elegant 19th-century Western-style stone house, originally built as a summer retreat for an American diplomat. The food, too, is Western style; specialties of the house include fresh rainbow trout from Lake Chūzen-ji, roast lamb with pepper sauce, and melt-in-your-mouth filet mignon made from local Tochigi beef. High ceilings, hardwood floors, and an air of informality make this a very pleasant place to dine. The restaurant opens at 11 AM in the summer and 11:30 AM in winter; it always closes at 7:30. ⊠ *2339–1 Sannai, Nikkō* ☎ *0288/ 53–3751* ⊟ *AE, DC, MC, V* ⊘ *Closed Wed.*

$$–$$$ ✕ **Sawamoto.** Charcoal-broiled *unagi* (eel) is an acquired taste, and there's no better place in Nikkō to acquire it than at this restaurant. The place is small and unpretentious, with only five plain-wood tables, and service can be lukewarm, but Sawamoto is reliable for a light lunch or dinner of unagi on a bed of rice, served in an elegant lacquered box. Eel is considered a stamina builder: just right for the weary visitor on a hot summer day. ⊠ *1019 Bandu, Kami Hatsuishi-machi, Nikkō* ☎ *0288/ 54–0163* ⊟ *No credit cards* ⊘ *No dinner.*

Where to Stay

Nikkō

★ **$$–$$$$** ▦ **Nikkō Kanaya Hotel.** This family-run operation is a little worn around the edges after a century of operation, but it still has the best location in town: across the street from Tōshō-gū. The main building is a delightful, rambling Victorian structure that has hosted royalty and other important personages—as the guest book attests—from around the world. The long driveway that winds up to the hotel at the top of the hill is just below the Sacred Bridge, on the same side of the street. The hotel is very touristy; daytime visitors browse through the old building and its gift shops. The helpful staff is better at giving area information than the tourist office. Rooms vary a great deal, as do their prices. The more expensive rooms are spacious and comfortable, with wonderful high ceilings; in the annex the sound of the Daiya-gawa murmuring below the Sacred Bridge lulls you to sleep. Horseback riding and golf are available nearby. ⊠ *1300 Kami Hatsuishi-machi, Nikkō, Tochigi-ken 321-1401* ☎ *0288/54–0001* ⊅ *77 rooms, 62 with bath* ᗽ *2 restaurants, coffee shop, pool, bar* ⊟ *AE, DC, MC, V.*

¢ ▦ **Turtle Inn Nikkō.** This Japanese Inn Group member provides modest, cost-conscious Western- and Japanese-style accommodations with or without a private bath. Simple, cheap breakfasts and dinners are served in the dining room, but you needn't opt for these if you'd rather eat out. Rates go up about 10% in high season (late July and August). To get here, take the bus bound for Chūzenji from either railway station and get off at the Sōgō Kaikan-mae bus stop. The inn is two minutes from the bus stop and within walking distance of Tōshō-gū. ⊠ *2–16 Takumi-chō, Nikkō, Tochigi-ken 321-1433* ☎ *0288/53–3168* ⊅ *7 Western-style rooms, 3 with bath; 5 Japanese-style rooms without bath* ⊕ *www.turtle-nikko.com* ᗽ *Restaurant, Japanese baths, Internet* ⊟ *AE, MC, V.*

Chūzen-ji

$$$$ ▦ **Chūzen-ji Kanaya.** A boathouse and restaurant on the lake give this branch of the Nikkō Kanaya on the road from the village to Shōbu-ga-hama the air of a private yacht club. Pastel colors decorate the simple, tasteful rooms, which have floor-to-ceiling windows overlooking the lake or grounds. ✉ *2482 Chū-gūshi, Chūzen-ji, Nikkō, Tochigi-ken 321-1661* ☎ *0288/51–0001* ⤴ *60 rooms, 54 with bath* ♿ *Restaurant, boating, waterskiing, fishing* ▤ *AE, DC, MC, V* ⏐⊙⏐ *MAP.*

Shōbu-ga-hama

$$ ▥ **Nikkō Prince Hotel.** On the shore of Lake Chūzen-ji, this hotel, part of a large Japanese chain, is within walking distance of the Dragon's Head Falls. With many of its accommodations in two-story maisonettes and rustic detached cottages, the Prince chain markets itself to families and small groups of younger excursionists. The architecture favors high ceilings and wooden beams, with lots of glass in the public areas to take advantage of the view of the lake and Mt. Nantai. ✉ *Chū-gūshi, Shōbu-ga-hama Nikkō, Tochigi-ken 321-1692* ☎ *0288/55–1111* ⊕ *www.princehotels.co.jp* ⤴ *60 rooms with bath* ♿ *Restaurant, 2 tennis courts, pool, downhill skiing, bar, lounge* ▤ *AE, DC, MC, V* ⏐⊙⏐ *MAP.*

Nikkō Essentials

BY BUS

⚠ **There is no bus service between Tōkyō and Nikkō.** Local buses leave Tōbu Nikkō Station for Lake Chūzen-ji, stopping just above the entrance to Tōshō-gū, approximately every 30 minutes from 6:15 AM until 7:01 PM. The fare to Chūzen-ji is ¥1,100, and the ride takes about 40 minutes. The last return bus from the lake leaves at 7:39 PM, arriving back at Tōbu Nikkō Station at 9:17.

BY CAR

■ **TIP→** It's possible, but unwise, to travel by car from Tōkyō to Nikkō. The trip will take at least three hours, and merely getting from central Tōkyō to the toll-road system can be a nightmare. If you absolutely *must* drive, take the Tōkyō Expressway 5 (Ikebukuro Line) north to the Tōkyō Gaikandō, go east on this ring road to the Kawaguchi interchange, and pick up the Tōhoku Expressway northbound. Take the Tōhoku to Utsunomiya and change again at Exit 10 (marked in English) for the Nikkō–Utsunomiya Toll Road, which runs into Nikkō.

BY TAXI

Cabs are readily available in Nikkō; the one-way fare from Tōbu Nikkō Station to Chūzen-ji is about ¥6,000.

BY TRAIN

The limited express train of the Tōbu Railway has two direct connections from Tōkyō to Nikkō every morning, starting at 7:30 AM from Tōbu Asakusa Station, a minute's walk from the last stop on Tōkyō's Ginza subway line; there are additional trains on weekends, holidays, and in high season. The one-way fare is ¥2,740. All seats are reserved. Bookings are not accepted over the phone; they can only be bought at Asakusa station. During summer, fall, and weekends, buy tickets a few days in advance. The trip from Asakusa to the Tōbu Nikkō Station takes about two hours, which is quicker than the JR trains. If you're visiting Nikkō on a day trip, note that the last return trains are at 4:29 PM (direct express) and 7:42 PM (with a transfer at 7:52 at Shimo-Imaichi).

If you have a JR Pass, use JR (Japan Railways) service, which connects Tōkyō and Nikkō, from Ueno Station. Take the Tōhoku–Honsen Line limited express to Utsunomiya (about 1½ hours) and transfer to the train for JR Nikkō Station (45 minutes). The earliest departure from Ueno is at 5:10 AM; the last connection back leaves Nikkō at 8:03 PM and brings you into Ueno at 10:48 PM. (If you're not using the JR Pass, the one-way fare will cost ¥2,520.)

More expensive but faster is the Yamabiko train on the north extension of the Shinkansen; the one-way fare, including the surcharge for the express, is ¥5,430. The first one leaves Tōkyō Station at 6:04 AM (or Ueno at 6:10 AM) and takes about 50 minutes to Utsunomiya; change there to the train to Nikkō Station. To return, take the 9:43 PM train from Nikkō to Utsunomiya and catch the last Yamabiko back at 10:53 PM, arriving in Ueno at 11:38 PM.

🔹 **Japan Railways** ☎ 03/3423-0111 ⊕ www.japanrail.com.

TOURS

From Tōkyō, Sunrise Tours operates one-day bus tours to Nikkō, which take you to Tōshō-gū and Lake Chūzenji for ¥13,500 (lunch included). The tour schedule varies widely from season to season, so check the Web site or call well in advance.

🔹 **Sunrise Tours** ☎ 03/5796-5454 ⊕ www.jtb.co.jp/sunrisetour.

VISITOR INFORMATION

You can do a lot of preplanning for your visit to Nikkō with a stop at the Japan National Tourist Organization office in Tōkyō. Closer to the source is the Tourist Information and Hospitality Center in Nikkō itself, about halfway up the main street of town between the railway stations and Tōshō-gū, on the left; don't expect too much in the way of help in English, but the center does have a good array of guides to local restaurants and shops, registers of inns and hotels, and mapped-out walking tours.

🔹 **Japan National Tourist Organization** ⊠ Tōkyō Kōtsū Kaikan, 10F, 2-10-1 Yūraku-chō, Chiyoda-ku, Tōkyō ☎ 03/3201-3331 ⊕ www.jnto.go.jp Ⓜ JR Yamanote Line (Higashi-guchi/East Exit) and Yūraku-chō subway line (Exit A-8), Yūraku-chō Station. **Nikkō Tourist Information and Hospitality Center** ☎ 0288/54-2496.

KAMAKURA

Kamakura, about 40 km (25 mi) southwest of Tōkyō, is an object lesson in what happens when you set the fox to guard the henhouse.

For the aristocrats of the Heian-era Japan (794–1185), life was defined by the imperial court in Kyōto. In Kyōto there was grace and beauty and poignant affairs of the heart; everything beyond was howling wilderness. Unfortunately, it was the howling wilderness that had all the estates: the large grants of land, called *shōen,* without which there would be no income to pay for all that grace and beauty.

By the 12th century two clans—the Taira (*ta*-ee-ra) and the Minamoto, both offshoots of the imperial line—had come to dominate the Heian court and were at each other's throats in a struggle for supremacy.

The rivalry between the two clans became an all-out war. By 1185 Yoritomo and his half-brother, Yoshitsune (1159–89), had destroyed the Taira utterly, and the Minamoto were masters of all Japan. In 1192 Yoritomo forced the imperial court to name him shōgun. The emperor was left as a figurehead in Kyōto, and the little fishing village of Kamakura became the seat of Japan's first shogunal government.

The Minamoto line came to an end when Yoritomo's two sons were assassinated. Power passed to the Hōjō family, who remained in control, often as regents for figurehead shōguns, for the next 100 years. The end came suddenly, in 1333, when two vassals assigned to put down a revolt switched sides. The Hōjō regent committed suicide, and the center of power returned to Kyōto.

Kamakura reverted to being a sleepy seaside town until the end of World War II when it developed as a residential area for the well-to-do. Nothing secular survives from the days of the Minamoto and Hōjō; the warriors of Kamakura had little use for courtiers, or their palaces and gardened villas; the shogunate's name for itself, in fact, was the Bakufu—literally, the "tent government." As a religious center, however, the town presents an extraordinary legacy. The Bakufu endowed shrines and temples by the score in Kamakura, especially temples of the Rinzai sect of Zen Buddhism. Most of those temples and shrines are in settings of remarkable beauty. If you have the time for only one day trip from Tōkyō, you should spend it here.

Getting Around

There are three principal areas in Kamakura, and you can easily get from one to another by train. From Tōkyō head first to Kita-Kamakura for most of the important Zen temples, including Engaku-ji (Engaku Temple) and Kenchō-ji (Kencho Temple). The second area is downtown Kamakura, with its shops and museums and the venerated shrine Tsuru-ga-oka Hachiman-gū. The third is Hase, a 10-minute train ride southwest from Kamakura on the Enoden Line. Hase's main attractions are the great bronze figure of the Amida Buddha, at Kōtoku-in, and the Kannon Hall of Hase-dera. There's a lot to see in Kamakura, and to hit just the highlights will take you most of a busy day.

TIMING TIP

If your time is limited, you may want to visit only Engaku Temple and Tōkei Temple in Kita-Kamakura before riding the train one stop to Kamakura. If not, follow the main road all the way to Tsuru-ga-oka Hachiman-gū and visit four additional temples en route.

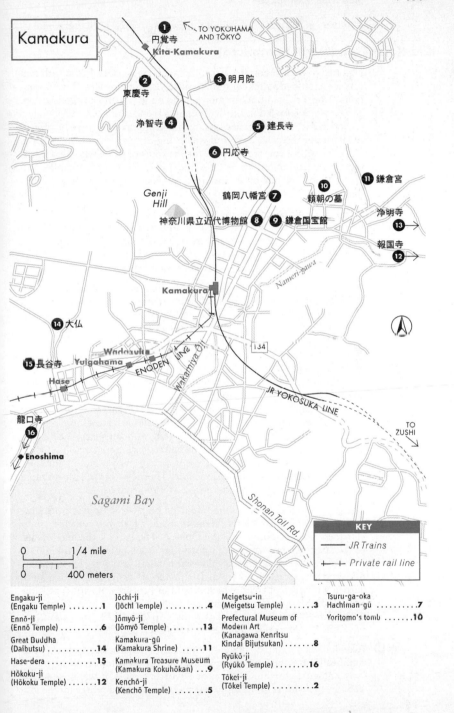

Kamakura

TO YOKOHAMA AND TŌKYŌ

1 円覚寺
Kita-Kamakura

2 東慶寺

3 明月院

4 浄智寺

5 建長寺

6 円応寺

Genji Hill

7 鶴岡八幡宮

10 頼朝の墓

11 鎌倉宮

8 神奈川県立近代博物館

9 鎌倉国宝館

13 浄明寺

12 報国寺

Nameri-gawa

Kamakura

14 大仏

Wadazuka

15 長谷寺   **Yuigahama**

Hase

ENODEN LINE

Wakamiya Ōji

134

JR YOKOSUKA LINE

TO ZUSHI

龍口寺
16

◆ **Enoshima**

Sagami Bay

Shonan Toll Rd.

KEY	
——	*JR Trains*
+—+	*Private rail line*

```
0        1/4 mile
|----|----|
0        400 meters
```

Numbers in the text correspond to numbers on the Kamakura map.

Kita-Kamakura (North Kamakura)

Hierarchies were important to the Kamakura Shogunate. In the 14th century it established a ranking system called Go-zan (literally, "Five Mountains") for the Zen Buddhist monasteries under its official sponsorship.

★ ❶ The largest, **Engaku-ji** (Engaku Temple), was founded in 1282, and it ranked second in the Five Mountains hierarchy. Here, prayers were to be offered regularly for the prosperity and well-being of the government; Engaku Temple's special role was to pray for the souls of those who died resisting the Mongol invasions in 1274 and 1281. The temple complex currently holds 18, but once contained as many as 50 buildings. Often damaged in fires and earthquakes, it has been completely restored

Engaku Temple belongs to the Rinzai sect of Zen Buddhism. Introduced into Japan from China at the beginning of the Kamakura period (1192–1333), the ideas of Zen were quickly embraced by the emerging warrior class. The samurai especially admired the Rinzai sect, with its emphasis on the ascetic life as a path to self-transcendence.

Among the National Treasures at Engaku Temple is the **Hall of the Holy Relic of Buddha** (Shari-den), with its remarkable Chinese-inspired thatched roof. Built in 1282, it was destroyed by fire in 1558 but rebuilt in 1563. The hall is said to enshrine a tooth of the Gautama Buddha himself, but it's not on display. In fact, except for the first three days of the New Year, you won't be able to go any farther into the hall than the main gate. Such is the case, alas, with much of the Engaku Temple complex: this is still a functioning monastic center, and many of its most impressive buildings are not open to the public. The accessible National Treasure at Engaku Temple is the **Great Bell** (Kōshō), on the hilltop on the southeast side of the complex. The bell—Kamakura's most famous—was cast in 1301 and stands 8 feet tall. It's rung only on special occasions, such as New Year's Eve. Reaching the bell requires a trek up a long staircase, but once you've made it to the top you can enjoy tea and traditional Japanese sweets at a small outdoor café. The views of the entire temple grounds and surrounding cedar forest are tremendous.

The two buildings open to the public at Engaku Temple are the **Butsunichi-an,** which has a long ceremonial hall where you can enjoy *sado* (Japanese tea ceremony), and the **Ōbai-in.** The latter is the mausoleum of the last three regents of the Kamakura Shogunate: Hōjō Tokimune, who led the defense of Japan against the Mongol invasions; his son Sadatoki; and his grandson Takatoki. To the side of the mausoleum is a quiet garden with apricot trees, which bloom in February. As you exit Kita-Kamakura Station, the stairway to Engaku Temple is in front of you. ✉ *409 Yama-no-uchi, Kita-Kamakura* ☎ *0467/22–0478* 🖰 *Engaku Temple ¥300* ☉ *Nov.–Mar., daily 8–4; Apr.–Oct., daily 8–5.*

★ ❷ **Tōkei-ji** (Tōkei Temple), a Zen temple of the Rinzai sect, holds special significance for the study of feminism in medieval Japan. More popularly known as the Enkiri-dera, or Divorce Temple, it was founded in 1285 by the widow of the Hōjō regent Tokimune as a refuge for the vic-

2

tims of unhappy marriages. Under the shogunate, a husband of the warrior class could obtain a divorce simply by sending his wife back to her family. Not so for the wife: no matter what cruel and unusual treatment her husband meted out, she was stuck with him. If she ran away, however, and managed to reach Tōkei Temple without being caught, she could receive sanctuary and remain there as a nun. After three years (later reduced to two), she was officially declared divorced. The temple survived as a convent through the Meiji Restoration of 1868. The last abbess died in 1902; her headstone is in the cemetery behind the temple, beneath the plum trees that blossom in February. Tōkei Temple was later reestablished as a monastery.

The **Matsugaoka Treasure House** (Matsugaoka Hōzō) of Tōkei Temple displays several Kamakura-period wooden Buddhas, ink paintings, scrolls, and works of calligraphy, some of which have been designated by the government as Important Cultural Objects. The library, called the Matsugaoka Bunko, was established in memory of the great Zen scholar D. T. Suzuki (1870–1966).

Tōkei Temple is on the southwest side of the JR tracks (the side opposite Engaku Temple), less than a five-minute walk south from the station on the main road to Kamakura (Route 21–the Kamakura Kaidō), on the right. ⊠ *1367 Yama-no-uchi, Kita-Kamakura* ☎ *0467/22–1663* 🖘 *Tōkei Temple ¥100, Matsugaoka Treasure House additional ¥300* ⊙ *Tōkei Temple Apr.–Oct., daily 8:30–5; Nov.–Mar., daily 8:30–4. Matsugaoka Treasure House Mon.–Thurs. 9:30–3:30.*

❸ Meigetsu-in (Meigetsu Temple) is also known as Ajisai-dera, the hydrangeas temple. When the flowers bloom in June, the gardens transform into a sea of color—pink, white, and blue—and visitors can number in the thousands. A typical Kamakura light rain shouldn't deter you; it only showcases this incredible floral display. Meigetsu-in features Kamakura's largest *yagura,* a tomb cavity enclosing a mural, on which 16 images of Buddha are carved. From Tōkei Temple walk along Route 21 toward Kamakura for about 20 minutes until you cross the railway tracks; take the immediate left turn onto the narrow side street that doubles back along the tracks. This street bends to the right and follows the course of a little stream called the Meigetsu-gawa to the temple gate. ⊠ *189 Yama-no-uchi, Kita-Kamakura* ☎ *0467/24–3437* 🖘 *¥300* ⊙ *Apr., May, and July–Oct., daily 9–4 June, daily 8:30–5; Nov.–Mar., daily 9–4.*

❹ In the Five Mountains hierarchy, **Jōchi-ji** (Jōchi Temple) was ranked fourth. The buildings now in the temple complex are reconstructions; the Great Kantō Earthquake of 1923 destroyed the originals. The garden is exquisite. Jōchi Temple is on the south side of the railway tracks, a few minutes' walk farther southwest of Tōkei Temple in the direction of Kamakura. Turn right off the main road (Route 21) and cross over a small bridge; a flight of moss-covered steps leads to the temple. ⊠ *1402 Yama-no-uchi, Kita-Kamakura* ☎ *0467/22–3943* 🖘 *¥200* ⊙ *Daily 9–4:30.*

★ **❺** Founded in 1250, **Kenchō-ji** (Kenchō Temple) was the foremost of Kamakura's five great Zen temples—and lays claim to being Japan's oldest Zen temple. It was modeled on one of the great Chinese monasteries of the time and built for a distinguished Zen master who had just arrived from China. Over the centuries, fires and other disasters have taken their toll on Kencho Temple, and although many buildings have been authentically reconstructed, the temple complex today is half its original size. Near the Main Gate (San-mon) is a **bronze bell** cast in 1255; it's the temple's most important treasure. The Main Gate and the Lecture Hall (Hattō) are the only two structures to have survived the devastating Great Kantō Earthquake of 1923. Like Engaku Temple, Kencho Temple is a functioning temple of the Rinzai sect, where novices train and laypeople can take part in Zen meditation. The entrance to Kencho Temple is about halfway along the main road from Kita-Kamakura Station to Tsuru-ga-oka Hachiman-gū, on the left. ⊠ 8 *Yama-no-uchi, Kita-Kamakura* ☎ *0467/22–0981* ▣ *¥300* ☉ *Daily 8:30–4:30.*

★ ❻ In the feudal period, Japan acquired from China a belief in Enma, the lord of hell, who, with his court attendants, judged the souls of the departed and determined their destination in the afterlife. Kamakura's otherwise-undistinguished **Ennō-ji** (Ennō Temple) houses some remarkable statues of these judges—as grim and merciless a court as you're ever likely to confront. To see them is enough to put you on your best behavior, at least for the rest of your excursion. Ennō Temple is a minute's walk or so from Kencho Temple, on the opposite (south) side of the main road to Kamakura. A few minutes' walk along the main road to the south will bring you to Tsuru-ga-oka Hachiman-gū in downtown Kamakura. ⊠ *1543 Yama-no-uchi, Kita-Kamakura* ☎ *0467/25–1095* ▣ *¥200* ☉ *Mar.–Nov., daily 9–4; Dec.–Feb., daily 9–3:30.*

Kamakura

When the first Kamakura shōgun, Minamoto no Yoritomo, learned he was about to have an heir, he had the tutelary shrine of his family moved to Kamakura from nearby Yui-ga-hama and ordered a stately avenue to be built through the center of his capital from the shrine to the sea. Along this avenue would travel the procession that brought his son—if there were a son—to be presented to the gods. Yoritomo's consort did indeed bear him a son, Yoriie (yo-*ree*-ee-eh), in 1182; Yoriie was brought in great pomp to the shrine and then consecrated to his place in the shogunal succession. Alas, the blessing of the gods did Yoriie little good. He was barely 18 when Yoritomo died, and the regency established by his mother's family, the Hōjō, kept him virtually powerless until 1203, when he was banished and eventually assassinated. The Minamoto were never to hold power again, but Yoriie's memory lives on in the street that his father built for him: Wakamiya Oji, "the Avenue of the Young Prince."

■ TIP→ **A bus from Kamakura Station (Sign 5) travels to the sights listed below, with stops at most access roads to the temples and shrines. However, you may want to walk out as far as Hōkoku-ji and take the bus back; it's easier to recognize the end of the line than any of the stops in between.** You can also go by taxi to Hōkoku-ji—any cab driver knows the way—and walk the last leg in reverse. Downtown Kamakura is a good place to stop for lunch and shopping. Restaurants and shops sell local crafts, especially the carved and lacquered woodwork called Kamakura-*bori*, on Wakamiya Oji and the street parallel to it, Komachi-dōri.

★ **7** The Minamoto shrine, **Tsuru-ga-oka Hachiman-gū,** is dedicated to the legendary emperor Ōjin, his wife, and his mother, from whom Minamoto no Yoritomo claimed descent. At the entrance, the small, steeply arched, vermilion **Drum Bridge** (Taiko-bashi) crosses a stream between two lotus ponds. The ponds were made to Yoritomo's specifications. His wife, Masako, suggested placing islands in each. In the larger **Genji Pond,** to the right, filled with white lotus flowers, she placed three islands. Genji was another name for clan, and three is an auspicious number. In the smaller **Heike Pond,** to the left, she put four islands. Heike (*heh*-ee-keh) was another name for the rival Taira clan, which the Minamoto had destroyed, and four—homophonous in Japanese with the word for "death"—is very unlucky indeed.

On the far side of the Drum Bridge is the **Mai-den.** This hall is the setting for a story of the Minamoto celebrated in Nō and Kabuki theater. Beyond the Mai-den, a flight of steps leads to the shrine's Main Hall (Hon-dō). To the left of these steps is a ginkgo tree that—according to legend—was witness to a murder that ended the Minamoto line in 1219. From behind this tree, a priest named Kugyō leapt out and beheaded his uncle, the 26-year-old Sanetomo, Yoritomo's second son and the last Minamoto shōgun. The priest was quickly apprehended, but Sanetomo's head was never found. Like all other Shintō shrines, the Main Hall is unadorned; the building itself, an 1828 reconstruction, is not particularly noteworthy.

To reach Tsuru-ga-oka Hachiman-gū from the east side of Kamakura Station, cross the plaza, turn left, and walk north along Wakamiya Oji. Straight ahead is the first of three arches leading to the shrine, and the shrine itself is at the far end of the street. ✉ *2–1–31 Yuki-no-shita* ☎ *0467/22–0315* 🏛 *Free* ⊙ *Daily 9–4.*

8 The **Prefectural Museum of Modern Art** (Kanagawa Kenritsu Kindai Bijutsukan) on the north side of the Heike Pond at Tsuru-ga-oka Hachiman-gū, houses a collection of Japanese oil paintings and watercolors, wood-block prints, and sculpture. ✉ *2–1–53 Yuki-no-shita* ☎ *0467/ 22–5000* 🏛 *¥800–¥1,200, depending on exhibition* ⊙ *Tues.–Sun. 9:30–4:30.*

9 The **Kamakura Treasure Museum** (Kamakura Kokuhōkan) was built in 1928 as a repository for many of the most important objects belonging to the shrines and temples in the area. Many of these are designated Important Cultural Properties. The museum, located along the east side of the Tsuru-ga-oka Hachiman-gū shrine precincts, has an especially fine collection of devotional and portrait sculpture in wood from the Kamakura and Muromachi periods; the portrait pieces may be among the most expressive and interesting in all of classical Japanese art. ✉ *2–1–1 Yuki-no-shita* ☎ *0467/22–0753* 🏛 *¥300* ⊙ *Tues.–Sun. 9–4.*

The man who put Kamakura on the map, so to speak, chose not to leave it when he died: it's only a short walk from Tsuru-ga-oka Hachiman-gū to the tomb, Minamoto no Yoritomo. If you've already been to Nikkō and have seen how a later dynasty of shōguns sought to glorify its own memories, you may be surprised at the simplicity of **Yoritomo's tomb**. To get here, cross the

(10)

> ## WHAT IS A BODHISATTVA?
>
> A Bodhisattva is a being that has deferred their own ascendance into Buddhahood to guide the souls of others to salvation. It is considered a diety in Buddhism.

Drum Bridge at Tsuru-ga-oka Hachiman-gū and turn left. Leave the grounds of the shrine and walk east along the main street (Route 204) that forms the T-intersection at the end of Wakamiya Oji. A 10-minute walk will bring you to a narrow street on the left—there's a bakery called Café Bergfeld on the corner that leads to the tomb, about 100 yards off the street to the north and up a flight of stone steps. ⌖ *Free* ☉ *Daily 9–4.*

(11) **Kamakura-gū** (Kamakura Shrine) is a Shintō shrine built after the Meiji Restoration of 1868 and dedicated to Prince Morinaga (1308–36), the first son of Emperor Go-Daigo. When Go-Daigo overthrew the Kamakura Shogunate and restored Japan to direct imperial rule, Morinaga—who had been in the priesthood—was appointed supreme commander of his father's forces. The prince lived in turbulent times and died young: when the Ashikaga clan in turn overthrew Go-Daigo's government, Morinaga was taken into exile, held prisoner in a cave behind the present site of Kamakura Shrine, and eventually beheaded. The **Treasure House** (Hōmotsu-den), on the northwest corner of the grounds, next to the shrine's administrative office, is of interest mainly for its collection of paintings depicting the life of Prince Morinaga. To reach Kamakura Shrine, walk from Yoritomo's tomb to Route 204, and turn left; at the next traffic light, a narrow street on the left leads off at an angle to the shrine, about five minutes' walk west. ✉ *154 Nikaidō* ☎ *0467/22–0318* ⌖ *Kamakura Shrine free, Treasure House ¥300* ☉ *Daily 9–4.*

(12) Visitors to Kamakura tend to overlook **Hōkoku-ji** (Hōkoku Temple) a lovely little Zen temple of the Rinzai sect that was built in 1334. Over the years it had fallen into disrepair and neglect, until an enterprising priest took over, cleaned up the gardens, and began promoting the temple for meditation sessions, calligraphy exhibitions, and tea ceremony. Behind the main hall are a thick grove of bamboo and a small tea pavilion—a restful oasis and a fine place to go for *matcha* (green tea). The temple is about 2 km (1 mi) east on Route 204 from the main entrance to Tsuru-ga-oka Hachiman-gū; turn right at the traffic light by the Hōkoku Temple Iriguchi bus stop and walk about three minutes south to the gate. ✉ *2–7–4 Jōmyō-ji* ☎ *0467/22–0762* ⌖ *Hōkoku Temple free, bamboo grove ¥200, tea ceremony ¥500* ☉ *Daily 9–4.*

(13) **Jōmyō-ji** (Jōmyo Temple) founded in 1188, is one of the Five Mountains Zen monasteries. It is nestled inside an immaculate garden that is particularly beautiful in spring, when the cherry trees bloom. Its only distinctive features are its green roof and the statues of Shaka Nyorai and Amida Nyorai, who represent truth and enlightenment, in the main hall. To reach it from Hōkoku-ji, cross the main street (Route 204) that brought you the mile or so from Tsuru-ga-oka Hachiman-gū, and take the first narrow street north. The monastery is about 100 yards from the corner. ⊠ 3–8–31 Jōmyō-ji ☎ 0467/22–2818 ⊒ Jōmyō Temple ¥100, tea ceremony ¥500 ⊗ Daily 9–4.

Hase

The single biggest attraction in Hase ("*ha-seh*") is the temple Kōtoku-in's **⓮ Great Buddha** (Daibutsu)—sharing the honors with Mt. Fuji, perhaps, as **Fodor$Choice** the quintessential picture-postcard image of Japan. The statue of the com-★ passionate Amida Buddha sits cross-legged in the temple courtyard, the drapery of his robes flowing in lines reminiscent of ancient Greece, his expression profoundly serene. The 37-foot bronze figure was cast in 1292, three centuries before Europeans reached Japan; the concept of the classical Greek lines in the Buddha's robe must have come over the Silk Route through China during the time of Alexander the Great. The casting was probably first conceived in 1180, by Minamoto no Yoritomo, who wanted a statue to rival the enormous Daibutsu in Nara. Until 1495 the Amida Buddha was housed in a wooden temple, which washed away in a great tidal wave. Since then the loving Buddha has stood exposed, facing the cold winters and hot summers, for more than five centuries.

■ TIP→ **It may seem sacrilegious to walk inside the Great Buddha, but for ¥20 you can enter the figure from a doorway in the right side and explore (until 4:15 PM) his stomach.** To reach Kōtoku-in and the Great Buddha, take the Enoden Line from the west side of JR Kamakura Station three stops to Hase. From the east exit, turn right and walk north about 10 minutes on the main street (Route 32). ⊠ 4–2–28 Hase, Hase ☎ 0467/22–0703 ⊒ ¥200 ⊗ Apr.–Sept., daily 7–6; Oct.–Mar., daily 7–5:30.

⓯ The only Kamakura temple facing the sea, **Hase-dera** is one of the most **Fodor$Choice** beautiful, and saddest, places of pilgrimage in the city. On a landing part-★ way up the stone steps that lead to the temple grounds are hundreds of small stone images of Jizō, one of the bodhisattvas in the Buddhist pantheon. Jizō is the savior of children, particularly the souls of the still-born, aborted, and miscarried; the mothers of these children dress the statues of Jizō in bright red bibs and leave them small offerings of food, heartbreakingly touching acts of prayer.

The **Kannon Hall** (Kannon-do) at Hase-dera enshrines the largest carved-wood statue in Japan: the votive figure of Jūichimen Kannon, the 11-headed goddess of mercy. Standing 30 feet tall, the goddess bears a crown of 10 smaller heads, symbolizing her ability to search out in all directions for those in need of her compassion. No one knows for certain when the figure was carved. According to the temple records, a monk named Tokudo Shōnin carved two images of the Jūichimen Kannon from a huge laurel tree in 721. One was consecrated to the Hase-dera in present-day Nara Prefecture; the other was thrown into the sea in order to go wherever the sea decided that there were souls in need, and that image washed up on shore near Kamakura. Much later, in 1342, Ashikaga

Take a Dip

THE SAGAMI BAY has some of the closest beaches to Tōkyō, and in the hot, humid summer months it seems as though the city's teeming millions pour onto these beaches in search of a vacant patch of rather dirty gray sand. Pass up this mob scene and press on instead to **Enoshima**. The island is only 4 km (2½ mi) around, with a hill in the middle. Partway up the hill is a shrine where the local fisherfolk prayed for a bountiful catch—before it became a tourist attraction. Once upon a time it was quite a hike up to the shrine; now there's a series of escalators, flanked by stalls selling souvenirs and snacks. The island has several cafés and restaurants, and on clear days some have spectacular views of Mt. Fuji and the Izu Peninsula. To reach the causeway from Enoshima Station to the island, walk south from the station for about 3 km (2 mi), keeping the Katase-gawa (Katase River) on your right. To return to Tōkyō from Enoshima, take a train to Shinjuku on the Odakyū Line. From the island walk back across the causeway and take the second bridge over the Katase-gawa. Within five minutes you'll come to Katase-Enoshima Station. Or you can retrace your steps to Kamakura and take the JR Yokosuka Line to Tōkyō Station.

Takauji—the first of the 15 Ashikaga shōguns who followed the Kamakura era—had the statue covered with gold leaf.

The **Amida Hall** of Hase-dera enshrines the image of a seated Amida Buddha, who presides over the Western Paradise of the Pure Land. Minamoto no Yoritomo ordered the creation of this statue when he reached the age of 42; popular Japanese belief, adopted from China, holds that your 42nd year is particularly unlucky. Yoritomo's act of piety earned him another 11 years—he was 53 when he was thrown by a horse and died of his injuries. The Buddha is popularly known as the *yakuyoke* (good-luck) Amida, and many visitors—especially students facing entrance exams—make a point of coming here to pray. To the left of the main halls is a small restaurant where you can buy good-luck candy and admire the view of Kamakura Beach and Sagami Bay. To reach Hase-dera from Hase Station, walk north about five minutes on the main street (Route 32) toward Kōtoku-in and the Great Buddha, and look for a signpost to the temple on a side street to the left. ⊠ *3–11–2 Hase, Hase* ☎ *0467/ 22–6300* 💰 *¥300* 🕙 *Mar.–Sept., daily 8–5:30; Oct.–Feb., daily 8–4:30.*

Ryūkō-ji & Enoshima

The Kamakura story would not be complete without the tale of Nichiren (1222–82), the monk who founded the only native Japanese sect of Buddhism and who is honored at **Ryūkō-ji** (Ryūkō Temple). Nichiren's rejection of both Zen and Jōdo (Pure Land) teachings brought him into conflict with the Kamakura Shogunate, and the Hōjō regents sent him into exile on the Izu Peninsula in 1261. Later allowed to return, he continued to preach his own interpretation of the Lotus Sutra—and to as-

2

sert the "blasphemy" of other Buddhist sects, a stance that finally persuaded the Hōjō regency, in 1271, to condemn him to death. The execution was to take place on a hill to the south of Hase. As the executioner swung his sword, legend has it that a lightning bolt struck the blade and snapped it in two. Taken aback, the executioner sat down to collect his wits, and a messenger was sent back to Kamakura to report the event. On his way he met another messenger, who was carrying a writ from the Hōjō regents commuting Nichiren's sentence to exile on the island of Sado-ga-shima.

Followers of Nichiren built Ryūkō Temple in 1337, on the hill where he was to be executed, marking his miraculous deliverance from the headsman. There are other Nichiren temples closer to Kamakura, but Ryūkō not only has the typical Nichiren-style main hall, with gold tassels hanging from its roof, but also a beautiful pagoda, built in 1904. To reach it, take the Enoden Line west from Hase to Enoshima—a short, scenic ride that cuts through the hills surrounding Kamakura to the shore. From Enoshima Station walk about 100 yards east, keeping the train tracks on your right, and you'll come to the temple. ☒ *3–13–37 Katase, Fujisawa* 🖀 *0466/25–7357* 🖃 *Free* ⊘ *Daily 6–4.*

Where to Eat

Kita-Kamakura

★ **$$$ $$$$** ✕ **Hachinoki Kita-Kamakura-ten.** Traditional *shōjin ryori* (the vegetarian cuisine of Zen monasteries) is served in this old Japanese house on the Kamakura Kaidō (Route 21) near the entrance to Jōchi Temple. There's some table service, but most seating is in tatami rooms, with beautiful antique wood furnishings. Allow plenty of time; this is not a meal to be hurried through. Meals, which are prix-fixe only, are served Tuesday–Friday 11–2:30, weekends 11–3. ☒ *7 Yama-no-uchi, Kita-Kamakura* 🖀 *0467/23–3722* 🖃 *DC, V* ⊘ *Closed Mon. Open weekends only in July and Aug.*

Kamakura

$$$ ✕ **Ginza Isomura Kamakuraten.** This branch of the family-style *kushiage* (freshly grilled skewers) restaurant overlooks Komachi-dōri, Kamakura's main shopping street. A place by the window is perfect for people-watching during lunchtime. Since it seats only 21, the place gets crowded during dinnertime, but if you're willing to wait you'll be rewarded with meat, fish, and seasonal vegetable kushiage that's made in front of you. ☒ *Komachiichibankan Bldg., 2F, 2–10–1 Komachi, Kita-Kamakura* 🖀 *0467/22–3792* 🖃 *AE, DC, MC, V* ⊘ *Closed Wed.*

$–$$$ ✕ **T-Side.** Authentic, inexpensive Indian fare and a second-floor location that looks down upon Kamakura's main shopping street, make this restaurant a popular choice for lunch and dinner. Curries are done well, the various *thali* (sets) are a good value, and the kitchen also serves some Nepalese dishes. T-Side is at the very top of Komachi-dōri on the left as you enter from Kamakura Station. ☒ *2–11–11 Komachi, Kita-Kamakura* 🖀 *0467/24–9572* ⊘ *Daily 10–10* 🖃 *V.*

¢ ✕ **Kaisen Misaki-kō.** This *kaiten-zushi* (sushi on a conveyor belt) restaurant on Komachi-dōri serves eye-poppingly large fish portions that hang over the edge of their plates. All the standard sushi creations, including tuna, shrimp, and egg, are prepared. Prices range from ¥170 to ¥500. The restaurant is on the right side of the road just as you enter Komachi-dōri from the east exit of Kamakura Station. ⊠ *1–7–1 Komachi, Kita-Kamakura* ☎ *0467/22–6228* ▭ *No credit cards.*

Hase

$$$–$$$$ ✕ **Kaseiro.** This establishment, in an old Japanese house, serves the best Chinese food in the city. The dining-room windows look out on a small, restful garden. Make sure you plan for a stop here on your way to or from the Great Buddha at Kōtoku-in. ⊠ *3–1–14 Hase, Hase* ☎ *0467/ 22–0280* ⊙ *Daily 11–7:30* ▭ *AE, DC, MC, V.*

Kamakura Essentials

BY BUS
A bus from Kamakura Station (Sign 5) travels to most of the temples and shrines in the downtown Kamakura area.

BY TRAIN
Traveling by train is by far the best way to get to Kamakura. Trains run from Tōkyō Station (and Shimbashi Station) every 10–15 minutes during the day. The trip takes 56 minutes to Kita-Kamakura and one hour to Kamakura. Take the JR Yokosuka Line from Track 1 downstairs in Tōkyō Station (Track 1 upstairs is on a different line and does not go to Kamakura). The cost is ¥780 to Kita-Kamakura, ¥890 to Kamakura (or use your JR Pass).

Local train service connects Kita-Kamakura, Kamakura, Hase, and Enoshima.

To return to Tōkyō from Enoshima, take a train to Shinjuku on the Odakyū Line. There are 11 express trains daily from here on weekdays, between 8:38 AM and 8:45 PM; nine trains daily on weekends and national holidays, between 8:39 AM and 8:46 PM; and more in summer. The express takes about 70 minutes and costs ¥1,220. Or you can retrace your steps to Kamakura and take the JR Yokosuka Line to Tōkyō Station. 🚆 **Japan Railways** ☎ 03/3423-0111 ⊕ www.japanrail.com.

TOURS
Bus companies in Kamakura do not conduct guided English tours. You can, however, take one of the Japanese tours, which depart from Kamakura Station eight times daily, starting at 9 AM; the last tour leaves at 1 PM. Purchase tickets at the bus office to the right of the station. There are two itineraries, each lasting a little less than three hours; tickets, depending on what the tour covers, are ¥2,250 and ¥3,390. Take John Carroll's book *Trails of Two Cities: A Walker's Guide to Yokohama, Kamakura and Vicinity* (Kodansha International, 1994) with you, and you'll have more information at your fingertips than any of your fellow passengers.

■ **TIP→** On the weekend the Kanagawa Student Guide Federation offers a free guide service. Students show you the city in exchange for the chance to practice their English. Arrangements must be made in advance through the Japan National Tourist Organization in Tōkyō. You'll need to be at Kamakura Station between 10 AM and noon.

Sunrise Tours runs daily trips from Tōkyō to Kamakura; these tours are often combined with trips to Hakone. You can book through, and arrange to be picked up at, any of the major hotels. Before you do, however, be certain that the tour covers everything in Kamakura that you want to see, as many include little more than a passing view of the Great Buddha in Hase.

🗹 **Japan National Tourist Organization** ✉ Tōkyō Kōtsū Kaikan, 10F, 2-10-1 Yūraku-chō, Chiyoda-ku, Tōkyō ☎ 03/3201-3331 ⊕ www.jnto.go.jp Ⓜ JR Yamanote Line (Higashi-guchi/East Exit) and Yūraku-chō subway line (Exit A-8), Yūraku-chō Station. **Kanagawa Student Guide Federation** ☎ 03/3201-3331. **Sunrise Tours** ☎ 03/5796-5454 ⊕ www.jtb.co.jp/sunrisetour.

VISITOR INFORMATION

Both Kamakura and Enoshima have their own tourist associations, although it can be problematic getting help in English over the phone. Your best bet is the Kamakura Station Tourist Information Center, which has a useful collection of brochures and maps. And since Kamakura is in Kanagawa Prefecture, visitors heading here from Yokohama can pre-plan their excursion at the Kanagawa Prefectural Tourist Association office in the Silk Center, on the Yamashita Park promenade.

🗹 **Enoshima Tourist Association** ☎ 0466/37-4141. **Kamakura Station Tourist Information Center** ☎ 0467/22-3350. **Kamakura Tourist Association** ☎ 0467/23-3050. **Kanagawa Prefectural Tourist Association** ☎ 045/681-0007 ⊕ www.kanagawa-kankou.or.jp.

YOKOHAMA

In 1853 a fleet of four American warships under Commodore Matthew Perry sailed into the bay of Tōkyō (then Edo) and presented the reluctant Japanese with the U.S. government demands to open diplomatic and commercial relations. The following year Perry returned and first set foot on Japanese soil at Yokohama—then a small fishing village on the mudflats of the bay, some 20 km (12½ mi) southwest of Tōkyō.

Two years later New York businessman Townsend Harris became America's first diplomatic representative to Japan. In 1858 he was finally able to negotiate a commercial treaty between the two countries; part of the deal designated four locations—one of them Yokohama—as treaty ports. With the agreement signed, Harris lost no time in setting up his residence in Hangaku-ji, in nearby Kanagawa, another of the designated ports. The presence of foreigners—perceived as unclean barbarians—offended the Japanese elite. Die hard elements of the warrior class, moreover, were willing to give their lives to rid the country of intruders. In 1859 the shogunate created a special settlement in Yokohama for the growing community of merchants, traders, missionaries, and other assorted adventurers drawn to this exotic new land of opportunity.

The foreigners (predominantly Chinese and British, plus a few French, Americans, and Dutch) were confined here to a guarded compound about

5 square km (2 square mi)—placed, in effect, in isolation—but not for long. Within a few short years the shogunal government collapsed, and Japan began to modernize. Western ideas were welcomed, as were Western goods, and the little treaty port became Japan's principal gateway to the outside world. In 1872 Japan's first railway was built, linking Yokohama and Tōkyō. In 1889 Yokohama became a city; by then the population had grown to some 120,000. As the city prospered, so did the international community and by the early 1900s Yokohama was the busiest and most modern center of international trade in all of east Asia.

Then Yokohama came tumbling down. On September 1, 1923, the Great Kantō Earthquake devastated the city. The ensuing fires destroyed some 60,000 homes and took more than 40,000 lives. During the six years it took to rebuild the city, many foreign businesses took up quarters elsewhere, primarily in Kōbe and Ōsaka, and did not return.

Over the next 20 years Yokohama grew as an industrial center—until May 29, 1945, when in a span of four hours, some 500 American B-29 bombers leveled nearly half the city and left more than half a million people homeless. When the war ended, what remained became—in effect—the center of the Allied occupation. General Douglas MacArthur set up headquarters here, briefly, before moving to Tōkyō; the entire port facility and about a quarter of the city remained in the hands of the U.S. military throughout the 1950s.

By the 1970s Yokohama was once more rising from the debris; in 1978 it surpassed Ōsaka as the nation's second-largest city, and the population is now inching up to the 3.5 million mark. Yokohama has extended its urban sprawl north to Tōkyō and south to Kamakura—in the process creating a whole new subcenter around the Shinkansen station at Shin-Yokohama. Modern Yokohama thrives instead in its industrial, commercial, and service sectors—and a large percentage of its people commute to work in Tōkyō. Is Yokohama worth a visit? Not, one could argue, at the expense of Nikkō or Kamakura. But the waterfront is fun and the museums are excellent.

Getting Around

Yokohama's central area is very negotiable and much of what the city has to offer centers on the waterfront—in this case, on the west side of Tōkyō Bay. The downtown area is called Kannai (literally, "within the checkpoint"); the international community was originally confined here by the shogunate. The center of interest has expanded to include the waterfront and Ishikawa-chō, to the south.

Think of Kannai as two adjacent areas. One is the old district, bounded by Basha-michi on the northwest and Nihon-ōdori on the southeast, the Keihin Tōhoku Line tracks on the southwest, and the waterfront on the northeast. This area contains the business offices of modern Yokohama. The other area extends southeast from Nihon-ōdori to the Moto-machi shopping street and the International Cemetery, bordered by Yamashita Kōen and the waterfront to the northeast; in the center is Chinatown, with Ishikawa-chō Station to the southwest. This is the most interesting part of town for tourists.

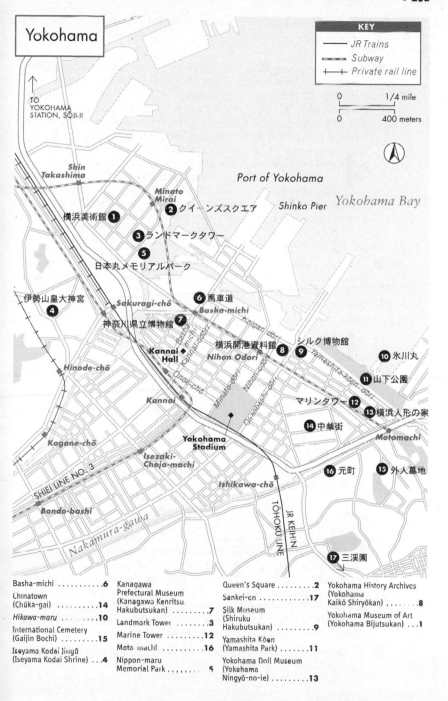

Yokohama

0 — 1/4 mile
0 — 400 meters

TO
YOKOHAMA
STATION, SŌJI-II

Shin
Takashima

Port of Yokohama

Yokohama Bay

横浜美術館 ❶

Minato
Mirai ❷ クイーンズスクエア

Shinko Pier

ランドマークタワー ❸

日本丸メモリアルパーク ❺

伊勢山皇大神宮
❹

Sakuragi-chō

馬車道 ❻
Basha-michi

神奈川県立博物館 ❼

Basha-michi
Kannai-dōri

Kannai ◆
Hall

横浜開港資料館 ❽ ❾ シルク博物館
Nihon Odori

氷川丸 ❿

Hinode-chō

Onoe-chō

Yamashita-kōen dōri

山下公園 ⓫

Kannai

Minato-dōri
Nihon-dōri
Ōsanbashi-dōri

マリンタワー ⓬

横浜人形の家 ⓭

Kogane-chō

**Yokohama
Stadium**

中華街 ⓮

Motomachi

*Isezaki-
Chōja-machi*

SHIEI LINE NO. 3

元町 ⓰

外人墓地 ⓯

Ishikawa-chō

Bando-bashi

Nakamura-gawa

JR KEIHIN

TŌHOKU LINE

三渓園 ⓱

Numbers in the text correspond to the Yokohama map.

What to See

❻ Running southwest from Shinko Pier to Kannai is **Basha-michi,** which literally translates into "Horse-Carriage Street." The street was so named in the 19th century, when it was widened to accommodate the horse-drawn carriages of the city's new European residents. This red-brick thoroughfare and the streets parallel to it have been restored to evoke that past, with faux-antique telephone booths and imitation gas lamps. Here you'll find some of the most elegant coffee shops, patisseries, and boutiques in town. On the block northeast of Kannai Station, as you walk toward the waterfront, is **Kannai Hall** (look for the red-orange abstract sculpture in front), a handsome venue for chamber music, Nō, classical recitals, and occasional performances by such groups as the Peking Opera. If you're planning to stay late in Yokohama, you might want to check out the listings. ⊠ *Naka-ku* Ⓜ *JR Line, Kannai Station; Minato Mirai Line, Bashamichi Station.*

★ **⓮** Yokohama's **Chinatown** (Chūka-gai) is the largest Chinese settlement in Japan—and easily the city's most popular tourist attraction, drawing more than 18 million visitors a year. Its narrow streets and alleys are lined with some 350 shops selling foodstuffs, herbal medicines, cookware, toys and ornaments, and clothing and accessories. If China exports it, you'll find it here. Wonderful exotic aromas waft from the spice shops. Even better aromas drift from the quarter's 160-odd restaurants, which serve every major style of Chinese cuisine: this is the best place for lunch in Yokohama. Chinatown is a 10-minute walk southeast of Kannai Station. When you get to Yokohama Stadium, turn left and cut through the municipal park to the top of Nihon-ōdori. Then take a right, and you'll enter Chinatown through the Gembu-mon (North Gate), which leads to the dazzling red-and-gold, 50-foot-high Zenrin-mon (Good Neighbor Gate). ⊠ *Naka-ku* Ⓜ *JR Line, Ishikawa-cho Station; Minato Mirai Line, Motomachi-Chukagai Station.*

❿ Moored on the waterfront, more or less in the middle of Yamashita Park, is the *Hikawa-maru.* It was built in 1929 by Yokohama Dock Co. and was launched on September 30, 1929. For 31 years, she shuttled passengers between Yokohama and Seattle, Washington, making a total of 238 trips. A tour of the ship evokes the time when Yokohama was a great port of call for the transpacific liners. The *Hikawa-maru* has a French restaurant, and in summer there's a beer garden on the upper deck. ⊠ *Naka-ku* ☎ *045/641–4361* 🎟 *¥800; multiple-entry ticket to Hikawa-maru and Marine Tower ¥1,300; multiple-entry ticket to Hikawa-maru, Marine Tower, and Yokohama Doll Museum ¥1,550* ☉ *Apr.–June, daily 9:30–7; July and Aug., daily 9:30–7:30; Sept. and Oct., daily 9:30–7; Nov.–Mar., daily 9:30–6:30* Ⓜ *JR Line, Ishikawa-chō Station; Minato Mirai Line, Motomachi-Chukagai Station.*

⓯ The **International Cemetery** (Gaijin Bochi) is a Yokohama landmark. It was established in 1854 with a grant of land from the shogunate; the first foreigners to be buried here were Russian sailors assassinated by xenophobes in the early days of the settlement. Most of the 4,500 graves on this hillside are English and American, and about 120 are of the Japanese wives of foreigners; the inscriptions on the crosses and headstones attest to some 40 different nationalities whose citizens lived and died in Yokohama. From Moto-machi Plaza, it's a short walk to the north end of the cemetery. ⊠ *Naka-ku* Ⓜ *JR Line, Ishikawa-chō Station; Minato Mirai Line, Motomachi-Chukagai Station.*

❹ **Iseyama Kodai Jingū** (Iseyama Kodai Shrine), a branch of the nation's revered Grand Shrines of Ise, is the most important Shintō shrine in Yokohama—but it's only worth a visit if you've seen most everything else in town. The shrine is a 10-minute walk west of Sakuragi-chō Station. ⊠ *64 Miyazaki-chō, Nishi-ku* ☎ *045/241–1122* ☞ *Free* ☉ *Daily 9–7* Ⓜ *JR Line, Sakuragi-chō Station; Minato Mirai Line, Minato Mirai Station.*

❼ One of the few buildings in Yokohama to have survived both the Great Kantō Earthquake of 1923 and World War II is the 1904 **Kanagawa Prefectural Museum** (Kanagawa Kenritsu Hakubutsukan) a few blocks north of Kannai Station (use Exit 8) on Basha-michi. Most exhibits here have no explanations in English, but the galleries on the third floor showcase some remarkable medieval wooden sculptures (including one of the first Kamakura shōgun, Minamoto no Yoritomo), hanging scrolls, portraits, and armor. The exhibits of prehistory and of Yokohama in the early modern period are of much less interest. ⊠ *5–60 Minami Naka-dōri, Naka-ku* ☎ *045/201–0926* ☞ *¥300, special exhibits ¥800* ☉ *Tues.–Sun. 9–4:30; closed last Tues. of month and day after a national holiday* Ⓜ *JR Line, Sakuragi-cho, Kannai Stations.*

🐾❸ The 70-story **Landmark Tower**, in Yokohama's Minato Mirai, is Japan's tallest building. The 69th floor observation deck has a spectacular view of the city, especially at night; the high-speed elevator carries you up at an ear-popping 45 kph (28 mph). The Yokohama Royal Park Hotel occupies the top 20 stories of the building. (☉ Daily 10–9, Sat. until 10 ☉ Jan. 1 and 3rd Tues. in Feb.) On the first level of the Landmark Tower is the **Mitsubishi Minato Mirai Industrial Museum**, with rocket engines, power plants, a submarine, various gadgets, and displays that simulate piloting helicopters—great fun for kids.

The Landmark Tower complex's **Dockyard Garden**, built in 1896, is a restored dry dock with stepped sides of massive stone blocks. The long, narrow floor of the dock, with its water cascade at one end, makes a wonderful year-round open air venue for concerts and other events; in summer (July–mid-August), the beer garden installed here is a perfect refuge from the heat. ⊠ *3–3–1 Minato Mirai, Nishi-ku* ☎ *045/224–9031* ☞ *Elevator to observation deck ¥1,000, museum ¥500* ☉ *Museum Tues.–Sun. 10–5* Ⓜ *JR Line, Sakuragi-chō Station; Minato Mirai Line, Minato Mirai Station.*

⓬ For an older generation of Yokohama residents, the 348-foot-high decagonal **Marine Tower**, which opened in 1961, was the city's landmark structure; civic pride prevented them from admitting that it falls lamentably short of an architectural masterpiece. The tower has a navigational beacon at the 338-foot level and purports to be the tallest lighthouse in the world. At the 328-foot level, an observation gallery provides 360-degree views of the harbor and the city, and on clear days in autumn or winter, you can often see Mt. Fuji in the distance. Marine Tower is in the middle of the second block northwest from the end of Yamashita Park, on the left side of the promenade. ⊠ *15 Yamashita-chō, Naka-ku* ☎ *045/ 641–7838* 🏷 *¥700; multiple-entry ticket to Marine Tower and Hikawa-maru ¥1,300; multiple-entry ticket to Marine Tower, Hikawa-maru, and Yokohama Doll Museum ¥1,550* ⏲ *Jan. and Feb., daily 9–7; Mar.–May and Nov. and Dec., daily 9:30–9; June, July, Sept. and Oct., daily 9:30–9:30; Aug., daily 9:30–10* Ⓜ *JR Line, Ishikawa-chō Station; Minato Mirai Line, Motomachi-Chukagai Station.*

⑯ Moto-machi, the street that follows the course of the Nakamura-gawa (Nakamura River) to the harbor, is where the Japanese set up shop 100 years ago to serve the foreigners living in Kannai. The street is now lined with smart boutiques and jewelry stores that cater to fashionable young Japanese consumers. ⊠ *Naka-ku* Ⓜ *JR Line, Ishikawa-chō Station; Minato Mirai Line, Motomachi-Chukagai Station.*

⑤ Nippon-maru Memorial Park is where the Ō-oka-gawa (Ō-oka River) flows into the bay. The centerpiece of the park is the *Nippon-maru*, a full-rigged three-masted ship popularly called the "Swan of the Pacific." Built in 1930, it served as a training vessel. The Nippon-maru is now retired, but it's open for guided tours. Adjacent to the ship is the **Yokohama Maritime Museum,** a two-story collection of ship models, displays, and archival materials that celebrate the achievements of the Port of Yokohama from its earliest days to the present. ⊠ *2–1–1 Minato Mirai, Nishi-ku* ☎ *045/221–0280* 🏷 *Ship and museum ¥600* ⏲ *Mar.–June, Sept., and Oct., daily 10–5; July and Aug., daily 10–6:30; Nov.–Feb., daily 10–4:30; closed Mon. (if Mon. is a holiday, closed Tues.). Closed day after a national holiday* Ⓜ *JR Line, Sakuragi-chō Station; Minato Mirai Line, Minato Mirai Station.*

The courtyard on the northeast side of the **Landmark Tower** connects
② to **Queen's Square,** a huge atrium-style vertical mall with dozens of shops (mainly for clothing and accessories) and restaurants. The complex also houses the Pan Pacific Hotel Yokohama and Yokohama Minato Mirai Hall, the city's major venue for classical music. ⊠ *2–3–1 Minato-Mirai, Nishi-ku* ☎ *045/222–5015* ⏲ *Shopping 11–8, restaurants 11–11* Ⓜ *JR Line, Sakuragi-chō Station; Minato Mirai Line, Minato Mirai Station* ⊕ *www.qsy.co.jp.*

★ **⑰** Opened to the public in 1906, **Sankei-en** was once the estate and gardens of Hara Tomitaro (1868–1939), one of Yokohama's wealthiest men, who made his money as a silk merchant before becoming a patron of the arts. On the extensive grounds of the estate he created is a kind of open-air museum of traditional Japanese architecture, some of which was brought

BLOOMIN' SEASON

Walking through Sankei-en is especially delightful in spring, when the flowering trees are at their best: plum blossoms in February and cherry blossoms in early April. In June come the irises, followed by the water lilies. In autumn the trees come back into their own with tinted golden leaves.

2

here from Kamakura and the western part of the country. Especially note-worthy is **Rinshun-kaku,** a villa built for the Tokugawa clan in 1649. There's also a tea pavilion, Chōshū-kaku, built by the third Tokugawa shōgun, Iemitsu. Other buildings include a small temple transported from Kyōto's famed Daitoku-ji and a farmhouse from the Gifu district in the Japan Alps (around Takayama). To reach Sankei-en, take the JR Kei-hin Tōhoku Line to Negishi Station and a local bus (number 54, 58, or 99) bound for Honmoku; it's a 10-minute trip to the garden. Or, go to Yokohama Station (East Exit) and take the bus (number 8 or 125) to Honmoku Sankei-en Mae. It will take about 35 minutes. ⊠ *58–1 Honmoku San-no-tani, Naka-ku* ☎ *045/621–0635* ⚏ *Inner garden ¥300, outer garden ¥300, farmhouse ¥100* ⊙ *Inner garden daily 9–4, outer garden daily 9–4:30.*

❾ The **Silk Museum** (Shiruku Hakubutsukan) pays tribute to the period at the turn of the 20th century when Japan's silk exports were shipped out of Yokohama. The museum houses an extensive collection of silk fabrics and an informative exhibit on the silk-making process. People on staff are very happy to answer questions. In the same building, on the first floor, are the main offices of the Yokohama International Tourist Association and the Kanagawa Prefectural Tourist Association. The museum is at the northwestern end of the Yamashita Park promenade, on the second floor of the Silk Center Building. ⊠ *1 Yamashita-chō, Naka-ku* ☎ *045/641–0841* ⚏ *¥500* ⊙ *Tues.–Sun. 9–4* Ⓜ *Minato Mirai Line, Nihon Ōdori Station, Exit 3.*

⓫ **Yamashita Kōen** (Yamashita Park) is perhaps the only positive legacy of the Great Kantō Earthquake of 1923. The debris of the warehouses and other buildings that once stood here were swept away, and the area was made into a 17-acre oasis of green along the waterfront. The fountain, representing the Guardian of the Water, was presented to Yokohama by San Diego, California, one of its sister cities. From Harbor View Park, walk northwest through neighboring French Hill Park and cross the walkway over Moto-machi. Turn right on the other side and walk one block down toward the bay to Yamashita-Kōen-dōri, the promenade along the park. ⊠ *Naka-ku* Ⓜ *JR Line, Ishikawa-chō Station; Minato Mirai Line, Motomachi-Chukagai Station.*

⓭ The **Yokohama Doll Museum** (Yokohama Ningyō-no-ie) houses a collection of some 4,000 dolls from all over the world. In Japanese tradition, dolls are less to play with than to display—either in religious folk customs or as the embodiment of some spiritual quality. Japanese visitors to this museum never seem to outgrow their affection for the Western dolls, to which they tend to assign the role of timeless "ambassadors of good will" from other cultures. The museum is worth a quick visit, with or without a child in tow. It's just across from the southeast end of Yamashita Park, on the left side of the promenade. ⊠ *18 Yamashita-chō, Naka-ku* ☎ *045/671–9361* ⚏ *¥300; multiple-entry ticket to museum, Marine Tower, and Hikawa-maru, ¥1,550* ⊙ *Daily 10–6; closed 3rd Mon. of month* Ⓜ *JR Line, Ishikawa-chō Station; Minato Mirai Line, Motomachi-Chukagai Station.*

8 Within the **Yokohama History Archives** (Yokohama Kaikō Shiryōkan), housed in what was once the British Consulate, are some 140,000 items recording the history of Yokohama since the opening of the port to international trade in the mid-19th century. Across the street is a monument to the U.S.–Japanese Friendship Treaty. To get here from the Silk Center Building, at the end of the Yamashita Park promenade, walk west to the corner of Nihon-ōdori; the archives are on the left. ☒ *3 Nihon-ōdori, Naka-ku* ☎ *045/201–2100* ☞ *¥200* ☉ *Tues.–Sun. 9:30–4:30* Ⓜ *Minato Mirai Line, Nihon O-dori Station.*

1 Minato Mirai 21 is the site of the **Yokohama Museum of Art** (Yokohama Bijutsukan), designed by Kenzō Tange, has 5,000 works in the permanent collection include paintings by both Western and Japanese artists, including Cézanne, Picasso, Braque, Klee, Kandinsky, Kishida Ryūsei, and Yokoyama Taikan. ☒ *3–4–1 Minato Mirai, Nishi-ku* ☎ *045/221–0300* ☞ *¥500* ☉ *Mon.–Wed. and weekends 10–5:30, Fri. 10–7:30 (last entry); closed Thurs. and day after a national holiday* Ⓜ *JR Line, Sakuragi-chō Station; Minato Mirai Line, Minato Mirai Station.*

OFF THE BEATEN PATH

SŌJI-JI – One of the two major centers of the Sōtō sect of Zen Buddhism, Sōji-ji, in Yokohama's Tsurumi ward, was founded in 1321. The center was moved here from Ishikawa, on the Noto Peninsula, after a fire in the 19th century. The Yokohama Sōji-ji is one of the largest and busiest Buddhist institutions in Japan, with more than 200 monks and novices in residence. Open to visitors are the **Buddha Hall,** the **Main Hall,** and the **Treasure House.** To get to Sōji-ji, take the JR Keihin Tōhoku Line two stops from Sakuragi-chō to Tsurumi. From the station walk five minutes south (back toward Yokohama), passing Tsurumi University on your right. Look out for the stone lanterns that mark the entrance to the temple complex. ☒ *2–1–1 Tsurumi, Tsurumi-ku* ☎ *045/581–6021* ☞ *¥300* ☉ *Daily dawn–dusk; Treasure House Tues.–Sun. 10–4.*

Where to Eat

★ **$$$$** ✕ **Kaseiro.** Chinese food can be hit or miss in Japan but not at Kaseiro. This elegant restaurant, with red carpets and gold-tone walls, is the best of its kind in the city, serving authentic Beijing cuisine, including Peking Duck and shark-fin soup. Both the owner and chef are from Beijing, and this restaurant is a well-known favorite among locals and travelers alike. ☒ *186 Yamashita-chō, Chinatown, Naka-ku* ☎ *045/681–2918* ⌂ *Jacket and tie* ☐ *AE, DC, V.*

$$$$ ✕ **Motomachi Bairin.** The area of Motomachi is known as the wealthy, posh part of Yokohama; restaurants here tend to be exclusive and expensive, though the service and quality justify the price. This restaurant is an old-style Japanese house complete with a Japanese garden and five private tatami rooms. The ¥10,000, 27-course banquet includes some traditional Japanese delicacies such as sashimi, shiitake mushrooms and chicken in white sauce, deep-fried burdock, and broiled sea bream. ☒ *1–55 Motomachi Naka-ku* ☎ *045/662–2215* ☐ *No credit cards* ☉ *Closed Mon.*

$$$$ ✕ **Serina Romanchaya.** The hallmarks of this restaurant are *ishiyaki* steak, which is grilled on a hot stone, and shabu-shabu—thin slices of beef cooked in boiling water at your table and dipped in one of several sauces; choose from sesame, vinegar, or soy. Fresh vegetables, noodles, and tofu are also dipped into the seasoned broth for a filling, yet healthful meal. ✉ *Shin-Kannai Bldg., B1, 4–45–1 Sumiyoshi-chō, Naka-ku* ☎ *045/681-2727* 🖃 *AE, DC, MC, V.*

★ **$$$–$$$$** ✕ **Aichiya.** One of the specialties at this seafood restaurant is fugu (blowfish). This delicacy, which is only served in winter, must be treated with expert care, because the organs contain a deadly toxin that must be removed before being consumed. The crabs are also a treat. ✉ *7–156 Isezaki-chō, Naka-ku* ☎ *045/251–4163* 🖃 *No credit cards* 🕑 *Closed Mon. No lunch.*

$$–$$$$ ✕ **Roma Statione.** Opened more than 40 years ago, Roma Statione, between Chinatown and Yamashita Park, remains a popular venue for Italian food. The owner, whose father studied cooking in Italy before returning home to open this spot, is also the head chef and has continued using the original recipes. The house specialty is seafood: the spaghetti *vongole* (with clam sauce) is particularly good, as is the spaghetti pescatora and the seafood pizza. An added bonus is the impressive selection of Italian wines. ✉ *26 Yamashita-chō, Naka-ku* ☎ *045/681–1818* 🖃 *No credit cards* Ⓜ *Motomachi-Chukagai station, Exit 1. Minato Mirai line.*

$$ ✕ **Chano-ma.** This stylish eatery serves modern Japanese cuisine. There are bedlike seats that you can lounge on while eating and a house DJ spins tunes during dinner. While you're there, make sure you try the miso sirloin steak or grilled scallops with tasty citron sauce drizzled on top, served with a salad. It gets crowded here on the weekends. At lunchtime you can take advantage of the ¥1,000 set lunch special. ✉ *Red Brick Warehouse Bldg. 2, 3F, 1–1–2 Shinkou, Naka-ku* ☎ *045/650–8228* 🖃 *AE, DC, MC, V* Ⓜ *Bashamichi station, Minato Mirai line. Sakuragi-cho, Kannai stations, JR Negishi line.*

🕲 **$$** ✕ **Yokohama Cheese Cafe.** This is a cozy and inviting casual Italian restaurant, whose interior looks like an Italian country home. There are candles on the tables and an open kitchen where diners can watch the cooks making pizza. On the menu: 18 kinds of Napoli-style wood-fire–baked pizzas, 20 kinds of pastas, fondue and other dishes that include—you guessed it—cheese. The set course menus are reasonable, filling, and recommended. ✉ *2–1–10 Kitasaiwai, Nisi-ku* ☎ *045/290–5656* 🖃 *DC, MC, V* Ⓜ *JR Yokohama station.*

Yokohama Essentials

AIRPORTS & AIRPORT TRANSFERS

From Narita Airport, a direct limousine-bus service departs once or twice an hour between 6:45 AM and 10:20 PM for Yokohama City Air Terminal (YCAT). The fare is ¥3,500. YCAT is a five-minute taxi ride from Yokohama Station. JR Narita Express trains going on from Tōkyō to Yokohama leave the airport every hour from 8:13 AM to 1:13 PM and 2:43 PM to 9:43 PM. The fare is ¥4,180 (¥6,730 for the first-class Green Car coaches).

The Airport Limousine Information Desk phone number provides information in English daily 9–6; you can also get timetables on its Web site. For information in English on Narita Express trains, call the JR Hi-gashi-Nihon Info Line, available daily 10–6.

🔋 **Airport Limousine Information Desk** ☎ 03/3665-7220 ⊕ www.limousinebus.co.jp. **JR Higashi-Nihon Info Line** ☎ 03/3423-0111.

BY BUS

Most of the things you'll want to see in Yokohama are within easy walking distance of a JR or subway station, but exploring by bus is a viable alternative. Buses are the best way to get to Sankei-en. The city map available in the visitor centers in Yokohama has most major bus routes, and the important stops on the tourist routes are announced in English. The fixed fare is ¥210. One-day passes are available for ¥600. Contact the Sightseeing Information Office at Yokohama Station (JR East exit) for more information and ticket purchases. ☎ 045/465-2077.

BY SUBWAY

One subway line connects Azamino, Shin-Yokohama, Yokohama, Totsuka, and Shōnandai. The basic fare is ¥200. One-day passes are available for ¥740. The Minato Mirai Line, a spur of the Tōkyū Tōyoko Line, runs from Yokohama Station to all the major points of interest, including Minato Mirai, Chinatown, Yamashita Park, Moto-machi, and Basha-michi. The fare is ¥180–¥200, and one-day unlimited-ride passes are available for ¥450.

BY TAXI

There are taxi stands at all the train stations. The basic fare is ¥660 for the first 2 km (1 mi), then ¥80 for every additional 350 meters (⅕ mi). Traffic is heavy in downtown Yokohama, however, and you will often find it faster to walk.

BY TRAIN

JR trains from Tōkyō Station leave approximately every 10 minutes. Take the Yokosuka, the Tōkaidō, or Keihin Tōhoku Line to Yokohama Station (the Yokosuka and Tōkaidō lines take 30 minutes; the Keihin Tōhoku Line takes 40 minutes and costs ¥450). From there the Keihin Tōhoku Line (Platform 3) goes on to Kannai and Ishikawa-chō, Yokohama's business and downtown areas. If you're going directly to downtown Yokohama from Tōkyō, the blue commuter trains of the Keihin Tōhoku Line are best.

The private Tōkyū Tōyoko Line, which runs from Shibuya Station in Tōkyō directly to Yokohama Station, is a good alternative if you leave from the western part of Tōkyō. ■ TIP➔ **The term "private" means that the train does not belong to JR and is not a subway line. If you have a JR pass you'll have to buy a separate ticket.** Depending on which Tōkyū Tōyoko Line you catch—the Limited Express, Semi Express, or Local—the trip takes between 25 and 44 minutes and costs ¥260.

Yokohama Station links all the train lines and connects them with the city's subway and bus services. Kannai and Ishikawa-chō are the two downtown stations, both on the Keihin Tōhoku Line; trains leave Yokohama Station every two to five minutes from Platform 3. From Sakuragi-chō, Kannai, or Ishikawa-chō, most of Yokohama's points of interest are within easy walking distance; the one notable exception is Sankei-en, which you reach via the JR Keihin Tōhoku Line to Negishi Station and then a local bus.

2

EMERGENCIES
The Yokohama Police station has a Foreign Assistance Department.
🚹 **Ambulance or Fire** ☎ 119. **Police** ☎ 110. **Washinzaka Hospital** ✉ 169 Yamate-chō, Naka-ku ☎ 045/623-7688. **Yokohama Police station** ✉ 2-4 Kaigan-dori, Naka-ku ☎ 045/623-0110.

ENGLISH-LANGUAGE MEDIA
BOOKS Yūrindō has a good selection of popular paperbacks and books on Japan in English. The Minato-Mirai branch is open daily 11–8; the store on Isezaki-chō opens an hour earlier.
🚹 **Yūrindō** ✉ Landmark Plaza 5F, 3-3-1 Minato-Mirai, Nishi-ku ☎ 045/222-5500 ✉ 1-4-1 Isezaki-chō, Naka-ku ☎ 045/261-1231.

TOURS
The sightseeing boat *Marine Shuttle* makes 40-, 60-, and 90-minute tours of the harbor and bay for ¥900, ¥1,400, and ¥2,000, respectively. Boarding is at the pier at Yamashita Park. Boats depart roughly every hour between 10:20 AM and 6:30 PM. Another boat, the *Marine Rouge,* runs 90-minute tours departing from the pier at 11, 1:30, and 4, and a special two-hour evening tour at 7 (¥2,500).
🚹 *Marine Shuttle* ☎ 045/671-7719. Port Service reservation center.

VISITOR INFORMATION
The Yokohama International Tourist Association arranges visits to the homes of English-speaking Japanese families. These usually last a few hours and are designed to give *gaijin* (foreigners) a glimpse into the Japanese way of life.

The Yokohama Tourist Office, in the central passageway of Yokohama Station, is open daily 9–7 (closed December 28–January 3). The head office of the Yokohama Convention & Visitors Bureau, open weekdays 9–5 (except national holidays and December 29–January 3), is in the Sangyō Bōeki Center Building, across from Yamashita Kōen.
🚹 **Yokohama Convention & Visitors Bureau** ✉ 2 Yamashita-chō, Naka-ku ☎ 045/221-2111. **Yokohama International Tourist Association** ☎ 045/641-4759. **Yokohama Tourist Office** ✉ Yokohama Station, Nishi-ku ☎ 045/441-7300.

FUJI-HAKONE-IZU NATIONAL PARK

Fuji-Hakone-Izu National Park, southwest of Tōkyō between Suruga and Sagami bays, is one of Japan's most popular resort areas. The region's main attraction, of course, is Mt. Fuji, a dormant volcano—it last erupted in 1707—rising to a height of 12,388 feet. The mountain is utterly captivating in the ways it can change in different light and from different perspectives. Its symmetry and majesty have been immortalized by poets and artists for centuries. ■ **TIP→ During spring and summer, Mt. Fuji often hides behind a blanket of clouds. Keep this in mind if seeing the mountain is an important part of your trip.**

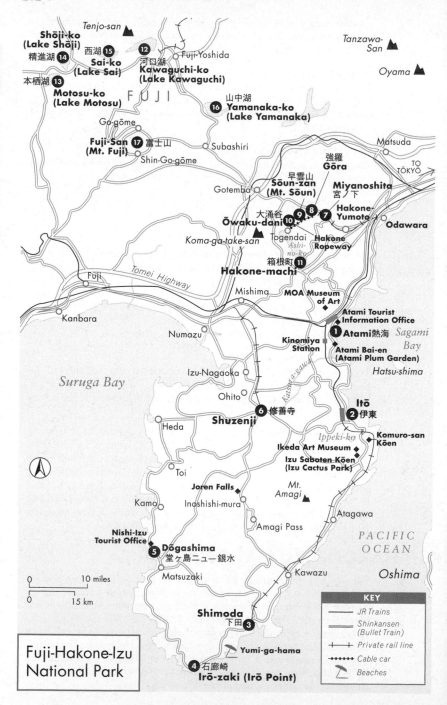

Tenjo-san ▲

Shōji-ko (Lake Shōji) 精進湖 ⑭
西湖 ⑮ **Sai-ko (Lake Sai)**
河口湖 ⑫ **Kawaguchi-ko (Lake Kawaguchi)**
Fuji-Yoshida

Motosu-ko (Lake Motosu) 本栖湖 ⑬

F U J I

山中湖 ⑯ **Yamanaka-ko (Lake Yamanaka)**

Go-gōme

Fuji-San (Mt. Fuji) ⑰ 富士山
Shin-Go-gōme
Subashiri

Tanzawa-San ▲

Oyama ▲

Matsuda

強羅 **Gōra**
早雲山 **Sōun-zan (Mt. Sōun)**
Miyanoshita 宮ノ下

Gotemba

TO TŌKYŌ

大涌谷 **Ōwaku-dani** ⑩ ⑨ ⑧ ⑦ **Hakone-Yumoto**
Togendai **Hakone Ropeway**
Koma-ga-take-san ▲
Ashi-no-ko
Odawara

Tomei Highway
Fuji

箱根町 ⑪ **Hakone-machi**

Mishima

MOA Museum of Art

Kanbara

Numazu

Kinomiya Station

Atami Tourist Information Office
① **Atami** 熱海
Atami Bai-en (Atami Plum Garden)

Sagami Bay

Hatsu-shima

Suruga Bay

Izu-Nagaoka

Ohito

⑥ 修善寺 **Shuzenji**
Heda

Itō ② 伊東

Ippeki-ko
Komuro-san Kōen

Ikeda Art Museum
Izu Saboten Kōen (Izu Cactus Park)

Toi

Joren Falls
Inoshishi-mura

Mt. Amagi ▲

Kamo

Amagi Pass

Atagawa

PACIFIC OCEAN

Nishi-Izu Tourist Office
⑤ **Dōgashima** 堂ヶ島ニュー銀水
Matsuzaki

Kawazu

Oshima

0 ———— 10 miles
0 ———— 15 km

Shimoda 下田 ③

④ 石廊崎 Yumi-ga-hama
Irō-zaki (Irō Point)

Fuji-Hakone-Izu National Park

KEY
——— JR Trains
——— Shinkansen (Bullet Train)
+—+ Private rail line
++++ Cable car
⤙ Beaches

Apart from Mt. Fuji, each of the three areas of the park—the Izu Peninsula, Hakone and environs, and the Five Lakes—has its own appeal. Izu is defined by its dramatic rugged coastline, beaches, and onsen. Hakone has mountains, volcanic landscapes, and lake cruises, plus onsen of its own. The Five Lakes form a recreational area with some of the best views of Mt. Fuji. And in each of these areas there are monuments to Japan's past. Although it's possible to make a grand tour of all three areas at one time, most people make each of them a separate excursion from Tōkyō.

Trains will serve you well in traveling to major points anywhere in the northern areas of the national-park region and down the eastern coast of the Izu Peninsula. For the west coast and central mountains of Izu, there are no train connections; unless you are brave enough to rent a car, the only way to get around is by bus.

Numbers in the text correspond to the Fuji-Hakone-Izu National Park map.

Izu Peninsula

Atami

❶ *48 min southwest of Tōkyō by Kodama Shinkansen.*

The gateway to the Izu Peninsula is Atami. Most Japanese travelers make it no farther into the peninsula than this town on Sagami Bay, so Atami itself has a fair number of hotels and traditional inns. When you arrive, collect a map from the **Atami Tourist Information Office** (☏ 0557/85–2222) at the train station to guide you to the sights below.

★ The **MOA Museum of Art** (MOA Bijutsukan) houses the private collection of the messianic religious leader Okada Mokichi. Okada (1882–1955), who founded a movement called the Sekai Kyūsei Kyō (Religion for the Salvation of the World), also acquired more than 3,000 works of art; some are from the Asuka period (6th and 7th centuries). Among these works are several particularly fine *ukiyo-e* (Edo-era woodblock prints) and ceramics. On a hill above the station and set in a garden full of old plum trees and azaleas, the museum also affords a sweeping view over Atami and the bay. ⊠ *26–2 Momoyama Atami, Shizouka-ken* ☏ *0557/84–2511* ⊞ *¥1,600* ☉ *Fri.–Wed. 9:30–5.*

The **Ōyu Geyser,** a 15-minute walk southeast from Atami Station, used to gush on schedule once every 24 hours but stopped after the Great Kantō Earthquake of 1923. Not happy with this, the local chamber of commerce rigged a pump to raise the geyser every five minutes. ⊠ *3 Kamijuku-cho Atami, Shizouka-ken.*

The best time to visit the **Atami Plum Garden** (Atami Bai-en) is in late January or early February, when its 850 trees bloom. If you do visit, also stop by the small shrine that's in the shadow of an enormous old camphor tree. The shrine is more than 1,000 years old and is a popular spot for people who are asking the gods for help with alcoholism. The tree is more than 2,000 years old and has been designated a National Monument. It is believed that if you walk around the tree once, another year will be added to your life. Atami Bai-en is always open to the public and is 15 minutes by bus from Atami or an eight-minute walk from Kinomiya Station, the next stop south of Atami served by local trains. ✉ *1169-1 Baien-cho, Atami, Shizouka-ken* ☎ *055/785–2222* 🖙 *Free.*

If you have the time and the inclination for a beach picnic, it's worth taking the 25-minute high-speed ferry (round-trip ¥2,340) from the pier over to **Hatsu-shima** (☎ 0557/81–0541 for ferry). There are nine departures daily between 7:30 and 5:20. You can easily walk around the island, which is only 4 km (2½ mi) in circumference, in less than two hours. Use of the **Picnic Garden** (open daily 10–3) is free.

WHERE TO STAY
★ $$$$

🏨 **Atami Taikansō.** The views of the sea must have been the inspiration for Yokoyama Taikan, the Japanese artist who once owned this villa. Now it is a traditional Japanese inn with exquisite furnishings and individualized service. The spacious rooms are classically Japanese, with ceiling-to-floor windows. The prices are high, but bear in mind that they include a multicourse dinner of great artistry, served in your room, and breakfast the next morning. There are also indoor and outdoor hot-springs baths. The inn is a 10-minute walk west from Atami Station. ✉ *7–1 Hayashi-ga-oka-chō, Atami, Shizuoka-ken 413-0031* ☎ *0557/81–8137* ⊕ *www.atami-taikanso.com* 🖙 *44 Japanese-style rooms with bath* 🍴 *Restaurant, pool, sauna, meeting rooms* ☰ *AE, DC, MC, V* 🍴*MAP.*

$$–$$$$

🏨 **New Fujiya Hotel.** Only the top rooms have a view of the sea at this modern, inland resort hotel that's a great base for sightseeing. Service is impersonal but professional, and a foreign visitor won't fluster the staff. The hotel is a five-minute taxi ride from Atami Station. ✉ *1–16 Ginza-chō, Atami, Shizuoka-ken 413-0013* ☎ *0557/81–0111* 🖙 *158 Western-style rooms with bath, 158 Japanese-style rooms with bath* 🍴 *3 restaurants, indoor pool, bar* ☰ *AE, DC, MC, V.*

Itō

2 *25 min south of Atami by JR local; 1 hr, 40 min southwest of Tōkyō via Atami by Kodama Shinkansen, then JR local.*

There are some 800 thermal springs in the resort area surrounding Itō, 16 km (10 mi) south of Atami. These springs—and the beautiful, rocky, indented coastline nearby—remain the resort's major attractions, although there are plenty of interesting sights here. Some 150 hotels and inns serve the area.

Itō traces its history of associations with the West to 1604, when William Adams (1564–1620), the Englishman whose adventures served as the basis for James Clavell's novel *Shōgun,* came ashore. Four years earlier Adams had beached his disabled Dutch vessel, *De Liefde,* on the shores of Kyūshū and became the first Englishman to set foot on Japan. The authorities, believing that he and his men were Portuguese pirates, put Adams in prison, but he was eventually befriended by the shōgun Ieyasu Tokugawa, who brought him to Edo (present-day Tōkyō) and granted him an estate. Ieyasu appointed Adams his adviser on foreign affairs. The English castaway taught mathematics, geography, gunnery, and navigation to shogunal officials and in 1604 was ordered to build an

80-ton Western-style ship. Pleased with this venture, Ieyasu ordered the construction of a larger oceangoing vessel. These two ships were built at Itō, where Adams lived from 1605 to 1610.

This history was largely forgotten until British Commonwealth occupation forces began coming to Itō for rest and recuperation after World War II. Adams's memory was revived, and since then the Anjin Festival (the Japanese gave Adams the name *anjin*, which means "pilot") has been held in his honor every August. A monument to the Englishman stands at the mouth of the river.

Izu Cactus Park (Izu Saboten Kōen) consists of a series of pyramidal greenhouses that contain 5,000 kinds of cacti from around the world. At the base of Komuro-san (Mt. Komuro), the park is 20 minutes south of Itō Station by bus. ✉ *1317–13 Futo* ☎ *0557/51–5553* 💴 *¥1,800* ⊙ *Mar.–Oct., daily 9–5; Nov.–Feb., daily 9–4.*

The **Ikeda 20th-Century Art Museum** (Ikeda 20-Seiki Bijutsukan), at Lake Ippeki, houses works by Picasso, Dalí, Chagall, and Matisse, plus a number of wood-block prints. The museum is a 15-minute walk north west from Izu Cactus Park. ✉ *614 Totari* ☎ *0557/45–2211* 💴 *¥900* ⊙ *Thurs.–Tues. 10–4:30.*

On the east side of **Komuro-san Kōen** (Mt. Komuro Park) are 3,000 cherry trees of 35 varieties that bloom at various times throughout the year. You can take a cable car to the top of the mountain. The park is about 20 minutes south of Itō Station by bus. ✉ *1428 Komuro-cho, Kawana, Ito-shi* ☎ *0557/45–1444* 💴 *Free; round-trip cable car to mountain top ¥400* ⊙ *Daily 9–4.*

WHERE TO STAY

$$$$ 🏨 **Hatoya Sun Hotel.** Located along a scenic coastline, Hatoya Hotel is in the Ito onsen resort area. The hotel has an aquarium bath, which has glass walls that let bathers gaze at tropical fish in an adjoining aquarium. The open-air hot springs look out onto the ocean where mountains are visible in the distance. Japanese buffet dinners are available every night. ✉ *572–12 Yukawa Tateiwa, Nagasaki-shi, Shizuoka-ken 414-0002* ☎ *055/736–4126* 🛏 *187 Japanese-style rooms with bath, 3 Western-style rooms with bath, 1 mixed Western-Japanese style room* ♨ *Minibar, restaurant, parking, bar, pool, sauna* ☰ *DC, MC, V.*

$$-$$$ 🏨 **Hanafubuki.** This traditional Japanese inn in the Jogasaki forest was given a modern makeover, but still retains classic elements like tatami mats, screen sliding doors and *chabudai* (low dining ables) with *zabuton* (cushion seating). The onsen are made of wood for rustic appeal. Meals are optional. ✉ *1041 Yawatano Isomichi, Ito-shi, Shizuoka-ken 413-0232* ☎ *055/754–1550* 🛏 *12 Japanese-style rooms, 2 Western-style rooms, 3 family rooms* ♨ *Restaurant, bar* ☰ *MC, V* ⊕ *www.hanafubuki.co.jp.*

EN ROUTE

South of Itō the coastal scenery is lovely, and there are several spa towns en route to Shimoda. Higashi-Izu (East Izu) has numerous hot-springs resorts, of which **Atagawa** is the most fashionable. South of Atagawa is **Kawazu,** a place of relative quiet and solitude, with pools in the forested mountainside and waterfalls plunging through lush greenery.

Shimoda

❸ *1 hr south of Itō by Izu Railways.*

Of all the resort towns south of Itō along Izu's eastern coast, none can match the distinction of Shimoda. Shimoda's encounter with the West began when Commodore Matthew Perry anchored his fleet of black ships off the coast here in 1853. To commemorate the event, the three-day Black Ship Festival (Kurofune Matsuri) is held here every year in mid-May. Shimoda was also the site, in 1856, of the first American consulate.

The **Shimoda tourist office** (☎ 0558/22–1531), in front of the station, has the easiest of the local English itineraries to follow. The 2½-km (1½-mi) tour covers most major sights. On request, the tourist office will also help you find local accommodations.

The first American consul to Japan was New York businessman Townsend Harris. Soon after his arrival in Shimoda, Harris asked the Japanese authorities to provide him with a female servant; they sent him a young girl named Saitō Okichi, who was engaged to be married. The arrangement brought her a new name, Tōjin (the Foreigner's) Okichi, much disgrace, and a tragic end. When Harris sent her away, she tried, but failed to rejoin her former lover. The shame brought upon her for working and living with a Westerner and the pain of losing the love of her life drove Okichi to drown herself in 1890. Her tale is recounted in Rei Kimura's biographical novel *Butterfly in the Wind*. **Hōfuku-ji** was Okichi's family temple. The museum annex displays a life-size image of her, and just behind the temple is her grave—where incense is still kept burning in her memory. The grave of her lover, Tsurumatsu, is at Tōden-ji, a temple about midway between Hōfuku-ji and Shimoda Station. ✉ *18–26 1-chōme* ☎ *0558/22–0960* ✍ *¥300* ⊙ *Daily 8–5.*

WHERE TO STAY

$$–$$$$

🏨 **Shimoda Prince Hotel.** This modern V-shape resort hotel faces the Pacific and is steps away from a white-sand beach. The decor is more functional than aesthetic, but the panoramic view of the ocean from the picture windows in the dining room makes this one of the best hotels in town. The Prince is just outside Shimoda, 10 minutes by taxi from the station. ✉ *1547–1 Shira-hama, Shimoda, Shizuoka-ken 415-8525* ☎ *0558/ 22–2111* ⊕ *www.princehotels.co.jp* ✍ *70 Western-style rooms with bath, 6 Japanese-style rooms with bath* ⚐ *2 restaurants, 3 tennis courts, pool, sauna, bar, nightclub, shops* 🟰 *AE, DC, MC, V.*

¢ 🏨 **Pension Sakuraya.** There are a few Western-style bedrooms at this family-run inn a few minutes' walk from Shimoda's main beach, but the best lodgings are the Japanese-style corner rooms, which have nice views of the hills surrounding Shimoda. The pleasant Japanese couple who runs the pension speaks English, and cheap meals are available in the dining room. ✉ *2584–20 Shira-hama, Shimoda, Shizuoka-*

> ### BATHING BEAUTIES
>
> If you love the sun, make sure you stop at **Yumi-ga-hama**. It's one of the prettiest sandy beaches on the whole Izu Peninsula. The bus from Shimoda Station stops here before continuing to Irō-zaki, the last stop on the route.

ken 415-0012 ☎ *0558/23–4470* ✆ *4 Western-style rooms with bath, 5 Japanese-style rooms without bath* ⊕ *http://izu-sakuraya.jp/english* ⟂ *Dining room, Japanese baths, laundry facilities, Internet* ⊟ *AE, DC, MC, V.*

Irō-zaki (Irō Point)

4 *40 min by bus or boat from Shimoda.*

If you visit Irō-zaki, the southernmost part of the Izu Peninsula, in January, you're in for a special treat: a blanket of daffodils covers the cape. From the bus stop at the end of the line from Shimoda Station, it's a short walk to the **Irō-zaki Jungle Park,** with its 3,000 varieties of colorful tropical plants. Beyond the park you can walk to a lighthouse at the edge of the cliff that overlooks the sea, from here you can see the seven islands of Izu. ✉ *546–1 Irō-zaki, Minami-Izu* ☎ *0558/65–0050* ✆ *¥900* ◷ *Daily 8–5.*

Dōgashima

5 *1 hr northwest of Shimoda by bus.*

The sea has eroded the coastal rock formations into fantastic shapes near the little port town of Dōgashima. A **Dōgashima Marine** (☎ 0558/52–0013) sightseeing boat from Dōgashima Pier makes 20-minute runs to see the rocks (¥920). In an excess of kindness, a recorded loudspeaker— which you can safely ignore—recites the name of every rock you pass on the trip. The **Nishi-Izu Tourist Office** (☎ 0558/52–1268) is near the pier, in the small building behind the bus station.

WHERE TO STAY

$$$$

🏨 **Dōgashima New Ginsui.** Surrounded by its very own secluded beach, every guest room overlooks the sea at the New Ginsui, which sits atop cliffs above the water. Service is first class, despite its popularity with tour groups. The Japanese-style rooms are given a modern makeover and the room rate includes a seafood kaiseki dinner served in your room and a buffet breakfast. For relaxation and pampering, visit the day spa or unwind in the outdoor hot spring. In a town overflowing with upmarket hotels, this is by far the best luxury resort on Izu's west coast and though it's a rule that we only include Web sites if they are in English, this one is worth a thousand words. ✉ *2977–1 Nishina, Nishi-Izu-chō, Shizuoka-ken 410-3514* ☎ *0558/52–2211* ✆ *121 Japanese-style rooms with bath* ⟂ *Restaurant, 2 pools, spa, nightclub, shops, laundry service, concierge, meeting rooms* ⊟ *AE, DC, MC, V* ⊕ *www.dougashima-newginsui.jp* ⚈ *MAP.*

Shuzenji

6 *2 hrs north of Shimoda by bus, 32 min south of Mishima by Izu-Hakone Railway.*

Shuzenji—a hot-springs resort in the center of the peninsula, along the valley of the Katsura-gawa (Katsura River)—enjoys a certain historical notoriety as the place where the second Kamakura shōgun, Minamoto no Yoriie, was assassinated early in the 13th century. Don't judge the town by the area around the station; most of the hotels and hot springs are 2 km (1 mi) to the west.

Know the Etiquette

GUESTS ARE EXPECTED TO arrive at ryokan in the late afternoon. When you do, put on the slippers that are provided and a maid will escort you to your room. Remember to remove your slippers before entering your room; never step on the *tatami* (straw mats) with shoes or slippers. Each room will be simply decorated—one small low table, cushions on the tatami, and a scroll on the wall, which will probably be *shōji* (sliding paper-paneled walls).

In ryokan with thermal pools, you can take to the waters anytime, although the pool doors are usually locked from 11 PM to 6 AM. In ryokan without thermal baths or private baths in guest rooms. The maid will ask what time you would like to bathe and fit you into a schedule. Make sure you wash and rinse off entirely before getting into the bath. Do not get soap in the tub. Other guests will be using the same bathwater, so it is important to observe this custom. After your bath, change into the yukata provided in your room. Don't worry about walking around in it—other guests will be doing the same.

Dinner is served around 6. At the larger, newer ryokan, meals will be in the dining room; at smaller, more personal ryokan, it is served in your room. When you are finished, a maid will clear away the dishes and lay out your futon. In Japan *futon* means bedding, and this consists of a thin cotton mattress and a heavy, thick comforter, which is replaced with a thinner quilt in summer. The small, hard pillow is filled with grain. The less expensive ryokan (under ¥7,000 for one) have become slightly lackadaisical in changing the quilt cover with each new guest; in an inoffensive a way as possible, feel free to complain—just don't shame the proprietor. Around 8 AM, a maid will gently wake you, clear away the futon, and bring in your Japanese-style breakfast, which will probably consist of fish, pickled vegetables, and rice. If this isn't appealing, politely ask if it's possible to have coffee and toast. Checkout is at 10.

Make sure you call or e-mail as far in advance as possible for a room—inns are not always willing to accept foreign guests because of language and cultural barriers. It is near impossible to get a room in July or August. Many top-level ryokan require new guests to have introductions and references from a respected client of the inn to get a room; this goes for new Japanese guests, too. On the other hand, inns that do accept foreigners without introduction sometimes treat them as cash cows, which means they might give you cursory service and a lesser room. If you don't speak Japanese, try to have a Japanese speaker reserve a room for you; this will convey the idea that you understand the customs of staying in a traditional inn.

If you've planned a longer visit to Izu, consider spending a night at **Inoshishi-mura,** en route by bus between Shimoda and Shuzenji. The scenery in this part of the peninsula is dramatic, and the dining specialty at the local inns is roast mountain boar. In the morning, a pleasant 15-minute walk from Inoshishi-mura brings you to **Joren Falls** (Joren-no-taki). Located on the upper part of the Kano River, these falls drop 82 feet into a dense forest below. This area has some nationally protected flora and fauna species and because of the cool temperature, hiking here is popular in summer.

WHERE TO STAY

★ $$$$

Ryokan Sanyōsō. The former villa of the Iwasaki family, founders of the Mitsubishi conglomerate, is as luxurious and beautiful a place to stay as you'll find on the Izu Peninsula. Antiques furnish the rooms—the best of which have traditional baths made of fragrant cypress wood and overlook exquisite little private gardens (note that these high-end rooms cost as much as ¥70,000). Breakfast and dinner are served in your room and are included in the rate. The Sanyōsō is a five-minute taxi ride from Izu-Nagaoka Station. ✉ *270 Mama-no-ue, Izunokuni-shi, Shizuoka-ken 410-2204* ☎ *0559/47–1111* ⌨ *3 Western-style, 30 Japanese-style, and 7 mixed Western-Japanese-style rooms with baths* ♨ *Japanese baths, bar, shops, meeting rooms* ▭ *AE, DC, MC, V.*

$$

Kyorai-An Matsushiro-kan. Although this small family-owned inn is nothing fancy, the owners make you feel like a guest in their home. They also speak some English. Japanese meals are served in a common dining room. Room-only reservations (without meals) are accepted only on weekdays. The inn is five minutes by bus or taxi from Izu-Nagaoka Station. ✉ *55 Kona, Izunokuni, Shizuoka-ken 410-2201* ☎ *0559/ 48–0072* ⌨ *14 Japanese-style rooms with bath, 2 without bath* ♨ *Dining room* ▭ *No credit cards* ⎮○⎮ *MAP.*

¢

Goyōkan. This family-run ryokan on Shuzenji's main street has rooms that look out on the Katsura-gawa, plus gorgeous stone-lined (for men) and wood-lined (for women) indoor hot springs. The staff speaks English and can make sightseeing arrangements for you. ✉ *765–2 Shuzenji-chō, Tagata-gun, Shizuoka-ken 410-24* ☎ *0558/72–2066* ⊕ *www. goyokan.co.jp* ⌨ *11 Japanese-style rooms without bath* ♨ *Refrigerators, sauna* ▭ *AE, DC, MC, V.*

Hakone

The national park and resort area of Hakone is a popular day trip from Tōkyō and a good place for a close-up view of Mt. Fuji (assuming the mountain is not swathed in clouds, as often happens in summer).

■ TIP→ **On summer weekends it often seems as though all of Tōkyō has come to Hakone with you. Expect long lines at cable cars and traffic jams everywhere.**

You can cover the best of Hakone in a one-day trip out of Tōkyō, but if you want to try the curative powers of the thermal waters or do some hiking, then stay overnight. Two of the best areas are around the old hot-springs resort of Miyanoshita and the western side of Koma-ga-take-san (Mt. Koma-ga-take).

The typical Hakone route, outlined here, may sound complex, but this is in fact one excursion from Tōkyō so well defined that you really can't get lost—no more so, at least, than any of the thousands of Japanese tourists ahead of and behind you. The first leg of the journey is from Odawara or Hakone-Yumoto by train and cable car through the mountains to Tōgendai, on the north shore of Ashi-no-ko (Lake Ashi). The long way around, from Odawara to Tōgendai by bus, takes about an hour—in heavy traffic, an hour and a half. The trip over the mountains, on the other hand, will take about two hours. Credit the difference to the Hakone Tozan Tetsudō Line—possibly the slowest train you'll ever ride. Using three switchbacks to inch its way up the side of the mountain, the train takes 54 minutes to travel the 16 km (10 mi) from Odawara to Gōra (38 minutes from Hakone-Yumoto). The steeper it gets, the grander the view.

❼ Trains do not stop at any station en route for any length of time, but they do run frequently enough to allow you to disembark, visit a sight, and catch another train. **Miyanoshita,** the first stop on the train route from Hakone-Yumoto, is a small but very pleasant and popular resort. As well as hot springs, this village has antiques shops along its main road and several hiking routes up the half-mile tall Mt. Sengen. If you get to the top, you'll be rewarded with a great view of the gorge.

★ The **Hakone Open-Air Museum.** (Hakone Chōkoku-no-mori Bijutsukan), which is a few minutes' walk from the Miyanoshita Station (directions are posted in English), houses an astonishing collection of 19th- and 20th-century Western and Japanese sculpture, most of it on display in a spacious, handsome garden. There are works here by Rodin, Moore, Arp, Calder, Giacometti, Takeshi Shimizu, and Kōtarō Takamura. One section of the garden is devoted to Emilio Greco. Inside are works by Picasso, Léger, and Manzo, among others. ✉ *1121 Ni-no-taira* ☎ *0460/ 2–1161* ⊕ *www.hakone-oam.or.jp* ✇ *¥1,600* ☾ *Mar.–Nov., daily 9–5; Dec.–Feb., daily 9–4.*

❽ **Gōra,** a small town at the end of the train line from Odawara and the lower end of the Hakone Tozan Cablecar, is a good jumping-off point for hiking and exploring. Ignore the little restaurants and souvenir stands here: get off the train as quickly as you can and make a dash for the cable car at the other end of the station. If you let the rest of the passengers get there before you, and perhaps a tour bus or two, you may stand 45 minutes in line.

❾ The Hakone Tozan Cablecar travels from Gōra to **Sōun-zan** (Mt. Sōun) and departs every 20 minutes; it takes 10 minutes (¥410; free with the Hakone Free Pass) to get to the top. It's ideal if you want to spend a day hiking. There are four stops en route, and you can get off and reboard the cable car at any one of them if you've paid the full fare. The **Hakone Museum of Art** (Hakone Bijutsukan), sister institution to the MOA Museum of Art in Atami, is at the second stop. The museum, which consists of two buildings set in a garden, houses a modest collection of porcelain and ceramics from China, Korea, and Japan. ✉ *1300 Gōra* ☎ *0460/2–2623* ⊕ *www.moaart.or.jp* ✇ *¥900* ☾ *Apr.–Nov., Fri.–Wed. 9:30–4:30; Dec.–Mar., Fri.–Wed. 9:30–4.*

★ At the cable-car terminus of Sōun-zan, a gondola called the **Hakone Rope-**
❿ way swings up over a ridge and crosses the valley called Ōwaku-dani, also known as "Great Boiling Valley," on its way to Tōgendai. The landscape here is desolate, with sulfurous billows of steam escaping through holes from some inferno deep in the earth. At the top of the ridge is one of the two stations where you can leave the gondola. From here, a

Hakone Freebies

MANY PLACES IN HAKONE accept the Hakone Freepass. It's valid for three days and is issued by the privately owned Odakyū Railways. The pass covers the train fare to Hakone and allows you to use any mode of transportation including the Hakone Tozan Cablecar, the Hakone Ropeway, and the Hakone Cruise Boat. In addition to transportation, Freepass holders get discounts at museums such as the Hakone Museum of Art, restaurants, and shops. The list of participants is pretty extensive and it always changes, so it's a good idea to check out the Web site for a complete list of participating companies and terms and conditions.

The Hakone Free Pass (¥5,500) and the Fuji-Hakone Free Pass (¥7,200) can be purchased at the **Odakyu Sightseeing Service Center** inside JR Shinjuku station, near west exit, or by credit card over the phone. Allow a couple of days for delivery to your hotel. If you have a JR Pass, it's cheaper to take a Kodama Shinkansen from Tōkyō Station to Odawara and buy the Hakone Free Pass there (¥4,130) for travel within the Hakone region only ☎ 03/5321–7887 ⊗ 8–8 ⊕ www.odakyu-group.co.jp.

¾-km (½-mi) walking course wanders among the sulfur pits in the valley. Just below the station is a restaurant; the food here is truly terrible, but on a clear day the view of Mt. Fuji is perfect. Remember that if you get off the gondola at any stage, you—and others in the same situation—will have to wait for someone to make space on a later gondola before you can continue down to Tōgendai and Ashi-no-ko (but again, the gondolas come by every minute). ✉ 1-15-1 Shiroyama, Odawara ☎ 046/532–2205 ⊕ www.hakoneropeway.co.jp ✈ ¥970 (without Free Pass) ⊗ Mar.–Nov., daily 8:45—5:15; Dec.–Feb., daily 9:15–4:15.

From Ōwaku-dani the descent by gondola to Tōgendai on the shore of **Ashi-no-ko** (Lake Ashi) takes 25 minutes. There's no reason to linger at Tōgendai; it's only a terminus for buses to Hakone-Yumoto and Odawara and to the resort villages in the northern part of Hakone. Head straight for the pier, a few minutes' walk down the hill, where boats set out on the lake for Hakone-machi. Look out for the **Hakone Sightseeing Cruise.** (✉ 1-15-1 Shiroyama, Odawara ☎ 046/532–6830 ✈ ¥300 ⊗ Summer, 40-minute intervals. Winter, 50-minute intervals. Mar.–Nov., daily 9:30–5; Dec.–Feb., daily 9:30–4 ⊕ www.hakone-kankosen.co.jp). The ride is free with your Hakone Free Pass; otherwise, buy a ticket (¥970) at the office in the terminal. A few ships of conventional design ply the lake; the rest are astonishingly corny Disney knockoffs. One, for example, is rigged like a 17th-century warship. There are departures every 30 minutes, and the cruise to Hakone-machi takes about 30 minutes.

⑪ The main attraction in **Hakone-machi** is the **Hakone Barrier** (Hakone Sekisho). The barrier was built in 1618 and served as a checkpoint to control traffic until it was demolished during the Meiji Restoration of

1868. An exact replica was built as a tourist attraction in 1965 and is only a few minutes' walk from the pier, along the lakeshore in the direction of Moto-Hakone. Last entry is 30 minutes before closing time. ✉ *Ichiban-chī, Hakone-machi* ☎ *0460/3–6635* ✍ *¥300* ☉ *Mar.–Nov., daily 9–5; Dec.–Feb., daily 9–4:30.*

Where to Stay

LAKE ASHI
★ $$–$$$$

Hakone Prince Hotel. The location of this resort complex is perfect, with the lake in front and the mountains of Koma-ga-take in back. The Hakone Prince draws both tour groups and individual travelers, and it's also a popular venue for business conferences. The main building has both twin rooms and triples; the Japanese-style Ryū-gū-den annex, which overlooks the lake and has its own thermal bath, is superb. The rustic-style cottages in the complex sleep three to four guests; these are only open mid-April–November. ✉ *144 Moto-Hakone, Hakone-machi, Kanagawa-ken 250-0522* ☎ *0460/3–1111* ⊕ *www.princehotels.co.jp* ✍ *142 Western-style rooms with bath, 116 Western-style cottages with bath* ⚘ *2 restaurants, coffee shop, dining room, room service, 7 tennis courts, 2 pools, Japanese baths, bar, lounge, shops* ▤ *AE, DC, MC, V* ¶◎¶ *CP.*

MIYANOSHITA
★ $$–$$$$

Fujiya Hotel. Built in 1878, this Western-style hotel with modern additions is showing signs of age, but that somehow adds to its charm. The Fujiya combines the best of traditional Western decor with the exceptional service and hospitality of a fine Japanese inn. There are both Western and Japanese restaurants, and in the gardens behind the hotel is an old imperial villa that serves as a dining room. Hot-spring water is pumped right into the guest rooms. ✉ *359 Miyanoshita, Hakone-machi, Kanagawa-ken 250-0522* ☎ *0460/2–2211* ⊕ *www.fujiyahotel.co.jp* ✍ *149 Western-style rooms with bath* ⚘ *3 restaurants, room service, 18-hole golf course, 2 pools, bar, convention center, meeting rooms, no-smoking rooms* ▤ *AE, DC, MC, V.*

¢

Lodge Fujimien. This traditional ryokan, complete with an on-site onsen, has all the trimmings of an expensive ryokan, for a fraction of the price. Spacious rooms are a little old and dark but have character in the layout, furniture, and traditional wall hangings, and on clear days, Mt. Fuji is visible from the balcony. The restaurant serves Japanese food, and its set meals are reasonably priced. Don't forget to prebook the daily dinner special in advance. Conveniently located near Minami Onsen-sou bus stop, Hakone's main sights are only a five-minute ride away. ✉ *1245 Sengoku-hara, Hakone, Kanagawa-ken 250-0631* ☎ *0460/4–8645* ✍ *21 Japanese-style rooms with bath, 5 Western-style rooms with bath* ⚘ *Restaurant, karaoke, hot spring, parking* ▤ *No cards.*

> ### WHAT THE YOLK?
>
> No, your eyes are not playing tricks on you. Those are in fact local entrepreneurs boiling eggs in the sulfur pits in Ōwaku-dani. Locals make a passable living selling the eggs, which turn black, to tourists at exorbitant prices. A popular myth suggests that eating one of these eggs can extend your life by seven years.

2

Fuji Go-ko (Fuji Five Lakes)

To the north of Mt. Fuji, the Fuji Go-ko area affords an unbeatable view of the mountain on clear days and makes the best base for a climb to the summit. With its various outdoor activities, such as skating and fishing in winter and boating and hiking in summer, this is a popular resort area for families and business conferences.

The five lakes are, from the east, Yamanaka-ko, Kawaguchi-ko, Sai-ko, Shōji-ko, and Motosu-ko. Yamanaka and Kawaguchi are the largest and most developed as resort areas, with Kawaguchi more or less the centerpiece of the group. You can visit this area on a day trip from Tōkyō, but unless you want to spend most of it on buses and trains, plan on staying overnight.

⓬ **Kawaguchi-ko** (Lake Kawaguchi), a 5- to 10-minute walk from Kawaguchi-ko Station, is the most developed of the five lakes, ringed with weekend retreats and vacation lodges. Excursion boats depart from a pier here on 30-minute tours of the lake. The promise, not always fulfilled, is to have two views of Mt. Fuji: one of the mountain itself and the other inverted in its reflection on the water. A gondola along the shore of Lake Kawaguchi (near the pier) quickly brings you to the top of the 3,622-foot-tall **Tenjō-san** (Mt. Tenjō). From the observatory here the whole of Lake Kawaguchi lies before you, and beyond the lake is a classic view of Mt. Fuji.

One of the little oddities at Lake Kawaguchi is the **Fuji Museum** (Fuji Hakubutsukan). The first floor holds conventional exhibits of local geology and history, but upstairs is an astonishing collection of—for want of a euphemism—phalluses (you must be 18 or older to view the exhibit). Mainly made from wood and stone and carved in every shape and size, these figures played a role in certain local fertility festivals. The museum is on the north shore of the lake, next to the Fuji Lake Hotel. ✉ *3964 Funatsu, Fujikawaguchiko-machi, Kanagawa-ken* ☎ *0555/ 73–2266* 🏠 *1st fl. ¥200, 1st and 2nd fl. ¥500* ☉ *Mar.–Oct., daily 9–4; Nov.–Feb., Sat.–Thurs. 9–4; closed 3rd Tues. of month.*

⓭ Buses from Kawaguchi-ko Station go to all the other lakes. The farthest west is **Motosu-ko** (Lake Motosu), the deepest and clearest of the Fuji Go-ko, which takes about 50 minutes.

⓮ Many people consider **Shōji-ko** (Lake Shōji), the smallest of the lakes, to be the prettiest—not least because it still has relatively little vacation-house development. The **Shōji Trail** leads from Lake Shōji to Mt. Fuji through Aoki-ga-hara (Sea of Trees). Beware. This forest has an underlying magnetic lava field that makes compasses go haywire.

⓯ **Sai-ko** (Lake Sai), between Lakes Shōji and Kawaguchi, is the third-largest lake of the Fuji Go-ko, with only moderate development. From the western shore there is an especially good view of Mt. Fuji. Near Sai-ko there are two natural caves, an ice cave and a wind cave. You can either take a bus or walk to them.

⓰ The largest of the Fuji Go-ko is **Yamanaka-ko** (Lake Yamanaka), 35 minutes by bus to the southeast of Kawaguchi. Lake Yamanaka is the closest lake to the popular trail up Mt. Fuji that starts at Go-gōme, and many climbers use this resort area as a base.

Where to Stay

KAWAGUCHI-KO

$$$–$$$$

🏨 **Fuji View Hotel.** This hotel on Lake Kawaguchi is a little threadbare but comfortable. The terrace lounge affords fine views of the lake and of Mt. Fuji beyond. The staff speaks English and is helpful in planning excursions. Many of the guests are on group excursions and take two meals—dinner and breakfast—in the hotel, but it's possible to opt for the room rate alone. Rates are significantly higher on weekends and in August. ✉ *511 Katsuyama-mura, Fuji-Kawaguchiko-machi, Yamanashi-ken 401-0310* 🕾 *0555/83–2211* ⊕ *www.fujiyahotel.co.jp* 🛏 *40 Western-style rooms with bath, 30 Japanese-style rooms with bath* ♨ *2 restaurants, 9-hole golf course, 3 tennis courts, boating* ▤ *AE, DC, MC, V* 🍴*MAP.*

> ### THE SHŌJI TRIANGLE
>
> The Aoki-ga-hara (Sea of Trees) seems to hold a morbid fascination for the Japanese. Many people go into Aoki-ga-hara every year and never come out, some of them on purpose. If you're planning to climb Mt. Fuji from this trail, go with a guide.

YAMANAKA-KO

$$

🏨 **Hotel Mount Fuji.** This is the best resort hotel on Lake Yamanaka and has all the facilities for a recreational holiday including on-site game and karaoke rooms and a nature walk on the grounds. The guest rooms are larger than those at the other hotels on the lake and are modeled after European hotels. The convenient location and large banquet halls make it a favorite among tour groups.The lounges are spacious, and they have fine views of the lake and mountain. Rates are about 20% higher on weekends. ✉ *1360-83 Yamanaka, Yamanaka-ko-mura, Yamanashi-ken 403-0017* 🕾 *0555/62–2111* ⊕ *www.mtfuji-hotel.com* 🛏 *150 Western-style rooms with bath, 1 Japanese-style room with bath* ♨ *3 restaurants, pool* ▤ *AE, DC, MC, V.*

¢

🏨 **Inn Fujitomita.** One of the closest lodging options to the Mt. Fuji hiking trails, this inexpensive inn is a launching point for treks around the Fuji Go-ko area. The inn might not be much to look at from the outside, but the interior is spacious and homey. The staff speaks English and can help you plan an itinerary for visiting the area sights. Meals, including vegetarian options, are available at a very low price. Shuttle service is provided from Fuji Yoshida Station and the Lake Yamanaka bus stop. ✉ *13235 Shibokusa, Oshinomura, Minami-Tsuru-gun, Ya-manashi-ken 401-105* 🕾 *0555/84–3359* ⊕ *www.tim.hi-ho.ne.jp/innfuji/* 🛏 *10 Japanese-style rooms, 3 with bath* ♨ *Dining room, 3 tennis courts, pool, fishing, laundry facilities; no TV in some rooms* ▤ *AE, DC, MC, V.*

Fuji-san (Mt. Fuji)

⓱

Fodor'sChoice
★

There are six routes to the summit of the 12,388-foot-high **Fuji-san** (Mt. Fuji), but only two, both accessible by bus, are recommended: from Go-gōme (Fifth Station), on the north side, and from Shin-Go-gōme (New Fifth Station), on the south. The climb to the summit from Go-gōme

Be Prepared

CLOSE UP

BEWARE OF FICKLE WEATHER around and atop the mountain. Summer days can be unbearably hot and muggy, and the nights can be a shocking contrast of freezing cold (bring numerous warm layers and be prepared to put them all on). Wear strong hiking shoes. The sun really burns at high altitudes, so wear protective clothing and a hat; gloves are a good idea, too. Bring enough food and water for the climb

(remember to take your garbage down with you) and bring a flashlight. Also, keep altitude sickness in mind. To avoid it, begin your assent at a slow pace and take frequent breaks. Use a backpack to keep your hands free and as a useful tool on the way down: instead of returning to Go-gōme, descend to Shin-Go-gōme on the volcanic sand slide called the **sunabashiri**—sit down on your pack, push off, and away you go.

takes five hours and is the shortest way up; the descent takes three hours. From Shin-Go-gōme the ascent is slightly longer and stonier, but the way down, via the *sunabashiri*, a volcanic sand slide, is faster.

The Climb

The ultimate experience of climbing Mt. Fuji is to reach the summit just before dawn and be able to greet the extraordinary sunrise. *Go-raikō* (The Honorable Coming of the Light), as the sunrise is called, has a mystical quality because the reflection shimmers across the sky just before the sun itself appears over the horizon. Mind you, there is no guarantee of seeing it: Mt. Fuji is often cloudy, even in the early morning.

The climb is taxing but not as hard as you might think scaling Japan's highest mountain would be. That said, the air *is* thin, and it *is* humiliating to struggle for the oxygen to take another step while some 83-year-old Japanese grandmother blithely leaves you in her dust (it happens). Have no fear of losing the trail on either of the two main routes. Just follow the crowd—some 196,000 people make the climb during the official season, which is July 1–August 26. ⚠ **Outside of this season, the weather is highly unpredictable and potentially dangerous, and climbing is strongly discouraged.** In all, there are 10 stations to the top; hiking purists start at the very bottom but if you want to save time and cheat a little, you can start at the fifth station. There are stalls selling food and drinks along the way, but at exorbitant prices, so bring your own.

Along the route are dormitory-style huts (about ¥7,000 with two meals, ¥5,000 without meals) where you can catch some sleep. ⚠ **These huts, which are open only in July and August, should be avoided at all costs. The food is vile, there's no fresh water, and the bedding is used by too many people and seldom properly aired. Sensible folk leave the Go-gōme at midnight with good flashlights, climb through the night, and get to the summit just before dawn. Camping on the mountain is prohibited.**

Fuji-Hakone-Izu National Park Essentials

BY BUS

Buses connect Tōkyō with the major gateway towns of this region, but except for the trip to Lake Kawaguchi or Mt. Fuji, the price advantage doesn't really offset the comfort and convenience of the trains. If you're interested only in climbing Mt. Fuji, take one of the daily buses directly to Go-gōme from Tōkyō; they run July through August and leave Shinjuku Station at 7:45, 8:45, 10:55, 4:50, 5:50, and 7:30. The last bus allows sufficient time for the tireless to make it to the summit before sunrise. The journey takes about 2 hours and 40 minutes from Shinjuku and costs ¥2,600. Reservations are required; book seats through the Fuji Kyūkō Highway Bus Reservation Center, the Keiō Highway Bus Reservation Center, the Japan Travel Bureau (which should have English-speaking staff), or any major travel agency.

To return from Mt. Fuji to Tōkyō, take an hour-long bus ride from Shin-Go-gōme to Gotemba (¥1,500). From Gotemba take the JR Tōkaidō and Gotemba lines to Tōkyō Station (¥1,890), or take the JR Line from Gotemba to Matsuda (¥480) and change to the private Odakyū Line from Shin-Matsuda to Shinjuku (¥750).

Direct bus service runs daily from Shinjuku Station in Tōkyō to Lake Kawaguchi every hour between 7:10 AM and 8:10 PM (¥1,700). Buses go from Kawaguchi-ko Station to Go-gōme (the fifth station on the climb up Mt. Fuji) in about an hour; there are eight departures a day (9:35, 10:10, 11:10, 12:10, 1:10, 2:10, 3:20, and 5:20) until the climbing season (July and August) starts, when there are 15 departures or more, depending on demand. The cost is ¥1,700.

From Lake Kawaguchi, you can also take a bus to Gotemba, then change to another bus for Sengoku; from Sengoku there are frequent buses to Hakone-Yumoto, Tōgendai, and elsewhere in the Hakone region. On the return trip, three or four buses a day make the two-hour journey from Lake Kawaguchi to Mishima (¥2,130), skirting the western lakes and circling Mt. Fuji; at Mishima you can transfer to the JR Shinkansen Line for Tōkyō or Kyōto. A shorter bus ride (70 minutes, ¥1,470) goes from Lake Kawaguchi to Gotemba with a transfer to the JR local line.

From Lake Kawaguchi, you can also connect to the Izu Peninsula. Take the bus to Mishima and from there go by train either to Shuzenji or Atami. From Shimoda, the end of the line on the private Izukyū Railway down the east coast of the Izu Peninsula, you must travel by bus around the southern cape to Dōgashima (¥1,360). From there, another bus takes you up the west coast as far as Heda and then turns inland to Shuzenji. From Shimoda, you can also take a bus directly north to Shuzenji through the Amagi Mountains (one departure daily at 10:45 AM, ¥2,180). The Tōkai Bus Company covers the west coast and central mountains of the Izu area well with local service; buses are not especially frequent, but they do provide the useful option of just hopping off and exploring if you happen to see something interesting from the window. Whatever your destination, always check the time of the last departure to make sure that you are not left stranded.

Within the Hakone area, buses run every 15–30 minutes from Hakone-machi buses to Hakone-Yumoto Station on the private Odakyū Line (40 minutes, ¥930), and Odawara Station (1 hour, ¥1,150), where you can take either the Odakyū Romance Car back to Shinjuku Station or a JR Shinkansen to Tōkyō Station. The buses are covered by the Hakone Free Pass.

🚌 Kawaguchi Contacts **Fuji Kyūkō Lake Kawaguchi Reservation Center** ☏ 055/572–2922. **Fuji Kyūkō Gotemba Reservation Center** ☏ 055/082–2555.

🚌 Tōkyō Contacts **Fuji Kyūkō Highway Bus Reservation Center** ☏ 03/5376–2222. **Keiō Highway Bus Reservation Center** ☏ 03/5376–2222. **Japan Travel Bureau** ☏ 03/3284–7605 ⊕ www.jtb.co.jp. **Tōkai Bus Company** ☏ 0557/36–1112 for main office, 0557/22–2511 Shimoda Information Center.

BY CAR

Having your own car makes sense only for touring the Izu Peninsula, and only then if you're prepared to cope with less-than-ideal road conditions, lots of traffic (especially on holiday weekends), and the paucity of road markers in English. It takes some effort—but exploring the peninsula *is* a lot easier by car than by public transportation.

■ TIP→ One way to save yourself some trouble is to book a car through the Nippon or Toyota rental agency in Tōkyō and arrange to pick it up at the Shimoda branch.

🚗 **Nippon Rent-a-Car** ☏ 03/3485–7196 English operator available on weekdays 10–5 ⊕ www.nipponrentacar.co.jp. **Toyota Rent-a-Car** ☏ 0070/800–0100 toll-free, 03/5954–8008 English operator available 8–8 ⊕ www.toyota-rl-tyo.co.jp/rentacar/syasyu/info-e.html.

BY TRAIN

Trains are by far the easiest and fastest ways to get to the Fuji-Hakone-Izu National Park area. The gateway stations of Atami, Odawara, and Kawaguchi-ko are well served by comfortable express trains from Tōkyō, on both JR and private railway lines. These in turn connect to local trains and buses that can get you anywhere in the region you want to go. Call the JR Higashi-Nihon Info Line (10–6 daily, except December 31–January 3) for assistance in English.

The *Kodama* Shinkansen from JR Tōkyō station to Atami costs ¥3,880 and takes 51 minutes; JR Passes are valid. The JR local from Atami to Itō takes 25 minutes and costs ¥320. Itō and Atami are also served by the JR Odoriko Super Express (not a Shinkansen train) also departing from Tokyo station; for correct platform, check the schedule display board. The Tōkyō–Itō run takes 1¾ hours and costs ¥4,190; you can also use a JR Pass. The privately owned Izukyū Railways, on which JR Passes are not valid, makes the Itō–Shimoda run in one hour for ¥1,570.

The Izu–Hakone Railway Line runs from Tōkyō to Mishima (1 hour, 36 minutes; ¥4,090), with a change at Mishima for Shuzenji (31 minutes, ¥500); this is the cheapest option if you don't have a JR Pass. With a JR Pass, a Shinkansen–Izu Line combination will save about 35 minutes and will be the cheapest option. The Tōkyō–Mishima Shinkansen leg (62 minutes) costs ¥4,400; the Mishima–Shuzenji Izu Line leg (31 minutes) costs ¥500.

Trains depart every 12 minutes from Tōkyō's Shinjuku Station for Odawara in the Hakone area. The ¥5,500 Hakone Free Pass, which you can buy at the station, covers the train fare. Reservations are required for the upscale Romance Car, with comfortable seats and big observation windows, to Hakone (an extra ¥870 with Hakone Free Pass). The Romance Car goes one stop beyond Odawara to Hakone-Yumoto; buy tickets at any Odakyū Travel Service counter or major travel agency, or call the Odakyū Reservation Center. Note that beyond Hakone-Yumoto, you must use the privately owned Hakone Tozan Tetsudō Line or buses.

The transportation hub, as well as one of the major resort areas in the Fuji Five Lakes area, is Kawaguchi-ko. Getting there from Tōkyō requires a change of trains at Ōtsuki. The JR Chūō Line Kaiji and Azusa express trains leave Shinjuku Station for Ōtsuki on the half hour from 7 AM to 8 PM (more frequently in the morning) and take approximately one hour. At Ōtsuki, change to the private Fuji-Kyūkō Line for Kawaguchi-ko, which takes another 50 minutes. The total traveling time is about two hours, and you can use your JR Pass as far as Ōtsuki; otherwise, the fare is ¥1,280. The Ōtsuki–Kawaguchi-ko leg costs ¥1,110. Also available are two direct service rapid trains for Kawaguchi-ko that leave Tōkyō in the morning at 6:08 and 7:10 on weekdays, 6:09 and 7:12 on weekends and national holidays.

The Holiday Kaisoku Picnic-gō, available on weekends and national holidays, offers direct express service from Shinjuku, leaving at 8:10 and arriving at Kawaguchi-ko Station at 10:37. From March through August, JR puts on additional weekend express trains for Kawaguchi-ko, but be aware that on some of them only the first three cars go all the way to the lake. Coming back, you have a choice of late-afternoon departures from Kawaguchi-ko that arrive at Shinjuku in the early evening. Check the express timetables before you go; you can also call either the JR Higashi-Nihon Info Line or Fuji-kyūukō Kawaguchi-ko Station for train information.

🚆 Fuji-kyūukō Kawaguchi-ko Station ☎ 0555/72-0017. **Hakone Tozan Railway** ☎ 0465/24-2115. **Izu-Hakone Railway** ☎ 0465/77-1200. **Izukyū Corporation** ☎ 0557/53-1111 for main office, 0558/22-3202 Izukyū Shimoda Station. **JR Higashi-Nihon Info Line** ☎ 03/3423-0111. **Odakyū Reservation Center** ☎ 03/3481-0130.

TOURS

Once you are on the Izu Peninsula itself, sightseeing excursions by boat are available from several picturesque small ports. From Dōgashima, you can take the Dōgashima Marine short (20 minutes, ¥920) or long (45 minutes, ¥1,240) tours of Izu's rugged west coast. The Fujikyū Kōgyō company operates a daily ferry to Hatsu-shima from Atami (25 minutes, ¥2,340 round-trip) and another to the island from Itō (23 minutes, ¥1,150). Izukyū Marine offers a 40-minute tour (¥1,530) by boat from Shimoda to the coastal rock formations at Irō-zaki.

Sunrise Tours operates a tour to Hakone, including a cruise across Lake Ashi and a trip on the gondola over Ōwaku-dani (¥15,000 includes lunch and return to Tōkyō by Shinkansen; ¥12,000 includes lunch and return to Tōkyō by bus). ■ **TIP→ These tours are an economical way to see the main sights all in one day.** Sunrise tours depart daily from Tōkyō's Hamamatsu-chō Bus Terminal and some major hotels.

🏢 **Dōgashima Marine** ☎ 0558/52-0013. **Fujikyū Kōgyō** ☎ 0557/81-0541. **Izukyū Marine** ☎ 0558/22-1151. **Sunrise Tours** ☎ 03/5796-5454 ⊕ www.jtb.co.jp/sunrisetour.

VISITOR INFORMATION

Especially in summer and fall, the Fuji-Hakone-Izu National Park area is one of the most popular vacation destinations in the country, so most towns and resorts have local visitor information centers. Few of them have staff members who speak fluent English, but you can still pick up local maps and pamphlets, as well as information on low-cost inns, pensions, and guesthouses.

🏢 **Atami Tourist Association** ✉ 12-1 Ginza-chō, Atami ☎ 0557/85-2222. **Fuji-Kawaguchiko Tourist Association** ✉ 890 Funatsu, Kawakuchiko-machi, Minami-Tsuru-gun ☎ 0555/72-2460. **Hakone-machi Tourist Association** ✉ 698 Yumoto, Hakone-machi ☎ 0460/5-8911. **Nishi-Izu Tourist Office** ✉ Dogashima, Nishi-Izu-chō, Kamo-gu ☎ 0558/52-1268. **Shimoda Tourist Association** ✉ 1 1 Soto-ga-oka, Shimoda-shi ☎ 0558/22-1531.

Points of Interest

SITES/AREAS	JAPANESE CHARACTERS
Atami	熱海
Atami Plum Garden (Atami Bai-en)	熱海梅園
Basha-michi	馬車道
Central Yokohama	横浜市街
Chinatown (Chūka-gai)	中華街
Chūgū Shrine (Chūgū-shi)	中宮祠
Chūzen Temple (Chūzen-ji)	中禅寺湖
Dōgashima	堂ヶ島
Dragon's Head Falls (Ryūzu-no-taki)	竜頭滝
Engaku Temple (Engaku-ji)	円覚寺
Ennō Temple (Ennō-ji)	円応寺
Enoshima	江ノ島
Fuji Five Lakes (Fuji Go-ko)	富士五湖
Fuji Museum (Fuji Hakubutsukan)	富士博物館
Fuji-Hakone-Izu National Park	富士箱根伊豆国立公園
Fuji-san (Mt. Fuji)	富士山
Futara-san Shrine (Futara-san Jinja)	二荒山神社
Garden Arboretum	ガーデン植物園
Gōra	強羅
Great Buddha (Daibutsu)	大仏
Hakone	箱根
Hakone Open-Air Museum (Hakone Chōkoku-no-mori Bijutsukan)	箱根彫刻の森美術館
Hakone-machi	箱根町
Hase	長谷
Hase Temple (Hase-dera)	長谷寺
Hikawa-maru	氷川丸
Hōfuku Temple (Hōfuku-ji)	宝福寺
Hōkoku Temple (Hōkoku-ji)	報国寺
Ikeda 20th-Century Art Museum (Ikeda 20-Seiki Bijutsukan)	池田20世紀美術館
Inoshishi-mura	いのしし村
International Cemetery (Gaijin Bochi)	外人墓地
Irō-zaki (Irō Point)	石廊崎

Irō-zaki Jungle Park	石廊崎ジャングルパーク
Iseyama Kodai Shrine (Iseyama Kodai Jingū)	伊勢山皇大神宮
Itō	伊東
Izu Cactus Park (Izu Saboten Kōen)	伊豆サボテン公園
Izu Peninsula (Izu-hantō)	伊豆半島
Jakkō Falls (Jakkō-no-taki)	寂光滝
Jigen Temple Hall (Jigen-dō)	慈眼堂
Jōchi Temple (Jōchi-ji)	浄智寺
Jōmyo Temple (Jōmyō-ji)	浄明寺
Kamakura	鎌倉
Kamakura Treasure Museum (Kamakura Kokuhōkan)	鎌倉国宝館
Kamakura Shrine (Kamakura-gū)	鎌倉宮
Kanagawa Prefectural Museum (Kanagawa Kenritsu Hakubutsukan)	神奈川県立博物館
Kegon Falls (Kegon-no-taki)	華厳滝
Kenchō Temple (Kenchō-ji)	建長寺
Kita-Kamakura (North Kamakura)	北鎌倉
Mt. Komuro Park (Komuro-san Kōen)	小室山公園
Lake Ashi (Ashi-no-ko)	芦ノ湖
Lake Kawaguchi (Kawaguchi-ko)	河口湖
Lake Motosu (Motosu-ko)	本栖湖
Lake Sai (Sai-ko)	西湖
Lake Shōji (Shōji-ko)	精進湖
Lake Yamanaka (Yamanaka-ko)	山中湖
Landmark Tower	ランドマークタワー
Marine Tower	マリンタワー
Meigetsu Temple (Meigetsu-in)	明月院
Miyanoshita	宮ノ下
MOA Museum of Art (MOA Bijutsukan)	MOA 美術館
Monument to Masatuna Matsudaira	松平正綱の杉並木寄進碑
Moto-machi	元町
Mt. Sōun (Sōun-zan)	早雲山
Mt. Tenjō (Tenjō-san)	天上山
Nikkō	日光

Nikkō Edo Village (Nikkō Edo Mura)	日光江戸村
Nippon-maru Memorial Park	日本丸メモリアルパーク
Ōwaku-dani	大涌谷
Prefectural Museum of Modern Art (Kanagawa Kenritsu Kindai Bijutsukan)	神奈川県立近代博物館
Queen's Square	クイーンズスクエア
Rinnō Temple (Rinnō-ji)	輪王寺
Ryūkō Temple (Ryūkō-ji)	龍口寺
Sacred Bridge (Shinkyō)	神橋
Sankei-en	三渓園
Shimoda	下田
Shōji Trail	精進（湖畔）トレイル
Shuzenji	修善寺
Silk Museum (Shiruku Hakubutsukan)	シルク博物館
Sōji Temple (Sōji-ji)	総持寺
Taiyū-in Mausoleum	大猷院廟
Tōkei Temple (Tōkei-ji)	東慶寺
Tōshō Shrine (Tōshō-gū)	東照宮
Treasury House (Hōmotsu-kan)	宝物館
Tsuru-ga-oka Hachiman-gū	鶴岡八幡宮
Umagaeshi	馬返し
Urami Falls (Urami-no-taki)	裏見滝
Yamashita Park (Yamashita Kōen)	山下公園
Yokohama	横浜
Yokohama Doll Museum (Yokohama Ningyō-no-ie)	横浜人形の家
Yokohama History Archives (Yokohama Kaikō Shiryōkan)	横浜開港資料館
Yokohama Museum of Art (Yokohama Bijutsukan)	横浜美術館
Yoritomo's tomb	頼朝の墓
Yumi-ga-hama	弓ヶ浜

RESTAURANTS

Aichiya	あいちや
Chano-ma	茶の間
Ginza Isomura Kamakuraten	ぎんざ磯むら 鎌倉店
Gyōshintei	尭心亭

Hachinoki Kita-Kamakura-ten	鉢の木北鎌倉店
Kaisen Misaki-kō	海鮮三崎港
Kaseirō	華正樓
Masudaya	ゆば亭ますだや
Meiji-no-Yakata	明治の館
Motomachi Bairin	元町梅林
Nantai	なんたい
Roma Statione	ローマステーション
Sawamoto	澤本
Serina Romanchaya	瀬里奈 浪漫茶屋
Yokohama Cheese Café	横浜チーズカフェ

HOTELS

Atami Taikansō	熱海大観荘
Chūzenji Kanaya Hotel	中善寺金谷ホテル
Dōgashima New Ginsui	堂ヶ島ニュー銀水
Fuji View Hotel	富士ビューホテル
Fujiya Hotel	富士屋ホテル
Goyōkan	五葉館
Hakone Prince Hotel	箱根プリンスホテル
Hanafubuki	花吹雪
Hatoya Sun Hotel	ホテルサンハトヤ
Hotel Mount Fuji	富士山ホテル
Inn Fujitomita	旅館ふじとみた
Kyoraian Matsushiro-kan	去来庵 松城館
Lodge Fujimien	ロッジ富士見苑
New Fujiya Hotel	ニュー富士屋ホテル
Nikkō Kanaya Hotel	日光金谷ホテル
Nikkō Prince Hotel	日光プリンスホテル
Pension Sakuraya	ペンション桜家
Ryokan Sanyōsō	旅館三養荘
Shimoda Prince Hotel	下田プリンスホテル
Turtle Inn Nikkō	タートルイン日光

Nagoya, Ise-Shima & the Kii Peninsula

WORD OF MOUTH

"We did the Toyota tour last year, and my husband has done it twice. . . . It is amazing—a tour you do not want to miss. Toyota treats you like you are a stock holder—your names are on a lighted board when you arrive."

—melen

Revised by
Jon Duvles

NAGOYA PUNCHES WELL ABOVE ITS WEIGHT. The present-day industries of Japan's fourth-largest city are a corollary of its *monozukuri* (art of making things) culture. This is manifested in the efficiency of Toyota's production lines, but traditional crafts including ceramics, tie-dyeing, and knife-making are still very much alive. Nagoya's GDP is greater than Switzerland's, but this economic prowess is matched by a capacity to pleasantly surprise any visitor.

Nagoya purrs along contentedly, burdened neither by a second-city complex nor by hordes of tourists, and it has an agreeable small-town atmosphere. A substantial immigrant population, by Japanese standards, including many South Americans working in local factories, provides international flavoring to the city's food and entertainment choices. Among the legacies of the city's hosting of the 2005 World Expo are a vastly improved tourism and transportation infrastructure.

On arrival, you will first notice the twin white skyscrapers sprouting from the ultramodern station, almost a city in itself. The even taller building opposite is the head office of the automaking giant Toyota, the driving force of the local economy. An extensive network of underground shopping malls stretches out in all directions below the wide, clean streets around Nagoya Station and in downtown Sakae. Above ground are huge department stores and international fashion boutiques.

Within two hours' drive of the city are the revered Grand Shrines of Ise, Japan's most important Shintō site, and to the south are the quiet fishing villages of Ise-Shima National Park. On the untamed Kii Peninsula, steep-walled gorges and forested headlands give way to pristine bays, and fine sandy beaches await in Shirahama. Inland is the remarkable mountain temple town of Kōya-san. Add to this some memorable *matsuri* (festivals), and this corner of Japan becomes far more than just another stop on the *shinkansen*.

See the glossary at the end of this book for definitions of the common Japanese words and suffixes used in this chapter.

ORIENTATION & PLANNING

Orientation

Nagoya is on a wide plain in the main urban and industrial corridor that runs along the south side of Honshū from Tōkyō as far west as Kōbe. The mountains of the southern Japan Alps rise just north and east of the city, and to the west is the lush Kii Peninsula.

Nagoya

An ancient transport, business, and cultural hub, Nagoya combines the best of old and contemporary Japan. Just to the north, along the edge of the Gifu and Nagano mountains, are cormorant fishing and craft centers. Modern industry encroaches on the city, but it is also an essential part of Nagoya's vibrancy.

Top Reasons to Visit

THE SHRINE OF SHRINES
South of Nagoya are the Grand Shrines of Ise. The shrines, rebuilt every two decades for the last 1,500 years, are the most sacred in Japan. Naikū, the Inner Shrine, is dedicated to the worship of Amaterasu, the sun goddess and highest Shintō deity.

CRAFTY SHOPPING
Nagoya has the world's largest producer of porcelain, Noritake, and the nearby towns of Seto, Tajimi, and Tokoname have famous ceramics traditions as well. Arimatsu offers tie-dyed fabric, Gifu makes paper lanterns and umbrellas, and in Seki samurai swords are still forged the traditional way.

SEE JAPAN AT WORK & PLAY
Nagoya, with its comfortable size, is the perfect place to sample contemporary Japanese culture. Factory tours are available at Toyota, Noritake, and major brewers Asahi and Kirin. Sports include the annual sumō tournament in July and Chunichi Dragons baseball games.

RELIVE JAPAN'S MODERNIZATION
In the green hills outside Inuyama city is Meiji-mura, an open-air architectural museum with more than 60 buildings from the Meiji era (1868–1912) that were brought from all over the country and lovingly reconstructed. Highlights include the foyer of Frank Lloyd Wright's stunning Imperial Hotel and a still-functioning kabuki theater.

EATING FISH FROM THE BIRD'S MOUTH
Ukai takes the twin Japanese obsessions of patience and idiosyncratic dining to their natural extreme. Cormorants attached to leashes capture *ayu* (sweetfish) lured to the surface by the light of a fire from a boat. Rings around the birds' necks prevent them from swallowing their catch, which are taken from their mouths by fishermen.

Ise-Shima National Park
Many people get no farther than the shrines at Ise, but just to the south is a world of bays ringed by fishing villages and oyster farms.

Kii Peninsula
Traveling west and inland on the Kii Peninsula, time slows down, with few roads and only one coastal railway line. The Kii Peninsula rewards patient explorers with beautiful wilderness and the shrines of the Kumano Kodo pilgrimage road.

Kōya-san
Kōya-San is the headquarters of the 1,200-year-old Shingon Buddhist sect, which has overnight temple accommodation. This small, isolated mountain town, dotted by 120 temples, is a calm and spiritual retreat.

Planning

Nagoya is between Tōkyō and Kyōto, and we recommend spending a couple of days exploring the sights. The city serves as a jumping-off point for traveling south and west to Ise-Shima and the Kii Peninsula. The weather can be changeable along the coastline of Ise-Shima, and if you're heading inland on the Kii Peninsula be prepared for hilly terrain.

The Best of Times

Spring is the most popular season, especially in mid-April when cherry trees bloom. Nagoya gets extremely humid in July and August, but in autumn the trees turn color under blue skies. Sea breezes make coastal areas bearable in summer. Cold winds blow into Nagoya from the ski grounds to the north during winter, but Wakayama and Mie prefectures remain mild.

Concerning Restaurants & Hotels

Restaurants in Nagoya and on the peninsulas are slightly less expensive than in Tōkyō. Your cheapest options are the noodle shops, *donburi* (rice bowl) chains, and *kaiten* (revolving) sushi and curry houses. Franchised restaurants often have English alongside Japanese on their menus, but don't expect the staff to know more than a few words.

Nagoya's lodging ranges from *ryokan* (traditional Japanese inns) and efficient business hotels to large luxury palaces. At Kōya-san, temple accommodation is a fascinating experience. Furnishings in temples are spartan but sufficient, and the food is strictly vegetarian. You may be invited to attend early-morning prayer service. In addition to holidays, hotels are busy in October owing to conferences held in Nagoya and autumn foliage outside the city. Unless otherwise noted, expect private baths, air-conditioning, and basic TV in all rooms. The large hotels in downtown Nagoya have English-speaking staff, but it's advisable to ask a tourist information center to make reservations for you outside the city.

For a short course on accommodations in Japan, *see* Accommodations *in* Essentials.

WHAT IT COSTS In yen				
$$$$	$$$	$$	$	¢
RESTAURANTS over 3,000	2,000–3,000	1,000–2,000	800–1,000	under 800
HOTELS over 22,000	18,000– 22,000	12,000– 18,000	8,000– 12,000	under 8,000

Restaurant prices are per person for a main course at dinner. Hotel prices are for a double room with private bath, excluding service and tax.

Transportation Station

In Nagoya subways are the easiest way to get around. Outside the city the extensive rail network will take you to most places of interest, although buses may be necessary on the remote Kii Peninsula.

AIR TRAVEL Nagoya's compact, user-friendly Chubu International Airport ⊕ www.centrair.jp (referred to locally as "Centrair"), serves overseas flights and is a hub for domestic travel.

BUS TRAVEL The main bus terminals in Nagoya are at Nagoya Station, Oasis 21 in Sakae, and Kanayama. Buses with green signs are going to Nagoya Station, pink indicates Sakae, and black Kanayama. Standard fares are ¥200

Festivals

NAGOYA AND SURROUNDING cities host a wide variety of *matsuri* (festivals) throughout the year. Running the gamut from chaotic to tranquil, beautiful to bizarre, these annual events bring the culture and traditions of the area to life in ways that castles, museums, and temples cannot. We have picked out a few of the best, but whenever you visit check with the Tourist Information Center or Nagoya International Center for upcoming festivals. All these events are free.

FEBRUARY

Hadaka (Naked) Festival. For 1,200 years, thousands of men aged 42 (an unlucky age in Japan) have braved the winter cold wearing nothing but *fundoshi* (loincloths). Their goal, in an event that regularly results in serious injury to participants, is to touch the *shin otoko* (the one truly "naked man") and transmit their bad spirits to him before he reaches Kōnomiya shrine and submits to cleansing rituals. Eagerness to achieve this task often leads to dangerous stampedes, but the crowds of more than 100,000 are well protected from harm. The festival is held in the first half of February—contact Nagoya City Tourist Information Center in JR Nagoya Station for details. Kōnomiya Station is 15-minutes north of Nagoya on the Meitetsu Gifu line, and the shrine is a 10-minute walk from the station.

MARCH

Hōnen Festival. The 1,500-year-old Tagata-jinja in Komaki is home to one of Japan's infamous male fertility festivals. On March 15 large crowds gather to watch and take pictures of a 6-ft, 885-lb *owasegata* (phallus) being carried between two shrines and offered to the *kami* (god) for peace and a good harvest. The festival starts at 10 and climaxes with face-size "lucky" rice cakes being tossed into the crowd just before 4. The closest station is Tagata-jinja-mae on the Meitetsu Komaki line. Change at Inuyama if you are traveling from Nagoya. The train takes one hour.

JULY

Owari Tsushima Tenno Festival. The main feature of this charming, low-key event is five boats decorated with 365 paper lanterns (for the days of the year) arranged into a circular shape and 12 more (representing the months) hanging from a mast. The festival occurs the evening of the fourth Saturday in July. Haunting traditional music accompanies the boats as they drift lazily around the river and the lanterns and fireworks reflect in the water. Tsushima is 25-minutes west of Nagoya on the Meitetsu Bisai line. Follow the crowds west from the station to the shrine and festival area.

AUGUST

Domannaka. Dozens of troupes of up to 150 dancers each arrive from all over Japan to take over Nagoya's streets and public spaces. Started in 1999, this energetic festival has rapidly gained popularity. It mixes hip-hop beats with spiced-up traditional dance moves and colorful costumes. Domannaka takes place over a weekend in late August. The exact dates and locations change from year to year, so get the latest details from Nagoya City Tourist Information Center in JR Nagoya Station.

for adults and ¥100 for children, and a joint subway and bus pass costs ¥850 per day.

CAR TRAVEL Wide main streets make Nagoya relatively easy to navigate. Road signs in the city often point to places out of town, however, so a detailed map is advised. Major highways connect Nagoya to Tōkyō, Nagano, Takayama, Kanazawa, Kyōto, and Nara.

SUBWAY TRAVEL Nagoya's subway system is user-friendly, with signs and announcements in English, and accesses almost all places of interest in the city. One-day passes cost ¥600. If you are staying a few days, there's a "Yurika" discount ticket for multiple trips. Yurika tickets can also be used on city buses and some Meitetsu trains.

TRAIN TRAVEL The JR trains are the easiest to jump on and off of, but they do not serve all destinations. Meitetsu and Kintetsu stations are lacking in English signage, though Meitetsu prints a handy English-language guide to their network and instructions on how to purchase tickets. You can pick up a copy at Meitetsu Nagoya Station or Chubu International Airport.

Visitor Information

❷ The **Nagoya International Center**, or Kokusai Senta, as it's locally known, is a wise stop on any Nagoya itinerary. Multilingual staff have a wealth of info on Nagoya and the surrounding area, and the center publishes a monthly newsletter, "Nagoya Calendar," which gives up-to-date advice, information, and event listings in English. It is one stop from JR Nagoya Station on the Sakura-dōri Subway Line or a seven-minute walk through the underground walkway that follows the line. ✉ *47–1 Sakura-dōri, Nagono 1-chōme, Nakamura-ku* ☎ *052/581–0100* ⊕ *www. nic-nagoya.or.jp* ⊗ *Tues.–Sun. 9–7.*

NAGOYA

By shinkansen, 1½–2 hrs west of Tōkyō, 1 hr east of Ōsaka, 40 min east of Kyōto.

In 1612, shōgun Ieyasu Tokugawa established Nagoya by permitting his ninth son to build a castle here. Industry and merchant houses sprang up in the shadow of this magnificent fortress, as did pleasure quarters for samurai. Supported by taxing the rich harvests of the surrounding Nōbi plain, the Tokugawa family used the castle as its power center for the next 250 years.

After the Meiji Restoration in 1868, when Japan began trade with the West in earnest, Nagoya developed rapidly. When the harbor opened to international shipping in 1907, Nagoya's industrial growth accelerated, and by the 1930s it was supporting Japanese expansionism in China with munitions and aircraft. This choice of industry was Nagoya's downfall; very little of the city was left standing after World War II.

Less than two months after the war, ambitious and extensive reconstruction plans were laid, and Nagoya began its remarkable comeback as an industrial metropolis. Today Nagoya is home to 2.2 million people living in a 520-square-km (200-square-mi) area.

Getting Around

When rebuilding Nagoya after the war, planners laid down a grid system, with wide avenues intersecting at right angles. Hisaya-odōri, a broad avenue with a park in its 328-foot-wide median, bisects the city. At Nagoya's center is an imposing 590-foot-high television tower (useful for getting your bearings). Nagoya-jō is north of the tower, Atsuta Jingū to the south, Higashiyama-kōen east, and the JR station west. The Sakae subway station serves as the center of the downtown commercial area.

❶ JR Nagoya Station is like a small city, with a variety of shops in, under, and around the station complex. The main **Nagoya City Tourist Information Center** (☎ 052/541–4301 ✆ daily 9–7) is in the station's central corridor. English-speaking staff can supply sightseeing information, subway maps, and details of upcoming events. Smaller information centers are in three other parts of the city—Sakae (✉ Oasis 21 bus station and shopping center ☎ 052/963–5252 ✆ daily 10–8), **Kanayama** (✉ North Exit of Kanayama Station ☎ 052/323–0161 ✆ daily 9–8), and **Nagoya Port** (✉ next to Nagoya-ko subway station ☎ 052/654–7000 ✆ daily 9–5).

What to See

❸ Nagoya-jō is notable for the castle's size and for the pair of gold-plated dolphins—one male, one female—mounted atop the *donjon* (principal keep). Built on land artificially raised from the flat Nagoya plain, the castle is protected by vast stone walls and two picturesque moats. The current castle is a 1959 reconstruction of the 1612 original, and an elevator whisks you between floors. Between the entrance, where you encounter a full-scale replica of the 2,673 pound female dolphin, and the top floor, which has 360-degree views of modern-day Nagoya, are five floors of exhibits. On the third floor is an evocative re-creation of Edo-era streets, complete with sound effects. Inside the east gate a traditional teahouse built of *hinoki* (Japanese cypress) stands in the **Ninomaru Tei-en** (Ninomaru Gardens), where a traditional tea ceremony costs ¥500. Nagoya-jō's east gate is one block north of the Shiyakusho (City Hall) subway station. ☎052/231–1700 ✐¥500 ✆ *Castle daily 9:30–4:30, garden daily 9:30–5.*

❹ Delicate colors and intricate hand-painted designs characterize the china of Noritake, the world's largest manufacturer of porcelain. Its **Noritake Garden** complex includes a craft center—effectively a mini-factory where workers demonstrate the 15-step manufacturing process from modeling to glazing to hand painting. You can even paint a design and transfer it to a piece of china. Workshops run 10–4 and cost ¥1,600 plus the price of shipping your piece once it has been fired (only plates can be shipped overseas). The upper floors house a small museum displaying "Old Noritake" works with art nouveau and art deco influences. Browsing is free in the "Celabo" area in the Welcome Center, which shows the diverse industrial applications of ceramics, from circuit boards to racing helmets. You aren't likely to find any bargains at the company shop, but you may discover pieces not available elsewhere.

Noritake Garden is a 15-minute walk north of JR Nagoya Station or five minutes from the Kamejima subway station. ✉ *1–36 Noritake-Shin-*

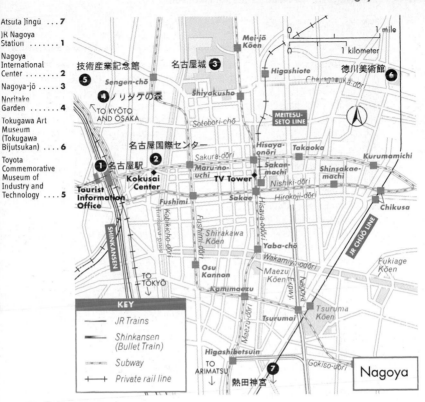

Nagoya

machi 3-chōme, Nishi-ku ☎ *052/561–7114 craft center, 052/561–7290 shop* ⊕ *www.noritake-elec.com/garden* ☯ *Craft center Tues.–Sun. 10–5, shop Tues.–Sun. 10–6* 🎫 *Craft center and museum ¥500. Joint entrance with Toyota Commemorative Museum ¥800.*

❺ Housed in the distinctive redbrick buildings of the company's original factory, the **Toyota Commemorative Museum of Industry and Technology** is dedicated to the rise of Nagoya's most famous company. Toyota's textile-industry origins are explored in the first of two immense halls, with an amazing selection of looms illustrating the evolution of spinning and weaving technologies over the last 200 years. The second, even larger hall focuses on the company's move into auto manufacturing. The museum's main aim is to interest today's Japanese schoolchildren in Nagoya's traditional *monozukuri* (art of making things) industrial culture, and the intimidatingly large halls are broken up into interactive display areas. In the Technoland room you can try out a wind tunnel, navigate a virtual reality maze, and use a massive lever to easily lift a 120-kg engine. The museum is a 20-minute walk north of JR Nagoya Station or 10 minutes from the Kamejima subway station. ✉ *1–35 Noritake-Shinmachi 4-chōme, Nishi-ku* ☎ *052/551–6115* ⊕ *www. tcmit.org* ☯ *Tues.–Sun. 9:30–5* 🎫 *Museum ¥500. Joint entrance with Noritake Garden ¥800.*

Play Ball!

CLOSE UP

IN NAGOYA you will find Japanese sports fans just as entertaining as the action on the field. Ask Tourist Information about upcoming events and where to buy tickets.

BASEBALL

The Chunichi Dragons play home games at the 40,500-capacity Nagoya Dome. Two leagues of six teams make up Japanese professional baseball, and the Dragons have won the Central League pennant six times and one Japan Series in 1954. In recent years the team is in a groove, reaching the Japan Series in 2004 and 2006. Fans here are a bit different—they sing well-drilled songs for each of the batters on their own team, but sit in stony silence when the opposing team is at bat. The season runs from April to October, and tickets for the upper-tier "Panorama" seats start at ¥1,500, rising to ¥5,800 for those behind home plate. Other than when a big team such as the Yomiuri Giants is in town, tickets are usually available at the stadium.

SOCCER

Perennial underachievers Nagoya Grampus Eight always seem to hang around mid-table in J-League Division One. Despite being a founder team of the J-League, and having had star players such as Gary Lineker and Dragan Stojkovic, Grampus have managed only a couple of Emperor's Cup wins. Still, remarkably loyal fans turn up in the thousands to cheer on the team. From March to December they play half their home games in Nagoya at the Mizuho Stadium, where the running track dissipates the atmosphere, and half at the futuristic 45,000-seat Toyota Stadium.

SUMŌ

In mid-July Nagoya's Prefectural Gymnasium, situated next to the castle, hosts one of the three sumō tournaments held outside Tōkyō each year. The arena holds 8,000 people, and you are almost guaranteed a good view of the *dohyō* (ring). Tickets, which cost from ¥2,800, are often available on the day of the tournament, but it's better to make advance reservations, particularly in the second half of the two-week event. The venue is a two-minute walk from Exit 7 of the Shiyakusho subway station. ⊠ *Aichi Prefectural Gymnasium 1-1 Ninomaru,Naka-ku* ☎ *052/962-9300 (ticket sales during the tournament)* ⊕ *www.sumo.or.jp* ☰ *AE, DC, MC, V.*

★ ❻ The **Tokugawa Art Museum,** (Tokugawa Bijutsukan) is most famous for having the seldom-displayed 12th-century hand scrolls of *The Tale of Genji,* widely recognized as the world's first novel. Still, it is the beautiful relics of the lifestyle of the premodern samurai class, the former aristocracy, that will fascinate most—swords and armor, tea-ceremony artifacts, Nō masks, clothing, and furnishings. If you're visiting specifically to see the scrolls, call the museum to make sure they are on display; if not, look for a later copy in Room 6.

Tokugawa Art Museum is a 10-minute walk south of Ōzone Station, which is on the Meijō subway line and the JR Chūō Line. ⊠ *1017 Tokugawa-chō, Higashi-ku* ☎ *052/935–6262* ⊕ *www.tokugawa-art-museum. jp* ☞ *¥1,200* ⊙ *Tues.–Sun. 10–5.*

7 A shrine has stood at the site of **Atsuta Jingū** for 1,700 years. After Ise, this is the country's most important Shinto shrine. The Hōmotsukan (Treasure House) holds one of the emperor's three imperial regalia—the Kusanagi-no-Tsurugi (Grass Mowing Sword). Nestled among 1,000-year-old trees, making it easy to spot from the train, the shrine is an oasis of tradition in the midst of modern industrialism. Sixty festivals and 10 religious events are held here each year—check with the tourist office to see what's going on.

From Nagoya Station take the JR Tokaidō Line south to Atsuta Station, then walk eight minutes southwest. ⊠ *Atsuta-ku* ☎ *052/671–4151* ⊕ *www.atsutajingu.or.jp* ⬛ *Shrine free, Treasure Museum ¥300* ☉ *Daily 9–4; closed last Wed. and Thurs. of month.*

Fodor'sChoice ★ Dropping in at an automobile factory might not be everyone's idea of holiday fun, but a **Toyota Plant Tour** makes all those dry books about *kaizen* (improvement) and the Japanese postwar economic miracle come to life. The tour starts at the **Toyota Kaikan** (Toyota Exhibition Hall). After exhibits on hybrid technology, safety, and motor sports, a company bus whisks you to one of several factories in the vicinity. The main assembly shop is something to behold—a hive of modern manufacturing activity where man and machine operate as one. Workers stand or sit on specially designed equipment that moves parallel to the production line so that it never has to pause, and every employee has the authority to stop the line if a fault is identified. In a remarkable feat of logistics, cars of all shapes and sizes are produced individually rather than in batches. English guides are available at the kaikan and factory for the 2–3 hour tour. A reservation made at least two weeks in advance is required.

The kaikan is about 90 minutes from Nagoya Station. Take the Tsurumai subway line to Toyota-shi, then Meitetsu Bus No. 4 toward Toyota Kinen Byoin, and get off at Toyota Honsha Mae. ⊠ *Toyota Kaikan Exhibition Hall 1, Toyota-cho* ☎ *0565/23–3922* ⊕ *www.toyota.co.jp/en/about_toyota/facility/toyota_kaikan* ☉ *Mon.–Sat. 9:30–5 (except national and summer holidays)* ⬛ *Free.*

Where to Stay & Eat

Nagoya's hotels are concentrated in three major areas: the district around JR Nagoya Station, downtown Fushimi and Sakae, and the Nagoya-jō area.

$$$$ ✕ **Kisoji.** Come here for reasonably priced (¥3,700) *shabu-shabu*—thinly sliced beef and vegetables that you boil in broth in the center of your table and then dip into various sauces before eating. Set courses run from ¥4,700 to ¥6,800. There are Western-style tables and chairs, but waitresses wear kimonos. You can drink all you want for 90 minutes for ¥1,680. Kisoji is two blocks northwest of the Sakae intersection. ⊠ *20–15 Nishiki 3-chōme, Naka-ku* ☎ *052/951–3755* ⬛ *AE, DC, MC, V.*

★ **$–$$$$** ✕ **Daibutsu Korokoro.** An *izakaya* (traditional) restaurant with several twists, the main one being the decor. This is how modern Japanese restaurants should look—dark wood, discreet lighting, and a maze of private

On the Menu

NAGOYA CUISINE IS CONSIDERED hearty, and is famous for its *aka miso* (red miso). Dishes featuring this sticky, sweet paste include *misonikomi udon*, thick noodles cooked in an earthenware pot of miso soup with chicken, egg, wood mushrooms, and green onions (you may want the chili pepper served on the side); *hitsumabushi*, chopped eel cooked in miso, and *miso katsu*, pork cutlet with miso-flavored sauce.

Other local specialties include *kishimen*, velvety smooth flat white noodles; *tebasaki*, deep-fried spicy chicken wings; and *uirō*, a sweet cake made of rice powder and sugar, eaten during the tea ceremony. The highly prized *kō-chin* is a specially fattened and uniquely tender kind of chicken.

dining rooms. In the middle of the restaurant is a 9½-foot-tall bronze Buddha. The tuna and salmon sushi set is fantastic; other interesting concoctions include citron tofu *gyōza* (dumplings) and croquettes of okra and cheese. The menu is in Japanese and English, and the restaurant is across from the main post office, 1½ blocks north of JR Nagoya Station's Sakura-dori exit. ⊠ *Kuwayama Bldg. B1, 2–45–19 Meieki, Naka-mura-ku* ☎ *052/581–9130* ▤ *AE, DC, MC, V.*

★ **$$–$$$** ✕ **Ibashō.** This fabulous old wooden restaurant serves a Nagoya specialty, *hitsumabushi,* or chopped eel smothered in miso sauce and served on rice. Ibashō is two blocks from Exit 1 of the Shin-Sakae subway station, and a hitsumabushi set meal is ¥2,300. The restaurant closes at 8 PM. It's closed Sunday and the second and third Monday of the month. ⊠ *3–13–22 Nishiki, Naka-ku* ☎ *052/951–1166* ▤ *No credit cards.*

$–$$$ ✕ **Jinmaru Nishina.** Locals come here to eat and drink at reasonable prices. Jinmaru Nishina is lively with groups of friends and office workers enjoying a night out. Everything from Korean-style kimchi dishes to Taiwan-style noodles is served, along with superb sashimi and draft beers. Jinmaru is behind the fire station, a four-minute walk from Exit 6 of the Fushimi subway station. ⊠ *Tōkyō Kaijō Bldg., 1st fl., 23–34 Sakae 1-chōme, Naka-ku* ☎ *052/203–5885* ▤ *AE, DC, MC, V.*

$–$$ ✕ **Yamamotoya Honke.** Nothing but *misonikomi-udon*—udon noodles in a hearty, miso-based broth with green onions and mushrooms—is served at this simple restaurant. A big, steaming bowl of this hearty, cold-chasing specialty costs just ¥924. It is halfway between the Fushimi and Yabo-chō subway stations. ⊠ *3–12–19 Sakae, Naka-ku* ☎ *052/241–5617* ▤ *No credit cards.*

$$$$ 🏨 **Nagoya Kankō Hotel.** The Imperial Family and professional ballplayers are among those served by Nagoya's oldest hotel. It's well located and provides the extra class and character you would expect for the price. The lobby's white-brick walls are balanced by soft-tone carpets and dark-wood furnishings. Rooms are spacious, and they look over the city center. The Kankō is five minutes by taxi from Nagoya Station. ⊠ *19–30 Nishiki 1-chōme, Naka-ku, Nagoya, Aichi-ken 460-8608* ☎ *052/231–7711* 🖷 *052/231–7719* ⊕ *www.nagoyakankohotel.co.jp* ➔ *375 rooms,*

Fodor's Choice ★

7 suites ⚓ 5 restaurants, room service, in-room safes, minibars, cable TV, gym, in-room data ports, massage, bar, shops, dry cleaning, laundry service, concierge, free parking ▤ AE, DC, MC, V.

★ **$$$-$$$$** ⌨ **The Westin Nagoya Castle.** A top-notch, reasonably priced hotel, the Westin has good amenities for its price range, including an indoor pool, fitness center, and sauna. The hotel stands on the bank of the Nagoya Castle moat, and your room might overlook the beautiful white castle, which is illuminated at night. Rooms on the other side overlook the downtown area. A free shuttle bus leaves from JR Nagoya Highway Bus Station on the hour from 10 to 8. ⊠ *3–19 Hinokuchi-chō, Nishi-ku, Nagoya, Aichi-ken 451-8551* ☎ *052/521–2121* 📠 *052/531–3313* ⊕ *www.castle.co.jp* 🛏 *195 Western-style rooms, 5 suites ⚓ 7 restaurants, minibars, cable TV, in-room data ports, indoor pool, gym, hair salon, sauna, 2 bars, shop, concierge, business services, meeting rooms, free parking, no-smoking rooms ▤ AE, D, DC, MC, V.*

$$ ⌨ **Fushimi Mont Blanc Hotel.** Centrally located and comparatively inexpensive, this business hotel is a good alternative to the luxury hotels. The rooms are small and simply furnished, but not wanting in any of the standard amenities, and the restaurant serves decent Japanese-style breakfasts and lunches for just ¥680. If necessary, request an Internet connection when making your reservation. The hotel is eight minutes from Nagoya Station by taxi. ⊠ *2-2-26 Sakae, Naka-ku, Nagoya, Aichi-ken 460-0003* ☎ *052/232–1121* 📠 *052/204–0256* ⊕ *www.montblanc-hotel.co.jp* ⚓ *2 restaurants, refrigerators, massage, meeting rooms* ▤ *AE, DC, MC, V.*

Nightlife

Sakae-chō has a high concentration of restaurants and bars. By day couples and families pack its streets, flitting between boutiques and department stores, but at night the area fills mostly with patrons of shady bars called "snacks." Unless you've got a lot of cash to burn, avoid such places.

Close to Exit 5 of the Fushimi subway station, toward the Hilton hotel, is the **Elephant's Nest** (⊠ 1–4 Sakae 3-chōme, Naka-ku ☎ 052/232–4360). This popular English-style pub has Guinness on tap, dart boards, and live soccer on the TV. The food is okay, too, including fish-and-chips. It's open 5:30–1 Sunday–Thursday and until 2 on Friday and Saturday. Happy Hour is from 5:30 to 7.

The young crowd gathers at the wild, seven-floor **iD Cafe** (⊠ Mitsukoshi Bldg., 1–15 Sakae 3-chōme, Naka-ku ☎ 052/251–0382). On weekday evenings entrance to this club costs ¥1,500, including three drinks. The price rises on weekends, as does the number of drinks.

Nova Urbana (⊠ Koasa Bldg. B1, 4–2–10 Sakae, Naka-ku ☎ 052/252–0127). A Brazilian restaurant-cum-bar-cum-club, Nova Urbana has something for everyone. The all-you-can-eat churrasco buffet, with barbecued beef, is great value at ¥2,380 for men or ¥1,980 for women, and you can drink all you want for an extra ¥1,500. There is live music, always with a Latin feel, and no one stays seated for long. Opening hours are 6 PM–3 AM Tuesday–Thursday, until 4 on Friday, 6 on Saturday, and midnight on Sunday and national holidays.

246 < **Nagoya, Ise-Shima & the Kii Peninsula**

SOUTH GIFU-KEN

Old Japan resonates in the foothills of the Hida Sanmyaku (Hida Mountains), just north of Nagoya. Ancient customs and crafts, such as cormorant fishing and umbrella-, lantern-, pottery-, and sword-making, are still practiced, and the nation's oldest castle, Inuyama-jō, has seen it all for almost 500 years. Gifu is the main center of *ukai* (cormorant fishing). Inuyama also offers the fishing experience, and it boasts a superior castle and, in Meiji-mura, an outstanding museum.

Gifu

❽ *20 min northwest of Nagoya on the JR Tōkaidō Line or Meitetsu Nagoya Line.*

Gifu's main attraction is its 1,300-year tradition of cormorant fishing. The city center spreads several blocks north from the JR and Meitetsu stations. Extensive rebuilding after World War II didn't create the prettiest place, but there is plenty going on. *Wagasa* (oiled paper umbrellas) are handmade in small family-owned shops, and *chōchin* (paper lanterns) and laquered *uchiwa* fans are also produced locally. If you are interested in seeing these items being made, ask Tourist Information for workshops that allow visitors. Gifu Park is 15 minutes by bus or 30 minutes on foot north from JR Gifu Station.

A city **Tourist Information Office** (☎ 058/262–4415 ☉ Daily 10–7) is on the second floor of the train station, just outside the ticket gates.

What to See

Ukai, or fishing with cormorants, can be seen for free from the banks of the Nagara-gawa, just east of Nagara Bridge at around 7:30 PM. Or you can buy a ticket for one of approximately 130 boats that ply the waters. Allow two hours for an ukai outing—an hour and a half to eat and drink (bring your own food if you haven't arranged for dinner on board) and a half hour to watch the fishing. Boat trips (¥3,300) begin at around 6 PM nightly from May to October; reservations, made through Gifu City Cormorant Fishing Sightseeing Office or the Tourist Information Center, are essential. There's no fishing when there's a full moon. (☎ 058/262–0104 Gifu City Cormorant Fishing Sightseeing Office, 058/262–4415 Tourist Information Office).

Gifu-jō is a castle perched dramatically on top of Mt. Kinka, overlooking the city center and Nagara River. The current building dates from 1951—the 16th-century structure was destroyed by an 1891 earthquake. A cable-car ride up from Gifu Park (¥600 one-way, ¥1,050 round-trip) gets you to the castle in 10 minutes, or you can walk the 2.3-km (1.5 mi)-path to the 329-m summit in about an hour. Take Bus 11 (Nagara–Sagiyama) to Gifu Park (¥300). ⊠ *Gifu-jō, Ōmiya-chō* ☎ *058/263–4853* 🎫 *¥200* ☉ *Daily 9–5.*

In Gifu Park, five minutes' walk south of the cable-car station, is **Gifu City Museum of History.** On the second floor you can dress up in traditional clothing and play old Japanese games such as *bansugoroku* (similar to backgammon). The nearby Nawa Insect Museum (¥500) houses

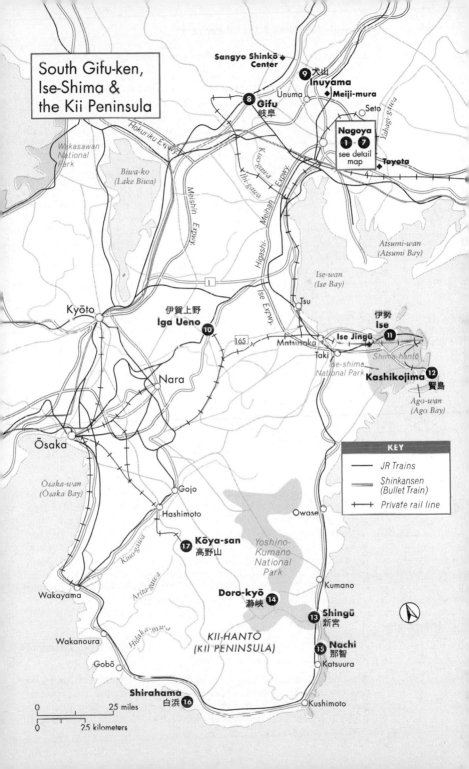

disturbingly large beetles, butterflies, and other bugs. ⊠ *18–1 2-chōme, Ōmiya-chō* ☎ *058/265–0010* ☞ *¥300* ⊗ *Tues.–Sun. 9–5.*

Japan's third-largest Buddha resides at **Shōhō-ji.** This incarnation of Shaka Nyorai (Great Buddha) is 45 feet tall and constructed of pasted-together paper *sutra* (prayers) coated with clay and stucco and then lacquered and gilded; it took 38 years to complete. From Gifu Park, walk two blocks south. ⊠ *8 Daibutsu-chō* ☎ *058/264–2760* ☞ *¥150* ⊗ *Apr.–Nov., daily 8:30–5; Dec.–Mar., daily 9–4.*

OFF THE BEATEN PATH **SANGYO SHINKŌ CENTER** (Seki Swordsmith Museum) – Seki has a 700-year-old sword-manufacturing heritage, and you'll appreciate the artistry and skill of Japanese swordsmiths at the Swordsmith Museum. Three types of metal are used to form blades forged multiple times and beaten into shape with a hammer. Demonstrations are held on January 2 and the first Sundays of March, April, June, and November. Special displays occur during the Seki Cutlery Festival the second weekend of October. Seki is 30 minutes northeast of Gifu via the Meitetsu Minomachi Line. ⊠ *4–6 Heiwa-dōri, Seki-shi* ☎ *0575/23–3825* ⊕ *www.sekikanko.jp* ☞ *¥200.*

Where to Stay & Eat

$–$$ ✕ **Junkissa-u.** Cormorants strut around the Japanese garden outside this restaurant, where the specialty is *ayu* (sweetfish). The owner boasts of upholding the 1,300-year-old local *ukai* (cormorant-fishing) tradition, and the ayu are prepared every way imaginable. Most popular is *ayu-no-narezushi,* a kind of reverse sushi with the ayu stuffed full of rice. ⊠ *94–10 Naka-Ukai, Nagara, Gifu-shi* ☎ *058/232–2839* ⊟ *No credit cards* ⊗ *No dinner.*

$$–$$$$ ☷ **Ryokan Sugiyama.** Across the Nagara River from the castle, Sugiyama is a tasteful blend of traditional and modern. The rooms are large, with tatami floors and elegant shōji doors—ask for one overlooking the river. The staff is polite in a mannered way, and the good food includes the ubiquitous ayu. The ryokan is a 15-minute taxi ride from Gifu Station or a 10-minute walk north of the ukai boat boarding area and the castle. ⊠ *73–1 Nagara, Gifu-shi, Gifu-ken 502-0071* ☎ *058/231–0161* 🖷 *058/233–5250* ☞ *46 rooms* ⊟ *AE, DC, MC, V* ⑩ *MAP.*

$$–$$$ ☷ **Hotel 330 Grand Gifu.** This tall, modern hotel has larger-than-average, Western-style rooms. Take one facing Kinkazan Park for excellent views toward Gifu Castle and the Nagara River. Hotel 330 is one block north and half a block west of Gifu Station. ⊠ *5–8 Nagazumi-chō, Gifu-shi, Gifu-ken 500-8175* ☎ *058/267–0330* 🖷 *058/264–1330* ☞ *147 rooms* ⚄ *Restaurant, cable TV, in-room data ports* ⊟ *AE, DC, MC, V.*

Inuyama

➒ *20 min east of Gifu by Meitetsu Kakamigahara Line, 30 min north of Nagoya by Meitetsu Inuyama Line.*

Inuyama sits along the Kiso River, on the border between Aichi and Gifu prefectures. A historically strategic site, the city changed hands several times during the Edo period. You can see cormorant fishing here; tickets are available from major hotels for ¥2,500–¥2,800. Call the **Tourist**

Information office (☎ 0568/61–6000) in the station for details. A good way to see the Kiso-gawa is on a tame raft. To travel the hour-long, 13-km (8-mi) river trip (¥3,400), take the train on the Meitetsu Hiromi Line from Inuyama to Nihon-Rhine-Imawatari. Once there, check out several companies before selecting the boat you prefer.

What to See

★ Inuyama's most famous sight is **Inuyama-jō**, also known as Hakutei-jō (White Emperor Castle). Built in 1537, it is the oldest of the 12 original castles in Japan. The castle is exceedingly pretty, and stands amid carefully tended grounds on a bluff overlooking the Kiso River. Climb up the creaky staircases to the top floor for a great view of the river, city, and surrounding hills. The gift shops at the foot of the castle hill are good for browsing. From Inuyama-Yūen Eki, walk southwest along the river for 15 minutes. ☎ 0568/61–1711 ¥500 ☉ Daily 9–5.

The pretty stretch of the **Kiso-gawa** that flows beneath cliff-top Inuyama-jō has been dubbed the Japanese Rhine. One well-established boating company that offers trips on the Kiso-gawa is **Nippon Rhine Kankō** ☎ 0574/28–2727.

FodorsChoice **Meiji-mura** is one of Japan's best museums. Situated in attractive countryside, this expansive site has more than 60 buildings originally constructed during the Meiji era (1868–1912), when Japan ended its policy
★ of isolationism and swiftly industrialized. The best way to experience the exhibits is to wander about, stopping to look at things that catch your eye. There's an English pamphlet you receive upon entry to help guide you. If you get tired of walking, transport options within Meiji-mura include a tram originally from Kyōto and a steam train from Yokohama. Among the exhibits are a surprisingly beautiful octagonal wood prison from Kanazawa, a kabuki theater from Ōsaka that hosts occasional performances, and the former homes of renowned writers Soseki Natsume, Ogai Mori, and Lafcadio Hearn. The entrance lobby of legendary American architect Frank Lloyd Wright's Imperial Hotel, where Charlie Chaplin and Marilyn Monroe were once guests, is arguably the highlight. It opened on the day of the Great Kanto Earthquake in 1923, 11 years after the death of Emperor Meiji, and though it is not strictly a Meiji-era building, its Mayàn-influenced detailing and sense of grandeur and history are truly unique. Buses run from Inuyama Station to Meiji-mura at six minutes past the hour from 10 to 3. The ride takes 20 minutes and costs ¥410. ⊠ 1 Uchiyama ☎ 0568/67–0314 ⊕ www.meijimura.com ¥1,600 ☉ Mar.–Oct., daily 9:30–5; Nov.–Feb., daily 9:30–4.

In Uraku-en, a traditional garden attached to the grounds of the Meitetsu Inuyama Hotel, sits the **Jo-an Teahouse**. The teahouse was constructed in Kyōto in 1618 and moved to its present site in 1971. Admission to the garden is pricey, so it's worth paying an extra ¥500 to be served green tea in the traditional style. Uraku-en is less than ½ km (¼ mi) from Inuyama-jō, behind the Meitetsu Inuyama Hotel. ⊠ 1 Gomon-saki ☎ 0568/61–4608 Teahouse and gardens ¥1,000 ☉ Mar.–Nov., daily 9–5; Dec.–Feb., daily 9–4.

Hiking

Tsugao-san. A hike to Tsugao-san reveals more pleasant scenery near the Inuyama-jō. Start on the paved riverside trail at the base of Inuyama-jō. Follow the trail east past the Japan Monkey Park, then north to Jakkō-in (built in 654), where the maples blaze in fall. Along the route are good views of the foothills stretching north from the banks of the Kiso-gawa. You can climb Tsugao-san or continue northeast to Ōbora Pond and southeast to Zenjino Station, where you can catch the Meitetsu Hiromi Line two stops back to Inuyama Station. The train passes through Zenjino four times an hour. From Inuyama-jō to Zenjino Station is an 8-km (5-mi) hike. Allow 2½ hours from the castle to the top of Tsugao-san; add another hour if you continue to Zenjino via Ōbora Pond.

Where to Stay

$$$–$$$$ ☒ **Meitetsu Inuyama Hotel.** On the south bank of the Kiso-gawa, this hotel has winning views of the river, castle, and hills. The lobby is bright and lively, and the hotel grounds, including Uraku-en, and hot-spring baths are relaxing. Sunny rooms have pleasant vistas; the best face the castle, which overlooks the hotel and is illuminated in the evening. The hotel is convenient for accessing local sights and can arrange tours. ☒ *107–1 Kita-Koken, Inuyama, Aichi-ken 484-0082* ☎ *0568/61–2211* 🖷 *0568/ 62–5750* 🛏 *92 Western-style rooms, 34 Japanese-style rooms* ⧄ *3 restaurants, bar, sauna* 🖃 *AE, MC, V.*

Iga Ueno

❿   *2 hrs southwest of Nagoya on the JR Kansai Line, 1hr 40 min east of Kyōto by JR, 1 hr east of Nara by JR, 2 hrs east of Ōsaka by JR.*

This small city halfway between Nagoya and Nara has some interesting claims to fame. Noted *haiku* poet Matsuo Bashō was born here in the 1640s, and it was home to one of Japan's leading ninja schools.

★ ♨   At the **Iga-Ryu Ninja Museum** the city makes the most of its major attraction. The Iga-Ryu school of *ninjutsu* (ninja arts) was one of the top two training centers for Japan's ancient spies and assassins in the 14th century. At the *ninja yashiki* (ninja residence), a guide dressed in ninja costume explains how they were always prepared for attack. The hidden doors and secret passages are ingenious, but it can't have been a relaxed existence. Energetic demonstrations of ninja weapons like throwing stars, swords, daggers, and sickles are fun (Dec.–Feb., weekends 11–3; Mar.–Nov., every second day 11–3), and for ¥200 you can try out the throwing star. Two exhibitions round out the tour. The first gives background on ninja history and techniques, and the second displays the disguises and encryption used by the Iga ninja, as well as the inventive tools that enabled them to walk on water and scale sheer walls. The museum is in Ueno Park, a 10-minute walk up the hill from Iga Ueno Station. ☒ *117 Uenomaronouchi* ☎ *0595/23–0311* 🖾 *¥700* ☉ *Daily 9–5.*

Iga Ueno-jō stands today because of one man's determination and wealth. The first castle built here was destroyed by a rainstorm in 1612, before it was completed. More than 300 years later, local resident Katsu Kawasaki financed a replica that sits atop vertiginous 98-foot stone walls—

be careful when it's windy. Kawasaki also paid for the Haiku Poetry Master's Pavilion, built in memory of Japan's famous wandering poet, Matsuo Bashō, which stands near the castle in Ueno Park. ☎ 0595/21–3148 📧 ¥500 ☉ Daily 9–5.

ISE-SHIMA NATIONAL PARK

Hanging like a fin underneath central Honshū, the Ise-Shima is a scenic and sacred counterweight to Japan's overbuilt industrial corridor. Ise-Shima National Park, which holds the supremely venerated shrines of Ise Jingū, extends east from Ise to Toba (the center of the pearl industry), and south to the indented coastline and pine-clad islands near Kashikojima. The bottom hook of the peninsula, around to Goza via Daiō, has some of the prettiest coves on the Ago Bay, each one home to oyster nets and small groups of fishing boats.

Ise

⓫ *80 min south of Nagoya by Kintetsu Limited Express (longer by JR local), 2 hrs east of Kyōto by private Kintetsu Line, 2 hrs east of Nara by JR, 2 hrs east of Ōsaka by Kintetsu.*

When you step off the train, you may feel that Ise is a drab city, but hidden in two forests of towering cedar trees are the most important and impressive Shintō shrines in Japan. Indeed, the city's income comes mainly from the pilgrims who visit Gekū and Naikū, the Outer and Inner shrines, respectively. Near the Inner Shrine you'll find an array of shops hawking souvenirs to the busloads of tourists and a few spots to eat such local specialties as *Ise udon* (udon noodles with a thick broth) and *akafuku* (sweet rice cakes). The busiest times at Ise Jingū are during the Grand Festival, held October 15–17 every year, when crowds gather to see the pageantry, and on New Year's Eve and Day, when hundreds of thousands come to pray for good fortune.

Getting Around

Ise has two stations five minutes apart, Ise-shi and Uji-Yamada, the main station. From either station it's only a 10-minute walk through town to the Outer Shrine. A frequent shuttle bus makes the 6-km (4-mi) trip between Gekū and Naikū; a bus also goes directly from the Inner Shrine to Ise Station.

Ise Tourist Information Center (☎ 0596/28–3705, 8:30–5) is across the street from the Outer Shrine, and has information about both Ise and the surrounding area.

What to See

Fodor'sChoice Astoundingly, **Ise Jingū** (Grand Shrines of Ise) is rebuilt every 20 years, ★ in accordance with Shintō tradition. To begin a new generational cycle, exact replicas of the previous halls are erected with new wood, using the same centuries-old methods, on adjacent sites. The old buildings are then dismantled. The main halls you see now—the 61st set—were completed in 1993 at an estimated cost of more than ¥4.5 billion. For Japanese, importance is found in the form of the buildings; the vintage of the materials is of little concern. You cannot enter any of the buildings, but the tantalizing glimpses of the main halls that you catch while walking the grounds add to the mystique of the site.

Deep in a park of ancient Japanese cedars, **Gekū,** dating from AD 477, is dedicated to Toyouke Ō-kami, goddess of agriculture. Its buildings are simple, predating the influx of 6th-century Chinese and Korean influence. It's made from unpainted *hinoki* (cypress), with a closely cropped thatched roof. You can see very little of the exterior of Gekū—only its roof and glimpses of its walls—and none of the interior. Four fences surround the shrine, and only the imperial family and their envoys may enter.

The same is true for the even more venerated **Naikū,** 6 km (4 mi) southwest of Gekū. Naikū is where the Yata-no-Kagami (Sacred Mirror) is kept, one of the three sacred treasures of the imperial regalia. The shrine, said to date from 4 BC, also houses the spirit of the sun goddess Amaterasu, who Japanese mythology says was born of the left eye of Izanagi, one of the first two gods to inhabit the earth. According to legend, Amaterasu was the great-great-grandmother of the first mortal emperor of Japan, Jimmu. Thus, she is revered as the country's ancestral goddess-mother and guardian deity. The Inner Shrine's architecture is simple. If you did not know its origin, you might call it classically modern. The use of unpainted cypress causes Naikū to blend into the ancient forest encircling it.

Both Grand Shrines exhibit a natural harmony that the more contrived buildings in later Japanese architecture do not. You can see very little of either through the wooden fences surrounding the shrines, but the reward is in the spiritual aura surrounding Naikū and Gekū. This condition, where the inner experience is assigned more importance than the physical encounter, is very traditional Japanese. Entry to the grounds of both shrines, which are open sunrise to sunset, is free. If you are pressed for time, head for the more impressive Naikū first.

Where to Stay & Eat

★ $$$$ ✕ **Restaurant Wadakin.** If you love beef, make a pilgrimage to Matsusaka, one train stop north of Ise. Wadakin claims to be the originator of Matsusaka beef's fame; the cattle are raised with loving care on the restaurant's farm out in the countryside. Sukiyaki or the chef's steak dinner will satisfy your cravings. ✉ *1878 Naka-machi, Matsusaka* ☎ *0598/21–1188* ▭ *No credit cards* ⊘ *Closed 4th Tues. of month.*

★ $ ▦ **Hoshide Ryokan.** This 85-year old traditional-style inn has wood-decorated tatami rooms and narrow squeaking corridors. The hosts are congenial and considerate—they provide dinner at a table for those tired of sitting on the floor, and vegetarian meals if requested in advance. Hoshide-kan is near the quaint Kawasaki area, 5 minutes' walk north from the Kintetsu station or 10 minutes from the JR station. Follow the main street and it's on the right just before the second set of signals. Ise will become a "bicycle town" in 2010, and if you want to explore the city on two wheels, the hotel rents them for ¥300 a day. ✉ *2–15–2 Kawasaki, Ise, Mie-ken 516-0009* ☎ *0596/28–2377* ▤ *0596/27–2830*

CLOSE UP

The Pearl Divers

AT TOBA, before Kokichi Mikimoto (1858–1954) perfected a method for cultivating pearls here in 1893, *Ama* (female divers: women were believed to have bigger lungs) would dive all day, bringing up a thousand oysters, but they wouldn't necessarily find a valuable pearl. Pearl oysters are now farmed, and the famous female divers are a dying breed. On the outlying islands, however, women do still dive for abalone, octopus, and edible seaweed. The **Mikimoto Pearl Museum** (Mikimoto Shinju no Hakubutsukan), on Pearl Island, 500 yards southeast from Toba Station, explores this history. ☎ *0599/25–2028* ⊕ *www.mikimoto-pearl-museum.co.jp* ¥1,500 ⊗ *Apr.–Oct., daily 8:30–5; Nov.–Mar., daily 9–4.*

Take one of two routes from Ise to Toba: a 45-minute bus ride from near Nai-kū, for ¥980, or the more scenic JR train, for ¥230. **Toba Tourist Information Center** (☎ 0599/25–2844), outside Exit 1 of Kintetsu Toba Station, has an English map of the main attractions. Open 9–5:30.

hoshide@amigo.ne.jp *10 Japanese-style rooms with shared bath* *Japanese baths* *AE, MC, V* *MAP.*

Kashikojima

★ 12 *50 min by bus or 30 min by train south from Toba, 2 hrs south by train on the Kintetsu Line from Nagoya.*

The jagged coastline at Ago-wan (Ago Bay), with calm waters and countless hidden coves, presents a dramatic final view of the Ise Peninsula. The best approach to Kashikojima is to catch a bus to Goza, the tip of the headland, and ride a ferry back across the bay. From the boat you'll get a close-up look at the hundreds of floating wooden rafts from which the pearl-bearing oysters are suspended.

Tucked behind a promontory, the fishing village of **Daiō** is an interesting stop on the journey around the headland. At a small fish market you can buy fresh squid, mackerel, and other seafood. Standing above the village is a 46-meter-tall lighthouse, **Daiōzaki tōdai,** open to visitors daily 9–5 for an entrance fee of ¥150. To reach this towering white structure, walk up the narrow street lined with fish stalls and pearl souvenir shops at the back of the harbor. From this lighthouse you can see **Anorizaki tōdai,** the oldest (1870) stone lighthouse in Japan, 11 km (7 mi) east.

Getting Around

To take a coastal route, get off the train at Ugata and take a bus to Nakiri; then change buses for one to Goza, where frequent ferries return across the bay to Kashikojima.

It's possible to follow the coast from Kashikojima to the Kii Peninsula, but there is no train, and in many places the road cuts inland, making the journey long and tedious. From Kashikojima or Toba you are better off taking the Kintetsu Line back to Ise to change to the JR Sangū

Line and travel to Taki, where you can take the JR Kisei Line south to the Kii Peninsula.

Where to Stay

$–$$ ▦ **Daiōsō.** Staying at this small family-run ryokan next to the harbor in Daiō allows you to enjoy the peaceful evening after the tourists have left and witness the early-morning activity of the fishermen. A good *izakaya* (traditional-style) restaurant is attached to the ryokan. Lunch and dinner are served every day, with fresh *Ise ebi* (lobster) the main attraction. The Japanese-style tatami rooms are clean and modern—try to get one overlooking the water. Daiō can be reached by bus from Ugata, and the harbor bus stop is just 20 meters from the ryokan. ✉ *244 Namigiri, Shima, Mie-ken 517-0603* ☎ *0599/72–1234* 🖷 *0599/72–0489* ✎ *daiohso@ekakinomacti.com* ➷ *7 Japanese-style rooms* ♨ *Restaurant* ⊟ *AE, DC, MC, V* ⑩ *MAP.*

★ **$–$$** ▦ **Ishiyama-sō.** On tiny Yokoyama-jima in Ago-wan, this small inn has painted its name in large letters on the red roof. Ishiyama-sō is a two-minute ferry ride from Kashikojima; phone the day before, and your hosts will meet you at the quay. The inn isn't fancy, but it offers rooms overlooking the sea. You'll find tea sets and *yukata* (Japanese bathrobes) in the rooms. Breakfast and dinner, included in the room rate, are served in the communal dining hall. ✉ *Yokoyama-jima, Kashikojima, Ago-chō, Shima-gun, Mie-ken 517-0502* ☎ *0599/52–1527* 🖷 *0599/52–1240* ✎ *i.i.k-nk@poem.ocn.ne.jp* ➷ *10 rooms, 4 with shower* ♨ *Japanese baths, TV* ⊟ *AE, MC, V* ⑩ *MAP.*

KII PENINSULA

Beyond Ise-Shima, the Kii Peninsula has magnificent marine scenery, coastal fishing villages, beach resorts, and the temple mountain of Kōyasan. Wakayama Prefecture, which constitutes much of the Kii Peninsula, has a population of only 1 million, and life here moves at a relaxed pace. From Shingū you can reach all three great shrines of the Kumano Kodo pilgrimage route. Nearby Yoshino-Kumano National Park has pristine gorges, holy mountains, and another ancient Buddhist site at Yoshino-san, where gorgeous hillside sakura flower in early April.

Shingū

⓭ *2 hrs southwest of Taki by JR Limited Express, 2 hrs southwest of Kashikojima by the Kintetsu and JR lines, 3½ hrs southwest of Nagoya by JR.*

Shingū is home to one of the three great shrines of the Kumano Kodo, **Hayatama-taisha** (daily 9–4:30). One of the few north–south roads penetrating the Kii Peninsula begins in town and continues inland to Nara by way of Doro-kyō (Doro Gorge). A drive on this winding, steep, narrow road, especially on a bus, warrants motion-sickness pills. The mossy canyon walls outside your window and the rushing water far below inspire wonder, but frequent sharp curves provide plenty of anxiety. Continue north on the road past Doro-kyō to reach **Hongū** (daily 9–4:30), which has attractive wooden architecture and a thatched roof.

Shingu Tourist Association Information Center (☎ 0735/22-5231 ⊘ Daily 9–5:30) is to the left as you exit the station.

Where to Stay

$$ ☒ **Shingū-Yū ai Hotel.** Better than the average business hotel, a nice façade, fair-size rooms, and a convenient location make this a good option if you're staying overnight in Shingū. It's next to the post office, a five-minute walk from the train station. ⊠ *3–12 I-no-sawa, Shingū-shi, Wakayama-ken 647-0045* ☎ *0735/22–6611* 🖷 *0735/22–4777* ⇋ *82 Western-style rooms* ⌂ *Restaurant* ▤ *AE, DC, MC, V.*

Doro-kyō

⑭ *30 min north of Shingū by JR bus.*

The wide ocean views of the coastal journey to Shingū give way to gorges and mountainsides of a deep mossy green when you pass through the tunnel five minutes north of the city. Up the Kumano River, the walls of the steep-sided Doro-kyō rise above you. Farther up, sheer 150-foot cliffs tower over the Kumano-gawa.

The best way to see this gorge is on a four-hour trip (¥5,100) upriver on a flat-bottomed, fan-driven boat. Outside seats on the boats are the best. You can book a trip that includes bus and boat at the Shingu information center. If you have a JR Pass, taking a 30-minute bus ride from Shingū Station to Shiko, the departure point for the boats going up river, will save you ¥1,120.

The boat trip doesn't venture much beyond Doro-hatchō before returning to Shiko. You can hire different boats (two hours round-trip, ¥3,280) to explore the two other gorges and rapids that extend for several miles upstream. Buses go back to Shingū from either Doro-hatchō or Shiko.

Nachi

⑮ *10 min southwest of Shingū by JR.*

Nachi-no-taki, the highest waterfall in Japan, drops 430 feet into a rocky river. At the bus stop near the falls a large torii gate marks the start of a short path that leads to a paved clearing near the foot of the falls. A 20-minute bus ride (¥600) from Nachi Station gets you here.

A 15-minute climb up the mossy stone path opposite the souvenir shops is **Nachi Taisha** (daily 9–4:30), reputed to be 1,400 years old and perhaps the most impressive of the Kumano Kodo shrines. For ¥200 you can ride an elevator to the top of the bright red pagoda for an on-high view of the waterfall.

Next to the shrine is the 1587 Buddhist temple Seiganto-ji, starting point for a 33-temple Kannon pilgrimage through western Honshū. Many visitors walk here from a point several kilometers away on the road to Nachi Station. The temple grounds offer mountain views to the southwest.

Five miles from Kushimoto, **Shio-no-misaki** is Honshū's southernmost point. Stationed high above the rocky cliffs is a white lighthouse that unfortunately closes before sunset (open 9–4, ¥150). Adjacent to the lighthouse is a good spot for picnics and walking on the cliff paths. The beach looks inviting, but sharp rocks and strong currents make swimming a bad idea.

Shirahama

⓰ *75 min west of Nachi, 3 hrs south of Ōsaka by JR train.*

Rounding the peninsula, 54 km (34 mi) northwest of Shio-no-misaki, Shirahama is a small headland famous for its pure white-sand beach. If you're wondering why it looks and feels so different from the other beaches, it's because this sand is imported from Australia. Hot springs are dotted along the beach and around the cape. The climate, which allows beach days even in winter, makes Shirahama an inviting base for exploring the area. While it can be intolerably busy in July and August, it is otherwise pretty laid-back. A 17-minute bus ride from the train station gets you to the beachside town.

Fodor'sChoice
★
Soak in the open-air at **Sakino-yu Onsen,** a hollow among the wave-beaten rocks facing the Pacific, where it's said that Emperors Saimei (594–661) and Mōmmu (683–707) once bathed. It's at the south end of the main beach, below Hotel Seamore. ▧ *¥300 ⊗ Thurs.–Tues. dawn–dusk.*

At the north end of the beach is **Shirara-yu Onsen,** where locals come and go all day to bathe and chat. The baths overlook the beach and ocean from the second floor of this old wooden building, and on the first floor is an open lounge area. You can rent or buy towels, but bring your own toiletries. It's a two-minute walk north of Shirara Minshuku. ▧ *¥300 ⊗ Daily 7 AM–11 PM.*

Where to Stay

$–$$ ▨ **Shirara Minshuku.** This friendly hotel right off the beach in Shirahama is a good alternative to the expensive resorts. The Japanese-style rooms are simple, and there is a natural hot-spring bath. The restaurant serves fresh local seafood in a variety of styles, including *funamori,* fresh sashimi served on a boat. ⊠ *1359 Shirahama-chō, Nishimuro-gun, Wakayama-ken 649-2211* ☎ *0739/42–3655* 🖷 *0739/43–5223* ⬎ *18 Japanese-style rooms* ⌂ *Restaurant* ▤ *AE, V.*

KŌYA-SAN

Kōya-san

★ **⓱** *2 hrs east of Wakayama (via Hashimoto) by JR, 90 min southeast of Ōsaka's Namba Station on the Nankai Dentetsu Line.*

This World Heritage Site is the headquarters of the Shingon sect of Buddhism, founded by Kūkai, also known as Kōbō Daishi, in AD 816. Every year a million visitors pass through Kōya-san's **Dai-mon** (Big Gate) to enter the great complex of 120 temples, monasteries, schools, and graves. Traveling to Kōya-san takes you through mountain wilderness, but the town itself is sheltered and self-contained. The main buildings are imposing, while the minor temples are in a wide range of styles and colors, each offering small-scale beauty in its decor or garden. Monks, pilgrims, and tourists mingle in the main street, the sneaker-wearing, motorcycle-riding monks often appearing the least pious of all.

Getting Around

If you approach Kōya-san by cutting across the Yoshino-Kumano National Park by bus from Shingū or Hongū on Route 168, get off the bus at Gojo and backtrack one station on the JR Line to Hashimoto; then take the Nankai Line.

By rail, the last leg of the trip is a five-minute cable-car ride (¥380) from Gokuraku-bashi Station. JR Passes are not valid for the cable car. The lift deposits you at the top of 3,000-foot Kōya-san, where you can pick up a map and hop on a bus to the main attractions, which are about 2½ km (1½ mi) from the station and 4 km (2½ mi) from each other on opposite sides of town. Two buses leave the station when the cable car arrives, which is every 20 or 30 minutes. One goes to Okuno-in Cemetery, on the east end of the main road, and the other goes to the Daimon, to the west.

Kōya-san Tourist Association office (✉ 600 Kōya-san, Kōya-chō, Ito-gun, Wakayama-ken ☎ 0736/56 2616) at the intersection in the center of town can be reached by bus for ¥300.

What to See

If time is limited, head for **Okuno-in,** a memorial park, first. Many Japanese make pilgrimages to the mausoleum of Kōbō Daishi or pay their respects to their ancestors buried here. Arrive early in the morning, before the groups take over, or even better, at dusk, when it gets wonderfully spooky.

Exploring this cemetery is like peeking into a lost and mysterious realm. Incense hangs in the air, and you can almost feel the millions of prayers said here clinging to the gnarled branches of 300-year-old cedar trees reaching into the sky. This *is* a special place. The old-growth forest is a rarity in Japan, and among the trees are buried some of the country's most prominent families, their graves marked by mossy pagodas and red-robed Bodhisattvas.

You can reach Okuno-in by way of the 2½-km (1½-mi) main walkway, which is lined with more than 100,000 tombs, monuments and statues. The lane enters the cemetery at Ichi-no-hashi-guchi; follow the main street straight east from the town center for 15 minutes to find this small bridge at the edge of the forest.

The path from Okuno-in-mae ends at the refined **Tōrō-dō** (Lantern Hall), named after its 11,000 lanterns. Two fires burn in this hall; one has reportedly been alight since 1016, the other since 1088. Behind the hall is the mausoleum of Kōbo Daishi. The hall and the mausoleum altar are extremely beautiful, with subtle lighting and soft gold coloring. ▦*Free* ⊙ *Lantern Hall Apr.–Oct., daily 8–5; Nov.–Mar., daily 8:30–4:30.*

On the southwestern side of Kōya-san, **Kongōbu-ji** is the chief temple of Shingon Buddhism. It was first built in 1592 as the family temple of

Hideyoshi Toyotomi, and rebuilt in 1861 to become the main temple of the Kōya-san community. The screen-door artwork and large-scale rock garden are noteworthy. 🖼¥500 ⊘ *Apr.–Oct., daily 8–5; Nov.–Mar., daily 8:30–4:30.*

The **Danjōgaran** (Sacred Precinct) boasts several outsize halls. The most striking is the **Kompon-daitō** (Great Central Pagoda). This red pagoda with an interior of brightly colored beams contains five large seated gold Buddhas. Last rebuilt in 1937, the two-story structure has an unusual style and rich vermilion color. From Kongōbu-ji walk down the temple's main stairs and take the road to the right of the parking lot in front of you; in less than five minutes you will reach Danjogaran. 🖼 *Each building ¥100 ⊘ Apr.–Oct., daily 8–5; Nov.–Mar., daily 8:30–4:30.*

The **Reihōkan** (Treasure Hall) has a collection of more than 5,000 well-preserved Buddhist relics, some dating back 1,000 years. The New Wing houses themed exhibitions of sculpture, painting, and artifacts. The Old Wing (confusingly marked "Exit") has a permanent exhibition of Buddha and Bodhisattva figures and calligraphic scrolls. The museum is across the road from the Danjōgaran. 🖼 ¥600 ⊘ *Daily 8:30–5:30.*

Where to Stay & Eat

Kōya-san has no modern hotels, however 53 of the temples offer Japanese-style accommodations—tatami floors, futon mattresses, and traditional Japanese shared baths. You eat the same food as the priests. Dinner and breakfast is *shōjin ryōri,* vegetarian cuisine that uses locally made tofu. Prices start from ¥9,500 per person, including meals. Only a few temples accept foreign guests, so an advance reservation is advisable, especially in October, when crowds come for the autumn leaves. Arrangements can be made through Kōya-san Tourist Association, the Nankai Railway Company office in Namba Station (Ōsaka), and the Japan Travel Bureau in most Japanese cities.

$–$$ 🏯 **Rengejō-in.** Rengejō-in is an especially lovely temple that is open to foreigners. Both the head priest and his mother speak English, and they serve excellent vegetarian meals. For the basic price you get a simple but stylish tatami room with a TV. Pay a bit extra and you get a larger room with garden views both front and back. From the cable-car terminus, take the bus and get off at the Ishinguchi stop. Rengejō-in is right across the street. ✉ *700 Kōya-san, 648-0211* ☎ *0736/56–2233* 🖷 *0736/56–4743* 💤 *46 rooms* ♨ *No room phones* ▤ *No credit cards.*

NAGOYA, ISE-SHIMA & THE KII PENINSULA ESSENTIALS

Transportation

BY AIR

Nagoya's Chubu International Airport ⊕ www.centrair.jp (referred to locally as "Centrair") is served by direct overseas flights from more than 30 cities worldwide, and is an important domestic hub for onward travel to more than 20 Japanese cities. Most major airlines have offices in downtown Nagoya, 45 km (28 mi) northeast of the airport.

CARRIERS For domestic travel, Japan Airlines (JAL) and All Nippon Airways (ANA) have offices in Nagoya.

All Nippon Airways ☎ 052/962-6211 ⊕ www.ana.co.jp. **Japan Airlines** ☎ 052/265-3369 ⊕ www.jal.co.jp.

AIRPORT TRANSFER The Meitetsu Airport Limited Express train makes the 28-minute run between Centrair and Nagoya Station for ¥1,200. This price includes a seat-reservation fee. Meitetsu also operates an airport bus, which costs ¥1,000 and takes 70 minutes.

Chūbu Kokusai Kūkō (Centrair) ☎ 0569/38-1195, daily 6:40 AM-10 PM ⊕ www.centrair.jp. **Meitetsu Airport Bus & Airport Limited Express** ⊠ Meitetsu Customer Center ☎ 052/582-5151, daily 8-7 ⊕ www.meitetsu.co.jp.

BY BUS

Highway buses operated by JR and Meitetsu connect Nagoya with major cities, including Tōkyō and Kyōto. The fare is half that of the *shinkansen* trains, but the journey takes three times longer.

JR buses crisscross Nagoya, running either north–south or east–west. The basic fare is ¥200—pay when you get on the bus. A one-day bus pass costs ¥600, and a combination bus/subway pass costs ¥850. Detailed information on bus travel can be collected at the Tourist Information Office in the center of Nagoya Station, and tickets are also available.

JR Tokai Bus ☎ 052/563-0489, daily 9-7 **Meitetsu Highway Bus** ☎ 052/582-0489, daily 8-7 **Nagoya City Transportation Bureau** ☎ 052/522-0111, daily 8-7 ⊕ www.kotsu.city.nagoya.jp.

BY CAR

The journey on the two-lane expressway from Tōkyō to Nagoya takes about five hours; from Kyōto allow 2½ hours. Japanese highways are jam-prone, with holiday season tailbacks out of Tōkyō sometimes reaching 60 miles in length. Signage is confusing, so be sure to get a car with satellite navigation or a good road map.

SUBWAYS

All Nagoya's stations have bilingual maps, and many trains have English announcements. The Higashiyama Line runs from the north down to JR Nagoya Station and then due east, cutting through the city center at Sakae. The Meijō Line runs in a loop, passing through the city center at downtown Sakae. A spur line, the Meitō, connects Kanayama to Nagoya Port. The Tsurumai Line runs north–south through the city, then turns from the JR station to Sakae to cross the city center. A fourth line, the Sakura-dōri, cuts through the city center from the JR station, paralleling the east–west section of the Higashiyama Line. The basic fare is ¥200. A one-day pass for Nagoya's subways costs ¥740, while a combination bus/subway pass is ¥850.

Nagoya City Transportation Bureau ☎ 052/522-0111, daily 8-7 ⊕ www.kotsu.city.nagoya.jp.

TAXIS

Taxis are parked at all major stations and hotels. Elsewhere it is still far easier to wave one down on the street than to call one of the Japanese-speaking reservation numbers. The initial fare is ¥610. A ride from Nagoya Station to Nagoya-jō costs about ¥1,200.

TRAIN TRAVEL

Three rail companies, JR Central Japan ⊕ www.jr-central.co.jp (on which you can use a rail pass), Meitetsu ⊕ www.meitetsu.co.jp, and Kintetsu, operate different lines that often intersect at major stations. Frequent bullet trains run between Tōkyō and Nagoya. The ride takes 1 hour, 52 minutes on the *Hikari* Shinkansen and 2½ hours on the slower *Kodama* Shinkansen, and costs ¥ 6,090. JR Passes are not accepted on the ultrafast *Nozomi,* which links Nagoya with Kyōto (43 minutes) and Ōsaka (1 hour). Less-expensive Limited Express trains proceed from Nagoya into and across the Japan Alps—to Takayama, Toyama, Matsumoto, and Nagano.

🚊 **JR Central Japan** ☎ 052/522-0111, daily 8-7 ⊕ www.jr-central.co.jp. **Kintetsu** ☎ 052/561-1604, daily 9-4. **Meitetsu** ✉ Meitetsu Customer Center ☎ 052/582-5151, daily 8-7 ⊕ www.meitetsu.co.jp.

Contacts & Resources

BANKS & EXCHANGE SERVICES

The post office in Nagoya Station can handle basic currency exchanges, and many banks are on the Sakura-dori side of the building. Sakae is the other major center for banks offering exchange facilities—Citibank is close to Exit 7 from the subway station. Most Japanese banks close at 4 on weekdays, and are open for only a few hours on Saturday morning. Major hotels can exchange money for guests.

🚊 **Citibank** ✉ Nagoya Branch, 3-14-15 Sakae, Naka-ku, Nagoya ⊙ Mon.-Fri. 9-3, Sat. 10-4, ATM daily 24 hrs ☎ 052/243-9252, Mon.-Fri. 9-5 ⊕ www.citibank.co.jp. **Post Office** ✉ Central Nagoya Ekimae Bunshitsu, 1-1-1 Meieki, Nakamura-ku, Nagoya ⊙ Mon.-Fri. 9-6 ☎ 052/564-2132.

EMERGENCIES

Nagoya is better set up than most Japanese cities in providing services for foreign residents and tourists, often in their own language. However, it is unlikely that local services outside the city will have English speakers on staff. If you are outside the city or cannot find an English speaker, try the Japan Helpline.

🚊 **Ambulance & Fire** ☎ 119. **Japan Helpline** ☎ 0120/461-1997. **Kokusai Central Clinic** ✉ Nagoya International Center Bldg. ☎ 052/561-0633. **National Hospital of Nagoya** ✉ 4-1-1 Sannomaru-ku, Naka-ku, Nagoya ☎ 0521/951-1111. **Police** ☎ 110.

INTERNET, MAIL & SHIPPING

Luxury and many business hotels offer Internet access; traditional ryokan and minshuku rarely do. Nagoya has Internet cafés (often combined with *manga* coffee shops) and Wi-Fi hot spots, especially in Sakae and Kanayama, but outside the city you may find less availability. Post offices abound, and major shipping companies have offices in Nagoya.

🏢**DHL** ✉Yusen Travel Co. Ltd., Nagoya Branch, 6F, 3-25-3 Meieki, Nakamura-ku, Nagoya ⊙weekdays 9:30-5 ☎0120/39-2580 ⊕www.dhl.com. **Federal Express** ✉Asaikosan 7, 1-9-57 Chitose, Atsuta-ku, Nagoya ⊙weekdays 8:30-8, Sat. 8:30-1 ☎0120/00-3200 ⊕www.fedex.com. **Post Office** ✉Central Nagoya Ekimae Bunshitsu 1-1-1 Meieki, Nakamura-ku, Nagoya ⊙weekdays 9-6 ☎052/564-2132.

MEDIA

BOOKS & MAGAZINES Maruzen, opposite the Maruei department store near the Sakae intersection, has a broad selection of English-language books and magazines. On the 11th floor of the Takashimaya Department Store in JR Nagoya Station, Sanseido has a smaller selection. Both shops stock copies of *Avenues* magazine, a long-running local quarterly with useful event listings.

🏢 **Maruzen** ✉3-23-3 Nishiki, Naka-ku, Nagoya ☎0521/261-2251. **Sanseido** ✉1-4 Meieki 1-chōme, Nakamura-ku ☎052/566-8877 ✉Takashimaya Department Store 11F, JR Nagoya Station.

TOUR OPTIONS

The Nagoya Yūran Bus Company runs five different bus tours of the city. The three-hour Panoramic Course tour (¥2,610) includes Nagoya-jō and Atsuta Jingū and has scheduled morning and afternoon departures. A full-day tour (¥6,270) will take you to sights around Nagoya. Trips also run up to Inuyama to watch *ukai* (¥7,680 round-trip). These tours have only a Japanese-speaking guide.

You can arrange a full-day tour to Ise and the Mikimoto Pearl Island at Toba from Kyōto or Ōsaka (¥24,800) through Sunrise Tours.

🏢JTB Sunrise Tours ☎052/211-3065. Nagoya Yuran Bus Company ☎052/561-4036.

Points of Interest

SITES/AREAS	JAPANESE CHARACTERS
Atsuta Shrine (Atsuta Jingū)	熱田神宮
Dai-mon (Big Gate)	大門
Daiō	大王
Danjōgaran (Sacred Precinct)	壇上伽藍
Doro-kyō	瀞峡
Gifu	岐阜
Gifu City Museum of History (Gifu-shi Rekishi Hakubutsukan)	岐阜市歴史博物館
Gifu-jō	岐阜城
Hayatama Great Shrine (Hayatama Taisha)	速玉大社
Head Shrine (Hongū)	本宮
Iga Ueno	伊賀上野
Iga-Ryu Ninja Museum	伊賀流忍者博物館
Iga Ueno Castle (Iga Ueno-jō)	伊賀上野城
Inuyama	犬山
Inuyama-jō	犬山城
Ise	伊勢
Ise Jingū (Grand Shrines of Ise)	伊勢神宮
Ise-Shima National Park	伊勢志摩国立公園
Jo-an Teahouse	茶室如庵
JR Nagoya Station	名古屋駅
Kashikojima	賢島
Kii Peninsula (Kii-hantō)	紀伊半島
Kimpusen Temple (Kimpusen-ji)	金峰山寺
Kiso River (Kiso-gawa)	木曽川
Kongōbu Temple (Kongōbu-ji)	金剛峰寺
Meiji-mura	明治村
Mikimoto Pearl Museum	ミキモト真珠の博物館
Mt. Kōya (Kōya-san) or Kōya-san (Mt. Kōya)	高野山
Nachi-no-taki	那智の滝
Nagoya	名古屋
Nagoya International Center	名古屋国際センター
Nagoya-jō	名古屋城
Noritake Garden	ノリタケの森
Okuno-in	奥の院

3

Reihō-kan (Treasure Hall)	霊宝館
Sakino-yu Onsen	崎の湯温泉
Sangyō Shinkō Center (Seki Swordsmith Museum)	産業振興センター
Shingū (Head Shrine) or Head Shrine	新宮
Shio-no-misaki	潮岬
Shirahama	白浜
Shirara Onsen (Shirara-yu)	しらら湯温泉
Shōhō Temple (Shōhō-ji)	正法寺
Tokugawa Art Museum (Tokugawa Bijutsukan)	徳川美術館
Tōrō-dō (Lantern Hall)	灯籠堂
Toyota Commemorative Museum of Industry (Sangyō Gijutsu Kinenkan)	産業技術記念館
Toyota Kaikan (Toyota Exhibition Hall)	トヨタ会館
Tugao-san (Mt. Tsugao) or Mt. Tsugao (Tsugao-san)	継鹿尾山

RESTAURANTS

Daibutsu Korokoro	だいぶつころころ
Ibashō	いば昇
Jinmaru Nishina	じんまる nishina
Kisoji	木曽路
Restaurant Wadakin	和田金
Yamamotoya Honke	山本屋本家

HOTELS

Daiō-sō	大王荘
Fushimi Mont Blanc Hotel	伏見モンブランホテル
Hoshide Kan	星出館
Hotel 330 Grande Gifu	ホテル 330 グランデ岐阜
Ishiyama-sō	石山荘
Meitetsu Inuyama Hotel	名鉄犬山ホテル
Nagoya Kankō Hotel	名古屋観光ホテル
Rengejō Temple (Rengejō-in)	蓮華定院
Ryokan Sugiyama	旅館すぎ山
Shingū-Yū ai Hotel	新宮ユーアイホテル
Shirara Minshuku	南紀白浜国民民宿しらら
South Gifu	岐阜南
The Westin Nagoya Castle	ウェスティンナゴヤキャッスルホテル

The Japan Alps & the North Chūbu Coast

WORD OF MOUTH

"[In Takayama] on our first afternoon, we visited the old historic section. On the second day we visited the morning markets and several temples outside the historic section, then we hired a guide for a half day to basically read signs and interpret for us. We asked her to really show us around the old section and take us to the major temples. It was well worth the $100US."

–KSC2003

"We took the bus from Takayama to Matsumoto. One of the best things we did in Japan. Stopped at ski/hot springs resort on the way for baths, walks, and lunch."

–Elainee

Updated by
Deidre May

ESCAPE FROM JAPAN'S CITIES to this central alpine region for snow-topped mountains, coastal cliffs, open-air hot springs, and superb hiking and skiing. Many traditional villages are virtually untouched by development. Towns within the North Chūbu region (Fukui, Ishikawa, Toyama, Niigata, Nagano, and Gifu prefectures) have largely maintained their distinctive architecture. In Ogi-machi and Hida Minzoku Mura, sturdy wooden houses with thatched roofs have open-hearth fireplaces. Famous temples such as Fukui's Zen Eihei-ji, Nagano's Zenkō-ji, and Kanazawa's Nichiren Myōryū-ji (locally called Ninja-dera—temple of the Ninja), are symbols of the region's religious history.

Traditional arts are celebrated at annual events like Sado-ga-shima's three-day Earth Celebration with Taiko group Kodō and the more solemn *okesa* (folk dances), and the riotous Seihakusai festival in Nanao on Noto Peninsula. Before the Tōkaidō highway was built along the Pacific coast and the Chūō train line connected Nagoya and Niigata, this region was extremely isolated, which led to the development of highly skilled craftsmanship. Japanese ceramics, pottery, art, and scrolls are exhibited at folklore museums, and you can watch craftspeople dye linens, paint silk for kimonos, carve wood, and hand-lacquer objects in workshops.

See the glossary at the end of this book for definitions of the common Japanese words and suffixes used in this chapter.

4

ORIENTATION & PLANNING

Orientation

The Japan Alps is not a defined political region; it's a name that refers to the mountains in Chūbu, the Middle District. Chūbu encompasses nine prefectures in the heart of Honshū, three of which-Gifu-ken, Nagano-ken, and Yamanashi-ken make up the central highlands. Between the Alps and the sea is a narrow coastal belt known as Hokuriku, comprised of Kanazawa, Fukui, and the rugged coastline of the Noto Peninsula. Heavy snowfall in winter and hot summers make this region ideal for growing rice. Niigata and Sado Island form the northeastern coast.

The Japan Alps

The Alps are divided into three ranges, the Northern Hida Mountains, the central Kiso range, and the Southern Alps of Akaishi. The northern region is the most popular for hiking and skiing, and is easily accessed from Matsumoto or Nagano. The jagged snowcapped peaks interspersed with high basins reach elevations of 9,850 feet. Mostly forested, they are covered with alpine flora in the warmer months. Hot springs are scattered throughout this volcanic region.

Kanazawa & the North Chūbu Coast

Ishikawa Prefecture stretches long and narrow from north to south; thus the topographies of the Noto and the southern Kaga are significantly different. Kanazawa, as the center of the administration, economy, and culture of Kaga, has mountains and fertile plains, and is also renown

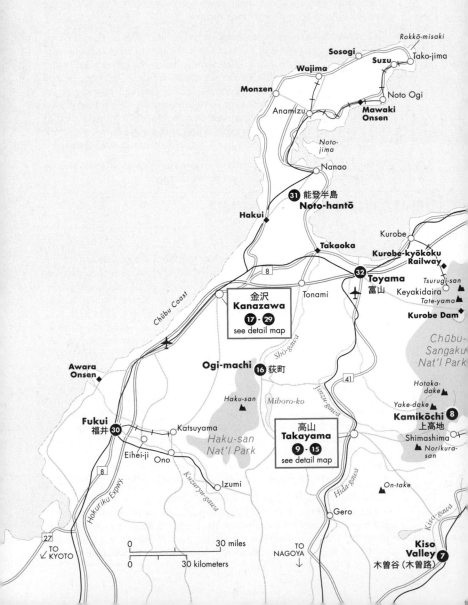

The Japan Alps

NIHON-KAI
(Sea of Japan)

Rokkō-misaki

Sosogi
Suzu
Tako-jima
Wajima
Monzen
Noto Ogi
Anamizu
Mawaki Onsen

Noto-jima

Nanao

31 能登半島
Noto-hantō

Hakui

Kurobe

Takaoka

Kurobe-kyōkoku Railway

32 Toyama
富山

Tsurugi-san

Keyakidaira
Tate-yama

Kurobe Dam

8

Tonami

金沢
Kanazawa

17 - 29
see detail map

Chūbu Coast

Chūbu-Sangaku Nat'l Park

Awara Onsen

Ogi-machi **16** 荻町

Shō-gawa

Miboro-ko

Jinzu-gawa

41

Hotaka-dake

Yake-dake

Kamikōchi **8**
上高地

Fukui
福井 **30**

Katsuyama

Haku-san

Shimashima

Norikura-san

Haku-san Nat'l Park

高山
Takayama

9 - 15
see detail map

Eihei-ji
Ono

Izumi

Kuzuryugawa

On-take

8

Hida-gawa

Hokuriku Expwy.

Gero

Kiso-gawa

27

TO
↙ KYOTO

TO
NAGOYA

Kiso Valley **7**
木曽谷（木曽路）

0   30 miles

0   30 kilometers

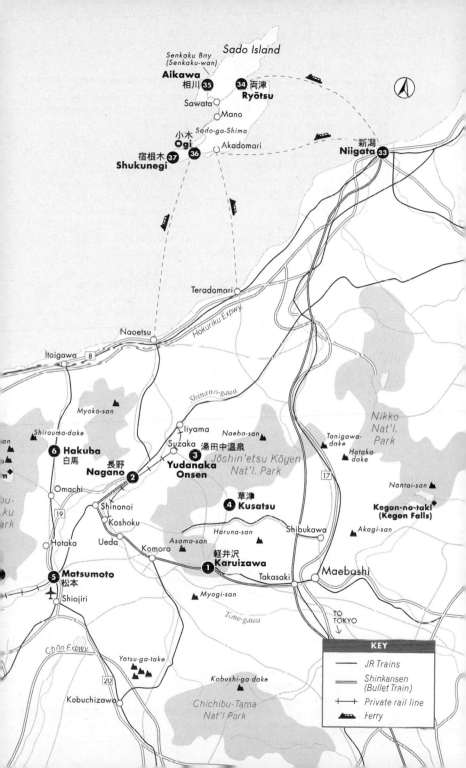

Top Reasons to Visit

AN ONSEN FOR ALL SEASONS
Near coastal regions, onsen tend to be salty and high in calcium, while those in mountain areas are usually higher in iron and sulfur. Both lay claim to various skin, bone, and mental health benefits, while relaxation and rejuvenation are guaranteed.

MOUNTAIN HIKES
With peaks reaching 11,000 feet, the Japan Alps offer staggering views and a serious workout. The breathtaking Kamikōchi area of Nagano is laced with trails through and around the snow peaks. In summer the highland slopes and valleys come alive with wildflowers.

SKI LIKE AN OLYMPIAN
The resort upgrades from the Nagano Winter Olympics continue attracting plenty of outdoor enthusiasts, particularly on weekends. Shiga

Kōgen, near Yudanaka, and Happa-one, near Hakuba, are among the best areas.

GLIMPSES OF FEUDAL JAPAN
Visit the former samurai quarters found amid the earthen walls and flowing canals of the Nagamachi section of Kanazawa. Also, the stately Matsumoto castle, surrounded by streets of merchant houses, evokes how people lived in a strictly hierarchical society.

FOLK ART
Handed down through generations, folk crafts still flourish today. Kanazawa is renown for dyed silk, gilded crafts, and pottery; Matsumoto has excellent wood craftsmanship. Lacquer is a specialty of the Noto Peninsula. In the restored Kiso Valley towns of Tsumago and Magome, artisans work while customers browse.

for traditional crafts. The northern part, the Noto-hantō Peninsula, has two contrasting coastlines. The Sea of Japan side is severely eroded, while the southern coast hems a becalmed bay.

Planning

To see everything—the Alps, the Noto-hantō (Noto Peninsula), the Chūbu Coast, and Sado-ga-shima—you need more than a week. Winter weather impedes travel (from Matsumoto, Kamikōchi can be reached only between May and October). Getting to the ski resorts, however, is not difficult. Temperatures vary widely from the coastal areas to the mountains. Hikers should bring warm clothes even in summer. The peak summer season is from mid-July to the end of August; the skiing season peaks over Christmas and New Year's; so book in advance or avoid these times. In more remote regions, only a few buses or trains run per day.

Numbers in the text correspond to numbers in the margin and on the Japan Alps, Takayama & Kanazawa maps.

The Best of Times

May, June, and September are the best months, when transportation is safe and reliable, and there aren't too many sightseers. At the height of summer the Alps and coastal regions are the getaway for those fleeing the stagnant heat of urban Japan—expect throngs of tourists and lofty prices. Winter's heavy snows makes driving around the Alps difficult or impossible. Unless you've got skiing to do, and a direct train to get there, winter is not ideal.

Concerning Restaurants & Hotels

Traditional Japanese *ryōtei* specialize in seasonal delicacies while casual eateries serve delicious home-style cooking and regional dishes. Western fare is easy to come by, especially in larger cities like Kanazawa, which is famed for the local Kaga cuisine.

Accommodations run the gamut from Japanese-style inns to large, modern hotels. Ryokan and minshuku (guesthouses) serve traditional Japanese food, and usually highlight regional specialties. Hotels in the bigger cities have a variety of Western and Japanese restaurants. Hotels listed in this chapter have private baths, air-conditioning, telephones, and TVs unless stated otherwise. Japanese Inns mostly include two meals in the room rate. In summer, hotel reservations are advisable.

WHAT IT COSTS In yen					
	$$$$	$$$	$$	$	¢
RESTAURANTS	over 3,000	2,000–3,000	1,000–2,000	800–1,000	under 800
HOTELS	over 22,000	18,000–22,000	12,000–18,000	8,000–12,000	under 8,000

Restaurant prices are per person for a main course at dinner. Hotel prices are for a double room, excluding service and tax.

Transportation Station

Travel in the Alps is largely restricted to the valleys and river gorges that run north and south. The only east-west route through the mountains, between Matsumoto and Takayama, is passable only from May through mid-October. It's easier to go along the coast and through the foothills of Fukui, Ishikawa, Toyama, and Niigata, except in winter when Fukui gets hit with furious blizzards. In Noto-hantō, buses and trains can be relied on for trips to key places.

AIR TRAVEL The major airport in the area is Komatsu Kūkō in Kanazawa, although there are daily flights from Fukuoka, Ōsaka, and Sapporo to Matsumoto and Toyama for those wanting to reach the Alps quickly. Since the opening of the airport in Wajima, you can reach the Noto Peninsula in one hour from Tōkyō.

BOAT TRAVEL To get to Sado Island, you will need to take the ferry or hydrofoil, which is no fun in harsh winter weather.

BUS & TRAIN TRAVEL Whether to take the bus or the train isn't usually a choice, because there is often only one form of public transportation. Not all train lines in Nagano Prefecture are JR, so budget in additional charges if you are traveling on a rail pass.

CAR TRAVEL To really explore the area, rent a car in Kanazawa or Toyama to make the loop of the Noto Peninsula at your own pace. Another good route is between Kanazawa and Takayama via Shirakawa-gō.

On the Menu

EVERY MICROREGION HAS ITS specialties and unique style of preparing seafood from the Nihon-kai. Seaweed, like vitamin-rich *wakame* and *kombu*, is a common ingredient, sometimes together with tiny clams called *shijimi*, in miso soup.

In Toyama spring brings tiny purple-hued baby firefly squid (*hotaru-ika*), which are boiled in soy sauce or sake and eaten whole with a tart mustard-miso sauce. Try the seasonal *ama-ebi* (sweet shrimp) and *masu-zushi* (thinly sliced trout sushi that's been pressed flat). In winter crabs abound, including the red, long-legged *beni-zuwaigani*.

Speaking of crabs, Fukui has huge (some 28 inches leg to leg) *echizen-gani* crabs. When boiled with a little salt and dipped in rice vinegar, they're pure heaven. In both Fukui and Ishikawa, restaurants serve *echizen-soba* (homemade buckwheat noodles with mountain vegetables) with sesame oil and bean paste for dipping.

The seafood-based *Kaga-ryōri* (Kaga cuisine) is common to Kanazawa and Noto-hantō. *Tai* (sea bream) is topped with mountain fern brackens, greens, and mushrooms. At Wajima's early-morning fish market near the tip of Noto-hantō and at Kanazawa's *omi-chō* market you have your choice of everything from abalone to seaweed, and nearby restaurants will cook it for you.

In Niigata Prefecture try *noppei-jiru*, a hot (or cold) soup with *sato-imo* (a type of sweet potato) as its base, and mushrooms, salmon, and a few other local ingredients. It goes well with hot rice and grilled fish. *Wappa-meshi* is steamed rice garnished with local ingredients, especially wild vegetables, chicken, fish, and shellfish. In autumn try *kiku-no-ohitashi*, a side dish of chrysanthemum petals marinated in vinegar. Like other prefectures on the Nihon-kai coast, Niigata has outstanding fish in winter—*buri* (yellowtail), flatfish, sole, oysters, abalone, and shrimp. A local specialty is *namban ebi*, raw shrimp dipped in soy sauce and wasabi. It's butter-tender and especially sweet on Sado-ga-shima. Also on Sado-ga-shima, take advantage of the excellent *wakame* (seaweed) dishes and *sazae-no-tsuboyaki* (wreath shellfish) broiled in their shells with a soy or miso sauce.

The area around Matsumoto is known for its wasabi and chilled *zarusoba* (buckwheat noodles), a refreshing meal on a hot day, especially with a cold glass of locally brewed sake. Eel steamed inside rice wrapped in bamboo leaves is also popular.

Sansai soba (buckwheat noodles with mountain vegetables) and *sansai-ryōri* (wild vegetables and mushrooms in soups or tempura) are specialties in the mountainous areas of Takayama and Nagano. Local river fish like *ayu* (smelt) or *iwana* (char) are grilled on a spit with *shōyū* (soy sauce) or salt. *Hoba miso* is a dark, slightly sweet type of miso roasted on a large magnolia leaf.

Nagano is also famous for *ba sashi* (raw horse meat), *sakura nabe* (horse-meat stew cooked in an earthenware pot), and boiled baby bees. The former two are still very popular; as for the latter, even locals admit they're something of an acquired taste.

Visitor Information

Offices of the JR Travel Information Center and Japan Travel Bureau are at major train stations. They can help you book local tours, hotel reservations, and travel tickets. You shouldn't assume English will be spoken, but usually someone speaks sufficiently well for your basic needs. Where public transportation is infrequent, such as the Noto-hantō and Sado-ga-shima, local tours are available; however, the guides speak only Japanese.

THE JAPAN ALPS

The Japan Alps cover a region known as Shinshu, between the north and south coasts of the Chūbu Area. There are 10 peaks above 9,800 feet attracting skiers and hikers. There are many parks and forests for less stenuous nature exploring.

Getting Around the Japan Alps

Roads and railways through the Japan Alps follow the valleys. This greatly lengthens trips such as the four-hour Matsumoto-Takayama ride via Nagoya. Route maps for Shinkansen and JR lines are at any train station or bookstore. Some routes only have a few services a day. The last train or bus may leave as early as 7 PM.

Buses are not as convenient as trains, but some scenic routes are recommended. Any bus station, always right by the train station, has maps and schedules. The local tourist-information office—also in or near the train station—will help you decipher timetables and fares.

Karuizawa

❶ *66 min by Shinkansen from Tōkyō's Ueno Station, 2 hrs by JR Limited Express to Nagano and to Kusatsu.*

When Archdeacon A.C. Shaw, an English prelate, built his summer villa here in 1886 at the foot of Mt. Asama in southeastern Nagano, he sparked the interest of fashionable, affluent Tōkyōites, who soon made it their preferred summer destination. Some became patrons of the arts, which led to the opening of galleries and art museums. Pamphlets on current exhibitions are at the tourist office.

Emperor Akihito met the Empress Michiko on a tennis court here in the 1950s. Two decades later John Lennon and Yoko Ono lolled at her family's *bessō* (summer house) and the Monpei Hotel. In Kyū-Karuizawa, near the Karuizawa train station, more than 500 branches of trendy boutiques sell, well, the same goods as their flagship stores in Tōkyō. Coming from Tōkyō, Karuizawa is a nice stop en route to the hot-spring towns of Kusatsu and Yudanaka or Matsumoto and Kamikochi. It is very crowded from mid-July to the end of August. Naka-Karuizawa Station, one stop (five minutes) away on the Shinano Tetsudō line, is a gateway to Shiraito and Ryūgaeshi waterfalls, the Yachō wild bird sanctuary, and hiking trails. The Kanazawa Tourist Information Service is inside the JR station (☎ 0267/42–2491).

Get Your Festival On

TAKAYAMA'S SPRING AND FALL festivals (April 14 and 15 and October 9 and 10) transform the usually quiet town into a rowdy, colorful party, culminating in a musical parade of intricately carved and decorated *yatai* (floats) and puppets. Flags and draperies adorn local houses, and at night the yatai are hung with lanterns. Book rooms well ahead and expect inflated prices. April's Sannō Matsuri is slightly bigger than October's Hachi-man Matsuri.

During Kanazawa's Hyaku-man-goku Matsuri (June 13–15), parades of people dressed in ancient Kaga costumes march through the city to the sound of folk music. Torchlit Nō (old-style Japanese theater) performances, ladder-top acrobatics by Kaga firemen, and singing and dancing in parks create a contagious atmosphere of merrymaking.

Of the *many* festivals on the Noto-hantō, the most impressive are Nanao's Seihakusai festival, a 400-year-old tradition where three huge 30-ton wooden *Hikiyama* (Towering Mountain) floats with unpivoted wheels, are hauled around the city streets by locals, held May 13–15, and Ishizaki Hoto Matsuri, held the first Saturday of August.

Hiking, Biking & Bird-Watching

Asama-san, an active volcano of more than 8,000 feet, threatens to put an end to the whole "Highlands Ginza" below. For a view of the glorious Asama-san in its entirety, head to the observation platform at **Usui-tōge** (Usui Pass). You can also see neighboring Myogi-san, as well as the whole Yatsugatake, a range of eight volcanic peaks. Walk northeast along shop-filled Karuizawa Ginza street to the end, past Nite-bashi, and follow the trail through an evergreen forest to the pass. A lovely view justifies the 1½-hour walk. Two to three buses leave per hour if you want a ride back.

Hiking paths at **Shiraito-no-taki and Ryūgaeshi-no-taki** (Shiraito and Ryūgaeshi falls) get crowded during the tourist season, but they are a good afternoon excursion in the off-season. To get to the trailhead at Mine-no-Chaya, take the bus from Naka-Karuizawa. The ride takes about 25 minutes. From the trailhead it's about a 1½-km (1-mi) hike to Shiraito. The trail then swings southeast, and 3 km (2 mi) farther are the Ryūgaeshi Falls. For a longer hike, walk back to town via Mikasa village. It's about an hour and 15 minutes. Or catch the bus bound for Karuizawa (10 minutes) from the parking lot.

Yachō-no-mori (Wild Bird Forest) is home to some 120 bird species. You can watch the birds' habitat from two observation huts along a 2½-km (1½-mi) forest course. To get to the sanctuary, take a five-minute bus ride from Naka-Karuizawa Station to Nishiku-iriguchi, and then walk up the small road for 400 meters. The narrow entrance is shortly after the café, restaurant, and onsen on the left. Alternatively, you can bike to the sanctuary's entrance in about 15 minutes. Bikes can be rented at Naka-Karuizawa Station for ¥800 per hour or ¥2,000 a day.

Where to Stay & Eat

$-$$ ✕ **Kastanie**. The tiled bar counter and wooden tables covered with red-and-white checked cloths are as inviting as the staff of this terraced restaurant a few blocks north of the Karuizawa station. Try the grilled vegetable Veronese spaghetti and the salmon and camembert pizza. Meat plates include herbed, grilled chicken (¥1,580) or sizzling rib-roast steak (¥2,630). Look for the sign hanging from the second floor. ✉ *Kitasaku-agun, Karuizawa-shi* ☎ *0267/42–3081* ⊘ *Thurs.–Tues. noon–10.*

$$ ☷ **Pension Grasshopper**. This guesthouse has Western-style beds with great views of Asama-san. The English-speaking owner, Kayo Iwasaki, whips up a delicious mix of Japanese and Western fare. If you opt out of the meal plan, the price is reduced by ¥2,675 per person, but you must specify this when booking. The house is in the suburbs; the management will transport you to and from the Shinano Oiwake station (two stops from Karuizawa). ✉ *5410 Kariyado, Karuizawa-chō, Kitasaku-gun, Nagano-ken 389-0111* ☎ *0267/46–1333* 🖷 *0267/46–1099* ⊕ *www5.ocn.ne.jp/~g-hopper/english.html* ⇌ *10 rooms without bath* ⚖ *Dining room, Japanese baths* ☰ *MC, V* ⦿ *EP, MAP.*

Nagano & Environs

97 min northwest of Tōkyō's Ueno Station by Shinkansen, 40 min northwest of Karuizawa by Shinkansen, 3 hrs northeast of Nagoya by JR Limited Express.

Nagano Prefecture is called the "Roof of Japan," home to the northern, central, and southern Japan Alps and six national parks that offer year-round recreational activities. Active volcanoes include Mt. Asama on the border between Nagano and Gunma Prefectures and Mt. Ontake in Nagano Prefecture, which is a destination for religious pilgrims.

Nagano

❷ Rimmed by mountains, Nagano has been a temple town since the founding of Zenko-ji temple in the 7th century. Before the 1998 Winter Olympics a new Shinkansen line was built connecting Tōkyō and Nagano, and new highways were added to handle the car and bus traffic. Suddenly the fairly inaccessible Alps region was opened to visitors. Yet as the excitement faded, a rather forlorn air descended. This lifts in season, when people swarm the surrounding mountains. You can pick up a free map of Nagano at the **City Tourist Office** (☎ 026/226–5626 ⊕ www. nagano-tabi.net/english), open daily from 9 to 6, inside the JR station.

★ Nagano's unusual **Zenkō-ji** is the final destination each year for millions of religious pilgrims. Since the 6th century this nonsectarian Buddhist temple has accepted believers of all faiths and admitted women when other temples forbade it. Each morning the head priest (Tendai sect) and head priestess (Jōdo sect) hold a joint service to pray for the prosperity of the assembled pilgrims (usually on tour packages). Line up outside to be blessed by the priest, who taps his rosary on each head. You then pass the incense burner, waving the smoke over yourself for good fortune and health. Inside, rub the worn wooden statue of the ancient doctor Binzuru (Pindola Bharadvaja in Sanskrit), for relief of aches and pains.

A faithful disciple of Buddha, Binzuru is famous for stories of his miraculous powers and ability to fly. After the service, descend into the pitch-black tunnel in the basement to find the iron latch on the wall—seizing it is said to bring enlightenment.

It's a 3-km (2-mi) walk from the station, or you can arrange a taxi through your hotel the night before. The starting time for the morning service ranges from 5:30 to 7 AM, depending on the season, a minute later or earlier each day. From 9:30 you can hop on the Gururin-go bus for the 10-minute trip (¥100) to the temple gate. ✉ *Motoyoshi 4–9–1* ☎ *026/234–3591* 🖭 *¥500* ⊘ *Inner sanctuary daily 5:30–4:30.*

Yudanaka Onsen

❸ Photographs of snow-covered white macaques cavorting in open-air thermal pools have made the Yudanaka Onsen famous. Northeast of Nagano, nine open-air hot springs are between Yudanaka Onsen and Shibu Spa Resort. The onsen where the monkeys soak is known as Jigoku-dani (Hell Valley), and is just east of Yudanaka and Shibu. Yudanaka is the last stop on the Nagano Dentetsu Line; the trip from Nagano takes 40 minutes and costs ¥1,230. Several spas string out from here. The area is not unlike Yellowstone National Park, with its bubbling, steaming, sulfurous volcanic vents and pools. Considerable development, however, including more than 100 inns and hotels, several streets, and shops, ends the comparison. The spas are the gateway to Shiga Kōgen (Shiga Heights), site of Olympic alpine skiing and the snowboarding slalom. The entire Yudanaka resort area and Shiga Kōgen ski area fall under the jurisdiction of Yamanouchi Town; the **Tourist Information Center** (☎ 0269/33–1107, 0269/33–2138 for reservations assistance) is just south of Yudanaka Station.

Kusatsu

★ ❹ The highly touted hot springs at Kusatsu contain sulfur, iron, aluminum, and even trace amounts of arsenic. Just inside the border of Gunma Prefecture, the springs are reached in summer by a bus route across Shiga Kōgen from Yudanaka, or from Karuizawa. The *yu-batake* (hot-spring field) gushes 5,000 liters of boiling, sulfur-laden water per minute before it's cooled in seven long wooden boxes and sent to more than 130 ryokan in the village. The open field is beautifully lit up at night. For more information call the **Kusatsu Information Center** (☎ 0279/88–3642 ⊕ www.kusatsu-onsen.ne.jp/eng/index.html) or consult their excellent Web site, which also explains the history of Kusatsu.

Netsu-no-yu (Fever Bath) is the main and often unbearably hot public bath next door to the yuba-take. You can watch one of six daily *yu-momi* shows (7 and 7:30 AM and 3, 3:35, 4, and 4:35 PM) between April and October, in which locals churn the waters with long wooden planks until the baths reach a comfortable temperature. ✉ *414 Kusatsu-chō* ☎ *0279/88–3613* 🖭 *¥500* ⊘ *Daily 7 AM–10 PM.*

For a dip in the open air, try the 5,500-square-foot milky bath at **Saino-kawara Dai-rotemburo** in the western end of Kusatsu village, with pleasing scenery by day and stars by night. The spa is a 15-minute walk west from the Kusatsu bus terminal. ✉ *521–3 Kusatsu-chō* ☎ *0279/*

88–6167 ☎ *¥500* ☉ *Apr.–Nov., daily 7 AM–8 PM; Dec.–Mar., daily 9 AM–8 PM.*

Where to Stay & Eat

$$–$$$$ ✕ **Restaurant Sakura.** A few blocks southwest of Zenkō-ji, the famous sake distiller Yoshinoya has a restaurant attached to the sake factory and warehouses. From 9 to 5 you can tour for free, ending with a sampling of fresh sake. Sakura has an open-air terrace and a glass-walled interior. The Sakura bentō, for ¥1,895, holds seasonal delights like the pungent Matsutake mushroom, and a small carafe of sake. ⊠ *941 Nishinomon-chō* ☎ *026/237–5000* ▤ *AE, MC, V* ☉ *Closed Wed.*

$$ ✕▨ **Nagano Sunroute Hotel.** A coffee table and two easy chairs are squeezed into each compact Western-style room, which is all you need if you're en route to other Alps destinations. **Rinsen,** a modern Japanese restaurant off the lobby, has stylish private rooms. The escalator across the street from JR Nagano Station leads to the reception area and tea lounge. ⊠ *1–28–3 Minami-Chitose, Nagano-shi, Nagano-ken 380-0823* ☎ *026/228–2222* ▤ *026/228–2244* ⤳ *143 rooms* ⟁ *Restaurant, coffee shop, tea shop, in-room data ports, no-smoking rooms.*

★ $$$–$$$$ ▨ **Hotel Fujiya** (Gohonjin Fujiya). The newest part of this famous hotel was rebuilt in 1923; the rest has been around since the 1660s. During its long life everyone from feudal lords to celebrities has stayed here—and left autographed plaques—en route to Zenkō-ji. Tatami rooms vary from small (¥9,450 per person, including meals) to the royal suite (¥28,000 per person, including meals), which has three rooms with sliding doors that open onto a garden. Several rooms have private baths, and the shared bath is unusually deep. Fujiya is not sophisticated, but it's wonderfully old-fashioned. No English is spoken, but the family, which has run the hotel since its dawning, is appreciative of respectful foreigners. It's on Chūō-dōri, two blocks below the temple. ⊠ *80 Daimon-chō, Nagano-shi, Nagano-ken 380-0841* ☎ *026/232–1241* ▤ *026/232–1243* ⊕ *www.thefujiyagohonjin.com* ⤳ *25 rooms, 3 with private bath* ⟁ *Dining room, Japanese baths* ▤ *AE, DC, MC, V* ▮⊙▮ *MAP.*

★ $ ▨ **Uotoshi Ryokan.** This small ryokan in the steamy bath village of Yudanaka has a 24-hour, hot springs-fed *hinoki* (cypress) bathtub. The rooms are rustic and cozy and come with either a Western or Japanese breakfast. You can try Japanese archery (*kyūdō*) if the the owner has free time. Dinners feature delicious mountain vegetables and Nihon-kai seafood (¥2,520–¥3,680). It's a seven-minute walk from Yudanaka Station, across the Yomase River and on the left. ⊠ *2563 Sano, Yamanouchi-machi, Shimo-Takai-gun, Nagano-ken 381-0402* ☎ *0269/33–1215* ▤ *0269/33–0074* ⊕ *www.avis.ne.jp/~miyasaka* ⤳ *8 Japanese-style rooms without bath* ⟁ *Restaurant, Japanese baths* ▤ *AE, MC, V* ▮⊙▮ *BP.*

Nightlife

From Chūō street, go two blocks west from the Karukayasan Mae intersection, and on the right is a narrow staircase leading up to **Kukai** (⊠ Mona Lisa Bldg., 2nd fl., 1391–1 Kitasekidō Machi ☎ 026/228–6335). The music is mostly jazz, making this a good place to relax with some wine (available by the glass) at a table overlooking the street. Light meals like pastas and salads are served until midnight.

Matsumoto

⑤ *1 hr southwest of Nagano on JR Shinonoi Line, 2 hrs and 40 min northwest of Tōkyō Shinjuku Station on JR Chūō Line, 2¼ hrs northeast of Nagoya on JR Chūō Line.*

Snowcapped peaks surround Matsumoto, where the air is cool and dry on the alpine plateau. Like Nagano, this city is a gateway to the Northern Alps. This former feudal castle town now thrives as a center for traditonal crafts, from *tensan,* fabric woven from silk taken from wild silkworms, to Matsumoto *shiki* or lacquerware, Azumino glass, and wood crafts. Old merchant houses stand along Nakamachi Street, south of the castle. Several historic educators, lawyers, and writers from this city have influenced Japan's sociopolitical system.

What to See in Old Town

To make the most of Matsumoto, grab a map at the **Tourist Information Center** (☎ 0263/32–2814) at the JR station, and head for the old part of town near the Chitose-bashi Bridge at the end of Hon-machi-dōri. *Kura* (warehouses), unusual in their use of irregular stone crisscross patterns, sit on the banks of the Metoba River. Matsumoto-jō and the Kaichi Primary School are on the other side.

★ **Matsumoto-jō** (Matsumoto Castle), nicknamed Karasu-jō (Crow Castle) for its black walls, began as a small fortress with moats in 1504. It was remodeled into its current three-turreted form from 1592 to 1614, just as Japan became a consolidated nation under a central government. The civil wars ended and the peaceful Edo era (1603–1868) began, rendering medieval castles obsolete. Its late construction explains why the 95-foot-tall *tenshukaku* (stronghold or inner tower) is the oldest surviving tower in Japan—no battles were ever fought here. Exhibits on each floor break up the challenging climb up very steep stairs to the top. If you hunker down to look through rectangular openings (broad enough to scan for potential enemies) on the sixth floor, you'll have a gorgeous view of the surrounding mountains. In the first week of June there is a *Taiko* (Japanese drums) festival and on October 3 and 4 the Matsumoto Castle Festival features a samurai parade.

In the southwest corner of the castle grounds, which bloom in spring with cherry trees, azaleas, and wisteria, the **Japan Folklore Museum** (Nihon Minzoku Shiryōkan ☎ 0263/32–0133) exhibits samurai wear, kimonos, and prefeudal and Edo-period agricultural implements. In January an ice-sculpture exhibition is held in the museum's park. The castle is a 20-minute walk from the station. ✉ *4–1 Marunouchi* ☎ *0263/32–2902* ✄ *Castle and museum ¥520* ⊙ *Daily 8:30–5.*

★ **Kaichi Primary School** (Kyū Kaichi Gakkō). Built in 1873, the former Kaichi Primary School houses more than 80,000 educational artifacts from the Meiji Restoration, when education was to become the unifying tool for the rapid modernization of postfeudal Japan. The displays in the former classrooms include school uniforms, wall charts (used prior to the introduction of textbooks), and 19th-century desks and writing slates. The building was used as a school until 1960. The building's bizarre style reflects the architecture of the period: a mishmash of diverse Occidental elements fashioned from Japanese materials. A big, fancy cupola sits atop the shingled roof; the white walls made of mortar are dotted with red, slatted windows; and the front door, hidden in the shadow of the blue, grandiose balcony, is protected by a skillfully carved dragon. ⊠ *2–4–12 Kaichi* ☎ *0263/32–5725* 🖭 *¥300* ☉ *Tues.–Sun. 8:30–5.*

Museums

The city's museums are west of the JR station. It's too far to walk, and there's no bus. You can take a ¥2,000 taxi ride or ride the Kamikōchi train (on the private Matsumoto Dentetsu Line) four stops to Oniwa Station. From there it's a 10-minute walk.

★ The **Japan Wood-Block Print Museum** (Nihon Ukiyo-e Hakubutsukan) is devoted to the lively, colorful, and widely popular *ukiyo-e* woodblock prints of Edo-period artists. Highlights include Hiroshige's scenes of the Tōkaidō (the main trading route through Honshū in feudal Japan), Hokusai's views of Mt. Fuji, and Sharaku's kabuki actors. Based on the enormous holdings of the wealthy Sakai family, the museum's 100,000 pieces (displays rotate monthly) include some of Japan's finest prints and represent the largest collection of its kind in the world. ⊠ *2206–1 Shimadachi, Koshiba* ☎ *0263/47–4440* 🖭 *¥1,000* ☉ *Tues.–Sun. 10–5.*

The **Japan Judiciary Museum** (Shihō Hakubutsukan), next to the Ukiyo-e Hakubutsukan, is Japan's oldest palatial wooden court building, and once housed the Matsumoto District Court. Displays pertain to the history of law enforcement from the feudal period to the modern era. ⊠ *2206–1 Shimadachi-Koshiba* ☎ *0263/47–4515* 🖭 *¥700* ☉ *Daily 9–4:30.*

What to See Around Matsumoto

The local train to the Daiō horseradish farm and the Rokuzan Art Museum journeys through vibrant green fields, apple orchards, and miles of rice paddies. The **Rokuzan Art Museum** (Rokuzan Bijutsukan) displays the work of Rokuzan Ogiwara, a sculptor who was influenced by Auguste Rodin and pioneered modern sculptural styles in Japan. He is especially known for his female figures and male figures in heroic poses. This ivy-covered brick building with a stunning bell tower is in Hotaka, 10 stops north of Matsumoto Station on the JR Ōito Line. From Hotaka Station it's a 10-minute walk to the museum. ⊠ *5095–1 Ōaza-hotaka* ☎ *0263/82–2094* 🖭 *¥700* ☉ *Apr.–Oct., Tues.–Sun. 9–5; Nov.–Mar., Tues.–Sun. 9–4.*

Daiō Wasabi Farm (Daiō Wasabi Nōjo). At the largest wasabi farm in the country, the green horseradish roots are cultivated in flat gravel beds irrigated by melted snow from the Alps. The chilly mineral water is ideal for the durable wasabi. You should try some of the farm's products, which range from wasabi cheese to wasabi chocolate and ice cream. You can pickle your own horseradish in one of the 20-minute workshops (¥1,000). The farm is 10 stops (one on the express) north along the JR Ōito Line from Platform 6 in Matsumoto Station. To reach the farm you can rent a bike, take a 40-minute walk along a path from the train station (the station attendant will direct you), or hop in a taxi for about ¥1,300. ⊠ *1692 Hotaka* ☎ *0263/82–8112* 🖭 *Free* ☉ *Daily 10–5:30.*

Where to Stay & Eat

$$-$$$$
Fodor'sChoice
★ ✕ **Kura.** For a surprisingly small number of yen you can feast in this 90-year-old Meiji-era warehouse in the center of town. Kura serves a large assortment of sushi and traditional fare: the *aji tataki* (horse-mackerel sashimi) and tempura are particularly tasty. The stoic owner expertly prepares your meal, but should his wife spot you relishing the food, you're in for some disarming hospitality—she has an arsenal of potent *ji-zake* (locally brewed sake) and a heart of gold. From the station, take a left onto Kōen-dōri. Take a left after the Parco department store, and you'll see the restaurant's whitewashed facade and curved black eaves on the left. ☒ *2–2–15 Chūō* ☎ *0263/33–6444* ▭ *AE, MC, V* ☯ *Closed Wed.*

$ ✕ **Dehli.** The house specialty is a fiery Japanese-style chicken curry that will send you to spice heaven. Look for the low eaves and black latticework of the traditional building on the south bank of the Metoba River, a five-minute walk east of Chitose-bashi bridge. The windows are covered with colorful rice paper, and a tiny menu is posted near the door. Catering to a lunchtime crowd, Dehli is open from mid-morning to 6:45 PM. ☒ *2–4–13 Chūō* ☎ *0263/35–2408* ☯ *Closed Wed.*

★ $$$$ 🏨 **Kikunoyu.** A stately hot-spring ryokan built in the *honmune-dukuri* or traditional private-house style, there's a characteristic gabled roof, ornamental board above the front gable (*suzume-odōri*), and bow windows. The spacious lobby has crossbeams made from the trunk of a zelkova tree. There are three hot-spring baths: *Kikuburo* is made of Italian marble with a large carved chrysanthemum, another is made of granite, and there is an open air bath. Ground-floor guest rooms face the garden, and some have private *hinoki* (cypress) baths. Artfully arranged meals on lacquer trays arrive in your room. A bowl of cakes called *yōkoso manju* and buckwheat tea welcome you upon arrival. It's a 20-minute bus ride from Matsumoto Station to **Asama Onsen,** which is northeast of the city at the foot of the Utsukushigahara highlands. ☒ *1–29–7 Asama-onsen, Matsumoto-shi, Nagano-ken 390-0303* ☎ *0263/46–2300* 🖷 *0263/ 46–0015* ⊕ *www.kikunoyu.com/* 🛏 *17 rooms* ▭ *V* ⛏ *MAP.*

$$$ 🏨 **Hotel Buena Vista.** One of Matsumoto's more expensive hotels, the Buena Vista has a glowing marble lobby, a coffeehouse, a café-bar, four restaurants (two Japanese, one Chinese, one French), *and* a sky lounge called **Bar Fuego** that serves Italian food. Corner rooms with two large picture windows need to be requested in advance. Single rooms snugly accommodate a small double bed, while standard doubles and twins have space for a table and chairs. The hotel is four blocks southeast of Matsumoto Station. ☒ *1–2–1 Hon-jō, Matsumoto, Nagano-ken 390-0814* ☎ *0263/37–0111* 🖷 *0263/37–0666* ⊕ *www.buena-vista.co.jp* 🛏 *200 rooms* ⚬ *5 restaurants, coffee shop, hair salon, massage, bar, no-smoking rooms* ▭ *AE, DC, MC, V.*

$$ 🏨 **Hotel New Station.** Although good-value business hotels are often sterile, this one has a cheerful staff and a lively restaurant that serves freshwater *iwana* (char)—an area specialty. The rooms are adequate, but small. To get a "full-size" room by Western standards, request a deluxe twin. Every room has a private bath, and there are also shared Japanese baths. To reach the hotel, take a left from the station exit and walk south for two minutes. ☒ *1–1–11 Chūō, Matsumoto, Nagano-ken 390-0811*

☏ *0263/35–3850* 🖷 *0263/35–3851* ⊕ *www.hotel-ns.co.jp/english.html*
🛏 *103 rooms* ⚐ *Restaurant, Japanese baths, meeting room, no-smoking rooms* ▤ *AE, DC, MC, V.*

Nightlife

Eonta (✉ Ōta 4-chōme 9–7 ☏ 0263/33–0505 ⊕ www.getnagano.com/en/Places/Nightlife ⊙ Thurs.–Tues. 4 PM–midnight) is a jazz bar that's been popular with locals since the 1970s. The owner plays songs from his 1,000-plus CDs. The corner with sofas is for those who listen only. Toasted sandwiches, light meals, and good coffee are served. It's in a quasi-dilapidated two-story building a few blocks southeast of the castle.

Off the small park north of the Hotel Buena Vista, **Half Time** (✉ Takeuchi San-box, 2nd fl., 1–4–10 Fukashi ☏ 0263/36–4985) is a smaller jazz joint that has tasty cocktails and snacks from 7 PM until the wee hours. Owner Akira Shiohara, who is quite a trumpet player, will even join in if you ask him. Two doors down, another bar, **People's** (✉ Washizawa Building, 2nd fl., 1–4–11 Fukashi ☏ 0263/37–5011), offers cheap Internet access (¥200 per hour), plus beer, cocktails, and Italian fare.

Hakuba

★ *1 hr north of Matsumoto on JR Limited Express or 1 hr 45 min on the JR Ōito Line and 1 hr 5 min by bus from Nagano.*

In the northwestern part of Nagano Prefecture, **Hakuba** Village lies beneath the magnificent Hakuba Range, the best of the northern Japan Alps. Hakuba means "white horse," because the main peak, Mt. Shirouma-dake (9,617 feet), resembles a horse. This is an all-year resort area for trekking, skiing, and climbing around the 9,500-foot mountains among rare alpine flora, insects, and wildlife. Gondola and chair lifts carry you up to ridges with panoramic views. More than 850 lodging facilities serve the 3.7 million annual visitors. Olympic alpine runs and ski jumps await winter sports fans, and summer visitors can still find snow, especially in the Grand Snowy Gorge.

Getting Around

The information center to the right as you exit the train station provides basic maps (mostly in Japanese). A bus to Happō-o-ne ski resort takes five minutes. The **Hakuba Village Office of Tourism** (☏ 0261/72–5000 ⊕ www.vill.hakuba.nagano.jp/e/access/index.html). Near the Alpico bus terminal and Happō bus stop is the **Happō-o-ne Tourism Association** (☏ 0261/72–3066). The staff can help you reserve a hotel room, but for the peak summer and winter seasons, you should book in advance.

What to See

Happō-o-ne Ski Resort (Happō-o-ne sukiba). Japan's first parallel jumping hills were constructed; with critical points of 393 feet and 295 feet, and each has a scaffold structure for the in-run and landing slope. These ski jumps are also used in spring and summer. The Champion and Panorama courses have starting points of an altitude of 5,510 feet, with separate courses for men (vertical drop 2,755 feet) and women (vertical drop 2,555 feet). The downhill course for super giant slalom starts lower. This ridge stretches to the east from Mt. Karamatsu (8,843 feet), with breathtaking views if the mist doesn't roll in. Even in summer a sweater or light jacket may be needed. You can reach the first cairn via three connecting gondolas (5 minutes to Happō Gondola Station, then 8 minute by gondola for Usagidaira and a further 10 minutes by alpine lift). From here the jewel-like Happō Pond is a 6-km (4-mi) hike. For more ambitious hikers, three more hours gets you to the top of Mt. Karamatsu-dake. It's a 5-minute bus ride from Hakuba to Happō and then a 15-minute walk through the resort of Swiss-like chalets and hotels to the gondola station. The round-trip fare is ¥2,270, and the lower gondola operates from 8 AM to 5 PM; the higher chairlift stops at 4:30 PM.

Mt. Shirouma-dake. Hiking at the bottom of Hakuba Grand Snowy Gorge (Daisekkei), one of Japan's largest gorges (3.5 km), which is snowy all year round, requires warm clothes even in midsummer, when temperatures can dip below freezing. More than 100 types of alpine flowers grace the nearby fields in the summer. From the trailhead at Sarukura Village heading west, it's 1 hour 45 minutes to the gorge through the forest. If you are lucky, you may see snow grouse, a protected species in Japan. For climbers who want to scale Mt. Shirouma, which takes six hours to the top (two huts are on the way for overnight stay), proper equipment is necessary. The trail southwest of Sarukura to Yarigatake— a shorter hike of 3 hours—leads to the highest outdoor hot spring, **Yari Onsen,** at an elevation of 6,888 feet (☎ 0261/72-2002 *➤ ¥300*). The onsen is part of an overnight lodge with rates from ¥8,500, which include two meals. Adequate hiking gear is necessary for the longer trails. Sarukura is a 40-minute bus ride from Hakuba Station. Equipment like snowshoes and crampons can be rented in Hakuba Village.

Tsugaike Natural Park (Tsugaike Shizen-en) is an alpine marshland with a wide variety of rare alpine flora from early June to late October and dazzling gold and crimson leaves from September to October. It is a three-hour walk to take in the entire park. Getting there requires a one-hour bus ride (early June to late October) from Hakuba Oike Station, two stops north of Hakuba Station.

Kiso Valley

★ **❼** *1 hr south of Matsumoto on JR Chūō Line.*

This deep and narrow valley is cut by the Kiso river and walled in by the central Alps to the east and the northern Alps to the west. From 1603 to 1867 the area was called Nakasendo (center highway), because it connected western Japan and Kyōto to Edo (present-day Tōkyō).

After the Tōkaidō highway was built along the Pacific coast and the Chūō train line was constructed to connect Nagoya and Niigata, the 11 old post villages, where travelers and traders once stopped to refresh themselves, became ghost towns. Two villages, **Tsumago** and **Magome,** have benefited from efforts to retain the memory of these old settlements. Beautiful houses have been restored along the sloping stone streets. Walking through these historical areas, you can almost imagine life centuries ago, when the rustic shops were stocked with regular supplies instead of the traditional crafts now offered for sale.

Getting Around

The central valley town of Nagiso is one hour south of Matsumoto on the JR Chūō Line. Tsumago is a 10 minute bus ride (¥270) from JR Nagiso Station. Magome is closer to JR Nakatsugawa Station, which is 12 minutes south on the same line. Both towns are served by buses from the Nagiso and Nakatsugawa stations, so you can take a bus to one village and return from the other. Local buses between Magome and Tsumago are infrequent.

The **Magome Tourist Information Office** (☎ 0264/59–2336) is open from April to November, daily 9–5; and from December to March, Monday to Saturday 9–5. The staff can help you reserve a hotel room. The **Tsumago Tourist Information Office** (☎ 0264/57–3123) has the same hours and services as the Magome tourist office.

Where to Stay

★ $$$$ ⬚ **Hatago Matsushiro-ya.** This small ryokan in Tsumago has been a guest-house since 1804. Delicately arranged dinners are served in your room. No English is spoken, so a Japanese speaker, perhaps from the tourist office, will need to make your reservation. Ten large tatami rooms share a single bath and four very clean but old-fashioned pit toilets. The ryokan is closed from Wednesday morning to Thursday morning. ✉ *807 Azumaterashita, Minami-Nagiso-machi, Kiso-gun, Nagano-ken 399-5302* ☎ *0264/57–3022* ⌁ *10 Japanese-style rooms without bath* ⌂ *Japanese baths; no room phones* ▤ *No credit cards* ⵙ *MAP.*

$$$$ ⬚ **Onyado Daikichi.** The windows in all six tatami rooms of this *minshuku* face the wooded valley. The chef prepares local specialties such as horse-meat sashimi, mountain vegetables, and fried grasshoppers. More familiar dishes are available as well. Owner Nobuka-san welcomes foreign guests, and even speaks a little English. There are shared Japanese baths. ✉ *Tsumago, Nagiso-machi, Kiso-gun, Nagano-ken 399-5302* ☎ *0264/57–2595* ⊟ *0274/57–2203* ⌁ *6 Japanese-style rooms without bath* ⌂ *Dining room, Japanese baths* ▤ *No credit cards* ⵙ *MAP.*

Kamikōchi

❽ *2 hrs west of Matsumoto by train (Dentetsu Line) and bus, 2 hrs east of Takayama by bus.*

The incomparably scenic route from Matsumoto to Takayama winds over the mountains and through Chūbu-Sangaku National Park (Chūbu-Sangaku Kokuritsu Kōen) via Kamikōchi. Travel is only possible after the last week of April or the first week of May, when plows have removed the almost 30 feet of winter snow. If you spend the night in Kamikōchi, which is surrounded by virgin forests of birch, larch, and hemlock, consider renting a rowboat at Taishō-ike (Taishō Pond) for the spectacular view of the snow-covered peaks.

Getting Around

No cars are allowed in Kamikōchi. Take the Matsumoto Electric Railway from Matsumoto Station to Shin-Shimashima, the last stop. The ride takes 30 minutes and departs once or twice an hour. At Shin-Shimashima Station, cross the road for the bus to Naka-no-yu and Kamikōchi. There's also a bus from Matsumoto to Kamikōchi, departing only twice a day at 8:55 and 10:15 AM. The road is closed from around November until April or May. You pay ¥2,400 for both legs of the trip at the start.

Hiking

As you approach Kamikōchi, the valley opens onto a row of towering mountains: Oku-Hotaka-san is the highest, at 10,466 feet. Mae-Hotaka-san, at 10,138 feet, is on the left. To the right is 9,544-foot Nishi-Hotaka-san. The icy waters of the Azusa-gawa flow from the small Taishō Pond at the southeast entrance to the basin.

There are many trails in the river valley around Kamikōchi. One easy three-hour walk east starts at **Kappa-bashi**, a small suspension bridge over the crystal-clear Azusa-gawa, a few minutes northeast of the bus terminal. Along the way is a stone sculpture of the British explorer Reverend Walter Weston, the first foreigner to ascend these mountains. Continuing on the south side of the river, the trail cuts through pasture to rejoin the river at Myōshin Bridge. Cross here to reach Myōshin-ike (Myōshin Pond). At the edge of the pond sits the small Hotaka Jinja Kappa-bashi (Water Sprite Bridge). To see the beautiful **Taishō-ike** (Taishō Pond), head southeast from Kappa-bashi for a 20-minute walk. You can rent a boat (¥800 per half hour), or continue 90 minutes farther east to **Tokusawa**, an area with camping grounds and great mountain views.

Kamikōchi is where the trails for some of the most famed alpine ascents begin; favorite peaks are Mt. Yariga-take and Mt. Hotaka-dake. An invaluable reference is Paul Hunt's *Hiking in Japan*, since most maps are in Japanese. Planning in advance is essential; climbs range from a few days to a week, and the trails can be crowded in summer.

Where to Stay

Hotels and ryokan close from mid-November to late April.

$$$$
Fodor'sChoice
★
Ⓗ **Imperial Hotel.** This rustic alpine lodge is owned by Tōkyō's legendary Imperial Hotel, and staff members are borrowed from that establishment for the summer. In the lounge low wooden beams support the beautifully crafted ceiling, while a central hearth warms the room. Guest rooms have sofas and gorgeous woodwork, and some have balconies. Western and Japanese restaurants are on the premises. Make reservations well in advance. You can see the red-tiled, gabled roof of the hotel from Kamikōchi's bus terminal in the center of town. ⊠ *Kamikōchi, Minami-Azumi-gun, Azumi-mura Nagano-ken 390-1516* ☎ *0263/ 95–2006, 03/3504–1111 Nov.–Mar., 212/692–9001 in U.S.* 🖷 *0263/ 95–2412* ⊕ *www.imperialhotel.co.jp* 🛏 *75 rooms* ♨ *3 restaurants, bar, lounge* ⊟ *AE, DC, MC, V.*

$$$–$$$$
Ⓗ **Taishō-ike Hotel.** This small mountain resort is perched on the rim of the brilliant-blue Taishō Pond. The lobby, restaurant, and bath have large windows with excellent views of the breathtaking landscape. Opt for the spacious Western-style rooms, with their comfortable beds and soft, puffy quilts. The Japanese rooms are not as nice as in a ryokan. Rooms at the back, without a view of the water, are ¥3,000–¥5,000 less.

✉ *Kamikōchi, Minami-azumi-gun, Nagano ken 390-1516* ☎ *0263/ 95-2301* 🖷 *0263/95-2522* ↩ *21 Western-style rooms, 6 Japanese-style rooms* ♦ *Restaurant, Japanese baths, shop; no room phones* ▭ *MC, V* ⦿ *MAP.*

Takayama

Fodor'sChoice ★ *2 hrs 10 min north of Nagoya by JR Limited Express, 4 hrs north of Matsumoto by JR via Nagoya, 2 hrs 20 min by bus from Matsumoto.*

Takayama, originally called Hida, is a tranquil town whose rustic charms are a result of hundreds of years of peaceful isolation in the Hida San-myaku (Hida Mountains). Downtown, shops and restaurants mingle with museums and inns along rows of traditional wood-lattice buildings. A peculiar-looking ball of cedar leaves suspended outside a storefront indicates a drinking establishment or brewery. Nicknamed "little Kyōto," Takayama has fewer crowds and wider streets, not to mention fresh mountain air and gorgeous scenery.

Takayama's hugely popular festivals, spring's Sannō Matsuri (April 14–15) and the smaller autumn Hachi-man Matsuri (October 9–10), draw hundreds of thousands of spectators for parades of floats. Hotels are booked solid during matsuri time, so if you plan to join the festivities, make reservations several months in advance.

Getting Around

Takayama has connections north to Toyama by JR train (four departures daily). The ride takes about two hours (with up to an hour waiting for connections) and costs ¥1,620. From Toyama trains go east to Niigata or west to Kanazawa and the Noto-hantō, via Ogi-machi. It's easy to get to Takayama by bus from Matsumoto—but only between May and early November—and it costs ¥3,100. A highly recommended detour to Kamikōchi increases the fare to ¥6,260.

Laid out in a compact grid, Takayama can be explored on foot or bicycle. Bikes at the rental shop south of the station cost ¥300 per hour.

The **Hida Tourist Information Office** (☎ 0577/32–5328 🖷 0577/33–5565 🌐 www.hida.jp/english) in front of the JR station is open from April to October, daily 8:30–6:30; and from November to March, daily 8:30–5. The staff provides maps and helps with accommodations, both in town and in the surrounding mountains.

What to See

★ ❾ **Takayama Jinya** (Historical Government House). This rare collection of stately buildings housed the 25 officials of the Tokugawa shogunate who administered the Hida region for 176 years. Highlights include an original storehouse (1606), which held city taxes in sacks of rice, a torture chamber, curiously translated as the "law court," and samurai barracks. Free guided tours in English are available upon request and take 30–50 minutes. In front of the house, fruit, vegetables, and local crafts are sold at the **Jinya-mae Asa-ichi**, open from April to October, daily 6–noon, and from November to February, daily 7–noon. From the JR station, head east on Hirokōji-dōri for a few blocks to the old section

of town. Before the bridge, which crosses the small Miya-gawa, turn right, pass another bridge, and the Takayama Jinya is on your right. ⌧ *1–5 Hachiken-machi* ☎ *0577/32–0643* ⌨ *¥420* ⊙ *Apr.–Oct., daily 8:45–5; Nov.–Mar., daily 8:45–4:30.*

⓾ The main hall of **Shōren-ji** in Shiroyama Kōen (Shiroyama Park) was built in 1504. It was moved here in 1961 from its original site in Shirakawa-gō, right before the area was flooded by the Miboro Dam. Beautifully carved, allegedly from the wood of a single cedar tree, this temple is an excellent example of classic Muromachi-period architecture. The temple sits on a hill surrounded by gardens, and you can see the Takayama skyline and the park below. ⌧ *Shiroyama Kōen* ☎ *0577/32–2052* ⌨ *¥200* ⊙ *Apr.–Oct., daily 8–5:30; Nov.–Mar., daily 8–5.*

⓫ The **Archaeology Museum** (Hida Minzoku Kōkokan) resides in an old house that once belonged to a physician who served the local daimyō. The mansion has mysterious eccentricities—hanging ceilings, secret windows, and hidden passages—all of which suggest ninja associations. Displays include wall hangings, weaving machines, and other Hida regional items. ⌧ *82 Kamisanno-machi* ☎ *0577/32–1980* ⌨ *¥500* ⊙ *Mar.–Nov., daily 8:30–5:30; Dec.–Feb., daily 9–5.*

★ ⑫ The **Folk-Craft Museum** (Kusakabe Mingeikan) is in a house from the 1880s that belonged to the Kusakabe family—wealthy traders of the Edo period. This national treasure served as a residence and warehouse, where the handsome interior, with heavy, polished beams and an earthy barren floor provides an appropriate setting for Hida folk crafts such as laquered bowls and wood carvings. ✉ *1–52 Ōjin-machi* ☎ *0577/ 32–0072* 💲 *¥500* ⊙ *Mar.–Nov., daily 8:30–5; Dec.–Feb., Sat.–Thurs. 8:30–4:30.*

★ ⑬ The **Takayama Float Exhibition Hall** (Takayama Matsuri Yatai Kaikan) is a community center that displays four of the 11th-, 17th-, and 18th-century *yatai* (festival floats) used in Takayama's famous Sannō and Hachiman festivals. More than two centuries ago Japan was ravaged by the bubonic plague, and yatai were built and paraded through the streets to appease the gods. Because this seemed to work, locals built bigger, more elaborate yatai to prevent further outbreaks. The delicately etched wooden panels, carved wooden lion-head masks for dances, and elaborate tapestries are remarkable. Technical wizardry is also involved, as each yatai contains puppets, controlled by rods and wires, that perform amazing feats like Olympic gymnasts. ✉ *178 Sakura-machi* ☎ *0577/ 32–5100* 💲 *¥820* ⊙ *Mar. Nov., daily 8.30–5; Dec.–Feb., daily 9–4:30.*

⑭ **Kokubun-ji** is the city's oldest temple, dating from 1588. It houses many objects of art, including a precious sword used by the Heike clan. In the Main Hall (built in 1615) sits a figure of Yakushi Nyorai, a Buddha who eases those struggling with illness. In front of the three-story pagoda is a wooden statue of another esoteric Buddhist figure, Kannon Bosatsu, who vowed to hear the voices of all people and immediately grant salvation to those who suffer. The ginkgo tree standing beside the pagoda is believed to be more than 1,200 years old. ✉ *1–83 Sowa-machi* ☎ *0577/32–1395* 💲 *¥300* ⊙ *Daily 9–4.*

⑮ **Hida Folk Village** (Hida no Sato) is a collection of traditional farmhouses
Fodor's Choice dating from the Edo era. The houses were transplanted from all over
★ the region, and their assembly employs ropes rather than nails. Many of the houses are A-frames with thatched roofs called *gasshō-zukuri* (praying hands). Twelve of the buildings are "private houses" displaying folk artifacts like tableware and weaving tools. Another five houses are folk-craft workshops, with demonstrations of *ichii ittōbori* (wood carving), *Hida-nuri* (Hida lacquering), and other traditional regional arts. To get to Hida Minzoku Mura, walk 1 km (½-mi) south from Takayama Station and take a right over the first bridge onto Route 158. Continue west for another ¾ km to the village. The route follows busy roads, so it's better to take a bus from Platform 6, on the left side of the bus terminal. ✉ *1–590 Kami-Okamoto-chō, 3 km (2 mi) west of Takayama* ☎ *0577/34–4711* 💲 *¥700* ⊙ *Daily 8:30–5.*

Where to Stay & Eat

★ **$$$$** ✕ **Kakushō**. This restaurant is known for applying *shōjin*, or temple food, which includes *sansai ryōri*, light dishes of mountain vegetables soaked in a rich miso paste and served with freshwater fish grilled with salt or soy sauce. Occasionally this treat is served atop a roasted magnolia leaf

CLOSE UP

Gassho-zukuri Farmhouses

GASSHO-ZUKURI MEANS "praying hands," and refers to the sloping gable roofs made by placing wooden beams together at a steep 60-degree angle to prevent snow from piling up. In the early 18th century, there were more than 1,800 of these mountain farmhouses between Nagoya and Kanazawa. The openness of the interior was multipurpose: a central hearth sent billows of smoke upward to cure meats and dry food placed on a metal grill suspended from the ceiling; the floor space was used to make gunpowder and *washi* (Japanese paper); and the triangular alcove on top was reserved for silkworm cultivation. Stables were connected to the living space, so no one had to go outdoors during the long, cold winter months.

Perhaps most intriguing of all, the houses were built without nails. Strips of hazel branches tied the beams together, giving the joints the flexibility to sway in the wind. Although modern Japanese no longer live in gassho-zukuri houses, many of these structures have been preserved in historic village settings. These villages, developed in the 1990s, have become increasingly popular tourist destinations, especially for domestic travelers. Of the 150 or so gassho-zukuri that remain, more than half are in the Hida Folk Village in Takayama and the Shirakawa-gō Gassho-zukuri Village in Ogi-machi.

and called *hōba-miso*. The owner, Sumitake-san, can translate the menu for you. From Miya-gawa, head east on the Sanmachi-dōri, crossing four side streets (including the one running along the river), walk up the hill, and take a left at the top. No English sign is out front, but a white *noren* (hanging cloth) hangs in the entrance way of this Edo-era house. You might want to steer toward the semiformal. It's directly across from a small pay parking lot. ✉ *2 Babachō-dōri* ☎ *0577/32–0174* ⌨ *Reservations essential* ▭ *AE, DC, MC, V.*

★ $$ ✕ **Suzuya**. Suzuya's secret recipes have been passed down over several generations. The specialty of the house is the superb and inexpensive sansai-ryōri, the time-honored mountain cuisine. Suzuya is in a traditional Hida-style house, and the dining room is intimate and wood-beamed. There's an English menu, and the staff is used to serving foreign guests. From the station, turn onto Kokubunji-dōri and take a right after five blocks. ✉ *24 Hanakawa* ☎ *0577/32–2484* ▭ *AE, DC, MC, V.*

$$$–$$$$ ▦ **Hida Plaza Hotel**. This is the best international-style hotel in town. Traditional Hida ambiance permeates the old wing, and beautiful wood accents the hotel's tastefully decorated restaurants. Tatami rooms are simple and elegant, and the large Western rooms have sofas. All rooms have wide-screen TVs, and many have views of the mountains. The newer wing is not as attractive, but its rooms are larger. Luxury appears in the form of mineral baths crafted of fragrant cypress wood. From the station, head north; the hotel is on the right. ✉ *2–60 Hanaoka-chō, Takayama, Gifu-ken 506-0009* ☎ *0577/33–4600* 🖷 *0577/33–4602* ⊕ *www.hida-hotelplaza.co.jp* ⇱ *136 Western-style rooms, 89 Japanese-*

style rooms, 2 suites & 4 restaurants, coffee shop, indoor pool, health club, Japanese baths, sauna, dance club, shops ⊟ *AE, DC, MC, V.*

★ **$$** 🎌 **Yamakyū.** Cozy, antiques-filled nooks with chairs and coffee tables become small lounges in this old Tera-machi minshuku. In the mineral-water baths a giant waterwheel turns hypnotically, complimented by recorded bird songs. Although there's an 11 PM curfew, dinner hours are more flexible than those of the typical minshuku, and the food, of astonishing variety, is superb. Fifteen of the rooms have private toilets. Yamakyū is east of the Enako-gawa, at the very top of San-machi dōri, a 20-minute walk from Takayama Station. ⊠ *58 Tenshō-ji-machi, Takayama, Gifu-ken 506-0832* ☎ *0577/32–3756* 🖷 *0577/35–2350* 🔊 *30 Japanese-style rooms without bath & Dining room, Japanese baths, shop* ⊟ *No credit cards* ◯ *MAP.*

Nightlife

Nightlife in sleepy Takayama revolves around locally produced beer and sake. Open for lunch until 3, and then again at 5:30, **Renga-ya** (⊠ 3–58–11 Hon-machi ☎ 0577/36–1339) is a brewery, bar, and restaurant. Head east on Kokubun-ji-dōri and turn left just before the river. It's one block down on the left. You'll see the brewery through the window.

Two blocks east and one block south of City Hall is a bar popular with the foreign locals called **Red Hill** (⊠ 1–4 Sowa-chō ☎ 0577/33–8139 ◷ Tues.–Sun. 7 PM–midnight). Close by is an upstairs reggae bar, **Bagus,** which offers a delicious chai from the varied drinks menu in English. (⊠ 1–31–3 Hatsuda ☎ 0577/36–4341 ◷ 7 PM–midnight).

Ogi-machi

⑯ *2 hrs northwest of Takayama by bus.*

It's speculated that Ogi-machi, an Edo-era hamlet deep within Shirakawa-gō village, was originally populated by survivors of the powerful Taira family, who were nearly killed off in the 12th century by the rival Genji family. The majority of the residents living here still inhabit gasshō-zukuri houses. Their shape and materials enable the house to withstand the heavy regional snow, and in summer the straw keeps the houses cool. Household activities center on the *irori* (open hearth), which sends smoke up through the timbers and thatched roof. Meats and fish are preserved (usually on a metal shelf suspended above the hearth) by the ascending smoke, which also prevents insects and vermin from taking up residence in the straw.

Getting Around

It's more convenient to drive to Ogi-machi, but it's possible to get there by public transportation. The bus to Ogi-machi departs from Nagoya at 9 AM daily, taking three hours and costing ¥3,500. You'll also find daily bus service from Ogi-machi to Kanazawa, departing at 8:40 AM and 2:40 PM. The trip also takes three hours, and costs ¥3,300, or ¥5,900 round-trip. Bus services stop from about the end of October until March or April, and it is best to reserve a seat through tourist offices in advance. From Takayama, buses go year-round four to six times daily for ¥2,400, ¥4,300 round-trip. Many old houses also function as minshuku. To stay in one, make reservations through the **Ogi-machi Tourist Office** (✉ 57 Ogi-machi, Shirakawa-mura ☎ 0576/96–1311), open daily 9–5. It's next to the Gasshō-shuraku bus stop in the center of town.

What to See

★ Opposite Ogi-machi, on the banks of the Shō-gawa, is **Shirakawa-gō Gasshō-zukuri Village**, an open-air museum with 25 traditional Gasshō-zukuri farmhouses. The houses were transplanted from four villages that fell prey the Miboro Dam, built upriver in 1972. Over the years a colony of artisans has established itself in the village. You can watch them creating folk crafts like weaving, pottery, woodwork, and hand-dyeing in a few of the preserved houses. Many of the products are for sale. ✉ *Ogi-machi, Shirakawa mura, Ōno-gun* ☎ *0576/96–1231.*

KANAZAWA & THE NORTH CHŪBU COAST

The center of culture and commerce in the Hokuriku region, Kanazawa ranks among Japan's best-loved cities. To the east are snow-capped mountains, including the revered (and hikeable) Haku-san. To the north stretches the clawlike peninsula of the Noto-hantō, where lush rolling hills and rice fields meet scenic coastlines. Farther north along the Nihon-kai are the hardworking industrial capitals of Toyama and Niigata, and offshore the secluded Sado Island.

Kanazawa

2 hrs northeast of Kyōto; 3 hrs north of Nagoya; 2½ hrs northwest of Takayama, changing trains at Toyama; 3 hrs 40 min southwest of Niigata-all by JR Limited Express. (Possible railway repairs between Toyama and Takayama may make the 3-hour direct bus between Kanazawa and Takayama a better option; there are two daily, and the cost is ¥3,300 one-way)

Twenty-first century Kanazawa presents an extraordinary union of unblemished Old Japan and a modern, trendsetting city. More than 300 years of history have been preserved in the earthen walls and flowing canals of Nagamachi, the former samurai quarter west of downtown; the cluster of Buddhist temples in Tera-machi on the southern bank of the Saigawa River; and the wooden facades of the former geisha district, located north of the Asano-gawa river. Modern art, fashion, music, and international dining thrive in the downtown core of Kōrinbō, and in the shopping districts of Tatemachi and Katamachi. The Japan Sea provides great seafood and a somewhat dreary climate. Fortunately, cold, gray, and wet weather is offset by friendly people.

In the feudal times of the Edo period, the prime rice-growing areas around Kanazawa (known then as the province of Kaga) made the ruling Maeda clan the second wealthiest in the country. Harvests came in at more than *hyaku-man-goku* (1 million *koku*, the Edo-period unit of measurement based on how much rice would feed one person for a year). This wealth funded various cultural pursuits such as silk dyeing, ceramics, and the production of gold-leaf and lacquerware products.

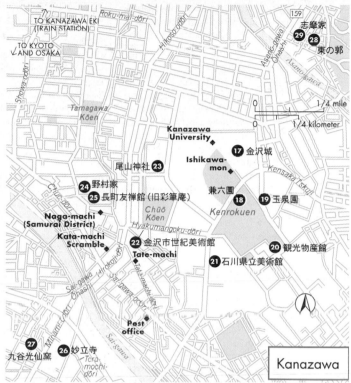

Kanazawa

This prosperity did not pass unnoticed. The fear of attack by the Edo daimyō inspired the Maeda lords to construct one of the country's most massive castles amid a mazelike network of narrow, winding lanes that made the approach difficult and an invasion nearly impossible. These defensive tactics paid off, and Kanazawa enjoyed 300 years of peace and prosperity. Nevertheless, seven fires over the centuries reduced the once-mighty Kanazawa-jō to castle walls and a single, impressive gate. The former castle grounds are now the site of Kanazawa University.

Getting Around

Ideal for tourists, the *shū-yū basu* (loop bus) departs every 15 minutes from 8:30 AM to 9 PM from Gate 0 of Kanazawa Station's east exit, and delivers you to the major tourist sites. Stops are announced in English and displayed on a digital board at the front of the bus. A single ride costs ¥200; the day pass is ¥500. You can purchase the pass from the Hokutetsu bus ticket office in front of Kanazawa Station.

Visitor Information

The **Kanazawa Information Office** (☎ 076/232–6200 ☐ 076/238–6210) has two desks at the train station and a volunteer staff that will help you find accommodations. It's open daily 9–7; an English speaker is on duty 1–6 from the **Kanazawa Goodwill Guide Network** (⊕ kggn.sakura.ne.jp), which offers free guide and interpreting services.

What to See

⑰ The area around the old **Kanazawa-jō** (Kanazawa Castle) is a suitable place to start exploring Kanazawa. Only the **Ishikawa-mon** (Ishikawa Gate) remains intact—its thick mossy stone base is topped with curving black eaves and white lead roof tiles. The tiles could be melted down and molded into ammunition in the case of a prolonged siege. To reach the castle, take any bus (¥200) from Gate 11 at the bus terminal outside the JR station.

> ### SAMURAI TOWN
>
> Behind the modern Kōrinbō 109 shopping center, Seseragi-dōri leads to **Naga-machi** (the Samurai District), where the Maeda clan lived. Narrow, snaking streets are lined with beautiful, golden adobe walls 8 feet high, footed with large stones and topped with black tiles.

★ ⑱ Across the street from the castle remains is Kanazawa's **Kenroku Garden** (Kenrokuen), the largest of the three most famous landscaped gardens in the country (the other two are Mito's Kairaku Garden and Okayama's Kōraku Garden). The Maeda lord Tsunanori began construction of Kenrokuen in 1676, and by the early 1880s it had become 25 sprawling acres of skillfully wrought bridges and fountains, ponds, and waterfalls. The garden changes with the seasons: spring brings cherry blossoms; brilliant azaleas foretell the arrival of summer; autumn paints the maples deep yellow and red; and in winter the pine trees are strung with long ropes, tied from trunk to bough, for protection against heavy snowfalls. Kenrokuen means "Garden of Six Qualities" (*ken-roku* means "integrated six"). The garden was so named because it exhibited the six superior characteristics judged necessary by the Chinese Sung Dynasty for the perfect garden: spaciousness, artistic merit, majesty, abundant water, extensive views, and seclusion. Despite the promise of its last attribute, the gardens attract a mad stampede of visitors—herded by megaphone—in cherry-blossom season (mid-April) and Golden Week (late April and early May). Early morning is the sensible time for a visit, when the grounds are peaceful and relaxing. ⊠ 1 Kenroku-chō ☎ 076/221–5850 ☑ ¥300, free 3rd Sun. of month ☉ Mar.–mid-Oct., daily 7–6; mid-Oct.–Feb., daily 8–4:30.

⑲ **Gyokusen Garden** (Gyokusenen), a tiny, intimate garden, was built by
Fodor'sChoice Kim Yeocheol, who later became Naokata Wakita when he married into
★ the ruling Kanazawa family. Yeocheol was the son of a Korean captive brought to Japan in the late 16th century. He became a wealthy merchant, using his fortune to build this quiet getaway. The garden's intimate tranquillity stems from the imaginative and subtle arrangement of moss, maple trees, and small stepping stones by the pond. Two waterfalls that gracefully form the Chinese character for *mizu* (water) feed the pond. The garden is markedly different from the bold strokes of Kenroku Garden. You can have tea here for ¥600. ☎ 076/221–0181 ☑ ¥500 ☉ Mid-Mar.–mid-Dec., Thurs–Tues 9–4.

⑳ At the **Ishikawa Prefectural Products Center** (Ishikawa-ken Kankō Bussankan), near Gyokusen Garden, you can see demonstrations of Yuzen dyeing, pottery, and lacquerware production. ☎ 076/224–5511

¥700, *includes admission to Gyokusen Garden* ⊙ *Apr.–Oct., daily 9–4:30; Nov.–Mar., Fri.–Wed. 9–4:30.*

㉒ The circular **21st-Century Museum of Contemporary Art** (21 Seiki Bijutsukan) was created to entwine a museum's architecture with the art exhibits, and for exhibition designers to take cues from the architecture. Transparent walls and scattered galleries encourage visitors to choose their own route. Previous exhibitions have included a Gerhard Richter retrospective, a video installation by Mathew Barney, and the work of Japanese photographer Araki Nobuyoshi. It's south of Kanazawa Park, next to City Hall. ☎ *076/220–2801* ⊕ *www.kanazawa21.jp/en/index. html* ⊠ *Depends on exhibition* ⊙ *Tues.–Fri. 10–6, weekends 10–8.*

㉑ The **Ishikawa Prefectural Art Museum** (Ishikawa Kenritsu Bijutsukan) displays the country's best permanent collection of *Kutani-yaki* (colorful overglaze-painted porcelain), dyed fabrics, and old Japanese paintings. ⊠ *2–1 Dewa-machi, southwest of Kenrokuen* ☎ *076/231–7180* ⊠ *¥350* ⊙ *Daily 9–4:30.*

㉓ Built in 1599, **Oyama Jinja** was dedicated to Lord Toshiie Maeda, the founder of the Maeda clan. The shrine's unusual three-story gate, **Shinmon**, was completed in 1875. Previously located atop Mt. Utatsu, it's believed that the square arch containing stained-glass windows once functioned as a lighthouse, guiding ships in from the Japan Sea to the Kanaiwa port, 6 km (4 mi) northwest. You're free to walk around the shrine. To get here from the JR station, take Bus 30 or 31 from Gate 8. ⊠ *11–1 Oyama-chō* ☎ *076/231–7210* ⊠ *Free.*

㉕ A few houses have been carefully restored in the Samurai District, including the **Saihitsuan Yūzen Silk Center** (Kyū-Saihitsuan), where you can watch demonstrations of Yūzen silk painting, a centuries-old technique in which intricate floral designs with delicate white outlines are meticulously painted onto silk used for kimonos. It's behind the Tōkyū Hotel, five blocks southwest of Oyama Jinja. ⊠ *1–3–28 Naga-machi* ☎ *076/264–2811* ⊠ *¥500* ⊙ *Fri.–Wed. 9–noon and 1–4:30.*

㉔ **Nomura-ke**, an elegant house in Naga-machi, was rebuilt more than 100 years ago by an industrialist named Nomura. Visit the Jōdan-no-ma drawing room made of *hinoki* (cypress), with elaborate designs in rosewood and ebony. Then pass through the sliding doors, adorned with the paintings of Sasaki Senkai of the illustrious Kano School, to a wooden veranda. Rest your feet here, and take in the stunning little garden with weathered lanterns among pine and maple trees, and various shrubs and bonsai. Stepping-stones lead to a pond dotted with moss-covered rocks and brilliant orange-flecked carp. In the upstairs tearoom you can enjoy a cup of *macha* (green tea) for ¥300 and a bird's-eye view of the gardens. ⊠ *1–3–32 Naga-machi* ☎ *076/221–3553* ⊠ *¥500* ⊙ *Apr.–Sept., daily 8:30–5:30; Oct.–Mar., daily 8:30–4:30.*

㉖ On the south side of the Sai-gawa is the intriguing and mysterious **Myōryū-ji**. Its popular name, Ninja-dera (Temple of the Ninja), suggests it was a clandestine training center for martial-arts masters who crept around in the dead of night armed with *shuriken* (star-shape blades). In fact, the temple was built to provide an escape route for the daimyō in

Fodor's Choice
★

case of invasion. Ninja-dera was built by Toshitsune in 1643, when the Tokugawa shogunate was stealthily knocking off local warlords and eliminating competition. At first glance, it appears a modest yet handsome two-story structure. Inside, however, you find 29 staircases, seven levels, myriad secret passageways and trap doors, a tunnel to the castle hidden beneath the well in the kitchen, and even a *seppuku* room, where the lord could perform an emergency ritual suicide. Unfortunately (or fortunately, considering all the booby traps), visitors are not permitted to explore the hidden lair alone. You must join a Japanese tour and follow along with your English pamphlet. ⊠ *1–2–12 No-machi* ☎ *076/ 241–0888* ⊟ *¥800* ⊘ *Mar.–Nov., daily 9–4:30; Dec.–Feb., daily 9–4.*

㉘ **Higashi-no-Kuruwa** (the Eastern Pleasure Quarter), near the Asano-gawa, was the high-class entertainment district of Edo-period Kanazawa. Now the pleasures are limited to viewing quaint old geisha houses recognizable by their wood-slat facades and latticed windows. Many have become tearooms, restaurants, or minshuku. If you are lucky, you might see a geisha scuttling to her appointment. Take the JR bus from Kanazawa Station (¥200) to Hachira-chō, just before the Asano-gawa Ōhashi. Cross the bridge and walk northeast into the quarter.

㉙ One elegant former geisha house, **Shima-ke**, is open to the public for tours. ⊠ *1–13–21 Higashi-yama* ☎ *076/252–5675* ⊟ *¥400* ⊘ *Tues.–Sun. 9–5.*

㉗ At the **Kutani Pottery Kiln** (Kutani Kōsen Gama), established in 1870, you can watch artisans making the local Kutani pottery, which is noted for its vibrant color schemes. ⊠ *5–3–3 No-machi* ☎ *076/241–0902* ⊟ *Free* ⊘ *Mon.–Sat. 8:30–noon and 1–5, Sun. 8:30–noon.*

Where to Stay & Eat

$$$$ ✗**Sugi no I.** This elegant restaurant in Teramachi, on the south bank of the Saigawa River close to the Sakura-bashi bridge, serves Kaga specialties like duck stew with wheat gluten called *jibu ni* and *gori no tsukuda ni,* tiny soy-simmered river fish on Kutani china, Oribe pottery, and lacquerware. There is a special ladies' course (that anyone can order) for ¥3,000. For a surcharge of ¥500 per person you can have a private room overlooking the garden. In traditional Japanese style, the meal finishes with rice, pickles, and soup; in autumn the broth is clear with herbs and a shrimp dumpling. Full-course dinners start at ¥15,000. ⊠ *Sugi no I, 3–11, Kyokawa Machi* ☎ *0762/43–2288* ⊜ *Reservations essential* ⊟ *AE, V.*

★ $$$–$$$$ ✗**Miyoshian.** Excellent *bentō* (box lunches) and fish and vegetable dinners have been made here for nearly 100 years in the renowned Kenroku Garden. Prices are still reasonable—the Kaga kaiseki course is less than ¥3,000. In the annex matcha tea is served with Japanese pastries from Morihachi, a confectioner with a 360-year history. ⊠ *1 Kenroku-chō* ☎ *076/221–0127* ⊟ *AE, MC, V* ⊘ *Closed Tues.*

★ $$–$$$$ ✗**Kincharyō.** The menu changes seasonally in the showpiece restaurant of the Kanazawa Tōkyū Hotel. The lacquered, curved countertop of the sushi bar is beautiful. Superb dinner courses range from tempura sets (¥4,042–¥8,085) to mixed kaiseki (9 items cost ¥5,775). In spring your meal may include *hotaru-ika* (firefly squid) and *iidako* (baby octopus) no larger than your thumbnail. The lunch *kaiseki bentō* costs from ¥1,300 to ¥3,600. ⊠ *Kanazawa Tōkyū Hotel, 3rd fl., 2–1–1 Kōrimbo* ☎ *076/231–2411* ☐ *AE, DC, MC, V.*

$–$$$$ ✕ Not far from the Ōmi-Chō market is **Fumuroya**, a store that specializes in wheat gluten, called *ofu*, and its adjacent lunch restaurant offers a set lunch for ¥3,100 of *jibu ni*, a stew made with chicken (instead of the usual duck), ofu, and shiitake mushrooms. ⊠ *2–3–1 Owari-chō* ☎ *0762/21–1377* ⚓ *Reservations essential* ☐ *V* ☯ *Mon.–Sat. 11:30–4. Closed the 2nd and 4th Mon. of each month.*

★ ¢–$ ✕ **Legian**. You might be surprised to find a funky Balinese eatery along the Sai-gawa. But if you try the *gado-gado* (vegetables in a spicy sauce), *nasi goreng* (Indonesian-style fried rice), or chicken *satay* (grilled on a skewer, with peanut sauce), you'll be happily surprised. Indonesian beer and mango ice cream are also available. It's open late (Monday–Thursday until 12:30 AM, Friday and Saturday until 4:30 AM), and after dinner things get interesting. From Kata-machi Scramble (the area's central intersection), turn right just before Sai-gawa bridge, and follow the narrow lane along the river. ⊠ *2–31–30 Kata-machi* ☎ *076/262–6510* ☐ *No credit cards* ☯ *Closed Wed.*

¢ ✕ **Noda-ya**. Slip into this little tea shop for a scoop of delicious *macha sofuto kurīmu* (green tea ice cream), or just a cup of tea. You can sit in the little garden in back or on benches out front. At the far end of the Tate-machi shopping street, Noda-ya is difficult to spot, but you can find it if you follow your nose—the scent of roasting green tea leaves is heavenly. The shop is open daily 9–8. ⊠ *3 Tate-machi* ☎ *076/22–0982* ☐ *No credit cards.*

★ $$$$ ▥ **APA Hotel Eki-mae**. This hotel is so close to the JR station it's practically inside it. A blue ceiling with sparkling stars watches over a Seattle's Best coffee shop and a modern lobby. Inside your small yet stylish room a charming origami crane perches atop a carefully pressed bathrobe. Each room has views over Kanazawa, and the sauna and onsen are free for guests. ⊠ *1–9–28 Hiroka, Kanazawa, Ishikawa-ken 920-0031* ☎ *076/231–8111* 🖷 *076/231–8112* ⊕ *www.apahotel.com* ⋗ *456 rooms* ⚅ *2 restaurants, coffee shop, refrigerators, massage, sauna, no-smoking rooms* ☐ *AE, DC, MC, V.*

★ $$$$ ▥ **Hotel Nikkō Kanazawa**. The exotic lobby of this 30-story hotel is more reminiscent of Singapore than Japan, with tropical plants, cherry-oak slatted doors, and colonial-style furniture. A winding staircase curls around a bubbling pond in the middle of the lobby and leads to a European brasserie, Garden House, which serves wonderful coffee and cake. The colorful top-floor lounge, Le Grand Chariot, has panoramic views over Kanazawa, sumptuous French cuisine, and soft piano music. Guest rooms begin at the 17th floor, and the Western-style ones are decorated with creamy pastels and blond-wood furnishings and have striking views—of the sea, city, or mountains. A JAL ticket counter is on the premises, and an underground passageway connects the hotel to the JR station. The hotel charges ¥2,100 for use of the pool and gym. ⊠ *2–15–1 Hon-machi, Kanazawa, Ishikawa-ken 920-0853* ☎ *076/234–1111* 🖷 *076/234–8802* ⊕ *www.jalhotels.com* ⋗ *256 rooms, 4 suites* ⚅ *4 restau* *rants, in-room fax, minibars, cable TV, in-room VCRs, in-room data ports, pool, gym, hot tub, sauna, 2 bars, lobby lounge, shops, laundry service, travel services, parking (fee), no-smoking rooms* ▤ *AE, DC, MC, V.*

★ $$$$ ⊞ **Ryokan Asadaya.** This small ryokan, established during the Meiji Restoration (1867), is the most lavish lodging in Kanazawa. The interior blends traditional elegance with innovative designs—a perfect metaphor for the age of Japan's transition into modernity. Antique furnishings and exquisite scrolls and paintings appear throughout the inn. Superb regional Kaga cuisine is served in your room or in the restaurant. ⊠ *23 Jukken-machi, Kanazawa, Ishikawa-ken 920-0906* ☎ *076/ 232–2228* 🖷 *076/252–4444* ⊕ *www.asadaya.co.jp/asadayaryokan_e. php* ⇗ *5 Japanese-style rooms* ⚒ *Restaurant* ▤ *AE* ⑩ *MAP.*

$$$-$$$$ ⊞ **Kanazawa New Grand Hotel.** Stepping into this hotel's sleek black-and-cream marble lobby is a refreshing break from the dreary concrete of the main drag outside. From the sky lounge, Dichter, and restaurant, Sky Restaurant Roi, which serves some of the city's best contemporary French cuisine, you get a great view of Oyama Shrine and the sunset. The spacious rooms, though far from new, are done in white-and-beige tones, and have sofas. Japanese-style rooms are slightly larger, but furnishings are spare. The hotel is a 15-minute walk from the station, if you head down Eki-mae-dōri and take a right on Hikoso-ōdōri. ⊠ *1–50 Takaoka-chō, Kanazawa, Ishikawa-ken 920-0864* ☎ *076/233–1311* 🖷 *076/233–1591* ⊕ *www.new-grand.co.jp* ⇗ *100 Western-style rooms, 2 Japanese-style rooms, 2 suites* ⚒ *5 restaurants, coffee shop, cable TV, in-room data ports, shops, no-smoking rooms* ▤ *AE, DC, MC, V.*

¢ ⊞ **Yōgetsu.** In a century-old geisha house in the Eastern Pleasure Quarter, Yōgetsu is a small, stylish minshuku. The owner is a welcoming hostess, and keeps a neat shared bath. The guest rooms are small and sparsely furnished, but rustic exposed beams add character. Only second-floor rooms are air- conditioned. ⊠ *1–13–22 Higashiyama, Kanazawa, Ishikawa-ken 920-0831* ☎ *076/252–0497* ⇗ *5 Japanese-style rooms without bath* ⚒ *Dining room, Japanese baths* ▤ *No credit cards* ⑩ *MAP.*

Nightlife

All-night fun can be found in the center of town. Be warned: these places don't take credit cards. Free billiard tables make **Apre** (⊠ 4th fl., Laporto Bldg., 1–3–9 Katamachi ☎076/221–0090) a scene on weekends (it's closed Monday). When it opens at 8 PM, the tables fill up, and the action is competitive. It's tricky to find, so don't hesitate to call for directions. **Pole-Pole** ("po-ray-po-ray" ⊠ 2–31–31 Kata-machi ☎ 076/260–1138) is a reggae bar run by the same jolly owner as Legian, and is just behind the restaurant. If you want to sit, arrive before midnight. The two dark cramped rooms get so full that the crowd spills out into the hallway. Pole-Pole is closed on Sunday but open until 5 AM the rest of the week.

Zizake (⊠ 1–7–23 Katamachi ☎ 076/263–6377 ◷ Mon.–Sat. 4 PM–midnight). From the Katamichi crossing, walking away from Kohrinbo you will find this sake shot bar about 100m on the left. As the pile of three sake casks outside the door attest, 64 varieties of sake are served, all from Ishikawa Prefecture and most priced ¥315–¥525, which gets you an ample tasting-size portion. The most expensive are the aged sakes which cost about ¥1,000. On the food menu are small dishes like the *morokyu*, crunchy-fresh cucumbers slathered with miso, and fresh sashimi served with tangy slivers of fresh *myoga*, a kind of ginger.

Fukui

㉚ *40 min southwest of Kanazawa by JR Limited Express, 2 hrs north of Nagoya by JR Limited Express.*

★ One of the two headquarters of Soto Zen, **Eihei-ji** is 19 km (12 mi) southeast of Fukui. Founded in 1244, the extensive complex of 70 temple buildings is spread out on a hillside surrounded by hinoki and *sugi* (cedar) trees more than 100 feet tall, some as old as the original wooden structures. This temple offers a rare glimpse into the daily practice of the 200 or so monks (and a few nuns) in training. They are called *unsui* or cloud water, the traditional name for mendicant monks wandering in search of a teacher. The rigorous training remains unchanged since Dogen started this monastery. Each monk only has one tatami mat (1 m by 2 m), to eat, sleep, and meditate on. The mats are lined in rows on raised platforms in a communal room. All activities, from using the bathroom to cleaning out the incense tray, are considered to be a meditation, and so visitors are expected to dress modestly and explore in silence. Students of Zen or those interested in meditation can do short retreats of one to three days and lodge at the temple (for ¥8,000 a night, including two meals), with two weeks' advance notice in writing. The easiest way to get to Eihei-ji from Fukui is by train. ⊠ *5–15 Shihi Eiheiji-chō, Yoshida-gun, Fukui 910-1294* ☎ *0776/ 63-3102* 💳 *¥500* ⊙ *Daily 5–5.*

Where to Sleep

¢-$ 🏨 **Hotel Akebono Bekkan.** Think of this small, two-story wooden hotel as a weekend retreat—the owners can arrange training sessions in Zen meditation and classes in pottery and papermaking. The Akebono Bekkan is actually the annex of a large, modern hotel, the Riverge Akebono, so you can enjoy the best of both worlds. Both Japanese and Western breakfasts are served, but only Japanese food is available at dinner. All the small tatami rooms have private toilets, but the bath is shared. The inn is next to Sakura Bridge, a 10-minute walk from Fukui Station. ⊠ *3–10–12 Chūō, Fukui-shi, Fukui-ken 910-0006* ☎ *0776/22-1000* 🖨 *0776/22-8023* ⊕ *www.riverge.com* 🛏 *10 Japanese-style rooms without bath* 🔥 *Restaurant, Japanese baths* 🖃 *AE, V.*

Noto-hantō (Noto Peninsula)

㉛ *Nanao, on east coast of peninsula, is 52 min northeast from Kanazawa by JR Limited Express. Wajima, on north coast of Noto-hantō, is 2¼ hrs northeast of Kanazawa by JR Limited Express.*

Thought to be named after an Ainu (indigenous Japanese) word for "nose," the Noto-hantō, a national park, juts out into the Nihon-kai and shelters the bays of both Nanao and Toyama. Steep, densely forested hills line the eroded west coast, which is wind- and wave-blasted in winter and ruggedly beautiful in other seasons. The eastern shoreline is lapped by calmer waters and has stunning views of Tate-yama (Mt. Tate), the Hida Mountains, and even of some of Nagano's alpine peaks more than 105 km (70 mi) away. This is a good place to explore by car, or even by bicycle. Although the interior routes can be arduous, the coastal roads are relatively flat. You can also combine train and bus trips or guided tours, which can be arranged in Kanazawa.

Getting Around

From Anamizu the private Noto Line goes northeast to Takojima, the region's most scenic route. The line to Wajima turns inland after Hakui and misses some of the peninsula's best sights. A quick sightseeing circuit of the Noto-hantō, from Hakui to Nanao, can be done in six to eight hours, but to absorb the peninsula's remarkable scenery, stay two or three days, stopping in Wajima and at one of the minshuku along the coast; arrangements can be made through tourist information offices in Kanazawa, Nanao, or Wajima.

What to See

In **Hakui**, a 40-minute train ride from Kanazawa, you can bike along the coastal path as far as beautiful Gan-mon (Sea Gate), some 26 km (16 mi) away, where you can stop for lunch. Just north of Chirihama, a formerly popular and now unkempt beach, the scenery improves. Rent bikes from **Kato Cycle** (☎ 0767/22–0539), for ¥800 per day across from Joyful Supermarket, west of the JR station in Hakui.

Myōjō-ji is a less visited but well-tended temple complex a few miles north by bus from Hakui (buses leave outside the train station). The temple, founded in 1294 and belonging to the Nichiren sect of Buddhism, has a five-story pagoda from the 1600s. A very large, colorful Buddha statue sits inside a squat wooden building. The influence of mainland Asia is visible in the garguantan, wooden guardian deities. A recorded announcement on the bus tells where to get off for Myōjō-ji. It's a 10-minute walk to the temple from the bus stop. ⊠ *1 Yo Taki-tani-machi* ☎ *0767/27–1226* 📷 *¥350* ☉ *Daily 8–5.*

EN ROUTE

Although you can take the inland bus directly north from Hakui to Monzen, the longer (70-minute) bus ride along the coast is recommended for its scenic value. The 16-km (10-mi) stretch between Fukuura and Sekinohana, known as the **Noto Seacoast** (Noto-Kongō), has fantastic wind- and wave-eroded rocks, from craggy towers to partly submerged checkerboard-pattern platforms. Among the best is **Gan-mon**, a rock cut through the center by water. Gan-mon is about 45 minutes north of Hakui and is a stop on tour-bus routes.

The Zen temple complex **Sōji-ji** at Monzen once served as the Soto sect's headquarters. Though a fire destroyed most of the buildings in 1818 and the sect moved its headquarters to Yokohama in 1911, this is still an important training temple. As at Eihei-ji in Fukui, lay practitioners may stay for a few days. Strolling paths traverse the lush grounds, where you can see some spectacular red maples and an elaborately carved gate. The Sōji-ji-mae bus stop is in front of the temple; use a bus from Monzen Station to reach it. It can also can be accessed from the Anamizu bus station on the Noto Chūō bus bound for Monzen (32 minutes). ⊠ *1–18 Monzen, Monzen-chō* ☎ *0768/42–0005* 🚍 *¥400* ⊙ *Daily 8–5.*

Only 16 km (10 mi) and one bus stop up the road from Monzen is **Wajima**. This fishing town at the tip of the peninsula is also known for its gorgeous lacquerware. Wajima's **tourist office** (☎ 0768/22–1503), at the station, is open daily 10–6.

To observe the traditional lacquerware manufacturing process, visit the **Lacquerware Hall** (Wajima Shikki Kaikan). The production of a single piece involves more than 20 steps, from wood preparation and linen reinforcement to the application of layers of lacquer, carefully dried and polished between coats. Wajima Shikki Kaikan is in the center of town on the north side of Route 249, just before Shin-bashi (New Bridge). From the station, turn left when you exit and walk straight (northwest) about four blocks until you hit Route 249. Turn left again—there's a Hokuriku Bank on the corner—and continue southwest along Route 249 for about four blocks. ☎ *0768/22–2155* 🚍 *¥200* ⊙ *Daily 8:30–5.*

The **asa-ichi**, or morning market, in Wajima is held daily 8–11:30, except on the 10th and 25th of each month. You can buy seafood, fruit, vegetables, local crafts, and lacquerware from elderly women wearing indigo *monpei* (field pants). The smaller *yū-ichi* (evening market) starts around 3 PM. Almost anyone can point you in the right direction. ⊠ *Asa-ichi dōri Kawai-chō* ☎ *0768/22–7653 mornings only.*

From Wajima an hourly bus runs to **Sosogi**, a small village 20 minutes to the northeast, passing the terraced fields of Senmaida, where rice paddies descend from the hills to the sea. You can continue around the peninsula's northern tip by bus, from Sosogi to **Rokkō-zaki** (Cape Rokkō), past a small lighthouse, and down to the northern terminus of the Noto Railway Line at Takojima. Unless you have a car, however, the views and scenery don't quite justify the infrequency of the public transportation.

The same hourly bus that runs between Wajima and Sosogi continues on to **Suzu** on the *uchi* (inside) coast. Just south of Suzu, near Ukai Station, is a dramatic offshore rock formation called *Mitsuke-jima,* a huge wedge of rock topped with lush vegetation, connected to the shore with a pebbly path popular with lovers. It is said that Kobo Daishi gave it the nickname of *Gunkan Island* or Battleship Island because it ressembles a warship sailing to attack.

Southeast of Suzu is the open-air **Mawaki Onsen**. Artifacts, including pottery from the *Jōmon* (straw-rope pattern) archaeological period (13,000 BC–300 BC) were found here. Mawaki is also well known for its wonderful hilltop view, which overlooks the rice fields and fishing villages along the edge of Toyama Bay. One bath-and-sauna complex is stone, the other is wood; on alternate weeks they open to men and women. A hotel is connected to the bath complex. To get here, hike up the hill or take a short taxi ride from Jomon Station on the Noto Line. Mawaki can also be reached in 2¼ hours by car from Kanazawa along a scenic toll road, or 2½ hours by train (with a change in Wakura). On your way south to Mawaki Onsen are numerous opportunities for hiking, swimming, and camping. ✉ *19–39 Mawaki* ☎ *0768/62–4567* 📠 *0768/62–4568* 🎫 *¥450* ⊙ *Mon. noon–10, Tues.–Sun. 10–10.*

A terrific brewery and log-cabin-style restaurant called the **Heart and Beer Nihonkai Club** (✉ 92 Aza-Tatekabe, Uchiura-machi ☎ 0768/72–8181) is five minutes by taxi from Matsunami Station (on the Noto Line). It's operated by two beer masters from eastern Europe in conjunction with an association that helps people with disabilities. Specials include delicious emu stew (¥1,200), raised on-site, and tasty Noto beef, along with some very good microbrewed beer (¥460). It's open from Thursday to Tuesday.

Nanao is best known for its festivals. **Seihakusai festival,** a 400-year-old tradition held May 3–5, is essentially three days of nonstop partying. Huge (26-foot) 10-ton floats resembling ships called *deka-yama* (big mountains) are paraded through the streets. At midnight the floats become miniature kabuki stages for dance performances by costumed children. Since Seihakusai festival is celebrated during Golden Week, when almost everyone in Japan is on vacation, it's a wild scene. The men pulling the floats are given generous and frequent libations of beer and sake, and the crowd also suffers no shortage of refreshments.

Takaoka, the southern gateway to the Noto Peninsula has Japan's third-largest **Daibutsu** (Great Buddha), standing 53 feet high and made of bronze. Also in Takaoka, a 400-m walk from the station, is **Zuiryū-ji**, a delightful Zen temple that doubles as a youth hostel. A sprawling park, **Kojō-kōen,** not far from the station, is particularly stunning in autumn, with its red-and-silver maples. Takaoka is mostly known for its traditions of copper-, bronze-, and iron-smithing, and remains a major bell-casting center.

Where to Stay

$$$$ 🏨 **Wakara Yonekyu.** A 6-minute ride from JR Wakura Onsen station gets you to this white seven-story bay-front hotel that combines ryokan traditional touches with modern facilities. At the spacious indoor and outdoor hot-spring baths you feel the ocean spray. A complimentary cup of matcha is served in the tea ceremony room. Room rates include two meals, usually local fish and beef and sometimes snow crab. ✉ *6–8–6, Kawaimachi Wajima city, Ishikawa-ken 928-0001* ☎ *0768/22–4488* 📠 *0768/22–8899* 💬 *39 rooms ♨ Restaurant, nightclub, bar,* ☐ *No credit cards* ⍥ *MAP.*

$$-$$$$ 🏨 **Mawaki Pō-re Pō-re.** This little hotel, built into a hillock, connects with the bath complex at Mawaki and has great views of the sea and surrounding hills. Breakfast is included, and the staff is kind. The Western-style rooms are done in blue and lilac; the Japanese-style rooms have shōji screens and are slightly larger and brighter but cost more. You're a minute away from the mineral baths. ✉ *19–110 Aza-Mawaki, Noto-machi, Fugeshi-gun, Ishikawa-ken 927-0562* ☎ *0768/62–4700* 📠 *0768/62–4702* 💬 *5 Western-style rooms, 5 Japanese-style rooms, 1 suite ♨ Restaurant* ☐ *No credit cards* ⍥ *BP.*

$$ 🏨 **Fukasan.** Conveniently near the morning market and only one street up from the harbor, this two-story wooden *minshuku*, or Japanese guesthouse, is infused with the warmth of the hosts, who have furnished the interior with locally made crafts. Included in the rate are two meals. ✉ *Kawaimachi 4–4 Wajima City, Ishikawa-ken 927-0562* ☎ *0768/ 22–9933* 🖷 *0768/22–9934* ⌁ *4 Japanese rooms* ⚭ *Restaurant* ▭ *No credit cards* ▯ *MAP.*

Toyama

 30 min southeast of Takaoka by JR local, 1 hr east of Kanazawa by JR Limited Express, 3 and 4 hrs north of Kyoto and Nagoya, respectively, by JR.

Busy, industrial Toyama is beautified by Toyama-jōshi Kōen (Toyama Castle Park), a spread of greenery with a reconstructed version of the original 1532 castle. **Toyama Bay** is the habitat of the glowing *hotaru ika,* or firefly squid. Their spawning grounds stretch for 15 km (9 mi) along the coast from Uozu to the right bank of Toyama City's Jouganji River and about 1.3 km from shore. From March until June, their spawning season, the females gather close to the seabed and come to the surface from dusk till midnight. From the early morning until dawn the sea magically glows from the squids' photophores, blue-white light-producing organs that attract their prey. This phenomenon has been designated a special natural monument. Sightseeing boats provide close-up views.

A slow open-air train called the **Kurobe-kyōkoku Railway** operates April through November along the river of the deepest valley in Japan, Kurobe-kyōkoku (Kurobe Gorge) to Keyakidaira. On the 20-km (12½-mi), 90-minute ride the old-fashioned tram chugs past gushing springs and waterfalls, and you might even see wild monkeys or *serow,* a native type of mountain goat. One of the best views is from the 125-foot-long and 128-foot-high bridge, Atobiki-kyo. Bring a windbreaker, even in summer, as it's a cold and damp ride. Kuronagi-onsen, Kanetsuri-onsen, and Meiken-onsen, which supply water to Unazuki-onsen, and other hot springs are along the trolley route. You can get off at any one of those springs and enjoy the spa. From June to November the Kurobe-Kyokoku trains leave Unazuki for Keyakidaira twice hourly from 7:30 to 3:40 and cost ¥1,440 one-way. To get to Unazuki from Toyama Station, take the JR line to Uozu Station and switch to the Chitetsu line (30 minutes). A 1-km (½-mi) walk from Keyaki-daira Station leads to the precipitous cliff over the Sarutobi-kyo valley and a view of the Kurobe River.

For more information on the Kurobe-kyōkoku Railway and hiking or camping in the Keyakidaira area, contact the **Tourist Information Office** (☎ 0764/32–9751) in Toyama Station.

Hiking

For experienced hikers there are some breathtaking vistas from the top of Mt. Takayama and other peaks in the area, however adequate planning is necessary and maps in English are hard to come by.

From Keyakidaira you can proceed on foot to two rotemburo (open-air spas) nearly 100 years old: **Meiken Onsen** is a 10- to 15-minute walk; **Babadani Onsen**, 35 to 40 minutes.

If you're a serious hiker, trails from Keyakidaira can lead you to the peak of **Shirouma-dake** (Mt. Shirouma), more than 9,810 feet high, in several hours. Nearby **Tate-yama** (Mt. Tate) also rewards experienced hikers with stunning views. You can also hike to Kurobe Dam, and to the cable car that leads up to a tunnel through Tate-yama to Murodō. If you have several days to spare, camping gear, and a map of mountain trails and shelters, you can go as far as Hakuba in Nagano.

The **National Parks Association of Japan** in Tōkyō is a good source of help on hiking and camping around Toyama. ⊠ *Toranomon Denki Bldg., 4th fl., 2–8–1 Toranomon; from Toranomon Station on Ginza subway line, take Exit 2 and walk 2 blocks straight before taking a right. The Toranomon Denki Building will be on left in 3rd block; Minato-ku, Tōkyō* ☎ *03/3502–0488.*

Niigata

㉝ *3 hrs from Toyama on JR Hokuriku line, 1½ hrs northwest of Tōkyō's Ueno Station by Shinkansen, 2 hrs 15 min northwest of Tōkyō on Toki local line.*

The coast between Kurobe and Niigata is flat and not so interesting. Two towns along the way, Naoetsu and Teradomari, serve as ferry ports to Ogi and Akadomari, respectively, on Sado-ga-shima. From Niigata ferries go to Sado-ga-shima and even Hokkaidō. In the skiing season people fly in to Niigata before traveling by train to the northern Alps for quick access to ski resorts. The **Tourist Information Office** (☎ 025/241–7914) to the left of the station can help you find a hotel and supply city maps and ferry schedules for Sado-ga-shima. It's open daily 8:30–7.

Northern Culture Museum (Hoppō Bunka Keikan) is on the banks of the Agano River on the Kamabara plain, a 40-minute bus ride from Niigata station. This former estate was established in the Edo period by the Ito family, who, by the 1930s, were the largest landowner in the Kaetsu area, with 3,380 hectares of paddy fields, more than 2,500 acres of forest, and 78 overseers who controlled no fewer than 2,800 tenants. The family also owned about 60 warehouses, which stored 1,800 tons of rice every autumn. Ito Mansion, built in 1887, was their home for generations until the Land Reform Act of 1946, which compelled landowners to sell off their paddy land holdings above 3 hectares. Their mansion with its valuable art collection became this museum, which has two restaurants and coffee shops. The house has 65 rooms, a special art gallery, gardens, a tearoom, and an annex for study called "Sanrakutei" where everything is triangular or diamond-shaped, from the pillars and furniture to even the tatami mats. The garden is laid out in the traditional style of the Kamakura and Muromachi periods (14th–15th centuries). Its five teahouses are in different parts of the garden (two of them built later), and numerous natural rocks—mostly from Kyōto—are artistically arranged around the pond. At Niigata ask the Tourist Information Office to point you in the direction of the right bus, which takes 40 minutes. Alternatively, by taxi it takes 25 minutes. ⊠ *2–15–25 Somi Niigata* ☎ *025/385–4003* ⊕ *www6.ocn.ne.jp/~ncm* ☒ *¥800* ☉ *Daily 9–4:30.*

Where to Stay & Eat

$$-$$$ ✕ **Marui** (141). *The* place for fresh fish. For starters, order the *nami nigiri* (standard sushi set) for ¥1,400, plus a bottle of chilled sake, the local Kitayuki brand, for ¥1,260. Then glance at what your neighbors have ordered and ask for what looks good. You can't go wrong with the freshest fish, abalone, sea urchin, and squid in town. Marui closes during mid-afternoon. It's one block off the Furu-machi arcade, around the corner from Inaka-ya. ✉ *8–1411 Higashibori-dōri* ☏ *025/228–0101* ▤ *No credit cards* ⊗ *Closed Sun.*

★ **$-$$$** ✕ **Inaka-ya.** Their specialty, *wappa-meshi* (rice steamed in a wooden box with toppings of salmon, chicken, or crab), makes an inexpensive and excellent lunch. The *yanagi karei hitohoshi-yaki* (grilled flounder), *nodo-kuro shioyaki* (grilled local whitefish), and *buri teriyaki* (yellowtail) will make your mouth water. Inaka-ya closes between lunch and dinner from 2 to 5, and is found in the heart of Furu-machi, the local eating and drinking district. ✉ *1457 Kyūban-chō, Furu-machi-dōri* ☏ *025/223–1266* ⚑ *Reservations not accepted* ▤ *No credit cards.*

$$-$$$$ ⬒ **Ōkura Hotel Niigata** is a sophisticated, first-class hotel on the Shinano-gawa, ½ km from the station. Rooms overlooking Shinano-gawa have the best views. A formal French restaurant in the penthouse overlooks the city. Breakfast and lighter meals are in the Grill Room. ✉ *6–53 Kawabata-chō, Niigata City, Niigata-ken 951-8053* ☏ *025/224–6111, 0120/10–0120 toll-free in Japan* ⬚ *025/224–7060* ⊕ *www.okura-niigata.com* ⟿ *300 Western-style and Japanese-style rooms* ♨ *3 restaurants, shops, business services* ▤ *AE, DC, MC, V.*

$$ ⬒ **Niigata Tōei Hotel.** For an inexpensive business hotel a block and a half from the station, this ranks the best. The ninth floor has a Japanese steak house and a lounge that closes unusually early (9 PM). In the beer garden on the roof from mid-June to the beginning of September ¥3,500 will get you 100 minutes of all-you-can-consume beer, *chū-hi*, a carbonated mixture of distilled spirits called *shochu* and fruity flavors, and snacks. From the Bandai exit from Niigata Station, head north on Higashi Ōdōri for three blocks, then take a left. ✉ *1–6–2 Benten, Niigata 951-0901* ☏ *025/244–7101* ⬚ *025/241–8485* ⟿ *133 rooms* ♨ *2 restaurants, cable TV, in-room data ports, bar, meeting room* ▤ *AE, D, MC, V.*

SADO ISLAND (SADO-GA-SHIMA)

1 hr by hydrofoil from Niigata, 2½ hrs by car ferry.

Sado is known as much for its unblemished natural beauty as for its melancholy history. Revolutionary intellectuals, such as the Buddhist monk Nichiren, were banished to Sado to endure harsh exile as punishment for treason. When gold was discovered on Sado during the Edo period (1603–1868), the homeless and poverty-stricken were sent to Sado to work as forced laborers in the mines. This long history of hardship has left a tradition of soulful ballads and folk dances. Even the bamboo grown on the island is said to be the best for making *shakuhachi*, the flutes that accompany the mournful music.

May through September is the best time to visit Sado. In January and February the weather is bitterly cold, and at other times storms can prevent sea and air crossings. Although the island is Japan's fifth largest, it's still relatively small, at 530 square km (331 square mi). Two parallel mountain chains running along the north and south coasts are split by a wide plain, and it is here that the island's cities are found. Despite the more than 1 million tourists who visit the island each year (more than 10 times the number of inhabitants), the pace is slow.

Getting Around

34 Sado's usual port of entry is **Ryōtsu**, the island's largest township. The town's center runs between Kamo-ko (Kamo Lake) and the coast, with most of the hotels and ryokan on the shore of the lake. Kamo-ko is connected to the sea by a small inlet running through the middle of town. Ryōtsu's Ebisu quarter has the island's largest concentration of restaurants and bars.

Frequent bus service is available between major towns on Sado-ga-shima. The 90-minute bus ride from Ryōtsu to Aikawa departs every 30 minutes and costs ¥740. Two-day weekend passes for unlimited bus travel are ¥2,000, and are available at the Ryōtsu and Ogi ports and in the towns of Sawata and Aikawa. During July and August there's a special one-day pass for ¥1,500. In hop-on, hop-off zones it is possible to flag the bus driver or get off anywhere on most routes, which is very convenient for sightseeing.

From May through November, four- and eight-hour tours of the island depart from Ryōtsu and Ogi. These buses have a magnetic attraction to souvenir shops. The best compromise is to use the tour bus for the mountain skyline drive (¥4,500) or the two-day skyline and historic-site combined tour (¥7,000), then rent a bike to explore on your own. You can make bus-tour reservations directly with the **Niigata Kōtsū Regular Sightseeing Bus Center** ☎ *0259/52–3200.*

Check out the island's extensive Web site, ⊕ www.mijintl.com, for information on ferry schedules, sightseeing routes, and lodging.

What to See

35 The simplest way explore Sado is to take the bus from Ryōtsu west to **Aikawa**. Before gold was discovered here in 1601 it was a town of 10,000 people. The population swelled to 100,000 before the gold was exhausted. Now it's back to a tenth that size.

Aikawa's **Sado Mine** (Sado Kinzan) has been a tourist attraction since operations halted in the 1980s. There are about 325 km (250 mi) of underground tunnels, some running as deep as 1,969 feet. Parts of this extensive digging are open to the public. Robots illustrate how Edo-period slaves worked in the mine. The robots are quite lifelike, and they demonstrate the appalling conditions endured by the miners. The mine is a tough 40-minute uphill walk or a five-minute taxi ride (about ¥900) from the bus terminal. The return is easier. ☎ *0259/74–2389* ▨ *¥700* ⊙ *Apr.–Oct., daily 8–5:10; Nov.–Mar., daily 8–sunset.*

Heartbeat of Sado Island

1

A HAWK FLIES OVERHEAD as the sky deepens to the indigo of the kimonos the two women are wearing. With an elegant flick, the batchi resounds against the stretched hide of the taiko drum and a rhythm begins. Soon all the members of **Kodō** bound onto the outdoor stage with their vibrant and distinctive blend of ensemble taiko, percussion, flute, song, and dance. The annual three-day **Earth Celebration**, held in August, kicks off.

On the second and third evenings Kodō are joined by artists they meet on tour, ranging from African and Asian drummers to a Romanian brass band, Fanfare Cio Carlia, and Carlos Nuñez, the Galician bagpipe revivalist. On stage collaborations offer surprises; cleated *geta* (Japanese clogs) were custom-made for New York tap star Tamango to dance with.

Kodō (which can mean heartbeat, child, or drum) was started in the '60s in a desire to revive Japanese folk music. About 20 core members live communally on Sado Island with their families, growing rice and vegetables organically. To play the largest odaiko, an 800-pound, double-headed drum, takes immense stamina; and all members train intensively.

Not only is this an opportunity to catch Kodō on their home turf, but there are fringe events, workshops, a flea market and local festivals, and a pier-side send-off when the ferry leaves. Tickets and accommodation should be booked well in advance through their Web site, ⊕ www.kodo.or.jp.

★ North of Aikawa is **Senkaku Bay** (Senkaku-wan), the most dramatic stretch of coastline on Sado-ga-shima. Information on sightseeing boats is available from **Senkaku Bay Tourism** (Senkaku-wan Kankō ☎ 0259/75-2221). From the water you can look back at the fantastic, sea-eroded rock formations and 60-foot cliffs. You get off the boat at Senkaku-wan Yuen (Senkaku Bay Park), where you can picnic, stroll, and gaze at the varied rock formations offshore. From the park, return by bus from the pier to Aikawa. To reach the bay, take a 15-minute bus ride from Aikawa to Tassha for the 40-minute sightseeing cruise. The one-way cruise boat runs April–November (¥700, glass-bottom boat ¥850).

The most scenic drive on Sado is the **Ōsado Skyline Drive**. No public buses follow this route. You must take either a tour bus from Ryōtsu or a taxi from Aikawa across the skyline drive to Chikuse (¥4,500), where you connect with a public bus either to Ryōtsu or back to Aikawa.

To reach the southwestern tip of Sado, first take a bus to Sawata from Aikawa or Ryōtsu, and then transfer to the bus for Ogi; en route you may want to stop at the town of **Mano**, where the exiled emperor Juntoku (1197–1242) is buried at the **Mano Goryō** (Mano Mausoleum).

36 The trip from Sawata to **Ogi** takes 50 minutes, the highlight being the beautiful *benten-iwa* (rock formations) just past Tazawaki. Take a window seat on the right-hand side of the bus. You can use Ogi as a port for returning to Honshū by ferry (2½ hours to Naoetsu) or on the hydrofoil (1 hour). Ogi's chief attractions are the **taraibune**, round, tublike boats used for fishing. You can rent one (¥500 for a 30-minute paddle) and with a single oar paddle your way around the harbor. Taraibune can also be found in Shukunegi on the Sawasaki coast, where the water is dotted with rocky islets and the shore is covered with rock lilies in summer.

★ ③⑦ **Shukunegi** has become a sleepy backwater town since it stopped building small wooden ships to traverse the waters between Sado and Honshū. It has, however, retained its simple lifestyle and traditional buildings that date back more than a century. You can reach Shukunegi from Ogi on a sightseeing boat or by bus. Both take about 20 minutes; consider using the boat at least one way for the view of the cliffs that an earthquake created 250 years ago.

Where to Stay & Eat

You can make hotel reservations at the information counters of Sado Kisen ship company at Niigata Port or Ryōtsu Port.

★ $-$$$ ✕ **Uoharu**. At the Ferry terminal in Ogi, ask to be directed toward the area clustered with restaurants. In a corner three-story building is a fish shop at ground level with a restaurant upstairs. You can either choose your fish fresh off ice or try one of the excellent lunches like the sashimi, abalone steak (*awabi,*) or sea urchin (*sazae*) sets from a menu with pictures. They close at 5 PM, but accept reservations for the evening. ✉ *Ogimachi 415-1* ☎ *0259/86–2085* ⊕ *www6.ocn.ne.jp/~uoharu/* ▭ *No credit cards* ⊗ *Daily 11–5.*

$$$$ ◫ **Sado Royal Hotel Manchō**. This is the best hotel on Sado's west coast. It caters mostly to Japanese tourists, and no English is spoken, but the staff makes the few visiting Westerners feel welcome. Request a room on the sea side for the stunning ocean view. Breakfast and dinner are included in the rate. ✉ *58 Shimoto, Sado-ga-shima, Aikawa Niigata-ken 952-1575* ☎ *0259/74–3221* 🖷 *0259/74–3738* ⤴ *90 rooms* ⟁ *Restaurant, Japanese baths* ▭ *DC, V* ⏀ *MAP.*

★ $ ◫ **Sado Seaside Hotel**. One kilometer from Ryōtsu Port, this is more a friendly inn than a hotel. If you telephone before you catch the ferry from Niigata, the owner will meet you at the dock carrying a green Seaside Hotel flag. The rooms and shared baths are spotless. Breakfast is ¥840, and a tasty mélange of regional delicacies for dinner costs ¥1,575. ✉ *80 Sumiyoshi, Sado-ga-shima, Ryōtsu Niigata-ken 952-0015* ☎ *0259/ 27–7211* 🖷 *0259/27–7213* ⊕ *www2u.biglobe.ne.jp/~sado/englishpage. htm* ⤴ *13 Japanese-style rooms, 5 with bath* ⟁ *Dining room, Japanese baths, laundry service* ▭ *AE, V.*

Getting There

BY FERRY   Sado Kisen has two main ferry routes, both with regular ferry and hydrofoil service. From Niigata to Ryōtsu the journey takes 2½ hours, with six or seven crossings a day; the one-way fare is ¥2,190 for ordinary second class, ¥3,100 for first class, and ¥6,210 for special class. The jetfoil (¥6,090 one-way, ¥10,990 round-trip within five days) takes one hour, with 10 or 11 crossings daily in summer, 3 in winter, and between 3 and 8 at other times of the year (depending on the weather). The bus from Bay No. 6 in front of the JR Niigata station takes 15 minutes (¥200) to reach the dock for ferries sailing to Ryōtsu.

Between Ogi and Naoetsu the hydrofoil cost is the same as the Niigata Ryōtsu crossing, but the Naoetsu ferry terminal is a ¥150 bus ride or ¥900 taxi ride from Naoetsu Station. Depending on the season, one to three ferries sail between Teradomari (a port between Niigata and Naoetsu) and Akadomari, taking two hours. The fare is ¥1,610 for second class and ¥2,500 for first class. The port is five minutes on foot from the Teradomari bus station, and 10 minutes by bus from the JR train station (take the Teradomari-ko bus).

⊞ Sado Kisen ☎ *025/245-1234 in Niigata.*

JAPAN ALPS & THE NORTH CHŪBU COAST ESSENTIALS

Transportation

BY AIR
The flight from Tōkyō's Haneda Kūkō to Komatsu Kūkō in Kanazawa takes one hour on Japan Airlines (JAL) or All Nippon Airlines (ANA); allow 40 minutes for the bus transfer to downtown Kanazawa, which costs ¥1,100.

Japan Air System (JAS) has daily flights between Matsumoto and Fukuoka, Ōsaka, and Sapporo. ANA has five flights daily between Tōkyō and Toyama.

Kyokushin Kōkū (Kyokushin Aviation) has small planes that take 25 minutes to fly from Sado-ga-shima to Niigata; there are five round-trip flights a day in summer and three in winter; the one-way fare is ¥7,350.
⊞ Kyokushin Kōkū ☎ *025/273-0312 in Niigata, 0259/23-5005 in Sado.*

BY CAR
Rental cars are available at all major stations. In Kanazawa try Eki Rent-a-Car at the east exit from the train station. In Wajima your best bet is Nissan Rent-a-Car at Wajima Station. An economy-size car costs about ¥8,000 per day or ¥50,000 per week. Reserve the car before you leave Tōkyō, Nagoya, or Kyōto—not many people speak English in rural Japan. Highways charge hefty tolls.

In winter certain roads through the central Japan Alps are closed. In particular, the main route between Matsumoto and Takayama via Kamikōchi is closed November–April.
⊞ Local Agencies Eki Rent-a-Car ✉ Kanazawa Station ☎ *076/265-6659.* **Nissan Rent-a-Car** ✉ *14-27 Shōwa-machi, Wajima* ☎ *0762/22-0177.*

BY TRAIN
Tōkyō–Nagano Shinkansen service has effectively shortened the distance to the Alps from the east: the trip on the Nagano Shinkansen takes only about 90 minutes. From Kyōto and Nagoya the Alps are three hours

away on the Hokuriku and Takayama lines. Unless you are coming from Niigata, you will need to approach Takayama and Kanazawa from the south (connections through Maibara are the speediest) on JR.

Contacts & Resources

BANKS & EXCHANGE SERVICES

Authorized foreign exchange banks for changing travelers cheques can be found in cities and larger towns. It's better to draw cash in advance if you visit remote areas.

In Kanazawa the **Hokkoku Credit Service** is located on the seventh floor of Korinbo Yamato. ⊠ *1–1–1 Korinbo* ⊙ *Daily 10–7.*

ATMs for foreign credit cards and with English instructions are at the JTB, Japan Travel Bureau office, two blocks north of JR Nagano Station.

In Matsumoto's Nose Ekimae Building in front of the station is the **Shinkin Bank Credit Service.** ⊠ *1–3–17 Chūō* ⊙ *Daily 10–7.*

Aeon Credit Service is in the Niigata Saty store ⊠ *2–1–10 Koshiminami* ⊙ *Daily 10–7.*

EMERGENCIES

In emergencies try to get a Japanese speaker to assist with calling for help.
🔲 Ambulance ☎ 119. Police ☎ 110. 24-hr Medical Emergency Help Line ☎ 0120/890-423.
🔲 Hospitals Kanazawa Sogo Kenko Center ⊠ 3-23 Ote-machi ☎ 076/222-0102 ⊙ Daily 7 PM-6 AM is an after-hours and public holiday emergency clinic at the Kanazawa General Health Center ☎ 076/222-9999. Kokumin Kenko Hoken Karuizawa Hospital ☎ 0267/45-5111. Nagano Sekijuji Hospital ⊠ 5-22-1 Wakasato ☎ 026/226-4131 Matsumoto Hospital ⊠ Yoshikawa Murai 1290 ☎ 0263/58-4567

INTERNET

Most hotels have data ports or an Internet station, but ryokan rarely do. In bigger cities around the main stations you can find internet cafés. Some are open 24-hours and double up as manga cafés. Usually the charge is about ¥400 an hour; some offer free access if you order a drink. Tourist information centers can point you toward the nearest one. Hotel lobbies and areas around the stations often have free wireless access.

Here's a sampling of Internet cafés: in the Katamichi district in Kanazawa, **biz café** (⊠ Katamachi 2–2–9 ☎ 076/233–1008 ⊕ www.e-katamachi.com/bizcafe ⊙ Thurs.–Tues. 10–6) charges 200¥ for Internet use on their IBM ThinkPads. You can also hook up your laptop.

A few blocks northwest of the Matsumoto station, on the second floor of the **Matsumoto City International & Information Center** (⊠ M-Wing Bldg. ☎ 263/34–3000 Ext. 1141 ⊙ Weekdays 9 AM–10 PM, weekends 9 AM–5 PM), which has a big ball outside, you can access the Internet for free. It's closed every 2nd and 4th Wednesday.

MAIL & SHIPPING

For fast, low-cost, door-to-door delivery to any address in Japan, **Takkyu-bin** is a service available at most convenience stores and stores displaying the logo of a cat carrying a kitten. Pickups are made six times a day. Especially useful are Ski Takkyubin and Airport Takkyubin, which deliver ski equipment to ski resorts and suitcases to airports.

International courier services are the most expensive way to ship packages or documents overseas, but they are also the fastest and most reliable. **Federal Express** (☎ 0120/003–200). **Nippon Express Company** (☎ 0120/152–259). **UPS Yamato** (☎ 0120/271–040).

MEDIA

In larger towns and cities some bookstores have a small selection of foreign books and newspapers. In more remote areas it may be impossible to find even a newspaper in English. *Kanazawa: The Other Side of Japan,* by Ruth Stevens, explores this city's culture and history. Ski enthusiasts should consult ⊕ www.snowjapan.com. In Kanazawa, across from the station, **Libro** (✉ 1&2F Rifare, 1–5–3 Honmachi ☎ 076/232–6202 ☉ Daily 10–8) has the largest foreign language section.

TOURS

Goodwill Guides is a network of volunteer guides who take foreigners on tours for free. You are only required to pay their expenses while they are with you, including a meal if you eat together. Bookings can be done through their Web site.

The Japan Travel Bureau runs a five-day tour from Tōkyō every Tuesday from April through October 26. The tour goes via Shirakaba-ko to Matsumoto (overnight), to Tsumago and Takayama (overnight), to Kanazawa (overnight), to Awara Onsen (overnight), and ends in Kyōto. The fare is ¥150,000, including four breakfasts and two dinners.

Contact the Niigata Kōtsū Information Center at the Ryōtsu bus terminal for a tour of Sado-ga-shima. It covers Skyline Drive, where public buses don't run. Tours, from May to November, depart daily from Ryōtsu and cost ¥6,440.

🛈 Tour Contacts Goodwill Guides ⊕ www.jnto.go.jp/eng/arrange/essential/list_volunteerGuides_a-n.html. **Japan Travel Bureau** ☎ 03/3281–1721. **Niigata Kōtsū Information Center** ☎ 0259/27–3141.

Points of Interest

SITES/AREAS	JAPANESE CHARACTERS
Aikawa	相川
Archaeology Museum (Hida Minzoku Kōkokan)	飛騨民族考古館
Asa-ichi	朝市
Daiō Wasabi Farm (Daiō Wasabi Nōjo)	大王わさび農場
Eihei-ji	永平寺
Eonta	えおんた
Folk-Craft Museum (Kusakabe Mingeikan)	日下部民芸館
Fukui	福井
Gyokusen Garden (Gyokusenen)	玉泉園
Hakuba	白馬
Hakuba Village (Hakuba-mura)	白馬村
Hakui	羽咋
Happō-o-ne Ski Resort	八方尾根スキー場
Higashi-no-Kuruwa (the Eastern Pleasure Quarter)	東の郭
Ishikawa Prefectural Art Museum (Ishikawa Kenritsu Bijutsukan)	石川県立美術館
Ishikawa Prefectural Products Center (Ishikawa-ken Kankō Bussankan)	石川県観光物産館
Japan Judiciary Museum (Shihō Hakubutsukan)	日本司法博物館
Japan Wood-Block Print Museum (Nihon Ukiyo-e Hakubutsukan)	日本浮世絵博物館
Kaichi Primary School (Kyū Kaichi Gakkō)	開智学校
Kamikōchi	上高地
Kanazawa	金沢
Kanazawa-jō (Kanazawa Castle)	金沢城
Karuizawa	軽井沢
Kenroku Garden (Kenrokuen)	兼六園
Kiso Valley (Kiso-ji)	木曽谷（木曽路）
Kodō	鼓童
Kokubun-ji	国分寺
Kurobe-kyōkoku Railway	黒部峡谷鉄道
Kusatsu	草津
Kutani Pottery Kiln (Kutani Kōsen Gama)	九谷光仙窯
Mano	真野

Matsumoto	松本
Matsumoto-jō (Matsumoto Castle)	松本城
Mawaki Onsen	真脇温泉
Meiken Onsen	名剣温泉
Mt. Asama (Asama-san)	
Mt. Shirouma-dake (Shirouma-dake)	浅間山
Myōjō-ji	妙成寺
Myōryū Temple (Myōryū-ji)	妙立寺
Naga-machi (the Samurai District)	長町
Nagano	長野
Nagano & Environs	長野とその周辺
Nanao	七尾
National Parks Association of Japan	国立公園協会
Near Asama Onsen	浅間温泉
Netsu-no-yu (Fever Bath)	熱の湯
Niigata	新潟
Nishi-no-Kuruwa (the Western Pleasure Quarter)	西の郭
Nomura Samurai Residence (Nomura-ke)	野村家
Northern Culture Museum (Hoppō Bunka Hakubutsukan)	北方文化博物館
Noto Seacoast (Noto-Kongō)	能登金剛
Noto-hantō (Noto Peninsula)	能登半島
Ogi	小木
Ogi-machi	荻町
Ōsado Skyline Drive	大佐渡スカイライン
Oyama Shrine (Oyama Jinja)	尾山神社
Rokkō-zaki (Cape Rokkō)	禄剛崎
Rokuzan Art Museum (Rokuzan Bijutsukan)	碌山美術館
Ryokan Kikunoyu	菊の湯
Ryōtsu	両津
Sado Island (Sado-ga-shima)	佐渡島
Sado Mine (Sado Kinzan)	佐渡金山
Sai-no-kawara Dai-rotemburo	西の河原大露天風呂
Saihitsuan Yūzen Silk Center (Kyū-Saihitsuan)	長町友禅館（旧彩筆庵）
San-machi-suji	三町筋
Senkaku Bay (Senkaku-wan)	尖閣湾

Legian	レギャン
Marui	丸伊
Miyoshi-an	三芳庵
Noda-ya	野田屋
Restaurant Sakura	さくら
Suginoi	杉の井
Suzuya	寿々や
Uoharu	魚春

HOTELS

APA Hotel Eki-mae	アパホテル金沢駅前
Fukasan	深三
Hatago Matsushiro-ya	旅籠松代屋
Hida Plaza Hotel	ひだホテルプラザ
Hotel Akebono Bekkan	ホテルアケボノ別館
Hotel Buena Vista	ホテルブエナビスタ
Hotel Fujiya (Gohonjin Fujiya)	御本陣藤屋旅館
Hotel New Station	ホテルニューステーション
Imperial Hotel	上高地帝国ホテル
Kanazawa New Grand Hotel	金沢ニューグランドホテル
Mawaki Pō-re Pō-re	真脇ポーレポーレ
Nagano Sunroute Hotel	ホテルサンルート長野
Niigata Tōei Hotel	新潟東映ホテル
Ōkura Hotel Niigata	ホテルオークラ新潟
Onyado Daikichi	御宿大吉
Pension Grasshopper	ペンショングラスホッパー
Ryokan Asadaya	旅館浅田屋
Sado Royal Hotel Manchō	佐渡ロイヤルホテル万長
Sado Seaside Hotel	佐渡シーサイドホテル
Taishō-ike Hotel	大正池ホテル
Uotoshi Ryokan	魚敏旅館
Wakura Yonekyu	和倉米久
Yamakyū	山久
Yōgetsu	陽月

Kyōto

WORD OF MOUTH

"In Kyoto, Kiyomizu is nice, and the roads leading up to it are lined with souvenir shops and a few restaurants. Stop often for browsing and have *kakikori* (shaved ice with colorful flavored syrup and, if it's fancy, ice cream, bean paste, or sweetened condensed milk)."

—KimJapan

"The Hana Touro festival in Kyoto was the absolute top highlight of our first trip (and it ranks still as the most incredible visual and musical night of my life). It happens from the beginning to about the third week of March."

—emd

By Deidre May   **YOU WALK THROUGH 11 CENTURIES OF JAPANESE HISTORY** when you walk through Kyōto. Of course, the city has been swept into the industrialized, high-tech age along with the rest of Japan—plate-glass windows dominate central Kyōto, and parking lots have replaced traditional town houses. But magnificent temples and shrines, perfect gardens, and the pursuit of traditional arts bring to life Kyōto's rich past. It was in Kyōto that Asian influences, particularly Chinese, were most deeply assimilated, polished, and reinvented into the distinctively Japanese culture that exists today.

Kyōto's history is full of contradictions: famine and prosperity, war and peace. Wars generated through internecine conflicts both political and spiritual raged while a refined artistic culture was nurtured. The city was razed countless times, and countless times it was rebuilt. Although Kyōto was Japan's capital for more than 10 centuries, the real center of political power was often elsewhere, be it Kamakura (1192–1333) or Edo (1603–1868). Until 710 Japan's capital moved with the accession of each new emperor. Then Nara was chosen as the permanent capital. This experiment lasted 74 years, during which Buddhists achieved tremendous political power. In an effort to thwart them, Emperor Kammu moved the capital to Nagaoka for a decade and then, in 794, to Kyōto (then called Uda). Poets were asked to compose verse about Uda, and they included the phrase *Heian kyō*, meaning "Capital of Peace," reflecting the hope and desire of the time.

From 794 to the end of the 12th century the city flourished under imperial rule. Shingon, an esoteric form of Buddhism considered less threatening than the Nara sects, also flourished. Buddhism developed a syncretic relationship with the older animism of Shintō, absorbing many of the Shintō gods. During this time the nobility, known as "cloud dwellers," cultivated an extraordinary culture of refinement called *miyabi*. This governed all aspects of court life, from dress to artistic pursuits and romance. Unfortunately, the use of wood for construction, combined with Japan's two primordial enemies, fire and earthquakes, has destroyed all the buildings from this era, except Byōdō-in in Uji. The short life span of a building in the 11th century is exemplified by the Imperial Palace, which burned down 14 times in 122 years.

Imperial power waned in the 12th century. Gradually, the Fujiwara nobility had grown to prominence by intermarrying with royal daughters. As their power increased, so did the might of the samurai class employed to protect the noble families' interests. Ensuing clashes between various clans led to the Gempei War (1180–85), and the samurai emerged victorius.

Centuries of shogunal rule followed and marked a change of cultural values. The *bushidō*, or warrior spirit, found a counterpart in the minimalism of Zen Buddhism's austerity. The past luxury of miyabi was replaced with Zen's respect for frugality and discipline. This period also brought devastating civil wars. Because the various feuding clans needed the emperor's support to claim legitimacy, Kyōto, the imperial capital, became the stage for bitter struggles.

The Ōnin Civil War (1467–77) was particularly devastating for Kyōto. Two feudal lords, Yamana and Hosokawa, disputed who should succeed the reigning shōgun. Yamana camped in the western part of the city with 90,000 troops, and Hosokawa settled in the eastern part with 100,000 troops. Central Kyōto was the battlefield, and many of the city's buildings were destroyed.

Not until the end of the 16th century, when Japan was brought together by the might of Nobunaga Oda and Hideyoshi Toyotomi, did Japan settle down. Then came the usurpation of power by Ieyasu Tokugawa, founder of the Tokugawa shogunate, which lasted for the next 264 years. Tokugawa moved the political center of the country to Edo. Kyōto remained the imperial capital—the emperor being basically a figurehead—and the first three Tokugawa shōguns paid homage to the city by restoring old temples and building new villas in the early 1700s. Much of what you see in Kyōto dates from this period. When Emperor Meiji was restored to power in the late 1860s, his capital and imperial court were moved to Edo (which was renamed Tōkyō). Commerce flourished, though, and Kyōto continued as the center of traditional culture. What's more, the move saved the city from being bombed flat in World War II.

Perhaps participating in the tea ceremony is an apt metaphor for approaching Kyōto. As you move through the tea garden toward the teahouse and proceed through each successive ritual, there is a sense of leaving the outer world behind, of progressively moving inward to reach the heart of the experience. In the same way, you cannot approach Kyōto directly. You must approach obliquely, making turns to get to its hidden center.

See the glossary at the end of this book for definitions of the common Japanese words and suffixes used in this chapter.

ORIENTATION & PLANNING

Orientation

In the southern part of Kyōto Prefecture, the city is surrounded by the natural fortress of the low Tamba Mountains to the north, west, and east. Unlike other Japanese cities, Kyōto was modeled on the grid pattern of the Chinese city of Xian. Accordingly, addresses in the city are organized differently than in other parts of the country. Residents will assure you that this makes the city easier to navigate; confounded tourists may disagree. Many of the streets are named, but east–west streets are numbered—the *san* in San-jō-dōri, for example, means "three." *Nishi-iru* means "to the west," and *higashi-iru,* means "to the east." *Agaru* is "to the north," and *sagaru* is "to the south." These directions are normally given in relation to the closest intersection. Thus, the restaurant Ogawa's address—Kiya-machi, Oike-agaru, Higashi-iru—means, "Kiya-machi street, north of Oike on the east side."

Eastern Kyōto
Higashiyama, as eastern Kyōto is known, is chockablock with temples and shrines, among them Ginkaku-ji, Heian Jingū, and Kiyomizu-dera.

CLOSE UP

Top Reasons to Visit

ARCHITECTURAL LEGACY
Over its 1,200-year history Kyōto has accumulated more than 1,600 Buddhist temples (30 are the headquarters for major sects spread throughout Japan), 200 Shintō shrines, and three imperial palaces. Despite modernization, about 27,000 traditional houses still remain. The preservation districts, with their dark slatted frontages and tile roofs, evoke the ancient city. Such districts include Sannen-zaka, a cobbled street at the foot of Kiyomizu-dera; Gion Shin-bashi, the area east of the Kamo-gawa and north of Shijō-dōri; and the canal street that leads to Kamigamo Jinja.

THE GARDEN AS ART FORM
Simplicity and symbolism are the perfected goals of Kyōto's gardens, from the tiniest *tsuboniwa* (courtyard gardens), which often measure less than 6 square feet, to the lavish *kayushiki* (stroll gardens) such as those at Katsura Rikyū and Tōfuku-ji. Influenced by the Chinese style, Kyōto's gardens symbolize heavenly paradise on earth. The timeless arrangement of sand and rocks in the *karesansui* (dry gardens) of Zen temples signifies the eternal quest for completeness; the most famous of these dry gardens is at Ryōan-ji.

CRAFTY SHOPPING
In Kyōto artisans polished their skills into a high art through centuries of producing elegant goods for the imperial family. Today traditional craftspeople still work in Kyōto, and even to the simplest household utensils exhibit this exceptional legacy. Kyōto has no shortage of art and antiques shops. Secondhand kimonos can be a steal at $100. Ceramics, lacquerware, and woven bamboo make great souvenirs, and flea markets provide the odds and ends.

LIVE CULTURE
The theatrical traditions of Kyōgen, Nō, and Kabuki influenced the development of the geisha. Professional dancers and performers, these women are revered as an embodiment of culture, from their opulent and finely woven kimonos, accessories, and hair ornaments to their skill at dancing, singing, and other traditional arts. In addition, you can also catch Kabuki and Nō productions.

FESTIVAL FEVER
Experience one of Kyōto's many festivals. Five spectacular events are the Aoi (Hollyhock) in mid-May, the monthlong Gion in July, the Jidai (Costume) in October, and the wondrous Daimon-ji (August) and Kurama (May and October) festivals. For more information *see* On the Calendar at the front of this book.

5

Gion—a traditional shopping neighborhood by day and a geisha entertainment district by night—is also here.

Western Kyōto & Arashiyama
Among western Kyōto's many temples and gardens are Ryōan-ji, Kinkaku-ji, and Myōshin-ji. The exquisite villa Katsura Rikyū is farther south en route to the rural hills of Arashiyama, with its temple, Tenryū-ji, and beautiful riverside parks.

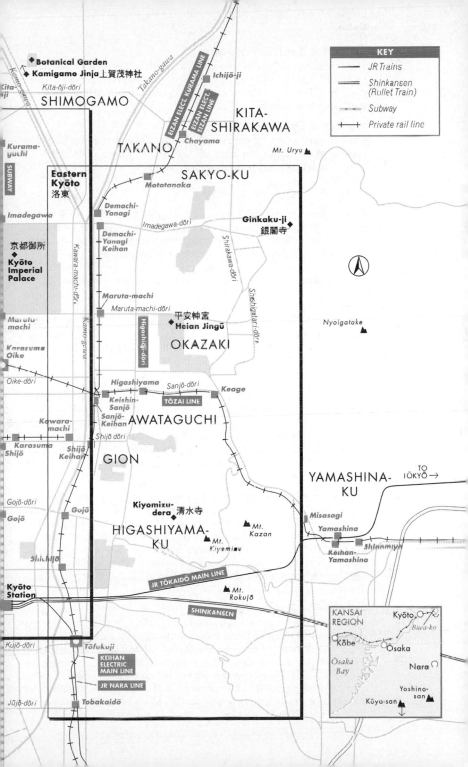

Central & Southern Kyōto

Here are the hotels, the business district, and the Kiya-machi entertainment area. Central Kyōto also has one of the oldest city temples, Tō-ji; the rebuilt Imperial Palace; and Nijō-jō, the onetime Kyōto abode of the Tokugawa shōguns.

Northern Kyōto

The main attractions of northern Kyōto are the mountaintop Buddhist enclave of Enryaku-ji on Hiei-zan and the charming countryside of Ōhara, which also has several peaceful temples.

Planning

Plan a minimum stay of three days, though five days to a week would be better. With hundreds of temples and shrines and several former imperial and shogunal residences, Kyōto has a lot to see, to say the least. Keep this in mind and don't run yourself ragged. Balance a morning at temples or museums with an afternoon in traditional shops, and a morning at the market with the rest of the day in Arashiyama or at one of the imperial villas. We highly recommended a visit to at least one of the mountaintop temple complexes, such as Enryaku-ji on Hiei-zan or Daigo-ji in central Kyōto. Note that you must apply in advance (anywhere from one to several days) to visit attractions that require permits, such as the Imperial Palace, the imperial villas Katsura Rikyū and Shūgaku-in, and Koinzan Saihō-ji.

Timing

Cherry-blossom time in spring (usually the first week in April) and the glorious autumn foliage in early November are remarkable, though the city can be crowded and expensive. Except for the depths of winter and the peak of summer heat in August, Kyōto's climate is mild enough—though often rainy, especially mid-June to mid-July—to make sightseeing pleasant for most of the year. In the high season (May–October) the large numbers of visitors can make accommodations scarce.

Religious buildings are generally open seven days a week, but many museums close Monday. If you're in Kyōto for the Gion Festival, held throughout July, go downtown on the 17th for the main parade. You can also walk around the streets downtown on the evenings leading up to the festival, when the floats are on display and there are street stalls. If you're here for the Jidai (Costume) Festival on October 22 be sure to head for Heian Jingū for the procession of about 2,000 people in costumes from every period of Kyōto's history.

Concerning Restaurants & Hotels

Attuned to subtle seasonal changes, Kyōto cuisine emphasizes freshness and contrast. From the finest ryōtei to the smallest *izakaya* (pub), the distinctive elements of gracious hospitality, subtle flavors, and attention to decor create an experience that engages all the senses. Although the finest traditional *kaiseki ryōri* is costly, this experience is highly recommended. Both elaborate establishments and casual shops usually offer set menus at lunchtime, at a considerably lower price than dinner.

No other Japanese city can compete with Kyōto for style and grace. For the ultimate experience of Kyōto hospitality, stay in a *ryokan*, a traditional Japanese inn. Though often costly, a night in a ryokan guarantees you beautiful traditional Japanese surroundings, excellent service, and elegant meals. *See* the Ryokan Etiquette box in this chapter to find out what's expected at these inns. Then have a Japanese person make the reservation for you; the ryokan will be more inclined to accept a Japanese person's request. Kyōto is a tourist city, so accommodations range from luxurious hotels to small guesthouses. Service in this city is impeccable; the information desks are well stocked, and concierges or guest-relations managers are often available in the lobby to respond to your needs.

WHAT IT COSTS In yen					
	$$$$	**$$$**	**$$**	**$**	**¢**
RESTAURANTS	over 3,000	2,000–3,000	1,000–2,000	800–1,000	under 800
HOTELS	over 22,000	18,000–22,000	12,000–18,000	8,000–12,000	under 8,000

5

Restaurant prices are per person for a main course at dinner. Hotel prices are for a double room with private bath, including service and 5% tax.

Transportation Station

Sights are all over Kyōto, mostly north of Kyōto Station, but many of them are clustered together, and you can walk from one to another. The city is fairly flat, which makes it ideal for biking. Where the sights are not near each other, you can use Kyōto's buses, which run on a grid pattern that's easy to follow. Notwithstanding traffic and armed with a bus map, you could cross and recross Kyōto without too much difficulty, stringing together sights of your own choosing.

AIR TRAVEL   International and some domestic flights land at Kansai International Airport, near Ōsaka. Ōsaka's Itami Airport handles most regional flights.

BUS TRAVEL   Buses in Kyōto are quick, reliable, and punctual, making them an excellent form of transportation. There are even some routes particularly designed for travelers that connect all the major sightseeing spots. Pick up route maps at the Kyōto Tourist Information Center.

SUBWAY TRAVEL   When traveling north–south in the city center or east–west, the subway can help save time, though the bus is generally the better choice.

TRAIN TRAVEL   In addition to Japan Rail there are five private railways serving Kyōto. These are best used to reach the sights in the outlying regions of the city and to make day trips to Ōsaka, Nara, Kōbe, Himeji, and even as far afield as Tōkyō, which is less than three hours by Shinkansen.

Visitor Information

The Kyōto Tourist Information Center is on the ninth floor of the Kyōto Station building, in the Kyōto International Prefectural Center. To get there, take the south elevator from the second floor of Isetan department store. The counter may be small, but commendable assistance comes from a friendly, knowledgeable staff. Only the staff at the Welcome Inn counter can help you make lodging reservations. The office is open daily 10 to 6 and closed the second and fourth Tuesday of each month.

The Japan Travel Bureau (JTB) and Keihan Travel Agency provide information on Japan Rail Passes, tours such as the Sunrise Tours JTB offers, and conferences and symposiums. The JTB Web site lists contact numbers outside of Japan.

7 **Japan Travel Bureau** ✉ Kyōto eki-mae, Shiokōji Karasuma Higashi-Iru, Shimogyō-ku ☎ 075/361-7241 ⊕ www.jtbgmt.com. **Keihan Travel Agency** ✉ 12 Mori-chō, Fushimi-ku ☎ 075/602-8162. **Kyōto Tourist Information Center** ✉ 9F JR Kyōto Station building, Kyōto International Prefectural Center, Karasuma-dōri, Shimogyō-ku ☎ 075/344-3300 ⊕ www.kyoto-kankou.or.jp.

EXPLORING KYŌTO

Eastern Kyōto

If you have time to visit only one district in the city, this is the one. Eastern Kyōto—known as Higashiyama (literally, "Eastern Mountain")—has some of Kyōto's most popular shrines and temples. Among the highlights is Ginkaku-ji, an elegant temple with two striking gardens. Kiyomizu-dera also stands out: built into a hillside, this temple has fine views of the city.

Getting Around

The sights of Eastern Kyōto can be visited by a combination of walking and taking the bus.

7 **Kyōto International Conference Center** (Kokuritsu Kyōto Kokusai Kaikan). On expansive grounds, the center has a library and information facilities, Internet stations, and rental halls for public performances. The bulletin board by the entryway is full of tips on housing opportunities, and events in Kyōto. The KICH also offers free or inexpensive lessons in tea ceremony, koto (a 13-string instrument), calligraphy, and Japanese. The book *Easy Living in Kyōto* (available free) gives helpful information for a longer stay. The Community House is just off the intersection at the foot of the road to Nanzen-ji. ✉ *2–1 Torii-chō, Awata-guchi, Sakyō-ku* ☎ *075/752-3010* ☑ *Free* ⊗ *Tues.–Sun. 9–9; when Mon. is national holiday, Community House stays open Mon. and closes following day.*

What to See

★ **21** **Chion-in.** To many, this is the most daunting temple gate in Japan, towering at the bottom of steep stairs that lead to one of Japan's larger temples, the headquarters of the Jōdo sect of Buddhism. On this site, in the original temple, Hōnen, the founder of the Jōdo sect, chose to leave this world by fasting to death in 1212. Like most Kyōto temples, it was repeatedly destroyed by fires and earthquakes; the oldest standing buildings are the Hon-dō (Main Hall, 1633) and the Daihōjō (Abbots' Quarters, 1639). The temple's belfry houses the largest bell in Japan, which was cast in 1633 and requires 17 monks to ring. To herald the New Year, the monks ring the bell—as well as bells at other temples in Kyōto—107 times before midnight and once after to release people from

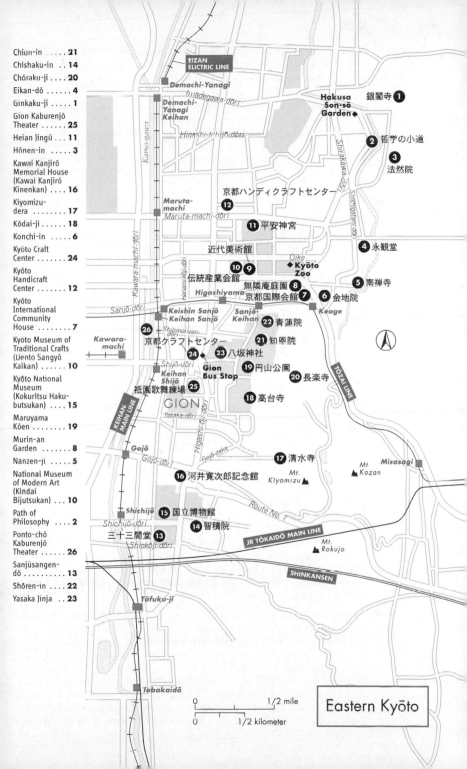

EIZAN
ELICTRIC LINE

Demachi-Yanagi

Demachi-
Yanagi
Keihan

Hakusa
Son-sō
Garden ◆

銀閣寺 **1**

哲学の小道 **2**

法然院 **3**

京都ハンディクラフトセンター **12**

平安神宮 **11**

Maruta-
machi

Maruta-machi-dōri

近代美術館

4 永観堂

Oike

◆ Kyōto
Zoo

10 **9**

伝統産業会館

無鄰菴庭園 **8**

5 南禅寺

Higashiyama

京都国際会館 **7**

6 金地院

Sanjō-dōri

Keishin Sanjō
Keihan Sanjō

Sanjō-
Keihan

Keage

22 青蓮院

26

Shimonzen-

Kawara-
machi

京都クラフトセンター

24 **23** 八坂神社

21 知恩院

Shijō-dōri

Keihan
Shijō

Gion
Bus Stop

19 円山公園

20 長楽寺

祇園歌舞練場 **25**

GION

Yasaka-dōri

18 高台寺

Gojō

Gojō-dōri

Gojō-zaka

17 清水寺

Mt.
Kiyomizu ▲

Mt
Kazan ▲

Misasagi

16 河井寛次郎記念館

Shichijō

15 国立博物館

Shichijō-dōri

14 智積院

三十三間堂

Shiokōji-dōri

13

Route No. 1

JR TŌKAIDŌ MAIN LINE

Mt.
▲ Rokujo

SHINKANSEN

Tōfuku-ji

Tobakaidō

0 _____ 1/2 mile

0 _____ 1/2 kilometer

Eastern Kyōto

the worldly desires of the old year. This ceremony is broadcast nationally. Leading to the Assembly Hall, the corridor behind the Main Hall, which houses the original Amida statue from Hōnen's time, is an *uguisubari* (nightingale floor). This type of floor is constructed to "sing" at every footstep to warn the monks of intruders. Walk underneath the corridor to examine the way the boards and nails are placed to create this inventive burglar alarm. From Kyōto Station take Bus 206 to the Gion stop. The temple is north of Maruyama Kōen. ⊠ *400 Hayashi-shitachō 3-chōme, Yamato-ōji, Higashi-hairu, Shimbashi-dōri, Higashiyama-ku* ☎ *¥400* ⊙ *Mar.–Oct., daily 9–4:30; Nov.–Feb., daily 9–4; not all buildings open to public.*

★ ⑭ **Chishaku-in.** The major reason for visiting this temple is for its famous paintings by Tōhaku Hasegawa and his son Kyūzo—known as the Hasegawa school. Some of the best examples of Momoyama-period (late-16th-century) art, these paintings were originally created for the sliding screens at Shōun-in, an earlier temple commissioned by Hideyoshi Toyotomi and built in 1591 on the same site. When his concubine, Yodogimi, bore him a son in 1589, Hideyoshi named him Tsurumatsu, or Crane Pine—two symbols of longevity. But the child died at age two, and Shōun-in was built for Tsurumatsu's enshrinement. The paintings were saved from the fires that destroyed Shōun-in and are now on display in the Exhibition Hall of Chishaku-in. In his later years Tōhaku Hasegawa painted exclusively for Zen temples, and his masterpieces ranged from lyrical monochrome ink creations to more colorful, bolder works, such as the screen paintings exhibited here. Rich in detail and in strong colors on a gold background, the screens display the seasons by using the symbols of cherry, maple, pine, and plum trees and autumn grasses.

From Kyōto Station take Bus 206 or 208 to the Higashiyama-Shichijō stop. Chishaku-in is on the east side of Higashi-ōji-dōri. ⊠ *Higashiyama-ku* ☎ *¥350* ⊙ *Daily 9–4:30.*

⑳ **Chōraku-ji.** A procession of stone lanterns lines the steep path to this tiny temple, which was founded by Emperor Kammu with the priest Saichō in 805. In the year 1185, after the Taira clan was almost annihilated by the Minamoto clan, Kenreimon-in, the mother of the deceased child emperor Antoku and the last survivor of the Taira, found refuge and became a nun here. Note the 11-faced statue of Kannon, the bodhisattva Avalokitesvara. Few bother to climb the hill to this temple, making it a tranquil place with a bird's-eye view of Kyōto. Flying squirrels make occasional appearances in summer. Chōraku-ji is east of Maruyama Kōen. ⊠ *Higashiyama-ku* ☎ *¥400* ⊙ *Daily 9–5.*

★ ❹ **Eikan-dō.** Nestled in the foothills, this temple complex has a beautiful garden with a large pond as a centerpiece, and the "borrowed scenery" of a mountain in the background. The buildings are 16th-century reconstructions, rebuilt after the originals were destroyed in the Ōnin Civil War in the 15th century. Officially this temple, founded in 855 by Priest Shinshō, is named Zenrin-ji, but it honors the memory of the 11th-century priest Eikan, and is popularly known as Eikan-dō. He was a man of the people, and he would lead them in a dance in celebration of Amida Buddha. According to tradition, the Amida statue came to life on one occasion and stepped down from his pedestal to join the dancers. Taken aback, Eikan slowed his dancing feet. Amida looked back over his shoulder to reprimand Eikan for slowing his pace. This legend explains why the unusual statue in the Amida-dō has its face turned to the side, as if glancing backward. A climb to the top of the pagoda affords superb views of the grounds below and Kyōto beyond. Autumn attracts throngs, not only to view the colorful maple trees but also to see the Buddhist treasures, such as paintings on *fusuma* (sliding doors), that are displayed in November. For this month the temple is lighted up until 9 PM. Eikan-dō is a 15-minute walk south of Hōnen-in on the Path of Philosophy. ⊠ *Higashiyama-ku* 📧 *Dec.–Oct.* *¥500, Nov. ¥1,000* ⊙ *Dec.–Oct., daily 9–5, last entry at 4:30; Nov., daily 9–9, last entry at 8:30.*

❶ Ginkaku-ji. Ginkaku-ji means "Temple of the Silver Pavilion," but the
FodorśChoice temple is not silver; it was only intended to be. Shōgun Yoshimasa
★ Ashikaga (1435–90) commissioned this villa for his retirement and decreed it would become a Zen temple after his death. Construction began in the 1460s, in the years leading up to the Ōnin Civil War, which was partially precipitated by a power struggle involving the Ashikaga line: Yoshimasa handed power over to his younger brother and then belatedly tried to install his young son as shōgun. In 1474, a few years before the Imperial House went bankrupt and his shogunate became powerless, Yoshimasa, seeing the end in sight, abdicated to give his full attention to the building of his villa and his taste for aristocratic pleasures. These included romance, moon gazing, and the tea ceremony, which he helped develop into a high art form. Though he never had time to complete the coating of the pavilion with silver foil, he constructed a dozen or so buildings. Many were designed for cultural pursuits, such as incense and tea ceremonies. On his death, the villa was converted into a Buddhist temple. However, with the decline of the Ashikaga family, Ginkaku-ji deteriorated, and many buildings were destroyed.

The remaining original buildings are **Tōgū-dō** (East Seeking Hall) and Ginkaku-ji itself. The four other structures on the grounds were built in the 17th and 19th centuries. Yoshimasa is thought to have lived in the front room of Tōgū-dō, and the statue of the priest is probably of Yoshimasa himself. The back room, called Dojin-sai (Comradely Abstinence), became the prototype for traditional tea-ceremony rooms. Ginkaku-ji is a simple and unadorned two-story building. Its appeal lies in the serene exterior shape, which combines Chinese elements such as bell windows with the developing Japanese Muromachi (1333–1568) architecture. The upper floor contains a gilt image of Kannon (goddess of mercy) said to have been carved by Unkei, a famous Kamakura-period sculptor; it's not, however ordinarily open to public view.

Ginkaku-ji overlooks the complex **gardens**, attributed to artist and architect Sōami (1465–1523). Yoshimasa based his villa on Kinkaku-ji, which belonged to his grandfather, Shōgun Yoshimitsu Ashikaga, who in turn had based his design on the moss gardens at Koinzan Saihō-ji. The central concept of all three designs is the juxtaposition of a dry Zen garden of raked sand, which is reshaped daily, with a verdant pond garden. The *karensui*, or dry garden, is composed of a 2-foot-high platform of raked sand that is supposed to evoke the sea and two sculpted mounds, the higher one symbolizing, perhaps, Fuji-san. The garden sparkles in the moonlight and has been aptly named the Sea of Silver Sand. You enter the garden on a shrub-lined path leading to the *karamon*, or Chinese gabled gate.

To reach Ginkaku-ji, take Bus 5 from Kyōto Station to the Ginkaku-ji-michi bus stop. Walk east on the street along the canal. Cross a north–south canal and Hakusa Son-sō Garden on your right; then go straight and Ginkaku-ji will be in front of you. ⊠ *Ginkaku-ji-chō, Sakyō-ku* ☞ *¥500* ☉ *Mid-Mar.–Nov., daily 8:30–5; Dec.–mid-Mar., daily 9–4:30.*

OFF THE BEATEN PATH

HAKUSASASON-SŌ GARDEN – Coming down the hill from Ginkaku-ji, a hundred yards before the street crosses a north–south canal, you can see a small villa, built in 1916, with an impeccable garden. This was the modest home of the late Hashimoto Kansetsu, who studied in the 20th century under the literati painter Seiho Takeuchi. Hashimoto, who often portrayed animals such as monkeys, later influenced the realism of the Shijo school by creating a unique style that combined various Japanese styles and also drew inspiration from Chinese classical literature and scenery. Some of his sketches and his collection of Greek and Persian pottery, calligraphy, and several paintings by Chinese and Japanese literati painters are exhibited. An exquisite stone garden and a teahouse are also open to the public. If you book at least two days in advance by fax (in Japanese), it's possible to experience the full tea ceremony, which starts at ¥2,800 per person for a group reservation of at least five. To get here, take Bus 5 from Kyōto Station to the Ginkaku-ji-michi stop. Walk east on the street along the canal. Just after the street crosses another canal flowing north–south, Hakusa Son-sō will be on the right. ⊠ *Higashiyama-ku* ☞ *¥800; with tea and sweets, an extra ¥800* ☎ *075/751–0446* 🖷 *075/751–0448* ☉ *Daily 10–5; last entry at 4:30.*

Fodor'sChoice ★ **Gion** (ghee-*own*). This is the legendary haunt of geisha, or *geiko*, as they are called in the ancient capital. In the early evening, in the glow of teahouse lanterns, you can see them scurrying along the cobbled backstreets on their high geta, white-faced, on the way to their appointments. In their wake their *maiko* follow—the young apprentice geisha identified by the longer sleeves of their kimonos.

The culture of the geisha and *ochaya* (teahouse) developed in the 16th and 17th century, partly due to the banning of women from the Kabuki stage, which remains unchanged. Female performers channeled their artistic talents, including singing, dancing, and playing musical instruments, into entertaining the male patrons of teahouses. The heart of the district is on Hanami-kōji-dōri. Heading north, the street intersects with Shinmonzen-dōri, which is famous for its antiques shops and art galleries. Here you can find collectors' items—at collectors' prices—which make for interesting browsing, if not buying. The shops on Shijō-dōri, which parallels Shinmonzen-dōri to the south, carry slightly more affordable paraphernalia of the geisha world, from handcrafted hair ornaments to incense to parasols. ⊠ *Higashiyama-ku.*

★ ㉕ **Gion Kaburenjō Theater.** Because Westerners have little opportunity to enjoy a geisha's performance in a private party setting—which requires a proper recommendation from and probably the presence of a geisha's respected client—a popular entertainment during the month of April is the Miyako Odori (Cherry-Blossom Dance), presented at this theater. Against sumptuous backdrops, geisha, wearing elaborate kimonos and makeup, enact a narrative in dance and song to the accompaniment of a *shamisen* (a three-string instrument), flute, and drums. Before the show there is a tea ceremony. There are also other performances in May and October, and tickets cost between ¥2,000 and ¥7,000. At the nearby **Gion Corner,** demonstrations of traditional performing arts take place nightly March–November (⇨ Nightlife & the Arts, *below*). ⊠ *Gion Hanami-kōji, Higashiyama-ku* ☎ *075/561–1115.*

⓫ **Heian Jingū.** One of the city's newest historical sites, Heian Jingū was built in 1894 to mark the 1,100th anniversary of the founding of Kyōto. The shrine honors two emperors: Kammu (737–806), who founded the city in 794, and Kōmei (1831–66), the last emperor to live out his reign in Kyōto. The new buildings are for the most part replicas of the old Imperial Palace, at two-thirds the original size. Still, the dignity and the relative spacing of the **East Hon-den** and **West Hon-den** (the Main Halls), and the **Daigoku-den** (Great Hall of State), in which the Heian emperor would issue decrees, conjure up an image of how magnificent the Heian court must have been. During New Year's, kimono-clad and gray-suited Japanese come to pay homage, trampling over the imposing gravel forecourt leading to the Great Hall of State.

There are three stroll gardens at Heian Jingū positioned east, west, and north of the shrine itself. They follow the Heian aesthetic of focusing on a large pond, a rare feature at a Shintō shrine. The steps of the stepping-stone path that crosses the water are recycled pillars from a 16th-century bridge that spanned the Kamo-gawa before an earthquake destroyed it.

The best times to visit the shrine are when the cherry blossoms are in full bloom (usually early April) and on June 1 or 2 for the nighttime **Takigi Nō performances,** so named because they're lighted by *takigi* (burning firewood); they take place on a stage in front of the Great Hall of State. During the October 22 Jidai Festival, a pageant of 2,000 people attired in costumes from every period winds its way from the Imperial Palace and ends here. From the Dōbutsu-en-mae bus stop, follow the street between the Kyōto Municipal Museum of Art and the National Museum of Modern Art directly to the shrine. ⊠ *Okazakinishi Tennō-chō, Sakyō-ku* ☎ *075/371–5649* 🖃 *Garden ¥600; Takigi Nō ¥3,300 at gate, ¥2,500 in advance* ☉ *Mid-Mar.–Aug., daily 8:30–5:30; Sept., Oct., and early Mar., daily 8:30–5; Nov.–Feb., daily 8:30–4:30.*

SHOP STOP

Kyōto Handicraft Center. Seven floors of everything Japanese—dolls, woodblock prints, kimonos, pottery, and even pearl jewelry—is on sale here. The center caters to tourists with its English-speaking staff. It's ⓬ good for browsing, and the pricing is fairly reasonable. From the Gion bus stop take Bus 202 or 206 five stops north on Higashi-ōji-dōri to the

Kumano Jinja-mae bus stop. From Kyōto Station use Bus 206; the center is across Maruta-machi-dōri from Heian Jingū. ✉ *Kumano Jinja Higashi, Sakyō-ku* ☎ *075/761–5080* ⊕ *www.khc-kyoto.jp* ⊘ *Mar.–Nov., daily 9:30–6; Dec.–Feb., daily 9:30–5:30.*

❸ Hōnen-in. Bamboo surrounds this tranquil temple and thatched-roof gate set against a mountain backdrop. Two long mounds of sand flanking the path are raked daily; the patterns on the left mound indicate the seasons, whereas the right mound is usually raked to represent waves (water symbolizes impermanence). The temple was built in 1680 on a site that in the 13th century simply consisted of an open-air Amida Buddha statue. Hōnen-in honors the priest Hōnen (1133–1212), the founder of the Jōdo sect, who brought Buddhism down from its lofty peak to the common folk by making the radical claim that all were equal in the eyes of Buddha. His ideas threatened other sects, especially the Tendai. The established Buddhist powers pressured then-emperor Gotoba to diminish Hōnen's influence over the masses. At about the same time, two of the emperor's concubines became nuns after hearing some of Hōnen's disciples, including Junsai, reputedly the handsomest monk in Japan, preaching. The incident provided Gotoba with an excuse to decry the Jōdo sect as immoral, with the charge that its priests were seducing noblewomen. Emperor Gotoba had Junsai and three other Hōnen disciples publicly beheaded and sent Hōnen into exile. Eventually, in 1211, Hōnen was pardoned and permitted to return to Kyōto, where a year later, at Chion-in, he fasted to death at the age of 79.

In the first week of April and all of November, the Hon-dō (Main Hall) is open, since this is a training monastery. Every morning, here, in front of the Amida statue, monks place 25 flowers, representing the 25 bodhisattvas who accompany the Amida Buddha to receive the souls of the newly deceased. From the Path of Philosophy, at the first large bridge as you walk south, turn off the path and take the road east. ✉ *Higashiyama-ku* ☜ *Free* ⊘ *Daily 7–4.*

⑯ Kawai Kanjirō Memorial House (Kawai Kanjirō Kinenkan). Kanjirō Kawai, one of Japan's most prolific and renowned potters, designed and lived in this rural Japanese-inspired house. He was one of the leaders of the Mingei (folk art) movement, which sought to revive interest in traditional folk arts during the 1920s and '30s, when all things Western were in vogue in Japan. On display are some of the artist's personal memorabilia and, of more interest, some of his exquisite and asymmetrical vases, bowls, and pots showcasing the various techniques he experimented with. He was a master of glazes; his trademark color was red copper, though he also used brilliant cobalt blue and brown iron glazes. An admirer of Western, Chinese, and Korean ceramics techniques, Kawai won many awards, including the Grand Prix at the 1937 Paris World Exposition. From Kyōto Station take Bus 206 or 208 to the Sanjūsangen-dō-mae stop and then head east to the end of Shichijō-dōri. The house is a five-minute walk north along Higashi-ōji-dōri. ✉ *Gojō-zaka, Higashiyama-ku* ☎ *075/561–3585* ☜ *¥900* ⊘ *Tues.–Sun. 10–5; when Mon. is national holiday, museum stays open Mon. and closes following day. Closed Aug. 10–20 and Dec. 24–Jan. 7.*

⑰ **Kiyomizu-dera.** For centuries visitors and pilgrims have climbed the cob-
Fodor'sChoice bled streets to Kiyomizu-dera, which stands prominently on a steep hill-
★ side with fine views of the city. Supported in part by 139 pillars, the temple
juts out over the valley. Finding the courage to set out on a daring, new
adventure is likened to "taking a leap from the veranda of Kiyomizu."
The cypress-shingle roof harmonizes with the cryptomeria-covered hills,
and below is the slender Sound of Feathers waterfall, believed to be the
original source of *kiyomizu,* or pure water, which is drunk to prevent
illness, using long-handled cups. The valley stroll garden is meant to suggest the southern paradise of the bodhisattva Kannon, the 11-faced goddess of mercy.

Built in 788, the original temple, which today belongs to the Hossō sect,
predates Kyōto by six years. Although Kiyomizu-dera honors the popular Kannon, to whom women pray for an easy childbirth, it has become
over time a sort of everyman's temple. You'll see evidence of this throughout the grounds, from the stacked rows of little Jizō Bosatsu statues (representing the god of travel and children) to the many *koma-inu* (mythical
guard dogs), donated by grateful patrons, marking the pathways.

The current structure dates from 1633; the militant monks of Hiei-zan
destroyed the original temple during one of their periodic bloody purges.
On the south side is a brilliant vermilion, three-tier pagoda decorated
with Chinese influences in the forms of colorful flowers, esoteric Buddhist symbols, and ornate metalwork above the grand wooden gate. On
the north side of the main hall is a small shrine called **Jishu-jinja,** dedicated to Okuni Nushi-no-mikoto, a land-ruling deity also considered
to be a powerful matchmaker. Many young people visit the shrine to
seek help in finding their life partners. They try to walk between two
stones placed 18 meters (59 feet) apart, with their eyes closed. It's said
that love will materialize for anyone who can walk in a straight line between the two.

Shops selling souvenirs, religious articles, and ceramics line Kiyomizu-
zaka, the street leading to the temple. There are also tea shops where
you can sample *yatsuhashi*—doughy, triangular sweets filled with cin-
namon-flavor bean paste—a Kyōto specialty. From Kyōto Station take
Bus 206 to the Kiyomizu-michi stop. From the Kawai Kanjirō Memorial House cross the major avenue, Gojō-dōri, and walk up Higashi-ōji-
dōri. The street to the right, Gojō-zaka, leads into Kiyomizu-zaka,
which you'll take to the temple. November 1–10, the garden of the superior of the temple is open to the public. ⊠ *Kiyomizu 1-chōme, Higashiyama-ku* 🖼 *¥300* ⏰ *Daily 6–6.*

**NEED A
BREAK?**

★

On the road to Kiyomizu-dera, just south of Ninen-zaka, is a wooden archway
covered in *senja-fuda,* adhesive name cards left by pilgrims on the entryways
to shrines and temples. The passage under the arch leads to a small courtyard
teahouse, **Bun-no-suke Jaya.** The specialty here is *amazake,* a sweet, nonal-
coholic beverage served with ginger and traditionally enjoyed by nuns. You can
also sip matcha and order fresh Kyōto sweets. The teahouse was founded by
Katsura Bun-no-suke, a renowned *rakugo* (comic storytelling) artist whose fame

5

waned with the advent of motion pictures. The interior is adorned with an eclectic collection of kites and folk dolls. ✉ *Kiyomizu 3-chō, Higashiyama-ku* ☎ *075/ 561-1972* ⊙ *Thurs.-Tues. 10-5:30.*

⑱ Kōdai-ji. This quiet temple established in the early 17th century provides a tranquil alternative to the crowds of nearby Kiyomizu-dera. The temple was built as a memorial to Hideyoshi Toyotomi by his wife, Kita-no-Mandokoro, who became a nun here after her husband died—a common practice at the time. The famous 17th-century landscaper Kobori Enshū designed the gardens, which include the Heart of Waves, where wavy raked gravel encircles a small mound. The teahouse above on the hill, designed by tea master Sen-no-Rikyū, has a unique umbrella-shape bamboo ceiling and a thatched roof. In November this temple is lighted up until 9 PM. From Kyōto Station take Bus 206 to the Higashiyama-yasui bus stop. ✉ *Higashiyama* 🚃 *¥500* ⊙ *Apr.–Nov., daily 9–4:30; Dec.–Mar., daily 9–4.*

★ ⑥ Konchi-in. Famous tea master and landscape designer Kobori Enshū completed the gardens in 1632, under commission by the Zen priest Sūden. One garden has a pond in the shape of the Chinese character *kokoro* (heart). The other is a dry garden with a gravel area in the shape of a boat; a large flat stone representing the home of the Daoist immortals, Mount Horai; and a backdrop of *o-karikomi* (tightly pruned shrubbery). The two rock groupings in front of a plant-filled mound are in the crane-and-tortoise style. Since ancient times these creatures have been associated with longevity, beauty, and eternal youth. In the feudal eras the symbolism of the crane and the tortoise became very popular with the samurai class, whose profession often left them with only the hope of immortality. Though not on the same grounds, this temple is part of the ⇨ **Nanzen-ji** complex. To get here, leave Nanzen-ji and take the side street to the left. ✉ *86 Fukuchi-chō, Nanzen-ji, Sakyō-ku* 🚃 *¥400* ⊙ *Mar.–Nov., daily 8:30–5; Dec.–Feb., daily 8:30–4:30.*

⑩ Kyōto Museum of Traditional Crafts (Kyōto Dentō Sangyō Fureai-kan). This museum displays a wide array of traditional Kyōto crafts, including lacquerware, pottery, jewelry, and kimonos. The museum hosts educational crafts-making demonstrations, and even has a shop with crafts souvenirs. A model interior of a traditional town house is in the basement. From the Dōbutsu-en-mae bus stop, head down the street leading to Heian Jingū. The museum is inside the torii on the west side, after the National Museum of Modern Art. ✉ *9–2 Seishōji-chō, Okazaki, Sakyō-ku* ☎ *075/761-3421* 🚃 *Free* ⊙ *Tues.–Sun. 9–5; last entry at 4:30.*

⑮ Kyōto National Museum (Kokuritsu Hakubutsukan). Exhibitions at this museum in a Meiji-era redbrick building change regularly, but you can count on an excellent display of paintings, sculpture, textiles, calligraphy, ceramics, lacquerware, metalwork, and archaeological artifacts from its permanent collection. The artwork is mainly Japanese, though some foreign pieces are shown. From Kyōto Station take Bus 206 or 208 to the Sanjūsangen-dō-mae stop. The museum is across Higashi-ōji-dōri from Chishaku-in. ✉ *Yamato-ōji-dōri, Higashiyama-ku* ☎ *075/541-1151* ⊕ *www.kyohaku.go.jp* 🚃 *¥500; additional fee for special exhibitions* ⊙ *Tues.–Sun. 9–4:30.*

⑲ Maruyama Kōen (Maruyama Park). Many people cut through this park, which lies near Yasaka Jinja and between Chion-in and Gion, when sightseeing. This is a popular venue for drinking sake outdoors during the cherry-blossom season, and vendors are usually around to supply refreshment. From Kyōto Station take Bus 206 to the Higashiyama stop; the park is north of Kōdai-ji. ✉ *Higashiyama-ku.*

⑧ Murin-an Garden. In a departure from traditional Japanese stroll gardens, Murin-an has expanses of English lawn that reflect the melding of Japanese and Western elements (this blending of styles is also visible in the architecture of the house). Backed by a sweep of hills beyond the shrubs, and unlike the restrained sense of harmony of most traditional Japanese gardens, Murin-an allows more freedom of movement along paths that pass converging streams and a miniature three-tier waterfall. The south side of the garden is almost always in shadow, creating wonderful contrasts. The garden is south of the Dōbutsu-en-mae bus stop. Enter from the side road on the other side of a canal. ✉ *Sakyō-ku* 🎫 *¥350* 🕐 *Daily 9–4:30.*

★ ⑤ Nanzen-ji. Like Ginkaku-ji, this former retirement villa was turned into a temple on the death of its owner, Emperor Kameyama (1249–1305). To counterbalance the might of the old Nara sects, military rulers historically favored this Zen sect and its associated philosophical and aesthetic tradition steeped in Chinese culture. By the 14th century this had become the most powerful temple in Japan, which spurred the Tendai monks to destroy it. The 15th-century Ōnin Civil War demolished the buildings again, but some were resurrected during the 16th century. Nanzen-ji has become one of Kyōto's most important temples, in part because it's the headquarters of the Rinzai sect of Zen Buddhism.

Monks in training are still taught in the Sō-dō building. You enter the temple through the enormous 1628 **San-mon** (Triple Gate), the classic "gateless" gate of Zen Buddhism that symbolizes entrance into the most sacred part of the temple precincts. From the top floor of the gate you can view Kyōto spread out below. Whether or not you ascend the steep steps, give a moment to the statue of Goemon Ishikawa. In 1594 this Robin Hood–style outlaw tried but failed to kill the daimyō Hideyoshi Toyotomi. He hid in this gate until his capture, after which he was boiled in a cauldron of oil. His story is still enacted in many Kabuki plays.

On through the gate is **Hōjō** (Abbots' Quarters), a National Treasure. Inside, screens with impressive 16th-century paintings divide the chambers. These wall panels of the *Twenty-Four Paragons of Filial Piety and Hermits* were created by Eitoku Kanō (1543–90) of the Kanō school—in effect the Kanō family, because the school consists of eight generations of one bloodline (Eitoku was from the fifth generation). Kobori Enshū created what's commonly known as the Leaping Tiger Garden, an excellent example of the karesansui style, attached to the Hōjō. The large rocks are grouped with clipped azaleas, maples, pines, and moss, all positioned against a plain white well behind the raked gravel expanse. The greenery effectively connects the garden with the lush forested hillside beyond.

5

Within Nanzen-ji's 27 pine-tree-covered acres sit several other temples, known more for their gardens than their architecture. One worth visiting is **Nanzen-in,** once the temporary abode of Emperor Kameyama. Nanzen-in has a mausoleum and a garden that dates from the 14th century; a small creek passes through it. From Nomura Art Museum, walk south along the main path to Nanzen-ji; the temple complex will be on your left. ⊠ *Nanzenji-Fukuchi-chō, Sakyō-ku* ☒ *Abbot's Quarters ¥400, entrance to San-mon or Nanzen-in ¥300* ⊙ *Mar.–Nov., daily 8:40–5; Dec.–Feb., daily 8:40–4:30.*

❾ National Museum of Modern Art (Kindai Bijutsukan). The museum is known for its collection of 20th-century Japanese paintings, which emphasizes artistic movements in the Kansai region, and its ceramic treasures by Kanjirō Kawai, Rosanjin Kitaōji, Shōji Hamada, and others. There are frequent exhibitions of contemporary artists. From the Dōbutsu-en-mae bus stop, walk down the street that leads to the Heian Jingū. The museum is on the left inside the torii. ⊠ *Enshōji-chō, Okazaki, Sakyō-ku* ☎ *075/761–4111* ☒ *¥420; additional fee for special exhibitions* ⊙ *Tues.–Sun. 9:30–5.*

❷ Path of Philosophy (Tetsugaku-no-michi). Cherry trees line this walkway along the canal. It has traditionally been a place for contemplative strolling since a famous scholar, Ikutaro Nishida (1870–1945), took his daily constitutional here. Now professors and students have to push their way through tourists whose interest lies mainly with the path's specialty shops. Along the path are several coffee shops and small restaurants. **Omen,** one block west of the Path of Philosophy, is an inexpensive, popular restaurant known for its homemade white noodles. From Kyōto Station take Bus 5 to the Ginkaku-ji-michi bus stop. Walk east on the street that follows the canal. Just after the street crosses a north–south canal, the path begins on your right. ⊠ *Sakyō-ku.*

㉖ Ponto-chō Kaburenjō Theater. Like Gion, Ponto-chō is known for its nightlife. At the north end of Pontochō-dōri, the Ponto-chō Kaburenjō presents the visually spectacular geisha song-and-dance performances in spring (May 1–24) and autumn (October 15–November 7). The theater sits on the west side of the Kamo-gawa between Sanjō and Shijō streets. ⊠ *Ponto-chō, Sanjō-sagaru, Nakagyō-ku* ☎ *075/221–2025.*

★ ⑬ Sanjūsangen-dō. Everyone knows this temple as Sanjūsangen-dō, even though it's officially called Rengeō-in. *Sanjūsan* means "33," which is the number of spaces between the pillars that lead down the temple's narrow, 394-foot-long hall. Enthroned in the middle of the hall is the 6-foot-tall, 1,000-handed Kannon—a National Treasure—carved by Tankei, a sculptor of the Kamakura period (1192–1333). One thousand smaller statues of Kannon surround the large statue, all covered in gold leaf, and in the corridor behind are the 28 guardian deities who protect the Buddhist universe. Notice the frivolous-faced Garuda, a bird that feeds on dragons. Are you wondering about the 33 spaces mentioned earlier? Kannon can assume 33 different shapes on her missions of mercy. Because there are 1,001 statues of Kannon in the hall, 33,033 shapes are possible. People come to the hall to see if they can find the likeness of a loved one (a deceased relative) among the many statues.

From Kyōto Station take Bus 206, 208, or 100 to the Sanjūsangen-dō-mae stop. The temple is to the south, just beyond the Kyōto Park Hotel. ✉ *657 Sanjusangen-dō Mawari-chō, Higashiyama-ku* 💴 ¥600 🕙 *Apr.–mid-Nov., daily 8–5; mid-Nov.–Mar., daily 9–4.*

Sannen-zaka and Ninen-zaka (Sannen and Ninen slopes). With their cobbled paths and delightful wooden buildings, these two lovely winding streets are fine examples of Old Kyōto. This area is one of four historic preservation districts in Kyōto, and the shops along the way sell local crafts and wares such as *Kiyomizu-yaki* (Kiyomizu-style pottery), Kyōto dolls, bamboo basketry, rice crackers, and antiques. From Kiyomizu-dera turn right halfway down Kiyomizu-zaka. Slightly farther down is a stately landmark: **Yasaka Pagoda,** the oldest extant wooden structure in Kyōto, last rebuilt in 1440. ✉ *Higashiyama-ku.*

★ ㉒ **Shōren-in.** Paintings by the Kanō school are on view at this temple, a five-minute walk north of Chion-in. Though the temple's present building dates only from 1895, the sliding screens of the Hon-dō (Main Hall) have the works of the 16th-century Muromachi-era painter Motonobu Kanō, second-generation Kanō—known for combining the Chinese ink-painting style with the more decorative Japanese style—and Mitsunobu Kanō of the sixth generation in the early 17th century. In the gardens an immense camphor tree sits at the entrance gate, and azaleas surround a balanced grouping of rocks and plants. It was no doubt more grandiose when the artist and architect Sōami designed it in the 16th century, but with the addition of paths through the garden, it's a nice place to wander. Occasionally, koto concerts are held in the evening in the Sōami garden (check with a Japan Travel Bureau office for concert schedules). From Kyōto Station take Bus 206 to the Higashiyama-Sanjō stop. ✉ *Higashiyama-ku* 💴 ¥500 🕙 *Daily 9–5.*

㉓ **Yasaka Jinja.** According to ancient Japanese geomancy, a city needs the protection of the four directional gods. Yasaka Shrine was built in the 7th century above an underground lake to ensure that the god who resides in the east—the blue water dragon—receives the fresh water needed to ensure healthy earth energy. The original enshrined Shintō deity, Susanō-no-Mikoto, later came to be associated with the Buddhist deva Gozu Ten-no, a protector against pestilence and god of prosperity. Also known as Gion Shrine, Yasaka hosts the Gion Festival, which started in 869 as a religious ritual to rid the city of a terrible plague that originated in Kyōto and swiftly spread all over Japan. The festival lasts the month of July and includes many events at the shrine. At New Year's, Kyōto residents flock here to buy amulets for good fortune. You can write up a prayer for prosperity and good health and tie it to the tree covered with little paper bows. From Kyōto Station take Bus 206 or 100 to the Gion bus stop; the shrine is just off Higashi-ōji-dōri. ✉ *625 Gion-machi, Kitagawa, Higashiyama-ku* 💴 *Free* 🕙 *Daily 24 hrs.*

SHOP STOP

㉔ **Kyōto Craft Center.** Kyōto residents come to this collection of stores to shop for fine contemporary and traditional crafts—ceramics, lacquerware, prints, and textiles. You can also purchase moderately priced souvenirs such as dolls, coasters, bookmarks, and paper products. From Kyōto Station take Bus 206 to the Gion stop. The center is on the corner of Shijō-dōri and Higashi-ōji-dōri. ✉ *Shijō-dōri, Gion-machi, Higashiyama-ku* ☎ *075/561–9660* ⊘ *Thurs.–Tues. 11–7.*

Western Kyōto & Arashiyama

As in eastern Kyōto, the city's western precincts are filled with remarkable religious architecture, including Kitano Tenman-gu, the eye-popping golden Kinkaku-ji, the sprawling temple complexes of Daitoku-ji and Myōshin-ji, and Ryōan-ji, with its inimitably simple gravel-and-stone garden. The Katsura Rikyū villa and Koinzan Saihō-ji, known as the Moss Temple, are highly recommended, though they require advance planning and plenty of time to reach and visit.

Beyond the city is the semirural hillside area of Arashiyama, which lies along and above the banks of the Ōi-gawa (the local name for the Katsura-gawa as it courses through this area). The pleasure of Arashiyama, the westernmost part of Kyōto, is the same as it has been for centuries. The gentle foothills of the mountains, covered with cherry and maple trees, are splendid. The sights are fairly spaced out, connected by a pathway that meanders along the hillside, through fields and a peaceful bamboo grove, and past several craft shops and restaurants. It's no wonder that the aristocracy of feudal Japan came here to escape famine, riots, and political intrigue.

Getting Around

The sights in the northern and western parts of this area can be reached easily using city buses. For Katsura Rikyū rail is best, and to reach Koinzan Saihō-ji you can take Bus 29 from Karasuma Shijō. A 20-minute train ride from Kyōto Station will bring you to Arashiyama, which you can explore on foot or by bicycle. Several bike-rental shops are near the station.

You need two full days to cover the western Kyōto and Arashiyama sights. If you only have one day, skip a few of the western Kyōto sights so you can make your way to Arashiyama in the afternoon. You can see most of Arashiyama in a relaxed morning or afternoon, with the jaunt south to Koinzan Saihō-ji and/or Katsura Rikyū—at the beginning or end of the tour. Just be sure to leave plenty of time to visit these last two sights, both of which also require permission in advance.

What to See in Western Kyōto

★ ❸ **Daitoku-ji.** The Daitoku-ji complex of the Rinzai sect of Zen Buddhism consists of 24 temples (several are open to the public) surrounded by trees in a spacious, walled enclosure. The original temple was founded in 1319, but fires during the Ōnin Civil War destroyed it in 1468. Most buildings you see today were built under the patronage of Hideyoshi Toyotomi in the late 16th century. However, it's thought that the priest Ikkyū oversaw much of Daitoku-ji's development. Ikkyū, known for his rather startling juxtapositions of the sacred and the profane—he was a priest and a poet—is reported to have said that "brothels are more suitable settings for meditation than temples." Despite leaving the temple to live a Zen lifestyle outside the monastery, he eventually became the abbot and helped shape the formalized tea ceremony.

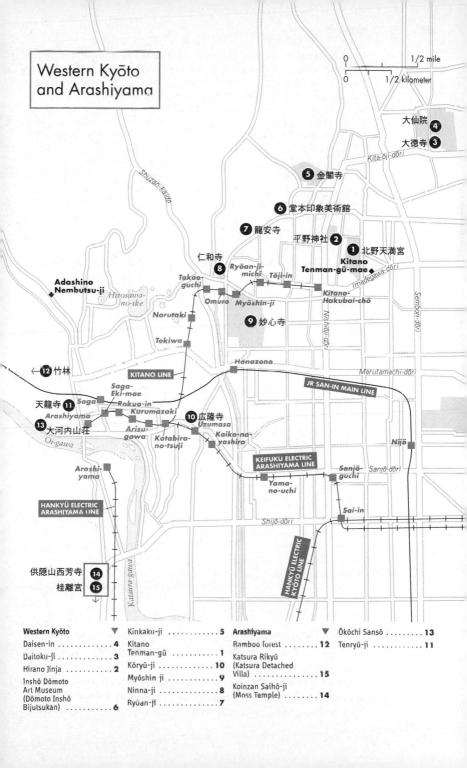

Western Kyōto and Arashiyama

1/2 mile

1/2 kilometer

大仙院 **4**

大徳寺 **3**

Kita-ōji-dōri

金閣寺 **5**

堂本印象美術館 **6**

龍安寺 **7**

平野神社 **2**

北野天満宮 **1**

Kitano Tenman-gū-mae ◆

Imadegawa-dōri

仁和寺 **8**

Takao-guchi

Ryōan-ji-michi

Tōji-in

Adashino Nembutsu-ji

Hirosawa-no-ike

Omuro

Myōshin-ji

Kitano-Hakubai-chō

Narutaki

妙心寺 **9**

Nishijin-dōri

Sembon-dōri

Tokiwa

Hanazono

Marutamachi-dōri

←**12** 竹林

KITANO LINE

JR SAN-IN MAIN LINE

Saga-Eki-mae

天龍寺 **11**

Saga

Rokuo-in

Kurumazaki

広隆寺 **10**

Arashiyama

大河内山荘 **13**

Arisu-gawa

Uzumasa

Oi-gawa

Katabira-no-tsuji

Kaiko-no-yashiro

Nijō

Arashi-yama

KEIFUKU ELECTRIC ARASHIYAMA LINE

Sanjō-guchi

Sanjō-dōri

Yamano-uchi

HANKYŪ ELECTRIC ARASHIYAMA LINE

Sai-in

Shijō-dōri

供隠山西芳寺 **14**

桂離宮 **15**

HANKYŪ ELECTRIC KYŌTO LINE

Katsura-gawa

The **Chokushi-mon** (Gate of Imperial Messengers) originally served as the south gate of Kyōto's Imperial Palace when it was constructed in 1590. Then Empress Meisho in the mid-17th century bequeathed it to Daitoku-ji. Note the curved-gable style of the gate, typical of the Momoyama period. The **San-mon** (Triple Gate) is noteworthy for the addition of its third story, designed by the most famous of tea masters, Sen-no-Rikyū (1521–91). In contrast to the extravagant tea ceremonies of Toyotomi, Sen-no-Rikyū developed the concept of *wabi*—seeking beauty in simplicity, and even poverty and loneliness—in connection with the tea ceremony. Sen-no-Rikyū, who is buried in the temple grounds, went on to commit seppuku; legend has it he was ordered to do so by Toyotomi, who was angry at a statue Sen-no-Rikyū supposedly erected of himself on the San-mon. Three subtemples in the complex are noteworthy: **Daisen-in**, Ryōgen-in, and Kōtō-in.

Ryōgen-in has five small gardens of gravel, stone, and moss. The A-Un garden has a stone with ripples emanating and is said to represent the union of duality, from the "a" sound said at birth to the "un" said at death, encompassing all in between. The fee for Ryōgen-in is ¥350, and the temple stays open 9–4:30. The subtemple **Kōtō-in** is famous for its long, maple-tree-lined approach and the single stone lantern central to the main garden. The fee is ¥400, and the temple stays open from 9 until 4:30 or 5 (enter 30 minutes before closing).

There are several ways to get to the temple from downtown Kyōto. Take the subway north from Kyōto Station to Kita-ōji Station, from which any bus going west along Kita-ōji-dōri will take you to the Daitoku-ji-mae stop. You can also take Bus 12 north up Horikawa-dōri and disembark soon after the bus makes a left on Kita-ōji-dōri. From western Kyōto Bus 204 (which runs up Nishi-ōji-dōri) and Bus 206 (which runs up Sembon-dōri) will also take you to the temple. The temple grounds are free, but there are admission costs for additional temples, and one or two are by appointment only. ✉ *Daitoku-ji-chō, Murasakino, Kita-ku* ☾ *Daily, temple hrs vary between 9 and 5.*

★ ❹ **Daisen-in**. Of all the subtemples at **Daitoku-ji**, Daisen-in is perhaps the best known—in part for its excellent landscape paintings by the renowned Sōami (1465–1523), as well as the famed Muromachi-era karesansui garden, attributed to Kogaku Sōkō (1465–1548), the founder of the temple. Circling the building, the rock-and-gravel gardens depict the flow of life in the movement of a raked river, swirling around the rocks over a waterfall, to finally run into the ocean of nothingness. *See* **Daitoku-ji**, *below*, for directions to Daisen-in. ✉ *Kita-ku* 🎟 *¥400* ☾ *Mar.–Nov., daily 9–5; Dec.–Feb., daily 9–4:30.*

┌─
│ **NEED A BREAK?**

Ichiwa has been serving tea and *aburi mochi*—skewered rice-flour cakes charcoal-grilled and dipped in sweet miso sauce—since the Heian Era (750–1150). You can enjoy the treats under the eaves of a 17th-century house as you watch visitors on their way to and from Imamiya Shrine. Ichiwa is just outside the shrine, northwest of Daitoku-ji. ✉ *69 Imamiya-chō, Murasakino, Kita-ku* ☎ *075/492-6852* ☾ *Thurs.–Tues. 10–sunset.*

② **Hirano Jinja**. The symbol of this shrine is the cherry blossom, and each spring the blossoms of this pale pink flower contrast with the vermilion lanterns that flank the path. This complex of four shrine buildings dates from the 17th century, but its ancestry is ancient. The shrine was brought from Nagaoka—Japan's capital after Nara and before Kyōto—to protect the budding new Heian-kyō, as Kyōto was then called. Take either Bus 50 or 52 from downtown Kyōto or Kyōto Station. The ride takes a little more than a half hour. The shrine is about a 10-minute walk north of the Kitano Tenman-gū-mae bus stop. ✉ *Miyamoto-chō 1, Hirano, Kita-ku* 🎫 *Free* ⊘ *Daily 6–5.*

⑥ **Inshō Dōmoto Art Museum** (Dōmoto Inshō Bijutsukan). The narrative paintings of the 20th-century artist Inshō Dōmoto, affectionately known as Insho-san, hold wide appeal because they depict scenes from everyday life and stories from world religions. The artist later experimented with abstract expressionism. Also on display are the fusuma, or sliding doors, he decorated. From the Kinkaku-ji-mae bus stop, take Bus 12 or 59 south for 10 minutes to Ritsumeikan-Daigaku-mae. ✉ *Kami-Yanagi-chō, Hirano, Kita-ku* ☎ *075/463–1348* 🎫 *¥500* ⊘ *Tues.–Sun 10–5.*

⑤ **Kinkaku-ji** (Temple of the Golden Pavilion). For a retirement home, the gold-sheathed Kinkaku-ji is pretty magnificent. Shōgun Yoshimitsu Ashikaga (1358–1409) had it constructed in 1,393 for the time when he would quit politics—the following year, in fact—to manage the affairs of state through the new shōgun, his 10-year-old son. On Yoshimitsu's death, his son followed his father's wishes and converted the villa into a temple named Rokuon-ji. The structure sits, following the Shinden style of the Heian period, at the edge of the lake. Pillars support the three-story pavilion, which extends over the pond and is reflected in the calm waters. To underscore this statement of his prestige and power, the shōgun had the ceiling of the third floor of the pavilion covered in gold leaf.

In 1950 a student monk with metaphysical aspirations torched Kinkaku-ji, burning it to the ground. (Yukio Mishima's book *Temple of the Golden Pavilion* is a fictional exploration of the mind of the student.) Kinkaku-ji was rebuilt in 1955 based on the original design, except that all three stories were covered with gold leaf, in accordance with the shōgun's original intention, instead of only the third-floor ceiling.

Marveling at this pavilion, you might find it difficult to imagine the era in which Shōgun Yoshimitsu Ashikaga lived out his golden years. The country was in turmoil, and Kyōto residents suffered severe famines and plagues—local death tolls sometimes reached 1,000 a day. The temple is a short walk from the Kinkaku-ji-mae bus stop. From Daisen-in the ride on Bus 12 takes about 10 minutes. ✉ *1 Kinkaku-ji-chō, Kita-ku* 🎫 *¥400* ⊘ *Daily 9–5.*

★ ① **Kitano Tenman-gū**. This shrine was originally dedicated to Tenjin, and emissaries were often sent here with offerings to appease this god of thunder. Then in the 10th century the nobility of Japan suffered various inexplicable calamities. Emperor Daigo had a dream that seemed to account for the misfortune: the spirit of noted poet and politician Michizane would not rest until he had been pardoned. For political reasons, when Emperor Daigo ascended to the throne, Michizane was accused of treason and sent into exile on Kyūshū, where he died. Because the dream identified Michizane with the god of thunder, Emperor Daigo decreed that Kitano Tenman-gū would be rededicated to the poet-politician. On top of that, Michizane's political rank was posthumously restored. When that was not enough, he was promoted to a higher position and later to prime minister.

The shrine's present structure dates from 1607. The main sanctuary is a complex mix of Buddhist and Shintō architecture; note the unusual *irimoya*-style roof, which has layered peaks that are typical of the ornate Momoyama period. A large **market** is held on the grounds on the 25th of each month. Stalls at the market sell food, antiques, old kimonos, and other collectibles. It's worth taking a detour one block east of the shrine to see the seven old ochaya, or teahouses, of **Kamishichiken,** the geisha district that predates Gion. Take either Bus 100 or 50 from Kyōto Station and get off at Kitano Tenman-gū-mae. The ride takes a little more than a half hour. ⊠ *Imakoji-agaru, Onmae-dōri, Kamigyō-ku* ⊠ *Shrine free; plum garden ¥500, including green tea* ☉ *Shrine Apr.–Oct., daily 5–5; Nov.–Mar, daily 5:30–5:30. Plum garden Feb.–Mar., daily 10–4.*

NEED A BREAK?

Want to freshen up before dinner? **Funaoka Onsen,** on the corner of Sembon and Imadegawa, several blocks north of Kitano Tenman-gū, was established in 1923. The spacious, communal bathing area has been renovated, but the changing rooms still have their original wood-relief ceilings and beautiful tiles. There are gender-separate indoor baths, as well as two outdoor baths—one made of cedar and one of rock—that are open to men and women on alternate days. Towels, soap, and shampoo are for sale. ⊠ *Sembon Imadegawa kado, Murosaki no Minami, Funaoka-chō, Kita-ku* ☎ 075/441–3735 ⊠ ¥350 ☉ Daily 3 PM–1 AM.

★ ❿ **Kōryū-ji.** One of Kyōto's oldest temples, Kōryū-ji was founded in 622 by Kawakatsu Hata in memory of Prince Shōtoku (572–621). Shōtoku, known for issuing the Seventeen-Article Constitution, a set of Confucian-inspired moral dictates, was the first powerful advocate of Buddhism after it was introduced to Japan in 552. In the **Hattō** (Lecture Hall) of the main temple stand three statues, each a National Treasure. The center of worship is the seated figure of Buddha, flanked by the figures of the Thousand-Handed Kannon and Fukukenjaku-Kannon. In the **Taishi-dō** (Prince Hall) is a wooden statue of Prince Shōtoku, thought to have been carved by him personally. Another statue of Shōtoku in this hall was probably made when he was 16 years old.

The most famous of the Buddhist images in the Reihō-den (Treasure House) is the statue of **Miroku Bosatsu,** who according to Buddhist belief is destined to appear on earth in the far-off future to save those unable to achieve enlightenment. Japan's first registered National Treasure, this rustic wooden statue is thought to date to the 6th or 7th century, carved, perhaps, by Shōtoku himself. Of all the Buddhas in Kyōto, this may be the most captivating. The epitome of serenity, the statue gently rests the fingers of its right hand against its cheek (one finger, sadly, was broken off when an ardent student clutched the statue in the late '60s).

From Kyōto Station take the JR San-in Main Line to Hanazono Station and then board Bus 61. From Shijō-Ōmiya Station, in central Kyōto, take the Keifuku Electric Arashiyama Line to Uzumasa Station. From central or western Kyōto, take Bus 61, 62, or 63 to the Uzumasa-kōryūji-mae stop. ⊠ *Hachigaoka-chō, Uzumasa, Ukyō-ku* 🖼 *¥600* ☉ *Mar.–Nov., daily 9–5; Dec.–Feb., daily 9–4:30.*

★ ❾ **Myōshin-ji.** Japan's oldest bell—cast in 698—hangs in the belfry near the South Gate of this 14th-century temple, and is still rung daily to regulate the schedules of the monks. Emperor Hanazono was confirmed enlightened by the founder of Daitoku-ji, Kokushi, after many years of cloistered Zen practice. Thus his villa was converted into a temple; the work required so many laborers that a sprawling complex of buildings was built to house them. In all, there are some 40 structures, though only four are open to the public. Beware of the dragon on the ceiling of Myōshin-ji's Hattō (Lecture Hall). Known as the "Dragon Glaring in Eight Directions," it looks at you wherever you stand.

Within the complex, the temple **Taizō-in** has a famous painting by Sanraku Kanō called *Four Sages of Mt. Shang,* recalling the four wise men who lived in isolation on a mountain to avoid the reign of destruction. The garden of Taizō-in is gentle and quiet—a good place to revive. The temple structure, originally built in 1404, suffered like the rest of the Myōshin-ji complex in the Ōnin Civil War (1467–77) and had to be rebuilt. Buses 61, 62, and 63 all stop at the Myōshin-ji-mae stop. ⊠ *Ukyō-ku* 🖼 *¥400 for Myōshin-ji; additional ¥400 for Taizō-in* ☉ *Daily 9:10–11:50 and 1–4.*

❽ **Ninna-ji.** The original temple was once the palace of Emperor Omuro, who started construction in 896. Nothing of that structure remains; the complex of buildings that stands today was rebuilt in the 17th century, though the *shinden* style recalls the Heian-era villas of the 11th century with its bisymmetrical layout of a main hall, or shinden, where the priest would live, flanked by buildings connected with roofed passageways. There's an attractive five-story pagoda (1637), and the Hon-dō (Main Hall), which was moved from the Imperial Palace, is also worth noting. The temple's focus of worship is the Amida Buddha. Take either Bus 26 or 59 to the Omuro-ninna-ji stop. ⊠ *Ukyō-ku* 🖼 *¥500* ☉ *Daily 9–4:30.*

❼ **Ryōan-ji.** The garden at Ryōan-ji, rather than the temple, attracts people from all over the world. Knowing that the temple belongs to the Rinzai sect of Zen Buddhism may help you appreciate the austere aesthetics of the garden. It's a karesansui, a dry garden: just 15 rocks arranged in three groupings of seven, five, and three in gravel. From the temple's veranda, the proper viewing place, only 14 rocks can be seen at one time. Move slightly and another rock appears and one of the original 14 disappears. In the Buddhist world the number 15 denotes completeness. You must have a total view of the garden to make it a meaningful experience—and yet, in the conditions of this world, that's not possible.

Fodor'sChoice ★

If possible, visit Ryōan-ji in the early morning before the crowds arrive and disturb the garden's contemplative quality. If you need a moment to yourself, head to the small restaurant on the temple grounds near an

5

ancient pond, where you can contemplate over an expensive beer. From a southbound 12 or 59 bus, the temple will be on your right. ⌂ *13 Goryōshita-machi, Ryōan-ji, Ukyō-ku* ⌐ ¥500 ⊘ *Mar.–Nov., daily 8–5; Dec.–Feb., daily 8:30–4:30.*

What to See in Arashiyama

The easiest ways to get to Arashiyama are by the JR San-in Main Line from Kyōto Station to Saga Station, or via the Keifuku Electric Railway to Arashiyama Station (which is just south of Saga Station).

⓬ **Bamboo forest.** Dense bamboo forests—with their rows upon rows of long, ringed, smooth stems—provide a feeling of composure and tranquillity. The sound of wind blowing through bamboo, of stems knocking against one another and leaves rustling, is revered in Japan. Nowadays, bamboo forests are few and far between. This one, on the way to Ōkōchi Sansō from Tenryū-ji, is a delight. ⌂ *Ukyō-ku.*

⓯ **Katsura Rikyū** (Katsura Imperial Villa). The setting for this villa is a perfect example of Japanese integration of nature and architecture. As is typical of the Heian period, the garden makes use of a wide variety of styles, with elements of the pond and island, karesansui, and tea gardens, among others. The garden is a study in the placement of stones and the progressive unfolding of the views that the Japanese have so artfully mastered in garden design.

Fodor'sChoice
★

Here you find Japan's oldest surviving stroll garden, dating to the 17th century, with pathways that take you through a repertoire of miniaturizations of landscapes: an encyclopedia of famous Japanese natural sites and literary references, such as the 11th-century *Tale of Genji*. Not satisfied to create simply beautiful pictures, landscape architect Kobori Enshū focused on the rhythm within the garden: spaces open then close, are bright then dark; views are visible and then concealed.

Look out at the garden from the three *shōin* (a type of house that incorporates alcoves and platforms for the display of personal possessions) and the four rustic tea arbors around the central pond, which have been strategically placed for optimal vistas. Bridges constructed from earth, stone, and wood connect five islets in the pond.

Built in the 17th century for Prince Toshihito, brother of Emperor Goyōzei, Katsura is in southwestern Kyōto on the banks of the Katsura-gawa, with peaceful views of Arashiyama and the Kameyama Hills. The villa is fairly remote from other historical sites—allow several hours for a visit. Katsura requires special permission for a visit. Applications must be made, preferably a day in advance, in person to the **Imperial Household Agency** (⌂ Kyōto Gyoen-nai, Kamigyō-ku ☎ 075/211–1215 ⊕ http://sankan.kunaicho.go.jp), open weekdays 8:45–4. You will need your passport to pick up a permit, and you must be at least 20 years of age. The time of your tour will be stated, and you must not be late. The tour lasts one hour and is in Japanese only, although an introduction video in English is shown in the waiting room before each tour begins. To reach the villa, take the Hankyū Railway Line from one of the Hankyū Kyōto Line stations to Katsura Station; then walk 15 minutes to the villa from the station's east exit or take a taxi for about ¥800. ☒ *Katsura Shimizu-chō, Ukyō-ku* ☏ *075/211–1215 inquiries only* ☒ *Free* ☉ *Tours week-days at 10, 11, 2, and 3; additional tours 1st and 3rd Sat. of month Dec.–Mar. and June–Sept., and every Sat. in Apr., May, Oct., and Nov.*

⑭ Kōinzan Saihō-ji (Moss Temple). Entrance into the temple precincts **Fodor'sChoice** transports you into an extraordinary sea of green: 120 varieties of moss ★ create waves of greens and blues that eddy and swirl gently around Kōin-zan Saihō-ji's garden and give the temple its popular name, Kokedera—the Moss Temple.

The site was originally the villa of Prince Shōtoku (572–621). During the Tempyō era (729–749) Emperor Shōmu charged the priest Gyogi Bosatsu to create 49 temples in the central province, one of which was this temple. The original garden represented Jōdo, the Pure Land, or west-ern paradise of Buddhism. The temple and garden, destroyed many times by fire, lay in disrepair until 1338, when the chief priest of nearby Mat-suno-jinja had a revelation here. He convinced Musō Soseki, a distin-guished Zen priest of Rinzen-ji, the head temple of the Rinzai sect of Zen Buddhism, to preside over the temple and convert it from the Jōdo to the Zen sect. Soseki, an avid gardener, designed the temple garden on two levels surrounding a pond in the shape of the Chinese charac-ter for heart. Present-day visitors are grateful for his efforts. The gar-den is entirely covered with moss and provides a unique setting for a contemplative walk. May and June, when colors are brightest due to heavy rains, are the best times to see the garden.

Another interesting aspect to your temple visit is the obligatory *sha kyo,* writing of sutras. Before viewing the garden, you enter the temple and sit at a small, lacquered writing table where you're provided with a brush, ink, and a thin sheet of paper with Chinese characters in light gray. After rubbing your ink stick on the ink stone, dip the tip of your brush in the ink and trace over the characters. A priest explains in Japanese the tem-ple history and the sutra you are writing. If time is limited you don't have to write the entire sutra; when the priest has ended his explana-tion, simply place what you have written on a table before the altar and proceed to the garden. To gain admission send a stamped, self-addressed postcard to: Saihō-ji Temple, 56 Matsuno Jinjatani-chō, Nishikyō-ku, Kyōto 615-8286. Include the date and time you would like to visit. You can write in English, and the response will also be in English. The post-card must reach the temple at least five days prior to your visit. It's also possible to arrange a visit through the Kyōto Tourist Information Cen-ter. To reach the temple, take the Hankyū Line from Arashiyama to Mat-suno Station. ☒ *¥3,000; have exact change.*

⑬ Ōkōchi Sansō. Walk the estate grounds of Ōkōchi's Mountain Villa to breathe in some contemplative peace—Denjirō Ōkōchi, a renowned silent-movie actor of samurai films, chose this location for his home because of the superb views of Arashiyama and Kyōto. Admission to the villa includes tea and cake to enjoy while you absorb nature's pleasures. ☒ *8 Tabuchiyama-chō, Ogurayama, Saga, Ukyō-ku* ☏ *075/872–2233* ☒ *¥900* ☉ *Daily 9–5.*

OFF THE
BEATEN
PATH

ADASHINO NEMBUTSU-JI – If you're in no rush to leave Saga Arashiyama after your visit to Ōkōchi Sansō, continue walking along the country lane past Nison-in, souvenir shops, and noodle restaurants for about half an hour. Eventually you climb a small hill up to an unusual temple: Adashino Nembutsu-ji. Here about 8,000 stone Buddhas are packed together like a silent congregation. Their enshrinement is believed to honor the destitute whose remains were abandoned in the Adashino area from the Heian to the Edo periods. The main hall, built in 1712, contains a statue of Amida Buddha carved by Tankei, a sculptor famous in the Kamakura Era (1185–1333). On August 23 and 24, at a Buddhist ceremony called Sentō-kuyō, more than 1,000 candles are lighted for the repose of the spirits of ancestors. A stirring time to be on this hillside is in late afternoon, when the shadows beneath the effigies lengthen. You can get back to Arashiyama or Kyōto stations on Bus 72 from the Toriimoto stop. ✉ *17 Adashino-chō, Toriimoto, Ukyō-ku* ☎ *075/861–2221* 🎟 *¥500* ◷ *Mar.–Nov., daily 9–4:30; Dec.–Feb., daily 9–4.*

★ ⑬ **Tenryū-ji.** For good reason is this known as the Temple of the Heavenly Dragon: in the 14th century Emperor Go-Daigo, who had brought an end to the Kamakura shogunate, was forced from his throne by Takauji Ashikaga. After Go-Daigo died, Takauji had twinges of conscience. That's when Priest Musō Sōseki had a dream in which a golden dragon rose from the nearby Ōi-gawa. He told the shōgun about his dream and interpreted it to mean the spirit of Go-Daigo was not at peace. Worried about this ill omen, Takauji completed Tenryū-ji in 1339 on the same spot where Go-Daigo had his favorite villa. Apparently the late emperor's spirit was appeased. Construction took several years and was partly financed by a trading mission to China, which brought back treasures of the Ming dynasty. In the Hattō (Lecture Hall), where today's monks meditate, a huge "cloud dragon" is painted on the ceiling. The temple was often ravaged by fire, and the current buildings are as recent as 1900; the painting of the dragon was rendered by 20th-century artist Shōnen Suzuki.

The **Sōgenchi garden** of Tenryū-ji dates from the 14th century and is one of the most notable in Kyōto. Musō Soseki, an influential Zen monk and skillful garden designer, created the garden to resemble Mt. Hōrai in China. It is famed for the arrangement of vertical stones in its large pond and as one of the first gardens to use "borrowed scenery," incorporating the mountains in the distance into the design of the garden.

If you visit Tenryū-ji at lunchtime, consider purchasing a ticket for Zen cuisine served at **Shigetsu** (☎ 075/882–9725), within the temple precinct. The ¥3,500 price includes lunch in the large dining area overlooking a garden, as well as admission to the garden itself. Here you can experience the Zen monks' philosophy of "eating to live" rather than "living to eat." While you won't partake in the monk's daily helping of gruel, a salted plum, and pickled radishes, you will try Zen cuisine prepared for festival days. The meal includes sesame tofu served over top-quality soy sauce, a variety of fresh boiled vegetables, miso soup, and rice. The *tenzo,* a monk specially trained to prepare Zen cuisine, creates a multicourse meal that achieves the harmony of the six basic flavors—bitter, sour, sweet, salty, light, and hot—required for monks to practice

Zen with the least hindrance to body and mind. The more elaborate courses cost ¥5,500 and ¥7,500. Advance reservations are required by a Japanese speaker. Take the JR San-in Main Line from Kyōto Station to Saga Station or the Keifuku Electric Railway to Arashiyama Station. From Saga Station walk west; from Arashiyama Station walk north. ⊠ *68 Susuki-no-bamba-chō, Saga-Tenryū-ji, Ukyō-ku* ☎ *075/882-9725* 🎫 *Garden ¥500; ¥100 additional to enter temple building* ⊙ *Apr.–Oct., daily 8:30–5:30; Nov.–Mar., daily 8:30–5.*

Central & Southern Kyōto

The two major sights in central Kyōto are the opulent Nijō Castle and the more modest Imperial Palace. The latter requires permission, and you must join a guided tour. Central Kyōto is a big shopping destination: west of the Kamo-gawa to Karasuma-dōri and on the north–south axis between Shijō-dōri and Oike-dōri, there are department stores, specialty shops, and restaurants. The most interesting southern Kyōto sights are three religious structures: Tōfuku-ji, Fushimi-Inari Taisha, and Byōdō-in, which is actually in the tea-producing city of Uji. Both Fushimi-Inari Taisha and the temple Daigo-ji in southern Kyōto are set on mountains with trails to explore.

Getting Around

The sights in central Kyōto can be reached by bus, but if you're traveling in a group it may be cheaper to use a cab rather than buying multiple bus fares. To reach the sights in southern Kyōto, take the train.

The temples and shrines in southern Kyōto are at a distance from one another, so traveling time can eat into your day. If you visit Tōfuku-ji, consider combining it with a visit to Fushimi-Inari Taisha, farther south.

Central Kyōto's sights are fairly close to one another and quickly accessible by bus or taxi. A morning could be taken up with the Imperial Palace and Nijō-jō. Remember that to visit the Imperial Palace you must make a reservation in advance. Also, the palace is closed Saturday afternoon and Sunday, and all day on the second and fourth Saturday of the month in winter and summer.

Kyōto Station. Kyōto's train station, opened in 1997, is more than just the city's central point of arrival and departure: the station houses a hotel, a theater, a department store, and dozens of shops and restaurants with great views of the city from the 16th floor. ⊠ *Shimogyō-ku.*

What to See

★ **Byōdō-in** (Temple of Equality). South of Kyōto in Uji-shi, this temple was originally the villa of a 10th-century member of the influential Fujiwara family. The **Amida-dō** is also known as the Phoenix Hall, thanks to its two protruding wings that make the building resemble the legendary bird; the hall is depicted on the ¥10 coin. Built in the 11th century by the Fujiwaras, it's considered one of Japan's most beautiful religious buildings—something of an architectural folly—where heaven is brought close to earth. Jōchō, one of Japan's most famous 11th-century sculptors, crafted a magnificent statue of Amida Buddha here; his hand mudra indicates that the Buddha rests in the highest of the nine paradises. The Aji Pond in front symbolizes the lotus lake of Amida's paradise. In the museum alongside you can see 52 small wooden *kuyo* or reverent bosatsu floating on clouds, playing celestial music.

Uji is a famous tea-producing district, and the slope up to the temple is lined with shops where you can sample the finest green tea and pick up a small package to take home. It's possible to set up a visit to a tea farm through the Kyōto Tourist Information Center. The shrines and temples surrounding the Uji River are also pleasant to explore. To get to Uji, take the JR Nara Line to Uji Station. Byōdō-in is a 12-minute walk east toward the river from the station. ⊠ *Ujirenge, Uji-shi* ☎ *0774/21-2861* 🖃 *¥500; additional ¥300 for Phoenix Hall* ☉ *Temple Mar.–Nov., daily 8:30–5:30; Dec.–Feb., daily 9–4:30. Phoenix Hall Mar.–Nov., daily 9–5; Dec.–Feb., daily 9–4.*

NEED A BREAK? **Opposite Byōdō-in, Taihō-an** is an authentic tea-ceremony building set in a delightful garden. Here you can enjoy a cup of green tea with a seasonal Japanese sweet, or if you book in advance, the full tea ceremony for ¥1,500. ⊠ *2 Ujitōgawa, Uji-shi* ☎ *0774/23-3334* ☉ *Thurs.–Tues. 10–sunset.*

★ **Daigo-ji.** The main temple of this mountain enclave founded in 874 is set in the foothills, and many smaller temples stand on the ridges above. Its five-story pagoda, which dates from 951, is reputed to be the oldest existing structure in Kyōto. By the late 16th century the temple had begun to decline in importance and showed signs of neglect. Then Hideyoshi Toyotomi paid a visit one April, when the temple's famous cherry trees were in bloom. Hideyoshi ordered the temple restored. The **Sanbō-in**, with its Momoyama-period thatched roof, has bold colorful paintings of nature and Chinese village scenes; the paintings, which incorporate gold leaf, were done by the Kanō school. The intriguing garden combines elements of the *chisen-kaiyu* (stroll garden with a pond) and the karesansui, or dry garden. From the temple you can continue up the mountain (about an hour's hike) to several subtemples. At the top, on a clear day, it's possible to make out the Ōsaka skyline in the far distance. To reach Daigo-ji, in the southeast suburb of Yamashina, take the Tōzai subway line to Daigo Station; follow the signs for a 10-minute walk to the nearby hills. ⊠ *22 Higashi Ōji-chō, Fushimi-ku* 🖃 *¥500* ☉ *Mar.–Oct., daily 9–5; Nov.–Feb., daily 9–4.*

★ **Fushimi-Inari Taisha.** One of Kyōto's oldest and most revered shrines, Fushimi-Inari honors the goddesses of agriculture (rice and rice wine) and prosperity. It also serves as the headquarters for all the 40,000 shrines representing Inari. The shrine dates back to the 8th century and is noted for its bronze foxes and for some 10,000 small torii, donated by the thankful, which create a vermilion tunnel that stretches far up the hill through quiet woods and past other smaller shrines. The full hike up the hill can take up to two hours, but a few noodle shops are open for lunch along the way. Take the JR Nara Line to Fushimi-Inari Station, from which it's a three-minute walk to the shrine. From Tōfuku-ji join the JR train at Tōfuku-ji Station and go one stop south, toward Nara. ⊠ *68 Fukakusa Yabu-no-uchi-chō, Fushimi-ku* 🖃 *Free* ☉ *Daily sunrise–sunset.*

Central Kyoto

0   1/2 mile

0   1/2 kilometer

SUBWAY

Imadegawa   Imadegawa-dōri

西陣織物 ❹

❸ 樂美術館

❶ 京都御所

Sembon-dōri

Horikawa-dōri

Karasuma-dōri

Kawara-machi-dōri

Kamo-gawa

Maruta-machi-dōri   Maruta-machi

Nijō-dōri

❷ 二条城

Karasuma-Oike

Nijō-jō Horikawa-dōri   Oike-dōri   TOZAI LINE   Kyōto Shiyakusho-mae

Nijō

Sanjō-dōri

Nijō Jinya ◆ 二条陣屋

TO DAIGO-JI

Hankyū-Ōmiya   Shijō-dōri   Karasuma   Kawara-machi

JR SAN-IN MAIN LINE

Shijō-Ōmiya   Shijō

Ōmiya-dōri

Horikawa-dōri

Karasuma-dōri

Takase-gawa

Gojō-dōri   Gojō

❺ 風俗博物館

Tanba-guchi

❻ 西本願寺   ❼ 東本願寺

Shichijō-dōri

Kawara-machi-dōri

Kamo-gawa

JR TOKAIDŌ MAIN LINE

京都駅 Kyōto Station

SHINKANSEN   Hachijō-dōri   TO BYŌDŌ-IN, FUSHIMI-INARI-TAISHA, AND TOFUKU-JI

❽ 東寺

Tōji

Gekkeikan Ōkura Kinenkan (Gekkeikan Ōkura Museum). Not far from Fushimi-Inari Taisha is an old sake-brewery district of white-walled warehouses dating back 400 years. Near the plentiful rice paddies of Shiga and the old trade canals that connected Kyōto, Ōsaka, and Uji, it's an ideal setting for sake brewing. Gekkeikan, founded in 1637, is one of the oldest breweries. The museum within the brewery displays utensils used to make sake. The brewery is a five-minute walk from Chūshojima Station, on the Keihan Line, or a 10-minute walk from Momoyama Goryō-mae Station, on the Kintetsu Kyōto Line. Reservations must be made in advance. ⊠ *247 Minamihama-chō, Fushimi-ku* ☎ *075/623–2056* ⊕ *www.gekkeikan.co.jp* ⊠ *¥300* ⊙ *Tues.–Sun. 9:30–4:30.*

★ ❼ **Higashi-Hongan-ji.** Until the early 17th century Higashi-Hongan-ji and Nishi-Hongan-ji were one temple. Then Shōgun Ieyasu Tokugawa took advantage of an internal feud within the Jōdo Shinshu sect of Buddhism and, to diminish its power, split it into two different factions. The original faction has the west temple, Nishi-Hongan-ji, and the later faction the eastern temple, Higashi-Hongan-ji.

The rebuilt (1895) structure of Higashi-Hongan-ji is the second-largest wooden structure in Japan, after Nara's Daibutsu-den. During construction of the temple, female devotees had their hair cut and woven into the strong thick rope—called *kezuna*—used to drag the heavy timber. A ragged section of one kezuna is on display inside the **Daishi-dō**, a double-roofed structure that is admirable for its curving, swooping lines. The temple contains fewer historical objects of interest than its rival, Nishi-Hongan-ji. From Kyōto Station walk 500 yards northwest; from the costume museum walk south on Horikawa-dōri. ⊠ *Shichijō-agaru, Karasuma-dōri, Shimogyō-ku* ⊠ *Free* ⊙ *Mar.–Oct., daily 5:50–5:30; Nov.–Feb., daily 6:20–4:30.*

★ ❺ **Kyōto Costume Museum** (Fūzoku Hakubutsukan). Marvel at the range of Japanese fashion, which starts in the pre-Nara era and works its way up through various historical eras to the Meiji period. The museum is one of the best of its kind, and provides an interesting perspective on Japan's history. Exhibitions, which change twice a year, use doll-size replicas to highlight a specific historical period. One room has two mannequins draped in Heian robes that can be tried on for free. From the Raku Art Museum, the Nishijin Textile Center, or Nijō-jō, take Bus 9 south on Horikawa-dōri. Disembark at the Nishi-Hongan-ji-mae bus stop. The museum is on the fifth floor of the Izutsu Building, at the intersection of Horikawa and Shin-Hanaya-chō, north of the temple on the other side of the street. ⊠ *Izutsu Bldg., Shimogyō-ku* ☎ *075/342–5345* ⊠ *¥400* ⊙ *Oct. 9–Sept. 2, Mon.–Sat. 9–5; closed Apr. 1–8, July 1–8, and Dec. 23–Jan. 6.*

❶ **Kyōto Imperial Palace** (Kyōto Gosho). Centrally located in a beautiful park, the present palace was completed in 1855, so it housed only two emperors, including the young emperor Meiji before the imperial household was moved to Tōkyō. The original, built for Emperor Kammu to the west of the present site, burned down in 1788. A new palace, modeled after the original, went up on the present site, but it, too, ended in flames. The Gosho is a large but simple wooden building that can hardly be described as palatial. On the one-hour tour you'll only have a chance for a brief glimpse of the Shishin-den—the hall where the inauguration of emperors and other important imperial ceremonies take place—and a visit to the Edo-era gardens, where you'll see a bridge made from zelkova wood. Though a trip to the Imperial Palace is on most people's agenda and it fills a lot of real estate, it's less interesting than some of Kyōto's older historical sites.

Guided tours, available in English, start at the Seisho-mon entrance. It's necessary to reserve ahead a few days in person at the office of the **Imperial Household Agency** (Kunaichō), which is on the palace grounds; you'll need to show your passport. The office is closed weekends. You can also apply for a tour online a few days in advance. To get to the palace, take the Karasuma Line of the subway in the direction of Kokusaikaikan. Get off at Imadegawa Station, and use the Number 6 Exit. Cross the street and turn right. Enter the palace through the Inui Go-mon gate on your left. ✉ *Kunaichō, Kyōto Gyoen-nai, Kamigyō-ku* ☎ *075/211–1215 information only* ⊕ *http://sankan.kunaicho.go.jp to apply for tour* 🎫 *Free* ☉ *Office weekdays 8:45–noon and 1–4. English-language tours weekdays at 10 AM and 2 PM; additional tours on 1st and 3rd Sat. of month, and every Sat. in Apr., May, Oct., and Nov.*

② Nijō-jō. Nijō Castle was the local Kyoto address for the Tokugawa shogunate. Dominating central Kyōto with its towering walls and moat, the castle is an intrusion, both politically and artistically. The man who built the castle in 1603, Ieyasu Tokugawa, the founder of the shogunate, did so to emphasize that political power had been completely removed from the emperor and that he alone determined the destiny of Japan. Accordingly, Tokugawa built and decorated his castle with such ostentation as to make the populace cower in the face of his wealth and power.

FodorśChoice ★

Ieyasu Tokugawa had risen to power through skillful political maneuvers and treachery. His military might was unassailable, and that's probably why his Kyōto castle had relatively modest exterior defenses. However, as he well knew, defense against treachery is never certain. The interior of the castle was built with that in mind. Each building had concealed rooms where bodyguards could maintain a watchful eye for potential assassins, and the corridors had built-in "nightingale" floors, so no one could walk in the building without making noise. Rooms were locked only from the inside; thus, no one from the outer rooms could gain access to the inner rooms without being admitted by someone within. The outer rooms were kept for visitors of low rank and were adorned with garish paintings that were meant to dazzle them. The inner rooms were for the important lords, whom the shōgun would impress with the refined, tasteful paintings of the Kanō school.

The opulence and grandeur of the castle were a snub to the emperor. They relegated the emperor and his palace to insignificance, and the Tokugawa family even appointed a governor to manage the emperor and the imperial family. The Tokugawa shōguns were rarely in Kyōto. Ieyasu stayed in the castle three times; the second shōgun stayed twice, including the time in 1626 when Emperor Gomizuno-o was granted an audience. After that, for the next 224 years, no Tokugawa shōgun visited Kyōto, and the castle started to fall into disrepair. Only when the Tokugawa shogunate was under pressure from a failing economy, and international pressure to open Japan to trade, did the 14th shōgun, Iemochi Tokugawa (1846–66), come to Kyōto to confer with the emperor. The emperor told the shōgun to rid Japan of foreigners, but Iemochi did not have the strength. As the shogunate's power continued to wane, the 15th and last shōgun, Yoshinobu Tokugawa (1837–1913), spent most of his time in Nijō-jō. Here he resigned, and the imperial decree was issued that abolished the shogunate after 264 years of rule. After the Meiji Restoration in 1868, Nijō-jō became the Kyōto prefectural office until 1884; during that time it suffered from acts of vandalism. Since 1939 the castle has belonged to the city of Kyōto, and considerable restoration has taken place.

You enter the castle through the impressive **Kara-mon** (Chinese Gate). Notice that you must turn right and left at sharp angles to make this entrance—designed to slow the advance of any attacker. From the Kara-mon, the carriageway leads to the **Ni-no-maru Goten** (Second Inner Palace), whose five buildings are divided into many chambers. The outer buildings were for visits by men of lowly rank, the inner ones (on higher levels) for those of higher rank. The most notable room, the **Ōhiroma** (Great Hall), is easy to recognize. In the room costumed figures reconstruct the occasion when the last Tokugawa shōgun returned the power of government to the emperor in the late 1860s. This spacious hall was where, in the early 17th century, the shōgun would sit on a raised throne to greet important visitors seated below him. The sliding screens of this room have magnificent paintings of forest scenes.

Also impressive is the garden, created by landscape designer Kobori Enshū shortly before Emperor Gomizuno-o's visit in 1626. Notice the crane-and-tortoise islands flanking the center island (called the Land of Paradise). The symbolic meaning is clear: strength and longevity. The garden was originally designed with no deciduous trees, for the shōgun did not wish to be reminded of the transitory nature of life by autumn's falling leaves. To reach the castle, take the bus or subway to Nijō-jō-mae. ⊠ *Horikawa Nishi-Iru, Nijō-dōri, Nakagyō-ku* ☎ *075/841–0096* 🎫 *¥600* ⊘ *Daily 8:45–5; last entry at 4.*

NEED A BREAK? After your visit to Nijō-jō, take a break at the traditional Japanese candy store **Mukashi Natsukashi**, on the corner of Ōmiya-dōri, three blocks west of the intersection of Horikawa-dōri and Oike-dōri. Browse the candy, grab a cold drink from a cedar bucket, and try the specialty of the house, *dorobo* (a crispy molasses-covered rice-flour snack). You can rest on the bench outside the shop while sampling your catch. ⊠ *Oshikoji-dōri, Ōmiya-dōri, Nakagyō-ku* ☎ *075/841–4464.*

Nijō Jin-ya. A short walk south of Nijō-jō is the less visited Nijō Jinya, a former merchant house built in the 17th century. The house later became an inn for traveling daimyo, or feudal lords. When Kyōto was the seat of the imperial crown, Nijō Jinya served as a safe venue for the daimyo to conduct secret meetings. The house is crammed with built-in safeguards against attack, including hidden staircases, secret passageways, and hallways too narrow to allow the wielding of a sword. Since the hour-long tour through the warren of rooms is in Japanese, we recommended hiring a translator. The staff at the **Utano Hostel** (☎ 075/462-2288) can make arrangements for a translator if you call at least three days in advance. Ask your concierge to call Nijō Jinya to make a reservation for you to tour the house. ✉ *Sembon Ōmiya-chō, Nakagyō-ku* ☎ *075/841-0972* 🖼 *¥1,000* ⊙ *Tours daily 10–4.*

★ ❻ **Nishi-Hongan-ji.** Set within a sprawling compound with courtyards and gardens, the buildings of this temple are excellent examples of Momoyama-style architecture. This was the center of the Jōdo Shinshu sect of Buddhism, founded in 1272 by the daughter of the sect's organizer, Shinran. The marvelous artifacts at this temple were confiscated by Ieyasu Tokugawa from Hideyoshi Toyotomi's Jurakudai Palace in Kyoto and from Fushimi-jō, in southern Kyōto.

Because much of what was dear to Hideyoshi Toyotomi was destroyed by the Tokugawas, it's only at Nishi-Hongan-ji that you can see the artistic works closely associated with his personal life, including the great **Kara-mon** (Chinese Gate) and the **Daisho-in,** both brought from Fushimi-jō, and the **Noh stage** from Jurakudai Palace.

Nishi-Hongan-ji is on Horikawa-dōri, a couple of blocks north of Shichijō-dori. Visits to some of the buildings are permitted four times a day by permission from the temple office. Tours of Daisho-in (in Japanese) are given occasionally throughout the year. ✉ *Shichijō-agaru, Horikawa-dōri, Shimogyō-ku* ☎ *075/371–5181* 🖼 *Free* ⊙ *Mar., Apr., Sept., and Oct., daily 5:30–5:30; May–Aug., daily 5:30* AM*–6* PM*; Nov.–Feb., daily 6–5.*

❹ **Nishijin Textile Center** (Nishijinori Kaiken). The Nishijin district, which still has some old machiya hugging the canals, hangs on to the artistic thread of traditional Japanese silk weaving. The Nishijin Textile Center hosts demonstrations of age-old weaving techniques on everything from old-fashioned hand-operated looms to computerized Jacquard looms. The center also hosts fashion shows and special exhibitions. With a reservation in advance, you can try on various different kimonos, including the 10-layer court attire. On the mezzanine you can buy kimonos and gift items such as *happi* (workmen's) coats and silk purses. The center is on the 9 and 12 bus routes, north of the Raku Art Museum, at the corner of Horikawa-dōri and Imadegawa-dōri. ✉ *Horikawa-dōri, Imadegawa-Minami-Iru, Kamigyō-ku* ☎ *075/451–9231* ⊕ *www.nishijin. or.jp* 🖼 *Free* ⊙ *Daily 9–5; closed Aug. 13–15, Dec. 29–Jan. 15.*

❸ **Raku Museum** (Raku Bijutsukan). Any serious collector of tea-ceremony artifacts is likely to have a Raku bowl in his or her collection. This museum displays more than 1,000 items, mostly tea bowls, made by members of the Raku family, whose pottery roots can be traced to the 16th century. As a potter's term in the West, *raku* refers to a low-temperature firing technique, but the word originated with this family, who made exquisite tea bowls for use in the shōgun's tea ceremonies. The museum is to the east of Horikawa-dōri, two blocks south of Imadegawa-dōri; take

MR. MONKEY WAS NO MONKEYMAN

HIDEYOSHI TOYOTOMI WAS quite a man. Though most of the initial work of unifying Japan in the late 16th century was accomplished by the warrior Nobunaga Oda (he was ambushed a year after defeating the monks on Hiei-zan), it was Hideyoshi who completed the job. Not only did he end civil strife, he also restored the arts. For a brief time (1582–98), Japan entered one of the most colorful periods of its history. How Hideyoshi achieved his feats is not exactly known. He was brought up as a farmer's son, and his nickname was Saru-san (Mr. Monkey) because he was small and ugly. According to one legend— probably started by Hideyoshi himself—he was the son of the emperor's concubine. She had been much admired by a man to whom the emperor owed a favor, so the emperor gave the concubine to him. Unknown to either of the men, she was soon pregnant with Hideyoshi. Whatever his origins (he changed his name frequently), he brought peace to Japan after decades of civil war.

Bus 9 or 12 to Ichi-jō-modōri-bashi. ⊠ *Aburakōji, Nakadachuri-agaru, Kamigyō-ku* ☎ *075/414–0304* ⊠ *¥700–¥1,000, depending on exhibition* ⊘ *Tues.–Sun. 10–4:30.*

★ **Tōfuku-ji.** In all, two dozen subtemples and the main temple compose this expansive complex, which maintains the magnificent scale of a medieval temple. Established in 1236, this temple of the Rinzai sect of Zen ranks as one of the most important in Kyōto, along with the Myōshin-ji and Daitoku-ji. The grand **San-mon** (Triple Gate) has intricate wood carvings of the historical Buddha and his disciples, attributed to the Heian-era sculptor of Buddhist images, Teicho. Arranged around the building are four contrasting gardens, both dry gravel and landscaped, including a stroll garden. Autumn, with the burnished color of the maple trees, is an especially fine time for visiting. There are at least three ways to get to Tōfuku-ji, which is southeast of Kyōto Station: Bus 208 from Kyōto Station, a JR train on the Nara Line to Tōfuku-ji Station, or a Keihan Line train to Tōfuku-ji Station. From the trains it's a 15-minute walk to the temple. Consider combining a visit here with one to Fushimi-Inari Taisha, farther south. ⊠ *Hon-machi 15-chōme, Higashiyama-ku* ☎ *075/ 561–0087* ⊕ *www.tofukuji.jp/english.html* ⊠ *¥400* ⊘ *Daily 9–4.*

❽ **Tō-ji.** Established by imperial edict in 796 and called Kyō-ō-gokoku-ji, Tō-ji was built to guard the city. It was one of the only two temples that Emperor Kammu permitted to be built in the city—he had had enough of the powerful Buddhists while in Nara. The temple was later given to the priest Kūkai (Kōbō Daishi), who founded the Shingon sect of Buddhism at the turn of the 9th century.

Fires and battles during the 16th century destroyed the temple buildings, but many were rebuilt, including in 1603 the Kon-dō (Main Hall), which blends Chinese and Japanese elements. The Kō-dō (Lecture Hall), on the other hand, has managed to survive the ravages of war since it was built in 1491. Inside this hall are 15 original statues of Buddhist gods, making up a mandala, considered masterpieces of the Heian Era (750–1150).

On the 21st of each month a market, known locally as Kōbō-san, is held. Antique kimonos, fans, and other artifacts can be found at bargain prices if you know your way around the savvy dealers. A smaller antiques market is held on the first Sunday of the month. From Kyōto Station take the Kintetsu Kyōto Line one stop to Tō-ji Station or walk 10 minutes west from the central exit of JR Kyōto Station. Bus 207 also runs past Tō-ji: either south from Gion, then west; or west from Karasuma-dōri along Shijō-dōri, then south. Get off at the Tō-ji-Higashimon-mae stop. ⊠ 1 Kujō-chōme, Minami-ku ⊠ Main buildings ¥500, grounds free ☉ Mar. 20–Sept. 19, daily 9–5; Sept. 20–Mar. 19, daily 9–4:30.

Northern Kyōto

The mountain Hiei-zan and the Ōhara region are the focal points in the northern suburbs of Kyōto. For several centuries Ōhara was a sleepy Kyōto backwater surrounded by mountains. Although it's now catching up with the times, it retains a feeling of Old Japan. Hiei-zan is a fount of Kyōto history. On its flanks the priest Saichō founded Enryaku-ji in the 8th century and with it the vital Tendai sect of Buddhism. It's an essential Kyōto sight, and walking on forested slopes among its 70-odd temples is a good reason to make the trek to Hiei-zan.

Getting Around
The sights in northern Kyōto are spread out and must be reached by a combination of train, bus, and cable car.

It's best to make this a day trip to allow for unhurried exploration of Ōhara and Hiei-zan. If you're booked on a tour to the Shūgaku-in Imperial Villa on the same day, then you'll probably only have time to explore either the sights of Ōhara (Jakkō-in, Jikkō-in, and Sanzen-in) or Hiei-zan.

What to See

Fodor'sChoice **Hiei-zan and Enryaku-ji.** From the observatory at the top of Hiei-zan a
★ serpentine mountain path leads to Enryaku-ji (a half-hour walk), which remains a vital center of the Tendai sect of Buddhism. Today Enryaku-ji has three main precincts: the Eastern Precinct, where the main building in the complex, the Kompon Chū-dō, stands; the Western Precinct; and the Yokawa district, a few miles north. At one time the complex consisted of 3,000 buildings and had its own standing army. These days, however, the monks are known as marathon monks—due to the extremely rigorous physical training that some still undergo— rather than their ancient appellation of military monks.

Enryaku-ji really began in 788. Emperor Kammu, the founding father of Kyōto, requested Priest Saichō (767–822) to establish a temple on Hiei-zan to protect the area. Hiei-zan was a natural barrier between the fledgling city and the northeastern Kin-mon (Devil's Gate), where devils were said to pass.

Unlike the older Nara sects that accepted a hierarchical society, Tendai espoused the belief that attaining Buddhahood was possible for anyone. The temple grew, and because police were not allowed on its mountain-top sanctuary, criminals flocked here, ostensibly to seek salvation. By the 11th century the temple had formed its own army to secure order on its estate. In time this army grew and became stronger than those of most other feudal lords, and the power of Enryaku-ji came to threaten Kyōto. No imperial army could manage a war without the support of Enryaku-ji, and when there was no war Enryaku-ji's armies would burn and slaughter monks of rival Buddhist sects, even destroying the Imperial Palace in 1177. Not until the 16th century was there a force strong enough to sustain an assault on the temple. With accusations that the monks had concubines and never read the sutras, Nobunaga Oda (1534–82), the general who helped unify Japan by ending more than a century of civil strife, attacked the monastery in 1571. In the battle many monks were killed, and most buildings were destroyed. Structures standing today were built in the 17th century.

The **Kompon Chū-dō** in the Eastern Precinct dates from 1642 and has a stunning copper roof in the *irimoya-zukuri* layered style. Its dark, cavernous interior conveys the mysticism for which the Tendai sect is known. Giant pillars and a coffered ceiling shelter the central altar, which is surrounded by religious images and sacred objects. Worshipers kneel on a side higher than the shadowy area containing the altars, which allows them to come face-to-face with the deity. The ornate oil lanterns that hang before the altar represent the four stages of enlightenment.

The Western Precinct is where Saichō founded his temple and where he is buried. An incense burner wafts smoke before his tomb, which lies in a small hollow. Cedar trees surround the main structures of Jōdo-in, Ninai-dō, and Shaka-dō, the oldest building in the complex. Sometimes you can hear chanting or catch sight of a monk sweeping the paths or clattering up the stone steps in wooden geta.

Take Kyōto Line Bus 16, 17, or 18 up the main highway, Route 367, to the Yase Yuenchi bus stop, next to Yase Yuen Station. You can see the entrance to the cable car on your left. It departs every 30 minutes, and you can transfer to the ropeway at Hiei for the remaining ride to the summit, where an observatory affords panoramic views of the mountains and of Biwa-ko. *Enryaku-ji ⊠ 4220 Sakamoto-hon-machi, Ōtsu-shi ⊕ www.hieizan.or.jp ⊠ Enryaku-ji ¥800, Hiei-zan cable car ¥530, ropeway ¥310 ⊙ Enryaku-ji Mar.–Nov., daily 8:30–4:30; Dec.–Feb., daily 9–4. Hiei-zan ropeway and cable car Apr.–Sept., daily 9–6; Oct.–Mar., daily 9–5; mid-July–late Aug., observatory stays open until 9 and the last cable car run is at 9:20 PM.*

Jakkō-in. In April 1185, after a two-year battle, the Taira clan met its end in a naval battle against the Minamoto clan. The Minamotos slaughtered the Tairas, turning the Seto Nai-kai (Inland Sea) red with Taira blood. Seeing that all was lost, the Taira women drowned themselves, taking with them the eight-year-old emperor Antoku. His mother, the beautiful, 29-year-old Kenreimon-in, leaped into the sea, but Minamoto soldiers snagged her hair with a grappling hook and hauled her back on board their ship. She was the sole surviving member of the Taira clan.

Taken back to Kyōto, Kenreimon-in shaved her head and became a nun. First she had a small hut at Chōraku-ji in eastern Kyōto; when that collapsed in an earthquake she was accepted at Jakkō-in. She lived in solitude in a 10-foot-square cell made of brushwood and thatch for 27 years, until her death ended the Taira line. You may need to ask for directions to her mausoleum, which is higher up the hill, away from the throng of visitors and along the path by the side of the temple. When Kenreimon-in came to Jakkō-in it was far removed from Kyōto. Now Kyōto's sprawl reaches this far and beyond, but the temple, hidden in trees, is still a place of solitude and a sanctuary for nuns. The main hall burned down in 1999 and has since been reconstructed, providing a contrast with the aged gate. From Kyōto Station take Kyōto Line Bus 17 or 18 for a 90-minute ride and get out at the Ōhara bus stop; the fare is ¥480. Walk 20 minutes or so along the road leading to the northwest. ⊠ *Sakyō-ku* 🖾 *¥500* 🕙 *Mar.–Nov., daily 9–5; Dec.–Feb., daily 9–4:30.*

★ **Jikkō-in.** At this small, little-frequented temple you can sit, relax, and have a taste of the powdered matcha of the tea ceremony. To enter, ring the gong on the outside of the gate and then wander through the carefully cultivated garden, with its natural waterfall, central pond, and tiny teahouse framed against the hills. In November the *fudan zakura* are in bloom, which means you can enjoy the novelty of cherry blossoms at the same time as the changing maple leaves. Inside the temple, the lintel holds 36 portraits of Chinese poets by the Kanō school. Take Kyōto Line Bus 17 or 18 for 90 minutes from Kyōto Station; the fare is ¥580. From the Ōhara bus stop, walk northeast for about seven minutes along the signposted road. Jikkō-in is 200 yards from Sanzen-in. ⊠ *Sakyō-ku* 🖾 *¥500* 🕙 *Daily 9–5.*

Kamigamo Jinja. Kamigamo, built along with its sister shrine Shimogamo Jinja in the 8th century by the Kamo family, has always been associated with Kamo Wakeikazuchi, a god of thunder, rain, and fertility. Now the shrine is famous for its Aoi (Hollyhock) Festival, which started in the 6th century when people thought that the Kamigamo deities were angry at being neglected. Held every May 15, the festival consists of 500 people wearing Heian-period costumes riding on horseback or in ox-drawn carriages from the Imperial Palace to Shimogamo Jinja (farther south on the Kamo-gawa) and then to Kamigamo. If you're in town for the festival, arrive at the Imperial Palace park before the festival starts for good photo opportunities. In the courtyard of the temple are two great cones of sand, *tate-zuna*, known as the twin peaks of heaven; this area is sacred for deities to descend to earth through them. The canal street that leads up to the shrine has many machiya, and some of these elongated town houses are more than 400 years old. To get to the shrine, take Bus 9 north from Kyōto Station or from a stop on Horikawa-dōri. Or take the subway north to Kitayama Station, from which the shrine is 20 minutes on foot northwest. ⊠ *Motoyama, Kamigamo, Sakyō-ku* 🖾 *Free* 🕙 *Daily 9–4:30.*

Miho Museum (Miho Bijutsukan). Built in and around a mountaintop and thoughtfully landscaped—its wooded setting in the hills of Shigariki north of Kyōto is part of the experience—the I. M. Pei–designed Miho Museum houses the remarkable Shumei-family collection of traditional Japanese art and Asian and Western antiquities. An Egyptian falcon-headed deity, a Roman fresco, a Chinese tea bowl, and a Japanese Bosatsu (Buddha) are among the superb pieces here. If the current exhibition sparks your interest, it may be worth the journey. An on-site restaurant sells *bentō* (boxed meals) with organic ingredients (it's best to call and make a reservation), and a tearoom serves Japanese and Western beverages and desserts. From Kyōto Station ride the JR Tōkaidō Line for 15 minutes to Ishiyama Station; from there the bus to the museum takes 50 minutes. Buses to Miho, ¥800 one-way, run on the hour from 9:10 AM to 1:10 AM and return hourly from 11 AM to 6 PM (with seasonal variations). ⊠ *300 Momodani, Shiga-ken, Shigariki* ☎ *0748/ 82–3411* ⊕ *www.miho.jp* ⌨ *¥1,000* ☉ *Mid-Mar.–mid-June and Sept.–mid-Dec., Tues.–Sun. 10–5; last entry at 4.*

★ **Sanzen-in.** This small temple of the Tendai sect was founded by the renowned priest Dengyō-Daishi (767–822). The temple is a *monzeki,* meaning the abbot has traditionally been of royal blood. The Hon-dō (Main Hall) was built by Priest Eshin (942–1017), who probably carved the temple's Amida Buddha. The Buddha is flanked by two seated attendants: the goddess of wisdom, Daiseishi, to the right and the goddess of compassion, Kannon, to the left. Unusual for a Buddhist temple, Sanzen-in faces east, not south. Note its ceiling, on which a painting depicts the descent of Amida, accompanied by 25 bodhisattvas, to welcome the believer.

Full of maple trees and moss, the gardens are serene in any season. In autumn the colors are magnificent, and the approach to the temple up a gentle slope—with the river on one side and small shops on the other—enhances the anticipation for the burnt-gold trees guarding the old, weathered temple. Snow cover in winter is also magical. Take Kyōto Line Bus 17 or 18 north for 90 minutes from Kyōto Station to Ōhara. From the Ōhara bus station walk northeast for about seven minutes along the signposted road. ⊠ *Raigōin-chō, Ōhara, Sakyō-ku* ⌨ *¥600* ☉ *Mar.–Nov., daily 8:30–4:30; Dec.–Feb., daily 8:30–4.*

Shūgaku-in Imperial Villa (Shūgaku-in Rikyū). Three palaces make up this villa complex with pleasant grounds that offer a view of northern Kyōto. The Upper and Lower villas were built in the 17th century by the Tokugawa family to entertain the emperor; the Upper Villa provides nice views of northern Kyōto. The Middle Villa was added later as a palace home for Princess Bunke, daughter of Emperor Go-mizunoo. The villa was transformed into a temple when Princess Bunke decided that a nun's life was her calling. Comparing the villas to the ostentatious might of Ieyasu Tokugawa's Nijō-jō on the other end of town illustrates how vastly the pure aesthetics of the imperial style differed from the shōgun's tastes.

Special permission is required to visit the villa, a few days in advance, from the **Imperial Household Agency** (⊠ Kunaichō, Kyōto Gyoen-nai,

Kamigyō-ku ☎ 075/211–1215 ⊕ http://sankan.kunaicho.go.jp). From Hiei-zan take the Eizan Railway from Yase Yuen Station to Shūgaku-in Station. The villa is a 15-minute walk from there. From downtown Kyōto the trip takes an hour on Bus 5 from Kyōto Station. Or ride 20 minutes north on a Keifuku Eizan Line train from the Demachi-Yanagi terminus, which is northeast of the intersection of Imadegawa-dōri and the Kamo-gawa. ✉ *Yabusoe Shūgaku-in, Sakyō-ku* 🎟 *Free* ⊙ *Tours, in Japanese only, weekdays at 9, 10, 11, 1:30, and 3; Sat. tours on 1st and 3rd Sat. of month; every Sat. Apr., May, Oct., and Nov.*

WHERE TO EAT

If you find yourself with an unintelligible menu, ask for the *o-makase*, or chef's recommendation; you can specify your budget in some instances. The custom of dining early, from 6 PM until 8 PM, still endures in very traditional restaurants, but many restaurants are open until 10 PM or 11 PM. If possible, let the hotel staff make reservations for you where necessary. For more formal restaurants try to book at least two days in advance; bookings are often not accepted for the following day if called in after 4 PM. Keep in mind that not all restaurants accept credit cards. For more on Japanese cuisine, *see* Understanding Japan.

Eastern Kyōto

Japanese

$$$$ ✕ **Kikunoi.** At this grand dame of *Kyōkaiseki ryōri*, third-generation chef-
Fodor'sChoice owner Yoshihiro Murata excels at expressing the mood and flavors of
★ the seasons. Once seated in a private dining room, you are brought a small *sakizuke* (appetizer), the first of up to 14 courses, each exquisitely presented and delicious, yet always with an underlying robustness. The most difficult dishes to make are often the most simple; Murata does not shy away from these and even generously shares his years of perfecting and innovating techniques on a monthly television program. In order to entice all the senses, sometimes he will even light a few pine needles on the dish to release an aroma. This restaurant is on the northern edge of Kōdai-ji. Evening courses start at ¥15,500, and lunch bentōs start at ¥4,200. ✉ *Makuzugahara, Maruyama, Gion, Higashiyama* ☎ *075/561–0015* ⊕ *www.kikunoi.jp/honten.htm* ⌕ *Reservations essential* ☰ *AE, DC, MC, V* ⊙ *No lunch Mon.*

$$$$ ✕ **Kikusui.** Near Nanzen-ji temple, Kikusui serves up traditional kaiseki ryōri and hot-pot sets with a view of an elegant Japanese garden. The colors of Nanzen-ji-michi are beautiful in the spring, when a large, umbrella-like cherry tree spreads a canopy of pink-and-white blossoms overhead. Autumn, when maples explode in fiery reds and oranges, is also lovely. You can sample the subtle flavors and beautiful colors of Kyōto's traditional cuisine by ordering the *kyō-no-aji* (mini kaiseki) at lunchtime for a reasonable ¥5,000. ✉ *31 Fukui-chō, Nanzen-ji, Sakyō-ku* ☎ *075/771–4101* ⌕ *Reservations essential* 🗍 *Jacket and tie* ☰ *AE, DC, V.*

$$$$ ✕ **Minokō.** The specialty at this former villa on the eastern fringe of Gion is *cha-kaiseki* cuisine—elegant multicourse meals that evoke the rituals

On the Menu

CLOSE UP

THE EXPERIENCE NOT TO MISS in Kyōto is *kaiseki ryōri*, the elegant full-course meal that was originally intended to be served with the tea ceremony and later served with sake at Edo-era merchant parties. All the senses are engaged: the scent and flavor of the freshest ingredients at the peak of season; the visual delight of a continuous procession of porcelain dishes and lacquered bowls, gracefully adorned with an appropriately shaped slice of fish or vegetable; the textures of foods unknown and exotic; the sound of water in a stone basin outside in the garden. Kaiseki ryōri is often costly yet always unforgettable.

For an initiation or a reasonably priced sample, the *kaiseki bentō* (box lunch) served by many *ryōtei* (high-class Japanese restaurants) is a good place to start. Box lunches are so popular in Kyōto that restaurants compete to make their bentō unique, exquisite, and delicious.

Compared with the style of cooking elsewhere in Japan, *Kyōto-ryōri* (Kyōto cuisine) is lighter and more delicate, stressing the natural flavor of ingredients over enhancement with heavy sauces and broths. *Obanzai* (Kyōto home cooking) is served at many restaurants at reasonable cost. The freshness and quality of the ingredients is paramount, and chefs carefully handpick only the best. *Sōsaku ryōri* (creative cuisine) is becoming popular as chefs find inspiration in other cultures while retaining light and subtle flavors.

Kyōto is also the home of *shōjin ryōri*, the Zen vegetarian-style cooking best sampled on the grounds of one of the city's Zen temples, such as Tenryū-ji in Arashiyama. Local delicacies like *fu* (glutinous wheat cakes) and *yuba* (soy-milk skimmings) have found their way into the mainstream of Kyōto ryōri, but were originally devised to provide protein in the traditional Buddhist diet.

---

of formal tea ceremonies. Upon arriving, you'll be led by Mrs. Yoshida, the gracious hostess, to a quiet room that overlooks a tea garden with stone lanterns and a trickling stream. Meanwhile, Mr. Yoshida oversees every detail of your meal. Not only are the secrets for creating subtle flavors passed down by kaiseki's master chefs but also the knowledge of the harvest and life cycles of plants and animals. Eggs are not used in summer, as it is believed this would be strenuous for the hens—an example of Minokō's approach to harmonious living. An informal box lunch called *chabako-bentō* is served for ¥6,000; it includes frothy matcha and a sweet. One of the curious turtles may leave the pond and edge closer to watch you dine. ⊠ *480 Kiyoi-chō, Shimogowara-dōri, Gion, Higashiyama-ku* ☎ *075/561–0328* ⚐ *Reservations essential* 🏛 *Jacket and tie* ▤ *DC, MC, V* ⊗ *Closed 2nd and 4th Wed. of each month.*

$$$$ ✕ **Tōzentei.** Halfway down Shinmonzen street (famous for antique stores) two asymmetrical potted plants frame the white walls and grey latticed windows of this intimate counter restaurant, in business since 2006. No imported flavors are used in the lunch course menus (starting at ¥3,150) of *kappō ryōri*, or Japanese traditional cuisine. That is not to say you won't be surprised, as *tōzen*, or enrapture, in the name implies. ✉ *Kita-ku* ☎ *075/711–5136* ⚐ *Reservations essential* 🞸 *AE, DC, MC, V* ☉ *No lunch Mon.*

$$$$ ✕ **Yugenbori**. North of Shijō-dōri in the heart of Kyōto's still-thriving

Fodor's Choice geisha district, this restaurant is in a teahouse a few steps down a cob-

★ bled path from the romantic Shira-kawa, a small tributary of the Kamogawa. The o-makase meal is an elegant sampler of Kyōto's finest kaiseki cuisine, with local delicacies presented on handmade ceramics. The shabu-shabu (thinly sliced beef, dipped briefly into hot stock) and *suppon* (turtle dishes) are excellent. Don't miss the *hōba* miso—bean paste with *kinoko* mushrooms and green onions, which are wrapped in a giant oak leaf and grilled at your table—on the à la carte menu. A cheaper option is the excellent box lunch for ¥2,500. ✉ *Sueyoshi-chō, Kiridoshikado, Gion, Higashiyama-ku* ☎ *075/551–3331* 🞸 *AE, DC, V.*

★ **$$$–$$$$** ✕ **Kyōto Gion Oishimbo**. In the hub of old Gion is a surprisingly reasonable restaurant where you can leisurely sample *obanzai*, classic home-style Kyōto cooking. Organic shiitake mushrooms star in many of the dishes, which range from tofu gluten steaks to duck carpaccio. Trust the chef and order one of the set menus like the Nattoku course for ¥3,700; these consist of a range of dishes from soup and sashimi to simmered, grilled, and salad dishes complemented by a glass of Seishū Oishinbo, the raw house sake. Tatami-matted rooms on the first floor overlook a small *tsuboniwa* (courtyard garden). ✉ *Hanamikōji-sagaru, Futatsujime Higashi-iru, Higashiyama-ku* ☎ *075/532–2285* ⚐ *Reservations essential* 🜲 *Jacket required* 🞸 *AE, D, DC, MC, V.*

$$$–$$$$ ✕ **Nontaro**. This sushi restaurant in the heart of the geisha district has been serving visitors to Gion for more than 40 years. You can order sushi à la carte or choose one of the o-makase (chef's choice) selections. If you're in the mood for something different, try the *kokesushi*—a giant sushi roll. ✉ *Hanamikō-ji Shijō-agaru, Higashiyama-ku* ☎ *075/561–3189* ⚐ *Reservations essential* 🞸 *AE, DC, MC, V* ☉ *Closed Sun.*

★ **$$$–$$$$** ✕ **Omen**. Just south of Ginkaku-ji, this is one of the best places to stop for an inexpensive home-style lunch before proceeding down the old canal—the walkway beneath the cherry trees known as the Path of Philosophy—on the way to Nanzen-ji. Omen is also the name of the house specialty: thick white noodles brought to your table in a basket with a bowl of hot broth and a platter of seasonal, organic vegetables, which are added to the broth a little at a time and sprinkled with roasted sesame seeds. Another famed Kyōto dish, *saba* (salted mackerel) sushi is also served. The monthly set menu costs ¥2,700. Like the food, the restaurant is country style, with a choice of counter stools, tables and chairs, or tatami mats. The waiters dress in happi coats and headbands; the atmosphere is lively and comfortable. Reservations are accepted only on weekdays. ✉ *74 Ishi-bashi-chō, Jōdo-ji, Sakyō-ku* ☎ *075/771–8994* 🞸 *No credit cards* ☉ *Closed Thurs.*

★ **$$** ✕ **Café Peace**. Delicious all-vegetarian cuisine with soy-based dishes is the main draw here. Choose between several kinds of homemade soup, spring rolls, noodle dishes, and curries. Meat lovers have sworn that the sweet-and-sour "pork" tastes like the real thing. The staff is hip, environmentally aware, and anti–animal testing. The restaurant has a great

5

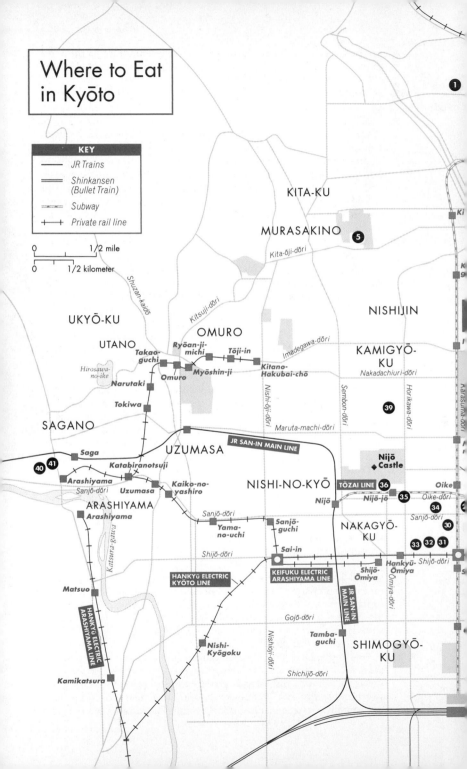

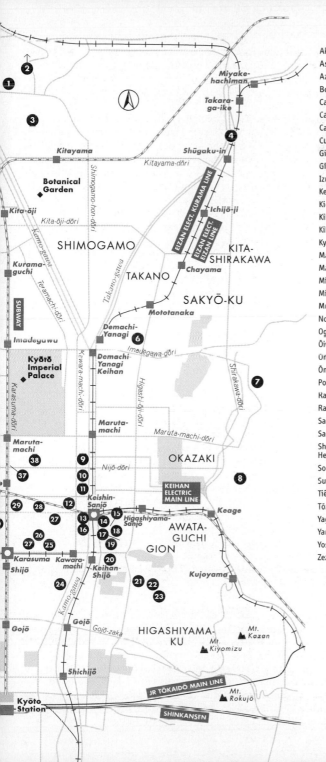

view of the mountains from its third-floor vantage point on the corner of Higashioji and Imadegawa and provides an event space on the fourth floor with regular yoga classes. ✉ *3F Domus Hyakumanben Bldg., Higashiōji dōri, Sakyō-ku* ☎ *075/707–6856* ⊕ *www.cafepeace.com* ⊟ *No credit cards* ⊗ *Closed Sun.*

$–$$ ✕ **Gion Kappa Nawate.** This late-night *robatayaki* (charcoal grill) izakaya, or casual bar-restaurant, can get a little rowdy. It's two blocks north of Shijō on Nawate street in the heart of Gion, and you don't need a reservation to find a seat at the long counter if there are no tables. Grilled chicken, meat (sometimes even duck), seafood, and other dishes, including vegetables and salads, are available cheaply. In cooler months try the simmered *oden* (hot pot). ✉ *Sueyoshi-cho, Nawate-dōri, Shijō agaru, Higashiyama-ku* ☎ *075/531–4048* ⊗ *No lunch.*

★ ¢ ✕ **Rakushō.** Flowering plum trees, azaleas, irises, camellias, and maple trees take seasonal turns adding color to this tea shop in a former villa. En route from Maruyama Kōen to Kiyomizu-dera, Rakushō is a pleasant place to enjoy a bowl of frothy matcha or freshly brewed coffee while gazing over the garden. You can order *warabi mochi*, rice-flour dumplings with the consistency of Jell-O, rolled in sweetened soybean powder. Rakushō closes at 6 PM. ✉ *Kōdai-ji Kitamon-mae-dōri, Washio-chō, Higashiyama-ku* ☎ *075/561–6892* ✍ *Reservations not accepted* ⊟ *No credit cards* ⊗ *Closed 4 days a month; call ahead.*

Western Kyōto

Japanese

★ $$$$ ✕ **Sagano.** Amid Arashiyama's lush, green bamboo forests, this quiet retreat serves one of the finest meals of *yudōfu* (cubes of bean curd simmered in broth) in Kyōto. The meal, which is the same for lunch and dinner, includes such local delicacies as tempura and *aburage* (deep-fried tofu) with black sesame seeds and seasonally changing dishes. At the sunken counter, waitresses in kimonos prepare the meal in front of you—with a backdrop of antique wood-block prints on folding screens—or you can walk through the garden to private, Japanese-style rooms in the back. If weather permits, you can dine on low tables in the courtyard garden beneath towering bamboo. Reservations are a good idea year-round, and particularly during fall foliage season, when the maple trees of Arashiyama are stunning. Arrive before 5:30 for dinner in the tatami rooms, before 6:30 for counter service. ✉ *45 Susuki-no-bamba-chō, Saga, Tenryū-ji, Ukyō-ku* ☎ *075/861–0277* ⊟ *No credit cards.*

Spanish

$$$–$$$$ ✕ **Bodegon.** A white-walled, tile-floored, wrought-iron, and blown-glass Spanish restaurant in Arashiyama brings paella to a neighborhood famous for its tofu. Bodegon sits unobtrusively along the main street that runs through the center of this scenic district, combining Spanish fare and wine with Kyōto hospitality. A wildly popular tourist area in daylight, Arashiyama rolls up its sidewalks after dark, and Bodegon is a good place to dine after sightseeing. ✉ *1 Susuki-no-bamba-chō, Saga, Tenryū-ji, Ukyō-ku* ☎ *075/872–9652* ⊟ *MC, V* ⊗ *Closed Thurs.*

Central Kyōto

Cafés

☼ $–$$ ✕ **Ask a Giraffe.** Shin Pu Kan is a three-story brick shopping center encircling a courtyard with a live performance stage. On the first floor, attached to George, an Italian interior goods shop, is the eclectic café Ask a Giraffe. Don't let the bright yellow interior divert you from the subtle flavors; here even a simple hamburger becomes a treat. The seasonal culinary updates are usually the best choices—this could mean grilled mackerel and lightly fried rice with greens or a winter stew. There are always sandwiches, vegetable salads, and pastas. Cakes are sweet infusions of goodness, and the coffee is very palatable. It's on Karasuma-dōri, two blocks down from Oike. ✉ *Shin Pu Kan, 1st fl., Karasuma-dōri, South of Anekōji-dōri.* ☎ *075/257–8028* ⚏ *Reservations accepted* ▭ *AE, DC, MC, V.*

$–$$ ✕ **Café bibliotic HELLO!.** The banana trees that mask this airy, two-story, renovated-town-house café are visible from several blocks away. There are three lunch options, which change regularly, from steak sandwiches to rice dishes and curries. Good coffee and a range of enticing drinks like the Moroccan chai or the seasonal strawberry, mint, and ginger smoothie complement the fresh desserts; these desserts vary with the season and the chef's whims, but tend to be drenched in fresh fruit, like the French toast with mango and coconut cream. And you can browse a wall of books. If you are exploring Teramachi-dōri north of Oike, this is a few blocks west. ✉ *Nijō-dōri, Yanaginobana Higashi iru, Nakagyō-ku* ☎ *075/231–8625* ▭ *No credit cards.*

¢–$$ ✕ **Café Sarasa.** In an area where trendy stores that recycle old kimonos stand shoulder to shoulder with traditional art supply shops, there's a lovely old café where you can sip café au lait. The beams and mud walls of this Edo-era house lend an earthy charm. Café Sarasa serves light meals—try the Okinawa-style fried rice with vegetable and tofu, or the Vietnamese-style pancakes. It's three blocks west of Teramachi-dōri and a little south of Sanjō. Look for a tiny bicycle shop and head up the stairs to the left of it. ✉ *2F Wood-Inn, 534 Asakuchi-chō, Tominokōji-dōri, Sanjō agaru, Nakagyō-ku* ☎ *075/212–2310* ▭ *No credit cards.*

Chinese

$$$$ ✕ **Zezekan Pocchiri.** This former Taisho-era warehouse with antique glass windows and an inner courtyard garden is a setting that befits the excellent Beijing-style dishes that take inspiration from Zen Buddhist cuisine. Evening courses from ¥5,200 start with five types of appetizers, including *gyōza* or pan-fried dumplings (very popular in Japan) followed by dishes like Szechuan-style (spicy) stir-fried tofu, a chicken stew, or lightly flavored sea bream. The ¥11,000 course is literally fit for an emperor—its wellspring being imperial-court cuisine; Peking Duck is followed by delicacies like spiny lobster stew and crab in winter. For lunch try the ¥4,000 Beijing Honzen course, including dim sum and a meat and fish dish. The bar (open until 11 PM) in the old *kura*, or storehouse, at back stocks a good selection of Chinese aperitifs and European wines, but there is a table charge. Look for the wall mural with many *pocchiri*, the sash clasp used by maiko to secure their *obis* (kimono sashes). ✉ *Nishikikōji-dōri,*

Muromachi-Nishi-iru, Tenjinyamacho 283-2 ☎ *075/257–5766* ⚞ *Reservations essential* 🕴 *Jacket and tie* ▤ *AE, DC, MC V.*

French

★ $$$$ ✗ **Ogawa.** The best in Kyōto-style nouvelle cuisine is served in this intimate spot across from the Takase-gawa canal. Finding a seat at the counter or the upstairs dining room is as difficult as getting tickets for opening night at the opera—but the food is worth the wait. With particularly Japanese sensitivity to using only the best ingredients at the peak of the season, proprietor Ogawa never bores you by serving the same meal twice. *Ayu*, a popular local river fish, is served in summer, salmon in fall, crab in winter, shrimp in spring. The marvelous desserts might include fresh papaya sherbet or mango mousse with mint sauce. The set meals are spectacular, but you can also opt for an hors d'oeuvres selection of three dishes, such as oyster gratin, crab-and-scallop stew, and *matsutake* (wild mushroom) tempura. ⊠ *Kiya-machi Oike-agaru Higashi-Iru, Nakagyō-ku* ☎ *075/256–2203* ⊕ *http://r-ogawa. com* ⚞ *Reservations essential* 🕴 *Jacket and tie* ▤ *AE, DC, MC, V* ☉ *Closed Tues.*

Indian

$–$$$$ ✗ **Kerala.** Using freshly imported spices, the Indian chefs cook up 20 different curries and dishes, including south-Indian-style tandoori chicken. This second-story restaurant opposite the Royal Hotel has a blend of modern and traditional Indian furnishings, and the reasonably priced evening set meals (on average ¥2,700) have a tandoori dish and a curry choice with the usual accoutrements. The vegetarian-friendly à la carte menu has some tasty choices like the *kulcha* Kerala bread stuffed with egg and almond. ⊠ *Ledic Bldg. 2F, Kawaramachi-dōri, Sanjō agaru, Nishi-gawa* ☎ *075/251–0141/2* ▤ *AE, DC, MC, V.*

Italian

★ $$$$ ✗ **Cucina Il Viale.** The signature dish is handmade pasta served with a scarlet tomato sauce that's bound to make the most travel-weary sourpuss smile. Rounding out the menu are antipasti—such as local, organic, and carefully picked Kyōto vegetables served with fine Italian ham—and main dishes like ultratender pork steak or grilled fish in balsamic vinegar with a hint of orange. Espresso and decadent desserts are also served; the litchi mousse alone is worth the visit. Lunch courses start from ¥1,575 and dinner courses from ¥3,990. ⊠ *Horikawa, Oike Nishi-iru, Nakagyō-ku* ☎ *075/812–2366* ⚞ *Reservations essential* ▤ *AE, V* ☉ *Closed Mon. No lunch Tues.*

Japanese

$$$$ ✗ **Giro Giro Hitoshina.** Below Shijō-dōri along the Takase-gawa canal the neon signage is abruptly replaced by discreet wooden doors with lanterns. Farther on, south of Matsubara Bridge and wedged between houses, is Giro Giro Hitoshina, its large canal-side window glowing. A square counter that surrounds the chefs fills the ground floor, but the upstairs has tables. The monthly changing 10-dish course is a showcase of sōsaku ryōri, the creative reinvention of traditional cuisine currently popular. À la nouvelle cuisine, tiny morsels are daubed onto an array of plates:

a few slender Spanish *aji* (horse mackerel) glide in a clear soup, followed by monkfish liver grilled on a leaf with miso; a mille-feuille tartlet encloses a scrumptious morsel of crab after beef sashimi. Drinks flow as fast as the waiters endlessly traversing between the two floors. ⊠ 420-7 *Nanba-chō, Nishi Kiya-machi-dōri, Higashigawa, Matsubarashita, Shimogyō-ku* ☎ 075/343–7070 ⚐ *Reservations essential* ⊟ AE, DC, MC, V ⊘ *Closed last Mon. of each month. No lunch.*

$$$$
Fodor'sChoice
★
✕ **Mankamerō.** Established in 1716, Mankamerō is the only restaurant in Kyōto that offers formal yusoku ryōri, the type of cuisine once served to members of the imperial court. A specially appointed—and ceremonially dressed—chef prepares the food using utensils made only for this type of cuisine. A dramatic dish is the "dismembered" fish; the chef elaborately arranges each part of the fish, which is then served to you on a series of pedestal trays. Prices are also quite elaborate—up to ¥30,000 per person for the full yusoku ryōri repertoire—though a wonderful *takekago* bentō (lunch of cubes of sashimi on ice, a clear soup, small bamboo boxes with steamed dishes, and a basket of seasonal delights) is within reach of wealthy commoners at ¥6,350. Mankamerō is on the west side of Inokuma-dōri north of Demizu-dōri. Look for the blue-tile roof above the entrance with a white noren with a fish drawn in the center. It closes at 8 PM. ⊠ *Inokuma-dōri, Demizu-agaru, Kamigyō-ku* ☎ 075/441–5020 ⚐ *Reservations essential* 🏛 *Jacket and tie* ⊟ AE, DC, MC, V ⊘ *Closed once a month; call ahead.*

★ $$$$
✕ **Mishima-tei.** This is the top choice for sukiyaki (stir-fried beef, vegetables, and noodles) in Kyōto. In the heart of the downtown shopping district, Kyōto housewives line up to pay premium prices for Mishima-tei's high-quality beef, sold by the kilogram over the counter at the meat shop downstairs. Mishima-tei was established in 1904, and climbing the staircase of this traditional wood-frame restaurant with its turn-of-the-20th-century atmosphere is like journeying into the past. Down the long dark corridors with polished wood floors, kimono-clad servers run about with trays of beef and refills of sake to dozens of private tatami-mat rooms where patrons sit around a sunken hearth or *hori-kotatsu*. Ask for a room that faces the central courtyard garden for the best view. Plan on dining by 7, as the service—and the preparation of your food—can be rushed toward the end of the evening. ⊠ *Tera-machi, Sanjō-sagaru, Higashi-Iru, Nakagyō-ku* ☎ 075/221–0003 ⚐ *Reservations essential* ⊟ AE, DC, MC, V ⊘ *Closed Wed.*

$$$$
✕ **Mukadeya.** Obanzai—Kyōto home-style cooking—is the specialty of this sophisticated, refurbished old villa. Dishes like bonito sashimi and pumpkin with gingery ground chicken are artfully laid out on lacquer trays. Lunch bentō start at ¥3,150, and the dinner course of ¥5,775 has 12 different dishes. Unlike many traditional houses where winding corridors lead to small interior rooms, here the open-plan renovation involves a courtyard garden and dark stone-tile *genkan* (foyer) that add expansiveness. You sit on legless chairs (a back and a seat) placed on tatami around low tables. In the evening a 10% service charge is added to the bill. ⊠ *381 Mukadeya-chō, Shinmachi-dōri, Nishiki-agaru, Nakagyō-ku* ☎ 075/256–9393 ⚐ *Reservations essential* 🏛 *Jacket and tie* ⊟ AE, MC, V ⊘ *Closed Wed.*

5

$$$$ ✕ **Ōmi.** The Ebisugawa-tei annex to the Hotel Fujita Kyōto is a restored Meiji-era villa that also houses this excellent steak restaurant. The specialty is the celebrated beer-fed and hand-massaged Ōmi beef. You'll be ushered through corridors to the dining room and seated around a *horikotatsu*, a recessed grill, with counter seating in a pristine tatami room. There's also an excellent seafood platter to choose from and a good lunch set menu on weekends. After your meal you can stop in at the basement bar of the Hotel Fujita for a drink beside the beautiful duck pond and waterfall. ✉ *Hotel Fujita Kyōto, Nijō-dōri, Kiya-machi Kado, Nakagyō-ku* ☎ *075/222–1511* ⌖ *Reservations essential* 🔺 *Jacket and tie* ▭ *AE, DC, MC, V* ⊘ *No lunch weekdays.*

$$$$ ✕ **Suishin.** Not far south of the Kaburenjo theater on the riverside street, a front of dark latticed wood conceals a vegetable lover's utopia. The dining area is deliberately raised so that diners sitting on the cushions are at eye level with the busy chefs in the open kitchen. Along one side are horikotatsu tables with a hole beneath that you can let your feet dangle in, and similar seating at the long bar—it makes tatami-matted dining possible without stiff knees. For a culinary journey through all the essential Kyōto dishes, opt for the Fushimi set at ¥4,000 or the slightly more expensive Goshō or "Imperial" course. Locally grown, organic vegetables are cooked lightly and combined with the freshest fish and slivers of meat. The flavors are so light they seem to float in your mouth. Trays are smoothly served and removed by the hostess in a kimono. Look for a black-and-white building on the west side with a lantern above the door. ✉ *Zaimoku-chō 181, Ponto-chō, Nakagyō-ku* ☎ *075/221–8596* ▭ *AE, DC, MC, V.*

$$$$ ✕ **Yoshikawa.** Adjacent to the well-reputed inn of the same name, this restaurant serves full-course kaiseki ryōri dinners (¥12,000) that include a lavish selection of sashimi, soup, rice, vegetables, baked fish, and tempura, the specialty of the house. Or you can try the tempura dinners (¥6,000), which include 13 different pieces of fish, meat, and vegetable tempura, plus rice and soup. Dinner is served in a tatami room. A better value is the ¥2,000 lunch served at the counter, where you can watch the chef fry up your meal. Tempura should be light and crisp—best right from the pot—and for this Yoshikawa is famous. English is spoken, and last orders are taken by 8:30. ✉ *Tomino-kōji, Oike-sagaru, Nakagyō-ku* ☎ *075/221–5544 or 075/221–0052* ⌖ *Reservations essential* 🔺 *Jacket and tie* ▭ *AE, DC, MC, V* ⊘ *Closed Sun.*

$$$–$$$$ ✕ **Manzaratei Nishiki.** The chef's talent for superbly adding elements of other cultures, namely Korean, French, and Italian, to Japanese traditional dishes has made this restaurant in a renovated two-story machiya very popular. Depending on the season, the ample menu has crab with vinegared miso, local (free-range) fried chicken and sausage, grilled fillet of beef, Korean-style pork, spring rolls with a *ponzu* (citrus) dressing, steamed rice with greens and sea bream, and a choice of salads. Since it's all in Japanese, opt for one of the generous multicourse menus, starting at ¥3,500. The staff will make you comfortable, and with counter space on both floors, those dining alone should feel at home, too. In the back is a small warehouse-turned-dining-room for groups, and in summer you can dine alfresco on the tiny terrace. It's one block north of

Shijō and three buildings west of Karasuma on the north side of the street. ✉ *Uradeyama chō 317, Nishikikōji, Nishi iri, Nakagyō-ku* ☎ *075/ 257–5748* ♨ *Reservations accepted* ▭ *AE, DC, MC, V* ☯ *No lunch.*

🕒 **$$$–$$$$** ✕ **Ōiwa.** Ōiwa, which is at the head of the Takase-gawa canal, serves *kushikatsu*—skewered meats and vegetables battered, deep-fried, and then dipped in a variety of sauces. The building is actually a kura, or warehouse. Kuras were traditionally separate from the main house and made of thicker walls covered in white plaster to protect valuables from fire. This particular kura once belonged to a kimono merchant family, and it's one of the first in Kyōto to have been turned into a restaurant. The Japanese chef trained in one of the finest French restaurants in Tōkyō, and his version of kushikatsu (usually considered a working man's snack with beer) has an unpretentious elegance. Order by the skewer or ask for the o-makase set course. There is a set menu for small children that includes five skewers for ¥840 ✉ *Kiya-machi-dōri, Nijō-sagaru, Nakagyō-ku* ☎ *075/231–7667* ⊕ *www.kushi-oiwa.co.jp* ▭ *No credit cards* ☯ *No lunch Wed. and weekends. Closed irregularly; call ahead.*

★ **$$$–$$$$** ✕ **Omen.** This branch of the famed noodle shop near Ginkaku-ji (*see* Eastern Kyōto) is convenient to the downtown shopping area—a perfect place to pop in for a delicious lunch. ✉ *Gokō-machi Shijō Agaru, Nakagyō-ku* ☎ *075/255–2125* ▭ *No credit cards* ☯ *Closed Thurs.*

$$$–$$$$ ✕ **Pontocho Rōbin.** For summer dining, the perfect location is an outdoor *yuka*, or dining platform, overlooking the river. The former teahouses on this quaint street have been replaced by exclusive restaurants, mostly serving expensive course menus. In a particularly well-restored two-story machiya, Rōbin has an à la carte menu and is open late. The "Rō" in the name is a bow to the unique 20th-century potter and artist Rōsanjin Kitaōji. In autumn the delicious *nabe* course is a pot of simmering stock with fresh vegetables, fish, and meat. Other course menus include delicacies like snow crab, and creative yuba dishes cost about ¥5,500 per person including dessert. ✉ *Wakamatsu-chō 137-4, Ponto-chō, Nakagyō-ku* ☎ *075/222–8200* ♨ *Reservations essential* ▭ *AE, DC, MC, V* ☯ *No lunch.*

$$$–$$$$ ✕ **Shinsen-en Heihachi.** When you order a pot of Japan's fattest *udon* (wheat noodles) here and look out over the remnants of Kyōto's first Imperial Palace garden, you'll be doing the Japanese equivalent of gazing at the White House Rose Garden. When Emperor Kammu established Heian-kyō in 794, he built a 33-acre Sacred Spring Garden containing pleasure pavilions for moon-viewing, of which a pond with a vermilion bridge and some small shrines remain today. The hot-pot dinners (¥10,000 for four people) are very popular, so it's best to book ahead. Also on offer are kaiseki ryōri and shabu-shabu. ✉ *Nijō-jō Minami-guwa, Nakagyo-ku* ☎ *075/841–0811* ▭ *AE, MC, V.*

¢–$$ ✕ **Ramen Santōka.** Nestled in one corner of a voguish restaurant plaza around a Zen gardenscape is an upscale (but reasonably priced) ramen restaurant. The delicious soups are made with the stock from choice pork, vegetables, and sometimes fish. You can choose from salty, soy sauce, or miso-based dishes topped with vegetables, slices of the slow-cooked pork, and a salty plum. Ramen Santōka stays open until 2 AM or until the soup runs out. You'll be seated along the convivial counter.

5

✉ *Kyōen, Sanjō and Kawabata, Higashiyama- ku* ☎ *075/532–1335* 🖃 *AE, DC, MC, V.*

Korean

$$–$$$ ✕ **Kicchan**. Spicy Korean food has long been favored in Japan, and at this cheerful renovated machiya you can sample this spicy fare while listening to the loud bantering between chef and waiters. Many dishes here are made with the chili condiment kimchee. One popular choice is actually Japanese: *okonomiyaki* is a thick pancake with vegetables and meat or seafood topped with a dark sauce. ✉ *Rokkaku-dōri, Muromachi-nishi-iru, Nakagyō-ku* ☎ *075/241–3390* 🖃 *No credit cards* ◔ *No lunch.*

¢–$$ ✕ **Somushi Kocha-ya**. Surrounded by a low roof, earthen walls, and a tiny garden, this Korean teahouse and organic restaurant is partly made from the wood of a Fukushima temple (the owner saved it when the temple was torn down) and filled with furnishings collected on travels. The interior is blissfully cool in summer, when diners are treated to vegetables and iced, spicy noodles. In winter you can warm up on the *ondol*, or Korean-style under-floor heating of the raised platform, while savoring rice porridge or soft, filled fritters, *jyon*, and curries. Traditional herb and spice teas with various health benefits are made on the premises. The restaurant is one block west of Karasuma on Shijō-dōri. ☎ *075/ 253–1456* 🖃 *AE, DC, MC, V* ◔ *Closed Wed.*

Vietnamese

$$–$$$ ✕ **Tiêm ân Hu'o'ng Việt**. Tucked away in a small street north of Karasuma Oike, this delightful eatery has celadon walls and dark Vietnamese furnishings reminiscent of a Hanoi residence. Order several dishes to share, and be sure to try the *ban xeo*—a huge pancake that you assemble yourself with vegetables, shrimp, and fragrant herbs and then dip into a spicy sauce—or the beef noodle soup *pho*. ✉ *Oshikōji-dōri, Karasama Oike-agaru, Nakagyō-ku* ☎ *075/253–1828* 🖃 *No credit cards* ◔ *Closed Tues.*

Northern Kyōto

Italian

★ $$–$$$$ ✕ **Azekura**. On the northern outskirts of Kyōto, not far from Kamigamo Jinja, Azekura serves superb Italian cuisine under the giant wooden beams of a 300-year-old sake warehouse. Originally built in Nara, the warehouse was moved to this former samurai estate more than 25 years ago by a kimono merchant. Lunch sets start at ¥1,800, and dinner at ¥4,300. Entrées include roast duck, lobster, and sautéed pork. An impressive selection of Italian wines is available. Azekura is a perfect stop when exploring the Shake-machi district around the shrine, where priests and farmers have lived for more than 10 centuries. ✉ *30 Okamoto-chō, Kamigamo, Kita-ku* ☎ *075/701–0162* ✑ *Reservations essential* 🖃 *No credit cards* ◔ *Closed Mon.*

Japanese

$$$$ ✕ **Akiyama**. Counter kaiseki lunches are popular, and each chef has a signature style of preparation and presentation. The broad counter inside this sturdy yet immaculate house seats 10, and the ¥3,150 lunch course is rustic yet refined. Liberal use is made of unpolished dark rice, roughly blended vegetables, mini hot pots, and choice sashimi like whorls of conger eel. Dessert could be a ball of mochi, pounded, steamed rice swirled in chocolate and roasted soybean paste. Dinners start at ¥6,300. Akiyama is some blocks west along the canal road, with its stately merchant houses, leading to Kamigamo Jinja; the roofed gate of the restaurant opens onto a garden that merges with the foliage of the hillside. This quiet neighborhood can be explored by bicycle. ⊠ 58 Kamigamōkamoto-cho, Kita-ku ☎ 075/711–5136 ⚱ Reservations essential ▤ AE, DC, MC, VC ☉ Closed Wed. and last Thurs. of the month.

★ $$$$ ✕ **Izusen.** In the garden of Daiji-in, a subtemple of Daitoku-ji, this restaurant specializes in shōjin ryōri, vegetarian Zen cuisine. The lunch set (¥3,150) is presented in sets of red-lacquer bowls of diminishing sizes, each one fitting inside the next as the meal is completed. Two Kyōto specialties, fu (wheat gluten) and yuba (soy milk skimmings), are served in soups and sauces that prove vegetarian cuisine to be as exciting as anything with meat. You can dine in tatami-mat rooms and in warm weather on low tables outside in the temple garden. Reservations are recommended in spring and fall. Izusen closes at 4 PM. ⊠ 4 Daitoku-ji-chō, Murasakino, Kita-ku ☎ 075/491–6665 ▤ No credit cards. ☉ No dinner.

★ $$$$ ✕ **Yamabana Heihachi-Jaya.** Somewhat off the beaten path in the northeastern corner of Kyōto, along the old road to the Sea of Japan, this roadside inn has provided comfort to many a weary traveler during its 400-year history. Heihachi-Jaya hugs the levee of the Takano-gawa and is surrounded by maple trees in a quiet garden with a stream. Apart from the excellent full-course kaiseki dinner, the famed duck hot pot in winter, and the delicious *mugitoro* bentō (a boxed lunch of mountain-potato salad served with barley rice), what makes this restaurant special is its clay sauna. Called a *kamaburo,* the sauna is a mound-shape clay steam bath heated from beneath the floor by a pinewood fire. Have a bath and sauna, change into a cotton kimono if you wish, and retire to the dining room (or to a private room) for a *very* relaxing meal. This is an unforgettable way to round off a day of exploring Hiei-zan and Ōhara. Heihachi-Jaya closes at 9 PM. ⊠ 8–1 Kawagishi-chō, Yamabana, Sakyō-ku ☎ 075/781–5008 ⚱ Reservations essential ▤ AE, DC, MC, V.

$$$–$$$$ ✕ **Sagenta.** Discovering the town of Kibune is one of the best parts of
Fodor'sChoice summer in Kyōto. A bump-and-rumble train ride into the mountains
★ north of Kyōto on the nostalgic little Eizan train leaves you on a mountain road that winds along a stream for about 2 km (1.2 mi) to Kibune. This road is lined with restaurants that place dining platforms across the stream in summer. Sagenta is the last of these restaurants, at the very top of the slope, and it serves kaiseki lunches year-round, as well as one-pot nabe (stew) dishes in fall and winter. A popular summertime specialty is *nagashi-somen,* or chilled noodles that flow down a bamboo spout from the kitchen to a boat-shape trough; you catch the noodles from the trough as they float past, dip them in a sauce, and eat them with mushrooms, seasonal green vegetables, and shrimp. To get there take the Eizan Electric Railway on the Kurama Line from Demachiyanagi Station to Kibuneguchi Station, and then walk up the hill for 30 min-

utes or arrange to have the restaurant shuttle bus pick you up. ⊠ 76 *Kibune-chō, Kurama, Sakyō-ku* ☏ *075/741–2244* ⚖ *Reservations essential* ☰ *AE, DC, MC, V* ⊘ *Closed periodically in winter.*

WHERE TO STAY

You can assume all hotel rooms have private bathrooms, air-conditioning, telephones, and televisions, unless noted otherwise. In expensive ($$$–$$$$) and moderately priced ($$) lodgings, rooms come with a hot-water thermos and tea bags or instant coffee, as well as *yukata* (cotton kimonos).

Book your stay at least a month in advance, or as early as three months ahead if you're traveling during peak spring and autumn seasons or around important Japanese holidays and festivals. Hotels in Kyōto often offer considerable discounts in summer. Keep in mind the following festival dates when making reservations: May 15, July 16–17, August 16, and October 22. Rooms will be scarce at these times. For a short course on accommodations in Japan, *see* Accommodations *in* Japan Essentials.

Central Kyōto

★ **$$$$** ✕▦ **Kinmata.** In the central courtyard water spouts out of the mouth of a dragon into a stone pond with colorful carp. This 200-year-old ryokan stands on a side street in the heart of the shopping district, but city sounds barely intrude upon this oasis of wooden passageways with low railings and sliding paper doors. Renowned for delicious seafood kaiseki ryōri, the inn serves dinner either in the privacy of your guest room or more cheaply in the quaintly old-fashioned, European-style restaurant. The inn is full of finely crafted woodwork and has a Meiji-era gas lamp and stone lantern near the entrance of the traditional, narrow facade. Booking well in advance is recommended. ⊠ *Gokomachi Shijō agaru, Nakagyō-ku* ☏ *075/221–1039* 🖷 *075/231–7632* ⤳ *7 rooms* ☰ *AE, DC, MC, V* ¶⊙] *MAP.*

$$$$ ▦ **Yoshikawa.** This quiet, unpretentious, traditional inn is within walking distance of the downtown shopping area. Opened in the 1950s, it features the *sukiya-zukuri* style: traditional Japanese architecture surrounded by a landscaped garden. Each tastefully decorated room has a cypresswood bath. As at most ryokan, the room rate includes two excellent meals. Guests are served kaiseki ryōri, including the specialty tempura, in their rooms. They will prepare a custom meal for vegetarians and vegans, too. ⊠ *Tomino-kōji, Oike-sagaru, Nakagyō-ku 604-8093* ☏ *075/221–5544* or *075/221–0052* 🖷 *075/221–6805* ⤳ *9 Japanese-style rooms* ⚭ *Restaurant, in-room data ports* ☰ *AE, DC, MC, V* ¶⊙] *MAP.*

$$$$ ▦ **ANA Hotel Kyōto.** The best thing about this hotel is its location, directly across from Nijō-jō. If your room faces the castle rather than another high-rise, you can be assured that you are indeed in Kyōto. The roof garden has spectacular 360-degree views of the city and surrounding mountains, and from the lobby you can see a delicate waterfall cascading into a courtyard pond. The sheer white, voluptuous beds make the rooms a bit snug, but with all this beauty around you, you won't

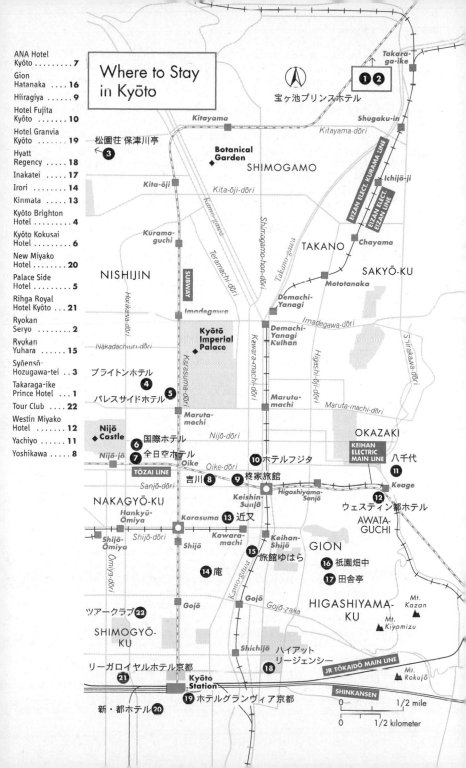

spend much time in them. ✉ *Nijō-jō-mae, Horikawa-dōri, Nakagyō-ku, Kyōto-shi 604-0055* ☎ *075/231–1155* 🖷 *075/231–5333* ⊕ *www.ana-hkyoto.com* ⮌ *303 rooms* ♨ *7 restaurants, pool, health club, bar* ▭ *AE, DC, MC, V.*

$$$$ ▦ **Hiiragiya.** For more than 150 years the Nishimura family has welcomed dignitaries and celebrities to this elegant inn. Founded in 1818 to accommodate provincial lords visiting the capital, the inn has hosted Charlie Chaplin, Elizabeth Taylor, and Yukio Mishima in addition to its 19th-century samurai visitors. The inn is representative of Kyōto in the way it skillfully combines ancient and modern. Where else could you find cedar baths with chrome taps? Not only does it turn on the lights, but it allows you to open and close the curtains by remote control. Rooms in the new wing are pricier; the one with a platform futon is in particular demand. A few blocks away is the Hiiragiya Bekkan, or Annex. The rooms may have fewer antiques and the dinner courses may not be as ornate, but these lodgings open out onto a beautiful garden and cost less. ✉ *Nakahakusan-chō, Fuyachō-Anekōji-agaru, Nakagyō-ku, Kyōto-shi 604-8094* ☎ *075/221–1136* 🖷 *075/221–1139* ⊕ *www.hiiragiya.co.jp* ⮌ *33 Japanese-style rooms, 28 with bath* ♨ *Laundry facilities, concierge, Internet* ▭ *AE, DC, MC, V* ▯◎▮ *MAP.*

$$$$ ▦ **Hotel Fujita Kyōto.** In the light of a full moon the waterfall in the garden sparkles while waterfowl play. The lobby is narrow and long, with comfortable gray armchairs against fading red carpeting. The Fujita has Japanese and Scandinavian decor throughout, and 18 rooms have Japanese-style furnishings. Not far from the nightlife center of Gion, this pleasant yet pricey hotel is along the Kamo-gawa. ✉ *Nishizume, Nijō-Ōhashi, Kamo-gawa, Nakagyō-ku, Kyōto-shi 604-0902* ☎ *075/222–1511* 🖷 *075/256–4561* ⊕ *www.fujita-kyoto.com* ⮌ *171 Western-style rooms, 18 Japanese-style rooms* ♨ *6 restaurants, bar* ▭ *AE, DC, MC, V.*

$$$$ ▦ **Irori.** With six centrally located, beautifully restored machiya that can house from 2 people (a little romantic hideaway) to 16 people, Irori offers the unique opportunity to experience life in a traditional Kyōto town house. The company is becoming a dynamic force in the preservation movement, with the intention of continuing to restore more of these precious buildings. One of the founders, Alex Kerr, is also an art dealer. He ensures that the houses are furnished exquisitely with rugs, scrolls, beautiful lamps, and even some sofas. All have beautiful wooden bathtubs. Aside from an English concierge service and the daily replenishing of towels and linens, the houses are occupied as private residences. The Origins Art program offers a range of workshops that last from half a day to several, usually custom made for groups of 10 or more, although smaller groups can inquire. Among the offerings are workshops on the tea ceremony, Nō drama, and calligraphy. ✉ *Sujiya-chō 144-6, Tominokōji-dōri, Takatsuji-agaru, Shimogyō-ku 600-8061* ☎ *075/352–0211* 🖷 *075/352–0211* ⊕ *www.kyoto-machiya.com* ♨ *Internet; no room TVs* ▯◎▮ *EP.*

♺ $$$$
Fodor'sChoice
★ ▦ **Kyōto Brighton Hotel.** The Brighton, on a quiet side street close to the Imperial Palace, is one of the city's best top-end Western-style hotels. Its simple, clean design gives it an airy and spacious quality lacking in most other Kyōto hotels. Hallways circle a central atrium with glass el-

evators, and plants hang from the banisters of every floor. Rooms are large by Japanese standards, with separate seating areas that include a couch and TV. Forever updating and upgrading its facilities, the hotel installed a water-purification system to keep the PH balance just right. An excellent concierge staff will help you plan your sightseeing. Be sure to visit the restaurant, Hotaru; the resident chef won the renowned (and nationally televised) *Iron Chef* contest for his inventive cuisine. Lunch kaiseki obentō at ¥3,700 include 12 dishes. ⊠ *Nakadachiuri, Shin-machi-dōri, Kamigyo-ku, Kyōto-shi 602-8071* ☎ *075/441–4411, 800/ 223–6800 in U.S.* 📠 *075/431-2360* ⊕ *www.brightonhotels.co.jp* ⇆ *183 rooms, 2 suites* ⚥ *5 restaurants, cable TV, pool, 2 bars, business services, no-smoking floors* ⊟ *AE, DC, MC, V.*

⏻ **$$$$** 🏨 **Rihga Royal Hotel Kyōto.** The rooms at this well-established, tasteful chain hotel vary in price according to size, but even the smallest rooms don't seem claustrophobic thanks to the delicate shōji windows. Family rooms for four people are available. On the 14th floor is Kyōto's only revolving restaurant, which offers splendid views of the city. There's also a branch of the famous Western Kyōto restaurant Kitchō on the premises. The hotel is a five-minute walk from Kyōto Station, and a shuttle bus leaves the Hachijō Exit every 15 minutes. There's a ¥1,050 charge to use the pool and sauna. ⊠ *Horikawa-Shiokōji, Shimogyō-ku, Kyōto-shi 600-8327* ☎ *075/341–1121, 800/877–7107 in U.S.* 📠 *075/341-3073* ⊕ *www.rihga.com* ⇆ *194 rooms* ⚥ *7 restaurants, pool, sauna, 3 bars, in-room data ports, no-smoking rooms* ⊟ *AE, DC, MC, V.*

⏻ **$$$–$$$$**
Fodor'sChoice
★
🏨 **Hotel Granvia Kyōto.** Elements of traditional Japanese interior design (dark wood, clean lines, and subdued beige tones) are combined with ultramodern touches (dark marble and the lobby's quirky geometrical floor lamps) at this popular hotel inside the Kyōto Station building. Rooms are spacious; a standard double room has two double beds, a desk, a little sitting area, and the best combination of Western- and Japanese-style bathrooms. The showerhead is mounted on the wall next to the bathtub, allowing you to shower outside the tub and then relax in the tub as the Japanese do. Take some time to walk between the north and south towers along the glassed walkway. On the 15th floor the sky lounge, which serves a fusion of French and Japanese nouvelle cuisine, has a panoramic view of the city. With a pick of 15 restaurants using the finest ingredients, including a branch of the famed Kitchō, choosing where to eat is challenging. There's a charge (¥1,000) to use the pool and gym, and no children are admitted to either. Cable television is available at a daily surcharge. Off-peak-season room rates drop considerably, so inquire about seasonal packages. ⊠ *Karasuma, Oshikoji-dōri-sagaru, Shimogyō-ku, Kyōto-shi 600-8216* ☎ *075/344–8888* 📠 *075/344–4400* ⊕ *www.granvia-kyoto.co.jp/c/index.html* ⇆ *539 rooms* ⚥ *15 restaurants, cable TV, pool, health club, in-room data ports, business services* ⊟ *AE, DC, MC, V.*

⏻ **$$$–$$$$** 🏨 **Kyōto Kokusai Hotel.** Across the street from Nijō-jō, Kokusai provides excellent views of the castle from the rooftop lounge and rooms on the west side, and is only a few yards from the entrance to the Nijō-jō-mae stop on the Tōzai subway line. Perhaps the best reason to choose this hotel is the Lounge Miyabi, where a large glass window looks out onto a beautiful courtyard garden. A stage with a thatched roof and lacquered flooring floats on the garden's pond. In the daytime you can relax with matcha and a sweet and watch a swan swim across the pond. At night, have your picture taken with a maiko. Then take your seat either inside or outside to watch her perform two dances on the floating stage. Though the rooms still retain an elegance with window-side armchairs, the silken duvets are decidedly outmoded. ⊠ *Nijō-eki-mae, Horikawa-dōri, Nakagyō-ku, Kyōto-shi 604-8502* ☏ *075/222–1111* 🖷 *075/231–9381* ➲ *277 rooms* ♨ *5 restaurants, bar* ▤ *AE, DC, MC, V.*

★ ⚅ ¢–$ 🏨 **New Miyako Hotel.** The 10-story white edifice has two protruding wings with landscaping and street lamps reminiscent of an American hotel. On the south side of Kyōto Station, it's convenient for train trips from the city. A friendly guest-relations manager in the bright marble lobby can help you plan your day. The south-wing rooms have been refurbished in bright tones against white, contrasting with the increasingly dated though cheaper rooms in the other wing. ⊠ *17 Nishi-Kujōin-chō, Minami-ku, Kyōto-shi 601-8412* ☏ *075/661–7111* 🖷 *075/661–7135* ⊕ *www.miyakohotels.ne.jp/newmiyako* ➲ *710 Western-style rooms, 4 Japanese-style rooms* ♨ *7 restaurants, cable TV, bar, in-room data ports, business services* ▤ *AE, DC, MC, V.*

★ ⚅ ¢–$ 🏨 **Palace Side Hotel.** A budget traveler's dream, this hotel is on the east side of the Imperial Palace, and it has excellent facilities, including a communal kitchen, laundry room, and two meeting rooms. Guest rooms are small, but they are spotless and perfectly acceptable; the art is mostly by local artists who stayed in the rooms in which their paintings hang. Larger family rooms are available (some have kitchens), and there are discounts for stays longer than three nights. Masseurs that specialize in Thai massage are on hand to bring you pain relief and relaxation. Breakfast is ¥1,050 per person, and you can eat at outdoor tables. ⊠ *Karasuma-dōri, Shimō-dachiuri-agaru, Kamigyō-ku 602-8011* ☏ *075/415–8887* 🖷 *075/415–8889* ⊕ *www.palacesidehotel.co.jp* ➲ *120 rooms* ♨ *Restaurant, some kitchenettes, Internet* ▤ *AE, DC, MC, V.*

¢ 🏨 **Tour Club.** Tatami mats cover the floors, Japanese paintings are on the walls, and there's even a little Zen garden in this hotel, formerly an apartment building. The rooms are like studio apartments, with futons, kettles, and private bathrooms. The communal kitchen, living room, laundry room, and Internet station encourage you to meet other guests and talk to the staff, who speak English and provide sightseeing advice. Tea and coffee are available for free, and there are bikes for rent. Tour Club is a 10-minute walk from Kyōto Station. ⊠ *362 Momiji-chō, Kitakōji-agaru, Higashinakasuji-dōri, Shimogyō-ku 600-8345* ☏ *075/353–6968* ⊕ *www.kyotojp.com* ➲ *11 rooms, 2 dormitories* ♨ *Internet; no room phones, no room TVs* ▤ *No credit cards* ⑩ *EP.*

Eastern Kyōto

★ ⚅ $$$$ 🏨 **Gion Hatanaka.** Alongside the southern gate of Yasaka Jinja, below Maruyama Park, stone stairs lead to a sukiya-style building with an attached four-story annex overlooking the tall trees that rim the shrine's grounds. The lobby has minimalist geometric lines to complement the sparse courtyard garden. Guest rooms have enclosed balconies where you can sip tea and gaze across the hills. The public baths are made from the pale umbrella pine and give off a woody fragrance. Smaller bathrooms are attached to the rooms. Opened in 2001, this ryokan offers the grace of Kyōto hospitality without the stiff formality. Flexible packages suit a variety of budgets; off-peak season you can stay without meals, and there are a range of meal packages. Some of the cheaper packages include a stay in the hotel combined with dinner in a nearby restaurant, and even the option of a river-platform restaurant in the summer (transport included). The elaborate kaiseki menus (served in the rooms), from the soup course served in a lacquer basket of petals to tart morsels of crab in a hollowed *sudachi* (a green citrus fruit), showcase the artful attention to detail with a hint of European influence. As the number of people sharing a room increases, the rate per person decreases, with special rates for children. There is wireless Internet access in the lobby. ⊠ *Yasaka Jinja, Minami-mon-mae, Gion, Higashiyama-ku* ☎ *075/541–5315* 🖷 *075/551–0533* ⊕ *www.thehatanaka.co.jp* ⟳ *21 Japanese rooms* ▤ *AE, DC, MC, V* ¶◉¶ *MAP.*

🄲 $$$$ 🄷 **Yachiyo.** Carefully shaped bushes, pine trees, and rocks, landscaped by the famed Ōgawa family, surround the woodwork and low-hanging tiled eaves of the special entrance to this ryokan, and the sidewalk from the gate curves into the doorway. Yachiyo is less expensive than its counterparts in the deluxe category but still provides attentive care. The inn's biggest draw is its proximity to Nanzen-ji, one of the most appealing temples in Kyōto. Rooms without baths are much less expensive than rooms with bath that overlook the garden or are in the newer building. Breakfast and dinner are included, but you can negotiate lower rates by choosing the yuba or shabu-shabu course over the elaborate kaiseki course and dining in the restaurant rather than in your room. A limited number of rooms with no meal plan are available. ⊠ *34 Nanzen-ji-fukuchichō, Sakyō-ku, Kyōto-shi 606-8435* ☎ *075/771–4148* 🖷 *075/771–4140* ⊕ *www.ryokan-yachiyo.com* ⟳ *25 rooms, 20 with bath* ♿ *Restaurant, Japanese baths* ▤ *AE, DC, MC, V* ¶◉¶ *MAP.*

$$$–$$$$ **Hyatt Regency.** On the southern end of the eastern foothills, not far from several famed sights, this luxury hotel boldly combines traditional aesthetics with state-of-the-art technology. Spacious rooms have granite baths and flat-screen televisions with DVD players, and some creative packages include acupuncture in the spa and fitness center, with meals custom-designed to your treatment. Touzan is an excellent Japanese-style restaurant that specializes in both char-grilled dishes and sushi but extends to hot pots in winter. Rooms with balconies double in price. ⊠ *644-2 Sanjusangendo-mawari, Higashiyama-ku 605-0941* ☎ *075/541–1234* 🖷 *075/541-2203* ⊕ *www.hyattregencykyoto.com* ⟳ *184 rooms* ♿ *3 restaurants, cable TV, gym, bar, in-room data ports* ▤ *AE, DC, MC, V* ¶◉¶ *EP.*

$$$–$$$$ 🄷 **Westin Miyako Hotel.** The Miyako, grande dame of Kyōto hotels, first
Fodor's Choice opened in the early 1900s. Perched atop Mt. Kacho near the eastern
★ temples, the hotel has a walking trail, several Japanese gardens, and indoor and outdoor pools (free for guests). Twenty Japanese-style rooms in two annexes retain the feel of a traditional ryokan. Western-

CLOSE UP

Ryokan Etiquette

UPON ENTERING, take off your shoes, as you would do in a Japanese household, and put on the slippers that are provided in the entryway. A maid, after bowing to welcome you, will escort you to your room, which will have tatami (straw mats) on the floor and will probably be partitioned off with shōji (sliding paper-paneled walls). Remove your slippers before entering your room; you should not step on the tatami with either shoes or slippers. The room will have little furniture or decoration—perhaps one small low table and cushions on the tatami, with a long, simple scroll on the wall. Often the rooms overlook a garden.

Plan to arrive in the late afternoon, as is the custom. After relaxing with a cup of green tea, have a long, hot bath. In ryokan with thermal pools you can take to the waters anytime, although the doors to the pool are usually locked from 11 PM to 6 AM. In ryokan without thermal baths or private baths in guest rooms, guests must stagger visits to the one or two public baths. Typically the maid will ask what time you would like your bath and fit you into a schedule. In Japanese baths, washing and soaking are separate functions: wash and rinse off entirely, and then get in the tub. Be sure to keep all soap out of the tub. Because other guests will be using the same bathwater after you, it is important to observe this custom. After your bath, change into a *yukata*, a simple cotton kimono provided in your room. Don't worry about walking around in what is essentially a robe—all other guests will be doing the same.

Dinner, which is usually included in the price, is served in your room at smaller and more personal ryokan; at larger ryokan, especially the newer ones, meals will be in the dining room. After you are finished, a maid will discreetly come in, clear away the dishes, and lay out your futon. In Japan *futon* means bedding, and this consists of a thin cotton mattress and a heavy, thick comforter. In summer the comforter is replaced with a thinner quilt. The small, hard pillow is filled with grain. In the morning a maid will gently wake you, clear away the futon, and bring in your Japanese-style breakfast, consisting of fish, miso soup, vegetables, and rice, although some ryokan have a Western option.

Because most ryokan staffs are small and dedicated, it is important to be considerate and understanding of their somewhat rigid schedules. Guests are expected to arrive in the late afternoon and eat around 6. Usually the doors to the inn are locked at 10, so plan for early evenings. Breakfast is served around 8, and checkout is at 10.

Not all inns are willing to accept foreign guests (though the ones listed in this chapter are amenable) because of language and cultural barriers. Also, top-level ryokan expect even new Japanese guests to have introductions and references from a respected client of the inn, which means that you, too, might need an introduction from a Japanese for very top-level ryokan. When you reserve a room, try to have a Japanese make the call for you; this will convey the idea that you understand the customs of staying in a traditional inn.

style rooms in the south wing are large and tastefully furnished. Other Western-style rooms that were not recently renovated are smaller and tired, but less expensive. A free shuttle bus runs to Kyōto Station via the downtown shopping district, a 20-minute ride. There is a satellite concierge at the Hachijō Exit of the station, where you can check in and drop off your bags. ✉ *Sanjō-Keage, Higashiyama-ku, Kyōto-shi 605-0052* ☎ *075/771–7111* 🖷 *075/751–2490* 🌐 *www.westinmiyako-kyoto.com* 🛏 *300 Western-style rooms, 20 Japanese-style rooms* ⚥ *9 restaurants, 2 pools, gym, 2 bars, in-room data ports, business services* 🖃 *AE, DC, MC, V.*

$$ 🏨 **Inakatei.** Not far from Kōdai-ji, along a stone-paved walking street, this small ryokan is nestled amidst other machiya in a preservation district of Gion along the eastern hills. Both floors have views of the charming garden with a small *chashitsu*, or teahouse. Reasonably priced ryokan that serve breakfast are proliferating, and this one offers a veritable feast of yūdofu (simmered bean curd), salmon, miso soup, rice, vegetables, and Japanese tea. There is no dinner. The only drawback is language; the booking must be made in Japanese, and you should make sure the owner knows what time you are coming. Arrive by taxi, since the driver will be able to find the side street. Inakatei particularly suits guests familiar with ryokan etiquette. ✉ *463 Ishibekōji, Gion, Shimogawara, Higashiyama-ku* ☎ *075/561–3059* 🛏 *6 rooms without bath* ⚥ *No room phones* 🍴 *FP.*

$–$$ 🏨 **Ryokan Yuhara.** Yuhara draws repeat visitors wishing to save a few yen while exploring Kyōto. The friendliness of the staff more than compensates for the spartan amenities. Especially rewarding is a springtime stay, when the cherry trees are in full bloom along the Takase-gawa, which the inn overlooks. This is a 15-minute walk from Gion and Ponto-chō. No meals are served and baths are communal. There is an 11 PM curfew. ✉ *188 Kagiya-chō, Shomen-agaru, Kiya-machi-dōri, Higashiyama-ku, Kyōto-shi 605-0909* ☎ *075/371–9583* 🛏 *8 Japanese-style rooms* ⚥ *Japanese baths* 🖃 *No credit cards.*

Northern Kyōto

$$$$ 🏨 **Ryokan Seryo.** After a long day of sightseeing there is nothing more pleasing than to relax in an outdoor hot spring (gender-segregated) up in the mountains. Seryo is in front of the famed Ōhara temple Sanzenin. Since this ryokan is in the countryside, the rooms are large with very plump futons on raised platforms and quaint balconies. The kaiseki dinner (served around 6 PM) includes wild mountain vegetables and wild boar nabe in the winter; breakfast is an opulent array of yūdofu, steamed egg custard (*chawan mushi*), and homemade yogurt. With two meals included, ¥21,000 per person is a good value. Usually the inn does not accept single travelers. It takes a 70-minute bus ride from Kyōto Station and then a 10-minute walk to get here. ✉ *22 Shorinin-cho, Ōhara, Sakyō-ku* ☎ *075/744–2301* 🖷 *075/744–2369* 🌐 *www.seryo.co.jp* 🛏 *10 Japanese-style rooms* 🍴 *MAP.*

$$$$ 🏨 **Takaraga-ike Prince Hotel.** Although some distance north of the center, this deluxe hotel is near the Kokusaikaikan subway station and the International Conference Hall. Its unusual doughnut shape provides each room with a view of the surrounding mountains and forests. Inside corridors overlook an inner garden. The top Royal floor, opened in 2007, offers a concierge service and refurbished rooms. The lower guest rooms are decorated in rose tones to complement the greenery outside, and all have large beds. At the authentic teahouse beside the pond, demonstrations of the tea ceremony can be arranged. Beaux Sejours serves sumptious buffets of slow-cooked food (like the tender roast beef), and even breakfast is buffet style. ⊠ *Takaraga-ike, Sakyō-ku, Kyōto-shi 606-8505* ☎ *075/712–1111, 800/542–8686 in U.S.* 🖷 *075/712–7677* ⊕ *www.princejapan.com* ⇒ *322 rooms* ♨ *4 restaurants, 2 bars, in-room data ports, Wi-Fi* ⊟ *AE, DC, MC, V* †◎† *BP.*

Western Kyōto

$$$$ 🏨 **Syōensō-Hozugawa-tei.** In the *onsen* (hot springs) village of Yunohana in the mountains of Tamba northwest of Kyōto, this hotel allows you to soak in your own *rotemburo* (outdoor bath) overlooking a private garden. If you're feeling adventurous you can get into the full swing of an onsen visit by joining other guests in one of the communal baths (separated by gender), including a rotemburo. Though the building is nondescript, the layers of sliding paper screens of the lobby's facade and the steps bordered on one side by a gently sloping waterfall suggest Old Kyōto. Kaiseki dinners are prepared with seasonal favorites, including Tamba boar in winter. An overnight stay at the hotel complements a trip to Arashiyama. For ¥600 you can take the scenic Sagano Torokko train, which leaves Saga Torokko Station in Arashiyama six minutes before the hour for the 20-minute ride to Kameoka, where Yunohana is located. Call ahead to ask the hotel shuttle bus to meet you at the station. To return to Arashiyama, take the Hosogawa-kudari boat the next day. Alternatively, you can take the JR line between Kameoka and Kyōto stations. ⊠ *Kameoka City, Yunohana-onsen, 621-0034* ☎ *0771/22–0903* 🖷 *0771/23–6572* ⊕ *www.syoenso.com* ⇒ *56 Japanese-style rooms, 7 with bath* ♨ *Restaurant, sauna* ⊟ *AE, MC, V* †◎† *MAP.*

NIGHTLIFE & THE ARTS

The Arts

Kyōto is known for its traditional performances—particularly dance and Nō theater. All dialogue is in Japanese, but sometimes there are synopses available. From time to time world-class musicians play the intimate venues, including David Lindley, Ron Sexsmith, and Michelle Shocked. The most convenient source for information is your hotel concierge or guest-relations manager, who may even have a few tickets on hand. For further information on Kyōto's arts scene check the music and theater sections of the monthly magazine **Kansai Time Out,** at bookshops for ¥300; you can also find information on the Web site www.kto.co.jp. Another source is the **Kyōto Visitor's Guide,** ⊕ www.kyotoguide.com, which devotes a few pages to "This Month's Theater." Look at the festival listings for temple and shrine performances. It's available free from the Kyōto Tourist Information Center on the ninth floor of the Kyōto Station building; the staff can also provide you with information.

Gion Corner

Some call it a tourist trap, but for others it's a comprehensive introduction to Japanese performing arts. The one-hour show combines court music and dance, ancient comic plays, Kyōto-style dance performed by maiko (apprentice geisha), and puppet drama. Segments are also offered on the tea ceremony, flower arranging, and koto music. Before attending a show, walk around Gion and Ponto-chō. You're likely to see beautifully dressed geisha and maiko on their way to work. It's permissible to take their picture—"*Shashin o totte mō ii desu ka?*"—but as they have strict appointments, don't delay them.

For tickets to **Gion Corner,** contact your hotel concierge or call the theater directly. The show costs ¥2,800—a bargain considering that it would usually cost 10 times as much to watch maiko and geisha perform. Two performances are held nightly at 7 and 8, March–November. No performances are offered August 16. ⊠ *Yasaka Hall, 1st fl., Gion, Higashiyama-ku* ☎ *075/561–1119* ⊕ *www.kyoto-gion-corner.info.*

Seasonal Dances

In the **Miyako Odori** in April and the **Kamo-gawa Odori** in May and October, geisha and maiko dances and songs pay tribute to the seasonal splendor of spring and fall. The stage settings are spectacular. Tickets to performances at the **Gion Kaburenjō Theater** (⊠ Gion Hanami-kōji, Higashiyama-ku ☎ 075/561–1115) cost from ¥2,000 to ¥7,000. Tickets at the **Ponto-chō Kaburenjō Theater** (⊠ Ponto-chō, Sanjō-sagaru, Nakagyō-ku ☎ 075/221–2025) cost between ¥2,000 and ¥4,000.

Kabuki

Kabuki developed in the Edo era as a theatrical art with lavish costumes and sets and dynamic all-male performances. Though Kabuki is faster paced than Nō, a single performance can easily take half a day. Devotees pack bentō to eat while watching shows. Kyōto hosts traveling Kabuki performances periodically, since most of the troupes are based in Tōkyō. Especially anticipated in Kyōto is the annual monthlong **Kaomise** (Face Showing) Kabuki Festival in December, featuring top Kabuki stars and introducing upcoming artists. Tickets range from ¥5,250 to ¥24,150 and need to be booked weeks in advance. The beautifully renovated **Minami-za** (⊠ Shijo Kamo-gawa, Higashiyama-ku ☎ 075/561–1155), the oldest theater in Japan, hosts performances year-round.

Nō

Kyōto is the home of Japan's most ancient form of traditional theater, Nō, which is more ritualistic and sophisticated than Kabuki. Some understanding of the plot of each play is necessary to enjoy a performance, which is generally slow-moving and solemnly chanted. The carved masks used by the main actors express a whole range of emotions, though the mask itself may appear expressionless until the actor "brings it to life." Nō performances are held year-round and range from ¥3,000 to ¥13,000. Particularly memorable are outdoor Nō performances, especially **Takigi Nō**, held outdoors by firelight on the nights of June 1–2 in the precincts of the Heian Jingū. For more information about performances, contact the Kyōto Tourist Information Center.

Kanze Kaikan Nō Theater. This is the older of Kyōto's Nō theaters, and it sometimes hosts Nō orientation talks. The theater does not offer programs in English. ⊠ *44 Enshōji-chō, Okazaki, Sakyō-ku* ☎ *075/771–6114.*

Ōe Nōgakudō. ⊠ *Oshikōji-dōri, Nakagyō-ku* ☎ *075/561–0622.*

Shin Kongo Nō Theater. ⊠ *Karasuma-dōri, Ichijō-sagaru, Kamigyō-ku* ☎ *075/441–7222.*

Nightlife

Though Kyōto's nightlife is more sedate than Ōsaka's, the areas around the old geisha quarters downtown thrive with nightclubs and bars. The Kiya-machi area along the small canal near Ponto-chō is as close to a consolidated nightlife area as you'll get in Kyōto. It's full of small watering holes with red lanterns (indicating inexpensive places) or small neon signs in front. It's also fun to walk around the Gion and Ponto-chō areas to try to catch a glimpse of a geisha or maiko stealing down an alleyway on her way to or from an appointment.

Café Independents. As its name suggests, this bar hosts a spectrum of indie rock, jazz, and blues artists, making it a good place to tap into the underground music scene. Trestle tables line the graffiti-covered walls of this basement venue with some tasty dishes on offer. ⊠ *1928 Bldg., Sanjō-dōri, Nakagyō-ku* ☎ *075/255–4312.*

Le Club Jazz. You can hear live jazz, blues, and soul gigs on Tuesday, and jam sessions every night from Thursday to Monday. There's a ¥2,000 cover charge, which includes two drinks on weekends. The club is diagonally opposite Café Independents. ⊠ *Sanjō Arimoto Bldg., 2nd fl., Sanjō-Gokōmachi Nishi-Iru, Kamigyō-ku* ☎ *075/211–5800.*

★ **Metro.** One of the best clubs in Kansai, Metro has an extremely wide range of regular events, from salsa to reggae, as well as frequent guest appearances by famous DJs from Tōkyō and abroad. ⊠ *Ebisu Bldg., 2nd fl., 82 Shimotsutsumi-chō, Maruta-machi-sagaru, Kawabata-dōri, Sakyō-ku* ☎ *075/752–4765* ⊕ *www.metro.ne.jp.*

★ **Tadg's.** North of the Minami-za theater in Gion, this convivial pub entertains patrons with Irish music and sporting events on TV. Have a chat with the locals to find out what's happening around town. The menu offers classic fish-and-chips, plus Irish stew and a beef-and-Guinness pie. ⊠ *236 Ōtobiru 2F, Nijuichiken-chō, Yamat-ōji, Kawabata Shijō-agaru* ☎ *075/525–0680* ⊕ *www.tadgspub.com.*

★ **Taku Taku.** This bar is an enduring live-music venue, tending toward rock and blues, that occasionally features some stellar performers. You can find it in an old kura, or storehouse, in the backstreets southwest of the

Takashimaya department store. ✉ *Tominokōji-dōri, Bukkōji-sagaru, Shimogyō-ku* ☎ *075/351–1321.*

Yoramu. Israeli sake aficionado Yoram has an extensive range of the delicate rice wine, from unfiltered to aged, fruity to dry, all available by the glass. A tasting set of three kinds of sake starts at ¥1,200. The dishes on the menu have all been chosen to complement the drink. The cozy bar is south of Nijō-dōri, east of Higashino-tōin-dōri. ✉ *Nijō-dōri, Nakagyō-ku* ☎ *075/213–1512.*

SHOPPING

Most shops slide their doors open at 10, and many shopkeepers partake of the morning ritual of sweeping and watering the entrance to welcome the first customers. Shops lock up at 6 or 7 in the evening. Stores often close sporadically once or twice a month, so it helps to call in advance if you're making a special trip. On weekends downtown can be very crowded.

A shopkeeper's traditional greeting to a customer is *o-ideyasu* (Kyōto-ben, the Kyōto dialect for "honored to have you here"), voiced in the lilting Kyōto intonations with the required bowing of the head. When a customer makes a purchase, the shopkeeper will respond with *o-okini* ("thank you" in Kyōto-ben), a smile, and a bow. Take notice of the careful effort and adroitness with which purchases are wrapped; it's an art in itself. American Express, MasterCard, Visa, and to a lesser degree traveler's checks are widely accepted.

Shopping Districts

Kyōto is compact and relatively easy to navigate. Major shops line both sides of **Shijō-dōri,** which runs east–west, and **Kawara-machi-dōri,** which runs north–south. Concentrate on Shijō-dōri between Yasaka Jinja and Karasuma Station as well as Kawara-machi-dōri between Sanjo-dōri and Shijō-dōri. Some of modern Kyōto's shopping districts are underground. **Porta,** under Kyōto Station, hosts more than 200 shops and restaurants in a sprawling subterranean arcade.

Roads leading to Kiyomizu-dera run uphill, yet you may hardly notice the steepness for all of the alluring shops that line the way. Be sure to peek in for unique gifts. Food shops offer sample morsels, and tea shops serve complimentary cups of tea. **Shin-Kyōgoku,** a covered arcade running between Teramachi-dōri and Kawara-machi-dōri, is another general-purpose shopping area with many souvenir shops.

Depāto

Kyōto *depāto* (department stores) are small in comparison to their mammoth counterparts in Tōkyō and Osaka. They still carry a wide range of goods and are great places for one-stop souvenir shopping. Wandering around the food halls (in all but Hankyū) is a good way to build up an appetite. Prices drop dramatically during end-of-season sales.

Note that all the stores close irregularly for a few days each month. You can call at the beginning of the month to find out about scheduled closures.

Daimaru mainly appeals to more expensive and conservative tastes, and is on the main Shijō-dōri shopping avenue. Its basement food hall is the best in town. ⊠ *Shijō-Karasuma, Shimogyō-ku* ☎ *075/211–8111* ☉ *Daily 10–7:30.*

Fujii Daimaru, which is directly opposite the Teramachi mall on Shijō-dōri, is a funkier branch of the old matron Daimaru. ⊠ *Shijō-Teramachi, Shimogyō-ku* ☎ *075/211–8181* ☉ *Daily 10–8:00.*

Hankyū, directly across from Takashimaya on Kawara-machi-dōri, has two revamped restaurant floors. Window displays show the type of food served, and prices are clearly marked. ⊠ *Shijō-kawara-machi, Shimogyō-ku* ☎ *075/223–2288* ☉ *Daily 10–7:30.*

Isetan, in the Kyōto Station building, has 13 floors, including a restaurant floor, a cosmetics floor, an amusement arcade, and an art gallery. It closes periodically on Tuesday. ⊠ *Karasuma-dōri, Shimogyō-ku* ☎ *075/352–1111* ☉ *Daily 10–7:30.*

Takashimaya, on Kawara-machi-dōri, is Japan's most established and sophisticated depāto, with designer and luxury goods at matching prices. You'll find accommodating English-speaking salespeople and a convenient money-exchange counter. The restaurant floor is rather grand, with a concierge service for diners. ⊠ *Shijō-kawara-machi, Shimogyō-ku* ☎ *075/221–8811* ☉ *Daily 10–7:30.*

Markets

Contact the **Kyōto Tourist Information Center** (⊠ 9F JR Kyōto Station building, Kyōto International Prefectural Center, Karasuma-dōri, Shimogyō-ku ☎ 075/344–3300 ⊕ www.kyoto-kankou.or.jp) for information about seasonal fairs from local area pottery sales to the national antiques fairs, usually held in May, June, and October.

Kyōto has a wonderful food market, **Nishiki-kōji,** which is north of Shijō-dōri and branches off the Teramachi-dōri covered arcade in central Kyōto. Look for delicious grilled fish dipped in soy sauce for a tasty snack or fresh Kyotō sweets. Try to avoid the market in late afternoon, when housewives come to do their daily shopping. The market is long and narrow; in a sizable crowd there's always the possibility of being pushed into the display of fresh fish. ⊠ Nishiki-kōji-dōri, Nakagyō-ku.

Temple Markets

Several temple markets take place in Kyōto each month. These are great places to pick up bargain kimonos or unusual souvenirs. They're also some of the best spots for people-watching. The largest and most famous temple market is the one at **Tō-ji** (⇨ Central & Southern Kyōto), which takes place on the 21st of each month. Hundreds of stalls display fans, kimonos, antiques, and trinkets, which attract many collectors. The temple also hosts a smaller antiques market on the first Sunday of the month. ✉ *1 Kujō-chō, Minami-ku.*

The vibrant flea market at **Kitano Tenman-gū** (↪ Western Kyoto & Arashiyama) overflows into the side streets surrounding the grounds on the 25th of each month, with kimono and Japanese crafts at reasonable prices. ✉ *Imakoji agaru, Onmae-dōri, Kamigyō-ku.*

A market specializing in homemade goods is held at **Chion-in** on the 15th of each month. To get to the Chion-in market, take Bus 206 from Kyōto Station to Hyakumanben. ✉ *400 Hayashi-shita-chō 3-chōme, Yamato-ōji, Higashi-hairu, Shimbashi-dōri, Higashiyama-ku.*

Traditional Items & Gift Ideas

Art & Antiques

Nawate-dōri between Shijō-dōri and Sanjō-dōri is noted for fine antique textiles, ceramics, and paintings. ✉ *Higashiyama-ku.*

Shinmonzen-dōri holds the key to shopping for art and antiques in Kyōto. It's an unpretentious little street of two-story wooden buildings between Higashi-ōji-dōri and Hanami-kōji-dōri, just north of Gion. What gives the street away as a treasure trove are the large credit-card signs jutting out from the shops. There are no fewer than 17 shops specializing in scrolls, *netsuke* (small carved figures to attach to Japanese clothing), lacquerware, bronze, wood-block prints, paintings, and antiques. Shop with confidence, because shopkeepers are trustworthy and goods are authentic. Pick up a copy of the pamphlet *Shinmonzen Street Shopping Guide* from your hotel or from the Kyōto Tourist Information Center. ✉ *Higashiyama-ku.*

Tera-machi-dōri between Oike-dōri and Maruta-machi is known for antiques of all kinds and tea ceremony utensils. ✉ *Nakagyō-ku.*

Bamboo

The Japanese wish their sons and daughters to be as strong and flexible as bamboo. Around many Japanese houses are small bamboo groves, for the deep-rooted plant withstands earthquakes. On the other hand, bamboo is so flexible it can bend into innumerable shapes. Bamboo groves used to flourish on the hillsides surrounding Kyōto, but the groves are in decline. The wood is carefully cut and dried for several months before being stripped and woven into baskets and vases.

Kagoshin has been in operation since 1862. Basket weavers here use more than 50 varieties of bamboo in intricate designs. ✉ *Ōhashi-higashi, Sanjō-dōri, Higashiyama-ku* ☎ *075/771-0209* 🕐 *Mon.–Sat. 9–6.*

Ceramics

Asahi-do, in the heart of the pottery district near Kiyomizu-dera, specializes in Kyōto-style hand-painted porcelain, and offers the widest selection of any pottery store in the area. ✉ *1–280 Kiyomizu, Higashiyama-ku* ☎ *075/531–2181* ⊙ *Daily 9–6.*

Tachikichi, on Shijō-dōri west of Kawara-machi, has five floors full of contemporary and antique ceramics. One floor is an art gallery that hosts exhibits of very fine ceramics by Japanese and international artists. In business since 1872, Tachikichi has an excellent reputation. ✉ *Shijō-dōri, Tominokōji, Nakagyō-ku* ☎ *075/211–3143* ⊙ *Thurs.–Tues. 10–7.*

Dolls

Ningyō were first used in Japan in the purification rites associated with the Doll Festival, an annual family-oriented event on March 3. Kyōto ningyō are made with fine detail and embellishment.

Nakanishi Toku Shōten has old museum-quality dolls. The owner, Mr. Nakanishi, turned his extensive doll collection into the shop two decades ago and has since been educating customers with his vast knowledge of the doll trade. ✉ *359 Moto-chō, Yamato-ōji Higashi-Iru, Furumonzen-dōri, Higashiyama-ku* ☎ *075/561–7309* ⊙ *Daily 10–5.*

Folk Crafts

For many, the prize souvenir of a visit to Kyōto is the **shuinchō,** a booklet usually no larger than 4 by 6 inches. It's most often covered with brocade, and the blank sheets of heavyweight paper inside continuously fold out. You can find them at gift stores or at temples for as little as ¥1,000 and use them as "passports" to collect ink stamps from places you visit while in Japan. Stamps and stamp pads are ubiquitous in Japan—at sights, train stations, and some restaurants. Most ink stamping will be done for free; at temples monks will write calligraphy over the stamp for a small fee.

Kuraya Hashimoto has one of the best collections of antique and newly forged swords and will ship them for you. ✉ *Nishihorikawa-dōri, Oike-agaru, southeast corner of Nijō-jō, Nakagyō-ku* ☎ *075/821–2791* ⊕ *www.japan-sword.com* ⊙ *Thurs.–Tues. 10–6.*

At **Ryūshido** you can stock up on calligraphy and *sumi* supplies, including writing brushes, ink sticks, ink stones, paper, paperweights, and water stoppers. ✉ *Nijō-agaru, Tera-machi-dōri, north of Nijō, Kamigyō-ku* ☎ *075/252–4120* ⊙ *Daily 10–6.*

Yamato Mingei-ten, on Kawara-machi-dōri near the BAL Building downtown, has an ever-changing selection of folk crafts, including ceramics, metalwork, paper, lacquerware, and textiles from all over Japan. ✉ *Kawara-machi, Takoyakushi-agaru, Nakagyō-ku* ☎ *075/221–2641* ⊙ *Wed.–Mon. 10–8:30.*

Incense

Kunyoku-dō, on Horikawa-dōri opposite Nishi-Hongan-ji, has been dealing in fine woods, herbs, and spices for 400 years. ✉ *Horikawa-dōri, Nishihonganji-mae, Shimogyō-ku* ☎ *075/371–0162* ⊙ *Daily 9–5:30, closed 1st and 3rd Sun. of month.*

Kyōto Crafts

TEMPLES, SHRINES, GARDENS can't be taken home with you. You can, however, pack up a few *omiyage* (mementos) for which this city is famous. The ancient craftspeople of Kyōto served the imperial court for more than 1,000 years, and the prefix *kyō-* before a craft is synonymous with fine craftsmanship.

Kyō-ningyō, exquisite display dolls, have been made in Kyōto since the 9th century. Constructed of wood coated with white shell paste and clothed in elaborate, miniature patterned-silk brocades, Kyōto dolls are considered the finest in Japan. Kyōto is also known for fine ceramic dolls and *Kyō-gangu,* its local varieties of folk toys.

Kyō-sensu are embellished folding fans used as accoutrements in Nō theater, tea ceremonies, and Japanese dance. They also have a practical use—to keep you cool. Unlike other Japanese crafts, which have their origin in Tang-dynasty China, the folding fan originated in Kyōto.

Kyō-shikki refers to Kyōto lacquerware, which also has its roots in the 9th century. The making of lacquerware, adopted from the Chinese, is a delicate process requiring patience and skill. Finished lacquerware products range from furniture to spoons and bowls, which are carved from cypress, cedar, or horse-chestnut wood. These pieces have a brilliant luster; some designs are decorated with gold leaf and inlaid mother-of-pearl.

Kyō-yaki is the general term applied to ceramics made in local kilns; the most popular ware is from Kyōto's Kiyomizu district. Often colorfully hand-painted in blue, red, and green on white, these elegantly shaped teacups, bowls, and vases are thrown on potters' wheels located in the Kiyomizu district and in Kiyomizu-danchi in Yamashina. Streets leading up to Kiyomizu-dera—Chawan-zaka, Sannen-zaka, and Ninen-zaka—are sprinkled with kyō-yaki shops.

Kyō-yuzen is a paste-resist silk-dyeing technique developed by 17th-century dyer Yuzen Miyazaki. Fantastic designs are created on plain white silk pieces through the process of either *tegaki yuzen* (hand-painting) or *kata yuzen* (stenciling).

Nishijin-ori is the weaving of silk. *Nishijin* refers to a Kyōto district producing the best silk textiles in all Japan, which are used to make kimonos. Walk along the narrow backstreets of Nishijin and listen to the persistently rhythmic looms.

Kimonos & Accessories

Shimmering new silk kimonos can cost more than ¥1,000,000—they are art objects, as well as couture—while equally stunning old silk kimonos can cost less than ¥3,000. You can find used kimonos at some local end-of-the-month temple markets.

Aizen Kōbō, two blocks west of the textile center on Imadegawa-dōri and a block south, specializes in the finest handwoven and hand-dyed indigo textiles. Pure Japanese indigo dye, with its famed rich color, may soften but will never fade. The shop is in a traditional weaving family home, and the friendly owners will show you their many dyed and woven goods, including garments designed by Hisako Utsuki, the owner's wife. ⊠ *Ōmiya Nishi-Iru, Nakasuji-dōri, Kamigyō-ku* ☎ *075/441–0355* ⊕ *http://web.kyoto-inet.or.jp/people/aizen* ⊘ *Mon.–Sat. 9–5:30.*

Jūsan-ya has been selling *tsugekushi* (boxwood combs) for more than 60 years. *Kanzashi,* the hair ornaments worn with kimonos, are also available. ⊠ *Shinkyōgoku Higashi-Iru, Shijō-dōri, Shimogyō-ku* ☎ *075/ 221–2008* ⊘ *Daily 10–6.*

Umbrellas protect kimonos from the scorching sun or pelting rain. Head for **Kasagen** to purchase authentic oiled-paper umbrellas. The shop has been around since 1861, and its umbrellas are guaranteed to last for years. ⊠ *284 Gion-machi, Kita-gawa, Higashiyama-ku* ☎ *075/ 561–2832* ⊘ *Daily 10–9.*

The most famous fan shop in all of Kyōto is **Miyawaki Baisen-an,** in business since 1823. It delights customers not only with its fine collection of lacquered, scented, painted, and paper fans, but also with the old-world atmosphere that emanates from the building that houses the shop. ⊠ *Tominokōji Nishi-Iru, Rokkaku-dōri, Nakagyō-ku* ☎ *075/ 221–0181* ⊘ *Daily 9–6.*

Lacquerware

Monju sells authentic lacquered trays, bowls, incense holders, and tea containers. Unlike the inexpensive, plastic, faux lacquerware sold at some souvenir shops, real lacquerware has a wooden base, which is then coated with natural lacquer made from the Asian sumac tree. Gold and silver powder is used in the more lavish *maki-e* lacquerware. You can even buy chopsticks with their own carrying case to use instead of the disposable ones supplied in restaurants. This shop is on Shijō-dōri in Gion. ⊠ *Hanamikōji Higashi-iru, Shijō-dōri, Higashiyama-ku* ☎ *075/ 525–1617* ⊘ *Fri.–Wed. 10:30–7:30.*

Novelties

Loft has five floors jam-packed with kitsch, from beauty products to anime merchandise. Kids and teenagers love browsing here, and you're sure to find some unusual souvenirs and gifts. ⊠ *Kawara-machi-nishi, Takoy-akushi-dōri, Nakagyō-ku* ☎ *075/255–6210* ⊘ *Daily 11–9.*

KYŌTO ESSENTIALS

Transportation

BY AIR

The closest international airport to Kyōto is Kansai International Airport (KIX), near Ōsaka. KIX does have domestic flights, particularly to major cities, but the majority of internal air traffic uses Ōsaka's Itami Airport. Flight time between Tōkyō and Ōsaka is about 70 minutes.

🚹 **Itami Airport** ☎ 06/6856–6781. **Kansai International Airport** ☎ 0724/55–2500 ⊕ www.kansai-airport.or.jp.

AIRPORT TRANSFERS From KIX to Kyōto Station, take the JR Haruka Limited Express, which departs every 30 minutes to make the 75-minute run and costs ¥3,490 including charges for a reserved seat; or use a JR Pass. Alternatively, a limousine bus service, available daily 9–9, takes 95–105 minutes between KIX and several Kyōto destinations, including the Hachijō Exit of Kyōto Station. The cost is ¥2,300 one-way and ¥3,800 round-trip. From Itami, buses depart for Kyōto approximately every 20 minutes from 8:10 AM to 9:20 PM. Some stop at major hotels, but most go straight to Kyōto Station. The trip takes 55–90 minutes and costs ¥1,280 or ¥1,370, depending on the Kyōto destination.

MK Taxi offers a shuttle bus that runs between Kyōto and both KIX and Itami. Though it's a door-to-door service, it takes longer because the shuttle bus picks up or drops off up to eight people. It's necessary to book at least two days in advance by telephone or online. If you are arriving you will be met as you clear customs. From KIX the cost is ¥3,000 per adult; it's ¥2,000 from Itami. There is an additional surcharge of ¥1,000 if you have more than one large bag. Taxis cost between ¥20,000 and ¥30,000 from KIX and Itami to Kyōto.

Airport Limousine ☎ 075/682-4400 ⊕ www.kate.co.jp. **JR Haruka Limited Express** ✉ JR West, Kyōto Station bldg , Karasuma-dōri ☎ 075/691-1000. **MK Taxi** ☎ 075/702-5489 ⊕ www.mk-group.co.jp/english/shuttle.

BY BIKE

Kyoto Tour Cycling Project (KCTP) Rentals start at ¥1,000 (¥1,500 for a mountain bike) per day and include a map of suggested routes. There are five pick-up/drop-off terminals around Kyōto. The Kyōto terminal also has a handy luggage counter. KCTP also offers several bike tours. ✉ 552-13 Higashi-Aburanokōji-chō, Aburanokōji-dōri, Shiokō-ji-sagaru, Shimogyō-ku ☎075/354-3636 ⊕www.kctp.net. **Rental Cycle Yasumoto Kawabata** rents bikes downtown for ¥1,000 per day from Monday to Saturday, 9 to 5. ✉ Kawabata-dōri, just north of Sanjō-dōri, Higashiyama-ku ☎ 075/751-0595.

BY BUS

Buses serve the entire city. Most city buses run 7 AM–9 PM daily, but a few start as early as 5:30 AM and run until 11 PM. The main bus terminals are Kyōto Station, Keihan Sanjō Station, Karasuma-Kitao-ji, and at the Shijō-dōri–Karasuma-dōri intersection. Many city buses and bus stops show destinations in both English and Japanese, but ask your hotel clerk beforehand to write down your destination in Japanese, along with the route number in case you need to ask someone. Pick up a bus map from the Kyōto Tourist Information Center or download it from ⊕ www.city.kyoto.jp/koho/eng/access/transport.html.

Within the city the standard fare is ¥220, which you pay when leaving the bus; outside the city limits the fare varies according to distance. Several special transportation passes are available, including the following: a one-day city bus pass for ¥500, valid for use inside the inner city area; Kyōto sightseeing one-day (¥1,200) or two-day (¥2,000) passes that cover travel on city buses, the subway, and private Kyōto Line buses, with restrictions on some routes; and the *torafika kyō* pass, which provides ¥3,300 worth of transport via city bus or subway for ¥3,000. Additionally, the ¥3,000 *surutto Kansai,* covers transportation on city buses, the subway, and all the major Kansai railways except the JR line, but is not discounted. All these passes are sold at travel agencies, main bus terminals, and information centers in Kyōto Station.

You can use a JR Pass on the local bus that travels between Kyōto Station and Takao (in northwestern Kyōto), passing close to Nijō Station.

BY SUBWAY

Kyōto has a 28-station subway system. The Karasuma Line runs north to south from Kokusai Kaikan to Takeda. The Tōzai Line runs between Nijō in the west and Roku-jizō in the east. Purchase tickets at the vending machines in stations before boarding. Fares increase with distance traveled and begin at ¥210. Service runs 5:30 AM–11:30 PM. Discounted passes are available for tourists (⇨ By Bus, *above*).

BY TAXI

Taxis are readily available in Kyōto. Fares for smaller-size cabs start at ¥640 for the first 2 km (1 mi), with a cost of ¥100 for each additional 500 meters (⅓ mi). Many taxi companies provide guided tours of the city, priced per hour or per route. Keihan Taxi has four-hour tours from ¥18,000 per car; MK Taxi runs similar tours starting at ¥18,800 for three hours. There are fixed fares for some sightseeing services that start and end at Kyōto Station. A 7½-hour tour of the city's major sights will cost in the region of ¥26,000 with any of the 17 taxi companies, including Keihan Taxi and MK Taxi.

🚕 **Keihan Taxi** ☎0120/113-103. **MK Taxi** ☎075/721-2237 ⊕www.mk-group.co.jp/english/index.html.

TRAIN TRAVEL

Frequent daily Shinkansen run between Tōkyō and Kyōto (2 hours, 40 minutes). The one-way fare, including charges for a reserved seat, is ¥13,200. Train service between Ōsaka and Kyōto (30 minutes) costs ¥540 one-way. From Shin-Ōsaka Station you can take the Shinkansen and be in Kyōto in 15 minutes; tickets cost ¥1,480. You may use a Japan Rail Pass on the Hikari and Kodama Shinkansen. The Keihan and the Hankyū limited express trains (40 minutes each) are less expensive than the JR, unless you have a JR Pass. The one-way Ōsaka–Kyōto fare is ¥400 or ¥460 on the Keihan Line and ¥390 on the Hankyū Line. They depart every 15 minutes from Ōsaka's Yodoyabashi and Umeda stations respectively.

In Kyōto the Keihan Line from Ōsaka is partly underground (from Shichijō Station to Demachi-Yanagi Station) and extends all the way up the east bank of the Kamo-gawa to Imadegawa-dōri. At Imadegawa-dōri a passage connects the Keihan Line with the Eizan Railway's Demachi-Yanagi Station. The Eizan has two lines, the Kurama Line, running north to Kurama, and the Eizan Line, running northeast to Yase. The Hankyū Line, which runs to the Katsura Rikyū, connects with the subway at Karasuma Station. From Shijō-Ōmiya Station the Keifuku Arashiyama Line runs to western Kyōto. JR also runs to western Kyōto on the San-in Main Line.

Contacts & Resources

BANKS & EXCHANGE SERVICES

Sumitomo, Sanwa, and Tōkyō Mitsubishi banks have foreign exchange facilities, which usually open at 10 AM on weekdays, all situated near the Karasuma-Shijō intersection. The central post office and other main post offices offer a currency exchange and traveler's check service, but only in certain currencies, including British pounds; American, Canadian, and Australian dollars; and euros. International credit cards can be used at most post office ATMs. International ATM machines are also in the Kyōto Tower Building (basement), opposite Kyōto Station's Central Exit. For over-the-counter cash advances without a PIN number: for Visa go to Sumitomo Bank's main branch on Karasuma-dōri just south of Sanjō-dōri, or the subbranch in the Hankyū department store; for MasterCard, head for Nanto Bank, at the Karasuma-Oike junction; and head to Sanwa Bank, at the intersection of Shijō-dōri and Karasuma-dōri, for American Express.

CONSULATES

The nearest American consulate is in Ōsaka.

EMERGENCIES

Both the Kyōto Shijō Hospital and the Sakabe Clinic have 24-hour emergency facilities.

🏥 Doctors **Daiichi Sekijūji (Red Cross Hospital)** ✉ Higashiyama Hon-machi, Higashiyama-ku ☎ 075/561-1121. **Japan Baptist Hospital** ✉ Kita-Shirakawa, Yamanomoto-chō, Sakyō-ku ☎ 075/781-5191. **Kyōto Shijō Hospital** ✉ 272-6 Shijō Horikawa-chō, Higashi-Horikawa-dōri, Shimogyō-ku ☎ 075/361-5471. **Sakabe Clinic** ✉ 435 Yamamoto-chō, Gokō-machi, Nijō-sagaru, Nakagyō-ku ☎ 075/231-1624.

🏥 Emergency Services **Ambulance** ☎ 119. **Police** ☎ 110.

ENGLISH-LANGUAGE MEDIA

BOOKS The eighth floor of Junkudō in the BAL Building on Kawara-machi-dōri has several shelves devoted to English books, while nearby Media Shop carries a wide range of coffee-table books and titles on art and architecture in English and Japanese. Random Walk is an English bookstore in the Teramachi arcade that focuses on books about Japan with a selection of paperbacks. Izumiya Book Center, across from Kyōto Station on the Shinkansen side, devotes a corner to English-language books.

🏪 Bookstores **Izumiya Book Center** ✉ Avanti Bldg., 6th fl., Minami-ku ☎ 075/671-8987. **Junkudō Bal** ✉, 8F BAL Bldg., Kawara-machi-dōri., Rokkaku-sagaru ☎ 075/253-6460 ⊙ Daily 11 AM–8 PM. **Media Shop** ✉ Vox Bldg., 1st fl., Kawara-machi-dōri, San-jō, Nakagyō-ku ☎ 075/255-0783. **Random Walk** ✉ Teramachi St., Takoyakushi-kudarū, Nakagyō-ku ☎ 075/256-8231.

NEWSPAPERS & MAGAZINES Established in 1977, the monthly *Kansai Time Out* publishes comprehensive events listings for Kōbe, Kyōto, Nara, and Ōsaka. It costs ¥300 and is available in major hotels and bookshops.

INTERNET

At the Kyōto Tourist Information Center in the Kyōto Station building, the Internet costs ¥100 per 15 minutes. On the south end of Shinkyōgo-ku arcade is Fujiyama, the haunt of *manga otaku* (computer geeks). Once you complete the obligatory membership form for ¥300, you can use the Internet for ¥200 per 30 minutes. It's open daily 9–9. A more laid-back option in the same area is Café Lulu, a casual second-floor restaurant with the ambience of a friend's living room. If you order something, you can use one of three computers for free. There is also wireless access.

🏠 **Café Lulu** ✉ Rokkaku St., east of Tomonikōji-dōri. ☎ 075/211-1575. **Fujiyama Café** ✉ 3rd Bldg., 557 Kyōto-shochiku, Nakanomachi, Shinkyōgo-ku, Shijō-agaru, Nagakyō-ku ☎ 075/221-2494. **Kyōto Tourist Information Center** ✉ 9F JR Kyōto Station bldg., Kyōto International Prefectural Center, Karasuma-dōri, Shimogyō-ku ☎ 075/344-3300 ⊕ www.kyoto-kankou.or.jp.

TOURS

EXCURSIONS Hozugawa Yūsen organizes excursions down a 15-km (9-mi) stretch (about 90 minutes) of the Hozu Rapids in flat-bottom boats, from Kameoka to Arashiyama, which cost ¥3,900. Sunrise Tours, a subsidiary of Japan Travel Bureau, conducts full- and half-day tours to Nara and Ōsaka. An afternoon tour to Nara costs ¥6,300. Morning and afternoon trips to Ōsaka, for ¥8,900 and ¥6,200, respectively, are not worth the cost, especially if you have a JR Pass.

🏠 **Hozugawa Yūsen** ☎ 0771/22-5846. **Sunrise Tours** ☎ 075/341-1413 ⊕ www.jtbgmt.com/sunrisetour/.

ORIENTATION Sunrise Tours organizes half-day morning and afternoon deluxe coach
TOURS tours highlighting different city attractions. Pickup service is provided from major hotels. A ¥5,300 morning tour commonly covers Nijō-jō, Kinkaku-ji, Kyōto Imperial Palace, Higashi-Hongan-ji, and the Kyōto Handicraft Center. A ¥5,300 afternoon tour includes the Heian Jingū, Sanjūsangen-dō, and Kiyomizu-dera. An ¥11,200 full-day tour covers all the above sights and includes lunch.

🏠 **Sunrise Tours** ☎ 075/341-1413 ⊕ www.jtbgmt.com/sunrisetour/kyoto.

SPECIAL- Several private companies offer guided tours of Kyōto. Joe Okada of
INTEREST TOURS Kyōto Specialist Guide Group will tailor a tour to fit your interests and budget. Your Japan Speciality Services is run by the editor-in-chief of the *Kyōto Visitor's Guide,* Ian Roepke, and offers half-day and full-day tours of Kyōto, including both familiar sights and lesser-known backstreet views. A seasoned guide who can shed insight into the mysterious world of the geisha, Peter MacIntosh of Kyōto Sights and Nights lends late-afternoon walks through the old teahouse districts of Gion. More exclusive evening tours include the walking tour followed by a light dinner or a full kaiseki dinner with geisha entertainment. Volunteer guides can be requested by calling ISC at the Utano Youth Hostel. Bookings must be made three days in advance. The Kyōto International Community House can arrange home visits.

🏠 **ISC** ✉ Utano Youth Hostel, Ukyō-ku ☎ 075/462-2288. **Kyōto International Community House** ✉ 2-1 Torii-chō, Awata-guchi, Sakyō-ku ☎ 075/752-3010. **Kyoto Sights** and Nights ☎ 090/5169-1654 ⊕ www.kyotosightsandnights.com. **Kyōto Specialist Guide Group** ✉ 1137 Amarube-shimo, Maizuru-shi ☎ 0773/64-0033. **Your Japan Speciality Services** ☎ 090/5642-4724 ⊕ www.kyoto-tokyo-private-tours.com.

WALKING TOURS   The Japan National Tourist Office (JNTO) publishes pamphlets with descriptions of five walking tours, including maps. The tours range in length from about 40 to 80 minutes. Pick up the pamphlets at the Kyōto Tourist Information Center in the Kyōto Station building.

Personable Kyōto-ite Johnnie Hajime Hirooka conducts walking tours of Kyōto, in English, that leave from Kyōto Station at 10:15 AM Monday through Thursday, early March through late November, rain or shine. Itineraries vary—he often takes people to sights they might not otherwise see. Walks take four hours and cost ¥2,000 per person, ¥1,000 for teenagers, and free for children.

🔢 **Johnnie Hajime Hirooka** ☎🖨 075/622-6803 ⊕ web.kyoto-inet.or.jp/people/h-s-love/. **Kyōto Tourist Information Center** ✉ 9F JR Kyōto Station bldg., Kyōto International Prefectural Center, Karasuma-dōri, Shimogyō-ku ☎ 075/344-3300 ⊕ www.kyoto-kankou.or.jp.

5

Points of Interest

SITES/AREAS	JAPANESE CHARACTERS
Adashino Nembutsu-ji	化野念仏寺
Bamboo forest	竹林
Byōdō-in (Temple of Equality)	平等院
Central & Southern Kyōto	洛中と洛南
Chion-in	知恩院
Chishaku-in	智積院
Chōraku-ji	長楽寺
Daigo-ji	醍醐寺
Daisen-in	大仙院
Daitoku-ji	大徳寺
Eastern Kyōto	洛東
Eikan-dō	永観堂
Fujii Daimaru	藤井大丸
Fushimi-Inari Taisha	伏見稲荷大社
Gekkeikan Ōkura Kinenkan (Gekkeikan Ōkura Museum)	月桂冠大倉記念館
Ginkaku-ji (Temple of the Silver Pavilion)	銀閣寺
Gion	祇園
Gion Kaburenjō Theater	祇園歌舞練場
Hakusasason-sō Garden	白沙村荘庭園
Heian Jingū	平安神宮
Hiei-zan Enryaku-ji	比叡山延暦寺
Higashi-Hongan-ji	東本願寺
Hirano Jinja	平野神社
Hōnen-in	法然院
Ichiwa	いち和
Inshō Dōmoto Art Museum (Dōmoto Inshō Bijutsukan)	堂本印象美術館
Jakkō-in	寂光院
Jikkō-in	実光院
Kamigamo Jinja	上賀茂神社
Katsura Rikyū (Katsura Imperial Villa)	桂離宮
Kawai Kanjirō Memorial House (Kawai Kanjirō Kinenkan)	河井寛次郎記念館

Kinkaku-ji (Temple of the Golden Pavilion)	金閣寺
Kitano Tenman-gū	北野天満宮
Kiyomizu-dera	清水寺
Kōdai-ji	高台寺
Kōinzan Saihō-ji (Moss Temple)	供隠山西芳寺
Konchi-in	金地院
Kōryū-ji	広隆寺
Kunyoku-dō	薫玉堂
Kyōto Costume Museum (Fūzoku Hakubutsukan)	風俗博物館
Kyōto Craft Center	京都クラフトセンター
Kyōto Handicraft Center	京都ハンディクラフトセンター
Kyōto Imperial Palace (Kyōto Gosho)	京都御所
Kyōto International Conference Center (Kokuritsu Kyōto Kokusai Kaikan)	国立京都国際会館
Kyōto Museum of Traditional Crafts (Kyōto Dentō Sangyō Fureai-kan)	京都伝統産業ふれあい館
Kyōto National Museum (Kokuritsu Hakubutsukan)	京都国立博物館
Kyoto Station	京都駅
Maruyama Kōen (Maruyama Park)	円山公園
Miho Museum (Miho Bijutsukan)	ミホミュージアム
Mukashi Natsukashi	昔なつ菓子
Murin-an Garden	無隣庵庭園
Myōshin-ji	妙心寺
Nanzen-ji	南禅寺
National Museum of Modern Art (Kindai Bijutsukan)	京都国立近代美術館
Nijō Jin-ya	二条陣屋
Nijō-jō	仁和寺
Ninna-ji	二条城
Nishi-Hongan-ji	西本願寺
Nishijin Textile Center (Nishijinori Kaikan)	西陣会館
Northern Kyōto	洛北
Oe Nogakudō Theater	大江能楽堂
Ōkōchi Sansō	大河内山荘
Path of Philosophy (Tetsugaku-no-michi)	鉄学の道

5

Ponto-chō Kaburenjō Theater	先斗町歌舞練場
Raku Museum (Raku Bijutsukan)	樂美術館
Ryōan-ji	龍安寺
Sanjūsangen-dō	三十三間堂
Sannen-zaka and Ninen-zaka (Sannen and Ninen slopes)	三年坂と二年坂
Sanzen-in	三千院
Shōren-in	青蓮院
Shūgaku-in Imperial Villa (Shūgaku-in Rikyū)	修学院離宮
Taiho-an	対鳳庵
Tenryū-ji	天龍寺
Tōfuku-ji	東福寺
Tō-ji	東寺
Western Kyōto & Arashiyama	洛西と嵐山
Yasaka Jinja	八坂神社
RESTAURANTS	
Akiyama	秋山
Ask a Giraffe	アスクアジラフ
Azekura	愛染倉
Bodegon	ボデゴン
Café bibliotic HELLO!	カフェビブリオティックハロー！
Café Peace	カフェピース
Café Sarasa	カフェさらさ
Cucina Il Viale	イルヴィアーレ
Divo Diva	ディボディバ
Gion Kappa Nawate	祇園かっぱ縄手本店
Giro Giro Hitoshina	技魯技魯ひとしな
Izusen	泉仙
Kerala	ケララ
Kicchan	きっちゃん
Kikunoi	菊乃井
Kyōto Gion Oishimbo	京都ぎおんおいしんぼ
Mankamerō	萬亀楼
Manzaratei Nishiki	まんざら亭Nishiki

Minokō	美濃幸
Mishima-tei	三嶋亭
Mukadeya	百足屋
Nontaro	呑太呂
Ogawa	おがわ
Ōiwa	大岩
Omen	おめん
Pontocho Rōbin	先斗町魯ビン
Rakushō	洛匠
Ramen Santōka	らーめん山頭火
Sagano	嵯峨野
Sagenta	左源太
Shinsen-en Heihachi	神泉苑 平八
Somushi Kocha-ya	素夢子 古茶家
Suishin	すいしん
Tiêm än Hu'o'ng Viêt	テイエム・フォーン・ヴィエット
Tōzentei	陶然亭
Yagenbori	やげんぼり
Yamabana Heihachi-Jaya	山花 平八茶屋
Yoshikawa	吉川
Zezekan Pocchiri	膳感漢ぽっちり
HOTELS	
ANA Hotel Kyōto	京都全日空ホテル
Gion Hatanaka	祇園畑中
Hiiragiya Ryokan	柊家旅館
Hotel Fujita Kyōto	ホテルフジタ京都
Hotel Granvia Kyōto	ホテルグランヴィア京都
Hyatt Regency	ハイアットリージェンシー京都
Inakatei	田舎亭
Iori	庵
Kinmata	斤又
Kyōto Brighton Hotel	京都ブライトンホテル
Kyōto Kokusai Hotel	京都国際ホテル
New Miyako Hotel	新・都ホテル

Palace Side Hotel	パレスサイドホテル
Rihga Royal Hotel Kyōto	リーガロイヤルホテル京都
Ryokan Seryo	芹生
Ryokan Yuhara	旅館ゆはら
Seryō	芹生
Syōensō-Hozugawa-tei	松園荘 保津川亭
Takaraga-ike Prince Hotel	宝ヶ池プリンスホテル
Tawaraya	俵屋
Westin Miyako Hotel	ウェスティン都ホテル
Yachiyo	八千代

Nara

WORD OF MOUTH

"Make the effort to get to Horyu-ji Temple. It's spectacular. There are frequent trains running to and from
Horyu-ji, and it's less than 15 minutes from Nara."
                                                    —PaoloCast

By Justin Ellis

NARA IS A PLACE OF SYNTHESIS, where Chinese art, religion, and architecture fused with Japanese language and Shintō traditions. The city was established in 710 and was then known as Heijō-Kyō (citadel of peace). Fujiwara-no-Fuhito, father-in-law of Emperor Mōmmu, was responsible for the city's creation. His grandson, the future Emperor Shōmu, later graced the new capital with its wealth of temples, pagodas, and shrines. Buddhism had come to Japan in the 6th century. Along with *kanji* (Chinese characters) and tea, it spread throughout the archipelago. Emperor Shōmu hoped that making the new capital the center of Buddhism would unite the country and secure his position as head of an emergent nation state.

The grandest of the Buddhist temples built in Nara during this era was Tōdai-ji, which Emperor Shōmu intended as a nexus for all the temples of his realm. But after 84 years the citadel of peace fell victim to the very intrigue that the Emperor had tried to suppress. In 794 the capital moved to Kyōto and Nara lost prominence, as did the Kegon sect that still manages Tōdai-ji today.

Now Nara is a provincial city whose most obvious role is a historical one, and Tōdai-ji is a monument rather than a political stronghold. Nara is a site of renewal and reinvention that has overcome typhoons, fires, and wars to remain a city of superlatives. Its position in the national consciousness as the birthplace of modern Japanese culture is well secured as it approaches its 1,300th anniversary in 2010.

See the glossary at the end of this book for definitions of the common Japanese words and suffixes used in this chapter.

ORIENTATION & PLANNING

Orientation

Almost at the center of the Japanese archipelago, Nara is on the Yamato plain, with Ōsaka to the west and Kyōto to the north. Much of what you'll come to Nara to see is in picturesque Nara Kōen (Nara Park), which is a short distance east of the two main stations. The commercial shopping district is south of Kintetsu Nara Station, while Sanjō-dōri, west of Nara Kōen and Nara-machi, has the two main tourist shopping areas. Hōryū-ji, Yakushi-ji, and Tōshōdai-ji, the major temples of western Nara, are all on one bus route or can be reached by JR train.

Nara-Kōen

The broad and undulating Nara Kōen was created out of wasteland in 1880. It nestles into the dense forest at the foot of Kasuga Mountain in the east, next to which are the cleared slopes of Wakakusa-yama. The park is home to some 1,200 tame deer, the focus of much local lore and legend.

Nara-machi

Nara-machi was the 'new' area of Nara at the beginning of the Edo period (1600–1868). Today its lanes and alleys are still lined by old wooden houses with latticed windows and whitewashed walls. Many of these old houses have been converted into galleries, museums, and shops.

Top Reasons to Visit

ARCHITECTURE

Nara is unrivaled in Japan for its wealth of classical temples, pagodas, and shrines—some are among the oldest wooden structures in the world. Crafted in the Chinese style, when Buddhism first appeared in Japan, they evoke the purity and vision of a new political order embarking on a religious and imperial odyssey.

HOSPITALITY & TRANQUILLITY

The unaffected, generous hospitality of Nara's citizens is famous all over Japan. That warmth and the city's serenity can best be experienced in a traditional, family-run inn.

SHOPPING

Among the merchant houses and traditional restaurants of Nara-machi's maze of streets, longtime locals in old wooden shops sell the crafts for which Nara is famous: *sumi* (ink sticks) for calligraphy and ink painting, Nara *sarashi-jofu* (fine hand woven, sun-bleached linen), and akahadayaki pottery.

LOCAL EATS

Nara is renowned for its *kaiseki*, a 7–12 course visual and culinary journey using the freshest seasonal ingredients. Kaiseki's humble but hearty cousin, *cha-gayu*, rice porridge flavored with green tea and served with seasonal vegetables, has been a Nara staple throughout the ages, as have tangy *nara-zuke*, vegetables pickled in sake.

TŌDAI-JI TEMPLE COMPLEX

Tōdai-ji Temple was conceived as the center of a religious and political network, and Nara's classical heart beats in the massive Daibutsu-den (Hall of the Great Buddha), home to the monumental Daibutsu (Great Buddha). The complex's oldest building, the 8th-century San-gatsu-dō, houses some of the finest examples of serene, 8th-century Tenpyo-era statues in Japan.

Western Nara

Hōryū-ji temple is known as the apotheosis of classical Japanese architecture. First built in the 7th century, it houses the oldest wooden structures in the world. Also in western Nara is Tōshōdai-ji temple, where Ganjin, the first Buddhist monk to come to Japan from China, taught Japanese monks and legitimized the spread of Buddhism throughout the country.

Planning

Most visitors miss the best that Nara has to offer on hurried day trips from Kyōto. To really appreciate Nara, allow yourself two days—one for central Nara and another for western Nara. On the first day, explore all the temples and shrines in Nara Kōen and spend a full morning or afternoon shopping and walking the streets of Nara-machi. On the second day, visit western Nara.

The Best of Times

Spring (March to May) and autumn (September to November) are the best times to visit Nara. The cherry blossoms peak in late March–early

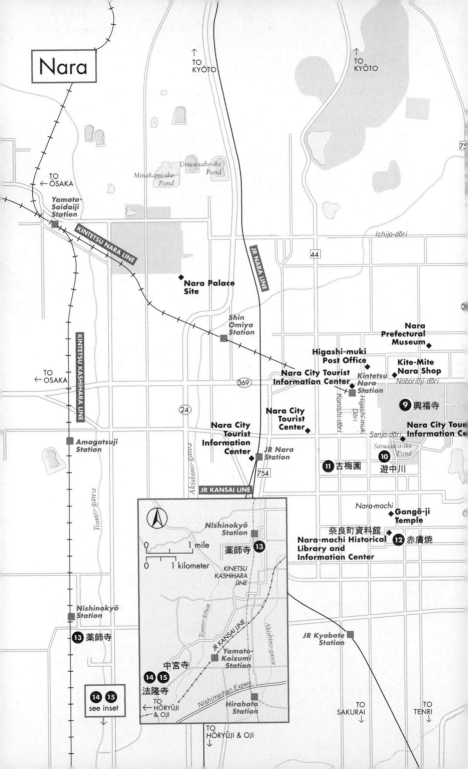

April, and the turning foliage is at its brightest in late October–early November. Summer (June to August) is hot and sticky. June is when Japan's rainy season either drizzles for a few days and disappears or creates weeks of torrential downpours. There are often light snowfalls in winter (December to February).

Concerning Restaurants & Hotels

It's a sin to visit Nara and not have a *kaiseki* dinner, an aesthetically arranged 7- to 12-course set meal using the freshest ingredients. It's usually an evening meal, but most kaiseki restaurants serve mini-kaiseki at lunchtime for day-trippers. Most traditional restaurants are small and have set courses. Nara retires early, and restaurants close around 10 PM, taking last orders around 9 PM. Small restaurants and *izakaya* (afterwork drinking haunts that serve an array of small dishes and drinks) are dispersed throughout the two main shopping streets, Higashi-muki Dōri (a pedestrian arcade) and Konishi-dōri, close to Kintetsu Nara Station. When ordering food, start by asking for an *osusume* (a suggestion) and go from there. Don't be embarrassed or afraid to communicate, even without Japanese, as people in Nara look after their visitors. But keep in mind that each time you eat some delicious sashimi or order tempura you add ¥600–¥900 to your bill. Learning a language can be expensive! Expect to pay about ¥750 for a large bottle of beer. Because English-speaking staff and English menus aren't givens, ask a staff member from your hotel to help make arrangements. Alternatively, stay in a *ryokan* (traditional inn), where a kaiseki dinner is included in the room rate.

Nara has accommodations in every style and price range. Since most people treat the city as a day-trip destination, at night the quiet streets are the domain of Nara's residents. All lodgings have air-conditioning, televisions, and communal baths unless noted otherwise. Some ryokan close on Sunday nights. Hotels in Central Nara around the main railway stations are often noisier than those closer to Nara Kōen and in Nara-machi. During spring and autumn and peak holiday periods, rooms are hard to find on weekend nights. Book well in advance if you plan to travel to Nara during these times.

For more on Japanese cuisine, *see* Understanding Japan *and* Dining *in* Essentials.

For a short course on accommodations in Japan, *see* Lodging *in* Essentials.

WHAT IT COSTS In yen				
$$$$	**$$$**	**$$**	**$**	**¢**
RESTAURANTS over 3,000	2,000–3,000	1,000–2,000	800–1,000	under 800
HOTELS over 22,000	18,000–22,000	12,000–18,000	8,000–12,000	under 8,000

Restaurant prices are per person for a main course. Hotel price categories are for two people and based on rack rates in high season and the European Plan (with no meals) unless otherwise noted. Tax (5%) and service charges are extra.

Getting Around Town

With relatively flat roads and an abundance of greenery, we recommend seeing Nara on foot. For people with less time, most of the main sites can be reached by bicycle, except for those along the eastern edge of the park, such as the San-gatsu-dō, the Ni-gatsu-dō, and Kasuga Taisha. For small groups, short taxi rides within Nara city cost only slightly more than buses. Expect to pay about ¥1,000 to get to Kasuga Taisha from either of the main train stations. Two local bus routes circle the main sites (Tōdai-ji, Kasuga Taisha, and Shin-Yakushi-ji) in the central and eastern parts of the city: Bus 1 runs counter-clockwise, and Bus 2 runs clockwise. This urban loop line costs ¥180. Both stop at JR Nara Station and Kintetsu Nara Station.

Visitor Information

The **Nara City Tourist Information Office** is on the first floor of Kintetsu Nara Station and is open daily 9–5. (✉ Kintetsu Nara Station, 29 Naka-machi, Higashi-muki, Nara-shi ☎ 0742/24–4858). Another Nara City Tourist Information Office, open daily 9–5, is at JR Nara Station (✉ JR Nara Station, 1 Banchi Sanjō, Hon-machi, Nara-shi ☎ 0742/22–9821).

Nara City Tourist Information Center is open daily 9–9, but the English-speaking staff are only on duty until 7 PM. The center is a 10-minute walk from both Kintetsu Nara Station and JR Nara Station and has free maps, sightseeing information in English, a souvenir corner, and a lounge. (✉ 23–4 Kami-sanjō-chō, Nara-shi ☎ 0742/22–3900).

For an overview of the arts and crafts of Nara Prefecture, visit the Kite-Mite Nara Shop on your way to Nara Kōen. A brochure in English is available. **Kite-Mite Nara Shop** (✉ 38-1 Noboriōji-chō, Nara-shi ☎ 0742/26–8823).

EXPLORING NARA

Nara Kōen

Nara Kōen has the city's popular tourist sites. Even so, it is wide enough to accommodate thousands of giggling school children and other Japanese tourists, yet still feel spacious and quiet. And—be warned—it is home to many divine messengers of god—the tame deer seen just about everywhere. Legend has it that Takenomikazuchi-no-mikoto, one of the five gods of Kasuga Shrine, once landed atop Mt. Mikasa-yama riding a white deer. Since then these animals have been regarded as sacred messengers of Takenomikazuchi-no-mikoto and have been designated National Treasures. They very quickly convey the message that they want something to eat. *Shika-senbei* (deer crackers) are for sale throughout the park.

What to See at the Tōdai-ji Temple Complex

The temple complex was conceived by Emperor Shomu in the 8th century as the seat of authority for Buddhist Japan. Construction was completed in 752, and even though the imperial household later left Nara, Tōdai-ji and its Great Buddha remained. An earthquake damaged it in

855, and in 1180 the temple was burned to the ground. Its reconstruction met a similar fate during the 16th-century civil wars. A century later only the central buildings were rebuilt; these are what remain today. Among the structures, the Daibutsu-den is the grandest, with huge beams that seemingly converge upward toward infinity.

To get to Tōdai-ji, board Bus 2 from the front of either the JR or Kintetsu Nara station and exit at Daibutsu-den. Cross the street to the path that leads to the Tōdai-ji complex. You can walk from Kintetsu Nara Station in about 15 minutes by heading east on Noborioji-dōri, the avenue running parallel to the station. In Nara Kōen turn left onto the pedestrians-only street, lined with souvenir stalls and restaurants, that leads to Tōdai-ji. A taxi from JR or Kintetsu Nara station costs about ¥1,000.

The following sites are close together, making this a walk of about three hours, allowing for time to feed the deer.

❸ **Daibutsu-den** (Hall of the Great Buddha). The Daibutsu-den is a rare ex-
Fodor'sChoice ample of monumentality in the land of the diminutive bonsai. Unfortu-
★ nately the *kutsu-gata* (shoe-shape) gilt ornaments that decorate the roof ridge of the Daibutsu-den did a lamentable job in their supposed ability to ward off fire. The current Daibutsu-den was restored in 1709 at two-thirds its original scale. At 157 feet tall and 187 feet wide, it's still considered the largest wooden structure in the world. If you want to ward off illness, follow the lead of those lighting incense at the huge bronze urn and waving it all over their bodies.

Inside the Daibutsu-den is the **Daibutsu**, a 53-foot bronze statue of the Buddha. His hand alone is the size of six tatami mats. The Daibutsu was originally commissioned by Emperor Shōmu in 743. After numerous unsuccessful castings, this figure was finally made in 749. A statue of this scale had never been cast before in Japan, and it was meant to serve as a symbol to unite the country. The Daibutsu was dedicated in 752 in a grand ceremony attended by the then-retired Emperor Shōmu, the imperial court, and 10,000 priests and nuns. The current Daibutsu is an amalgamation of work done in three eras: the 8th, 12th, and 17th-centuries.

Patience may be a virtue, but here there is a fast track to enlightenment. Apparently, if you can squeeze through the hole in the pillar behind the Daibutsu you've achieved it. In a cruel irony, wisdom is thus bestowed upon children with ease while their elders struggle on. ⊠ *Tōdai-ji Temple Complex, Nara Kōen, Central Nara* 🎫 *¥500* ⊙ *Jan., Feb., Nov., and Dec., daily 8–4:30; Mar., daily 8–5; Apr.–Sept., daily 7:30–5:30; Oct., daily 7:30–5.*

❷ **Kaidan-in.** A peaceful pebble garden in the courtyard of this small temple belies the ferocious expressions of the Four Heavenly Guardian clay statues inside. Depicted in full armor and wielding weapons, they are an arresting sight. *Kaidan* is a Buddhist word for the terrace on which monks are ordained; the Chinese Buddhist Ganjin (688–763) administered many induction ceremonies of Japanese Buddhists here. The current structure dates from 1731. Kaidan-in is in northwestern Nara Kōen, west of the Daibutsu-den. ⊠ *Tōdai-ji Temple Complex, Nara Kōen,*

Central Nara ☒ ¥500 ☉ *Apr.–Sept., daily 7:30–5:30; Oct., daily 7:30–5; Nov.–Feb., daily 8–4:30; Mar., daily 8–5.*

❶ Nandai-mon (Great Southern Gate). The soaring Tōdai-ji Gate, the entrance to the temple, is supported by 18 large wooden pillars, each 62 feet high and nearly 3⅓ feet in diameter. The original gate was destroyed in a typhoon in 962 and rebuilt in 1199. Two outer niches on either side of the gate contain fearsome wooden figures of Deva kings, who guard the great Buddha within. They are the work of master sculptor Unkei, of the Kamakura period (1185–1335). In the inner niches are a pair of stone *koma-inu* (Korean dogs), mythical guardians that ward off evil. ☒ *Central Nara.*

❹ Ni-gatsu-dō (Second Month Temple). Named for a ritual that begins in February and culminates in the spectacular sparks and flames of the Omizu-tori festival in March, the Ni-gatsu-dō was founded in 752. It houses important images of the Buddha that are, alas, not on display to the public. Still, its hilltop location and veranda afford a commanding view of Nara Kōen. ☒ *Tōdai-ji Temple Complex, Nara Kōen, Central Nara* ☒ *Free* ☉ *Jan., Feb., Nov., and Dec., daily 8–4:30; Mar., daily 8–5; Apr.–Sept., daily 7:30–5:30; Oct., daily 7:30–5:30.*

★ ❺ San-gatsu-dō (Third Month Temple). The San-gatsu-dō, founded in 733, is the oldest original building in the Tōdai-ji complex. It takes its name from the *sutra* (Buddhist scripture) reading ceremonies held here in the third month of the ancient lunar calendar (present-day February to April). You can sit on benches covered with tatami mats and appreciate the 1,200-year-old National Treasures that crowd the small room. The principal display is the lacquer statue of Fukūkensaku Kannon, the goddess of mercy, whose diadem is encrusted with thousands of pearls and gemstones. The two clay *bosatsu* (bodhisattva) statues on either side of her, the Gakkō (Moonlight) and the Nikkō (Sunlight), are fine examples of the *Tenpyo* period (Nara period), the height of classical Japanese sculpture. The English pamphlet included with admission details all the statues in the San-gatsu-dō. ☒ *Tōdai-ji Temple Complex, Nara Kōen, Central Nara* ☒ ¥500 ☉ *Jan., Feb., Nov., and Dec., daily 8–4:30; Mar., daily 8–5; Apr.–Sept., daily 7:30–5:30; Oct., daily 7:30–5.*

NEED A BREAK? At the foot of Wakakusa-yama and down some stone steps is **Wakakusa-yama Mizutani chaya**, a delightful old thatched-roofed farmhouse. You can order simple noodle dishes and *matcha* whisked green tea. Alternatively, enjoy a cold beer under the canopy of maple trees. (☒ 30 Kasugano-chō Nara-shi ☎ 0742/22-0627 ☉ Thurs.–Tues. 11–4:30)

What to See Elsewhere in Nara Kōen

Kasuga Taisha is Nara's main shrine and one of Japan's three most important ones, along with Ise Jingu in Mie Prefecture and Izumo Taisha in Shimane. In a secluded spot at the foot of Kasuga-yama, this is reputedly where the gods first appeared in Japan. It's a 15-minute walk from the San-gatsu-dō. Beyond the lanterns of Kasuga Taisha is a refreshing 30-minute walk through a small forest that leads to Shin-Yakushi-ji temple, a treasure house of Nara-period sculpture. From

FIRE FESTIVALS & LIGHT-UPS IN NARA

To light up doesn't mean to have a cigarette in Japan. In fact, most light-ups are at temples and shrines where, atypically, smoking is banned. Below are the more dramatic illuminations on the Nara festival calendar.

JANUARY

Wakakusa-yama Yaki (Grass Burning Festival). On the night before the second Monday in January, 15 priests set Wakakusa-yama's dry grass afire while fireworks illuminate Kōfuku-ji's Five-Story Pagoda in one of Japan's most photographed rituals. This rite is believed to commemorate the resolution of a boundary dispute between the monks and priests of Tōdai-ji and Kōfuku-ji. The fireworks start at 5:50 and the grass fire is lit at 6.

FEBRUARY

Mantoro (Lantern Festival). On February 3 the 2,000 stone and 1,000 bronze lanterns at Kasuga Taisha are lighted to mark the traditional end of winter called *setsubun*. Between 5 and 9.

MARCH

Shunie-Omizutori (Water Drawing Festival). From March 1 to 14 priests circle the upper gallery of the Ni-gatsu-dō (Second Month Hall) wielding 21-foot-long *taimatsu* (bamboo torches) weighing more than 80 kg, while sparks fall on those below. Catching the embers burns out sins and wards off evil. This festival is more than 1,200 years old, a rite of repentance to the Eleven-Headed Kannon, an incarnation of the Goddess of Mercy. March 1–12, 7:30–8; 13, 7–7:30; 14, for 10 minutes from 6:30.

JULY–OCTOBER

Light-up Promenade. Sights including Yakushi-ji, Kōfuku-ji, and Tōdai-ji are illuminated at night. July, August, and September 7–10, October 6–10.

AUGUST

Toka-e. From August 1 to 15 Nara Kōen is aglow with more than 7,000 candles. From 7 to 9:45.

Chugen Mantoro (Mid-year Lantern Festival). For more than 800 years the thousands of lanterns at Kasuga Taisha have been lighted to guide ancestors back to earth on their annual pilgrimage, Obon. August 14–15 from 7 to 10.

Shin-Yakushi-ji it is a 30-minute walk back to central Nara Kōen, where the Five-Story Pagoda of Kōfuku-ji Temple leads you to its main hall and the magnificent statues therein. A couple of hours' strolling in the alleys of Nara-machi provides a change of pace from temple-hopping and is a good way to end the day.

★ ❻ **Kasuga Taisha.** Famous for the more than 2,000 stone *mantoro* (lanterns) that line the major pathways, Kasuga Taisha is at once a monument to those who have paid tribute to the shrine's Shintō gods by dedicating a lantern, and to the Shintō tradition of worshipping nature. The lighting of the lanterns on three days of the year attracts large crowds that whisper with reverential excitement. February 3 is the Mantoro Festival, celebrating the beginning of spring, and August 14 15 is the Chugen Mantoro Festival, when the living show respect to their ancestors by lighting the way back to earth for them on their annual visit. As people take photographs with their mobile phones, the new messengers (men with loudspeakers) direct the well-behaved crowds. Kasuga Taisha was founded in 768

> ### DEER-SAFE TIP
>
> Behind the Ni-gatsu-dō is a lovely rest area where free water and cold tea are available 9 AM–4 PM. Although no food is sold here, it's a quiet spot to picnic, unhindered by the antlered messengers.

and for centuries, according to Shintō custom, the shrine was reconstructed every 20 years on its original design—not merely to renew the materials but also to purify the site. It's said that Kasuga Taisha has been rebuilt more than 50 times; its current incarnation dates from 1893. After you pass through the *torii* (orange gate), the first wooden structure you'll see is the **Hai-den** (Offering Hall); to its left is the **Naorai-den** (Entertainment Hall). To the left of Naorai-den are the four **Hon-den** (Main Shrines). They are designated as National Treasures, all built in the same Kasuga style and painted vermillion and green—a striking contrast to the dark wooden exterior of most other Nara temples.

To get to Kasuga Taisha from Nara Kōen, walk east past the Five-Story Pagoda until you reach a torii. This path will lead you to the shrine. ✉ *160 Kasuga-no-chō, Nara-shi* ☎ *0742/22–7788* 🎫 *Kasuga Shrine Museum ¥420; shrine's outer courtyard free; inner precincts with 4 Honden structures and gardens ¥500* ⊙ *Museum daily 9–4; inner precincts Jan., Feb., and Dec., daily 7–4:30; Mar. and Nov., daily 7–5; Apr., daily 6:30–5:30; May–Sept., daily 6:30–6; Oct., daily 6:30–5:30.*

❾ Kōfuku-ji. The **Kōfuku-ji temple's** Five-Story Pagoda dominates the skyline. Built in 1426, it's an exact replica of the original pagoda built here in 730 by Empress Kōmyō, which burned to the ground. At 164 feet it is the second-tallest in Japan, a few centimeters shorter than the pagoda at Tō-ji Temple in Kyōto. To the southwest of the Five-Story Pagoda, down a flight of steps, is the **Three-Story Pagoda**. Built in 1114, it is renowned for its graceful lines and fine proportions.

While the Five-Story Pagoda is Kōfuku-ji's most eye-catching building, the main attraction is the first-rate collection of Buddhist statues in the **Tōkondō** (Great Eastern Hall). A reconstruction dating from the 15th-century, the hall was built to speed the recovery of the ailing Empress Genshō. It is dominated by a statue of Yakushi Nyorai (Physician of the Soul), and is flanked by Four Heavenly Kings and Twelve Heavenly Generals. In contrast to the highly stylized and enlightened Yakushi Nyorai, the seated figure on the left is a statue of a mortal, Yuima Koji. A lay devotee of Buddhism, Yuima was respected for his eloquence but perhaps more revered for his belief that enlightenment could be accomplished through meditation even while mortal passions were indulged. Although Kōfuku-ji temple is no longer a religious mecca, you may see older Japanese writing on *ema* (votive plaques) left by pilgrims to ensure the happiness and safety of their families. The exquisite incense and the patina of the gold leaf on the drapery of the Yakushi Nyorai create a reflective experience.

Ironically, the architecturally contrasting concrete-and-steel **Kokuhōkan** (National Treasure House), north of Kōfuku-ji, houses the largest and most varied collection of National Treasure sculpture and other works of art. The most famous is a statue of Ashura, one of the Buddha's eight protectors, with three heads and six arms.

Kōfuku-ji is a five-minute walk west of Nara Kokuritsu Hakubutsukan (Nara National Museum) in the central part of Nara Kōen, and it's an easy 15-minute walk from the JR or Kintetsu station. ⊠ 48 Noboriōji-chō, Nara-shi ☎ 0742/22–7755 ☜ Great Eastern Hall ¥300, National Treasure House ¥500 ☉ Daily 9–5.

❽ Nara National Museum (Nara Kokuritsu Hakubutsukan). The original museum, built in 1895, houses the museum's permanent collection of sculpture from Japan, Korea, and China. The main focus is on the Nara and Heian periods. The West Wing has paintings, calligraphy, ceramics, and archaeological artifacts from Japan, some dating back to the 10th-century BC. The East Wing is used for temporary exhibitions. During the driest days of November the Shōsō-in Repository, behind the Tōdai-ji, displays some of its magnificent collection. ⊠ 50 Noboriōji-chō ☎ 0742/22–7771 ☜ ¥420 ☉ Tues.–Sun., daily 9:30–5; enter by 4:30.

❼ Shin-Yakushi-ji. This temple was founded in 747 by Empress Kōmyō (701–760) in gratitude for the recovery of her sick husband, Emperor Shōmu. Only the Main Hall, which houses many fine objects from the Nara period, remains. In the center of the hall is a wooden statue of Yakushi Nyorai, the Physician of the Soul. Surrounding this statue are 12 clay images of the Twelve Divine Generals who protected Yakushi. Eleven of these figures are originals. The Generals stand in threatening poses, bearing spears, swords, and other weapons, and wear terrifying expressions. ⊠ 1289 Takabatake-fukui-chō ☜ ¥600 ☉ Daily 9–5.

Nara-machi

Nara-machi is a maze of lanes and alleys lined with old warehouses and *machiya* (traditional wooden houses) that have been converted into galleries, shops, and cafes. A lot of locals still live here, so the smell of grilled mackerel at lunchtime or roasted tea in the afternoon wafts through the air. Many of the old shops deal in Nara's renowned arts and crafts, such as akahadayaki pottery, ink, and linen. A free map, available from any Nara City Tourism Information Office, guides you to the main shops, museums, and galleries, as do English signposts. Nara-machi is a good change of pace from temple viewing.

We've noted usual hours, but stores can close irregularly. Ask at the Nara City Tourist Information Center if you'd like to check before you set out. From the southwest corner of Sarusawa-ike, with the pond notice board on your left, walk straight until you come to a main road, on the other side of which is the centre of Nara-machi.

What to See

⑫ Akahadayaki. A potter's wheel is in the window of Akahadayaki, where beautiful ceramic candleholders, *tokaki,* illuminate the rooms with leaf and geometric patterns. The *tokaki* and ceramics at Akahadayaki are all handmade, original designs. ✉ *18 Shibashinya-chō, Nara-machi* ☎ *0742/23–3110* ⏱ *Thurs.–Tues. 10:30–5.*

⑪ Kobaien. Nara accounts for about 90% of Japan's *sumi*-ink production, and for 400 years Kobaien has made fine ink sticks for calligraphy and ink painting. More recently, some types of sumi-ink have been used for tattooing. ✉ *7 Tsubai-chō, Nara-machi* ☎ *0742/23–2965* ⏱ *Weekdays 9–5.*

NEED A BREAK? **Koshi-no-ie is a well-to-do merchant's house that has been thoroughly restored. It's like a quick trip through the Edo period.** ☎ **0742/34–4739** ⏱ **Tues.–Sun. 9–5.**

⑩ "Yū" Nakagawa. "Yū" Nakagawa specializes in hand-woven, sun-bleached linen textiles, a Nara specialty known as *sarashi-jofu.* This shop sells *noren* (two-panel curtains put on business entranceways to show that they are open), handbags, slippers, and other linen crafts incorporating traditional Nara motifs. ✉ *31–1 Genrin-in-chō, Nara-machi* ☎ *0742/22–1322* ⏱ *Daily 11–6.*

6

Western Nara

Hōryū-ji is home to some of the oldest wooden buildings in the world. Just east of Hōryū-ji is Chūgū-ji, with one of the finest sculptures in Japan, the 7th-century Miroku Bodhisattva. A short bus ride back toward Nara brings you to Yakushi-ji and Tōshōdai-ji temples, both religious and political centers during the Nara period. To visit all four temples in one day, go to Hōryū-ji by the JR Main Line first (Chūgū-ji is a 10-minute walk from Hōryū-ji) and proceed to Tōshōdai-ji and Yakushi-ji by bus.

What to See

⑭ Hōryū-ji. Hōryū-ji is the jewel in the crown of classical Japanese architecture. In the morning, elderly locals on their way to work pray in front of the temple with an intensity the younger generation usually displays toward manga and *purikura* (photo stickers). Founded in 607 by Prince Shōtoku (573–621),

Fodor'sChoice ★

SUBSTITUTE MONKEYS

Nara-machi Shiryōkan (Nara-machi Historical Library and Information Center). So just what are those red cloth animals on pieces of rope outside houses in Nara-machi? They are called *migawarizaru,* substitute monkeys. They bear the inscription "*kana-ianzen mubyosokusai,*" or "good health and safety for the family." Typically, there is one monkey for every member of a household, and each is supposed to suffer illness and accidents on behalf of its owner. The Nara-machi Shiryōkan displays artifacts from Nara-machi from the Edo period (1600–1868) to the present. It's near Gangō-ji temple. ✉ 12 *Shibashinya-chō, Nara-machi* ☎ *0742/22 5509* ⏱ *Tues.–Sun. 10–4.*

Hōryū-ji's original wooden buildings are among the world's oldest. The first gate you pass through is the **Nandai-mon,** which was rebuilt in 1438 and is thus a relatively young 500 years old. The second gate, **Chū-mon** (Middle Gate), is the 607 original. Unlike most Japanese gates, which are supported by two pillars at the ends, central pillars support this gate. Note their entasis, or swelling at the center, an architectural feature from ancient Greece that traveled as far as Japan. Such columns are found in Japan only in the 7th-century structures of Nara.

After passing through the gates, you enter the temple's western precincts. The first building on the right is the **Kon-dō** (Main Hall), a two-story reproduction of the original 7th-century hall, which displays Buddhist images and objects from as far back as the Asuka period (552–645). The Five-Story Pagoda to its left was disassembled in World War II to protect it from air raids, after which it was reconstructed with the same materials used in 607. Behind the pagoda is the **Daikō-dō** (Lecture Hall), destroyed by fire and rebuilt in 990. Inside is a statue of Yakushi Nyorai (Physician of the Soul) carved from a camphor tree.

From the Daikō-dō, walk past the Kon-dō and Chū-mon; then turn left and walk past the pond on your right. You come to two concrete buildings known as the **Daihōzō-den** (Great Treasure Hall), which display statues, sculptures, ancient Buddhist religious articles, and brocades. Of particular interest is a miniature shrine that belonged to Lady Tachibana, mother of Empress Kōmyō. The shrine is about 2½ feet high; the Buddha inside is about 20 inches tall.

Tōdai-mon (Great East Gate) opens onto Hōryū-ji's eastern grounds. The octagonal **Yumedono** (Hall of Dreams) was so named because Prince Shōtoku used to meditate in it.

To get here, take a JR Kansai Main Line train to Hōryū-ji Station (¥210). The temple is a short shuttle ride or a 15-minute walk. Alternatively, bus 52, 60, or 97 to Hōryū-ji is a 50-minute ride from the JR Nara station or Kintetsu Nara Station (¥760). The Hōryūji-mae bus stop is in front of the temple. ⊠ *1–1 Ikaruga-chō, Hōryū-ji, Ikoma-gun, Nara-ken, Western Nara* ☎ *0745/75–2555* ☒ *¥1,000* ⊙ *Feb. 22–Nov. 3, daily 8–5; Nov. 4–Feb. 21, daily 8–4:30; last entry 30 min before closing.*

⓯ **Chūgū-ji.** Chūgū-ji was originally the home of Prince Shōtoku's mother in the 6th-century and is now a Buddhist nunnery. This temple houses an amazing wooden statue of the Miroku Bodhisattva, the Buddha of the Future. His gentle countenance has been a famous image of hope since it was carved, sometime in the Asuka period (552–645). Chūgū-ji is a few minutes' walk north of the Yumendono. ⊠ *1–2 1-chōme Ikaruga-chō, Hōryū-ji, Kita Ikoma-gun, Nara-ken, Western Nara* ☎ *0745/75–2106* ☒ *¥500* ⊙ *Apr.–Sept., daily 9–4:30; Oct.–Mar., daily 9–4.*

★ ⓭ **Yakushi-ji.** The two pagodas that tower over Yakushi-ji temple are an analogy of past and present Japan. Yakushi-ji's **East Pagoda** dates from 1285, and has such an interesting asymmetrical shape that it inspired Boston Museum of Fine Arts curator Ernest Fenollosa (1853–1908), an early Western specialist in Japanese art, to remark that it was as beau-

Try, Try, Try Again

Tōshōdai-ji was built in 751 for Ganjin, a Chinese priest who traveled to Japan at the invitation of Emperor Shōmu. At that time Japanese monks had never received formal instruction from a Buddhist monk. The invitation was extended by two Japanese monks who had traveled to China in search of a Buddhist willing to undertake the arduous and perilous journey to Japan.

It seemed that Ganjin would never make it to Japan. On his first journey some of his disciples betrayed him. His second journey resulted in a shipwreck. During the third trip his ship was blown off course, and on his fourth trip government officials refused him permission to leave China. Before his next attempt, he contracted an eye disease that left him blind. He persevered nonetheless, and finally reached Japan in 750. Ganjin shared his knowledge of Buddhism with his adopted country and served as a teacher to many Japanese abbots as well as Emperor Shōmu. He is also remembered for bringing the first sampling of sugar to Japan. Every June 6, to commemorate his birthday, the **Miei-dō** (Founder's Hall) in the back of the temple grounds displays a lacquer statue of Ganjin that dates from 763.

The main entrance to Tōshōdai-ji is called the Path of History, since in Nara's imperial days dignitaries and priests trod this route; today it is lined with clay-walled houses, gardens, and the occasional shop selling crafts or nara-zuke.

At the temple's entrance entastic pillars support the **Nandai-mon** (Great South Gate). Beyond the Nandai-mon is the **Kon-dō** (Main Hall), a superb example of classical Nara architecture. It is due to be under restoration until autumn 2009. Inside the hall is a lacquer statue of Vairocana Buddha, the same incarnation of Buddha that is enshrined at Tōdai-ji. The halo surrounding him was originally covered with 1,000 Buddhas; now there are 864. In back of the Kon-dō sits the **Daikō-dō** (Lecture Hall), formerly an assembly hall of the Nara Imperial Court, the only remaining example of Nara palace architecture.

Tōshōdai-ji is a 10-minute walk from the rear gate of Yakushi-ji along the Path of History. From central Nara or Hōryū-ji, take Bus 52 or 97 to the stop in front of Tōshōdai-ji. ✉ 13–46 Gojō-chō, Nara-shi, Western Nara ☎ 0742/33-7900 ✆ ¥600 ⊙ Daily 8.30–5.

tiful as "frozen music." Its simple, dark brown beams with white ends contrast starkly with its flashier, vermillion-painted 20th-century neighbor, the **West Tower**, built in 1981. For many, the new goes against the "imperfect, impermanent, and incomplete" principles of the old *wabi-sabi* aesthetic; but we think the contrast dynamizes Yakushi-ji right into the 21st-century. Officially named one of the Seven Great Temples of Nara, Yakushi-ji was founded in 680 and moved to its current location in 718. From central Nara take either the Kintetsu Line train, changing at Yamato-Saidaiji to Nishinokyō, or Bus 52 or 97 to Yakushi-ji; from Hōryū-ji or Chūgū-ji, take Bus 97 to Yakushi-ji-mae. ✉ 457 Nishinokyō-chō, Nara-shi, Western Nara ☎ 0742/33–6001 ✆ ¥500 ⊙ Daily 8:30–5.

WHERE TO EAT

★ $$$$ ✗ **Onjaku.** Hidden down a quiet street just south of Ara-ike in Nara Kōen is this intimate restaurant serving exquisitely presented traditional kaiseki meals. Within the faded wooden walls, a common architectural motif in Nara, you can sit at a rustic counter or in one of two serene tatami rooms. Choose from one of the two set meals on offer. ✉ *1043 Kita-temma-chō, Nara Kōen area* ☎ *0742/26–4762* ⌚ *Reservations essential* ⊟ *No credit cards* ⊙ *Closed Tues.*

★ $$$$ ✗ **Tsukihitei.** Deep in the forest behind Kasuga Taisha, Tsukihitei has the perfect setting for kaiseki. From the walk up a wooded path to the tranquillity of your own tatami room, everything is conducive to experiencing the beautiful presentation and delicate flavors—as Hellen Keller did when she dined at Tsukihitei in 1948. When reserving a table, enlist the help of a good Japanese speaker to select a set meal for you, and allow yourself to be regaled. The lunch sets cost between ¥10,000 and ¥15,000. ✉ *158 Kasugano-chō, Nara Kōen area* ☎ *0742/26–2021* ⌚ *Reservations essential* ⊟ *AE, DC, MC, V.*

★ $$$$ ✗ **Uma no Me.** In a little 1920s farmhouse just north of Ara-ike pond in Nara Kōen this delightful restaurant with dark beams and pottery-lined walls serves delicious home-style cooking. Everything is prepared from scratch. Recommended is the ¥3,500 lunch course with seasonal vegetables, tofu, and fried fish. As there is only one set meal, ordering is no problem. ✉ *1158 Takabatake-chō, Nara Kōen area* ☎ *0742/23–7784* ⌚ *Reservations appreciated* ⊟ *No credit cards* ⊙ *Closed Thurs.*

★ $$$$ ✗ **Yanagi-ja-ya.** Though unassuming from the outside, once you enter the revered Yanagi-ja-ya you're transported to a bygone age. In a secluded tatami room overlooking a garden you'll be served elegantly simple bento meals of sashimi, stewed vegetables, and tofu in black-lacquer boxes. Lunch costs ¥4,000–¥6,000. ✉ *49 Noboriōji-chō, Nara Kōen area* ☎ *0742/ 22–7460* ⌚ *Reservations essential* ⊟ *No credit cards* ⊙ *Closed Wed.*

$$$$ ✗ **Yanagi-ja-ya.** At this branch of this Nara institution in Nara Kōen, just past the Five-Story Pagoda, you may find yourself just popping in to try some *warabi mochi* for morning or afternoon tea. Delicious morsels made from warabi (bracken fern root) are tossed in soybean flour and sweetened with brown sugar syrup. ✉ *48 Teraoji-chō, Nara Kōen area* ☎ *0742/ 22–7560* ⌚ *Reservations essential* ⊟ *No credit cards* ⊙ *Closed Mon.*

$$–$$$$ ✗ **Tō-no-chaya.** One of Nara's most distinctive meals is *cha-gayu* (green tea–flavored rice porridge). During the day Tō-no-chaya serves a light meal of this special dish, with sashimi and vegetables, plus a few sweetened rice cakes for dessert. The restaurant was named Tō-no-chaya, which means "tearoom of the pagoda," for its views of see the Five-Story Pagoda of Kōfuku-ji. Bento-box meals are served 11:30–4. You must reserve ahead for cha-gayu in the evening. ✉ *47 Noboriōji-chō, Nara Kōen area* ☎ *0742/22–4348* ⊟ *No credit cards* ⊙ *Closed Tues.*

$$–$$$$ ✗ **Yamazakiya.** Pungent nara-zuke will lure you into this well-known shop and adjoining restaurant. Inside, white-capped prep cooks busily prepare packages of pickles that you can try with cha-gayu or a meal of tempura. The set menus are on display, making ordering simple. This is a good place to escape the crowds on Higashi-muki Dōri, the main

shopping street. Nara Kintetsu Station and Nara Kōen are within a five-minute walk. ⊠ *5 Minami-machi-chō Higashi-muki Dōri, Nara Kōen area* ☏ *0742/27–3715* ▤ *DC, V* ☻ *Closed Mon.*

Nara-machi

$$$–$$$$ ✕ **Harishin.** Harishin's Kamitsumichi bento, with a selection of sashimi, tofu, fried shrimp, vegetables, and homemade plum liqueur, is a bargain for ¥2,625. Harishin is traditional and quite rustic. You sit in either a large tatami room overlooking a garden or around a large *irori* (hearth). ⊠ *15 Nakashinya-chō, Nara-machi* ☏ *0742/22–2669* ▤ *AE, D, MC, V* ☻ *Closed Mon. No dinner.*

$$–$$$ ✕ **Tempura Asuka.** If you choose from the selection of set meals, make sure you pick one with tempura—the house specialty. Other fare ranges from a light tempura-soba lunch to an elaborate kaiseki dinner. Lunch options start at ¥1,050. As with other less formal Nara-machi restaurants, you can sit at the counter, at a table overlooking the garden, or in a tatami room. ⊠ *11 Shōnami-chō, Nara-machi* ☏ *0742/26–4308* ▤ *AE, DC, MC, V* ☻ *Closed Mon.*

$$–$$$ ✕ **Hirasō.** At Hirasō you can try *kakinoha-zushi*, sushi wrapped in a persimmon leaf. What's more, you can take it away in a light wooden box wrapped with precision. Most set menus at Hirasō include *cha-gayu* (rice porridge flavored with green tea), which is usually made with mushrooms or seasonal vegetables. Another featured Nara delicacy is *kakisugu*, dried persimmon, dusted with *kudzu* (flour made from the East Asian kudzu vine) and cooked tempura style. Hirasō has tables and chairs, but the tatami alcoves are more intimate. It's open all day, and take-out sushi is available from 10 to 8:30. ⊠ *30-1 Imamikado-chō* ☏ *0742/22–0866* ▤ *AE, DC, MC, V* ☻ *Closed Mon.*

Western Nara

$$$–$$$$ ✕ **Van Kio.** This large restaurant is famous for its *tamatebako* set meal. Different foods are put into beautiful paper boxes, sealed inside an earthenware bowl, and then theatrically smashed open with a wooden mallet. Apparently this custom is utilized on first dates with some success. Other specialties from the menu (in English) include the Renge set lunch, eight *obanzai* (samples) of local Japanese food arranged on spoons including *kakinoha-zushi* (sushi wrapped in a persimmon leaf). From the sumptuous dining room you look out onto a garden bordered by Japanese stone lanterns in different shapes and sizes—all for sale. It's a short walk from Yakushi-ji's south gate. ⊠ *410 Rokujō-chō, Western Nara* ☏ *0742/33–8942* ▤ *MC, V* ☻ *Closed Mon.*

WHERE TO STAY

$$$$ ▥ **Edo-San.** You can't get closer to the deer than this. Individual cottages, some with thatched roofs in the greenery of Nara Kōen, is what Edo-San is all about. Indulge in a kaiseki dinner served in your cottage while you gaze through a large round window out into the park. One cottage has a private bath, and there's a communal bath for other guests. The one drawback is its proximity to a noisy major road. ⊠ *1167 Takabatake-chō Nara-shi, Nara-ken 630-8103* ☏*0742/26–2662* ☐*0742/*

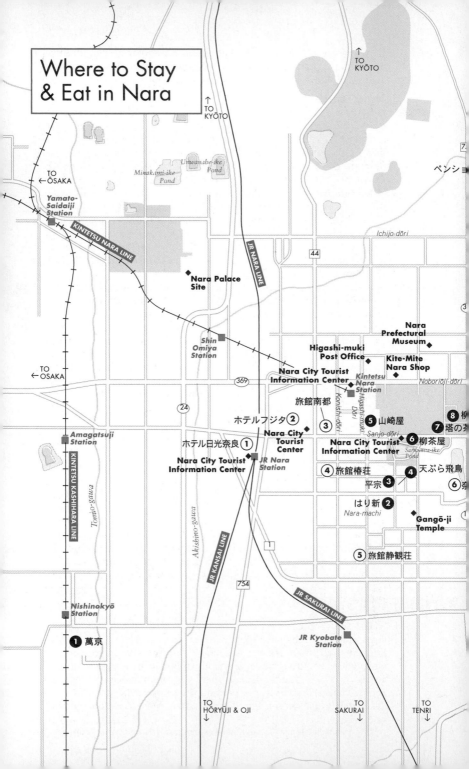

Where to Stay & Eat in Nara

TO ← OSAKA

↑ TO KYŌTO

↑ TO KYŌTO

ペンシ

TO ← OSAKA

Yamato-Saidaiji Station

KINTETSU NARA LINE

Minakami-ike Pond

Unwanabe-ike Pond

Ichijo-dōri

JR NARA LINE

44

◆ Nara Palace Site

Shin Omiya Station

◆ Nara Prefectural Museum

Higashi-muki Post Office ■

Kite-Mite Nara Shop

Nara City Tourist Information Center

Kintetsu Nara Station

Noboriōji-dōri

369

旅館南都

24

ホテルフジタ ②

③

Konishi-dōri

Higashi-muki Dōri

⑤ 山崎屋

Sanjo-dōri

⑧ 柳

⑦ 塔の茶

Amagatsuji Station

KINTETSU KASHIHARA LINE

ホテル日光奈良 ①

Nara City Tourist Center

Nara City Tourist Information Center ⑥ 柳茶屋

Sanuika-ike Pond

Nara City Tourist Information Center

JR Nara Station

④ 旅館椿荘

平宗 ③

④ 天ぷら飛鳥

⑥ 奈

Tomio-gawa

Akishino-gawa

はり新 ②

Nara-machi

◆ Gangō-ji Temple

JR KANSAI LINE

⑤ 旅館静観荘

754

Nishinokyō Station

JR SAKURAI LINE

① 萬京

JR Kyobate Station

TO HŌRYŪJI & OJI ↓

TO SAKURAI ↓

TO TENRI ↓

26–2663 ⊕ *www.edosan.jp* ↪ *10 Japanese-style cottages* ⟁ *Free parking* ⊟ *AE, DC, MC, V* ¶○¶ *MAP.*

★ **$$$$** 🏨 **Kankasō.** At once exquisitely refined and delightfully friendly, Kankaso exemplifies the best of Japanese hospitality. Beautiful gardens surround this peaceful ryokan near Tōdai-ji, and inside, elegant ikebana arrangements adorn the alcove. Each room is decorated with scrolls and pottery. Although the building has been renovated over the centuries, its 1,200-year-old central beam testifies to its longevity. The communal baths look out onto the gardens. A delicious kaiseki dinner is included, as is breakfast. ✉ *10 Kasugano-chō, Nara-shi, Nara-ken 630-8212* 🕾 *0742/26–1128* 🖷 *0742/26–1301* ⊕ *www.kankaso.jp* ↪ *9 Japanese-style rooms* ⟁ *In-room safes, some refrigerators, massage, shop, laundry service, free parking* ⊟ *MC, V* ¶○¶ *MAP.*

$$$$
FodorśChoice
★
🏨 **Nara Hotel.** No wonder the Emperor stays here. Built in 1909, when Western architecture was all the rage, the hotel has high ceilings, wide hallways, and sumptuous beds fit for, well, an emperor. The filigree-pattern light shades and silver-painted room heaters are all original. Although most rooms have a good view of the gardens or the temples, those in the new wing are not as grand as the turn-of-the-20th-century-style rooms in the old wing. Dinner is a very special event in the old-fashioned Edwardian-style dining room, where French food is served. ✉ *1096 Takabatake-chō, Nara-shi, Nara-ken 630-8301* 🕾 *0742/26–3300* 🖷 *0742/23–5252* ⊕ *www.narahotel.co.jp* ↪ *129 rooms, 3 suites* ⟁ *Restaurant, tea shop, minibars, in-room data ports, massage, bar, lobby lounge, laundry service, free parking, no-smoking rooms* ⊟ *AE, DC, MC, V.*

$$$–$$$$ 🏨 **Tsubakisō.** Friendly service and an internal garden make for a relaxed stay in this quiet mix of old and new. Rooms in the newer wing have suites with private baths, whereas rooms in the old wing share a communal bath. A *cha-gayu* (rice porridge flavored with green tea) breakfast is served in the dining room overlooking the garden. Prices include a kaiseki dinner and breakfast, and there are reduced prices for longer stays. Tsubakisō is down a quiet side street in central Nara, about a 10-minute walk from either of the main train stations. ✉ *35 Tsubai-chō, Nara-shi, Nara-ken 630-8343* 🕾 *0742/22–5330* 🖷 *0742/27–3811* ↪ *7 Japanese-style rooms, 3 with bath* ⟁ *Minibars, some in-room data ports, parking (fee)* ⊟ *AE, MC, V* ¶○¶ *MAP.*

$$–$$$ 🏨 **Hotel Fujita Nara.** Centrally situated between JR Nara Station and Nara Kōen, this modern hotel is often the best deal in town. Rates vary depending on the season, and drop considerably outside the April and May, October and November peak periods. The rooms are spacious and decorated in pastel tones. The pale-pink wave-shape lighting arrangement in the atrium harks back to the '80s. The restaurant, Hanakagami, serves Japanese cuisine. ✉ *47–1 Shimo Sanjō-chō, Nara-shi, Nara-ken 630-8236* 🕾 *0742/23–8111* 🖷 *0742/22–0255* ⊕ *www.fujita-nara.com* ↪ *115 rooms, 3 suites* ⟁ *Restaurant, massage, bar, lobby lounge, refrigerators, some in-room broadband, some in-room data ports, some free parking, no-smoking rooms* ⊟ *AE, DC, MC, V.*

$$–$$$ 🏨 **Hotel Nikko Nara.** Nara's largest hotel provides comfort in plush surroundings. Rooms have large windows and are generally quite bright. The thick carpets and wooden flooring in the bathrooms of the larger twins give a feeling of solidity not always found in hotels of a similar price range. Close to downtown restaurants, the hotel is atop a shopping arcade next to Nara JR Station. The lobby, however, is on the third floor and can be difficult to find. Given its location, the rooms are remarkably quiet. All rooms have private baths, and there's a communal bath as well. ✉ *8–1 Sanjō-honmachi, Nara-shi, Nara-ken 630-8122* ☎ *0742/35–8831* 🖷 *0742/35–6868* ⊕ *www.nikkonara.jp* 🛏 *330 rooms, 1 suite ☖ Restaurant, café, refrigerators, some in-room data ports, Japanese baths, massage, shop, dry cleaning, laundry service, meeting rooms, parking (fee), no-smoking rooms* ▤ *AE, D, MC, V.*

$$ 🏨 **Pension Nara Club.** On a street of old houses with traditional gardens, this small hotel is reminiscent of a European pension. The small, plainly decorated rooms have simple, dark-wood furniture and private bathrooms. Here you're away from the hustle and bustle, while it's only a scenic 20-minute walk from Tōdai-ji. A meal plan is available. ✉ *21 Mikado-chō, Nara-shi, Nara-ken 630-8204* ☎ *0742/22–3450* 🖷 *0742/22–3490* ⊕ *www. naraclub.com* 🛏 *8 rooms ☖ Free parking; no-smoking* ▤ *AE, V.*

$$ 🏨 **Ryokan Nanto.** The quietest ryokan on the city side of Nara Kōen, Nanto has airy tatami rooms of a simplicity fit for a Zen-practicing samurai. Internal dry rock gardens are throughout the maze-like collection of rooms, which makes finding the communal bath an adventure. Most rooms have toilets, some have baths, and there are large rooms for families and small groups. A Japanese breakfast is included. Ryokan Nanto is halfway between Kintetsu Nara Station and JR Nara Station. ✉ *29 Kamisanjō-chō, Nara-shi, Nara-ken 630-8228* ☎ *0742/22–3497* 🖷 *0742/23–0882* ⊕ *www.basho.net/nanto* 🛏 *13 Japanese-style rooms, 3 with bath ☖ Dining room, massage, lobby lounge, parking (fee)* ▤ *D, MC, V* ﾟＯﾟ *CP.*

Nara-machi

$ 🏨 **Ryokan Seikansō.** Of the many inexpensive, small ryokans in Nara-machi, this family-run establishment is the best pick for its spotlessness and attentive service. The quiet neighborhood contributes to the inn's relaxed atmosphere. Simple rooms overlook a large central garden. It's very popular so it's best to book far in advance. ✉ *29 Higashikitsuji-chō, Nara-shi, Nara-ken 630-8327* ☎ *0742/22–2670* 🖷 *0742/22–2670* 🛏 *9 Japanese-style rooms ☖ Free parking; no a/c* ▤ *AE, MC, V.*

NARA ESSENTIALS

Transportation

AIRPORTS & TRANSFERS

The nearest airports are in Ōsaka. All international and a few domestic flights use Kansai International Airport (KIX). Most domestic flights use Itami Airport. The hourly airport limousine bus from KIX takes 90 minutes and costs ¥1,800. From Itami, buses leave hourly, take 55 minutes, and cost ¥1,440.

BY BUS

The most economical way to explore Nara is by bus. Two local routes circle the main sites (Tōdai-ji, Kasuga Taisha, and Shin-Yakushi-ji) in the central and eastern parts of the city: Bus 1 runs counterclockwise, and Bus 2 runs clockwise. This urban loop line costs ¥180. Both stop at JR Nara Station and Kintetsu Nara Station. Bus 97 west to Hōryū-ji (with stops at Tōshōdai-ji and Yakushi-ji) takes about 50 minutes and costs ¥760; you can catch it in front of either station. Pick up a bus map at the Nara City Tourist Center.

BY TAXI
The rate is ¥610 for the first 1½ km (1 mi) and ¥90 for each additional 1,300 feet. From Kintetsu Nara Station to Kasuga Taisha it is about ¥900; to Hōryū-ji, about ¥5,000.

BY TRAIN
From Kyōto, the private Kintetsu Railway's Limited Express trains are the best way to get to Nara. They leave every half hour for the 33-minute trip (¥1,110). Three JR trains from Kyōto run every hour. The express takes 45 minutes (change at Yamato-Saidai-ji); the two locals take 70 minutes. All JR trains cost ¥740 without a JR Pass.

From Ōsaka's Kintetsu Namba Station, Nara is a 31-minute ride on a Limited Express (¥1,040). Trains leave every hour. Ordinary Express trains (¥540) leave every 20 minutes, and the trip takes 35 minutes. The JR Line from Tennō-ji Station takes 50 minutes and costs ¥450; from JR Namba it costs ¥540 and takes 40 minutes; from Ōsaka Station it takes one hour and costs ¥780.

From Kōbe, take the JR Tōkaidō Line rapid train from San-no-miya Station to Ōsaka and transfer to one of the trains listed above.

To get to Hōryū-ji Temple in western Nara, take a JR main line train from JR Nara Station. The ride to Hōryū-ji Station takes 11 minutes and costs ¥210.

Contacts & Resources

BANKS & EXCHANGE SERVICES
Most banks in Nara are on Sanjō-dōri to the east and west of the Nara City Tourist Information Center. The most convenient place to exchange U.S. dollars and traveler's checks is at the Hotel Fujita Nara. Some of the staff speak English. A passport and an address in Japan are required. **Hotel Fujita Nara** (✉ 47–1 Shimo-sanjō-chō, Nara-shi, Nara-ken 630-8236 ☎ 0742/23–8111 🖷 0742/22–0255 ⊕ www.fujita-nara.com).

An ATM in a convenience store accepts international cards (Visa, MasterCard, American Express, Diners Club, JCB, PLUS, CIRRUS and Maestro) one block south of Kintetsu Nara Station between Higashi-muki Dōri and Konishi-dōri. **Daily Yamazaki Convenience Store** (✉ 1 Mikado-chō Konishi-dōri, Nara-shi, Nara-ken 630–8225 ☉ Weekdays 8–9, weekends and public holidays 9–5).

EMBASSIES & CONSULATES
The nearest U.S. consulate is in Ōsaka.

EMERGENCIES
There is a *koban* (Police Box) at Kintetsu Nara Station, identified by the red light over its doorway. Police sometimes speak English, but if

not, ask the people around you if they do, and usually someone can be found. Doctors at major hospitals, many having studied overseas, can often treat minor ailments in English with the help of a dictionary. Emergency services telephone operators usually don't speak English.

🚑 **Ambulance** ☎ 119. **Nara National Hospital** ✉ 1–50–1 Higashi-kidera-chō, Nara-shi, Nara-ken 630-8305 ☎ 0742/24–1251. **Kintetsu Nara police station** ✉ Nishi Mikado-mae, Nara-shi, Nara-ken 630-8305 ☎ 0742/22–5612. **Police** ☎ 110.

INTERNET, MAIL & SHIPPING

Most large hotels in Nara have some rooms with data ports, while smaller and more traditional accommodations often have no Internet access but may have a computer for public use. Below are two Internet cafés in the city.

Superman is on the fifth floor of a game center on Sanjō-dōri west of the Nara City Tourist Information Center. **Superman** (✉ 478–1 Sanjō-chō, Nara-shi, Nara-ken ☎ 0742/25–5500 ◷ 10 AM–midnight).

Internet Café Suien is inside the Asyl Hotel, two blocks west of Kintetsu Nara Station. **Internet Café Suien** (✉ Hotel Azyl 1–58 Aburazaka-chō, Nara-shi, Nara-ken 630-8014 ☎ 0742/22–2577 ⊕ www.worldheritage.co.jp ◷ 7:30 AM–11 PM)

Nara Central Post Office (✉ 5–3–3 Ōmiya, Nara-shi, Nara-ken 630-8115 ☎ 0742/35–1605 ◷ Daily 24 hours). The main post office is quite far west in Shin-Ōmiya. Several local branches are close to Kintetsu Nara Station.

Higashi-muki Post Office is on the north side of Noborioji-dōri (the main road in front of Kintetsu Nara Station) in the first block on Higashi-muki Kita-dōri. An ATM here accepts international cards (✉ 24 Higashi-muki Kita-dōri, Nara-shi, Nara-ken 630-8214 ☎ 0742/26–3904 ◷ weekdays 9–5. ATM hrs weekdays 9–7, weekends 9–5.

TOURS

The Japan Travel Bureau conducts daily bus tours to Nara. The five-hour (¥6,300) guided tour in English departs from Kyōto at 1:40. Reservations must be made one day in advance.

The Student Guide Service and the YMCA Guide Service are free and leave from the JR Nara Station's Nara City Tourist Information Office and Kintetsu Nara Station. Reservations need to be made one day in advance. The guides are volunteers, so you should cover the day's expenses. Entrance fees are waived for guides, however.

The Japan National Tourist Office (JNTO) publishes the leaflet "Walking Tour Courses in Nara" for a recommended self-guided two-hour tour of Nara Kōen and nearby temples and shrines; other tours start with a bus ride from the city center. There is no JNTO office in Nara.

🚑 **Japan Travel Bureau** ☎ 075/341–1413. **Student Guide Service** ✉ Nara City Sarusawa Tourist Information Office, 49 Nobori-ōji-chō, north side of Sarusawa ike ☎ 0742/26–4753. **YMCA Guide Service** ☎ 0742/45–5920.

Points of Interest

SITES/AREAS	JAPANESE CHARACTERS
Akahadayaki	赤膚焼
Chūgū-ji	中宮寺
Daibutsu-den (Hall of the Great Buddha)	大仏殿
Hōryū-ji	法隆寺
Kaidan-in	戒檀院
Kasuga Taisha	春日大社
Kobai-en	古梅園
Kōfuku-ji	興福寺
Nandai-mon (Great Southern Gate)	南大門
Nara Kōen	奈良公園
Nara-machi	奈良町
Nara-machi Shiryōkan (Nara-machi Historical Library and Information Center)	奈良町資料館
Nara National Museum (Nara Kokuritsu Hakubutsukan)	奈良国立博物館
Ni-gatsu-dō (Second Month Temple)	二月堂
San-gatsu-dō (Third Month Temple)	三月堂
Shin-Yakushi-ji	新薬師寺
Tōdai-ji Temple Complex	東大寺
Tōshōdai-ji	唐招提寺
Wakakusa-yama Mizutani-chaya	若草山水谷茶屋
Western Nara	奈良西部
Yū Nakagawa	遊中川
Yakushi-ji	薬師寺
Yougendō	涌玄堂
RESTAURANTS	
Harishin	はり新
Hirasō	平宗
Onjaku	温石
Tempura Asuka	天ぷら飛鳥
Tō-no-chaya	塔の茶屋
Tsukihi-tei	月日亭
Uma no Me	馬の目
Van Kio	萬京

Yamazakiya	山崎屋
Yanagi-jaya	柳茶屋
HOTELS	
Edo-San	江戸三
Hotel Fujita Nara	ホテルフジタ奈良
Hotel Nikko Nara	ホテル日航奈良
Kankasō	観鹿荘
Nara Hotel	奈良ホテル
Pension Nara Club	ペンション奈良倶楽部
Ryokan Nanto	旅館南都
Ryokan Seikansō	旅館静観荘
Tsubakisō	旅館椿荘

6

Ōsaka

WORD OF MOUTH

"It was unbelievable—the Tigers fans were so much louder in the Osaka Dome than in Tōkyō. Every seat in the fan section was taken. We chanted for the batters, banged our bats, and the guy across the aisle was praying with prayer beads—these are serious fans. . . . At the stretch (I think it is 6th inning instead of 7th) the woman in front of us tapped me and pointed up to the big video screen in the Dome and . . . they put us up on the screen. I looked at myself and thought, "no one will ever believe this, and I look like a fool!"

–emd

Updated by
Justin Ellis

PEOPLE IN ŌSAKA DON'T SAY KONNICHI-WA, they yell *Mo kari makka?* (Are you making any money?). Ōsaka became a merchant town at the end of the 16th century, when traders and businessmen were at the bottom of the feudal hierarchy. Denied the cultural pursuits of the aristocracy, Ōsaka impresarios spent their millions patronizing *bunraku* puppetry and *kamigata kabuki* into art forms. They spent even more on enhancing Ōsaka's reputation as the "kitchen of Japan," but always made sure they got their money's worth. Today Osaka is still a culinary mecca, and the city's notoriously forthright *oba-chan* (grandmothers) drive a hard bargain at the market.

From the ashes of World War II Ōsaka's entrepreneurs worked hard to regain the city's reputation as Japan's commercial center; this is where Oodles of Noodles, Panasonic, and the Suntory whisky in your hotel minibar hail from. Ōsaka is proud of its past, but it envisions itself as the hub of Japan's robotics industry.

Ōsaka's streets are a kaleidoscope of *irachi*—life in the fast lane. Spend some time here and it soon becomes obvious why Ōsaka is home to Japan's funniest comedians: it's a city of candid personalities who shun the superficial and infuse even the grayest precincts with unexpected charm. So if someone yells out *Mo kari makka?*, just yell back *Botchi botchi den na* (I'm doing okay!).

See the glossary at the end of this book for definitions of the common Japanese words and suffixes used in this chapter.

7

ORIENTATION & PLANNING

Orientation

Ōsaka City is at the heart of the Kansai region (west Japan), at the mouth of the Yodo river on Ōsaka Bay. Ōsaka Prefecture is bordered by Nara Prefecture in the east, Kyōto Prefecture in the north, Hyōgo Prefecture in the northwest and Wakayama Prefecture in the south. The main areas of the city, Kita (north) and Minami (south), are divided by two rivers: the Dojima-gawa and the Tosabori-gawa. Between Kita and Minami is Naka-no-shima, an island and the municipal center of Ōsaka. The bay area, to the west of the city center, is home to the Ōsaka Aquarium, the Suntory Museum, and Universal Studios Japan (USJ). The Shinkansen stops at Shin-Ōsaka, three stops (about five minutes) north of Ōsaka Station on the Midō-suji subway line. To the north of Shin-Ōsaka is Senri Expo Park.

Kita: North of Chūō Dōri

Kita (north) is Ōsaka's main economic and administrative center and site of Ōsaka's largest stations: JR Ōsaka and Hankyū Umeda. The Kita area is crammed full of shops, department stores, and restaurants. South of Ōsaka Station is the city's most exclusive nightlife district, Kitashinchi, and south of here is Naka-no-shima, home to the Museum of Oriental Ceramics. One more mile southeast are Ōsaka-jō (Ōsaka Castle) and Ōsaka Kōen (Ōsaka Park)

Top Reasons to Visit

THE WORLD OF TOMORROW
The narrow streets of Dōtombori buzz with energy in the heart of Ōsaka's frenzied neonscape. From domestic robots to parts for the Space Shuttle—Ōsaka is on the cutting edge of high-tech.

JAPAN'S KITCHEN
Ōsaka has been *nihon no daidokoro* (Japan's kitchen) since the 17th century. The tradition continues, but now the cuisine borrows from all over the world. *Okonomiyaki* and *takoyaki*, (tasty, grilled seafood snacks) are the city's specialties, and for an action-loving populace they are quickly prepared and can be eaten on the go.

PARTY 'TIL THE RISING SUN
Ōsaka's vibrant street fashion is next season's preview: easily espied on a night out in adrenalized Shin-sai-bashi. With so much bonhomie from the locals, it won't be long before you're getting down in a fashionable club or belting out hits in a subterranean karaoke bar.

ŌSAKA AQUARIUM
One of the world's largest aquariums, the Ōsaka Kaiyūkan is an epic voyage through the depths of the marine world. The king penguins are enchanting, and the whale shark in the huge central tank never fails to intimidate.

ARCHITECTURE
Skyscrapers vie with 4th-century burial mounds on Ōsaka's 1,500-year-old architectural skyline. In the 21st century the environmentally attuned work of minimalist master Ando Tadao continues to redefine the Japanese cityscape: and all from his office in downtown Ōsaka.

Minami: South of Chūō Dōri

The restaurants and bars of Dōtombori-dōri attract Ōsaka's youth to Minami (south), as does Ōsaka's largest collection of department stores. The main stations in this area are Namba, Shin-sai-bashi and Namba Nankai. The National Bunraku Theater, Shochikuza Theater, America-mura, Minami-horie, Dōguya-suji and Den Den Town are all in Minami. South of Minami is Tennō-ji with its park and attractions, including the Municipal Museum of Art. Sumiyoshi Taisha (Sumiyoshi Grand Shrine) is a 10-minute train ride south of Tennō-ji.

Planning

Ōsaka's vitality and diversity can be appreciated in two days; three if you want to see everything on the checklist. Spend mornings and afternoons visiting museums and temples and early evenings browsing shops and department stores, which usually close at around 8:30. After that it's time for the bars, restaurants, and entertainment.

Your first stop should be Osaka Castle, Ōsaka-jō, and the surrounding park, Ōsaka-kōen. From here make your way to the Museum of Oriental Ceramics on Naka-no-shima. In the late afternoon browse the gadget stores of Den Den Town and go to the Dōguya-suji arcade for cooking

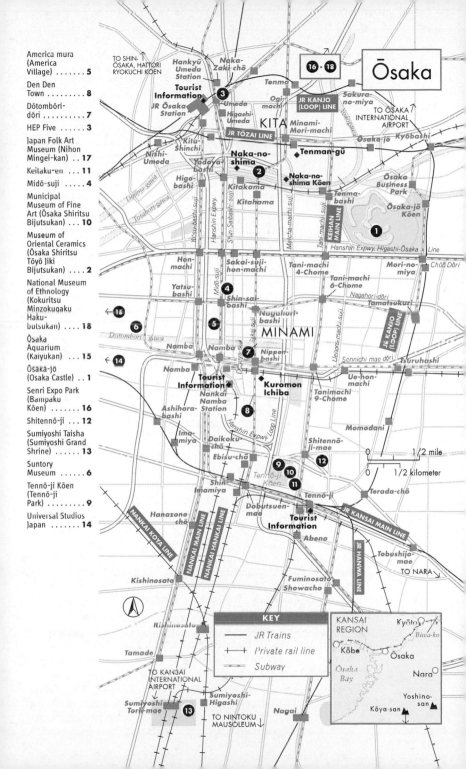

Ōsaka

utensils. For fashion, wander America-mura and Minami-horie, then head to Dōtonbori-dōri for dinner. Alternatively, spend an afternoon at a *bunraku* performance to enjoy the subtleties of Japanese puppetry. Performances start at 4 PM and finish with enough time to go for a walk along Dōtombori-dōri before dinner.

The sights south of the city center can be seen in one day. Start at Tennō-ji Park, visiting the Municipal Museum of Fine Art and its collection of classical Japanese art. Northeast of the park is Shitennō-ji (commonly referred to as Tennō-ji), Japan's first temple. South of Tennō-ji is Sumiyoshi Taisha, one of Japan's three greatest shrines. To wrap up your stay, instead of heading to Dōtombori-dōri after dark, go to central Ōsaka.

Ōsaka is an excellent base from which to explore the surrounding Kansai region—Kyōto, Nara, and Kōbe are each 30 minutes away by train. Ōsaka is also the most convenient jumping-off point for a trip to the mountainside monasteries of Kōya-san, two hours away on the Nankai private rail line. Most museums are closed Monday. One exception is Senri Expo Park, which closes (along with its museums) on Wednesday. Museums stay open on Monday national holidays, closing the following day instead. Likewise, Senri Expo Park stays open on Wednesday holidays, closing Thursday instead.

The Best of Times

Spring (March to May) and fall (September to November) are the best times to visit Ōsaka. The cherry blossoms flower in late March–early April, and the autumn leaves are brightest in late October–early November. The summer (June to August) is very hot and sticky. This and an erratic rainy season, mostly in June, justify the extent of Ōsaka's labyrinthine underground shopping malls.

Concerning Restaurants & Hotels

Ōsaka has a broad range of Japanese food, from the local snack foods, *okonomiyaki* and *takoyaki* to full kaiseki restaurants. The seafood from the Seto Inland Sea is always fresh, as is the tender beef used at the many Korean barbecue restaurants in Ōsaka's Korea Town, Tsuruhashi. French and Mexican foods are also popular in Ōsaka.

The department stores around Ōsaka Station are "gourmet palaces," each with several floors of restaurants. The Hankyū Grand Building and the Daimaru at JR Ōsaka Station have the best selection. Under Ōsaka Station is the Shin-Umeda Shokudokai—a maze of narrow alleys lined with *izakaya* (lively after-work drinking haunts). The beer and hot snacks comfort many an overworked salaryman on the commute home.

For some energetic dining neonside, head to Dōtombori-dōri and Soe-mon-chō (*so*-eh-mon cho), two areas along Dōtombori-gawa packed with restaurants and bars. Kimono clad *mama-sans* serve the city's expense-accounters at Kita-shinchi, in south Kita-ku, the city's most exclusive dining quarter.

Ōsaka is known more as a business center than as a tourist destination, so hotel facilities are usually excellent but their features are rarely distinctive, except at the high-end of the scale. The city has modern accommodations for almost every taste. Choose accommodations based on location rather than amenities.

WHAT IT COSTS In yen				
$$$$	**$$$**	**$$**	**$**	**¢**
RESTAURANTS over 3,000	2,000–3,000	1,000–2,000	800–1,000	under 800
HOTELS over 22,000	18,000–22,000	12,000–18,000	8,000–12,000	under 8,000

Restaurant prices are per person for a main course. Hotel price categories are based on the range between the least and most expensive standard double rooms in nonholiday high season, based on the European Plan (with no meals) unless otherwise noted. Taxes (5%–15%) are extra.

Getting Around Town

Ōsaka's subway system is extensive and efficient. Midō-suji is the main line, which runs north-south and has stations at Shin-Ōsaka, Umeda (next to Ōsaka Station), Shin-sai-bashi, Namba, and Tennō-ji. Tickets cost between ¥200 and ¥400. The JR Loop Line (Kanjo-sen) circles the city above ground and intersects with all subway lines. Fares range from ¥120 to ¥190, or you can use your JR Pass. Taxis are plentiful and rates are reasonable. Expect to pay ¥1,500 for trips between Ōsaka Station and Shin-sai-bashi/Namba. Within localities, walking is recommended.

Visitor Information

The main visitor information center is at JR Ōsaka Station. To get there from the Midō-suji exit, turn right and walk about 50 yards. The office is beneath a pedestrian overpass, next to the city bus station. The Shin-Ōsaka center is at the JR local line exit at Shin-Ōsaka Station. For the Namba center, take Exit 24 at Namba Station in front of Starbucks; for the Tennō-ji center, take the east exit of JR Tennō-ji Station. The Universal City center is a two-minute walk from JR Universal City Station. They are all open daily 8–8 and closed December 31–January 3, except for Universal City, which opens at 9.

Ōsaka Station Tourist Information Center ✉ 3-1-2 Umeda, JR Ōsaka Station Kita-ku ☎ 06/6345-2819. Namba Station Tourist Information Center ✉ 2-2-3 Namba, B1 Midō-suji Grand Bldg., Chūō-ku ☎ 06/6211-3551. Tennō-ji Station Tourist Information Center ✉ 10-45 Hidenin-chō 1F JR Tennō-ji Station Bldg., Tennō-ji-ku ☎ 06/6774-3077. Shin-Ōsaka Tourist Information Center ✉ JR Shin-Ōsaka Station, Higashi-Yodo-gawa-ku ☎ 06/6305-3311. Universal City Tourist Information Center ✉ 6-2-61 Shimaya, Universal City Walk, Konohara-ku ☎ 06/4804-3824. Kansai Tourist Information Center ✉ 1F Passenger Terminal Bldg., Kansai International Airport ☎ 0724/56-6025.

EXPLORING ŌSAKA

Kita: North of Chūō Dōri

Culture by day and glamour by night: Kita is the place to come for the museums of Naka-no-shima, the city's deluxe department stores, and the "gourmet palaces" in and around Ōsaka Station. At night take in

Venice of the East

WHEN TŌKYŌ WAS BUT A fishing village and Kyōto a mountain hamlet, big things were happening in Ōsaka. The Ōsaka-Nara region was the center of the emerging Japanese (Yamato) nation into the ninth century, and in 645 Emperor Kotoku (596–654) made Ōsaka his capital. He called it Naniwa, but the city's imperial ascendancy was brief. Until the 8th century capital cities were relocated upon an emperor's death. As a result, Ōsaka was the royal seat for a fleeting nine years. Despite changes in its political fortunes, Ōsaka developed as a trade center, a role its waterways had destined it to play. Exchange wasn't limited to commerce. Buddhism and Chinese characters filtered into the fledgling Japanese society through Ōsaka to Nara, and from Nara to the rest of the country. By 1590 Toyotomi Hideyoshi (1536-98), the first *daimyo* (warlord) to unite Japan, had completed construction of Ōsaka Castle to protect his realm against the unruly clans of Kyōto. He designated Ōsaka a merchant city to consolidate his position. After Toyotomi died, Tokugawa Ieyasu's (1543-1616) forces defeated the Toyotomi legacy at the Battle of Sekigahara in 1600. Ōsaka's strategic importance was again short-lived, as Tokugawa moved the capital to Edo (now Tōkyō) in 1603. Ōsaka grew rich supplying the new capital with rice, soy sauce, and sake as Edo transformed its agricultural land into city suburbs. All copper produced in Japan was exported through Ōsaka, and the National Rice Exchange was headquartered in Dōjima, near Kita-shinchi. "70% of the nation's wealth comes from Ōsaka," was the catchphrase of the era. Some of Japan's business dynasties were

founded during the economic boom of the 17th century, and they prevail today—Sumitomo, Konoike, and Mitsui among them. By the end of the Genroku Era (1688–1704) Ōsaka's barons were patronizing *bunraku* puppetry and *kamigata kabuki* (comic kabuki). Chikamatsu Monzaemon (1653–1724), writer of the *The Forty-Seven Ronin,* penned the tragedies which quickly became classics. Ihara Saikaku (1642–93) immortalized the city's merchants in the risqué *Life of an Amorous Man* and the *The Great Mirror of Male Love.* When Tōkyō became the official capital of Japan in 1868 there were fears that the "Venice of the East" would suffer. But expansion of the spinning and textile industries assured prosperity, and earned Ōsaka a new epithet–"*Manchester* of the East." As a consequence of the Great Kantō Earthquake in 1923, Ōsaka became Japan's main port and by 1926 the country's largest city. Chemical and heavy industries grew during World War I, and were prime targets for American bombers during World War II. Much of Ōsaka was flattened, and more than a third of the prefecture's 4.8 million people were left homeless. During the postwar years many Ōsaka companies moved their headquarters to Tōkyō. Even so, Ōsaka was rebuilt and went on to host Asia's first World Expo in 1970. It has since fashioned itself as a city of cutting-edge techonology and lifestyle. The Ōsaka City Government plans to revive the "Water City" appellation for Ōsaka, but for now the heritage of the city's waterways lives on in its place names: *bashi* (bridge), *horie* (canal), and *semba* (dockyard).

the view from the Umeda Sky Building or the Ferris wheel at the HEP Five department store before you explore Ōsaka's nonpareil entertainment district: Kita-shinchi.

What to See

Hattori Ryokuchi Kōen. Come for the park's open-air **Museum of Old Japanese Farmhouses** (Nihon Minka Shūraku Hakubutsukan), and wander about full-size traditional rural buildings such as the the giant *gassho-zukuri* (thatch-roofed) farmhouse from Gifu Prefecture. The park also has horseback-riding facilities, tennis courts, a youth hostel, and an open-air stage, which hosts concerts and other events in the summer. There's even an outdoor Kabuki theater! An English-language pamphlet is available. Take the Midō-suji subway line from Umeda to Ryokuchi Kōen Station. The park is a 10-minute walk away. ⊠ *1–1 Hattori Ryokuchi, Toyonaka-shi* ☎ *06/6862–4946 park office, 06/6862–3137 museum* ⛩ *Park free, museum ¥500* ⊙ *Daily 9:30–5; last entry at 4:30.*

❸ HEP Five. With 11 floors of restaurants, shops, and entertainment facilities, HEP Five (Hankyū Entertainment Plaza) appears to be just another Ōsaka shopping palace. What makes HEP Five special is the enormous Ferris wheel on its roof. ⊠ *3 min southeast of Hankyū Umeda terminus, Kita-ku* ☎ *06/6366–3639* ⛩ *Ferris wheel ¥500* ⊙ *Building and Ferris wheel daily 11–11, shops daily 11–9.*

⓱ Japan Folk Art Museum (Nihon Mingei kan). The exhibits of "beauty from day-to-day life" at this museum in Senri Expo Park explore the diversity and intricacy of Japanese handicrafts from Hokkaidō to Okinawa. The textiles, wooden crafts, and bamboo ware in simple displays evoke Japan's traditional past; they make quite a contrast to Ōsaka's modernity. ⊠ *10–5 Bampaku Kōen, Senri Expo Park, Senri, Suita-shi* ☎ *06/6877–1971* ⛩ *¥700* ⊙ *Thurs.–Tues. 10–5; last entry at 4:30.*

❷ Museum of Oriental Ceramics (Ōsaka Shiritsu Tōyō Jiki Bijutsukan). You **Fodor'sChoice** don't have to be a ceramics connoisseur to be thoroughly absorbed by ★ the beauty and refinement of the works displayed here. The museum is within Naka-no-shima Kōen, the city's oldest park (opened in 1891), and houses more than 900 pieces of Chinese, Korean, and Japanese ceramics. The collection, one of the finest in the world, includes 15 works that have been designated National Treasures or Important Cultural Properties. To get here take the Sakai suji subway line to Kita-hama or the Midō-suji subway line to Yodoya-bashi and walk north across the Tosabori-gawa to the museum. ⊠ *1–1 Naka-no-shima, Kita-ku* ☎ *06/6223–0055* ⛩ *¥500* ⊙ *Tues.–Sun. 9:30–5; last entry at 4:30.*

⓲ National Museum of Ethnology (Kokuritsu Minzokugaku Hakubutsukan). The National Museum of Ethnology exhibits textiles, masks, and contraptions from around the world with sensitivity and respect. Displays on the Ainu (the original inhabitants of Hokkaidō) and other aspects of Japanese culture are particularly informative. Information sheets explaining the sections of the museum are available on request and supplement the English-language brochure included with admission. The museum is on the east side of the main road that runs north–south through Senri Expo Park. ⊠ *Senri Expo Park, Senri, Suita-shi* ☎ *06/6876–2151*

CLOSE UP

To the Gods of Sake & Conviviality

IN GLAMOROUS KITA-SHINCHI Akashiya is known for its earthiness, and its *akashiya*–takoyaki balls in a light broth. Even more novel than the number of people they can squeeze into this tiny space is the opportunity to get behind the counter and make the takoyaki yourself. And while you contemplate another glass of *Samurai* and take in the sumō blaring from the television, outside shiny black taxis contend with Porsches and Mercedes on the narrow street. As the salaried venture homeward, the seductive denizens of the Kita-shinchi demi-monde emerge from cramped apartments in pencil-thin stilettos and sequined evening gowns. Behind closed doors ice is chipped from huge blocks to slink into the cascade of whisky and soda to be served that evening. Back at Akashiya, Numata-san is introducing himself with a business card in one hand and devouring sushi with chopsticks in the other. He's down from Tōkyō on business, and soon will be speeding past Mt. Fuji on the Shinkansen—home in time to tuck his children into bed. As the shutters rattle down at Akashiya, *mama-sans* in kimonos are curb-side bowing farewell to their unsteady clientele. Across the way a lady prays at a shrine. She is undoubtedly paying her respects to the Kita-shinchi deities of sake and conviviality.

Akashiya (✉ 1-3-23 Dōjima, Ōsaka-ya, 1F Kita-shinchi Bldg.,Kita-ku ☎ 06/6341-3910 ✆ Tues.–Sun. 5 PM–2 AM).

⊕ *www.minpaku.ac.jp/english/* ✉ ¥420 ✆ *Thurs.–Tues. 10–5; last entry at 4:30.*

⏱ ⑮ **Ōsaka Aquarium** (Kaiyūkan). This eye-catching red, gray, and blue build-
Fodor'sChoice ing is the best aquarium in Japan. More than 11,000 tons of water hold
★ a multitude of sea creatures, including whale sharks, king penguins, giant spider crabs, jellyfish, and sea otters. You can stroll through 15 different re-created environments, including the rivers and streams of Japanese and Ecuadorian forests, the icy waters around Antarctica, the dark depths of the Japan Sea, and the volcanically active Pacific Ring of Fire. To get here, take the Chūō subway line to Ōsaka-kō Station; the aquarium is a five-minute walk northwest from the station. ✉ *1–1–10 Kaigan-dōri, Minato-ku* ☎ *06/6576-5501* ⊕ *www.kaiyukan.com/eng/index.htm* ✉ ¥*2,000* ✆ *Tues.–Sun. 10–8; last entry at 7.*

❶ **Ōsaka-jō** (Ōsaka Castle). It may seem ironic for a business center that
Fodor'sChoice Ōsaka's best-known attraction is its castle, a symbol of feudalism that
★ held merchants at the bottom of the social hierarchy. Originally built in the 1580s, today the five-story ferro-concrete reconstruction (completed in 1931) presides over the wide Ōsaka Kōen, which encloses the castle moat. Toyotomi Hideyoshi, the first warlord to unite Japan, was showing off with this castle. It was intended to intimidate his rivals and show his commitment to Ōsaka and attract merchants from all over Japan.

The Young & Headless

1

AT THE AGE OF SEVEN, Toyotomi Hideyori was under attack from his father's longtime nemesis. Even so, in 1603 a political marriage was made between Hideyori and Tokugawa's granddaughter, the six-year-old Senhime. Senhime and Hideyori endured a precarious existence in Ōsaka Castle but had a son in 1608, thus binding the two most powerful clans in Japan. However, in 1615 Senhime's restive father, Tokugawa Hidetata, came to challenge his coming-of-age rival. Senhime was removed to Tōkyō, where in vain she pleaded for clemency to save Hideyori's life. With no hope of victory, Hideyori and his cohort performed ritual suicide and sent the castle up in flames. The ill-fated Kunimatsu, who was to head the new Toyotomi-Tokugawa dynasty, was taken by Tokugawa troops and beheaded. Senhime spent her later years as a Buddhist nun and died aged 69 in Tōkyō.

Inside the castle there is a museum with artifacts of the Toyotomi family and historical objects relating to Ōsaka prior to the Tokugawa shogunate. Unless you are a Hideyoshi aficionado, these exhibits are of limited interest; the castle's magnificent exterior and the impressive view from the eighth floor of the donjon are the reasons to see Ōsaka-jō. If your timing is right, you might catch the cherry blossoms (late March-early April) and **Nishi-no-maru Teien** (Nishi-no-maru Garden) at their best.

From Ōsaka-jō Kōen-mae Station it's about a 10-minute walk up the hill to the castle. You can also take the Tani-machi subway line from Higashi-Umeda Station (just southeast of Ōsaka Station) to Tani-machi 4-chome Station. From here it's a 15-minute walk. ⊠ *1–1 Ōsaka-jō, Chūō-ku* ☎ *06/6941–3044* ☞ *Castle ¥600, garden additional ¥210* ☉ *Sept.–mid-July, daily 9–5, last entry at 4:30; mid-July–Aug., daily 9–8; last entry at 7:30.*

⑯ Senri Expo Park (Bampaku Kōen). On the former site of Expo '70—one of the defining events in Ōsaka's postwar history—this 647-acre park contains sports facilities, an enormous statue by Okamoto Taro called the *Tower of the Sun*, a garden with two teahouses, other gardens, a vast amusement park called Expo Land that's popular with families and young couples, the **National Museum of Ethnology**, the **Japan Folk Art Museum**, and two smaller museums. To get to the park, take the Midō-suji subway line to Senri-Chūō Station (20 minutes from Umeda); then take the Expo Land bus to Nihon Teien-mae Station (30 minutes) or the monorail to Bampaku Kōen-mae (10 minutes). ⊠ *Senri, Suita-shi* ☎ *06/6877–3339 for Expo Land* ☞ *Gardens ¥150–¥310 each, Expo Land ¥1,100; see separate entries for other facilities,* ☉ *Mar.–late Dec., Thurs.–Tues. 9–5.*

Tenman-gū. This 10th-century shrine is the main site of the annual **Tenjin Matsuri**, held July 24 and 25, one of the three largest and most enthusiastically celebrated festivals in Japan. Dozens of floats are paraded through the streets, and more than 100 vessels, lighted by lanterns, sail along the canals amid fireworks. The festival started as an annual procession to bestow peace and prosperity on the shrine's faithful. It is dedicated to Sugawara no Michizane, the Japanese patron of scholars. Sugawara was out of favor at court when he died in 903; two years later plague and drought swept Japan—Sugawara was exacting revenge from the grave. To appease Sugawara's spirit he was deified as Tenjin-sama. He is enshrined at Tenman-gū. On the 5th, 15th, and 25th of each month students throughout Japan visit Tenman-gū shrines to pray for academic success. Tenman-gū is a short walk from either JR Tenman-gū Station or Minami-Mori-machi Station on the Tani-machi-suji subway line. ✉ *2–1–8 Tenjin-bashi, Kita-ku* ☎ *06/6353–0025* 🎫 *Free* ◷ *Apr.–Sept., daily 5:30 AM–sunset; Oct.–Mar., daily 6 AM–sunset.*

🕐 ⑭ **Universal Studios Japan.** The 140-acre Universal Studios Japan (USJ) combines the most popular rides and shows from Universal's Hollywood and Florida movie-studio theme parks with special attractions designed specifically for Japan. Popular rides include those based on *Jurassic Park, Spider-Man,* and *E.T.* The Japan-only Snoopy attraction appeals to the local infatuation with all things cute, as do the daily parades of Hello Kitty. Restaurants and food outlets abound throughout the park, and the road from JR Universal City Station is lined with names like Hard Rock Cafe and Bubba Gump Shrimp, local fast-food chain MOS Burger, and Ganko Sushi.

Tickets are available at locations throughout the city, including branches of Lawson convenience stores and larger JR stations, as well as at USJ itself. Due to high demand on weekends and during holiday periods, tickets must be bought in advance and are not available at the gate. The park is easily reached by direct train from JR Ōsaka Station (about 20 minutes) or by changing to a shuttle train at JR Nishi-kujo Station on the Loop Line. ✉ *2–1–33 Sakurajima, Konohana-ku* ☎ *06/6465–3000* ⊕ *www.usj.co.jp* 🎫 *¥5,800* ◷ *Daily 10–10.*

Minami

Tradition by day and neon by night, Minami is the place to come for Ōsaka history: Japan's oldest temple, a breathtaking collection of Japanese art in the Municipal Museum of Fine Art, and a mausoleum bigger than the pyramids. And then youth culture takes over when it comes to nightlife neonside: this is where future fashionistas forge the haute couture of tomorrow. Amid all this modernity are two bastions of Ōsaka tradition: the National Bunraku and Shin-Kabukiza Kabuki theaters.

What to See

❺ **America-mura** (America Village). Though it takes its name from the original shops that sold cheap American fashions and accessories, Amemura (*ah*-meh *moo*-ra), as it's called, is now a bustling district full of trendy clothing stores, record stores, bars, cafés, and clubs that cater to teenagers and young adults. Shops are densely packed, and it's virtually impossible to walk these streets on weekends. To see the variety of styles and fashions prevalent among urban youth, Ame-Mura is *the* place to go in Ōsaka. ⊠ *West side of Midō-suji, 6 blocks south of Shin-sai-bashi Station, Chūō-ku.*

⑧ **Den Den Town.** All the latest video games, computers, cameras, phones, mp3 players, and other electronic gadgets are discounted here. "Den Den" is derived from the word *denki,* which means electricity. ⊠ *2 blocks east of Namba Station, Naniwa-ku.*

★ ⑦ **Dōtombori-dōri.** Neon lights and sake nights lure Ōsakans to Dōtombori-dōri's bars, restaurants, and shops. The street runs alongside Dōtombori-gawa, and it's the best place to experience Ōsaka nightlife. Presiding over the river is the Glico man: Ōsaka's most famous neon athlete. Ebisu-bashi, the main bridge spanning the river, is a popular romantic spot and where young fans gather when major sports events take place. The atmosphere can crescendo with exuberant fans diving in—much to the annoyance of the police. As if Dōtombori didn't already have the density of downtown Cairo, "a Waterfront Theater Palace" (platforms for strolling and eating) is being built in front of the buildings that front the river! ⊠ *From Umeda, take Midō-suji subway line to Namba and walk north 2 blocks up Midō-suji. Chūō-ku.*

Fujii-dera. An 8th-century, 1,000-handed statue of Kannon, the goddess of mercy, is this temple's main object of worship. The seated figure is the oldest Buddhist sculpture of its kind, and it's only on view on the 18th of each month. To get here, take the Midō-suji subway line to Tennō-ji Station, then transfer to the Kintetsu Minami–Ōsaka Line and take it to Fujii-dera Station. The temple is a few minutes' walk away. ⊠ *1–16–21 Fujii-dera, Fujii-dera-shi* ☎ *0721/938–0005* ⊠ *Free* ⊘ *Statue on view 18th of month.*

⑪ **Keitaku-en.** Jihei Ogawa, master gardener of the late Meiji period, spent 10 years working the late Baron Sumitomo's circular garden into a masterpiece. The woods surrounding the pond are a riot of color in spring, when the cherry blossoms and azaleas bloom. Keitaku-en is adjacent to Shiritsu Bijutsukan in Tennō-ji Kōen. ⊠ *Tennō-ji-ku* ⊠ *Included in Tennō-ji Kōen admission* ⊘ *Tues.-Sun. 9:30–4:30; last entry at 4.*

④ **Midō-suji.** Ōsaka's Champs Élysées, the ginko-tree-lined Midō-suji boulevard is Ōsaka's most elegant thoroughfare and home to its greatest concentration of department stores. To the east of Midō-suji is the Shin-sai-bashi-suji arcade, one of Ōsaka's best shopping and entertainment streets. If you're in town on the second Sunday in October, try to

---

THE MASTER OF MINIMALISM

Ōsaka native Ando Tadao is Japan's most famous architect, and a global figurehead of the minimalist movement. The Suntory Museum is the self-trained architect's Ōsaka masterpiece, but you can also see his work at the JR Universal City Station on the Yumesaki Line and at the cinematheque in Tennō-ji Park. The Suntory Museum has regular exhibitions about art and culture from around the world. **Suntory Museum** ⊠ *1-5-10 Kaigan-dōri, Minato-ku* ☎ *06/6577-0001* ⊕ *www.suntory.com/culture-sports/smt/* ⊠ *¥420* ⊘ *Thurs.-Tues. 10–5; last entry at 4:30.*

7

catch the annual Midō-suji Parade, with its colorful procession of floats and musicians. The Shin-sai-bashi stop (Exit 7) on the Midō-suji subway line is in the heart of the city's shopping districts. ⊠ *Chūō-ku.*

⑩ Municipal Museum of Fine Art (Ōsaka Shiritsu Bijutsukan). The building isn't too impressive, but the exceptional collection of 12th- to 14th-century classical Japanese art is. Other collections include the works of Edo-period artist Ogata Korin, more than 3,000 examples of modern lacquerware, and a collection of Chinese paintings and artifacts. Take the Loop Line or the Midō-suji subway line to Tennō-ji Station, or the Tani-machi subway to Shitennō-ji-mae. The museum is in Tennō-ji Kōen, southwest of Shitennō-ji. ⊠ *1–82 Chausuyama-chō, Tennō-ji-ku* 🕾 *06/6771–4874* 🖃 *¥300* ☉ *Tues.–Sun. 9:30–5; last entry at 4:30.*

Nintoku Mausoleum. The 4th-century mausoleum of Emperor Nintoku is in the city of Sakai, southeast of Ōsaka. The mausoleum was built on an even larger scale than that of the pyramids of Egypt—archaeologists calculate that the central mound of this site covers 1.3 million square feet. Construction took more than 20 years and required a total workforce of about 800,000 laborers. Surrounding the emperor's burial place are three moats and pine, cedar, and cypress trees. You can walk around the outer moat to get an idea of the size of the mausoleum and the grounds. However, entry into the mausoleum is not allowed. From Tennō-ji Station, take the JR Hanwa Line to Mozu Station (a half-hour ride). From there the mausoleum is a five-minute walk. ⊠ *7 Daisen-chō, Sakai-shi* 🕾 *0722/41–0002.*

⑫ Shitennō-ji (Shitennō Temple). Tennō-ji, as this temple is popularly known, is one of the most important historic sights in Ōsaka and the oldest temple in Japan. Founded in 593, architecturally it's gone through hell, having been destroyed by fire many times. The last reconstruction of the Main Hall (Kon-dō), Taishi-den, and the five-story pagoda in 1965 has maintained the original design and adhered to the traditional mathematical alignment. What has managed to survive from earlier times is the 1294 stone torii that stands at the main entrance. (Torii are rarely used at Buddhist temples.)

The founder, Umayado no Mikoto (573–621), posthumously known as Prince Shōtoku (Shōtoku Taishi), is considered one of early Japan's most enlightened rulers for his furthering of Buddhism and his political acumen. He was made regent over his aunt, Suiko, and set about instituting reforms and establishing Buddhism as the state religion. Buddhism had been introduced to Japan from China and Korea in the early 500s, but it was seen as a threat to the aristocracy, who claimed prestige and power based upon their godlike ancestry. On the 21st of every month the temple has a flea market that sells antiques and baubles; go in the morning for a feeling of Old Japan.

Three train lines will take you near Shitennō-ji. The Tani-machi-suji subway line's Shitennō-ji-mae Station is closest to the temple and the temple park. The Loop Line's Tennō-ji Station is several blocks south of the temple. The Midō-suji subway line also has a Tennō-ji stop, which is next to the JR station. ⊠ *1–11–18 Shitennō-ji, Tennō-ji-ku* 🕾 *06/ 6771–0066* 📠 *¥200* ⊙ *Apr.–Sept., daily 8:30–4:30; Oct.–Mar., daily 8:30–4.*

OFF THE
BEATEN
PATH

THE KOREAN EXPERIENCE – Koreans are the largest ethnic minority in Japan, and their highest concentration is in Ōsaka. Known as *zainichi*, after decades, in some cases centuries, of "assimilation" they have only recently begun to proclaim their traditional heritage and use their Korean names. By 2004 a wave of Korean *tarento* (talent) ruled TV and cinema screens across Japan. The most popular was Bae Yong-jun, affectionately known as *Yon-sama*. You may not be able to see Yon-sama in person, but you'll get an eyeful of him from the posters outside restaurants in Tsuruhashi, Ōsaka's Korea Town. **Gyuto** is one such restaurant. Well known as a dating spot, the reasonably priced Kōbe beef set menus for dinner are around ¥3,500 per person. Gyuto has a funky interior and is 50 yards from the west exit of JR Tsuruhashi Station. (⊠ 2–5 Shimoajihara-chō Tennō-ji-ku 🕾 06/6775–0710 🖃 AE, DC, MC, V)

⓭ **Sumiyoshi Taisha** (Sumiyoshi Grand Shrine). In a city of former mariners it's no surprise that locals revere Sumiyoshi Taisha, since it's dedicated to the guardian deity of sailors. According to legend, the shrine was founded by Empress Jingū in 211 to express her gratitude for her safe return from a voyage to Korea. Sumiyoshi Taisha is one of three shrines built prior to the arrival of Buddhism in Japan (the other two are Ise Jingū in Mie Prefecture and Izumo Taisha in Tottori Prefecture). According to Shintō custom, shrines were torn down and rebuilt at set intervals to the exact specifications of the original. Sumiyoshi was last replaced in 1810. Sumiyoshi is also famous for its taiko-bashi (arched bridge), given by Yodogimi, the consort of Toyotomi Hideyoshi, who bore him a son.

Every June 14 starting at 1 PM, a colorful rice-planting festival takes place here with traditional folk performances and processions. Sumiyoshi Matsuri, a large and lively festival, is held from July 30 to August 1. A crowd of rowdy young men carries a 2-ton portable shrine from Sumiyoshi Taisha to Yamato-gawa and back; this is followed by an all-night street bazaar. To reach the shrine, take the 20-minute ride south on the Nankai Main Line from Nankai Namba Station to Sumiyoshi Kōen Station. ⊠ *2–9–89 Sumiyoshi, Sumiyoshi-ku* 🕾 *06/6672–0753* 📠 *Free* ⊙ *Apr.–Oct., daily 6–5; Nov.–Mar., daily 6:30–5.*

➒ **Tennō-ji Kōen** (Tennō-ji Park). This park contains not only the **Municipal Museum of Fine Art** and the garden of **Keitaku-en,** but also the **Tennō-ji Botanical Gardens** (Tennō-ji Shokubutsuen). Also within the park is a prehistoric burial mound, **Chausuyama Kofun,** that was the site of Tokugawa Ieyasu's camp during the siege of Ōsaka-jō in 1614–15. Take the Loop Line from Ōsaka Station to Tennō-ji Station. The park is on the left side of the road going north to Shitennō-ji. ⊠ *6–74 Chausuyama-chō, Tennō-ji-ku* 🕾 *06/6771–8401* 📠 *¥150, park only* ⊙ *Tues.–Sun. 9:30–4:30; last entry at 4.*

SHOPPING ŌSAKA

Ōsaka has a vast network of underground shopping malls, the human equivalent of rabbit warrens. They are a great escape from the erratic rainy season and the summer heat. Signage is in both English and Japanese in many places, and if you're ever not sure of your bearings, all you have to do is pop up to ground level, like some sort of urban submariner.

For street-cred threads, head to **America-mura,** where tiny boutiques are crammed with the designs of tomorrow's fashionistas. A little to the west is **Minami-horie** where the fashionistas have moved up a notch and are now enjoying brand recognition. A stroll in either area will give you an inkling about what will be in the department stores a year from now.

Evisu Tailor—jean designer to the stars: Madonna included. Anyone wearing a pair of handmade raw-denim Evisus is recognized by the conspicuous seagull logo on the back pockets. The main shop is in Minami-semba, a 10-minute walk north of Minami-horie. ⊠ *4–13–6 Minami-semba, Chūō-ku* ☎ 06/6243–1992.

Master-piece. The shoulder bags and satchels at Master-piece are a combination of leather, velvet, and suede, and are an Ōsaka trademark. Take a little Ōsaka groove home. ⊠ *1–18–23 Minami-horie, Nishi-ku* ☎ 06/6243–1992.

SOZ is the brainchild of Hideki Tominaga, an Ōsaka native. He has created the the Mini Carpenter Block—an art toy of colorful, interlocking, plastic pieces that develops creativity. The cutest of his creations is Mr. Pen, whom you may want to buy after seeing the king penguins at the Ōsaka Aquarium. The SOZ showroom is open Monday, Wednesday, and Saturday from 11 to 5. (SOZ products are also available at the Suntory Museum.) Take Exit 28 from Hon-machi Station. ⊠ *1–14–20 Utsubo Hon-machi, 2F Ultra Bldg., Nishi-ku* ☎ 06/6754–2166.

There are specialized wholesale areas throughout the city, and many have a few retail shops as well. One such area is **Dōguya-suji,** just east of Nankai Namba Station and the Takashimaya department store. This street is lined with shops selling nothing but kitchen goods—all sorts of pots, pans, utensils, and glassware are piled to the rafters. Though most customers here are in the restaurant trade, laypeople shop here, too. Feel free to wander around: there's no obligation to buy. A trip here could be combined with a visit to nearby **Den Den Town,** known for its electronic goods. Also in this neighborhood, east of the main entrance to Dōguya-suji, is **Kuromon Ichiba,** the famous market district where chefs select the treats—fruits, vegetables, meat, and much more—cooked up at the city's restaurants that evening.

Department Stores & Shopping Complexes

All major Japanese *depāto* (department stores) are represented in Ōsaka. Hankyū is headquartered here. They're open 10–7, but usually close one day a month, on a Wednesday or Thursday. The food hall in the basement of Hanshin department store is the city's best. The following are some of Ōsaka's leading depātos: **Daimaru** (✉ 1–7–1 Shin-sai-bashi-suji, Chūō-ku ☎ 06/6343–1231). **Hankyū** (✉ 8–7 Kakuta-chō, Kita-ku ☎ 06/6361–1381). **Hanshin** (✉ 1–13–13 Umeda, Kita-ku ☎ 06/6345–1201). **Takashimaya** (✉ 5–1–5 Namba, Chūō-ku ☎ 06/6631–1101).

Hilton Plaza West and East have internationl brands like Max Mara, Dunhill, Chanel, and Ferragamo. Herbis Ent Plaza is a local high-end shopping complex connected to the Hilton Plaza West complex. These three shopping complexes are opposite Ōsaka Station. To the east of the Hankyū Grand Building is NU Chayamachi—a collection of small boutiques, both local and foreign, and some good cafes. **Hilton Plaza East** (✉ 1–8–6 Umeda, Kita-ku ☎ 06/6348–9168). **Hilton Plaza West** (✉ 2–2–2 Umeda, Kita-ku ☎ 06/6342–0002). **Herbis Ent Plaza** (✉ 2–2–22 Umeda, Kita-ku ☎ 06/6343–7500). **NU Chayamachi** (✉ 10–12 Chayamachi, Kita-ku ☎ 06/6373–7371).

Crafts

At one time famous for its traditional crafts—particularly *karaki-sashimono* (ornately carved furniture), fine Naniwa Suzuki pewterware, and *uchihamono* (Sakai cutlery)—Ōsaka lost much of its traditional industry during World War II. The simplest way to find Ōsakan crafts is to visit one of the major department stores.

Nihon Kōgeikan Mingei Fukyubu (Japan Folkcraft Collection). Folk crafts from all over the country, including ceramics, basketry, paper goods, folk toys, and textiles, are sold at this store near the Umeshin East Hotel in the popular gallery district, within walking distance of the U.S. consulate. Open Monday–Saturday 10–5:30. ✉ *4–7–15 Nishi-Tenma, Kita-ku* ☎ *06/6362–9501.*

Electronics

Although some Japanese electronic goods may be cheaper in the United States than in Japan, many electronics products are released on the Japanese market 6 to 12 months before they reach the West.

Den Den Town. This district has about 300 retail shops that specialize in electronics products, as well as stores selling cameras and watches. Shops are open 10–7 daily. Take your passport, and make your purchases in stores with signs that say TAX FREE in order to qualify for a 5% discount. The area is near Ebisu-chō Station on the Sakai-suji subway line (Exit 1 or 2), and Nippon-bashi Station on the Sakai-suji and Sennichi-mae subway lines (Exit 5 or 10).

Yodobashi Camera. If you haven't the time to spend exploring Den Den Town, head to this enormous electronics department store in Umeda. Don't be put off by the name: they sell far more than just cameras. On the north side of JR Ōsaka Station, opposite the Hotel New Hankyū, the store is impossible to miss. It's open daily 9:30–9. ✉ *1–1 Ōfuka-chō, Kita-ku* ☎ *06/4802–1010.*

SPORTS

Baseball

Kyocera Dōmu Ōsaka (Ōsaka Dome). The Orix Buffaloes are the local team, but it is the Hanshin Tigers from Nishi-no-miya, between Kōbe and Ōsaka, that prompt young men to jump into the Dōtombori river in excitement. The Hanshin department store has 10% discounts when the Tigers win, and you can see their black-and-yellow colors all over the city. Ōsaka Dome looks like a spaceship, and has pleasing-to-the-eye curved edges in a city dominated by the grey cube. Tickets cost as little as ¥1,600. Buy them at the gate, at branches of Lawson convenience store in the city, or by telephone from Ticket Pia. ⊠ *Next to Ōsaka Dōmu-mae Chiyozaki subway station on Nagahori Tsurumi-ryokuchi line, Taishō-ku* ☎ *06/6363–9999 Ticket Pia.*

Soccer

There has been a soccer boom in Japan since the World Cup was co-hosted by South Korea and Japan in 2002. Two J. League soccer teams, Gamba Ōsaka and Cerezo Ōsaka, play in Ōsaka. Tickets start at ¥1,500 for adults, and the season runs from March to November.

The Gamba Ōsaka play at **Bampaku EXPO Memorial Stadium** (⊠ 5–2 Senri Bampaku Kōen, Suita-shi ☎ 06/6202–5201) in the north of the city. Access is via the Ōsaka Monorail to Kōen Higashi-guchi Station. The Cerezo Ōsaka play at the **Nagai Stadium** (⊠ 2–2–19 Nagai-Higashi, Sumiyoshi-ku ☎ 06/6692–9011) in south Ōsaka, close to Nagai Station on the JR Hanwa Line or Midō-suji subway line.

Sumō

The sumō scene has become a hotbed of international rivalry as Bulgarians, Estonians, and some Russians with attitude have been edging the local talent out of the *basho* (ring). From the second Sunday through the fourth Sunday in March, one of Japan's six sumō tournaments takes place in the **Ōsaka Furitsu Taiikukaikan** (Ōsaka Prefectural Gymnasium). Most seats, known as *masu-seki,* are prebooked before the tournament begins, but standing-room tickets (¥1,000) and a limited number of seats (¥3,000) are available on the day of the event. The ticket office opens at 9 AM, and you should get in line early. The stadium is a 10-minute walk from Namba Station. ⊠ *3–4–36 Namba-naka, Naniwa-ku* ☎ *06/ 6631–0120.*

WHERE TO EAT

Kita: North of Chūō-dōri

★ **$$$$** ✕ **Isshin.** Only 16 seats grace this *kappo* restaurant to the east of Kita-shinchi. Ordering the *omakase* (chef's suggestion) dispenses with menu anxiety. The quality and quantity reflect Ōsaka's reputation for good food at reasonable prices. Sashimi, tempura, crab, and whatever is in season will be on the menu with a range of premium sakes to accompany them. Isshin is east of Midō-suji and Shin-midō-suji near the American con-

On the Menu

CLOSE UP

ŌSAKANS ARE PASSIONATE about food. As the old saying goes, *Ōsaka wa kuida-ore*—in Ōsaka you eat so much you fall over. They expect restaurants to use the freshest ingredients—for centuries the nearby Seto Inland Sea has allowed all classes easy access to fresh seafood. Ōsakans continue to have discriminating palates and demand their money's worth.

Ōsakan cuisine is flavored with a soy sauce lighter in color and milder in flavor than the soy used in Tōkyō. One local delicacy is *okonomiyaki*, something between a pancake and an omelet, filled with cabbage, mountain yams, pork, shrimp, and other ingredients. *Ōsaka-zushi* (Ōsaka-style sushi), made in wooden molds, has a distinctive square shape. *Unagi* (eel)

remains a popular local dish; grilled unagi is eaten in summer for quick energy. *Fugu* (blowfish) served boiled or raw is a winter delicacy.

The thick white noodles known as *udon* are a Japanese staple, but Ōsakans are particularly fond of *kitsune* udon, a local dish (now popular throughout Japan) in which the noodles are served with fried tofu known as *abura-age*. Another Ōsaka invention is *takoyaki*, griddle dumplings with octopus, green onions, and ginger smothered in a delicious sauce. Sold by street vendors in Dōtombori, these tasty snacks also appear at every festival and street market in Kansai. If you don't want to fall over, try and leave the table *hara-hachi bunme*, 80% full.

---

sulate. Go down the street with the convenience store on your right and Isshin is about 100 yards on the left. ⊠ *4–12–2 Nishi-Tenma, B1 Oshima Bldg., Kita-ku* ☎ *06/4709–3020* ➡ *AE, DC, MC, V.*

★ **$$$–$$$$** ✕ **Lois Café Chinois.** Nestled into a quiet corner of one of Ōsaka's underground shopping malls, Lois Café Chinois is a sanctuary of softly lighted elegance—Shanghai 1930s-style. The menu is Chinese food for a Japanese clientele: an array of steamed dumplings, noodles, spring rolls, and Peking duck, but lighter than continental fare. If you only need a pick-me-up, one of their huge parfaits for afternoon tea will dispense with the need for dinner. There is a no-smoking area. ⊠ *Hankyū Sanbangai B2 North Bldg. 1–1–3 Shibata, Kita-ku* ☎ *06/6359–1930* ➡ *AE, DC, MC, V.*

$$$ ✕ **La Baie.** The city's premier hotel restaurant serves extremely good French
Fodor'sChoice food. The wood-paneled La Baie is more akin to a Georgian nobleman's
★ dining room than a formal restaurant—smart but relaxed. Service is impeccable, and wines are specially chosen to complement three of the four full-course menus available. The special weekday ladies' menu is a good introduction to the Ritz Carlton's culinary refinement. Warmed chocolate biscuit with whipped amaretto is the signature dessert. ⊠ *2–5–25 Umeda, Kita-ku* ☎ *06/6343–7020* ⚠ *Reservations recommended* 🎩 *Jacket required* ➡ *AE, DC, MC, V.*

$$–$$$ ✕ **Mimiu.** It's the birthplace of *udon-suki*—thick, noodle stew with Chinese cabbage, clams, eel, yams, shiitake mushrooms, *mitsuba* (a three-leaved green), and other seasonal ingredients simmered in a pot over a burner at your table. Mimiu is on the 10th floor of the Hanshin department store opposite Ōsaka Station. ⊠ *1–13–13 Umeda, Kita-ku* ☎ *06/6345–6648* ⌒ *Reservations not accepted* ⊟ *V.*

$$ ✕ **Negiyaki Yamamoto.** It would be a sacrilege to leave Ōsaka without trying *okonomiyaki.* Ōsaka's specialty pancake of grilled cabbage, seafood, and pork topped with barbecue sauce is even tastier when cooked in front of you. A cold beer is the only accompaniment necessary. The waiting lines outside Yamamoto Negiyaki attest that it is the best place in town. Go mid-afternoon to avoid a wait. ⊠ *Umeda East 3–25 Kadota-chō, Kita-ku* ☎ *06/6131–0118.*

¢–$$ ✕ **Los Inkas.** Hugely popular with the local Latin community, Los Inkas is always busy, and the up-tempo music makes it a good place for a party. Many dishes are Peruvian, though other Latin cuisines, including Mexican, are represented. Menu highlights include *ceviche mixto,* shrimp, octopus, and fish marinated in lime juice and spices; and *lomo saltado,* beef, vegetables, and french fries sautéed together. ⊠ *2F Kodama Leisure Bldg., 1–14 Dōyama-chō, Kita-ku* ☎ *06/6365–5190* ⊟ *No credit cards* ⊘ *Closed Mon.*

$ ✕ **Satoyama Cafe.** Japan is returning to its macrobiotic roots, and Satoyama Café is in with the trend. The healthy lunch sets include a selection of small vegetable dishes, brown rice, pickles, and a main dish for under ¥1,000. It's in an old brick-building legal office with high ceilings and a small garden. Take the Yotsu-bashi Line to Higo-bashi Station, Exit 3. ⊠ *1F Yamauchi Bldg. 1–1–4 Tosabori, Nishi-ku* ☎ *06/6459–1155* ⌒ *Reservations not accepted* ⊟ *MC, V.*

South of Chūō-dōri

★ $$$$ ✕ **La Tour.** This French restaurant in the Swissôtel Nankai Ōsaka has heavy French cutlery, Rothko lithographs, and dark-red upholstery to match their culinary aspirations. Bouillabaisse is the house specialty, accompanied by excellent service. ⊠ *Swissôtel Nankai Ōsaka, 1–60 Namba 5-chōme, Chūō-ku* ☎ *06/6646–5126* ⌒ *Reservations essential* ⊟ *AE, DC, MC, V.*

$$$$ ✕ **Ume no Hana.** Healthy prix-fixe, multicourse menus of tofu-based cuisine—particularly refreshing on hot summer days—are the specialty here. This is a good spot to take a break from shopping in Shin-sai-bashi, and during the day you can order one of the cheaper lunch sets. The private dining rooms are in a traditional Japanese style with pottery and ikebana. Reserve ahead on weekends and in the evening. ⊠ *11F Shin-sai-bashi OPA Bldg., 1–4–3 Nishi-Shin-sai-bashi, Chūō-ku* ☎ *06/6258–3766* ⊟ *AE, DC, MC, V.*

$$$–$$$$ ✕ **Kani Dōraku.** The most famous restaurant on Dōtombori-dōri—the enormous mechanical crab is a local landmark—Kani Dōraku has fine crab dishes at reasonable prices. For lunch a crab set, with large portions of crab, costs around ¥4,000; crab for dinner costs more than ¥6,000. An English-language menu is available. Reserve ahead on weekends. ⊠ *1–6–18 Dōtombori, Chūō-ku* ☎ *06/6211–8975* ⊟ *AE, DC, MC, V.*

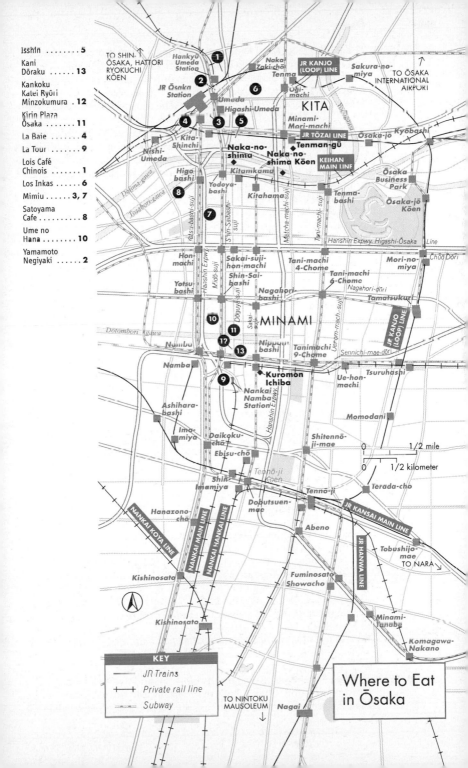

Where to Eat in Ōsaka

KEY

— JR Trains

+ Private rail line

‑‑ Subway

$$-$$$$ ✕ **Kankoku Katei Ryori Minzokumura.** Popular with Korean celebrities, this restaurant eschews glitz for tradition. *Katei* means "home-style" in Japanese, and the Korean hot pot teppanyaki, sumbiyaki, and seafood hot pot set menus won't break the bank. It opens early (3 PM) and closes late (4 AM). ⊠ *1–22 Soemon-chō, Unagidani, Chūō-ku* ☎ *06/6212-2640* ▭ *AE, DC, MC, V.*

★ $$–$$ ✕ **Kirin Plaza Ōsaka.** The black-and-chrome facade of the Takamatsu Shin–designed Kirin Plaza was controversial when unveiled, but today defines the Dōtombori skyline. Inside is a branch of the Kirin City beerhall chain, which has a working microbrewery in full view. The restaurant, on the third floor, serves mixed Japanese and Western dishes such as avocado tempura and hot salads. There are contemporary art exhibitions on the upper floors and a great view of the neonscape from the restaurant. ⊠ *3F Kirin Plaza Bldg., 7–2 Soemon-chō, Chūō-ku* ☎ *06/ 6212–6572* ▭ *V.*

WHERE TO STAY

North of Chūō-dōri

$$$$ 🏨 **ANA Hotel Ōsaka.** One of Ōsaka's oldest deluxe hotels, the ANA overlooks Naka-no-shima Kōen. The 24-story building is a handsome white-tile structure with some unusual architectural features like great fluted columns in the lobby. There's also an enclosed courtyard with trees. The main bar is a throwback to a 1950s English gentlemen's club. Guest rooms feature shades of chocolate, tan, and cream. Each room has a trouser press, and the cups are traditional Japanese ceramics. ⊠ *1–3–1 Dōjima-hama, Kita-ku, Ōsaka 530-0004* ☎ *06/6347–1112,* 🖷 *06/6347–9208* 🌐 *www.anahtlŌsaka.co.jp/english* 🛏 *493 rooms* ⚲ *5 restaurants, coffee shop, minibars, refrigerators, cable TV with movies, in-room broadband, in-room safes, indoor pool, health club, massage, sauna, business services, meeting rooms, parking (fee)* ▭ *AE, DC, MC, V.*

$$$$ 🏨 **Hotel New Otani Ōsaka.** Indoor and outdoor pools, a rooftop garden, tennis courts, and a sparkling marble atrium make this amenities-rich hotel a popular choice for Japanese and Westerners. The modern rooms, large by Japanese standards, afford handsome views of Ōsaka-jō and the Neya-gawa (Neya River). Rooms have light color schemes accented with geometric patterns and Japan-inspired modern prints. The New Otani is like a minicity within Ōsaka Business Park. Spend an evening in the Teppanyaki restaurant on the 11th floor enjoying Ōsaka-jō in all its floodlit glory. ⊠ *4–1 Shiromi 1-chōme, Chūō-ku, Ōsaka 540-8578* ☎ *06/6941–1111* 🖷 *06/6941–9769* 🌐 *www.Ōsaka. newotani.co.jp* 🛏 *525 rooms, 53 suites* ⚲ *9 restaurants, minibars, refrigerators, cable TV, in-room broadband, some in-room safes, 2 tennis courts, indoor-outdoor pool, health club, hair salon, bicycles, 2 bars, Internet, business services, meeting rooms, parking (fee)* ▭ *AE, DC, MC, V.*

★ $$$$ 🏨 **Rihga Royal Hotel.** Royal means Emperor, and the royal family stays here when visiting Ōsaka. Built in the 1930s, the Royal contains more than 20 restaurants, bars, and karaoke rooms, and no fewer than 60

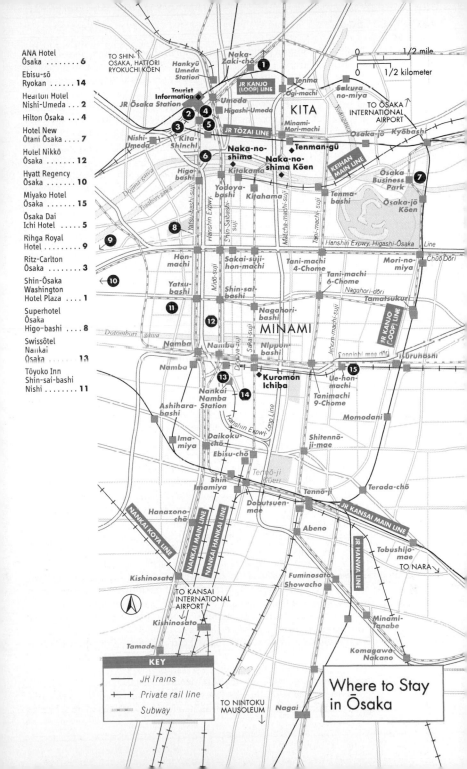

Where to Stay in Ōsaka

KEY

— JR Trains

+ Private rail line

= Subway

shops—in addition to nearly 1,000 rooms. The West Wing has standard rooms for business travelers, the Tower Wing standard and executive floors. Each executive floor has a nature theme, so depending on your mood stay on the forest, sky, flower, or sea floors. A stay in the VIP tower means free access to the swimming club's two sun-roof pools (other guests pay ¥2,000). A shuttle bus goes to the Umeda and Yodoya-bashi stations. ⊠ *5–3–68 Naka-no-shima, Kita-ku, Ōsaka 530-0005* ☎ *06/6448–1121* ⊟ *06/6448–4414* ⊕ *www.rihga.com* ↪ *980 rooms, 53 suites* ⊘ *20 restaurants, cable TV with movies, in-room broadband, in-room safes, 3 pools (1 indoor), health club, hair salon, massage, sauna, steam room, 2 bars, shops, babysitting, concierge, business services* ⊟ *AE, DC, MC, V.*

$$$$ ⬚ **The Ritz-Carlton, Ōsaka.** Smaller than Ōsaka's other top hotels, the

Fodor'sChoice   Ritz-Carlton combines a homey feel and European elegance in the city's

★   most luxurious place to stay. King-size beds with goose-down pillows and dark-wood furnishings grace the guest rooms, and the bathrooms have plush bathrobes and towels. Stay on a Club floor for the special lounge. A rarity in Japan, the room price at the Ritz Carlton includes use of the pool, Jacuzzi, and gym. All rooms have an IT panel through which you can connect your computer and audiovisual equipment to the flat-screen television. All this comes, you understand, at a price— the Ritz-Carlton is Ōsaka's most expensive hotel. ⊠ *2–5–25 Umeda, Kita-ku, Ōsaka 530-0001* ☎ *06/6343–7000,* ⊟ *06/6343–7001* ⊕ *www. ritzcarlton.com* ↪ *292 rooms* ⊘ *4 restaurants, lobby lounge, cable TV with movies, in-room broadband, pool, health club, bar, concierge floor, business services, parking(fee)* ⊟ *AE, DC, MC, V.*

★ **$$$–$$$$**   ⬚ **Hilton Ōsaka.** Glitz and glitter lure tourists and expense-accounters to the Hilton Ōsaka, the city's most convenient hotel, across from JR Ōsaka Station in the heart of the business district. It's a typical Western-style hotel, with an orgy of marble and brass. The high-ceiling lobby is dramatic and stylish, and the hotel's arcade contains designer boutiques. The five executive floors have a lounge for complimentary continental breakfasts and evening cocktails, and the decor is 21st century art deco with a Japanese streak. ⊠ *8–8 Umeda 1-chōme, Kita-ku, Ōsaka 530-0001* ☎ *06/6347–7111* ⊟ *06/6347–7001* ⊕ *www.hilton. co.jp/Ōsaka* ↪ *525 rooms* ⊘ *7 restaurants, café, coffee shop, minibars, refrigerators, cable TV with movies, in-room broadband, some in-room safes, indoor pool, health club, massage, sauna, shops, business services, meeting rooms, parking (fee)* ⊟ *AE, DC, MC, V.*

$$$–$$$$ ⬚ **Ōsaka Dai Ichi Hotel.** As Japan's first cylindrical skyscraper—known as the Maru-Biru (Round Building)—the Dai Ichi stands out. The rooms are wedge shaped, and half are small singles usually occupied on weekdays by businesspeople. At the restaurant in the basement you can try your hand at cooking takoyaki at your table. It's conveniently across from Ōsaka Station and next to the Hilton Ōsaka. ⊠ *1–9–20 Umeda, Kita-ku, Ōsaka 530-0001* ☎ *06/6341–4411* ⊟ *06/6341–4930* ⊕ *www. daiichihotels.com* ↪ *448 rooms* ⊘ *6 restaurants, refrigerators, in-room broadband, bar, shops* ⊟ *AE, DC, MC, V.*

$$ ⬚ **Hearton Hotel Nishi-Umeda.** A few minutes' walk from JR Ōsaka Station, the Hearton is a more affordable alternative. Unless you're really on a budget, however, opt for one of the larger twin rooms; the smaller rooms are barely big enough for you to swing the proverbial cat in. From Ōsaka Station walk west and go around the Gran Via hotel to the street crossing. Go through the food-court arcade and the hotel is at the end. ⊠ *3–3–55 Umeda, Kita-ku, Ōsaka 530-0001* ☎ *06/6342–1111* 🖷 *06/6342–1122* ⊕ *www.hearton.co.jp/english* ☎ *471 rooms* ⚴ *Restaurant, coffee shop, refrigerators, in-room broadband, cable TV with movies, dry cleaning, bicycles* ☱ *AE, DC, MC, V.*

$$ 🏨 **Shin-Ōsaka Washington Hotel Plaza.** Part of a no-nonsense chain of business hotels throughout the country, the Washington is the smartest of its kind. Rooms are not large, but are clean and comfortable. Among the highlights are the China Table Chinese restaurant for the food and city views, and the blend of urban groovers from Tokyo and businessmen in the foyer. Convenient to JR Shin-Ōsaka Station, from which the Shinkansen arrives and departs. Exit 7 Shin-Ōsaka subway. ⊠ *5–5–15 Nishi-Nakajima, Yodo-gawa-ku, Ōsaka 532-0011* ☎ *06/6303–8111* 🖷 *06/6308–8709* ⊕ *http://shinŌsaka.wh-at.com* ☎ *490 rooms* ⚴ *4 restaurants, refrigerators, in-room broadband, parking (fee), no-smoking floors* ☱ *AE, DC, MC, V.*

★ $ 🏨 **Superhotel Ōsaka Higo-bashi.** A member of the popular nationwide chain of business hotels, this Superhotel is in a quiet leafy neighborhood a five-minute walk south of Naka-no-shima. There are just two set prices, for singles or doubles, and they include an international buffet breakfast. That means thick slices of toast and miso soup. The friendly staff give all female guests a complimentary amenities pack on arrival. Exit 7 Higo-bashi Station on the Yotsu-bashi line. ⊠ *1–20–1 Edo-bori, Nishi-ku, Ōsaka 550-0002* ☎ *06/6448–9000* 🖷 *06/6448–2400* ☎ *80 rooms* ⚴ *In-room broadband; no room phones* ☱ *V* ⦿ *CP.*

South of Chūō-dōri

$$$$ 🏨 **Hotel Nikkō Ōsaka.** A striking white tower in the colorful Shin-sai-bashi Station area, the Nikkō is within easy reach of Ōsaka's nightlife. Price depends on amenities, as the twin and double rooms are all the same size. Opt for a room on one of the L floors for a couple of thousand yen extra. The decor is red, black, and gray, and the rooms have plush beds with double spring mattresses. Black-and-white photographs of Midō-suji-dōri ornament the walls. Ask for a no-smoking room if you prefer not to be assaulted by the smell of stale cigarettes. From Exit 8 Shin-sai-bashi Station on the Midō-suji Line, you walk directly into the hotel. ⊠ *1–3–3 Nishi-Shin-sai-bashi, Chūō-ku, Ōsaka 542-0086* ☎ *06/6244–1111* 🖷 *06/6245–2432* ⊕ *www.hno.co.jp* ☎ *640 rooms, 5 suites* ⚴ *3 restaurants, coffee shop, minibars, refrigerators, cable TV with movies, in-room broadband, 3 bars, shops, Internet, meeting rooms, parking (fee)* ☱ *AE, DC, MC, V.*

$$$$ 🏨 **Hyatt Regency Ōsaka.** If Universal Studios Japan is on your itinerary, the Hyatt, in the Nankō development area, is quite convenient, and Kansai International Airport is a 45-minute bus ride away. The hotel is a 20-minute subway ride from the city center, however. Modern comforts abound: guest rooms are spacious, especially deluxe doubles and junior suites, which are larger than the typical Japanese apartment. Some rooms on the upper floors have grand views of Ōsaka Bay. ✉ *1–13 Nankō-Kita, Suminoe-ku, Ōsaka 559-0034* ☎ *06/6612–1234* 🖷 *06/6614–7800* ⊕ *www.hyattregencyŌsaka.com* 🖙 *500 rooms, 7 suites* ⚒ *11 restaurants, minibars, refrigerators, cable TV with movies, in-room broadband, indoor-outdoor pool, health club, massage, sauna, spa, 2 bars, Internet, business services, meeting rooms, free parking* ▤ *AE, DC, MC, V.*

$$$$ 🏨 **Miyako Hotel Ōsaka.** Even though rooms at the Miyako are on the small side, they are light and airy, with wood-paneled headboards. The bathrooms, meanwhile, are large by Japanese standards. Backlighted modern artworks and ceramics adorn the busy foyer and other public areas. All rooms have tables. The private Kintetsu Line Ue-hon-machi Station next door runs trains to Nara and Kyōto. The National Bunraku Theater and Shitennō-ji are also fairly close. ✉ *6–1–55 Ue-hon-machi, Tennō-ji-ku, Ōsaka 543-0001* ☎ *06/6773–1111* 🖷 *06/6773–3322* ⊕ *www.radisson.com/Osaka.jp* 🖙 *575 rooms, 2 suites* ⚒ *10 restaurants, coffee shop, cable TV, in-room broadband, indoor pool, health club, racquetball, 2 bars, lounge, shops, concierge floor, airport shuttle* ▤ *AE, DC, MC, V.*

$$$$ 🏨 **Swissôtel Nankai Ōsaka.** With mellow contemporary art and European-style furnishings, the standard rooms at this high-end hotel, a member of the Raffles International Group, are some of the best in the city. The Executive Club offers additional privacy and a private lounge for breakfast, cocktails, and nightcaps. Be sure to have a drink in Tavola 36, the hotel's top-floor Italian sky lounge, complete with a DJ booth. Take the third-floor exit at Nankai Namba Station to get to the Swissôtel. ✉ *1–60 Namba 5-chōme, Chūō-ku, Ōsaka 542-0076* ☎ *06/6646–1111* 🖷 *06/6648–0331* ⊕ *www.swissotel-Ōsaka.co.jp* 🖙 *535 rooms, 11 Western-style suites, 2 Japanese-style suites* ⚒ *11 restaurants, cable TV with movies, in-room broadband, indoor pool, health club, hot tub, massage, sauna, shops, concierge floor* ▤ *AE, DC, MC, V.*

$ 🏨 **Ebisu-sō Ryokan.** Ōsaka's only member of the inexpensive Japanese Inn Group is a partly wooden structure with 15 Japanese-style rooms. It's a very basic but quiet, no-frills operation run by two delightful old ladies who will direct you to the abundance of restaurants and cafés nearby. Close to the electrical-appliance and computer center of Den Den Town and the National Theater, Ebisu-sō Ryokan is a five-minute walk from Ebisu-chō Station (Exit A-2) on the Sakai-suji subway line. ✉ *1–7–33 Nippon-bashi-nishi, Naniwa-ku, Ōsaka 556-0004* ☎ *06/6643–4861* 🖙 *15 Japanese-style rooms without bath* ▤ *AE, MC, V.*

¢–$ 🏨 **Tōyoko Inn Shin-sai-bashi Nishi.** A 10-minute walk west of the Shin-sai-bashi subway station and close to the laid-back cafés of Minami Horie, the Tōyoko Inn is a good-value, comfortable business hotel. Thought has gone into the facilities for the budget traveler. Computers with free Internet access are in the foyer, and you can make free local calls from the house phone. The prices include a light breakfast of rice balls, miso soup, and coffee. ✉ *1–9–22 Kita-Horie, Nishi-ku, Ōsaka 550-0014* ☎ *06/6536–1045* 🖷 *06/6536–1046* ⊕ *www.toyoko-inn.com/eng* 🖙 *144 rooms* ⚒ *Refrigerators, room TV with movies, in-room data ports, Internet, no-smoking rooms* ▤ *AE, DC, V* ⦿ *CP.*

NIGHTLIFE & THE ARTS

The Arts

National Bunraku Theater. Bunraku became an art form in Ōsaka—so seeing a performance here is paying homage to the likes of Chikamatsu Monzaemon, the Shakespeare of Japan. The theater is open in January, March, April, June, July, August, and November. Each run starts on the third of the month and lasts about three weeks. Ōsaka's tourist offices will have the current schedule, which is also printed in *Kansai Time Out* and the quarterly tourist booklet *Meet Ōsaka*. Tickets are ¥4,400 and ¥5,600; performances usually begin at 11 AM and 4 PM. From the Namba subway station, take the Sennichi-mae subway line one stop east to Nippon-bashi Station. Exit 7 will bring you right outside the theater, ✉ *12–10 Nippon-bashi 1-chōme, Chūō-ku* ☎ *06/6212–2531* ⊕ *www.Ōsaka.isp.ntt-west.co.jp*

Shōchiku-za Kabuki Theater. Ōsaka's Kabuki theater, built in 1923 as Japan's first Western-style theater, rivals Tōkyō's Kabuki-za. Technology has been cleverly incorporated into Shōchiku-za alongside traditional theater design. The house hosts kabuki for about half the year, with major performances most months. The rest of the year it hosts musicals and other concerts. Tickets range from ¥4,000 to ¥20,000, ✉ *1–9 19 Dōtombori, Chūō-ku* ☎ *06/6214–2211, 06/6214–2200 for reservations.*

PUPPET THEATER

Ōsaka is the home of *bunraku* (puppet drama), which originated during the Heian period (794–1192). In the late 17th and early 18th centuries the local playwright Chikamatsu Monzaemon elevated bunraku to an art form. Bunraku puppets are about two-thirds human size. Three completely visible puppeteers move the puppets. At the National Bunraku Theater the story is chanted in song by the *joruri* (chanter), with music played on a three-stringed "banjo," the *shamisen*. Try and catch a performance of *Sonezaki Shinju* (*The Love Suicides at Sonezaki*), set where Kita-shinchi stands now.

Nightlife

Ōsaka has a diverse nightlife scene. The Kita (North) area surrounds JR Umeda Station; and the Minami (South) area is between the Shinsai-bashi and Namba districts and includes part of Chūō-ku (Central Ward). Many Japanese refer to Minami as being "for kids," but there are plenty of good restaurants and drinking spots for more seasoned bon vivants. Ōsaka's hip young things hang out in America-mura, in the southern part of Chūō-ku, with its innumerable bars and clubs. Kita draws a slightly more adult crowd, including businesspeople.

Bars

Café Absinthe. After browsing the fashions in Minami-horie's boutiques, pop into Café Absinthe in neighboring Kita-horie for Mediterranean food and good music. Live performances usually start at around 9. The music and the crowd are very international and very laid-back. ✉ *1–16–18 Kita-horie, Nishi-ku* ☎ *06/6534–6635.*

Dance Clubs

Club Joule. Club Joule caters to trance, psychedelic, reggae, and hip-hop fans during the week and house clubbers on weekends. A café-style seating area upstairs is a good place to recuperate between dances—or an ideal location for those who'd rather just watch the action. Shin-sai-bashi Station Exit 7. ✉ *2F/ 3F Brutus Bldg., 2–11–30 Nishi-Shin-sai-bashi, Chūō-ku* ☎ *06/6214–1223.*

Club Karma. If you're looking for serious techno or all-night dancing, Club Karma hosts all-night drum 'n' bass/techno events on weekends and on nights before national holidays (cover from ¥2,500). On non-event nights it's a scenester bar serving good food to hip music. ✉ *1F Kasai Bldg., 1–5–18 Sonezaki-shinchi, Kita-ku* ☎ *06/6344–6181.*

Mother Hall. Mother Hall doesn't host club events every night, but when it does they're packed. This is a large-scale club that can accommodate up to 1,500 people for trance, house, and other electronic music. ✉ *B1 Swing Yoshimoto Bldg., 12–35 Namba, Chūō-ku* ☎ *06/ 4397–9061.*

Sazae. This is the city's slickest dance club, with a state-of-the-art sound system and regular appearances by big-name international DJs. There are weekly drum 'n' bass, reggae, disco, hip-hop, and progressive house nights as well as a gay event once or twice a month. ✉ *16–4 Chaya-machi, Kita-ku* ☎ *06/6486–3388.*

Jazz

Blue Note. Jazz fans should head to Umeda and this high-end club where the cream of the international and national jazz scenes plays two sets nightly. Tickets aren't cheap: expect to pay anywhere from ¥5,000 to ¥12,000. ✉ *B2 Herbis Plaza Ent 2–2–22 Umeda, Kita-ku* ☎ *06/ 6342–7722.*

Mr. Kelly's. This club on the ground floor of the Sun Garden Hotel regularly features a jazz trio plus a guest vocalist. The cover charge starts at ¥3,000 for a double-bill. ✉ *2–4–1 Sonezaki Shinchi, Kita-ku* ☎ *06/ 6342–5821.*

Rock & Alternative

Bears. This tiny basement, full at 70 people, is the city's single most interesting venue for live music. It's ground zero for the region's avant-garde musical underground, including such performers as Haco and Empty Orchestra. Events start and finish early, so get here by 6:30. There's something on every evening. ✉ *B1 Shin-Nihon Namba Bldg., 3–14–5 Namba-naka, Naniwa-ku* ☎ *06/6649–5564.*

Club Quattro. Up-and-coming Japanese rock bands and popular Western bands play here. The sound system is excellent. ✉ *8F Shin-sai-bashi Parco Bldg., Shin-sai-bashi-suji 1–9–1, Chūō-ku* ☎ *06/6281–8181.*

ŌSAKA ESSENTIALS

To research prices, get advice from other travelers, and book travel arrangements, visit www.fodors.com.

Transportation

BY AIR

International carriers flying into Ōsaka include Air Canada and Northwest Airlines from North America, and Japan Airlines from the United Kingdom. Flights from Tōkyō operate throughout the day and take 65 minutes. Japan Airlines (JAL) and All Nippon Airways (ANA) have domestic flights to major cities.

🛪 Carriers **Air Canada** ☎ 0120/048-048. **All Nippon Airways** ☎ 0120/02-9222. **Japan Airlines** ☎ 0120/255-931 international, 0120/25-5971 domestic. **Northwest Airlines** ☎ 0120/120-747.

AIRPORTS & TRANSFERS All international flights arrive at Kansai International Airport (KIX), which also handles connecting domestic flights to major Japanese cities. The airport, constructed on reclaimed land in Ōsaka Bay, is laid out vertically—the buildings that is, not the runways. The first floor is for international arrivals, the second floor is for domestic departures and arrivals, the third floor has shops and restaurants, and the fourth floor is for international departures.

About 60% of domestic flights still use Ōsaka's old airport, confusingly called Ōsaka International Airport; it's more commonly known as Itami Airport, as it is situated in the city of Itami, a half hour or so northwest of Ōsaka.

KIX was designed to serve the entire Kansai region (Kōbe, Kyōto, and Nara), not just Osaka, so there's good train service out of the airport. There are four main access routes to Ōsaka: to Shin-Ōsaka take the JR Kansai Airport Express Haruka for the 45-minute run (¥3,180); to Tennō-ji Station, the same JR train will take about 29 minutes (¥2,470); to JR Kyō-bashi Station take the Kansai Airport Rapid train for a 70-minute run (¥1,160); and, to Nankai Namba Station take the private Nankai Rapid Limited Express for a 29-minute trip (¥1,390). There's no English-language hotline for JR schedules, but tourist information offices and hotel staff should be able to help.

The airport is not large: as soon as you exit customs you are in the arrivals lobby, where you'll find English-language tourist information and direct access to limousine buses. An airport bus limousine service runs between KIX and many of Ōsaka's downtown hotels. The very comfortable bus takes about 60 minutes and costs ¥1,300–¥1,800.

Buses from Itami Airport operate at intervals of 15 minutes to one hour (depending on your destination), daily 6 AM–9 PM, and take passengers to seven locations in Ōsaka: Shin-Ōsaka Station, Umeda, Namba (near the Nikkō and Holiday Inn hotels), Ue-hon-machi, Abeno, Sakai-higashi, and Ōsaka Business Park (near the New Otani Hotel). Buses take 25–50 minutes, depending on the destination, and cost ¥490–¥620. Schedules, with exact times and fares, are available at the information counter at the airport.

Taxis to the city from Kansai International Airport are expensive; between Itami Airport and hotels in central Ōsaka, taxis cost approximately ¥7,500 and take about 40 minutes.

BY SUBWAY

Ōsaka's subway system offers the most convenient means of exploring the city. There are seven lines, of which Midō-suji is the main one; it runs between Shin-Ōsaka and Umeda in 6 minutes, Shin-Ōsaka and Shin-sai-bashi in 12 minutes, Shin-Ōsaka and Namba in 14 minutes, and Shin-Ōsaka and Tennō-ji in 20 minutes.

A very useful Ōsaka subway map is available in city tourist offices, most hotels, and from the Japan National Tourist Organization in the United States or in Tōkyō (⇨ Visitor Information *in* Japan Essentials).

The JR Loop Line circles the city aboveground and intersects with all subway lines. Fares range from ¥120 to ¥190, or you can use your JR Pass.

FARES & SCHEDULES Subways run from early morning until nearly midnight at intervals of three to five minutes. Fares begin at ¥200 and are determined by the distance traveled. You can purchase a one-day pass (¥850)—which provides unlimited municipal transportation on subways, the New Tram (a tram line that runs to the port area), and city buses—at the commuter ticket windows in major subway stations and at the Japan Travel Bureau office in Ōsaka Station. JR trains are not included in this ticket.

BY TAXI

You'll have no problem hailing taxis on the street or at taxi stands. (A red light in the lower left corner of the windshield indicates availability.) The problem is Ōsaka's heavy traffic. Fares are metered at ¥550–¥640 for the first 1 m (2 km), plus ¥90 for each additional 500 yards. Few taxi drivers speak English, so it's advisable to have your destination written in Japanese characters to show to the driver. It's not customary to tip, and many taxis now accept credit cards. Late at night, generally after midnight, there's a 20% surcharge.

BY TRAIN

Hikari shinkansen trains from Tōkyō Station to Shin-Ōsaka Station take about three hours and cost ¥13,950. You can use a JR Pass for the *Hikari* but not for the faster *Nozomi* shinkansen trains, which cost ¥14,720 and are about 30-minutes faster. Shin-Ōsaka Station, on the north side of Shin-Yodo-gawa, is linked to the city center by the JR Kōbe Line and the Midō-suji subway line. On either line the ride, which takes 6–20 minutes depending on your mid-city destination, costs ¥180–¥230. Train schedules and fare information can be obtained at the Travel Service Center in Shin-Ōsaka Station. A taxi from Shin-Ōsaka Station to central Ōsaka costs ¥1,500–¥2,700.

TRAVEL AGENCIES

Academy Travel and No. 1 Travel sell cheap air tickets, and staff members are well versed in English.

🖪 **Academy Travel** ⊠ 4F Takada II Bldg., 2-6-8 Jūsō Higashi, Yodo-gawa-ku ☎ 06/6303-3538. **No. 1 Travel** ⊠ 11F Nisshin Bldg., 8-8 Taiyūji-chō, Kita-ku ☎ 06/6363-4489.

Contacts & Resources

BANKS & EXCHANGE SERVICES

Major currencies can be exchanged and traveler's checks cashed at the TIS office in front of the central exit at JR Ōsaka Station. It is open Monday–Saturday 10:30–7:30, Sunday and national holidays 10:30–6:30. Namba City Mitsubishi-Tōkyō UFJ Bank has a currency shop on the second floor of Namba Nankai Station in front of the central exit. It's open 10–7:30 on weekdays and 10–5 on weekends and national holidays. The ATM (8–9 weekdays, 9–5 weekends) at the Central Post Office accepts international cards, as does the Citibank in Shin-sai-bashi. The Citibank Shin-sai-bashi branch is open weekdays 9–3, and the ATM is open 24 hours. It is a five-minute walk from Exit C7 from Shin-sai-bashi Station on the Midō-suji Line.

Citibank (⊠ 2-1-2 Nishi Shin-sai-bashi, 1F/ 2F Midō-suji Diamond Bldg., Minami-ku ☎ 06/6213-2731). **Mitsubishi-Tōkyō UFJ Bank** (⊠ 2F Namba City, Nankai Namba Station, Minami-ku ☎ 06/6643-6815). **Ōsaka Central Post Office** (⊠ 2-4 Umeda 3-chōme, Kita-ku ☎ 06/6341-7870 ⏱ 7-11). **TIS** (⊠ 3-1 Umeda, Ōsaka Station, Kita-ku ☎ 06/4797-9685).

BUSINESS ASSISTANCE

Contact Information Service System Co., Ltd., for business-related assistance, including quick-print business cards and interpreting. For laptop repair, try Sofmap.

🖪 **Information Service System Co., Ltd.** ⊠ Hotel Nikkō Ōsaka, 1-3-3 Nishi-Shin-sai-bashi, Chūō-ku ☎ 06/6245-4015. **Sofmap** ⊠ 3-2-135 Umeda, Kita-ku ☎ 06/4797-4300.

CONSULATES

U.S. ⊠ 2-11-5 Nishi-Tenma, Kita-ku ☎ 06/6315-5900.

EMERGENCIES

There is a *kōban* (police box) between the Ōsaka Station Tourist Information Center and the city bus terminal under the pedestrian walkway. For medical advice in English, call the AMDA International Medical Center Kansai.

🖪 **Doctors & Hospitals AMDA International Medical Center Kansai** ⊠ Yubinkyo-ku Ōsaka Chikko, Minato-ku 552-0021 (Postal address only) ☎ 06/4395-0555. **Sumitomo Hospital** ⊠ 2-2 Naka-no-shima 5-chōme, Kita-ku ☎ 06/6443-1261. **Tane General Hospital** ⊠ 1-2-31 Sakai-gawa, Nishi-ku ☎ 06/6581-1071. **Yodo-gawa Christian Hospital** ⊠ 9-26 Awaji 2-chōme, Higashi, Yodo-gawa-ku ☎ 06/6322-2250.

🖪 **Emergency Services Ambulance** ☎ 119. **Metropolitan Police Office Service** ☎ 06/6943-1234. **Police** ☎ 110.

7

ENGLISH-LANGUAGE MEDIA

BOOKS Kinokuniya Book Store is open daily 10–10, except for the third Wednesday of the month. It's across the street from the Midō-suji entrance of Ōsaka Station in the Hankyū Station complex. Random Walk Ōsaka is west of Midō-suji in America-mura and is open daily from 10 to 8. Take Exit 7 from Shin-sai-bashi Station on the Midō-suji Line.

🗊 **Kinokuniya Book Store** ⊠ Hankyū Samban-gai 1-1-3, Shibata, Kita-ku ☎ 06/6372-5821. **Random Walk Ōsaka** ⊠ 1-5-17 Nishi-Shin-sai-bashi, Chūō-ku ☎ 06/6251-8862.

NEWSPAPERS & *Kansai Time Out* (⊕ www.kto.co.jp) is a monthly publication listing events
MAGAZINES in Kōbe, Kyōto, Nara, and Ōsaka and has topical articles written for travelers and residents. It costs ¥300, and is available at all major bookstores in the region. *Kansai Scene* (⊕ www.kansaiscene.com) is a free monthly magazine catering mainly to Ōsaka residents and travelers, and is available at major hotels and bars.

INTERNET, MAIL & SHIPPING

There is a FedEx Kinko's branch at Ōsaka Station to the right of the tourist information center up the stairs. All tourist information offices have lists of Internet cafés in their areas. Wi-Fi was not widely available in Ōsaka at the time of publication. **FedEx Kinko's Ōsaka Station East Branch** (⊠ 3–1–1 Umeda 2F Float Ct., Kita-ku ☎ 06/6341–7870 ☉ Daily 7–11).

The Ōsaka Central Post Office is on the southwestern side of Ōsaka Station opposite the Hilton Hotel. It has a 24-hr service window. **Ōsaka Central Post Office** (⊠ 2–4 Umeda 3-chōme, Kita-ku ☎ 06/6341–7870 ☉ Daily 7–11).

SIGHTSEEING TOURS

The Aqua Liner runs a 60-minute tour (¥1,600–¥1,880) through Ōsaka's waterways, departing daily from April to September every hour from 10 to 4. There are also evening tours from 6 to 7 on Friday, Saturday, Sunday, and national holidays departing from three piers, at Ōsaka-jō, Tenma-bashi, and Yodoya-bashi. These are the only tours of Ōsaka conducted in both Japanese and English.

Japan Travel Bureau Sunrise Tours runs afternoon tours in English daily to Kyōto (¥8,000) and Nara (¥9,000). Pickup service is available at several hotels.

Japan's Home Visit System, which enables foreign visitors to meet local people in their homes for a few hours to learn about the Japanese lifestyle, is available in Ōsaka. Apply in advance through the Ōsaka Tourist Information Center at either JR Shin-Ōsaka Station or JR Ōsaka Station.

🗊 **Aqua Liner** ☎ 06/6942-5511. **Japan Travel Bureau Sunrise Tours** ☎ 03/5796-5454, 075/341-1413.

TELEPHONES

🗊 **Directory & Operator Assistance** Directory assistance in English is available weekdays 9-5. No service on national holidays or December 29-January 3. **NNT Directory Assistance in English** ☎ 0120/364-463.

Points of Interest

SITES/AREAS	JAPANESE CHARACTERS
America-mura (America Village)	アメリカ村
Den Den Town	でんでんタウン
Dōtombori-dōri	道頓堀通り
Fujii-dera	藤井寺
Hattori Ryokuchi Kōen	服部緑地公園
HEP Five	ヘップファイブ
Japan Folk Art Museum (Nihon Mingei-kan)	日本民芸館
Keitaku-en	慶沢園
Midō-suji	御堂筋
Municipal Museum of Fine Art (Ōsaka Shiritsu Bijutsukan)	大阪市立美術館
Museum of Oriental Ceramics (Ōsaka Shiritsu Tōyō Jiki Bijutsukan)	大阪市立東洋陶磁美術館
National Museum of Ethnology (Kokuritsu Minzokugaku Hakubutsukan)	国立民族学博物館
Nintoku Mausoleum (Nintoku Tenno Ryō Kofu)	仁徳天皇陵古墳
Ōsaka Aquarium (Kaiyūkan)	海遊館
Ōsaka-jō (Ōsaka Castle)	大阪城
Senri Expo Park (Bampaku Kōen)	万博公園
Shitennō-ji (Shitennō Temple)	四天王寺
Sumiyoshi Taisha (Sumiyoshi Grand Shrine)	住吉大社
Tenman-gū	天満宮
Tennō-ji Kōen (Tennō-ji Park)	天王寺公園
Universal Studios Japan	ユニバーサルスタジオジャパン
RESTAURANTS	
Akashiya	明石屋
Café Absinthe	カフェアブサン
Gyuto	牛斗
Isshin	一新
Kani Dōraku	かに道楽
Kankoku Katei Ryōri Minzokumura	韓国家庭料理民俗村
La Baie	ラ・ベ
Lois Café Chinois	ロイスカフェ シノワ

7

Los Inkas	ロスインカス
Mimiu	美々卯
Negiyaki Yamamoto	ねぎ焼 やまもと
Satoyama Cafe	里山カフェ
Ume no Hana	梅の花
HOTELS	
ANA Hotel Ōsaka	大阪全日空ホテル
Ebisu-sō Ryokan	えびす荘旅館
Hearton Hotel Nishi-Umeda	ハートンホテル西梅田
Hilton Ōsaka	ヒルトン大阪
Hotel New Otani Ōsaka	ホテルニューオータニ大阪
Hotel Nikkō Ōsaka	ホテル日航大阪
Hyatt Regency Ōsaka	ハイアットリージェンシー大阪
Kirin Plaza Ōsaka	キリンプラザ大阪
Minzokumura	民俗村
Miyako Hotel Ōsaka	都ホテル大阪
Rihga Royal Hotel Ōsaka	リーガロイヤルホテル大阪
The Ritz-Carlton, Ōsaka	リッツカールトン大阪
Ōsaka Dai Ichi Hotel	大阪第一ホテル
Shin-Ōsaka Washington Hotel Plaza	新大阪ワシントンホテルプラザ
Superhotel Ōsaka Higo-bashi	スーパーホテル大阪肥後橋
Swissôtel Nankai Ōsaka	スイスホテル南海大阪
Tōyoko Inn Shin-sai-bashi Nishi	東横イン心斎橋西

Kōbe

8

By Allison
Burke

KŌBE RESONATES WITH A COOL, HIP VIBE, a condition of its internationalism and its position between mountains and sea. With more than 44,000 *gaijin* (foreigners) living in the city, representing more than 120 countries, Kōbe may be Japan's most diverse city. It has great international cuisine, from Indonesian to French. It also has some of the best Japanese cuisine, specializing in Kōbe beef.

Kōbe's diversity is largely attributable to its harbor. The port was a major center for trade with China dating back to the Nara period (710–784). Kōbe's prominence increased briefly for six months in the 12th century when the capital was moved from Kyōto to Fukuhara, now western Kōbe. When Japan acquiesced to opening five ports, and on January 1, 1868, international ships sailed into Kōbe's harbor. American and European sailors and traders soon settled in Kōbe, and their culture and technology spread throughout the city. Cinema and jazz made their debut in Kōbe and that legacy is ongoing. Many original residences have survived, and the European structures contrast strikingly with the old Japanese buildings and modern high-rises.

Prior to 1995, Kōbe was Japan's busiest port. But on January 17, 1995, an earthquake with a magnitude of 7.2 hit the Kōbe area, killing more than 6,400 people, injuring almost 40,000, and destroying more than 100,000 homes. Communication lines were destroyed, damaged roads prevented escape and relief, and fires raged throughout the city. Since the earthquake, Kōbe has made such a recovery that visitors can hardly imagine such a catastrophe occurred so recently.

The city now pulses with the activity of a modern, industrialized city. The colorful skyline reflects off the night water, adding to Kōbe's reputation as a city for lovers. Don't come to Kōbe looking for traditional Japan; appreciate its urban energy, savor its international cuisine, and take advantage of its shopping.

See the glossary at the end of this book for definitions of the common Japanese words and suffixes used in this chapter.

ORIENTATION & PLANNING

Orientation

Kōbe lies along the Seto Inland Sea in the center of Honshu, a little west of Ōsaka and several hours east of Hiroshima. Smaller than Tōkyō and Ōsaka, Kōbe is more accessible and less formidable. It is large enough, however, to keep you occupied with new attractions and events no matter how frequently you visit.

Divided into approximately 10 distinctive neighborhoods, the city extends from the business-oriented region near the harbor to the lower slopes of Mt. Rokkō. Penned in by natural boundaries, Kōbe expanded its territory with three man-made islands in the harbor.

Downtown

San-no-miya Station, in the city center, marks the heart of Kōbe's entertainment and nightlife. Every night passersby linger to hear musicians

Top Reasons to Visit

THE BEEF

Kōbe beef is world famous for the highly marbleized texture that makes it supremely tender. It's easy to find a good steak house, and you would be sorely missing out by skipping a taste.

THE NIGHT VIEW

The nighttime neon lights reflecting off the quiet ocean opposite the black of the mountains make Kōbe famous as a city for romantic moments. Seen from Harborland, the Ferris wheel and distant Akashi bridge alternate colors, adding to Kōbe's nighttime magic.

LUMINARIE

For two weeks before Christmas, millions of lights arch across Kōbe's streets, forming glittering tunnels. The Japanese tourists are as much of an attraction as the lights; hordes block the streets raising their *keitai* (cell phones) to snap pictures. This event began as a commemoration of the 1995 Hanshin-Awaji Earthquake, and now attracts approximately 5 million visitors each year.

EAST MEETS WEST

When the port opened to international trade in 1868, Western fashion, cuisine, technology, and entertainment began to filter into the country. Jazz, international dining, and a larger than normal proportion of *gaijin* (foreigners) are lasting legacies of Kōbe's history.

NADA NO SAKE

The sake breweries of Nada, a district in western Kōbe, use the high-quality ingredients of *miyamizu* (mineral rich water) and a higher-quality rice called Yamada Nishiki, grown near Mt. Rokkō, especially for sake brewing. A large number of sake museums and breweries are in Nada, many offering free tastings and gift shops.

8

in a small park just north of the station. The quieter region of Kitano-cho is 15 minutes north, and Moto-machi can be reached in 10 minutes on the JR line west. Most of the business district lies south of San-no-miya, near the harbor.

Kintano-chō

Kōbe's original European and American settlers built elegant residences, now known as *ijinkan*, on the city's northern slopes. Many of the preserved ijinkan have been turned into museums. Small boutiques, international cafés, and a few antiques shops seduce visitors to meander along Kitano-zaka and Pearl Street.

North of Kōbe

The impressive Nunobiki Falls are surprisingly accessible from downtown, just behind the Shin-Kōbe station. Rokkō-san (*san* means "mountain") is a little farther out, providing great views and cool mountain air. Arima Onsen is on the other side of Rokkō-san. Arima has winding streets of gift shops and restaurants, and is one of Japan's oldest hot-springs destinations.

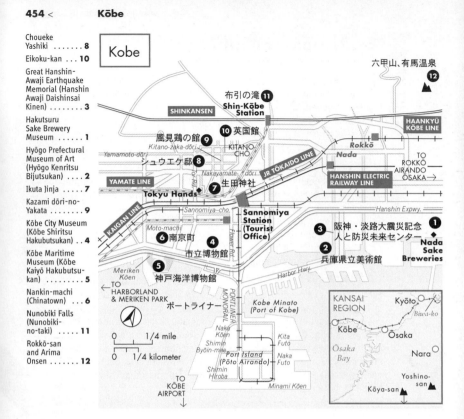

Planning

The big attractions of Kōbe can be covered in a day or two. Hit the Great Hanshin-Awaji Earthquake Museum and the Kōbe City Museum in the morning. Follow this with a stroll around Kitano-cho and a café stop, and wind down the day at Harborland for dinner. On a second day head up Rokkō-san and to the resort town of Arima, where you can soak in mineral hot springs and wander the quaint streets.

The Best of Times

Except for the cold days of winter and the humid days of midsummer, Kōbe enjoys a mild climate tempered by the Seto Nai-kai. Spring, especially at cherry-blossom time, and autumn are the best seasons to visit.

Concerning Restaurants & Hotels

Kōbe is the place to find international cuisine, especially dishes from Southeast Asia. Excellent restaurants are found practically anywhere, but especially north of San-no-miya Station and in the Kitano area.

Kōbe is an industrialized city that caters to business travelers. There are many comfortable, well-situated business hotels. Unless otherwise noted, all hotel rooms have air-conditioning, private bathrooms, and televisions.

WHAT IT COSTS In yen					
	$$$$	$$$	$$	$	¢
RESTAURANTS	over 3,000	2,000–3,000	1,000–2,000	800–1,000	under 800
HOTELS	over 22,000	18,000–22,000	12,000–18,000	8,000–12,000	under 8,000

Restaurant prices are per person for a main course. Hotel price categories are for two people and based on rack rates in high season and the European Plan (with no meals) unless otherwise noted.

Getting Around Town

Three rail lines, JR, Hankyu, and Hanshin, cut straight through the city from one side to the other, and converge at San-no-miya Station. Most of the city is a 10-minute walk from a train station, making trains the most convenient way to get around.

The shinkansen (bullet train) stops at the Shin-Kōbe Station, just North of San-no-miya. The two are connected by the Seishin-Yamate Line that extends north from San-no-miya Station to the Shin-Kōbe station. Shin-Kōbe also connects to Arima. The City Loop bus starts at San-no-miya and circles through Meriken Park, Harborland, and Kitano before returning to San-no-miya. Taxis are easy to find at San-no-miya Station, but can also be found at any *noriba*, or taxi stand.

Visitor Information

Kōbe Tourist Information Center. The TIC offers detailed maps, in English, of all the neighborhoods, with attractions and streets clearly marked. Also pick up a "Kōbe Guide" and a "Visitor's Welcome Book," which has coupons on museums, activities, and hotels. English-speaking staff can help book rooms, find tours, and give recommendations. By the west exit of JR San-no-miya Station, the Kōbe Information Center is open daily 9–7. Another branch is at the JR Shin-Kōbe station, open daily 10–6.

The Japan Travel Bureau can arrange for hotel reservations, train tickets, package tours, and more throughout the country.

🚹 **Japan Travel Bureau** ✉ JR San-no-miya Station ☎ 078/231–4118. **Kōbe Information Center** ✉ JR San-no-miya Station ☎ 078/322–0220 ✉ Shin-Kōbe Station ☎ 078/241–9550. **Kōbe Tourist Information Center** ✉ At west exit of JR San-no-miya Station ☎ 078/271–2401.

EXPLORING KŌBE

Downtown Kōbe

In 1868, after nearly 200 years of isolation, the Kōbe port opened to the West, and Kōbe became an important gateway for cultural exchange. Confined to a small area by its natural boundaries, the city has kept its industrial harbor within the city limits. The harbor's shipping cranes project incongruously against the city's sleek skyscrapers, but the overall landscape manages to blend together beautifully. The harbor is approximately a 15-minute walk southwest of the San-no-miya area.

What to See

❸ Great Hanshin-Awaji Earthquake Memorial (Hanshin Awaji Daishinsai
Kinen). In 1995 the Great Hanshin-Awaji Earthquake killed 6,433 people and destroyed much of the harbor and vast areas of the city. Using
documentary footage and audio, an introductory film shows the fright-
ening destruction wrought upon this modern city. A re-created post-quake
display, film screenings, and high-tech exhibits convey the sorrows and
memories of the event. This excellent museum has English pamphlets
and electronic guides, and English-speaking volunteers are on hand. It's
a 10-minute walk from the south exit of JR Nada Station, one stop east
of JR San-no-miya Station. ⊠ 1–5–2 Wakinohama Kaigan-dōri, Chūō-
ku 🕾 078/262–5050 ⊕ www.dri.ne.jp 🎟 ¥500 ⊙ Daily 9:30–5:30.

❷ Hyōgo Prefectural Museum of Art (Hyōgo Kenritsu Bijutsukan). This
striking concrete edifice was designed by acclaimed architect Tadao
Andō. Andō works primarily with concrete, and is known for his use
of light and water, blending indoors and outdoors and utilizing flowing geometric paths in his designs. He has innumerous works in Japan,
and designed the Museum of Modern Art in Fort Worth, Texas, and the
Pulitzer Foundation for the Arts building in St. Louis. The permanent
exhibition features art from prominent 20th-century Japanese painters
Ryōhei Koiso and Heizō Kanayama, Kōbe natives who specialized in
Western techniques. The museum rotates its vast collection, displaying
fantastic modern works from Japanese artists as well as sculptures by
Henry Moore and Auguste Rodin. It also hosts international exhibitions.
It's a 10-minutes walk from the south exit of JR Nada Station, one stop
east of JR San-no-miya Station. ⊠ 1–1–1 Wakinohama Kaigan-dōri,
Chūō-ku 🕾 078/262–0901 ⊕ www.artm.pref.hyogo.jp 🎟 ¥500 ⊙ Daily
10–6.

❼ Ikuta Jinja. Legend has it that this shrine was founded by Empress Jingū
in the 3rd century, making it one of Japan's oldest. An impressive orange torii, rebuilt after the 1995 earthquake, stands amid the bustle of
modern Kōbe, welcoming tourists and religious observers alike. Every
year two Noh plays, *Ebira* and *Ikuta Atsumori*, at Ikuta's Autumn Festival (Akimatsuri) retell parts of the 12th-century *Genpei* war. It's
around the corner from Tokyu Hands, about 450 yards west of San-
no-miya Station. ⊠ 1–2–1 Shimoyamate-dōri Chūō-ku.

★ ❹ Kōbe City Museum (Kōbe Shiritsu Hakubutsukan). This museum specializes in work from the 16th and 17th centuries, focusing on reciprocal
cultural influences between East and West. The first floor has a variety
of displays on the West's impact on Japan in the second half of the 17th
century. Other exhibits document the influence of Western hairstyles for
women and the arrival of electric and gas lamps. The museum also has
an impressive collection of woodcuts, old maps, archaeological artifacts,
and Namban-style art, namely prints, silkscreens, and paintings from
the late 16th to 17th centuries, usually depicting foreigners in Japanese
settings. The historical exhibits are fascinating, but it is the artwork from
this period that is the real draw.

From San-no-miya Station, walk south on Flower Road to Higashi-
Yuenchi Kōen. Walk through the park to the Kōbe Minato post of-

fice, across the street on the west side. Then head east along the street in front of the post office toward the Oriental Hotel. Turn left at the corner in front of the hotel, and the City Museum is in the old Bank of Tōkyō building at the end of the block. ⊠ *24 Kyō-machi, Chūō-ku* ☎ *078/391–0035* ☞ *¥200; more for special exhibitions* ☉ *Tues.–Sun. 10–5.*

5 **Kōbe Maritime Museum and Kawasaki Good Times World** (Kōbe Kaiyō Hakubutsukan). The Maritime Museum is the stunning building with a billowing roofline of metal-pipe sails. It showcases detailed ship models, opening with a 9-meter model of the HMS *Rodney,* the British flagship that led a 12-ship flotilla into Kōbe Harbor on January 1, 1868. A model of the *Oshoro Maru,* one of Japan's earliest sailing ships, is adorned with pearls, rubies, gold, and silver. **Kawasaki Good Times World** is also inside the museum. High-tech displays and interactive models showcase the Kawasaki company's products and history from Jet Skis to the Shinkansen bullet train. Visitors can ride a helicopter flight simulator and see a robot work at a Rubic's cube. Admission is included in the fee for the Kōbe Maritime Museum. ⊠ *2 Meriken Kōen, Hatoba-chō, Chūō-ku* ☎ *078/391–6751* ☞ *¥600, ¥900 including admission to Port Tower* ☉ *Tues.–Sun. 10–5.*

SAKELICIOUS!

Hakutsuru Sake Brewery Museum Nada, one of Kōbe's westernmost neighborhoods, is famous for its sake. A number of museums and breweries are here—many offering free sake tasting!—but the best is the Hakutsuru Sake Brewery Museum. At the door you are confronted by a sake barrel of immense proportions. Traditional tools and devices, videos in English, and life-size figures of traditionally clad brewers demonstrate the sake-brewing process. The tour ends with free tasting and a gift shop. It's a five-minute walk south from Hanshin Sumiyoshi Station. ⊠ *4-5-5 Sumiyoshiminami-machi, Higashinada-ku* ☎ *078/822-8907* ☞ *Free* ☉ *Tues.-Sun. 9:30-4:30.*

6 **Nankin-machi.** If you're heading to Meriken Park or Harborland, consider a short stop in Kōbe's Chinatown. The area was originally a center for Chinese immigrants to Kōbe, though it is now mostly popular with Japanese tourists for souvenirs and food. It's a lot more Japan-like than one would expect China to be. To find Nankin-machi from Motomachi Station, walk on the port side and enter the neighborhood through the large fake-marble gate.

Harborland & Meriken Park. A trip to Kōbe is incomplete without a waterside visit. Within Meriken Park broken slabs of thick concrete and crooked lightposts are preserved as part of the Port of Kobe Earthquake Memorial Park. Across the grassy park the Kōbe Maritime Museum's roofline of white metal poles, designed like the billowing sails of a tall-ship, contrast beautifully with the crimson Port Tower. The top of the tower provides a 360-degree view of Kōbe. A walkway connects to **Mosaic,** Harborland's outdoor shopping mall. You can eat dinner at any of the restaurants on the waterfront. The nighttime view is stunning, with Port Tower and the Maritime Museum lighted. Nearby, a small Ferris wheel rotates lazily, the colors of its flashing lights bouncing off the sides of nearby ships. Meriken Park and Harborland are a 10-minute walk south of Moto-machi station.

The Islands. Three man-made islands rest in the middle of the harbor. Rokkō Island is home to numerous foreign companies, a number of shopping plazas, and the Sheraton hotel, and is where foreigners now tend to settle. Port Island features conference centers, an amusement park, and the Portopia Hotel. Port Island is linked with downtown by a fully computerized monorail—with no human conductor—that extends south to the Kōbe airport.

Kitano-chō

Wealthy foreigners, including Americans, English, and Germans, settled in the Kitano area in the late 19th century, bringing Western-style domestic architecture. Their homes are referred to in Kōbe as *ijinkan,* and the district is extremely popular with Japanese tourists, who enjoy the rare opportunity to see old-fashioned Western houses. Some residences are still inhabited by Westerners, but more than a dozen 19th-century ijinkan in Kitano-chō are open to the public. A few of them are worth exploring, but seeing them all can be repetitive. The curious mélange of Japanese and Western Victorian and Gothic architecture makes for an good neighborhood walk. The streets are littered with small boutiques, cafés, and a few antiques shops. Try **Nanae** for antiques and the **Bistrot Café de Paris** for a bite of French cuisine.

To get to Kitano-chō, walk 15 minutes north along Kitano-zaka-dōri from San-no-miya Station or 10 minutes west along Kitano-dōri from Shin-Kōbe Station. Yamamoto-dōri (nicknamed Ijinkan-dōri) is Kitano's main east–west street, and the ijinkan are on the small side streets ascending the hill. Tourist information centers offer detailed area maps with all attractions marked in English.

What to See

★ ❽ **Choueke Yashiki** (Choueke ["choo-eh-keh"] Mansion). This ijinkan should be your first priority. Built in 1889, this is the only currently inhabited house open to the public. It's chock-full of Namban woodblock prints, most dating 1861–62, and memorabilia from East and West. Mrs. Choueke is on hand to show you her treasures. ⊠ *Yamamoto-dōri, also known as Ijinkan-dōri, Chūō-ku* ☎ *078/221–3209* ⊠ *¥500* ⊙ *Wed.–Mon. 9–5.*

❿ **Eikoku-kan** ("*eh*-ee-ko *koo*-kan," English House). This typical old-fashioned Western house was constructed in 1907 by an Englishman named Baker, and served as a makeshift hospital during World War II. Now it's a house museum by day and an English pub by night. Antique baroque and Victorian furnishings dominate the interior, there are several downstairs bars and, as if belonging to a decadent member of the royal family, a bottle of champagne in the bathtub. A classic black Jaguar in the driveway and an enormous moose head on the wall complete the English atmosphere. ⊠ *2–3–16 Kitano-dōri, Chūō-ku* ☎ *078/241–2338* ⊠ *¥700* ⊙ *Daily 9–5.*

⑨ Kazamidori-no-Yakata (Weathercock House). More elaborate than any other Kōbe ijinkan, this one, built by a German trader in 1910, stands out strikingly in red brick at the north end of Kitano-chō. It is listed as an Important Cultural Property (Japan is fond of titles that evoke great importance!). The interior reflects various traditional German architectural styles, including that of a medieval castle. Its architecture makes this the most famous ijinkan, however the interiors are spartan, with few additional attractions. ⊠ *3–13–3 Kitano-dōri, Chūo-ku* ☎ *078/242–3223* ✉ *¥300* ◷ *Wed.–Mon. 10–5.*

North of Kōbe

Thanks to Kōbe's mountain backdrop, hiking is a popular local pastime. From Shin-Kōbe Station it's a short climb to the Nunobiki Falls. For a good mountain day hike, try going up Rokkō-san; from Hankyū Kōbe Line Rokkō Station you can take a bus or taxi to Rokkō Cable-Shita cable-car station ("Shita" means down or bottom). From there you can either hike all the way up the mountain or take the cable car partway. You may see wild boar—harmless unless provoked—in the forested mountains.

⑪ Nunobiki Falls (Nunobiki no taki). In the bustle of this modern city, you wouldn't think that one of Japan's most impressive waterfalls is just behind the train station. Nunobiki Falls has four gushing cascades in the forests of Mt. Rokkō. References to their beauty appear in Japanese literature since the 10th century. They are a 20-minute walk from behind the Shin-Kōbe station. After the falls you can pick up the Shin-Kōbe Ropeway, which stops just above the falls before continuing on to the Nunobiki Herb Park. The stopping point provides a beautiful view of the city, especially at night. Follow the signs to the falls from the station or ask directions from the Ropeway staff. ⊠ *Chūo-ku.*

⑫ Rokkō-san and Arima Onsen. Three cable cars scale Mt. Rokkō, providing spectacular views of the city. For convenience, take the Shin-Kōbe Ropeway up to the Nunobiki Herb Park. It departs just east of the Shin-Kōbe station. Time the trip so you'll descend soon after dusk, when the city lights shine against the black sea.

The Rokkō cable also has staggering views of lush forests. On the mountain are various recreational areas, including the oldest golf course in Japan, designed in 1903 by the English merchant Arthur H. Gloom, and the summer houses of Kōbe's wealthier residents.

To get to Rokkō-san, take the Hankyū Kōbe Line from Hankyū

DISAPPEARING DOLLS

If you make it to Arima, the *Arima ningyo fude* (Arima doll brush) makes a nice souvenir. Made for calligraphy, the brushes have handles wrapped in colorful silk thread, and a little doll pops out of the handle when writing. The doll disappears when the brush is laid down. Legend has it that long ago Emperor Kōtoku greatly desired a son. After he visited Arima Springs his wish was granted and a son was born. Made for more than 1,300 years, the dolls symbolize the birth of Prince Arima. The brushes are hand-made locally, and their beautiful designs make them popular gift items.

8

San-no-miya Station to Hankyū Rokkō Station (¥180). From there take a taxi or a bus to Rokkō Cable-shita Station. A funicular railway travels up the mountain to Rokkō-sanjo Station (¥570). You can return to Kōbe by cable car or by rail. Take the Kōbe Dentetsu to Tanigami Station and change for the subway back to San-no-miya (¥900).

The Japanese were already enjoying the thermal waters at **Arima Onsen** before the 7th century. Arima is on the north slope of Rokkō-san and consists of a maze of tiny streets and traditional houses. Some 30 ryokan use the thermal waters' reputed curative powers to attract guests. Although the water gushes up freely from springs, some ryokan charge as much as ¥10,000 for use of their baths. Go instead to the public bath, **Arima Onsen Kaikan,** in the center of the village near the bus terminal. Here ¥520 gets you a soak in the steaming waters. Arima Onsen Kaikan is open daily 8 AM–10 PM (closed the first and third Tuesday of the month). Take the subway north from JR Shin-Kōbe Station, transferring at Tanigami and ending at Arima (¥900).

SHOPPING

Major Shopping Districts

Kōbe's historic shopping area is known as **Moto-machi.** It extends west for 2 km (1 mi) from JR Moto-machi Station. Much of the district is under a covered arcade, which starts opposite the Daimaru department store and runs just north of Nankin-machi. Moto-machi is more of a functional shopping area, selling housewares (including antiques), imported foods, and electronics, with restaurants scattered between.

Nearly connected to the Moto-machi arcade, the **San-no-miya Center Gai** arcade extends from the department store Sogo to the Moto-machi area for 1 km (½ mi). Because it's next to San-no-miya Station, this is a good stop for a bite to eat. Center Gai has a hipper vive than the **Moto-machi** district. Next to Sogo is a branch of the Loft department store, home to crafts and lifestyle accessories spread over four floors. The building also houses a branch of the Kinokuniya bookstore, which has a small English-language selection.

Piazza Kōbe and **Motokō Town** are two names for one long shopping district full of used goods running under the JR train tracks from San-no-miya to Moto-machi.

Specialty Stores

Naniwa-ya sells excellent Japanese lacquerware at reasonable prices, and has been in operation since before World War I. ⊠ *3–8 Moto-machi-dōri 4-chōme, Moto-machi* ☎ *078/341–6367* ⊙ *Thurs.–Tues. 11–6.*

> ### BOUTIQUE ROW
>
> Kōbe's trendy crowd shops in the exclusive stores on **Tor Road,** which stretches north–south on a tree-lined slope into Kitano-chō. Fashionable boutiques selling Japanese designer brands and imported goods alternate with chic cafés and restaurants. The side streets are fun to poke about.

Sakae-ya has traditional Japanese dolls, from Oshie (three-dimensional pictures made of silk) to kimekomi dolls (animals representing the zodiac calendar) to the traditional samurai and kimono-clad ladies. The tiny shop is packed with cloth for doll-making, cupboards for hiding doll-making supplies, and, of course, dolls. ⊠ *8–5 Moto-machi-dōri 5-chōme, Moto-machi* ☏ *078/341–1307* ⊙ *Tues.–Sun. 10–5:30.*

Tasaki Shinju. The main shop of this pearl company not only sells pearls but also exhibits astounding works of "pearl" art, including a model of the "Akashi Pearl Bridge" and a rooster with an impossibly long pearl tail. ⊠ *Tasaki Bldg., 6–3–2 Minatojima, Naka-machi, Port Island* ☏ *078/303–7667* ⊙ *Daily 10–6.*

Nanae is a darling and inexpensive antiques shop in Kitano-chō with a large collection of high-quality used *yukata* (lightweight summer kimonos) that shoppers can try on and a collection of ceramics and other antiques. Nanae, the owner, enjoys explaining the history behind the pieces. ⊠ *2–14–26 Yamamoto-dōri, Chūō-ku* ☏ *078/222–8565* ⊙ *Daily 10–7.*

Santica Town. This underground shopping mall, with 120 shops and 30 restaurants, extends for several blocks beneath Flower Road south from San-no-miya Station. It's closed the third Wednesday of the month. ⊠ *1–10–1 San-no-miya, Chūō-ku, Kōbe-shi, Hyōgo-ken 650-0021* ☏ *078/291–0001* ⊙ *Daily 10–8.*

WHERE TO EAT

$$$$ ✕ **A-1.** A-1 has a relaxed atmosphere and serves thick slices of Kōbe beef. The *teppanyaki* (broiled on a hot plate) steak is cooked in a spice, wine, and soy marinade and served with charcoal-grilled vegetables and crisp garlic potatoes. Their "small" is enough to fill you up, and costs ¥5,400. Four shops are about town, but the main one is conveniently north of Hankyū San-no-miya Station, across from the B-Kōbe hotel. ⊠ *Lighthouse Bldg., ground floor, 2–2–9 Shimoyamate-dōri, Chūō-ku* ☏ *078/331–8676* ☰ *AE, DC, V.*

$$$$ ✕ **Aragawa.** Japan's first steak house is famed for its superb hand-fed Kōbe beef from one farm in the nearby city of Sanda. The melt-in-your-mouth *sumiyaki* (charcoal-broiled) steak is worth its weight in yen—and it's only served with mustard and pepper. (Don't even think about asking for other condiments.)

Fodor's Choice ★

REARED ON BEER

Around the world, **Kōbe beef** is legendary for its extreme succulence and taste. The process of raising the cows would seem like a tall tale, except that it's true. Cows receive daily massages, and in summer they ingest a diet of sake and beer mash. They are descended from an ancient line of *wagyu* (Japanese cows) known to be genetically predisposed to higher marbling. True Kōbe beef comes from only 262 farms in the Tajima region of Hyogo Prefecture (of which Kōbe is the capital), most of which raise an average of five animals. The best beef restaurants are mostly in the central Chūō-ku district, and Kōbe beef is on the menu at the top hotels.

The dining room's dark-wood paneling and lovely chandelier give it a European air. Be prepared to spend ¥20,000 for your main course. ⊠ *2–15–18 Nakayamate-dōri, Chūō-ku* ☎ *078/221–8547* ⌂ *Jacket and tie* ▤ *AE, DC, MC, V* ⊗ *Closed Sun.*

★ **$$$$** ✕ **Ōnishi.** Ōnishi has a well-deserved reputation, both with Japanese locals and longtime foreign residents, for serving fine Kōbe beef. Steaks are cooked by master chefs in the middle of an enournous counter–hot plate around which diners sit. Baseball players and sumō wrestlers are among the celebrity patrons. ⊠ *3F Yūberu Bldg, Higashimon St. 1–4–6 Nakayamate-dōri, Chūō-ku* ☎ *078/332–4029* ▤ *No credit cards* ⊗ *Tues.–Sun. 5 PM–3 AM.*

$$$$ ✕ **Tōtenkaku.** This Chinese restaurant has been famous among Kōbe residents since 1945 for its Peking duck, flown in fresh from China. Built at the turn of the 20th century, Tōtenkaku is in one of Kōbe's *ijinkan*, the F. Bishop House. Tall ceilings, red carpets, luxurious curtains, and artwork from China—the building itself is worth the proverbial cost of admission. You can keep the price down by ordering one of the Chinese noodle specialties to fill you up, or by going at lunchtime, when you can have a set meal for just ¥1,800. ⊠ *3–14–18 Yamamoto-dōri, Chūō-ku* ☎ *078/231–1351* ▤ *AE, DC, MC, V.*

$$$$ ✕ **Wakkoku.** Wakkoku is a swank but affordable restaurant in the shopping plaza underneath the Oriental hotel. The beef is sliced thin and cooked before you on a teppanyaki grill along with fresh vegetables and served with pepper, mustard, and soy sauce for dipping. The food is delicious. Wakkoku uses three-year-old cows that have never been bred, which assures their highest-quality beef of unbelievable tenderness. Lunch sets start at ¥2,700 and go up to ¥5,000. The pricier option uses the highest-quality meat, a small but noticeable difference. ✉ *Kitano-chō 1-chōme, Chūō-ku* ☎ *078/262–2838* ▭ *AE, DC, V.*

$$$–$$$$ ✕ **Bistrot Café de Paris.** This lively café offers delectable French cuisine and features a popular outdoor terrace—a true rarity in Japan at a prime location. The menu ranges from couscous to bouillabaisse. Midway up the hill on Kitano-zaka, it's great for people-watching and is a good stop while cruising the Kitano district. Lunch sets run around ¥2,500, dinners around ¥3,600. ✉ *1–7–21 Yamamoto-dōri, Chūō-ku* ☎ *078/241–9448* ▭ *No credit cards.*

★ **$$–$$$** ✕ **Star Child's Hamburger and Soul Music.** Star Child's combination bar-restaurant is a hidden gem. While serving the best burgers in town, it also has awesome avocado sandwiches and crispy french fries. It's hip and funky, and plays excellent music. More laid-back than other Kōbe hangouts, Star Child's is a good place for a bite to eat and relaxing with a few drinks. ✉ *Across street from Sone on Kitano-zaka 1–22 5 Nakaya mate-dōri, 2F* ☎ *078/252–1101* ☼ *6 PM–3 AM.*

¢–$$$ ✕ **Warung Bali.** The dulcet sounds of the gamelong drift about Warung Bali, a tasty Indonesian restaurant serving Balinese food. The *tempeh goring* and tofu with peanut sauce are simply amazing. Owner and chef Made Widjaja is on hand to do more than inspire Japanese to eat *nasi campur* with their hands; he speaks fluent English and can custom-make dishes, a relief for vegetarians dining in Japan. ✉ *Ōnaga Bldg., 1st fl., 2–4–5 Kitanagata Dōri, Chūō-ku* ☎ *078/321–6080* ▭ *No credit cards.*

★ **$$** ✕ **Raja.** Raja's mellow ambiance is matched by delicious Indian food, reputedly made by the first Indian chef in Kōbe. Among their home-style Indian food of spicy curries and samosas, vegetarians can find something *mecha oishii* (very delicious). Raja attributes the excellence of their tandoori chicken to using the highest grade charcoal available in Japan. Oddly located on the west end of Chinatown, near Moto-machi. ✉ *Sanonatsu Bldg., basement, 2–7–4 Sakae-machi, Chūō-ku* ☎ *078/ 332–5253* ▭ *AE, DC, V.*

$–$$ ✕ **Rough Rare.** This funky, laid-back, two-story café attracts a young, stylish clientele. A DJ booth is upstairs, and the tables are cleared away for dancing on weekends. Pasta, burgers, salads, and *omuraisu* (a Japanese omelet filled with ketchup-flavored rice) are served. The food isn't gourmet, but the restaurant is just plain cool. ✉ *18–2 Akashi-chō, near Daimaru department store, Chūō-ku* ☎ *078/333–0808* ▭ *No credit cards.*

¢–$$ ✕ **Teepee.** The only evidence that this spot situated in the southeast corner of Chinatown is an Italian restaurant is the menu, which includes some of the best pizzas in town, along with pastas, salads, and other Italian dishes. Tall cream walls with large wooden beams and a patio give Teepee a Southwestern look, and with Neil Young on the stereo the atmosphere is definitely casual. ✉ *KCS Bldg., 3rd fl., 1–2–26 Sakae-machi, Chuo-ku* ☎ *078/327–7177* ▭ *No credit cards.*

8

WHERE TO STAY

★ $$$$ 🏨 **Hotel Okura Kōbe.** A 35-story hotel on the wharf in Meriken Kōen, this is one of the city's best. Beautifully furnished, the hotel lives up to the Okura chain's reputation for excellence. Rooms were designed by David Hicks, who has designed interiors for the British royal family. The hotel has a well-equipped health club and stunning views of the bay from the beautiful French Emerald Restaurant on the 35th floor. ⊠ *Meriken Kōen, 2–1 Hatoba-chō, Chūō-ku, Kōbe-shi, Hyōgo-ken 650-8560* ☎ *078/333–0111* 🖷 *078/333–6673* ⊕ *www.Kōbe.hotelokura.co.jp* ✈ *489 rooms & 5 restaurants, coffee shop, room service, minibars, cable TV, in-room data ports, indoor and outdoor pools, gym, 2 bars* ▤ *AE, DC, MC, V.*

$$$$ 🏨 **Portopia Hotel.** A dazzling modern hotel with every facility imaginable. Rooms overlook the port, and the restaurants and lounges on the top floors have panoramic views of Rokkō-san and Ōsaka Bay. Ask for a room in the south wing if you want a balcony and ocean view. The Portopia suffers from being on man-made Port Island and can only be reached by the Portliner monorail or by taxi, but is very convenient to the new Kōbe Airport. Its subpar location is somewhat countered by the fact that everything from food—Chinese, Japanese, and French—to clothing is available inside the hotel. ⊠ *6–10–1 Minatojima Naka-machi, Chūō-ku, Kōbe-shi, Hyōgo-ken 650-0046* ☎ *078/302–0111* 🖷 *078/302–6877* ⊕ *www.portopia.co.jp* ✈ *761 rooms & 8 restaurants, 2 coffee shops, lounge, bar, room service, cable TV, in-room data ports, tennis court, 2 pools (1 indoor), health club, hair salon, sauna, shops* ▤ *AE, DC, MC, V.*

$$$$ 🏨 **Shin-Kōbe Oriental Hotel.** The tallest building in Kōbe, this stunning
Fodor's Choice luxury hotel stands out prominently at night, a brightly lighted needle-
★ thin tower jutting into the sky. The entire hotel is sumptuous, spacious, and chic. Guest rooms have pastel fabrics and are furnished with a desk, a coffee table, and two reading chairs. Corner rooms on higher floors have superb views over Kōbe. Beneath the lobby are five floors of shops and restaurants including Wakkoku. It is a five-minute walk from Kitano-cho, the Shin-Kōbe Ropeway is just outside, and several hiking trails, including one to Nunobiki Falls, pass very close to the hotel. It's directly connected to Shin-Kōbe Station, where the shinkansen arrives, and is three minutes from downtown by subway. ⊠ *Kitano-chō 1-chōme, Chūō-ku, Kōbe-shi, Hyōgo-ken 650-0002* ☎ *078/291–1121* 🖷 *078/291–1154* ⊕ *www.orientalhotel.co.jp* ✈ *600 rooms & 7 restaurants, tea lounge, bar, room service, minibars, cable TV, in-room data ports, indoor pool, gym, hair salon, sauna, shops* ▤ *AE, DC, MC, V.*

$$$–$$$$ 🏨 **Hotel Monterey Kōbe.** With its Mediterranean-style courtyard fountains and European furnishings, the Hotel Monterey takes you off Kōbe's busy streets and into modern Italy. It was modeled after a monastery in Florence. The rooms are beautiful and spacious, with terra-cotta floors and tiled bathrooms. The hotel is in a fantastic location, just east of Ikuta Jinja in the heart of San-no-miya. ⊠ *2–11–13 Shimoyamate-dōri, Chūō-ku, Kōbe-shi, Hyōgo-ken 650-0011* ☎ *078/392–7111* 🖷 *078/322–2899* ✈ *162 rooms & 2 restaurants, in-room data ports* ▤ *AE, DC, MC, V.*

\$\$ 🏨 **San-no-miya Terminal Hotel.** In the terminal building above JR San-no-miya Station, this hotel is extremely convenient, particularly if you need to catch an early train. The rooms are pleasant and large for the price, but the hotel doesn't have much in the way of facilities. Shops and restaurants abound in the station complex, however. ✉ *8 Kumoi-dōri, Chūō-ku, Kōbe-shi, Hyōgo-ken 651-0096* ☎ *078/291–0001* 🖷 *078/291–0020* ⊕ *www.sth-hotel.co.jp* 🛏 *190 rooms* ♿ *Cable TV, Wi-Fi* ▤ *AE, DC, MC, V.*

\$ 🏨 **Shin-Kōbe Sun Hotel.** This old-fashioned business hotel was built in the early boom years after World War II. The rooms are a little tired, but the hotel has a nice, large, Japanese-style public bath, the staff is very friendly, and the building is quiet. Served 7–9, breakfast (Japanese or Western) is included in the bill. The hotel is a 10-minute walk from the San-no-miya station, halfway up the hill toward the JR Shin-Kōbe station. ✉ *2–1–9 Nunobiki-chō, Chūō-ku, Kōbe-shi, Hyōgo-ken 651-0097* ☎ *078/272–1080* 🖷 *078/272–1088* 🛏 *125 rooms* ♿ *Restaurant, refrigerators, Wi-Fi, TV, Japanese bath, no-smoking rooms* ▤ *AE, DC, V* ⭘ *CP.*

¢ 🏨 **Superhotel Kōbe.** This business hotel features rooms built according to a formula, with just two set prices for singles and doubles. The bathrooms are tiny, and don't expect stunning interior design. But you get a functional space with a comfortable bed in central Kōbe, halfway between the city's two main train stations, San-no-miya and Shin-Kōbe. ✉ *2–1–11 Kanō-chō, Chūō-ku, Kōbe-shi, Hyōgo-ken 650-0001* ☎ *078/261–9000* 🖷 *078/261–9090* 🛏 *80 rooms* ♿ *TV, in-room data ports; no room phones* ▤ *MC, V.*

NIGHTLIFE

Kōbe's compactness is an advantage—virtually all the best bars are within walking distance of each other. Kōbe is regarded as the center of Japan's thriving jazz scene.

Booze Up Bar. Entering Booze Up feels like stepping onto the retro set of a Quentin Tarantino movie. Soul and funk LPs are artfully blended one to the other on dual turntables. Tasty pizzas and pastas are served up alongside good cocktails. Can ya dig it? Just northwest of Tokyu Hands. ✉ *2–15–3 Shimoyamate-dōri* ☎ *078/322-2873.*

Polo Dog. Polo Dog is regularly packed with foreigners, both longtime residents and travelers passing through, and usually has live music on weekends, when it gets loud. The bar serves burgers, salads, and excellent garlic french fries. It's arrayed with '50s and '60s Americana and known for having the cheapest drinks in town. ✉ *One street south of Center Gai, near Flower Road. K Bldg., 2nd fl., 1–3–21 San-no-miya-chō* ☎ *078/331–3944.*

Ryan's. Guinness and Kilkeney are on tap, and Irish stew and fish-and-chips are on the menu at Ryan's Irish pub, the only Irish-owned and -operated bar in Japan. One of the most popular Western-style watering holes in Kōbe, Ryan's attracts a young crowd and has live music Friday and Saturday. ✉ *Rondo Bldg., 7th fl., north side of San-no-miya Station* ☎ *078/391–6902.*

Sone. The city's most famous jazz club, in existence since 1961, Sone is run by the Sone family. Four sets of live music are played every night, starting at 6:50, and the action often centers around a piano trio with rotating guest vocalists. The musicians are a mix of Japanese and visiting foreigners. Spacious and relaxed, Sone serves pizza, pasta, and salads. There's a cover charge of ¥900 ☒ *1–24–10 Nakayamate-dōri* ☎ *078/221–2055.*

KŌBE ESSENTIALS

To research prices, get advice from other travelers, and book travel arrangements, visit www.fodors.com.

Transportation

BY AIR

Kansai International Airport (KIX) is south of Ōsaka, and approximately 40 minutes from Kōbe. It handles the region's international flights and some domestic flights to and from Japan's larger cities. The Kōbe Airport, handling mainly domestic flights, is 18 minutes from JR San-no-miya Station via the Portliner.

AIRPORT TRANSFERS   Excellent public transport from the airports makes using taxis impractical. From Ōsaka International Airport, take the JR Kansai Airport Express Haruka to Shin-Ōsaka and change to the JR Tōkaidō Line for Kōbe's JR San-no-miya Station, a 75-minute (¥3,520) trip. For a quicker trip, ignore the train and take the comfortable limousine bus (70 minutes; ¥1,800), which drops you off in front of San-no-miya Station.

From Ōsaka Itami Airport, buses to San-no-miya Station leave from a stand between the airport's two terminals approximately every 20 minutes 7:45 AM–9:10 PM. The trip takes about 40 minutes (¥1,020).

BY PORTLINER

The **Portliner** was the first digitally driven monorail in the world, and departs from San-no-miya Station every six minutes from 6:05 AM until 11:40 PM on its loop to and around Port Island. The ride affords a close-up view of Kōbe Harbor and extends south to the Kōbe Airport. A trip from San-no-miya to the airport takes 18 minutes and costs ¥320 one-way. ☒ *¥480 round-trip to Port Island.*

BY SUBWAY

Kōbe's main subway line runs from Tanigami in the far north of the city, and passes through Shin-Kōbe and San-no-miya stations before continuing west to the outskirts of town. Another line runs along the coast from San-no-miya and links up with the main line at Shin-Nagata Station. Fares start at ¥180 and are determined by destination. The San-no-miya–Shin-Kōbe trip costs ¥200.

BY TRAIN

The Hikari Shinkansen runs between Tōkyō and Shin-Kōbe Station in about 3½ hours. If you don't have a JR Pass, the fare is ¥14,470.

The trip between Ōsaka Station and Kōbe's San-no-miya Station takes 20 minutes on the JR Tōkaidō Line rapid train, which leaves at 15-minute intervals throughout the day; without a JR Pass the fare is ¥390. The Hankyū and Hanshin private lines run between Ōsaka and Kōbe for ¥310.

Within Kōbe, Japan Rail and the Hankyū and Hanshin lines run parallel from east to west and are easy to negotiate. San-no-miya and Moto-machi are the principal downtown stations. Purchase tickets from a vending machine; you surrender them upon passing through the turnstile at your destination station. Fares depend on your destination.

Contacts & Resources

BANKS & EXCHANGE SERVICES
There are two currency exchange stations just outside of the west and center exits of JR San-no-miya Station, open 11–7 (☎ 078/291–0070). Look for big signs reading CURRENCY EXCHANGE. Most major banks and some post offices have exchange services, usually displaying the sign AUTHORIZED MONEY EXCHANGE. Counter service runs 9–3 PM, but often exchange services don't open until 10 AM, when the exchange rate is set. Major bank offices are scattered throughout the city, the major names being Sumitomo Mitsui Bank (☎ 078/291–0070) and Mitsubishi Bank (☎ 078/391–8141).

EMERGENCIES
Daimaru Depāto has a pharmacy that's a three-minute walk from JR Moto-machi Station.

🚩 **Emergency Services Ambulance** ☎ 119. **Police** ☎ 110.

🚩 **Hospitals Kōbe Adventist Hospital** ✉ 4–1 Arinodai 8-chōme, Kita-ku ☎ 078/981–0161. **Kōbe Kaisei Hospital** ✉ 3–11–15 Shinohara-Kita-machi, Nada-ku ☎ 078/871–5201.

🚩 **Pharmacy Daimaru Depāto** ✉ 40 Akashi-chō, Chūō-ku ☎ 078/331–8121.

ENGLISH-LANGUAGE MEDIA
Kansai Time Out (www.kto.co.jp) is a monthly publication listing events in Kōbe, Kyōto, Nara, and Ōsaka. It costs ¥300 and is available at major hotels and bookshops throughout the region.

Kinokuniya stocks a small selection of new English-language novels as well as guidebooks, books on Japan, and Japanese study guides. For a wider selection of English reading material, head to Wantage Books, the only secondhand English-language bookshop in the Kansai region.

🚩 **Bookstores Kinokuniya** ✉ 8–1–8 Onoe-dōri ☎ 078/265–1607. **Wantage Books** ✉ 1–1–13 Ikuta-chō ☎ 078/232–4517.

INTERNET, MAIL & SHIPPING
A bunch of Internet cafés are just north of San-no-miya Station. Most are combination *manga* (comic-book) cafés. Media Café Popeye is halfway between the San-no-miya and Moto-machi stations, just north of the railway tracks. South of Moto-machi Station, look for Comic Busters in the Otom Garden building. **Media Café Popeye** (✉ 2–1–6 Kitanagasa-dōri, Chūō-ku ☎ 098/325–8677).

8

Comic Busters (✉ 1–11–17 3F Moto-machi-dōri, Chūō-ku ☎ 078/391–1333).

Most post-office branches are open 9–5 weekdays. The main post office is open 9–9 daily. **Kōbe Central Post Office, International Mail Section** (✉ 6–2–1 Sakaemachi-dōri, Chūō-ku ☎ 078/360–9600). A FedEx Kinko's on the first floor in the JR San-no-miya station (daily 7 AM–10 PM, 078/291–4311) also handles international mail.

TOURS

The City Transport Bureau has several half-day and full-day tours of major attractions around the city. The tours are conducted in Japanese. Buses depart from the south side of the Kōbe Kotsu Center Building, near San-no-miya Station. Information and tickets, which start at ¥2,700, are obtained at the Shi-nai Teiki Kankō Annaisho (Sightseeing Bus Tour Information Office), on the second floor of the Kōbe Kotsu Center Building. The buses leave from the San-no-miya Bus Terminal, to the east of JR San-no-miya Station.

Authorized taxi services run tours (¥4,200 per hour) that cover 11 different routes and take from two to five hours. Reserve at the Kōbe Tourist Information Center (also known as "Hello Kōbe"), near the west exit of JR San-no-miya Station. Several voluntary guide services are available, such as Kōbe Systemized Goodwill Guides Club (SGG) and Kōbe Student Guide. Guides are free, but please pay for all travel expenses, meal expenses, and building admissions. It's best to reserve a few days in advance. Kōbe Student Guide, ⊕ www.geocities.co.jp/Berkeley/3136/ ✎ ksg-ml@ml-b8.infoseek.co.jp

▰ Shi-nai Teiki Kankō Annaisho ☎ 078/231–4898. **Systemized Goodwill Guides Club (SGG)** ☎ 078/785–2898.

Points of Interest

SITES/AREAS	JAPANESE CHARACTERS
Choueke Yashiki (Choueke ["shoo-eh-keh"] Mansion)	シュウエケ邸
Eikoku-kan (British Mansion)	英国館
Great Hanshin-Awaji Earthquake Memorial (Hanshin Awaji Daishinsai Kinen)	阪神・淡路大震災記念 人と防災未来センター
Hakutsuru Sake Brewery Museum	白鶴酒造資料館
Harborland & Meriken Park	ハーバーランドとメリケン・パーク
Hyōgo Prefectural Museum of Art (Hyōgo Kenritsu Bijutsukan)	兵庫県立美術館
Ikuta Jinja	生田神社
Kazamidori-no-Yakata (Weathercock House)	風見鶏の館
Kitano-chō	北野町
Kōbe City Museum (Kōbe Shiritsu Hakubutsukan)	神戸市立博物館
Kōbe Maritime Museum and Kawasaki Good Times World (Kōbe Kaiyō Hakubutsukan)	神戸海洋博物館
Nankin-machi	南京町
Nunobiki Falls (Nunobiki-no-taki)	布引の滝
Rokkō-san and Arima Onsen	六甲山と有馬温泉

RESTAURANTS	
Aragawa	あら皮
Bistrot Café de Paris	ビストロカフェドパリ
Ōnishi	大西
Raja	ラジャ
Rough Rare	ラフレア
Star Child's Hamburger and Soul Music	スターチャイルド
Teepee	ティピ
Tōtenkaku	東天閣
Wakkoku	和黒
Warung Bali	ワルン・バリ

HOTELS	
Hotel Monterey Kōbe	ホテルモントレー神戸
Hotel Okura Kōbe	ホテルオークラ神戸
Portopia Hotel	ポートピアホテル
San-no-miya Terminal Hotel	三宮ターミナルホテル
Shin-Kōbe Oriental Hotel	新神戸オリエンタルホテル
Shin-Kōbe Sun Hotel	新神戸サンホテル
Superhotel Kōbe	スーパーホテル神戸

8

Western Honshū

By John Malloy
Quinn

LIKE DISPARATE SIBLINGS BORN OF A SET OF COMMON GENES, the two coasts of Western Honshū have distinctly different personalities. Taken together, however, they embody the ancient and modern—those two seemingly bipolar time frames that exist in a more profound juxtaposition in Japan than perhaps in any other other country in the world. While the southern coast, or San-yō, has basically gone along with Japan's full-steam-ahead efforts to set the pace for the entire modern world, the San-in coast, on the north side of the rugged Chūgoku San-chi or Central Mountains, has been largely left off the "Things to Exploit" list, thanks to its remoteness. Adding to the intrigue, touches of convenient modernity have made inroads in the fairly large and pleasantly humming San-in city of Matsue, yet you'll still encounter deep pockets of dramatic Old World charm along the largely developed San-yō.

Neither coast is short of history, religious significance, beauty, or culinary delights. Hiroshima survived one of history's most terrible events to become a disarmingly forward-looking city. Hagi is a scenic bayside town that for 500 years has been the center of Hagi-yakii ceramics, a light-colored and smooth-textured earthenware glazed with mysteriously translucent and crackled milky colors. Matsue attracted and enchanted the famous Greek-Irish writer Lafcadio Hearn, who did much in the 1890s to open Western eyes to the exotic realm he found in Japan—a realm that, foreign and inscrutable as it was, accepted him as well.

See the glossary at the end of this book for definitions of the common Japanese words and suffixes used in this chapter.

ORIENTATION & PLANNING

Orientation

9

Western Honshū is bisected east to west by a chain of rugged mountains called the Chūgoku San-chi. Although they are attractive in all seasons, they still make going north–south a difficult proposition. Travel along the north coast, or San-in, is incredibly slow, so if you are pressed for time, to get to Hagi or Tsuwano, Yamaguchi is a good base; for Matsue, Kurashiki and Okayama work best.

San-yō

San-yo comprises the southern coastline of Western Honshū, and the major cities are Okayama and Hiroshima. If you go to Hiroshima expecting to see a city dressed in a state of perpetual mourning, you will be surprised. While you can verify what abysmal misery man has wrought, you can also see that it was certainly not the end for this amazing city. The entire stretch is heavily populated, industrialized, and congested. However, bright spots are Kurashiki, near Okayama, and Miyajima, near Hiroshima.

San-in

San-in may come closest to providing the best of what Japan has to offer. Hagi and Tsuwano can make you giddy that you found them—and also make you never want to leave—and Matsue, though larger than it used

Top Reasons to Visit

PHOTOGENIC ICONS
In a tidal basin beside the tiny island of Miyajima, the vermilion Ō-torii, or big gate, rises from the Inland Sea. One of Japan's most recognizable sights, it declares the entire island sacred and blessed by the sea gods. An hour from Matsue is the austere shrine of Izumo Taisha. Built 1,500 years ago, this Shintō shrine reputedly ensures marital happiness.

FABULOUS SEAFOOD
Great seafood abounds, from the famous oysters of Hiroshima (*kaki-gai* in Japanese) and anago or conger eel of Miyajima, to the succulent *uni-don*, or sea urchin on a bed of rice, popular in Hagi, and the *mamakari*, a sardine-like fish found in Kurashiki and Okayama. In Matsue are freshwater fish and little black shijimi clams from Lake Shinji.

LESSONS OF THE PAST
The charred Atomic-Bomb Dome of Hiroshima delivers a powerful visual sermon. Although its monuments to human disaster are held in great reverence and respect, the city has determined to embrace the future in a very big way. Here you will find an energy and multinational vibe that rivals that of Tōkyō and Ōsaka.

GARDENS
In the lively capital city of Okayama—sunniest of all Japan's prefectures—is one of Japan's top three gardens, the spacious and dazzling Kōrakuen, which surrounds the stunning black U-jō, or "Crow Castle."

THEY'RE GOOD PEOPLE
The people here are among the friendliest and most unhurried in Japan. You may get stared at for being a foreigner, but locals who spot you looking at a map will whip out their cell phones to call their friends and parents to make sure they're giving you good advice.

to be, can still change your life, as it did for Lafcadio Hearn, the Greek-Irish writer who came here 116 years ago and made a living by telling the rest of the world what a great place it was.

Planning

Travel along San-yō is easy, and the weather is usually mild. If you seek adventure up along San-in, you'll need time for slow trains, layovers, incomplete or changeable information, and the like. It is possible to get from Yamaguchi up to Matsue in a day, but you'll have more fun if you take a couple of days or more. Slow down and enjoy the mellow pace in the realms of Hagi and Tsuwano. Sure, these towns are a genuine pain to get to—but they also hold treasures that you won't find anywhere else, precisely because they are so hard to get to.

The Best of Times
The San-yō is the sunniest region in Japan, and almost anytime is a good time to visit. The northern shore, or San-in, gets a stronger dose of winter than the southern one, but it has a wonderfully long spring. Like most of Japan, Western Honshū gets dreadfully muggy by midsummer, but

Western Honshū

NIHON-KAI (Sea of Japan)

Oki Archipelago

Kyōto

Maizuru

Miyazu-wan (Miyazu Bay)

Ama-no-hashidate

Fukuchiyama

Kasumi

Kinosaki

Kōbe

Nishi-Akashi

Himeji

Ōsaka

Ōsaka-wan (Ōsaka Bay)

Kansai Int'l Airport

Wakayama

Awaji-shima

Tottori

Chizu

Misasa Onsen

三朝温泉

Kurayoshi

Daisen-zan

Daisen

Yonago

Bizen

Okayama

岡山

18

Kurashiki

倉敷

19

Shodo-shima

Seto Ōhashi

Takamatsu

Kino-kawa

Tokushima

SHIKOKU

Matsuyama

Kotohira

Ikeda

Yoshino-gawa

Tsuyama

Ni'imi

Sōja

Asahi River

Fukuyama

SETO-NAI-KAI (Inland Sea)

Tadotsu

松江 Matsue **17**

Yasugi

Bingo-Ochiai

Miyoshi

Izumo

16 Izumo Taisha

出雲大社

Ōtc

Shikijiki

Hiroshima

広島

1 - 11

see detail map

宮島 Miyajima **12**

JR SAN-IN MAIN LINE

Gōtsu

Hamada

Masuda

Susa

Hagi 萩 **14**

Nagato

Hōhoku

Toyota

Tsuwano

津和野 **15**

山口 Yamaguchi **13**

Shin-Yamaguchi

Ogōri

Shimonoseki

Okura

40 miles

40 kilometers

Western Honshū

the wind off the Nihon-kai cools the San-in coast. Summer festivals and autumn colors are spectacular throughout the region, and attract many tourists, so reserve well ahead if you are traveling then.

Concerning Restaurants & Hotels

Western Honshū is one of the best regions to sample local Japanese seafood, with regional specialties from the Nihon-kai (Japan Sea) and Seto Nai-kai (Inland Sea). Oysters in Hiroshima, sea eel on Miyajima, and sashimi and sushi on the San-in coast are superb. Matsue's location makes a variety of both freshwater and saltwater fish available. Most reasonably priced restaurants have a visual display of the menu in the window, if not on the menu pages. If you cannot order in Japanese and no English is spoken, after you secure a table lead the waiter to the window display and point. If you're adventurous, it is always fun to ask, "Osusumu?" which means, "What do you recommend?"

Accommodations cover a broad spectrum, from pensions and *minshuku* (private residences that rent rooms) to large, modern resort hotels that have little character but all the facilities of an international hotel. Large city and resort hotels have Western and Japanese restaurants. In summer or on holiday weekends hotel reservations are necessary.

Unless otherwise noted, rooms have private baths, air-conditioning, and basic TV service. For a short course on accommodations in Japan, *see* Lodging *in* Essentials.

WHAT IT COSTS In yen				
$$$$	**$$$**	**$$**	**$**	**¢**
RESTAURANTS over 3,000	2,000–3,000	1,000–2,000	800–1,000	under 800
HOTELS over 22,000	18,000–22,000	12,000–18,000	8,000–12,000	under 8,000

Restaurant prices are per person for a main course at dinner. Hotel prices are for a double room with private bath, excluding service and tax.

Transportation Station

BUS TRAVEL In the major cities local buses or streetcars are a good way to get around. You won't likely need highway buses, except for making the one-hour run between Yamaguchi and Hagi (knocking three hours off the train-travel time). Two companies operate bus routes: JR and Bōchō bus lines; Japan Rail Passes are only valid for use on the JR buses. During peak travel times, call ahead and reserve seats for these buses. Local tourist information offices will help reserve tickets for non-Japanese speakers.

CAR TRAVEL All the major cities and most of the towns listed here will have at least a basic choice of car-rental outlets. If you know a little Japanese, can handle both middle-of-nowhere navigation and hectic urban traffic situations, you might consider renting a car and exploring Western Honshū at your own pace—but you'll also need a good Japanese map atlas.

TRAIN TRAVEL Traveling in San-yō means hopping on and off JR's Shinkansen and local trains on the Tōkaido railway line that follows the southern shore of

Western Honshū from Tōkyō to Shimonoseki. The Nozomi SuperExpress cuts significant time off the longest hauls, but the JR Rail Pass is not accepted on it. The Hikari is plenty fast enough, and it can get you from Tōkyō to Hiroshima in four hours. Less than an hour farther on the Kodama Shinkansen puts you in Shin-Yamaguchi, from where you can visit Hagi (a bus is highly recommended for this) and take trains up to Tsuwano or Matsue. From there, a train can get you down to Kurashiki and Okayama for a grand loop of the whole region. It is always advisable to reserve seats on the popular routes between big cities and to holiday destinations during peak season. Most stations now have tourist offices with English-speakers that can help with this.

Visitor Information

Most major towns and nowadays even the small ones have tourist information centers that offer free maps and brochures. They can also help you secure accommodations. Except for the internationally known places, though, you should not assume that extensive English is spoken.

THE SAN-YŌ REGION

San-yo means "sunny side of the range," and the southern region along the Inland Sea is celebrated for its mild and clear climate. Although it's highly developed and you can't see or appreciate much of its beauty from the train or the highway, it's wonderfully easy to hop off and get a closer look at it. Major sights of scenic and historic note heading westward are Okayama, Kurashiki, Hiroshima, and Miayajima. Shin-Yamaguchi is a great place to jump off the Shinkansen if you are heading to the well-hidden towns of Hagi and Tsuwano, and with a nice mineral bath at Yuda Onsen only a short taxi or train ride or long walk away, nearby Yamaguchi City makes a perfect place to base and/or branch out from.

Hiroshima

1 hr 21 min west of Ōsaka, 4 hrs from Tōkyō by shinkansen, ¥18,065

On August 6, 1945, at 8:15 AM, a massive chunk of a heavy and unstable metal was made to hold more atoms than it was physically able to, and with the energy left over, the fabric of space itself ignited and glowed—for only an instant. For that brief moment, however, it became as hot as the surface of the sun in Hiroshima, until then a rather ordinary workaday city in wartime Japan. Half the city was leveled by the resulting blast, and the rest was set ablaze. Rain impregnated with radioactive fallout then fell, killing many that the fire and 1,000-mph shock wave had not. By the end of this mind-boggling disaster, more than 140,000 people died.

In modern Hiroshima's Peace Memorial Park, the monuments to that day abound, but only one original site bears witness to that enormous release of atomic energy 60 years ago: the A-Bomb Dome. Its gloomy shadows are now surrounded by a vibrant, entirely rebuilt city. As if to show just how earnestly Hiroshima has redefined itself, only a short walk to the east lies Nagarekawa-chō, the city's raucous nightlife district.

Getting Around

The streetcar (tram) is an easy form of transport in Hiroshima. Enter the middle door and take a ticket from the automatic dispenser. Pay the driver at the front door when you leave. All fares within city limits are ¥150. A one-day pass is ¥600, available for purchase at the platform outside JR Hiroshima Station. There are seven streetcar lines; four either depart from the JR station or make it their terminus. Stops are announced by a recording, and each stop has a sign in *rōmaji* posted on the platform. Buses also joust among the traffic of Hiroshima's hectic streets; the basic fare is ¥180. Information in English can be gathered at any of the Hiroshima Tourist Info Centers.

Taxis can be hailed throughout the city. The fare for the first 1½ km (1 mi) is ¥570 for small taxis, ¥620 for larger ones, then ¥70 for every 300 meters (335 yards).

Two excellent, English-speaking **Tourist Information Offices** are in JR Hiroshima Station: the south exit office is the main one, 082/261–1877, the other is at the Shinkansen (north) exit, ☎ 082/263–6822. ☉ Both are open daily 9–5:30. The main tourist office, **Hiroshima City Tourist Association** (☎ 082/247–6738 ☉ Apr.–Sept., daily 9:30–6; Oct.–Mar., daily 8:30–5) is in the Peace Memorial Park, next to the Motoyasu fork of the river, between the Children's Peace Memorial and the Flame of Peace. Also in the park, in the southwest corner between the Ōta River and the Peace Memorial Museum, is the **International Conference Center Hiroshima** (☎ 082/242–7777 ☉ May–Nov., daily 9–7; Dec.–Apr., daily 10–6), which offers ample useful English information.

What to See

The **Peace Memorial Park** (Heiwa Kinen Kōen) contains the key World War II sites in Hiroshima. It's situated in the northern point of the triangle formed by two of Hiroshima's rivers, the Ōta-gawa (also called Hon-kawa) and Motoyasu-gawa. From Hiroshima Station it's a 20-minute walk southwest, or take Streetcar 2 or 6 to the Gembaku-Dōmu-mae stop and cross over Motoyasu-gawa on the Aioi-bashi. The park entrance is in the middle of the bridge, and from there to Peace Memorial Museum are statues and monuments. Head straight for the museum (a 10-minute walk from the bridge); you can linger at the monuments on your way back. A less dramatic approach from Hiroshima Station is to take the Hiroshima Bus Company's red-and-white Bus 24 to Heiwa Kōen, only a two-minute walk to the museum, or to take Streetcar 1 to Chūden-mae for a five-minute walk to the museum.

Fodor'sChoice
★ ❶

The **A-Bomb Dome** (Gembaku Dōmu) is a poignant symbol of man's self-destructiveness. It was the city's old Industrial Promotion Hall, and it stands in stark contrast to the new Hiroshima, which hums along close by. Despite being directly below the bomb blast, the building did not collapse into rubble like the rest of the city. Eerie, twisted, and charred, the sturdy domed structure of iron and concrete has stood darkly brooding next to the river, basically untouched since that horrible morning. A visit to A-Bomb Dome is a sobering reminder of nuclear destruction, and at

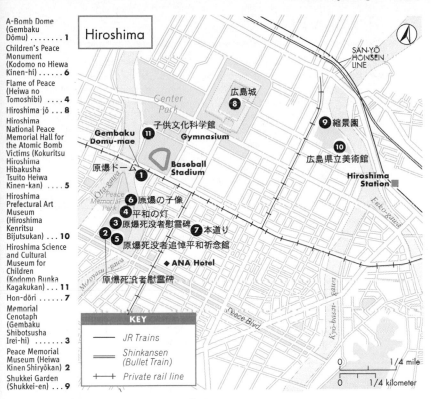

dusk the sad old building's foreboding, derelict appearance can be emotionally overwhelming. The site is just outside the official northeast boundary of Peace Memorial Park. Take Streetcar 2 or 6 from Hiroshima Station to the Gembaku-Dōmu-mae stop. ⊠ *Heiwa Kinen Kōen.*

❷ A visit to the **Peace Memorial Museum** (Heiwa Kinen Shiryōkan) may be too intense an experience for some. Through displays of models, charred fragments of clothing, melted ceramic tiles, lunch boxes, and watches— and hideously surreal photographs—Hiroshima's story of death and destruction is told. The heat-ray-photographed human shadow permanently imprinted on granite steps can take you well beyond sadness, and the Dalí-esque watch forever stopped at 8:15 is chilling. Most exhibits have brief explanations in English, and more detailed information is on audiocassettes, which you can rent for ¥150. ⊠ *Heiwa Kinen Koen* 🖀 *082/241–4004* 🖾 *¥50* 🕑 *Apr.–July, daily 9–5:30; Aug. 1–15, daily 8:30–6:30; Aug. 16–Nov., daily 8:30–5:30; Dec.–Mar., daily 9–4:30.*

❸ The **Memorial Cenotaph** (Gembaku Shibotsusha Irei-hi), designed by Japanese architect Kenzo Tange, resembles the primitive A-frame houses of Japan's earliest inhabitants. Buried inside is a chest containing the names of those who died in the destruction and aftermath of the atomic bomb. On the exterior is the inscription (translated), REST IN PEACE, FOR

1,000 Paper Cranes

PAUSE BEFORE the **Children's Peace Monument** (Genbaku-no-ko Zō) before leaving the park. Many consider this the most profound memorial in Peace Memorial Park. The figure is of a Sadako, a young girl who at age 10 developed leukemia as a result of exposure to the atomic radiation that lingered long after the blast. She believed that if she could fold 1,000 paper *senbazuru* (cranes)—a Japanese symbol of good fortune and longevity—her illness would be cured. She died before finishing the thousand, and it is said that her schoolmates finished the job for her. Her story has become a folktale of sorts, and it inspired a nationwide paper crane-folding effort among schoolchildren that continues to this day. The colorful chains of paper cranes—delivered daily from schools all over the world—are visually and emotionally striking. ✉ *Heiwa Kinen Kōen.*

THE ERROR SHALL NOT BE REPEATED. The cenotaph stands before the north side of the Heiwa Kinen Shiryōkan. ✉ *Heiwa Kinen Kōen.*

❹ The **Flame of Peace** (Heiwa no Tomoshibi) burns behind the Memorial Cenotaph. The flame will be extinguished only when all atomic weapons are banished. In the meantime, every August 6, the citizens of Hiroshima float paper lanterns down the city's rivers for the repose of the souls of the atomic-bomb victims. ✉ *Heiwa Kinen Kōen.*

❺ The **Hiroshima National Peace Memorial Hall for the Atomic Bomb Victims** (Kokuritsu Hiroshima Hibakusha Tsuitō Heiwa Kinen-kan) recounts the stories of known victims of the atomic devastation. In addition to the extensive archives of names, a collection of victims' photos lends immediacy to one of the most shocking moments in history. Heartbreaking first-hand accounts and memoirs of survivors are available for viewing. ✉ *1–6 Nakajima-chō, Heiwa Kinen Kōen, Hiroshima, 730-0811 ☎ 082/543–6271 🖷 082/543–6273 🖾 Free ☉ Apr.–July, daily 9–6; Aug. 1–15, daily 8:30–7; Aug. 16–Nov., daily 8:30–6; Dec.–Mar., daily 9–5.*

❼ Around **Hon-dōri**, Hiroshima's central district, are hundreds of shopkeepers. Take the tram that runs from the main station to stop T-31 (Hondōri), or simply walk east across the north bridge out of Peace Park. The big department stores are at the east end of the arcade, near the Hatchobori streetcar stop: Sogō (closed Tuesday) is open 10–8; Fukuya (closed Wednesday) and Tenmaya (closed Thursday) are open from 10 to 7:30; and Mitsukoshi (closed Monday) is open 10–7. Many restaurants, including a big, gorgeous bakery of the popular Andersen's chain (one block down on the right from T-31), and a range of modern hotels are also found here.

❽ **Hiroshima-jō** was originally built by Terumoto Mōri on the Ōta-gawa delta in 1589. He named the surrounding flatlands *Hiro-Shima,* meaning wide island, and it stuck. The Imperial Japanese Army used the castle as headquarters in World War II, and with its significant depot of munitions it was one of the targets of the bomb. It was destroyed in the blast. In 1958 the five-story donjon was rebuilt to its original specifications. It's unlike many castles in Japan, with lots of brown wood paneling, and it stands in intriguing contrast to the modern city that has been created around it. Inside are exhibits from Japan's feudal Edo Period (17th–19th centuries). It's a 15-minute walk north from the A-Bomb Dome. ⊠ *21–1 Moto-machi, Naka-ku* ☎ *082/221–7512* 🖂 *Castle and museum ¥360* ⊗ *Apr.–Sept., daily 9–5:30; Oct.–Mar., daily 9–4:30.*

❾ The garden laid out in 1630 by Lord Naga-akira Asano, **Shukkei-en** (literally, shrunken scenery garden), resembles one once found around a lake in Hangzhou, China, which the *daimyō* wanted to re-create for leisurely strolls. The water is dotted with tiny rocky islets sprouting gnarled pine trees. Small bridges cross above lots of colorful carp, a fish venerated for its long and vigorous life. Shukkei-en is east of Hiroshima-jō castle on the banks of the Kyō-bashi-gawa. Return to the JR station on Streetcar 9; at the end of the line transfer to Streetcar 1, 2, or 6. If you purchase a combined ticket (¥600) for the garden and the Prefectural Art Museum, you must visit the museum first and enter the garden from the museum. ⊠ *2–11 Kamiya-chō, Naka-ku, 730-0014* ☎ *082/221–3620* 🖂 *¥250* ⊗ *Apr.–Sept., daily 9–6; Oct.–Mar., daily 9–5.*

❿ **Hiroshima Prefectural Art Museum** (Hiroshima Kenritsu Bijutsukan), next to the Shukkei Garden, is a visual treat. Standouts include two particularly surrealistic pieces; one a typically fantastical piece by Salvador Dalí called *Dream of Venus,* the other Ikuo Hirayama's much closer-to-home *Holocaust at Hiroshima.* Hirayama, who became one of Japan's most acclaimed artists, was a junior-high-school student at the time the A-bomb was dropped. ⊠ *Moto-machi, Naka-ku* ☎ *082/222–5346* 🖂 *¥500; museum and park ¥600* ⊗ *Tues.–Sun. 10–6.*

⓫ The hands-on **Hiroshima Science and Cultural Museum for Children** (Kodomo Bunka Kagakukan) is a good diversion for the kids. The joyful noise of excited children alleviates the somberness of Peace Memorial Park. Kids get a kick out conducting their own hands-on science "experiments." To get here, leave the park via Aioi-bashi at the North Entrance and walk north and east, keeping the river on your left and the baseball stadium on your right. A planetarium is next door. ⊠ *5–83 Moto-machi, Naka-ku* ☎ *082/222–5346* 🖂 *Center free, planetarium ¥500; kids ¥250.* ⊗ *Tues.–Sun. 9–5.*

Where to Stay & Eat

$$$$ ✕ **Kakifune Kanawa** (Kanawa Oyster Boat). Hiroshima is known for its oysters. Kanawa, on a barge moored on the Motoyasu-gawa, near Peace Memorial Park, is Hiroshima's most famous oyster restaurant. *Kaiseki ryōri* (Japanese haute cuisine) is also a draw. Dining is on tatami mats, with river views. ⊠ *3–1 Chisaki Ohtemachi, moored on river at Heiwa-bashi, Naka-ku, 730-0051* ☎ *082/241–7416* ⊟ *AE, DC, MC, V* ⊗ *Closed Sun. Apr.–Sept., 1st and 3rd Sun. Oct.–Mar.*

$–$$$ ✕ **Hiroshima Station.** If you don't have enough time to go out on the town for lunch or dinner, try the beer garden–restaurant area in the station's

9

basement, and the second and sixth floors of the Asse Department Store. You'll find restaurants of all types, from in-and-out cheapies to elegant eateries—many are branches of famous establishments elsewhere in the city. Enter the Asse complex from the south exit of the JR Hiroshima station. **Asse Department Store** ⊠ *JR Hiroshima Station Bldg. 9–1 Matsubara-chō, Higashi-ku* ☎ *082/248–2391* ⊘ *Daily 10–9.*

$–$$$ ✕ **Suishin.** Famous for its *kamameshi,* or rice casseroles, this restaurant serves the freshest fish from the Seto Nai-kai—fugu, or puffer-fish, oysters, and eel, to name but a few. If you prefer your fish cooked, try the rockfish grilled with soy sauce. Suishin has an English-language menu, and a simple set-up with only a counter bar and four tables. ⊠ *6–7 Tatemachi, Naka-ku* ☎ *082/247–4411* ⊟ *AE, DC, MC, V* ⊘ *Closed Wed.*

¢–$$ ✕ **Okonomi Mura** (Village of Okonomiyaki). In this enclave 20 shops serve *okonomi-yaki,* literally, "as you like it." Okonomi-yaki is best described as an everything omelet, topped with bits of shrimp, pork, squid, or chicken, cabbage, and bean sprouts. Different areas of Japan make different okonomi-yaki; in Hiroshima the ingredients are layered rather than mixed, and they throw in lots of fried noodles. Seating in these shops, which are generally open late, is either at a wide counter in front of a grill or at a table with its own grill. This complex is near the Hon-dōri shopping area, just west of Chūō-dōri. ⊠ *Shintenchi Plaza, 5–13 Shintenchi, 2nd–4th fls., Naka-ku* ⊟ *No credit cards.*

★ $$$$ 🏨 **ANA Hotel Hiroshima.** The reliable and popular ANA Hotel remains ╲ one of the very best in town. The hotel is within walking distance of the Peace Museum and the nightlife of Nagarekawa. The Unkai restaurant, on the fifth floor, has good Japanese food and looks over a garden of dwarf trees, rocks, and a pond with colorful carp. ⊠ *7–20 Naka-machi, Naka-ku, Hiroshima, Hiroshima-ken 730-0037* ☎ *082/241–1111* 🖷 *082/241–9123* ➦ *427 Western-style rooms, 4 Japanese-style rooms* ♿ *5 restaurants, indoor pool, health club, sauna, beer garden (May–Aug.), shops* ⊟ *AE, DC, MC, V.*

$$–$$$$ 🏨 **Hotel Granvia Hiroshima.** Connected by walkways to Hiroshima's JR station, this nice, relaxing hotel is convenient and welcoming to weary travelers. The Japanese restaurant Seto-uchi on the second floor offers a sampling of good traditional fare, and the expansive multilevel lobby is great for people-watching. ⊠ *1–5 Matsubara-machi, Minami-ku, Hiroshima, Hiroshima-ken 732-0822* ☎ *082/262–1111* 🖷 *082/262–4050* ➦ *407 rooms* ♿ *6 restaurants, coffee lounge, roof garden, bar, shops.* ⊟ *AE, DC, MC, V* ❙◎❙ *EP, MAP.*

$$ 🏨 **Comfort Hotel Hiroshima.** This affordable hotel stands near Peace Memorial Park, and it's a short walk from the happening nightspots. Rooms, though standard, are comfortable, and guests have free Internet access in the lobby. ⊠ *3–7–9 Otemachi, Naka-ku, Hiroshima, Hiroshima-ken 730-0051* ☎ *082/545–7811* 🖷 *082/545–7812* ➦ *258 Western-style rooms* ⊟ *AE, DC, MC, V.*

Tours

A number of sightseeing tours are available, including tours of Hiroshima and cruises on the Seto Nai-kai, in particular to Miyajima, the island with the famous tidal-basin torii.

To arrange for a sightseeing taxi ahead of time, telephone the **Hiroshima Station Tourist Information Center** (☎ 082/261–1877). A two-hour tour is approximately ¥8,400. Because these taxi drivers are not guides, you should rent a taped recording describing key sights in English. These special taxis can be picked up from a special depot in front of Hiroshima Station at the Shinkansen entrance.

A 4-hour, 40-minute tour of the city's major sights operated by **Hiroshima Bus Company** (☎ 082/243–7207 ☎ 082/243–0272) costs ¥3,500. Tours leave at 9 AM and 2 PM. An eight-hour tour of both the city and Miyajima costs ¥9,470, and includes lunch. It leaves at 9:30 AM. You depart from in front of Hiroshima Station's Shinkansen entrance. All tours are in Japanese, but the sights are gaijin-friendly.

Hiroshima Peace Culture Foundation International Relations and Cooperation Division (☎ 082/242–8879 ☎ 082/242–7452) has a home-visit program. To make arrangements, go the day before you wish to visit a Japanese home to the International Center on the ground floor of the International Conference Center in Peace Memorial Park. Although not required, bringing an inexpensive gift such as flowers or treats from your home country helps to ensure a successful visit.

Miyajima

⑫ *10 min from Miyajima-guchi (¥400, 25 min by JR Sanyo Line) or by JR ferry, ¥340 round-trip*

Miyajima's easily recognizable and majestic orange Ō-torii, or big gate, is made of several stout, rot-resistant camphor-tree trunks, and is famed for the illusion it gives of "floating" over the water. The torii is one of Japan's most enduring scenic attractions, but most of the time it actually presides over brownish tidal sand flats, so you want to time your visit for when the tide is in.

Behind the sea-gate is the elegant shrine Itsukushima Jinja. For a few hundred yen you can walk the labyrinthine wooden boardwalks out over the tidal basin and pick your spots to snap those perfect photos.

To get to the shrine and to see the torii, go right from the pier on the path that leads through the village, which is crowded with restaurants, hotels, and souvenir shops. As you pass through the park, expect to be greeted by herds of fearless deer. Don't show or let them smell any food, or else you'll become too popular—and they like to butt those who disappoint them!

Getting Around

The easiest, least expensive way to get to Miyajima is to take the train on the JR San-yo Line from Hiroshima Station to Miyajima-guchi Station. From Miyajima-guchi Station, a three-minute walk takes you to the pier where ferries depart for Miyajima. The train takes about 25 minutes (¥400) and departs from Hiroshima every 15–20 minutes. The first train leaves Hiroshima at 5:55 AM; the last ferry returns from Miyajima at 10:05 PM. There are two boats, but the JR Rail Pass is only valid on the JR-operated boat (¥340 return without Rail Pass). Allow a minimum of three hours for the major sights of Miyajima, or just one hour to get photos of Ō-torii and the shrine.

Inside the ferry terminal (common to both lines), tucked in the entrance to a novelty and snack shop, is the English-speaking **Miyajima Tourist Association** (☎ 0829/44–2011), open daily 9–7.

What to See

★ **Ō-torii** stands nearly 50 feet tall at the entrance to the cove where the ancient Shintō shrine is. This, the 18th version, was built in 1875, and has become one of the nation's most popular symbols. Hotels and ferry operators have tide charts so you can maximize your photo opportunities; otherwise you may gasp in surprise to find the mythic gate suspended over drab sand flats.

If you stay overnight on the island, and if the weather cooperates, you're guaranteed to get some photos to die for, because the gate is lit up in spectacular fashion, and looks hallucinatory set against the black night air and calm reflecting water. The nearby five-story pagoda and the shrine are also lighted.

Itsukushima Jinja was founded in 593 and dedicated to the three daughters of Susano-o-no-Mikoto, the Shintō god of the moon—also of the oceans, moon-bent as they are. The shrine was continually repaired and rebuilt, and the present structure is a 16th-century copy of 12th-century buildings. The orange woodwork next to the glaring white walls is visually addictive, especially when complemented by blue skies and seas. The deck has gorgeous views of the torii. ¥300 ◷ Mar.–Oct., daily 6:30–6; Nov.–Feb., daily 6:30–5:30.

Atop a small hill overlooking Itsukushima Jinja, **Go-jū-no-tō** (Five-Storied Pagoda) is laquered in bright orange, like the shrine and gate, and dates from 1407.

Many people spend only half a day on Miyajima, but if you have more time, take a stroll through **Momijidani Kōen** (Red Maple Valley Park), inland from Itsukushima Jinja. A cable car goes a mile up nearly to the summit of **Misen-dake** (Mt. Misen). It's a short hike from the upper terminus to the top of the mountain, where you can look out over Seto Nai-kai and all the way to Hiroshima. Cable car ¥900 one-way, ¥1,500 round-trip; park free.

Where to Stay & Eat

★ $$$–$$$$ **Ryokan Jūkei-sō**. This charming and relatively modernized hillside ryokan has been around for more than a century. It also has the best views available anywhere on the island. Every room is blessed with a panorama of Ō-torii, the shrine, and the pagodas—and all are photogenically backed by the sea, lush trees, or mountains. The English-speaking owners provide excellent service and food. It's off the quiet east side of the bay, and getting here is a nice stroll—or ask the Tourist Info Office inside the ferry terminal to call for you, and a van will pick you up. A private (no extra charge) outdoor bath on a sheltered overhanging corner has great views, so don't forget to reserve your 30-minute slot of pure Zen when you check in. Down in the basement there are more baths—separate sexes, open 24 hours. While soaking you can stare at what is probably the most impressive noncommercial aquarium you'll ever see. ✉ *50 Miyajima-chō, Hiroshima, Hiroshima-ken 739-0533* ☎ *0829/44–0300* 📠 *0829/44–0388* ↩ *12 Japanese-style rooms* ♨ *Restaurant, Japanese baths* ➘ *AE, DC, MC, V* ⦿ *EP, MAP.*

$$–$$$$ ✕⊡ **Iwasō Ryokan.** For traditional elegance, it's easy to like this venerable Japanese inn. The new rooms are nice, but the older rooms have more character. Two quaint cottages on the grounds have suites decorated with antiques. Prices vary widely according to the size of your room, its view, and the kaiseki dinner you select, so be sure to get it all ironed out when you make reservations. Breakfast and dinner are included in the rates, and can be made Western style. Nonguests can also enjoy the food. ✉ *345 Miyajima-chō, Hiroshima, Hiroshima-ken 739-0500* ☎ *0829/44–2233* 📠 *0829/44–2230* ↩ *42 Japanese-style rooms, 33 with bath* ♨ *Restaurant, Japanese baths* ➘ *AE, DC, V* ⦿ *EP, MAP.*

Yamaguchi

⑬ *54 min west of Hiroshima, ¥5,440, by JR Shinkansen and local Yamaguchi Line; 4 hrs 24 min west of Tōkyō by JR Shinkansen to Shin-Yamaguchi, then 22 min by JR Yamaguchi Line, ¥20,860.*

Convenient access to the Shinkansen at nearby Shin-Yamaguchi (which has no other notable attractions), unbeatable connections to territory's most remote hinterlands, and some disarmingly nice hospitality and local charm make Yamaguchi City a logical base for striking out for Hagi and Tsuwano—especially if accommodations are booked in those romantic hideaways. This capital city has a rare and well-preserved five-story pagoda, a slightly famous park, a decent shopping mall that isn't wall-to-wall people, and a lot of lush greenery descending from the mountains. The countless healing sulfurous baths of Yuda Onsen are only a short ¥500 cab ride or one train stop away.

Should you need a map of Yamaguchi, restaurant or hotel recommendations and assistance, or useful onward travel information, head to the English-speaking **Tourist Information Office** (☎ 083/933–0090), open daily 9–6, on the second floor of the JR Yamaguchi Station.

Shin-Yamaguchi also has a helpful English-speaking **Tourist Information Office** (☎ 083/972–6373), open daily 9–6, on the second floor by the station's north (Shinkansen) exit.

Where to Eat

$$–$$$$ ✕ **Tojima-zushi.** A favorite with locals for a nice night out, this simple but intimate spot has invigorating and delicious fresh sushi. A few minutes' walk along the boulevard from the station's exit is a covered shopping arcade. Turn right, then take the next cross street to the left and look for the sign up above, a few doors down on the left. ☎ 083/922–1835 ➘ *No credit cards* ⊗ *Wed.–Mon. 11:30–2:30 and 5–10:30.*

Where to Stay

$$ ⊡ **Sunroute International Hotel Yamaguchi.** The staff handles your every request with grace. Rooms are adequate, the views of those gorgeous green mountains are good, and the price is right. It's on a right-hand corner a few blocks up the big street heading straight from the station exit. ✉ *1–1 Nakagawara-chō, Yamaguchi-shi, Yamaguchi-ken 753-0088* ☎ *083/923–3610* 🖷 *083/923–2379* 📞 *80 Western-style rooms, 1 Western-style suite* 🔥 *Restaurant, bar, shop* 🗐 *AE, DC, MC, V.*

THE SAN-IN REGION

If you are looking for adventure in a "real Japan" setting, you have come to the right place. Though the endless narrow ridges of steep mountains can make access from the developed south difficult, slow, and expensive, this hard fact of geography has kept the entire north stretch of Western Honshu delightfully isolated. Any effort pays off in great scenery, local crafts, seafood, history, and people.

Getting Around
The JR San-in Main Line from Shimonoseki to Kyōto is the second-longest in Japan, at 680 km (422 mi). It has the most stations of any line, which means too many stops and long traveling times. Only two Limited Express trains a day cover the entire Shimonoseki–Kyōto route in either direction. Local trains and buses run between major towns on the San-in coast, but still nowhere near as often or as quickly as in San-yō.

Hagi

3 hrs 42 min north of Yamaguchi by JR train (¥4,180, add 12–20 min if from Shin-Yamaguchi); 1 hr by JR bus (Rail Pass OK) from Yamaguchi, ¥1,680; 1 hr by Bōchō Bus from Shin-Yamaguchi, ¥1,970.

⑭ Hagi is virtually surrounded by two forks of the Abu-gawa—the river's south fork, Hashimoto-gawa, and the river's northeast fork, Matsumoto-gawa. Rising in great semi-circles behind the town are symmetrical waves of shadowy mountains, and before it stretches a sparkling blue sea.

Hagi is rich with history, and owing to its remoteness retains the atmosphere of a traditional castle town, though its castle was a casualty of the Meiji Restoration. Turning away from feudalism to support the new order, the city was of critical importance in the 1865 to 1867 movement to restore power to the emperor. Japan's first prime minister, Hirobumi Ito (1841–1909), was a Hagi native.

Hagi is also famous for Hagi-yaki, a type of earthenware with soft colors and milky, translucent glazes ranging from beige to pink. The esteemed local ceramics industry began in the 16th century when a Mōri general brought home captive Korean potters (perhaps his consolation for a failed invasion) to create pottery for their new masters. The visually soothing Hagi-yaki is second to Raku-yaki as the most coveted pottery in Japan, and it does not come cheap—except during the annual price-friendly Hagi-yaki Festival every May 1–5.

Getting Around

The fastest way to Hagi is by JR Bus (Rail Pass OK), crossing the mountains in just 1 hour for ¥1,680 from Yamaguchi City. The bus departs from the front of the train station. A JR bus also leaves from the Shinkansen exit of Shin-Yamaguchi for an 80-minute ride for ¥1,970. Buses run one per hour between 6 AM and 7 PM. Some buses stop at Hagi Station, the Hagi Bus Center, or Higashi-Hagi Station; all stop at the last two. Return buses follow the same plan. The ideal way to explore Hagi is by bicycle, and you can rent a bike for ¥1,000 per day near the stations or shopping arcades. A local bus system (red bus) loops around town for ¥100 a ride; ¥500 for a full day.

City information is available from English-speaking staff at the **Hagi City Tourist Bureau** (☎ 0838/25–1750 ☉ Daily 9–5:45) next to Hagi Station. For local information at Higashi-Hagi Station, try **Hagi Tourist Office** (☎ 0838/22–7599 🖷 0838/24–2202) in the building to the left of the station, on the left side of the shopping arcade. The **City Tourist Office** (✉ 495–4 Emukai, Hagi-shi, 758-0053 ☎ 0838/25–3131 ☉ Mon.–Sat. 9–5) is downtown in Hagi City Hall.

What to See

If you've just arrived by bus, you won't be impressed by the run-down buildings around the Hagi Bus Center. That's okay. Head three short blocks north, then left onto Tamachi Mall (see below), and head west through the quaint older sections of town for 15 minutes to see the park and castle ruins. If you need to make a Tourist Info stop first, head south two blocks and then west two more, to Hagi City Hall.

Tamachi Mall is the busiest street in Hagi, with some 130 shops selling local products from Yamaguchi Prefecture. The shopping mood is addictive, the wares gorgeous, the shopkeepers friendly—so the money can go quickly. Tamachi Mall is six blocks southwest from the Hagi Grand Hotel, across the Matsumoto-gawa from Higashi-Hagi Station. ✉ *Central Hagi.*

Shizuki Kōen, bounded on three sides by the sea, is at Hagi's westernmost end. This large, lovely park contains the Hagi-jō ruins and Hana-no-e Teahouse. ✉ *Ō-aza Horiuchi* ☎ *0838/25–1826* 🖳 *¥210, includes admission to Hagi-jō grounds, Mōri House, and Hana-no-e Teahouse ☉ Apr.–Oct., daily 8–6:30; Nov.–Feb., daily 8:30–4:30; Mar. daily 8:30–6.*

Hagi-jō was one of many castles destroyed by the Meiji government around 1874 as being a symbol of backward ways. The dramatic seaside location with a stupendous mountain backdrop must have made the castle a superb sight in its day, but we can only imagine, since the walls and moats are all that remain.

9

★ The **Hana-no-e Teahouse** is a bare-bones oasis of Zen, set amid meditative gardens and judiciously pruned greenery. The attendants make the classic, slightly bitter *matcha* (¥500) tea for you while you reflect upon the the transiency of life—or where you'd like to go next.

Mōri House, south of the park, is a long narrow building once home to samurai foot soldiers in the late 18th century. The rooms are sparse and placed one next to the other. This arrangement allowed the soldiers to assemble just outside in rank and file at a moment's notice.

Stop in at **Jō-zan Gama** (Jō-zan Kiln), near Shizuki Kōen, perhaps the best place to browse through and purchase magnificent pottery. Usually you are welcome to enter the studios and see the kilns. Classes or a chance

> ## SAMURAI LIVING
>
> **Horiuchi** is the old samurai section of town. From Shizuki Kōen, recross the canal (on the middle bridge) to the east side and head toward downtown. The tomb of **Tenju-in** is a memorial to Terumoto Mōri, who in the early 16th century founded the tenacious clan that ruled the Choshu area for 13 generations. Next you come to the **Outer Gate of Mōri**; the **Toida Masuda House Walls** are on your right as you head south. Dating from the 18th century, these are the longest mud walls in the area, and they thrust you back in time. At the next chance, turn right and head west to the ancient, wooden **Fukuhara Gate**.

to make your own may be available. Bicycles can be rented here as well. ⊠ *Hagi-jo-ato, Horiuchi* ☎ *0838/25–1666* ⊗ *Daily 8–5.*

Where to Stay & Eat

$$$–$$$$ ✕ **Nakamura.** Set-menu courses at this reliable and popular traditional restaurant typically offer a variety of fish, mountain vegetables, miso soup, and steamed rice. Nakamura has tatami and Western seating but no English-language menu. You can select your food from the tempting window display. ⊠ *Furu-Hagi-chō* ☎ *0838/22–6619* ⊜ *Reservations not accepted* ⊟ *No credit cards* ⊗ *Daily 11–2 and 5–8.*

$$–$$$$
Fodor'sChoice
★
✕ **Chiyo.** A *tsubaki* course, at ¥3,150, includes squid and scallops cooked before you with butter on a sizzling-hot river stone, and such goodies as *fugu* (blowfish)—as sashimi or cooked, tempura-style—stuffed with foie gras. Zingy homemade pickles reset your palate for each successive treat. Women beautifully dressed in formal wear serve you in a classically elegant manner, and off to the right of the intimate 10-seat counter are views of the mossy green and flowery window garden. ⊠ *20–4 Ima, Furu-Hagi* ☎ *0838/22–1128* ⊟ *AE, DC, MC, V* ⊗ *Closed Mon. No dinner Sun.*

$–$$ ✕ **Fujita-ya.** Colorful characters come to this casual restaurant for beer and sake, *soba* (thin wheat noodles), and hot tempura served on fragrant handmade cypress trays. ⊠ *Kumagai-chō* ☎ *0838/22–1086* ▭ *No credit cards* ⊘ *Closed 2nd and 4th Wed. of month.*

$$$$ ⊞ **Hokumon Yashiki.** An elegant ryokan with fine touches of understated luxury, the Hokumon Yashiki pampers you in a style the ruling Mōri clan was surely accustomed to. The inn overlooks a garden in the samurai section of town, near the castle grounds. Meals are served in your room. ⊠ *210 Horiuchi, Hagi, Yamaguchi-ken 758-0057* ☎ *0838/22–7251* 🖷 *0838/25–8144* ⮐ *42 Japanese-style rooms without bath, 5 Western-style rooms* ⚭ *Japanese baths* ▭ *No credit cards* ⅋◎⅋ *MAP.*

$$$–$$$$ ⊞ **Hagi Tanaka Hotel.** It's one station north of town and behind the marina. It's enticingly close to the hypnotic Mt. Kasa, its baths tap an onsen, and delectable morsels from the bay are served for dinner in your room. You won't have to tear yourself away from the views until you line up for the buffet breakfast (either Japanese or Western) in the morning. Guest rooms are all Japanese style, and face either the bay or the mountains. Don't expect any English—but then, you already know how to eat and relax, right? ⊠ *707–10 Koshigahama, Hagi, Yamaguchi-ken 758-0011* ☎ *0838/25–0001* 🖷 *0838/24–1111* ⮐ *92 Japanese-style rooms* ⚭ *Lounge, indoor/outdoor Japanese baths, shops* ▭ *AE, DC, MC, V.*

$ ⊞ **Urban City Hotel Hasegawa.** If you want a cheap, decent place to crash near the Hagi Bus Center, this business hotel is adequate—and right across the street. ⊠ *17 Karahi-machi, Hagi, Yamaguchi-ken 758-0044* ☎ *0838/ 22–0450* 🖷 *0838/22–4884* ⮐ *18 rooms, 6 Japanese style* ⚭ *Restaurant, bar.* ▭ *AE, DC, MC, V.*

Tsuwano

2 hrs 43 min northeast of Hagi by JR, ¥1,620; 1 hr 13 min northeast of Yamaguchi by JR Yamaguchi Line, ¥950; 1 hr northeast of Shin-Yamaguchi by JR Super Oki Express, ¥2,770; 1 hr by Bōchō Bus from Yamaguchi, ¥1,060.

⑮   This hauntingly beautiful town, tucked into a narrow north–south val-
Fodor's Choice   ley at the foot of conical Aono-yama and its dormant volcanic moun-
★   tain friends may be the most picturesque hamlet in all Japan. If you catch it on a clear day, the view from the old castle ruins simply takes your breath away. Even when it's cloudy, the mist hangs ghostlike among the trees and ridges. The stucco-and-tile walls are like those in Hagi and

Kurashiki, and the clear carp-filled streams running beside the streets can induce even tired, jaded travelers to take a stroll or bike ride backward through time.

It's easy to see how a gifted spirit and intellect could soar here. The towering Japanese literary figure Ōgai Mori, novelist and poet, was born (in 1862) and lived here—until he went off and enrolled at Tōkyō University's preparatory program in Medicine at the astonishing age of 12!

Getting Around

Though JR trains from Yamaguchi are quick and easy, JR train routes from Hagi to Tsuwano involve a change and long layovers in Masuda. You can also take a bus from Hagi's **Bōchō Bus Center** (☎ 0856/72–0272) directly to Tsuwano, which takes around two hours. (¥2,080).

In Tsuwano all sights are within easy walking distance. You can rent a bicycle from one of the four shops near the station plaza (two hours ¥500; all day ¥800).

Tsuwano's **Tourist Information Office** (☎ 0856/72–1771) is inside the Photograph Gallery to the right of the railway station. It's open daily 9–5 and has free brochures; staff members will help you reserve accommodations. As with most places in town, little English is spoken here.

What to See

The **Taikodani Inari Jinja** (Taiko Valley Inari Shrine) is one of the five most revered Inari shrines in Japan. Inari shrines are connected with the fox, a Shintō symbol of luck and cleverness. People come to pray for good fortune in business and health. A series of 1,174 red wooden gates are suspended above steps that climb up the western side of the valley to the shrine, and the journey is a nice hike. From the station, follow the stream-side Tono-machi-dōri past the Katorikku Kyōkai (Catholic church), but before crossing the river turn right onto the small lane. The lane leads to the tunnel-like approach through the gates to the structure high on a cliffside. The shrine is nothing astounding, but the views out over the valley are. You can also take a bus that approaches by a back road; the Tourist Information Office can help with this. **Yasaka Jinja** is another shrine on the site, where every July 20, 24, and 27 sees the Heron Dance Festival.

Tsuwano Castle was another casualty of the Meiji Restoration in the late 19th century, but from the derelict ruins of **Tsuwano-jō** (☉ Daily 10–5) there is an awesome panoramic view of the dormant volcanic cone of Aono-yama to the east, surrounding similar peaks, and the entire valley stretching out below. To get up here you can hike a marked trail that leads from Taikodani Inari Jinja or take a chairlift from below the Inari shrine for ¥450 round-trip. The chairlift takes only 5 minutes, and from the top it's about a 15-minute hike to the castle foundations.

The **Old House of Ōgai Mori** is spartan, but perhaps worth a visit if only to commemorate the achievements of this gifted genius who called Tsuwano his home. Ōgai Mori (1862–1922), son of the head physician to the *daimyō* (lord) of Shimane, became a doctor at the young age of 19, and who, in spite of courting trouble for his outspoken criticism of

Japan's backward ways compared to the West, went on to become the author of such acclaimed novels as *The Wild Geese* and *Vita Sexualis*. He was also a prominent figure in the fledgling government behind the Meiji Restoration. From Tsuwano Station it's a 12-block walk south along the main road, or take the bus and get off at Ōgai Kyūkyo-mae. ☎ 08567/2–3210 ☒ ¥500 ⊙ *Tues.–Sun. 9–5.*

OFF THE BEATEN PATH

OTOMETŌGE MARIA SEIDŌ. Between 1868 and 1870, in an effort to disperse Christian strongholds and cause them extreme hardship—in the hope that the believers would recant their faith—the Tokugawa shogunate sent 153 Christians from Nagasaki to Tsuwano, where they were imprisoned and tortured. Many gave in, but 36 died for their faith. Otometōge Maria Seidō (St. Mary's Chapel at the Pass of the Virgin) was built in 1951 to commemorate the plight of the 36 martyrs, which is portrayed in the stained-glass windows. The chapel is a 1-km (½-mi) walk from Tsuwano Station. Go right out of the station, make another right at the first street (which leads to Yōmei-ji), and just after crossing the tracks turn right again and walk up the hill. Every May 3 a procession begins at the church in town and ends in the chapel courtyard, where a large outdoor mass is celebrated.

Where to Stay & Eat

$$$–$$$$
Fodor$Choice
★

✕ **Yūki.** Carp dishes—yes, carp—and delectable mountain vegetables maintain Yūki's highly venerated reputation. They have ayu, or river smelt, and other things, but for only ¥2,800 you can get the Tsuwano *teishoku,* or gourmet carp course, which offers a smattering of everything a big fat carp can become: there's chewy carp sashimi (with a wonderful lemony-mustard-thyme dipping sauce), tender deep-fried carp, carp steeped so long in soy sauce, sake, and brown sugar that it is dense and even slightly dry but very delicious, and carp boiled in a tangy miso soup until it's almost flaky. This is bona-fide stamina food, and it is way better than you might think—these are not like the carp you and your uncles pulled out of those old muddy ponds! The dining room is chock-full of old farm and country-life implements, and there's even a carp-filled stream burbling at your feet, running right through the center of it! Come early, as they close at around 7 PM. ☒ 271–4 Hon-chō-dōri ☎ 0856/72–0162 ☐ No credit cards ⊙ Closed Thurs.

¢–$$
✕ **Aoki.** An old-fashioned, rustic-decor sushi restaurant with a few tables on tatami mats and a long bar counter with stools, Aoki has a

BATHING & THE VOLCANO

Tsuwano puts its geothermal gifts to good use at the spa at **Nagomi-no-Sato**. Inside and out, the tubs have great views of the surrounding gumdrop-shape volcanic peaks. It's west of everything else in town, across the river from the Washibara Hachiman-gū (a shrine where traditional horseback archery contests are held every April 2), but still not too far to get to by rented bike. ☒ 257-Ō-*aza Washibara* ☎ 0856/72-4122, 0120/26-4753 toll free ☒ ¥500 ⊙ Hot springs daily 10–8 except 2nd and 4th Thurs. of month; restaurant daily 10–10, except 1st and 3rd Thurs.

9

cheerful staff and reasonable prices. It's also within easy walking distance of Tsuwano Station. Try the *jyo-nigiri* (deluxe sushi set); it will likely include a slice or two of tasty, chewy koi, or local carp. That and a frosty mug of beer set you back only ¥1,900. They stay open until 10 PM. ⊠ *Takaoka-dōri* ☎ *0856/72–0444* ⊟ *No credit cards* ⊘ *Closed Thurs.*

$$ 🏠 **Tsuwano Lodge.** Relax and revel in style at this lodge tucked among **Fodor'sChoice** the rice paddies and bamboo groves along the way to the Washibara ★   Hachiman-gū shrine. The owners are friendly (but don't speak much English), the rooms are basic but tasteful, and the food is diverse, healthy, and prepared with flair. Perhaps best of all, there's a rooftop *rotemburo* (outside bath) full of sulfur- and calcium-laden water—good for the skin, hair, and nails. ⊠ *Rte. 345, Washibara, Kanoashi-gun, Shimane-ken, Tsuwano-chō 699-5613* ☎ *0856/72–1683* 🖷 *0856/72–2880* ⌁ *8 Japanese-style rooms without baths* ♨ *Dining room, Japanese baths* ⊟ *No credit cards* ❑ *EP, MAP.*

$$ 🏠 **Wakasagi-no-Yado.** Despite the limited English of the family that runs this small but satisfactory inn, they're eager to help overseas tourists and will meet you at Tsuwano Station, only an eight-minute walk away. Typical of *minshuku*, there's a common bath. A Japanese or Western breakfast is served, included in the rates. ⊠ *Mōri, Kanoashi-gun, Tsuwano-chō Shimane-ken 699-0056* ☎🖷 *0856/72–1146* ⌁ *8 Japanese-style rooms without bath* ♨ *Japanese baths* ⊟ *No credit cards* ❑ *BP.*

Izumo Taisha

🔟 *1 hr west of Matsue by Ichibata Dentetsu (electric railway), ¥790.*

Oldest of all Japan's Shintō shrines, this site has been of significance—second only to the great shrine at Ise—since the 6th century. The main building was last rebuilt in 1744. It might have been the largest wooden building in the country at one time, but since the 13th century, each time it was rebuilt it was scaled to only half its former size, and it is now only 24 meters tall. Nature has arrayed a shrine of its own to compliment the ornate but somehow subdued structures: a lofty ridge of forested peaks rises behind, a boulevard of fragrant ancient pines lines the approach, and lush green lawns flank both sides. Pilgrims come to pray for success in courtship and marriage.

Getting Around

The easiest way is to go from Matsue Shinji-ko Onsen. Buses run often between it and Matsue station for ¥200. It takes one hour on the Ichibata Dentetsu (electric railway, ¥790), from Matsue Shinji-ko Onsen Station. After about 50 minutes you'll need to change trains at Kawato Station for the final 10-minute leg to Izumo Taisha-mae Station. You can also get there by taking the JR train from Matsue Station to Izumo, then transferring to the JR Taisha Line and taking that to Taisha Station, where you can either take a 5-minute bus ride to Taisha-mae Station or walk to the shrine in about 20 minutes.

What to See

Although **Izumo Taisha** is Japan's oldest Shintō shrine, the *hon-den* (main building) dates from 1744, and most of the other buildings from 1874.

The architectural style, with its saddled crests and ornamental roof fixtures resembling crossed swords, is said to be unique to the Izumo region, but some similarities with the main Shintō shrine of Ise Jingū on the Kii Peninsula can be noted. The taisha is dedicated to a male god, Okuninushi, the creator of the land and god of marriage and fortune. Instead of clapping twice, as at other shrines, you should clap four times—twice for yourself, and twice for your current or future partner. According to folklore, if you successfully throw a 5-yen coin so that it sticks up into the sacred hanging strands of the enormously thick 5-ton, 25 foot-long twisted straw rope, or shimenawa, suspended above the entrance to the main building, you will be doubly assured of good luck in marriage (which may say something about the difficulties of marriage).

Two rectangular buildings on either side of the compound are believed to house the visiting millions of Shintō gods during the 10th lunar month of each year. In the rest of Japan the lunar October is referred to as Kaminazuki, "month without gods," while in Izumo, October is called Kamiarizuki, "month with gods." The shrine is a five-minute walk north, to the right along the main street, from Izumo Taisha-mae Station. ⊠ *Izumo Taisha, Izumo-shi* ☎ *0853/53–2298* 🎫 *Free* ☉ *Daily 8:30–5:30*

Matsue

⑰

Fodor'sChoice
★

2 hrs 34 min northeast of Tsuwano by JR Super Oki Express, ¥5,870; 2 hrs 17 min northwest of Kurashiki, Okayama by JR Yakumo Limited Express, ¥5,550.

Matsue is a city blessed with such overwhelming beauty and good food that you will be stuck on what to look at and what to do first. It's where the lake named Shinji-ko empties into the lagoon called Nakaumi-ko, which connects directly with the Sea of Japan. This makes Matsue a seafood lover's paradise, bursting with fresh fish and specializing in both kinds of eel, all kinds of shrimp, shellfish, carp, sea bass, smelt, whitebait, and famous black shijimi clams from Shinji-ko. The water also provides the city with a lovely network of canals.

Matsue also attracts and holds onto some of the country's most welcoming and interesting people, both foreign and native. This remote realm is a traveler's favorite, and once you've come here you'll surely be back—it's that kind of place. In the 1890s the famed journalist-novelist Lafcadio Hearn came here and promptly fell in love—with the place, and then a local woman—and let the entire world know about it.

Getting Around

Most sights in Matsue are within walking distance of each other. Where they are not, the buses fill in. The bus station faces the train station.

Matsue Tourist Information Office (⊠ 665 Asahi-machi ☎ 0852/21–4034 🖷 0852/27–2598). The office is outside JR Matsue Station and open daily 9–6. You can collect free maps and brochures. The Shimane Tourist Association offers a substantial discount for foreigners who visit its tourist attractions; the current list includes the castle, the Hearn Memorial Hall (both 50% off), and some art museums, including the otherwise expensive Louis C. Tiffany Museum and English Garden (30% off). You need only present your passport or foreigner's registration card at the entrance to these places.

What to See

★ Start a tour of Matsue at the enchanting and shadowy **Matsue-jō** and walk in the castle park, **Shiroyama Kōen,** under aromatic pines. Constructed of pine, the castle was completed in 1611. The castle not only survived the Meiji upheavals intact, it was never ransacked during the Tokugawa shogunate. Perhaps it's the properties of the wood, or the angles, or the mysterious tricks of light and shadows, but this castle feels alive.

Despite its foreboding aspect, the castle seems to beckon you inside. Built by the daimyō of Izumo, Yoshiharu Horio, for protection, Matsue-jō's donjon (main tower), at 98 feet, is the second-tallest among originals still standing in Japan. Crouching below the lofty pines, Matsue-jō is slightly spooky at all times. The castle is fabulously preserved, with six interior levels belied by a tricky facade that suggests only five. The lower floors display a collection of samurai swords and armor. The long climb to the castle's uppermost floor is worth it, for the view encompasses the city, Lake Shinji, the Shimane Peninsula, snowy Daisen, and the mountains.

The castle and park are a 1-km (½-mi) stroll northwest from the station, or take the Lakeline Bus from Terminal 7 in front of the station and get off at Ote-mae; the fare is ¥150. ☎ 0852/21–4030 ☜ ¥550 ⊘ Apr.–Sept., daily 8:30–6; Oct.–Mar., daily 8:30–4:30.

Meimei-an Teahouse, built in 1779, is one of Japan's best-preserved teahouses. For ¥400 you can contemplate the mysteries of Matsue-jō, and for ¥400 more, you get tea and a sweet. To get here, leave Shiroyama Kōen, the castle park, at its east exit and follow the moat going north; at the top of the park a road leads to the right, northwest of the castle. The teahouse is a short climb up this road. ✉ Kitahori-cho ☎ 0852/ 21–9863 ⊘ Daily 9–5.

Samurai Mansion (Buke Yashiki), built in 1730, belonged to the well-to-do Shiomi family, chief retainers to the daimyō. Note the separate servant quarters, a shed for the palanquin, and slats in the walls to allow cooling breezes to flow through the rooms. Buke Yashiki is on the main road at the base of the side street on which Meimei-an Teahouse is located (keep the castle moat on your left). ✉ 305 Kitahori-cho ☎ 0852/ 22–2243 ☜ ¥300 ⊘ Apr.–Sept., daily 8:30–6; Oct.–Mar., daily 8:30–4:30.

The **Lafcadio Hearn Residence** (Koizumi Yakumo Kyūkyo), next to the Tanabe Bijutsukan, has remained unchanged since the famous writer left Matsue in 1891. Born of an Irish father and a Greek mother, Lafcadio Hearn (1850–1904) spent his early years in Europe and moved to the United States to become a journalist. In 1890 he traveled to Yokohama, Japan, and made his way to Matsue, where he began teaching, and met and married a samurai's daughter named Setsu Koizumi. He later took posts in Kumamoto, Kōbe, and Tōkyō. Disdainful of the materialism of the West, he was destined to be a lifelong Japanophile and resident. He became a Japanese citizen, taking the name Yakumo Koizumi. His most famous works were *Glimpses of Unfamiliar Japan* (1894) and *Japan: An Attempt at Interpretation* (1904). ☎ 0852/23–0714 ✉ ¥250 ⊗ Daily 9–4:30.

The **Lafcadio Hearn Memorial Hall** (Koizumi Yakumo Kinenkan) has a good collection of the author's manuscripts and other artifacts that reflect his life in Japan. It's adjacent to Koizumi Yakumo Kyūkyo. Two minutes from the Memorial Hall is the Hearn Kyūkyo bus stop, where a bus goes back to the center of town and the station. ☎ 0852/21–2147 ✉ ¥300 ⊗ Apr.–Sept., daily 8:30–6; Oct.–Mar., daily 8:30–4:30.

When dusk rolls around, you'll want to position yourself well. You won't get a better sunset than the one seen every night over **Shinji-ko**. As locals do, you can watch it from Shinji-ko Ōhashi, the town's westernmost bridge, but the best spot is south of the bridge, along the road, down near water level in **Shiragata Kōen**, the narrow lakeside park just west of the NHK Building and the hospital. This is a great place to kick back and enjoy some micro-brews and portable sushi while that big orange ball dunks itself in the lake.

Matsue English Garden re-creates the scale, arrangement, and style of a traditional English garden. There's an outdoor rest area, fountain plaza, sunken garden, indoor garden, "white" garden, pergola, cloister courtyard, landscape garden, rose terrace, and laburnum arch. If you've covered everything else, try this place—it's quite stunning, and it was put together in only five years by a jovial English gardener named Keith Gott. Although the admission is high, it also gets you into the **Louis C. Tiffany Museum,** where the country's largest private Tiffany collection is housed. An ornate and authentic "Paris Salon" is next door. The complex is out on the lakeshore northwest of town, at Nishi-Hamasada, 40 minutes from JR Matsue Station by Lakeline Bus; get off at Tiffany Bijitsukan-Mae. It's one stop (5 minutes) west of Matsue Shinji-ko Onsen Station by the Ichibata Railway, so it can be seen on the way to or from Izumo Taisha. ✉ 369 Nishi-Hamadasa-chō ☎ 0852/36–3030 ✉ ¥2,000 ⊗ Apr.–Sept., daily 9–5; Oct.–Mar., daily 9–4.

Where to Stay & Eat

$$–$$$ ✕ **Kawakyō**. This is the best place to try the seven famous delicacies from
Fodor'sChoice Shinji-ko: *suzuki* (or *hosho-yaki*), sea bass wrapped in *washi* (paper) and
★ steam-baked over hot coals; *unagi* (freshwater eel) split, broiled, and basted in sweet soy sauce; *shirao*, a small whitefish often served as sashimi or cooked in vinegar-miso; *amasagi* (smelt), teriyaki-grilled or cooked in tempura; *shijimi*, small black-shelled clams served in miso or other soup; *koi*, string-bound, washi-wrapped, steam-baked carp; and *morogeebi*, steamed shrimp. Especially good is the hosho-yaki. The staff is very outgoing, as is the regular crowd. Don't forget to request one of the delicious *ji-zake* (locally made sake) samplers. Reservations are a good idea. Kawakyō is in the block just east of the middle (Matsue Ōhashi) bridge, a block north of the river. ✉ 65 Suetsugu Honmachi ☎ 0852/22–1312 ▤ No credit cards ⊗ Mon.–Sat. 6–10:30. No lunch.

$–$$ ✕ **Yakumo-an**. A colorful garden surrounds the dining area at this traditional house that serves good soba. Recommended dishes include the *sanshurui soba* (three kinds of soba) for ¥750. Take the top dish and, leaving the garnishes in, pour the broth into it, then dunk the noodles as you go. Drink the leftover broth, too; it's full of B vitamins and good for your metabolism. ⊠ *Just west of Tanabe Bijutsukan, north of castle* ☎ *0852/22–2400* ⊟ *No credit cards* ⊗ *Daily 9–4:30.*

¢–$$ ✕ **Ōhashi**. If you're pressed for time but need to grab some decent lunch, try some warigo soba, a local buckwheat noodle specialty. Ōhashi is right inside the Shamine department store next to the station, and has a filling, healthy Yakumo Gozen set course for ¥1,000. ⊠ *472–2 Asahi-machi* ☎ *0852/26–6551* ⊟ *No credit cards* ⊗ *Daily 10:30–8.*

★ $$$$ ✕🏨 **Naniwa Issui**. A swanky ryokan near the Matsue Shinji-ko Onsen Station (for easy Izumo Taisha access), Naniwa Issui is envied for its amazing views out over the big lake—and for its onsen. The seven mind-blowing super-deluxe rooms on the fourth floor have private rotemburos to soak in out on the balconies—and the newest, largest big-screen entertainment centers available. Naniwa offers impeccable service and fabulous Matsue seafood cuisine. In season, the delightful lounge-side garden becomes a beer and cocktail patio. ⊠ *63 Chidori-chō, Matsue, Shimane-ken 690-0852* ☎ *0852/21–4132* 🖷 *0852/21–4162* 🛏 *29 Japanese-style rooms* ♨ *Restaurant, Japanese baths, shop* ⊟ *DC, MC, V* ¶❍❘ *MAP.*

★ $–$$ 🏨 **Ryokan Terazuya**. The same family has maintained a tradition of heartwarming hospitality at this charming riverside ryokan since 1893. Rooms are cozy but air-conditioned, and the location is perfect for watching sunsets. The food is superb and of an astounding variety—virtually all the local seafood and vegetable specialties, both raw and cooked, are served. English is spoken, and your kind hosts may even demonstrate sushi-making and tea ceremony. ⊠ *60–3 Tenjin-machi, Matsue, Shimane-ken 690-0064* ☎ *0852/21–3480* 🖷 *0852/21–3422* 🛏 *9 Japanese-style rooms without baths* ♨ *Japanese baths* ⊟ *No credit cards* ❍❘ *EP, MAP.*

$ 🏨 **Minshuku Kamoi**. This hotel is only a block and a half west of the north exit from Matsue Station. The rooms are modern, with basic chain hotel–style furnishings, and have LAN access. ⊠ *498–10 Asahi-machi, Matsue, Shimane-ken 690-0003* ☎ *0852/60–1045* 🖷 *0852/60–1046* 🛏 *190 rooms* ♨ *Internet* ⊟ *DC, MC, V.*

Nightlife

★ **Filaments** (⊠ 5 Hakkenya-chō ☎ *0852/24–8984*), burns brightly all night, every night. Osamu-san, the easy-going proprietor, speaks wonderful English, and loves to meet people who wander by. His collection of music covers every taste—and every available surface—and keeps everyone endlessly amused and humming—if not dancing about wildly. Pick up something interesting, and he'll put it on for you—immediately. The drinks are good and cheap (from ¥500), and snacks are served at prices from ¥650 to ¥1,000. Filaments is on a corner just a block south of the river near the second of the four main bridges.

Okayama

❶⓮ *3 hrs 17 min west of Tōkyō by JR Shinkansen, ¥16,660; 2 hrs 27 min southeast of Matsue by JR Yakumo Express, ¥5,870.*

The city of Okayama claims to have the most sunny days in Japan. A beautiful black castle is set amid a spacious and luxuriant garden, justly rated among Japan's top three. Hop on one of the frequent streetcars plying Momotaro-dōri, the main boulevard heading east from the Shinkansen station (¥100); ride three stops east; and walk southeast to the castle, park, and museums. For ¥520 you can buy a combined park-castle ticket.

The Shinkansen station makes Okayama an attractive base for visiting the quaint charms of Kurashiki—only a 15-minute local JR train hop to the west. The city also serves as a gateway to the remote and beautiful realm of Matsue, 2½ hours, ¥5,670 by JR train to the northwest.

Should you need a map of Okayama or city information, head to the **Tourist Information Office** (☎ 086/222–2912), open daily 9–6, on the first floor near the east exit of the JR station.

What to See

★ **Kōraku Garden** (Kōrakuen) is one of the country's finest gardens, with charming tea arbors, green lawns, ponds, and hills that were created three centuries ago on the banks of the Asahi-gawa. Gardens in Japan, whether dry, wet, or a combination of both, are constructed with many elements in mind, but the goal is always to engender feelings of peace and tranquillity. They are a form of visual meditation, so to speak. Kōrakuen scores high in all relevant areas. The maple, apricot, and cherry trees give the 28-acre park plenty of flowers and shade. The riverside setting, with Okayama-jō in the background, is delightful. The garden's popularity increases in peak season (April through August), but this is perhaps the largest park in Japan—you won't feel as hemmed in by crowds. Bus 20 (¥160) from Platform 2 in front of the JR station goes directly to Kōrakuen. ⊠ *1–5 Kōrakuen* ☎ *086/272–1148* ✉ *¥350* ☉ *Apr.–Sept., daily 7:30–6; Oct.–Mar., daily 8–5.*

Painted an unexpectedly attractive shadowy black, and set off dramatically by lead tiles and contrasting white vertical-slat shutters, **Okayama-jō** is known locally as U-jō ("Crow Castle"). Though the castle was built in the 16th century, only the "moon-viewing" outlying tower survived World War II. A ferroconcrete replica was painstakingly constructed to scale in 1966. The middle floors now house objects that represent the region's history, including a collection of armor and swords and a palanquin you can climb into to have your photo taken. Unlike many other castles with great views, this one has an elevator to take you up the six floors. A five-minute walk across the bridge brings you from the south exit of Kōrakuen to the castle. Boats are for rent on the river below. ⊠ *2–3–1 Marunouchi* ☎ *086/225–2096* ✉ *¥300* ☉ *Daily 9–5.*

The **Museum of Oriental Art** (Orient Bijutsukan) has on display at least 2,000 items from its impressive collection. Special exhibitions vary, but they generally show how Middle Eastern art reached ancient Japan via the Silk Road, and items range from Persian glass goblets and ornate mirrors to early stringed instruments. To reach the museum from the JR station, take the streetcar (¥140) bound for Higashiyama directly north for 10 minutes. The museum is across Asahi-gawa from Kōrakuen (about a 10-minute walk). ☎ *086/232–3636* ✉ *¥300* ☉ *Tues.–Sun. 9–5.*

9

Where to Stay & Eat

$$–$$$$ ✕ **Musashi.** Healthy, vegetable-laden Okayama-style cuisine is what you'll find at this delightful eatery. For lunch we recommend the unbeatable *bara-zushi teishoku,* or bits and pieces of sushi with vegetables set, a feast for only 1,000 yen. Musashi is a few minutes' walk straight out along the boulevard from the east exit of JR Okayama Station, on the left just past Tully's Coffee Shop. ✉ *1–7–18 Nodaya-chō, 700-0815* ☎ *086/222–3893* ▭ *AE, DC, MC, V* ☾ *Mon.–Sat. 10:30–2:30 and 5–10:30.*

$$$$ 🏨 **Hotel Granvia Okayama.** This large, luxurious hotel makes a superb, comfortable base for exploring the area. Bright white marble and luxurious wood dominate the lobby. The bilingual staff is cheerful and welcoming. The spacious rooms have the sheen of opulence. It's connected to the JR Okayama station—stay on the second (Shinkansen) level and follow the signs toward the south end. ✉ *1–5 Ekimoto-chō, Okayama-shi, Okayama-ken 700-8515* ☎ *086/234–7000* 🖶 *086/234–7099* ☎ *323 Western-style rooms, 3 Western-style suites, 2 Japanese-style suites* ♨ *7 restaurants, coffee shop, bar, shops* ▭ *AE, DC, MC, V.*

Kurashiki

★ *3 hrs 17 min west of Tōkyō or 1½ hrs west of Ōsaka by Shinkansen to Okayama, then 15 min by local train.*

From the 17th through the 19th centuries, this vital shipping port supplied Ōsaka with cotton, textiles, sugar, reeds, and rice. Those days are long past, and today Kurashiki thrives on income from tourism. If your view were limited to what you see just outside the station, you'd be forgiven for thinking Kurashiki is just another over-industrialized modern Japanese city. We strongly recommend, however, venturing 10 minutes on foot southeast of the station to Bikan Chiku, a neighborhood of canals, bridges, shops, restaurants, ryokans, and museums.

You can see most of Kurashiki's sights in a day, but it's worth staying longer, perhaps in a splendid old ryokan, to fully appreciate the time-machine aspect of the place. The white-stucco walls of old warehouses are accented smartly with charred pine-plank paneling and leaden-gray, burnt-brown, and carbon-black tiles crisscrossed with raised diagonals or squares of stark white mortar. These structures follow the willow-shaded canals and cobblestone streets linked by graceful stone bridges. The Bikan district is artfully lit up at night, and a stroll down the willow-draped canals after a sumptuous meal can be an unforgettably romantic journey.

Note that virtually the entire town shuts down on Monday.

Kurashiki Tourist Information Office (☎ 086/426–8681 🖶 086/422–0542 ☾ Apr.–Oct., daily 9–6; Nov.–Mar., daily 9–5:15), on the right outside the second-floor south exit from the JR station, open daily 9–7, has knowledgeable locals who provide useful maps and information. Another office is in the Bikan district, on the first bend of the canal, on the right a block past the Ōhara Museum of Art, just across the bridge from the

Ryokan Tsurugata. They sell tickets for the 20-minute canal-boat tours (summer only) for ¥300, and provide info on the museums located around the Bikan area.

What to See

★ **Ōhara Art Museum** (Ōhara Bijutsukan), in the old town, is a museum not to be missed. In 1930, noted art collector and founder Magosaburo Ōhara built this Parthenon-style building to house a collection of Western art with works by El Greco, Corot, Manet, Monet, Rodin, Gauguin, Picasso, Toulouse-Lautrec, and many others. They were shrewdly acquired for him by his friend Kojima Torajiro, a talented Western-style artist whom he dispatched to Europe for purchases. The museum is wonderfully compact, and can be appreciated in a single morning or an afternoon. Two wings exhibit Japanese paintings, tapestries, wood-block prints, and pottery—including works by Shoji Hamada and Bernard Leach—as well as modern and ancient Asian art, much of it also brought home from trips made by Torajiro at Ōhara's behest. ⊠ *1–15–Chūo* ☎ *086/422–0005* 🎫 *¥1,000* ⊙ *Tues.–Sun. 9–5.*

Where to Stay & Eat

$–$$$$ ✕ **Kiyū-tei.** For the best reasonably priced grilled steak in town, come to this attractive Kurashiki-style restaurant. The entrance to the restaurant is through a nearly hidden courtyard behind a gate across the street from the entrance to the Ōhara Museum. ⊠ *1–2–20 Chuo* ☎ *086/ 422–5140* 🝙 *AE, DC, MC, V* ⊙ *Closed Mon.*

$–$$$ ✕ **Hamayoshi.** Only three tables and a counter make up this intimate restaurant specializing in fish from the Seto Nai-kai. Sushi is one option; another is *mamakari,* a kind of vinegared sashimi sliced from a small fish caught in the Inland Sea. Other delicacies are *shako-ebi,* a type of spiny prawn, and lightly grilled *anago,* or sea eel. No English is spoken, but the owner will help you order and instruct you on how to enjoy the chef's delicacies. Hamayoshi is on the main street leading from the station, just before the Kurashiki Kokusai Hotel. ⊠ *Achi 2–19–30* ☎ *086/421–3430* 🝙 *No credit cards* ⊙ *Closed Mon.*

¢–$ ✕ **KuShuKuShu (9494).** Cool music and loud laughter can be heard from here when all else on the streets is locked up tight. Unwind to an eclectic mix of traditional white stucco, black wooden beams, bright lights, and jazz. Scores of tasty à la carte snacks, such as grilled meats or cheese and salami plates, and low-priced beer add to the fun. It's tucked along the east side of the covered Ebisu-dōri shopping arcade halfway between the station and Kanryu-ji. ⊠ *Achi 2–16–41* ☎ *086/421–0949* 🝙 *No credit cards* ⊙ *No lunch.*

$$$$ ✕🝤 **Ryokan Kurashiki.** Refurbished in a newly polished old-style splendor, this is perhaps the most luxurious place to submit yourself to the ritual of pleasures sought by wealthy Japanese at a traditional ryokan more than 300 years ago. Limited English is spoken, but for navigation of the deeper intricacies, you'll want a command of Japanese. Next door to all this opulence is an affordable coffee shop, Coffee Kan. ⊠ *4–1 Honmachi, Kurashiki, Okayama-ken 710-0054* ☎ *086/422–0730* 🖷 *086/ 422–0990* 🛏 *18 rooms, 9 with bath* ⚲ *Restaurant, Japanese baths* 🝙 *AE, DC, MC, V* 🍽 *MAP.*

$$$–$$$$ ✕🏨 **Ryokan Tsurugata.** Treat yourself to a stay—or perhaps just a fantastic dinner—at this charming 260-year-old ryokan. Rooms are intimate and secluded, but it's best to come for the fabulous—and filling—traditional dinners that incorporate the best local delicacies, from fish to fruit. The suite overlooking the 400-year old garden is especially captivating. The same friendly and hospitable folks who run the Kurashiki Kokusai Hotel (see below) own and manage the Ryokan Tsurugata, so some English is spoken and foreigners are welcome—and rather pampered. You'll need patience when requesting reservations, since the number of available rooms is limited and the demand is high. The hotel is across the bridge from the Ōhara Art Museum. ⊠ *1–3–15 Chūō, Kurashiki, Okayama-ken 710-0046* ☎ *086/424–1635* 🖷 *086/424–1650* 🛏 *11 Japanese-style rooms, 3 with private bath* ⚿ *Japanese baths* ▤ *AE, DC, MC, V* ⦿*l MAP.*

$$–$$$ 🏨 **Kurashiki Kokusai Hotel.** The town's best Western-style hotel welcomes guests with a black-tile lobby and dramatic Japanese wood-block prints. Ask for a room in the newer annex at the back of the building overlooking the garden. The location of the Kokusai is ideal—just around the corner from Bikan Chiku and the Ōhara Museum, a 10-minute walk on the main road leading southeast from the station. ⊠ *1–1–44 Chūō, Kurashiki, Okayama-ken 710-0046* ☎ *086/422–5141* 🖷 *086/ 422–5192* 🛏 *106 Western-style rooms, 4 Japanese-style rooms* ⚿ *Restaurant, bar, shop, free parking* ▤ *AE, DC, MC, V.*

¢ 🏨 **Toyoko Inn.** One of Kurashiki's newest and most popular hotels, this place offers great value a convenient three minutes away from the station's south exit. They have free Internet access. ⊠ *2–10–20 Achi, Kurashiki, Okayama-ken 710-0055* ☎ *086/430–1045* 🖷 *086/430–1046* 🛏 *154 Western-style rooms* ⚿ *Continental breakfast, in-room LAN sockets* ▤ *AE, DC, MC, V.*

WESTERN HONSHŪ ESSENTIALS

Transportation

BY AIR

Hiroshima Kūkō is the region's major airport, with many daily flights to Haneda Kūkō in Tōkyō and direct daily flights to Kagoshima, Okinawa, Sendai, and Sapporo. Other airports in Western Honshū—at Izumo, Tottori, and Yonago—have daily flights to Tōkyō. JAS and ANA fly out of Iwami Airport, which serves Hagi, Tsuwano, and Masuda, to Tōkyō and Ōsaka. For airline phone numbers, *see* Air Travel *in* Essentials.

Seven daily flights connect Hiroshima and Tōkyō's Haneda Kūkō, and there are flights to Kagoshima, on Kyūshū, and to Sapporo, on Hokkaidō. There are also many flights to Singapore, Hong Kong, Seoul, and other regional hubs.

BY BOAT & FERRY

Hiroshima is a ferry hub. Seto Nai-kai Kisen Company runs eight boats daily to Miyajima (¥1,460 one-way, ¥2,800 round-trip). Two important connections are to and from Matsuyama on Shikoku—16 hydrofoil ferries a day take one hour (¥6,000), and 12 regular ferries a day take three hours (¥4,340 first class, ¥2,170 second class); and to and from Beppu on Kyūshū; one daily, ¥8,500, three hours.

🛈 Boat & Ferry Information **Seto Nai-kai Kisen Company** ✉ 12–23 Ujinakaigan 1-chōme, Minami-ku, Hiroshima ☎ 082/253-1212 🖷 082/505-0134.

BY TRAIN

By far the easiest way to travel to Western Honshū and along its southern shore is by Shinkansen from Tōkyō, Kyōto, and Ōsaka. Major Shinkansen stops are Okayama, Hiroshima, and Shin-Yamaguchi. It takes approximately four hours on the Shinkansen to travel to Hiroshima from Tōkyō, less than half that from Ōsaka.

JR express trains run along the San-yō and San-in coasts, making a loop beginning and ending in Kyōto. Crossing from one coast to the other in Western Honshū requires traveling fairly slowly through the mountains. Several train lines link the cities on the northern Nihon-kai coast to Okayama, Hiroshima, and Shin-Yamaguchi on the southern coast.

Contacts & Resources

BANKS & EXCHANGE SERVICES

In Hiroshima: **Hiroshima Bank** (✉ 1–3–8 Kamiya-chō, Naka-ku, Hiroshima ☎ 082/247 5151).

In Hagi: **Yamaguchi Bank** (✉ 16–1 Higashi Tamachi, Hagi-shi, Yamaguchi-ken 758-0047 ☎ 0832/22–0380).

In Matsue: **San-in Godo Bank** (✉ 10 Sakana-chō, Matsue, Shimane ☎0120/31–5180); Shimane Bank, (✉2–35 Tōhon-chō ☎085/224–4000).

In Okayama: **Chugoku Bank** (✉ 1–15–20 Marunouchi, Okayama ☎ 086/223–3111).

In Yamaguchi City: **Yamaguchi Bank** (✉ JR Yamagcuhi Station Bldg, 2–5–5 Yamaguchi-chi, Yamaguchi-ken ☎ 08/922–1750).

EMERGENCIES

🛈 Ambulance ☎ 119. Police ☎ 110.

INTERNET

In Hiroshima, connected to the JR Hiroshima station, there's Futaba £ Café GIGA, 082/568–4792, offering 24 hour Internet access, games, and movies. Their downtown (Kamiya-chō) branch is also 24-hours; 082/542–5455.

In Matsue there is Wi-Fi and more at Café Diner Sign, 494–1 Asahi-machi, 085/231–0900.

For packages, the Higashi-machi post office is outside Hiroshima Station's south exit, open 9–5.

Points of Interest

SITES/AREAS	JAPANESE CHARACTERS
A-Bomb Dome (Gembaku Dōmu)	原爆ドーム
Children's Peace Monument (Genbaku-no-ko Zō)	原爆の子像
Flame of Peace (Heiwa no Tomoshibi)	平和の灯
Grand Gate (Ō-torii)	大鳥居
Go-jū-no-tō (Five-Storied Pagoda)	五重の塔
Hagi	萩
Hiroshima	広島
Hiroshima Castle (Hiroshima-jō)	広島城
Hiroshima National Peace Memorial Hall for the Atomic Bomb Victims (Kokuritsu Hiroshima Hibakusha Tsuitō Heiwa Kinen-kan)	原爆死没者追悼平和祈念館
Hiroshima Science and Cultural Museum for Children (Kodomo Bunka Kagakukan)	子供文化科学館
Hon-dōri	本道り
Horiuchi	堀内
Itsukushima Shrine (Itsukushima Jinja)	厳島神社
Izumo Taisha and Hinomisaki Point	出雲大社と日御碕
Jō-zan Gama (Jō-zan Kiln)	城山窯
Kōraku Garden (Kōrakuen)	後楽園
Kurashiki	倉敷
Lafcadio Hearn Memorial Hall (Koizumi Yakumo Kinenkan)	小泉八雲l記念館
Lafcadio Hearn Residence (Koizumi Yakumo Kyūkyo)	小泉八雲旧宅
Lake Shinji (Shinji-ko)	宍道湖
Louis C. Tiffany Garden Museum	ルイス C。. テイフアニー庭園美術館
Maria Seidō Chapel (Otometōge Maria Seidō)	乙女峠マリア聖堂
Matsue	松江
Matsue Castle (Matsue-jō)	松江城
Matsue English Garden	松江イングリッシュ　ガーデン
Meimei-an Teahouse	明々庵
Memorial Cenotaph (Gembaku Shibotsusha Irei-hi)	原爆死没者慰霊碑
Miyajima	宮島
Momijidani Kōen (Red Maple Valley Park)	紅葉谷公園

Museum of Oriental Art (Orient Bijutsukan)	岡山市立オリエント美術館
Nagomi-no-Sato Onsen	なごみの里温泉
Ōhara Art Museum (Ōhara Bijutsukan)	大原美術館
Old House of Ogai Mori	森鴎外旧宅・森鴎外記念館
Okayama	岡山
Okayama Castle (Okayama-jō)	岡山城
Peace Memorial Museum (Heiwa Kinen Shiryōkan)	平和記念資料館
Peace Memorial Park (Heiwa Kinen Kōen)	平和記念公園
Samurai Mansion (Buke Yashiki)	武家屋敷
The San-in Region	山陰地方
The San-yō Region	山陽地方
Shizuki Park (Shizuki Kōen)	指月公園
Shukkei-en	縮景園
Taikodani Inari Jinja (Taiko Valley Inari Shrine)	太鼓谷稲荷神社
Tamachi Mall	田町モール
Tsuwano	津和野
Yamaguchi	山口

RESTAURANTS

Aoki	あおき
Fujita-ya	藤田屋
Hamayoshi	浜吉
Hiroshima Station	広島駅
Kakifune Kanawa (Kanawa Oyster Boat)	かき船かなわ
Kawakyō	川京
Kiyū-tei	亀遊亭
KuShuKuShu (9494)	くしゅくしゅ
Musashi	武蔵
Nakamura	中村
Ōhashi (soba shop)	大橋
Okonomi Mura (Village of Okonomiyaki)	お好み村
Suishin	酔心
Tojima-zushi	とじま寿司
Yakumo-an	八雲庵
Yuki	遊亀

9

HOTELS

ANA Hotel Hiroshima	広島全日空ホテル
Comfort Hotel Hiroshima	コンフォートホテル広島
Hagi Tanaka Hotel	萩たなかホテル
Hokumon Yashiki	北門屋敷
Hotel Granvia Hiroshima	ホテルグランヴィア広島
Hotel Granvia Okayama	ホテルグランヴィア岡山
Iwasō Ryokan	岩惣
Kurashiki Kokusai Hotel	倉敷国際ホテル
Minshuku Kamoi	民宿カモ井
Naniwa issui	なにわ一水
Ryokan Jūkei-sō	聚景荘
Ryokan Kurashiki	旅館倉敷
Ryokan Terazuya	旅館寺津屋
Ryokan Tsurugata	旅館鶴形
Sunroute Kokusai Hotel Yamaguchi	サンルート国際ホテル山口
Toyoko Inn	松江ワシントンホテル
Toyoko Inn (Kurashiki Eki Minamiguchi)	東横イン倉敷駅南口
Toyoko Inn (Matsue Ekimae)	東横イン松江駅前
Tsuwano Lodge	津和野ロッジ
Urban City Hotel Hasegawa	ビジネスホテル長谷川
Wakasagi-no-Yado	民宿若さぎの宿

Shikoku

WORD OF MOUTH

"I really liked Matsuyama on Shikoku Island. There's a famous hot spring there, but what I really liked was its laid-back feel, plus there's an area of densely packed restaurants and bars for some nice nightlife."

—bkkmei

"The best place we have seen (I have been there with my daughter Letizia) is Naoshima Island with its incredible modern-art museums and open-air installations."

—Gianni

By Joshua
Bisker

LEAVE MODERNIZED JAPAN BEHIND: cross the sea to rushing rivers, sky-high mountains, historic villages, funky cities, local craftworks, brilliant summer festivals, and a thousand terrific sights found only on Shikoku. Child-rearing and small scale, back-breaking agriculture dominate life below the factory-ridden northern coast, but you'll find diverse cuisines, festivals, special products, and even various dialects of Japanese thanks to a long history outside the country's mainstream.

If you didn't know Shikoku's key products were textiles, fish, lumber, and ships, you'd swear they were grizzled old farmers and tiny, adorable children. Every autumn, country people in their sixties, seventies, eighties, and even nineties toil through the harvest, while herds of school children bobble through their rice fields in matching yellow hats. In summer, white-robed *o-hemro-san* stand out against the green: pilgrims walking Shikoku's famous pilgrimage path, an 88-temple circuit established by the Buddhist saint Kōbō Daishi in the 8th century. It takes two or three months to walk, and you can ease a pilgrim's burden by offering *o-settai,* a few coins or some other charity, as he walks the road to enlightenment.

Shikoku's simple lifestyle may feel exotic to a traveler, but from the local perspective it's visitors who appear exotic and strange. Meeting foreigners still verges on the fantastical for people here, and outside Shikoku's four major cities you may be treated more like a celebrity (or a space alien) than a faceless tourist. Connecting with people will be more personal here than in Tōkyō or Kansai, and every encounter can be an adventure: locals on Shikoku will actually shout out loud when they see you—Ah! Gaijin-san!—and welcome you into their towns.

ORIENTATION & PLANNING

Orientation

Shikoku has four prefectures—Kagawa in the northeast, Tokushima below it, Ehime in the west, and Kōchi along the entire bottom shore. Your trip will almost certainly start at one of the island's northern cities: coming from Kansai your most likely access is via Takamatsu in eastern Shikoku; from Hiroshima or Western Honshu it's Matsuyama in western Shikoku; in both cases you'll want to move through or around the mountains of central Shikoku before gaining the other coast. Use the cities for access to small towns and natural getaways.

This chapter assumes you begin with Takamatsu and finish heading out toward Hiroshima by bus, ferry, or bicycle. Coming through the other way you'd miss the nicer part of the cycling trip, but you end up in convenient Kansai.

Takamatsu & Eastern Shikoku

In Kagawa and Tokushima prefectures, natural spectacles like the giant whirlpools in Tokushima and artistic attractions like Takamatsu's Noguchi Garden Museum springboard you to small towns nearby.

CLOSE UP

Top Reasons to Visit

EXPLORE THE SCENERY

Raft down the river Yoshinogawa, hike up craggy Mt. Tsurugi, and swim in Kōchi's crystal seas. Walk through Takamatsu's traditional Ritsurin-kōen, Kōchi's botanical gardens, the Noguchi sculpture park at Yashima, and an island of art on Naoshima. Best of all, bicycle across the Seto Inland Sea on bridges stretching all the way to Honshu!

DO AS THE NATIVES DO

Roll up your sleeves and shine your dancing shoes—discover Japan by doing. Try a martial art at Matsuyama's Budōkan, make soba noodles in the Iya Valley, dye fabrics and fingers near Tokushima, and learn a two-step or two in time for the summer dances.

FESTIVAL FRENZY

Festivals large and small mark every weekend between April and October. Mud festivals, fire festivals, lantern festivals, and boat festivals lead up to bigger events—battles between gargantuan mobile shrines, mountain-top fireworks displays, demon-bull parades, and—biggest in the nation—the summer dance festivals Yosakoi and Awa Odori.

GET PERSONAL

You might be the first foreigner this old farmer has ever spoken with, so make his day! He'll make yours, too, and you're guaranteed a good photo, a great story, and an armful of juicy, hand-picked mikans.

THE REAL JAPAN

You'll hear a hundred times that Shikoku is "the real Japan," but decide the reason for yourself: is it time-forgotten towns like Uchiko and Nishi-Iya, unique landmarks like Dōgo Onsen or Kompira-san, or just the untold acres of rice?

Central Shikoku

Mile-high mountains kept central Shikoku off travel itineraries for centuries, and the area has escaped the taints of homogenization and heavy industry. Come visit two great escapes: the forest paradise of Iya—gorges and tiny villages best explored on a rafting trip down the vibrant Yoshino river—and rowdy, fun-loving Kōchi City near the sun-kissed southern surf.

10

Matsuyama & Western Shikoku

Matsuyama mixes small-town character with an exciting urban landscape. Come for Japan's best eating, fashion, and in-city sights outside of Honshū. See the superb clifftop castle and dreamlike Dōgo Onsen, the oldest exploited hot spring in Japan, and explore a melting pot of cuisines in the city's downtown before venturing into the surrounding mountain villages.

Planning

Shikoku's rewards lie off the beaten path and involve the challenges of a road less traveled. Disabled access is limited, and public transportation imperfect. English competence is minimal, but locals will be very excited to socialize with you. Avoid scaring them off with too much Eng-

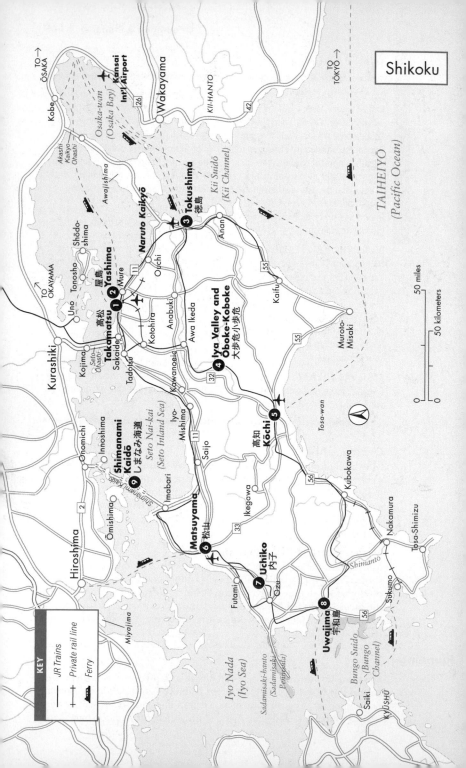

On the Menu

EVERY CORNER OF SHIKOKU has a special dish, cuisine, or crop. Ehime is famous for *mikan*—clementines—and between November and March you can't walk a country mile without a farmer handing you a bag. Ehime is also the nation's main cultivator of *tai*, or red snapper; tai-meshi is rice that's cooked with chunks of the fish, usually in a flaming tin pot. Kagawa-ken's *sanuki-udon* is widely thought to be the nation's best, and Tokushima-ken's delicious *Iya-soba*, made from the valley's hearty strand

of buckwheat flour, is especially tasty if you've pounded the dough yourself at a *soba dojo*. Naruto grows the best *satsumaimo*, purple Japanese sweet potatoes, and *imo-taki* are popular across the island in autumn: potato baking parties for watching the full moon. The most renowned cuisine styles are in Kōchi: tosa-ryōri and sawachi-ryōri, different ways of serving enormous amounts of delicious fish, particularly slices of lightly seared *katsuo*.

lish. "Hello, what's your name?" is the best way to begin integrating with people, and kids may be better in-roads than their shy parents. They'll be tickled to finally use the English they're studying in school.

The Best of Times

Shikoku's unspoiled scenery offers some perfect locations to bask in the fleeting glory of cherry blossoms in spring and foliage in autumn. Summer is festival time throughout the country, but Shikoku has the best of the bunch: the epic dance festivals **Yosakoi** in Kōchi, held August 9–12, and Tokushima's **Awa Odori**, August 12–15.

Concerning Restaurants & Hotels

Three of Shikoku's four main cities—Takamatsu, Kōchi, and especially Matsuyama—specialize in a variety of cuisines at very reasonable prices. In smaller towns expect places to close at 8 PM. Accommodations on Shikoku range from *ryokan* and *minshuku* in old homes to international hotels and lavish onsen resorts. Unless otherwise noted, all hotel rooms have private baths, phones, and air-conditioning. Large city and resort hotels serve Western and Japanese food. Reservations are essential during major festivals, and Japanese holiday periods.

For a short course on accommodations in Japan, *see* Lodging *in* Essentials.

WHAT IT COSTS In yen					
	$$$$	$$$	$$	$	¢
RESTAURANTS	over 3,000	2,000–3,000	1,000–2,000	800–1,000	under 800
HOTELS	over 22,000	18,000–22,000	12,000–18,000	8,000–12,000	under 8,000

Restaurant prices are per person for a main course at dinner. Hotel prices are for a double room with private bath, excluding service and tax.

Transportation Station

Trains and buses are the main modes of travel, though in rural areas they can be infrequent and irregular. Missing a train doesn't always mean just waiting for the next one: the next one might not come until April. Check schedules and find out when taxi rides between local-access and express-access train stations will save you time. Ask Tourist Information Centers (not JR ticket windows) to help you plan. Driving is a great way to explore the old rural countryside.

AIR TRAVEL All Nippon Airways (ANA) and Japan Airlines (JA) provide domestic flights to and from Shikoku's four major cities: Takamatsu, Kōchi, Matsuyama, and Tokushima.

BOAT TRAVEL Cities and a number of small ports have ferry or hydrofoil access from Tōkyō, Kansai, Western Honshū, and Kyūshū. International ferry routes run between Matsuyama, Korea, and Russia.

BUS TRAVEL Buses link the major cities and provide access to far-off coastal points and mountains, and offer direct travel between Matsuyama and Tokushima or Kōchi. Short-range and overnight buses also connect to cities on Honshu.

CAR TRAVEL Shikoku's narrow roads present challenges, but having your own transportation provides an escape into the island's mountainous interior and small towns everywhere.

TRAIN TRAVEL Shikoku is belted around by a single rail track with branches going off to the interior. Since it is just a single track in most places, expect irregular schedules and long waits for local trains as express ones hurtle by.

Visitor Information

Major tourist information centers in Shikoku's main cities could offer the only skilled English speakers you meet, so use them for advice, transportation info, reservations, recommendations, and local news. Community events and festivals are happening all the time: a one-horse town over the ridge may be celebrating its four-hundredth annual lantern festival tomorrow night, but you'll never know unless you ask.

A nationwide service for English-language assistance or travel information is available daily 9–5. Dial toll-free for information. When using a yellow, blue, or green public phone (do not use red phones), insert a ¥10 coin, which will be returned.

English-language hotline (☎ 0120/444–800 or 0088/224–800). **Kōchi** (☎ 088/882–1634). **Matsuyama** (☎ 089/931–3914). **Takamatsu** (☎ 087/851–2009). **Tokushima** (☎ 088/656–3303).

TAKAMATSU & EASTERN SHIKOKU

Takamatsu

❶ *1 hr from Okayama by JR.*

Coming to Shikoku almost certainly means a trip through easy-going Takamatsu, where chatty locals bustle through the arcades and dozens of bicycles rest casually over bright NO BICYCLE PARKING signs along the boardwalk. Despite a relaxed atmosphere, Takamatsu hums with urban verve; a short walk down the city's wide, sunlit boulevards brings you to funky shops, artsy cafés, exciting nightlife, and a bevy of dazzling cultural sights and museums.

Getting Around

You're most likely to set off from Takamatsu's northern tip, where the JR station meets bus platforms and a ferry port just north of the grassy, highly missable castle park. Two buildings glitter in the open square, the **Signal Tower,** with cafés on the first floor and free Internet on the third, and the plush and popular ANA Clement Hotel. A squat **Information Office** (☎ 087/851–2009) is great for maps, train tables, and advice; some staff speak English quite well. If you need more info, try **IPAL,** a cultural exchange office in the central **Chūō-kōen** (ask for the map of their favorite lunch spots).

Bike rental is available near the JR station. Outside a small police headquarters is an elevator down: for ¥100 you've got yourself a bike! A bicycle is the best way to explore Takamatsu. It will save you an enormous amount of time walking or waiting in the spread-out cityscape.

What to See

The number one attraction in Takamatsu is the great garden park **Ritsurin-kōen**, a breathtaking and peaceful retreat from the world around. Though not officially recognized as one of Japan's three best gardens, Ritsurin-kōen offers a more intimate and immersive experience than the others. Leave yourself a few hours to explore, and though you get a handy trail map as you enter, remember to walk your own path while you explore. Just around the next bend are great surprises: an embankment of irises in full bloom in June; a sea of ferns surrounding a thatch-roofed lookout; a thousand turtles surfacing in a pond to say hello; a pavilion serving bitter green tea; and koi the size of torpedoes eating breadsticks and fish food out of your fingertips. This 120-acre haven was once the summer estate of nobility, and though the ancient clans have crumbled with time, the park has lost none of its magic or beauty. ☎ 087/833–7411 ☜ ¥400 ◷ June–Aug., daily 7–7; Sept.–May, daily 7–5.

Just south of the decaying castle park, the **Kagawa-ken History Museum** (Kagawa-ken Rekishi Hakubutsukan) emphasizes interactive learning with hands-on exhibits—everything from sword-making to woodblock-printing to the craft of producing (and playing with) Japanese toys—and an engaging permanent collection. You won't need a lick of Japanese to enjoy walking in a Neolithic hut, crawling with a magnifying glass on the giant photo map of Kagawa, dressing up in full samurai armor and lush ceremonial kimonos. The museum staff will help you don the costumes and will take a Polaroid picture for you, and it's all included in the entry fee. ⊠ 5–5 Tamamo cho ☎ 087/822–0002 ☜ ¥400 ◷ Tues.–Sun. 9–4:30, Fri. until 7.

Where to Eat

$$$ ╳ **Uo Ichiba.** The simmering energy of a cantina thrives in this upscale three-floor restaurant. Flags and banners hang above tanks full of eels

10

Chichu Art Museum

THE RIDE FROM Takamatsu to Naoshima isn't long, but you'll step off the ferry onto a very distant shore. Radical art and architecture intersect with windswept hills and heavy forests, and outdoor sculpture gardens, modern concrete museums, and labyrinthine underground exhibition halls offer endless surprises in wood, metal, canvas, stone, and oil. The mission of the **Chichu Art Museum**, completed in 2004, is to re-explore the relationship between nature and humanity through art, and the **Benessee Art Site**, a huge project with works of art in and around the island, and **Benessee House**, containing permanent indoor exhibits, will give you plenty to explore for yourself. Stay in a *ryokan* or in the art-filled Benessee hotels designed by Tadao Andō. The island is nothing like the rest of Shikoku, but then it's not quite like anything else in the world. ⊕ www.naoshima-is.co.jp.

and fish waiting to be selected for your plate, and the chefs do a dazzling job preparing this freshest, most sumptuous seafood. Other Japanese fare is also top-notch. Dinner is lively, but the set menus at lunch are considerably cheaper. Located just across from Kawaroku Hotel off Marugame-machi arcade. ⊠ *Hyaken-machi 9–5* ☎ *087/826–2056.*

$$–$$$ ✕ **Tenkatsu.** Find your favorite fish in the pool at Tenkatsu and it will be on your plate a minute later. Forgo the tatami tables to sit close to the action at the big black countertop. The interior design doesn't overwhelm, but the food makes up for it. Plastic displays and a picture menu help you choose the dish (choosing the fish is rather more intuitive). Nabe pots in autumn and winter are house favorites. ⊠ *Nishizumi Hiroba, Hyōgo-machi* ☎ *087/821–5380* 🗖 *AE, DC, MC, V.*

★ **$$** ✕ **Ginza Salon.** This lovely little *shokudo*-cum-bistro balances a swanky-chic atmosphere with cuisine so comforting that you'll imagine it's always been your favorite place. The food has all the same elements but none of the tired tastes of normal Japanese cuisine, and the antique tables and plush chairs create a perfect setting for their delicious lunch plates, colorful dinner menu, and excellent handmade pastries. The reasonable prices, as well as the bus girl's silly French maid uniform, will make you wish you could lunch here every day. Look for a colorful splash of chairs outside the entrance in the northernmost arcade. ⊠ *Hyōgo-machi 2–4–11* ☎ *087/823–7065* ⊘ *Daily 11 AM–1 AM.*

$ ✕ **King's Yawd.** It's the best Jamaican place in town, but maybe that goes without saying. The jerk chicken and tropical cocktails are everything you didn't hope to find on this side of the globe. King's Yawd becomes a popular nightspot late into almost every evening, but without getting too loud. Watch Jamaican movies projected onto the red and yellow walls, and spend live-music or party nights dancing under a giant tapestry of Haile Selassie. To get here, go south through the arcade Maruga-machi. When it hits the big road Kawara-machi, cross, go left, and look out for the glowing Jamaican flag. ⊠ *4th fl. of Kawara-machi Bldg., Kawara-machi-dōri 1–9–9* ☎ *087/837–2660* ⊘ *Closed Sun.*

Where to Stay

★ $$$–$$$$ ✕▦ **Kiyomi-sanso Hanajyukai.** Over-look city and sea from a flower-covered mountainside at Hanajyukai from the luxurious warmth of a rooftop onsen. This lush resort caters to rich Japanese tourists, and they know how to make you feel like royalty. All rooms are Japanese-style and include breakfast and an elegant dinner. A bit far from the city center, away from Yashima. ⊠ *3–5–10 Nishitakara-chō* ☎ *087/ 861–5580* 🖷 *087/834–9912* ⇱ *48 Japanese-style rooms* ⚴ *Restaurant, cable TV* ▭ *AE, DC, MC, V* ⎮⦿⎮ *MAP.*

> ### SKIKOKU BLUES
>
> **Benny's.** For a change of pace (and music), go upstairs to Benny's. Sofas encourage mingling with the friendly clientele, and local bands play most nights of the week (Benny himself plays blues harmonica, and will happily solo for you). All drinks are ¥500. ⊠ *6th fl. of Kawara-machi Bldg., just above King's Yawd.*

$$$–$$$$ ▦ **ANA Hotel Clement Takamatsu.** Sparkling in the sky before the JR station, Hotel Clement looks like paradise. If Western-style rooms and super-easy city access are priorities, then this is the place for you. It's part of a national chain of luxury hotels with all the trappings: modern, bright rooms, gift shops and cafés, restaurants, and a faux-classy skybar. Strangely, there's no onsen or bath, but (strangely again) there is a Shintō shrine on the second floor. ⊠ *1 1 Hamamo-chō* ☎ *087/811– 1111* 🖷 *087/800–2222* ⊕ *www.anahotels.com/eng/index.html* ⇱ *500 rooms* ⚴ *Salon, rooftop garden, karaoke* ▭ *AE, DC, MC, V.*

$ ▦ **Hotel Kawaroku/Elstage.** The nice rooms might surprise you after seeing the ugly brick exterior, but you'll forgive a place with a rough history: in operation since 1877 but destroyed during World War II, the hotel was rebuilt in a distinctly modern, "ugly" style. The interior more or less escaped this second devastation (excepting the gruesome lobby and unsmiling reception staff), and the rooms are spacious and comfortable. The large Japanese-style rooms look prettier than Western ones. Steer clear of the recent annex, Her Stage, a ghastly business hotel. ⊠ *1–2 Hyakken-chō* ☎ *087/821–5666* 🖷 *087/821–7301* ⇱ *21 Western-style rooms, 49 Japanese-style rooms* ⚴ *Restaurant, cable TV, Japanese baths* ▭ *AE, V.*

10

Yashima

❷ *20 min by JR or Kotoden tram from Takamatsu.*

An east-lying district of Takamatsu, Yashima is home to two captivating attractions: the historical preserve **Shikoku Mura** and the **Isamu Noguchi Garden Museum,** a superb sculpture park (technically in a neighboring district, Mure). Local Kotoden trains leave Kawara machi Terminal and head to Yashima and Yakuri (two stops farther down). Coming by car or bike from the **Chūō-kōen,** go east along Route 11 past the love hotels and pachinko parlors and make a left at the McDonald's to arrive at Shikoku Mura. Each way takes between 25 and 30 minutes.

★ Bamboo groves conceal a trove of ancient treasures at the mountainside park **Shikoku Mura.** Dozens of historical buildings and bridges from around Shikoku have been brought to this expansive forest park and lovingly restored. English information boards provide a surprisingly interesting history for each location, and a web of well-kept pathways lets you wander freely without feeling either shepherded or lost. It's a large place, and if you go as a group a good meeting spot is **Shikoku Mura Gallery,** nestled on the hillside above an ancient sugar mill. The gallery has a lovely collection, with works by Picasso, Chagall, Monet, and literary notable Natsume Soseki. ☎ 087/843–3111 ☞ ¥800 ☉ Apr.–Oct., daily 8:30–5; Nov.–Mar., daily 8:30-4:30.

NEED A BREAK? The udon restaurant and café at the bottom of the mountain are good for a pick-me-up. Both are in restored old buildings, a riverside house with a waterwheel and a British colonial.

Fodor'sChoice
★
Isamu Noguchi Garden Museum (Isamu Noguchi Teien Hakubutsukan). This extensive sculpture park is a wonderland in stone, and being in the embrace of Noguchi's creativity is an unforgettable experience. The sensitivity, creativity, and playfulness of the Japanese-American sculptor is so powerful here that you'll feel as if he is guiding you through himself. The site was once his studio and home, and now holds hundreds of works in stone and other mediums. Visiting requires at least two weeks' advance reservation, which you can do through their Web site. To get here, take a 10-minute taxi ride from Yashima Station or go two stops farther on the Kotoden Line to Yakuri before hopping in a cab. ✉ 3–5–19 Mure, Mure-chō ☎ 087/870–1500 ☎ 087/845–0505 ⊕ www. isamunoguchi.or.jp/index.htm ☞ ¥2,100 ☉ Tues., Thurs., and Sat. at 10, 1, and 3 by appointment.

Kotohira

55 min by JR or Kotoden tram from Takamatsu.

The first half of your climb up the sacred mountain is a chaos of vendors' wares and tourists' chatter. But the final half of the ascent is filled with the rewards of pilgrimage: the echo of your footsteps, a splash of blue sea through a break in the trees, a hummed *konnichiwa* from above you on the trail. The stairways leading up the mountain Kompira-san are famous—785 steps to the impressive main shrine and 583 more to the final lookout—and finishing the climb, breathless at the summit, you will see why this path to enlightenment is so well worn.

On the way down you may want to rest at the Shōin, an Edo-period hall with artifacts and screens painted by Okyo Maruyama; ¥400. When you reach the bottom, congratulate yourself with a tour through the **Kinryō Sake Museum and Brewery,** marked by an enormous sake bottle fountaining into the street in front of the temple stairs: sample the wares for ¥100 a shot.

The town sits almost smack in the middle of Shikoku and it's easy to access: Takamatsu is probably the closest city but you can also go directly to Kōchi. Change trains at Tadōtsu for Matsuyama or Awa-Ikeda for Tokushima or Iya. Kotohira is an express stop on the JR lines and the terminus of Takamatsu's Kotoden local line, and the town's stations are down the road from each other. Ditch your bags in coin lockers before you head toward the mountain.

Tokushima

❸ *1 hr 10 min by JR from Takamatsu and from Awa Ikeda.*

Tokushima is a trove of fabulous sights and unique local attractions. Most visitors stay near the city's center, but the best place to be is **Naruto,** an oceanside townlet famous for **giant whirlpools** that churn and thunder in the rocky straights below the cliffs. Nearby, the ambitious **Otsuka Museum** attracts huge crowds for its bizarre and breathtaking archive of the world's art. In surrounding hamlets you can try your hand at local crafts like **indigo-dyeing** and **paper-making** as they've done it for centuries, and back in the city proper you'll learn to dance the **Awa Odori,** either in a special performance hall or with the million others dancing the streets every summer during the **Awa Odori Festival.** The major sights can be covered in a well-planned day or two. After an overnight in Tokushima you can be in the mountains and gorges of **Iya** the next evening.

Getting Around

Tokushima makes up for an inconvenient public transport system with **TOPIA** (⊠ 6th fl. of Clement Plaza above JR Station ☎ 088/656–3033 ⊕ www.topia.ne.jp/e_index/e_index.htm ⊙ Daily 10–6), the best tourist information center in western Japan. The English-speaking staff provide bus schedules, train times, tide calendars (necessary for seeing the whirlpools at their best), price charts, and good advice. A solid attack plan will keep you from losing time to infrequent trains and buses. Taxi rides will save you hours of waiting.

What to See

The thunderous roar of **giant whirlpools** fills the cliffs around the Naruto Kaikyō (the Naruto Straits), splitting the peaceful sky and green mountainsides asunder with a chaos of furious, frothing sea. See the whirlpools from a glass-bottomed gantry 45 meters above the water or from the deck of a tour boat, down in the belly of the beast.

The walkway, called **uzu-no-michi,** gives a great view of the pools and the seacoast, but when you see the water you'll wish you had chosen the boats. There are a few companies with different-size boats and marginally different prices (¥1,500–¥2,500), but all the rides are exhilarating.

Two of the best boat tours are Wonder Naruto and Aqua Eddy. Which you choose will depend on when you arrive, and what time the pools reach their active peak on that day. Check www.uzusio.com/sche.html for schedules. The changing tide is what forms the whirlpools, forcing the sea through the rocky bottleneck, so any day has two prime hours to see the action. The straights froth angrily for a good hour on each end of the peaks. Buses leave Tokushima for Naruto on the hour 9–3, taking 63 minutes and costing ¥690; the return has more varied times, so check the schedule. The boat quay at Naruto Kan-kōkō is a few stops before the end of the line, about an eight-minute walk from uzu-no-michi. There are also trains to Naruto Station; catch a bus or taxi from there to the coast.

★ From **uzu-no-michi** a boardwalk rings the high coastline; walk south for 10 minutes and you'll come to the **Otsuka Bijutsukan** (Otsuka Museum of Art), a strange and ambitious new museum. It's the largest exhibition space

Dancing the Shikoku

THE AWA ODORI FESTIVAL happens every summer over Ōbon, festival of the dead, and if you miss it you can still get a dose at the **Awa Odori Kaikan.** *Odori* means "dance," and at the Kaikan silk-robed professionals perform the famous local step nightly. But shine your shoes: when the troupe leader starts talking to the audience, he's looking for volunteers. Everyone will be thrilled to see you try, so stand up! They'll give you some fragmented English directions and thankfully, it's a very easy dance. The first volunteering round is for men, the second for women; each has different steps to learn. You might get a prize for participating, and one special award goes to the biggest fool on the floor—this honor is a staple of the festival, and it's not always the foreigners who win.

The best show is at 8 PM. Arrive early and browse the gift shop or treat yourself to a ropeway ride up the mountain for a lovely view of the city. ⊠ 20, 2-chōme Shinmachibashi ☎ 088/611-1611 ⊡ Afternoon dance ¥500, evening dance ¥700. Ropeway ¥1,000 round-trip. ⊙ Gift shop daily 9–6. Performances at 2, 3, 4, and 8; also at 11 on weekends. Closed 2nd and 4th Weds. of month

---

in Japan, but you'll only see Western art here . . . sort of. A thousand great works of art have been reproduced on ceramic tiles and arranged by era and location. Well-known and obscure pieces are on display, and the collection is far more than a Greatest Hits of Art. Surround yourself with a room full of Rubens alters, stand alone in the Sistine Chapel or before Picasso's *Guernica,* or wander through replicated French churches, Greek tombs, a banquet hall from Pompeii, and countless other sights you thought were one-of-a-kind. And this is the difficulty of Otsuka; these sights are one-of-a-kind, and seeing them here can be unnerving, as you feel moved by the power of a thousand stunning pictures of pictures. It is a surreal and stunning experience. ⊠*Located in National Park in Naruto-chō* ☎088/687-3737 ⊕ *www.o-museum.or.jp* ⊡¥3,150; children (through high-school age) ¥510. ⊙ Tues.–Sun., 9:30–5, last entry at 4.

At Ai-no-Yakata, **The House of Indigo,** try the ancient craft of dyeing cloth in cauldrons of blue-black, pungent indigo. Someone at the desk will show you a price chart for items—cotton handkerchiefs are only ¥500, silk scarves close to ¥2,000. Towels come out splendidly, but you have to ask for the separate price chart (the word is *ta-o-ru*). It's fun, and you'll be delighted with what you make. Snoop around the 400-year-old craft center when you're finished. One of the proprietors performs daily on the *shaku-hachi,* a thick bodied wooden flute, and he'll play anytime you ask. From Tokushima Station hop a 20-minute bus to Higashi Nakatomi. Walk down the hill behind you and follow the indigo signs. ☎ 088/692-6317 ⊡ ¥300 ⊙ Daily 9–5.

Trek out to the Awagami **Hall of Awa Handmade Paper** (Awa Washi Dentō) to make your own postcards and browse their phenomenal gift shop; it goes from sheets of softer-than-silk wrapping paper to peerless fans and parasols. It's also something of a pain to get to. Trains to Awa-

Yamakawa Station take an hour, then walk 15 minutes to the hall. ☎ 0883/42–6120 ➱ ¥300 ⊙ Tues.–Sun., 9–5.

Where to Stay & Eat

Tokushima is well served by slick bars and restaurants; the two best are easily Wine and its upstairs neighbor Shanghai Fang. For lodging in the city itself, your best bet is at one of the chain hotels near the **Awa Odori Kaikan** or the station. The expensive resort hotels like Tokushima Grand Hotel Kairakuen and even the Washington Hotel feel old and worn-out, and they don't deal well with non-Japanese-speaking guests.

$$–$$$ ✕ **Chinese Kitchen Shanghai Fang.** Shanghai Fang offers a funkier mixture of spaces and environs in a smaller space than **Wine's** with tons of character. Wine wins for cuisine, but you'll come for the feel as much as the meal. Ask to look around, and you'll want to sit at each table you see; perhaps you'll take the tall and skinny private room beneath the stairwell, the sumptuously secluded love seat beside the door, a thick dark-wood table on flagstones, or the sunken floor tables ringed by water and rocks. The ¥3,000 course is not revolutionary, but still delicious. ☎ 088/624–5838.

$$–$$$ ✕ **Wine.** Excellent Japanese cuisine balances traditional with experimental. Across three floors are dozens of different spaces to sit: cushioned floor nooks, sit-down tables, private latticed-in chambers, and an astonishing variety of styles that never clash in this superbly decorated restaurant. They'll help you decipher the Japanese menu, but you can't go wrong with the ¥2,500 set course; eight different dishes give a wide range of eats and even the staples—sashimi, salads—are excellent. ⊠ Konya-machi, Kinenman Part II ☎ 088/624–5838 ☰ MC, V.

★ $$$$ ▦ **Renaissance Resort Naruto.** Stretching along the sandy beaches at Naruto, this new Renaissance Resort is peerless for comfort, service, luxury, and access to the sights and surroundings of Naruto. Pick your favorite room from a variety of Western and Japanese arrangements with unique character; the Resort's Japanese Web site has pictures of every room. Ask to be beachside and the sound of the surf will lull you to sleep. In daylight you'll forgo swimming in the rough waves, but there's a fun restaurant on the dunes. ⊠ 16–45 Oge Tosadomariura, 772-0053 ☎ 088/687–2580 ✍ 088/687–2211 ⊕ www.renaissance-naruto.com ◁ 208 ♨ Pool, 2 hot springs ☰ AE, D, MC, V.

$$ ▦ **Tokyu Inn.** Tokushima's hotel trade thrives on one annual festival event, so rooms are abundant but lacking in flair. There's nothing terribly special about this straightforward service hotel, but it's comfy and clean. ⊠ 1–24 Moto-machi ☎ 088/626–0109 ✍ 088/626–0686 ⊕ www.tokyuhotels.co. jp/en/TI/TI_TOKUS/index.html ◁ 148 rooms ☰ AE, D, MC, V.

CENTRAL SHIKOKU: IYA VALLEY & KŌCHI

Iya Valley & Ōboke-Koboke Gorges

❹ 45 min by train from Awa-Ikeda, 1½ hrs by car from Tokushima or Matsuyama.

Fodor's Choice

★

At the exact center of Shikoku the old roads yield a hidden paradise. The roaring river Yoshino-gawa cuts through tall verdant mountains and the gray stone gorges **Ōboke** and **Koboke,** while over the next ridge, ancient **vine bridges** sway high above the thundering turquoise spray. Dive into the wilderness or relax in the area's fabulous hot springs and spend the night in a luxurious spa hotel. Trek deeper into the **Iya Valley** and hike the sloping sides of Mt. Tsurugi, or try your hand at making delicious **Iya soba,** tōfu, or a number of local crafts.

Getting Around

The Yoshino-gawa is an amazing river, and it's easy to access and enjoy. Express trains go to **Awa-Ikeda** in northern Tokushima-ken, where local trains run south to **Ōboke Station.** Once there, local buses can bring you to the sights, but going by car is best. Take Shikoku's big northern highways to the Kawanoe interchange and follow signs toward Kōchi. Stay on the Kōchi Expressway until exiting at the Ōtoyo IC (if you're coming from Kōchi to begin with, go straight to Ōtoyo). Follow Route 32 through Ikeda to Ōboke for rafting and sightseeing.

What to See

Fodor's Choice ★ Hitting the wild river and rocky gorges should be your top priority, and doing it couldn't be more hassle-free: **rafting** and **canyoning** trips are run by **Happy Raft,** a friendly adventure-tour group on the best river in Japan. The international staff are fun-loving but safety-conscious, and they'll show you the river in a way that's great for first-timers and veterans alike. Spend a wet and happy morning here before moving on through the valley, or try a longer combination trip—you can overnight at the inexpensive Happy Guest House in between. Half-day trips start at ¥7,000, full days from ¥13,500, and prices are reasonable for combo rafting and canyoning trips with lodging and dining included. ⊕ *www. outdoorjapan.com/gear_services/outdoorad_happy_raft.html.*

Kazura-Bashi. Iya's most famous features are the three vine bridges, **kazura-bashi,** that span the gorges, one 20 minutes from Ōboke station and a pair near Mt. Tsurugi. The bridges date back 800 years, to the aftermath of the momentous Gempei War, when the defeated Taira clan fled to these valleys after losing the throne and shogunate to the rival Minamoto clan. If the refugees were attacked, they could cut the bridges' vines at a moment's notice. These days, thin steel wires reinforce the precarious planks, and fresh vines are restrung every three years, but it still feels death-defying to cross the boards over the rivers. From Route 32 or Route 45 follow the signs to Kazura-bashi. Skip the ¥500-yen lot next to the big tourist center and park for free right next to the bridge. The tall waterfall down the path is free, and the bridge is ¥500.

Where to Stay & Eat

★ **$$$** ✕⬚ **Hikyō-no-yu.** The finest resort in the area, thanks to lavish hot spring baths, a great view of the mountains, and a sumptuous *irori*-style restaurant: each table is a traditional raised hearth where fresh river fish and mountain vegetables are cooked in front of you while other delicacies are served. The three buildings of this opulent resort dominate a mountain face in Nishi-Iya, impossible to miss along Route 45 as you follow signs toward Kazura-bashi from Route 32. Bus service available from Ōboke Station. ✉ *401 Oi-no-Uchi Nishiyamamura, Miyoshi,*

CLOSE UP

Make Like Indiana Jones

IF A DAY OR TWO spent rafting, canyoning, and bridge walking (with a night at the onsen) leaves you wanting more, grab your bullwhip and fedora and head farther into the valley. Mt. Tsurugi, the "Fufu" Bashi (so-called "husband and wife" vine bridges), a handful of onsen-hotels and craft workshops await you. Driving there is not complicated per se—follow signs toward Higashi-Iya and Tsurugi-san—but the narrow mountain roads are challenging, and you'll want someone to mark the way for you on a map. The *taiken,* literally *experiences,* offered by local artisans are unique activities.

We recommend making delicious buckwheat noodles, *soba,* especially since this region is famous for it. Hiring a local sherpa to climb Tsurugi-san with you is a good choice, too. For a full listing of these taiken, check ⊕ http://iya.jp/takumi/e.htm. Translation assistance is offered by Chiiori House, a sustainable living project run by author Alex Kerr, itself a phenomenal location. But remember, the trouble with hidden paradises is that they're *hidden.* A car, some basic Japanese ability and some gusto will help you get the most out of being here. ⊕ www.chiiori.org.

Tokushima-ken 778-0101 ☎ *0883/87–2300* 🖷 *0883/87–2313* 📞 *8 Western-style rooms, 15 Japanese-style rooms* ♿ *Hot spring, dining room, TV* 🖃 *AE, D, MC, V* 🍴 *MAP.*

Kōchi

⑤ *50 min from Kōchi by Nampu Line train, or 1½ hrs by JR, 3 hrs by JR bus or train from Matsuyama, 2 hrs from Nakamura to the southwest. About 2 hrs from Tokushima or Takamatsu.*

Kōchi has a reputation for being different. The locals are rough-talking, boisterous, and social, and their spirited city has an attitude far from the Japanese mainstream. The famous **Yosakoi Dance Festival,** one of Japan's most popular summer events, is an explosion of parades and performances that fills the city for days. For weeks before and after, the streets shake with excitement, making summer the best time to visit. Kōchi smacks of a brash, square-shouldered gumption simply not found anywhere else in Japan, and it richly rewards a short swagger through.

10

Getting Around

The helpful **Tourist Information Booth** at the station lends bicycles free of charge from 10 to 5 any day of the week, but the city center at **Hari-maya-bashi** is only a 10-minute walk south. Streetcars go from the station to just about anywhere you want to go for ¥180, and the tram lines are easily navigable. A taxi ride from Kōchi Station to Harimaya-bashi runs about ¥550. There you are in striking distance to half the city's best attractions. Other hot spots lie farther out: a compact but cultured **Art Museum** and the green mountain **Godai-san,** home to a large **temple** and a breathtaking **botanical garden.**

What to See Downtown

Harimaya-bashi is the bridge at the center of Kōchi's best-known story, retold in a Yosakoi song, about the Buddhist priest espied here buying a hairpin for a lover, breaking his vow of celibacy for an affair that ended in tragedy. The arched red bridge still spans a canal downtown; see what's for sale there these days, or else try shopping in the twisting, tunneled **arcades** and the shops and side streets that sprout off from them. Locals come out to dine, chat, and dance (yes, dance) in parks and at outdoor cafés until the wee hours: even in this, Kōchi is a world apart from the general Japanese stigma against eating, lounging, and horsing around in public. When the stores and bars finally close, there's always a ramen cart on a corner brimming with commerce, so pull up a stool and dig in! Kōchi people won't pay you a lot of mind until you start talking to them, but many are multilingual, affable, and easy to engage.

★   The best place to mingle with the locals is at their two popular markets. Kōchi goes for culinary treasure over material stuff, and while the busy, hivelike **Hirome-ichiba** has interesting pottery, jewelry, and photographs, everyone's really here for the food. This exciting maze of mini-restaurants and food counters has enough strange, delicious foods that you couldn't try everything in a year. Displays, pictures, and abundant people traffic will help you ask for what you want, and you can always point to someone else's plate across the broad wooden tables. Open daily 11–11, it's at the western end of the main arcade, close to the the castle. Look for the mass of bicycles hemming in a squat coffee stand beside the entrance, a big orange-and-green sign above the hangar-bay door, and a large crowd of well-fed locals.

Nichiyō-ichi market offers a mile of bizarre fruits and vegetables (some looking like they're from other planets), tasty walking-food, local crafts, and kitsch, and an army of fellow browsers. It's not the place for good souvenir shopping, but why not try some *yuzu-an* in a pastry pocket? A Kōchi specialty replaces red-bean *anko* in normal desserts with a paste made from sour yellow yuzu fruit grown in the prefecture. Nichiyō-ichi runs along broad, palm-lined Ōtetsuji-dōri, parallel to the arcade and just north of it, and goes from Harimaya-bashi right up to the gates of the castle, early morning to mid-afternoon every Sunday.

★   **Kōchi Castle.** Go west through the markets and arcades downtown to find the barrel-chested body of **Kōchi-jo.** Kōchi-jō has a slightly different feel from other Japanese castles, more rough-hewn and well lived-in. The view from the topmost watchtower is splendid, and walking up the enormous steps or through the daimyō's receiving chambers is like being transported to the Edo period. From the station, hop a green Yosakoi Gurarin bus for a short ¥100 ride. Walking from Harimaya-bashi should take fifteen minutes. ⊠ *1–2–1 Marunouchi* ☎ *088/872–2776* 🔊 *¥400* ⊙ *Daily 9–5; last entry at 4:30.*

☺   **Yokoyama Memorial Manga Museum.** (Yokoyama Ryuichi Kinen Mangakan). The playful, modern Mangakan celebrates the life and work of Japan's first great cartoonist, Yokoyama Ryuichi. Many people here don't remember his name either, but his most popular character, Fuku-chan, is still widely loved. The Mangakan offers a window into a talented creator's life and work, and it's a lot of fun: the cartoons inspire and delight, and no language skill is required to enjoy most of the visual humor. Look through World War II propaganda cartoons (from the other side), interactive print stations, dioramas, model railroads, and tons of comic strips. ⊠ *On 3rd–5th floors of Cul-Port, Kōchi Culture Plaza; 2–1 Kutanda* ☎ *088/883–5029* ✆ *¥400* ☉ *Tues.–Sun. 9–7.*

What to See Outside the City Center

Ⓒ The city's best attraction lies away from downtown Kōchi. The **Makino**
Fodor'sChoice **Botanical Garden**, (Makino Shokubutsuen), an Eden-like valley of flow-
★ ers and trees hidden atop the mountain Godaisan. Different trails for each season show off the best nature has to offer. Hours disappear as you walk through the azaleas, camellias, chrysanthemums, and thousands of other plants in this huge and lovingly tended landscape (don't miss the giant ferns, so big you can actually sit in them). You're encouraged to leave the paths and explore on your own, for "to commune with nature we need to make ourselves free and jump into her," wrote botanist Tomi-taro Makino, for whom the garden was planted. You'll find more of his quotes, recollections, philosophy, and drawings in a fascinating museum inside the park. ☎ *088/882–2601* ✆ *¥500* ☉ *Tues.–Sun. 9–5.*

The prefecture may be known for its great surfing and swimming beaches, but the city's **Katsurahama** is not one of them. Rocks and breakers prohibit any fun in the water, and the pebbly sand isn't comfortable for picnicking, but the view from a cliff-top shrine is great (moon-watching from this spot is depicted in many ukiyo-e prints). Katsurahama is best known for the giant statue of **Sakamoto Ryoma**, Kōchi's local-born historic hero, staring grimly out to sea from his big black pedestal. Ryoma was a radical and a revolutionary during the turbulent times before the Meiji Restoration, and the political changes he instigated were big enough to get him killed; at the **Sakamoto Ryoma Memorial Museum**, jut-ting fabulously over the sand and surf, you can see the blood-splashed screen from the room where he was assassinated, and learn about his life and politics. You'll finally know who the cowboyish samurai is plas-tered on every street corner in Kōchi. One stop before Katsurahama on an orange Kenkotsu bus, the trip takes 40 minutes. (Sakamoto Ryoma Kinenkan.) ⊠ *830 Urado-Shiroyama* ☎ *088/841–0001* ⊕ *www.Kōchi-bunkazaidan.or.jp/~ryoma/english1.htm* ✆ *¥400* ☉ *Daily 9–5.*

10

OFF THE
BEATEN
PATH

MUROTO POINT (Muroto Misaki) – A surreal coastline of rocks, steep precipices, and surf awaits you at far-off cape Misaki. The road east follows a rugged shoreline cut by inlets and indentations along a rockscape out of Dr. Seuss, where the Pacific Black Current has shaped enormous terraces going down to the sea. It's about a 2½-hour drive along the coast road out to the cape, or a long bus ride to the black-sand beaches at Murotomisaki-mae. A concrete promenade lets you walk the farthest tip of sea-sculpted land.

Where to Stay & Eat

$$$–$$$$ ✕ **Tosa Ryori Tsukasa**. Set courses range from bento-box to jaw-dropping sashimi feasts: *sawachi ryōri*, lavish fish platters that are a Kōchi specialty. The staff recommend the katsuo—*sasuga Kōchi*, "just as you'd expect from

Kōchi"—but consider the *shabu-shabu* meat and veggie sets, which your servers will teach you to cook on a special table in your private tatami room. Be careful with seating; the main area on the first floor is a bland cafeteria, so arrange for a tatami room instead. ✉ *1–2–15 Harimaya-chō, around corner from Tosahan* ☎ *088/873–4351* ▭ *AE, DC, MC, V.*

$$–$$$$ ✕ **Tosahan.** If you want to see Kōchi's refined side, try a *Tosa Ryōri* course at Tosahan. Dark-wood beams, tatami floors, and red-paper lanterns create a rich atmosphere. A picture menu and displays make ordering easy. Katsuo is the specialty, along with *nabe* hot pots, and anything you get will be more or less perfect. Look for the giant backlit poster of Ryoma, Kōchi's claim-to-fame samurai, glowering at you a few blocks into Obiya-machi arcade. ✉ *1–2–2 Obiya-machi Arcade* ☎ *088/821–0002* ▭ *AE, DC, MC, V.*

¢–$ ✕ **Faust.** A delightful café restaurant is just off the arcades' main drag. Sit outdoors and people-watch on the cobbled lane or head indoors to the fancy, intimate third floor. The first floor is dinerlike, the second acceptable, but sitting in the literati-chic upper level and getting to order from the same cheap, delicious menu is having your cake and eating it too. The cake, incidentally, is excellent. ✉ *1–2–22 Hon-machi* ☎ *088/873–4111.*

¢–$ ✕ **Myoujin-Suisam.** Inside Hirome-ichiba, just follow your nose, but don't leave without trying the *katsuo tataki,* Kōchi's regional fish specialty. Look for the orange flames erupting from this stall's window. Fresh cuts of katsuo are seared to perfection by a cook perilously close to being engulfed by the flames that he feeds big handfuls of straw. Most katsuo for Kōchi come from the port town **Kure** to the southwest, and this shop belongs to the captain of Kure's largest fishing vessel. The fish is served on beds of rice or drizzled with citrusy Pons sauce, and you'll never get enough of it. ✉ *Inside Hirome-ichiba* ☉ *Daily 11–11.*

$$$$ 🏨 **Jyōseikan.** "Fit for a king" is an expression we take for granted, but watch yourself—Jyōseikan is where the Emperor stays when the royal family comes to Kōchi. A monumental, somewhat dated exterior gives way to a grand interior with spacious bedrooms (some strangely decorated), exquisite tatami suites, and a sauna and bath with wonderful prospects of the city and castle. Two stops west of Harimaya-bashi by tram. ✉ *2–5–34 Kami-machi, Kōchi-shi, Kōchi-ken 780-0901* ☎ *088/ 875–0111* 🖷 *088/824–0557* ⊕ *www.ryokan.or.jp/shikoku/details/Kōchi/ e-jyoseikan.html and www.jyoseikan.co.jp* ↦ *72 Japanese-style rooms* ⅋ *Restaurant, coffee shop* ▭ *AE, DC, MC, V.*

$$$ 🏨 **Hotel Shin-Hankyu.** There's no question that you'll be in the lap of luxury, but you might be anywhere in the world. Shin-Hankyu is a topnotch chain hotel, and you may feel like you've left Kōchi when you step inside the lobby. It is spacious and modern, with a lovely cake-and-tea shop on the ground floor and slightly expensive restaurants on the second. Western-style guest rooms are pleasant and roomy, and the staff is extremely helpful to foreign guests. ✉ *4–2–50 Hon-machi* ☎ *088/873–1111* 🖷 *088/873–1145* ⊕ *http://hotel.newhankyu.co.jp/ Kōchi-e/index.html* ↦ *238 Western-style rooms with 4 doubles, 4 Japanese-style rooms* ⅋ *4 restaurants, pool, health club, bar, no-smoking rooms* ▭ *AE, DC, MC, V.*

$$ 🏨 **Washington Hotel.** The location on Ōtetsuji-dōri puts you right by the castle, on top of the Sunday market, and in the best spot to get home from a night out feasting and rollicking your way through town. There's a small restaurant inside for the unadventurous. The Washington is warm without being exceptional, and the rooms are a good size. Fifteen minutes from the JR station. ⊠ *1–8–25 Otetsuji* ☎ *088/823–6111* 🖷 *0888/ 25–2737* 🖘 *172 rooms* ♨ *Restaurant* 🖃 *AE, V.*

MATSUYAMA & WESTERN SHIKOKU

Matsuyama

6 *2 hrs west of Takamatsu by JR, 1 hr from Awa-Ikeda. Buses and trains to Kōchi or Tokushima each take about 3 hrs. Hiroshima is 1½ hrs by hydrofoil, 3 by ferry, or 4 by bus. Overnight ferries to Beppu, Ōsaka, Kōbe, Seoul, and Vladivostok. All roads lead to Matsuyama.*

Shikoku's largest city, Matsuyama prides itself on a great history, friendly disposition, fantastic cultural attractions, and a love for fine food, intense fashion, and haiku. You'll be quickly captivated by the sights and feel of the city, and you can join in the fun; bathe at Dōgo Onsen, Japan's oldest hot spring, hit the fashion avenue downtown, or go restaurant crawling through the best spots on the island. Denizens say It's *sumi-yasui*, easy living here, and you'll find Matsuyama is one of the most rewarding stops along your route.

Getting Around

Matsuyama is easy to get around in, served by a good tram network and an enormous central landmark, **Matsuyama Castle** and the moat surrounding it. Orientation is not difficult, though it's a large and not particularly well-organized city; the hastiness with which sections have been developed—and the antiquity of other areas—has left many grimy sectors and dead zones, but for visitors the action is concentrated around a few locations.

No. 5 trams run from the JR station to Dōgo Onsen, and most of the city's best spots are on the way. Hand the conductor ¥150 when you exit at the huge orange facade of Laforet, a Tōkyō-based department store. The stop is **Ōkaidō-mae** on the street Ichiban-chō, in front of the city's busy arcades and the restaurant mile surrounding them. Away from the arcades, a five-minute walk past the Starbucks will bring you to Matsuyama Castle's ropeway. It's especially nice at night thanks to waist-high streetlights and tall fishbowl lampposts.

If you need help, the **City Tourist Information Office** has maps and brochures (⊠ Matsuyama Station ☎ 089/931–3914), but for real assistance head to EPIC. The **Ehime Prefectural International Center** is a great resource for advice on the city and region. The desk staff will bend over backward to help you with event info, transport tips, hotel reservations, and even rental bikes (for a refundable ¥1,000 deposit). (Ehime-ken Kōryū Kyōkai Kokusai Sentā ☎ 089/917–5678 ⊕ www.epic.or.jp/index.html).

What to See

★ Mention Matsuyama to anyone, and **Dōgo Onsen** will be the first place they recommend. It has been the city's number one attraction since time

10

A Shopping Tour

MATSUYAMA IS the fashion capital of Shikoku, and a stroll down its main shopping arcade, **Ōkaidō,** will leave you reeling from the getups, ranging from gorgeous to grotesque. Nowhere else outside of Tōkyō does fad-fashion get this high a priority. Stores are suitably fashion trendy—though look out for a secondhand ceramics shop, unassuming but treasure-filled, just past the Häagen-Dazs—becoming more numerous on the arcade's second street, **Gintengai.** Both arcades are great for people-watching, but they empty out once the stores close. Ōkaidō begins at the Starbucks on Ichiban-chō and goes south for a kilometer until turning right into the Gintengai; Gintengai empties out by a large Takashimaya department store and the city bus and tram terminal, **Shi-eki** (a block north to Kinokunia, English books on the fourth floor). Walk a few blocks farther, following the tram lines past a Mr. Donuts and an Indian place, Ladkey's, with good lunch specials, and you'll hit the castle moat and the town's best lunch place, Amitie, just across from the **Art Museum.** The tram stop here is Bijutsukan-mae.

Ōkaidō, **Gintengai,** and Shi-eki complete a square adjacent the moat. Inside are clothing stores, cafés, and other shops. You won't discover any hidden temples or ancient pathways, but there's plenty of good shopping and city life. Walk a square of the same area on the *other* side of Ōkaidō and you'll hit a staggering number of great restaurants. The best street to follow is parallel to the main arcade and one block east; head into **Ōkaidō** from Laforet and go left at the first lights (this is Niban-chō), then make a right and you'll be in foody heaven. No spot on the strip is terribly expensive, and each place has a lot of character and great food. For coffee afterward, head in the opposite direction along Niban-chō, one block past a red London bus to **Sakura.** The coffees and cakes are wonderful, but the pink, cherry-blossom beer is better in someone else's glass.

---

began for this nation: Dōgo is the oldest hot spring in Japan, with a history stretching back almost 3,000 years. The oldest written texts mention it as a favorite of gods, emperors, and the poorest peasants, and it's still in daily use by locals and tourists. The main wooden building at present-day Dōgo dates from 1894 and looks like a fairy-tale castle. The only thing that's changed significantly is the view, and bathing here lets you strip down and wash away, so to speak, the cares and concerns of the world.

A ¥620 ticket gets you a bath with frills. Upstairs you are given a basket with towels and a *yukata,* a light-weight robe, and pointed to the bath, Kami-no-Yu: Water of the Gods. The gods apparently like it simple. The great granite tub is not like the modern multibath complexes. Remember your onsen procedure: go into the bathroom with your teeny prop towel, and wash and rinse yourself (and rinse your towel!) before getting into the bath. Don't worry about bathing faux pas like dropping your towel in the water. On laid-back Shikoku, and especially at Dōgo, no one gives it much bother. Even tattoos are usually no problem. After you bathe, don the soft yukata and relax upstairs. Your ticket includes green tea and *sembei* crackers, served in a serene public tatami room. Relaxing in this second-story terrace is one of the great joys of coming to Dōgo. Stay as long as you like, sipping free tea refills, or explore the upstairs quarters where writer Natsume Soseki stayed and worked during his time in Matsuyama. (Dōgo was about the only thing he liked about the city, although they claim him as a local icon.) The baths are open 6:30 AM to 11 PM.

Ishiteji. Ishiteji is like an ancient, Buddhist-theme amusement park. With more fun things to see and do than at any other holy site, it's without a doubt the best temple on Shikoku. As sprawling and unkempt as the city around it, it awaits you with surprises, like temple cats, too numerous to count. Ghastly statues and lovely bridges wait in the forest, a scrambling rock pathway leads up the back of the mountain, and two spooky caves are yours to explore (even most locals don't know about them). The obvious draws are wonderful, too—a pagoda and huge temple buildings, painted panels, and golden statues, a giant mandala on the stairway to the main shrine, a wood-carved Kami with a sword you can heft, a huge bronze bell to ring for a hundred yen, a cauldron of ash to light incense in. Pass a stone dragon at the entrance and a strip of *omiyage* merchants, and you'll see a table for making origami cranes; they'll be added to the heavy, colorful bunches hanging around pillars everywhere, and in return you can take home a white placard on which the monks have written a sutra. Don't miss the cave behind the main temple building. The darkness is not total, but it feels impossibly long, and when you finally emerge on the other side—past startling wooden statues and 88 stone Buddhas (one for each temple on the pilgrimage)—you'll be confronted by a 100-foot statue of the Kobo Daishi striding across the mountains. (Remember those huge sandals you saw at the gate? They're his.) ⊙ *Shops and caves close between 4 and 5.*

OFF THE BEATEN PATH

Japan's finest martial-arts stadium is the **Ehime Ken-Budōkan**, 15 minutes by local train from JR. Watch or try a class in any number of arts, any time of day. The Ken-Budōkan is next to **Botchan Stadium**, where you can watch Ehime's minor-league baseball team, the Mandarin Pirates, or—even more fun—see a high-school game: Japan is nuts for high-school baseball, and Ehime's teams have been national competitors the last few years, so home games are well attended. Get schedules and information at EPIC.

Matsuyama Castle. Large, well-kept, and mighty, Matsuyama-jō is one of the cooler castles in Japan. Inside you can watch footage of the post–World War II reconstruction; the hand labor is astonishing, from the shaping and joining of wood to the stamping out of straw wattle for the walls. There's no concrete, no rebar, and only enough nails to hold down the floorboards. Dark-wood passageways carry the smell of old smoke, from the numerous fires the castle has suffered. For daytime visits, ride the ropeway up and wander around with a delightful wax-paper parasol. Hit the lovely garden just west of the castle, and exit from there to Ichiban-chō, a few blocks west of Laforet. ⊠ *5 Maru-no-uchi, Matsuyama-shi* ☎ *089/921–4873* ⌨ *Castle ¥500. Ropeway ¥500 round-trip, or a ¥1,000 comprehensive ticket.* ⊙ *Tues.–Sun. 9–4:30.*

10

Where to Stay & Eat

$$$$ ✕ **Kawasemi.** *Kaiseki ryōri* is a style of cuisine so highly ritualized that it's considered a traditional art. At tables or in private tatami booths, you'll savor delicate morsels of marinated seafood, slivers of poached fish, vegetables, and savory coulis arranged with care and artistry fit for serving an emperor. The gloomy black-and-gray interior finds harmony with stunning ikebana arrangements. Look on Niban-chō for a second-floor sign with CLUB written in purple, two blocks east of Ōkaidō. Lunches cost about ¥1,000, though dinners soar endlessly higher. ✉ *2–5–18 Niban-chō* ☎ *089/933–9697* ⊟ *AE, MC, V.*

$–$$ ✕ **Amitie.** The alleys and side streets east off Ōkaidō offer an endless number of great dinner spots, but for lunch this is our favorite. Excellent cuisine without being snooty, funky without being low-brow or grimy. Sit upstairs and strike up conversation with your neighbors; the convivial hosts and softly worn wooden interior engender affability. It's outside Bijutsukan-mae tram stop, across the moat from the Art Museum.

$$$$ 🏨 **ANA Hotel Matsuyama.** The biggest international hotel downtown, the ANA is just next to Laforet on Ichiban-chō. Ask for a room on the 11th or 12th floor that overlooks the Bansuiso Mansion, an imitation French château, floodlighted at night. The hotel has shopping arcades, several restaurants, and a rooftop beer garden. ✉ *3–2–1 Ichiban-chō* ☎ *089/ 933–5511* 🖷 *089/921–6053* ⤴ *327 rooms* ↻ *4 restaurants, hair salon, beer garden* ⊟ *AE, DC, V.*

$$$$ 🏨 **Funaya Ryokan.** You couldn't get a higher recommendation: Funaya has been an on-and-off imperial favorite since 1626. Western rooms are lovely, Japanese-style ones are classier, and the finest of both look out on the lush central garden. Take a hot-spring bath before dining; breakfast and dinner are included in the rate. Two minutes from the Dōgo tram terminal. ✉ *1–33 Dōgo Yu-no-machi* ☎ *089/947–0278* 🖷 *089/ 943–2139* ⤴ *28 Japanese-style rooms, 26 Western-style rooms* ↻ *Pool, sauna* ⊟ *AE, DC, MC, V* ⦿ *MAP.*

Uchiko

❼ *30 min south of Matsuyama by train.*

Walking the cobbled hills of Uchiko feels like traveling back in time. Along the old shopping street, **Yokaichi,** the only change in centuries has been the height of plants against the beige-orange walls. Go straight out of the station and follow a wooden sign pointing left. You won't need more than a morning to poke through the fun shops, full of good, cheap *omiyage*: straw pinwheels, tea leaves, sour *tsukemono*, and local sake. The highlight is a waxworks, where an old man and his sons hand-make distinctive candles (the smaller ones are as surprisingly inexpensive as the larger are surprisingly costly).

There are a few sights—old merchant houses and an impressive turn-of-the-century kabuki theater, **Uchiko Za**—but Uchiko is more of a meandering town. A path between houses reveals a hillside of peach trees and wildflowers; open doorways lead to secluded gardens with men playing *shōgi*, or the occasional restaurant. One thing is not to be missed however: at the very end of the road you'll crest a final hill and see a mountainous statue of the **sleeping Buddha** reclining across the lap of enlightenment. It's the last thing you'd expect to find in this sleepy town—especially since it isn't marked on a single tourist map or guidebook anywhere else.

Uwajima

8 *1½ hrs south of Matsuyama by train, 3½ hrs west of Kōchi.*

Abroad, Uwajima is known for its sumō-style bullfights. Domestically, its claim to fame is a notorious **sex museum** with displays that would make Hugh Hefner blush. A **tourist info office** across from the station (opposite the bull statue) is open 9–5, and can lend you a bike (stickers with Uwajima's demon-bull are ¥50 and great souvenirs). ☎ *089/522-3934.*

The museum is located at a Shinto fertility shrine, **Taga Jinja**, not far from the station. It's easy to zip past the entrance, but once there you can tell you've arrived. No, that's no giant squid. Just beyond is the museum, called **Deko Boko Jindou**, literally a place honoring "things that poke out, things that go in." The three-floor collection is astonishing. What is that samurai doing with his . . . ? It's best to leave the kids at the castle for this one (it's up the arcade and to the right). ⊠ *Deko 1340* ☎ *089/522–3444* ≣ *¥800* ⊙ *Daily 8–5.*

Uwajima's other attraction is the **togyu**, a sport in which two bulls lock horns and push, à la sumō, for control of the ring. The bullfights date back 400 years, and if you can make it during one of the six annual tournaments you'll have a great time. January 2, the third Sunday in March, the first Sunday in April, July 24, August 14, and the second Sunday in November. The stadium is at the foot of Maru-yama, a 30-minute walk from Uwajima Station.

The Shimanami Sea Road

9 *Beginning in Imabari, 40 min north of Matsuyama by train.*

Your Shikoku excursion will begin and end with trips over the water, and the best way to come or go from Western Honshu is the **Shimanami Kaidō**: ten long bridges create an unbroken thoroughfare between Imabari (just north of Matsuyama) and Onomichi (just east of Hiroshima), across islands in the Seto Nai-kai, Japan's inland sea. Most of these places were totally inaccessible before the bridges were completed in 1999, so the scenery is unspoiled and serene: fishing villages, kaki orchards, seaweed pastures, pearl farms, and a stretch of sparkling sea. Driving, busing, and ferrying from Imabari to Hiroshima are all delightful, and going across with a rental bike is unforgettable.

FodorśChoice
★

Biking the Shimanami Kaidō is a safe, exciting experience that anyone with a reasonable level of fitness can accomplish. The bridges were built with cyclists in mind: a separate cycling track runs along each one, so you won't deal with car traffic for almost the entire ride. The bridges are flat, and the cycling isn't strenuous. Don't get discouraged by the big corkscrew pathways up from Imabari to the Kurushima Ōhashi, or the unattractive hills on the first island, Ōshima. After that it's clear sailing.

10

Biking straight to Onomichi takes about six hours, but you don't have to cycle the whole way: leave the bikes on any of the islands' rental stations and ferry the rest of the way across. Your hotel can send your luggage ahead, so it is the perfect way to travel. For renting bikes, try Imabari's **Sunrise Itoyama** (✉ 2–8–1 Sunaba-chō, Imabari-shi ☎ 089/841–3196). Rental bikes are ¥500 a day plus a ¥1,000 refundable deposit. The shop is open from May to September, daily 8–8. Between October and March it's 8–5. The shop workers won't speak much English, so it's best to go through Imabari's helpful International Organization, **ICIEA** (☎ 0898/34–5763 ⊕ http://iciea.imabari-cc.ac.jp/e_index.html ☉ Daily 8:30–5:15).

On the third island from Imabari, **Ōmishima**, stands the **Ōyamazumi Jinja**, 1,200 years a shrine to battle. In the 8th century victorious warriors started leaving their weaponry here as thanks for divine favor. The museum holds more than two-thirds of the nation's designated national treasures in swords, spears, breastplates, and helmets. ✉ 3327 Miya-ura, Ōshima-chō ☎ 089/782–0032 ⌗ ¥1,000 ☉ Daily 8:30–4:30.

OFF THE BEATEN PATH

CAPE ASHIZURI-MISAKI AND THE SHIMANTO-GAWA RIVER – Great beaches and a clean, roaring river wait at Shikoku's southwest tip. From Matsuyama, trains will take you as far south as Uwajima. Buses finish the journey to Nakamura (trains run directly from Kōchi). Called the last clean river in Japan, the beautiful Shimanto-gawa is easy to see through various boat tours, including dining-inclusive trips and some where you can watch (but not try) old fishing styles. Tourist Info Office staff at JR are eager, if not terribly multilingual. The best beach on Shikoku, Ōkinohama, is an hour south, but you'll need your own transportation or good luck catching buses. Squeaky white sand and clear, crashing waves make it unbeatable for surfing, swimming, and sun. This area is a favorite of everyone who visits, but getting there takes some doing.

SHIKOKU ESSENTIALS

Transportation

BY AIR

All Nippon Airways and Japan Airlines provide domestic flights to and from Shikoku's four major cities. Takamatsu exchanges 7 daily flights with Tōkyō and 10 with Ōsaka; Tokushima 5 daily from Tōkyō and 10 from Ōsaka; Kōchi 5 daily from Tōkyō and 23 from Ōsaka. Matsuyama has 6 daily from Tōkyō and 6 from Ōsaka.

🛃 **Carriers All Nippon Airways (ANA)** ☎ 800/235–9262 in U.S. and Canada, 0120/02–9222 in Japan ⊕ www.anaskyweb.com. **Japan Airlines (JAL)** ☎ 800/525–3663 in U.S. and Canada, 0120/255–971 in Japan ⊕ www.jal.co.jp.

BY BOAT & FERRY

The Kansai Kisen (Kansai Steamship) to Takamatsu takes 5½ hours from Ōsaka's Bentenfuto Pier and 4½ hours from Kōbe's Naka-Tottei Pier. The boat leaves Ōsaka at 8:30 AM and 2:20 PM and Kōbe at 9:50 AM and 3:40 PM. It arrives at Takamatsu at 2 PM and 8:10 PM. From Ōsaka, the cost is ¥2,500 and up; it's slightly less from Kōbe.

Nankai Ferry connects Tokushima with Wakayama City, offering convenient access to Kansai International Airport. The journey takes two hours and costs ¥2,000 one-way, ¥3,800 round-trip.

Ferry companies have been offering fewer voyages along their less-traveled sea routes, and some services have closed. Look for up-to-date info at ⊕ www.japancycling.org/v2/aguide/shikoku/ferry.shtml. Hourly high-speed boat service between Matsuyama and Hiroshima costs ¥5,700 on Ishizaki Kisen. The trip takes one hour. A three-hour ferry by Seto Nai-kai Kisen costs ¥4,260 for first class, ¥2,130 for second class. Avoid the overnight Diamond Ferry that runs to Kōbe.

🔢 **Ishizaki Kisen** ☎ 089/953-1003. **Kansai Kisen** ☎ 06/573-0530 Japanese only. **Nankai Tokushima Shuttle Line** ☎ 088/664-3330 Japanese only. **Seto Nai-kai Kisen** ☎ 082/253-1212.

BY BUS

Buses connect with Honshū at Matsuyama and Takamatsu. Matsuyama to Hiroshima, by way of Onomichi, takes 3 hrs and costs ¥3,200 on Shimanami Liner. There are six departures per weekend day (three on weekdays) between 9 AM and 8 PM. JR Bus Shikoku connects Takamatsu with Tōkyō, Ōsaka, Kyōto, Nagoya, and Kōbe.

🔢 **Shimanami Liner** ☎ 0898/25-4873. **JR Bus Shikoku** ☎ 0878/25-1717.

BY CAR

The easiest and cheapest rental-car service is ToCoo, a middle-man company that reserves cars at branch connections in all of Shikoku's airports and cities. Reservations are made through the Web site. Major places are connected by large, two-lane toll roads. Signs are in English but exits are far apart.

🔢 **ToCoo** ⊕ www2.tocoo.jp

BY TRAIN

Rail access is through Tadotsu via Okayama (four hours from Tōkyō; one hour from Ōsaka). Transfer there from JR Hikari Shinkansen to a JR Limited Express train bound for Takamatsu (one hour), Matsuyama, or Kōchi (three hours).

Express trains are efficient and speedy, running between Takamatsu and Matsuyama in 2 hours, 45 minutes; Takamatsu to Kōchi in 3 hours, Takamatsu to Tokushima in less than 90 minutes. Matsuyama to Kōchi is quicker by bus.

Contacts & Resources

EMERGENCIES

🔢 **Ambulance** ☎ 119. **Police** ☎ 110.

Points of Interest

SITES/AREAS	JAPANESE CHARACTERS
Art Museum	愛媛県立美術館
Awa Odori	阿波踊り
Awa Odori Kaikan	阿波踊り会館
Benessee Art Site	ベネッセ アートサイト
Benessee House	ベネッセハウス
Botchan Stadium	坊ちゃんスタジアム
Chichu art museum	地中美術館
Chiiori House	ちいおりプロジェクト
Deko Boko Jindou	凸凹人道
Dōgo Onsen	道後温泉
Hall of Awa Handmade Paper (Awa Washi Dentō)	阿波和紙伝統産業会館
Harimaya Bashi	播磨屋橋
Hirome-Ichiba	ひろめ市場
Isamu Noguchi Garden Museum (Isamu Noguchi Teien Hakubutsukan)	イサム・ノグチ庭園美術館
Ishiteji	石手寺
Iya	祖谷
Iya Valley and Ōboke-Koboke Gorges	祖谷と大歩危小歩危
Katsurahama	桂浜
Kazura-Bashi	かずら橋
Ken-Budōkan	愛媛県武道館
Kōchi	高知
Kōchi Castle	高知城
Kotohira	琴平
Matsuyama	松山
Matsuyama Castle	松山城
Muroto Point (Muroto Misaki)	室戸岬
Ōkinohama	沖の浜
Otsuka Bijitsukan (Otsuka Museum of Art)	大塚美術館
Ōyamazumi Jinja	大山祇神社
Ritsurin-kōen	栗林公園
Sakamoto Ryoma	坂本竜馬
Shikoku Mura	

Shikoku Mura Gallery	四国村ギャラリ
Shimanami Sea Road (Shimanami Kaidō)	しまなみ海道
Shimantogawa	四万十川
Sleeping Buddha	涅槃像
Taga Jinji	多賀神社
Takamatsu	高松
Tōgyū (bullfighting)	闘牛
Tokushima	徳島
Uchiko	内子
Uchiko Za	内子座
Uwajima	宇和島
Yashima	屋島
Yokaichi	内子・よか市
Yokoyama Ryuichi Kinen Mangakan	横山降一記念まんが館
Yosakoi	よさこい

RESTAURANTS

Amitie	アミティエ
Benny's	ベニズ
Chinese Kitchen Shanghai Fang	上海ファング
Faust	ファウスト
Ginza Salon	ギンザサロン
Kawasemi	川瀬見
King's Yawd	キングズヤード
Kinryo Sake Brewery	西野金陵株式会社
Myoujin-Suisam	明神水産
Tenkatsu	天勝
Tosa Ryōri Tsukasa	土佐料理　司高知本店
Tosahan	土佐藩
Uo Ichiba	魚市場
Wine	和いん

HOTEL

ANA Hotel Clement Takamatsu	全日空ホテルクレメント高松
ANA Hotel Matsuyama	松山全日空ホテル
Funaya Ryokan	ふなや旅館

10

Hikyō-no-yu	秘境の湯
Hotel Kawaroku/Elstage	ホテル川六／エルステージ
Hotel Shin-Hankyu	新阪急ホテル
Kiyomi-sanso Hanajyukai	喜代美山荘 花樹海
Renaissance Resort Naruto	ルネッサンス リゾート 鳴門
Tōkyū Inn	東急イン
Washington Hotel	ワシントンホテル

Kyūshū

WORD OF MOUTH

"In Fukuoka, an interesting area at night that attracts many local residents, are the *yatai*, open-air food stalls. These are set up in the evening, are open until the early morning hours, and serve reasonably priced food such as yakitori, ramen, oden, etc., as well as beer and sake. There are many along the Naka-gawa River near the Nakasu entertainment district, where the bars and clubs are located."

—curiousgeo

By John Malloy
Quinn

KYŪSHŪ COULDN'T BE MORE VARIED, with active yet accessible volcanoes, thermal spas, endless fields of rice and potatoes, forested mountains capped by winter snows, busy harbors, and seaside resorts.

Ruins and artifacts thousands of years old suggest that Kyūshū was the gateway for human contact between Japan and the rest of Asia. The most rapid anthropological changes occurred from about 300 BC to AD 300, when rice became widely cultivated and complex pottery and tools began to appear, thus conveniently framing the Yayoi Period. Continuous trade with China brought prosperity and culture to the region, and advanced ceramics were introduced—and then produced—by Korean masters that were employed and enslaved by the local fiefdoms of the 16th and 17th centuries.

It was also through Kyūshū that Western knowledge, weapons, religion, and cooking methods made inroads into Japan. Nagasaki saw the arrival of vast fleets of European merchants and missionaries in the mid-1500s, and a frenzy of trading in ideas and goods continued unabated until the Tokugawa Shōgunate shut the door in the early 1600s, in the spasms of a panic induced by the alarming phenomenon of Christianity. The Portuguese and other Catholics fond of preaching to the natives were expelled and permanently barred, but the Dutch, considered more money-minded, were permitted to stay—under scrutiny. They were housed within the enclave of Dejima, a man-made island in Nagasaki Harbor, where they were constantly guarded and watched. This was the only point of contact the West would have with Japan until Perry's forceful visit more than 200 years later.

Today Kyūshū is a fascinating mix of old and new, and of nature and culture. Much of the remote and rugged interior—such as that surrounding Mt. Aso's fuming cone—is still untrammeled, yet the amenities of modern life are well supplied in cities and seaside resorts, in areas that have been inhabited for 10,000 years.

See the glossary at the end of this book for definitions of the common Japanese words and suffixes used in this chapter.

ORIENTATION & PLANNING

Orientation

Kysūshū is close to the Korean Peninsula. It's considerably west of Tōkyō and a little south. A good route starts with a flight or Shinkansen run into Fukuoka in the north, moves down to Nagasaki on the west coast by express train, winds eastward by bus or train to the central city of Kumamoto, with a possible side trip to Aso-san (Mt. Aso), and a jaunt south to the city of Kagoshima via the new high-speed train, then further south by local train to the hot-sand resort area of Ibusuki. If time permits, back up through Kumamoto, and go on northeastward by direct bus to the hot-springs resort of Yufuin.

Top Reasons to Visit

DIVERSE CITIES

While free-wheeling Fukuoka has the best nightlife, Nagasaki evokes a vividly old-world port-city charm. Kumamoto's grand ancient castle retains the city's rustic airs, despite streets teeming with traffic, and Kagoshima is meant for relaxing among its blossoms and palm trees.

GASTRONOMY DOMAIN

Fukuoka is home to Japan's most sought-after noodles: Hakata ramen; filament-thin egg noodles in a broth richly flavored with pork-bones. Nagasaki has *chanpon*, a buttery noodle soup containing everything from octopus and squid to carrots, cabbage, and celery. Kagoshima's *kuro-buta tonkatsu*, or Black Pig pork cutlet, is breaded and fried and served with special sauce, cabbage, and pickles made from the world's largest white radishes.

INSIDE THE VOLCANO

Mt. Aso, in the center of the island, is notoriously active, as is Sakura-jima, a fire-spewing dragon growling and spitting ash across the bay from Kagoshima. Hot springs are found throughout Kyūshū, and in the Satsuma Peninsula you can be buried in a berm of hot sand while the magma churns not far below.

INTO THE WILD

With its lava flows, outlying islands, rugged mountain landscapes, thickly forested interior, and gigantic national parks, Kyūshū is an adventurer's dream. Many peaks are accessible, the views are incredible, and except for time, most trails don't require more than a good pair of shoes and a jug of water.

REMOTE ACCESS

A very sleek high-speed train links Kumamoto with Kagoshima within an hour, and from there, in another hour, you can be on or under the hot sand, basking in sunshine down at the palm-lined, wave-lapped, breezy beaches of Ibusuki.

Fukuoka

Fukuoka has one of the most convenient airports in the world: you can be downtown in 5–10 minutes by subway for ¥250! Fabulous dining, shopping, and nightlife are what this vibrant city has to offer.

Nagasaki

Consistently rated by the Japanese as one of their country's most enjoyable destinations, for centuries Nagasaki was Japan's only port open to the West. Though it was largely obliterated by the plutonium bomb that marked the end of World War II, the city was rebuilt to re-create its rich and colorful international past.

Kumamoto

Kumamoto's massive 17th century castle and luxuriant garden of Suizen-ji Jōju-en are the highlights of this old fortress town; they are a peaceful contrast to the broad boulevards chock-full of vehicles.

Kagoshima

Kagoshima, with its mild climate and easy-going vibe, is fond of comparisons to Naples, Italy—but the smoking, rumbling cone of Sakura-jima

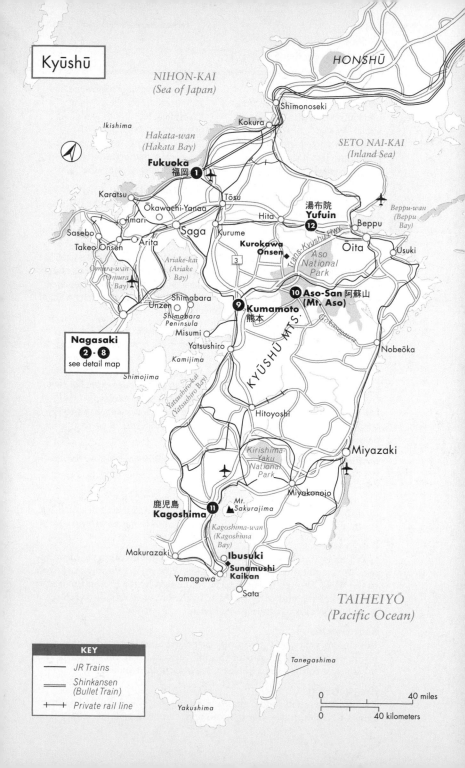

out in the bay makes Pompeii the more apt comparison. Hot-sand baths and lovely beaches are along the southern reaches of the prefecture.

Aso-san (Mt. Aso)

Aso is a chain of five volcanic peaks, and Naka-dake is the only one currently active. These mountains, the lakes, and the almost unnaturally green fields surrounding them are part of Aso National Park. Aso-san is remote, but inns and hot springs dot the area.

Yufuin

Yufuin is a delightful and popular hot-springs resort beneath the dramatic twin-peaked mountain Yufu-dake. Galleries, microbreweries, museums, and trendy eateries are scattered among the charming inns.

Planning

Travel in Kyūshū is pretty easy nowadays. If you come between May and October, consider packing rain gear, since sideways rain can render umbrellas useless. As for attire, businesses and restaurants are casual throughout Kyūshū, and sweating salarymen are likely the only people you'll see suffering neckties and jackets. In all the big cities you can find people who can speak and understand some English.

The Best of Times

In early spring it's pleasantly warm and the greenery is at its astounding best. May and June usher in heavy rains, and July and August are very muggy. September is summery, but watch for typhoons, which like to blow in until late October. Autumn colors are very nice, particularly in the north, and they appear in late October or early November. In January and February the mountains of central Kyūshū receive a little snowfall, and that's when the Siberian cranes show up for the gentle winter the region enjoys.

Concerning Restaurants & Hotels

Fresh fish is served everywhere on Kyūshū. Appetites run hearty here, so there's lots of meat, too. Local specialties abound, and are often reasonably priced. In the bigger cities like Fukuoka, Nagasaki, Kumamoto, and Kagoshima—and along the trendy new streets of Yufuin—you'll find plenty of Western-style restaurants.

You can find the usual American hotel chains, with all the familiar extras, in Fukuoka and Nagasaki. The rural areas surrounding Aso and Kagoshima have inns with stunning views of the surrounding peaks. In Yufuin nearly all hotels and *ryokan* (traditional inns) offer welcome baths of thermal mineral water. Unless otherwise noted, all hotel rooms have private baths, basic television service, and air-conditioning.

Reservations are essential during the long national holidays, particularly Golden Week (late April–early May), Ōbon (mid-August), and New Year's (first week of January)—when Japanese tourists flock to the island.

WHAT IT COSTS In yen				
$$$$	$$$	$$	$	¢
RESTAURANTS over 3,000	2,000–3,000	1,000–2,000	800–1,000	under 800
HOTELS over 22,000	18,000–22,000	12,000–18,000	8,000–12,000	under 8,000

Restaurant prices are per person for a main course at dinner. Hotel prices are for a double room, excluding 5% tax and tip.

Transportation Station

Travel in Kyūshū is for the most part straightforward, with trains providing the bulk of the transport. Highway buses are useful for certain routes. Frequent and inexpensive ferries ply the bays and ports, linking Kyūshū with offshore islands. During holiday seasons you'll want to reserve seats on express trains, but with most buses and ferries turning up 20 minutes prior to departure you should get on board with no trouble.

AIR TRAVEL Air routes link Kyūshū's major cities with Tōkyō and Ōsaka. Fukuoka, Nagasaki, and Kagoshima have the most frequent and useful daily connections, and offer some international flights. When using domestic carriers like ANA you need not enter and return from the same city: it's easy to fly into Fukuoka and out of Kagoshima, for example.

BUS TRAVEL Buses make useful connections around Kyūshū—and if you don't have a JR Rail Pass, they are are often much cheaper than the trains. For example, the bus between Nagasaki and Kumamoto is half the price and takes about the same time—and you don't have to make any changes or wait for connections, as you do with trains. A highway bus makes a trip between Kumamoto to Yufuin, either direct or with a stopover at the Aso-san crater.

CAR TRAVEL Car rental is a good idea in Kyūshū if you have lots of time, and if you explore the more out-of-the-way places such as Aso-san. All the major rental outfits have offices in the big cities near the JR stations. The roads in Kyūshū are sometimes wider than in other regions, but don't expect them to be any less jammed with speeding trucks or lumbering tour buses!

TRAIN TRAVEL High-speed train service now links Kumamoto with Kagoshima, via a quick and easy change in Yatsushiro. The new Tsubame (Swallow) train is chic, posh, spacious, and uncrowded. Express trains making the popular run between Fukuoka and Nagasaki are jammed on weekends and holidays, so book at least a day ahead.

Visitor Information

Every major city has tourist information offices near shopping, sightseeing, and eating areas, and one or more near the high-speed train exit of each JR train station. Generally, one English speaker is on duty during peak travel hours. The bigger hotels usually have front desk employees who speak and understand some English; they are good sources for information on local sights and restaurant recommendations. For the full range of brochures, detailed travel and connection questions, and timetables, see the tourist info offices.

On the Menu

CLOSE UP

THE MOST CELEBRATED DISH in Fukuoka is *tonkotsu ramen*, a strongly flavored pork-bone based soup with extra-thin noodles, scallions, and strips of roasted pork. Usually it gets heaps of garlic, chili pepper, and toppings of various sorts. Wherever you are on Kyūshū, ramen can never be too far, and it's always good.

Popular in Nagasaki, *shippoku* consists of elaborately prepared dishes that blend the flavors of Asia and Europe. Served Chinese style on a revolving round tabletop and perfect for large groups, shippoku is not a solitary affair. Another Nagasaki favorite, *chanpon*, consists of Chinese-style noodles, vegetables, and shellfish in a thick soup. *Sara* udon has the chanpon ingredients fried crispy instead of boiled.

Ba-sashi (raw horse meat) is a Kumamoto specialty. If you are hungry for a horse, all you need to know is that it tastes better than beef, and you feel the power *instantly*. Perhaps an easier-to-swallow delicacy is *karashi renkon*, slices of lotus root stuffed with mustard and/or cayenne and deep-fried. Compared to the subdued flavors of most Japanese cuisine, these dishes attest to the region's bolder palate.

In Kagoshim, don't pass up a chance to try the famed *kurobuta tonkatsu*, or breaded fried pork loin from locally bred black pigs. There's also *satsuma-age*, a fried-fish cake stuffed with ingredients like garlic, cheese, meat, potato, or burdock root. *Imo-jōchū*, a much-loved local spirit distilled from sweet potatoes, helps wash down these goodies—or start a fire.

In Yufuin trendy European-style cafés and eateries of all price ranges crowd the streets. Many people also dine in their hot-spring lodgings, where the culinary focus is usually fresh game and vegetables.

FUKUOKA

❶ *1½ hrs west of Tōkyō by plane, 5 hrs west of Tōkyō or 2½ hrs west of Ōsaka by Shinkansen.*

Fukuoka is a good base to begin exploring Kūshū. To get a sense of the city, walk along the meandering Naka-gawa river. The new Canal City shopping complex, a 15-minute walk west of Hakata Station, is full of great people-watching, shops, and dining. You'll find a bit of everything, from global coffee and fast-food outlets to famous local ramen.

If you are a night owl, you will find plenty happening in the west-central downtown area known as Tenjin, in alley after alley, at truly surprising hours. Friday nights only begin at midnight, with a hearty bowl of *tonkotsu* (pork-bone soup) ramen, a rich and tasty staple that locals seem to depend on for legendary all-night stamina.

The Naka-gawa divides the city. Everything west of the river is known as Fukuoka, while everything east—including the station and airport—is referred to as Hakata. Don't be overly confused: Hakata is just a ku, or district—the whole place is still Fukuoka.

Getting Around

Fukuoka was rebuilt after World War II with wide, tree-lined avenues arranged on an easy-to-navigate Western-style grid. The subway system connects the downtown attractions with a convenient extension to the international airport. The two major transportation hubs are Hakata Station and Tenjin Station. Tenjin, in the heart of downtown Fukuoka, is the terminal for both subway lines. The Kūkō Line runs to Hakata Station and on to Fukuoka Airport, and the Hakozaki Line runs out toward the bay. Fares start at ¥200.

A low-cost bus (¥100) operates in the city center. Most city buses leave from **Hakata Kōtsū Bus Center** (☎ 092/431–1171) across the street from Hakata Station, and from Tenjin Bus Center.

Sightseeing buses leave from **Tenjin Bus Center** (☎ 092/734–2500 or 092/771–2961) and from Hakata Kōtsū Bus Center. Very few tours are given in English, so ask at your hotel or the tourist information office for the recommended ones. A four-hour tour costs approximately ¥2,400.

The **Fukuoka International Association** (✉ Rainbow Plaza, IMS Bldg., locals call it "Eemuzu Biru," 8th fl., 1–7–11 Tenjin, Chūō-ku ☎ 092/733–2220 ☉ Daily 10–8; closed every 3rd Tues.) has an English-speaking staff, and English-language newspapers and periodicals are available for visitors to read. **Fukuoka Station Information** (✉ JR Fukuoka Station, 1 F, Central Gate ☎ 092/731–5221 ☉ Daily 8–8) offers information on travel, sightseeing, and accommodations.

What to See

The monk Eisai (1141–1215) returned from a long stint in China to introduce Zen Buddhism to Japan, and—so the story goes—planted the first tea-bush seeds. He established Japan's first Zen temple, **Shōfuku-ji,** which the inscription on the main gate by Emperor Gotoba commemorates. In Zen tradition, the grounds and structure reflect the calm, austere nature of this deeply meditative philosophy. The bronze bell in the belfry was designated an Important Cultural Property by the Japanese government. The temple is a 15-minute walk northwest from Hakata Station, or a five-minute Nishitetsu bus ride from the station to the nearby Oku-no-dō stop (you can pick up the bus on the main road in front of Hakata Station's west exit). ✉ 6–1 *Gokushō-machi, Hakata-ku* ☎ 092/291–0775 ⬜ *Free* ☉ *Daily 9–5.*

The lake at **Ōhori Kōen** was once part of an impressive moat surrounding Fukuoka's castle. A leisurely 1-mi path follows the perimeter of the lake. In early April the pink and white flowers of the park's 2,600 cherry trees present a dazzling display. Within the park is the **Fukuoka City Art Museum,** which houses a few notable works by Dalí, Miró, Chagall, and Warhol. Across from it is a traditional Japanese garden. From Hakata Station, take the subway to Ōhori Kōen Station; it's a 20-minute ride. ✉ *Chūō-ku* ☎ 092/714–6051 ⬜ *Park free, museum ¥200, garden ¥240* ☉ *Museum and garden Tues.–Sun. 9–4:45.*

To see where the hipsters do serious shopping and while away the hours, stroll around the amazing **Canal City.** Restaurants range from upscale dining to take-out, and there are countless cafés, shops, and hotels and a huge cinema. One end is a futuristic half-dome structure tiered with balconies and many levels of shops and eateries, in eye-catching salmon pink and pastel blue. Due to tantalizing sightlines, liberal use of glass, and clever angles employed in the entire structure, wherever you wander, it seems as if you can see into everything else. To get here, follow the street leading from the west exit of Hakata Station; it's a 15-minute walk. ⊠ *1–2 Sumiyoshi, Hakata-ku* ☎ *092/282-2525* ⊕ *www.canalcity.co.jp/english.*

Where to Stay & Eat

$$$ ✕ **Bassin.** Inside the fancy Plaza Hotel Tenjin, Bassin (locals pronounce it "Bah-san") has wooden counters and furniture set off against cream-colored walls, and art deco lamps. Try the garden salad with seaweed dressing or the marinated tofu. Unique dishes include grilled chicken in a burdock-root sauce, and stewed turtle meat with summer vegetables. More elaborate Japanese courses run ¥3,500–¥7,000. ⊠ *1–9–63 Daimyō, Chūō-ku* ☎ *092/739-3210* ▤ *AE, DC, MC, V.*

¢ ✕ **Deko.** Deko has no English menu, but the daily special, or *teishoku,* is a reliable choice. The central low tables of this boisterous bar are Japanese style; regular tables and chairs are in the back. The salmon-and-basil spring rolls are an excellent appetizer. It's between the Hakata train station and Yakuin subway station on Sumiyoshi-dōri. ⊠ *1–24–22 Takasago, Rasa Bldg., B1, Chūō-ku* ☎ *092/526-7070* ▤ *AE, DC, MC, V.*

★ ¢ ✕ **Hōrin.** To prepare for a big night in Tenjin, this is a convenient, delicious, and inexpensive place to grab some tonkotsu ramen. For less than ¥800 you can dive into a big bowl of thin noodles in a steamy pork-based soup garnished with sliced pork, chopped onions, slivers of ginger, and whatever other toppings you choose. As at Ichi-ran (below), the most recommended and popular topping is the sliced *kikurage* (black mushrooms)—high in protein, full of B vitamins, and said to boost the immune system. It's on a corner, just off the south side of Kōkutai-dōri, two blocks west of Haruyoshi Bridge, on the way to all-night fun in the Tenjin district. ⊠ *3–21—15 Haruyoshi, Chūō-ku* ☎ *092/738-5811* ▤ *No credit cards.*

★ ¢ ✕ **Ichi-ran.** Folks in Fukuoka wait in long lines to get their fix of distinctive extra-thin noodles swimming in a rectangular black box of pork-bone broth topped with tasty slices of *char-shu,* or roasted pork, *negi* (green onions), and sprinkles of *togarashi* (red pepper). Additional toppings such as *kikurage* (sliced black mushrooms), extra pork, or boiled eggs can be added for 100 yen each. The clerk gives you an order form (with English choices too), and you indicate exactly how you like it, from fat content to the amount of garlic. You then buy a ticket from the machine inside the door. Hang onto it until you are seated at a private cubicle with a curtain concealing all but the smells of the intoxicating substance you are about to receive. You place your ticket and order form on the counter below the curtain, and moments later the goods appear. The noodles taste best when ordered slightly chewy, and the soup is flavorful enough with a light fat content. There are several branches, including one in the basement of the Hakata Station complex, but the best one is in Canal City. ⊠ *1–2–22–B1F, Sumiyoshi, Hakata-ku* ☎ *092/263-2201* ▤ *No credit cards.*

★ $$$$ ⊞ **Fukuoka Grand Hyatt Hotel.** Far and away the best digs in town, the Grand Hyatt overlooks the fantastic Canal City entertainment complex. Those craving extravagance tempered with sophistication won't be disappointed. Mauve accents, green lighting, huge white stone pillars, and blonde wood panels set the relaxing mood of the lobby, which descends into one of the most arresting views of any bar in the world. Beyond an invisible and immense wall of glass, a fountain plays, and on the other side is the eye-riveting concave hemisphere of Canal City's Sun Dome. The hotel's opulent rooms peer out over either a long sci-fi view of the inside of Canal City or the Naka River and the rest of town. ⊠ *1–2–82 Sumiyoshi, Canal City, Hakata-ku, Fukuoka, Fukuoka-ken 812-0018* ☎ *092/282–1234* 🖷 *092/282–2817* ⊕ *www.fukuoka.grand.hyatt.com* ⇨ *370 rooms, 14 suites* ⚷ *4 restaurants, pool, health club (guests only; ¥3,000), hair salon, 2 bars, no-smoking rooms, in-room data ports* ⊟ *AE, DC, MC, V.*

$$ ⊞ **Canal City Fukuoka Washington Hotel.** This is no ordinary Washington Hotel; it's a full snazzy class above the others members of the chain. It's in Canal City, and the rooms have views either across the courtyard of the hallucinatory mall or out over the city. The lobby has free Internet, and hundreds of shops and eateries are steps away. ⊠ *1–2–20 Sumiyoshi, Hakata-ku, Fukuoka, Fukuoka-ken 812-0018* ☎ *092/282–8800* 🖷 *092/282–0757* ⇨ *423 rooms* ⚷ *2 restaurants, refrigerators, cable TV, in-room fax, no-smoking rooms* ⊟ *AE, DC, MC, V.*

$$ ⊞ **Hakata Tōkyū Inn** is an upscale Western-style hotel by the Naka-gawa, with large picture windows and free satellite TV. For dinner, try the hotel's bar-grill, Sora, on the top floor; the views of the Nakasu district are fantastic, and a decent crowd gathers for evening cocktails. Head east from Exit 16 of the Tenjin subway station; take your first left, and the hotel is on the right. ⊠ *1–16–1 Tenjin, Chūō-ku, Fukuoka, Fukuoka-ken 810-8584* ☎ *092/781–7111* 🖷 *092/781–7198* ⊕ *www.tokyuhotels. co.jp/en* ⇨ *217 rooms* ⚷ *Restaurant, refrigerators, cable TV, in-room data ports, bar, no-smoking rooms* ⊟ *AE, DC, MC, V.*

$ ⊞ **Tōyoko Inn Hakata Nishinakasu.** This Western-style hotel is a nice inexpensive choice for those staying downtown around the Naka-gawa. The lobby has a sunny lounge area with good views of the street for people-watching while you sip your coffee or surf the Internet for free. It's only one block west of the Haruyoshi Bridge along Kōkutai-dōri, on the right (north) side of the street. ⊠ *1–16–1 Nakasu, Chūō-ku, Fukuoka, Fukuoka-ken 810-0002* ☎ *092/739–1045* 🖷 *092/739–1046* ⊕ *www.toyoko-inn.com* ⇨ *260 rooms* ⚷ *Café, refrigerators, in-room data ports* ⊟ *AE, DC, MC, V.*

Nightlife

Fukuoka is forever in the throes of an ongoing party—perhaps in a heroic endeavor to put off the inevitable hangover—but the surest places for memorable nightlife action are the Nakasu and Tenjin areas, which run along the Naka-gawa. Nakasu is on the east side of the river, Tenjin on the west side.

For consorting with the in crowd, try the bar and café known as **Propeller Drive** (⊠ 1–13–30 Imaizumi, Chūō-ku ☎ 092/715–6322). It is open late every night, and you are practically guaranteed to see some of the prettiest and most stylishly dressed women in the world—as well as a few confident guys who are not intimidated by this. It's fancy, but there's no cover charge. All three floors have white-stucco walls, the second floor has a wonderful overhang with tables along a lovely long stucco railing, and everywhere, countless mirrors reflect the light of crystal chandeliers. The signature cocktail is the Love Swallow, a tasty rum-based drink built around a strawberry frozen in a perfect sphere of ice. Teetotalers will be pleased with the mango lassi, and a highly recommended snack is the pasta with bacon and spinach cream sauce.

Shopping

Fukuoka is known for two traditional folk crafts: Hakata *ningyō* (dolls) and Hakata obi (kimono sashes). Made of fired clay and hand-painted with bright colors and distinctive expressions, Hakata ningyō are primarily ornamental figures representing children, women, samurai, and geisha. The obi are made of a local silk that has a slightly coarse texture; other products made of this silk, such as bags and purses, make excellent souvenirs.

Kyūshū has a rich tradition of ceramics. Though not as colorful or exotic as Hagi-yaki, the shops and kilns of Arita and other towns of Saga Prefecture, in particular, continue to produce fine pottery, especially delicate-looking but surprisingly tough porcelain.

The seventh floor of the department store **Iwataya** (✉ 2–11–1 Tenjin, Chūō-ku ☎ 092/721–1111) carries the most complete selection of local merchandise, including Hakata dolls, silk, and ceramics. From the Tenjin subway station, take Exit W-5 and follow the street straight for two blocks. Traditional Edo-style restaurants and shops selling quaint souvenirs line the **Kawabata Shopping Arcade** (Kawabata Shōtengaii) stretching along the Naka-gawa from the Nakasu-Kawabata subway station to Canal City.

Getting There

BY AIR **Fukuoka Airport** (☎ 092/483–7003) is Kyūshū's main airport. It's just two stops away—only five minutes—from Fukuoka's Hakata train station on the Kūkō subway line. All Nippon Airways (ANA), Japan Airlines (JAL), and Skymark Airlines (SKY) fly the 1½-hour route to Fukuoka Airport from Tōkyō's Haneda Airport. JAL also flies once daily (1¾ hours) between Tōkyō's Narita International Airport and Fukuoka Airport. ANA and JAL have 12 direct flights (1¼ hours) between Osaka and Fukuoka. *See* Essentials for airline phone numbers.

BY BUS The **Kyūshū Kyūkō Bus Company** (☎ 092/734–2500 or 092/771–2961) makes the two-hour trip between Fukuoka's Tenjin Bus Center and Nagasaki. Frequent buses make the four-hour trip between Fukuoka (departing from Hakata Kōtsū Bus Center and Tenjin Bus Center) and Kagoshima.

BY TRAIN JR Shinkansen trains travel between Tōkyō and Hakata Station in Fukuoka (5½ hours) via Ōsaka and Hiroshima. The regular fare is ¥22,320, and there are 15 daily runs. Regular JR express trains also travel this route, but take at least twice as long.

NAGASAKI

1 hr 47 min southwest of Fukuoka by JR Express Kamome, ¥4,910.

Nagasaki is strung together on a long series of hillocks in a scenic valley following the Urakami River down into a harbor. The city was left with no suitably intact reminders of the atomic bombing, and there were apparently no compunctions about rebuilding up to the edges of a tiny ground-zero circle with a monument at its center. Still, relatively new as it all may be, everything here speaks primarily of Nagasaki's international history, from the city's lively and compact Chinatown to the European-style mansions and Catholic churches in the hillsides.

In the mid-16th century Portuguese missionaries—including Saint Francis Xavier, came ashore to preach throughout Kyūshū. This new and altruistic religion—coinciding with the arrival of firearms—threatened to spread like an epidemic through impoverished masses of the feudal system, and in 1597, to give bite to a new decree by Shogun Toyotomi to stifle worship, 26 followers were publicly crucified in Nagasaki. This cruel display was followed not long after by Tokugawa's nationwide edict making it a deadly crime to be Christian.

All foreigners were expelled except the Dutch, who were allowed to live on the island known as Dejima. Of the local population, only merchants and prostitutes had direct interactions with them. The Dutch took over the considerable brokerage of trade that the Portuguese had formerly handled between China and Japan, and the whole city prospered with this tiny loophole out in the harbor. This odd situation lasted until 1859, when insular Japan was forced to open up to the outside world.

Once other ports became popular, the city lost much of its special status, but Mitsubishi decided to concentrate its arms manufacturing and shipbuilding capabilities here; this and bad weather over the primarily target of Kokura in northern Kyūshū made Nagasaki the default target for the second atomic bomb dropped in 1945.

The city isn't small, but as it lies in a long winding valley you get a small slice at a time. Similarities with San Francisco have been touted, and the comparison is not far off—although the posters in streetcars advertising whale-bacon and racy comics quickly remind you of where you are!

Getting Around

While most of the interesting sights, restaurants, and shopping areas are south of Nagasaki Station, the Peace Park and the Atomic Bomb Museum are to the north, about 10–15 minutes by tram or taxi.

Nagasaki is small enough to cover on foot, otherwise the streetcar system is the most convenient mode of transportation. Stops are posted in English, and lines extend to every attraction in town. You can purchase a one-day streetcar pass (¥500) at tourist offices and major hotels. Otherwise, pay ¥100 as you get off the streetcar at any stop. If you wish to transfer from one streetcar to another, get a *norikae kippu* (transfer ticket) from the driver of the first one. Local buses are not as convenient, and the routes, timetables, and fares are complicated.

Nagasaki

平和公園
原爆資料館

②③

Ken-ei
Bus Center

Tourist
Office

**Nagasaki
Station**

**City/Tourist
Information**

JR NAGASAKI HONSEN LINE

NISHI NAKA
MASHI-DORI

**Post
Office**

Asahi Ōhashi

NAGASAKI
ELECTRIC
RAILWAY

*Gotō-
machi*

Urakami gawa

Rte. 202

*Nagasaki-kō
(Nagasaki
Harbor)*

**Nagasaki
Port Terminal**

Hamaichi-dōri

Rte. 34

Ōhato

Kankō-dōri

Dōjima

Nakashima gawa

**Dejima
Wharf**

④
出島

Tsuki-machi

SHINCHI
CHŪKAGAI
(SHINCHI
CHINATOWN)

Doza-dōri

*Shimin
Byōin-mae*

Matsugae

*Ōura
Kaigan-dōri*

*Ōura-
Tenshudo-shita*

⑤ オランダ坂

Ishi-bashi

⑥ 孔子廟

1/8 mile

1/8 kilometer

グラバー園
⑦

⑧ 大浦天主堂

KEY	
——	*JR Trains*
+++	*Streetcar*

A few privately run rickshaws hang out on the streets of Chinatown. The minimum cost is ¥1,000 per person, and you can call ahead to arrange a pickup at your hotel.

One-hour **cruises** (☎ 095/824–0088) of Nagasaki Harbor depart from Nagasaki-kō (Nagasaki Port) at 10:30, noon, 1:30, 3, and 4:30; the cost is ¥1,200.

The **City Tourist Information Center** (✉ Inside Nagasaki Station, 1–1 Onoue-machi ☎ 095/823–3631 ⊕ www1.city.nagasaki.nagasaki.jp), provides English assistance, maps, and brochures; it's open daily 8–8. The **Nagasaki Prefectural Tourist Information Center** (✉ Nagasaki Ken-ei Bus Terminal Bldg., 2nd fl., 3–1 Daikoku-machi ☎ 095/828–7875) is across the street from Nagasaki Station. Use the pedestrian bridge on the second floor of the station to reach it. English travel information for the entire prefecture, including maps and bus schedules, is available daily 9–5:45.

What to See

❷ Heiwa Kōen (Peace Park) was built on the grounds of an old prison destroyed in the atomic blast. In the middle is a large statue of a godlike man sitting with one arm stretched to the sky (where the bomb came from) and one to the land (where it fell). A short distance down the hill, **Hypocenter Kōen** marks the bomb's "hypocenter." A solitary pillar was erected to mark the exact epicenter, and there is curiously little distance separating this from anything else. Traffic rumbles by not far below, and apartment buildings and a hotel or two look down from the hill directly behind. If you came upon it during a stroll, the feeling might almost be: Oh, what's in this little clearing over here? But a dreadfully heavy awareness tends to descend upon all here, so the mood becomes a somber one. From Nagasaki Station take either Streetcar 1 or 3 for the 10-minute ride to the Matsuya-machi stop. 🎟 *Free* ⊙ *Park never closes.*

❸ The spiral staircase of the **Atomic Bomb Museum** (Gembaku Shiryōkan) takes you down into a dark collection of video loops, dioramas, and exhibits that demonstrate the devastating effects of the bomb. English audio tours are available, though what you see is already too much to handle. The continuous, unblinking film footage is absolutely nauseating at several points, and a melted and blasted wall clock, as surreal as any painting, sears its way into your conscience. Out in the brightly lighted hallway, across from life-size mock-ups of the two atomic bombs, is a strange exhibit under a caption that reads "Japan's Wartime Aggression in the Pacific," which has a perfunctory list of conflicts, and includes an odd picture of Chinese peasant women training with pistols—though there's no mention of the atrocity that Tōkyō's Yasukuni Shrine calls "The Nanjing Strategy." To get to the museum, take Streetcar 1 from Nagasaki Station to the Hamaguchi stop. ✉ *7–8 Hirano-machi* ☎ *095/844–1231* ⊕ *www1.city.nagasaki.nagasaki.jp* 🎟 *¥200, audio tour ¥150* ⊙ *Sept.–Apr., daily 8:30–5:30; May–Aug., daily 8:30–6.*

When the government expelled foreigners from Japan in the mid-17th century, Dutch traders were the only Westerners allowed to remain— **❹** but they were relegated to and confined on the artificial island of **Dejima** in Nagasaki Harbor. Here you can see a 450-year-old mix of Dutch

August 9, 1945

11

ON AUGUST 9, 1945, two days after the blast at Hiroshima, Nagasaki fell victim to a second atomic bomb because of bad weather—the plane, named *Bock's Car,* was supposed to drop the "Fat Man," a plutonium bomb, on the war industries of Kukora. A delay in hooking up with *Bock's Car*'s B-29 escorts meant that when they reached Kukora bad weather had rolled in and blocked their view of the target. So they headed over to the secondary target, Nagasaki, and dropped the bomb there.

More powerful than the bomb dropped on Hiroshima, the "Fat Man's" runaway fission released the heat- and light-wave radiation of a small sun, and delivered a blast pressure of *tons per square inch,* which explains why virtually nothing was left standing, or even recognizable, within miles. Nagasaki's hilly topography helped save a number of residential areas from total destruction, and incredibly, some didn't lose electricity. Meanwhile, 6.7 square km (2.59 square mi) were obliterated, 74,884 people were killed in the blast or shortly thereafter, and another 74,909 were injured. Radioactivity caused the deaths of an estimated 70,000 others within five years.

housing styles. Take Streetcar 1 to the Dejima stop. ☒ *6–3 Dejima-machi* ☎ *095/821–7200* ✆ *¥500* ⊘ *Daily 8–6.*

❺ **Oranda-zaka** (Holland Slope) is a good place to wander on the way to Chinatown and Glover Garden. It's a cobblestone incline with restored wooden houses originally built by Dutch residents in the late 19th century. Many have become shops and tearooms in summer. To get here, follow the street on the southeast side of the Chinese Mansion.

❻ The **Chinese Mansion** (Kōshi-byō), a bright-red Confucian shrine, was built in 1893 by the Chinese residents of Nagasaki. The small museum displays artifacts on loan from Beijing's National Museum of Chinese History and the Palace Museum of Historical Treasures. The closest streetcar stop is Ishi-bashi; look for the signs leading to the shrine. ☎ *095/ 824–4022* ✆ *¥525* ⊘ *Daily 8:30–5.*

❼ **Glover Garden** contains an impressive assortment of 19th-century West-
Fodor's Choice ern houses. Wooden verandas, Greco-Roman porticos and arches, and
★ other random elements of European architecture adorn these houses, which are often crowned with Japanese-style roofs. The main attraction is the former mansion (1863) of Thomas Glover, a prominent Scottish merchant who introduced the first steam locomotive and industrialized coal-mining in Japan. Escalators whisk you up the steep hillside to the gardens, where you can admire the views of Nagasaki and the harbor. Take Streetcar 5 to Ōura Tenshudo-shita and follow the signs, ☎ *0958/ 22–8223* ✆ *¥600* ⊘ *Oct.–July, daily 8–6; Aug. and Sept., daily 8–6.*

❽ **Ōura Catholic Church** (Ōura Tenshu-dō) survived the bomb that leveled much of the city farther up the valley. It was constructed in 1865 to commemorate the death of 26 Christians crucified in 1597, victims of Toyotomi's gruesome message of religious intolerance. It's the oldest Gothic-style building in Japan. Below the entrance to Glover Garden, the church is a five-minute walk from the Ōura Tenshu-dō-shita streetcar stop. ⊠ *Minami Yamate 5–3, Dejima-machi* ☎ *0958/23–2628* ⇨ *¥300* ⊙ *Mar.–Nov., daily 8–6; Dec.–Feb., daily 8:30–5.*

Where to Stay & Eat

$$$$ ✕ **Kagetsu**. This quiet hilltop retreat is Nagasaki's most prestigious restaurant. Dishes are served as *kaiseki* (Kyōto-style multicourse meals) or *shippoku*, an elaborate course blending Asian and European elements. Lunch runs from ¥5,200 to ¥10,500; dinners start at ¥11,000. The interior wooden beams date to 1618, when Kagetsu was reputedly a high-class brothel. According to another local legend, Meiji Restoration leader Ryōma Sakamoto once took a chunk out of a wooden pillar with his sword during a brawl, leaving a still visible gash. ⊠ *2–1 Maruyama-chō* ☎ *095/822–0191* ⊟ *DC, MC, V.*

¢–$$$ ✕ **Dejima Wharf**. Warm nights draw crowds to the outdoor terraces of this trendy two-story wooden complex on the pier next to Nagasaki Port. You'll find a sprawl of tantalizing seafood restaurants downstairs; a quiet pub serving pasta dishes, pizza, and cocktails at the north end of the second floor; and a family restaurant with burgers and Japanese noodle and rice dishes on the south end of the second floor. ⊠ *Dejima Wharf* ☎ *095/828–3939* ⊟ *AE, DC, MC, V.*

★ ¢–$$ ✕ **Kairakuen**. This ornate Chinese restaurant is a local favorite, and it's easy to see, smell, and taste why. They serve the best *chanpon*—Chinese-style noodles and vegetables in an invigorating soup—in town. Mama-san speaks English if given the chance, and Papa-san sits like Buddha and watches over the customers. It's just inside the entrance to Chinatown, on the left. (Take the streetcar to Tsukimachi and walk a couple of blocks south.) ⊠ *10–16 Shinchi-machi* ☎ *095/822–4261* ⊟ *MC, V.*

$ ✕ **Karuda**. Authentic pizza and pasta are the mainstays at this Italian restaurant in the Shian-bashi entertainment quarter (east of Chinatown). From rustic wooden tables upstairs you watch the narrow streets below. Take-out is also available. From the Shian-bashi tram stop, head two blocks north into the arcade and another two blocks east. ⊠ *1–20 Kajiya-machi* ☎ *095/826–1302* ⊟ *No credit cards.*

★ $$$$ 🏨 **Hotel New Nagasaki**. Glossy marble and massive slabs of granite dominate this popular and upscale hotel. Standard twin rooms are large and comfortable, with enough space for a couple of easy chairs and a table. Light colors, pastel carpets, and tasteful gold accents keep things looking chic. It's unbeatably convenient, right next to Nagasaki Station and the new, always lively Amu Plaza shopping center. ⊠ *14–5 Daikoku-machi, Nagasaki-shi, Nagasaki-ken 850-0057* ☎ *095/826–8000* 🖷 *095/823–2000* ⊕ *www.newnaga.com* ⇨ *130 rooms* ⌂ *3 restaurants, cable TV, in-room data ports, indoor pool, gym, sauna, shops* ⊟ *AE, DC, MC, V.*

$$$$ 🏨 **Sakamoto-ya**. Established in 1895, this wooden ryokan is the oldest lodging in town, and it seems to have changed very little over time. It's small and has extremely personalized service and fragrant Japanese *hi-*

noki (cypress) bathtubs. The cost of the rooms varies according to size and location, but charges always include breakfast and dinner. The restaurant specializes in *shippoku,* which takes its name from Chinese kanji meaning dinner table, available for ¥3,500. ✉ *2–13 Kanaya-machi, Nagasaki-shi, Nagasaki-ken 850-0037* ☎ *095/826–8211* 🖷 *095/ 825–5944* ☎ *14 Japanese-style rooms* ♿ *Restaurant, Japanese baths* ⊟ *AE, DC, MC, V* †⊙† *MAP.*

$$ 🖵 **Holiday Inn Nagasaki.** For value and location—with a dash of style and sophistication—this is the place. Leather chairs, vintage sofas, antique telephones, and dark oil paintings in the lobby are reminiscent of an old European drawing room. Free international newspapers are at the entrance, and the hotel staff provides advice in perfect English. Rooms are spacious, with rare king-size beds. Look for the familiar sign on Kankō-dōri, the busy, main strip of downtown Nagasaki, at the Shian-bashi tram stop. ✉ *6–24 Dōza-machi, Nagasaki-shi, Nagasaki-ken 850-0841* ☎ *095/828–1234* 🖷 *095/828–0178* ⊕ *www.ichotelsgroup. com* ☎ *87 rooms, 6 suites* ♿ *Restaurant, room service, refrigerators, lounge, car rental, no-smoking rooms* ⊟ *AE, DC, MC, V.*

$–$$ 🖵 **Hotel WingPort.** Computer rentals and in-room Internet access make the WingPort popular with business travelers. Guest quarters are nice but small—unless you splurge for the super or deluxe twins—and the hotel is a two-minute walk from Nagasaki Station (across the pedestrian bridge on the narrow road past the convenience store). ✉ *9–2 Daikoku-machi, Nagasaki-shi, Nagasaki-ken 850-0057* ☎ *095/833–2800* 🖷 *095/833–2801* ☎ *200 rooms* ♿ *Restaurant, in-room data ports* ⊟ *AE, DC, MC, V.*

Shopping

Castella sponge cake, the popular souvenir of Nagasaki, was introduced by the Portuguese in the mid-16th century. The original recipe called for just eggs, flour, and sugar, but it's been tinkered with over time. Every sweet shop and souvenir store in town has its own specially flavored recipe, but you're advised to stick with the good old plain, a delightful treat with coffee or tea and raspberries.

The bakery **Fukusaya** (✉ *3–1 Funadaiku-machi* ☎ *095/821–2938*) has been in business since the Meiji period. When you say "castella" in this town, most people think of this shop and its distinctive yellow packaging. There's a branch on the first floor of the New Nagasaki Hotel, next to Nagasaki Station.

Not far from Dejima, **Hamano-machi** is the major shopping district in downtown Nagasaki. This covered arcade stretches over four blocks and contains numerous department stores, cake shops, cafés, pharmacies, and fashion boutiques.

Amu Plaza (Amu Puraza). Towering over Nagasaki Station, this is where everyone converges as the sun sets. The newest shops and restaurants are here, and a multi-theater movie complex is inside. It's thoroughly modern, and a striking contrast to the city's old-fashioned style.

Getting There

BY AIR   Nagasaki Airport is approximately one hour by bus or car from Nagasaki. A regular shuttle bus travels between Nagasaki Airport and Nagasaki Station and costs ¥1,200. All Nippon Airways and Japan Airlines fly daily from Haneda Airport in Tōkyō to Nagasaki Airport (1¾ hours). From Ōsaka the flights are about 1¼ hours. *See* Essentials for airline phone numbers and Web sites.

BY BUS   The **Kyūshū Kyūkō Bus Company** (☏ 092/734–2500) runs buses between Fukuoka's Tenjin Bus Center and **Nagasaki Bus Terminal** (✉ 3–1 Daikoku-machi ☏ 095/826–6221); the trip takes two hours. The **Nagasaki Ken-ei Bus Company** (☏ 095/823–6155) can get you to Unzen (¥1,900), a string of hot springs on the Shimabara Peninsula, in two hours, and direct to Kumamoto in three hours for ¥3,600.

BY TRAIN   The JR Kamome Express train costs ¥4,910 and takes 1 hour 47 minutes from Fukuoka's Hakata Station to **Nagasaki Station** (✉ 1–1 Onouemachi, Nagasaki- shi ☏ 095/826–4336). To get to Kumamoto from Nagasaki, take the JR Kamome to Tosu (two hours) and switch to the Tsubame Relay (one hour). Note that unless you have a free ride with a RailPass, at ¥6,770, it's going to be nearly double the cost of the bus.

KUMAMOTO

❾ *1 hr 20 min south of Fukuoka by JR Limited Express, ¥3,440.*

Kumamoto is nearly midway along the west coast of Kyūshū. From here you can go to Unzen to the west, Aso-san to the east, and Kagoshima to the south on the new high-speed train line.

The town has many sights of its own, including the nationally famous Suizen-ji Garden, but the most renowned is the castle once deemed impregnable. Kiyomasa Katō ushered in the 17th century with the construction of the mighty fortress (it was even bigger than the current replica), and he and his son held sway here until the 1630s. The Hosokawa clan then took over, and for the next couple of centuries Kumamoto was a center of the Tokugawa governmental authority. In 1877, the real "Last Samurai," Saigō Takamori, and his army of rebels brought their doomed rebellion here to battle untested Meiji government conscripts holed up inside. In the ensuing tussle much of the castle and its compound were destroyed. Supposedly, it was during this fearsome siege of 50-odd days that raw horseflesh was first eaten—and discovered to be so worth doing that it continues as a local stamina food to this day.

A number of notable folks had homes in town, including the writers Lafcadio Hearn and Sōseki Natsume, both of whom lived here for brief periods while teaching English.

Getting Around
In most Japanese cities the hive of activity is around the station. However, very little of interest surrounds JR Kumamoto Station—the bulk of the attractions are to the northeast, squeezed in between the Tsuboi

In Footsteps of the "Last Samurai"

CLOSE UP

AS TOM CRUISE noted about his film *The Last Samurai*, it was not the character he portrayed, Nathan Algren, who was the true hero of the story, but rather the samurai he'd come to admire, his captor, Katsumoto, played by Ken Watanabe. The character Katsumoto was based on an enigmatic man from Kagoshima named Saigō Takamori, a central figure in the effort to restore the Emperor, who turned away when he felt betrayed by his cause. A physically and mentally imposing man influenced strongly by the conscience-honing philosophies of Confucianism and Zen, Takamori understood that dramatic changes would be necessary to ensure the success of Japan's transition from feudal state to modern society. Among them was the need for a well-trained, tested, and respected army. To further this end, he devised a scheme to provoke a war with the "hermit kingdom" of Korea. So audacious was his plan—it involved his own sacrifice to bring it off—that although it gained a high degree of secret support unknown to him, officially he was rebuked for it, whereupon he withdrew to the hills to school a band of disgruntled out-of-work samurai that later became the Satsuma Rebellion. With the unlikely exception of the character of Algren, the movie provided the fairly accurate basis of events. Key battles were in Kumamoto—the only successful siege of the mighty castle ever was by Takamori and his men—and Kagoshima, where it all came to an end in late 1877.

---

and Shira rivers. Most of what constitutes downtown huddles near the old castle.

This city is spread out, and buses get stuck in traffic, so your best bet is to hop a streetcar. Two tram lines (Nos. 2 and 3) connect the major areas of the city. Grab a ticket from the automatic dispenser when you board, and pay as you get off. A fare chart is posted at the front, to the left of the driver. From the Kumamoto Eki-mae streetcar stop in front of the train station it's a 10-minute ride downtown (¥150). One-day travel passes, good for use on streetcars (and city buses), are available for ¥500 from the City Tourist Information Office.

The **City Tourist Information Office** (✉ JR Kumamoto Station, 3–15–1 Kasuga ☎ 096/352–3743), open daily 8:30 to 7, can provide maps and information in English. The city's Web site (⊕ www.visitkumamoto.com) also has good descriptions of major sights.

What to See

★ Towering, ominous **Kumamoto Castle** (Kumamoto-jō) was completed in 1607, designed and built by Kiyomasa Katō (1562–1611), the area's feudal lord or *daimyō*. Gracefully curved roofs rest atop the gorgeous white-and-black keep. The wide stone base has *mushagaeshi*, concave walls with stout platform overhangs, situated under slanted windows perfect for unleashing rock falls, one of many clever features to prevent intrusion. The castle nonetheless suffered a fatal attack in the Battle of Seinen, when rebellious samurai led by Saigō Takamori, furious over their obsolescence under the imperial Meiji government, went up against government troops holed up inside for six blood-drenched weeks during the Satsuma Rebellion of 1877. Most accounts have it that Takamori and his rebels actually breached, sacked, and burned the castle before running off to Kagoshima, although one source claims that a fire broke out and spread a day or so before the battle even began.

The costly reconstruction of the massive castle didn't make noticeable headway until 1960, when it opened to the public. Though much has been done, the scope of the task is mind-boggling, and efforts continue. The top floor commands an excellent view of Kumamoto, and exhibits include samurai weapons and armor arrayed to evoke images of the fearless warriors charging into battle. To get here, board Streetcar 2, get off at the Kumamoto-jō-mae stop, and walk up the tree-lined slope. Volunteer guides conduct tours in English, or you can take a self-guided audiocassette tour for ¥300. ☎ *096/352–5900* 🖅 *¥500; ¥640 for combined admission to castle and Hosokawa Mansion; purchase ticket at castle* ☉ *Apr.–Oct., daily 8:30–5:30; Nov.–Mar., daily 8:30–4:30.*

The **Hosokawa Mansion** (Kyū-Hosokawa Gyōbu-tei) was built in 1646 for the Hosokawa family, who took power at the behest of Tokugawa in 1611—and whose local lineage produced Japan's briefly reigning but still wildly popular former Prime Minister Morihiro Hosokawa (served 1993–9). English-speaking guides lead a detailed tour, pointing out architectural features such as hidden doors and booby traps. To get here, follow the signs from the main castle entrance. ⊠ *3–1 Furukyō-machi* ☎ *096/352–6522* 🖅 *¥300; ¥640 for combined admission to mansion and Kumamoto Castle; purchase ticket at castle* ☉ *Apr.–Oct., Tues.–Sun. 8:30–5:30; Nov.–Mar., Tues.–Sun. 8:30–4:30.*

Created in the mid-17th century, **Suizen-ji Jōju-en** (Suijzen-ji Garden) was originally part of the sprawling villa of the ruling Hosokawa family. An undulating hummock of lush green grass representing Japan—there's even a Fuji-san-like cone in about the right place—is beside a pond surrounded by a network of stone bridges. The garden is dotted with impeccably trimmed bushes and trees. A tiny old teahouse gives welcome respite from the tour-bus groups. Also on the grounds is Izumi Jinja (Izumi Shrine), which houses the tombs of several eminent Hosokawa clan members. To get to the garden, take Streetcar 2 or 3 east from the castle to the Suizen-ji Jōju-en-mae stop. ⊠ *1–1 Tetorisai-machi* ☎ *096/38–2111* 🖅 *¥400* ☉ *Mar.–Nov., daily 7:30–6; Dec.–Feb., daily 8:30–5.*

Where to Stay & Eat

$$$$ ✕ **Loire.** Deluxe French dishes are served at this elegant, spacious restaurant on the 11th floor of the Kumamoto Castle Hotel. Windows provide a dramatic view of the castle, which is flooded in pale-green light at night. Slices of smoked black pig with fresh fruit make a wonderful hors-d'oeuvre, and the lamb chops are superb—as is the sea bass. Sumptuous

11

desserts start at only ¥630. Choose between fixed courses, or order things à la carte. ✉ *4–2 Jōtō-machi* ☎ *096/326–3311* ☰ *AE, DC, MC, V.*

★ **$$–$$$$** ✗ **Suganoya.** When in Kumamoto, do as the locals do—eat some *ba-sashi*—raw horsemeat! What do you think gave the Last Samurai that legendary stamina during that castle siege? If you order the Nishiki Set ¥6,300, you can get served in all its forms, from a starter of raw tidbits with garlic and ginger and assorted dunking sauces to a finale of hari-hari nabe, a soup of thinly sliced delicately flavored meat (horse, of course!) and vegetables cooked rare in a folded-paper vessel that doesn't burn. Sit at the bar for a delightful atmosphere of frenzy, or kick back at one of the secluded tables. ✉ *2–12 Jō-tō-machi, Lion Parking Biru 2F* ☎ *096/355–3558* ☉ *Daily 11:30–2 and 4:30–8:30* ☰ *AE, DC, V.*

$ ✗ **Aoyagi.** When you enter, you'll be greeted by elegant women dressed in full kimono. But don't just stand there, there's work to be done! The extensive menu includes regional favorites—*ba-sashi* (raw horse meat) and *karashi renkon* (lotus root stuffed with fiery chili powder or mustard and fried)—in addition to various types of sushi and tofu dishes. You can sit at the counter and admire the skilled chefs or relax in a quiet booth. It's tucked behind the Daiei department store, not far from the Shi-yakusho-mae streetcar stop. ✉ *1–2–10 Shimotori-chō* ☎ *096/353–0311* ☉ *Mon.–Sat. 6–11 PM. Closed Sun.* ☰ *AE, DC, V.*

★ **$$–$$$$** 🏨 **Kumamoto Hotel Castle.** Just across from the castle, things are dark-wooded and traditional enough to be mysterious, but the service is excellent and modern. They'll even help you plan out a timetable for a journey to Aso-san, and continue to check into it while you get yourself ready, and then be forthright enough to tell you that persistent cloud cover and showers are likely to make your arduous day-trip a dubious adventure. Rooms come in an amazing variety of layouts, all with ornate puffy furnishings in luscious creamy colors. ✉ *4–2 Jōtō-machi, Kumamoto-shi, Kumamoto-ken 860-8565* ☎ *096/326–3311* 🖷 *096/326–3324* 📞 *185 rooms* ♨ *5 restaurants, 2 bars, cable TV* ☰ *AE, DC, MC, V.*

$$$ 🏨 **Hotel New Ōtani Kumamoto.** It's not as over-the-top as its big-city counterparts, but it's endowed with the same crisp service and all the amenities. Weary travelers will be happy to know it's just to the left (north) of Kumamoto Station. The small bright lobby does interesting things with color, space and geometry. ✉ *1–13–1 Kasuga, Kumamoto-shi, Kumamoto-ken 860-0047* ☎ *096/326–1111* 🖷 *096/326–0800* ⊕ *www. newotani.co.jp/en* 📞 *130 rooms* ♨ *4 restaurants, room service, sauna (men only), piano bar* ☰ *AE, DC, MC, V.*

$ 🏨 **Tōyoko Inn Karashima Kōen.** This adequate but inexpensive hotel offers a rare bonus: a free in-room movie channel in the otherwise basic Western-style rooms. There's also a simple but tasty complimentary Japanese breakfast—*onigiri* (rice balls wrapped in seaweed), miso soup, and coffee—in the lobby. To get here, take the streetcar to Karashima-cho. ✉ *1–24 Kōyaima-machi, Kumamoto-shi, Kumamoto-ken, 860-0012* ☎ *096/322–1045* 🖷 *096/322–2045* ⊕ *www.toyoko-inn.com/e hotel/00077/index.html* 📞 *153 rooms* ♨ *Restaurant, cable TV, laundry facilities, Internet, no-smoking rooms* ☰ *AE, DC, MC, V* ◉ *CP.*

Shopping

Kumamoto's most famous product is *Higo zōgan,* or Higo inlay. A unique form of metalwork originally employed in the decoration of swords, scabbards, and gunstocks of the Hosokawa clan, it consists of black steel delicately inlaid with silver and gold, and it is now used to make fashionable jewelry that does not come cheap—a simple pendant can run ¥8,000, and prices for large pieces reach ¥700,000 and more. Other local products include gold paper lanterns, dolls, tops, and fine cutlery.

Dentō Kōgei-kan (Kumamoto Traditional Crafts Center ⊠ 3–35 Chibajō ☎ 096/324–4930), open Tuesday–Sunday 9–5, is the best place to buy *zōgan* and regional handicrafts. It's in a redbrick building across from the Akazu-mon entrance to the castle.

Getting There

BY AIR   The Kyūshū Sankō bus makes the 50-minute run from Kumamoto Airport to JR Kumamoto Station for ¥670. Flights on All Nippon Airways and Sky Net Asia (SNA) connect Tōkyō's Haneda Airport with Kumamoto Airport (1¼ hours). ANA flies the hour-long route from Ōsaka's Itami Airport eight times a day. *See* Essentials for airline phone numbers and Web sites.

BY BUS   The Nagasaki Ken-ei Bus (from Nagasaki Ken-ei Bus Terminal) costs ¥3,600 and takes three hours to **Kumamoto City Kōtsū Center** (⊠ 3–10 Sakura-machi ☎ 096/354–6411). Before reaching Kumamoto the bus stops in Unzen (¥1,900, two hours). **Kyū-Sankō buses** (☎ 096/355–2525) leaving from Kumamoto City Kōtsū Center take 3 hours 15 minutes to Kagoshima, for ¥3,600. There's also a bus route linking the onsen paradise of Yufuin and Kumamoto in 4½ hours for ¥3,850, and from April to October a trip via Aso-san (90-minute stop for Aso sightseeing) can be done for ¥7,550 in about six hours. Call (Kyū-Sankō at) 096/354–4845 for reservations (recommended).

BY TRAIN   The JR Tsubame Express from Fukuoka's Hakata Station stops at **Kumamoto Station** (⊠ 3–15–1 Kasuga ☎ 096/211–2406) and takes 1¼ hours, ¥3,940. From Nagasaki, take JR to Tosu and change to the train for Kumamoto (2¾ hours, ¥7,170).

ASO-SAN (MT. ASO)

⑩ *1 hr 10 min east of Kumamoto by JR Hōhi Line, ¥2,180, then 40 min by bus, ¥470.*

Aso-san comprises the world's largest caldera, 128 km in circumference, up to 15 mi wide in places, formed after a massive lava-dome collapse around 100,000 years ago. Inside the crater are seven settlements and countless cows and horses. The emerald-green grasses that nourish them thrive in the wildly fertile volcanic soil. The crater area, officially named the Aso-Kujū (Mt. Aso National Park), contains five volcanic cones; one is still active. Naka-dake is the living beast, and it sticks up out of the side of the taller Taka-dake just east of the crater's center. There's no mistaking the sulfurous stench of the mighty belches that gust freely from its mouth.

Aso-san is an excellent stopover on the way to Yufuin from Kumamoto. It can be a day-trip—but start early; though you have until 9 for the last Kumamoto-bound train, the last bus back from the ropeway to distant Aso Station is at 5. If you want to spend more time in the park, stay in one of the many mountain pensions clustered in the southern half.

Stop by the **Aso Station Information Center** (⊠ inside JR Aso Station ☎ 0967/34–0751 ☉ Thurs.–Tues. 9–5) to get your bearings and check conditions. The mountain's emissions occasionally take the lives of tourists, and park officials will shut things down when the alarm is raised.

Exploring Aso-san

Fodor'sChoice The view from the top of 5,000-foot **Naka-dake** is reason enough to visit ★ Mt. Aso National Park. Inside the crater a churning ash-gray lake bubbles and spits scalding, reeking steam. Naka-dake's rim is a 30-minute walk from the bottom of the **Aso Nishi Cable Car** (⊠ Furubōchū, Aso-chō ☎ 0967/34–0411) at Asosan-jō; the cable car (¥410 one-way) takes you up in four minutes. You can skirt around some of the lip, but the northern reaches have been out of bounds since 1997, when toxic fumes seeped out and killed two tourists. If rumbling turns to shaking, and steam and smoke turn to sizeable ash fall, know where the bunkerlike shelters are located. These were built after a dozen people perished in a sudden eruption some 50 years ago.

Kusasenri, a 35-minute ride from the JR Aso Station on the Kyūshū Sankō bus line, is a bowl-shaped meadow where cows and horses graze on the lush grass and wade in shallow marshes. If you have time, hike along an easy trail that goes 5½ km (3½ mi) around the base of Kijima-dake. It takes an hour or so, and provides excellent views of the otherworldly terrain. You could also march the 3 km (2 mi) straight across the rugged lava plain to the foot of Naka-dake. For several trails of other lengths and difficulty in the area, pick up the "Aso Trekking Route Map" at the information center in JR Aso Station.

The **Aso Volcano Museum** (Aso Kazan Hakubutsukan) is across from the Kusasenri parking lot and rest area. Want to see what's happening inside the volcano? Two impervious cameras were inserted into the most active part of the volcano, and museum visitors can watch what they are seeing. Another display shows how Japan sits on the busiest tectonic plate junction in the world—and how these fault lines are visible from space. ⊠ *Kusasenri Aso-cho* ☎ *0967/34 2111* ▭ *¥840* ☉ *Daily 9–5*.

Where to Stay

There are more than 50 lodging outfits in and around Aso National Park; the following are particularly worth recommending.

$$$ ▣ **Yamaguchi Ryokan.** From the outdoor baths of this rustic lodge you can watch mineral water meander down the rocky cliffs of the green

mountainside. Don't be shy—mixed bathing is often practiced here. Two meals are included, and dinner is served in your Japanese-style room. The lobby has a raftered ceiling and a toasty old-fashioned furnace. It's a cozy place to enjoy a cup of coffee or tea. From Kumamoto, take the JR Hōhi Line to Tateno and switch to the Minami Aso Tetsudō Line. ⊠ *2331 Kawayō, Aso-gun, Chōyō-mura Kumamoto-ken 860-1404* ☎ *0967/67–0006* 📠 *0967/67–1694* 🛏 *35 Japanese-style rooms* 🖃 *AE, DC, MC, V* 🍽 *MAP.*

$$ 🏨 **Pension Angelica.** The main appeal of this manor in the woods is the hospitality of the Tatsuji family. White lacy bedspreads decorate the bright guest rooms, which have tall windows overlooking flower bushes. The kitchen creates culinary wonders, from fresh bread to Mediterranean dishes. At craft time, you can learn to make *washi* (Japanese paper) or clay figurines. From Kumamoto, take the JR Hōhi Line to Tateno and switch to the Minami Aso Tetsudō Line. Get off at Takamori and call the pension, which will have someone pick you up; the hosts asks that you get there before dinner, served at 6:30. ⊠ *1–1800 Shirakawa, Minami-aso-mura, Aso-gun, Kumamoto-ken 869-1502* 📠 *0967/62–2223* 🌐 *www5.ocn.ne.jp/~angelica* 🛏 *7 rooms, 2 with bath* 🍴 *Restaurant, Japanese baths, bar, lounge, no-smoking rooms* 🖃 *No credit cards* 🍽 *MAP.*

Getting There

BY BUS **Kyūshū Sankō and Kumakita Sankō buses** (☎ 096/355–2525 or 0968/857–1000) make frequent runs between Kumamoto City Kōtsū Center, the Aso Nishi cable-car station at Asosan-jō, and Kurokawa Onsen. The Kyūshū bus continues from Kurokawa Onsen to Yufuin and Beppu.

BY TRAIN The JR Hōhi Line runs between Kumamoto Station and **JR Aso Station** (⊠ Kurokawa, Aso-chō ☎ 0967/34–0101) in from 56 minutes (express; ¥2,180) to 80 minutes (local; ¥1,810). From JR Aso Station you must board a bus (40 minutes; ¥620) to get to the Aso Nishi cable-car station at Aso-san-jō. The JR Hōhi Main Line also connects JR Aso Station to Yufuin in 155 minutes for ¥3,950. It's 2¼ hrs northeast of Kagoshima by JR, ¥8,330.

KAGOSHIMA

🅫 *1 hr south of Kumamoto by Relay Tsubame and Tsubame High-Speed Express, ¥5,850; 2 hrs 10 min south of Hakata/ Fukuoka by JR Tsubame and Relay Tsubame Express, ¥8,920.*

Kagoshima is a laid-back, flowery, palm-lined southern getaway on the Satsuma Peninsula blessed with mild weather, outgoing people, and a smoking volcano out in the bay. Ancient relics believed to date back to 9,000 BC indicate that humans have been in the area a very long time. It became a center of trade with Korea and China, and was an important fortress town from the mid-16th century until the Meiji Restoration. This is where Saigō Takamori and his rebel followers (reduced to a few hundred from 40,000) made their last stand against the new Emperor on September 24, 1877, chased here after having sacked Kumamoto Castle. Facing 300,000 well-supplied troops, they had no chance, and Takamori was injured in the fight. Rather than face capture, he ordered one of his own men to cut off his head. Takamori was posthumously pardoned and honored as a national hero. His bronze statue stands near the museum, and the site of the final showdown is commemorated on 450-foot Shiro-yama, to the southeast of downtown.

> ## MALL BREAK
>
> The lively Amu Plaza complex attached to the Chūō Station will keep you busy with shopping and food opportunities, and, if you get bored, a cineplex. A giant Ferris wheel is on top, for one of the best views in town!

Today the area is famous not only for its history but for the world's smallest mandarin oranges (only an inch across) and the largest white daikon radishes—grown in the rich volcanic soil, they can span 3 feet and weigh in at more than 100 lbs. There's also *kurobuta*, a special breed of black pig that locals convert into breaded and fried cutlets called *tonkatsu*.

Getting Around

For the past hundred years the easiest way to get around Kagoshima has been by streetcar. A ¥160 fare will take you anywhere on the trusty old network. One-day travel passes for unlimited rides on streetcars (and buses) cost ¥600. You can buy one at the Chūō Kagoshima Station Tourist Office, or on a streetcar or bus. Buses get around, but are run by five competing outfits on a complicated system.

The **Chūō Kagoshima Station Tourist Office** (✉ 1–1 Chūō-machi ☎ 099/253–2500) is on the second floor of the station's Sakura-jima (formerly East) Exit. An English-speaking person is on hand to arm you with maps and info or help you make hotel reservations. It's open daily 8:30–6.

What to See

★ Across Kinkō Bay rises **Sakura-jima,** and you can often see it spewing thick plumes of dust and smoke. Its last big eruption was in 1955, but the far side of the cone sometimes lets loose with explosive burps that light the night sky red and cover the town in a blanket of ash. There are scattered lodgings and hot springs, as well as winding paths up to old lava plateaus with great views over the crater or back toward town.

A **24-hour ferry** connects **Kagoshima Port** (✉ 4–1 Shin-machi, Hon-kō ☎ 099/223–7271) with **Sakura-jima Port** (✉ 61–4 Sakura-jima Yokoyama-chō ☎ 099/293–2525), at the foot of the volcano itself. There are four to six ferries per hour, with fewer connections after 10 PM. The one-way fare is ¥150, and the trip takes only 10–15 minutes. To get to the pier from Kagoshima Chūō Station, take Bus 4 or 6 for the short ¥180 ride.

There are two recommended in-depth **tours** of the area (Japanese guides only): one departs from Chūō Station Bus Stop 9 at 8:50 AM and includes the city and the volcano; 6 hours 10 minutes, ¥4,000, operated by **JR**

Kyūshū Bus (☎ 099/247–5244), and another offers a tour of the volcano island; tours depart from Bus Stop 8 daily at 9:30 AM, take six hours, and cost ¥1,900, run by **Kagoshima-kotsu Bus** (☎ 099/247–2333).

**OFF THE
BEATEN
PATH**

IBUSUKI TENNEN SUNAMUSHI ONSEN –This laid-back seaside resort on the southern tip of the Satsuma Peninsula may provide your one chance to try a therapeutic hot-sand bath. Exit Ibusuki Station and follow the signs to the NATURAL HOT SAND BATHING SPOT, a 15–20 minute walk or five-minute cab ride to the beach. You buy your ticket and rent a *yukata,* or cotton robe—the small towel is yours to keep—on the second floor of the main "Saraku" Sand Bath Hall, and then go down into the locker rooms (separate sexes) to remove your clothes and change into the robe before heading to the beach. Stand in line and wait for an assistant to call you over. They'll scoop a place for you and show how to wrap your head and neck in the towel. They will then bury you in hot, mildly sulfur-smelling sand with their shovels. It'll get squirmy, but stay in the Zen zone for at least 10 minutes. Fifteen will give you a full charge—if you can take it! Aside from giving you a powerful dose of joint-penetrating heat, the stimulating, sweaty experience is also guaranteed to cleanse your pores and soften your skin. It's a highly scenic one hour trip south of Kagoshima on the Ibusuki Nanohana local train line. ⊠ *5–25–18 Yū-no-hama, Ibusuki-shi* ☎ *099/223–3900* 🖅 *¥1000, including towel and robe rental* ⊙ *Daily 8:30–noon and 1–8:30.*

Where to Stay & Eat

★ **$$$** ✕ **Kumaso-tei.** Enjoy the best of Satsuma specialties in a maze of private and semiprivate Japanese-style rooms. There's an English photo menu, and deluxe set meals range from ¥3,150 to ¥5,250. Highlights include *kibinago* (raw herring), *satsuma-age* (fish cakes filled with potato or burdock root), *kurobuta-tonkotsu* (breaded, fried pork loin from locally bred black pigs). From the Tenmonkan-dōri streetcar stop, walk four blocks north through the covered arcade and turn left; the restaurant will be on the right. ⊠ *6–10 Higashi Sengoku-cho* ☎ *099/222–6356* 🖃 *AE, DC, MC, V.*

$$ ✕ **Amami Restaurant Keihan.** This restaurant specializes in *keihan,* a dish from the southern Kyūshū island of Amami Ōshima, where sliced chicken, cooked egg, seaweed, green onions, and mushrooms are arranged on rice. Broth is poured over it to create a hearty, flavorful feast. From the Tenmonkan-dōri streetcar stop, head north, take the first right, and walk two blocks. After crossing the wide street, Tengoku-dōri, turn right at the first block. ⊠ *Yamahira Bldg. 2F, 5–19 Naka-cho* ☎ *099/223–2855* 🖃 *AE, DC, V* ⊙ *Closed 3rd Tues. of month.*

$$–$$$$ 🏨 **Shirōyama Kanko Hotel.** Also called Castle Park Hotel in brochures, the hotel is on Shirō-yama, site of Takamori's last stand. High enough to provide enviable views but not too far away to be inconvenient, this hotel is famous for its rotemburo baths and fantastic views of both the town and the volcano. It's a 10-minute taxi ride from the JR Chūo Kagoshima Station. ⊠ *1–41 Shinshoin-cho, Kagoshima-shi, Kagoshima-ken 890-8586* ☎ *099/224–2211* 🖷 *099/224–2200* 🛏 *365 Western rooms* ♿ *4 restaurants, bar, garden* 🖃 *AE, DC, MC, V* ⅰ◎ⅰ *EP.*

11

$$ ⬛ **Furusato Kankō Hotel.** This hotel is on Sakura-jima, and the *rotem-*
Fodor's Choice *buro* (outdoor bath) offers amazing views. There's a thermal lap pool,
★ also a saltwater pool (¥210 fee). Two meals are included in the rate. Every
room has a view of the water; five have miniature gardens. There's even
a Zen room for meditation. A free shuttle (15 minutes) runs every half
hour between the hotel and the Sakura-jima ferry port. ✉ *1076–1 Fu-*
rusato-chō, Kagoshima-shi, Kagoshima-ken 891-1592 ☎ *099/221–*
3111 📠 *099/221–2345* 🛏 *40 Japanese-style rooms* ♨ *Restaurant,*
pool, bar ▤ *AE, DC, MC, V* ◐❘ *MAP.*

$–$$ ⬛ **Sun Days Inn Kagoshima.** This sleek business hotel offers excellent value,
style, and convenience. You're within five minutes by taxi from the Chūo
Kagoshima train station, Tenmon-kan nightlife district, and the Sakura-
jima ferry port. Deluxe "DX" rooms with lounge furniture cost ¥25,000.
✉ *9–8 Yamanokuchi-chō, Kagoshima-shi, Kagoshima-ken 892-0844*
☎ *099/227–5151* 📠 *099/227–4667* 🛏 *351 Western-style rooms*
♨ *Restaurant, café, lounge, no-smoking rooms* ▤ *AE, MC, V.*

Getting There

BY AIR   The flight between Tōkyō's Haneda Airport and Kagoshima Airport takes
1¾ hours. From Ōsaka the flight takes about 1¼ hours. The **Airport Lim-**
ousine (☎ 099/256–2151) picks up passengers every 10 minutes (until
9 PM) at Bus Stop No. 2 outside the Kagoshima Airport. From downtown, catch it in the terminal in the Nangoku Nissei Building, across
the street from the East (Sakura-jima) Exit from JR Chūo Kagoshima
Station. The 40-minute trip costs ¥1,200.

BY BUS   Frequent buses make the four-hour trip for ¥5,300 from Fukuoka (departing from Hakata Kōtsū Bus Center and Tenjin Bus Center) to **Chūo**
Kagoshima Station (✉ 1–1 Chūō-chō ☎ 099/256–1585).

BY TRAIN   The JR Tsubame and Relay Tsubame Limited Express trains connect in
Shin-Yatsushiro, and arrive at **Chūo Kagoshima Station** (✉ 1–1 Chūo-chō
☎ 099/256–1585) from Fukuoka's Hakata Station in 2¼ hours and from
Kumamoto in 1¼ hours.

YUFUIN

★ ⑫   *2 hrs 10 min southeast of Fukuoka by Yufuin-no-Mori Express on JR*
Kyudai Line, ¥4,400.

Southwest of the majestic twin peaks of Yufu-dake, this tranquil village
resembles a checkered quilt. Forests nestle up to clusters of galleries, local
crafts shops, and rustic lodgings. Most of the year Yufuin is a relatively
peaceful area, but things heat up in July and August with the arrival of
national music and film festivals.

Yufuin has suffered from fewer of the pitfalls of modern tourism than
the nearby and overdeveloped Beppu. But it wasn't an accident. City
planners and investors went to Europe and came back with ideas about
how to set up a quaint and lovely spa town—and how not to. This small
town has blossomed into a quieter, more sedate getaway than its
hideously garish counterpart to the east. Relatively unadorned natural

baths can be found here, and a thriving arts-and-crafts industry—not to mention fantastic food.

Getting Around

To enjoy the best of Yufuin in a day, start by picking up an English map at **Yufuin Tourist Information Office** (⊠ In Yufuin Station, 8–2 Kawakita ☎ 0977/84–2446), open daily 9 to 7. For more detailed information, visit the **Yufuin Tourist Center** (⊠ 2863 Kawakami ☎ 0977/85–4464), open daily 9–6 and a five-minute walk from the station. Bicycles can be rented from either office.

What to See

From Yufuin Station, take the 5-minute taxi ride north to **Kūsō-no-Mori**—a collection of art galleries along the foot of Yufu-dake. Work your way back south toward the train station via the **Yu-no-tsu** neighborhood—a long shopping street lined with traditional Japanese wooden buildings—where you can mill in and out of artsy craft shops and souvenir stalls, or relax in one of the many coffee shops or tearooms. In winter steam rises from the surface of **Kinrin-ko** (Lake Kinrin), a thermal lake in the east end of town. Warm up with a dip in one of the many bathhouses along its shores.

On most days an artist is painting at the large wooden table in the center of the **Yutaka Isozaki Gallery.** Small cards with inspirational messages and illustrations such as persimmons and wildflowers make original souvenirs (¥300–¥2,000). For a unique memento of old Japan you can sift through clothing made from antique kimonos at the rear of the gallery or piles of antique cotton and silk textiles in **Folk Art Gallery Itoguruma,** the little shop to the right of the entrance. ⊠ *1266–21 Kawakami* ☎ *0977/85–4750* ⊙ *Daily 9–6.*

Where to Stay & Eat

★ $$$$ ✕ **Budōya.** Part of the pricey Yufuin Tamanoyu hotel, which was until 1975 a lodging for Zen Buddhist monks, this restaurant retains an air of solemnity. The first level has stone floors, thick wooden tables, and windows overlooking a thicket of wildflowers and tall grass. Upstairs, rooms have tatami floors and bamboo-mat ceilings. For a splurge, try the *amiyaki* course (¥6,000), with tender charcoal-grilled beef, seasonal vegetables, and homemade *kabosu* (lime) sherbet. Open daily noon–3 and 5–8:30. ⊠ *Yunotsubo, Yufuin-cho, Oita-gun* ☎ *0977/84–2158* ▤ *AE, DC, MC, V.*

$$$–$$$$ ✕ **Moustache.** Started by a Japanese chef who wanted to create a European atmosphere in the shadow of Yufu-dake, Moustache is a café and restaurant with a flair for hearty, country French–style fare. Food can be ordered in set courses or à la carte. The *masu,* or sea trout, is highly recommended. Open from 11:30 to 8:30, closed Mondays. ⊠ *1264-7 Kawakami, Yufuin-cho, Oita-gun* ☎ *0977/84–5155* ▤ *AE, DC, MC, V.*

$$$–$$$$ ▦ **Onyado Yufu Ryōchiku.** In winter, when not submerged in the mineral waters here, you can toast yourself by the burning coals in the *irori* (sunken hearth) in the lobby of this 1925 inn. Breakfast and dinner are included and are served in your room. The inn is among the shops and galleries near the thermally heated Lake Kinrin, which gives off steam much of the year. ⊠ *1097–1 Kawakami Ōita-gun, Ōita-ken, Yufuin-chō 879-*

5102 ☎ *0977/85–2526* 🖨 *0977/85–4466* 📶 *8 Japanese-style rooms without bath* 🛁 *Indoor/outdoor mineral baths* 🍴 *MC, V* 🍴 *MAP.*

$$–$$$$ 🏨 **Pension Momotarō.** The owners of this interesting and very rustic pension make every effort to make you feel at home—they'll even take you to the station when you depart. Both Western-style and Japanese-style rooms are available in the main building, and four charming A-frame cottages are on the premises—each with hot spring water piped into the bath and shower! Rates include two meals, which can include duck, pheasant, and river smelt. ✉ *1839–1 Kawakami, Ōita-gun, Ōita-ken, Yufuin-chō 879-5102* ☎ *0977/85–2187* 🖨 *0977/85–4002* 📶 *6 Western-style rooms, 4 Japanese-style rooms, 4 chalets* 🛁 *Dining room, indoor/outdoor mineral baths* 🍴 *No credit cards* 🍴 *MAP.*

Getting There

BY AIR The closest airport is **Ōita Airport** (✉ 3600 Itohara, Musashi-machi, Higashi Kunisaki-gun ☎ 0978/67–1174). The flight to Ōita Airport from Tōkyō's Haneda Airport takes 1½ hours; the flight from Ōsaka's Itami Airport takes one hour. **Ōita Kōtsu Bus Company** (☎ 097/534–7455) runs the hourly airport shuttle to the Kitahama Bus Station in Beppu. The trip takes about 45 minutes and costs ¥1,450. Reservations are not required. From Beppu, take a local bus or JR train to Yufuin.

BY BUS The *Kujūgō*, run by **Kyūshū Ōdan Teiki Kankō Bus** (☎ 096/355–2525) travels between Kumamoto and Beppu three times times daily (8:40 AM, 9:50 AM, and 2:30 PM) on the Trans-Kyūshū Highway, stopping in Yufuin along the way. The one-way fare from Kumamoto to Yufuin (3¾ hours) is ¥3,450.

BY TRAIN
JR Yufuin-no-Mori Express trains run six times daily between Fukuoka's Hakata Station and **Yufuin Station** (✉ 8–2 Kawakita ☎ 0977/84–2021); they take 2 hours 40 minutes and cost ¥3,630. From Kumamoto, JR Airake Express trains run to Yufuin, taking 3 hours 9 minutes for ¥4,790. From Kagoshima, it takes 4 hours 20 minutes and costs ¥10,320.

KYŪSHŪ ESSENTIALS

Contacts & Resources

BANKS & EXCHANGE SERVICES
In Fukuoka, outside the West Exit from Hakata Statiion, there are a number of major banks that exchange currency. In Tenjin there are a few big ones at the intersection of Watanabe-dōri and Meiji-dōri.

CONSULATE
🔳 United States **U.S. Consulate** ✉ 2–5-26 Ōhori, Chūō-ku, Fukuoka ☎ 092/751-9331.

EMERGENCIES
🔳 Emergency Services **Ambulance** ☎ 119. **Police** ☎ 110.
🔳 Hospital **Fukuoka Nakagawa Hospital** ✉ 17-17 Mukaishin-machi 2-chōme, Minami-ku, Fukuoka ☎ 092/565-3531. **Kagoshima City Hospital** ✉ 20-17 Kajiya-chō ☎ 099/

224-2101. **Kumamoto Chūō Hospital** ✉ 96 Tamukae ☎ 096/370-3111. **Nagasaki University Hospital** ✉ 7-1 Sakamoto-machi 1-chōme ☎ 095/847-2111. **Nakamura Hospital** ✉ 8-24 Akiba-chō, Beppu-shi ☎ 0977/23-3121.

INTERNET, MAIL & SHIPPING

In Fukuoka you can connect to the Net at one of six Kinko's copy centers for ¥500 an hour. One is in front of Hakata Station, in the Dai-ichi Seimei Bldg, 092/473–2677, and another is near Tenjin Station and Kego Park in the Hummingbird Bldg., 092/722–4222. Both are open 24-hours.

In Kumamoto the Hotel New Otani has an Internet terminal in the lobby, and it's 10 minutes for ¥100.

A post office is nearly always in or near every major train station, and at least one is in every downtown district. To send something internationally, you may want to ask for an EMS (equivalent of Fed-Ex here) or "You-Pack"; they have set rates for convenient sizes and weights, and often it's cheaper and simpler than regular metered air mail. A handy link to locate the nearest (or any) post office in Japan is: www. yuubinkyoku.com/english/index.html.

TOURS

A sightseeing bus, **Kyūshū Sankō** (☎ 096/325–0100), makes a four-hour scenic trip (¥3,790) that starts at Fugen-dake and Shimabara, then ferries across Ariake Bay to Kumamoto-kō (Kumamoto Port) before ending the journey at Kumamoto City Kōtsū Center.

Points of Interest

SITES/AREAS	JAPANESE CHARACTERS
Amu Plaza Nagasaki (Amu Puraza)	アミュプラザ長崎
Aso Volcano Museum (Aso Kazan Hakubutsukan)	阿蘇火山博物館
Aso-san (Mt. Aso)	阿蘇山
Atomic Bomb Museum (Gembaku Shiryōkan)	原爆資料館
Canal City	キャナルシティ
Chinese Mansion (Kōshi-byō)	孔子廟
Dejima	出島
Fukuoka	福岡
Fukuoka City Art Museum	福岡市美術館
Hamano-machi	浜野町
Heiwa Kōen (Peace Park)	平和公園
Hosokawa Mansion (Kyū-Hosokawa Gyobu-tei)	旧細川刑部邸
Hypocenter Park	原爆落下中心地
Ibusuki Tennen Sunamushi Onsen	指宿天然砂むし温泉
Kagoshima	鹿児島
Kawabata Shopping Arcade (Kawabata Shōtengai)	川端道商店街
Kinrin-ko (Lake Kinrin)	金鱗湖
Kumamoto	熊本
Kumamoto Castle (Kumamoto-jō)	熊本城
Kusasenri	草千里
Kūsō-no-Mori	空想の森
Nagasaki	長崎
Naka-dake	中岳
Ōhori Kōen	大濠公園
Oranda-zaka (Holland Slope)	オランダ坂
Ōura Catholic Church (Ōura Tenshu-dō)	大村天主堂
Propeller Drive	プロペラドライブ
Sakura-jima	桜島
Shōfuku-ji	正福寺
Suizen-ji Jōju-en (Suijzen-ji Garden)	水前寺公園
Yufuin	湯布院
Yutaka Isozaki Gallery	由夛加磯崎ギャラリー

RESTAURANTS

Amami Restaurant Keihan	奄美レストランけいはん
Aoyagi	青柳
Bassin	バサン
Budōya	葡萄屋
Dejima Wharf	出島ワーフ
Deko	デコ
Hōrin	鳳凛
Ichi-ran	一蘭
Kagetsu	花月
Kairakuen	会楽園
Karuda	カルダ
Kumaso-tei	熊襲亭
Loire	ロワール
Moustache	レストランムスタッシュ
Sugano-ya	菅乃屋

HOTELS

Canal City Fukuoka Washington Hotel	キャナルシティ福岡ワシントンホテル
Fukuoka Grand Hyatt Hotel	福岡グランドハイアットホテル
Furusato Kankō Hotel	ふるさと観光ホテル
Hakata Tōkyū Inn	博多東急イン
Holiday Inn Nagasaki	ホリデーイン長崎
Hotel New Nagasaki	ホテルニュー長崎
Hotel New Ōtani Kumamoto	ホテルニューオータニ熊本
Hotel WingPort	ホテルウィングポート
Kumamoto Hotel Castle	熊本ホテルキャッスル
Onyado Yufu Ryōchiku	御宿由府両築
Pension Angelica	ペンションアンジェリカ
Pension Momotarō	ペンシヨン桃太郎
Sakamoto-ya	坂本屋
Shirōyama Kanko Hotel	城山観光ホテル
Sun Days Inn Kagoshima	サンデイズイン鹿児島
Tōyoko Inn Hakata Nishinakasu	東横イン博多西中洲
Tōyoko Inn Karashima Kōen	東横イン唐島公園
Yamaguchi Ryokan	山口旅館

Okinawa

THE KINGDOM OF RYŪKYŪ

WORD OF MOUTH

"Cannot imagine why anyone would opt for driving around often gridlock-prone Naha (where Spam and other U.S.-processed foods were often listed as don't miss souvenirs!). Having said that, there is a great locally produced ice cream that had interesting flavors—my favorites were local citrus-lime (*sequwasa*) and brown-sugar."

—W9London

By John Malloy
Quinn

OKINAWA MEANS "ROPE ALONG THE OPEN SEA," a fitting name for this chain of 140-plus coral-fringed, subtropical islands stretching more than 700 km (435 mi) into the Pacific Ocean. Once part of the ancient seafaring kingdom of Ryūkyū, the islands were ruled by the local Shō Dynasty, near the present-day capital of Naha, from the 15th century until the early 17th century. During this time the indigenous Ryūkyūans enjoyed a favorable climate and a thriving trade with China. Ryūkyū lacquerware and textiles were exchanged for Chinese pottery and herbs, and spices from Southeast Asia.

Ryūkyū successfully navigated the straits between Chinese and Japanese domination until 1609, when the capital was invaded and conquered by the powerful Shimazu clan from Kyūshū. From this moment forward, island inhabitants were required to pay taxes to Japan. In the late 1870s the Meiji government took control and renamed the islands Okinawa Prefecture. Over time, the Ryūkyūan language was forcibly replaced with Japanese, and the two cultures were purposely integrated. The Meiji government instituted major tax and land-distribution reforms, and eventually introduced military conscription.

Although hundreds of miles from the main Japanese islands, Okinawa bore the brunt of the final years of World War II. Squeezed between the American forces and the Japanese army, Okinawa lost as many as 100,000 native civilians. Following Japan's defeat, and continuing today, the islands host the majority of U.S. troops protecting this corner of the Pacific region. Although the U.S. military presence here is controversial, it provides a tremendous monetary boost to an otherwise poor region.

Tourism and other industries have not easily taken root in Okinawa, yet Okinawa has long been considered Japan's Hawaii, with gorgeous beaches, a warm climate—the average yearly temperature is 72°—and friendly locals. If you love beaches, you could hardly choose a better destination. Almost all the beaches here are heaped with generous helpings of white sand made of pulverized coral that is soft and small-grained up at the tide line and loose and large-grained near and under the water. The sand on some beaches, as on Taketomi and one or two on Iriomote, is actually made from the tiny, dried, and sun-bleached, starshape skeletons of dead aquatic critters; this sand is called *hoshi-suna* (star-sand). Among the most unforgettable experiences of a trip to Okinawa, especially the southern islands, is spectacular diving and snorkeling, even some jungle trekking—all within a few hours of Tōkyō.

See the glossary at the end of this book for definitions of the common Japanese words and suffixes, such as -hama (beach), used in this chapter.

ORIENTATION & PLANNING

Orientation

Okinawa prefecture makes up southernmost Japan, a line of islands stretching like a tail. The main group of islands extends from 200 km (125 mi) southwest of Kyūshū to within 100 km (62 mi) of Taiwan. Part of the main island's importance to the U.S. military is that it is equi-

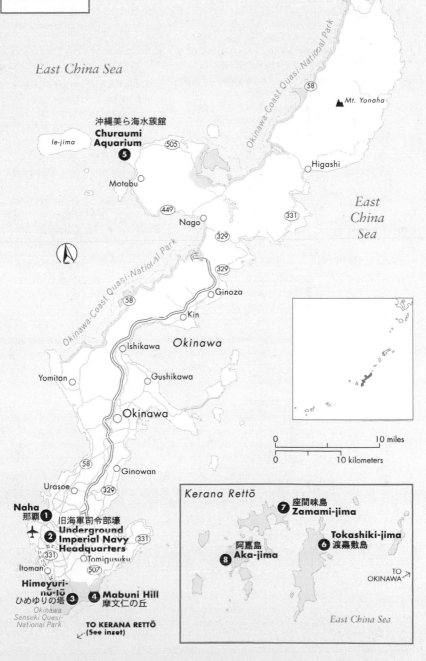

Okinawa

East China Sea

Okinawa-Coast Quasi-National Park

▲ Mt. Yonaha

le-jima

沖縄美ら海水族館
Churaumi Aquarium ⑤

(505)

Motobu

Higashi

East China Sea

(449)

Nago

(331)

(329)

Okinawa-Coast Quasi-National Park

(329)

Ginoza

(58)

Kin

Ishikawa

Okinawa

Yomitan

Gushikawa

Okinawa

(58)

Ginowan

Urasoe

(329)

Naha
那覇 ①
旧海軍司令部壕
Underground Imperial Navy Headquarters ②

(331)

○Tomigusuku

Itoman

(507)

Himeyuri-nō-tō
ひめゆりの塔 ③ ④ **Mabuni Hill**
摩文仁の丘

Okinawa Senseki Quasi-National Park

TO KERANA RETTŌ
↙(See inset)

0 ___ 10 miles
0 ___ 10 kilometers

Kerana Rettō

⑦ 座間味島
Zamami-jima

Tokashiki-jima
⑥ 渡嘉敷島

阿嘉島
⑧ **Aka-jima**

TO
OKINAWA →

East China Sea

Top Reasons to Visit

BEACHES

Some say the best beaches are on Miyako-jima, some say they're on islands in the Keramas, and others argue for the beaches of Ishigaki, Taketomi, or Hateruma-jima. The truth is that virtually anywhere you go in Okinawa, you can find world-class beaches. Even Hontō (the main island) has nice ones, especially to the north, and a few on Miyako-jima rival anything in the Caribbean.

WORLD WAR II MEMORIALS

Okinawa was the site of the final and bloodiest battle of the War in the Pacific, and the largest amphibious landing ever. Outside Naha, these evocative memorials, where the final fighting took place, are in a strangly picturesque and peaceful landscape.

WHALE-WATCHING

In the winter months humpback whales make their way through these waters and you can either watch from land or get up close on a boat tour.

ADVENTURE MAGNET

Island-hopping around Okinawa can provide the intrepid traveler plenty of opportunities for adventure, from swimming with the manta rays to trekking through the swamps and deep jungle of the mountainous Yaeyama-shotō islands.

THE WORLD BELOW

Atop a ridge that divides some of the globe's deepest waters, Okinawa is a great destination for snorkelers and divers, especially in the waters off the southern islands of Miyako-jima, Ishigaki-jima, and Iriomote-jima. Healthy coral and an amazing variety of colorful fish and mollusks thrive in clear, warm seas of deep violet-blue to emerald-green.

distant from such "strategic" destinations as Seoul, Taiwan, Shanghai, and the Phillipines.

Okinawa Hontō

Known as just "Okinawa," this is the most built-up island and the base for the majority of U.S. troops. This is where the battle of Okinawa took place and the location of the major World War II memorials.

Kerama Rettō

A fast ferry ride from Naha, the prefecture capital on Okinawa Hontō, these islands have great beaches and coral reefs to explore. This is a specturally beautiful area, with seas of see-through blue and rocky outcrops emerging boldly from the water.

Miyako-shotō

A group of small islands about 175 mi south of Okinawa Hontō, Miyako-Shotō is where the comparisons to Hawaii ring true, and days of beach relaxation and snorkeling roll by.

Yaeyama-shotō

The remote Yaeyama Islands, the southernmost islands of the Okinawa chain, are for those who like to get off the beaten path. Explore the national park Iriomote-jima, the faraway beaches, and the village that maintains the Ryūkyū style of long ago.

Planning

The town of Naha is worth one day, as are the Kerama Islands nearby, but you should focus your trip on the southern islands of Miyako, Ishigaki, and lush, primitive Iriomote-jima. The south has the best beaches, reef diving, and exotic culture of the region. Plan on riding a few ferries and some small planes.

The Best of Times

Okinawa enjoys winters most folks dream about. Temperatures in January average 60°. Some coming for the diving prefer the winter months, believing the water is more transparent. Winter is also when Okinawa has fewer crowds and cheaper prices. From late January to the end of March whale-watching is a popular activity, especially on Zamami Island, an easy day trip from Naha's port.

May and June are the rainiest months—avoid Okinawa during this time. In July the rains taper off—though squalls can form at any time—temperatures average 82°, and prices jump. August sees the worst of the heat, crowding, and prices. September through October is typhoon season, when, as the locals say, "the weather is . . . well, it's up to God." Although you may have glorious, perfect weather, it's wise to leave extra days at both ends of a fall trip to allow for flight or ferry cancellations due to high winds or heavy rainfall. On November 1–3, Shuri-jō (Shuri Castle) hosts a festival showcasing court dances, traditional music, and a big parade.

Concerning Restaurants & Hotels

You can find nearly every kind of cuisine in Okinawa, from American burgers to traditional noodle shacks and cheap, smoky taverns. There are also trendy, upscale establishments, especially in the cities and resort hotels. In most cases, thanks to the large American military presence, someone nearby probably speaks a little English.

Accommodations in Naha range from a youth hostel and cheap hotels to luxurious, internationally known resorts. Rooms may be scarce and outrageously expensive around New Year's, Golden Week (April 29 to May 5), and in August, especially during the mid-month Obon holiday.

For a short course on accommodations in Japan, *see* Accommodations *in* Essentials.

WHAT IT COSTS In yen					
	$$$$	$$$	$$	$	¢
RESTAURANTS	over 3,000	2,000–3,000	1,000–2,000	800–1,000	under 800
HOTELS	over 22,000	18,000–22,000	12,000–18,000	8,000–12,000	under 8,000

Restaurant prices are per person for a main course at dinner. Hotel prices are for a double room with private bath, excluding service and 5% tax.

On the Menu

OKINAWANS ARE AMONG the longest-lived people on earth. The islands abound in fresh seafood and vegetables, from the exotic, colorful, delicious fish called *goma-aigo*, found in the waters off Ishigaki-jima, to the bitter gourds known as *goya*, which are ubiquitous in the region and reputedly chock-full of antioxidants and toning agents.

You'll quickly discover that the food in Okinawa is more adventurous than in the rest of Japan. Many dishes incorporate Southeast Asian and Chinese flavors. Although beef is fairly cheap, the natives prefer pork; you'd have to go deep into the Ozarks to find people getting as much mileage out of their beloved dead swine. In the markets pressed pigs' faces hang on hooks, the face parts sold as snacks; and in restaurants you can order sliced marinated pig ears, smoked pig tongue, and pig feet in every variety of flavor. You can also find thick, fatty, savory chunks of meat floating in bowls of *sōki soba* (thin, white noodles in a hearty broth).

On the outer islands, goat or sea-snake stew is served. Don't pass up the delectable *rafutē*: slabs of pork bacon that have been slow-cooked in a mix of *awamori* (rice liquor), soy sauce, locally grown brown sugar, and ginger root.

Okinawa loves blending things, and *goya champur* is a stir-fried dish of bitter gourd, meat, and vegetables. The word "champur" is Malay–Indonesian for "mix." The locals are so fond of this word and its implications (even if unaware of its origins) that they proudly refer to the entire mélange that is Okinawa culture as "chanpuru." *Taco rice* is a weird but delicious mix of Tex-Mex-style seasoned ground beef and shredded lettuce, onion, and tomato, served on top of white Japanese rice, usually with spicy salsa. Taco rice is said to have been made popular by GIs after World War II.

Spice freaks can indulge in the local hot sauce, *koregusu*, a gasoline-color, magma-flavor liquid that is the result of cramming as many local red chili peppers (*koregusu* in Ryūkū) as can fit into a small bottle full of high-octane awamori. Go ahead, fire a squirt or two into your noodles or onto your plate of goya champur.

Among interesting sea delicacies on a menu will be *umi-budo* (sea grapes). These are a type of seaweed that squirt and crunch in the mouth like caviar, but with a much less fishy taste.

For drinks, the locals are fond of their rice liquor—awamori—distilled to three levels of potency: strong (25%–30% alcohol), stronger (40%–50%), and downright deadly (60%). Most locals drink it straight up or on the rocks, then remain silent until they regain the ability of speech. Awamori blends with just about anything. You may even want to try the bizarre "healthy liver tonic drink": awamori mixed with water and *ukon* (turmeric powder) over ice. Whether or not it prevents hangovers or cleanses the blood and liver, its slightly medicinal taste wins over most skeptics.

The local beer, Orion, is good but quite light; for more flavor, Naha has some tasty microbrews.

For dessert don't hesitate to try fresh-squeezed sugarcane juice, purple sweet-potato ice cream, or a kind of limeade-like juice called *shikuwasā*. It's all good!

Transportation Station

Naha Airport works well as an entry point. There are frequent, regularly scheduled flights and ferries to the southern islands. Scooters and bicycles are good ways to transport yourself around the smaller islands.

BY AIR   You can fly into Okinawa from most major Japanese airports. If you come from the United States, you will have to stop over in mainland Japan, Hong Kong, Seoul, Shanghai, or Taipei.

BY BUS   Until buses learn to swim, you will not be island hopping on them. Many of the islands do have bus routes, however, that take you near the sights.

CAR TRAVEL   A good map is indispensable. A handy and in-depth English reference, *Okinawa by Road* (Kume Publishing Co), is available at the airport and in bookstores in Okinawa and Tōkyō.

FERRY TRAVEL   Ferries are best for travel between a main island and surrounding islets, rather than for travel from one main island to another (except Iriomotejima and Ishigaki-jima, which are closer together).

Visitor Information

Okinawa Prefectural Government Tourism and Resort Bureau (✉ 1–2–2 Izumizaki, Naha 900-8570 ☏ 098/866–2764). **Naha Airport Information Desk** (☏ 098/857–6884). **Okinawa Tourist Information Office** (✉ Kokusai-dōri ☏ 098/868–4887).

OKINAWA HONTŌ

2½ hrs from Tōkyō by air, 2 hrs from Ōsaka by air; 44–48 hrs from Tōkyō by ferry, 34–40 hrs from Ōsaka by ferry.

Okinawa Hontō, the largest and most populous island of the Nansei (Southwest) group, is usually just referred to as Okinawa. Naha is the prefecture capital. Although Okinawa Hontō is not endowed with as many pristine reefs and primitive landscapes as the islands farther south, its northern shores between Moon Beach and Inbu Beach boast some lovely beaches (and expensive resorts). Off the rocky Motobu Peninsula diving opportunities abound. Also, the rugged Kerama Islands and their beaches and corral are a boat ride from Naha.

Southern Okinawa Hontō has numerous historically significant sights and war memorials dedicated to the devastating Battle of Okinawa (1945). About 25,000 American troops are also based on this island.

Naha

❶   The modern capital city of Naha, population 307,000, is the main entry point for travelers to Okinawa and is well connected to islands farther south. The main cultural sight in Naha, which was also the ancient Ryūkyū capital, is the wonderfully reconstructed Shuri-jō, a World Heritage Site. A strong pottery tradition also thrives here, and many shops specialize in that craft, as well as textile arts. Lively food markets selling gastronomic eye-openers should be explored, and Naha has the largest variety of dining and drinking establishments in the prefecture.

CLOSE UP

Legend of the Shiisā

A POPULAR OKINAWAN LEGEND tells of an angry and vicious dragon that once besieged the islands. One day the desperate islanders placed a shiisā statue that belonged to a local boy on the beach just as the monster was approaching. The tiny lion roared and out leapt a living lion large enough to fight and drown the dragon. Its body was changed into a new string of offshore islands, and afterward there were no more attacks.

To this day, homes and businesses often display two shiisā lions—one with its mouth open to scare off evil spirits and the other with its mouth closed to keep in good spirits. The lions are thought of as good-luck talismans, and they are popular keepsakes sold by dozens of souvenir shops on Kokusai-dōri in Naha.

Getting There & Around

Japan TransOcean Air (JTA ☎ 0120/25–5971 ⊕ www.japanair.com), an arm of Japan Airlines, flies to Naha from several Japanese cities. **ANK** (☎ 0120/02–9222), a regional arm of All Nippon Airways, offers similar flights. Naha's monorail system goes to downtown Naha from the airport, and most hotels are near monorail stops. If traffic is moving, a taxi will cost around ¥1,500 and take about 15 minutes between the airport and downtown.

Naha's main points of interest, like Shuri Castle, are connected by monorail, most for ¥200–¥290. Trains begin running at 6 AM, and the last trains in each direction depart at 11:30 PM. Buses in Naha are slow and not recommended. The downtown area can be covered on foot, and if you get tired, flag down a taxi. Fares start at ¥550. You can arrange for basic transport or tours in English through **Okinawa Prefectural Taxi Association** (☎ 098/855–1344). Tours of the Shuri Castle area take four hours and cost ¥12,000 and up, depending on the car you reserve. **Naha Kojin (taxi cooperative)** (☎ 098/868–1145) offers similar tours.

What to See

Kokusai-dōri. "International Street" runs a mile from the center of town out toward Shuri-jō. A lively street lined with endless shops, Kokusai-dōri is abuzz with shoppers, revelers, and tourists. You'll encounter salsa dance bars, American-style steak-and-lobster restaurants, even Starbucks. The souvenir shops sell everything from snake-skin banjos and ceramic *shiisā* (lion figurines) to jugs of awamori (rice liquor).

You'll see all types of people—tattooed and pierced adolescents in baggy clothes; short-skirted high-school girls eating ice cream while talking on their cell phones; gaggles of smartly dressed office ladies on tour from Tōkyō or Ōsaka ready to spend their bonuses in record time; American GIs looking for diversion from base life; and packs of staggering salarymen, singing badly on their way to the next karaoke bar. Follow the crowds. Something interesting is bound to happen.

CLOSE UP

Pottery Row

Tsuboya pottery district. More than 300 years of ceramic tradition are celebrated here, where nearly 20 workshops still crank out the goods. Legend has it that the guru of aluminosilicates himself, famous Japanese potter Hamada Shōji, lurked about here in the 1920s and '30s and came away with inspiration for his work. As you amble, notice the bits of broken pottery randomly, whimsically jammed into walls in Gaudi-esque embellishment. Most workshops are open to visitors, so you can observe the various stages of pottery-making and purchase the finished wares. Popular items include wedge-shape soy-sauce or oil decanters and shiisā lions of all sizes and colors.

The small Tsuboya Pottery Museum (Tsuboya Yakimono Hakubutsukan,

✉ 1-9-32 Tsuboya ☎ 098/862-3761) has exhibits illustrating the history of the region's earthenware production, including representative pieces from all periods. There's a reproduction of the interior of a traditional Okinawan house, showing Tsubo-yaki tableware and kitchen utensils. The museum is open Tuesday through Sunday 10-6, and admission costs ¥315. There are no English explanations, and you can admire the entire collection in about an hour. Next to the museum is an intact 19th-century climbing kiln, called a *nobori-gama*.

To get to the pottery district, walk east on Heiwa-dōri until it turns into Yachimun-dōri. ✉ *Between Yachimun-dōri and Rte. 330.*

12

To get to the main stretch, walk one block south of the Kenchō-mae monorail station, past the post office and Kumoji Palette shopping center, then turn left. For maps and additional sightseeing information, step into the **Okinawa Tourist Information Center** (✉ Okie Ōdōri at Ichiba-dōri ☎ 098/868-4887).

★ **Ichiba-dōri and Heiwa-dōri shopping arcades.** Halfway up Kokusai-dōri, on the right, just past the building called Opa and roughly across from the large Mitsukoshi department store, is a set of streets great for wandering. The first of these shopping arcades is Ichiba-dōri, and the next one to the right is Heiwa-dōri. Both are crammed with funky, hole-in-the-wall eateries and bars; shops selling discount clothing, hardware, and gadgets; and, best of all, the numerous and the sometimes shocking but always entertaining **markets.** Here ghoulish pressed, pickled, and smoked pigs' faces stare down like Halloween masks from hooks everywhere, and rainbow-color fish that dart about the reefs now rest on ice. Tropical fruit and lengths of sugarcane are ready to be sliced or juiced on the spot. A foray into Naha's labyrinthine markets is a treat for the senses, and they're mostly air-conditioned, so you can escape for a chill-session when it's unbearably muggy outside.

★ **Shuri-jō.** The superbly reconstructed Shuri Castle and main buildings demonstrate the strong Chinese influence in the Ryūkyū style. Bright red walls and roof tiles contrast with the gray-white stone blocks of the massive outer walls. In the 5,000-square-foot central courtyard the rows of red-and-white tiles indicate where the various ranks of officials lined up for ceremonies. Nearby are high-walled, narrow streets with original paving stones from the 1500s. The original 15th-century castle was once part of a sprawling estate: the Ryūkyū royal compound. During World War II the Japanese Imperial Army made the complex its headquarters, and it was destroyed in the Battle of Okinawa. Shuri-jō is a 15-minute walk from Shuri Station, the last stop on the monorail; follow the signs from the station. ⊠ *1–2 Kinjo-chō, Shuri* ☎ *098/886–2020* ⊠ *¥800* ⊗ *Mar.–Nov., daily 9–5:30; Dec.–Feb., daily 9–5.*

Where to Eat

★ $$$$ ✕ **Sam's Anchor Inn**. With a nautical theme and smiling waitresses in sailor uniforms, Sam's is always crowded with hungry, steak-loving GIs. Sam's is pricier than many places on bustling Kokusai-dōri, but it delivers good, hearty set meals of steak and seafood. If you've got the appetite, don't miss the steak-and-lobster combo. Lunches are an excellent value, with set meals for less than ¥3,500. From the Kencho-mae monorail station, take a right on the busy Kencho-mae-dōri, then go left at the next street, which is Kokusai-dōri. Walk two blocks, and Sam's is on the left. ⊠ *3-3–18 Kumoji, 2F* ☎ *098/862–9090* ⊟ *AE, MC, V.*

¢–$$ ✕ **Helios Pub**. A microbrewery and pub, Helios serves up four tasty brews along with hearty snacks like tender oxtails stewed in black beer, a goya champur omelet with rice, and herb-seasoned bratwurst sausages. Wood floors and beams, brick pillars, and hanging sheaves of barley form the decor. From Kencho-mae Station, cross Kencho-mae-dōri, go right one block, then turn left at Kokusai-dōri. It's 8½ blocks up, on the left side. ⊠ *1–2–25 Makishi* ☎ *098/863–7227* ⊟ *D, MC, V.*

★ ¢–$ ✕ **Gosso Gozzo**. Enter, step across flat stones with water running between them, then pass vats of steaming tofu, and take your seat in the darkened and ye olde-looking (Japanese-style) dining room. Choose from an Okinawan menu that includes the sliced octopus served in creamy sweet-and-sour dill-weed sauce; various forms of tofu (one is as old and stinky as blue cheese); and umi-budo, or sea grapes, a type of sea vegetable netted and plucked from the bar's aquarium. Or try the pickled pigs' ears. For your beverage, order the delectable, locally made Niheide beer or the smooth local sake called *nama genshu*. Gosso Gozzo is a couple of blocks from the Kencho-mae monorail station. From the station, cross the busy street and follow the canal until you get to Lawson's convenience store, then turn right. Take the first left onto a tiny side street, and it's on the left side in the middle of the block. ⊠ *3–12–18 Kumoji* ☎ *098/860–5211* ⊟ *No credit cards* ⊗ *No lunch.*

¢ ✕ **Tacos-ya**. Among the funky, little, hole-in-the-wall eateries on busy Kokusai-dōri, Tacos-ya is a perfect pit stop for lunch. Tiny, tasty tacos are unbelievably cheap, and the taco rice—spicy ground beef, shredded lettuce, and diced tomatoes on rice—is a filling delight for only ¥550. And where else in Japan can you get a chilled Corona for only ¥400? ⊠ *2–18–13 Matsuo* ☎ *098/862–6080* ⊟ *No credit cards.*

Where to Stay

$$$$ ▥ **Okinawa Harbor View Hotel**. One of Naha's finest, this spiffy ANA-operated hotel caters to the higher-end market, from the pool's careful

nighttime lighting scheme to the dark woods of the lobby. Rooms are distinctive and elegant, with cream walls, and pastel furnishings. The restaurants' meals start at ¥2,000, and you can head to the rooftop bar for a cocktail. The nearest monorail stop is the Asahibashi Station; from there head southeast on Tsubokawa-dōri to the third major intersection, then turn left. ⊠ *2–46 Izumizaki, Naha 900-0021* ☎ *098/ 853–2110* 🖷 *098/835–9696* ⊕ *www.harborview.co.jp* ➲ *352 rooms* ⚬ *4 restaurants, pool, hair salon, massage, sauna, bar, lobby lounge, shop, laundry service, business services, convention center, meeting rooms* ▤ *AE, D, DC, V.*

$–$$ ▦ **Hotel Sun Palace.** An earth-tone tile exterior and rounded, bougainvillea-filled balconies greet you as you approach this appealing riverside hotel. Inside, the rooms are not overly attractive but quite acceptable. However, it's the reasonable prices, good service, and convenient location that make the Sun Palace an excellent choice. From the Kencho-mae monorail station, cross the bridge spanning the Kumoji River, then turn right. ⊠ *2–5–1 Kumoji, Naha 900-0015* ☎ *098/863–4181* ⊕ *www.palace-okinawa.com* 🖷 *098/861–1313* ➲ *67 Western-style rooms, 8 Japanese-style rooms* ⚬ *Restaurant, in-room data ports, shop* ▤ *D, MC, V.*

$–$$ ▦ **Roynet Hotel Naha Kumoji.** The Roynet offers 10 floors of crisp new rooms and facilities. As in many chain hotels, the rooms are a bit cramped and they're not big on character, but each has a large square window and a writing desk. You can rent a PC for ¥800 a night, a color printer for ¥500. The hotel is four blocks from the Miebashi monorail station. ⊠ *2–23–12 Kumoji, Naha 900-0015* ☎ *098/869–0077* 🖷 *098/ 862–0088* ⊕ *www.roynet.co.jp/naha* ➲ *239 rooms* ⚬ *Restaurant, in-room data ports, Internet, business services* ▤ *MC, V.*

¢ ▦ **Hyper Hotel Naka.** While it's nothing fancy and the rooms are small, the Hyper Hotel is good for travelers on a budget. Beds are wider than in most business hotels, and desks are in each room. Family rooms have a raised bunk bed. It's five minutes by taxi from the airport, along Route 221, across from the big Jusco department store. ⊠ *5–11–1 Kanagusuku, Naha 901-0155* ☎ *098/840–1000* 🖷 *098/858–1001* ➲ *89 rooms* ⚬ *Restaurant, laundry service, Internet, business services* ▤ *MC, V* ❢❢ *CP.*

Nightlife

For nightlife in Naha, you need only follow the crowds up and down Kokusai-dōri, or duck into side streets and give someplace a try. There's something for everyone, and at all hours. Folks are congenial, the draft-beer mugs are big, and the prices are tame by Tōkyō standards.

Rock in Okinawa (⊠ 3–11–2 Makishi ☎ 098/861–6394) hosts live rock shows nearly every night of the year. It's open from 7 PM to 7 AM nightly, and the cover charge is generally ¥1,000 to ¥2,000. Rock in Okinawa is on Kokusai-dōri, near the Heiwa-dōri arcade and the Kokusai shopping center.

Club Cielo (⊠ 1–1–1 Matsuo, 6F ☎ 098/861–9955) is an upscale, rooftop, strut-your-stuff dance club, where it behooves you to dress well. Patrons are allowed entrance only between 9 PM and midnight, although the party never stops. Cover charges range from ¥1,500 to

¥2,000. Club Cielo is in the Best Denki Building on Kokusai-dōri, diagonally across from the Palette Kumoji shopping center.

The War Memorials

After the largest naval build-up in history congregated off Okinawa, American troops, supported by an immense naval bombardment, landed on Okinawa's beaches on Easter Sunday, April 1, 1945. Thus began the bloodiest battle of the Pacific campaign—a battle that would last 82 days, during which time America's President Franklin Delano Roosevelt would die and Germany would officially surrender. The battle claimed more lives than the atomic bombs of Hiroshima and Nagasaki combined. The numbers are staggering: more than 12,000 Americans dead and 38,000 wounded; more than 107,000 Japanese conscripts dead and an estimated 100,000 civilians (many pressed into some sort of military duty) dead.

The fighting got heavier as the battle wore on. The initial landing found surprisingly light resistance. The Japanese army had fortified the interior of the island in ringed formations, stationed in caves and trenches in order to draw out the action and wear the American forces down. Fierce fighting would gain the Americans tiny increments of land, and the battle began to take on the characteristics of the trench warfare of World War 1. In late May the rains began, turning battlefields into muddy pits of waste and dead bodies. Some 26,000 Americans succumbed to combat stress, otherwise known as shell shock, and were removed from the front lines during the fight.

As the battle marched into June, Japanese forces began retreating south to the Kiyamu Peninsula. The Japanese soldiers were commanded to fight to the death. Rather than face capture, many blew themselves up with hand grenades. Only 465 Japanese troops were captured by early June, whereas 62,548 had been killed. Many Japanese soldiers, along with civilians, died in collapsed caves blown apart by the Americans and sometimes themselves. Even after the main Japanese forces had been thoroughly defeated, and the Japanese General Ushijima, likening himself to a samurai, stabbed himself in ritual suicide on June 22, brutal fighting continued against pockets of Japanese fighters for two more weeks.

Getting There & Around

Since public buses are infrequent and bus tours are in Japanese, the best way to get to the war memorials is by renting a car or hiring a taxi. You can hire a taxi with an English-speaking driver for about ¥18,000 for six hours. Book one day ahead via the front desk of your hotel, the tourist information office, or call the **Okinawa Prefectural Taxi Association** (☎ 098/855–1344) or **Naha Kojin (taxi cooperative)** (☎ 098/868–1145).

What to See

❷ Underground Imperial Navy Headquarters (Kyū Kaigun Shireibu-gō). The cold, clammy tunnels are where a dramatic end came to Admiral Ōta and 174 of his men on June 13, 1945. He and six of his top officers killed themselves to escape capture or death by American forces. The grenade blasts that killed the rest of Ōta's men left visible shrapnel damage on the walls. An information desk has pamphlets in English, but the staff is

12

unlikely to speak anything but Japanese. It's 25 minutes from the Naha Bus Terminal via buses No. 33, 46, or 101 (¥220). Get off at the Tomigusuku-Jōshi Kōen-mae (Tomigusuku Castle Park) bus stop, and walk 10 minutes uphill to the ticket gate. ⊠ *236 Aza Tomishiro, Tomishiro-shi* ✆ *¥420* ☎ *098/850–4055* ☉ *Daily 8:30–5.*

❸ **Himeyuri-nō-tō.** On June 19, 1945, more than 200 high-school students, mostly girls, and their teachers committed mass suicide rather than submit to the encroaching American army. The women had been recruited to help the Imperial Army in war efforts, but were left to fend for themselves during the Japanese retreat. Fearing they would suffer a worse fate if captured, they chose to kill themselves. Adjacent to the site is the **Himeyuri Peace Prayer & Memorial Museum.** Himeyuri-no-tō is 60 minutes from Naha via bus No. 32 or 89 (¥550), with a change in Itoman to bus No. 82 (¥270). Buses depart hourly and continue on to Mabuni Hill after Himeyuri-no-tō ☎ *No phone.*

❹ **Mabuni Hill** (Mabuni-no-Oka). Mabuni Hill and its monuments encompass a gorgeous, grassy view now, but in the late spring of 1945 it was the site of the worst battle of World War II in the Pacific, where the remainder of the Imperial Army was cornered and defeated. The cliffs were dubbed the "Suicide Cliffs" by the Americans. The 119 memorials, rows of inscribed stone tablets scattered about the hillside, list the names of every known person who died in the Battle of Okinawa: Japanese soldiers, civilians, and American soldiers as well. The nearby **Peace Memorial Hall** (Heiwa Kinen Shiryōkan) is presided over by a large Buddha statue in a white tower. You can find pamphlets in English, and the location of any name listed on the tablets can be accessed via a computer directory. Mabuni Hill is about 80 minutes from Naha via bus No. 32 or 89 (¥870) and No. 82. ⊠ *448–2 Mabuni, Itoman-shi* ☎ *098/997–3011* ✆ *¥500* ☉ *Tues.–Sun. 9–5.*

Elsewhere on Okinawa Hontō

Scattered along the west coast of Okinawa Honto north of Naha are flashy beach resorts usually booked solid with package-tour travelers from Tōkyō or Ōsaka: Sunset Mihama, Moon Beach, Manza Beach, Emerald Beach, and Okuma Beach, listed from south to north. Although pleasant enough, the beaches at these resorts aren't nearly as beautiful as those on the southern islands of Miyako-jima and Ishigaki-jima, and on the Kerama Islands. The impressive Churaumi Aquarium, however, with its 22½-foot whale sharks and fleet of giant manta rays, is worth visiting.

★ ☺ ❺ **Churaumi Aquarium** (Churaumi Suizokukan). Churaumi means "beautiful sea" in the regional dialect, and this $150 million aquarium is one of the world's best and largest. The Churaumi features a unique 7,500-ton, 10-meter-deep tank big enough to give play space to a trio of whale sharks, four giant mantas, and schools of tuna, grouper, and other fish from the nutrient-rich Kuroshio (Black Current), which flows past Okinawa. It's the world's first tank deep enough to allow viewing whale sharks feeding in their natural, vertical position. Other tanks hold dangerous sharks, a pioneering coral-breeding experiment, deep-water species, and other wondrous inhabitants of the sea.

Take bus No. 20 or 120 from Naha Terminal to Nago (¥1,740; 2 hours, 20 minutes). In Nago change to bus No. 65 or 70 to Kinenkōen-mae and get off at the south or central gates of the Ocean Expo Park (¥790, 65 minutes). ⊠ *424 Ishikawa, Motobu-chō* ☎ *098/048–3748* ⊕ *www.chample.tv/churaumi/index_en.html* ✉ *¥1,800* ☉ *Dec.–Feb., daily 9–4; Mar.–July 19, daily 9–5; July 20–Aug., daily 8:30–6:30; Sept.–Nov., daily 9–5.*

Bull-Fighting

An interesting local pastime is a type of bull-fighting called *tōgyū*, where, instead of going up against a nimble man with a flashy cape, the bulls fight each other. As in sumō, the winner is the one who pushes the loser from the ring. There are a dozen or so places to watch bullfights around the islands; the most popular and busy venues are in Gushikawa and Okinawa City, both on the main island. Bullfights are held about twice a month, with tournaments held in November and May at the stadium in Gushikawa, not too far from Naha.

KERAMA RETTŌ

35 km (22 mi) west of Naha by ferry.

The Kerama Islands have many pristine beaches, and divers rate the coral and clear water off their coasts highly. Three main islands are in the group: Takashiki, Zamami, and Aka-jima, plus many more small uninhabited islets. You can experience the best of the Keramas in a day trip or two from Naha. Eating and drinking establishments are scattered over the three main islands, so you won't lack for sustenance.

Getting There & Around

From Naha's Tomari Port you can catch ferries to all three main islands. The Ferry Kerama reaches Tokashiki-jima in 70 minutes. The fare is ¥1,360, and there are generally two departures daily. Call **Tokashiki-son Renrakusho** (☎ 098/868–7541) to confirm schedules.

To get to Zamami-jima you have two choices: the high-speed *Queen Zamami* ferry reaches the island in 55 minutes, stopping at Aka-jima along the way. The fare is ¥2,750 per person, and there are two or three departures daily. The slower *Zamami-maru* ferry reaches the island in two hours, and makes one run daily, also via Aka-jima. The fare is ¥1,860. Call **Zamami-son Renrakusho** (☎ 098/868–4567) for schedules.

Once you're on one of the islands, you can rent bicycles or scooters from vendors at the piers. Bicycles rent for about ¥500 per hour, scooters ¥3,000 per day. Zamami-jima also has a car-rental agency, **Zamami Rent-a-Car** (☎ 098/987–3250), extending from the jetty at the east end of the village. Prices range from ¥3,000 an hour to ¥8,000 a day. You can also walk to many places of interest.

DIVING **Fathoms Diving** (☎ 090/8766–0868 mobile), run by an American expat, former U.S. Marine Richard Ruth, offers guided diving tours from Naha out to the Keramas.

Tokashiki-jima

❻ The largest of the Kerama Islands, and the closest one to Okinawa Hontō, Tokashiki-jima gets the most tourist traffic from Naha. Two lovely beaches with clean, white sand are on the west side: Tokashiki Beach, in the center of the coast, and Aharen Beach, toward the south.

12

Zamami-jima

❼ At the harbor you can duck into the **tourist information office** (☎ 098/ 987–2277) in the cluster of buildings to the left of the ferry exit for information in English on boat tours, bike rentals, and diving outfitters. The tourist office is open daily 8:30–5.

SNORKELING For great snorkeling, try **Furuzamami Beach**, a short walk south of the harbor and village. In summer there are snorkel rentals and showers. There's also a restaurant, and shuttle buses run to and from the pier and other beaches.

WHALE- On Zamami-jima late January through March is prime whale-watch-
WATCHING ing season, and during those months you can join two-hour boat tours for ¥5,000. Weather permitting, the **Zamami Whale Watching Association** (☎ 098/987–2277) sends out boats from Zamami port daily at 10:30 AM. From land, the north shore gives you the best chance of seeing whale tails and fin-slapping humpback antics—bring your best binoculars.

Aka-jima

❽ Aka-jima doesn't get much traffic, but those who make it here won't say that's a bad thing! Beautiful and quiet **Nishibama Beach**, near the northern tip of the island, offers good snorkeling and diving, with equipment rental locations. From the pier, walk over the hill to the east. The gently sloping beach west of the pier is also pretty and has places to eat and rent snorkel gear.

MIYAKO-SHOTŌ

300 km (186 mi) southwest of Okinawa Hontō.

Some intensive beach therapy can be engaged in here. In the southwest corner of the main island, Miyako-jima, is Maehama, perhaps Japan's finest beach, and across the bridge on the adjacent tiny island of Kurima-jima lies the gorgeous, secluded beach Nagama-hama. Throughout the Miyako islands you can find bright white sand and emerald, turquoise, and cobalt waters. If you're traveling to Miyako-jima in July or August, or during a Japanese holiday, book your lodging ahead of time.

Getting There & Around

Japan TransOcean Air (JTA) and **ANK** fly from Naha (45 minutes, 11 flights daily) and Ishigaki-jima (another Okinawan island) to Miyako-shotō. From the airport to Hirara a taxi costs about ¥1,300.

Ferries from Naha reach Miyako-jima in 8¼ hours; a one-way ticket costs about ¥5,000. Some ferries go on to Ishigaki-jima, an additional five-hour, ¥2,700 trip. All trips are overnighters, and require at least two weeks' advance booking. From Hirara Port ferries make day trips to nearby Irabu-jima, Shimoji-jima, Tarama-jima, and Minna-jima. Tickets can be bought in the Hirara ferry terminal. Boats generally leave every half hour for the 10-minute trip to Irabu-jima (¥410). Boats to the other islands depart less often.

Buses on Miyako-jima depart from two terminals in Hirara and travel the coastal roads around the island. Buses to the north of the island and Ikema-jima (35 minutes from Hirara) depart from the Yachiyo bus station, a few blocks north of the central post office along Route 83. Buses heading south to Maehama (25 minutes from Hirara) and Cape Higashihenna (50 minutes from Hirara) depart from the Miyako Kyōei terminal, about a kilometer east of the downtown post office on McCrum-dōri. Buses run every couple of hours from morning to early evening.

> **CAUTION**
>
> Although following the coastal roads is straightforward enough, driving in the interior of Miyako-jima requires time and patience, and should not be attempted after dark. Signage is confusing, and the endless sugarcane fields look identical.

Taxi use on Miyako-jima is convenient and reasonable. A taxi for the 10-km (6.2-mi) trip to Maehama Beach should cost ¥5,000 or less. **Miyako Taxi** (☎ 098/072–4123) has English-speaking drivers. For car rentals, reserving in advance is essential. **Nippon Rent-a-Car** (☎ 098/072–0919, 0120/17–0919 toll-free) will pick you up at the airport or ferry terminal. Rates average ¥5,500–¥6,000 per day. Perhaps the best option for getting around the island is by scooter (¥3,000–¥4,000 per day) or motorbike (¥6,500 per day). **Nippon Rent-a-Car** also rents motorbikes, and you can arrange for one to be dropped at your hotel.

Hirara

❾ On the main island of Miyako-jima, sprawling, unremarkable Hirara, population 48,000, doesn't have much to see but offers plenty of budget accommodations. Whether you arrive by plane or ferry, stop in at the **tourist information desk** (☎ 098/072–0899 airport, 098/073–1881 ferry), open daily 9–5, for help on travel, tour, and lodging arrangements.

DIVING & SNORKELING **The Goodfellas Club** (☎ 098/073–5483) on Route 390 just east of Route 192 in south Hirara offers diving trips in the waters around Miyako-jima. You can rent or buy snorkeling equipment at one of the many shops in Hirara or near the beaches.

Beaches

⓬ **Boraga Beach.** Here, on the southern shore of the island, a swimming pool filled with water from a cold natural spring is next to some picturesque stretches of sand. Snorkel gear and kayak rental are arranged through the pool complex, which includes a refreshment stand.

❿ **Maehama Beach.** Maehama, or as you may see on local signs, Yonaha
Fodor'sChoice Maehama, is regarded by many as Japan's best beach, and it lives up to
★ its reputation. White sand stretches for miles on a smooth, shallow shelf extending far into the warm, clear water. Eventually the sand gives way to forests and canyons of coral that provide shelter and playgrounds for

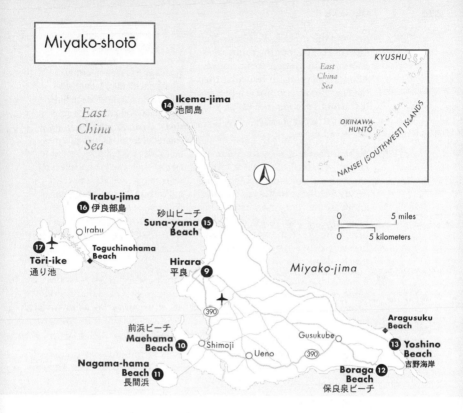

Miyako-shotō

Ikema-jima 池間島 ⑭

East China Sea

KYUSHU

East China Sea

OKINAWA-HUNTŌ

NANSEI (SOUTHWEST) ISLANDS

Irabu-jima 伊良部島 ⑯

砂山ビーチ
Suna-yama Beach ⑮

○ Irabu

Toguchinohama Beach ◆

Tōri-ike 通り池 ⑰

Hirara 平良 ⑨

Miyako-jima

390

前浜ビーチ
Maehama Beach ⑩

○ Shimoji

Aragusuku Beach ◆

Gusukube ○

390

Yoshino Beach 吉野海岸 ⑬

Nagama-hama Beach 長間浜 ⑪

○ Ueno

Boraga Beach 保良泉ビーチ ⑫

0 ___ 5 miles
0 ___ 5 kilometers

beautiful, luminescent aquatic creatures. A tiny slice of Maehama can keep you entertained all day, but it actually stretches for 7 km (4.4 mi). At the Tokyu Resort are water-sports equipment rentals and a marina. The beach is 25 minutes from Hirara via bus.

⑪ **Nagamahama Beach.** A lovely and often deserted beach on the west side of tiny Kurima-jima, Nagamahama can be reached via the bridge just southeast of Maehama. This is a fantastic place to spend the day snorkeling and picnicking on the fine white sand.

⑮ **Sunayama Beach.** This beach has an enormous sand dune (*suna-yama* means "sand mountain"), out of which juts a marvelously rugged natural stone arch. The snorkeling is as good as at Maehama, and the beach is only a few kilometers (15 minutes by bus) north of Hirara.

OFF THE BEATEN PATH **HIGASHI-HENNA MISAKI** (Cape Higashi-henna) – If you're in the southern corner of Miyako-jima and you have a couple of hours to spare, take a leisurely walk out to see Cape Higashi-henna's surreal landscape. A twisty, narrow road atop a spine of rock leads through a thatch of green grass out to a lonely, perfectly lovely lighthouse. The 2-km (1.2-mi) peninsula retains an impressive, end-of-the-earth-feeling; and in spring the ground is covered with trumpet lilies. The transparent water is too shallow and the shore is too rocky for safe snorkeling, but the multicolor coral can be viewed from above. Allow about one hour to walk from the Bora bus stop at Boraga Beach. If you rent a scooter in Hiraga, you can ride to the end of the road next to the lighthouse.

⑬ Yoshino Beach. The water here is said to have the highest concentration of colorful fish in all of Miyako-shotō; needless to say, it's an awesome spot to snorkel. The beach is just north of Higashi-henna-misaki. Aragusuku Beach, just north of Yoshino Beach, is nearly identical.

OF JETS & CAVERNS

Tōri-ike. Travel even farther, across one of the several small bridges from Irabu-jima to Shimoji-jima, and proceed to its west side, beyond the oversize runway where All Nippon Airways sometimes trains its jumbo-jet pilots to take off and land the unbelievably noisy things, and you can check out Tori-ike, a deep, mysteriously dark cenote connected by underwater caverns to the sea. It's a justly celebrated spot for diving.

---

⑭ Ikema-jima. Connected to the northwestern corner of Miyako-jima by a bridge, this small island, ringed by a scenic coastal road, has fine views above and below the sea. A distinctive rock formation shaped like a whale tail poised to slap the water lies offshore (and is prominent in postcards). The island is 35 minutes by bus from Hirara.

⑯ Irabu-jima. This small, rural island, only a 15-minute boat ride (¥410) from Hirara port, has two more gorgeous and secluded beaches: **Toguchi-no-hama** and **Sawada-no-hama.**

Where to Stay & Eat

$ ✕ **Chūzan.** This local tavern serves inexpensive Okinawa favorites such as gōya champur; Korean-style *bibimbap,* a delicious, tangy, healthy dish of kimchi, bean sprouts, spinach, and other vegetables stirred into rice; and a plate of *katsuo* (bonito) sashimi big enough for two or three people. A couple of blocks east from the port, it's on the left side of McCrum-dōri before it meets Route 83. ✉ *McCrum-dōri, Miyako-jima, Hirara* ☎ *098/073–1959* ▤ *No credit cards* ☉ *No lunch.*

★ ¢–$ ✕ **Gōya.** The wooden walls of this rustic establishment are full of alcoves holding treasures and knickknacks from dolls to farm implements to ancient jugs full of fresh awamori (rice liquer). Partially enclosed tatami-style rooms offer intimate dining and drinking experiences, while the beer hall–style area in front of the stage makes socializing easy. There's live music nightly, and cheap, filling, delicious food. Tasty gōya chips, rafute (bacon slow-cooked in a mix of awamori, soy sauce, brown sugar, and ginger root), and garlicky *gyoza* (fried meat dumplings) should be accompanied by large mugs of icy cold Orion beer. Gōya is 10 minutes from downtown Hirara by taxi. ✉ *570–2 Nishizato, Rte. 78 just past Rte. 390, Miyako-jima, Hirara* ☎ *098/074–2358* ▤ *No credit cards* ☉ *Closed Wed. No lunch.*

$$$$ ▦ **Hotel Atoll Emerald.** Every room at this contemporary high-rise hotel next to the pier has ocean views. The Atoll Emerald is the nicest and most convenient hotel in downtown Hirara. The rooms are large, and

each has a big picture window, and corner deluxe rooms enjoy two of them. Suites are enormous, with L-shape sectional sofas. ⊠ *108–7 Shimozato, Miyako-jima, Hirara 906-0013* ☏ *098/073–9800* 🖷 *098/073– 0303* ⊕ *www.atollemerald.jp* ➷ *133 Western-style rooms, 4 Japanese- style rooms, 4 Western-style suites* 🖒 *4 restaurants, pool, hair salon, sauna (men only), bar, lobby lounge, shops, laundry facilities, business serv- ices, convention center* ▭ *AE, D, MC, V.*

$$$$ 🏨 **Miyakojima Tōkyū Resort.** One of Japan's finest hotels—regally situ-
Fodor'sChoice ated on Japan's finest beach—the Miyakojima Tokyū Resort delivers
★ everything you could want from a beach vacation. Rooms are spacious and beautiful (newer ones are in the Coral Wing), and most have su- perb views over one of the most incredible beach scenes in the world. Significant discounts can be had by booking air-hotel packages through any major travel agency. ⊠ *914 Yonaha, Shimoji-chō, Miyako-jima, 906- 0305* ☏ *098/076–2109* 🖷 *098/076–6781* ⊕ *www.tokyuhotels.co.jp* ➷ *205 Western-style rooms, 40 Japanese-style rooms, 3 Western-style suites* 🖒 *5 restaurants, tennis courts, 2 pools, dive shop, snorkeling, wind- surfing, boating, jet skiing, marina, waterskiing, fishing, bicycles, bar, video game room, shop, laundry service, business services, convention center* ▭ *AE, D, MC, V* ⦿ *BP.*

$–$$ 🏨 **Miyako Central Hotel.** On Route 78, a few blocks from the pier, this tidy, narrow, eight-story hotel caters to the economically minded. You can get a spartan room or a spacious deluxe twin at an affordable price. It's within walking distance of downtown, near the bus depot, ferry port, dive outfits, and car-rental agencies. Several nightspots are also within walking distance. ⊠ *225 Nishizato, Miyako-jima, Hirara 906-0012* ☏ *098/073–2002* 🖷 *098/073–5884* ⊕ *www.cosmos.ne.jp/~mcentral* ➷ *62 rooms* 🖒 *Restaurant, meeting room* ▭ *AE, V.*

Nightlife

Miyako-jima has a notoriously hard-drinking nightlife. A common boast is that Miyako-jima has more bars per person than in any other part of the country, which, given the Japanese fondness for drinking, likely means that Miyako-jima has one of the highest concentration of bars in the world. Countless nightspots adorn Hirara, especially in the blocks just east of the piers.

Bar Alchemist (⊠ 215–3 Shimozato, Hirara ☏ 090/4582–4278) is a good vibes bar with a piano, a telescope, and an endearing, eccentric owner. It's a couple of blocks south of the ferry terminal on the seafront road, upstairs above the A Dish restaurant. It's closed on Monday, but other nights you might find live music.

South Park (⊠ 638–Shimozato, Hirara ☏ 098/073–7980) bills itself as an "American shot bar." Cocktails are only ¥700, and shots begin at ¥600. South Park is a bit of a hike east of the piers, near where Route 243 crosses Route 190. From the post office downtown, walk south five blocks then east for two blocks. It's closed Monday; the rest of the week it opens at 6 PM.

YAEYAMA-SHOTŌ

430 km (267 mi) southwest of Okinawa Hontō.

Starting 100 km (62 mi) southwest of Miyako-jima, the string of lush, mountainous islands called the Yaeyama-shotō (Manifold Mountain Islands) stretches nearly to Taiwan. On the jungled, swampy, and mysterious Iriomote-jima there is a fascinating national park and unsurpassed diving and manta-viewing offshore. Ishigaki-jima has the highest mountain (1,725 feet) in Okinawa, jungles, and more lovely beaches. On the minuscule island of Taketomi-jima there's an adorable, traditional, Ryūkyū-style village that's like stepping into a past age, and everyone's happy to keep it that way. At Hateruma-jima, Japan's southernmost reach, the water is clearer than glass and gets frighteningly deep in a hurry, and at Yonaguni-jima, Japan's western end, wild ponies roam, giant moths flap about like white bats at night, and mysterious Atlantis-like ruins lie on the seabed off the southern shore.

Ishigaki-jima

Ishigaki-jima, the main island of and gateway to the entire Yaeyama region, is known for its black-pearl industry, pineapples, white-sand beaches, and emerald waters. It's also the only island in the Yaeyama chain with a sizable town. Unlike Hirara on Miyako-jima, Ishigaki is not sprawling, and it's easy to explore on foot. Consisting of a harbor—with great connections to the rest of the Yaeyamas and, occasionally, even Taiwan—and a couple of main streets lined with shops, diving outfitters, hotels, bars, and restaurants, you can scout out downtown Ishigaki in an hour or two.

Getting There & Around

Both **JTA** and **ANK** airlines make the 55-minute flight from Naha to Ishigaki-jima. **Arimura Sangyō** (☎ 098/860–1980, 03/3562–2091 in Tōkyō) runs ferries from Naha to Ishigaki-jima via Miyako-jima four times a month, and tickets cost ¥6,130–¥20,330. **R.K.K** (☎ 098/868–1126, 03/3281–1831 in Tōkyō) runs ferries between Naha, Miyako-jima, and Ishigaki-jima four times a month. The trip from Naha to Ishigaki runs 13–16 hours and costs ¥6,130–¥15,330. Several ferries depart daily from the town Ishigaki to the surrounding islands, including Iriomote-jima, Taketomi-jima, and Kuro-shima.

The best ways to get around are by car and scooter. **Ai-Ai** (☎ 098/083–9530), at the corner of Yui-dōri, one block northeast of the post office on Sanbashi-dōri, rents bikes and scooters.

Toyota (☎ 098/082–0100) and **Nippon Rent-a-Car** (☎ 098/082–3629) have branches at the airport. **Nissan Rent-a-Car** (☎ 098/083–0024) is to the left of the bus station on Sanbashi-dōri, near the piers and fish market. Ishigaki-jima has a couple of buses that circle the coastal roads, but the service is infrequent.

The **tourist information office** (☎ 098/082–2809) is in the complex of municipal buildings next to the library (which has free Internet access) and

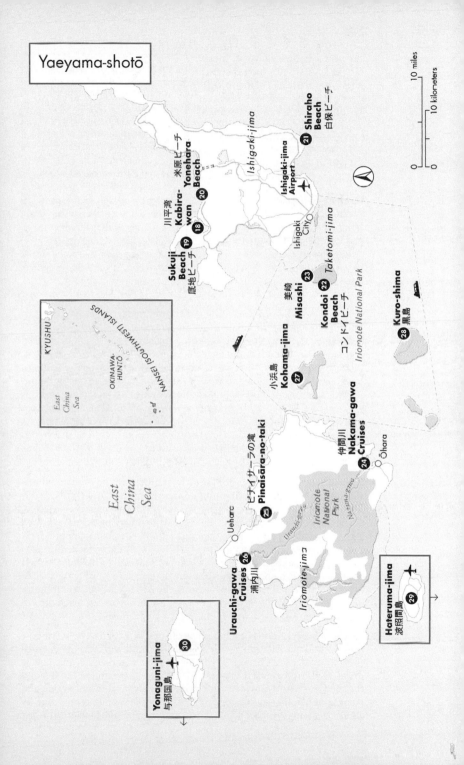

across from Shinei Kōen, a few blocks east of the long-distance ferry terminal and a few blocks west of the bus terminal. It's open Tuesday through Saturday 8:30–5, and some English is spoken. Pamphlets in English about Ishigaki-jima and the rest of the islands are for the taking, plus maps and lists of dive shops and places to explore.

Diving & Snorkeling

The scuba-diving and snorkeling around Ishigaki-jima is superb; you can find plenty of outfitters, such as **Tom Sawyer** (☎ 098/083–4677), based in downtown Ishigaki-shi. Trips include the coral reefs near Kabira-wan, Yonehara, and Cape Hirakubo. Lunch-inclusive outings cost around ¥12,000.

> ## CLAM COLOSSICUS
>
> **Sukuji Beach.** A 1-km (0.6-mi) walk from Kabira Bay, lovely, shallow Sukuji Beach will startle you with its amazing variety of reef life. Perhaps only the Great Barrier Reef has more giant clams, and here many are embedded into the coral only a few meters deep, so nearly anyone with snorkel gear can swim down and see them. This area is fairly developed, with equipment rentals and resorts, and there's a Club Med at the far western end. Sukuji is 30–35 minutes by car from Ishigaki-shi. ⊠ *Rte. 207 off Rte. 79.*

⑱ Kabira-wan (Kabira Bay). This beautiful, sheltered bay with hues of green and blue against fine, white sand is the center of Japan's black-pearl cultivation industry. Swimming is discouraged (due to the pearl farming), but you may walk the road to **Sukuji Beach** on the back side of the peninsula for a swim and snorkel. In addition to numerous tacky tourist shops and eateries, Kabira is the starting point for many glass-bottom boat tours. A 30-minute ride costs about ¥1,000. You can avoid the masses and get a good view at the elevated observation deck that overhangs the water. The bay is 30 minutes northwest by car or 40 minutes by bus (¥580) from downtown Ishigaki. ⊠ *Rte. 207 off Rte. 79.*

㉑ Shiraho Beach. Rare and beautiful reefs of blue coral lie submerged offshore from the village of Shiraho, on the southeast corner of Ishigaki-jima. A proposal to build an airport over the beach has so far been rejected, but if the airport is ever built the reefs will end up under the runway. The village has many lodging, restaurant, and equipment-rental facilities. You need to hire a boat (around ¥2,000, including snorkeling gear) to get safely past the breakers; try **Minshuku Maezato** (☎ 098/086–8065) next to the Shiraho post office. A bus heading east from Ishigaki-shi can drop you at the Shōgaku-mae bus stop; the trip takes about 30 minutes and costs ¥350. If you're driving or taking a taxi, you can reach the village via Route 390. ⊠ *10 km (6.2 mi) east of Ishigaki-shi.*

⑳ Yonehara Beach. At this beach, maybe the best one for snorkeling on the island, you have to waddle with fins (get the kind with decent heel protection) over a shelf of old, dead coral before you reach a spectacular drop-off. The clear water drops suddenly into a startling abyss. Beyond the shelf is a world crowded with multicolor tropical fish hovering and darting about the young coral below. Snorkel gear is rented out by shops on the main road, and there are camping and toilet facilities. Yonehara is about one hour north from Ishigaki-shi by bus, at a cost of ¥720. ⊠ *Rte. 79, 5 km (3 mi) east of Kabira-wan.*

Where to Stay & Eat

$–$$$ ✗ **Sushi Bar Tatsu.** Some of the best fish you'll ever taste swims just off-shore, and ends up on plates in this lively, Hawaiian-style restaurant. In fact, the sushi master once lived in Hawaii. Recommended for sushi or sashimi is a local rainbow-color fish called *gōma aigo*; its firm and tasty flesh will make an addict out of you. Tatsu is at the intersection of Shiyakusho-dōri and Shimin-kaikan-dōri, three blocks northwest of Shimei Kōen. ⊠ *10–28 Shinei-chō, Ishigaki-shi* ⊟ *No credit cards* ☾ *Closed Sun.*

$–$$ ✗ **Iso.** Near the harbor and behind the post office, this traditional Okinawan café serves local cuisine at reasonable prices. Most dishes are based on pork. The lunch special is only ¥600. ⊠ *9 Ōkawa, Ishigaki-shi* ☎ *098/082–7721* ⊟ *No credit cards.*

$$$$ ▥ **Hotel Miyahira.** Not far from the piers and downtown streets, the Miyahira is an upscale standby with a squat, orange-tile, Ryūkyū-style exterior and lots of shiisā lions for good measure. The interior is done up in a comfortable Western style. Breakfast is available for ¥400; for the dinner plan, add ¥2,100. ⊠ *4 9 Misaki-chō, Ishigaki-shi 907-0012* ☎ *098/082–6111* ⊠ *098/083–3236* ⊕ *www.miyahira.co.jp* ⇆ *158 Western-style rooms* ♿ *6 restaurants, pool, Internet, car rental* ⊟ *AE, MC, V* ⵏⵔ *EP, MAP.*

$$$$ ▥ **Ishigaki Grand Hotel.** This hotel next to the pier has a bright, attractive lobby and a gracious staff. Breakfast is included, and often all-you-can eat and drink buffet dinners are available. Rooms are simple but clean and sufficiently appointed. A nice spa on the ninth floor for guests. ⊠ *1 Tonoshiro, Ishigaki-shi 907-0004* ☎ *098/082–6161* ⊠ *098/082–2981* ⊕ *www.ishigaki-grand-hotel.com* ⇆ *64 Western-style rooms and suites, 10 Japanese-style rooms and 1 deluxe suite* ♿ *2 restaurants, Japanese baths, sauna* ⊟ *AE, MC, V* ⵏⵔ *CP.*

¢–$ ▥ **Hyper Hotel Ishigaki.** A member of the Hyper chain, this hotel offers wider-than-standard beds, fluffy duvets, and it's a block east of the ferry dock. Best of all, the prices are unbeatable for Western-style rooms that include all the basic amenities. It's a good choice for families or groups; a third person in one room costs only ¥1,000 more. ⊠ *1–2–3 Yashima-cho, Ishigaki-shi 907-0011* ☎ *098/082–2000* ⊠ *098/082–3933* ⊕ *www.hyper-ishigaki.co.jp* ⇆ *94 rooms* ♿ *Laundry facilities* ⊟ *MC, V* ⵏⵔ *CP.*

Taketomi-jima

8 km (5 mi) west of Ishigaki-jima.

On tiny Taketomi-jima you can imagine you are on a distant planet. Cute, compact houses with red-tile roofs and white coral–block walls sit contentedly amid a riot of greenery and blossoms. Even the sand is unique—the star-shape grains are the dried calcinous skeletons of tiny aquatic creatures. Just 300 folks call this speck home, but since it's only a 10-minute ride from Ishigaki-jima, boatloads of people visit each day. Ferries leave on the half hour and the trip costs ¥580 each way. Once you're on the islet you can wander around, swim, and snorkel in the clear, shallow water. Flat, less than a mile across at its widest point, and with a circumference of less than 9 km (6 mi), it's perfect for bicycling. A **visitor center** is a block east of the ferry pier. Little or no English is spoken, but you can pick up a map of the island.

㉒ Kondoi Beach. Perhaps the best beach on Taketomi, Kondoi is a prime spot to examine the island's famous star sand. Signs tell you not to take any, but someone is making money selling tons of it at the shops. You can see the islands of Iriomote, Kohama, and Kuroshima. Kondoi-misaki (Cape Kondoi) is a 30- to 40-minute walk from the ferry pier, halfway down the west coast of the island.

㉓ Misashi. The water around the island's northern tip is the best for snorkeling. Offshore rocky outcrops attract and shelter colorful gatherings of undersea critters. Walk northwest for 20 minutes along the beach or road from the ferry terminal; like everything on tiny Taketomi, it's not far.

Where to Stay & Eat

After the last ferry back to Ishigaki-jima, Taketomi becomes an intimate little community on the edge of the earth. The lodgings are not sophisticated, but a night on this quiet island is an unforgettable experience. The inns serve dinner, and a couple of small restaurants are within a block of the pier. There's even a pub, called Chirorin-mura, a block south of the Unbufuru lookout, at the southern end of the village.

¢ ✕🍴 **Minshuku Izumiya**. Popular for its lovely flower garden, this inn offers meals as part of the package. Those seeking more privacy can rent the separate traditional-style house across the sandy lane. ✉ *Taketomi-chō* ☎ *098/085–2250* ✍ *7 Japanese-style rooms without bath, villa* ♿ *No room phones, no room TVs* ☰ *No credit cards* ✵🍽 *MAP*.

¢ ✕🍴 **Nohara-sō**. A very informal place to stay, Nohara-sō is about good food and super-friendly service. It's a block or so east of the pier, just past the visitor center. Two meals and the use of snorkeling gear are included in the rates. ✉ *Taketomi-chō* ☎ *098/085–2252* ✍ *7 Japanese-style rooms without bath* ♿ *No room phones, no room TVs* ☰ *No credit cards* 🍽 *MAP*.

Iriomote-jima

30 km (19 mi) west of Ishigaki-jima.

You might not expect Japan to have a remote pocket of subtropical rain forest, but Japan is nothing if not full of the unexpected. Arguably the most secluded and unexplored region in the country, Iriomote-jima is an adventure lover's paradise. You can see plants and animals here not found anywhere else, such as the *yamaneko,* a lynxlike wildcat; knobby-kneed trees called *sakishima suōnoki*; and deadly vipers called *habu*.

If instead of scaring you it thrills you to share the muck and weeds with deadly snakes and slimy leeches, then chances are Iriomote-jima is the place for you. With languid rivers winding through mangroves and vines, waterfalls that attract swimmers and butterflies alike, and jungle trails that may or may not take you to the other side of the island before night falls and the bats begin to flutter, how could an adventurer like you be disappointed? Iriomote's jungle is the kind of place you go to if you want to test your mettle before auditioning for *Survivor*. Just remember to pack a knife, a compass, a camera, a journal, some yen, swamp-strength bug repellent, a snake-bite- and first-aid kit, salt or a flame source to fight off the leeches, and plenty of food and water.

Only about 4,000 people live on Iriomote, most along the northeast coastal road. Much of the island is a protected national park, and no roads head into the interior. The entire southwest third of the island is isolated and wild, with not even a coastal road and almost no settlements.

Getting Around

Ferries from Ishigaki-jima to the port of Funaura, in north-central Iriomote-jima, take about 40 minutes. There are nine sailings daily, and the fare is ¥2,000. Bus service connects Funaura with the towns of Ōhara and Shirahama, at the end of the 60-km (37-mi) coastal road, for ¥1,050. Buses run only twice daily and take about 80 minutes each way.

A **tourist information center** (☎ 098/082–9836), staffed part time is in Funaura next to the ferry pier. Although the staff won't speak much or any English, they can provide you with information on the few hostels and inns in and between the towns of Funaura and Uehara, on the northern coast, and near the remote southern port of Ōhara. They can also point you in the right direction if you want to hire a dive outfitter, or rent a bike, scooter, or car and driver.

No money-withdrawal facilities are on Iriomote-jima, so make sure you bring enough money for your entire stay.

What's to See

★ **Manta Way.** One of earth's rarest spectacles can be observed in Manta Way, the nickname for the strait between the east coast of Iriomote-jima and the neighboring Kohama-jima. Here manta rays often cruise in vast fleets, gracefully flapping along and feeding on plankton. April to June is the best time for manta-watching. Farther out, experienced divers can explore pinnacles of coral jutting up from the deep blue. Any of the minshuku or hostels on Iriomote can help arrange transport and dives.

㉔ Nakama-gawa Cruises (☎ 0980/85–5304). The second-longest river on the island can be explored on cruises that depart from the port of Ōhara, take about an hour, and cost ¥1,260. The trips offer you an Amazon-like experience with fewer tourists than at the Urauchi-gawa up north.

㉕ Pinaisāra-no-taki. These waterfalls, the tallest in the prefecture, can sometimes be seen from boats coming into Funaura. To get to the best viewpoints, either take a kayak or wade through the lagoon, depending on the tide, and climb a path to the top of the falls. Beware of leeches and especially the poisonous *habu* (water moccasins). A film canister of salt will save you from an attack of thirsty leeches; make plenty of noise to frighten away the snakes. The best option is to hire a local guide, such as Mr. Susumu Murata at ☎ 098/085–6425.

★ ㉖ **Urauchi-gawa Cruises.** A boat tour along this river is the sole reason many day-trippers come to the island, and though touristy, it's worthwhile. Boat operators wait for at least four riders, then for ¥1,500 per person they take you upriver as far as possible. You then disembark and hike a footpath to the waterfalls known as Mariudo-no-taki and Kanpirē-no-taki, where there are many suitable swimming spots, and lots of butterflies swarming in the mists. Allow three hours for the round-trip. Kayak rentals can also be negotiated from the boat operators. The first boats depart at 9 AM and the last depart at 4 PM. Since this is the most popular activity for visitors to Iriomote-jima, you'll find plenty of boats as well as frequent buses to Urauchibashi, the mouth of the river, 20 minutes west of Funaura.

A 15-km (9.3-mi) **cross-island trail** connects the falls of the Urauchi-gawa to a point near Ōhara, but this hike is a serious and rigorous undertaking. End to end, the hike will take 6–8 hours, and should not be attempted if you're alone or unprepared.

Where to Stay & Eat

Gourmet cuisine doesn't exist on Iriomote, but there is a place called Restaurant Urauchi with decent food and prices near where the Urauchi river boats leave, and there's a bare-bones market in Uehara. The lodgings can be booked with two meals, which is a good idea. All send minibuses out to meet the incoming ferries to provide free transport for guests. Pension Iriomote is a nice place to stay, with reliably good food in a great beach-side location on the back side of the headland west of Funaura, ☏ 098/085–6555, ¥16,000 with two meals. Not far from Pension Iriomote and farther along the road to Shirahama, Pension Hoshinosuna is a small enclave on the end of a pleasant beach, with diving operations and adjacent camping grounds (spaces ¥300; tent rental ¥500). ☏ 098/085–6448; fax 098/085-6828. ¥19,000 with 2 meals. In Ōhara, try Nature Lodge La Teada, ☏ 098/085–5555; 🖷 098/085–5988, ¥13,000 with two meals. They also have a few cottages (¥24,000).

Kohama-jima & Kuro-shima

㉗ Between Iriomote-jima and Taketomi-jima lies the small island of **Kohama-jima.** There a few places to stay, but most people visit on a short day trip from Ishigaki-jima. High-speed boats from Kohama to Ishigaki are frequent, cost ¥1,050, and take 30 minutes. The most popular activities are diving along Manta Way, and biking around to the beaches. Bikes can be rented near the dock.

㉘ Due south of Kohama-jima is the tiny island of **Kuro-shima** also blessed with fabulous diving. Chances are high you'll come across some Napoleon fish (reputed to be highly poisonous) among the colorful canyons of coral offshore. There's good snorkeling at Nishi-no-hama, just east of where the boat lets you off, and another beach with a U-shape reef is at the south end of the island. Bikes are available at the pier for the 3 km (2 mi) zigzag ride. In addition to great diving and snorkeling, the island is famous for raising the bulls used in Okinawa Hontō's unusual form of bullfighting called *tōgyū.* Like Kohama, Kuro-shima has a few inns, but since boats (¥1,150) from Ishigaki are fairly frequent and take only 30 minutes, most visitors make the crossing for a day trip.

Hateruma-jima & Yonaguni-jima

29 Hateruma-jima, Japan's southernmost point, is surrounded by some of the clearest water on the planet. Coral shelves drop away into a vertiginous indigo, and underwater visibility nears the edge of human vision. Just west of the pier at the amazing, gorgeous Nishi-no-hama, or Nishi Beach, is a sort of a snorkel-swim park. Facilities include bathrooms and a campground.

The island is only 5 km (3 mi) long, and rented bikes and scooters are the best way to get around. Speedboats from Ishigaki-jima to Hateruma-jima depart three times daily, and the one-hour trip costs ¥3,050 one-way; buy tickets at the counter inside Ishigaki's ferry terminal.

30 Underneath the waters off **Yonaguni-jima,** Japan's westernmost point, is an enormous series of ancient stone structures believed to have been a great temple that dates back to 8,000–10,000 BC, which would make it the oldest—by 5,000 years—human structure of this sort. The site has become popular among divers, especially since schools of photogenic hammerhead sharks often invade the area in winter. Marlin fishing here is also highly rated. Yonaguni-jima is known for wonders above ground, too: unusual rock formations, the Yonaguni atlas mouth, the world's largest moth species with a 24-cm (9½-in) wingspan (don't worry, they're not scary but beautifully colored with intricate designs), and wild Yonaguni ponies.

To get to Yonaguni-jima, you can fly via JTA from Ishigaki-jima in 30 minutes for ¥10,400. Two flights leave per day. Twice a week there's ferry service, but the trip takes 4½ hours. A one-way ticket costs ¥3,700.

Where to Stay

$$ ▦ **Hotel Irifune.** This hotel in the main village of Sonai, on Yonaguni's north coast, is nothing to rave about, but the management offers guided dive expeditions, and at ¥14,000 for two in a Western-style room with private bath, including meals, the price is right. Also, there are a few Japanese-style rooms with shared bath, and these run ¥12,000 for two. ✉ *Sonai* ☎ *0980/87–2311* 🛏 *8 Western-style rooms, 3 Japanese-style rooms without bath* ▤ *No credit cards* ❑ *MAP.*

OKINAWA ESSENTIALS

Transportation

BY AIR

There are no direct nonmilitary flights to Okinawa from the United States. International connections are available from Taipei, Taiwan; from Hong Kong and Shanghai, China; and from Seoul, Korea. Domestic flights from mainland Japan to Okinawa include those from Kagoshima (1 hour 20 minutes; ¥22,000 one-way) and Fukuoka (1 hour 35 minutes; ¥23,100) in Kyūshū, from Tōkyō (2 hours 30 minutes; ¥35,200), from Ōsaka (2 hours; ¥29,100), and from Nagoya (2 hours 15 minutes; ¥33,300).

🚩 Ishigaki-jima From mainland Japan, flights take 3 hours from Ōsaka, and 3½ hours from Tōkyō.

🚩 Miyako-shotō Japan TransOcean Air (JTA) ☎ 0120/25-5971 ⊕ www.japanair.com, an arm of Japan Airlines, operates flights to Miyako-jima from Naha and Ishigaki-jima (another Okinawan island), Tōkyō, Ōsaka, and Fukuoka. ANK ☎ 0120/02-9222, a regional arm of All Nippon Airways, offers similar flights. From Tōkyō's Haneda Airport there are two 3-hour flights per day, and a ticket costs ¥48,700. From Ōsaka there's one 2½-hour flight per day, and a ticket costs ¥42,100.

BY CAR

🚩 Naha Japaren ☎ 098/861-3900. Kūko Rent-a-Car ☎ 098/859-1111. Nippon ☎ 098/868-4554. Orion Rent-A-Car ☎ 098/867-0082. Toyota ☎ 098/857-0100.

BY FERRY

🚩 Miyako-shotō Arimura Sangyō in Tōkyō runs ferries 8 to 10 times a month. R.K.K in Tōkyō runs ferries 5 times a month, and the trips may take up to 10 hours. From the ferry terminal, taxi fare to central Hirara runs about ¥500.

🚩 Arimura Sangyō ☎ 098/860-1980 03/3562-2091. R.K.K ☎ 098/868-1126 03/3281-1831.

Contacts & Resources

EMERGENCIES

🚩 Adventist Medical Center ✉ 868 Kouchi, Nishihara-chō ☎ 098/946-2833. Police ☎ 110. Urasoe Sōgō Byōin (General Hospital) ✉ 4-16-1 Iso, Urasoe-shi ☎ 098/878-0231. U.S. Naval Hospital ✉ Camp Lester, Bldg. 6000 ☎ 098/643-7509.

ENGLISH-LANGUAGE MEDIA

The U.S. Armed Forces Radio Network at 648 on the AM dial broadcasts the news, a lot of cheesy infomercials, and a little music.

For a small selection of books, magazines, and newspapers, visit the bookshop on the seventh floor of the Palette Kumoji department store, at the bottom of Kokusai-dōri in Naha.

Points of Interest

12

SITES/AREAS	JAPANESE CHARACTERS
Boraga Beach	保良泉ビーチ
Churaumi Aquarium (Churaumi Suizokukan)	沖縄美ら海水族館
Hateruma-jima	波照間島
Higashi-henna Misaki (Cape Higashi-henna)	東平安名崎
Himeyuri-nō-tō	ひめゆりの塔
Ichiba-dōri and Heiwa-dōri shopping arcades	市場通りと平和通り
Ikema-jima	池間島
Iriomote-jima	西表島
Ishigaki-jima	石垣島
Kabira-wan (Kabira Bay)	川平湾
Kerama Rettō	慶良間列島
Kohama-jima	小浜島
Kokusai-dōri	国際通り
Kondoi Beach	コンドイビーチ
Kuro-shima	黒島
Mabuni Hill (Mabuni-no-Oka)	摩文仁の丘
Maehama Beach	前浜ビーチ
Misashi	美崎岬
Miyako-shotō	宮古諸島
Nagamahama Beach	長間浜ビーチ
Naha	那覇
Okinawa Hontō	沖縄本島
Pinaisāra-no-taki	ピナイサーラの滝
Shiraho Beach	白保ビーチ
Shuri-jō Castle Park (Shuri-jō Kōen)	首里城公園
Sukuji Beach	底地ビーチ
Sunayama Beach	砂山ビーチ
Taketomi-jima	竹富島
Tōri-ike	通り池
Tsuboya pottery district	中山
Underground Imperial Navy Headquarters (Kyū Kaigun Shireibu-gō)	旧海軍司令部壕
Yaeyama-shotō	八重山諸島

Yonaguni-jima	与那国島
Yonehara Beach	米原ビーチ
Yoshino Beach	吉野ビーチ
RESTAURANTS	
Chūzan	郷家
Gosso Gozzo	ごっそごっつぉ
Gōya	壺屋
Helios Pub	ヘリオスパブ
Iso	磯
Sushi Bar Tatsu	たつ
Tacos-ya	タコス屋
HOTELS	
Hotel Atoll Emerald	ホテルアトールエメラルド
Hotel Irifune	
Hotel Miyahira	ホテルミヤヒラ
Hotel Sun Palace	ホテルサンパレス
Hyper Hotel Ishigaki	ハイパーホテル石垣
Hyper Hotel Naka	ハイパーホテル那覇
Ishigaki Grand Hotel	石垣グランドホテル
Minshuku Izumiya	
Miyako Central Hotel	ミヤコセントラルホテル
Miyakojima Tōkyū Resort	宮古島東急リゾート
Nohara-sō	
Okinawa Harbor View Hotel	沖縄ハーバービューホテル
Roynet Hotel Naha Kumoji	ロイネットホテル那覇久茂地

Tōhoku

WORD OF MOUTH

"Sendai is a big city but a rather pleasant one, with among other things a very nice central covered shopping arcade, a few good museums, and excellent access to the Pacific Ocean coast. . . . I've been to Matsushima, and the bay there is really spectacular, and the fish fresh is delicious."

—Florence

By John Malloy Quinn

TŌHOKU TRANSLATES AS "EAST-NORTH," and a visit can do more than shift your physical coordinates. Though the Shinkansen has made getting up here easier, it is still a world away from the crowded south. The mountain villages are more remote, the forests more untamed, and the people more reserved—but don't be fooled, they are quite friendly if you show them you appreciate the pace, look, and feel of things.

Wild as Tōhoku can be, Sendai sets things in balance, right on the doorstep of the great northeastern wilderness. This attractive modern city of a million, with wide, shady boulevards and covered walkways and shopping complexes, puts on perhaps the country's biggest festival, Tanabata, every summer in early August, in honor of an ancient legend of star-crossed lovers. It attracts more than 3 million people, and it caters to them surprisingly well.

Beyond Sendai you won't find another city as large or lively until you hit Sapporo in Hokkaidō, but all around the countryside looms larger than ever. Ride the Akita Shinkansen to places like Lake Tazawa, Japan's deepest lake—a powder-blue reflection of sky that sits nestled in a caldera surrounded by virgin stands of bright-green beech draped in sweet-smelling vines, and steep hills studded with blue-green pines. Samurai history lives on virtually everywhere, but especially in the well-preserved dwellings and warehouses that now play host to curious tourists in Kakunodate. The town also has hundreds of lovely, ancient *shidarezakura,* or dangling cherry trees.

Tōhoku cherishes its forever-frontier status, and has plenty of low-key cities and timeless small towns full of folks who work hard in the cool summers and somehow bide their time through the fierce winters. Many ski areas collect neck-high powder snow, making for great skiing and snowboarding. There are also broad, river-riven plains that stretch between mountains and ocean, and they yield a bounty of treats, from apples and tomatoes to the rice and pure water that become some of the best dry, crisp karakuchi sake in the land. As a bonus, you're sure never to be far from an *onsen,* or hot spring—there seems to be one in each and every municipality!

See the glossary at the end of this book for definitions of the common Japanese words and suffixes used in this chapter.

ORIENTATION & PLANNING

Orientation

Tōhoku, like the rest of Honshū, is riven by a series of dramatic chains of densely forested mountains. While their rugged beauty will take your breath away, they can make travel difficult. If you allow for this, you won't be overly frustrated. Tōhoku is comprised of six prefectures, and stretches from the overly developed Fukushima, a short train ride from Tōkyō, to remote and rugged Aomori, which is within striking distance of Hokkaidō. This broad swath of territory encompasses mountain

CLOSE UP

Top Reasons to Visit

LAKES

Japan's two deepest lakes, Tazawa-ko, at 423 meters (1,400 feet), and Towada-ko, at 327 meters (1,080 feet) are sky-blue and never freeze. Towada-ko has some stocked trout, but the vulcanism below Tazawa-ko makes the water too acidic for a large fish population.

COASTAL BEAUTY

Many (perhaps too many) know about Matsu-shima Bay and its 250 little islands near Sendai but the coast is postcard-pretty virtually anywhere in Tōhoku. The views are particularly pleasing along the stretch from Akita City down to Atsumi Onsen, Yamagata, where the mountains march down into the Sea of Japan.

FRESH SEAFOOD & WILD VEGETABLES

Tōhoku abounds in some of the freshest food you'll ever eat. An astonishing variety of seafood and freshwater fish is presented in many ways, all of them tasty. Wild mountain vegetables, called sansai, are a specialty of the region, and turn up alongside many dishes.

COUNTRY LIFE

In Tōhoku much attention is still devoted to agrarian concerns in rustic settings. The region claims some of the cleanest water in the country, and the abundance of it helps produce the high-quality rice, noodles, apples, cherries, tomatoes, and beef and dairy cattle that make for a fine gastronomic visit.

MOUNTAIN ADVENTURES

The many fine mountain playgrounds are made all the more appealing by the relative absence of people using them. Outstanding destinations include Towada-Hachimantai National Park, Tazawa-ko, Iwaki-san, Yamadera, Dewa-sanzan, and Zao-san—which is, along with Appi, great for skiing.

13

ranges, primitive forests, stunning seacoasts, well-preserved feudal villages, sacred glaciated peaks and secluded temples, relaxing hot springs, and bottomless lakes in the craters of volcanoes.

Sendai

Sendai has made itself into what many other cities of a million people would envy: a fun-loving, livable, navigable, stylish haven of great shopping, friendly people, and fine eateries. Every year, with great fanfare, Sendai hosts the immense and colorful Tanabata Matsuri, a four-night, three-day festival that swells the town to three times its normal size.

Northern Tōhoku

By branching out from the Shinkansen hub of Morioka, you'll come across traditional iron-ware teakettles, grand old castles, lovingly preserved samurai houses, sparkling lakes, and huge national parks with mountains to climb, hiking trails for all abilities, large virgin forests, and hot springs galore.

West Coast Tōhoku

In the west, mountains give way to fertile plains that extend to the shore of the Sea of Japan. You'll find a castle here and there, but everywhere

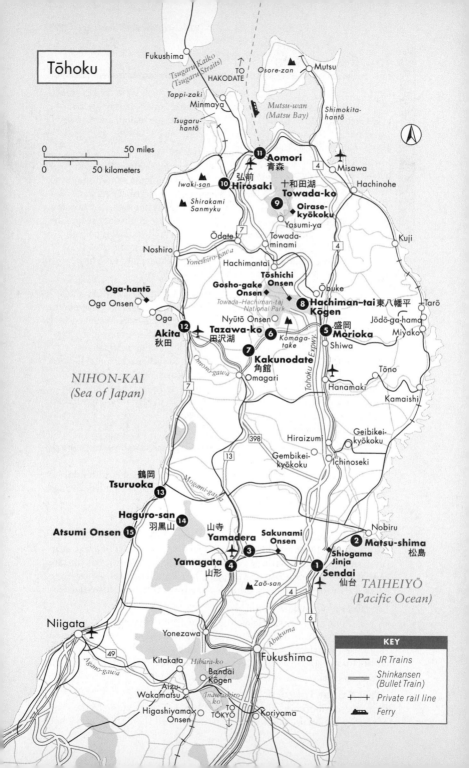

you'll encounter the best of foods, local women celebrated for their legendary fairness, mountains often buried in powder snow, and endless onsen.

Planning

To enjoy Tōhoku to the fullest, travel lightly, tack on a day or two for the unexpected, and bring something for cooler and wetter turns in the weather. You won't find many speakers of English or other Western languages, so it pays to drop into the tourist information offices (located within nearly every major train station) as soon as you arrive. Usually, one of the staff will speak English, and you'll save yourself a lot of frustration later on. One of the best features of the region is the incredible friendliness of those who live here, and even if they can't say much in reply, they will be eager to help.

The Best of Times
In the north and west, where winters are most severe, transportation slows down significantly, even grinding to a halt during prolonged sieges of snowfall. Along the Pacific and around Sendai things are decidedly milder. Fall colors in the region are fantastic, and spring brings spectacular blossoms of cherry and other fruit trees. Summer is cooler and less humid than in most of Japan.

It would be a hectic rush, but festival freaks could conceivably see all of Tōhoku's big summer festivals in a whirlwind visit, starting with Hirosaki's Neputa Matsuri (August 1–7), Aomori's Nebuta Matsuri (August 3–7), Akita's Kantō Matsuri (August 5–7), and the grand-daddy of them all, Sendai's Tanabata Matsuri (August 6–8). Things get fully booked well ahead, so secure arrangements as soon as plans allow. Don't be caught unaware—this includes train tickets as well, especially for reserved seats on shinkansen, which can be bought up to a month before the date of travel.

Craving for Savings?
Northern Tōhoku (Aomori, Iwate, and Akita prefectures) has an excellent way for foreigners staying in Japan one year or less to see the sights of the prefecture: the Northern Tōhoku Welcome Card gets you discounts on public buses (50%), at hotels (10%), and at museums (discount varies). The card is available upon presentation of your passport after filling out a short application form. Inquire at the JNTO office in Tōkyō, the information office at Aomori Airport, JR Aomori Station, or Hrosaki Station. The list of facilities offering the discount is limited, and they have blackout periods for high seasons. For complete information in English, visit the Web site at www.northern-tōhoku.gr. jp/welcome.

Concerning Restaurants & Hotels
Tōhoku's a great place for fresh food, whether it be from the fields, mountains, forests, or seas. Restaurants range from local sake shacks to upscale sushi bars and steak houses, and dress may be street-casual to office attire, but rarely formal. Menus may not always be in English, but nearly every shop will have its window displays full of lifelike represen-

tations of the menu. Remember this before you take off your shoes and wiggle your knees across the tatami mats to wedge them under that low table-top. In the cities plastic works well enough, but out in the countryside few if any places will accept credit cards.

Hotels in Tōhoku run the gamut from miniscule to behemoth, and often reflect local character. No matter the size or place, reserve in advance for the busy summer season. Many hotels in the larger cities have the standard amenities, and as is common in Japan, provide free toothbrushes, hair articles, robes, slippers, plentiful towels, hair dryers, and more. Most larger Western-type lodgings offer a choice of Japanese or Western breakfast (and sometimes room style, as well), and though it is not always included in the rates, breakfast is seldom more than ¥1,500 per person, or ¥1,800–2,000 for buffet. Casual clothes are usually fine, but as in most Asian countries, short pants on men are not widely seen.

WHAT IT COSTS In yen				
$$$$	**$$$**	**$$**	**$**	**¢**
RESTAURANTS over 3,000	2,000–3,000	1,000–2,000	800–1,000	under 800
HOTELS over 22,000	18,000–22,000	12,000–18,000	8,000–12,000	under 8,000

Restaurant prices are per person for a main course at dinner. Hotel prices are for a double room with private bath, excluding service and 5% tax.

Transportation Station

Most of the island's trains and buses ply north–south routes on either side of the mountains. Though trains are a viable means of getting around up here, in some cases a bus will save time. The most important travel routes fan out from Sendai and Morioka in the east, and from Akita City and Tsuruoka on the Japan Sea coast in the west. Routes are often highly scenic, but there are also many tunnels and occasional boring stretches where the road or track cuts away from the coast or into a steep ravine. A journey in Tōhoku is all about life at a different pace, so expect those out-of-the-way places to be hard to reach. In winter, prepare for frequent delays or closings due to heavy snows or high winds.

BUS TRAVEL From Morioka to Hirosaki, highway buses (JR Buses accept Rail Passes) are more convenient (and twice as fast) for getting to Akita than trains. From Tsuruoka to Yamagata, it's the same story (but it's a private bus line, not JR, and one of the terminals is in a modern shopping mall). Most buses pick you up or leave you near the station. Note: Overhead space is laughably limited.

CAR TRAVEL Driving in Tōhoku may be a good way for getting to the remote spots, but presents much of the same problems as driving in other parts of Japan, and then some: absence of proper signage (especially in English), inclement weather, following tour buses on narrow, winding roads, and getting nearly run off the highways by big trucks driven by daredevils.

On the Menu

VISITORS SEEKING culinary excellence and diversity will not be disappointed in Tōhoku. Restaurants in the region serve the freshest assortment of seafood, in sushi, sashimi, grilled, broiled, and boiled versions, as well as a bounty of seaweed and generous offerings of wild mountain vegetables—sansai—and mushrooms—kinoko—in season. Hinaijidori, or special local chicken, is a year-round treat, and so is the marbled, exquisitely tender beef known as Yonezawa-gyu—very expensive, but well worth it!

In Sendai, don't be afraid to try the local delicacy—grilled or braised beef tongue, gyu-tan, which tastes like a juicy and less chewy version of well-seasoned beef jerky. In Morioka, try the reimen, or cold, chewy ramen-

type egg noodles served in a big bowl with a slice of beef, a helping of kimchi, half a boiled egg, slices of cucumber, and a large wedge of watermelon. In Akita they are fond of inaniwa udon noodles that are flatter, whiter, and tenderer than the usual. In Kakunodate they mix sakura, or cherry blossoms, into the flour, and the result is mildly sweet noodles, as edible as they are pink! Don't miss the truly unique kiritampo, or hot pot made with chicken, local vegetables, and distinctive tubular rice cakes that have been formed and cooked onto sticks of bamboo or cedar. Yamagata has its distinctive rounded, chewy soba and incomparable beef. The local sake is uniformly excellent throughout the region, thanks to the quality rice and water.

13

TRAIN TRAVEL While Sendai is an easy 1 hour 40 minutes ride from Tōkyō, shinkansen lines don't go farther north than the west-coast city of Akita (via Morioka, with stops at Tazawa-ko and Kakunodate), and Hachinohe, on the northeast coast (also via Morioka, 45 minutes past Sendai). A shinkansen line also goes to Yamagata City, and train and bus routes extend from there to Tsuruoka and beyond. Overhead racks are adequate for small packs, but you should stow larger items in spaces at the ends of cars. In Japan no one is ever likely to touch your bags, even if left unattended.

Visitor Information

Individual towns have offices that provide local information. The largest and most helpful tourist centers, which provide information on all of Tōhoku, are at the Sendai and Morioka stations. In Tōkyō each prefecture has an information center with English brochures and maps.

🔢 Tourist Information JNTO Tourist Information Center in Tōkyo (TIC) ✉ Tōkyō Kotsu Kaikan, 2-10-1 Yurakucho, Chiyoda-ku ☎ 03/3201-3331 Ⓜ Yūraku-chō Line, Yūraku-chō station [Exit A-4B]. Prefecture information offices in Tokyo ☎ 03/3211-1775 for Akita ☎ 03/5276-1788 for Aomori ☎ 03/3524-8282 for Iwate ☎ 03/3504-8713 for Yamagata

SENDAI

❶ *By Shinkansen, 1 hr 40 min north of Tōkyō. ¥10,790 one-way*

Sendai is Tōhoku's largest city (population 1 million) and manages to have a big-city feel—with all the attendant trappings—while being as easy-going as a small town. Devastated by World War II, it has since become a thoroughly modern and well-planned city with wide boulevards and a surprising amount and variety of greenery. It's the economic and educational capital of the region, hosting a broad range of industries and universities. In recent decades the city has become a magnet for international students, teachers, and workers, and this has helped foster Sendai's energetic and affable atmosphere.

Sendai's origins can largely be traced to the "one-eyed dragon," Date Masamune (1567–1636). Affectionately nicknamed for his childhood loss of an eye from smallpox and his valor in battle, Date Masamune established a dynasty in Sendai that maintained its position as one of the three most powerful *daimyō* (feudal lord) families during the shōgun period. In addition to his military skills, he constructed a canal linking two rivers, improving the transport of rice.

A convenient entry-point for striking out into the region, Sendai has noteworthy sights, and is a fun place to spend a day or two poking around, shopping, and enjoying good restaurants.

Getting Around

Walkers and people-watchers will love Sendai—it seems as if the whole city is within a quick stroll. Thousands of shops, bars, restaurants, and cafés line glittering arcades that stretch in all directions. Spiffy hotels and glitzy department stores are well located. Not far from the station, and slicing cleanly through the downtown entertainment area, are three broad avenues: Aoba-dōri, Hirose-dōri, and Jōzen-ji-dōri. There's also Chūō-dōri shopping street—and all of these conveniently intersect and are linked by the wide shopping arcade of Ichiban-chō.

To use city buses, consult the bus and subway information office, near the subway station in front of the JR station. Here you can pick up English-language brochures with bus departure points, stops, and fares for the major sights. Sendai Loople, a limited-access bus, stops at Zuihō-den (20 minutes from the station) and Aoba Castle (30 minutes) and returns to the station in about an hour. A full-day pass costs ¥600; buses depart from the west exit of JR Sendai Station every half hour from 9 to 4.

At present, the new Sendai subway runs roughly north–south only, and its stations are far from the most interesting sights. It's really only of use to resident commuters.

The **Sendai Tourist Information Office** (☎ 022/222–4069) on the second floor of Sendai JR Station has English-speakers who will gladly recommend hotels and restaurants. They also provide essential maps with walking and bus routes. **Sendai International Center** (☎ 022/224–1919 hotline, 022/265–2471 general assistance) is across the street from the Sendai

Tanabata Matsuri (Tanabata Festival)

TŌHOKU'S TANABATA FESTIVAL, one of the largest in Japan, is held every year from August 6 to 8 (heralded by massive fireworks over the river the night of the 5th), when Sendai's population triples. The festival is believed to have evolved from a Chinese legend of a weaver girl (the star Vega in her afterlife) and her cowherd boyfriend (the star Altair, in his). As lovers tend to do, they slowly went mad, and began to spend their time idly, living as if in a dream. The jealous ruler became irate and banished them to the far sides of his kingdom (the Milky Way). But he relented, perhaps remembering some foolish love affair of his own, and allowed them to meet on one day a year: the seventh day of the seventh month.

Why the people here celebrate this quintessentially cosmic love story on the sixth day of the eighth month is probably more closely linked with a need to give restive subjects time off to party in a time of great heat. Whatever the background, the festival creates a great reservoir of energy. Colorful streamers flutter from every perch in town. To walk along the arcades with the endless streamers brushing down against your face, neck, and shoulders—as you bump against and smile back at other enraptured souls also seduced by the whole grand pageant—is to feel glad to be alive and in Sendai at such a wonderful time.

From 5 PM the evening of the 6th, parades, dances, events, and demonstrations of festival spirit are held nightly through the 8th, along a short stretch of Jozenji dōri between Kotodai Park and Bansui dōri. The tourist information office in Sendai Station can help with more details, also contained in countless pamphlets.

Municipal Museum. The office operates an English-language hotline to deal with questions about the city and prefecture.

What to See

Views of the city and ruined stone walls await those who hike or take a bus up Aoba-yama to **Aoba Castle** (Aoba-jō). A restored guardhouse and ruins are all that remain today. The Date dynasty kept its residence here for nearly three centuries after beginning construction of the once grand castle around 1600. Sadly, it was all pulled down during the Meiji Restoration. **Gokoku Jinja** (Gokoku Shrine) is now the main feature of the area. Near the observation terrace is a statue of the city's founder and favorite ruler, Date Masamune, mounted on a horse. In clear weather the Pacific Ocean can be seen far off to the right. Take a bus from Stop No. 9 in front of JR Sendai Station, or ride the Sendai Loople tourist bus (daily pass ¥600, one ride ¥250) to get here. ✉ *Free* ☎ *022/222-0128* ⊙ *Daily dawn–dusk.*

The **Sendai Municipal Museum** (Sendai-shi Hakubutsukan), at the foot of the hill beneath Aoba Castle, displays cultural artifacts, including pottery, paintings, and armor relating to the history of the Date family and the city, and hosts special exhibitions. ✉ *26 Kawauchi, Aoba-ku, Sendai* ☏ *022/225–3075* ✆ *¥400* 🕓 *Tues.–Sun. 9–4:45, last entry at 4:15; closed last day of each month, the day following special exhibits, and national holidays.*

No cold gray slab of stone, **Zuihō-den**, the grand mausoleum of Date Masamune, the most revered ruler of ancient Sendai, was made in the showy style of the Momoyama period (16th century), where figures of people, birds, and flowers are carved and inlaid in natural colors. Looking like the world's fanciest one-story pagoda, there is so much gold leaf that in the right light it practically glows. Having burned during the fire-bombing in 1945, Zuihō-den was reconstructed in a five-year period beginning in 1974. During the excavation, Date Masamune's well-preserved remains were found and have been reinterred in what appears to be a perfect replica of the original hall. To get here, take Bus 11 from JR Sendai Station to the Otamaya-bashi stop (20 minutes), or take the Loople Bus (¥250) to the Zuihō-den stop. The mausoleum is a short walk up the hill. From Aoba Castle it's a 30-minute walk down Aoba-yama and across the Hirose-gawa (Hirose River). ✉ *23–2 Otamayashita, Aoba-ku, Sendai* ☏ *022/262–6250* ✆ *¥550* 🕓 *Feb.–Nov., daily 9–4:30; Dec. and Jan., daily 9–4.*

Ōsaki Hachiman Jinja was one of the few structures World War II left standing in Sendai. Built in Yonezawa in 1527, the shrine pleased Date Masamune so much that he had it brought to Sendai in 1607. Nestled among trees, it is an elegant structure, with bright-metal ornamentation over subdued black lacquer. The main building has been designated a National Treasure. It's in the northwest section of the city, about 10 minutes from downtown (or Aoba-yama) by taxi and 15 minutes from the Zuihō-den area. You can also take Bus 15 from JR Sendai Station for ¥220. ✉ *4–6–1 Hachiman, Aoba-ku, Sendai* ☏ *022/234–3606* ✆ *Free* 🕓 *Daily dawn–dusk.*

For a bit of garden Zen, go to **Rinnō-ji** (Rinnō Temple). This is a quintessentially Japanese garden, with stream, lotus-pond, gnarled pines, azalea bushes, irises, and bamboo. In June the garden is a blaze of color, but with so many visitors then it's not as tranquil. It's a 20-minute walk from Ōsaki Hachiman Jinja, northwest of the city center. Use Bus 24 if you are coming directly from JR Sendai Station. ✉ *1–14–1 Kitayama, Aoba-ku, Sendai* ☏ *022/234–5327* ✆ *¥300* 🕓 *Daily 8–5.*

Visitors who want to see the sights from on high can do so from the observatory deck on the top floor of the 30-story **SS (Sendai Sumitomo) 30 Building** (✉ 4–6–1 Chūō ☏ 022/267–4465 ✆ Free 🕓 Daily 7 AM–1 AM).

Where to Eat

Sendai has hundreds of great restaurants, but the highest concentrations are found along the parallel streets Ichiban-chō, Inari-kōji, and Kokubun-chō. Most places display their menus in their windows, along with the prices. Also, within the JR station is the underground mall called Restaurant Avenue, which includes small branches of established restaurants.

$$$–$$$$ ✕ **Gintanabe Bekkan.** A favorite with locals, this establishment prepares fresh fish with great variety—all delicious. The sashimi *moriawase* (assorted sashimi) at ¥4,000 is an excellent selection for two people. From the Ichiban-chō exit of Mitsukoshi department store, turn left, take a right at the first narrow street, walk two short blocks, then turn left and walk 50 yards. It's the restaurant with the tub-shaped fish tank. ✉ *2–9–34 Kokubun-chō* ☎ *022/227–3478* 🖃 *AE, DC, MC, V* ☺ *No lunch.*

$$$–$$$$ ✕ **Jirai-ya.** A curtain next to a big red paper lantern leads to this inviting Sendai gem where *kinki* (deepwater white fish) are paired with tempura of fresh local vegetables. Try *kinoko-jiru* (mushroom soup), a local dish popular in autumn. It's just off Ichiban-chō, near Hirose-dōri. ✉ *2–1–15 Kokubun-chō* ☎ *022/261–2164* 🖃 *MC, V* ☺ *Closed Sun.*

$–$$$ ✕ **Beko Masamune.** Fancy a taste of the local delicacy? ¥1300 gets you the cow's-tongue set, grilled with your choice of miso, soy sauce, or salt, a bowl of tasty oxtail soup, and a healthy mix of rice and steamed barley—or skewers of chicken or sirloin for the less adventurous. Earthen walls, dark passages, and intimate lighting conjure up a romantic setting. It's a few minutes' walk from the station, at the entrance of the Clis Road/ Hapina Nakakacho (Chūo-dōri) arcade, on the second floor—look for the red sign with the black cow's head. ✉ *2–4–19 Kokubun-cho, Aoba-ku* ☎ *022/217–1124* 🖃 *No credit cards* ☺ *Daily 11:30–2 and 5–11:30.*

$$ ✕ **Aji Tasuke.** This small shop is a local institution that serves excellent and inexpensive Japanese meals. A ¥1,450 *shokuji* (meal) gets you the full set of grilled beef tongue and pickled cabbage, oxtail soup, and a bowl of barley mixed with rice. From the Ichiban-chō exit of Mitsukoshi department store turn left, walk to the first narrow street, turn right, then go left at the next corner; Aji Tasuke is 50 yards ahead on the left, next to a small shrine. ✉ *4–4–13 Ichiban-chō* ☎ *022/225–4641* 🖃 *No credit cards* ☺ *Closed Tues.*

$–$$ ✕ **Go Shu In Sen.** A good place for cheap seafood, you can't beat their lunch sets. ¥770 gets you the grilled fish of the day, and just ¥1,350 buys you *unaju*, or eel grilled in sweet soy sauce on rice. Go Shu In Sen is in the basement of the Shonai Bank Building, a couple of minutes from the JR station, on Aoba-dōri, near where it meets Atago Kamisugi-dōri. ✉ *3–1–24 Chuo, Aoba-ku* ☎ *022/225–6868* 🖃 *No credit cards* ☺ *Daily 11–11.*

Where to Stay

$$$ ✕🖾 **Hotel Metropolitan Sendai.** This upscale hotel adjacent to the railway station offers great value for its price range, and the service makes you feel like this could be your town if you only stayed a bit longer. Enjoy reasonably large Western-style guest rooms. The restaurants are all good (the Japanese one on the second floor, where the breakfast buffet is also served, has a fabulous glass-front view for people-watching), and simpler fare is available in the coffee shop. ✉ *1–1–1 Chūo, Aoba-ku, Sendai, Miyagi-ken 980-8477* ☎ *022/268–2525* 🖨 *022/268–2521* 🌐 *www.jrhotelgroup.com/eng/hotel/* ⚑ *300 rooms with bath* ⚓ *5 restaurants, lounge, coffee shop, indoor pool, gym, cable TV.* 🖃 *AE, DC, MC, V* 🍴 *EP.*

$$$ ✕⊞ **Sendai Kokusai Hotel.** The outside may be blockish, unimaginative concrete, but inside lurks one of Sendai's most stylish hotels. The Kokusai stands next to the SS 30 complex, and is a short walk from the station or downtown. Choose between swanky French, Chinese, or Japanese restaurants on the fifth floor, and a British-style pub on the first. ✉ *4–6–1 Chūō, Aoba-ku, Sendai, Miyagi-ken 980-0021* ☎ *022/268–1112* 🖷 *022/ 268–1113* ⊕ *www.tobu-skh.co.jp/english/english.htm* ⇆ *234 rooms with bath* ⚗ *6 restaurants, coffee shop, cable TV, bars, shop, business services, meeting rooms* ▤ *AE, DC, MC, V* ⫶⊙⫶ *EP.*

$ ⊞ **Comfort Hotel Sendai East.** A three-minute walk east from JR Sendai Station, this very Western-looking rectangular hotel is one of the newest in town. The business-ready and functional rooms come at an unbeatable price, with lots of parking nearby. From the station, walk east past the east bus terminal, and turn at the first left. It's in the third block, on the left, across from the MiniStop convenience store. ✉ *1–345 Nakake-chō, Miyagino-ku, Sendai, Miyagi-ken 983-0864* ☎ *022/792– 8711* 🖷 *022/792–8712* ⇆ *202 rooms with bath* ▤ *AE, DC, MC, V* ⫶⊙⫶ *BP.*

$ ⊞ **Hotel Shōwa.** Tucked inside one of the best shopping arcades in town, only a five-minute walk from JR Sendai Station, this business hotel is convenient for sightseeing and getting to the best downtown restaurants. The simple, clean rooms are reasonably priced. From the station, walk to the Chūō-dōri arcade and turn left. In the second block on the right, take one flight up to the hotel entrance. ✉ *2–6–8 Chūō, Aoba-ku, Sendai, Miyagi-ken 980-0021* ☎ *022/224–1211* 🖷 *022/224–1214* ⇆ *117 rooms with bath* ▤ *AE, DC, MC, V.*

Shopping

Sendai is the unofficial capital of the Tōhoku region, and you can find many of the regional crafts here, including kabazaiku cherry-bark items and *washi* (handmade paper), which are made outside Miyagi Prefecture. Heading west out of the station, follow the elevated walkways across the busy street below to where the shopping begins in earnest.

The best variety of shops may be found along the popular and chic CLIS Road arcade or the Sun Mall Ichiban-chō, (which it intersects after a few blocks heading west), but if you are pressed for time, drop down into the shopping center that lies beneath Sendai Station, where **Shimanuki** (✉ B1F, Sendai Station, 1–1–1 Chūō, Aoba-ku, Sendai ☎ 022/267–4021) is tops for folk crafts and snacks from around Tōhoku. Open daily 10:30–7:30. Their main store (✉ 3–1–17 Ichiban-chō ☎ 022/223–2370) is also open daily 10:30–7:30.

The Asaichi, or Farmer's Market, is an east–west alley positioned midway in the big block that sits roughly between JR Sendai Station's west exit and the SS 30 Sumitomo Sendai Building. It's busy from early morning to night, and you'll be able to see, hear, smell, and taste it all.

Getting to Sendai

By Air

Sendai is well-connected, with numerous daily flights to and from every major airport in Japan, and destinations in Asia and the Pacific as well.

For airline phone numbers, *see* Air Travel *in* Essentials.

By Bus

The **Tōhoku Kyūkō Express night bus** (☎ 03/3529–0321 in Tōkyō, 022/262–7031 in Sendai) from Tōkyō to Sendai is inexpensive (¥6,210) and takes approximately six hours. Five departures leave Tōkyō Station (Yaesu-guchi side) between 11 PM and midnight. The bus from Sendai departs from the train station at 11 PM and arrives in Tōkyō at 5 AM. Reservations are required for all buses.

By Train

From Tōkyō, the *Hayate* Shinkansen rockets to Sendai in just 1 hour 40 minutes, for ¥10,790. From Sendai it reaches Morioka in 45 minutes, for an additional ¥6,490.

SIDE TRIPS FROM SENDAI

Matsu-shima

❷ *25 min northeast of Sendai by JR, ¥400.*

Matsu-shima and its bay are the most popular coastal resort destinations in Tōhoku. Matsu-shima owes this distinction to the Japanese infatuation with oddly shaped rocks, which the bay has in abundance. Hordes come to see the 250 small, pine-clad islands scattered about the bay. Long ago it was such a sublime and tranquil scene that it was fondly written of by the 17th-century haiku poet Bashō. Overpopularity and a bit of pollution aside, the bay is still beautiful, and it makes for a worthwhile side trip from Sendai. If you can avoid weekends or holidays and obtain a good viewpoint—consider renting a cycle from one of the shops and pedaling up into the hills—you can indeed feel your cares float away, and the islands themselves may seem to bob and sway on the gentle breeze-driven swells. The key sights are within easy walking distance of each other. For maps and info, visit the tourist office at the end of the Matsushite Kaigan Pier. Many restaurants are in the area, but they are overpriced and often full of pushy tour-bus groups. This makes returning to Sendai a good option! However, if you fancy a stay, the hotels listed below have good food.

Just to the right as you step off the boat on the pier in Matsu-shima is the small temple of Godai-do. Constructed in 1609 at the behest of Date Masamune, the temple is on a tiny islet connected to the shore by two small arched bridges. Animals are carved in the timbers beneath the temple roof and among the complex supporting beams.

Zuigan-ji, Matsu-shima's main temple, dates from 828, but the present structure was rebuilt to meet Date Masamune's tastes in 1609. Zuigan-ji is perhaps the most representative Zen temple in the Tōhoku region. The main hall is a large wooden structure with elaborately carved wood panels and paintings (now faded) of some of Date's favorite totems: flowers, birds, and trees. The relaxing—outside of holidays—temple grounds are full of trees, including two plum trees brought back from Korea in 1592 by Date Masamune after a failed military venture. The natural caves surrounding the temple are filled with Buddhist statues that novices carved from the rock face as part of their training. Zuigan-ji is down the street from Godai-dō, across Route 45 and the central park. ☎ *022/211–1344* ✉ *¥700* ⏰ *Apr.–Sept., daily 8:30–5; Oct.–Mar., daily 9–4.*

From Godai-dō it's a short walk across the 250-yard pedestrian bridge near the Matsu-shima Century Hotel to the islet of **Fukurajima**. For the ¥200 toll you can walk away from the crowds to enjoy a picnic in the park with views across the bay.

Where to Stay

$$$–$$$$ ✕🏨 **Matsu-shima Century Hotel.** This hotel sits on the island-studded bay. The communal hot-spring bath has perhaps the best view of all—but the one from the coffee shop is not bad, either. Many rooms are lavish, especially the Japanese ones; some even have sea-view balconies. Indulge in the oysters, in season. ✉ *8 Sensui, Matsu-shima Aza, Matsu-shima-chō, Miyagi-ken 981-0213* ☎ *022/354–4111* 🖨 *022/354–4191* 🛏 *192 Western-style and Japanese-style rooms with bath* ♿ *2 restaurants, coffee shop, pool, hot spring, sauna* ☰ *AE, DC, MC, V.*

$$ ✕🏨 **Folkloro Matsu-shima Hotel.** This reasonably priced and popular hotel is a 10-minute walk from the station. There is no dinner restaurant, but you can enjoy your breakfast on a terrace overlooking the bay. When you come out of the (Matsu-shima Kaigan) station, make a right, go under the tracks, then turn right again and climb the hill—it's on the left. For 3,000 yen more, the larger "family" rooms can be a good splurge—a few of them have nice ocean views. ✉ *17 Sanjukari, Matsu-shima Aza, Matsu-shima-chō, Miyagi-ken 981-0213* ☎ *022/353–3535* 🖨 *022/353–3588* 🛏 *29 Western-style rooms with bath* ♿ *2 restaurants, coffee shop, pool, hot spring, sauna* ☰ *No credit cards.*

$$$$ 🏨 **Hotel Ichinobo.** This posh, expensive resort hotel with the feel of a family-run ryokan has a gorgeous garden that stays lighted up at night. All the large, bright rooms overlook the bay—as do the delightfully relaxing Tea Room, the public baths, and the well-heated outdoor pool up on the fifth floor. ✉ *1–4 Takagi Aza Hama, Matsu-shima-chō, Miyagi-ken 981-0215* ☎ *022/353–3333* 🖨 *022/353–3339* 🛏 *20 Western-style rooms with bath, 104 Japanese-style rooms with bath* ♿ *Restaurant, coffee shop, pool* ☰ *AE, DC, MC, V* 🍴 *EP.*

Yamadera

❸ *By JR Senzan Line, 46 min west of Sendai, ¥980.*

If you'd like to see one of Japan's most revered—and scenic—temple complexes, come up here on an easy day trip from Sendai—or, from Yamagata City, it's only 15 minutes, ¥230.

If you are expecting just another mundane temple, you will certainly be surprised. Yamadera is like something conjured out of the ethereal mists of an ancient Japanese charcoal painting. Built in the year 860, Yamadera's ambitious complex of temples is perched high on the upper slopes of **Hōju-san** (Mt. Hōju), with divine vistas. Belonging to the Tendai Buddhists, who believe in the existance of "Buddha-nature" within all living things, Yamadera attracts a steady stream of pilgrims. To get here, walk through the village from the station, cross the bridge, and turn right. Just inside the entrance is **Kompon Chū-dō,** the temple where the sacred Flame of Belief has burned constantly for 1,100 years.

Near Kompon Chū-dō is a statue of the Japanese poet **Matsuo Bashō** (1644–94), whose pithy and colorful haiku related his extensive wanderings throughout Japan. About a visit to the temple, he wrote how he felt the stillness soaking into the stones while hearing a cicada's piercing cry.

The path continues up a lot of steps—nearly 1,100 of them, well-tended though they be. At the summit is **Oku-no-in,** the hall dedicated to the temple founder, Jikaku Daishi. But if you've come this far, keep going. Of all the temples hanging out over the valley, the view from **Godai-do** is the best. The path becomes crowded in summer and slippery in winter. Allow one to one and a half hours for a leisurely climb up and a careful tramp down. On the way back to the station, pick up refreshments at the shop to the right of the bridge, where you can sit and see the river. There's a tourist info office (no English, though) by the bridge. ☎ 023/695–2816 ✑ ¥300 ☯ *Open daily 8–5.*

EN ROUTE **Sakunami Onsen** is a highly relaxing hot-spring stop off the train between Yamadera and Sendai. It's only 42 minutes, ¥570, from Sendai Station, close enough to be an alternative spot to spend the night.

Where to Stay

$$$$ ✕⌂ **Iwamatsu Ryokan.** Situated along a waterfall, this ryokan has rooms that look out on trees and the stream. The original *rotemburo*—or open-air bath—is mixed-sex bathing. At dinner local specialties are served. Expect some spit-roasted and salted river smelt, or *ayu*—an algae-eating fish with skin and flesh so sweet that a bucket of them smells like a ripe watermelon—and tasty sansai, or mountain vegetables, such as fern bracken, baby bamboo, and any number of types of mushrooms. Breakfast buffet is a large selection of Japanese and Western foods. The inn has shuttle-bus service from JR Sakunami Station, and regular bus service from JR Sendai Station. ✉ *16 Sakunami Motoki, Aoba-ku, Sendai-shi, Miyagi-ken 989-3431* ☎ *022/395–2211* 🖶 *022/395–2020* ➪ *102 Japanese-style rooms with bath* ♨ *Restaurant, tea shop, dance club* ▭ *AE, MC, V* ⌂ *MAP.*

Yamagata

 1 hr west of Sendai by JR Senzan Line, ¥1110; 2 hrs 7 min by (non JR) bus from Tsuruoka if you're coming from Akita or Atsumi Onsen, ¥2150.

Pottery Farm

IF YOU'RE INTERESTED in pottery, go to **Hirashimizu** on the outskirts of Yamagatan. This small enclave of traditional buildings and farmhouses is a step back in time. About six pottery families each specialize in a particular style. Two of them, the Shichiemon and Heikichi, offer pottery lessons, and participants can have the results fired and glazed and, two to four weeks later, mailed back home. The best-known pottery is that of the Seiryū-gama (Seiryū kiln). Their works have been exhibited in America and Europe, so the prices are high. The potteries are generally open daily 9–3, but may honor irregular holidays, so check with the tourist information office at the train station. From Bus Stop 5, in front of JR Yamagata Station, board the bus bound for Geijutsu Kōka Daigaku, (Kokai University of Art; whose bijitsu-kan, or Art Museum, has not only good art but great panoramic views of the mountains) for an 11-minute ride (¥210); a taxi is about ¥2,000.

Yamagata is the capital of the prefecture of the same name (and the "Sister City" of Boulder, Colorado). It's a community of a quarter-million souls who enjoy one of the most visually stunning locations in Japan. Everywhere you look are lovely mountains with an endless play of light and shadow on their flanks. Connoisseurs of soba and mountain vegetables will be delighted, as will fans of perfectly marbled beef. Yamagata Prefecture is the only prefecture to be 100% thermal—having at least one onsen, or hot spring, in each of its 44 municipalities.

You can pick up free maps and brochures from the **Yamagata Tourist Information Office** (☎ 023/631–7865) opposite the ticket turnstiles inside Yamagata JR Station; it's open daily 9–5:30.

At the **Hana-gasa Festival** (August 5–7), some 10,000 dancers from the region dance through the streets in traditional costume and *hana-gasa*, hats so named for the safflowers (locally called *benibana*) decorating them. It's based on an old ritual to promote fertility and a rich harvest. Floats are interspersed among the dancers, and stalls provide food and refreshments.

Most people come to Yamagata for **Zaō-san** (Mt. Zaō), where nearly 1.5 million alpine enthusiasts ski its 14 slopes between December and April. In summer hikers walk among the colored rocks around **Zaō Okama,** a mineral-tinted (copper-oxide green, but color varies) caldera lake nearly a quarter-mile across. A cable-car lift rises from **Zaō Onsen,** the mountain's resort town, climbing 1,562 feet from the base lodge; another makes the final ascent, an additional 1,083 feet. Each ride takes 7 min and costs ¥1,400; ¥2,500 return, and a total of ¥5,000 if you ride the whole way up and down. Even nonskiers make the wintertime trip to see the *juhyō*, a forest of snowy monsters caused by heavy snowfall sticking to the conifers, after which the wind sculpts them all winter long. Zaō Onsen is 19 km (12 mi) from Yamagata Station, a 45-minute trip (bus only). English info can be had from the Zaō Onsen Info Office, daily 9–5 ☎ 023/694–9328.

Where to Stay & Eat

★ **$$$–$$$$** ✕ **Sagorō.** If you have never indulged in some strictly top-end sukiyaki, shabu-shabu, or steak—or if you have and want to feel that way again—Sagorō will serve you a full dose of some excellent Yonezawa beef. This will not only inebriate you for the entire evening, but you will gush for days about its impossible tenderness, its impeccably perfect marbling of such ineffably sweet fat, and so on. Although most dishes are pricey, a plate of *shōga-yaki* (beef sauteed in ginger sauce; ¥1,700), *oshinko moriawase* (pickled vegetables; ¥700), rice, and soup can make for a fairly reasonable meal—that is, if you can sit, Zen-like, and endure the sights, smells, and sounds all around you. Go three blocks east from the station. Turn left. Look for the meat shop and you'll see the black bull on the sign above the street next to it. Take the stairs up one flight to heaven. ✉ *1–6–10 Kasumi-chō* ☎ *023/631–3560* ⏰ *Mon.–Sat. 11:30–2 and 5–9* ═ *No credit cards.*

$$–$$$ ✕ **Mimasu.** The highlights are good sushi, tempura, and *donburi*—bowls with cutlets, tempura, and chicken on top of rice. Lunch specials include *danjurō bentō*, a filling medley of tasty seasonal vegetables and fish. Within Nanoka-machi, Mimasu is a 15-minute walk from the station, or a short walk from the Yamagata Washington Hotel. ✉ *2–3–7 Nanoka-machi* ☎ *023/632–1252* ⏰ *Closed 2nd Wed. of month* ═ *No credit cards.*

¢–$$ ✕ **Mitsuya.** A short walk from the station will put you in front of some fine and slightly chewy Yamagata soba, or buckwheat, noodles. Everything is good, but in summer try the hiyashi-dori soba (with cold chicken)—better than it sounds, don't worry! Head south (right) from the east exit, and keep to the street that follows along the tracks until you can cross over them and turn to the right. Then it's just a hop to the traditional black-wood and white-stucco building on the left. ✉ *1–75 Kami-machi, Yamagata-shi* ☎ *023/644–4973* ⏰ *Wed.–Mon. 11–8* ═ *No credit cards.*

¢–$$ ✕ **Shōjiya.** Yamagata is famous for soba, and this is one of the best places to try it. For lunch or a light dinner, try the simple *kake* soba (served in a hot broth; ¥650), tempura soba (¥1,300), or *nameko* soba (with mushrooms; ¥900). Point to the picture menu if you have to. It's a 10-minute walk from the JR station. Go south, or right, from the east exit, and turn left at the first track-crossing you come to. Mitsuya is the equally good soba shop in the other direction, across the tracks. ✉ *14–28 Saiwai-chō* ☎ *023/622–1380* ═ *No credit cards* ⏰ *Closed Mon.*

$$$ ⛨ **Hotel Metropolitan Yamagata.** Yamagata's best—and best-located—hotel is on your right as you exit the east side of the station. The decor is snappy and stylish, with lots of wood paneling and old-fashioned chairs. The staff are breezily efficient. The Mogami-tei restaurant on the second floor is widely famous for its quality beef—shabu-shabu style rates the best here. Higher-floor rooms have views worth camping in front of. To top things off, you're within walking distance of the best downtown restaurants. ✉ *1–1–1 Kasumi-chō, Yamagata, Yamagata-ken 990-0039* ☎ *023/628–1111* 🖷 *012/628–1166* ⊕ *www.jrhotelgroup.com/eng/hotel/* ➭ *116 rooms with bath* ♨ *3 restaurants* ═ *AE, DC, V.*

$$ 🏨 **Ryokan Sendaiya.** Only a 10-minute walk from the station, near a park and a shrine, this four-story wooden building is a member of the ever-reliable, always reasonable Japan Inn Group, and has been impressing folks in the know for years now. There's a coin laundry for guests, also large communal hot-spring baths (but none in the rooms), and the meals are decent and cheap: ¥840 for Japanese breakfast, ¥630 for Western; ¥1,680 for dinner (Japanese only). Exit the east side of the station, and turn left (north). When you pass the NHK Building, turn right, and make the next left. It's on the left about the middle of the block. ✉ *10–26 Kinomi-chō, Yamagata, Yamagata-ken 990-0044* ☎ *023/ 642–0913* 🖷 *023/642–0939* 📇 *17 rooms without bath* ⚬ 🖃 *MC, V.*

$$ 🏨 **Yamagata Washington Hotel.** This downtown Yamagata business hotel is on a busy street full of shops and bars, and practically right across from the large-windowed Tully's Coffee Shop, perhaps the best people-watching, upscale java-stop in town. Rooms are run-of-the-mill, but cheap and clean. Rooms are on the third to the eighth floors, which makes it quieter than you might think they'd be. It's a long walk or short taxi ride from the station. ✉ *1–4–31 Nanoka-machi, Yamagata, Yamagata-ken 990-0042* ☎ *023/625–1111* 🖷 *023/624–1512* 📇 *223 rooms with bath* ⚬ *Restaurant, coffee shop* 🖃 *AE, DC, MC, V.*

NORTHERN TŌHOKU

Morioka

❺ *By JR Shinkansen, 45 min from Sendai, ¥6490, or from Tokyo, 2 hrs 25 min, ¥14,040.*

Morioka is a busy commercial and industrial city ringed by mountains. A nice park surrounds a ruined castle, and an ancient cherry tree has thrived by rooting itself into the crack of a huge granite slab in front of the district courthouse. But the city's major attraction is Nambu-tetsu, a special type of cast iron that forged into functional and highly ornamental wares. The most popular are heavy iron kettles. They are expensive, but as anyone who can tell their *matcha* from their *hojicha* teas knows, once conditioned, they will actually soften the water—yes, it's chemically explainable but downright magical all the same—and they will go on doing it forever if properly cared for. Dozens of shops throughout the city sell Nambu-tetsu, but the main shopping streets are Saien-dōri and Ō-dōri, which pass right by Iwate Kōen (Iwate Park).

Getting Around

To get to downtown Morioka from the JR Morioka Station, take Bus 5 or 6 from the terminal in front of the station. A convenient loop bus for tourists called Denden-mushi goes to the shopping area on the far side of the river past the park, departing every 20 minutes 9–6 from Bus Stop 15 or 16 in front of JR Morioka Station (¥100 for one ride, ¥300 for the day pass).

April 20–November 23, the **Iwate Kankō Bus Company** (☎ 019/651–3355) runs a morning and afternoon half-day tour of Morioka with Japanese-speaking guides. The 10:30–12:55 tour costs ¥2,000, and the 1:45–5 tour costs ¥2,500. All departures are from JR Morioka Station.

The **Northern Tōhoku Tourist Information Center** (☎ 019/625-2090) is on the second floor of JR Morioka Station, and the English-speaking staff has maps and other information on the three prefectures of Iwate, Akita, and Aomori. The office can help arrange accommodations from ritzy city splurges to rustic bath retreats. It's open daily 9–5:30.

What to See

Iwate Kōen (Iwate Park), is large enough to get lost in, with varied landscapes, an astonishing variety of artfully placed flowers and trees, shady groves, streams, and colors for every season. It's a good place for a romantic walk. In 1597 the 26th Lord of Nambu had a fine castle built here, but all that remains are ruined walls. To reach the park from JR Morioka Station, cross Kai-un-bashi and walk straight down the middle of the three roads that make a fork.

At the **Kamasada Iron Casting Studio**, Nobuho Miya is the affable and patient resident master caster. He speaks good English, and will gladly take your order (samples of all wares including traditional iron tea-kettles are displayed, and catalogs are for the taking). Your piece will be produced in two months' time and can be shipped anywhere. To get there, go half a block down the tiny street that extends in front of the venerable and well-known Azuma-ya soba restaurant (see below). ✉ 2–5 *Konya-chō Morioka, Iwate-ken 020-0885* ☎ *019/622–3911* 🖷 *019/622–3912* ☉ *Daily 10–5, but if your time is limited, call, fax, or e-mail ahead. He is sometimes pouring a cast in his foundry out back.*

Have a look around **Kōgensha**, which specializes in quality folk crafts like lacquerware, kites, dyed fabrics, and pottery. The main shop is composed of several small buildings around a courtyard. You can walk through the courtyard to a *kissaten* (coffee shop) and farther on to the river. Along the wall to the left are poems by famous local poet Kenji Miyazawa. To get to Kōgensha from Morioka Station, walk left to the stoplight in front of the Hotel Metropolitan Morioka, turn right, and cross the river on Asahi-bashi. Take the first left into a funky little street that leads to the main shop, 50 yards down on the left. There's also a branch shop across the street that sells basketry and wooden bowls. ✉ *2–18 Zaimoku-chō* 🖷 *019/622–2894* ☉ *Daily 10–6; closed 15th of each month and several days in mid-Aug.*

Where to Stay & Eat

★ **$$$–$$$$** ✕ **Ban-ya Nagasawa.** Everyone in town recommends this restaurant for *buri*, or yellowtail, and grilled shellfish such as scallops and abalone. You'll be eating mushrooms in fall, wild vegetables in spring, and drink-

HORSING AROUND

If you happen to be in town on the second Saturday in June, a small festival called **Chagu-chagu Umakko**—named for the noise the big horses' bells make—features 100 locally bred and gaily decorated Nambu-koma horses brought from nearby Takizawa Village to parade around in front of the station. The horses clomp through the streets between 9:30 and 1:30 that day only.

13

ing local sake all the time. To reach Banya Nagasawa from the train station, follow Ō-dori to the Iwate Bank and turn right at the statue of Takuboku Ishikawa. The restaurant is 2½ blocks ahead on the right, across from the Hotel New Carina. From the station you could also follow Saien-dōri to the Saien police box and turn left; the restaurant will be on your left. ⊠ *1–11–23 Saien* ☎ *019/622–6152* ▭ *MC, V* ⊘ *Closed Sun. and mid-Aug.*

$$–$$$ ✕**Azuma-ya**. Hearty soba comes from plentiful northern Japanese grain, and Azuma-ya is Morioka's place to eat these healthy buckwheat noodles. The second level is devoted to the courageous and hearty of appetite, where *wanko* soba courses—where you can attack and devour all the soba you desire—start at ¥2,500. Down on the first floor, delicious tempura soba is only ¥1,200. The *maneki-neko* (decorative beckoning cats) are mascots to keep customers coming back, and they seem to be doing their job. Azuma-ya is near the bus center, along the small street across the busy road from the Nakasan department store, on the other side of the river from Iwata Park; 10 minutes from the train station by taxi. ⊠ *1–8–3 Naka-no-hashi-dōri* ☎*019/622–2252* ▭ *No credit cards* ⊘ *Closed 1st and 3rd Tues. of month.*

$$–$$$ ✕**Daido-En**. Reimen are clear, slippery noodles made from flour, starch, and water. They came from Korea, and are frequently combined with spicy kimchee. Here, the reimen is spicy, all right, and it comes with half a boiled egg, green onions, cucumber pickles, a slice or two of meat—and a fat wedge of watermelon! Quality local beef is available for attable yaki-niku grilling, too. It's in the entertainment district, halfway between the station (three blocks) and Iwate Park. ⊠*2–6–19 Saien* ☎*019/654–5588* ▭ *No credit cards* ⊘ *Open daily 11–3 AM.*

$$$–$$$$ ▥ **Morioka Grand Hotel**. This pleasingly secluded hotel is near the top of a wooded hill with a breezy lookout over the rolling green hills that surround the otherwise ordinary-looking city. The staff is extremely polite and attentive, and the very large corner double and deluxe twin rooms have enough space to toss a Frisbee in. Some bathrooms are set up like a royal chamber. Virtually the entire front of the structure is glass, and the elegant breakfast and lunch lounge and wine-bar and steak house have equally distracting views and reasonable prices. It's a ¥1,000, 10-minute taxi ride up from the station, and a 20–30-minute walk down to the action in town if you don't mind meandering around some jungly switchbacks and wending your way along the easy-flowing Nakatsu River. ⊠ *1–10 Atagoshita, Hanamaki, Morioka, Iwate-ken 020-8501* ☎ *019/625–2111* 🖷 *019/625–1003* ⊕ *www.j-hotel.or.jp/hotel/moriokagrandhotel/en/index.html* ⮑ *27 total rooms: 5 Japanese-style (¥16,800–29,400), 13 twins, 7 doubles, 1 suite (¥73,500)* ♨ *2 restaurants, bar.* ▭ *AE, DC, V.*

$$$ ▥ **Hotel Metropolitan Morioka**. Both wings of this hotel have an English-speaking staff, restaurants, and a bar. Just to the left of the station plaza, the older wing has basic rooms and good service. From the old wing, cross the street facing the hotel and walk right one block to the new wing, where rooms are larger and cost an additional ¥2,000 and up. As a guest you can use the Central Fitness Club facilities for ¥525, including a 25-meter pool, weight machines, a sauna, and a Jacuzzi.

✉ *1–44 Morioka Eki-mae-dōri, new wing: 2–27 Morioka Eki-mae Kita-dōri, Morioka, Iwate-ken 020-0034* ☎ *019/625–1211* 📠 *019/ 625–1210* ⊕ *www.jrhotelgroup.com/eng/hotel/* 🛏 *134 Western-style rooms in old wing, 121 Western-style rooms in new wing* ♿ *5 restaurants, 2 bars, meeting rooms* ☰ *AE, DC, MC, V.*

$ 🏨 **Ryokan Kumagai.** This place is very welcoming to foreigners, and is a member of the affordable Japanese Inn Group. Expect basic tatami rooms, and there's a small dining area where Japanese and Western breakfasts and Japanese dinners are optional. It's traditional old-style, so no rooms have private baths. Located between the station and the center city, the inn is a 10-minute walk from JR Morioka Station—cross the river and walk along Kaiun-bashi-dōri two blocks and turn right (a gas station is on the left and a bank is on the right). Cross over one block, and the ryokan is on the left. ✉ *3–2–5 Ōsawakawara, Morioka, Iwate-ken 020-0025* ☎ *019/651–3020* 📠 *019/626–0096* 🛏 *11 Japanese-style rooms without bath* ♿ *Dining room, Japanese baths* ☰ *AE, MC, V* ▮◯▮ *MAP.*

Getting to Morioka

BY AIR Morioka (whose Hanamaki Airport is 40 minutes by bus, ¥560, from downtown) has 8 flights daily from Tokyo's Haneda (1 hour 10 minutes, ¥12,900–27,500) and 2–3 flights daily from both Ōsaka Airports (1 hour 30 minutes, ¥31,000–¥33,000) by ANA and JAL. There are also flights to Nagoya, Fukuoka, and Sapporo's Chitose Airport. For airline phone numbers, *see* Air Travel *in* Essentials.

Tazawa-ko & Kakunodate

The lake area of Tazawa-ko (Lake Tazawa) and the traditional town of Kakunodate are good side trips into Tōhoku's wilder interior, approachable from either Morioka or the west-coast city of Akita. For a little thermal relaxation in a very rustic setting, forge on to the old spa town of Nyūtō Onsen, just north of Lake Tazawa.

Tazawa-ko

★ ❻ *31 min west of Morioka (¥2180), 56 min east of Akita (¥3,480) by JR Komachi Shinkansen.*

The clear waters and forested slopes of Tazawa-ko (Lake Tazawa), Japan's deepest lake, create a mystical quality that appeals so much to the Japanese. According to legend, the great beauty from Akita, Takko Hime, sleeps in the water's deep as a dragon. The lake never freezes over in winter because Takko Hime and her dragon husband churn the water with their passionate lovemaking. At a depth of 1,397 feet, Tazawa-ko neither turns over nor freezes, and though as clear as sapphire glass, the startling powder-blue water is too acidic to support but a few hardy fish. A wonderfully scenic 20-km-long two-lane road, great for biking, rings this crater lake. Near the bus stop and roadhouse there may be some traffic, but it is generally sporadic, and once you get away from there it clears up. Halfway around is a good stop for ice cream or coffee. Riding over the twisty flats and gentle grades through fragrant and dense mixed forest, there are several spots where the indicator posts show depths of 345 meters or more, only a couple yards from the lake's edge. Clearly, all you see around you is perched precariously on the lip of a flooded cliff-walled abyss! In summer the perfume from the vines and vegetation lining the shady road is intoxicating. In winter the Tazawa area is a popular powder skiing destination, the lake stealing the show in every view from the nearby ski slopes.

A 15-minute bus ride (¥350) from the JR Tazawa-ko Station gets you to the Tazawa-ko-han center on the eastern lakeshore. A very small and shallow swimming area is a short distance to the northwest along the road. A 30-minute bus ride from JR Tazawa-ko Station via Tazawa-ko-han goes up to Tazawa-ko Kōgen, or Plateau, for ¥580. The journey offers spectacular views of the lake. You can rent your own paddleboat or rowboat, and a motorboat takes 40-minute cruises on the lake from late April to November (¥1,170). You'll want sunscreen and a hat or sunshade. There's also regular bus service around the lake (sometimes only halfway around in winter), and bicycles are available for rent (¥500 a day; ¥300 for 2 hours, usually sufficient for the loop) at the Tazawa-ko-han bus terminal and at many lodgings in the area.

The **Tazawa-ko Tourist Information Office** (☎ 0187/43–2111) to the left of the JR Tazawa-ko Station has maps and bus schedules; it's open daily 8:30–5:30.

Nyūtō Onsen, accessible by bus from Tazawak-ko, are small, unspoiled, mountain hot-spring spas in some of the few traditional spa villages left in Tōhoku. Most of these villages have only one inn, and you'll have to take your meals there. It's advisable to arrange accommodations before you arrive if you plan to stay the night, and the Tazawa-ko tourist info office can help arrange this.

Komaga-take (Mt. Komaga) stands a few miles east of Lake Tazawa. At 1,637m or a mile high, it's the highest mountain in the area—and one of the easiest to climb. Between June and October a bus from Tazawa-ko Station runs up to the eighth station, from where it takes an hour to hike to the summit. If you hike after rainshowers in June or July, you can walk through blooming alpine flowers.

Kakunodate

★ **❼** *14 min southwest of Tazawa-ko by JR Komachi Shinkansen, ¥1760, or 45 min from Morioka, ¥2970.*

The small, enchanting town of Kakunodate was founded in 1620 by Ashina Yoshikatsu, the local lord, who chose it for its defensible position and reliable water sources. It has remained an outpost of traditional Japan and it may be the best place for seeing cherry blossoms in the spring. The whole town is full of *shidarezakura*, or weeping cherry trees, their pink flowers gracing the dark-wood gates, walls, and roofs of ancient samurai houses. Along the banks of Hinokinai-gawa (Hinokinai River), these living jewel factories dangle a 2-km-long (1¼-mi-long) pink curtain. The **Kakunodate Tourist Information Center** (☎ 0187/54–2700), is in an old *kura*-style (warehouselike) building, adjacent to the tea shop by the station, and the English-speaking staff have maps and information about the samurai houses and walks in town, and can recommend nearby lunch or dinner options. Open daily 9–6.

What to See

Several well-preserved samurai houses date from the founding of the town. The most renowned and interesting is **Aoyagi-ke (Aoyagi Manor)**, with its sod roof. Part of this intricate, rambling estate is still lived in. Inside the old kura or warehouses that have been turned into museums are all kinds of historical artifacts to pore over, such as farm implements, old bicycles, and samurai battle armor and accoutrements of siege warfare. The cherry tree in the garden is nearly three centuries old. Within a 15-minute walk northwest from the station. ✉ *26 Higashi Katsuraku-chō* ☎ *0187/54–3257* 💴 *¥500* ⊙ *Apr.–Nov., daily 8:30–5; Dec.–Mar., daily 9–4.*

> ## BARK SHOPPING
>
> Kakunodate is the best place in Tōhoku to pick up mountain-cherry bark-veneer items—everything from glowing red lampshades to business-card holders. This is important to remember, since anything you're likely to find in the hokey souvenir shops in the prefectural capital of Akita will be overpriced and fake.

Denshō House (Denshōkan), a hall in front of a cluster of samurai houses, serves as a museum and a workshop for the local cherry-bark veneer handicrafts that became the new source of income for samurai when they suddenly found themselves fresh out of jobs. There are more varieties of this auburn wood, with its warm glow and eye-riddled, mysteriously beautiful surface, than you might think. Don't be put off by the imposing exterior of the Denshō House—go right on in and watch master craftsmen at work, or relax over coffee upstairs. You can buy what they make here, often at better prices than in the shops on the street. The Satake-Kita family armor and heavily Kyōto-influenced ancient heirlooms are exhibited in adjacent parts of the building. You can also learn about life in old-time winters, with displays of plaited-maple sleighs and some truly inventive and adaptive tools and togs for fighting snow. ✉ *10–1 Omote Shimo-chō* ☎ *0187/54–1700* 💴 *¥300* ⊙ *Apr.–Nov., daily 9–4:30; Dec.–Mar., daily 9–4:00. Closed Dec. 28–Jan. 4.*

Where to Stay

$$ 🏨 **Forukurōro (Folklore) Kakunodate.** This inexpensive and very friendly small hotel has bright, clean rooms with private baths. Deluxe twins have a sofa and additional space. A simple buffet breakfast and unbeatable convenience are included in a low-price night here. An attached soba shop is to the right on the first floor. The hotel is the first building on your left outside the station exit. ✉ *14 Nakasugasawa, Iwaze-aza, Kakunodate-machi, Akita-ken 014-0314* ☎ *0187/53–2070* 🖶 *0187/53–2118* 🛏 *26 rooms with bath* ▤ *MC, V* ❍❙ *CP.*

Towada–Hachiman-tai National Park

90 min–2 hrs northwest of Morioka by bus.

For walking among the splendid virgin beech, pine, and cedar forests covering the verdant valleys and mountainsides deep in the heart of Tōhoku, you could not pick a better destination. The mountains afford sweeping panoramas over the park's gorges and valleys, crystal-clear lakes like Towada-ko, gnarled and windswept trees, and volcanic mountain cones. The park borders on Aomori, Iwate, and Akita prefectures and spreads over 330 square mi. Hot springs and tiny villages lost in time are secreted away here, and the fresh tree-scented air promotes a feeling of true wilderness. Fall foliage can be spectacular and sometimes draws boisterous crowds. Buses run along a network that links all the main spots, but service is frequently suspended during winter storms. The Northern Tōhoku tourist info center could prove invaluable in helping you research, plan, and carry out a successful trip.

Hachiman-tai Kōgen (Plateau)

❽ Two hours 10 minutes by bus from Morioka Station, **Hachimantai Plateau**, situated roughly between Lakes Tozawa and Towada, is a hummock of scantily covered geological activity suspended between volcano tops, and the geysers and mudboils remind you of all that goes on below the supposedly solid earth. But remember, there are wonderful onsen near such geo-thermally active places!

Though remote and rustic, intrepid travelers will find some truly unique onsen resorts to soak in and linger at among the wilds. One of the most visited resting spots is **Goshogake Spa**, two hours 10 minutes from Tazawa-ko bus station, three buses daily, late April–late October. You can hike the 2-km (1.2-mi) nature trail, and then be steamed, boiled, or braised—try the old-fashioned steam-box baths where only your head protrudes—in a wide assortment of mineral baths situated among the bubbling mud and vaporous swamps.

Hachiman-numa (Hachiman Marsh), was originally a crater lake of a shield volcano. There's a paved road around the rim, and in July and August alpine wildflowers are in bloom. From the Hachiman-tai-chōjō bus stop off the Aspite Line it's a 20-minute walk up the path.

Tōshichi Onsen, a year-round spa town—elevation 4,593 feet at the foot of Mokko-san, off the Aspite Line, before Goshogake if coming from Morioka—is a popular spring skiing resort. On the north side of Tōshichi is **Hōraikyō**, a natural garden with dwarf pine trees and alpine plants scattered among strange rock formations. In early October the autumn colors are fantastic.

Towada-ko

❾ The area around **Towada-ko** (Lake Towada) is almost too popular in autumn. The lake fills a volcanic cone 1,096 feet deep, making it third-deepest in Japan. The crater holding it raises the level like a giant goblet 400 meters above the surrounding topography, giving it a dramatic illusory aspect. There are boat tours, and near Yasumiya Village facilities include a campsite. The lake is on the border of Aomori and Akita prefectures, and it's not nearly as convenient as Tazawa-ko. The town of Towada-minami (Towada South) is 20 minutes north of Hachiman-tai on the JR Hanawa Line. From here buses leave on the hour to Lake Towada; the bus fare is ¥1,110.

At the village resort of **Yasumi-ya** —the word *yasumi* means "holiday"— pleasure boats run across the lake to the village of Nenokuchi. The one-hour trip costs ¥1,320. Boats run every 30 minutes from mid-April to early November, and then less frequently until January 31, then not at all, due to extreme cold.

An excellent choice for a walk is to the **Oirase-kyōkoku** (Oirase [oh-ee-ra-seh] Gorge), northeast of the lake at Nenokuchi. The carefully tended trail to the gorge follows the stream for a total of 9 km (5½ mi; about 2 hours and 40 minutes). A two-lane road parallels the river, and you can catch buses at intervals of about 2 km (1¼ mi). Buses go north to Aomori and south to Nenokuchi and Yasumi-ya. Though very popular, especially in fall, this takes you through one of the most pristine areas of Tōhoku. Be prepared for cold mist or rain, take a map of the river and bus stops, and find out the bus schedule before you start out.

WHERE TO STAY

$$–$$$$

 Towada Kankō Hotel. This hotel makes a good base for enjoying the lake, one that is not overrun by tour buses. Western-style rooms have comfortable beds and a separate tatami area. Elaborate, traditonal, multi-variety kaiseki-style Japanese dinners are served in your room, and include local pickles, stews made with kiritampo grilled rice, fish or chicken, mushrooms, and wild vegetables. Japanese breakfast is served in the dining room. ✉ *Towada-ko, Yasumi-ya, Aomori-ken 018-5501* ☎ *0176/75–2111* 🖷 *0176/75–2327* ➳ *72 rooms with bath* ⚓ *Café, dining room, bar* ⊟ *AE, DC, MC, V* ⏇ *MAP.*

Getting to Towada-ko

The fastest way to Towada-ko is by one of the three daily buses directly from Morioka Station (2 hours 15 minutes, ¥2420). The last stop on the bus is Hachiman-tai Kankō Hotel. There's also bus service from Morioka to Matsukawa, Tōshichi, and Goshogake Onsen. See the Northern Tōhoku Tourist Information Office for more info on routes, schedules, activities, and places to stay in Towado-Hachimantai National Park.

Hirosaki

★ ❿ *2 hrs 15 min northwest of Morioka by JR express highway bus, ¥2700, from north-exit bus terminal of Morioka Station, or 4–5 hrs by JR trains (slow local trains, many changes required).*

Hirosaki is one of Northern Tōhoku's most attractive cities. Its only real cultural attraction is a small but very photogenic reconstructed castle. Still, the town has a very appealing, easy-going nature. Hirosaki is compact and walkable, but finding your bearings in the ancient castle town can prove difficult. The streets were designed to disorient invaders before they could get to the battlements. So pick up a map at the tourist information office.

The **Hirosaki Tourist Information Office** (☎ 0172/32–0524) is on the right side of the train station as you exit; it's open January 4–March, daily 8–5, and April–December 28, daily 8:45–6.

What to See

Hirosaki Castle (Hirosaki-jō) is situated atop a high stone base, and guarded by deep moats over which a red wooden bridge crosses in a picturesque curve. The original castle, completed in 1611, was set ablaze 16 years later by a lightning bolt. The present castle, of a smaller scale, dates back to 1810. When the more than 5,000 *someiyoshino* cherry trees blossom, or when the maples turn, the setting is gorgeous. A snow-lantern festival with illuminated ice sculptures is held in early February. The castle is a 30-minute walk from the station on the northwest side of town, across the river. Take the ¥100 bus from the No. 2 stop and get off at the Shiyakusho-mae, or City Hall stop. ☒ 2–1 *Shimo-Shirogane-chō, Hirosaki, Aomori-ken* ☏ 0172/33–8733 ☒ *Grounds free, castle ¥300* ☉ *Grounds daily 7 AM–9 PM; castle Apr.–Nov., daily 9–5.*

> ## FOLLOW THE PARADE
>
> The first week of August Hirosaki outdoes itself with the **Neputa Festival**. Each night, following various routes, internally illuminated fan-shaped floats brightly painted with mythological scenes and characters (borrowed from Chinese legends) parade through town. The festival is thought to have its origins in the preparation, 400 or more years ago, for some horrible battle, as a big send-off to the warriors. In any case, the blood-quickening thrum of the humongous drums will get you celebrating without the swordplay.

The **Hirosaki Sightseeing Information Center** (☒ 2–1 Shimo-Shirogane-chō, Hirosaki Koen Mae, Hirosaki, Aomori-ken ☏ 0172/26–3600 ☐ 0172/26–3601 ☉ Daily 8:45–6), south of the castle grounds, displays local industry, crafts, and regional art (free) and provides tourist information.

On the northeast corner of the castle grounds, **Tsugaru-han Neputa Mura (Tsugaru Peninsula Neputa Village)** exhibits the giant drums and floats used in the Neputa Festival. If you miss the real thing, come here to see the 40-foot fan-shape floats as they sleep off their hangovers from the mad mid-summer revelry. In the workshop you can paint your own traditional kite, paper-and-frame goldfish, and *kokeshi* (traditional wooden dolls) to take home as souvenirs. ☏ 0172/39–1511 ☒ ¥500 ☉ *Apr.–Nov., daily 9–5; Dec.–Mar., daily 9–4.*

Where to Stay & Eat

$$–$$$$ ✕ **Kikufuji.** Tasty, healthy and authentic dishes from the region are Kikufuji's specialty, from delicious vegetable stews like *kenoshiru* to the freshest seafood. The scallops brought in from the Mutsu Bay coast are superb, so try the *hotate-no-sugate-yaki*, or scallops cooked in the shell. Many *teishoku*, or meal-set assortments, cover all the bases. Excellent dry, cold local varieties of sake are also available. It's a short taxi ride from JR Hirosaki Station, or a long walk out along the main NW-SE diagonal, near the stream-crossing, and not far from the tall, freaky sci-fi building that is the new Naka-san department store. ☒ 1 Sakamoto-chō, Hirosaki, Aomori ☏ 0172/36–3300 ☐ 0172/36–3319 ☉ Daily 11–10 ☐ No credit cards.

$$$ ✕ **Anzu**. Performances of live Tsugaru-jamisen—the shamisen is a Japanese banjo—and the odd, wailing Tsugaru vocals are the main attraction at this Japanese restaurant. Jams take place evenings at 7, 9, and 10:30. Arrive an hour early to sit on cushions on the floor, in local style, and enjoy a menu of seasonal vegetables, sashimi, grilled scallops, grilled fish and rice, and soup for a reasonable ¥3,000. ⌧ *44–1 Oyakata* ☎ *0172/32–6684* ▭ *No credit cards.*

$$$ ✕ **Yamauta**. Hirosaki's most interesting eatery serves sashimi, grilled fish, yakitori, and other grilled meat for ¥380–¥2,700 and has live shamisen music every hour. The restaurant gets its musical character from its owner; he was once national shamisen champion and now uses the premises as a school for aspiring shamisen artists. Yamauta is closed one day a month, but the day varies. A five-minute walk past City Hirosaki Hotel from the train station. ⌧ *1–2–7 Ō-machi* ☎ *0172/36–1835* ▭ *No credit cards.*

SHAMISEN

Literally meaning "three-tastes-strings," and sometimes called jamisen if preceded by a suffix such as Tsugaru (Tōhoku dialect), the shamisen is somewhat like the American banjo in sound and playing manner. The sound-amplification board is traditionally made of dog or cat skin, and it is usually played with a large comblike plectrum made of tortoise shell or ivory. In Tōhoku, (as well as in southern Japan, especially Okinawa), styles are bent to suit local moods and ears. The shamisen has recently been exposed to young Japanese audiences by popular bands like the Yoshida Brothers, who forgo tradition and play the instrument with the ferocity of a rock guitar.

$$–$$$$ 🏨 **Hotel New Castle**. This decent business hotel is a block and a half from Hirosaki Castle. The restaurants serve formal and elegant Japanese meals. It's a 25-minute walk or short taxi ride northwest of the station. ⌧ *24–1 Kamisayashi-machi, Hirosaki, Aomori-ken 036-8354* ☎ *0172/36–1211* 📠 *0172/36–1210* ➠ *52 Western-style rooms, 2 suites, 4 Japanese-style rooms.* ♨ *2 restaurants* ▭ *AE, DC, MC, V.*

$$–$$$ 🏨 **City Hirosaki Hotel**. This modern hotel on the left next to the JR Hirosaki Station is well situated, and the lively coffee shop on the first floor is terrific for people-watching. The locally respected restaurant-bar–steak house on the 12th floor has a lunch buffet for ¥1,500 and a fancy dinner set for ¥3,000. Next door is a ritzy boutique mall with a private fitness center where the in-crowd goes. ⌧ *1–1–2 Ō-machi, Hirosaki, Aomori-ken 036-8004* ☎ *0172/37–0109* 📠 *0172/37–1229* ⊕ *www.tokyuhotels.co.jp/en* ➠ *141 rooms with bath* ♨ *2 restaurants, bar* ▭ *AE, DC, MC, V.*

Aomori

⓫ *33 min (¥1,860) by JR express or 49 min (¥650) by JR local train from Hirosaki; 2 hrs 14 min (¥6,560) by JR express from Morioka.*

Aomori is not as busy as it once was, before the train tunnel linked Honshū and Hokkaidō, and there's not a lot to see. Still, they enjoy delicious seafood, fruit, and vegetables, and they throw a frenzied festival every summer when normal gets thrown to the wind: the Nebuta Matsuri.

The **Aomori Tourist Information Center** (☎ 017/723–4670) is in the JR Bus Building just outside Aomori Station. English maps and brochures for the city and prefecture are available, and you can apply for the discount Tōhoku Welcome Card if you haven't done so online (see beginning of chapter). Open daily 8–5:30.

What to See

Aomori's main event is its **Nebuta Festival** (August 2–7), not to be confused with Hirosaki's Neputa Festival (residents tend to get annoyed when they are). Both are held in early August, and both have large, illuminated floats of gigantic samurai figures paraded through the streets at night. Aomori's festival is one of Japan's largest, and is said to celebrate the euphoria of post-battle victory, and is thus encouraged to be noisier and livelier. Dancers, called *heneto*, run alongside, dancing crazily, and you're encouraged to join in. You will not likely see such nonstop, full-throttle partying as this for a while—a year, at least!

If you can't visit during the Nebuta Festival, head to the **Nebuta-no-Sato, or Nebuta Village Museum,** in the southeast part of town, where glowing papier-mache sculptures painted with the fierce countenances of warriors used in Aomori's festival are displayed. To get here, take the JR bus bound for Lake Towada from Bus Stop 8 or 9 (30 minutes; ¥450), just outside the train station. ☎ 017/738–1230 ☜ ¥630 ⊘ July–Sept., daily 9–8 (closed during Nebuta Festival in early Aug.); mid-Apr.–June, Oct., and Nov., daily 9–5:30.

Local flavor abounds at the **Auga** market complex, where fish, shellfish, preserved seaweed, smoked fish, and fish eggs—in short, all manner of marine organisms—are hawked by hundreds of shopkeepers. It's one block east of JR Aomori Station, in the basement level of a modern building with distinctive crimson pillars, across from the Aomori Grand Hotel. ⊘ Daily 5 AM–6:30 PM.

Where to Stay & Eat

$$–$$$$ ✕ **Hide-zushi.** You're in a major seafood city, and if you want some of the best available from that cold, clean water, then this is the place to get it. Excellent service, bright surroundings, and sea urchin, salmon roe, scallops, squid, tuna, and crab await your whetted appetite. ✉ 1–5 Tsutsumi-machi ☎ 017/722–8888 ▤ AE, MC, V ⊘ Closed Sun.

$$–$$$$ ✕ **Nishimura.** It'd be hard to walk out of this Japanese restaurant hungry: the *danna* course (¥3,000), for example, includes abalone and sea-urchin soup, seaweed and fish, a mixed hot pot, and fried eggplant. From JR Aomori Station, walk east one block on Shinmachi-dōri, and then take the first left. Nishimura is on your right after two blocks. ✉ 1–5–19 Yasukata ☎ 017/773–2880 ▤ AE, MC, V ⊘ Closed Sun.

$$–$$$ ▦ **Hotel JAL City Aomori.** Opened in 1996, this nine-story upscale hotel curves around the corner as if it belonged in 1960s Miami Beach. The lobby is dominated by stone floors and walls and a gallerylike track-lighting scheme. The rooms are bright and spacious enough. The La Sera restaurant is good for buffets, brunches, and its pub. Only a six-minute walk east of the station, the hotel is on the corner of ASPAM-dōri. ✉ 4–12 Yasukata 2-chōme, Aomori-shi, Aomori-ken 030-0803 ☎ 017/732–

2580 ☎ 017/735–2584 ➥ 165 Western rooms, 2 suites ☼ 2 restaurants, bar, fitness center, spa, banquet room, business center ☰ AE, DC, MC, V ⧉ E.P.

$$ ⊞ **Aomori Grand Hotel.** The rates are good, and it's only one block southeast of the train station, just past the bus depot and tourist information office. The lounge for morning coffee has comfortable armchairs, and the Belle View Restaurant and Sky Bar on the 12th floor, where most of the interior decorating budget seems to have been spent, can provide an enjoyable afternoon or evening overlooking the harborscape. Rooms are comfortable, though without much flourish. ⊠ 1–1–23 Shin-machi, Aomori-shi, Aomori-ken 030-0801 ☎ 017/723–1011 ☐ 017/734–0505 ➥ 134 Western-style rooms, 2 Japanese-style suites, 2 Western suites ☼ 3 restaurants, bar ☰ AE, DC, MC, V.

Getting to Aomori

BY AIR Aomori has 10 daily flights from Tōkyō's Haneda Airport by JAS (JAL affiliate) and six by All Nippon Airways: 1 hour 15 minutes, ¥25,500 one-way, ¥42,900 round-trip. Aomori also has two JAL flights from Nagoya, two from Ōsaka, and two from Sapporo's Chitose Airport. For airline phone numbers, *see* Air Travel *in* Essentials.

TŌHOKU WEST COAST

Akita

12 *33 min (¥1,860) by JR express or 49 min (¥650) by JR local train from Aomori City, or 2 hrs (¥4,780) from Hirosaki by JR Kamoshika Limited Express (3–4 trains daily); 2 hrs 47 min–3 hrs 30 min by JR local train; 3 hrs 52 min (¥17,150) from Tōkyō by JR Komachi Shinkansen.*

The Dewa Sanchi (Dewa Mountains), marked by Mt. Taihei, march off to the east, and the Sea of Japan lies at the edge of the fertile plains that extend to the west. Akita's history began during the turbulent Nara Period, with Dewa-no-saku, a fortress built on a hill in Takashimizu by the powerful Yamato clan in 733. The area, set up to guard trade routes, soon gained strategic importance, and during the Heian era soldiers and their families began spreading the development outward. The Ando and Satake families each built major bastions in the Yuwa and Kawabe districts after the Battle of Sekigahara, 400 years ago. These municipalities, now merged, are considered to be the foundations of modern Akita City. Today the prefectural capital (population 320,000) is a lively, likeable city full of delicious food from the mountains, plain, rivers, and sea.

The countryside is devoted to producing what locals feel is the best rice in Japan—they certainly make good sake with it. Additionally, the fruits and vegetables grown here are unbelievably cheap and flavorful. The combination of climate, pure water, and healthy food is said to make the women of Akita the fairest in the land—a matter of prefectural, even national pride. In the Japanese media, "scientific" studies have been trotted out since the 19th century as proof of the Akita bijin (Akita beauty) phenomenon.

The **Akita Tourist Information Office** (☎018/832–7941 ☉ Daily 9:30–5) is on the second floor just across from the exit from the Shinkansen tracks at the station, and supplies many colorful English-language pamphlets and lots of friendly advice.

What to See

Senshū Kōen, or Senshū Park. Once the site of the now-ruined Kubota Castle, this large, shady respite from the sun is a pleasant haven of green leaves and strolling paths, with cherry blossoms and azaleas adding color in season. Large koi and goldfish swim lazily about the streams, ponds, and moats, while ducks gather around. A reconstructed former castle tower with an elevated lookout floor (▣ ¥100; ☉ Daily 9 AM–4:30 PM.) stands in the northwest corner of the park. In clear weather you can see all the way to the seacoast and distant ponderous hump of Oga Peninsula to the west and the stunning series of blue-green mountain ridges marching endlessly to the east. The park is a 10-minute walk west of the train station on Hiroko-ji-dōri.

> ### BIG BAMBOO
>
> The **Kantō Festival** (August 3–6) celebrates ancient fertility rites with young men balancing 36-foot-long bamboo poles (kantō) hung with as many as 46 lighted paper lanterns on its eight cross-bars—and weighing up to 110 pounds—against a special pouched strap on their waist, hip, back, or shoulder. The lanterns represent sacks full of rice, and a bountiful harvest is fervently prayed for and celebrated in anticipation of its arrival.

Under the distinctive copper-covered Japanese palace–style roof of the **Hirano Masakichi Museum of Fine Art** (Hirano Masakichi Bijutsukan) is an impressive and varied collection, including paintings by Tsuguji Fujita (1886–1968) and an excellent selection of Western art, with works by Toulouse-Lautrec and Picasso and a fantastic array of Goya etchings. The most eye-catching is Fujita's enormous *Events in Akita*. Fujita took just 15 days to complete the painting of three local festivals merged into a single scene, rendered on one of the world's largest canvases at the time, measuring 11 feet by 66 feet. The interior galleries provide an airy and minimalist aesthetic that allows the art to speak for itself. ▢ *3–7 Meitoku-chō* ☎*018/833–5809* ▣*¥610* ☉ *Early Jan.–Apr. and Oct.–late Dec., Tues.–Sun. 10–5; May–Sept., Tues.–Sun. 10–5:30; last entry 30 min before closing.*

The avenue known as **Kawabata-dōri** is where people come in the evening to sample the regional hot-pot dishes *shottsuru-nabe* (salty fermented sandfish stew) and kiritampo-nabe, drink *ji-zake* (locally brewed sake), and to enjoy the bars. It's six blocks west of the Atorion Building, across the Asahi-gawa (Asahi River) and slightly south.

EN ROUTE As you approach the flat rice-growing plains that surround and supply Akita, the train goes through Hirosaki and past the 5,331-foot **Iwaki-san** (Mt. Iwaki), presiding over the countryside. If you fancy seeing the view from on top, a bus from Hirosaki (many daily, 50 minutes, ¥950) travels to Dake Onsen, at the foot of the mountain, and from there a sightseeing bus travels up the Iwaki Skyline toll road (open late

April–late October) to the Hachigōme, or Eighth Station, for ¥880. The final ascent, with a 360-degree view from a mile up, is by cable car, for ¥750.

South of Mt. Iwaki, straddling Aomori Prefecture's border with Akita, are the **Shirakami Sanmyaku,** (Shirakami Mountains), site of the world's largest virgin beechwood forest. This is on UNESCO's list of World Heritage Sites. In keeping with the goal of preservation, access is provided by just a few tiny roads. The area is truly pristine and great for hiking.

13

Where to Stay & Eat

★ $$–$$$$ ✕ **Hinaiya.** This restaurant is named after the local breed of chicken that goes into *Hinai-jidōri* kiritampo-nabe, a hot pot made with kiritampo, or rice that's cooked, pasted onto sticks (usually cedar or bamboo), then grilled over a charcoal fire. The rice is then simmered in a pot with chicken and broth, seasonal vegetables, burdock, green onions, and mushrooms (¥1,800). To get to Hinaiya, in the heart of the Kawabata entertainment district, walk one block from the river on Suzuran-dōri; it's on the second floor. Noisy, fun-loving Hinaiya is conducive to partying, and even the fish swimming in the big tank seem oblivious to their fate. ⊠ *4–2–2 Ō-machi* ☎ *018/823–1718* ▭ *DC, MC, V.*

$$$ ✕ **Dai-ichi Kaikan.** The third-floor restaurant of this complex specializes in Akita cuisine such as kiritampo-nabe: ¥2,000 for the hot pot alone or ¥3,500 for the full-course set. The *inaniwa gozen* is a tray with noodles, chicken, dried ray, seaweed, wild vegetables, noodles, and *tsukemono* (pickled vegetables). Don't be squeamish, even if you have never seen some of the ingredients before. ⊠ *5–1–17 Kawabata* ☎ *018/823–4141* ▭ *MC, V.*

$$$–$$$$ 🏨 **Akita Castle Hotel.** Opposite the moat and a 10-minute walk west from the train station, this hotel has the best location in town and highly polished service. The dancing fluorescent jellyfish in the arty display in the glassy center of the lobby will catch your eye. The Western-style doubles are spacious, and the three Japanese-style rooms are huge. Both the bar and the French restaurant overlook the moats of Senshū Kōen and the distant mountains. Japanese and Chinese restaurants have this same enviable vantage. While in summer the dense trees block views of the castle buildings behind them, the tranquil shades of green soothe the soul. ⊠ *1–3–5 Naka-dōri, Akita-shi, Akita-ken 010-0001* ☎ *018/ 834–1141* 🖶 *018/834–5588* ⬚ *179 Western-style rooms with bath, 3 Japanese-style rooms with bath* ⊛ *3 restaurants, bar* ▭ *AE, DC, MC, V.*

$$$ 🏨 **Metropolitan Hotel Akita.** This terra-cotta-colored hotel is just outside the west side of JR Akita Station, and is perfect for shopping, people-watching, or striking out for anywhere nearby. The lobby is small, but you're right next to some fine street-side coffee and snack shops, and rooms here offer good value—deluxe versions have great views and an extra 12 square feet for an additional ¥1,000 (single) or ¥3,000 (twin). Breakfast is only ¥1,260, served in a sunny café on the third floor. ⊠ *7–2–1 Naka-dōri, Akita-shi, Akita-ken 010-8530* ☎ *018/831–2222* 🖶 *018/831–2290* ⬚ *60 Western-style rooms* ⊛ *Restaurant, coffee shop, bar* ▭ *AE, MC, V.*

$$–$$$ ☷ **Akita View Hotel.** The largest hotel in town, with an enormous lobby and a five-lane swimming pool, the Akita View is on the right side of Seibu department store. You're right in the thick of all the shops under the arcade extending from the station, and many restaurants are nearby. A three-minute walk east will bring you to JR Akita Station, and a 10-minute walk will take you to the edge of the entertainment district. ✉ *2–6 Naka-dōri, Akita-shi, Akita-ken 010-8621* ☎ *018/832–1111* ☈ *018/ 832–0037* ⌕ *192 rooms with bath* ♨ *2 restaurants, coffee shop, indoor pool, gym, bar, shops* ☰ *AE, DC, MC, V.*

Getting to Akita

BY AIR ANA and JAL fly to Akita four to six times daily from Tōkyō's Haneda Airport in 65 minutes for ¥23,700, twice daily from Ōsaka's Kansai Airport, and twice daily from Chitose Airport in Sapporo. They also fly from the Nagoya and Fukuoka Airports. For airline phone numbers, *see* Air Travel *in* Essentials.

Tsuruoka & Dewa-Sanzan

Tsuruoka is 2½ hrs south of Akita by JR Uetsu Line, ¥2,210, or 39 min from Atsumi Onsen, ¥480; buses from Tsuruoka run to Haguro-san Center in 40 minutes for ¥680, to the summit of Haguro in 55 min for ¥990, and to Ga-san, 90 min (¥1650) in summer.

South of Akita along the Nihon-kai coast are small fishing villages where nets hang to dry only inches from train windows, vast plains of rice fields lead to faraway hills, rushing rivers and clear streams are full of fish, and, closer to Atsumi Onsen, you will be confronted with lofty forested mountains coming down to the endless crashing waves. Along ❸ the way is the town of **Tsuruoka**, once a castle stronghold of the Sakai family, which serves as as a (bus) gateway to Yamagata City and the three mountains of Dewa-Sanzan that are held sacred by the *yama-bushi*, the popular name given to members of the ascetic and nature-loving Shugendō sect of "mountain warrior" Buddhists.

Getting Around

It's easiest to get to the base of Haguro by bus (55 minutes), either from Bus Stop 2, in front of JR Tsuruoka Station, or from Stop 5, at Shō-Kō (Shō-nai Kō-tsu) Mall (it's not a JR bus); there are four departures in winter and at least hourly departures in summer. A fare of ¥680 will take you from the station to the Haguro Center village at the entrance to the peak itself. Most buses from Tsuruoka to Haguro Center continue to the summit, Haguro-san-chō, which is not much farther, but the fare jumps to ¥990 (it covers a toll charge on a private road).

The **Tsuruoka Tourist Information Office** (☎ 0235/25–7678 ☼ Daily 9–5) is just to the right from the station exit. They might not speak much English, and most pamphlets about Dewa Sanzan are in Japanese, but they can help with bus schedules and lodging arrangements.

What to See

❹ The climb up **Haguro-san** (Mt. Haguro) begins in Haguro Center, at the red **Zaishin Gate** (Zaishin-mon), then goes up 2,446 or so stone steps to the summit. The strenuous ascent cuts through ancient cedar trees that rise to dominate the sky. You'll pass an aged 14th-century five-story pagoda sitting alone in the forest. A tea shop, open from April through November, is situated at a perfect stop to take in the view. The trail is just over a mile, or 1.7 km in all, and it may take you an hour to reach the 414-meter (1,400-foot) summit with its thatch-roof shrine **Dewa San-zan Jinja.** You may happen upon one of the mysterious ceremonies held there—the initiation ritual of a *yamabushi* (a "mountain warrior" who seeks power from ascetic practices and close bonds to nature) lasts nine grueling days, and it is said that if an apprentice wants to complete his training he must first prove that he can engage and destroy an imaginary demon. Seventeen to 19 buses a day (¥680) take 40 minutes to Haguro Center from JR Tsuroka Station; many of the buses go all the way to the summit in another 15 minutes for an extra ¥330. It is possible to stay overnight on the mountain at the temple-lodge of Sai-kan, which is attached by a long stairway to the Dewa-Sanzan Jinja; see below.

Haguro-san is the only mountain with year-round access, but if you want to visit the other holy peaks, buses leave JR Tsuruoka Station at 6 and 7 AM in summer for the 90-minute trip (¥1,650) to the Ga-san Hachigome (8th Station) stop, from where you can hike three hours past the glaciers and wildflowers to the 1,984-m (6,500-foot) summit of Ga-san, or Moon-mountain. From the top you can see the whole gorgeous gallery of mountains that is Yamagata, including one called Dewa-Fuji (after Mt. Fuji) for its shape, and to the Sea of Japan to the west.

The last of the trio of peaks, Yudono-san, is 1,504 m (5,000 feet) high, and is generally the last on pilgrims' rounds. You can descend on foot in a few hours from Ga-san but it involves some exertion, kanji-sign navigational ability, and slippery metal ladders, and you'll want to talk with the tourist info folks about current conditions. Buses make the 80-minute (¥1,490) run between Tsuruoka and Sen-in-zawa, a trailhead for a short climb to the summit, where you must make a small monetary donation and be purified in a secret ritual that you are forbidden to photograph or tell anyone about. Once cleansed, don't miss the last bus back down to Tsuruoka, which leaves promptly at 4:30.

In summer only, Shonai Kotsu buses also depart from Yamagata Bus Terminal (confer with the Tourist Information Office), with stops at all three sacred mountains.

Note that many of the bus companies conducting the trips to the mountains and towns in this area are not affiliated with JR, but they are generally not expensive.

Where to Stay & Eat

Spending the night around Tsuruoka, you can stay in town or up on Haguro-san, or best of all make your way to Atsumi Onsen (see below). If you're hanging around Tsuruoka, here are some places in town.

$$–$$$ ✕ **Kanazawa-ya.** An excellent place to eat soba, Kanazawa-ya offers *ten-zaru* (tempura served with cold soba noodles) and *kamo nanban* soba (duck meat with soba in hot broth) that are delicious. From the station, walk straight to the corner of Marica and Mister Donut, then turn left, and walk past the highway. Kanazawa-ya is on the left. ⊠ *3–48 Daihōji-machi, Tsuruoka* ☎ *0235/24–7208* ⊟ *No credit cards* ⊗ *Closed Wed.*

$$ ⊞ **Sai-kan.** This temple lodge connected to Dewa Sanzan Jinja by a long stairway allows you to enjoy the shrine and scenery at the summit after most tourists have gone. The large tatami-mat rooms can be separated by *fusuma* (sliding paper doors on wood frames) to create smaller guest rooms. Vegetarian meals of local goodies are served. The place is a madhouse at festival times, but because Sai-kan can handle 300 guests, one more person can probably flop down a futon and squeeze in. ⊠ *Tōge, Haguro-machi, Higashi Tagawa-gun, Yamagata-ken 997-0211* ☎ *0235/62–2357* ⊠ *0235/62–2352* ⟿ *300 futons* � ♨ *No a/c, no room phones, no room TVs* ⊟ *No credit cards* ⟦◎⟧ *MAP.*

$$ ⊞ **Tōkyō Dai-ichi Hotel Tsuruoka.** The rooms and views are pleasant, and an open-air bathhouse and sauna for guests are on the roof. The hotel connects to a shopping mall, and the travel connections are unbeatably convenient. It's a three-minute walk from JR Tsuruoka Station and next to the Shōnai Kōtsū Mall and the bus terminal from which buses depart for Haguro-san and Yamagata City (¥2,150, 2 hours 7 minutes). ⊠ *2–10 Nishiki-machi, Tsuruoka-shi, Yamagata-ken 997-0031* ☎ *0235/24–7611* ⊠ *0235/24–7621* ⊕ *www.daiichihotels.com/hotel/tsuruoka/* ⟿ *124 rooms with bath* ♨ *4 restaurants, coffee shop, Japanese baths, bar, meeting rooms* ⊟ *AE, MC, V.*

Atsumi Onsen

39 min south of Tsuruoka (¥480) by JR Uetsu Line.

⑮ Whether you have just climbed one or the whole trio of Dewa's holy mountains, the idea of a long soak in some truly fine mineral waters while listening to a rushing river or pounding surf may sound good to you. We have found a place that is so special that even if you have no interest other than reaching the ultimate Zen moment of pure relaxation, it would still be well worth your while to drop everything, wherever you are, and come here immediately.

Densely forested mountains rear up from the wave-battered seacoast and range themselves at staggering angles along and behind a lovely river valley. As you lean as far back as possible to take it all in, you will be forgiven for blinking and wondering if you dreamed your way into another world. People come here not only to look around in awe but also to soak in and drink the famous regenerative waters. There are many choices, but there is hardly a better place, nor any more luxurious, than at the Tachibana-ya.

★ $$$$ ⊞ **Tachibana-ya.** Come in, take off your shoes, and sit back while they pour you some tea and deliver the briefing. Your expansive room is stuffed with simple elegance, and the exquisite bath is equipped with a *hinoki*, or cedar-cypress bathtub. The faucets dispense the naturally sweet and curative waters, raised from submerged vaults, the same waters that fill the green-stone indoor and outdoor baths down below. In front, the large expanse of glass behind the slidable shoji screens looks out upon a river valley steep and green, and the only decisions you need make during your stay are how many hours you'd like to soak before and after whatever time you would like your banquets served by your room's very own personal attendant. All of this and more soul repair is just a short ¥1,000 taxi ride or 10-minute ¥200 bus ride from JR Atsumi Onsen Station. ⊠ *Atsumi 3-chōme, Tsuruoka-shi, Yamagata-ken 999-7204* ☎ *0235/43–2211* 🖷 *0235/43–3681* ⊕ *www.tachibanaya.jp/* ⤴ *78 Japanese-style rooms* ⚒ *Bars, shop, coffee shop* ⊟ *AE, DC, MC, V.* ⫯ *MAP.*

13

TŌHOKU ESSENTIALS

To research prices, get advice from other travelers, and book travel arrangements, visit www.fodors.com.

Transportation

BY BUS
Buses take over where trains do not run, and in most instances they depart from JR train stations. You should be able to find someone at the train station to direct you to the appropriate bus. Particularly useful bus routes are the ones from Morioka to Hirosaki, and another between Tsuruoka and Yamagata City; they save lots of time if not also money.

BY CAR
All major towns have car-rental agencies. Hertz is the one most frequently represented. Note that maps are not provided by car-rental agencies; be sure to obtain bilingual maps in Tōkyō or Sendai. Other car-rental companies are usually limited to Toyota or Nissan Rent-A-Car. These outfits usually have offices near major train stations, and even smaller ones. All you need is a valid International Driver's License (available from AAA in the US) and your home state or country's license.

🆔 Agency **Hertz Domestic Reservation Center** ☎ 0120/48–9882 toll-free in Japan ⊕ www.hertz.com.

BY CAR
Although a car can be handy, the cost of gas, tolls, and car rental makes driving expensive. Additionally, except on the Tōhoku Expressway, which links Tōkyō with Aomori, few road signs are in rōmaji. However, major roads have route numbers. If you're going to drive, be sure to obtain a road map on which the towns are written in rōmaji and kanji.

It's also considerably slower to drive than to ride on the Shinkansen. The approximate driving times from Tōkyō (assuming you can clear the metropolitan area in two hours) are 5 hours to Fukushima, 6 hours to Sendai, 8–10 hours to Morioka, and 10–11 hours to Aomori.

BY TRAIN
The most efficient way to get to Tōhoku from Tōkyō is on the Tōhoku Shinkansen trains, all of which the JR Pass covers. The Hayate, which makes the fewest stops, and the slower Yamabiko Shinkansen run to Sendai, Morioka, and Hachinohe; the Tsubasa runs to Yamagata; and

the Komachi goes to Akita. North of Hachinohe, conventional trains continue on to Aomori (an additional 70 minutes).

Elsewhere in Tōhoku, JR local trains are slower and less frequent (every two hours rather than every hour during the day) when they cross the region's mountainous spine. Most railways are owned by Japan Railways, and many buses are run by them, too, so your JR Rail Pass will work. Be aware that most trains stop running before midnight.

Contacts & Resources

BANKS & EXCHANGE SERVICES

For foreign exchange, you'll have to rely on main banks and central post offices, but outside of the narrow 9 AM–3 PM normal weekday business hours, you'll most likely be stuck with the inflated rates available at major hotel front desks.

In Akita City: Akita Bank ✉ *3–2–1 Sanno Akita -shi* ☎ *018/863–1212* ✉ *Hokuto Bank* ☎ *018/833–4211* ✉ *Central Post Office* ☎ *018/862–3504*. **In Aomori:** Aomori Bank ✉ *1–9–30 Hashimoto Aomori-shi* ☎ *017/777–1111*. **In Hirosaki:** Aomori Bank ✉ *6–1 Fujimi-chō, Hirosaki-shi* ☎ *017/223–6321*. **In Morioka:** Bank of Iwate ✉ *1–2–3 Chūo-dōri, Morioka, Iwate* ☎ *019/623–1111*. **In Sendai:** Sendai Chūo Post Office, ✉ *1–7 Kitamemachi, Aoba-ku, Sendai* ☎ *022/223–8241*. **In Yamagata:** Yamagata Bank ✉ *3–1–2 Nanoka-machi, Yamagata-shi* ☎ *023/623–1221*.

EMERGENCIES

In Japan people don't like to help accident victims, and whether for fear of liability claims or due to a general distaste for involvement with strangers, they prefer to let police handle matters of emergency or law enforcement. If you're in any sort of mishap, don't expect to receive much help or assistance—but you can be reasonably sure that someone who saw it will have called the local police. Officers who may respond will often seem quite gruff at first, but may be won over toward some measure of pity if you remain polite and obliging.

🚩 **Sendai City Hospital** ✉ 3–1 Shimizukōji, Wakabayashi-ku, Sendai, Miyagi-ken 984-8501 ☎ 022/266–7111. **(Morioka) Iwate Medical College Hospital** ✉ Uchimaru 19-1, Morioka-shi, Iwate-ken 020-8505 ☎ 019/651–5111. **Yamagata City Hospital** ✉ 1-3-26 Nanoka-machi, Yamagata 990-8533 ☎ 023/625–5555. **Ambulance** ☎ 119. **Police** ☎ 110.

INTERNET, MAIL & SHIPPING

You should now have little or no trouble getting on the Internet in towns of any size. Scattered around every major station are Internet cafés, and many hotels and ryokans have a handy PC or two hooked up in the lobby so guests can check e-mail, weather forecasts, and news. Many offer this benefit for free, while others charge ¥100 for each 10 minutes online. Simply insert your coin(s) and click away.

TOURS

The easiest way to tour the peninsula, which is 45 km (28 mi) northwest of Akita, is by using Akita Chūō Kōtsu bus lines. Full-day tours in Japanese cost ¥5,150 (7 hours 45 minutes), and ¥6,450 (8 hours 40 minutes) (not including meals); they depart from JR Akita Station's west exit from July to early November.

In summer the local Japan Travel Bureau at the train station in each major tourist area, or at major hotels, can make arrangements for scenic bus tours. The offices in Tōkyō, Kyōto, and Sendai arrange tours, some in English. 🚌 **Akita Chūō Kōtsū bus lines** ☎ 018/823-4411. **Japan Travel Bureau** ☎ 03/5796-5454 in Tōkyō, 075/371-7891 in Kyōto, 022/221-4422 in Sendai.

13

Points of Interest

SITES/AREAS	JAPANESE CHARACTERS
Akita	秋田
Aoba Castle (Aoba-jō)	青葉城
Aomori	青森
Aoyagi-ke (Aoyagi Manor)	青柳家
Atsumi Onsen	あつみ温泉
Denshō House (Denshōkan)	伝承館
Fukurajima	福浦島
Godai-dō	五大堂
Goshogake Spa	後生掛温泉
Hachiman-numa (Hachiman Marsh)	八幡沼
Hachimantai Plateau	八幡平
Haguro-san (Mt. Haguro)	羽黒山
Hirano Masakichi Museum of Fine Art (Hirano Masakichi Bijutsukan)	平野政吉美術館
Hirashimizu	平清水
Hirosaki	弘前
Hirosaki Castle (Hirosaki-jō)	弘前城
Hōju-san (Mt. Hōju)	宝珠山
Iwaki-san (Mt. Iwaki)	岩木山
Iwate Kōen (Iwate Park)	岩手公園
Kakunodate	角館
Kamasada Iron Casting Studio	釜定南部鉄器
Kawabata-dōri	川反通り
Kōgensha	光原社
Komaga-take (Mt. Komaga)	駒ヶ岳
Matsu-shima	松島
Morioka	盛岡
Nebuta Festival	ねぶた祭り
Neputa Festival	ねぷた祭り
Northern Tōhoku	北東北
Nyūtō Onsen	乳頭温泉
Oirase-kyōkoku	奥入瀬峡谷
Ōsaki Hachiman Jinja	大崎八幡神社

13

Rinnō-ji (Rinnō Temple)	輪王寺
Sakunami Onsen	作並温泉
Sendai	仙台
Sendai Municipal Museum	仙台市博物館
Senshū Kōen, or Senshū Park	千秋公園
Shirakami Sanmyaku (Shirakami Mountains)	白神山脈
Tazawa-ko	田沢湖
Tazawa-ko & Kakunodate	田沢湖と角館
Tōshichi Onsen	藤七温泉
Towada-Hachiman-tai National Park	十和田八幡平国立公園
Towada-ko	十和田湖
Tsugaru-han Neputa Mura	津軽藩ねぷた村
Tsuruoka	鶴岡
Tsuruoka & Dewa-Sanzan	鶴岡と出羽三山
Yamadera	山寺
Yamagata	山形
Yasumi-ya	休屋
Zaō-san (Mt. Zaō)	蔵王山
Zuigan-ji	五大堂
Zuihō-den	瑞鳳殿
RESTAURANTS	
Aji Tasuke	味太助
Anzu	杏
Azuma-ya	東家
Ban-ya Nagasawa	番屋ながさわ
Beko Masamune	べこ政宗
Daido-En	大同苑
Dai-ichi Kaikan	第一会館
Gintanabe Bekkan	銀たなべ別館
Go Shu In Sen	御酒印船
Hide-zushi	秀寿司
Hinaiya	秋田比内や
Jirai-ya	地雷也
Kanazawa-ya	金沢屋

Kikufuji	菊富士
Mimasu	三桝
Mitsu-ya	三津屋
Nishimura	西むら
Sagorō	佐五郎
Shōjiya	庄司屋
Yamauta	山唄
HOTELS	
Akita Castle Hotel	秋田キャッスルホテル
Akita View Hotel	秋田ビューホテル
Aomori Grand Hotel	青森グランドホテル
City Hirosaki Hotel	シティ弘前ホテル
Comfort Hotel Sendai East	コンフォートホテル仙台東口
Folkloro Matsu-shima Hotel	フォルクローロ松島ホテル
Forukurōro (Folklore) Kakunodate	フォルクローロ角館
Hotel Ichinobo	ホテルーの坊
Hotel JAL City Aomori	ホテルJALシテイ青森
Hotel Metropolitan Morioka	ホテルメトロポリタン盛岡
Hotel Metropolitan Sendai	ホテルメトロポリタン仙台
Hotel Metropolitan Yamagata	ホテルメトロポリタン山形
Hotel New Castle	ホテルニューキャッスル
Hotel Shōwa	ホテル昭和
Iwamatsu Ryokan	岩松旅館
Matsu-shima Century Hotel	松島センチュリーホテル
Metropolitan Hotel Akita	メトロポリタンホテル秋田
Morioka Grand Hotel	盛岡グランドホテル
Ryokan Kumagai	旅館熊ヶ井
Ryokan Sendaiya	旅館仙台屋
Sai-kan	出羽三山神社斉館
Sendai Kokusai Hotel	仙台国際ホテル
Tachibana-ya	たちばなや
Tōkyō Dai-ichi Hotel Tsuruoka	東京第一ホテル鶴岡
Towada Kankō Hotel	十和田観光ホテル
Yamagata Washington Hotel	山形ワシントンホテル

Hokkaidō

WORD OF MOUTH

"I think it would be hard for the kids to choose what they enjoyed the most—certainly as keen skiers they absolutely loved the beautiful powder skiing at Niseko."

—ozgal

By Amanda
Harlow

HOKKAIDŌ IS JAPAN UNTAMED. Wild mountains, virgin forests, sapphire lakes, and surf-beaten shores keep cities and towns at bay. Hokkaidō, as a distinct part of Japan, was born during the Meiji Restoration (1868–1912), when the Japanese government settled its border regions to ward off economic and political interests of Russia and Europe. Until then the large northern island had been left to the Ainu people, hunter-gatherers who traded with the Japanese and the Russians, and who believed in natural spirit worship.

Then the Meiji Emperor decided to colonize the north. In the 1870s, after studying American and European agriculture, city design, and mining, his government sent 63 foreign experts to harness Hokkaidō resources, and introduced a soldier-farmer system to spur mainlanders north to clear the land and settle. Hokkaidō was ripe with natural resources—coal and gold mines, huge herring fishing fleets, and fertile land conducive to dairy farming, potato growing, horse breeding, and even cold-climate, hardy rice. The legacy lives on—small holdings with silos and red- or blue-roof barns dot the rolling farmland and wide landscapes give stretches of Hokkaidō an American flavor.

On the losing end of the 19th-century Japanese colonization were the Ainu, who died in the thousands from previously unencountered diseases, forced labor, and conflict with the Japanese. Forced name changes and intermarriage threatened a whole way of life. Thanks to political and cultural activism in recent decades, the Ainu has clawed its way back to a grudging level of official and public acceptance.

Hokkaidō's Japanese people—who call themselves *Dosanko* after the region's draft horses, are open-minded and individualistic. They readily come to the rescue of foreign travelers with a warmth and directness that make up for language problems. Even now Japanese seeking an alternative way of life head north to Hokkaidō to start new lives as farmers, artists, outdoor adventure guides, and guesthouse owners.

Because Hokkaidō consists more of countryside than of culture-rich cities, the number of foreigners who visit has traditionally been small, although many Japanese visitors are attracted to this unusual, less traditional-looking area of the country. Many locally promoted attractions—flower fields and dairy farms—may be of less interest to people from Western countries than mountain scenery, wildlife, and volcanically active areas. Visitors from other Asian countries and Australian skiers are a common sight.

This is also one of Japan's more politically active borders. In 2006 a Russian patrol boat shot a Nemuro fisherman dead and fined his captain for poaching and border incursion. All over Hokkaidō, signboards and petitions support Japan's claim to the southern four of the Kuril Islands, which Russia snatched up in the final days of World War II. The Russian business presence is noticeable in Hokkaidō's eastern fishing ports, used-car export yards, and adult entertainment districts.

It's easy to romanticize Japan's northernmost island as largely uncharted territory. But Hokkaidō's big-city dwellers compare the latest fashions

Top Reasons to Visit

THE BEER

Kampai! or Cheers! with a glass of Hokkaidō's finest—Sapporo Beer, brewed since 1876 using foreign and local hops and barley mixed with pure Hokkaidō water. Local microbreweries such as Otaru and Hakodate are favorites too. Beer, not sake, is king in Hokkaidō, and Sapporo has a three-week Beer Garden Festival in July.

THE SLOPES

Deep powder snow and uncrowded lift lines are hallmarks of Hokkaidō's ski resorts. Japanese winter sports enthusiasts head here December to May, now joined by Australian powderheads at arguably Japan's best winter playground. Major resorts Niseko, Rusutsu, and Furano lead the way, but every small community has its local *suki-jo* where toddlers learn early how to excel.

THE VALLEY OF HELL

. . . and other sulfur-spewing springs. At Noboribetsu, Toya, Akan, and Shiretoko, the forces below burst forth into steaming yellow vents and craters which fuel the region's many hot springs. In 2000 thousands of people evacuated as Mount Usu at Toya erupted again; the latest ash-flow destruction is now a tourist sight.

THE LAST FRONTIER

Salmon-fishing bears and red-crested cranes, alpine flowers, and vast forests hold modern Japan at bay. Viewed from a car, this region has vistas of mountains and plains, but it's best to hike or bike the natural wonders.

WINTER WONDERLAND

Dark, frigid winter nights are brightend by exuberant winter festivals on frozen lakes and in parks. Giant ice and snow sculptures glisten under floodlights and fireworks explode. Out east, icebreakers cut through Arctic ice floes and bundled-up passengers spy seals and eagles.

14

---

while drinking cappuccinos in American coffee-shop chains, and the countryside is crisscrossed by road and rail networks. But small-town life in Hokkaidō is still quiet (often owing to economic stagnation), and for the adventurous visitor wild beauty and open spaces abound—the island is a geological wonderland: lava-seared mountains hide deeply carved ravines; hot springs, gushers, and steaming mud pools boil out of the ground; and crystal-clear lakes fill the seemingly bottomless cones of volcanoes. Half of Hokkaidō is covered in forest. Wild, rugged coastlines hold back the sea, and all around the prefecture islands surface offshore. The remnants of Hokkaidō's bear population, believed to number about 2,000, still roam the forests, snagging rabbits and scooping up fish from mountain streams. Hokkaidō's native crane, the *tanchō-zuru,* is especially magnificent, with a red-cap head and a white body trimmed with black feathers. Look for it on the ¥1,000 note and in the marshes of Kushiro, on the Pacific coast.

See the glossary at the end of this book for definitions of the common Japanese words and suffixes used in this chapter.

ORIENTATION & PLANNING

Orientation

Hokkaidō is Japan's northernmose island. Mountains topping 6,500 feet were formed, and are still formed, by volcanic activity. The island is dotted with deep caldera lakes and pockets of rich farmland. Summers are cooler and less humid, winters colder and snowier than elsewhere in Japan.

Hakodate
Gateway to Hokkaidō for train travelers, this bustling port and tourist city has 19th-century clapboard buildings built for early foreign residents, rattling streetcars, and the best public fish market in the region.

Sapporo
Hokkaidō's capital, voted most attractive city nationwide in 2006, is modern, green, clean, and easy to get around. At its heart is Ōdōri Park, the site of the Snow Festival in February and the Beer Festival in July. Barbecued lamb, crabs, and potatoes are among the city's specialties, and the Susukino nightlife area is a blaze of neon and noise.

Otaru & Niseko
A historic harbor town once dubbed the Wall Street of the North, Otaru is now popular for its short canal, cafés, shops, and restaurants; and artists crafting glass in small studios. Niseko is a winter-sports area with the best powder snow for skiers and snowboarders December to April, and in summer there are adventure sports such as river rafting and mountain biking.

Shikotsu-Tōya National Park
Soaring mountains and deep lakes offer an escape into nature two hours from Sapporo. At Tōya Onsen in the south the mountains steam and grow around a crater lake where visitors hike the recently solidified ash flows that engulfed a village, while at Shikotsu, campers, hikers, and fishing enthusiasts relax around one of Japan's deepest, prettiest lakes.

Eastern Hokkaidō
Eastern Hokkaidō is where nature rules. Bears and eagles on the Shiretoko Peninsula won world protection status with UNESCO designation as a natural Heritage Site, and the red-crested *tancho* cranes stalk the renowned Kushiro wetlands in the south. Farther north, Ainu people at Lake Akan share their culture through song and swirling dances and the eastern shores are gripped by Arctic ice floes in January and February.

Central & Northern Hokkaidō
The Daisetsu Mountains form the glorious, snow-capped center of Hokkaidō. Cable cars lift visitors to flower-filled plateaus, and hiking trails promise days of magical panoramic views. Small guesthouses fete walkers with lamb barbecues, beer, and hot springs. To the far north are Rebun and Rishiri islands, wild places with a short summer of rare flowers and creamy *uni* sea urchin.

Of Slopes & Powder

UP TO 40 FEET of powder snow makes Hokkaidō the best skiing and snowboarding destination in Japan. While only Niseko, two hours from Sapporo, has skiing above the tree line and runs are short by North American standards, there is great variety with so many areas within easy reach by public transport. The most spacious areas are Niseko and Rusutsu, two hours west of Sapporo; Kokusai and Kiroro, one hour west of Sapporo; and Furano, Tomamu, and Sahoro, two hours east of Sapporo. Trails are well groomed, lift lines outside the Christmas–New Year's peak season are short, and backcountry exploring wondrous.

Many ski schools (notably Kiroro, Rusutsu, Furano, and Kokusai) and the adventure-tour companies in Niseko have English-speaking guides and teachers. A day's lift pass averages ¥4,500, but ski packages

that include bus transportation are a better option and often include lunch and/or hot-spring tickets. Hotels and sports shops in Sapporo have discount lift coupons, too. All *su-ki-jo* have beginner courses, and if you are downtown in Sapporo, a taxi can get you to Mount Moiwa in 20 minutes. "Expert" courses are not as hard as in other countries. The biggest danger to novices would likely be mountaintop temperatures reaching minus 15°C (5°F).

Reservations for short ski tours to Hokkaidō from Tōkyō or Ōsaka should be made a week in advance. Reliable domestic delivery companies forward equipment to hotels, but Hokkaidō trains, taxis, and rental cars are fitted to transport winter gear. Equipment and wear can be rented at the resorts, but call ahead to check availability of larger boot sizes.

14

Planning

Hokkaidō's expansiveness is daunting. The main sights—calderas, remote onsen, craggy coasts, dramatic mountains—are everywhere. Rather than rushing to see everything, consider balancing the natural with the urban, the inland with the coastal, and figure in the seasonal appropriateness of sights, activities, and access.

The Best of Times

Hokkaidō has Japan's most dramatic seasons. Festivals predominate in summer and winter. May and early summer bring lilacs and alpine flowers. The cherry trees in Hokkaidō are the last to offer up *sakura* (cherry blossoms) in Japan, in late April and early May. Glorious weather from May to October lures Japanese drowning in the muggy air of Honshū. Hotel rooms become more difficult to book in summer, and the scenic areas are crowded with tour groups and Japanese families. Late September brings brief but spectacular golden foliage, reaching a peak in early October. The crisp fall gives way to chilly drizzle in November and early December. Winter makes travel more difficult (some minor roads and attractions are closed), and especially on the east coast the weather is frigid. It's no less beautiful a time, however, with snow

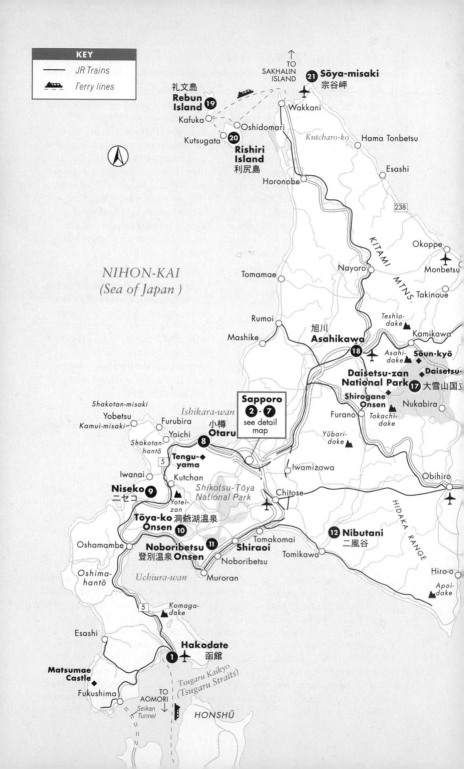

Sapporo
2 - 7
see detail map

Hokkaidō

OHOTSUKU-KAI
(Sea of Okhotsk)

Kunashiri-tō

14 **Shiretoko National Park**
知床国立公園

網走
Abashiri   **Utoro**

13

Shari

Rausu

Shiretoko-hantō

Engaru

Bihoro

Kusshuro-ko

Kitami

Shari-dake

Kawayu Onsen

Nemuro Kaiko
(Nemuro Straits)

Shikotan-tō

Bihoro Tōge

Akan-ko   **15** **Akan National Park**
阿寒国立公園

Mashū-ko

Nemuro Bay

Habomai-tō

Nemuro

Kushiro Marsh   **16** 釧路湿原

Attoko

Ikeda

Kushiro

TAIHEIYŌ
(Pacific Ocean)

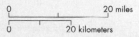

covering everything in mounds of white and ice floes crowding the Ohotsuku-kai. If you're here during the second week in February, don't miss the dazzling Snow Festival in Sapporo.

Concerning Restaurants & Hotels

Eat at local Japanese restaurants for Hokkaidō's regional food, which includes delicious seafood and lamb. Many reasonably priced restaurants have a visual display of their menu in the window. If you cannot order in Japanese and no English is spoken, lead the waiter to the window display and point.

Accommodations that are easily booked in English tend to be modern, characterless hotels built for Japanese tour groups. Gorgeous lobbies and cookie-cutter rooms are the norm. Room air-conditioning is unusual, except in large hotels, but the cool Hokkaidō summers render it unnecessary. More attractive and comfortable hotels are appearing as younger Japanese seek out lodging with more personality. Guesthouses, or pensions are a cheaper and friendlier option, with welcoming owners who strive to impress with the catch of the day or wild vegetables on the dinner menu. Most guesthouses have Western-style beds. Although booking in Japanese is the norm, simple English faxes or e-mails via a Web site can work too. Dinner reservations are required. Youth hostels are also a good option; in the towns and cities they are usually clean and modern, and in the national parks, although older, they are excellent touring bases. A good Web site in English is provided by the **Hokkaidō Youth Hostel Association** (☎ 011/825–3389 ⊕ www.youthhostel.or.jp/English).

Outside Sapporo and Hokkaidō's other commercial cities, hot-spring hotels charge on a per-person basis including two meals, excluding service and tax. In those cases, the rates listed below are for two people with two meals each, and the Modified American Plan (MAP) is noted in the service information. If you don't want dinner, you can often renegotiate the price. Isolated resort areas may present the limited choice of dining at your hotel or risking the local equivalent of fast food: ramen or Japanese-style curry.

WHAT IT COSTS In yen				
$$$$	**$$$**	**$$**	**$**	**¢**
RESTAURANTS over 3,000	2,000–3,000	1,000–2,000	800–1,000	under 800
HOTELS over 22,000	18,000–22,000	12,000–18,000	8,000–12,000	under 8,000

Restaurant prices are per person for a main course at dinner. Hotel prices are for a double room, excluding service and 5% tax.

Transportation

The best way to explore Hokkaidō is by train and car. Most car-rental companies allow different pick-up and drop-off locations and will meet customers at trains, ferries, and local flights. Long-distance buses are a good way to cut driving miles off a Hokkaidō journey, but check that the service uses the expressways and isn't stopping at every village.

CLOSE UP

On the Menu

HOKKAIDŌ IS KNOWN for its seafood—the prefecture's name means "the Road to the Northern Sea." *Shake* (salmon), *ika* (squid), *uni* (sea urchin), *nishin* (herring), and *kai* (shellfish) are abundant, but the real treat is the fat, sweet scallop, *kaibashira*, collected from northernmost Wakkanai. The other great favorite is crab, which comes in three varieties: *ke-gani* (hairy crab), *taraba-gani* (king crab), and Nemuro's celebrated *hanasaki-gani* (spiny king crab).

Jingisukan is thinly sliced mutton cooked on a dome-shape griddle.

The name comes from the griddle's resemblance to helmets worn by Mongolian cavalry under Genghis Khan. Vegetables—usually onions, green peppers, and cabbage—are added to the sizzling mutton, and the whole mix is dipped in a tangy brown sauce. Ramen is extremely popular and inexpensive. Local residents favor miso ramen, which uses a less delicate variety of fermented soybean paste than miso soup. Ramen with *shio* (salt) or *shōyu* (soy sauce) soup base is also widely available.

14

AIR TRAVEL Domestic carriers Japan Airlines, All Nippon Airways, and the budget Air Do connect major Japanese airports with Sapporo (New Chitose), Asahikawa, Hakodate, Abashiri (Memambetsu), and Kushiro. Flying across Hokkaidō is a good way to cross the distances, particularly eastern and northern regions. In winter sudden changes in weather can divert or cancel flights, so plan adequate time for connections.

BOAT TRAVEL Ferry services from Honshū connecting to Tomakomai, Hakodate, and Otaru are a leisurely way to arrive, while around Hokkaidō boats connect the islands of Rebun and Rishiri to the northern tip of Japan. In the far east they offer the best bear-viewing off the Shiretoko Peninsula.

BUS TRAVEL Long-distance buses connect the major cities and airports and reach into the national parks at resorts such as Tōya, Noboribetsu, Sounkyo, and Utoro. Although slower than train travel, buses are convenient to smaller communities. The main companies are Chūō, Donan, and Jotetsu. Only Chuo has English information.

CAR TRAVEL Driving is the best way to explore Hokkaidō (despite mountain bends and snow), because wide roads and English signage help guide you to wilder places. Toll highways link only Sapporo with Oshamambe, Asahikawa, and Obihiro. Otherwise, two-lane roads are the norm, and farm vehicles can slow travel.

TRAIN TRAVEL Japan Railways Hokkaidō helps visitors enjoy the big country in comfort, with a three- or five-day Hokkaidō Rail Pass and good English-language information at major stations. While there are no *Shinkasen* yet, super express trains connect Sapporo south to Hakodate (and onto Honshū), and north and east to Asahikawa, Kushiro, Abashiri, and Wakkanai. Train and car packages are available.

Visitor Information

The Hokkaidō Tourist Association (⊠ 1–8–3 Marunōchi, Chiyoda-ku, Tōkyō ☎ 03/3214–2481) has an office in Tōkyō, on the second floor of the Kokusai Kankō Kaikan Building, near the Yaesu exit from Tōkyō Station. The Japan National Tourist Organization's Tourist Information Center (TIC) in Tōkyō has free maps and brochures on Hokkaidō. **Tourist Information Center** (TIC ⊠ Tōkyō International Forum Bldg., Fl. B-1, 3–5–1 Marunōchi, Chiyoda-ku, Tōkyō ☎ 03/3201–3331). On Hokkaidō, the best places for travel information in English are Sapporo and Hakodate.

Bus and train travel information centers are at major train stations.

HAKODATE

❶ *3 hrs north from Tōkyō to Morioka by JR Shinkansen, then 2 or 3 hrs north from Morioka to Aomori by JR Limited Express, then 2½ hrs north to Hakodate by JR Rapid via the Seikan Tunnel. 3 hrs south of Sapporo by express train.*

Facing out on two bays, Hakodate is a 19th-century port town, with clapboard buildings on sloping streets, a dockside tourist zone, streetcars, and fresh fish on every menu. In the downtown historic quarter, a mountain rises 1,100 feet above the city on the southern point of the narrow peninsula. Russians, Americans, Chinese, and Europeans have all left their mark; this was one of the first three Japanese ports the Meiji government opened up to international trade in 1859. The main sights around the foot of Mount Hakodate can be done in a day, but the city is best appreciated with an overnight stay for the illumination in the historic area, the night views from either the mountain or the fort tower, and the fish market at dawn.

Getting Around

Streetcars cost ¥200–¥250, and municipal buses cost ¥200–¥260. The sightseeing area is hilly, so save foot power by using a one- or two-day bus and streetcar pass (¥1,000/1,700), and borrow an audio walking guide (deposit ¥500) from the tourist center.

For sightseeing, hotel, and onward traveling information in English, stop at the **Hakodate City Tourist Information Center** (☎ 0138/23–5440) inside the station building. It's open April–October, daily 9–7, and November–March, daily 9–5.

What to See

Morning Market (Asai-ichi). Bright red crabs wave giant claws from old fishing boats filled with water, squid darting furiously around restaurant tanks, and piles of dried octopus parts to sample—it's all at Hokkaidō's largest public fish market one block from Hakodate Station. It's open at dawn if you can face a fish-on-rice breakfast. *Asai-ichi,* which also has a fruit and vegetable section, stays active until mid-afternoon. ⊠ *Asai-ichi, Wakamatsu-cho, Hakodate.*

The Moto-machi Historic Area. Overlooking the western bay at the foot of Mount Hakodate is a 2 km-square area of wide, sloping streets lined with the 19th century churches, consulates, shops, and homes of the Japanese and foreigners who first opened up this part of Japan to commerce. Only the main historic buildings have English information, but many others have been converted into shops and cafés. Return here at night when the illuminated buildings, particularly in winter, show why Hakodate is a favorite Japanese romantic movie and TV drama location.

The most interesting historic buildings and museums, namely the arch-Victorian Old Public Hall, with the Emporer's Toilet, the British Consulate, a nice place for tea and scones, and the Museum of Northern Peoples, can be visited on a combined ticket: ¥300 for one site, ¥500 for two, ¥720 for all three. They're open from April to October, daily 9–7, and from November to March, daily 9–5.

14

NEED A BREAK?

More than 100 kimono-clad dolls watch guests with their coffees, teas, and traditional desserts in the tiny, two-room **Kitchen and Cafe Hana** (✉ 2–21 Funami-chō ☎ 0138/24–4700), in a house near the gates of the Old Public Hall. Shoes off at the door, please.

Hakodate Russian Orthodox Church (Harisutosu Sei Kyōkai). A green Byzantine dome and tower rise above this beautiful white church. The present building dates from 1916, and donations help with the upkeep of Hakodate's most exotic attraction. The Episcopal and Catholic churches are on either side. ✉ 3–13 Moto-machi ☎ 0138/23–7387.

Hakodate History Plaza (Hakodate Puraza). On the cobbled waterfront of Moto-machi, redbrick warehouses now bustle with 21st-century tourism: shops, restaurants, bars, harbor boat trips, street entertainers, and glass-blowing studios. In December it offers a giant Canadian Christmas tree and nightly fireworks. This is a good place to wind down, although most bars close at 10:30 PM. The Plaza is a 1.5-km (1-mi) walk from Hakodate Station. ✉ 14–16 Suehiro-chō, about 750 feet northwest of the Jūji-gai streetcar stop ☎ 0138/23–0350.

Where to Stay & Eat

$–$$ ✗ **Michi-no-iie.** What do squid eyes taste like? Imagine the dog's chew toy, all slimy and gristly, add in an exploding juice ball—and you have the eye light of the ika-sashi ika-sumi don set at ¥1,800. Your squid is pulled flapping from the tank and returns minutes later sliced, with squid-ink black rice, delicious slivers of still-twitching flesh, soup, pickles, and two big black eyes. Wash it down with gray-squid ice cream for dessert. Luckily, the restaurant has plenty of other seafood, and a picture menu for easy selection. It's on the Morning Market's closest corner to the station, first restaurant on the right in the eating alleyway. ✉ Donburi Yokocho Ichiba, Asai-ichi ☎ 0138–22–6086 ▭ No credit cards.

¢–$$ ✗ **Hakodate Beer Hall.** This seaside hall in Hakodate History Plaza serves seafood specialties such as squid, octopus, and tofu shabu shabu (cooked tableside by dipping into boiling water and then into a sauce) for ¥1,300 and three local brews (wheat beer, ale, and the slightly more bitter "alt" beer). Its spaciousness and conviviality are typical of Hokkaidō, and while it's in a tourist complex, locals like the wide range of Hokkaidō's seasonal specialties. ⊠ *5–22 Ote-machi* ☎ *0138/23–8000* 🖃 *AE, V.*

$$$–$$$$ ✕🖃 **Hakodate Kokusai Hotel.** This bustling modern hotel occupies three buildings a short walk from the station–Morning Market area and the History Plaza warehouses. Standard rooms in pastel shades have views of the ugly waterside highway or—much better—the city. *Tennpan* chefs slice and dice in Vue Mer on the top floor. If you're coming from Sapporo, check with Japan Rail about rail-hotel combination packages for good deals at this hotel. ⊠ *5–10 Ohtemachi, Hakodate 040-0064* ☎ *0138/23–5151* 🖳 *0138/23–0239* ⊕ *www.hakodate.ne.jp/kokusai-hotel* ⌁ *304 Western-style rooms, 6 Japanese-style rooms* ☖ *4 restaurants, room service, minibars, cable TV, hair salon, 3 bars, shop, laundry service, free parking* 🖃 *AE, MC, V.*

$$$ 🖳 **Pension Kokian.** A 100-year-old former seaweed shop with a modern annex behind the waterfront warehouses has small Western motel–style rooms, each with sink units and shared bathrooms. The traditional restaurant in the old building prepares the best of the morning's catch. ⊠ *13–2 Suehiro-chō, Hakodate 040-0053* ☎ *0138/26–5753* 🖳 *0138/22–2710* ⊕ *www.hakodate.or.jp/hotel/kokian* ⌁ *17 Western-style rooms* ☖ *Restaurant, bar; no a/c* 🖃 *AE, DC, V.*

★ ¢–$ 🖳 **Pension Puppy Tail.** Decoupage decorations and garlands of silk flowers overwhelm, but the family welcome is big. The owner, Fukui-san, speaks English, and can pick guests up from the station. Breakfast (¥1,000) and dinner (¥2,000) should be reserved the day before. Faxed reservations are best. The kitschy name? The Fukui family thought their red setter's tail looked like the Hakodate part of the Hokkaidō map. Rooms in the newer annex have private bathrooms. It's a 10-minute walk north of the station on Route 5. ⊠ *30–16 Wakamatsu-cho, Hakodate 040-0063* ☎ *0138/23–5858* 🖳 *0138/26–8239* ⊕ *www.p-puppytail. com* ⌁ *6 Western-style rooms, 13 Japanese-style rooms* ☖ *Dining room, Japanese baths* 🖃 *No credit cards.*

SAPPORO

3 hrs north of Hakodate by JR.

Voted Japan's Most Attractive City in a 2006 nationwide survey—Sapporo is a good planning base for any trip to Hokkaidō's wilder regions, with plenty of English-language information and transport connections. Hokkaidō's capital is also worth a few days' stay for its major snow (February), dance (June), and beer (July and August) festivals.

With 1.8 million inhabitants, it's four times larger than Asahikawa, the prefecture's next-largest city. It continues to expand as Hokkaidō's unemployed from the economically depressed farms in the central plains and industrial and fishing towns on the coast migrate here for work.

Downtown has English signs and uncongested streets. In 1870 the governor of Hokkaidō visited President Grant in the United States and requested that American advisers visit Hokkaidō to help design the capital on the site of an Ainu village. (The name *Sapporo* is derived from a combination of Ainu words meaning "a river running along a reed-filled plain.") As a result, Sapporo was built on a grid system with wide avenues and parks. It's distinctly lacking in pre-Meiji historic sights. On the other hand, you can walk the sidewalks without being swept away by a surge of humanity.

Numbers in the text correspond to numbers in the margin and on the Sapporo map.

Getting Around

Sapporo is easy to find your way around in. Eki-mae Dōri, (Station Road) runs south of the station, crossed east–west by Ōdōri Kōen (park), then continues south through the shopping district to the nightlife area Susukino and beyond to Nakajima Park. East–west streets are called *jō*, and those running north–south are *chōme*. They are numbered consecutively, and each block is approximately 100 yards square. Addresses use the cardinal points: north, south, east, and west are *kita, minami, higashi,* and *nishi,* respectively. Ōdōri Park divides city addresses north and south and the Sosei River (buried under road and park reconstruction until 2009) is the east–west divide.

Downtown sights are easily covered on foot in a few hours, using Ōdōri Subway Station as the center point. In winter underground shopping malls linking the subway station with both Susukino and the TV Tower become bustling thoroughfares. In summer, rent a bicycle (¥1,000 per day from near Sapporo Station). **Rent-A-Cycle Sapporo,** half a kilometer east of the station (in the small street behind the post office), has bikes for ¥1,000 a day or ¥1,500 for two days. (⊠ Kita -2-jo, Higashi 2, Sapporo ☎ 011/223–7662 ⊙ Daily 8:30–5).

Taxi meters start at ¥550 or ¥600, depending on the company. Check the basic fare, which is posted on the door, before you get in. An average fare, such as from the JR station to Susukino, runs about ¥800 ($7). In winter most taxies are fitted with ski and board roof-racks, and drivers are adept at stowing even the bulkiest winter gear.

③ Sapporo International Communication Plaza (Sapporo Kokusai Kōryū Puraza). This center is the best place for suggestions on travel in Hokkaidō and for meeting people who speak English. You can also have something translated from Japanese into English. The center has a salon with books, newspapers, and brochures in English and is meant for informal socializing. Ask foreign residents and Japanese about their favorite restaurants and nightspots. For up-to-date information on local cultural events, pick up a free copy of *What's On in Sapporo* at the salon information counter. The Clock Tower faces the building. ⊠ 3rd fl., Kita 1-jō Nishi 3, Chūō-ku, Ōdōri ☎ 011/221–2105 ⊕ www.plaza-sapporo. or.jp ⊙ Mon.–Sat. 9–5:30.

④ Plaza i. English-speaking staff members at the Ōdōri or JR station desks are extremely helpful in distributing free brochures, maps, and flyers on events in town, and will send and receive faxes. They can assist with accommodations throughout the area. The "Hokkaidō Trekking and Onsen Guide" and the "Hokkaidō Camping Guide" at ¥400, and hiking map booklets at ¥100 each have excellent English-language infor-

14

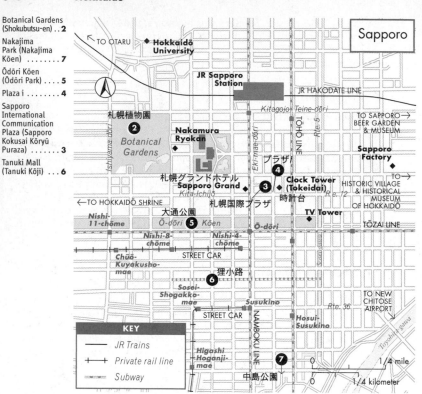

mation. ⊠ *Kita 1-jō Nishi 3, JR Sapporo Station, south exit (west), Chūō-ku, Ōdōri* ☏ *011/211–3678 or 011/209–5030* 🖷 *011/219–0020 or 011/209–5021* ⊕ *www.plaza-sapporo.or.jp* ⊘ *Daily 9–5:30.*

What to See

❺ **Ōdōri Kōen** (Ōdōri Park). This 345-foot-wide green belt bisects the city center. In summer everyone buys soy sauce–or butter-covered corn and potatoes from food vendors and sits down to watch the street performers, skateboarders, and each other. Sapporo Beer Festival lasts three weeks in July, when every block becomes an outdoor beer garden and thousands of drinkers enjoy open-air stage shows. Sapporo Snow Festival is one week in February, when volunteers create blockwide life-like snow sculptures and 2 million marveling visitors slip and slide around. ⊠ *Ōdōri.*

❻ **Tanuki Mall** (Tanuki Kōji). A *tanuki* is a raccoon dog, which is known in Japanese mythology for its cunning and libidinous nature. The Tanuki Kōji covered arcade got its name because the area used to be frequented by prostitutes. Now a different breed of merchant is eager to lighten the wallets of passersby. The arcade is crowded with small shops selling clothing, footwear, electronics, records, and Ainu-inspired souvenirs of Hokkaidō. Tanuki Kōji has considerably lower prices than the area's

CLOSE UP

Sapporo Festivals

ONE OF JAPAN'S best-known annual events, held for a week beginning February 5 or 6, is the **Sapporo Snow Festival**. More than 300 lifelike ice sculptures as large as 130 feet high by 50 feet deep by 80 feet wide are created each year. Memorable statues include baseball star Matsui, cavorting whales, dinosaurs, and the Taj Mahal.

The festival began in 1950 with six statues commissioned by the local government to entertain Sapporo citizens depressed by the war and the long winter nights. Now the event is so large that the sculptures are spread around three different sections of the city: Ōdōri Kōen, Makomanai, and Susukino. You'll also find ice slides for children. Everyone looks on as international teams of amateur and professional ice sculptors hired by major local businesses have four days to sculpt their creations. Although statues are roped off, taking photographs is no problem. The festival attracts more than 2 million visitors each year, so book your stay well in advance.

During the **Yosakoi Festival** every June, Sapporo's streets stage Japan's version of Carnival. More than 40,000 performers go wild in brightly colored costumes and face paint as they run, jump, and chant their way through the city streets. Dance teams wave flags and snap *naruko* (wooden clappers) in the wake of giant trucks mounted with powerful sound systems and *taiko* drummers in loincloths. Ticketed seats are available in the stands along the route in Ōdōri Kōen and at an outdoor stage, but they aren't necessary. Most people just perch wherever they can get a vantage point. Dance teams also perform in Susukino at night. A boisterous Japanese take on hip-hop crossed with aerobics, Yosakoi is far more exciting than the traditional *bon ōdōri* community dancing.

The Yosakoi Festival is based on the Koichi Festival in Shikoku. Dancers perform to music based on *soran*, a Hokkaidō fisherman's folk song. Yosakoi usually starts the second week of June, and the main events take place over a long weekend.

14

---

department stores. It's also the place to find Hokkaidō specialties from melon confections to dried salmon and seaweed. ⊠ *Minami 3-jō, extending from Nishi 1 to 7, Chūō-ku.*

Clock Tower (Tokeidai). For millions of Japanese, this little white-clapboard Russian-style meeting house defines Sapporo, because it is used as the city's symbol on souvenir packaging. Now almost lost among the modern office blocks, it was the 1878 drill hall for the pioneer students of Sapporo Agricultural College (now Hokkaidō University). Inside are photographs and documents of city history and a clock from Boston. More entertainment is had outside, watching tourists backing up on a busy intersection to fit in everything into the camera frame. ⊠ *Kita 1-jō Nishi 2, Chūō-ku* 🎫 ¥200 🕐 *Tues. Sat. 9 5.*

❷ **Botanical Gardens** (Shokubutsu-en). With more than 5,000 plant varieties, the gardens are a cool summer retreat, both for their green space and their shade. Nonplant highlights include a small Ainu Museum with a grisly but fascinating 13-minute film of an Ainu bear-killing ceremony in Asahikawa in 1935, and a large taxidermied huskie dog shares a room with bears and an Ezo wolf. This glassy-eyed hound is—was—Taro, one of the canine survivors of the abandoned 1958 Antarctic expedition, a story brought to non-Japanese audiences in the Disney movie *Eight Below*. After his ordeal, Taro retired to Hokkaidō University and died in 1970. ⊠ *Kita 3-jō Nishi 8, Chūō-ku* ☎ *May–Oct., gardens and greenhouse ¥400; Nov.–Apr., gardens free, greenhouse ¥110* ⊙ *Apr.–Sept., daily 9–4; Oct.–Nov., daily 9–3:30; Dec.–Mar., weekdays 9–5.*

❼ Nakajima Kōen (Nakajima Park). This green escape is a 10-minute walk beyond Susukino's lights and contains **Hōheikan**, a white-and-blue Russian-influenced 19th-century imperial guest house, **Hassō-an Teahouse**, a simple 17th-century teahouse in a Japanese garden, a boating lake, and the concert hall Kitara, home of the Pacific Music Festival, started in 1990 by Leonard Bernstein.

Elsewhere in Sapporo

★ ⓒ **Historical Village of Hokkaidō** (Kaitaku-no-mura). Step out of your shoes and into the 19th century at the herring-fleet dormitory where 60 fishermen appear to have just folded up their futons and left for a day's work, or the village clinic where Dr. Kondo seems to have vanished, leaving his scary-looking birthing table and books behind. It's easy to spend a few hours walking in and out of 60 homes, shops, farms, and offices brought from all over Hokkaidō in a park museum that shows how ordinary people lived and worked. A ride down main street in a horse-drawn trolley (summer) or sleigh (winter) costs ¥200. Ask for the excellent, free, blue-colored English guide at the ticket counter. The village is about 10 km (6 mi) outside Sapporo; easiest access is an hour bus ride (¥260) from Sapporo Station on a Japan Rail Bus or a 10-minute taxi ride from Shin-Sapporo Station. ⊠ *1–50–1 Konopporo, Atsubetsu-chō, Atsubetsu-ku* ☎ *011/898–2692* ☎ *¥830* ⊙ *Tues.–Sun. 9:30–4:30.*

Historical Museum of Hokkaidō (Kaitaku Kinenkan). From mammoth molars on through Ainu and samurai-farmers, to bulky 1950s home electronics—the history of Hokkaidō is meticulously exhibited in glass-case and map displays, which are dry compared to the people's history in the Historical Village 10 minutes away. But this is a thorough overview of how Meiji Japan realized it had a northern island rich in coal, fish, and agricultural oportunities. The village and museum are linked by a free shuttle bus on Sundays, and the public bus from Sapporo stops at the museum first. ⊠ *Konopporo, Atsubetsu-chō, Atsubetsu-ku* ☎ *011/898–0456* ☎ *¥450* ⊙ *Tues.–Sat. 9:30–4:30.*

Hokkaidō Shrine (Hokkaidō Jingu). Wash your hands and mouth at the stone basin first, then step up the gray stone steps. This 1871 Shintō shrine houses three gods deemed helpful in Hokkaidō's development: the gods of land and nature, of land development, and of healing. Sapporo families bring babies, children, anxious students, young engaged couples, even cars for Shintō ceremonies. In May this is Sapporo's main *hanami* (cherry-blossom) venue. It's a 15-minute walk from Maruyama Subway Station and shares the park with the zoo. ⊠ *Maruyama Kōen, Chūō-ku.*

The Beer

SAPPORO MEANS BEER to drinkers around the world, and what would a visit to the city of the same name be without a little beer research?

Head to Sapporo Beer Museum, 2 km (1 mi) northeast of Sapporo Station for a cursory history lesson in the redbrick former factory, and then to the neighboring Biergarten, where waiters in a cavernous noisy hall will rush to get a glass of the golden brew into your hands. Raise your glass— *Kampai*!

If you are in town in July and early August, join Sapporo Beer and other companies at the Sapporo Beer Garden festival in Ōdōri Park in the city center: every night for three weeks hundreds of revelers sit out under the trees with beer kegs and snacks, while musicians provide distraction on outdoor stages. The faithful can do the factory tour and tasting at Hokkaidō Brewery at Eniwa, near New Chitose Airport, where guides (Japanese-language only) show the brewing process.

Brewmaster Seibei Nakagawa spent two years at the Berliner Brauerai studying German know-how and returned ready to put it all into practice. The first brewery was at the current Sapporo Factory shopping mall, and Sapporo Reisi (cold) Beer, with a red-and-black label bearing the red star symbol of the Kaitakushi first went on sale in 1877.

Toriaizu biru! (First, beer!) is chorused at parties, beer-hall barbecues, and campsite cookouts. Sapporo Beer dominates the market, but microbreweries offer interesting alternatives. Look for local brews *ji-biru*, particularly Otaru (factory tour available), Hakodate, and Taisetsu.

14

Sapporo Beer Garden and Museum (Sapporō Biiru en). Redbrick buildings overshadowed by a giant shopping mall make up the public face of Sapporo's most famous export. The original brewery buildings are at another nearby mall, Sapporo Factory, and now brewing takes place near Chitose Airport. At the north-of-downtown site a small museum with mostly Japanese-only information shows the development of bottle and label designs, and beer-poster pin-up ladies over the ages. For ¥100 for one kind or ¥400 for three, visitors can taste the brews—Black Label is most popular, Classic is only available in Hokkaidō, and the original brew of Kaitakushi uses local hops.

In the evening the cavernous Sapporo Biergarten is filled with the cries of "*Kampai!*"—"Bottoms up!"—as serious drinkers tackle the *tabe-nomi hodai* (all you can eat and drink) feast of lamb barbecue and beer (¥3,570 per head). Recent menu additions include fish and vegetable dishes in a bid to attract more female customers.

Free tours of Hokkaidō Brewery, the brewing center a 20-minute local train ride from Chitose Airport, are available all year. Tours (only in Japanese, but English signage) last 60 minutes and start at 9, 10, and 11 AM and 1, 2 and 3 PM. Visitors receive a free beer at tour end. No reservations are necessary except for large groups.

To get to the Sapporo Beer Garden and Museum, take a 15-minute Sapporo Walk circular bus from the station or Ōdōri area (the same bus also stops at Sapporo Factory mall) or a ¥1,000 taxi ride. Hokkaido Brewery is served by Chūō Bus and trains stopping at Sapporo Beer Teien Station on the Chitose-Sapporo line. ⊠ *Sapporo Beer Garden and Museum, Kita 7-jō Higashi 9, Higashi-ku* ☎ *011/731–4368 museum, 011/ 742–1531 restaurant* ⊕ *www.sapporobeer.jp* 🎫 *Free* ☉ *Museum Sept.–May, daily 9–5; June–Aug., daily 8:40–6, last entry 80 min before closing; beer garden May–Sept., daily 11–9:30; Oct.–Apr., daily 11–8:45.* ⊠ *Hokkaidō Brewery, 542-1 Toiso, Eniwa City* ☎ *0123/ 32–5811* 🎫 *Free* ☉ *Daily 9–11:45 and 1–3:50, no tours on weekends Nov. to Apr. and public holidays.*

Sapporo Winter Sports Museum. Leap off a ski jump into the freezing air and land like a pro—or not. A realistic simulator has visitors comparing jump distances and style in the museum with a body-on approach at the base of the Olympic Ōkura Jump. The 1972 Winter Oympics and other Japanese sporting successes in skating, curling and many forms of skiing are celebrated with displays interesting even to non-sporting types. Outside the museum, take the chairlift to the top of the real jump 300 meters above the city with a chilling view of what jumpers face before take-off. Take a 15-minute bus ride from Maruyama Bus Terminal, City Bus Nishi 14 (¥200). ⊠ *1274 Miyanomori, Chūō-ku* ☎ *011/ 641–1972* 🎫 *¥600* ☉ *May–Oct., daily 9–6; Nov.–Apr., daily 9:30–5.*

Where to Eat

The greatest concentration of restaurants for nighttime dining is in the entertainment district of Susukino; good daytime choices are in the downtown department stores and the JR station. Formal dining rooms and coffee shops in all the major hotels serve Western-influenced foods, Italian and French fare being the most common. Most larger hotels have one Japanese restaurant and a Chinese restaurant.

Hokkaidō is known for its ramen, and Sapporo for its miso ramen. The city has more than 1,000 ramen shops, so it's not hard to find a noodle lunch. Tourist information still trumpets **Ramen Yoko-chō,** a small alley in Susukino packed with three dozen tiny ramen shops. Now it's only popular with map-clutching older Japanese. Younger Japanese use their mobile phones and the Internet for the latest "best" ramen and form hour-long lines outside the restaurant of the moment.

$$$–$$$$ ✕ **Daruma.** Below the sign with a roly-poly red doll, this 40-year-old establishment serves the freshest lamb barbecue *jingisukan* (¥700 a plate). At the end of the meal you're given hot tea to mix with the dipping sauce remaining from your meat. You drink the tea and sauce together: delicious! Be sure to wear your least favorite clothes, and don a paper bib. ⊠ *Crystal Bldg., Minami 5 Nishi 4, Chūō-ku* ☎ *011/552–6013* ⊜ *Reservations not accepted* ☰ *No credit cards* ☉ *Closed Mon.* ⊠ *Noguchi Bldg., Minami 6 Nishi 4, Susukino* ☎ *011/533–8929* ⊜ *Reservations not accepted* ☰ *No credit cards* ☉ *Closed Tues.*

★ **$$$–$$$$** ✕ **Kani Honke.** This crab-eating haven serves raw, steamed, boiled, and baked crustaceans from the Hokkaidō (or Russian) seas. The waitress will tell you whether the *ke-gani* (hairy crab), *taraba* (king crab), or *tzuwai-kani* (snow crab) is in season. The menu is in English and has photographs, so it's easy to choose from the set dinners, which start at ¥2,000. Wooden beams, tatami mats, and traditional decorations provide an authentic setting for the feast. There are two restaurants, one near the station and the other in Susukino. ⊠ *Station branch, Kita 3, Nishi 2* ☎ *011/222-0018* ⊠ *Susukino, Minami 6, Nishi 4* ☎ *011/551-0018* ⊟ *AE, DC, MC, V.*

★ $$$–$$$$ ✕ **Sushi-zen.** The fresh fish is so good that even the sushi-adverse may fall in love with it. Sushi-zen operates three restaurants and a delivery service. To taste the best at bargain prices, visit the Maruyama branch the third Wednesday of every month—when the trainee chefs' sushi is available for ¥200 apiece. ⊠ *Kita 1 Nishi 27, Maruyama, Chūō-ku* ☎ *011/644-0071* ⊠ *109 Bldg., Minami 4 Nishi 5, Chūō-ku* ☎ *011/521-0070* ⊠ *Minami 7 Nishi 4, Chūō-ku* ☎ *011/531-0069* ⊟ *AE, DC, MC, V* ⊘ *Closed Wed.*

¢–$$ ✕ **Zazi.** A casual downtown coffee shop with an English menu, this hangout is popular with students and expat customers. Favorites include the Power Lunch (¥1,000 for two fried eggs, sausages, potatoes, salad, and bread), generous spaghetti plates, one pot stews for ¥630, and homemade cakes. Only one busy cook works in the kitchen, so don't expect a speedy lunch. The restaurant opens at 10 AM. ⊠ *Minami 2-jō, Nishi 5, Chūō-ku* ☎ *011/221 0071* ⊟ *No credit cards.*

¢–$ ✕ **Keiyaki.** It's a mystery why some ramen restaurants are famous and millions are not. This ordinary-looking 10-stools-at-the-plastic-counter joint in Susukino has had lines of the faithful outside it for more than four years (an era in ramen shop terms) and is still chopping, boiling, and serving it's six-item menu: miso, *cha-shu* (pork slice), *negi* (long onion), butter corn, *karai* (spicy) *niniku* (garlic). There's even a branch in the Ramen Museum in Yokohama. At headquarters you order while standing in line outside, pay when you claim a counter spot, and then wait for the cook to hand down the steaming bowl (topped generously with vegetables) from the raised and hidden kitchen. Ahhh. Maybe then you'll deduce the secret of good ramen. ⊠ *Minami 6, Nishi 3, Susukino* ☎ *011/552-4601* ⊟ *No credit cards* ⊘ *Daily 11–11.*

Where to Stay

★ $$$$ ✕▢ **JR Tower Hotel Nikko Sapporo.** Sapporo's skyscraper over the station puts the city at your feet from small, modern rooms with cream and brown furnishings and throw pillows. Corner-room prices buy more space. Guests get a discount at the 22nd-floor super spa, where deep pools and big windows let you soak naked with a view in the hope that no office worker has a telescope. Tancho and Sky J (stylish ¥2,000 lunch buffet) on the 35th floor serve delicately arranged Japanese food and Continental cooking. Japanese chef Mikuni has a French restaurant and coffee shop in the Nikko, too. ⊠ *Sapporo Station JR Tower, Kita 5 Nishi 2, Chūō-ku, Sapporo 060-0005* ☎ *0120/58-2586 or 011/251-2222* 🖷 *011/251-6370* ⊕ *www.nikkohotels.com* ⇆ *350 Western-style rooms* ♨ *3 restaurants, café, patisserie, hair salon, massage, sauna, bar, Internet* ⊟ *AE, DC, MC, V.*

★ **$$$$** 🖼 **Sapporo Grand Hotel.** Classic European style with white-gloved bell-hops, first-rate service, and modern conveniences like room refrigerators tastefully hidden away in wooden cabinets, Sapporo's grand old hotel has welcomed guests since 1934. In the heart of downtown, the three buildings (Main, Annex, and East) almost fill a city block. Rooms in the older Main Building feel like gentlemen's-club rooms, with striped wall paper and small armchairs—and rooms in the restyled East Wing exhibit more modern flair. Standard rooms are average size, and closet space is limited. Specify when booking for requirements such as in-room broadband, room windows that open, or a double bed. In the Memorial Library check out photographs of VIP guests—Margaret Thatcher's thank you letter and the 1955 lunch menu for the visiting New York Yankees. ✉ *Kita 1-jō Nishi 4, Chūō-ku, Sapporo 060-0001* ☎ *011/261–3311* 🖨 *011/231–0388* ⊕ *www.mitsuikanko.co.jp/sgh* 🛏 *560 Western-style rooms* ⚮ *8 restaurants, 3 coffee shops, 2 bars, room service, in-room safes, minibars, cable TV, shops, Internet, business center, travel services, 3 no-smoking floors* ▭ *AE, DC, MC, V.*

★ **$$$–$$$$** 🖼 **Hotel Ōkura.** In the shopping heart of the city, one block from the Ōdōri subway station, the Ōkura gets the balance between style and the personal connection just right. Public areas are small, so the staff gets to know you quickly, while upstairs the rooms are spacious. Artful lighting, interior blinds, and a color scheme of browns and creams set a Japanese mood missing in many large hotels. Dining highlights include Cantonese dishes in Toh-Li—the ¥3,700 lunch set for couples is a good inexpensive choice—and the ¥3,600 afternoon tea with your own cake stand of goodies. 24-hour advance reservations are essential for the tea. ✉ *Nishi 5 Minami 1, Chūō-ku, Sapporo 060-0061* ☎ *011/221–2333* 🖨 *011/221–0819* ⊕ *www.hotelokura.co.jp/sapporo* 🛏 *147 Western-style rooms* ⚮ *3 restaurants, coffee shop, cable TV, hair salon, bar, shop, Internet, no-smoking floor* ▭ *AE, DC, MC, V.*

$$$ 🖼 **Nakamuraya Ryokan.** The small, family-run hotel is on a tree-lined street between government buildings near the botanical gardens. A large paper parasol decorates the lobby. Popular multibox lunches and dinner-in-your-room service help foreign guests enjoy quintessential Japanese hospitality, although anyone with multiple luggage may find the storage space limited. All six tatami rooms have small private bathrooms, and the large communal bath is a welcome comfort in winter. Now housed in a modern building, Nakamuraya Ryokan has been a business since 1898: the little boy in the sepia photograph in the lobby is the current owner's father. Basic English is spoken. ✉ *Kita 3-jō Nishi 7, Chūō-ku, Sapporo 060-0003* ☎ *011/241–2111* 🖨 *011/241–2118* 🛏 *29 Japanese-style rooms* ⚮ *Restaurant, minibars, Japanese baths* ▭ *AE, MC, V* ❍ *MAP.*

$ 🖼 **Hotel Maki.** Need a "Welcome back!" after sightseeing? Help with booking hotels ahead? The Inada family does their best with simple English. Hotel Maki is a change of style from the sterility of big-city hotels. Half the big tatami-mat rooms have private baths, and all have toilets and washbasins. There's also a general bath. The hotel is a favorite with out-of-town baseball and ski teams, who wolf down the extensive Japanese-style breakfast available for ¥900. It's in a quiet area five streetcar stops from Susukino or 10 minutes from Horohirabashi subway station. Simple English faxed reservations are best. ✉ *1–20 Minami 13 Nishi 7, Chuo ku, Sapporo 064-0913* ☎ *011/521–1930* 🖷 *011/531–6747* 🛏 *15 Japanese-style rooms* ⌂ *Dining room, Japanese baths; no a/c* ═ *No credit cards* ¶◉¶ *MAP.*

Nightlife

★ **Susukino**, Sapporo's entertainment district, is seven by seven mind-boggling blocks of neon and noise with more than 4,000 bars, nightclubs, and restaurants. Bars stay open late, some until 5 AM, though restaurants often close before midnight. Susukino mainly extends south of Route 36, although there are bars in the streets just north of the main road, too. The seedier alleys are mostly west of Station-mae-dori, but all of Susukino is safe.

On the Ōdōri side of Route 36, the road separating Susukino and Ōdōri, is **Slainte** (✉ Playtown Fuji Bldg., 8th fl., Minami 3-jō Nishi 3, Ōdōri ☎ 011/222–6801), with 13 seats at a quiet counter bar and a dangerously placed dartboard. You can find Japanese and foreign beers on tap, and 12 kinds of Irish whiskey. Slainte is open every evening 5–midnight. At **Saloon Maco** (✉ Asano Bldg., 2nd fl., Minami 3-jō Nishi 4, Ōdōri ☎ 011/222–1828), Stetson wearing Japanese staff (and drinkers) sing country and pop karaoke, fortified by a no-time-limit *nomi hodai* (all-you-can-drink plan) for ¥2,000. Pasta and salad dishes go for under ¥1,000. Look behind the JRA Building to find this bar.

Brian Brew (✉ FA-S3 Bldg., Minami 3-jō Nishi 3 ☎ 011/219–3556 ⊙ Daily 11:30 AM–1 AM) is an Irish pub serving Guinness and Kilkenny and foods for expats such as fish-and-chips and meat pies, open at lunchtime, too. Sporting events on big screen TVs.

British rock and roll is played in five nightly sets (first at 9.30 PM) by bar owner Kazuaki and his band at **Brits Beat Club** (✉ Green Bldg. No. 4, 2nd fl., Minami 5-jō Nishi 3, Susukino ☎ 011/531–8808 ⊕ www.brits.jp). The small bar serves cheap Brit fare, such as fish-and-chips and cottage pie, while the band plays everything from Beatles to Blur. There's a steep ¥2,100

DARS 101

Bars come in several kinds: clubs stocked with hostesses who make small talk (¥5,000 and up per hour, proving that talk is *not* cheap); *sunakku* bars (the word sounds like "snack," which translates into fewer hostesses and expensive *ōdoburu*–hors d'oeuvres); izakaya, for both Japanese and Western food and drink; bars with entertainment, either karaoke or live music; and "soapland" and *herusu* (health) massage parlors–generally off-limits to non-Japanese without an introduction. Signs that say NO CHARGE only mean that there's no charge to be seated; beware of hidden extras. Many bars add on charges for peanuts, female companionship, song, cold water, hand towels, etc. The term "free drink" refers to an all-you-can-drink special that costs money.

14

cover charge, and the bar is open nightly 8–4. Cheaper and popular with young, foreign English teachers is **Locotonte**. Friday night DJs make you sweat (¥2,000 men; ¥1,500 women) on a small dance floor to hip-hop and house music. (✉ Susukino Kaikan Bldg., 4th fl Minami 7-jō Nishi 4, Susukino ☎ 011/553–3728).

On Susukino's main street across from the temple, drinkers perch on high bar stools before the big windows at **Rad Brothers** (✉ Minami 7-jō Nishi 3 ☎ 011/561–3601). Perching on more expensive chairs a block away, and sipping Spanish wine are customers at **BAR españa** (✉ Minami 6 jō Nishi 3 ☎ 011/532–0001), which opens to the street if weather permits and offers a range of bar-eats and Mediterranean-inspired foods. There's a ¥500 cover charge.

Sapporo Essentials

AIR TRAVEL
No nonstop flights go from the United States to Hokkaidō. Passengers arriving in Japan on international flights with All Nippon Airways (ANA) and Japan Airlines (JAL) can get domestic discounted connections to Chitose. The Hokkaidō-based Air Do (rhymes with "who") often has the least expensive flights between Tōkyō and Sapporo. The company No. 1 Travel caters to foreigners and can offer good deals on domestic travel.

🛪 Airlines & Contacts **Air Do** ☎ 011/200–7333. **Japan Air System** ☎ 0120/711–283 international, 0120/511–283 domestic. **Japan Airlines** ☎ 0120/255–931 international, 0120/255–971, 011/232–3690 domestic. **Japan Travel Bureau** ☎ 011/241–6201. **No. 1 Travel** ☎ 011/251–3314 or 03/3205–6073 🖷 011/251–4607 ⊕ www.no1-travel.com.

AIRPORTS & TRANSFERS
Sapporo's New Chitose Airport (Shin-Chitose Kūkō), 40 km (25 mi) south of the city, is Hokkaidō's main airport. More than 30 domestic routes link Chitose to the rest of Japan, and flights from Chitose to other parts of Asia are increasing. Some local flights also depart from Okudama Airport, 5 km north of downtown.

🛪 Airport Information **New Chitose Airport** ☎ 0123/23–0111.

AIRPORT TRANSFERS Japan Railways (JR) runs every 20 minutes or so between the airport terminal and downtown Sapporo. (Shin-Chitose Kūkō Station is the final eastbound stop from Sapporo; do not get off at the Chitose or Minami Chitose stations if you want the airport) The trip is usually made by rapid-transit train (¥1,040, 40 minutes). Hokuto Bus runs a shuttle bus (¥820) that connects with ANA flights at Chitose and its hotel, the ANA Zennikku, in Sapporo, first stopping at the Renaissance and Sunroute hotels. Chūō Bus (¥820) runs a shuttle between the airport and Sapporo's Grand Hotel, also stopping at Ōdōri Kōen, JR Sapporo Station, and the Korakuen, Royton, and Keio Plaza hotels. These buses reach the airport in less than an hour, though you should allow more time in winter. Taxis are available, but ridiculously expensive.

🚌 **Hukuto Bus** ☎ 011/377–3855.

BUS TRAVEL

Local bus fares begin at ¥200. Buses follow the grid system and run until shortly after 11 PM. Sapporo buses have no English schedules, and bus-stand information is in Japanese. However, two circular routes connect many of the main sites. The Factory Line—bus stops are confusingly marked "Sapporo Walk"—connects downtown shops, the train station, the fish market, Sapporo Factory, and the Sapporo Beer Garden. The Sansaku or Stroller Bus (May to October only) connects downtown with Maruyama Park and Okurayama Jump Hill. Rides on both cost ¥200 each time or ¥750 for a day pass. In summer a ¥1,200 day pass gives unlimited rides on both circular bus lines as well as a one-way ticket to Shin-Chitose Airport. Tickets are available on the buses or from Chūō Bus counter at the JR station or bus terminal.

⨍ Bus Information Chūō Bus ☎ 011/231-0500.

CAR TRAVEL

Public transportation makes renting a car for Sapporo sightseeing unnecessary, but it's a good place to rent for setting out into the national parks. Major car companies are clustered around Sapporo Station, on arrival reservations for next day departure are possible outside Golden Week in early May and school summer holidays in August.

ROAD
CONDITIONS
Check the latest weather, construction information, and plan driving routes and times with the information-packed English Web site of Northern Road, a group of regional government road research groups. ⊕ northern-road.jp/navi/english.

⨍ Road Conditions ☎ 011/281-6511.

STREETCARS

Sapporo has a streetcar service with a flat fare of ¥170. However, it's confined to a single line connecting Susukino with Moiwa-yama in the city's southwest corner—well away from most of the sights mentioned in this section. The city has made its streetcars available for parties, and you may see the vehicles trundling across town with revelers on board.

SUBWAYS

Sapporo's subways have rubber wheels that run quietly, and most signs include English. There are three lines: the Namboku Line runs south from JR Sapporo Station past Susukino to Nakajima Kōen; the Tōzai Line bisects the city from east to west. These two cross at Ōdōri Station. The third, the Tōhō Line, enters central Sapporo from the southeast, then parallels the Namboku Line from Ōdōri Station to the JR station before branching off into the northeastern suburbs.

The basic fare, covering a distance of about three stations, is ¥200. A one-day open ticket (*ichi-nichi-ken*) for ¥1,000 provides unlimited subway (¥800 for the subway alone), bus, and streetcar access; a ¥700 Eco-ticket (*ekokippu*), intended to encourage residents to leave their cars at home, covers the same three types of public transport on the 5th and 20th of every month. Tickets are available at subway stations and at the Ōdōri Station Underground Commuters' Ticket Office, open weekdays 8:30–7, weekends 10–5:30. Prepaid cards (¥1,000, ¥3,000, ¥5,000, and ¥10,000 at vending machines) automatically debit the appropriate amount when you've reached your destination and give you a 10% discount. Subway trains stop running at midnight.

TRAIN TRAVEL

All JR trains arrive at the central station, on the north side of downtown Sapporo. Trains depart for Honshū about every two hours. The route sometimes involves a change of trains in Hakodate. As many as six trains per hour run to and from Otaru and east. Every half hour from 7 AM to 10 PM trains run north to Asahikawa.

EMERGENCIES

🚑 **Ambulance** ☎ 119. **Hokkaidō University Hospital** ⊠ Kita 14-jō Nishi 5, Sapporo ☎ 011/716-1161. **Nighttime Emergency Hospital** ⊠ Ōdōri Nishi 16, Ōdōri, Sapporo ☎ 011/641-4316. **Police** ☎ 110. **Sapporo City General Hospital** ⊠ Kita 11-jō Nishi 13, Sōen Station, Sapporo ☎ 011/726-2211.

TOURS

Escorted tours with English interpreters are available from Nippon Travel Agency Company. Buses or taxis are used depending on customer numbers, and prices range from ¥5,000 for a two-hour city tour to a ¥25,500-a-head traditional dinner and night-view plan. Nextage Inc. also offers taxi or minibus personalized tours from Sapporo (with or without guides) bookable via its Web site. Skybus, popular with skiers and boarders for airport to Niseko runs or airport to Sapporo door-to-door service connections, also has charter rates for sightseeing tours.

🚆 **Nippon Travel Agency** ☎ 011/207-5533. **Nextage Inc.** ☎ 011/210-7255 ⊕ www11.ocn. ne.jp. **Skybus** ⊕ www.skybus-jp.com.

OTARU & NISEKO

West of Sapporo, Meiji-era stone warehouses line a canal lighted at night by glowing lamps and bustling by day with rickshaw runners and sightseeers. An easy day trip by train from Sapporo, Otaru is a small, touristy port city facing the Japan Sea. Its herring-fishing heyday between the 1870s and 1930s created the riches that built the banks, warehouses, and grand houses that give the city its historical visage.

The Niseko area lies over the mountains and extends into the hinterland, where the perfect cone-shaped Mount Yōtei is surrounded by farms (fruits, potatoes, pumpkins, corn), villages, and hot springs. In winter this is one of Japan's leading ski areas, while from May to October outdoors enthusiasts enjoy river rafting and hiking. Niseko is best experienced by car over two or three days. Adventure tours should be booked in advance.

Otaru

★ ❽ *50 min west of Sapporo by JR, 40 km (25 mi) west of Sapporo by car.*

Otaru nets its wealth in tourists these days, rather than herring, but the canal where barges used to land the shimmering silver catch is still the center of action for the thousands of domestic and Asian visitors reeled in by images of a romantic weekend retreat. Gaijin from countries with 19th-century stone buildings may be less impressed by the tourist strip along the canal, but rent a bike or walk away from the main drag and you can explore quaint neighborhoods and interesting buildings.

Getting Around
Otaru makes a good base for touring around Hokkaidō by car. **Toyota Car Rental** (☎ 0134/27-0100), open daily 8 AM to 8 PM, is near Otaru Station. **Nippon Rentacar** (☎ 0134/32-0919), open daily 8:30 AM to 7 PM, is downtown. Neither agency has an English-speaking staff, so ask the tourist office or your hotel to help with reservations.

The **Otaru Tourist Office** (☎ 0134/29-1333) is to the left of the ticket gates inside the station. It's open daily 9–6, and has room availability lists from hotels. English is basic, but they try hard. The **Unga Plaza Tourist Office** (☎ 0134/33-1661), by the canal, has city information and leaflets for further travel. From the station, walk down the main street for eight blocks; the office is in the stone buildings on the left before the canal.

What to See
The canal and **Sakai-machi Street Historic District** are sandwiched between a contemporary shopping area and a busy port eight blocks downhill from the station. A one day pass (¥750) on the replica trolley is a useful energy-saver; and sun-burned rickshaw runners offer tours starting at ¥3,000 for two people. A 25-minute, ¥550 boat trip from the harbor dock just beyond the canal or a 20-minute, ¥200 bus ride from the station (Bus No. 3) to the Otaru Aquarium area, which includes a rocky peninsula and historic fishing houses, is a good way to start sightseeing. Alternatively, rent a bicycle (about ¥400 an hour) on the right three blocks south of the station and enjoy the quiet, but hilly backstreets.

In the port you'll see Russian, Chinese, and Korean (North as well as South) ships loaded up with used cars, bicycles, and refrigerators, ferries heading off to Niigata, and sightseeing boats in summer. The Russian presence is quite noticeable—one telephone booth even has a helpful area code list for sailors calling home.

☕ **Otaru Canal Glass Factory** (✉ Ironai 2-1-19 ☎ 0134/29-1112 ⊕ www. otaru-glass.com/english/index 🎫 Free to factory shop ☉ Oct.–Mar., daily 9.30–6; Apr.–Sept., daily 9–7). Blow your own beer glass in the heat of the sandblasting room, shot through with the color of your choice (beer glasses ¥2,310 and tumblers ¥1,890). 19th-century Otaru craftsmen made glass buoys and gas lamps for the fishing fleets. Ten minutes is all you need to make your drinking vessel. Reservations in advance are necessary, and creations are ready the next day after cooling, or can be forwarded both domestically and internationally for a ¥2,000 extra charge. Children over 10 are welcome to try their hand in the furnace room.

★ **Herring Mansion** (Nishin Goten). Herring fishermen ate, slept, and dreamt of riches in this 1897 working base of a fishery boss and his crew. On display are kitchen appliances, nets, and mislaid personal items of the men who toiled. Photographs of the Otaru coastline lined with ships and beaches piled high with fish reveal how the herring heydays brought riches to some, and put a serious dent in the Pacific fish stocks. ⊠ *3–228 Shukutsu* ☎ *0134/ 22–1038* 🖂 *¥200* ⊙ *Apr.–Nov., daily 9–5.*

Where to Stay & Eat

$$–$$$ ✕ **Otaru Souko No. 1.** "Prost!" with a brimming glass of one of Otaru's own microbrews—Japanese favorite Pilsener, the darker Dunkel, or the fruity Weiss, all made from German barley. Grilled crab legs *taraba-gani-no-aburi-yaki* help the beer go down for ¥2,394, or try a Hokkaidō twist on the Japanese classic by cooking thin strips of lamb in a beer broth, called *Ramu-shabu-donkeru* (¥1,764). The 60-minute all-you-can-drink plan costs ¥2,100, and a 30-minute musical stage show performs twice a night in the Bavarian-themed, canal-side stone-warehouse beer hall. ⊠ *5–4 Minato-machi* ☎ *0134/21–2323* 🖃 *AE, MC, V.*

THE HOUSE THAT HERRING BUILT

Aoyama Villa (Aoyama Bettei). Gorgeous, gold-painted sliding doors and dark lacquered floors testify to the huge wealth of fishing millionaires the Aoyamas. Teenage daughter Masae came home from a trip to another rich family in Honshū with big ideas about how her family could spend its fortune, and in 1917 her father commissioned the chief imperial carpenter and a team of top craftsmen to create a home and garden of sumptuousness rare in Hokkaidō. Take bus No. 3 from the station to the Shukutsu 3-chōme bus stop, then walk up the hill for about half a mile. ⊠ *Shukutsu 3-63* ☎ *0134/24–0024* 🖂 *¥1,000* ⊙ *Apr.-Oct., daily 9-6; Nov.-Mar., daily 9-5.*

¢–$$$ ✕ **Takeda.** Crab legs dripping juice, and darkly gleaming red salmon eggs piled high on a bowl of rice are just some of Otaru's famous raw-fish options at this small family restaurant in the middle of the noisy fish market, just up the steps to the left of the station. The *Omakase-don* at ¥2,500 somehow gets eight kinds of fish into one bowl, while anyone hoping to still manage some sightseeing after lunch may prefer crab soup (¥ 200) and one portion of fish (¥400). Open 7–4. ⊠ *Sankaku Market, Otaru Station* 🖃 *No credit cards.*

$$ ✕ **Kita Hōru.** You probably can't write postcards in the gloom, but chances are you won't want to. In the cavernous dining room of a former herring warehouse, oil lamps and their reflection off the glassware dimly illuminate the heavy circular tables and beer-barrel seating. Fish and rice dishes are the mainstays, or you can order coffee and cakes from the atmosphere-jarring self-service machine at the entrance. ⊠ *7–26 Sakai-machi* ☎ *0134/33–1993* 🖃 *No credit cards.*

¢ ✕ **Kita-no Ice Cream.** Beer ice cream anyone? Maybe you'd prefer sake ice cream—or squid, cherry-blossom, or pumpkin? This Otaru institution serves up 20 varieties from a shop in an 1892 warehouse in an alleyway one block from the canal. ⊠ *Ironai 1-chōe* ☎ *0134/23–8983* 🖃 *No credit cards.*

★ $$$–$$$$ ✕🖾 **Otaru Hilton.** The 18 floors of this hotel rise above the redbrick Wing-Bay complex, one of the largest shopping malls in Japan, with innumerable shops, seven movie theaters, a hot spring, restaurants galore, and a Ferris wheel outside. Otherwise the location is unattractive; the hotel is between the railroad and a harbor wall, 2 km (1 mi) on foot from the historic district. Western-style rooms in calming hues of gold, blue, and brown have large twin or double beds, and most overlook the marina. Amenities include excellent meals by guest chefs from other hotels in the group (the on-site Marina Restaurant is a favorite with local foodies), and a trolley stop just outside. Early booking and a best-rate guarantee can produce competitive rates, depending on the season. ⊠ *11–3 Otaru Chikkō, Otaru 047-0008* ☏ *0134/21–3111, 0120/48–9852 toll-free* 🖷 *0134/21–3322* ⊕ *www.hilton.com* ➥ *289 Western-style rooms* ⚲ *3 restaurants, café, patisserie, cable TV, 2 bars, Internet, no-smoking floors* ▤ *AE, DC, MC, V.*

★ **$$$–$$$$** 🏨 **Authent Hotel.** A former department store was reborn as an elegant city-center hotel in the heart of the downtown shopping area. The lobby's cream upholstery and yellow walls are echoed in the rooms, which have larger than usual bathrooms. Kaio is a small *teppanyaki* restaurant, and the 11th-floor piano bar has city views from the curved front of the building. ⊠ *15–1, Inaho 2, Otaru 047-0032* ☏ *0134/24–8100* 🖷 *0134/27–8118* ⊕ *www.authent.co.jp* ➥ *190 Western-style rooms, 5 Japanese-style rooms* ⚲ *3 restaurants, café, Japanese baths, bar, piano bar, 2 shops, Internet, no-smoking rooms* ▤ *AE, DC, MC, V.*

$–$$$$ 🏨 **Hotel Furukawa.** Dark wooden beams, shadowy corridors, and antiques transform a modern canal-side building into a comfortable, old-fashioned Japanese inn—a rarity in Otaru. The traditionally clad staff bows low on the raised straw matting in the reception area, and the first-floor restaurant has an outdoor terrace for sunset drinks with a canal view. The charm of the public areas is slightly marred by the small, faintly tobacco-smelling rooms that look out over the canal (and the road) or back to the city, but the eighth-floor Japanese bathroom has a one-person-sized whisky barrel perfect for outdoor soaking. ⊠ *1–2–15 Ironai, 047–0031* ☏ *0134–29–2345* 🖷 *0134/25–3331* ➥ *43 Western-style rooms, 1 Japanese-style room, 2 suites* ⚲ *Restaurant* ▤ *AE, MC, V.* ⒣ *EP.*

Niseko

★ ➈ *2 hrs, 10 min southwest of Otaru by JR.*

For the best skiing in Hokkaidō, head for Niseko. This is boomsville for Australian leisure developers with foreign-owned holiday homes and apartments shooting up everywhere, particularly in Hirafu village. Direct flights between Chitose and Cairns from November to April have revitalized Niseko, which had its heyday with Japanese skiers in the 1970s.

Between the skiing and boarding on Mt. Annupuri and the conical Mt. Yōtei is a gentle landscape of hot springs, dairy and vegetable farms, artists' workshops, and hiking trails. The Japanese love the outdoor farm and nature attractions, but the adventure-sport opportunities are the real reason to come. Outdoor-adventure companies run by Australian and Canadian expats offer year-round thrills, including rafting (best from April to May), backcountry skiing, mountain biking, and bungee jumping. The Niseko area is hands-down the best place to discover the Hokkaidō countryside, and it's easy to find an English-speaking guide.

The town of Kutchan is the gateway to the Niseko area, and is served by trains from Sapporo. From Kutchan you can switch to trains heading for the villages of Hirafu or Niseko, where many pensions and hotels offer pick-up services from the stations. The best hotels and almost all adventure companies are at Hirafu village.

Getting Around

Niseko is a 2½-hour drive from New Chitose Airport. From November to May public buses go from the airport to the Niseko ski resorts several times a day. In July and August Chūō Bus Company has two buses a day. The one-way trip costs ¥2,300.

From Sapporo you can drive to Niseko in two hours. Trains depart hourly for Kutchan; the trip takes two hours and costs ¥1,790. You may have to switch trains in Otaru. From Kutchan seven trains a day go to the Hirafu and Niseko villages, where most hotels and guesthouses are. Hotel staffs can pick up guests at the stations, and most will drive guests to the trailheads and ski lifts. You can also rent a car in Niseko. **Nippon Rental Car** (✉ 247–7 Aza-Soga ☎ 0136/43–2929) is open from April to October, daily 9–6, and from November to March, daily 9–5. **Mazda Rent–A–Car 9–5** (✉ 74–4 Aza-Honchō ☎ 0136/44–1188) is open daily 9–5. Both agencies are a five-minute walk from the station.

To the right of the ticket gate at the JR Kutchan Station is the excellent **Kutchan Tourist Association Tourist Office** (Kutchan Kankō Kyōkai no Kankō Annai-sho ✉ Minami 1-jō Nishi 4-chōme, Kutchan-chō ☎ 0136/22–5151). The **Niseko Tourism Office** (✉ JR Niseko Station ☎ 0136/44–2468 ⊕ www.niseko.gr.jp) also has maps and information.

Hiking

Head for **Yōtei-zan** (Mt. Yōtei). Climbing this Fuji look-alike takes four hours. Two trails lead up the mountain: the more challenging **Hirafu Course** and the easier but still arduous **Makkari Course**. Regardless of your approach, you'll find wildflowers in summer, and elderly Japanese chomping on bamboo shoots that grow wild on the hills. A hut at the top provides crude lodging. To get to the trails, take the bus from JR Kutchan Station 20 minutes to Yōtei To-zan-guchi (hiking trail entrance) for the Hirafu Course or 40 minutes to the Yōtei Shinzan Kōen stop for the Makkari Course.

Skiing

From November to May skiers and snowboarders enjoy 61 courses covering 47 km (30 mi) of powder in the Niseko area. There are five ski resorts, but the big three are Grand Hirafu, Higashiyama, and Annupuri. You can ski them all with a Niseko All-Mountain Pass costing ¥4,800 for one day or ¥8,800 for two days. Only the very top is above the tree line, and reaching Hirafu's big, off-trail bowl entails a 30-minute trek above the top chairlift. Nondrivers coming from Sapporo can buy package ski tours, including lunch and transportation by bus, for about ¥4,500. You can book tours at almost any city hotel. If you're driving to Niseko, check Sapporo convenience stores for discount lift tickets.

Annupuri Resort (☎ 0136/58–2080) has wide, gently sloping runs that are kind to beginners and shaky intermediates. Day passes cost ¥4,400. **Higashiyama Resort** (☎ 0136/44–1111), based at the Prince Hotel, has a super-fast cable car that takes you to beautifully designed forested courses. You descend through the trees to the mountain base. Day passes cost ¥4,000. **Grand Hirafu** (☎ 0136/22–0109) is the largest of the Niseko ski resorts, with 34 courses, 27% of which are classed "expert." The longest run is more than 5 km (3 mi) long. A day pass costs ¥4,900. Check out **www.niseko.ne.jp**, **www.grand-hirafu.jp** and **www.snowjapan. com** for snow reports and other information on skiing in Niseko.

Outfitters

Niseko Adventure Centre (☎ 0136/23–2093 ⊕ www.nac-web.com). In addition to river trips, mountain biking, and winter sports, the center has an indoor rock-climbing wall at its village-center base. **Scott Adventures** (☎ 0136/21–3333 ⊕ www.sas-net.com) has rafting trips popular with school groups. The company also arranges hot-air ballooning, fishing, snowshoeing, and dogsled riding with a team of huskies.

Where to Stay & Eat

¢–$$ ✕ **Izakiya Bang Bang.** *Yakitori* (sizzling meats on wood skewers) and other Hokkaidō favorites, such as salmon and herring, keep company with menu imports like spare ribs and tacos. Your dining neighbors could become tomorrow's skiing or adventure-tour buddies, and your pension's staff may enjoy their evenings off here. In Hirafu Village, Izakiya Bang Bang is definitely the place to be. English translations are on the menu. ✉ *188–27 Aza Yamada, Hirafu* ☎ *0136/22–4292* ⊕ *www.niseko.or. jp/bangbang* ☰ *MC, V* ⊗ *Closed Wed. No lunch.*

¢–$$ ✕ **Jo-Jo's.** Platters overflow with juicy hamburgers and generous salads, followed by home-baked cakes smothered in cream—power food for adventurists. A spacious laid-back restaurant on the second floor of the Niseko Adventure Center, it's all soaring beams and big windows looking out to Yōtei-zan. Open all day and busy with adventure guides and their nervous or elated customers. On the right, off the main road arriving in Hirafu village from Kutchan. ✉ *53–79 Aza Yamada, Hirafu, Kutchan* ☎ *0136/23–2093.*

$$$–$$$$ ⌂ **Hotel Niseko Alpen.** Slap-dab at the base of Grand Hirafu ski slopes is a modern hotel with English speakers to help plan a Niseko stay. The rooms are disappointingly like airport sleepover places, but nobody comes to Niseko to sit in a hotel room. The hotel hot springs have an outdoor pool with views of Yōtei-zan, and guests with any energy left after skiing, rafting, hiking, or mountain biking can use the 25-meter indoor pool or the stone-bed sauna. Front-desk staff can supply special modems for in-room broadband Internet connection. ✉ *Yamada 204, Hirafu, Kutchan* ☎ *0136/22–1105* ☐ *0136/23–2202* ⊕ *www.grand-hirafu.jp* ⊅ *72 Western-style rooms, 39 combination rooms* ⚑ *2 restaurants, tea lounge, pool, sauna, spa, shops* ☰ *AE, DC, MC, V* ⎮⊙⎮ *EP, MAP.*

$ ⌂ **Grand Papa.** In keeping with Niseko's wishful claim to be the St. Moritz of Asia, this Alpine-style pension in Hirafu village has lots of dark wood and red carpeting. The owners are exceptionally friendly. Nikawara-san is a woodcut artist and alpenhorn player, Yoko used to be a British

Airways flight attendant, and son Kohei is a ski instructor. Rooms are simple, and only three have private bathrooms. Everyone heads to Yukou hot spring (¥600) just minutes away on foot; the truly exhausted use the pension's shared public bath. After a dinner of Swiss cheese fondue, retire to Grand Papa's snug bar. ✉ *163 Hirafu, Niseko 044-0081* ☎ *0136/23–2244* 🖷 *0136/23–2255* ⊕ *niseko-grandpapa.com* ⤶ *17 Western-style rooms, 3 with bath; 2 Japanese-style rooms without bath* ♨ *Dining room, mountain bikes, bar, Internet* 🖃 *MC, V* 🍽 *BP.*

¢–$ 🏠 **Ryū's Inn**. Stay at this tiny, simply furnished house in the middle of the fields near the Higashiyama ski area if you want to be adopted by owners Ryū and Eriko Yasui. Ryū, who once worked in London's Dorchester Hotel, is a passionate Niseko promoter, and he'll drive you to his favorite hot springs, recommend restaurants, and tell you about Niseko's craft workshops. Dinners are by reservation, and there is a shared bathroom. ✉ *744–2 Soga, Niseko 048-1522* ☎ *0136/44–3265* ⊕ *www. niseko.gr.jp* ⤶ *4 Western-style rooms with shared bath* ♨ *Dining room, Japanese baths, ski storage, bar, free parking; no a/c, no room phones, no room TVs* 🖃 *AE, MC, V* 🍽 *BP.*

SHIKOTSU-TŌYA NATIONAL PARK

Mountains, forests, caldera lakes, hot-spring resorts, and volcanoes are virtually in Sapporo's backyard. Less than an hour from Sapporo, Route 230 passes the large hot-spring village Jozankei, then the mountains close in, the road climbs to Nakayama Pass at 2,742 feet. On a clear day the view from the top is classic Hokkaidō—farmland with the stately Mount Yōtei in its midst, and on the horizon to the south Lake Tōya's volcanic crater and Noboribetsu hot springs, where the earth steams, rumbles, and erupts.

Tōya-ko

★ *2½ hrs southwest of Sapporo by bus.*

At lunchtime on March 28, 2000, Usu-zan volcano exploded for the first time in 23 years and shot a 10,500-foot-high cloud of ash and smoke into the skies over the quiet resort town of Lake Tōya. About 16,000 farmers, hoteliers, and townspeople evacuated. Earth tremors cracked open the north–south expressway and ash flows engulfed the outskirts of the town. Lake Tōya exploded into the headlines. Amazingly, by July everyone came back, cleaned up their town, and reopened for business with still smoking craters in their midst.

Getting Around

Usu-zan is one of several peaks on Lake Tōya's crater, a huge volcanic rim that dominates the landscape. Route 230 from Sapporo drops over the northern edge, and Route 453 from Lake Shikotsu and Noboribetsu and roads from the coast come in from the south. Volcanic activity is centered around the small town of Tōya-ko Onsen, and a few kilometers around the lake at Shōwa Shin-zan. A road rings the water, dotted with campsites and hot springs, and pleasure boats go out to three small islands where deer beg for snacks.

Direct buses from Sapporo to Tōya-ko Onsen via Nakayama Tōge take 2½ hours (¥2,700). **Jōtetsu Bus** (☎ 011/572–3131) runs between Sapporo and Tōya-ko Onsen; reservations are necessary. **Dōnan Bus** (☎ 011/261–3601) makes the Sapporo to Tōya-ko Onsen trip daily. Tōya-ko Onsen is on the JR Sapporo–Hakodate Line. Disembark from the train at JR Tōya Station for a 15-minute bus ride to the lake.

What to See

⑩ **Tōya-ko Onsen.** Fireworks enjoyed over sake from a rooftop hot spring after a gargantuan dinner—this is why thousands of Japanese come to the one-street town year-round. From April 28 to October 31 the 30-minute, nightly fireworks are the highlight of any stay. A waterside walk in front of the wall of hotels is quiet before the bus groups arrive late afternoon. Sightseeing boats leave the pier for the 20-minute crossing to the islands. Bike rentals near the bus station cost ¥900 for two hours and ¥1,200 for three, the latter just enough time to cycle the circumference of the lake.

★ ☺ **Nishiyama Crater Trail.** A brand-new fire station, a school, and houses stand at crazy angles amid the solidified ash flows where the 2000 eruption reached the edges of Tōya-ko Onsen. Walkways wind up into the still steaming hills. Although hardly as exciting as Hawaiian lava-flow hikes, it's an impressive scene of what can happen when you live next to a volcano. Buses from Tōya Station to the onsen stop at the trailhead. The trail is accessible from the coast or from the lakeside above the village. ⊠ *3–4–5 Takashaga-dōri, between Abuta and Tōya-ko* ⊠ *Free* ☺ *Apr.–Nov., daily.*

☺ **Volcanic Science Museum** (Abuta Kazan Kagaku-kan). Smashed cars and heat-mangled kitchen appliances are part of Tōya's ever-expanding collection of volcanic memorabilia. The museum is old-fashioned and has the feel of a local collection of damaged homes and possessions. It's on the second floor of the Dōnan Bus Terminal in the center of Tōya-ko Onsen. ☎ *0142/75–4400* ⊠ *¥600* ☺ *Daily 9–5.*

OFF THE BEATEN PATH

SHŌWA SHIN-ZAN was the mountain that grew out a farmer's wheatfield in 1943. Kept secret by authorities during the war as a potentially unlucky symbol, it continued growing to its present height of 1,319 feet, and its name means "new mountain of the Shōwa era." It is privately owned by the family of the village postmaster who monitored its growth. A cable-car ride (¥1,450) up the eastern flank of Mount Usu (734 meters) provides great views of Shōwa Shin-zan, Lake Tōya and the sea in Funka (Eruption) Bay. Whatever you do, avoid the Bear Ranch at the base, a depressing tourist attraction and a disgrace in a region which won World Heritage status for its efforts to preserve the bears' habitat.

Where to Stay & Eat

$$–$$$ ✕ **Biyōtei.** A European-style restaurant in the heart of the village, Biyōtei has a stone floor, low beams, log table legs, and a garden full of gnomes. The menu is in English, and the sizzling hamburger platters are the best choices. The village is quiet during the day, and apart from large hotel coffeeshops and a few local noodle joints, this is the only restaurant. ⊠ *38 Rte. 2, Tōya-ko Onsen* ☎ *0142/75–2311* ⊟ *No credit cards.*

$$$$
Fodor'sChoice
★
✕⬚ **The Windsor Hotel.** Visible for miles around—the hotel looks like a giant luxury cruise ship perched on the rim of the Tōya volcano—the Windsor is the best hotel in Hokkaidō for location and service. The blue rooms have views of the lake and Tōya-ko Onsen's volcanic activity, while the rust-color rooms look out to the sea. French chef Michel Bras uses Hokkaidō fish, meats, and vegetables in his only restaurant outside of France. The simple, 14-table room has wooden floors and wicker chairs overlooking the lake. Unusual in Japan, the Windsor asks guests to refrain from smoking in all restaurants and most rooms. Foreign staff speak English, French, and Japanese. ⊠ *Shimizu, Abuta-cho 049-5722* ☎ *0120/29–0500 or 0142/73–1111* 🖷 *0142/73–1210* ⊕ *www.windsor-hotels.co.jp* ⌁ *395 Western-style rooms, 3 Japanese-style rooms* ⌂ *14 restaurants, patisserie, cable TV, 2 18-hole golf courses, 3 tennis courts, indoor pool, gym, Japanese baths, sauna, spa, mountain bikes, downhill skiing, 2 bars, piano bar, shops, babysitting, Internet, business services, meeting rooms, airport shuttle, helipad* ▭ *AE, D, DC, MC, V.*

★ ¢–$
⬚ **Pension Ohno.** A family-run guesthouse next to the Lakeside Park bus stop, ½ km (¼ mi) east of Tōya-ko Onsen, Pension Ohno is a calm alternative to the lodgings in the touristy village. Cozy cottage-style rooms have large beds and private bathrooms; the small on-site indoor hot spring is open round-the-clock, and the dining room overlooks the lake, where guests can enjoy feasts of salmon or beef before heading down to the water's edge for fireworks. No English is spoken. ⊠ *56–2 Aza Sobetsu-chō Onsen-chō, Abuta-chō 052-0103* ☎ *0142/75–4128* 🖷 *0142/75–3880* ⌁ *11 Western-style rooms* ⌂ *Restaurant* ▭ *MC, V* ⧖⧗ *MAP.*

Noboribetsu Onsen

⑪ *1 hr 20 min east of Tōya-ko by bus, 1 hr 40 min south of Sapporo by bus.*

GRRR! A bright red, 32-foot-tall, concrete demon brandishing a club points the way from the highway interchange to Noboribetsu Onsen, Hokkaidō's most famous spa. The town claims that some 34,300 gallons of geothermally heated water are pumped out every hour, making it the most prodigious hot spring in Asia.

Don't come here expecting a quaint little hot-spring town—this is Japanese tourism at its garish heights. The natural beauty of the steep-sided, wooden valley is dominated by ugly, mammoth hotels and tatty town buildings housing souvenir shops. Buses swing in every evening with hundreds of visitors for a boisterous one-night stay. At the top of the town a cobbled street leads to the Valley of Hell entrance, where the landscape is still dramatically scarred by nature, not Japanese architects. If you are coming from Sapporo, you can get more for your yen if you arrange a tour through your hotel, Japan Railways, or the Plaza i tourist office.

Getting Around

Noboribetsu City is one hour south of Sapporo by JR Limited Express. From the JR station in Noboribetsu, a shuttle bus serves Noboribetsu Onsen. Don't confuse Noboribetsu Onsen with Noboribetsu, an industrial city that is 13 minutes by bus from its namesake spa town.

CLOSE UP

Hokkaidō's First Inhabitants

ONCE UPON A TIME In *Ainumosir* (human being peaceful land), *aynu* (human beings) lived in *kotan* (villages), raising their families on a diet of *ohaw* (salmon, meat, or plants) and *sayo* (millet and other grains). They honored the god *Okikurmikamu*, and told *yukar* (epic poems) to remember the interwoven lives of human and the spirit world, particularly of bears and owls. Sometimes they traded kelp, salmon, and herring with the *sisam*, the neighbors north or south.

Around the 15th century life changed. The southern *sisam*—the Japanese—began arriving in greater numbers and building trading posts along the far south coast. As the Japanese moved north and solidified their presence on the island, the *aynu*—regarded as "hairy people"—became forced laborers.

In 1869 the new Meiji Government lumped Ainu together with Japanese as "commoners," and the Ainu language and lifestyle were outlawed. Along with intermarriages, this nearly obliterated the original culture. The Hokkaidō Former Aborigine Protection Law sliced up land ownership, and many Ainu lost out to *wajin*, the Japanese immigrants.

But the Ainu have fought back. By the 1980s Ainu were calling for basic human rights, drawing support from indigenous groups in other countries. Efforts were boosted when the United Nations made 1993 the Year of Indigenous Peoples, and a propaganda victory was achieved in 1994 when leading activist Shigeru Kayano of Nibutani was elected the first Ainu to Japan's House of Councillors. In May 1997 the national government passed belated legislation acknowledging the existence of Ainu and requiring the local and national governments to respect their dignity as a distinct race by promoting Ainu culture and traditions. The act stopped short of designating Ainu as an indigenous ethnic group, due to concerns about aboriginal rights to land and natural resources.

Visitors to Hokkaidō may find it hard to recognize full-blooded Ainu outside the tourist centers of Shiraoi, Nibutani, and Akan. Some 24,000 people declare themselves Ainu, but activism has not yet made this a universally proud heritage. Most Japanese have little knowledge or interest in Ainu affairs, beyond buying a cute wooden carving in a souvenir shop. Otherwise well-informed, worldly Japanese hosts may be surprised, and a little embarrassed, by foreign guests' interest in Ainu. Kayano's death in 2006 was hardly noted by the national media.

But the sad tourist parks are being revamped as cultural centers. Ainu language is taught at 14 locations, and Shiro Kayano is continuing his father's monthly Ainu radio broadcasts (FM-Pipaushi; available on the Internet).

The **Foundation for Research and Promotion of Ainu Culture** (FRPAC ☎ 011/271-4171 ⊕ www.frpac.or.jp) at Presto 1.7 (7th floor), Kita-1-jō Nishi 7-chōme, Sapporo, has English-language information. The best places to learn more about Ainu culture, politics, and people are the Nibutani Ainu Culture Museum and Kayano Shigeru Nibutani Archive; Poroto Kotan and Ainu Museum, Shiraoi; and Akan Ainu Kotan cultural performances.

14

Dōnan Bus (☎ 011/261–3601) travels from Sapporo to Noboribetsu Onsen; the trip takes 100 minutes (¥1,900; reservations advised). From June to late October three buses per day make the 1¼-hour run between Tōya-ko Onsen and Noboribetsu Onsen; only one bus runs per day the rest of the year (¥1,530; reservations necessary). Heavy snows keep the road closed until spring.

What to See

★ ☺ **Valley of Hell** (Jigokudani). In this volcanic crater that looks like a bow-shape valley boiling water spurts out of thousands of holes, sounding like the heartbeat of the earth itself—although, with its strong sulfur smell, you might describe it differently. Whereas hot springs elsewhere in Japan—Unzen on Kyūshū is a notable example—were used to dispose of zealous foreign missionaries during periods of zealous xenophobia, these natural cauldrons were once favored by suicidal natives. Moms shouldn't worry, though; the walkways to photo-op points have handrails and are very safe. Local maps detail several short hikes around the area. Even if the town itself disappoints, the Valley of Hell is worth a stop. Admission is free.

Where to Stay & Eat

$ ✕ **Dosanko-Tei.** Fish and meat dishes, all served with pickles, miso soup, and rice in a family-run restaurant (look for the orange lanterns outside) on the main street, one of the few eating places open during the day. The sign in the window reads, "Spoken English," but you'll probably be taken outside to point at the plastic displays in the window. Inside, farm implements and crafts adorn the walls. ✉ *Noboribetsu 49* ☎ *0143–84–2393* ☷ *No credit cards.*

$–$$ ✕☷ **Dai-ichi Takimoto-kan.** More than 1,000 guests a night enjoy the 12 different thermal pools in this prime example of a Japanese mass-tourism venue. It's like a giant youth hostel, and it's always fully booked. A vast dining room, the Attaka-tei, serves average Japanese and Western food, including a suitably sprawling dinner buffet of 75 dishes. Nonguests can bathe for ¥2,000 (¥3,000 on weekends). ✉ *55 Noboribetsu Onsen, Noboribetsu 059-0551* ☎ *0143/84–2111* 🖷 *0143/84–2202* ⊕ *www.takimotokan.co.jp* ✎ *393 Western-style rooms, 8 Japanese-style rooms* ఊ *3 restaurants, dining room, room service, indoor pool, 3 bars, pub, dance club, video game room, shops, laundry service* ☷ *AE, DC, MC, V* ꧁ *MAP.*

$$$$ ☷ **Ryotei Hanayuraya.** This is most foreigners' idea of a peaceful hot-spring hotel: floor-to-ceiling lobby windows look out on a small canyon and river, and the hotel hot springs on the top floor bubble gently among rocks and trees. Spend a little more and enjoy your own, private, one-person cypress wood bath on your balcony, followed by a traditional dinner delivered to the door. This relatively small, modern hotel is unvisited by the tour groups (but connected to a larger hotel, so you can use its bar and souvenir shop). No English speakers are on staff but reservations can be made in English through the hotel group's Web site. Guests can reserve seats on a free shuttle bus from Sapporo. ✉ *100 Noboribetsu Onsen, Noboribetsu 059-0551* ☎ *0143/84–2322* 🖷 *0143/*

84–2035 ⊕ http://tohoresort.com ⇥ 58 rooms ♧ Restaurant, a/c.; no no-smoking rooms ⊟ AE, DC, MC, V ⋈ MAP.

Nibutani

★ ⑫ *45 min east of Tomakomai by bus, 2 hrs southeast of Sapporo by car.*

Nibutani is one of the last places in Hokkaidō with a sizable Ainu population—or at least part Ainu, as few pure-blooded Ainu are left. The tiny village, which looks no different from any other, has two museums and a handful of souvenir shops. It's a long way from Sapporo, but it's where you can find the best collection of Ainu art and artifacts in Hokkaidō.

Getting Around

Nibutani is hard to reach by public transport. It involves an early train from Sapporo, a change, and then a local bus—all costing about ¥6,000 round-trip. The Tourist Office in Sapporo has information on the current public transport connections if this is your only option. Otherwise, you're better off renting a car for the day.

What to See

FodorśChoice **Nibutani Ainu Culture Museum** (Nibutani Ainu Bunka Hakubutsukan).
★ This museum is an excellent resource for information about the Ainu, and it's sadly unknown to many Japanese. Ainu artifacts, such as shoes of salmon skin, water containers made from animal bladders, and heavy blue-and-black embroidered coats are displayed, as well as implements used in *iyomante,* an Ainu ritual that sent the spirit of the bear back to the nonhuman world. A brief bilingual pamphlet is available, and some translated booklets are on sale. A selection of videos lets you listen to eerie traditional Ainu chants and songs. ⊠ *Off Rte. 237, Nibutani 55, Biratori-chō* ☎ *01457/2–2892* ⊠ *¥400, ¥700 joint ticket with Kayano Shigeru Nibutani Ainu Archive* ⊙ *Mid-Jan.–mid-Dec., Tues.–Sun. 9:30–4:30.*

Kayano Shigeru Nibutani Ainu Archive (Kayano Shigeru Nibutani Shirrō-kan). This museum puts a spotlight on artifacts, particularly Ainu clothing and items used in sacred rites collected by the late prominent Ainu activist and Nibutani resident Shigeru Kayano. Until his death in 2006, Kayano traveled extensively, and the archive contains presents to the Ainu from other indigenous peoples. The museum is across the main road from the Culture Museum. ⊠ *Nibutani 54, Biratori-chō* ☎ *01457/2–3215* ⊠ *¥400, ¥700 joint ticket with Nibutani Ainu Culture Museum* ⊙ *Mid-Jan.–mid-Dec., Tues.–Sun. 9:30–4:30.*

EASTERN HOKKAIDŌ

Bears and eagles rule the mountains of Shiretoko National Park. Farther inland are the mysterious lakes of the Akan National Park, where Ainu people hold on to their pre-Japanese culture with spirit worship, music, and dance. South, around Kushiro, are the vast wetland breeding grounds of the striking *tanchō-zuru* (red-crested crane). On the eastern coast flowers carpet the land in the short summer, while in winter creaking ice floes nudge against the shore, providing a temporary home to seals and seabirds. Unfortunately, the ice is getting thinner and the viewing season shorter—this is the front line of global warming.

Japan's last frontier is also a region of international politics. Japan and Russia are engaged in bitter disputes over islands and fishing and mineral rights. Russian sailors hang around fishing ports and bars in small towns, and signboards across the region proclaim "Return the Northern Territories!" This is Japan's campaign to reclaim islands, some just kilometers off its eastern shore, that were lost after World War II.

There are regional airports in Kushiro and Memanbetsu, and express trains reach Abashiri and Kushiro. The largest city is Kushiro, which is famous for its morning fish market, but more beautiful touring bases include Akan Onsen and Abashiri, and the small fishing town of Utoro, halfway up the Shieroko Peninsula, is Japan's easternmost outpost.

Abashiri

13 *5½ hrs east of Sapporo via Asahikawa by JR Limited Express.*

An excellent touring base for eastern Hokkaidō, Abashiri is a small town in the shadow of Tento-zan. On the town outskirts are shallow coastal lakes with flowers and seabirds. Bicycles can be rented for slow sightseeing. Winters are harsh: the whaling fleet sets out from here on "research" trips ("research" is the official word, common parlance would call it "hunting") under Japan's interpretation of IWC rules, which keeps Japan at loggerheads with conservationists. Visitors bundle up for boat tours through the *ryūhyō* (ice floes) that jam up on its shores and stretch out to sea as far as the eye can see.

Getting Around

The significant distance from Sapporo to Abashiri makes it advisable to take one of the four daily express trains out (a five-hour trip), then rent a car or take a bus to get to the surrounding parks and towns. A single bus runs to all the worthwhile sights in Abashiri. A day pass costs ¥900, and the bus departs hourly from **JR Abashiri Station** (✉ Shinmachi 2-chōme 2-banchi).

Some staff members at the **Abashiri Tourist Office** (☎ 0152/43–4261 ⊕ abashiri.jp), adjoining the JR station, speak English. This is where to find information about transportation and lodging in the area.

What to See

Ice-floe sailing with bird and seal spotting is possible late January to April from boats leaving **Aurora Terminal** (☎ 0152/43–6000) at the east end of the port. The *Aurora 1* and the *Aurora 2* let you inspect the ryūhyō at close range for ¥3,000. Travel agencies in Tokyō and Sapporo and JR Hokkaidō offer ice-floe/hot-spring package tours that always include this boat trip.

Hokkaidō Museum of Northern Peoples (Hoppō Minzoku Hakubutsukan). Look at the world from a northern perspective through its indigenous people, such as the Ainu, Inuits, and Sami (or Lapps). Displays compare and contrast the kitchen implements, clothes, and hunting snares and nets of various cultures from northern Japan, the neighboring Russian island of Sakhalin, and the northern parts of America and Eurasia. If the museum's layout seems a little bizarre, it's because the building was designed to resemble a flying swan. The museum is 5 km (3 mi)—a 10-minute drive—from JR Abashiri Station on the Dōdo Taikan Yama Kōen-sen, a local road. ☎ 0152/45–3888 ➧ ¥250 ☉ Tues.–Sun. 9:30–4:30.

★ ☺ **Prison Museum** (Abashiri Kangokuku Hakbutsukan). Spartan cells line the central corridors in five wooden prison blocks, showing how the convicts who built much of early Hokkaidō lived out their years. Used between 1912 and 1984, the prison is now a park museum with the blocks, watch towers, and farm buildings preserved. Only the most heinous criminals were banished to this forbidding northern outpost, the Alcatraz of Japan. English information is entertainingly lost in translation, but anguished-looking mannequins illustrate the grimness of life behind bars. ✉ 1–1 Yobito ☎ 0152/45–2411 ⊕ www.ryuhyo.com/kangoku2 ➧ ¥1,050 ☉ Apr.–Oct., daily 8–6; Nov.–Mar., daily 9–5.

Where to Stay & Eat

$–$$ ✕ **Nakazushi.** Rotarian Kanio Nakano presides over the Ohotsuku-kai's freshest catch in a small restaurant run for more than 40 years by the same family. Depending on the season, Nakano-san has salmon roe on rice, sea urchin, and the plump, juicy Abashiri scallop. *Tsuchi ku jira* (Baird's beaked whale) is sometimes on the menu. Although Nakano-san doesn't speak English, he's aware of the whale-meat debate, and can make substitutions if you let him know your no-whale preference through gestures. ✉ *Minami 2-jō Nishi 2, Abashiri* ☎ *0152/43–3447* ➦ *No credit cards.*

★ $$–$$$$ ▨ **Hotel Abashiri-ko-so.** Waterbirds and mist drift by the windows of the big but friendly hotel on the shore of Lake Abashiri, a few kilometers from town. It has the usual noise of Japanese resort hotels—game corners, tour groups, and karaoke rooms. But beyond the doors you can enjoy the peace of a lakeside walk, then a hot spring, and finally retire to your room and relax over a multicourse crab dinner. The combination rooms have raised beds and tatami sitting areas. Reservations can be made in English via the Web site. ✉ *Abashiri Kohan Onsen, Abashiri 099-2421* ☎ *0152/48–2245* ➧ *0152/48–2828* ⊕ *www.abashirikoso. com* ➧ *37 Western-style rooms, 20 Japanese-style rooms, 100 combination rooms* ⟁ *3 restaurants, sauna, 2 bars, shops* ➦ *AE, MC, V* ⊠⟁ *MAP.*

$$–$$$ ▨ **Abashiri Central Hotel.** Luxurious from the moment you enter, this downtown hotel seems a world away from small-town Abashiri. Rooms in yellows and blues overlook a main road out front or parking at the back. Fish from the local icy waters are a specialty of the Grand Glacier restaurant, which serves Japanese, Chinese, and French food. The weekday lunch buffet is only ¥1,000. English speakers are on staff. ✉ *7, Minami 2-jo Nishi 3, Abashiri 093-0012* ☎ *0152/44–5151* ➧ *0152/ 43–5177* ⊕ *www.abashirich.com* ➧ *94 Western-style rooms, 2 Japanese-style rooms* ⟁ *Restaurant, café, bar.*

Shiretoko National Park

★ 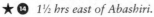 *1½ hrs east of Abashiri.*

The destination in Hokkaido for visitors with time to reach it—the spectacular Shiretoko Peninsula is worlds away from modern Japan. Brown bears hook salmon out of tumbling rivers, Blackiston's fish owls and Steller's sea eagles glide the skies. A steaming hot river tumbles to the sea. However, with the UNESCO designation came mass tourism; the Japanese bid to control and preserve has resulted in high metal fences, strict rules and limited shuttle-bus access to the last few kilometers of peninsula road—which can give an unwelcome Jurassic Park tone to the visit.

Most tour buses whisk their captives in and out in 24 hours—with an overnight stay in a big hotel in Utoro's hotel zone and quick photo-stops at Shiretoko Five Lakes, the nature center, and maybe a boat tour. Time your sightseeing at these places during the noon–1 tour lunch break or late in the day, and head for the places off the tour route. The magic of Shiretoko is found just beyond the bus park hordes. Local weather, even in summer, is fickle. A Shiretoko stay (and hiking plans) can be marred by mists and rain.

If you visit outside the summer crush—June and September are good times—Shiretoko is a remarkable, untouched pocket of wilderness in a heavily industrialized and technologically advanced nation. Read *Audrey Hepburn's Neck* (1996, Simon & Schuster, Inc.), a novel by Alan Brown, for a tale of a 20th-century childhood on Shiretoko.

Getting Around

From Sapporo to Abashiri it's a five-hour express train, then a local train to Shari, and finally a 55-minute bus ride to Utoro. Depending on the season, about seven daily bus connections go from Shari to Utoro. Buses from Abashiri and the airports in Kushiro and Membanbetsu also connect to Utoro. Several car-rental companies are at Kushiro and Abashiri, and only one (Nippon Rent a Car) at Shari.

The village of Utoro is the center of visitor activity. It's a simple working fishing village, with a hotel zone built on a bluff above the center. From the end of April to the end of October, a one-hour, ¥900 shuttle-bus trip links the town with the Nature Center and Shiretoko Five Lakes. Beyond here, the 12-km (7-mi) dirt road to Kamuiwaka is open to shuttle buses July 29–August 29. In winter the roads beyond Utoro are closed. Be careful of wildlife when driving, Shiretoko is full of grazing deer who favor cleared roadside verges.

Apart from hiking, a boat is the best way to see the wildest parts. Late April to October, several boat companies in Utoro harbor offer one- to three-hour trips (¥3,000–¥8,000) out along the peninsula, beneath soaring 600-foot cliffs to the tip of the cape. Early-morning and late-afternoon trips on a small boat offer the best chances to see bears come down to the beaches and the river outlets and forage for food. A stay of at least one night is recommended for hiking, hot springs, wildlife spotting, and silence.

What To See

Fodor'sChoice

★

🕐

Kamuiwakka Onsen. *Kamui* means "spirit" or "god" in the Ainu language, and there's something wondrous, almost other-worldly, about this tumbling hot river on the north shore under Iō-zan (Mt. Iō). Water rushes down the mountain through a series of falls and pools, creating a rotemburo with an ocean view. The pools are free—just strip and hop in. Best to wear shoes if you want to scramble up over slippy rocks to the pools higher upstream. Strict access rules have put this wonderful place almost out of reach except from one month in summer. Bear and park-patrol activity is high—so if you plan to hike the 12 km (7 mi) along the road from Five Lakes to Kamuiwakka, tred carefully.

Shiretoko Go-ko (Five Lakes). Twenty minutes east of Utoro by car—and on every tour bus route in the region—a collection of small lakes hides in the forest on a precipice above the ocean. It takes just over an hour to walk round all five on boardwalk paths. Most tour groups only reach the first two, and the others are sometimes closed due to bears. The lakes are pretty, but not essential viewing if you are on a tight schedule. Better to make time for a boat trip.

Mt. Rausu. Snow-covered from October to June and towering 5,448 feet along the spine of the peninsula, Mt. Rausu provides the real getaway from the crowds. The most accessible trailhead is 5 km (3 mi) east of Utoro behind the Hotel Chi-no-hate, you walk 1 hour 20 minutes to a 1,920-foot rocky outcrop, then another two hours to the top. From there trails head west (two hours) along the peninsula to meet the Utoro-Rausu highway at Shiretoko Pass or over the ridge and down to Rausu (three hours), or finally—and much more difficult—a serious-hikers-only trail (eight hours) along the ridge to the 5,127-foot Mt. Iō and then down to Kamuiwakka Onsen. Check weather conditions before hiking, sign the trailhead books, and fix a bear bell to your backpack.

Aching muscles can be soaked in open-air hot springs waiting at the end of the hike: **Iwaobetsu Onsen,** just below the Hotel Chi-no-hate car park, is four steaming rocky pools in a forest with no changing hut and a strong likelihood of sitting naked with strangers. Near the trailhead and camp-site on the Rausu side look for **Kuma-no-yu,** two boiling pools separated for men and women with some unfortunate concrete and rusty pipes, but fenced in for privacy.

Where to Stay

$$$–$$$$

🏨 **Hotel Chi-no-hate.** The name means "End of the World," and this quiet hotel in the forest 7 km (4 mi) from Utoro is the last accommodation before the wilds of the park, and at the trailhead for Mount Rausu. Large rooms overlook the car park and trees, and the public areas are old-fashioned and worn. After a quiet set dinner of Japanese food, guests in hotel cotton kimonos cross the car park to the pools of Iwaobetsu Onsen. Everyone heads to bed early for dawn-starting hikes. No English is spoken. The village bus stops here once a day. ✉ *52 Utoro Onsen, Shari-chō* ☎ *0152/24-2331* 📠 *0152/24-2280* 🛏 *41 rooms, 35 Japanese-style and 5 Western-style* ⚭ *Coffee lounge, shop, bar* 🚫 *No credit cards* ☾ *Closed Nov.–Apr.*

14

$$$–$$$$ 🏨 **Shiretoko Daiichi Hotel.** Beneath vast sunset ceiling murals replica antique furniture stands toe-deep in plush carpets decorated with regional flowers—this is a Japanese hotel stay at its most luxurious. At the very top of Utoro's hotel area, where all hotels are on the sea, the hot-spring sunset views are sensational. Mountain-facing windows look over the smallholdings around Utoro, where bear and deer steal vegetables at dusk. Meals are over-the-top buffets, and English-speakers are on duty in the evening at the tour desk. Reserve in English through the Web site. ✉ *306 Utoro Onsen, Shari-chō, 362-0003* ☎ *01522/4–2334* 🖷 *01522/4–2261* ⊕ *www.shiretoko-1.co.jp/* ⇩ *238 rooms, 178 Japanese-style, 41 Western-style* ⚿ *3 restaurants, shops, sauna, 2 bars, in-room broadband, 5 no-smoking rooms, 5 barrier-free rooms* ▤ *AE, DC, MC, V* ¶❙ *MAP.*

$$ 🏨 **Iruka (Dolphin) Hotel.** This hotel is a diver's and wildlife photographer's family guesthouse, on the waterside in Utoro. Vast fish dinners are served in the bright modern dining room and on the wooden deck overlooking Utoro Bay. Guests can use the tiny outdoor hot spring. Yamamoto-san speaks some English and is qualified to take guests diving under the ice floes in winter. From the small tatami rooms at dusk, keep an eye out for local foxes that curl up on the hoods of the still-warm cars in the car park. It's the first house in the village as you arrive from Abashiri. ✉ *5 Utoro, Shari-chō* ☎ *0152/4–2888* 🖷 *01522/4–2788* ⊕ *www.iruka-hotel.com* ⇩ *13 rooms* ⚿ *Fans, dive shop* ¶❙ *MAP.*

$ 🏨 **Iwaobetsu Youth Hostel.** It is old and unlovely outside, but inside is an efficient working hostel with wood floors and worn furnishings. Hikers and bikers sit down to salmon roe and rice dinners, then attend the evening meeting fortified with Mountain Grape wine. A little English is spoken, and the staff can rent mountain bikes and arrange sea-kayaking tours (¥8,000 for three hours). It's by the river, 4 km (2½ mi) out of Utoro on the road to the Five Lakes, where deer graze in the car park and bears are tempted by the nearby salmon hatchery. The road opposite the hostel leads to Chi-no-hate, Iwaobetsu, and Mount Rausu. ✉ *Aza Iwaobetsu, Utoro* ☎ *0152/4–2311* 🖷 *01522/4–2312* ⊕ *www.youthhostel.or.jp.*

Akan National Park

⑮ *1 hr southeast of Abashiri by car.*

Volcanoes rise from primeval forests, and lakeside beaches bubble with hot springs in this national park that is unfairly out-shone by its neighbors Daisetsu and Shiretoko. In Akan's northern forests, strange, cylindrical algae bob to the surface of Lake Akan. Ainu men pluck and blow eerie music from traditional instruments while women dancers duck and weave in honor of the red-crested white cranes that fly in every winter to breed on the wetland on the park's southern border. In summer it's a hiker's heaven of trails and hot springs; in winter the lakes freeze over and ice festivals spill out onto the frozen expanses.

Getting Around

There are buses to Akan-ko from Kushiro airport and station. You can also catch a bus from Akan-ko to Abashiri if you change buses in Bihoro. By car from Kitami, west of Abashiri, a road heads south to the small town of Tsubetsu, where it joins Route 240, entering Akan National Park near Akan-ko. From the southern part of Daisetsu-zan National Park at Nukabira, a road to Kamishihoro continues to Ashoro, which connects with Route 241; this runs directly to Akan.

What to See

★ **Akan-ko** (Lake Akan). Chugging tour boats with noisy Japanese commentaries and even speedboats disturb the waters below smoking volcanoes Me-Akan and O-Akan (Mr. and Mrs. Akan). But out on Churui Island silence is green among Lake Akan's strangest inhabitants, *marimo,* as they nestle peacefully in display tanks. These rare spherical colonies of green algae that may be as small as a ping-pong ball or as large as a soccer ball (the latter taking up to 500 years to form). The only other areas marimo can be found are in Yamanaka-ko (Lake Yamanaka), near Fuji-san, and in a few lakes in North America, Siberia, and Switzerland. These strange algae act much like submarines, bobbing to the lake surface when bright sunshine increases their photosynthesis but staying submerged in inclement weather, when light levels drop.

> ## SMELT FISHING
>
> Lake Akan in winter is dotted with ice holes. Fishermen crouch in sub-zero temperatures to hook *wakasagi* (pond smelt) from the depths. Visitors can slide across the lake and try their luck, fortified with *ama-sake,* a delicious—but alcoholic—drink made from sweet-end brown rice. The successful can head back to the shore where stallholders are on hand to mince the catch for a raw meal or fry or grill it. Grilled wakasagi often appears on the winter menus of Hokkaidō izakayas. *Wakasagi* fishing costs ¥800 for adults and ¥400 for kids. The gear includes a chair and your own personal ice hole.

Enjoy the lake from a canoe with the help of the **Akan Adventure Center,** which offers two- or eight-person Canadian canoes for a 45-minute beginner course (¥2,100), a 90-minute adventure course (¥5,300) or for the strong-of-arm the 2½-hour Yaitai Island course (¥8,400). Reserve one day in advance, 0154/67–2081, or in simple English e-mail via www.akan.co.jp. The center is in Akan Kohan, near the Ainu village and next to Pension Yamaguchi on the north end of the town street.

Akan-kohan. The small town on the lakeshore is a major stop on regional bus tours, with giant hotels blocking off the lake from the main road running through the town. Kitschy souvenir shops sell endless rows of carved bears made by Ainu residents, and bottles containing *marimo* that may never grow. At the northern end of the town is the Ainu village, one cobbled street lined by shops and restaurants, with the Culture Performance Center and a small museum at the top. May to October there are excellent 30-minute, traditional dance performances five times a day, and the 9 PM show features *yukara,* chanted epic poems. Performances cost ¥1,100.

★ ⑯ **Kushiro Marsh** (Kushiro Shitsugen). Graceful red-crested cranes preen and breed in protected Kushiro Marsh, which constitutes 60% of Japan's marshland. These rare cranes whose feathers were thought to bring good luck, were ruthlessly hunted at the beginning of the 20th century and were even believed extinct until a handful of survivors were discovered in 1924. They have slowly regenerated and now number about 650. The crane—long-legged, long-billed, with a white body trimmed in black and a scarlet cap on its head—is a symbol of long life and happiness. Legends hold that the birds live 1,000 years, and they have made it to a rather impressive 80 years of age in captivity. They pair for life, making them the symbol of an ideal couple, and they are frequently cited in Japanese wedding speeches.

November to March is the best season for wild-crane watching, because this is when the birds fly in from Russia, China, and Korea and gather at feeding stations such as Tsurumidai, off Route 53. In summer the birds that stay retreat deep into the swamps to raise their chicks and can only be spotted with binoculars. The **Akan International Crane Center** (Akan Kokusai Tsuru Centa) and the adjoining Tancho-no-Sato, **Crane Home** (✉ 23–40 Akan-chō ☎ 0154/66–4011) are both about one hour south of Lake Akan, near the Tancho-zuru bus stop on the Akan-kohan–Kushiro bus route. Here you can watch a feeding and visit the center's units for egg hatching, chick rearing, and bird medical care.

Canoe paddlers on the Kushiro River have a chance to see cranes and other birds: rental companies are at Lake Toro, off Route 391, and by the Norroko-go, a slow, sightseeing train from Kushiro (July and August only). The marshland comprises 183 square kilometers, and viewing areas with wooden walkways and observation towers are located off Route 53 and 359.

Where to Stay & Eat

$ ✕⚐ **Minshuku Yamaguchi.** The mynah bird, Tarō, may screech a welcome as you enter this small home. This is like staying with elderly relatives. While the Yamaguchis don't speak English, they proudly welcome foreign guests to their slightly faded rooms and mineral-stained shared baths. Japanese meals include tempura made from local fish like *wakasagi* and mountain vegetables. Look for the impressive flower display out front, just past the Ainu village end of the town. ✉ 5–3–2 *Akan-ko Onsen, Akan-chō 085-0467* ☎ *0154/67–2555* ⚐ *10 Japanese-style rooms without bath* ⚐ *Dining room, Japanese baths; no room phones* ⚌ *No credit cards* ⚐ *MAP.*

$$$$ ⚐ **Lake Spa Takada.** This is a small European-style hotel on the lakeside by the boat dock. It's fronted by a wooden deck of flower planters and garden umbrellas—a good spot to sit back and watch resort life. Rooms are small and quiet. Dinners in the Western-style dining room are impressive spreads with Lake Akan trout, venison, and seasonal vegetables. At the roof's small outdoor hot spring you look out over the lake. English is spoken. and the owners have family living in Australia, so bushman hats are on sale in the lobby shop. ✉ *1–6–11 Akan-ko Onsen* ☎ *0154/67–4157* ⚐ *0154/67–4158* ⊕ *www.lakespa-takada.com/* ⚐ *10 rooms, 7 Japanese-style; 3 Western-style* ⚌ *AE, MC, V* ⚐ *MAP.*

CENTRAL & NORTHERN HOKKAIDŌ

Breathtaking and often snowy Daisetsu-zan is Japan's largest national park—with Mount Asahi-dake at 7,311 feet, Hokkaidō's highest peak. Roads in the region skirt the mountains north and south, and cable cars lift visitors onto mountain plateaus with steaming volcanic vents, alpine flower meadows, and awe-inspiring views. Allow at least two days for reaching the area and enjoying its grandeur. Asahikawa is the largest city and the transport gateway to the park. Travelers with more time should trek north to Sōya-misaki, Japan's northernmost point, and the stark beauty of the Rebun and Rishiri islands.

14

Daisetsu-zan National Park

⑰ *50 min east of Asahikawa by car.*

Fodor'sChoice
★

The geographical center of Hokkaidō and the largest of Japan's national parks, Daisetsu-zan contains the very essence of rugged Hokkaidō: vast plains, soaring mountain peaks, hidden gorges, cascading waterfalls, wildflowers, forests, hiking trails, wilderness, and onsen. Daisetsu-zan, which means great snow mountains, refers to the park's five major peaks, whose altitudes approach 6,560 feet. Their presence dominates the area and channels human access into the park; only a few roads pass through. The rest dead-end in formidable terrain.

Getting Around

Sōun-kyō is two hours northheast of Asahikawa by car. You can catch a bus directly to Sōun-kyō Onsen (¥1,900) from in front of Asahikawa's JR station. If you are using a JR Pass, you can save money by taking the train to Kamikawa Station and transferring to the Dohoku Bus for the 30-minute run to Sōun-kyō. Bicycles can be rented for ¥1,000 a day in the village at the Northern Hotel, and a short cycling trail along the old road by the river is a peaceful way to enjoy the gorge. Rock falls have closed the road 3 km (2 mi) from the onsen. From July to September a ¥390 bus ride connects the village with the Daisetsu dam and lake.

The **Sōun-kyō tourist office** (☎ 01658/5–3350), in the bus terminal, provides hiking maps and information on sightseeing and lodging. English is spoken here.

What to See

★ **Sōun-kyō** (Sōun-kyō Gorge). As you follow the main route through the park, the first place to go is this 24-km (15-mi) ravine extending into the park from its northeast entrance. For an 8-km (5-mi) stretch, sheer cliff walls rise on both sides of the canyon as the road winds into the mountains. In winter and early spring forbidding stone spires loom as if in judgment; in other seasons they thrust through glorious foliage. Sōun-kyō Onsen is at the halfway point of the ravine.

Sōun-kyō Onsen village tries hard to be attractive. In summer, the pedestrianized main street is full of flower planters, and the guest houses and souvenir shops do their best to add charm to what is basically a modern and concrete Alpine village–wannabee. Activities take place in resort hotels, not in the village, and during the day most people are hiking through the park. From Late January to March the frozen river is illuminated for the Ice Waterfall Festival.

Hiking

★ ☾ **Kuro-dake.** Technology helps even the most reluctant up the mountains: a cable car and chair lift (¥2,200 round-trip) rise up the side of the gorge above the village to 4,264 feet. Hikers trudge on an hour more to the top of Kuro-dake, 2,244 feet higher. From here numerous well-marked trails lead either across volcanic gravel or low shrub plateaus. Crimson foliage sets the slopes ablaze in September. Between June and mid-October the cable car starts at 6 AM, and experienced hikers can cross the range to Asahi-dake and take its cable car down to Asahi-dake Onsen in one long day. But Daisetsu's beauty is best enjoyed slowly, and you may encounter deer, foxes, and bears.

On the park's west side two **spa towns** serve as summer hiking centers and winter ski resorts. **Shirogane Onsen,** at 2,461 feet, has had especially good skiing since its mountain, Tokachi-dake, erupted in 1962, creating a superb ski bowl. It erupted again in 1988. At **Asahi-dake Onsen** you can take a cable car (¥2,800 round-trip) up Asahi-dake to an altitude of 5,250 feet, and hike for two hours to the 7,513-foot summit. In late spring and early summer the slopes are carpeted with alpine flowers. Serious skiers come for Japan's longest ski season.

Where to Stay & Eat

You have no option but to lodge at **Sōun-kyō Onsen** if you want to stay in the northern part of the park. Rates tend to be 20% lower in winter. Because Sōun-kyō's hotels are almost exclusively ryokan, where meals are included, other dining opportunities in town are limited. A list of hotels and onsen is on the English page of www.sounkyo.net.

$$–$$$$ ✕⌨ **Chōyōtei.** Perched on a bluff halfway up the side of the gorge, this hotel has the best views of any in the park. Unfortunately, the hotel is also an eyesore, and spoils some of Sōun-kyō's beauty. It's full of tour groups, and nobody will notice your arrival or departure—but the hotel has sumptuous baths. Rooms facing the gorge merit the price, but rooms at the back have parking lot vistas. Dinner is in the huge buffet restaurant, or you can make reservations for a traditional *kaiseki* dinner (¥21,000 for two people) in a smaller restaurant. ⊠ *Sōun-kyō Onsen, Kamikawa 078-1701* ☎ *01658/5–3241* 🗗 *5 Western-style rooms, 257 Japanese-style rooms* ♨ *3 restaurants, minibars, bar, recreation room, video game room, shops* ▭ *AE, DC, MC, V* ¶⚫¶ *MAP.*

$$–$$$ ✕⌨ **Yamanoue.** This modern guest house is in the center of the village's flower-filled pedestrian area. The owner is a keen fisherman, so dinners can include freshwater fish, plus a wild mushroom soup served from the giant cauldron in the dining room. Sake liqueurs made from fruits such as mountain grape may enhance (or hinder) the next day's hiking power. Clean tatami rooms are upstairs with shared washing areas. Use of the hot spring next door is free. No English is spoken, but faxed reservations in simple English are okay. ⊠ *Sōun-kyō Onsen, Kamikawa 078-*

1701 🕾 *01658/5–3206* 🖨 *01658/5–3207* 🖵 *14 Japanese-style rooms without bath* ⚄ *Dining room, Japanese baths* ═ *MC, V* 🍴 *MAP.*

¢ 🖼 **Sōun-kyō Youth Hostel.** Between the big hotels—but at a fraction of the price and with a more personal welcome—this 40-year-old hostel is a good base for mountain hiking. Dorm rooms have eight wide bunk beds, and there are tatami or bunk-bed family rooms. There are small Japanese baths and you can rent mountain boots. The hostel is closed from October to May. ⊠ *Sōun-kyo Onsen, Kamikawa* 078-1701 🕾 *01658/5–3418* 🖨 *01658/5–3186* 🖵 *12 rooms* ⚄ *Dining room, Japanese baths, Internet; no room phones, no room TVs* ═ *No credit cards.*

Asahikawa

⑱ *1½ hrs northwest of Sapporo by tollway, 1 hr 20 min by train.*

Asahikawa, Hokkaidō's second-largest city, is the principal entrance to Daisetsu-zan National Park. Cosmopolitan it is not; daytime life centers around a pedestrian shopping area and at night the entertainment district is raucously full of men from the farming hinterland. Travelers pass through its station, bus terminal, or airport on their way to more beautiful places, but a small Ainu museum and a winter festival in February are worthwhile if the schedule dictates a one-night stay.

Kawamura Kaneto Ainu Memorial Hall (Kawamura Kaneto Ainu Kinenkan). A slightly ramshackle, dusty museum in the suburbs, which although unexciting does have the moral advantage of being owned by a genuine Ainu, a man named Kaneto Kawamura, whose family has lived in the Asahikawa area for seven generations. There's no English information, but photographs of his family and Ainu ceremonies, a small collection of artifacts, and a traditional house are interesting. To get here, take Bus 24 (¥170) from Platform 14, which is two blocks north of the JR station, and get off at Ainu Kinenkan-mae. ⊠ *11 Hokumon-chō* 🕾 *0166/ 51–2461* 🖨 *¥500* 🕓 *July and Aug., daily 8–6; Sept.–June, daily 9–5.*

Where to Stay & Eat

Far from the sea and from Hokkaidō's breadbaskets, Asahikawa is not known for its cuisine, with two notable exceptions: ramen and *tonkatsu* (breaded, deep-fried pork cutlet). Asahikawa ramen features a distinctively salty pork broth prized by ramen connoisseurs. Several noodle shops pepper the area around the station.

$–$$ ✕ **Takada-ya.** *Tonkatsu* and soba noodles, tempura and noodles, even curry with noodles in a traditionally decorated restaurant favored by shoppers and business people alike. At lunchtime there's a no-smoking rule to allow full appreciation of the soba. Diners are seated in booths and entertained with quiet jazz, and free *ban-cha* (roasted green tea) are served with all meals. It's on the main street three blocks from the station, opposite the Okuno department store. No English, but the menu has pictures. ⊠ *3-jō, 8-chōme Heiwa-dōri* ═ *No credit cards.*

¢–$$ ✕ **The Den.** Barman Mark cooks up burgers, Thai curry, and Tex-Mex at this friendly expat hang out. It's a good place to make foreign contacts north of Sapporo. You can find 12 different beers from around the globe, plus a pool table, live music, and parties. The bar closes at 1 AM most nights, and at 3 AM on Friday and Saturday. The Den is two blocks down the main street in front of the station, and turn left at the statue of the man playing saxophone for a cat. ⊠ *Yoshitake 2 Bldg. (5F), 2-jō 7-chōme* ☎ *0166/27–0999* ⊕ *www.thedenasahikawa.com* ⊟ *MC, V* ⊘ *No lunch.*

$$ ⊡ **Washington Hotel.** This is a bright, busy hotel opposite the station, with small motel-type rooms for anyone forced to stay the night in Asahikawa. The first-floor restaurant Bonjour is a popular lunch spot for Asahikawa ladies for its pasta and salad sets. In the evening the 12th-floor Japanese restaurant Ginza is used for business dinners by local companies. Make reservations in English through the Web site. ⊠ *7 Miyashita-dōri, Asahikawa* ☎ *0166/23–7111* ☎ *0166/26–6767* ⊕ *www. wh-rsv.com* ↩ *260 Western-style rooms* ⚒ *2 restaurants, 10 no-smoking rooms* ⊟ *AE, MC, V* ¶◎¶ *CP.*

The Northern Cape

Wakkanai is 5¾ hrs north of Sapporo by JR Limited Express, 1 hr north of Okadama Airport, or 45 min north from New Chitose Airport.

Japan's northernmost point is windy and empty. In the short summer season tiny alpine flowers bloom in coastal grasslands and on rocky outcrops overlooking the sea. In winter the Arctic ice floes lock the land for months of darkness. This is only a place to come when you've already seen Daisetsu and Shiretoko. Long-term residents and repeat visitors come this far north for the hiking, the flowers, and the peace found in such edge-of-the-world places.

Getting Around

From June through August, Air Nippon flies from Shin-Chitose Airport directly to Rishiri Airport on Rishiri-tō. At other times there are flights to Wakkanai, and then bus and ferry connections to the islands.

Higashi-Nihon Ferry (☎ 0162/23–3780) has boats that make the daily two-hour crossing to Rebun-tō and the one-hour, 40-minute crossing to Rishiri-tō. In summer there are four or five daily ferries, in winter two. Fares to Rebun are ¥3,780 for first class and ¥2,100 second class. Fares to Rishiri are ¥3,360 and ¥1,880. A ferry between the two islands costs ¥730.

What to See

⑲ **Rebun Island** (Rebun-tō) is the older of two Nihon-kai islands created by an upward thrust of the earth's crust. Along the east coast there are numerous fishing villages where fleets of *uni* boats fish just offshore; prickly sea urchins are spotted through bottomless boxes held over the side of the boat and then raked in.

On the west coast is an eight-hour hiking trail, and cliffs stave off the surging waters of the Nihon-kai. Inland, more than 300 species of wild alpine flowers blanket the mountain meadows in such profusion in mid-June that each step seems to crush a dozen of the delicate blossoms, including the white-pointed *usuyo-kiso,* which is found only on Rebun. Its name roughly translates as "dusting of snow."

★ ⑳ **Rishiri Island** (Rishiri-tō). The island is the result of a submarine volcano whose cone now towers 5,640 feet out of the water. The scenery is wilder than on Rebun-tō, and though it's a larger island Rishiri-tō has fewer inhabitants. The rugged terrain makes it hard to support life and figures for hardier climbing—the intermediate **Kutsugata Course** (four hours to the top), on the west side of the island, takes you past patches of wildflowers, including the buttercuplike *botan kimbai* and the vibrant purple *hakusan chidori,* and numerous bird species.

㉑ **Sōya-misaki** (Cape Sōya). This is the end of Japan. Behind lies a world of sushi, cherry blossoms, and bowing—ahead across frigid waters is Russia's Sakhalin Island. This lonely but significant spot is the site of several monuments marking the end of Japan's territory, as well as a memorial to the Korean airliner downed by the Soviet military north of here in 1982. A public bus makes the hour-long run between Wakkanai and Cape Sōya six times a day.

Where to Stay & Eat

$$$ ⌂ **Pension Ūnii**. This sky-blue building is at the top of the cliffs above Rebun's ferry terminal. No English is spoken, but the family welcomes foreigners. Rooms have private bathrooms, and the two meals included in the rate feature ingredients that swam only hours earlier. Gargantuan dinners alternate from Western-style to Japanese-style for guests who stay more than one night, although the switch from cutlery to chopsticks may be your only clue as to which is which. ☒ *Kafuku-Irifune, Rebun-chō 097-1201* ☎ *01638/6–1541* ☞ *9 Western-style rooms, 1 Japanese-style room* ⌂ *Dining room* ⊟ *No credit cards* ⦿ *MAP.*

$$–$$$ ⌂ **Hera-san-no Ie.** This is a good base for Rishiri hikes. Hera's House, as the name translates, typifies the warm, casual atmosphere that makes Hokkaidō so loved by Japanese hippies. The house is at the entrance to the Peshi-misaki hiking trail. ☒ *Oshitomari, Rishiri-Fuji-chō 097-0400* ☎ *01638/2–2361* ☞ *8 Japanese-style rooms without bath; 3 Western-style rooms* ⌂ *Dining room; no a/c* ⊟ *No credit cards* ⦿ *MAP.*

HOKKAIDŌ ESSENTIALS

Transportation

BY AIR

Japan Airlines (JAL), Japan Air System (JAS), and All Nippon Airways (ANA) link Hokkaidō to Honshū by direct flights from Tōkyō's Haneda Kūkō to Hakodate, Sapporo (New Chitose Airport), Asahikawa Airport, Abashiri (Memambetsu Airport), Nemuro (Nakashibetsu Airport), and Kushiro Airport. Two flights a day depart from Tōkyō's Narita International Airport. Other major cities on Honshū have flights to Sapporo, as do several places in the Asian and Pacific region. The cost by air from Tōkyō to Sapporo can be as low as ¥12,000, compared with ¥22,430 by train. Fly-stay packages from Tōkyō offer excellent deals for short trips. Some air travelers arriving in Japan on European flights can, with a change of planes at Tōkyō, fly at no extra charge to Sapporo. If you're flying from overseas to Sapporo via Tōkyō, book the do mestic portion when you buy your international ticket; otherwise you will fork out for what is, per mile, one of the most expensive domestic tickets in the world. Local start-up Air Do (rhymes with "who"), is starting to rectify this situation.

The two domestic airlines—Japan Air System (JAS) and All Nippon Airways (ANA)—have local companies connecting Sapporo with Hakodate, Kushiro, Wakkanai, and the smaller Memambetsu, Naka-Shibetsu, and Ohotsuku-Mombetsu airports in eastern Hokkaidō. Hokkaidō Air System is part of JAS. Air Hokkaidō and Air Nippon are part of ANA. There's also daily service between Wakkanai and both Rebun and Rishiri islands. **ⓘ Info Air Hokkaidō and Air Nippon** ☎ 0120/029-222. **Hokkaidō Air System** ☎ 0120/ 511-283.

BY BOAT & FERRY

This is the least expensive way to travel to Hokkaidō. First-class fares are typically more than double the second-class rate. From Tōkyō the luxury ferry *Sabrina Blue Zephyr* sails three or four times weekly to Kushiro (32 hours), and is operated by the Kinkai Yūsen Company, with rates of ¥9,400.

Higashi Nihon Ferry's express *Unicorn* makes two round-trips daily from Aomori to Hakodate. The express ferry takes two hours (to the train's 2½) but costs only ¥1,420 second class. Higashi-nihon boats also make the journey from Hachinohe to Tomakomai in nine hours (¥3,970); from Hachinohe to Muroran in eight hours (¥3,970); from Sendai to Tomakomai in 16½ hours (¥9,020); and from Aomori to Muroran in seven hours (¥3,460). Shin Nihon Ferry travels from Niigata to Otaru in 18 hours (¥5,250. Taiheiyo Ferry routes include Sendai to Tomakomai (18 hours, ¥7,600) and Nagoya to Tomakomai (36 hours, ¥10,200).

ⓘ Info Higashi Nihon Ferry ☎ 0177/82-3631 in Aomori, 0138/42-6251 in Hakodate, 0178/28-3985 in Hachinohe, 0144/34-5261 in Tomakomai, 0143/34-5261 in Muroran, 022/ 25-7221 in Sendai. **Kinkai Yūsen Company** ☎ 0154/52-4890. **Shin Nihon Ferry** ☎ 025/ 273-2171 in Niigata, 0134/22-6191 in Otaru. **Taiheiyō Ferry** ☎ 022/25-7221 in Sendai, 052/203-0227 in Nagoya.

BY BUS

Buses cover most of the major routes through the scenic areas, and all the excursions in this chapter may be accomplished by bus. There's no English-language telephone service for buses in Hokkaidō. Plaza i in Sapporo will supply bus-route and schedule information and make telephone bookings if required.

BY CAR

Hokkaidō is the best place in Japan for driving. Most major companies have offices at Chitose Airport, in major cities, and in smaller centers in tourist areas. JR Hokkaidō arranges train/car/stay packages, although reservations can only be made in English at major stations such as Sapporo and Hakodate. Car rental, depending on the season, can cost as little as ¥6,000 per day.

The staffs at local offices do not speak English. Reservations are best made through company Web sites or through the Tocoo Web site for Mazda, Nissan, and Northwing. Japanese are cautious drivers, though a combination of wide straight roads, light traffic, treacherous weather conditions, and Honshū visitors' unfamiliarity with all of the above gives Hokkaidō the worst traffic fatality figures in Japan. Beware of speed traps: in apparently rural areas a hidden village can dictate urban speed limits of 50 to 60 kph. Most signage is in English. When booking, request an English navigation system.

Local Agency Orix Rent-a-Car ✉ Minami 4 Nishi 1, Chūo-ku, Sapporo ☎ 011/241-0543. **ToCoo Car Rental** ☎ 03/5333-0246 ⊕ www2.tocoo.jp/.

BY TRAIN

14

The train journey from Tōkyō to Sapporo can take as little as 10 hours. This trip involves a combination of the Shinkansen train to Morioka (2½ hours), the northernmost point on the Tōhoku Shinkansen Line, and a change to an express train for the remaining journey to Hakodate (4 hours, 20 minutes) and then on to Sapporo (3¼ hours). The JR Pass covers this route (the cost is ¥22,430 without the pass). The Hokutosei sleeper train provides greater comfort and eliminates the need to change trains, but the voyage takes 17 hours. The fare is ¥23,520 (¥9,450 for JR Pass holders). Forget about local trains from Tōkyō, the combined travel time to Sapporo is 30 hours, not including the required overnight stop in Aomori. Travelers with more time than cash would do better on the ferry.

Japan Railways (JR) has routes connecting most major Hokkaidō cities. JR Hokkaidō offers foreign visitors a three- or five-day Hokkaidō Rail Pass, purchasable at major stations. Three days cost ¥14,000 and five days ¥18,000, Green superior cars cost ¥6,000 extra. Japan Rail's English-language information line provides price and schedule information for JR lines nationwide.

Train Information Japan Railway Information Line ☎ 03/3423-0111. JR Hokkaidō Twinkle Plazas at main stations ☎ 011/209-5030 ⊕ www.jrhokkaido.co.jp/global /.

Contacts & Resources

BANKS & EXCHANGE SERVICES

Outside major cities there are no exchange services. Hokkaidō towns are small, and local banks are not user-friendly for foreign visitors. Sapporo, Hakodate, Asahikawa, and Kushiro have banks with exchange counters and automatic teller machines. Credit card use is not widespread, apart from large hotels and gas stations.

Banks in Sapporo are concentrated on Eki-mae Dōri the wide main street linking the station and the Ōdōri shopping area. Banking hours are weekdays 10–3.

The Hokkaidō Bank Money Exchange Plaza (✉ Ōdōri, Nishi 4, Sapporo ☎ 011/233-1167 ☉ Weekdays 10–7, Sat. 10–5).

Consulate U.S. Consulate ☎ Kita 1-jō Nishi 28, Chūo-ku, Maruyama Park, Sapporo ☎ 011/641-1115.

EMERGENCIES

Traveler emergencies are most likely to happen when driving, hiking, or engaging in winter sports in Hokkaidō. Driving conditions in November and early December are hazardous, but locals are quick to aid stranded drivers, and many carry chains and winch cables in their vehicles. Distances between gas stations in rural areas can be long. In spring and fall hikers should heed bear warning signs at trailheads, and solo travelers should inform guesthouse staff about their hiking plans and sign in at trailhead visitor books.

Beyond major cities English is not widely spoken, but police and other emergency service staffs are generally unfazed by a foreign face. In Otaru or towns in eastern Hokkaidō police have been known to ask to see foreigners' passports if local Russian-Japanese tensions are on the upswing. Note that some mountain areas, and particularly Shiretoko National Park, are out of range for most mobile telephone servers.
🚺**Ambulance** ☎ 119. **Police** ☎ 110.

ENGLISH-LANGUAGE MEDIA

BOOKS   Outside Sapporo, finding English-language books is difficult, so you may want to browse in the expansive Kinokuniya near the west exit of Sapporo station first; foreign magazines are on the first floor near the escalators, and fiction, nonfiction, and English-language teaching books are on the second floor. The children's section also has many Japanese titles in translation.
🚺**Kinokuniya** ✉ Kita-5 jō Nishi 6, Sapporo station, Sapporo ☎ 011/231-2131 ⊙ Daily 10-9.

INTERNET, MAIL & SHIPPING

Sapporo is the best place for e-mail checking for those with laptops. Many major hotels allow nonguests to use their business centers for a fee. There are some Internet cafés, although few are well prepared for non-Japanese-speaking customers.

Outside Sapporo, public Internet connection chances are limited. Rural guesthouse owners will often allow short access to their personal computers, or foreign staff at English-language schools in small cities and towns may share their keyboard in exchange for the novel you finished reading on the plane.
🚺 **ComicLand Internet Cafe** ✉ Ōdōri Nishi 4, near Exit 10 from Ōdōri subway station, Sapporo ☎ 011/200-3003 ⊙ Until 3 AM. **Sapporo Main Post Office** ✉ Kita-5 jō Higashi 1 6, 2 blocks from Sapporo Station, Sapporo ☎ 011/251-3957 ⊙ Daily 9-5, but 24-hour window for registered mail.
🚺 **DHL** ☎ 011/894-8315.

TOURS

The Japan Travel Bureau runs tours of Hokkaidō from Tōkyō, lasting from a few to several days. These include airfare, hotel, and meals, and stop at major cities and scenic areas. Bookings should be made at least 10 days in advance. Although your guide may speak some English, the tours are geared to domestic travelers and are conducted in Japanese.
🚺 **Japan Travel Bureau** ☎ 03/5620-9500 in Tōkyō.

Points of Interest

SITES/AREAS	JAPANESE CHARACTERS
Abashiri	網走
Akan National Park	阿寒国立公園
Akan ko (Lake Akan)	阿寒湖
Akan-kohan	阿寒湖畔
Aoyama Villa (Aoyama Bettei)	旧青山別邸
Asahikawa	旭川
Botanical Gardens (Shokubutsu-en)	北大植物園
Central & Northern Hokkaidō	道央と道北
Clock Tower (Tokeidai)	時計台
Daisetsu-zan National Park	大雪山国立公園
Eastern Hokkaidō and Okhotsk	朝陽亭
Hakodate	函館
Hakodate History Plaza (Hakodate Puraza)	函館歴史プラザ
Hakodate Russian Orthodox Church (Harisutosu Sei Kyōkai)	函館ハリストス正教会
Herring Mansion (Nishin Goten)	鰊御殿
Historical Museum of Hokkaidō (Kaitaku Kinenkan)	開拓記念館
Historical Village of Hokkaidō (Kaitaku-no-mura)	北海道開拓の村
Hokkaido University Museum	北海道大学総合博物館
Hokkaidō Museum of Northern Peoples (Hoppō Minzoku Hakubutsukan)	北方民族博物館
Hokkaidō Shrine (Hokkaidō Jingu)	北海道神宮
Iwaobetsu Onsen	岩尾別温泉
Kamuiwakka Onsen	カムイワッカ温泉
Kawamura Kaneto Ainu Memorial Hall (Kawamura Kaneto Ainu Kinen-kan)	川村兼人アイヌ記念館
Kayano Shigeru Nibutani Ainu Archive (Kayano Shigeru Nibutani Shirrō-kan)	萱野茂二風谷アイヌ資料館
Kuma-no-yu	熊ノ湯
Morning Market	朝市
Mount Rausu	羅臼岳
Mt. Eniwa (Eniwa-dake)	恵庭岳
Mt. Kurodake (Kuro-dake)	黒岳
Nakajima Kōen (Nakajima Park)	中島公園

Nibutani	二風谷
Nibutani Ainu Culture Museum (Nibutani Ainu Bunka Hakubutsukan)	二風谷アイヌ文化博物館
Niseko	ニセコ
Nishiyama Crater Trail	西山火口群散策路
Noboribetsu Bear Park	のぼりべつクマ牧場
Noboribetsu Onsen	登別温泉
Nukumorino-yado Furukawa	ぬくもりの宿ふる川
Odōri Kōen (Odōri Park)	大通公園
Otaru	小樽
Otaru & Niseko	小樽
Otaru Canal Glass Factory (Otaru Unga Kōgeikan)	小樽運河工藝館
Plaza i	プラザi
Poroto Kotan	ポロトコタン
Prison Museum (Abashiri Kangokuku Hakbutsukan)	網走監獄博物館
Rebun Island (Rebun-tō)	礼文島
Rent-A-Cycle Sapporo	レンタサイクル札幌
Rishiri Island (Rishiri-tō)	利尻島
Sapporo	札幌
Sapporo Beer Garden and Museum (Sapporō Biiru-en)	札幌ビール園と博物館
Sapporo International Communication Plaza (Sapporo Kokusai Kōryū Puraza)	札幌国際プラザ
Sapporo Winter Sports Museum	札幌ウィンタースポーツミュージアム
Shikotsu-Tōya National Park	支笏・洞爺国立公園
Shiretoko Go-ko (Five Lakes)	知床五湖
Shiretoko National Park	知床国立公園
Shōwa Shin-zan	昭和新山
Sōun-kyō (Sōun-kyō Gorge)	層雲峡
Sōun-kyō Onsen	層雲峡温泉
Sōya-misaki (Cape Sōya)	宗谷岬
Tanuki Mall (Tanuki Kōji)	狸小路
The Foundation for Research and Promotion of Ainu Culture	アイヌ文化振興・研究推進機構

The Northern Cape	道北
Tōya-ko	洞爺湖
Tōya-ko Onsen	洞爺湖温泉
Valley of Hell (Jigokudani)	地獄谷
Volcanic Science Museum (Abuta Kazan Kagaku-kan)	虻田町立火山科学館
Yōtei-zan (Mt. Yōtei)	羊蹄山

14

RESTAURANTS

Biyōtei	びようてい
Daruma	だるま
Dosanko-tei	道産子亭
Hakodate Beer Hall	函館ビアホール
Izakiya Bang Bang	居酒屋ばんばん
Kani Honke	かに本家
Keiyaki	けやき
Kita Hall	北ホール
Kita-no Ice Cream	北のアイスクリーム
Michi-no Iie Shokudo	道乃家食堂
Nakazushi	中鮨
Otaru Souko No. 1	小樽倉庫No. 1
Ramen Yoko-chō	ラーメン横丁
Sushi-zen	すし善
Susukino	すすきの
Takada-ya	高田屋
Takeda	たけだ
The Den	ザ・デン
Zazi	ザジ

HOTELS

Abashiri Central Hotel	
Authent Hotel	網走セントラルホテル
Chōyōtei	オーセント・ホテル
Dai-ichi Takimoto-kan	東北海道とオホーツク
Grand Papa	東北海道とオホーツク
Hakodate Kokusai Hotel	グランパパ

Hera-san-no Ie	ペンションへらさんの家
Hotel Abashiri-ko-so	原さんのうち
Hotel Chi-no-hate	ホテル地の涯
Hotel Furukawa	ふる川
Hotel Maki	ふる川
Hotel New Hakodate	ホテルニューハコダテ
Hotel Niseko Alpen	ホテル ニュー ハコダテ
Hotel Ōkura	ホテル ニセコ アルペン
Iruka Hotel	いるかホテル
Iwaobetsu Youth Hostel	岩尾別ユースホステル
JR Tower Hotel Nikko Sapporo	JRタワーホテル日航札幌
Lake Spa Takada	
Minshuku Yamaguchi	山口民宿
Nakamuraya Ryokan	中村屋旅館
Otaru Hilton	小樽ヒルトン
Pension Kokian	ペンションうーにー
Pension Ohno	ペンションおおの
Pension Puppy Tail	ペンションパピーテール
Pension Ūnii	ペンションうーにー
Ryotei Hanayura-ya	旅亭 花ゆら
Ryū's Inn	リューズイン
Sapporo Grand Hotel	知床第一ホテル
Shiretoko Daiichi Hotel	知床第一ホテル
Sōun-kyō Youth Hostel	層雲峡ユースホステル
The Windsor Hotel	ワシントンホテル
Washington Hotel	ワシントンホテル
Yamanoue	山の上

UNDERSTANDING JAPAN

JAPANESE CUISINE

Meal Essentials

THE BASIC FORMULA FOR a traditional Japanese meal is deceptively simple. It starts with soup, followed by raw fish, then the entrée (grilled, steamed, simmered, or fried fish, chicken, or vegetables), and ends with rice and pickles, with perhaps fresh fruit for dessert, and a cup of green tea.

There are a few twists to the story. Beyond the raw fish, it's the incredible variety of vegetation used in Japanese cooking that surprises the Western palate: *take-no-ko* (bamboo shoots), *renkon* (lotus root), and the treasured *matsutake* mushrooms (which grow wild in jealously guarded forest hideaways, sometimes selling for more than $60 apiece), to name a few.

There are also ground rules. Absolute freshness is first. To a Japanese chef this is an unparalleled virtue, and much of a chef's reputation relies on the ability to obtain the finest ingredients at the peak of season: fish brought in from the sea this morning (not yesterday) and vegetables from the earth (not the hothouse).

Simplicity is next. Rather than embellishing foods with heavy spices and rich sauces, the Japanese chef prefers flavors that enhance, not elaborate, accent rather than conceal. Without a heavy dill sauce, fish is permitted a degree of natural fishiness— a garnish of fresh red ginger offsets the flavor rather than disguising it.

The third prerequisite is beauty. Simple, natural foods must appeal to the eye and the palate. Green peppers on a vermilion dish or an egg custard in a blue bowl. Rectangular dishes for a round eggplant. So important is the seasonal element in Japanese cooking that maple leaves and pine needles accent an autumn dish. Or two small summer delicacies, a pair of freshwater *ayu* fish, are grilled with a purposeful twist to their tails to make them "swim" across a crystal platter.

Japanese Haute Cuisine

Kaiseki refers to the most elegant style of Japanese food, and *ryōri* means cuisine. Rooted in the banquet feasts of the aristocracy, by the late 16th century kaiseki ryōri had developed into a meal to accompany ceremonial tea. The word *kaiseki* derives from the word for a heated stone (*seki*) that Buddhist monks placed inside the folds (*kai*) of their kimonos to stave off the cold in unheated temple halls.

Cha-kaiseki, the meal served with tea (*cha*), takes the edge off your hunger at the beginning of a formal ceremony and counterbalances the astringent character of the thick green tea. In the tea ceremony, balance is the guiding principle.

The formula for the basic Japanese meal derived originally from the rules governing formal kaiseki—not too large a portion, just enough; not too spicy, but perhaps with a savory sprig of trefoil to offset the bland tofu. A grilled dish is served before a steamed one, a steamed dish before a simmered one; a square plate is used for a round food.

Kaiseki ryōri appeals to all the senses at once. The poem on a hanging scroll and the flowers in the alcove set the seasonal theme, a motif picked up in the pattern of the evening's dishware. The colors and shapes of the vessels complement the foods served on them. The visual harmony is as vital as the balance and variety of flavors of the foods themselves. The finest ryōtei will never serve a fish or vegetable out of season—no matter how marvelous a winter melon today's modern greenhouses can guarantee. Melons are for rejoicing in the summer's bounty . . . period.

Kaiseki ryōri found its way into a much earthier realm when it became the fashionable snack with sake in the teahouses of the geisha quarters during the 17th and 18th centuries. The characters for the word *kaiseki* are different in this context; they refer to aristocratic "banquet seats." To partake in the most exclusive of these evenings in a teahouse in Kyōto requires a personal introduction and a great deal of money, though these days many traditional restaurants serve elegant kaiseki meals (without the geisha) at more reasonable prices.

An excellent way to experience this incomparable cuisine on a budget is to visit a kaiseki restaurant at lunchtime. Many of them offer *kaiseki bentō* lunches at a fraction of the dinner price, exquisitely presented in lacquered boxes, as a sampler of their full-course evening meal.

Zen-Style Vegetarian Cuisine

Shōjin ryōri is the Zen-style vegetarian cuisine. Protein is provided by an almost limitless number of dishes made from soybeans—such as *yu-dōfu*, or boiled bean curd, and *yuba*, sheets of pure protein skimmed from vats of steaming soy milk. The variety and visual beauty of a full-course shōjin ryōri meal offer new dimensions in gourmet vegetarian dining. *Goma-dōfu*, or sesame-flavored bean curd, is a delicious treat, as is *nasu-dengaku*, grilled eggplant covered with a sweet *miso* sauce.

Many fine restaurants—particularly in the Kyōto area—specialize in shōjin ryōri, but at one of the many temples throughout Japan open to visitors you can try these special meals within actual temple halls, often overlooking a traditional garden.

On the Menu

Sushi and tempura are the best-known Japanese dishes, but they are not the only ones. *Sashimi* consists of very fresh, thinly sliced seafood that is served with a soy sauce-wasabi paste, thinly sliced ginger root, or *ponzu*, and a simple garnish like shredded daikon radish. Though most seafood is served raw, some sashimi ingredients, like octopus, are sometimes cooked. Less common, but not unusual, sashimi ingredients are vegetarian items such as *yuba* (bean-curd skin) and raw red meats, such as beef or horse.

Sukiyaki is a popular beef dish sautéed with vegetables in an iron skillet at the table. The tenderness of the beef is the determining factor, and the best sukiyaki houses often run their own butcher shops—the Japanese are justifiably proud of their notorious beer-fed and hand-massaged beef.

Shabu-shabu is more popular with tourists than with the Japanese. It's similar to sukiyaki in that it is prepared at the table with a combination of vegetables, but it differs in that shabu-shabu is swished briefly in boiling water, while sukiyaki is sautéed in oil and, usually, a slightly sweetened soy sauce. The word *shabu-shabu* refers to the swishing sound.

Nabemono, or one-pot dishes, are not so familiar to Westerners, but nothing tastes better on a cold winter's night. Simmered in a light, fish-based broth, these stews can be made of almost anything: chicken (*tori-nabe*), oysters (*kaki-nabe*), or the sumō wrestler's favorite, the hearty *chanko-nabe* . . . with something in it for everyone. Nabemono is a popular family or party dish. Restaurants specializing in nabemono have a casual, country atmosphere.

Feasting on a Budget

Many wonderful restaurants provide excellent meals and service without draining your bank account. To find them, don't be afraid to venture outside your hotel lobby or try a spot that has no English menu; use the point and order method. Many restaurants post menus out front that clearly state the full price (some do add a 10% tax, and possibly a service charge, so ask in advance).

The Bentō. This traditional and extemely portable Japanese box lunch is available for takeout everywhere. It has rice, pickles, grilled fish or meat, and vegetables in an almost limitless variety of combinations to suit the season.

Soba & Udon. Soba and udon (noodle) dishes are lifesaving treats for stomachs (and wallets) unaccustomed to exotic flavors (and prices). Small shops serving soba (thin, brown buckwheat noodle) and udon (thick, white-wheat noodle) dishes can be found in every neighborhood in the country. Both can be ordered plain (ask for *o-soba* or *o-udon*), in a lightly seasoned broth flavored with bonito and soy sauce, or in combination with things like tempura shrimp (*tempura soba* or *udon*) or chicken (*tori-namban soba* or *udon*). For a refreshing change in summer, try *zaru soba,* cold noodles to be dipped in a tangy soy sauce. *Nabeyaki-udon* is a hearty winter dish of udon noodles, assorted vegetables, and egg served in the pot that cooked it.

Robatayaki. Perhaps the most expensive of the inexpensive options is the robatayaki (grill). It's easy to order because the food to be grilled is lined up behind glass at the counter. Popular choices are *yaki-zakana* (grilled fish), particularly *karei-shio-yaki* (salted and grilled flounder) and *asari saka-mushi* (clams simmered in sake). Try the grilled Japanese shiitake mushrooms, *ao-tō* (green peppers), and the *hiyayakko* (chilled tofu sprinkled with bonito flakes, diced green onions, and soy sauce). Yakitori can be ordered in most robatayaki shops, though many inexpensive drinking places specialize in this popular barbecued chicken dish.

Okonomiyaki is somewhat misleadingly called the Japanese pancake. It is actually a mixture of vegetables, meat, and seafood in an egg-and-flour batter grilled at your table, much better with beer than with butter. It's popular for lunch or as an after-movie snack.

Another popular drinking snack is **kushi-age,** skewered bits of meat, seafood, and vegetables battered, dipped in bread crumbs, and deep-fried. Many small restaurants serve only kushi-age at a counter, and many of the robatayaki serve it as a side dish.

Oden, a winter favorite, is a variety of meats and vegetables slowly simmered in vats, and it goes well with beer or sake. This may be ordered piece by piece (*ippin*) from what you see steaming away behind the counter or *moriawase,* in which case the cook serves up an assortment.

Regional Differences

Tōkyō people are known for their candor and vigor, as compared with the refined restraint of people in the older, more provincial Kyōto. This applies as much to food as to language, art, and fashion. Foods in the Kansai district (including Kyōto, Nara, Ōsaka, and Kōbe) tend to be lighter, the sauces less spicy, the soups not as hardy as those of the Kantō district, of which Tōkyō is the center. How many Tōkyōites have been heard to grumble about the "weak" soba broth in Kyōto? You go to Kyōto for the delicate and formal kaiseki, to Tōkyō for sushi.

Nigiri zushi (note that the pronunciation of "sushi" changes to "zushi" when combined with certain words), with slices of raw fish on bite-size balls of rice (the form with which most Westerners are familiar), originated in the Kantō district, where there is a bounty of fresh fish. *Saba zushi* is the specialty of landlocked Kyōto. Actually the forerunner of nigiri zushi, it is made by pressing salt-preserved mackerel onto a bed of rice in a mold.

Every island in the Japanese archipelago has its specialty, and within each island every province has its own *meibutsu ryōri,* or specialty dish. In Kyūshū try *shippoku-ryōri,* a banquet-style feast of different dishes in which you eat your way up to a large fish mousse topped with shrimp. This dish is the local specialty in Nagasaki, for centuries the only port through which Japan had contact with the West.

On the island of Shikoku, try *sawachi-ryōri,* an extravaganza of elaborately prepared platters of fresh fish dishes, which is the specialty of Kōchi, the main city on the Pacific Ocean side of the island. In

Hokkaidō, where salmon dishes are the local specialty, try *ishikari-nabe,* a hearty salmon-and-vegetable stew.

Tips on Dining

• There's no taboo against slurping your noodle soup, though women are generally less boisterous about it than men.

• Pick up the soup bowl and drink directly from it, rather than leaning over the table to sip it. Take the fish or vegetables from it with your chopsticks. Return the lid to the soup bowl when you are finished. The rice bowl, too, is to be picked up and held in your left hand while you eat from it.

• Don't point, lick, or gesture with chopsticks. Also, never take food from a common serving plate with the ends of the chopsticks you've had in your mouth. Never use your chopsticks to take food from someone else's chopsticks, as this denotes a funerary custom. Don't stick your chopsticks upright in your food when you're done using them; instead, allow them to rest on the side of your dish or bowl.

• When drinking with a friend, don't pour into your own glass. Take the bottle and pour for the other person. She will in turn reach for the bottle and pour for you. The Japanese will attempt to top off your drink after every few sips.

• The Japanese don't pour sauces on their rice in a traditional meal. Sauces are intended for dipping foods lightly, not for dunking or soaking.

• Among faux pas that are considered nearly unpardonable, the worst perhaps is blowing your nose. Excuse yourself and leave the room if this becomes necessary.

• Although McDonald's and Häagen-Dazs have made great inroads on the custom of never eating in public, it's still considered gauche to munch on a hamburger (or an ice-cream cone) as you walk along a public street. In particular, avoid eating on trains or you will attract disapproving stares.

— Diane Durston

KANPAI!

WHETHER YOU'RE OUT WITH FRIENDS, clients, or belting out a tune at the local karaoke bar, you're sure to have a drink at least once during your stay. Things may look a little different, even before you start knocking back a few, so take note of the liquors of this island nation. And remember, shout *Kanpai!* (sounds like "kaan-pie") instead of *Cheers!* when you raise your glass.

Beverage of the Samurai

Sake, pronounced *sa*-kay, is Japan's number one alcoholic beverage. There are more than 2,000 different brands of sake produced throughout Japan. Like other kinds of wine, sake comes in sweet (*amakuchi*) and dry (*karakuchi*) varieties; these are graded *tokkyū* (superior class), *ikkyū* (first class), and *nikkyū* (second class) and are priced accordingly. (Connoisseurs say this ranking is for tax purposes, and is not necessarily a true indication of quality.)

Best drunk at room temperature (*nurukan*) so as not to alter the flavor, sake is also served heated (*atsukan*) or with ice (*rokku de*). It's poured from *tokkuri* (small ceramic vessels) into tiny cups called *choko*. The diminutive size of these cups shouldn't mislead you into thinking you can't drink too much. The custom of making sure that your companion's cup never runs dry often leads the novice astray.

Junmaishu is the term for pure rice wine, a blend of rice, yeast, and water to which no extra alcohol has been added. Junmaishu sake has the strongest and most distinctive flavor, compared with various other methods of brewing, and is preferred by the sake *tsū*, as connoisseurs are known.

Apart from *nomiya* (bars) and restaurants, the place to sample sake is the izakaya, a drinking establishment that usually serves dozens of different kinds of sake, including a selection of *jizake,* the kind produced in limited quantities by small regional breweries throughout the country.

Heavenly Spirits

Shōchū is made from grain and particularly associated with the southern island of Kyūshū. It's served either on the rocks or mixed with water and can be hot or cold. Sometimes a wedge of lemon or a small pickled apricot, known as *umeboshi,* is added as well. It can also be mixed with club soda and served cold.

Havin' a Biiru

Japan has four large breweries: Asahi, Kirin, Sapporo, and Suntory. Asahi and Kirin are the two heavyweights, constantly battling for the coveted title of "Japan's No. 1 Brewery," but many beer fans rate Suntory's Malts brand and Sapporo's Yebisu brand as the tastiest brews in the land. Although there are some microbreweries across Japan, locally produced brews can still be hard to find.

JAPANESE GARDENS

MANY OF THE PRINCIPLES THAT influence Japanese garden design come from religion. Shintoism, Taoism, and Buddhism, the three major religious influences in Japan, all stress the contemplation and re-creation of nature as part of the process of achieving understanding and enlightenment.

From Shintoism, Japan's ancient religion, comes *genus loci* (the spirit of place) and the search for the divine presence in remarkable natural features: special mountains, trees, rocks, and so forth. You can see the Taoist influence in islands, which act as a symbolic heaven for souls who achieve perfect harmony. Here sea turtles and cranes—creatures commonly represented in gardens—serve these enlightened souls.

Buddhist gardens function as settings for meditation, the goal of which is enlightenment. Shōgun and samurai were strongly drawn to Zen Buddhism, so Zen gardens evolved as spaces to use almost exclusively for meditation and growth. The classic example is the *karesansui* (dry landscape) consisting of meticulously placed rocks and raked gravel.

The first garden designers in Japan were temple priests. Later, tea masters created gardens to refine the tea ceremony experience. A major contribution of the tea masters was the *roji,* the path or dewy ground that leads through the garden to the teahouse. The stroll along the roji prepares participants for the tea ceremony emotionally and mentally.

Gradually gardens moved out of the exclusive realm to which only nobles, *daimyō,* (feudal lords), wealthy merchants, and poets had access, and the increasingly affluent middle class began to demand professional designers. In the process, aesthetic concerns came to override those of religion.

In addition to genus loci, karesansui style, and the roji mentioned above, here are a few terms that will help you more fully experience Japanese gardens.

Change & movement. Change is highlighted in Japanese gardens with careful attention to the seasonal variations that plants undergo: from cherry blossoms in spring to summer greenery to autumn leaf coloring to winter snow clinging to the garden's bare bones. A water element, real or abstract, often represents movement, as with the use of raked gravel or a stone "stream."

Mie gakure. The "reveal-and-hide" principle dictates that from no point should all of a garden be visible, that there is always mystery and incompleteness; viewers move through a garden to contemplate its changing perspectives.

Miniaturized landscapes. The depiction of celebrated natural and literary sites has been a frequent design technique in Japanese gardens—Fuji-san, represented by a truncated cone of stones; Ama-no-Hashidate, the famous spit of land, by a stone bridge; or a mighty forest by a lone tree.

Shakkei. "Borrowed landscape" extends the garden's boundaries by integrating a nearby mountain, grove of trees, or a sweeping temple roofline, and framing and capturing the view by echoing it with elements of similar shape or color inside the garden.

Symbolism. Abstract concepts and mythological legends are part of the garden vocabulary. The use of boulders in a streambed can represent life's surmountable difficulties, a pine tree can stand for stability, or islands in a pond for a faraway paradise.

THE TEA CEREMONY

THE TEA CEREMONY is a precisely choreographed program that started more than 1,000 years ago with Zen monks. The ritual begins as the server prepares a cup of tea for the first guest. This process involves a strictly determined series of movements and actions, which include cleansing each of the utensils to be used. One by one, the participants slurp up their bowl of tea, then eat the sweet cracker served with it. Finally, comments about the beauty of the bowls used are exchanged. The entire ritual involves contemplating the beauty in the smallest actions, focusing on their meaning in the midst of the uncertainty of life.

The architecture of a traditional teahouse is also consistent. There are two entrances: a service entrance for the host and server and a low door that requires that guests enter on their knees, in order to be humbled. Tearooms often have tatami flooring and a flower arrangement or artwork in the alcove for contemplation and comment. The three best-known schools of tea ceremonies are the Ura Senke, the Omote Senke, and the Musha Kōji, each with its own styles, emphases, and masters.

Most of your tea experiences will be geared toward the uninitiated: the tea ceremony is a rite that requires methodical initiation by education. If you don't go for instruction before your trip, keep two things in mind: first, be in the right frame of mind when you enter the room. Though the tea ceremony is a pleasant event, some people take it quite seriously, and boisterous behavior is frowned upon. Instead, make conversation appropriate to a mood of serenity. Second, be sure to sit quietly through the serving and drinking—controlled slurping is expected—and openly appreciate the tools and cups afterward, commenting on their elegance and simplicity. This appreciation is the ritual's important final step. Above all, pay close attention to the perfect elements of the ceremony, from the art at the entryway and the kimono of the server to the quality of the utensils.

Want to experience this ancient and highly ritualized art form first hand? Stop by the Hotel Ōkura Tōkyō in the heart of Roppongi (⇨ Where to Stay *in* Chapter 1), where one-hour and full-day sessions are available. ☎ *03/3582–0111, 0120/003–751 toll-free* 🌐 *www.okura.com/tokyo* ⏲ *Mon.–Sat. 11–4*

— David Miles

POTTERY & LACQUERWARE

Pottery

Ranging from clean, flawlessly decorated porcelain to rustic, spirited "mugs," Japanese ceramics maintain a strong following worldwide. The form has significantly influenced methods in the West. The popularity of Raku firing techniques, adapted from those of the Japanese pottery clan of the same name, is one example.

Japanese ceramic styles are regionally defined. Arita yaki (ceramic ware from Arita on Kyūshū), Tobe yaki, Kutani yaki, and Kyōto's Kyō yaki and Kiyomizu yaki are all porcelain ware. True to the nature of porcelain—a delicate fine-particled clay body—these styles are either elaborately decorated or covered with images. Stoneware decoration tends to have an earthier but no less refined appeal, befitting the rougher texture of the clay body. Mashiko yaki's brown, black, and white glazes are often applied in splatters. Celebrated potter Shōji Hamada (1894–1978) worked in Mashiko.

Other regional potters use glazes on stoneware for texture and color—mottled, crusty Tokoname yaki; speckled, earth-tone Shigaraki yaki made near Kyōto; and the pasty white or blue-white Hagi yaki come to life with the surface and depth of their rustic glazes. Bizen yaki, another stoneware, has no liquid glaze applied to its surfaces. Instead, pots are buried in ash, wrapped in straw, or colored in the firing process by the potters' manipulations of kiln conditions.

Unless your mind is set on the idea of kiln-hopping in pottery towns like Hagi, Bizen, and Arita, you can find these wares in department stores. If you do go on a pilgrimage, call local kilns and tourist organizations to verify that what you want to see will be open and to ask about yearly pottery sales. Reading: Inside Japanese Ceramics (Weatherhill, 1999) by Richard L. Wilson.

Lacquerware

Japanese lacquerware had its origins in the Jōmon period (8,000–300 BC), but as early as the Nara period (AD 710–84) most of the techniques we recognize today were being used. For example, maki-e (literally, "sprinkled picture") refers to several different techniques that use gold or silver powder in areas coated with liquid lacquer.

The production of lacquerware starts with draining, evaporating, and filtering the sap from lacquer trees. Successive layers of lacquer are carefully painted on basketry, wood, bamboo, woven textiles, metal, and even paper. The lacquer strengthens the object, making it durable for eating, carrying, or protecting fragile objects, such as fans. Lacquerware can be mirrorlike if polished; often the many layers contain inlays of mother-of-pearl or precious metals inserted between coats, creating a complicated design of exquisite beauty and delicacy.

The best places to see lacquerware are Horyu-ji in Nara—the temple has a beautiful display—and Wajima in Ishikawa. For a taste of what is available closer to Tōkyō—along with a range of other unique crafts from Japan—head to Bingoya Folk Craft Shop, just past Shinjuku on the Oedo subway line.

Another option is the Japan Folk Crafts Museum, which is two stops from Shibuya on the Keio Inokashira line at Komada-Todaimae station. Not only is this a must-see for fans of Japanese folk craft, it is also the best museum in the Shibuya area, featuring pottery, textiles and lacquerware.

— David Miles and Barbara Blechman

AN IMMERSION COURSE

JAPANESE CULTURAL PHENOMENA often confound first-time visitors, but few rituals are as opaque as those surrounding bathing. Baths in Japan are as much about pleasure and relaxation as they are about washing and cleansing. Traditionally, communal bathhouses served as centers for social gatherings, and even though most modern houses and apartments have bathtubs, many Japanese still prefer the pleasures of communal bathing—either at onsen while on vacation or in public bathhouses closer to home.

Japanese bathtubs are deep enough to sit in upright with (very hot) water up to your neck. It's not just the size of the tub that will surprise you; the procedures for using them are quite different from those in West. You wash yourself in a special area outside the tub first. The tubs are for soaking, not washing—soap must not get into the bathwater.

Many hotels in major cities have only Western-style reclining bathtubs, so to indulge in the pleasure of a Japanese bath you need to stay in a Japanese-style inn or find an *o-furo-ya* (public bathhouse). The latter are clean and easy to find. Japanese bath towels, typically called *ta*-o-ru, are available for a fee at onsen and bathhouses. No larger than a hand towel, they have three functions: covering your privates, washing before and scrubbing while you bathe (if desired), and drying off (wring them out hard and they dry you quite well). If you want a larger towel to dry off, you have to bring one along.

You may feel apprehensive about bathing (and bathing *properly*) in an o-furo, but if you're well versed in bathing etiquette, you should soon feel at ease. And once you've experienced a variety of public baths—from the standard bathhouses found in every neighborhood to idyllic outdoor hot springs—you may find yourself a devotee of this ancient custom.

The first challenge in bathing is acknowledging that your Japanese bath mates will stare at your body. Take solace, however, in the fact that their apparent voyeurism most likely stems from curiosity.

When you enter the bathing room, help yourself to two towels, soap, and shampoo (often included in the entry fee), and grab a bucket and a stool. At one of the shower stations around the edge of the room, use the handheld showers, your soap, and one of your towels to wash yourself thoroughly. A head-to-toe twice-over will impress onlookers. After rinsing, you may enter the public bath. You can use your one dry towel to cover yourself, or you can place it on your head (as many of your bath mates will do) while soaking. The water in the bath is as hot as the body can endure, and the reward for making it past the initial shock of the heat is the pleasure of a lengthy soak in water that is never tepid. All you need to do is lean back, relax, and experience the pleasures of purification.

— David Miles

RITUAL & RELIGION

THERE IS A SAYING that the Japanese are Shinto when they're born, Christian when they marry, and Buddhist when they die. This does not mean they start life as devotees of one religion and change faiths at specific milestones, rather it illustrates their utilitarian view of religion and ritual in daily life and how individuals move back and forth between the different faiths easily.

In Western culture people tend to stay aligned with one religious faith, but the Japanese take advantage of everything that every religion has to offer as suits the occasion. The birth of a child is most often commemorated with a Shintō ceremony. While not strictly Christian, Western-style weddings (complete with a chapel and white dress) are very popular. Finally, funerals are usually solemn Buddhist events. Nearly every home has a small shrine dedicated to the gods of Shintō, at the same time maintaining an area for Buddhist devotion.

Buddhism

Originating in 6th-century BC India, Buddhism traveled through China, Korea, and eventually to Japan. The foundation of Buddhism is that the only way to be free of the suffering caused by human desire is to realize your true "Buddha nature" through the practices of the Buddhist sect you follow. All Buddhists believe in reincarnation, with the eventual goal of reaching nirvana (the Buddhist equivalent of heaven) in the afterlife. Every sentient being (from an ant to an aardvark) has Buddha Nature and is on this same path. That's why many strict Buddhists are vegetarians.

Good and bad karma determine your progress in the spiritual journey, and can either hurry you on to nirvana or doom you to repeating innumerable lifetimes on earth. Doing good deeds and living according to Buddhist tenets like "boundless love and compassion for all sentient beings" accumulate good karma. Selfishness, anger, and greed garner bad karma. To reach nirvana, you may receive guidance from a Bodhisattva—a being that has achieved nirvana but chooses to return to earth to help those still mired in struggle. These Bodhisattvas can appear in any form and offer anything from simple, momentary advice to lifelong guidance.

Buddhist beliefs were initially welcomed by Japan's ruling nobles, but not by common people because of the religion's complex structure and theories. Different sects evolved that made Buddhism more accessible to everyday folk.

Pure Land Buddhism (Jodo Shinshu) emerged in 1175. Similar to Christianity, Pure Land stresses a form of salvation upon death if you follow the rules and believe strongly in Amida the Buddha of Compassion. Anyone who calls his name, "Namu Amida Butsu," with sincere faith, trust, and devotion, will be granted an eternal life of happiness in the Pure Land.

In 1191 Zen came from China and became popular among the military class, forming a major part of Bushido or the samurai warrior code. Zen Buddhism stresses that each individual must realize his or her own Buddha-hood, accessible through daily practice of meditation, traditional arts like flower arranging, calligraphy, and karate or mundane tasks like chopping wood and carrying water.

Nichiren Buddhism came along in 1253. Its founder condemned other sects and proclaimed that everyone is guaranteed Buddha-hood in the afterlife by chanting the title of the Lotus Sutra "Nam Myoho Renge Kyo" daily while seated before a devotional object. His confrontational attitude twice led to exile, but he was eventually allowed to return.

Shintō

Shintō translates as the "kami way," and kami means god or spirit. Shintō believes that all things animate and inanimate contain representative spirits. Stones, trees, mountains, waterfalls, even the Japanese islands have spirits, which are honored and worshipped in myriad shrines along with other natural phenomena like the sun, animals, ancestral spirits, the spirits of national heroes, and those who died for the state or community.

This ancient and indigenous faith relates directly to the creation of the islands and lineage of the emperor. As Shintō mythology outlines creation, in the beginning, from the *kami* of the center of heaven (*ame-no-minaka-nushi-no-kami*) came the kami of birth and growth (*taka-mimusubi-no-mikoto* and *kami-musubi-no-mikoto*). Then appeared the creative couple Izanagi-no-mikoto and Izanami-no-mikoto, who gave birth to the Japanese islands and the many kami in them. Of these, three were the most important—the sun goddess (Amaterasu-o-Mikami), her brother in charge of the Earth (Susa-no-o-no-mikoto), and the Moon Goddess (Tsuki yomi no mikoto) who ruled the realm of darkness.

The grandson of the sun goddess (Ninigi-no-mikoto) was instructed to rule the people of Japan with three divine treasures—a mirror, a sword, and a string of jewels. His great-grandson, Emperor Jimmu Tennō (literally "Jimmu of heaven") assumed human form, and all subsequent emperors of Japan have claimed descent from this divine being.

Shintō has since evolved strange symbolism, exotic rites and ceremonies, colorful festivals, and a mystical atmosphere in its shrines. Shintō shrines are erected on sites where some manifestation of the local kami has been observed; they are not meant to propagate faith or teach doctrine. Shrines are commonly fronted by a gateway called a torii, that marks the boundary between the mundane and the divine. The shrines are usually composed of an inner compartment where the kami dwells, with a space in front for offerings adorned with folded strips of white paper in a zigzag (*gohei*) pattern as a symbolic offering. Actual offerings of salt, rice, water, fruit, flowers, and sake are placed on tables in front of the kami dwellings.

Basic Shrine & Temple Etiquette

If you are visiting a temple or shrine during a festival, just follow along with what all the other nonclergy visitors are doing. Japanese people are very good at group behavior, and the mindset can be quite contagious. If no group behavior is going on, follow these simple rules to avoid being viewed as a clumsy foreigner:

- Stay out of roped-off areas. The boundaries have been set out for good reason—some areas of shrines and temples are accessible to monks and priests only.

- Remove your shoes when entering the structure. You should see a group of slippers for visitors at the entrance. They are there for your use.

- Bow slightly before entering the doorway and upon leaving—always facing the main altar or shrine area.

- When standing before the altar, make some sort of offering: in most Buddhist temples you can buy a stick of incense to light and place in the censor. At Shintō shrines you may notice a rope attached to a bell. Pull the rope to ring the bell, clap your hands twice, and drop a few coins in the offering box.

- Don't take flash photographs without asking permission. Many shrines and temples house ancient scrolls or icons that can be damaged by the flash. You could ask in simple Japanese if photography is permitted (Sha-shin o totte mo eee desu ka?).

- In general, behave as if you were in a museum or cathedral, avoiding loud and disrespectful behavior.

— Jim Klar

THE EVOLUTION OF TŌKYŌ

IN THE 12TH CENTURY, Tōkyō was a little fishing village called Edo (pronounced *eh-doh*). Over the next 400 years it was governed by a succession of warlords and other rulers. One of them, Dōkan Ōta, built the first castle in Edo in 1457. That act is still officially regarded as the founding of the city, but the honor really belongs to Ieyasu (ee-eh-*ya*-su), the first Tokugawa shōgun, who arrived in 1590. On the site of Ōta's stronghold, he built a fortress of his own—from which, 10 years later, he was effectively ruling the whole country.

By 1680 more than a million people lived here, and a great city had grown up out of the reeds in the marshy lowlands of Edo Bay. Tōkyō is best understood as a *jō-ka-machi*—a castle town. Ieyasu had fought his way to the shogunate, and he had a warrior's concern for the geography of his capital. Edo Castle had the high ground, but all around it, at strategic points, he gave large estates to allies and trusted retainers. These lesser lords' villas also served as garrisons—outposts on a perimeter of defense.

Farther out, Ieyasu kept the barons he trusted least, and whom he controlled by bleeding their treasuries. He required them to keep large, expensive establishments in Edo; to contribute generously to the temples he endowed; to come and go in alternate years in great pomp and ceremony; and, when they returned to their estates, to leave their families—in effect, hostages—behind.

All the feudal estates, villas, gardens, and temples lay south and west of Edo Castle in an area known as Yamanote, where everything was about order, discipline, and ceremony. Every man had his rank and duties, and very few women were within the castle's garrisons. Those duties were less military than bureaucratic, and Ieyasu's precautions worked like a charm. The Tokugawa dynasty enjoyed some 250 years of nearly unbroken peace.

But Yamanote was only the demand side of the economy: somebody had to bring in the fish, weed the gardens, weave the mats, and entertain the bureaucrats. To serve the noble houses, common people flowed into Edo from all over Japan. Their allotted quarters of the city were jumbles of narrow streets, alleys, and cul-de-sacs in the low-lying estuarine lands to the north and east. Often the land assigned to them wasn't even there; they had to *make* it by draining and filling the marshes (the first reclamation project in Edo dates from 1457). The result was Shitamachi—literally "downtown"—the part below the castle. Bustling, brawling Shitamachi was the supply side: it had the lumberyards, markets, and workshops; the wood-block printers, kimono makers, and moneylenders. The people gossiped over the back fence in the earthy, colorful Edo dialect. They went to Yoshiwara—a walled and moated area on the outskirts of Edo where prostitution was under official control. (Yoshiwara was for a time the biggest licensed brothel area in the world.) They supported the bathhouses and kabuki theaters and reveled in their spectacular summer fireworks festivals. The city and spirit of the Edokko—the people of Shitamachi—have survived, while the great estates uptown are now mostly parks and hotels.

The shogunate was overthrown in 1867 by supporters of Emperor Meiji. The following year the emperor moved his court from Kyōto to Edo and renamed it Tōkyō: the Eastern Capital. By now the city was home to nearly 2 million people, and the geography was vastly more complex than what Ieyasu had seen. As it grew, it became many smaller cities, with different centers of commerce, government, entertainment, and transportation. In Yamanote, the commercial emporia, office buildings, and public halls made up the architecture of an emerging modern state. The workshops of Shitamachi multiplied, some becoming small wholesalers and family-run factories.

Still, there was no planning, no grid. The neighborhoods and subcenters were worlds unto themselves, and a traveler from one was soon hopelessly lost in another.

The fire-bombings of 1945 left Tōkyō, for the most part, in rubble and ashes. That utter destruction could have been an opportunity to rebuild on the rational order of cities like Kyōto, Barcelona, or Washington. No such plan was ever made. Tōkyō reverted to type: it became once again an aggregation of small towns and villages. One village was much like any other; the nucleus was always the *shōten-gai*, the shopping arcade. Each arcade had at least one fishmonger, grocer, rice dealer, mat maker, barber, florist, and bookseller. You could live your whole life in the neighborhood of the shōten-gai.

People seldom moved out of these villages. The vast waves of new residents who arrived after World War II—about three-quarters of the people in the Tōkyō metropolitan area today were born elsewhere—just created more villages. People who lived in the villages knew their way around, so there was no particular need to name the streets. Houses were numbered in the order in which they were built, rather than in a spatial sequence. No. 3 might well share a mailbox with No. 12. People still take their local geography for granted—the closer you get to the place you're looking for, the harder it is to get coherent directions. Away from main streets and landmarks even a taxi driver can get hopelessly lost.

Fortunately, there are the *kōban*: small police boxes, or substations, usually with two or three officers assigned to each of them full-time, to look after the affairs of the neighborhood. You can't go far in any direction without finding a kōban. The officer on duty knows where everything is and is glad to point the way. (The substation system, incidentally, is one important reason for the legendary safety of Tōkyō: on foot or on white bicycles, the police are a visible presence, covering the beat. Burglaries are not unknown, of course, but street crime is very rare.)

Tōkyō is still really two areas, Shitamachi and Yamanote. The heart of Shitamachi, proud and stubborn in its Edo ways, is Asakusa; the dividing line is Ginza, west of which lie the boutiques and department stores, the banks and engines of government, the pleasure domes and cafés. Today there are 13 subway lines in full operation that weave the two areas together.

FILMS & LITERATURE

Films

Akira Kurosawa, Japan's best-known film-maker, began directing in 1943. His film *Rashōmon* (1950), a 12th-century murder mystery told by four different and untrustworthy narrators, sparked world interest in Japanese cinema. Among his classic-period films are *Seven Samurai* (1954), *The Hidden Fortress* (1958) (also the inspiration for Star Wars), *Yōjimbō* (1961), *Red Beard* (1965), *Dersu Uzala* (1975), and *Kagemusha* (1980). The life-affirming *Ikiru* (1952) deals with an office worker dying of cancer. *The Bad Sleep Well* (1960), meanwhile, portrays a nightmare of (then) contemporary Japanese corporate corruption. Two of Kurosawa's most honored films were adapted from Shakespeare plays: *Throne of Blood* (1957), based on *Macbeth*, and *Ran* (1985), based on *King Lear*. Many of Kurosawa's films star the irrepressible Toshiro Mifune, whose intense character is constantly exploding against a rigid social structure.

Other seminal samurai pics include Teinosuke Kinugasa's *Gate of Hell* (1953), which vividly re-creates medieval Japan and won an Oscar for best foreign film, and *The Samurai Trilogy* (1954), directed by Hiroshi Inagaki, which follows the adventures of a legendary 16th-century samurai hero, Musashi Miyamoto.

In 1962 an immensely popular movie series began about Zatoichi, a blind swordsman who wanders from town to town seeking work as a masseur but instead always finds himself at the center of some bloody intrigue that forces him to kill lots of people. Beginning with *The Tale of Zatoichi*, some 25 movies were made in 11 years. The legend continued in two later films released in 1989 and 2003, both called *Zatoichi*.

A new group of filmmakers came to the forefront in postwar Japan including Kon Ichikawa, Hiroshi Teshigahara, and Shōhei Imamura. Ichikawa directed two powerful antiwar movies, *The Burmese Harp* (1956) and *Fires on the Plain* (1959). Teshigahara is renowned for the allegorical *Woman in the Dunes* (1964), based on a novel by Kōbō Abe. *The Ballad of Narayama* (1983), about the death of the elderly, and *Black Rain* (1989), which deals with the atomic bombing of Hiroshima, are two powerful films by Imamura.

Other Japanese filmmakers worth checking out are Jūzō Itami, Masayuki Suo, Kitano Takeshi, and Iwai Shunji. Itami won international recognition for *Tampopo* (1986), a highly original comedy about food. His other films include *A Taxing Woman* (1987), which pokes fun at the Japanese tax system, and *Mimbō* (1992), which dissects the world of Japanese gangsters. Suo's *Shall We Dance?* (1996) is a bittersweet comedy about a married businessman who escapes his daily routine by taking ballroom dancing lessons. (The 2004 film with the same name, starring Richard Gere, Susan Sarandon, and Jennifer Lopez, was based on Suo's original.) Iwai Shunji's *Love Letter* (1995) is a touching story about a girl who receives a lost letter from her boyfriend after he has died.

Akin to the samurai films are Japanese gangster flicks. Though they date back to such Kurosawa classics as *Drunken Angel* (1948) and *Stray Dog* (1949), an edgy gangster genre emerged in the 1990s led by Beat Takeshi Kitano, who wrote, directed, and starred in *Boiling Point* (1990), *Sonatine* (1993), and *Fireworks* (1997). Tasheki is the hard-faced, silent, bad-ass type, and Clint Eastwood fans will appreciate his films. There are many Japanese gangster films, including a whole exploitative subset that mixes extreme violence with basically soft-core porn.

Those interested in Japanese animated or anime movies, should start with the Academy Award–winning picture *Spirited Away* (2002), which is available in English. *Kiki's Delivery Service* (1989), starring Kirsten Dunst as the voice of Kiki, is another good choice.

Recently, Japanese horror has also enjoyed international popularity. Focusing more on anticipation and psychological horror than blood-spurting special effects—though some can be quite gruesome, such as the hair raising *Audition* (1999)—Japanese horror tends to leave an eerie feeling that's hard to get rid of. Many involve unseen, unstoppable, or difficult-to-understand threats, like ghosts, poltergeists, and inalterable, tragic destiny. The horror hits, *Ringu* (1998) and *Ju-on: The Grudge* (2003) and their American remakes *The Ring* (2002) and *The Ring Two* (2005) and *The Grudge* (2004) and *The Grudge 2* (2006) are representative of this genre.

Japan has also been the subject of numerous Western movies. For a look at wartime Japan, Steven Spielberg's *Empire of the Sun* (1987) explores the Japanese occupation of China and the Japanese treatment of the Western colonists they replace. The classic *Bridge on the River Kwai* (1957) also explores Japan's treatment of British prisoners of war. Clint Eastwood's *Flags of Our Fathers* and *Letters from Iwo Jima,* both released in 2006, examine the Battle of Iwo Jima from the American and Japanese perspectives, respectively.

For something lighter, see the schlocky Bond flick *You Only Live Twice* (1967), which shows Tōkyō during the heady growth years of the late sixties. It features Sean Connery undergoing plastic surgery to disguise himself as a Japanese person; the screenplay is by Roald Dahl. First-time visitors to Tōkyō will likely empathize with Sofia Coppola's *Lost in Translation* (2003), about the alienation experienced by an American visitor to Tōkyō. It is a compelling and accurate view of life in contemporary Tōkyō.

Literature

Fiction & Poetry. The great classic of Japanese fiction is the *Tale of Genji,* written by Murasaki Shikibu, a woman of the imperial court around 1000 AD. Genji, or the Shining Prince, has long been taken as the archetype of male behavior. From the same period, Japanese literature's golden age, *The Pillow Book of Sei Shōnagon* is the stylish and stylized diary of a woman's courtly life.

For a selection of Edo-period ghost stories, try Akinari Ueda's *Ugetsu Monogatari: Tales of Moonlight and Rain,* translated by Leon Zolbrod. The racy prose of late-17th-century Saikaku Ihara is translated in various books, including *Some Final Words of Advice* and *Five Women Who Loved Love.*

Modern Japanese fiction is widely available in translation. One of the best-known writers among Westerners is Yukio Mishima, author of *The Sea of Fertility* trilogy and *The Temple of The Golden Pavilion*. His books often deal with the effects of postwar Westernization on Japanese culture. Two superb prose stylists are Junichirō Tanizaki, author of *The Makioka Sisters, Some Prefer Nettles,* and the racy 1920s *Quicksand*; and Nobel Prize–winner Yasunari Kawabata, whose superbly written novels include *Snow Country* and *The Sound of the Mountain*. Kawabata's *Thousand Cranes,* which uses the tea ceremony as a vehicle, is an elegant page-turner. Jirō Osaragi's *The Journey* is a lucid, entertaining rendering of the clash of tradition and modernity in postwar Japan. Also look for Natsume Sōseki's charming *Botchan* and delightful *I Am a Cat.*

Other novelists and works of note are Kōbō Abe, whose *Woman in the Dunes* is a 1960s landmark, and Shūsaku Endō, who brutally and breathlessly treated the early clash of Japan with Christianity in *The Samurai*. Seichō Matsumoto's *Inspector Imanishi Investigates* is a superb detective novel with enlightening details of Japanese life. For a fictional retelling of the nuclear devastation of Hiroshima read Ibuse Masuji's classic novel *Black Rain*.

The "new breed" of Japanese novelists are no less interesting. Haruki Murakami's *Wild Sheep Chase* is a collection of often bizarre and humorous stories, and *Hard Boiled Wonderland and the End of the World* paints a vivid and fantastical picture of the frenetic changes of modern Japan. Murakami's *The Wind-up Bird Chronicle,* a dense and daring novel, juxtaposes the banality of modern suburbia with the harsh realities of 20th-century Japanese history. Along with Murakami's books, Banana Yoshimoto's *Kitchen* and other novels are probably the most fun you'll have with any Japanese fiction. Kōno Taeko's *Toddler-Hunting* and Yūko Tsushima's *The Shooting Gallery* are as engrossing and well crafted as they are frank about the burdens of tradition on Japanese women today. Nobel Prize–winner Kenzaburō Ōe's writing similarly explores deeply personal issues, among them his compelling relationship with his disabled son. His most important works are *A Personal Matter* and *Silent Scream.*

For books by Westerners, there's a host of titles. The emotional realities of Japan life for foreigners are engagingly rendered in *The Broken Bridge: Fiction from Expatriates in Literary Japan,* edited by Suzanne Kamata. The enormously popular tale *Memoirs of a Geisha,* by Arthur Golden, recounts the dramatic life of a geisha in the decades surrounding World War II. For a humorous and absorbing account of the Gaijin condition, try Will Ferguson's *Hokkaido Highway Blues: Hitchhiking Japan.*

Haiku, the 5-7-5-syllable form that the monk Matsuo Bashō honed in the 17th century, is the flagship of Japanese poetry. Bashō's *Narrow Road to the Deep North* is a wistful prose-and-poem travelogue that is available in a few translations. But there are many more forms and authors worth exploring. Three volumes of translations by Kenneth Rexroth include numerous authors' work from the last 1,000 years: *One Hundred Poems from the Japanese, 100 More Poems from the Japanese,* and *Women Poets of Japan* (translated with Akiko Atsumi). *Ink Dark Moon,* translated by Jane Hirshfield with Mariko Aratani, presents the remarkable poems of Ono no Komachi and Izumi Shikibu, two of Japan's earliest women poets. The Zen poems of Ryōkan represent the sacred current in Japanese poetry; look for *Dew Drops on a Lotus Leaf.* Other poets to look for are Issa, Buson, and Bonchō. Two fine small volumes that link their haiku with those of other poets, including Bashō, are *The Monkey's Raincoat* and the beautifully illustrated *A Net of Fireflies.*

History & Society. Fourteen hundred years of history are a lot to take in when going on a vacation, but a good survey makes the task much easier: read George Sansom's *Japan: A Short Cultural History.*

Yamamoto Tsunetomo's *Hagakure (The Book of the Samurai)* is an 18th-century guide of sorts to the principles and ethics of the "Way of the Samurai," written by a Kyūshū samurai. Dr. Junichi Saga's *Memories of Silk and Straw: A Self-Portrait of Small-Town Japan* is his 1970s collection of interviews with local old-timers in his hometown outside Tōkyō. Saga's father illustrated the accounts. Few books get so close to the realities of everyday life in early modern rural Japan.

John Hersey's *Hiroshima* records the stories of survivors, and is essential reading. George Feifer's *Tennozan: The Battle of Okinawa and the Atomic Bomb* recounts the grueling final battle of World War II. John W. Dower is an important historian about Japan whose best known books are *War Without Mercy: Race and Power in the Pacific War,* followed by *Embracing Defeat: Japan in the Wake of World War II,* which won the Pulitzer Prize.

Or pick up any book by Japanese writer Saburo Ienaga, who died in 2002 at age 89. He had long court battles with the Japanese government, arguing that government textbooks distorted Japan's responsibility for bringing on World War II and euphemizing atrocities. Though he lost many legal battles, he was more interested in the moral ones. He was in large part the catalyst for forcing the Japanese government to finally apologize for the 1937 Nanking massacre in the early 1980s, and later in the 1990s to acknowledge imprisoning Chinese and Korean women as sex-slaves to the Japanese Army and the existence of Unit 731, responsible for the deaths of thousands of prisoners in biochemical experiments. One of his major books is *The Pacific War: World War II and the Japanese, 1931-1945*.

Karel van Wolferens *The Enigma of Japanese Power* is an enlightening book on the Japanese sociopolitical system, especially for diplomats and businesspeople intending to work with the Japanese. Alex Kerr's *Lost Japan* examines the directions of Japanese society past and present. This book was the first by a foreigner ever to win Japan's Shinchō Gakugei literature prize. Elizabeth Bumiller's 1995 *The Secrets of Mariko* intimately recounts a very poignant year in the life of a Japanese woman and her family.

The biography of Ainu activist Shigeru Kayano, *Our Land Was a Forest*, has been translated into English by Westview Press.

If you're interested in the ancient traditions of the tea ceremony, check out *The Book of Tea*, by Kakuzo Okakura.

Art & Architecture. A wealth of literature exists on Japanese art. Much of the early writing has not withstood the test of time, but R. Paine and Alexander Soper's *Art and Architecture of Japan* remains a good place to start. A more recent survey, though narrower in scope, is Joan Stanley-Smith's *Japanese Art*.

The multivolume *Japan Arts Library* covers most of the styles and personalities of the Japanese arts. The series has volumes on castles, teahouses, screen painting, and wood-block prints. A more detailed look at the architecture of Tōkyō is Edward Seidensticker's *Low City, High City*. Kazuo Nishi and Kazuo Hozumi's *What Is Japanese Architecture?* treats the history of Japanese architecture and uses examples of buildings you will see on your travels.

Religion. Anyone wanting to read a Zen Buddhist text should try *The Platform Sutra of the Sixth Patriarch*, one of the Zen classics, written by an ancient Chinese head of the sect and translated by Philip B. Yampolsky. Another Buddhist text of great importance is the *Lotus Sutra*; it has been translated by Leon Hurvitz as *The Scripture of the Lotus Blossom of the Fine Dharma: The Lotus Sutra*. Stuart D. Picken has written books on both major Japanese religions: *Shintō: Japan's Spiritual Roots* and *Buddhism: Japan's Cultural Identity*.

Travel Narratives. Three travel narratives stand out as introductions to Japanese history, culture, and people. Donald Richie's classic *The Inland Sea* recalls his journey and encounters on the fabled Seto Nai-kai. Leila Philip's year working in a Kyūshū pottery village became the eloquent *Road Through Miyama*. Peter Carey's *Wrong About Japan* follows the author and his 12-year-old son on their journey through Japan and the world of manga and anime.

Language. There's an overwhelming number of books and courses available for studying Japanese. *Japanese for Busy People* uses conversational situations (rather than grammatical principles) as a means of introducing the Japanese language. With it you will also learn the two syllabaries, *hiragana* and *katakana*, and rudimentary *kanji* characters.

JAPAN AT A GLANCE

Fast Facts

Capital: Tōkyō
National anthem: *Kimigayo (The Emperor's Reign)*
Type of government: Constitutional monarchy with a parliamentary government
Administrative divisions: 47 prefectures
Independence: 660 BC (traditional founding)
Constitution: May 3, 1947
Legal system: Modeled after European civil law system with English-American influence; judicial review of legislative acts in the Supreme Court
Suffrage: 20 years of age; universal
Legislature: Bicameral Diet or Kokkai with House of Councillors (247 seats, members elected for six-year terms, half reelected every three years, 149 members in multiseat constituencies and 98 by proportional representation); House of Representatives (480 seats, members elected for four-year terms, 300 in single-seat constituencies, 180 members by proportional representation in 11 regional blocs)
Population: 127.5 million
Population density: 340 people per square km (880 people per square mi)
Median age: Female: 44.7, male: 41.1
Life expectancy: Female: 84.7; male: 77.96
Literacy: 99%
Language: Japanese
Ethnic groups: Japanese 99%; other (Korean, Chinese, Brazilian, Filipino) 1%
Religion: Shintō and Buddhist 84%; other 16%

Geography & Environment

Land area: 374,744 square km (144,689 square mi), slightly smaller than California
Coastline: 29,751 km (11,487 mi)
Terrain: Mostly rugged and mountainous
Islands: Bonin Islands (Ogasawara-gunto), Daitō-shotō, Minami-jima, Okino-tori-shima, Ryūkyū Islands (Nansei-shoto), and Volcano Islands (Kazan-retto)
Natural resources: Fish, mineral resources
Natural hazards: Japan has about 1,500 earthquakes (mostly tremors) every year; tsunamis; typhoons, volcanoes
Environmental issues: Air pollution from power plant emissions results in acid rain; acidification of lakes and reservoirs degrading water quality and threatening aquatic life; Japan is one of the largest consumers of fish and tropical timber, contributing to the depletion of these resources in Asia and elsewhere

Economy

Currency: Yen
Exchange rate: 110 yen
GDP: $3.6 trillion
Per capita income: 4 million yen ($35,610)
Inflation: -0.4%
Unemployment: 5.3%
Work force: 66.7 million; services 70%; industry 25%; agriculture 5%
Major industries: Chemicals, electronic equipment, machine tools, motor vehicles, processed foods, ships, steel and nonferrous metals, textiles
Agricultural products: Dairy products, eggs, fish, fruit, pork, poultry, rice, sugar beets, vegetables
Exports: $447.1 billion

Major export products: Chemicals, motor vehicles, office machinery, semiconductors
Export partners: U.S. 28.8%; China 9.6%; South Korea 6.9%; Taiwan 6.3%; Hong Kong 6.1%
Imports: $346.6 billion

Major import products: Chemicals, foodstuffs, fuels, machinery and equipment, raw materials, textiles
Import partners: China 18.3%; U.S. 17.4%; South Korea 4.6%; Indonesia 4.2%; Australia 4.1%

Political Climate

Japan has more than 10,000 political parties, mostly small, regional bodies without mass appeal. The Liberal Democratic party (LDP) has held the majority in the legislature since 1955, when the party was formed, with a brief ouster in the 1990s. The LDP is considered a conservative party and has supported close ties with the U.S., especially concerning security. The Democratic Party of Japan and New Komeito form the largest opposition groups. Economically, deregulation and growth in the free market are important policy issues. Japan's aging population is also becoming a crucible for politicians, as they balance a dwindling labor force and increasing pensions and benefits for the elderly.

Did You Know?

- Japanese engineers have built a car that can go 11,193 miles on one gallon of fuel, a world record. The car performs best at 15 mi per hour and engineers are adapting the technology for commercial production. Japan is also home to the world's first environmentally friendly rental car company. Kobe-Eco-Car in Kobe has rented electric vehicles, compressed natural gas vehicles, and hybrid cars since it was founded in 1998.

- With an average life expectancy of 77.96 years for men and 84.7 years for women, the Japanese live longer than anyone else on the planet.

- To take any of the 2,200 daily trips on the East Japan Railway is to ride the world's busiest train system. It carries 16 million passengers over 4,684 mi of track, stopping at a dizzying 1,707 stations.

- The largest sumō wrestling champion in the history of the sport isn't Japanese, but American. Chad Rowan, born in Hawaii, reached the top ranking of yokozuna, in 1983. He was 6 feet 8 inches and 501 pounds.

- The Japanese prime minister earns an annual salary of 69.3 million yen ($676,000), the highest of any prime minister in the world.

- Japan's *Yomiuri Shimbun* has more readers than any other newspaper on earth. Its combined morning and evening circulation is 14.3 million, 10 times more than that of the *New York Times*.

- Japan is the third-largest consumer of cigarettes. The Japanese smoke about 325 billion cigarettes each year, about 100 billion less than Americans and more than a trillion less than the Chinese.

- Japan has the highest density of robots in the world.

TŌKYŌ AT A GLANCE

Fast Facts

Type of government: Metropolitan prefecture with democratically elected governor and assembly. There are 47 prefectures in Japan; Tōkyō is the largest. Wards and other subsidiary units have local assemblies.
Population: 12.544 million (city), or 10% of Japan's total population.
Population of Foreign Residents: 360,000
Population density: 5,736 people per square km; Tōkyō is the most densely populated prefecture in Japan.

Households: 5.866 million; average 2.14 persons per household.
Demographic composition by age: Juveniles (ages 0–14), 1.446 million (11.9%); working age population (ages 15-64), 8.539 million (70.2%); and the elderly (65 years old and over), 2.176 million (17.9%).
Language: Japanese (official)

Geography & Environment

Latitude: 35°N (same as Albuquerque, New Mexico; Kabul, Afghanistan; Memphis, Tennessee).
Longitude: 139°E (same as Adelaide, Australia).
Elevation: 17 meters (59 feet).
Land area: 2,187 square km or 0.6% of the total area of Japan.
Terrain: Tōkyō sits on the Kantō plain, at the head of Tōkyō Bay, near the center of the Japanese archipelago. Edogawa River is to the east, mountains are to the west, and Tamagawa River is to the south. Mt. Fuji, Japan's highest mountain, rises up 12,388 feet about 60 mi (100 km) west of Tōkyō.

Natural hazards: Earthquakes, typhoons
Environmental issues: Tōkyō has banned trucks that don't meet strict emissions standards and ordered filters placed on many other diesel vehicles. As a result, the air quality has improved. Studies are being conducted on the so-called "heat island" effect, which is the raising of temperatures by air-conditioners and other exhausts emitted by buildings in the dense downtown area. Also, finding landfills for the city's garbage is a growing problem.

Economy

Unemployment: 6.1%
Work force: 6.2 million; clerical, technical, and management occupations 46.3%; sales and services 29.2%; manufacturing and transportation-related occupations 24%; agriculture, forestry and fisheries 0.5%

Major industries: Automobiles, banking, cameras and optical goods, consumer items, electronic apparatus, equipment, financial services, furniture, publishing and printing, textiles, transport.

Did You Know?

- The average Tōkyō residence is only slightly larger than a two-car garage in the U.S.

- Tōkyō has the lowest population of children aged 0 to 14 of any area of Japan.

- Japanese inventors have created a material that absorbs nitrogen and sulfur oxide gases, reducing smog. The product is now in use on bridges, buildings, and highways across Tōkyō.

- Tōkyō has the second largest home-less population in Japan. In 2003, the city counted 5,927 people. About half are estimated to be sleeping in parks and on the streets, the rest are in government shelters.

- There are eight U.S. military bases within Tōkyō, covering more than 6 square mi.

- Tōkyō's daytime population is 2.7 million people higher than its night-time population. The change is most dramatic in the city's downtown wards—Chiyoda, Chuo, and Mi-nato—which have only 268,000 persons by night and 2.3 million by day.

- The ginkgo is the most common tree in Tōkyō and has even been adopted as the city's symbol. It's fan-shaped green leaves turn yellow every fall.

- Tōkyō has served as the capital of Japan only since 1868; before that, Kyōto was the capital for more than 1,000 years.

- More than 2 million people pass through Shinjuku Station, Japan's busiest railway station, every day.

- Tōkyō suffers from an overabundance of *jidou hanbaiki* (vending machines) with 2.7 million beverage vending machines alone.

- Tōkyō is home to the world's tallest Buddha—standing 2½ times taller than the Statue of Liberty. Cast from bronze, it measures 394 feet high, and was completed in 1993. The joint Japanese and Taiwanese project, which took seven years to make, weighs 984 tons.

- The Mega-Float island at Yokosuka Port, Tōkyō Bay, is the largest artificial island in the world at 3,280 feet 10 inches long, 396 feet 12 inches wide, and 9 feet 10 inches deep. It opened to the public on August 10, 1999.

CHRONOLOGY

10,000 BC– Neolithic Jōmon hunting and fishing culture leaves richly
AD 300   decorated pottery.

AD 300   Yayoi culture displays knowledge of farming and metallurgy
          imported from Korea.

after 300 The Yamato tribe consolidates power in the rich Kansai plain and
          expands westward, forming the kind of military aristocratic society
          that will dominate Japan's history.

ca. 500   Yamato leaders, claiming to be descended from the sun goddess,
          Amaterasu, take the title of emperor.

538–52   Buddhism is introduced to the Yamato court from China by way of
          Korea, and complements the indigenous Shintō religion.

593–622   Prince Shōtoku encourages the Japanese to embrace Chinese culture
          and has Buddhist temple Hōryū-ji built at Nara in 607 (its existing
          buildings are among the world's oldest surviving wooden structures).

Nara Period

710–784   Japan has first permanent capital at Nara; great age of Buddhist
          sculpture, piety, and poetry.

Fujiwara or Heian (Peace) Period

794–1160 The capital is moved from Nara to Heian-kyō (now Kyōto), where
          the Fujiwara family dominates the imperial court. Lady Murasaki's
          novel *The Tale of Genji*, written circa 1020, describes the elegance
          and political maneuvering of court life.

Kamakura Period

1185–1335 Feudalism enters, with military and economic power in the provinces
          and the emperor a powerless, ceremonial figurehead in Kyōto.
          Samurai warriors welcome Zen, a new sect of Buddhism from China.

1192   After a war with the Taira family, Yoritomo of the Minamoto family
          becomes the first shōgun; he places his capital in Kamakura.

1274 and The fleets sent by Chinese emperor Kublai Khan to invade Japan are
1281   destroyed by typhoons, praised in Japanese history as kamikaze, or
          divine wind.

Ashikaga Period

1336–1568 The Ashikaga family assumes the title of shōgun and settles in Kyōto.
          The Zen aesthetic flourishes in painting, landscape gardening, and tea
          ceremony. Nō theater emerges. The Silver Pavilion, or Ginkaku-ji, in
          Kyōto, built in 1483, is the quintessential example of Zen-inspired
          architecture. The period is marked by constant warfare but also by
          increased trade with the mainland. Ōsaka develops into an important
          commercial city, and trade guilds appear.

1467–77 The Ōnin Wars initiate a 100-year period of civil war.

1543 Portuguese sailors, the first Europeans to reach Japan, initiate trade relations with the lords of western Japan and introduce the musket, which changes Japanese warfare.

1549–51 St. Francis Xavier, the first Jesuit missionary, introduces Christianity.

Momoyama Period of National Unification

1568–1600 Two generals, Nobunaga Oda and Hideyoshi Toyotomi, are the central figures of this period. Nobunaga builds a military base from which Hideyoshi unifies Japan.

1592 and Hideyoshi invades Korea. He brings back Korean potters, who
1597 rapidly develop a Japanese ceramics industry.

Tokugawa Period

1600–1868 Ieyasu Tokugawa becomes shōgun after the battle of Sekigahara. The military capital is established at Edo (now Tōkyō), spurring phenomenal economic and cultural growth. A hierarchical order of four social classes—warriors, farmers, artisans, then merchants—is rigorously enforced. The merchant class, however, is increasingly prosperous and effects a transition from a rice to a money economy. Merchants patronize new, popular forms of art: Kabuki, haiku, and the ukiyo-e school of painting. The latter part of this era is beautifully illustrated in the wood-block prints of the artist Hokusai (1760–1849).

1618 Japanese Christians who refuse to renounce their foreign religion are persecuted.

1637–38 Japanese Christians are massacred in the Shimabara uprising. Japan is closed to the outside world except for a Dutch trading post in Nagasaki harbor.

1853 U.S. commodore Matthew Perry reopens Japan to foreign trade.

Meiji Restoration

1868–1912 Opponents of the weakened Tokugawa Shogunate support Emperor Meiji and overthrow the last shōgun. The emperor is "restored" (with little actual power), and the imperial capital is moved to Edo, which is renamed Tōkyō (Eastern Capital). Japan is modernized along Western lines, with a constitution proclaimed in 1889; a system of compulsory education and a surge of industrialization follow.

1902–05 Japan defeats Russia in the Russo-Japanese War and achieves world-power status.

1910 Japan annexes Korea.

1914–18 Japan joins the Allies in World War I.

1923 The Great Kantō Earthquake devastates much of Tōkyō and Yokohama, killing 142,807 people, destroying more than 400,000 buildings and leaving at least 2 million people homeless.

1931 As a sign of growing militarism in the country, Japan seizes the Chinese province of Manchuria.

1937 Following years of increasing military and diplomatic activity in northern China, open warfare breaks out (and lasts until 1945); Chinese Nationalists and Communists both fight Japan.

1939–45 Japan, having signed anti-Communist treaties with Nazi Germany and Italy (1936 and 1937), invades and occupies French Indochina.

1941 The Japanese attack on Pearl Harbor on December 7 brings the United States into war against Japan in the Pacific.

1942 Japan's empire extends to Indochina, Burma, Malaya, the Philippines, and Indonesia. Japan bombs Darwin, Australia. U.S. defeat of Japanese forces at Midway turns the tide of the Pacific war.

1945 Tōkyō and 50 other Japanese cities are devastated by U.S. bombing raids. The United States drops atomic bombs on Hiroshima and Nagasaki in August, precipitating Japanese surrender.

1945–52 The American occupation under General Douglas MacArthur disarms Japan and encourages the establishment of a democratic government. Emperor Hirohito retains his position.

1953 After the Korean War, Japan begins a period of great economic growth.

1964 Tōkyō hosts the Summer Olympic games.

late 1960s Japan develops into one of the major industrial nations in the world.

mid-1970s Production of electronics, cars, cameras, and computers places Japan at the heart of the emerging "Pacific Rim" economic sphere and threatens to spark a trade war with the industrial nations of Europe and the United States.

1989 Emperor Hirohito dies.

1990 Coronation of Emperor Akihito. Prince Fumihito marries Kiko Kawashima.

1991 Mount Unzen erupts for the second time since 1792, killing 38 people.

1992 The Diet approves use of Japanese military forces under United Nations auspices.

1993 Crown Prince Naruhito marries Masako Owada.

1995 A massive earthquake strikes Kōbe and environs. Approximately 5,500 people are killed and 35,000 injured; more than 100,000 buildings are destroyed.

Members of a fringe religious organization, the Aum Shinri Kyō, carry out a series of poison-gas attacks on the transportation networks of Tōkyō and Yokohama, undermining, in a society that is a model of decorum and mutual respect, confidence in personal safety.

1997 The deregulation of rice prices and the appearance of discount gasoline stations mark a turn in the Japanese economy toward genuine privatization.

1998 The Japanese economy is crippled from slumps throughout Asia. Banks merge or go bankrupt, and Japanese consumers spend less and less.

1999 Japanese toys, films, and other accoutrements of pop culture find themselves in the international spotlight like never before. The economy, however, continues to suffer as politicians debate economic measures that foreign economists have been recommending for years. Small businesses are most affected, and the attitude of the average Japanese is grim.

A nuclear accident 112 km (70 mi) northeast of Tōkyō injures few but raises many questions about Japan's vast nuclear-power industry.

2001 In support of the U.S. war against terrorism in Afghanistan, the Japanese government extends noncombat military activities abroad for the first time since World War II by sending support ships to the Indian Ocean under a reinterpretation of the existing post-1945, pacifist constitution. Asian leaders express concern for the first Japanese military presence abroad since 1945.

2002 North Korea admits to the kidnapping of 11 Japanese civilians in the 1970s and '80s for use as language teachers. Japan negotiates the return of several of its citizens.

2003 Prime Minister Koizumi sends Japanese combat troops to Iraq in the first deployment of Japanese troops since World War II.

2006 The Bank of Japan (BOJ) raises interest rates for the first time in six years, from 0% to 0.25%, marking an end to a decade of economic stagnation. The decision brings Japan's monetary policy in line with those of the U.S. and Europe, where central bankers contain inflation by raising rates.

Shinzo Abe is elected as the country's youngest postwar prime minister and the first to be born after World War II.

ABOUT JAPANESE

Japanese sounds and spellings differ in principle from those of the West. We build words letter by letter, and one letter can sound different depending where it appears in a word. For example, we see *ta* as two letters, and *ta* could be pronounced three ways, as in *tat, tall,* and *tale.* For the Japanese, *ta* is one character, and it is pronounced one way: *tah.*

The *hiragana* and *katakana* (tables of sounds) are the rough equivalents of our alphabet. There are four types of syllables within these tables: the single vowels *a, i, u, e,* and *o,* in that order; vowel-consonant pairs like *ka, ni, hu,* or *ro;* the single consonant *n,* which punctuates the upbeats of the word for bullet train, *Shinkansen* (shee-n-ka-n-se-n); and compounds like *kya, chu,* and *ryo.* Remember that these compounds are one syllable. Thus Tōkyō, the capital city, has only two syllables—*tō* and *kyō*—not three. Likewise pronounce Kyōtō *kyō-tō,* not *kee-oh-to.*

Japanese vowels are pronounced as follows: *a*–ah, *i*–ee, *u*–oo, *e*–eh, *o*–oh. The Japanese *r* is rolled so that it sounds like a bounced *d.*

No diphthongs. Paired vowels in Japanese words are not slurred together, as in our words *coin, brain,* or *stein.* The Japanese separate them, as in mae (ma-eh), which means in front of; kōen (ko-en), which means park; byōin (byo-een), which means hospital; and tokei (to-keh-ee), which means clock or watch.

Macrons. Many Japanese words, when rendered in *romaji* (roman letters), require macrons over vowels to indicate correct pronunciation, as in Tōkyō. When you see these macrons, double the length of the vowel, as if you're saying it twice: to-o-kyo-o. Likewise, when you see double consonants, as in the city name Nikkō, linger on the Ks—as in "bookkeeper"—and on the O.

Emphasis. Some books state that the Japanese emphasize all syllables in their words equally. This is not true. Take the words *sayōnara* and *Hiroshima.* Americans are likely to stress the downbeats: *sa-yo-na-*ra and *hi-ro-shi-*ma. The Japanese actually emphasize the second beat in each case: sa-*yō-*na-ra (note the macron) and hi-*ro*-shi-ma. Metaphorically speaking, the Japanese don't so much stress syllables as pause over them or race past them: Emphasis is more a question of speed than weight. In the vocabulary below, we indicate emphasis by italicizing the syllable that you should stress.

Three interesting pronunciations are in the vocabulary below. The word *desu* roughly means "is." It looks like it has two syllables, but the Japanese race past the final *u* and just say "dess." Likewise, some verbs end in *-masu,* which is pronounced "mahss." Similarly, the character shi is often quickly pronounced "sh," as in the phrase meaning "pleased to meet you:" *ha*-ji-me-*mash(i)*-te. Just like *desu* and *-masu,* what look like two syllables, in this case *ma* and *shi,* are pronounced *mahsh.*

Hyphens. Throughout *Fōdor's Tōkyō,* we have hyphenated certain words to help you recognize meaningful patterns. This isn't conventional; it is practical. For example, *Eki-mae-dōri,* which literally means "Station Front Avenue," turns into a blur when rendered Ekimaedōri. And you'll run across a number of sight names that end in *-jingū* or *-jinja* or *-taisha.* You'll soon catch on to their meaning: Shintō shrine.

Structure. From the point of view of English grammar, Japanese sentences are structured back to front, ie subject-object-verb instead of subject-verb-object as in English. An English speaker would say "I am going to Tōkyō," which in Japanese would translate literally as "Tōkyō to going."

Note: placing an "o" before words like tera (otera) and shira (oshira) makes the word honorific. It is not essential, but it is polite.

ESSENTIAL PHRASES

Basics

Yes/No	*ha-i/ii*-e	はい／いいえ
Please	o-ne-*gai* shi-masu	お願いします
Thank you (very much)	(*dō*-mo) a-*ri*-ga-tō go-*zai*-ma su	(どうも)ありがとう ございます
You're welcome	*dō* i-ta-shi-ma-shi-te	どういたしまして
Excuse me	su-mi-ma-*sen*	すみません
Sorry	*go*-men na-*sai*	ごめんなさい
Good morning	o-*ha*-yō *go*-zai-ma-su	お早うございます
Good day/afternoon	kon-*ni*-chi-wa	こんにちは
Good evening	kom-*ban*-wa	こんばんは
Good night	o-*ya*-su-mi na-*sai*	おやすみなさい
Goodbye	sa-*yō*-na-ra	さようなら
Mr./Mrs./Miss	-san	一さん
Pleased to meet you	*ha*-ji-me-*mashi*-te	はじめまして
How do you do?	*dō*-zo yo-*ro*-shi-ku	どうぞよろしく

Numbers

The first reading is used for reading numbers, as in telephone numbers, and the second is often used for counting things.

1	*i*-chi / hi-*to*-tsu	一／一つ	17	*jū*-shi-chi	十七
2	ni / fu-*ta*-tsu	二／二つ	18	*jū*-ha-chi	十八
3	san / *mit*-tsu	三／三つ	19	*jū*-kyū	十九
4	shi / *yot*-tsu	四／四つ	20	*ni*-jū	二十
5	go / i-*tsu*-tsu	五／五つ	21	*ni*-jū-i-chi	二十一
6	ro-ku / *mut* tsu	六／六つ	30	*san*-jū	三十
7	*na*-na / *na*-na-tsu	七／七つ	40	yon-jū	四十
8	*ha*-chi / *yat*-tsu	八／八つ	50	go-jū	五十
9	kyū / *ko*-ko-no-*tsu*	九／九つ	60	*ro* ku-jū	六十
10	jū / tō	十／十	70	na-na-jū	七十
11	*jū*-i-chi	十一	80	*ha*-chi-jū	八十
12	*jū*-ni	十二	90	kyū jū	九十
13	*jū*-san	十三	100	*hya*-ku	百
14	*jū*-yon	十四	1000	sen	千
15	*ju*-go	十五	10,000	*i*-chi-man	一万
16	*jū*-ro-ku	十六	100,000	*jū*-man	十万

Days of the Week

Sunday	*ni*-chi *yō*-bi	日曜日
Monday	*ge*-tsu *yō*-bi	月曜日
Tuesday	*ka* yō-bi	火曜日
Wednesday	*su*-i *yō*-bi	水曜日
Thursday	*mo*-ku *yō*-bi	木曜日
Friday	*kin* yō-bi	金曜日
Saturday	*dō* yō-bi	土曜日
Weekday	hei-ji-tsu	平日
Weekend	shū-ma-tsu	週末

Months

January	*i*-chi *ga*-tsu	一月
February	*ni* ga-tsu	二月
March	*san* ga-tsu	三月
April	*shi* ga-tsu	四月
May	*go* ga-tsu	五月
June	*ro*-ku *ga*-tsu	六月
July	*shi*-chi *ga*-tsu	七月
August	*ha*-chi *ga*-tsu	八月
September	*ku* ga-tsu	九月
October	*jū* ga-tsu	十月
November	*jū*-i-chi *ga*-tsu	十一月
December	*jū*-ni *ga*-tsu	十二月

Useful Expressions, Questions, and Answers

Do you speak English?	*ei*-go ga wa-*ka*-ri-ma-su *ka*	英語が わかりますか。
I don't speak Japanese.	*ni*-hon-go ga wa-*ka*-ri-ma-*sen*	日本語が わかりません。
I don't understand.	wa-*ka*-ri-ma-*sen*	わかりません。
I understand.	wa-*ka*-ri-ma-shi-*ta*	わかりました。
I don't know.	*shi*-ra-ma-*sen*	知りません。
I'm American (British).	wa-*ta*-shi wa a-*me*-ri-ka (i-*gi*-ri-su) jin *desu*	私はアメリカ (イギリス) 人 です。
What's your name?	o-*na*-ma-e wa *nan* desu *ka*	お名前は何ですか。
My name is . . .	. . . to *mo*-shi-*ma*-su	……と申します。
What time is it?	i-ma *nan*-ji desu *ka*	今何時ですか。

How?	*dō* yat-te	どうやって。
When?	*i*-tsu	いつ。
Yesterday/today/ tomorrow	ki-*nō*/kyō/*ashi*-ta	きのう／きょう／あした
This morning	*ke*-sa	けさ
This afternoon	*kyo* no go-go	きょうの午後
Tonight	*kom*-ban	こんばん
Excuse me, what?	su-*mi*-ma-*sen, nan* desu ka	すみません、何ですか。
What is this/that?	*ko*-re/*so*-re wa *nan* desu *ka*	これ／それは何ですか。
Why?	*na*-ze desu *ka*	なぜですか。
Who?	*da*-re desu *ka*	だれですか。
I am lost.	*mi*-chi ni ma-yo-i-*mash*-ta	道に迷いました。
Where is [place]	[place] wa *do*-ko desu *ka*	.....はどこですか。
. . . train station?	e-ki	駅
. . . subway station?	chi-*ka*-te-tsu-no eki	地下鉄の駅
. . . bus stop?	*ba*-su *no*-ri-*ba*	バス乗り場
. . . taxi stand?	*ta*-ku-shi-i *no*-ri-*ba*	タクシー乗り場
. . . airport?	kū-kō	空港
. . . post office?	*yū*-bin-*kyo*-ku	郵便局
. . . bank?	*gin*-kō	銀行
. . . the [name] hotel?	[name] ho-*te*-ru	ホテル
. . . elevator?	e-re-bē-tā	エレベーター
Where are the restrooms?	*to*-i-re wa *do*-ko desu *ka*	トイレはどこですか。
Here/there/over there	*ko*-ko/*so*-ko/*a*-so-ko	ここ／そこ／あそこ
Left/right	hi-*da*-ri/*mi*-gi	左／右
Straight ahead	mas-*su*-gu	まっすぐ
Is it near (far)?	chi-*ka*-i (*to*-i) desu *ka*	近い (遠い) ですか。
Are there any rooms?	*he*-ya ga a-ri-masu *ka*	部屋がありますか。
I'd like [item]	[item] ga ho-*shi*-i no desu ga	.....がほしいのですが。
. . . Newspaper	*shim*-bun	新聞
. . . Stamp	*kit*-te	切手
. . . Key	*ka*-gi	鍵
I'd like to buy [item]	[item] o kai-*ta*-i no desu ke do	.....を買いたいのですけど。

a ticket to [destination]	[destination] *ma*-de no *kip*-pu	.....までの切符
Map	*chi*-zu	地図
How much is it?	i-*ku*-ra desu *ka*	いくらですか。
It's expensive (cheap).	ta-*ka*-i (ya-*su*-i) de su *ne*	高い (安い) ですね。
A little (a lot)	su-*ko*-shi (*ta*-ku-san)	少し (たくさん)
More/less	*mot*-to o-ku/ *su*-ku-*na*-ku	もっと多く／少なく
Enough/too much	*jū*-bun/ō-su-*gi*-ru	十分／多すぎる
I'd like to exchange . . .	. . . *ryō*-ga e shi-*te* i-*ta*-da-ke-masu *ka*	.....両替して 頂けますか。
dollars to yen	*do*-ru o *en* ni	ドルを円に
pounds to yen	*pon*-do o *en* ni	ポンドを円に
How do you say . . . in Japanese?	ni-*hon*-go de . . . wa *dō* *i*-i-masu *ka*	日本語で.....は どう言いますか。
I am ill/sick.	wa-*ta*-shi wa *byō*-ki desu	私は病気です。
Please call a doctor.	*i*-sha o *yon*-de ku-da-*sa*-i	医者を呼んで 下さい。
Please call the police.	*ke*-i-sa-tsu o *yon*-de ku-da-*sa*-i	警察を 呼んで下さい。
Help!	*ta*-su-*ke*-te	助けて！

Useful Words

Airport	kūkō	空港
Bay	wan	湾
Beach	-hama	浜
Behind	ushiro	後ろ
Bridge	hashi or -bashi	橋
Bullet train, literally "new trunk line"	Shinkansen	新幹線
Castle	shiro or -jō	城
Cherry blossoms	sakura	桜
City or municipality	-shi	市
Department store	depāti (deh-pah-to)	デパート
District	-gun	郡
East	higashi	東
Exit	deguchi or -guchi	出口
Festival	matsuri	祭

Feudal lord	daimyō	大名
Foreigner	gaijin	外人
Garden	niwa	植物園
Gate	mon or torii	門 or 鳥居
Gorge	kyōkoku	峡谷
Hill	oka	丘
Hot-spring spa	onsen	温泉
In front of	mae	前
Island	shima or -jima/-tō	島
Japanese words rendered in roman letters	rōmaji	ローマ字
Lake	mizumi or -ko	湖
Main road	kaidō or kōdō	街道／公道
Morning market	asa-ichi	朝市
Mountain	yama or -san	山
Museum	hakubutsukan	博物館
North	kita	北
Park	kōen	公園
Peninsula	-hantō	半島
Plateau	kōgen	高原
Pond	ike or -ike	池
Prefecture	-ken/-fu	県／府
Pub	izakaya	居酒屋
River	kawa or -gawa	川
Sea	umi or -nada	海
Section or ward	-ku	区
Shop	mise or -ya	店
Shrine	jinja or -gu	神社／　宮／
South	minami	南
Street	michi or -dō	道
Subway	chikatetsu	地下鉄
Temple	tera or ji/ in	寺
Town	machi	
Train	densha	電車
Train station	eki	駅
Valley	tani	谷
West	nishi	西

MENU GUIDE

Restaurants

Basics and Useful Expressions

A bottle of . . .	. . . *ip*-pon	.....一本
A glass/cup of . . .	. . . *ip*-pai	.....一杯
Ashtray	*ha*-i-*za*-ra	灰皿
Plate	*sa*-ra	皿
Bill/check	kan-*jō*	かんじょう
Bread	pan	パン
Breakfast	*chō*-sho-ku	朝食
Butter	ba-*tā*	バター
Cheers!	kam-*pai*	乾杯！
Chopsticks	*ha*-shi	箸
Cocktail	*ka*-ku-*te*-ru	カクテル
Does that include dinner?	*yū*-sho-ku ga tsu-ki-ma-su-ka	夕食が付きますか。
Excuse me!	su-mi-ma-*sen*	すみません。
Fork	*fō*-ku	フォーク
I am diabetic.	wa-*ta*-shi wa tō-*nyō*-byō de su	私は糖尿病です。
I am dieting.	*da*-i-et-to *chū* desu	ダイエット中です。
I am a vegetarian.	sa-i-*sho*-ku *shū*-gi-sha de-su	菜食主義者です。
I cannot eat [item]	[item] wa *ta*-be-ra-re-ma-*sen*	.....は食べられません。
I'd like to order.	*chū*-mon o shi-*tai* desu	注文をしたいです。
I'd like [item]	[item] o o-ne-*gai*-shi-ma su	.....をお願いします。
I'm hungry.	o-na-ka ga *su*-i-te i-*ma su*	お腹が空いています。
I'm thirsty.	*no*-do ga ka-*wa*-i-te i-*ma su*	喉が渇いています。
It's tasty (not good)	*o*-i-shi-i (ma-*zu*-i) desu	おいしい (まずい) です。
Knife	*na*-i-fu	ナイフ
Lunch	*chū*-sho-ku	昼食
Menu	me-nyū	メニュー
Napkin	*na*-pu-*kin*	ナプキン
Pepper	ko-*shō*	こしょう
Please give me [item]	[item] o ku-da-*sa*-i	.....を下さい。

Salt	*shi*-o	塩
Set menu	*te*-i-sho-ku	定食
Spoon	su *pūn*	スプーン
Sugar	sa-to	砂糖
Wine list	*wa*-i-n *ri*-su-to	ワインリスト
What do you recommend?	o-su-su-me *ryō*-ri wa *nan* desu *ka*	お勧め料理は何ですか。

Meat Dishes

gyōza	ギョウザ	Pork spiced with ginger and garlic in a Chinese wrapper and fried or steamed.
hambāgu	ハンバーグ	Hamburger pattie served with sauce.
hayashi raisu	はやしライス	Beef flavored with tomato and soy sauce with onions and peas over rice.
kara-age	からあげ	Chicken deep-fried without batter
karē-raisu	カレーライス	Curried rice. A thick curry gravy typically containing beef is poured over white rice.
katsu-karē	カツカレー	Curried rice with tonkatsu.
niku-jaga	肉じゃが	Beef and potatoes stewed together with soy sauce.
okonomi-yaki	お好み焼き	Sometimes called a Japanese pancake, this is made from a batter of flour, egg, cabbage, and meat or seafood, griddle-cooked then covered with green onions and a special sauce.
oyako-domburi	親子どんぶり	Literally, "mother and child bowl"—chicken and egg in brother over rice.
rōru kyabetsu	ロール・キャベツ	Rolled cabbage; beef or pork rolled in cabbage and cooked.
shabu-shabu	しゃぶしゃぶ	Extremely thin slices of beef are plunged for an instant into boiling water flavored with soup stock and then dipped into a thin sauce and eaten.
shōga-yaki	しょうが焼	Pork cooked with ginger.
shūmai	シュウマイ	Shrimp or pork wrapped in a light dough and steamed (originally Chinese).
subuta	酢豚	Sweet and sour pork, originally a Chinese dish.

sukiyaki	すき焼き	Thinly sliced bef, green onions, mushrooms, thin noodles, and cubes of tōfu are simmered in a large iron pan in front of you. These ingredients are cooked in a mixture of soy sauce, mirin (cooking wine, and a little sugar. You are given a saucer of raw egg to cool the suki-yaki morsels before eating. Using chopsticks, you help yourself to anything on your side of the pan and dip it into the egg and then eat. Best enjoyed in a group.
sutēki	ステーキ	Steak.
tanin-domburi	他人どんぶり	Literally, "strangers in a bowl"—similar to oyako domburi, but with beef instead of chicken.
tonkatsu	トンカツ	Breaded deep-fried pork cutlets.
yaki-niku	焼き肉	Thinly sliced meat is marinated then barbecued over an open fire at the table.
yaki-tori	焼き鳥	Pieces of chicken (white meat, liver, skin, etc.) threaded on skewers with green onions and marinated in sweet soy sauce and grilled.

Seafood Dishes

age-zakana	揚げ魚	Deep-fried fish.
aji	あじ	Horse mackerel
ama-ebi	あまえび	Sweet shrimp
asari no sakamushi	あさりの酒蒸し	Clams steamed with rice wine.
buri	ぶり	Yellowtail
dojo no yanagawa nabe	どじょうの 柳川なべ	Loach cooked with burdock root and egg in an earthen dish. Considered a delicacy.
ebi furai	海老フライ	Deep-fried breaded prawns.
ika	いか	Squid
iwashi	いわし	Sardines
karei furai	かれいフライ	Deep-fried breaded flounder.
katsuo no tataki	かつおのたたき	Bonito cooked slightly on the surface. Eaten with cut green onions and thin soy sauce.
maguro	まぐろ	Tuna
nizakana	煮魚	Soy-simmered fish

saba no miso ni	さばのみそ煮	Mackerel stewed with soy-bean paste.
samma	さんま	Saury pike
sashimi	刺身	Very fresh raw fish served sliced thin on a bed of white radish with a saucer of soy sauce and horseradish. Eaten by dipping fish into soy sauce mixed with horseradish.
sawara	さわら	Spanish mackerel
shake	しゃけ	Salmon
shimesaba	しめさば	Mackerel marinated in vinegar.
shio-yaki	塩焼	Fish sprinkled with salt and broiled until crisp.
tako	たこ	Octopus
ten-jū	天重	Deep-fried prawns served over rice with sauce.
teri-yaki	照り焼き	Fish basted in soy sauce and broiled.
una-jū	うな重	Eel marinated in a slightly sweet soy sauce is charcoal-broiled and served over rice. Considered a delicacy.
yaki-zakana	焼き魚	Broiled fish

Sushi

aji	あじ	horse mackerel
ama-ebi	甘えび	sweet shrimp
anago	あなご	conger eel
aoyagi	あおやぎ	round clam
chirashi zushi	ちらし寿司	In chirashi zushi, a variety of seafood is arranged on the top of the rice and served in a bowl.
ebi	えび	shrimp
futo-maki	太巻	Big roll with egg and pickled vegetables.
hamachi	はまち	yellowtail
hirame	ひらめ	flounder
hotate-gai	ほたて貝	scallop
ika	いか	squid
ikura	いくら	Salmon roe on rice wrapped with seaweed.
kani	かに	crab

kappa-maki	かっぱ巻	Cucumber roll
kariforunia-maki	カリフォルニア巻	California roll, containing crabmeat and avocado. This was invented in the U.S. but was re-exported to Japan and is gaining popularity there.
kazunoko	かずのこ	Herring roe
kohada	こはだ	Gizzard (shad)
maguro	まぐろ	Tuna
maki zushi	巻き寿司	Raw fish and vegetables or other morsels are rolled in sushi rice and wrapped in dried seaweed. Some popular varieties are listed here.
miru-gai	みる貝	Giant clam
nigiri zushi	にぎり寿司	The rice is formed into a bite-sized cake and topped with various raw or cooked fish. The various types are usually named after the fish, but not all are fish. Nigiri zushi is eaten by picking up the cakes with chopsticks or the fingers, dipping the fish side in soy sauce, and eating.
saba	さば	Mackerel
shake	しゃけ	Salmon
shinko-maki	新香巻	Shinko roll (shinko is a type of pickle)
sushi	寿司	Basically, sushi is rice, fish, and vegetables. The rice is delicately seasoned with vinegar, salt, and sugar. There are basically three types of sushi: nigiri, chirashi, and maki.
tai	たい	Red snapper
tako	たこ	Octopus
tamago	卵	Egg
tekka-maki	鉄火巻	Tuna roll
toro	とろ	Fatty tuna
uni	うに	Sea urchin on rice wrapped with seaweed.

Vegetable Dishes

aemono	和えもの	Vegetables dressed with sauces.
daigaku imo	大学いも	Fried yams in a sweet syrup

gobō	ごぼう	Burdock root
hōrenso	ほうれん草	Spinach
kabocha	かぼちゃ	Pumpkin
kimpira gobō	きんぴらごぼう	Carrots and burdock root, fried with soy sauce.
kyūri	きゅうり	Cucumber
negi	ねぎ	Green onions
nimono	煮もの	Vegetables simmered in a soy- and sake-based sauce.
oden	おでん	Often sold by street vendors at festivals and in parks, etc., this is vegetables, octopus, or egg simmered in a soy fish stock.
o-hitashi	おひたし	Boiled vegetables with soy sauce and dried shaved bonito or sesame seeds.
renkon	れんこん	Lotus root
satoimo	さといも	Taro root
sumono	酢のもの	Vegetables seasoned with ginger.
takenoko	たけのこ	Bamboo shoots
tempura	天ぷら	Vegetables, shrimp, or fish deep-fried in a light batter. Eaten by dipping into a thin sauce containing grated white radish.
tsukemono	漬物	Japanese pickles. Made from white radish, eggplant or other vegetables. Considered essential to the Japanese meal.
yasai itame	野菜いため	Stir-fried vegetables.
yasai sarada	野菜サラダ	Vegetable salad

Egg Dishes

bēkon-eggu	ベーコン・エッグ	Bacon and eggs
chawan mushi	茶わんむし	Vegetables, shrimp, etc., steamed in egg custard.
hamu-eggu	ハム・エッグ	Ham and eggs
medama-yaki	目玉焼	Fried eggs, sunny-side up
omuraisu	オムライス	Omelet with rice inside, often eaten with ketchup.
omuretsu	オムレツ	Omelet
sukuramburu eggu	スクランブル・エッグ	Scrambled eggs
yude tamago	ゆで卵	Boiled eggs

Tōfu Dishes

Tōfu, also called bean curd, is a white, high-protein food with the consistency of soft gelatin.

agedashi dōfu	あげだしどうふ	Lightly fried plain tōfu dipped in soy sauce and grated ginger.
hiya-yakko	冷やっこ	Cold tōfu with soy sauce and grated ginger.
mābō dōfu	マーボーどうふ	Tōfu and ground pork in a spicy red sauce. Originally a Chinese dish.
tōfu no dengaku	とうふの田楽	Tōfu broiled on skewers and flavored with miso.
yu-dōfu	湯どうふ	Boiled tōfu

Rice Dishes

chāhan	チャーハン	Fried rice; includes vegetables and pork.
chimaki	ちまき	A type of onigiri made with sticky rice.
gohan	ごはん	Steamed white rice
okayu	おかゆ	Rice porridge
onigiri	おにぎり	Triangular balls of rice with fish or vegetables inside and wrapped in a type of seaweed.
pan	パン	Bread, but usually rolls with a meal.

Soups

miso shiru	みそ汁	Miso soup. A thin broth containing tōfu, mushrooms, or other morsels in a soup flavored with miso or soy-bean paste. The morsels are taken out of the bowl and the soup is drunk straight from the bowl without a spoon.
suimono	すいもの	Soy sauce flavored soup, often including fish and tofu.
tonjiru	とん汁	Pork soup with vegetables.

Noodles

hiyamugi	ひやむぎ	Similar to somen, but thicker.
rāmen	ラーメン	Chinese noodles in broth, often with *chashu* or roast pork. Broth is soy sauce, miso or salt flavored.

soba	そば	Buckwheat noodles. Served in a broth like udon or, during the summer, cold on a bamboo mesh and called *zaru soba*.
sōmen	そう麺	Very thin wheat noodles, usually served cold with a tsuyu or thin sauce. Eaten in summer.
supagetti	スパゲッティ	Spaghetti. There are many interesting variations on this dish, notably spaghetti in soup, often with seafood.
udon	うどん	Wide flour noodles in broth. Can be lunch in a light broth or a full dinner called *nabe-yaki udon* when meat, chicken, egg, and vegetables are added.
yaki-soba	やきそば	Noodles fried with beef and cabbage, garnished with pickled ginger and vegetables.

Fruit

āmondo	アーモンド	Almonds
anzu	あんず	Apricot
banana	バナナ	Banana
budō	ぶどう	Grapes
gurēpufurūtsu	グレープフルーツ	Grapefruit
hoshi-budō	干しぶどう	Raisins
ichigo	いちご	Strawberries
ichijiku	いちじく	Figs
kaki	かき	Persimmons
kiiui	キーウィ	Kiwi
kokonattsu	ココナッツ	Coconut
kuri	くり	Chestnuts
kurumi	くるみ	Walnuts
mango	マンゴ	Mango
meron	メロン	Melon
mikan	みかん	Tangerine (mandarin orange)
momo	桃	Peach
nashi	梨	Pear
orenji	オレンジ	Orange
painappuru	パイナップル	Pineapple
papaiya	パパイヤ	Papaya
piinattsu	ピーナッツ	Peanuts

purūn	プルーン	Prunes
remon	レモン	Lemon
ringo	りんご	Apple
sakurambo	さくらんぼ	Cherry
suika	西瓜	Watermelon

Dessert

aisukuriimu	アイスクリーム	Ice cream
appuru pai	アップルパイ	Apple pie
kēki	ケーキ	Cake
kōhii zeri	コーヒーゼリー	Coffee-flavored gelatin
kurēpu	グレープ	Crepes
purin	プリン	Caramel pudding
shābetto	シャーベット	Sherbert
wagashi	和菓子	Japanese sweets
yōkan	ようかん	Sweet bean paste jelly

Drinks

Alcoholic

bābon	バーボン	Bourbon
biiru	ビール	Beer
burandē	ブランデー	Brandy
chūhai	チューハイ	Shōchū mixed with soda water and flavored with lemon juice or other flavors.
kakuteru	カクテル	Cocktail
nama biiru	生ビール	Draft beer
nihonshu (sake)	日本酒（酒）	Sake, a wine brewed from rice.
atsukan	あつかん	warmed sake
hiya	ひや	cold sake
sake	酒	Rice wine
shampen	シャンペン	Champagne
shōchū	焼酎	Spirit distilled from potatoes.
sukocchi	スコッチ	Scotch
uisukii	ウィスキー	Whisky
wain	ワイン	Wine
aka	赤	Red
shiro	白	White
roze	ロゼ	Rose

Non-alcoholic

aisu kōhii	アイスコーヒー	Iced coffee
aisu tii	アイスティー	Iced tea
gyū-nyū/miruku	牛乳／ミルク	Milk
jasumin cha	ジャスミン茶	Jasmine tea
jūsu	ジュース	Juice, but can also mean any soft drink.
kō-cha	紅茶	Black tea
kōhii	コーヒー	Coffee
kokoa	ココア	Hot chocolate
kōra		Coca-cola
miruku sēki	ミルクセーキ	Milk shake
miruku tii	ミルクティー	Tea with milk
nihon cha	日本茶	Japanese green tea
remon sukasshu	レモンスカッシュ	Carbonated lemon soft drink
remon tii	レモンティー	Tea with lemon
remonēdo	レモネード	Lemonade
ūron cha	ウーロン茶	Oolong tea

Japan Essentials

PLANNING TOOLS, EXPERT INSIGHT, GREAT CONTACTS

There are planners, and there are those who fly by the seat of their pants. We happily place ourselves among the planners. Our writers and editors try to anticipate all the issues you may face before and during any journey, and then they do their research. This section is the product of their efforts. Use it to get excited about your trip to Japan, to inform your travel planning, or to guide you on the road should the seat of your pants start to feel threadbare.

GETTING STARTED

We're really proud of our Web site: Fodors. com is a great place to begin any journey. Scan Travel Wire for suggested itineraries, travel deals, restaurant and hotel openings, and other up-to-the-minute info. Check out Booking to research prices and book plane tickets, hotel rooms, rental cars, and vacation packages. Head to Talk for on-the-ground pointers from travelers who frequent our message boards. You can also link to loads of other travel-related resources.

■ RESOURCES

ONLINE TRAVEL TOOLS

Japan is a constantly updating, changing country—so start out at ⊕ www.fodors. com to research the latest on prices and places and to book plane tickets, hotel rooms, rental cars, vacation packages, and more. In addition, you can post your pressing questions in the Travel Talk section. Other planning tools include a currency converter and weather reports, and there are loads of links to travel resources.

Cultural resources and travel-planning tools abound for the cybertraveler to Japan. For a good overview go to the Web site of the Japan National Tourist Office (JNTO ⊕ www.jnto.go.jp). Aside from the expected information about regions, hotels, and festivals, this has off-beat info such as the location of bargain-filled ¥100 shops in Tokyo and buildings designed by famous architects. Another good source for all-Japan information and regional sights and events is Japan-guide.com (⊕ www.japan-guide.com).

Japan Rail Pass (must be bought outside the country) and cuts costs on Japan's super-efficient trains. Japan Rail has countrywide info at ⊕ www.japanrail.com and details about the Rail Pass at ⊕ www. japanrailpass.net, the latter also has links to regional networks. JR Regions now offer regional rail passes that can only be bought by short-term visitors both outside and inside Japan. These are cheaper than the country-wide Pass and are useful for shorter stays in specific regions.

Check out train routes, times, and costs with either Jorudan's invaluable "Japanese Transport Guide" ⊕ www.jorudan.co.jp/ english or Hitachi's "Hyperdia-timetable" ⊕ grace.hyperdia.com/cgi-english/ hyperWeb.cgi, both of which have simple, uncluttered interfaces. You enter the station from where you're departing and your destination, and the planners present you with the travel times, fares, and distances for all possible routes.

Local Info. RATP (⊕www.subwaynavigator. com). maintains a useful subway navigator, which includes the subway systems in Ōsaka, Tōkyō, and Sapporo. The Metropolitan Government Web site (⊕ www.metro.tokyo.jp) is an excellent source of information on sightseeing and current events in Tōkyō.

Informed Travel. To arrive with all the what's hot, what's not tips check out the Web sites of Japan's three major English-language daily newspapers, the *Asahi Shimbun* (⊕ www.asahi.com), *Daily Yomiuri* (⊕ www.yomiuri.co.jp/dy), and the *Japan Times* (⊕ www.japantimes.co.jp). Expats share insider knowledge on the magazine sites *Metropolis* (⊕ http://metropolis.co.jp) and *Tokyo Journal* (⊕ www.tokyo.to/ index.html). Both have up-to-date arts, events, and dining listings. In the Kansai region, *Kansai Time Out* (⊕ www.kto. co.jp) is definitely worth a look.

Language. Avoid being lost in translation with the help of Japanese-Online (⊕www. japanese-online.com), a series of online language lessons that will help you pick up a bit of Japanese before your trip. (The site also, inexplicably, includes a sampling of typical Japanese junior-high-school math problems.)

All About Japan Cherry Blossoms Timing your trip to catch the blossoming of Japan's national flower is tricky, but compare past year dates, best party sites, and blossom types at ⊕ http://gojapan.about.com/cs/cherryblossoms/a/sakurafestival.htm.

Gardens Painstaking designs of stone, plants, light, and water, Japanese gardens are famous for their form and symbolism. A college professor's Web site at ⊕ http://learn.bowdoin.edu has photographic tours of more than 20 famous gardens and explanations about their history and design elements.

Mount Fuji Symbol of Japan, stately Fuji-san may or may not emerge from the haze or clouds during your trip, and it's long overdue for eruption, so keep an eye on it with the 24-hour live camera at ⊕ http://live-fuji.jp/fuji/livee.htm.

Sumō Fat men pushing each other around? The Japan Sumō Association sets you straight with everything from the moves, the rankings, and even translated interviews with the wrestlers. Tournament ticket information (but not booking), too. ⊕ www.sumo.or.jp/eng.

Sushi Order Japan's tastiest with confidence by checking translations on the Tokyo Food Page at ⊕ www.bento.com/tokyofood.html.

Kabuki The Kabuki-zan Theater in Tōkyō has history, stories, and sounds of the ancient art form (with good information about costumes and makeup) at its Web site ⊕ www.shochiku.co.jp/play/kabukiza/theater/index.html.

World Heritage Sites Ancient temples, peace museums, and misty mountains—Japan has a good share of places designated by UNESCO. Check them out at ⊕ http://web-jpn.org/plaza/about.html, a site sponsored by the Ministry of Foreign Affairs, which includes some quirky J-trends info such as massage chairs and beauty products for middle-aged men.

Currency Conversion Google ⊕ www.google.com does currency conversion. **Oanda.com** ⊕ www.oanda.com allows you to print out a handy table with the current day's conversion rates. **XE.com** ⊕ www.xe.com is a good currency conversion Web site.

Time Zones Timeanddate.com ⊕ www.timeanddate.com/worldclock gives you the correct time anywhere in the world.

Weather Japan Meteorological Agency ⊕ www.jma.go.jp/jma/indexe.html has daily and weekly forecasts as well as latest information on tsunami, earthquakes, volcanoes, and other natural events. **Accuweather.com** ⊕ www.accuweather.com is an independent weather-forecasting service with especially good coverage of hurricanes. **Weather.com** ⊕ www.weather.com is the Web site for the Weather Channel.

VISITOR INFORMATION

The Japan National Tourist Organization (JNTO) has offices in Tōkyō and Kyōto. Away from the main offices, the JNTO-affiliated International Tourism Center of Japan also has more than 140 counters/offices nationwide. Look for the sign showing a red question mark and the word "information" at train stations and city centers. Needing help on the move? For recorded information 24 hours a day, call the Teletourist service.

Japan National Tourist Organization (JNTO) Japan: ✉ 2-10-1 Yūrakuchō 1-chōme, Chiyoda-ku, Tōkyō ☎ 03/3502-1461 ✉ 9F, JR Kyōto Station Bldg., Hachijō-guchi, Minami-ku, Kyōto ☎ 075/344-3300. **United States:** ✉ 1 Rockefeller Plaza, Suite 1250, New York, NY 10020 ☎ 212/757-5640 ✉ 401 N. Michigan Ave., Suite 770, Chicago, IL 60611 ☎ 312/222-0874 ✉ 1 Daniel Burnham Ct., San Francisco, CA 94109 ☎ 415/292-5686 ✉ 515 S. Figueroa St., Suite 1470, Los Angeles, CA 90071 ☎ 213/623-1952.

Teletourist Service Tōkyō ☎ 03/3201-2911. **Tourist Information Centers (TIC) Tōkyō International Forum B1** ✉ 3-5-1 Marunouchi, Chiyoda-ku, Tōkyō ☎ 03/3201-3331 ✉ Main Terminal Bldg., Narita Airport, Chiba Prefecture ☎ 0476/34-6251 ✉ 2F, JR Kyōto Station Bldg., Hachijō-guchi, Minami-ku, Kyōto ☎ 075/343-6655 ✉ Kansai International Airport, Ōsaka ☎ 0724/56-6025.

∎ THINGS TO CONSIDER

GEAR

Pack light, because porters can be hard to find and storage space in hotel rooms may be tiny. What you pack depends more on the time of year than on any dress code. For travel in the cities, pack as you would for any American or European city. At more expensive restaurants and nightclubs men usually need to wear a jacket and tie. Wear conservative-color clothing at business meetings. Casual clothes are fine for sightseeing. Jeans are as popular in Japan as they are in the United States, and are perfectly acceptable for informal dining and sightseeing.

Although there are no strict dress codes for visiting temples and shrines, you will be out of place in shorts or immodest outfits. For sightseeing leave sandals and open-toe shoes behind; you'll need sturdy walking shoes for the gravel pathways that surround temples and fill parks. Make sure to bring comfortable clothing that isn't too tight to wear in traditional Japanese restaurants, where you may need to sit on tatami-matted floors. For beach and mountain resorts pack informal clothes for both day and evening wear. Central and southern Japan are hot and humid June to September, so pack cotton clothing. Winter daytime temperatures in northern Japan hover around freezing, so gloves and hats are necessary, and clip-on shoe spikes can be bought locally.

Japanese do not wear shoes in private homes or in any temples or traditional inns. Having shoes you can quickly slip in and out of is a decided advantage. Take wool socks (checking first for holes!) to help you through those shoeless occasions in winter.

All lodgings provide a thermos of hot water and bags of green tea in every room. For coffee you can call room service, buy very sweet coffee in a can from a vending machine, or purchase packets of instant coffee at local convenience stores. If you're staying in a Japanese inn, they probably won't have coffee.

Sunglasses, sunscreen lotions, and hats are readily available, and these days they're not much more expensive in Japan. It's a good idea to carry a couple of plastic bags to protect your camera and clothes during sudden cloudbursts.

Take along small gift items, such as scarves or perfume sachets, to thank hosts (on both business and pleasure trips), whether you've been invited to their home or out to a restaurant.

PASSPORTS

A passport verifies both your identity and nationality—a great reason to have one. U.S. passports are valid for 10 years. You must apply in person if you're getting a passport for the first time; if your previous passport was lost, stolen, or damaged; or if your previous passport has expired and was issued more than 15 years ago or when you were under 16. All children under 18 must appear in person to apply for or renew a passport. Both parents must accompany any child under 14 (or send a notarized statement with their permission) and provide proof of their relationship to the child.

There are 13 regional passport offices, as well as 7,000 passport acceptance facilities in post offices, public libraries, and other governmental offices. If you're renewing a passport, you can do so by mail. Forms are available at passport acceptance facilities and online.

The cost to apply for a new passport is $97 for adults, $82 for children under 16; renewals are $67. Allow six weeks for processing, both for first-time passports and renewals. For an expediting fee of $60 you can reduce this time to about two weeks. If your trip is less than two weeks away, you can get a passport even more rapidly by going to a passport office with the necessary documentation. Private expediters can get things done in as little as 48 hours, but charge hefty fees for their services.

■ TIP→ Before your trip, make two copies of your passport's data page (one for someone at home and another for you to carry separately). Or scan the page and e-mail it to someone at home and/or yourself. Hotels in Japan require foreign guests to show passports at

Trip Insurance Resources

INSURANCE COMPARISON SITES		
Insure My Trip.com		www.insuremytrip.com.
Square Mouth.com		www.quotetravelinsurance.com.
COMPREHENSIVE TRAVEL INSURERS		
Access America	866/807-3982	www.accessamerica.com.
CSA Travel Protection	800/873-9855	www.csatravelprotection.com.
HTH Worldwide	610/254-8700 or 888/243-2358	www.hthworldwide.com.
Travelex Insurance	888/457-4602	www.travelex-insurance.com.
Travel Guard International	715/345-0505 or 800/826-4919	www.travelguard.com.
Travel Insured International	800/243-3174	www.travelinsured.com.
MEDICAL-ONLY INSURERS		
International Medical Group	800/628-4664	www.imglobal.com.
International SOS	215/942-8000 or 713/521-7611	www.internationalsos.com.
Wallach & Company	800/237-6615 or 504/687-3166	www.wallach.com.

check in, but police are unlikely to ask foreign visitors for on-the-spot identification, although crime crackdowns on nightlife areas of big cities and political tensions with North Korea or Russia can alter local circumstances in some areas.

U.S. Passport Information **U.S. Department of State** ☎ 877/487-2778 ⊕ http://travel. state.gov/passport.

U.S. Passport & Visa Expediters **A. Briggs Passport & Visa Expeditors** ☎ 800/806-0581 or 202/464-3000 ⊕ www.abriggs.com. **American Passport Express** ☎ 800/455-5166 or 603/559-9888 ⊕ www. americanpassport.com. **Passport Express** ☎ 800/362-8196 or 401/272-4612 ⊕ www. passportexpress.com. **Travel Document Systems** ☎ 800/874-5100 or 202/638-3800 ⊕ www.traveldocs.com.

TRIP INSURANCE

What kind of coverage do you honestly need? Do you even need trip insurance at all? Take a deep breath and read on.

We believe that comprehensive trip insurance is especially valuable if you're booking a very expensive or complicated trip or if you're booking far in advance. Who knows what could happen six months down the road? Visiting Japan means the extra factors of language and an official love of paperwork. Health care is expensive. Whether or not you get insurance depends on how comfortable you are assuming all that risk yourself.

Comprehensive travel policies typically cover trip-cancellation and interruption, letting you cancel or cut your trip short because of a personal emergency, illness, or, in some cases, acts of terrorism in your destination. Such policies also cover evacuation and medical care. Some cover you for trip delays because of bad weather or mechanical problems as well as for lost or delayed baggage. Another type of coverage to look for is financial default—that is, when your trip is disrupted because a tour operator, airline, or cruise line goes out of business. Generally you must buy this when you book your trip or shortly thereafter, and it's only available to you if your operator isn't on a list of excluded companies.

If you're going abroad, consider buying medical-only coverage at the very least. Neither Medicare nor some private insurers cover medical expenses anywhere outside of the United States besides Mexico and Canada. Medical-only policies typically reimburse you for medical care (excluding that related to preexisting conditions) and hospitalization abroad, and provide for evacuation. You still have to pay the bills and await reimbursement from the insurer, though.

Expect comprehensive travel insurance policies to cost about 4% to 7% of the total price of your trip (it's more like 12% if you're over age 70). A medical-only policy may or may not be cheaper than a comprehensive policy. Always read the fine print of your policy to make sure that you are covered for the risks that are of most concern to you. Compare several policies to make sure you're getting the best price and range of coverage available.

BOOKING YOUR TRIP

ONLINE

You really have to shop around. A travel wholesaler such as Hotels.com or Hotel-Club.net can be a source of good rates, as can discounters such as Hotwire or Priceline, particularly if you can bid for your hotel room or airfare. They do, however, tend to work only with hotel chains (which makes them useless for getting hotel reservations outside of major cities) or big airlines (so that often leaves out upstarts like jetBlue and some foreign carriers like Air India). Also, with discounters and wholesalers you must generally prepay, and everything is nonrefundable. And before you fork over the dough, be sure to check the terms and conditions, so you know what a given company will do for you if there's a problem and what you'll have to deal with on your own.

■ TIP→ To be absolutely sure everything was processed correctly, confirm reservations made through online travel agents, discounters, and wholesalers directly with your hotel before leaving home.

Booking engines like Expedia, Travelocity, and Orbitz are actually travel agents, albeit high-volume, online ones. And airline travel packagers like American Airlines Vacations and Virgin Vacations—well, they're travel agents, too. But they may still not work with all the world's hotels.

An aggregator site will search many sites and pull the best prices for airfares, hotels, and rental cars from them. Most aggregators compare the major travel-booking sites such as Expedia, Travelocity, and Orbitz; some also look at airline Web sites, though rarely the sites of smaller budget airlines. Some aggregators also compare other travel products, including complex packages—a good thing, as you can sometimes get the best overall deal by booking an air-and-hotel package.

The range of online booking services for Japan is expanding, although most of the accommodation booked this way is large and impersonal and staff in the hotel may not speak any English. Also check the location carefully to avoid incurring unforeseen extra costs and hassles in trying to reach the sights from a suburban hotel. **Online Accommodations** **Japan Hotel.net** ⊕ www.japanhotel.net has a wide range from big city luxury to out-of-the-way family guesthouses. **Japan Online Booking** ⊕ www.japan-onlinebookinghotel.com connects to all the major hotels in main visitor destinations. **Budget Japan Hotels** ⊕ www.budgetjapanhotels.com offers big discounts on cheaper rooms at major hotels. **Hotelbook.com** ⊕ www.hotelbook.com focuses on independent hotels worldwide. **Hotel Club** ⊕ www.hotelclub.net is good for two- and three-star hotels in Japan. **Hotels.com** ⊕ www.hotels.com is a big Expedia-owned wholesaler that offers rooms in hotels all over the world. **Quikbook** ⊕ www.quikbook.com offers "pay when you stay" reservations that allow you to settle your bill when you check out, not when you book.

WITH A TRAVEL AGENT

If you use an agent—brick-and-mortar or virtual—you'll pay a fee for the service. And know that the service you get from some online agents isn't comprehensive. For example Expedia and Travelocity don't search for prices on budget airlines like JetBlue, Southwest, or small foreign carriers. That said, some agents (online or not) *do* have access to fares that are difficult to find otherwise, and the savings can more than make up for any surcharge.

A knowledgeable brick-and-mortar travel agent can be a godsend if you're booking a cruise, a package trip that's not available to you directly, an air pass, or a complicated itinerary including several overseas flights.

A top-notch agent planning your trip to Japan will make sure you have all the necessary domestic travel arrangements reserved in advance and check ahead for reservations for sumō tournaments, geisha shows or the one-day-a-month temple opening. And when things don't work out the way you'd hoped, it's nice to have an agent to put things right.

■ TIP➔ Remember that Expedia, Travelocity, and Orbitz are travel agents, not just booking engines. To resolve any problems with a reservation made through these companies, contact them first.

Check deals that allow add-on days to a package and then use this time to take a more personal, traditional side trip, which you can book on the ground with local tourist centers.

Agent Resources American Society of Travel Agents ☎ 703/739–2782 ⊕ www.travelsense. org.

Japan Travel Agents Nippon Travel Agency ✉ Shimbashi Ekimae Bldg., Number 1, Shimbashi, Minato-ku, Tōkyō ⊕ www.nta.co.jp/ English/index.htm ✉ 1025 W. 190th St., Suite 300, Gardena, CA ☎ 310/768–0017.

JTB Sunrise Tours ✉ 2–3–11 Higashi-Shinagawa, Shinagawa-ku, Tōkyō ☎ 03/5796–5454 ⊕ www.jtbusa.com.

IACE Travel ✉ Kounan Okamoto Bldg. (3F), Kounan, Minato-ku, Tōkyō ☎ 03/5282–1522 ⊕ www.iace-usa.com ✉ 18 E. 41st St., New York ☎ 800/872–4223.

■ ACCOMMODATIONS

Overnight accommodations in Japan run from luxury hotels to *ryokan* (traditional inns) to youth hostels and even capsules. Western-style rooms with Western-style bathrooms are widely available in large cities, but in smaller, out-of-the-way towns it may be necessary to stay in a Japanese-style room—an experience that can only enhance your stay.

Outside cities and major towns, most lodgings quote prices on a per-person basis with two meals, exclusive of service and tax. If you do not want dinner at your hotel, it is usually possible to renegotiate the price. Stipulate, too, whether you wish to have Japanese or Western breakfasts, if any. When you make reservations at a noncity hotel, you are usually expected to take breakfast and dinner at the hotel—this is the rate quoted to you unless you specify otherwise. In this guide, properties are assigned price categories based on the range between their least and most expensive standard double rooms at high season (excluding holidays).

Most hotels and other lodgings require you to give your credit-card details before they will confirm your reservation. If you don't feel comfortable e-mailing this information, ask if you can fax it (some places even prefer faxes). However you book, get confirmation in writing and have a copy of it handy when you check in.

Be sure you understand the hotel's cancellation policy. Some places allow you to cancel without any kind of penalty—even if you prepaid to secure a discounted rate—if you cancel at least 24 hours in advance. Others require you to cancel a week in advance or penalize you the cost of one night. Small inns and B&Bs are most likely to require you to cancel far in advance. Most hotels allow children under a certain age to stay in their parents' room at no extra charge, but others charge for them as extra adults; find out the cutoff age for discounts.

■ TIP➔ Assume that hotels operate on the European Plan (**EP**, no meals) unless we specify that they use the Breakfast Plan (**BP**, with full breakfast), continental Plan (**CP**, Continental breakfast), Full American Plan (**FAP**, all meals), or Modified American Plan (**MAP**, breakfast and dinner) or are all-inclusive (**AI**, all meals and most activities).

APARTMENT & HOUSE RENTALS
In addition to the agents listed below, English-language newspapers and magazines such as the *Hiragana Times*, *Kansai Time Out* or *Metropolis*, or the *City-Source English Telephone Directory* may be helpful in locating a rental property. Note that renting apartments or houses in Japan is not a common way to spend a vacation, and weekly studio-apartment rentals may be fully booked by local business travelers.

CONTACTS

Moveandstay (✉ Sabaai Concept Co., Ltd., 163 Ocean Insurance Bldg., Unit 17H, Surawongse Rd., Suriyawongse, Bangrak, Bangkok, Thailand 10500 ☎ 02/235-6624 🖷 02/235-6626 ⊕ www.moveandstay.com/Tokyo/default.asp). **Sakura House–Apartments** (✉ Nishi-Shinjuku K1 Bldg. (2F), 7-2-6 Nishi-Shinjuku, Shinjuku-ku, Tōkyō 160-0023 ☎ 03/5330-5250 🖷 03/5330-5251). **Tsukasa Weekly/Monthly Mansion** (✉ 22-37 Higashi Gotanda 5-chōme, Shinagawa-ku, Tōkyō 142-0062 ☎ 03/3440-3939 🖷 03/3784-1167 ✉ 1-3-2 Tokui-machi, Chūō-ku, Ōsaka 540-0025 ☎ 06/6949-4471 🖷 06/6942-9373); Japanese guarantor required. **The Mansions** (✉ 3-8-5 Roppongi, Minato-ku, Tōkyō 106-0032 ☎ 03/5414-7070 🖷 03/5414-7088 ✉ 2-1-3 Azabudai, Minato-ku, Tōkyō 106-0041 ☎ 03/5575-3232 🖷 03/5575-3233 ⊕ www.themansions.jp).

RENTAL LISTINGS

Metropolis (✉ 3F Maison Tomoe Bldg., 3-16-1 Minami-Aoyama, Minato-ku, Tōkyō 107-0062 ☎ 03/3423-6932 🖷 03/3423-6931 ⊕ www.metropolis.japantoday.com). **Kansai Time Out** (✉ 1-1-13 Ikuta-chō, Chūō-ku, Kōbe 651-0092 ☎ 078/232-4517 🖷 078/232-4518 ⊕ www.kto.co.jp).

HOME VISITS

Through the home visit system travelers can get a sense of domestic life in Japan by visiting a local family in their home. The program is voluntary on the homeowner's part, and there's no charge for a visit. The system is active in many cities throughout the country, including Tōkyō, Yokohama, Nagoya, Kyōto, Ōsaka, Hiroshima, Nagasaki, and Sapporo. To make a reservation, apply in writing for a home visit at least a day in advance to the local tourist information office of the place you are visiting. Contact the Japan National Tourist Organization (⇨ Visitor Information, *above*) before leaving for Japan for more information on the program.

HOSTELS

Hostels offer bare-bones lodging at low, low prices—often in shared dorm rooms with shared baths—to people of all ages, though the primary market is young travelers, especially students. Most hostels serve breakfast; dinner and/or shared cooking facilities may also be available. In some hostels you aren't allowed to be in your room during the day, and there may be a curfew at night. Nevertheless, hostels provide a sense of community, with public rooms where travelers often gather to share stories. Many hostels are affiliated with Hostelling International (HI), an umbrella group of hostel associations with some 4,500 member properties in more than 70 countries. Other hostels are completely independent and may be nothing more than a really cheap hotel.

Membership in any HI association, open to travelers of all ages, allows you to stay in HI-affiliated hostels at member rates. One-year membership is about $28 for adults; hostels charge about $10–$30 per night. Members have priority if the hostel is full; they're also eligible for discounts around the world, even on rail and bus travel in some countries.

Hostels in Japan run about ¥2,000–¥3,000 per night for members, usually ¥1,000 more for nonmembers. The quality of hostels varies a lot, though the bad ones are never truly terrible, and the good ones offer memorable experiences, particularly in the national parks, where staff are knowledgeable about hiking and wildlife. Most offer private rooms for couples or families, though you should call ahead to be sure. Note that hostels tend to be crowded during school holidays, when university students are traveling around the country, and at other times they may be busy accommodating retiree hiking groups. Booking ahead is pretty essential. **Hostelling International–USA** ☎ 301/495-1240 ⊕ www.hiusa.org. **Japan Youth Hostels, Inc.** ✉ Kanda Amerex Bldg. (9Fl.) 3-1-16 Misaki-chō, Chiyoda-ku, Tōkyō 100-0006

Online Booking Resources

AGGREGATORS

Kayak	www.kayak.com	looks at cruises and vacation packages
Mobissimo	www.mobissimo.com	compare airfare, car-rental, and hotel costs
Qixo	www.qixo.com	compares cruises, vacation packages, travel insurance
Sidestep	www.sidestep.com	compares vacation packages and lists travel deals
Travelgrove	www.travelgrove.com	compares cruises and vacation packages

BOOKING ENGINES

Cheap Tickets	www.cheaptickets.com	discounter
Expedia	www.expedia.com	large online agency; booking fee for airline tickets
Hotwire	www.hotwire.com	discounter
lastminute.com	www.lastminute.com	specializes in last-minute travel; link to a U.S. site
Luxury Link	www.luxurylink.com	auctions and offers on the high-end side of travel
Onetravel.com	www.onetravel.com	discounter for hotels, car rentals, airfares, packages
Orbitz	www.orbitz.com	booking fee for airline tickets; clear breakdown of fees and taxes
Priceline.com	www.priceline.com	discounter that allows bidding
Travel.com	www.travel.com	allows you to compare its rates with other booking engines
Travelocity	www.travelocity.com	booking fee for airline tickets; good problem resolution

OTHER RESOURCES

Bidding for Travel	www.biddingfortravel.com	good place to figure out what you can get and for how much

☎ 03/3288-1417. Check www.jyh.or.jp/English/index/html for regional Web sites.

HOTELS

Full-service, first-class hotels in Japan resemble their counterparts all over the world, and because many of the staff members speak English, these are the easiest places for foreigners to stay. They are also among the most expensive, tending to fall into the $$$ and $$$$ categories.

Business hotels are a reasonable alternative. These are clean, impersonal, and functional. All have Western-style rooms that vary from small to minuscule; service is minimal. However, every room has a private bathroom, albeit cramped, with tub and handheld shower, television (no English-language channels), telephone, and a hot-water thermos. Business hotels are often conveniently near the railway station. The staff may not speak English, but the rates fall into the $ and $$ categories.

Finding smaller, more personal hotels or guesthouses when you have no Japanese-language skills is hard, but it's worth doing an Internet search (using the word "pension" or "minshuku" for your destination, because enterprising owners of some smaller hotels have English Web sites.

Some useful words when checking into a hotel: air-conditioning, *eakon;* private baths, *o-furo;* showers, *shawā;* double beds, *daburubeddo;* twin beds *tsuinbeddo;* separate beds, *betsu;* pushed together, *kuttsukerareta;* queen bed, *kuīn saizun-no-beddo;* king bed, *kingu saizu-no-beddo.*

All hotels listed have private bath unless otherwise noted.
Daiichi Hotels ☎ 03/3596-8633 Tōkyō, 06/6486-3311 Ōsaka ⊕ www.daiichihotels.com. **Tōkyū Hotels** ☎ 03/3462-0109 ⊕ www.tokyuhotels.co.jp/en. **Washington Hotels** ☎ 03/3433-4253 ⊕ www.wh-rsv.com/english/index.html.

INEXPENSIVE ACCOMMODATIONS

JNTO publishes a listing of some 700 accommodations that are reasonably priced. To be listed, properties must meet Japanese fire codes and charge less than ¥8,000 (about $70) per person without meals. For the most part, the properties charge ¥5,000–¥6,000 ($44–$54). These prop-

erties welcome foreigners (many Japanese hotels and ryokan do not like to have foreign guests because they might not be familiar with traditional-inn etiquette). Properties include business hotels, *ryokan* of a very rudimentary nature, *minshuku* (Japanese bed-and-breakfasts), and pensions. It's the luck of the draw whether you choose a good or less-than-good property. In most cases rooms are clean but very small. Except in business hotels, shared baths are the norm, and you are expected to have your room lights out by 10 PM.

Many establishments on the list of reasonably priced accommodations—and many that are not on the list—can be reserved through the nonprofit organization **Welcome Inn Reservation Center.** Reservation forms are available from your nearest JNTO office (⇨ Visitor Information, *above*). The Japanese Inn Group, which provides reasonable accommodations for foreign visitors, can be reserved through this same service. The center must receive reservation requests at least one week before your departure to allow processing time. If you are already in Japan, the Tourist Information Centers (TICs) at Narita Airport and Kansai International Airport and in downtown Tōkyō and Kyōto can make immediate reservations for you at these Welcome Inns.

Reservations Japanese Inn Group Ryokan Asakusa Shigetsu ✉ 1-31-11 Nishi-Asakusa, Taitō-ku, Tōkyō 111-0032 ☎ 03/3252-1717 ⊕ www.jpinn.com. **Welcome Inn Reservation Center** ✉ Tōkyō Kotsu Kaikakan Bldg. (10th fl.), 2-10-1 Yuraku-chō, Chiyoda-ku, Tōkyō ✉ Kyōto Tourist Information, Kyōto Station ⊙ Closed 2nd and 4th Tues. Telephone reservations are not accepted. www.itcj.jp.

MINSHUKU

Minshuku are private homes that accept guests. Usually they cost about ¥6,000 (about $54) per person, including two meals. Although in a ryokan you need not lift a finger, don't be surprised if you are expected to lay out and put away your own

---

WORD OF MOUTH

Did the resort look as good in real life as it did in the photos? Did you sleep like a baby, or were the walls paper thin? Did you get your money's worth? Rate hotels and write your own reviews in Travel Ratings or start a discussion about your favorite places in Travel Talk on www.fodors.com. Your comments might even appear in our books. Yes, you, too, can be a correspondent!

bedding in a minshuku. Meals are often served in communal dining rooms at fixed times. Minshuku vary in size and atmosphere; some are private homes that take in only a few guests, while others are more like no-frills inns. Some of your most memorable stays could be at minshuku, as they offer a chance to become acquainted with a Japanese family and their hospitality.

Japan Minshuku Center ✉ Toka Bldg., 103 3-11-8 Hirai, Edogawa-ku, Tōkyō ☎ 03/3683-3396 ⊕ www.minshuku.co.jp.

RYOKAN

If you want to sample the Japanese way, spend at least one night in a ryokan (inn). Usually small, one- or two-story wooden structures with a garden or scenic view, they provide traditional Japanese accommodations: simple rooms in which the bedding is rolled out onto the floor at night.

Ryokan vary in price and quality. Some older, long-established inns cost as much as ¥80,000 ($700) per person, whereas humbler places that are more like bed-and-breakfasts are as low as ¥6,000 ($54). Prices are per person and include the cost of breakfast, dinner, and tax. Some inns allow you to stay without having dinner and lower the cost accordingly. However, this is not recommended, because the service and meals are part of the ryokan experience. It is important to follow Japanese customs in all ryokan. For more information, *see* the Ryokan Etiquette box *in* Chapter 5.

Japan Ryokan Association ✉ Asahi-Seimei-Otemachi Bldg. (16F), Otemachi 2-6-1, Chiyoda-ku, Tōkyō ☎ 03/3231-5310. **JNTO** (⇨ Visitor Information, *above*).

TEMPLES

You can also arrange accommodations in Buddhist temples. JNTO has lists of temples that accept guests. A stay at a temple generally costs ¥3,000–¥9,000 ($27–$80) per night, including two meals. Some temples offer instruction in meditation or allow you to observe their religious practices, while others simply offer a room. The Japanese-style rooms are very simple, and range from beautiful, quiet havens to not-so-comfortable, basic cubicles.

■ AIRLINE TICKETS

Most domestic airline tickets are electronic; international tickets may be either electronic or paper. With an e-ticket the only thing you receive is an e-mailed receipt citing your itinerary and reservation and ticket numbers. The greatest advantage of an e-ticket is that if you lose your receipt you can simply print out another copy or ask the airline to do it for you at check-in. You usually pay a surcharge (up to $50) to get a paper ticket, if you can get one at all. The sole advantage of a paper ticket is that it may be easier to endorse over to another airline if your flight is canceled and the airline with which you booked can't accommodate you on another flight.

■ **TIP→** Discount air passes that let you travel economically in a country or region must often be purchased before you leave home. In some cases you can only get them through a travel agent.

Both of Japan's major carriers offer reduced prices for flights within the country, which are real cost- and time-savers if your trip includes destinations such as Kyūshū or Hokkaidō, though tickets must be booked outside Japan and there are restrictions on use in peak times. JAL offers the Yōkoso Japan Airpass; ANA has the Visit Japan Fare. Cathay Pacific offers a pass that includes 18 cities throughout Asia.

Air Pass Info Visit Japan Fare ☎ 800/235-9262 All Nippon Airways in U.S. ⊕ www.anaskyweb.com or www.ana.co.jp. **All Asia Pass** ☎ 800/233-2742 Cathay Pacific ⊕ www.cathay-usa.com or www.cathay.ca. **Yōkoso Japan Airpass** ☎ 800/525-3663 Japan Airlines ⊕ www.jal.co.jp.

▌ RENTAL CARS

When you reserve a car, ask about cancellation penalties, taxes, drop-off charges (if you're planning to pick up the car in one city and leave it in another), and surcharges (for being under or over a certain age, for additional drivers, or beyond a specific distance from your point of rental). All these things can add substantially to your costs. Request car seats and extras such as GPS when you book.

Driving in Japan is unnecessary for travelers (and many locals), because the train network is efficient and far-reaching. Stations serve as information points and transport hubs nationwide. City streets are narrow and crowded with bikes and pedestrians, and inter-city toll highways expensive. However, exploring rural areas, and particularly national parks in Hokkaidō, is easier by car. Signage on major routes is in English, but car navigation systems are in Japanese. Book ahead in holiday seasons. Rates in Tōkyō begin at ¥6,300 a day and ¥37,800 a week, including tax, for an economy car with unlimited mileage.

In Japan you need an international driver's permit, available from the American Automobile Association. By law, car seats must be installed if the driver is traveling with a child under six.

CAR-RENTAL INSURANCE

Everyone who rents a car wonders whether the insurance that the rental companies offer is worth the expense. No one—including us—has a simple answer. It all depends on how much regular insurance you have, how comfortable you are with risk, and whether or not money is an issue.

When renting a car in Japan, it's probably best to say "Yes" to every kind of insurance on offer, because in the event of an accident you will certainly need all the help you can get with the other driver, damaged property owner, the police, and hospitals. Rental cars come with mandatory insurance, *kyosei hoken,* which covers the vehicle itself; you pay about $10

a day extra for CDW *jibaiseki hoken* to cover injuries, damage, and theft. Japanese custom dictates profuse apologies by both parties at the roadside, and exchange of contact and insurance information and calling in the police for anything more than a minor collision. It is also customary for the wronged person to get an apology in the form of money, cookies, or fruit during a follow-up visit from the wrong-doer (and sometimes his or her boss!).

If you own a car, your personal auto insurance may cover a rental to some degree, though not all policies protect you abroad; always read your policy's fine print. Some credit cards offer CDW coverage, but it's usually supplemental to your own insurance and rarely covers SUVs, minivans, luxury models, and the like. If your coverage is secondary, you may still be liable for loss-of-use costs from the car-rental company. But no credit-card insurance is valid unless you use that card for *all* transactions, from reserving to paying the final bill. All companies exclude car rental in some countries, so be sure to check about Japan.

■ TIP→ Diners Club offers primary CDW coverage on all rentals reserved and paid for with the card. This means that Diners Club's company—not your own car insurance—pays in case of an accident. It *doesn't* mean your car-insurance company won't raise your rates once it discovers you had an accident.

In most cases it's cheaper to add a supplemental CDW plan to your comprehensive travel-insurance policy (⇨ Trip Insurance *under* Things to Consider *in* Getting Started, *above*) than to purchase it from a rental company. That said, you don't want to pay for a supplement if you're required to buy insurance from the rental company. However, the staff at local car-rental agencies may not speak more than basic English, so any documents proving existing coverage may get little more than a cursory glance, and if in doubt buy local insurance, keep or make copies of all paperwork, and resign yourself to a reclaim battle when you get home.

■ TIP→ You can decline the insurance from the rental company and purchase it through a third-party provider such as Travel Guard (www.travelguard.com)—$9 per day for $35,000 of coverage. That's sometimes just under half the price of the CDW offered by some car-rental companies.

■ VACATION PACKAGES

Packages *are not* guided excursions. Packages combine airfare, accommodations, and perhaps a rental car or other extras (theater tickets, guided excursions, boat trips, reserved entry to popular museums, transit passes), but they let you do your own thing. During busy periods packages may be your only option, as flights and rooms may be sold out otherwise. To get a chance of a hotel in favorite destinations such as Kyōto in cherry blossom season, this could be the way to go. Packages will definitely save you time. They can also save you money, but—and this is a really big "but"—you should price each part of the package separately to be sure. And be aware that prices advertised on Web sites and in newspapers rarely include service charges or taxes, which can up your costs by hundreds of dollars.

■ TIP→ Some packages and cruises are sold only through travel agents. Don't always assume that you can get the best deal by booking everything yourself.

Each year consumers are stranded or lose their money when packagers—even large ones with excellent reputations—go out of business. How can you protect yourself? First, always pay with a credit card; if you have a problem, your credit-card company may help you resolve it. Second, buy trip insurance that covers default. Third, choose a company that belongs to the United States Tour Operators Association, whose members must set aside funds to cover defaults. Finally, choose a company that also participates in the Tour Operator Program of the American Society of Travel Agents (ASTA), which will act as mediator in any disputes. You can

also check on the tour operator's reputation among travelers by posting an inquiry on one of the Fodors.com forums.

Japan is daunting for first-time visitors and anyone without Japanese language skills, so a package tour is a great way to get into the country and find your feet. However, beware of expensive optional tours such as tea ceremonies, kabuki tours, and night views. Local tourist offices can probably tell you how to have the same experience more economically.

Organizations American Society of Travel Agents (ASTA) ☎ 703/739-2782 or 800/965-2782 ⊕ www.astanet.com. **United States Tour Operators Association** (USTOA) ☎ 212/599-6599 ⊕ www.ustoa.com.

■ GUIDED TOURS

Guided tours are a good option when you don't want to do it all yourself. You travel along with a group (sometimes large, sometimes small), stay in prebooked hotels, eat with your fellow travelers (the cost of meals is sometimes included in the price of your tour, sometimes not), and follow a schedule. But not all guided tours are an if-it's-Tuesday-this-must-be-Tokyo experience. A knowledgeable guide can take you places that you might never discover on your own, and you may be pushed to see more than you would have otherwise. Whenever you book a guided tour, find out what's included and what isn't. A "land-only" tour includes all your travel (by bus, in most cases) in the destination, but not necessarily your flights to and from or even within it. Also, in most cases prices in tour brochures don't include fees and taxes. And remember that you'll be expected to tip your guide (in cash) at the end of the tour.

Tōkyō, and Kyōto feature on almost every tour of Japan, Hiroshima, Nara, and Nikkō being the normal secondary destinations. Read brochures carefully and try to see through the inevitable pictures of cherry trees and geisha—to check whether what is planned fits your idea of a holiday. Is it temple after temple? Does the tour include experiences such as sushi and sumō—or are they only pricey options? Is the domestic travel by bullet train, plane, or bus? Japan can be quite a culture shock, so resist the temptation to pack in too much, and go for tours that include half days of freedom, because just stepping outside the hotel into the local streets is likely to provide some umimagined sights and experiences.

Along with the usual destinations, General also goes to the Inland Sea, some ancient onsen towns and World Heritage sites; Kintetsu promises to get you closer to the world of geisha in Kyōto. IACE and Nippon Express Travel USA have tours that look to modern Japan by taking in the Tōkyō Anime Festival and the Comic Market (side trip to techie-paradise Akihabra) and architecture old and new. Even the big companies try to get visitors off the beaten track: Explorient goes to the Kisō Valley near Nagoya.

Recommended Companies Exlororient Travel Services ✉ 75 Maiden La., Suite 805, New York ☎ 800/785-1233 ⊕ www. explorient.com. **General** ☎ 800/221-2216 ⊕ www.generaltours.com. **IACE** ☎ 866/735-4223 ⊕ www.iace-asia.com. **JALPAK International** ☎ 800/525-3663 ⊕ www.japanair. com. **Kintetsu** Branch offices in New York, Chicago, Los Angeles, San Jose, New Jersey, and San Francisco ☎ 800/422-381 ⊕ www. Kintetsu.com. **Nippon Express Travel USA** ☎ 212/319-9021 New York, 415/412-1822 San Francisco ⊕ www.nipponexpresstravel.us.en/japan.

SPECIAL-INTEREST TOURS

ART
Japan is overflowing with art—from pottery and painting to the precise skills of flower arranging and calligraphy. Many tours include museums and art galleries, but only some get you right into the artists' studios with English-langauge help to understand their skills and the chance to try your hand.

Absolute Travel ☎ 800/736-8187 ⊕ www. absoluteasia.com. **Smithsonian Journeys** ✉ Box 23182, Washington, DC ☎ 877/338-8687 ⊕ www.smithsonianjourneys.com.

BIKING
Most airlines accommodate bikes as luggage, provided they're dismantled and boxed. Biking is popular in Japan, but local bike-rental shops may not have frames large enough for non-Japanese bikers. **One Life Japan** ✉ Chyo-ou 2-14-10 No. 202,, Nakano-ku, Tōkyō ☎ 03/3231-5310 or 03/3361-1338 ⊕ www.onelifejapan.com/.

DIVING
Okinawa, Kyūshū, and the islands and peninsular south of Tōkyō are all popular diving areas. If you are a novice diver, make sure that a dive leader's "English spoken" means real communication skills. Dive Japan has lists of dive services and locations. **Dive Japan** ⊕ www.divejapan.com.

ECOTOURS
Whales, monkeys, bears, and cranes—Japan does have fauna and flora to appreciate slowly, but English-language tours are limited. Naturalist Mark Brazil, who writes extensively about wild Japan, leads ecotours through Zegrahm Eco Expeditions. **Zegrahm Eco Expeditions** ☎ 800/628-8747 ⊕ www.zeco.com.

GOLF
Japan's love affair with golf does not make it any easier for non-Japanese-speaking visitors to reserve a game unless introduced by a club member. Japan Golf Tours takes guided groups from the United States, and Golf in Japan, put together by golfing expats, helpfully lists over 2,000 courses that welcome foreign golfers. **Golf in Japan** Expat advice for visiting golfers. ⊕ www.golf-in-japan.com/. **Japan Golf Tours** ✉ 4 Elmwood La., Asheville, N.C. ☎ 827/277-6841 ⊕ www.japan-golf-tours.com.

HIKING

Japan has well-marked trails, bus-train connections to trailheads, and hidden sights to be discovered. Millions of Japanese are avid and well-equipped hikers. English information is growing, so check local tourist offices for details.

Outdoor Japan Bilingual magazine and Web site for all outdoor activities (⊕ www. outdoorjapan.com/). **Hike Japan,** run by an experienced British hiker, has a range of tours in all seasons ⊕ www.hikejapan.com.

LANGUAGE PROGRAMS

No better way to learn the language than to immerse yourself by studying Japanese in Japan, with classes, a homestay, and cultural tours on which to put the new-found skills into action. The Japanese Embassy information and culture section (JICC) Web site has good links to schools and procedures for study abroad programs.

Japan Information and Culture Center (JICC) ⊠ Lafayette Center III, 1155 21st St., N.W. Washington, DC ☎ 877/338-8687 ⊕ www.us. emb-japan.go.jp. **World Link Education** ☎ 800/621-3085 ⊕ www.wle-japan.com.

WINTER SPORTS

Japanese ski areas are smaller than those in North America and Europe, but excellent powder and après-ski features like hot springs are pulling in Australian and Asian visitors. Resorts in Nagano and Hokkaidō are most popular. Boarding is cooler than skiing for young Japanese.

Ski Japan has tours, information, and weather reports ⊕ www.skijapanguide.com.

■ CRUISES

Nagasaki, Ōsaka, and Kōbe are among the Japanese ports welcoming foreign cruise ships. Japanese are not big cruise-takers, although domestic ferry companies connect all the islands.

Cruise Lines Clipper Cruise Lines ☎ 800/ 456-8100 ⊕ www.intrav.com. **Crystal Cruises** ☎ 310/785-9300 or 800/446-6620 ⊕ www. crystalcruises.com. **Princess Cruises** ☎ 661/ 753-0000 or 800/774-6237 ⊕ www.princess. com.

TRANSPORTATION

TRAVEL TIMES FROM TOKYO			
TO	By Air	By Car or Bus	By Train
Osaka	1¼ hours	7–8 hours	2½ hours
Hiroshima	1½ hours	10 hours	5 hours
Kyoto	1¼ hour	7 hours	2½ hours
Fukuoka	2 hours	14 hours	6 hours
Sapporo	1½ hours	15 hours	10 hours
Naha (Okinawa)	3 hours	NA	NA

■ TIP➔ Ask the local tourist board about hotel and local transportation packages that include tickets to major museum exhibits or other special events.

∎ BY AIR

Flying time to Japan is 13¾ hours from New York, 12¾ hours from Chicago, and 9½ hours from Los Angeles. Japan Airlines' GPS systems allow a more direct routing, which reduces its flight times by about 30 minutes. Your trip east, because of tailwinds, can be about 45 minutes shorter.

You can fly nonstop to Tokyo from Chicago, Detroit, New York, Los Angeles, San Francisco, Portland (OR), Seattle, Minneapolis, and Washington, D.C. You can also fly nonstop to Ōsaka from Chicago, Detroit, Pittsburgh, and San Francisco. Because of the distance, fares to Japan tend to be expensive, usually between $900 and $1,200 for a seat in coach. But it's possible to get a ticket for as low as $700 from a discount-travel Web site, depending on the time of year.

All domestic flights in Japan are no-smoking.

Airlines & Airports Airline and Airport Links.com ⊕ www.airlineandairportlinks.com has links to many of the world's airlines and airports.

Airline Security Issues Transportation Security Administration ⊕ www.tsa.gov has answers for almost every question that might come up.

AIRPORTS
The major gateway to Japan is Tōkyō's Narita Airport (NRT), 80 km (50 mi) northeast of the city. International flights also use Kansai International Airport (KIX) outside Ōsaka to serve the Kansai region, which includes Kōbe, Kyōto, Nara, and Ōsaka. In 2005 Centrair Airport (NGO) near Nagoya opened to take even more of the strain off Narita. Fares are generally cheapest into Narita, however. A few international flights use Fukuoka Airport, on the island of Kyūshū; these include Continental flights from Guam, JAL from Honolulu, and flights from other Asian destinations. Shin-Chitose Airport, outside Sapporo on the northern island of Hokkaidō, handles some international flights, mostly to Asian destinations such as Seoul and Shanghai. Most domestic flights to and from Tōkyō are out of Haneda Airport.

Tōkyō Narita's Terminal 2 has two adjoining wings, north and south. When you arrive, your first task should be to convert your money into yen; you need it for transportation into Tōkyō. In both wings ATMs and money-exchange counters are in the wall between the customs inspection area and the arrival lobby. Both terminals have a Japan National Tourist Organization tourist information center, where you can get free maps, brochures, and other visitor information. Directly across from the customs-area exits at both terminals are the ticket counters for airport limousine buses to Tōkyō.

If you have a flight delay at Narita, take a local Keisei line train into Narita town 15 minutes away, where a traditional shopping street and the beautiful Narita-san Shinsho-ji Temple are a peaceful escape from airport noise.

If you plan to skip Tōkyō and center your trip on Kyōto or central or western Honshū, Kansai International Airport (KIX) is the airport to use. Built on reclaimed land in Ōsaka Bay, it's laid out vertically. The first floor is for international arrivals; the second floor is for domestic departures and arrivals; the third floor has shops and restaurants; and the fourth floor is for international departures. A small tourist information center on the first floor of the passenger terminal building is open daily 9–5. Major carriers are Air Canada, Japan Airlines, and Northwest Airlines. The trip from KIX to Kyōto takes 75 minutes by JR train; to Ōsaka it takes 45–70 minutes.

Airport Information Centrair (Chubu) Airport (NGO) ☎ 0569/38–1195 ⊕ www.centrair.jp/en/index.html. **Fukuoka Airport (FUK)** ☎ 092/483–7007 ⊕ www.fuk-ab.co.jp. **Haneda Airport (HND)** ☎ 03/5757–8111 ⊕ www.tokyo-airport-bldg.co.jp. **Kansai International Airport (KIX)** ☎ 0724/55–2500 ⊕ www.kansai-airport.or.jp. **Narita Airport (NRT)** ☎ 0476/34–5000 ⊕ www.narita-airport.or.jp. **New Chitose Airport (CTS)** ☎ 0123/23–0111.

GROUND TRANSPORTATION

Narita Airport is famously inconvenient for accessing the country it serves, and everyone has to head into Tōkyō first. It takes about 90 minutes—a time very dependent on city traffic—and costs around $20. If you are arriving with a Japan Rail Pass and staying in Tōkyō for a few days it is best to pay for the transfer into the city and activate the Rail Pass for travel beyond Tōkyō.

Directly across from the customs-area exits at both terminals are the ticket counters for buses to Tōkyō. Buses leave from platforms just outside terminal exits, exactly on schedule; the departure time is on the ticket. The Friendly Airport Limousine offers the only shuttle-bus service from Narita to Tōkyō.

Japan Railways trains stop at both Narita Airport terminals. The fastest and most comfortable is the Narita Limited Express (NEX), which makes 23 runs a day in each direction. Trains from the airport go directly to the central Tōkyō station in just under an hour, then continue to Yokohama and Ōfuna. Daily departures begin at 7:43 AM; the last train is at 9:43 PM. The one-way fare is ¥2,940 (¥4,980 for the first-class Green Car and ¥5,380 per person for a private compartment that seats four). All seats are reserved, and you'll need to reserve one for yourself in advance, as this train fills quickly.

The Keisei Skyliner train runs every 20–30 minutes between the airport terminals and Keisei-Ueno station. The trip takes 57 minutes and costs ¥1,920 ($17). The first Skyliner leaves Narita for Ueno at 9:21 AM, the last at 9:59 PM. There's also an early train from the airport, called the Morning Liner, which leaves at 7:49 AM and costs ¥1,400. From Ueno to Narita the first Skyliner is at 6:32 AM, the last at 5:21 PM.

Airport Transport Service Co. ☎ 03/3665–7232 in Tōkyō, 0476/32–8080 for Terminal 1, 0476/34–6311 for Terminal 2. **IAE Co.** ☎ 0476/32–7954 for Terminal 1, 0476/34–6886 for Terminal 2. **Japan Railways** ☎ 03/3423–0111 for JR East InfoLine ⊙ Weekdays 10–6. **Keisei Railway** ☎ 03/3831–0131 for Ueno information counter, 0476/32–8505 at Narita Airport.

TRANSFERS BETWEEN AIRPORTS

Transfer between Narita and Haneda, the international and domestic airports, is easiest by the Friendly Limousine Bus, which should take 75 minutes and costs $30. Train transfers involve two changes. **Friendly Airport Limousine** ☎ 03/3665–7220 ⊕ www.limousinebus.co.jp/e/index.html.

FLIGHTS

Japan Airlines (JAL) and United Airlines are the major carriers between North America and Narita Airport in Tōkyō; Northwest, American Airlines, Delta Airlines, and All Nippon Airways (ANA) also link North American cities with Tōkyō.

Most of these airlines also fly into and out of Japan's number two other international airports, Kansai International Airport, located south of Ōsaka and Centrair, near Nagoya.

Air Canada ☎ 888/247–2262, 0120/04–8048 in Japan ⊕ www.aircanada.ca. **All Nippon Airways** ☎ 800/235–9262, 0120/02–9222 in Japan for domestic flights, 0120/02–9333 in Japan for international flights ⊕ www. anaskyweb.com or www.ana.co.jp. **American** ☎ 800/433–7300, 0120/00–0860 in Japan ⊕ www.aa.com. **British Airways** ☎ 03/ 3593–8811 in Japan ⊕ www.british-airways. com. **Continental** ☎ 800/525–0280 ⊕ www. continental.com. **Delta Airlines** ☎ 800/221– 1212 for U.S. reservations, 800/241–4141 for international reservations ⊕ www.delta.com. **Japan Airlines** ☎ 800/525–3663, 0120/ 25–5931 international in Japan, 0120/25–5971 domestic in Japan ⊕ www.jal.co.jp. **Korean Air** ☎ 800/438–5000, 03/5443–3311 in Japan ⊕ www.koreanair.com. **Northwest** ☎ 800/ 447–4747, 03/3533–6000 or 0120/12–0747 in Japan ⊕ www.nwa.com. **United Airlines** ☎ 800/864–8331 for U.S. reservations, 800/ 538–2929 for international reservations ⊕ www.united.com.

BY BOAT

Ferries connect most of the islands of Japan. Some of the more popular routes are from Tōkyō to Tomakomai or Kushiro in Hokkaidō; from Tōkyō to Shikoku; and from Tōkyō or Ōsaka to Kyūshū. You can purchase ferry tickets in advance from travel agencies or before boarding. The ferries are inexpensive and are a pleasant, if slow, way of traveling. Private cabins are available, but it's more fun to travel in the economy class, where everyone sleeps on the carpeted floor in one large room. Passengers eat, drink, and enjoy themselves in a convivial atmosphere. There is little English information for local ferries, apart from three companies serving the Inland Sea between Ōsaka/Kōbe and Kyūshū (see below). For information on local ferries, *see* the Essentials sections at the end of the individual chapters.

Hankyu Ferry ⊕ www.han9f.co.jp/. **Kansai Ferry** ⊕ www.kanki.co.jp/foreign/index.htm. **Meimon Taiyo Ferry** ⊕ www.cityline.co.jp/ en.

▌ BY BUS

Japan Railways (JR) offers a number of long-distance buses that are comfortable and inexpensive. You can use Japan Rail Passes (⇨ By Train, *below*) on some, but not all, of these buses. Routes and schedules are constantly changing, but tourist information offices will have up-to-date details. It's now possible to travel from Ōsaka to Tōkyō for as little as ¥5,000 one-way. Buses are generally modern and very comfortable, though overnight journeys are best avoided. Nearly all are now no-smoking. Foreign travelers are not often seen on these buses, and they remain one of the country's best-kept travel secrets. Japan Rail Passes are not accepted by private bus companies. City buses outside of Tōkyō are quite convenient, but be sure of your route and destination, because the bus driver probably won't speak English.

Local buses have a set cost, anywhere from ¥100 to ¥200, depending on the route and municipality, in which case you board at the front of the bus and pay as you get on. On other buses cost is determined by the distance you travel. You take a ticket when you board at the rear door of the bus; it bears the number of the stop at which you boarded. Your fare depends on your destination and is indicated by a board at the front of the bus. Japan Railways also runs buses in some areas that have limited rail service. Remember, these buses are covered by the JR Pass, even if some JR reservation clerks tell you otherwise. Bus schedules can be hard to fathom if you don't read Japanese, however, so it's best to ask for help at a tourist information office. The Nihon Bus Association and the personal Web site

Japan Buses has information about routes and which companies have English Web information.

Reservations are not always essential, except at peak holiday times and on the most popular routes, like Tōkyō–Ōsaka. **Bus Information** JR Kantō Bus ☎ 03/3516-1950. **Nishinihon JR Bus** ☎ 06/6466-9990. **Nihon Bus Association** ⊕ www.bus.or.jp/e/index.html. **Japan Buses** ⊕ www.japanbuses.com/index.html.

■ BY CAR

You need an international driving permit (IDP) to drive in Japan. IDPs are available from the American Automobile Association. These international permits, valid only in conjunction with your regular driver's license, are universally recognized; having one may save you a problem with local authorities.

Major roads in Japan are sufficiently marked in roman type, and on country roads there's usually someone to ask for help. However, it's a good idea to have a detailed map with town names written in *kanji* (Japanese characters) and *romaji* (romanized Japanese).

Car travel along the Tōkyō–Kyōto–Hiroshima corridor and in other built-up areas of Japan is not as convenient as the trains. Roads are congested, gas is expensive (about ¥250 per liter), and highway tolls are exorbitant (tolls between Tōkyō and Kyōto amount to ¥10,550). In major cities, with the exception of main arteries, English signs are few and far between, one-way streets often lead you off the track, and parking is often hard to find.

That said, a car can be the best means for exploring cities outside the metropolitan areas and the rural parts of Japan, especially Kyūshū and Hokkaidō. Consider taking a train to those areas where exploring the countryside will be most interesting and renting a car locally for a day or even half a day.

GASOLINE
Gas stations are plentiful along Japan's toll roads, and prices are fairly uniform across

Car Rental Resources

AUTOMOBILE ASSOCIATIONS

U.S.: American Automobile Association (AAA)	315/797-5000	www.aaa.com; most contact with the organization is through state and regional members
National Automobile Club	650/294-7000	www.thenac.com; membership is open to California residents only

LOCAL AGENCIES

Japan Railways has a car-rental service, with good train/rental packages. Check with Travel Service Centers at major stations for details. No English Web or telephone service yet. CooCom, Tokyo 03/5333-0246 www2.tocoo.jp/english is an excellent, reliable Web site that offers easy booking with Mazda and Nissan and Northwing offices nationwide.

MAJOR AGENCIES

Alamo	800/522-9696	www.alamo.com
Avis	800/331-1084	www.avis.com
Budget	800/472-3325	www.budget.com
Hertz	800/654-3001	www.hertz.com
National Car Rental	800/227-7368	www.nationalcar.com

the country. Credit cards are accepted everywhere and are even encouraged—there are discounts for them at some places. Self-service stations have recently become legal, so if you pump your own gas you may get a small discount. Often you pay after putting in the gas, but there are also machines where you put money in first and then use the receipt to get change back. Staff will offer to take away trash and clean car windows. Tipping is not customary.

PARKING
There is little on-street parking in Japan. Parking is usually in staffed parking lots or in parking towers within buildings. Expect to pay upwards of $3 per hour. Parking regulations are strictly enforced, and illegally parked vehicles are towed away. Recovery fees start at $300 and increase hourly.

ROAD CONDITIONS
Roads in Japan are often narrower than those in the United States, but they're well maintained in general. Driving in cities can be troublesome, as there are many narrow, one-way streets and little in the way of English road signs except on major arteries. Japanese drivers stick to the speed limit, but widely ignore bans on mobile phone use and dash-board televisions, and ignore rules on baby seats. Wild boars are not uncommon in rural districts, and have been known to block roads and ram into cars in the mountainous city of Kōbe and in Kyūshū, especially at night. From December to April northern areas are snow covered.

ROADSIDE EMERGENCIES
Emergency telephones along highways can be used to contact the authorities. A nonprofit service, JHelp.com, offers a free, 24-hour emergency assistance hotline. Car-rental agencies generally offer roadside assistance services. Mobile phones are now so widespread that local drivers can call for help from the middle of nowhere.
Emergency Services Police ☎ 110. **Fire** ☎ 119. **JHelp.com** ☎ 0570/00-0911.

RULES OF THE ROAD
In Japan people drive on the left. Speed limits vary, but generally the limit is 80 kph (50 mph) on highways, 40 kph (25 mph) in cities. Penalties for speeding are severe. By law, car seats must be installed if the driver is traveling with a child under six, while the driver and all passengers in cars must wear seat belts at all times. Driving while using hand-held phones is illegal.

Many smaller streets lack sidewalks, so cars, bicycles, and pedestrians share the same space. Motorbikes with engines under 50 cc are allowed to travel against automobile traffic on one-way roads. Fortunately, considering the narrowness of the streets and the volume of traffic, most Japanese drivers are technically skilled. They may not allow quite as much distance between cars as you're used to. Be prepared for sudden lane changes by other drivers. When waiting at intersections after dark, many drivers, as a courtesy to other drivers, turn off their main headlights to prevent glare.

2006 saw a nationwide crackdown on drunk driving, following a spate of horrific, headlining-grabbing accidents, so it's wisest to avoid alcohol entirely if you plan to drive.

▌ BY TRAIN

Riding Japanese trains is one of the pleasures of travel in the country. Efficient and convenient, trains run frequently and on schedule. The Shinkansen (bullet train), one of the fastest trains in the world, connects major cities north and south of Tōkyō. It is only slightly less expensive than flying, but is in many ways more convenient because train stations are more centrally located than airports (and, if you have a Japan Rail Pass, it's extremely affordable).

Other trains, though not as fast as the Shinkansen, are just as convenient and substantially cheaper. There are three types of train services: *futsū* (local service), *tokkyū* (limited express service), and *kyūkō* (express service). Both the tokkyū and the kyūkō offer a first-class compartment known as the Green Car. Smoking is allowed only in designated carriages on long-distance and Shinkansen trains. Local and commuter trains are entirely no-smoking.

Because there are no porters or carts at train stations, it's a good idea to travel light when getting around by train. Savvy travelers often have their main luggage sent ahead to a hotel that they plan to reach later in their wanderings. It's also good to know that every train station, however small, has luggage lockers, which cost about ¥300 for 24 hours.

If you plan to travel by rail, get a Japan Rail Pass, which offers unlimited travel on Japan Railways (JR) trains. You can purchase one-, two-, or three-week passes. A one-week pass is less expensive than a regular round-trip ticket from Tōkyō to Kyōto on the Shinkansen. You must obtain a rail pass voucher prior to departure for Japan (you cannot buy them in Japan), and the pass must be used within three months of purchase. The pass is available only to people with tourist visas, as opposed to business, student, and diplomatic visas.

When you arrive in Japan, you must exchange your voucher for the Japan Rail Pass. You can do this at the Japan Railways desk in the arrivals hall at Narita Airport or at JR stations in major cities. When you make this exchange, you determine the day that you want the rail pass to begin, and, accordingly, when it ends. You do not have to begin travel on the day you make the exchange; instead, pick the starting date to maximize use. The Japan Rail Pass allows you to travel on all JR-operated trains (which cover most destinations in Japan) but not lines owned by other companies.

GROUND TRANSPORTATION

FROM NARITA	To	Fares	Times	Notes
Friendly Airport Limousine (buses)	Various $$$$ hotels in Tōkyō & JR Tōkyō and Shinjuku train stations	¥2,400– ¥3,800 ($21–$35)	Every hour until 11:30 PM in traffic	70–90 min, can be longer
Friendly Airport Limousine (buses)	Tōkyō City Air Terminal (TCAT)	¥2,900 ($26)	Every 10–20 min from 6:55 AM to 11 PM	
Narita Limited Express (NEX)	Central Tōkyō station, then continue to Yokohama and Ōfuna	One-way fare ¥2,940; Green Car ¥4,980; private compartment (four people) ¥5,380 per person	Daily departures begin at 7:43 AM; the last train is at 9:43 PM	All seats are reserved
kaisoku (rapid train on JR's Narita Line)	Tōkyō station, by way of Chiba	¥1,280; ¥2,210 Green Car	16 departures daily, starting at 7 AM	Trip takes 1 hour 27 min
Keisei Skyliner train	Keisei-Ueno station	¥1,920 ($17)	Every 20–30 min, 9:21 AM–9:59 PM	All seats are reserved
Taxi	Central Tōkyō	¥20,000 (about $180) or more		

The JR Pass is also valid on buses operated by Japan Railways (⇨ By Bus, *above*). You can make seat reservations without paying a fee on all trains that have reserved-seat coaches, usually long-distance trains. The Japan Rail Pass does not cover the cost of sleeping compartments on overnight trains (called blue trains), nor does it cover the newest and fastest of the Shinkansen trains, the *Nozomi,* which make only one or two stops on longer runs. The pass covers only the *Hikari* Shinkansen, which make a few more stops than the Nozomi, and the *Kodama* Shinkansen, which stop at every station along the Shinkansen routes.

Japan Rail Passes are available in coach class and first class (Green Car), and as the difference in price between the two is relatively small, it's worth the splurge for first class, for real luxury, especially on the Shinkansen. A one-week pass costs ¥28,300 coach class, ¥37,800 first class; a two-week pass costs ¥45,100 coach class, ¥61,200 first class; and a three-week pass costs ¥57,700 coach class, ¥79,600 first class. Travelers under 18 pay lower rates. The pass pays for itself after one Tōkyō–Kyōto round-trip Shinkansen ride. Contact a travel agent or Japan Airlines to purchase the pass.

Many travelers assume that rail passes guarantee them seats on the trains they wish to ride. Not so. If you're using a rail pass, there's no need to buy individual tickets, but you should book seats ahead. You can reserve up to two weeks in advance or just minutes before the train departs. If you fail to make a train, there's no penalty, and you can reserve again.

Seat reservations for any JR route may be made at any JR station except those in the tiniest villages. The reservation windows or offices, *midori-no-madoguchi,* have green signs in English and green-stripe windows. If you're traveling without a Japan Rail Pass, there's a surcharge of approximately ¥500 (depending upon distance traveled) for seat reservations, and

if you miss the train you'll have to pay for another reservation. When making your seat reservation you may request a no-smoking or smoking car. Your reservation ticket shows the date and departure time of your train as well as your car and seat number. Notice the markings painted on the platform or on little signs above the platform; ask someone which markings correspond to car numbers. If you don't have a reservation, ask which cars are unreserved. Unreserved tickets can be purchased at regular ticket windows. There are no reservations made on local service trains. For traveling short distances, tickets are usually sold at vending machines. A platform ticket is required if you go through the wicket gate onto the platform to meet someone coming off a train. The charge is ¥140 (the tickets are ¥130 in Tōkyō and Ōsaka).

Most clerks at train stations know a few basic words of English and can read roman script. Moreover, they are invariably helpful in plotting your route. The complete railway timetable is a mammoth book written only in Japanese; however, you can get an English-language train schedule from the Japan National Tourist Organization (JNTO ⇨ Visitor Information, *above*) that covers the Shinkansen and a few of the major JR Limited Express trains. JNTO's booklet *The Tourist's Handbook* provides helpful information about purchasing tickets in Japan.

Japan Railways Group ⊠ 1 Rockefeller Plaza, Suite 1622, New York, NY 10020 ☎ 212/332–8686 🖷 212/332–8690.

Buying a Pass Japan Airlines (JAL) ⊠ 655 5th Ave., New York, NY 10022 USA ☎ 212/838–4400. **Japan Travel Bureau** (JTB) ⊠ 810 7th Ave., 34th fl., New York, NY 10019 ☎ 212/698–4900 or 800/223–6104. **Nippon Travel Agency** (NTA) ⊠ 111 Pavonia Ave., Suite 317, Jersey City, NJ 07310 ☎ 201/420–6000 or 800/682–7872.

Train Information JR Hotline ☎ 03/3423–0111 is an English-language information service, open weekdays 10–6.

ON THE GROUND IN JAPAN

■ BUSINESS SERVICES & FACILITIES

FedEx Kinko's offices throughout Japan will help with business services, and the Japan Convention Service can arrange interpretation and conference planning. The Japan National Tourist Office has extensive contacts for business travelers. Major hotels have business centers.

FedEx Kinko's ⊕ www.english.fedexkinkos.co.jp. **Japan Convention Service** ⊕ www.jcs-pco.com. **Japan External Trade Organization** ⊠ Ark Mori Bldg., 6F 12-32, Akasaka 1-chōme, Minato-ku, Tōkyō ⊕ www.jetro.go.jp.

■ COMMUNICATIONS

INTERNET

Phone jacks are the same in Japan as in the United States. Many hotels have ADSL or Ethernet connections for high-speed Internet access. Ethernet cables are usually available to buy at hotels if you don't bring your own. Wireless Internet access (Wi-Fi) is increasingly available for free at certain coffee shops and in many hotel lobbies across the country. There are Internet cafes in many cities, often doubling as manga libraries where you can rent a relaxation room with massage chair, computer, and desk.

Cybercafés ⊕ www.cybercafes.com lists over 4,000 Internet cafés worldwide.

PHONES

The good news is that you can now make a direct-dial telephone call from virtually any point on earth. The bad news? You can't always do so cheaply. Calling from a hotel is almost always the most expensive option; hotels usually add huge surcharges to all calls, particularly international ones. Calling cards usually keep costs to a minimum, but only if you purchase them locally.

The country code for Japan is 81. When dialing a Japanese number from outside Japan, drop the initial "0" from the local area code.

CALLING WITHIN JAPAN

Public telephones are a dying species in cell-phone-happy Japan. But there are usually public telephones near convenience stores, stations, and of course in hotel lobbies. Phones accept ¥100 coins as well as prepaid telephone cards. Domestic long-distance rates are reduced as much as 50% after 9 PM (40% after 7 PM). Telephone cards, sold in vending machines, hotels, and a variety of stores, are tremendously convenient.

Operator assistance at 104 is in Japanese only. Weekdays 9–5 (except national holidays) English-speaking operators can help you at the toll-free NTT Information Customer Service Centre.

Directory Assistance ☎ 104. **NTT Information Customer Service Centre** ☎ 0120/36-4463.

CALLING OUTSIDE JAPAN

Many gray, multicolor, and green phones have gold plates indicating, in English, that they can be used for international calls. Three Japanese companies provide international service: KDDI (001), Japan Telecom (0041), and IDC (0061). Dial the company code + country code + city/area code and number of your party. Telephone credit cards are especially convenient for international calls. For operator assistance in English on long-distance calls, dial 0051.

The country code for the United States is 1. **Access Codes** Japan has several telephone companies for international calls, so make a note of all the possible access code numbers to use to connect to your U.S. server before departure. **AT&T Direct** ☎ 800/222-0300. **MCI WorldPhone** ☎ 800/444-4444. **Sprint International Access** ☎ 800/877-4646.

CALLING CARDS

Telephone cards for ¥1,000 ($9) can be bought at station kiosks or convenience stores and can be used in virtually all public telephones. For international calls, look for phones that accept KDDI prepaid cards valued between ¥1,000 and ¥7,000. Cards are available from convenience stores.

MOBILE PHONES

Japan is the world leader in mobile-phone technology, but overseas visitors cannot easily use their handsets in Japan because it is a non-GSM country. Best to rent a phone from one of the many outlets at Narita, Kansai, and Nagoya airports. Softbank sells 3G SIM cards so you can use your own number in Japan. Most company rental rates start at ¥525 ($5) a day, excluding insurance. Check the airport Web sites for the current companies. Phones can be ordered online or by fax, or rented for same-day use.

Softbank ⊕ www.softbank-rental.jp. **G-call** ⊕ www.g-call.com. **JALABC Rental Phone** ⊕ www.rental-mobile.com/en/domestic/.

▌ CUSTOMS & DUTIES

You're always allowed to bring goods of a certain value back home without having to pay any duty or import tax. But there's a limit on the amount of tobacco and liquor you can bring back duty-free, and some countries have separate limits for perfumes; for exact figures, check with your customs department. The values of so-called "duty-free" goods are included in these amounts. When you shop abroad, save all your receipts, as customs inspectors may ask to see them as well as the items you purchased. If the total value of your goods is more than the duty-free limit, you'll have to pay a tax (most often a flat percentage) on the value of everything beyond that limit.

Japan has strict regulations about bringing firearms, pornography, and narcotics into the country. Anyone caught with drugs is liable to be detained, refused reentry into Japan, and deported. Certain fresh fruits, vegetables, plants, and animals are also illegal. Nonresidents are allowed to bring in duty-free: (1) 400 cigarettes or 100 cigars or 500 grams of tobacco; (2) three 760-ml bottles of alcohol; (3) 2 ounces of perfume; (4) other goods up to ¥200,000 value.

Getting through customs at a Japanese airport goes more smoothly if you are well dressed, clean-shaven, and as conventional-looking as possible. Visitors arriving off flights from other Asian countries are particularly scrutinized for narcotics. **Information in Japan Ministry of Finance, Customs and Tariff Bureau** ✉ 3-1-1 Kasumigaseki, Chiyoda-ku, Tōkyō, 100-8940 ☎ 03/3581-4111 ⊕ www.customs.go.jp/index_e.htm. **U.S. Information U.S. Customs and Border Protection** ⊕ www.cbp.gov.

▌ DAY TOURS & GUIDES

The Japan Guide Association will introduce you to English-speaking guides. You need to negotiate your own itinerary and price with the guide. Assume that the fee will be ¥25,000–¥30,000 for a full eight-hour day. The Japan National Tourist Organization can also put you in touch with various local volunteer groups that conduct tours in English; you need only to pay for the guide's travel expenses, admission fees to cultural sites, and meals if you eat together.

The Japan National Tourist Organization (JNTO) sponsors a Good-Will Guide program in which local citizens volunteer to show visitors around; this is a great way to meet Japanese people. These are not professional guides; they usually volunteer both because they enjoy welcoming foreigners to their town and because they want to practice their English. The services of Good-Will Guides are free, but you should pay for their travel costs, their admission fees, and any meals you eat with them while you are together. To participate in this program, make arrangements for a Good-Will Guide in advance through JNTO in the United States or through the tourist office in the area where you want the guide to meet you. The program operates in 75 towns and cities, including Tōkyō, Kyōto, Nara, Nagoya, Osaka, and Hiroshima.

Recommended Tours/Guides Japan Guide Association ☎ 03/3213-2706. **Japan National Tourist Organization** ✉ Tōkyō International Forum B1, 3-5-1 Marunouchi, Chiyoda-ku ☎ 03/3201-3331 Ⓜ Yūraku-chō Line, Yūraku-chō station [Exit A-4B].

▮ EATING OUT

The restaurants we list are the cream of the crop in each price category. Food, like many other things in Japan, can be expensive. Eating at hotels and famous restaurants is costly; however, you can eat well and reasonably at standard restaurants that may not have signs in English. Many less expensive restaurants have plastic replicas of the dishes they serve displayed in their front windows, so you can always point to what you want to eat if the language barrier is insurmountable. A good place to look for moderately priced dining spots is in the restaurant concourse of department stores, usually on the bottom floor. Properties indicated by the symbols ✕🏠 are lodging establishments whose restaurant warrants a special trip.

In general, Japanese restaurants are very clean (standards of hygiene are very high). Tap water is safe, and most hotels have Western-style restrooms, although restaurants may have Japanese-style toilets, with bowls recessed into the floor, over which you must squat.

If you're in a hurry, a visit to one branch of the MOS Burger, Freshness Burger, or First Kitchen will fit the bill. These nationwide chains offer familiar hamburgers, but they also have local variations. Yoshinoya is another popular chain, serving grilled salmon, rice and miso soup for breakfast (until 10), and then hearty portions of rice and beef for the rest of the day.

Local and regional specialties are discussed at the beginning of each chapter in this book; for more general information on dining in Japan, *see* Understanding Japan at the end of this book.

For information on food-related health issues, *see* Health *below.*

MEALS & MEALTIMES

Office workers eat lunch from noon to 1 PM, so eat later to avoid crowds. Many restaurants have lunchtime specials until 2:30 PM aimed at housewives. Note that many restaurants in rural towns are closed by 9. Unless otherwise noted, the restaurants listed in this guide are open daily for lunch and dinner.

PAYING

Beyond major hotels and smart city dining, credit cards may not be accepted, so check before ordering.

RESERVATIONS

For upmarket, evening dining in major cities ask hotel staff to make reservations—not only will this guarantee a table, but it gives the management time to locate an English menu or staff with some language skills.

▮ ELECTRICITY

The electrical current in Japan is 100 volts, 50 cycles alternating current (AC) in eastern Japan, and 100 volts, 60 cycles in western Japan; the United States runs on 110-volt, 60-cycle AC current. Wall outlets in Japan accept plugs with two flat prongs, as in the United States, but do not accept U.S. three-prong plugs.

Consider making a small investment in a universal adapter, which has several types of plugs in one lightweight, compact unit. Most laptops and mobile phone chargers are dual voltage (i.e., they operate equally well on 110 and 220 volts), so require only an adapter. These days the same is true of small appliances such as hair dryers. Always check labels and manufacturers' instructions to be sure. Don't use 110-volt outlets marked FOR SHAVERS ONLY for high-wattage appliances such as hair dryers.

Steve Kropla's Help for World Travelers ⊕ www.kropla.com has information on electrical and telephone plugs around the world. **Walkabout Travel Gear** ⊕ www.walkabouttravelgear.com has a good coverage of electricity under "adapters."

▌EMERGENCIES

Assistance in English is available 24 hours a day on the toll-free Japan Helpline.

The following embassies and consulates are open weekdays, with one- to two-hour closings for lunch. Call for exact hours.
U.S. Embassy and Consulate ✉ 1-10-5 Akasaka, Minato-ku, Toranomon ☏ 03/322-4500 ⊕ http://tokyo.usembassy.gov/ Ⓜ Namboku Line, Tameike-Sannō station [Exit 13].
General Emergency Contacts Ambulance and Fire ☏ 119. **Japan Helpline** ☏ 0120/46-1997 or 0570/00-0911. **Police** ☏ 110.

▌HEALTH

Japan is a safe, clean country for travelers with good drinking water and no major water- or insect-borne diseases. Drugs and medications are widely available at drug stores, although the brand names and use instructions will be in Japanese, so if on regular medication, take along enough supplies to cover the trip. Condoms are sold widely, but they may not have the brands you're used to. Speak with your physician and/or check the CDC or World Health Organization Web sites for health alerts, particularly if you're pregnant or

traveling with children or have a chronic illness.

For information on travel insurance, shots and medications, and medical-assistance companies *see* Shots & Medications *under* Things to Consider *in* Before You Go, *above.*

SPECIFIC ISSUES IN JAPAN

Japan is basically a safe country for travelers. The greatest danger is the possibility of being caught up in an earthquake and its resulting tsunami. Earthquake information is broadcast (in Japanese) as news flashes on television within minutes, and during major disasters national broadcaster N.H.K. broadcasts information in English on radio and television. Minor tremors occur every month, and sometimes train services are temporarily halted. Check emergency routes at hotels and higher ground if staying near coastal areas.
General Information & Warnings U.S. Department of State ⊕ www.travel.state.gov.

Tap water is safe everywhere in Japan. Medical treatment varies from highly skilled and professional at major hospitals to somewhat less advanced in small neighborhood clinics. At larger hospitals you have a good chance of encountering English-speaking doctors who have been partly educated in the West.

Mosquitoes can be a minor irritation during the rainy season, though you are never at risk of contracting anything serious like malaria. If you're staying in a *ryokan* or anyplace without air-conditioning, anti-mosquito coils or an electric-powered spray will be provided. Dehydration and heatstroke could be concerns if you spend a long time outside during the summer months, but isotonic sports drinks are readily available from the nation's ubiquitous vending machines.

OVER-THE-COUNTER REMEDIES
It may be difficult to buy the standard over-the-counter remedies you're used to, so it's best to bring with you any medi-

cations (in their proper packaging) you may need. Medication can only be bought at pharmacies in Japan, but every neighborhood seems to have at least one. Ask for the *kusuri-ya*. Pharmacists in Japan are usually able to manage at least a few words of English, and certainly are able to read some, so have a pen and some paper ready, just in case. In Japanese, aspirin is *asupirin* and Tylenol is *Tairenōru*. Following national regulations, Japanese drugs contain less potent ingredients than foreign brands, so the effects can be disappointing, check advised dosages carefully.

∎ HOURS OF OPERATION

General business hours in Japan are weekdays 9–5. Many offices also open at least half the day on Saturday, but are generally closed on Sunday.

Banks are open weekdays from 9 to at least 3, some now staying open until 4 or 5. As with shops, there's a trend toward longer and later opening hours.

Gas stations follow usual shop hours, though 24-hour stations can be found near major highways.

Museums generally close on Monday and the day following national holidays. They are also closed the day following special exhibits and during the week-long New Year's celebrations.

Department stores are usually open 10–7, but close one day a week, varying from store to store. Other stores are open from 10 or 11 to 7 or 8. There's a trend toward longer and later opening hours in major cities, and 24-hour convenience stores, many of which now have ATM facilities, can be found across the entire country.

HOLIDAYS

As elsewhere, peak times for travel in Japan tend to fall around holiday periods. You want to avoid traveling during the few days before and after New Year's; during Golden Week, which follows Greenery Day (April 29); and in mid-July and mid-August, at the time of Ōbon

festivals, when many Japanese return to their hometowns (Ōbon festivals are celebrated July or August 13–16, depending on the location). Note that when a holiday falls on a Sunday, the following Monday is a holiday.

January 1 (*Ganjitsu*, New Year's Day); the second Monday in January (*Senjin-no-hi*, Coming of Age Day); February 11 (*Kenkoku Kinen-bi*, National Foundation Day); March 20 or 21 (*Shumbun-no-hi*, Vernal Equinox); April 29 (*Midori-no-hi*, Greenery Day); May 3 (*Kempō Kinen-bi*, Constitution Day); May 5 (*Kodomo-no-hi*, Children's Day); the third Monday in July (*Umi-no-hi*, Marine Day); the third Monday in September (*Keirō-no-hi*, Respect for the Aged Day); September 23 or 24 (*Shūbun-no-hi*, Autumnal Equinox); the second Monday in October (*Taiiku-no-hi*, Sports Day); November 3 (*Bunka-no-hi*, Culture Day); November 23 (*Kinrō Kansha-no-hi*, Labor Thanksgiving Day); December 23 (*Tennō Tanjōbi*, Emperor's Birthday).

∎ MAIL

The Japanese postal service is very efficient. Air mail between Japan and the United States takes between five and eight days. Surface mail can take anywhere from four to eight weeks. Express service is also available through post offices.

Although there are numerous post offices in every city, it's probably best to use the central post office near the main train station, because the workers speak English and can handle foreign mail. Some of the smaller post offices are not equipped to send packages. Post offices are open weekdays 9–5 and Saturday 9–noon. Some central post offices have longer hours, such as the one in Tōkyō, near Tōkyō Eki (train station), which is open 24 hours year-round. Most hotels and many convenience stores also sell stamps.

The Japanese postal service has implemented the use of three-numeral-plus-four postal codes, but its policy is similar to that in the United States regarding ZIP-plus-fours; that is, addresses with the three-numeral code will still arrive at their destination, albeit perhaps one or two days later. Mail to rural towns may take longer.

It costs ¥110 (98¢) to send a letter by air to North America. An airmail postcard costs ¥70 (63¢). Aerograms cost ¥90 (81¢).

To get mail, have parcels and letters sent "poste restante" to the central post office in major cities; unclaimed mail is returned after 30 days.

SHIPPING PACKAGES

FedEx has drop-off locations at branches of Kinko's in all major cities. A 1-kg/2.20-lb package from central Tōkyō to Washington, DC, would cost about ¥7,200 ($64), and take two days to be delivered.

The Japanese postal service is very efficient, and domestic mail rarely goes astray. To ship a 5-kg/11.02-lb parcel to the United States costs ¥10,150 ($91) if sent by airmail, ¥7,300 ($65) by SAL (economy airmail), and ¥4,000 ($36) by sea. Allow a week for airmail, 2 to 3 weeks for SAL, and up to 6 weeks for packages sent by sea. Large shops usually ship domestically, but not overseas.
Express Services FedEx ☎ 0120/00-320 toll-free, 043/298-1919 ⊕ www.fedex.com/jp_english.

▌ MONEY

Japan is expensive, but there are ways to cut costs. This requires, to some extent, an adventurous spirit and the courage to stray from the standard tourist paths. One good way to hold down expenses is to avoid taxis (they tend to get stuck in traffic anyway) and try the inexpensive, efficient subway and bus systems; instead of going to a restaurant with menus in English and Western-style food, go to places where you can rely on your good old index finger to point to the dish you want, and try food that the Japanese eat.

ITEM	AVERAGE COST
CUP OF COFFEE	¥250-600
Glass of Wine	¥500
Glass of Beer	¥300-600
Sandwich	¥300
One-Mile Taxi Ride in Capital City	¥660
Museum Admission	¥1,000

Prices throughout this guide are given for adults. Substantially reduced fees are almost always available for children, students, and senior citizens.

■ TIP➔ Banks never have every foreign currency on hand, and it may take as long as a week to order. If you're planning to exchange funds before leaving home, don't wait until the last minute.

ATMS & BANKS

Your own bank will probably charge a fee for using ATMs abroad; the foreign bank you use may also charge a fee. Nevertheless, you'll usually get a better rate of exchange at an ATM than you will at a currency-exchange office or even when changing money in a bank. And extracting funds as you need them is a safer option than carrying around a large amount of cash.

■ TIP➔ PIN numbers with more than four digits are not recognized at ATMs in many countries. If yours has five or more, remember to change it before you leave.

ATMs at many Japanese banks do not accept foreign-issue cash or credit cards. Citibank has centrally located branches in most major Japanese cities and ATMs that are open 24 hours. UFJ and Shinsei banks are members of the Plus network, as are some convenience store cash machines. Post offices have ATMs that accept Visa, MasterCard, American Express, Diners Club, and Cirrus cards. Elsewhere, especially in more rural areas, it's difficult to find suitable ATMs. PIN numbers in Japan are comprised of four digits. In Japanese an ATM is commonly referred to by its English acronym, while PIN is *anshō bangō*. Because of a spate of ATM crimes allegedly involving "foreigners" asking for help, Japanese bank customers may react badly to requests for assistance. Instead, contact bank staff by using the phone next to the ATM. Many machines also have English on-screen instructions.

CREDIT CARDS

Throughout this guide, the following abbreviations are used: **AE**, American Express; **DC**, Diners Club; **MC**, MasterCard; and **V**, Visa.

It's a good idea to inform your credit-card company before you travel, especially if you're going abroad and don't travel internationally very often. Otherwise, the credit-card company might put a hold on your card owing to unusual activity—not a good thing halfway through your trip. Record all your credit-card numbers—as well as the phone numbers to call if your cards are lost or stolen—in a safe place, so you're prepared should something go wrong. Both MasterCard and Visa have general numbers you can call (collect if you're abroad) if your card is lost, but you're better off calling the number of your issuing bank, since MasterCard and Visa usually just transfer you to your bank; your bank's number is usually printed on your card.

If you plan to use your credit card for cash advances, you'll need to apply for a PIN at least two weeks before your trip. Although it's usually cheaper (and safer) to use a credit card abroad for large purchases (so you can cancel payments or be reimbursed if there's a problem), note that some credit-card companies *and* the banks that issue them add substantial percentages to all foreign transactions, whether they're in a foreign currency or not. Check on these fees before leaving home, so there won't be any surprises when you get the bill.

■ TIP→ Before you charge something, ask the merchant whether or not he or she plans to do a dynamic currency conversion (DCC). In such a transaction the credit-card *processor* (shop, restaurant, or hotel, not Visa or MasterCard) converts the currency and charges you in dollars. In most cases you'll pay the merchant a 3% fee for this service in addition to any credit-card company and issuing-bank foreign-transaction surcharges.

Dynamic currency conversion programs are becoming increasingly widespread. Merchants who participate in them are supposed to ask whether you want to be charged in dollars or the local currency, but they don't always do so. And even if they do offer you a choice, they may well avoid mentioning the additional surcharges. The good news is that you *do* have a choice. And if this practice really gets your goat, you can avoid it entirely thanks to American Express; with its cards, DCC simply isn't an option.

MasterCard and Visa are the most widely accepted credit cards in Japan. When you use a credit card you'll be asked if you intend to pay in one installment as most locals do, say *hai-ikkai* (Yes, one time) just to fit in, even if you plan differently once you get home. Many vendors don't accept American Express. Cash is still king in Japan, and older Japanese consider it shameful to use a card.

Reporting Lost Cards American Express
☏ 800/992-3404 in U.S., 336/393-1111 collect from abroad, 0120/02-0120 for Japan office ⊕ www.americanexpress.com. **Diners Club** ☏ 800/234-6377 in U.S., 303/799-1504 collect from abroad, 0120/07-4024 for Japan office ⊕ www.dinersclub.com. **MasterCard** ☏ 800/622-7747 in U.S., 636/722-7111 collect from abroad, 00531/11-3886 for Japan office ⊕ www.mastercard.com. **Visa** ☏ 800/847-2911 in U.S., 410/581-9994 collect from abroad, 0120/13-3173 for Japan office ⊕ www.visa.com.

CURRENCY & EXCHANGE

The unit of currency in Japan is the yen (¥). There are bills of ¥10,000, ¥5,000, ¥2,000, and ¥1,000. Coins are ¥500, ¥100, ¥50, ¥10, ¥5, and ¥1. Japanese currency floats on the international monetary exchange, so changes can be dramatic.

At this writing the exchange rate was ¥117 for U.S. $1.

■ TIP➔ Even if a currency-exchange booth has a sign promising no commission, rest assured that there's some kind of huge, hidden fee. And as for rates, you're almost always better off getting foreign currency at an ATM or exchanging money at a bank.

TRAVELER'S CHECKS & CARDS

Some consider this the currency of the cave man, and it's true that fewer establishments accept traveler's checks these days. Nevertheless, they're a cheap and secure way to carry extra money, particularly on trips to urban areas. American Express issues traveler's checks in the United States; you can also avoid hefty surcharges by cashing Amex checks at Amex offices. Whatever you do, keep track of all the serial numbers in case the checks are lost or stolen.

Traveler's checks are widely accepted at major businesses in cities, though not in small businesses or rural areas.

American Express now offers a stored-value card called a Travelers Cheque Card, which you can use wherever American Express credit cards are accepted, including ATMs. The card can carry a minimum of $300 and a maximum of $2,700, and it's a very safe way to carry your funds. Although you can get replacement funds in 24 hours if your card is lost or stolen, it doesn't really strike us as a very good deal. In addition to a high initial cost ($14.95 to set up the card, plus $5 each time you "reload"), you still have to pay a 2% fee for each purchase in a foreign currency (similar to that of any credit card). Further, each time you use the card in an ATM you pay a transaction fee of $2.50 on top of the 2% transaction fee for the conversion—add it all up and it can be considerably more than you would pay when simply using your own ATM card. Regular traveler's checks are just as secure and cost less.

American Express ☎ 888/412-6945 in U.S., 801/945-9450 collect outside of U.S. to add value or speak to customer service ⊕ www.americanexpress.com.

■ RESTROOMS

The most hygienic restrooms are found in hotels and department stores, and are usually clearly marked with international symbols. You may encounter Japanese-style toilets, with bowls recessed into the floor, over which you squat facing the top. This may take some getting used to, but it's completely sanitary as you don't come into direct contact with the facility. If you can't face a squat, check out the last cubical in the row because it may be a Western-style toilet.

In many homes and Japanese-style public places, there will be a pair of slippers at the entrance to the restroom. Change into these before entering the room, and change back when you exit.

Many public toilets don't have toilet paper, though there are dispensers where packets can be purchased for ¥50 (45¢) or so. Similarly, paper towel dispensers and hand dryers are not always installed, so a small handkerchief is useful for drying your hands.

Find a Loo The Bathroom Diaries ⊕ www.thebathroomdiaries.com is flush with unsanitized info on restrooms the world over—each one located, reviewed, and rated.

■ SAFETY

Even in its major cities Japan is a very safe country, with one of the lowest crime rates in the world. You should, however, avoid Ura-Kabuki-chō in Tōkyō's Shinjuku district and some of the large public parks at nighttime.

■ TIP➔ Distribute your cash, credit cards, IDs, and other valuables between a deep front pocket, an inside jacket or vest pocket, and a

LOCAL DO'S & TABOOS

CUSTOMS OF THE COUNTRY

In the United States being direct, efficient, and succinct are highly valued traits. In Japan this style is often frowned upon. Most Japanese do not use first names casually, so use last names with the honorific *-san* after the name in social situations. Make sure you don't express anger or aggression. These traits are equated with losing face in Japan, something you do not want to happen. Also stick to neutral subjects in conversations; private lives are kept private. There is no "fashionably late" in Japan, so be on time. Eating in public and overt physical affection is also frowned on by older Japanese.

GREETINGS

Japanese of all ages and backgrounds bow in greeting each other (even on the telephone!), and foreign visitors who at least bob the head will get a smile of recognition. However, Japanese know all about handshaking now, and the visitor's head may crash with an outstretched hand.

SIGHTSEEING

There's no strict dress code for visiting temples and shrines, but you will feel out of place in shorts or outfits with modest skin coverage. Casual clothes, including jeans, are fine for sightseeing. Remember to remove your shoes when entering temples. There are usually slippers by the entrance for you to change into.

OUT ON THE TOWN

Men are expected to wear a jacket and tie at more expensive restaurants and nightclubs. Women should wear a dress or skirt. If you've been invited out to dinner, either in a private home or restaurant, it's customary to bring a small token for your host. If you are in a home, remember to remove your shoes and put on the slippers that are usually waiting for you. When eating, it's okay to ask for a fork if you're not comfortable with chopsticks. If you do use chopsticks, do not use the end of the chopstick that has been in your mouth to pick up food from communal dishes. And never leave you're chopsticks sticking straight up in your food. This is a big no-no. Rest them on the edge of your bowl or plate instead.

Drinking is something of a national pastime in Japan. If you're not up to the task, never refuse a drink (it's considered very rude). Instead, sip away, making sure you're glass is half full. Whatever you do, do not pour your own glass. Companions traditionally pour drinks for each other and pouring your own is pointing out that your companions are not attentive. In the same vein, if you see an empty glass, fill it.

DOING BUSINESS

Make sure you allow adequate time for travel—being late for a business function is not appreciated. Wear conservative-color clothing and bring along *meishi* (business cards). Meishi are mandatory in Japan, and it is expected that when you bow upon meeting people you will also hand them a card; only English is okay, but if you have one side in Japanese and one in English, your business associates will be very impressed. Remember to use last names with the honorific—san when addressing people. Also, hierarchy matters to the Japanese, so make sure your job title and/or rank is indicated on your card. You may see your associates putting the cards on the table in front of them, this is so they can remember your name easily. Follow suit; never shove the cards you have just received in your pocket or bag.

It's not customary for Japanese business people to bring their spouses along to dinners, so never assume it's okay to bring yours. If you want to bring your spouse along, ask in a way that eliminates a direct refusal.

If you are a woman traveling on business in Japan, it's good to note that many Japanese women still don't have careers, and Japanese businessmen may not know how to interact with a Western businesswoman. Be patient, and if need be, gently remind them to treat you the same as they would a man.

hidden money pouch. Don't reach for the money pouch once you're in public.

∎ TAXES

A 5% national consumption tax is added to all hotel bills. Another 3% local tax is added to the bill if it exceeds ¥15,000 (about $134). You may save money by paying for your hotel meals separately rather than charging them to your bill.

At first-class, full-service, and luxury hotels, a 10% service charge is added to the bill in place of individual tipping. At more expensive ryokan, where individualized maid service is offered, the service charge is usually 15%. At business hotels, minshuku, youth hostels, and economy inns, no service charge is added to the bill.

There's an across-the-board, nonrefundable 5% consumption tax levied on all sales, which is included in the ticket price. Authorized tax-free shops will knock the tax off purchases over ¥10,000 if you show your passport and a valid tourist visa. A large sign is displayed at such shops. A 5% tax is also added to all restaurant bills. Another 3% local tax is added to the

bill if it exceeds ¥7,500 (about $67). At more expensive restaurants a 10%–15% service charge is added to the bill. Tipping is not customary.

∎ TIME

All of Japan is in the same time zone, which is 14 hours ahead of New York, and 17 hours ahead of San Francisco. Daylight saving time is not observed.

∎ TIPPING

Tipping is not common in Japan. It's not necessary to tip taxi drivers, or at hair salons, barbershops, bars, or nightclubs. A chauffeur for a hired car usually receives a tip of ¥500 ($4.50) for a half-day excursion and ¥1,000 ($9) for a full-day trip. Porters charge fees of ¥250–¥300 (about $2.50) per bag at railroad stations and ¥200 ($1.80) per piece at airports. It's not customary to tip employees of hotels, even porters, unless a special service has been rendered. In such cases, a gratuity of ¥2,000–¥3,000 ($18–$26) should be placed in an envelope and handed to the staff member discreetly.

INDEX

PHOTO CREDITS

NOTES

NOTES

NOTES

NOTES

NOTES

ABOUT OUR WRITERS

Shikoku reviser **Joshua Bisker** graduated Oberlin College and soon found himself in a small town in Shikoku, where he was employed for two years instructing Japanese children in the value of irreverence and spontaneity.

When he's not hitting the pavement for *Variety* or his on-line column, *Sake-Drenched Postcards,* **Brett Bull** works behind a drafting table at a construction company in Tōkyō. He contributed to the Tōkyō Where to Stay and Shopping sections.

While teaching English in the castle town of Himeji, **Allison Burke** received her black belt in Aikido. Allison studied Japanese, wore traditional *happi* coats in her town's local festivals, and trekked about Japan. She updated the Kōbe Chapter.

Nicholas Coldicott is the editor in chief of a creative agency in Tōkyō. In his spare time he's a funk-and-soul DJ. He revised the Tōkyō Nightlife & the Arts section.

Jon Davies has lived near Nagoya since 2002. He's editor of *Avenues* magazine and contributes articles and photography to numerous publications. He revised the Nagoya, Ise-Shima & the Kii Peninsula chapter and the introductory essays.

Justin Ellis, an Australian native, is a contributor to *Kansai Time Out* and the *Kyoto Journal.* Familiar with Japanese history, Justin was thrilled to cover Nara and Osaka.

Hokkaidō updater **Amanda Harlow** left the south of England and settled in Japan in 1993, eventually stopping in Hokkaidō, where she works proofreading, teaching, and narrating government videos about clearing snow from roads.

Oscar Johnson cut his teeth at the *Los Angeles Times, The Namibian,* and other newspapers before taking to Tōkyō in 2002. He's since written for *The Asahi Shimbun/International Herald Tribune, Metropolis,* and *Jselect* magazines. Oscar contributed to the introductory essays.

A 47-year-old devotee of Zen Buddhism and Japanese martial arts, **Jim Klar** spent two years in Nara teaching English. He currently resides in sunny Cleveland, Ohio, with his wife and son. He wrote "Ritual Religion" in the Understanding Japan chapter.

Kyōtō updater **Deidre May** left her native South Africa, where she directed an animated television series, and came to Japan. She now lives in an old Japanese house in northeastern Kyōtō, at the site of one of the original Buddhist enclaves. She is a contributor and editor for the *Kyoto Journal.*

Oliver Ormrod has traveled extensively in Japan and Korea. He holds a BA in Asian Studies and an MA in intercultural communications. He contributed to the Arts & Culture and Facts & Figures sections.

In 2002 **Katherine Pham Do** left Australia for Japan, where she is currently developing a television series on Japanese cuisine. She updated the Tōkyō and Tōkyō Side Trips Where to Eat sections.

Canadian **Krista Kim Pickard** founded a beauty concierge company, *Noblesse Concierge,* in Tōkyō. She writes for *Korea Herald, DestinAsian,* and *Metropolis* magazines and for the *Japan Times.* She updated the Tokyo chapter.

Boulder native **John Malloy Quinn** helped open and run a small school on the Noto Peninsula, where he lived from 1993 to 2000. Currently he lives in a sunny rooftop perch in Tōkyō's Setagaya Ward. John updated the Tōhoku, Western Honshu, Kyushu, and Okinawa chapters and has written for Fodor's since 1999.